HISTORY OF THE CHURCH

VI

HISTORY OF THE CHURCH

Edited by

HUBERT JEDIN

and

JOHN DOLAN

Volume VI

THE CHURCH
IN THE AGE OF
ABSOLUTISM AND
ENLIGHTENMENT

by

Wolfgang Müller

Quintín Aldea

Johannes Beckmann

Louis Cognet

Patrick J. Corish

Oskar Köhler

Heribert Raab

Burkhart Schneider

Bernhard Stasiewski

Translated by

Gunther J. Holst

Crossroad · New York

1981

The Crossroad Publishing Company

18 East 41st Street, New York, NY 10017

Translated from the *Handbuch der Kirchengeschichte*

Vol. V: *Die Kirche im Zeitalter des Absolutismus und der Aufklärung*

© Verlag Herder KG Freiburg im Breisgau 1970

English translation © 1981 by The Crossroad Publishing Company

Library of Congress Cataloging in Publication Data

Kirche im Zeitalter des Absolutismus und der Aufklärung.

English.

The Church in the age of absolutism and enlightenment.

(History of the Church; v. 6)

Translation of: Die Kirche im Zeitalter des

Absolutismus und der Aufklärung.

Includes bibliographies and index.

1. Church history—17th century.   2. Church history—

18th century.   I. Müller, Wolfgang, 1905–

II. Series: Handbuch der Kirchengeschichte.   English; v. 6.

BR145.2.J413   1980, vol. 6   [BR440]   270s   81-5056

ISBN 0-8245-0010-5   [270.7]   AACR2   Previously: 0-8164-0445-3

CONTENTS

CONTENTS

PART TWO: THE ESTABLISHED CHURCH AND THE ENLIGHTENMENT

CONTENTS

PREFACE

As the list of contributors to this volume demonstrates, it was necessary to take into account the increasing complexity of the life of the Church in the period treated by calling upon more experts from other countries. The number of contributors could not but make it more difficult to maintain the uniformity within the total concept of this work. Therefore the editor and the coordinators have decided to preface this volume with an introduction to facilitate its synthesis.

At this time we announce with great sadness the death of Louis Cognet on 29 July 1970. The stamp of his greatness appears in this volume. Although it was only two years ago that he was invited to collaborate with us, he has produced an account of the life of the Church in France during and following the *Grand Siècle* to the great revolution which far surpasses any such account of similar size available in Germany till now. Drawing on his most profound expertise, he has done this with admirable precision. He was able to read the proofs of the chapters he authored, but prevented from seeing this volume appear in print.

Hubert Jedin

PREFACE TO THE ENGLISH EDITION

Few periods in the history of the Church offer such a striking variety of currents and counter currents, of triumphs and failures, as in what is known as the Age of the Baroque. Not only had a reformed, triumphant, and centralized Curia to maintain its counter offensive against a Protestantism increasingly vitalized and supported by the new maritime powers, it was now also faced with growing resistance from within on the part of an episcopate and princes who saw its once needed direction as being tantamount to interference. This was especially true in France where the decrees of Trent were only belatedly accepted. It can be said that all the movements that plagued the Church from the Reformation to the Revolution—Gallicanism, Jansenism, episcopalism, and absolutism—originated in Europe's most Catholic nation.

While Jansenism and Gallicanism held center stage, it was the nascent Enlightenment, spreading from Protestant Europe, that posed the real challenge to the post-Reformation Church. Many of its earlier disciples were from among the educated clergy and many of its basic principles—the idea of progress, religious freedom, recognition of the basic rights of man—form the very foundation of modern society. It was the alleged divorce of the use of reason from a humble dependence on God that turned the Church against it. It was perhaps Protestantism's adaptation to the new movement that made it, rather than Catholicism, the more dynamic of the Christian bodies in eighteenth-century Europe. Evangelism and Pietism would wait another two centuries to touch the Church of Rome seriously.

While the Church declined in religious leadership, it also continued to lose what was left of its prestige in political Europe. The failure of Louis XIV to restore the Catholic Stuarts to the English throne was as indicative of this as was the dissolution of the Jesuits in 1773 by Clement XIV. We might add to this list the disintegration of the Baroque. Perhaps nothing more strikingly demonstrates the secularized temper of the time and the profound cultural change than the fact that there is hardly a major painter, sculptor, or architect after 1700 who was primarily a religious artist.

John P. Dolan

INTRODUCTION

The century and a half of church history after the Peace of Westphalia, treated in this volume, is a particular epoch in the formation of the "modern world," but regarding the Church this period is difficult to characterize in a general way if the requisite criteria are gleaned from its own historical existence.

Concerning the relationship between the Church and the temporal world it must be stated that in the area of political forces the Church lost its participation and its leadership in the intellectual development of Europe. This loss, while especially marked in the case of the Catholic Church because of its significance within the context of Western history and its intrinsic predisposition for a universal world order, was also sustained by the Protestant and the Eastern Churches. Not only was Christianity split into denominations, it also began to lose more and more of its congruence with the society in which it lived. To be sure, "published" history commonly overlooked the fact that in this period of roughly 150 years and far beyond broad segments of the general population remained anonymous and continued to live within the Christian tradition until even the last retreats of traditional Christianity were confronted with the "modern world." This volume occasionally makes reference to the endurance of this order of life, grown throughout the centuries, which has been obscured to the view of history by the spectacular events of the "great" and mighty aspects of history, which were, however, shaped by a mere small segment of actors. To sharpen that view is one of the tasks of church history which must make use of the recently developed sociohistorical methods for that purpose.

The complexity of the period from 1648–1789, customarily designated as "the Age of Absolutism and Enlightenment," is equally significant in its bearing on church history. The assertion that the Church lost its role of intellectual leadership is indeed justified. Yet one must hasten to add that in the construction and interior design of churches and monastic establishments the period of the Baroque has given the general public a number of magnificent representations of a spirit which melded mathematical rationality and an awareness of the Christian faith. If one considers Voltaire as a representative of the spirit of his time, one must also be aware—regardless of cultural differences—that Johann Sebastian Bach and George Frederick Handel, both masters in the field of church music, represented high points in the history of music, and that such architects and artists as B. Neumann and Tiepolo were his contemporaries. Our general view of the history encompassing that century and a half is excessively determined by phenomena which "even then" presaged the arrival of modern society, whereas elements which tended to retain and preserve any religious creations in art and music have been undervalued. The degree of this distortion is heightened by the fact that the history of the Church of this period (even in church historiography itself) is treated too much within the framework of political history, while the history of Christian spirituality, both in Catholicism and Protestantism, has been neglected. This volume therefore pays particular attention to the latter element.

A final task for the determination of church history within the universal history of this period was the need to modify the prevailing opinion formed by nineteenth-century church historians concerning the age of Enlightenment. Its growing anti-Church and even anti-Christian tendencies are unequivocal. But the so-called Second Enlightenment in our present age has permitted us to see the strong effect exerted by the unbroken existence of Christian tradition upon the intellectual movements of the seventeenth and eighteenth century, regardless of all their polemical rhetoric (Chap. 19). To be sure, the "crisis of European intellectuality" was underway, but the old categories of order and the spirituality of the masses stayed alive.

The shift in the relationship between church history and general history is hardly more apparent than in the fact that the Thirty Years' War and the Peace of Westphalia were of necessity natural topics for discussion in Volume V, *Reformation and Counter Reformation,* while the present volume can only highlight the international relations and changes in the European balance of power. The last religious war lost its denominational character in 1635 when France under Cardinal Richelieu intervened formally against the Catholic powers. In the period after 1648 the fight of France for European hegemony relegated the denominational issue to a role of mere political propaganda. A case in point was the war between France and Holland (1672–78) in which Pope Clement X let himself be deceived regarding the intentions of Louis XIV (Chap. 7); in the Peace of Nijmegen (1678/79), in which France consolidated its hegemony at the expense of Spain and the Empire, the legate of Innocent XI merely played a minor role. Even before that, in the negotiations for the Peace of the Pyrenees between France and Spain (1659) the Holy See was completely excluded. On the other hand, an alliance of a different kind united the Emperor and the Protestant powers of Holland and England against France, which had invaded the Palatinate in 1688. Louis XIV, all the while, was giving the appearance of furthering the aims of the Catholic Church by supporting James II of the Stuarts and then, after James's flight, making the subsequent unsuccessful Irish rebellion (1690) an object of his political calculations (Chap. 12). The Pope was not officially represented at the Peace of Rijswijk (1697). "The Rijswijk Clause," stipulating that Catholic towns, whenever they came under Protestant dominion, would have to be tolerated, continued to be a recurring problem given the subsequent shifts in the balance of power. This was the case in the Peace of Utrecht (1713) and Rastatt (1714), in the Spanish War of Succession and again during Prussia's expansion in the Silesian wars and the Polish partitions (Chap. 24).

The fact that its residual political power over the Papal States would merely serve to embarrass the Holy See is demonstrated in exemplary fashion by the Spanish War of Succession. After Innocent XII had pleaded the cause of the Bourbon candidate and Clement XI had tried in vain to stay out of the conflict, war broke out between the troops of Emperor Joseph II and those of the Pope (1708). In retrospect this is reduced to a mere momentary specter which had nothing at all to do with the dualism of the highest representatives of Catholic Christianity (Chap. 9). What was left were the disputes with the radical regalism of the Spanish Bourbons (Chap. 11). Reduced to a state of helpless neutrality, Benedict XIV had to watch the farce performed by the history of the Western Empire some fifty years before its end in the Austrian War of Succession (1740–48) between Maria Theresa and the Wittelsbachs, who by the grace of France were able to furnish an Emperor in the person of Charles VII (1742). Benedict XIV was just as impotent when Frederick II reached out for Silesia (Chap. 31). And once again the conflict was ended by an alliance between the house of Habsburg and the Protestant powers of England and Holland against France.

The fact that the rights of the Papal States were ignored in war as well as in the bargaining surrounding the conclusion of peace was the lesser of the evils in comparison to their domestic shortcomings. These could simply not be overcome, because in an era of the modern state their political structure had become anachronistic. Yet the greatest damage to the Church itself was done by the rivaling influence of the Catholic powers of France, Spain and the Habsburgs on the papal elections from one pontificate to the other. Since the time of Constantine the Great these elections, to be sure, had been more or less exposed to the varying conditions of temporal history, not least among them the rivalries of Italian families. But diplomatic moves in an age of totally secularized abolutism—regardless of the political divine right ideology of the respective rulers—largely determining the election of the highest dignitary of Catholic Christianity was a perversion of the relationship between political and eccesiastical power in the former *corpus christianum.* While there were no unworthy persons on the throne of Saint Peter in this period and, indeed, Innocent XI (1676–89) and Benedict XIV (1740–58), one as pontiff, the other as scholar, were far above average, there is reason to doubt whether the political circumstances allowed the optimal candidate to prevail in each case (Chaps. 7–9, 30–32). Closing this volume with the suppression of the Society of Jesus (1773) during the pontificate of Clement XIV, brought about by the pressure of the Catholic powers, emphasizes a characteristic feature of this period.

But even though the papacy—in accordance with the facts—does recede into the background in the organization and structure of this book, we must emphasize one achievement which was significant for all of Europe and yet often too little recognized: the diplomatic initiative and financial support of the Popes in resisting and repulsing the Turks. In 1664 when Vienna was threatened by them, Alexander VII was politically in a very weak position opposite Louis XIV. Yet he asked for the King's help and, indeed, French troops had a part in the victory on the Raab River. But this victory could not be exploited because Leopold I justifiably distrusted the subsequent attitude of Louis XIV. Clement X deserves considerable credit for the victory of John Sobieski (1673), at a time when Louis XIV was conducting his Dutch war of conquest (Chap. 7). Above all others it was his successor Innocent XI who deserves a place of honor in the history of Europe. In the face of international adversities he worked undeterred towards the alliance which brought about the successful turn of events for central eastern Europe in the Turkish War 1683–99 (Chap. 8). The fact that this decisive victory initiated the rise of the Austro-Hungarian power was the motive for Louis XIV's inconstant policy towards the Turks and his formation of a front on the Rhine which paralyzed Emperor Leopold I. Following the example of France, from where the Crusades had once emanated, Spain, the land of *reconquista,* also betrayed Prince Eugene's victory at Peterwardein (1716) when it led its fleet, financed in large part by the Pope to be used against the Turks, in an attack against the imperial possessions in Italy (Chap. 9). A final chapter in the common history of Europe which was coauthored by the papacy was ended in the last third of the eighteenth century when Turkey was on the brink of collapse: In 1763 Austria entered into a defensive alliance with Turkey against the combination formed by Prussia and Russia upon the death of Augustus III, King of Poland.

The period discussed in this volume no longer had a Catholic Europe in the sense of a universal historical subject. For this reason the present volume could discuss connections common to all of Europe only from the viewpoint of a history of the papacy, while the major accents had to be put on the presentations of the individual countries. This necessitated dividing the volume among a number of authors. A guiding topic had to be the seventeenth- and eighteenth-century established Church (Chaps. 11, 18, 24). Overlaps with the history of the papacy were unavoidable, as was a separate discussion of Gallicanism (Chap. 4), because the latter could not be separated from its close connection with the Jansenism of this period if we were to demonstrate the complexity of the prevailing situation in which Jansenists were as anti-Gallican as the papacy, which in turn condemned the theology of Jansenism. At the same time the Gallican court was playing off its anti-Jansenism politically against the papacy and its policy, leading to the revocation of the Edict of Nantes (1685) against the Calvinists. Ecclesiopolitical embarrassments were thus added to the temporal political plights of the Popes. The concept of the "established Church" must be differentiated according to the various countries as well as the progressive theories and radicalism of the canon law of the established Churches. Connected with the established Churches is their religious evaluation, for which there is no common denominator even though the factor of political secularization is undeniable. A historical judgment must take into account the prevailing contradiction between the concept of a modern state and a Church historically endowed with political freedoms as well as the tensions between an extreme episcopalism and an extreme papalism.

The episcopalism of the Church of the Empire, like Gallicanism, had its roots in the late Middle Ages. The history of the Church of the Empire within the span of this volume (Chaps. 10, 23, 26) therefore provides an especially informative view of the historical situation in which the Church had to exist for these 150 years because it was a case of a "carry-over" from the period of Otto the Great into totally different conditions. No matter how scant the political reality one may be willing to grant the imperial patriotism of the ecclesiastic princes, especially since the Emperor had made Austria conspicuous, the memory of the Empire, which can still be experienced in the residences and monasteries, is a magnificent phenomenon—sentimentality aside—if history is not merely taken to represent the history of power. But the conflicts are obvious: In spite of all the attempts at reform there were the prevailing contradictions between the strange dual structure of the ecclesiastical principality and the Tridentine program; the tensions with the papal nuncios which intensified the more the threats to the ecclesiastical states receded after the Peace of Westphalia and church reform proceeded, raising the self-assurance of the ecclesiastic princes of the Empire whose episcopalism till the middle of the eighteenth century was rooted in the religiopolitical fundament of their existence, in the loyalty to the Empire. The radically Gallican theories of Enlightenment of those regarding the canon law of the established Church did not come into the episcopalism of the Empire until the turn to Febronianism. If we add the modernization of the ecclesiastical territories in the sense of enlightened absolutism, it becomes obvious that the history of these strange institutions was approaching its end long before the general secularization in 1803, which had actually been underway since 1648.

If in view of these ecclesiastical phenomena, "overtaken" by world history and yet respectable in their persistence, we search for elements pointing to the future we encounter the history of spirituality and foremost the history of religiosity in seventeenth-century France (Chaps. 1–3,5), which was deliberately chosen to start the present volume. Corresponding to the intellectual connections, this presentation reaches back to draw a line from Pierre de Bérulle (d. 1629), the founder of the French Oratory and friend of Saint Francis de Sales (d. 1622)—both of them religious inspirers of Saint Vincent de Paul (d. 1660)—through the Basque Jean Duvergier de Hauranne, abbot of Saint-Cyran (often called by that name; d. 1643), to the leader of Jansenism in its classical time, Antoine Arnauld (d. 1694), the brother of Mother Angélique, Abbess of the Cistercian convent Port-Royal in Paris. Originally the French Augustinianism of Bérulle had nothing to do with the problem of grace which was at the center of the Augustinianism of Cornelius Jansen (d. 1638) in Louvain. The basic common bond of all these religious movements and also the root of Blaise Pascal's (d. 1662) involvement on the side of Port-Royal was their protest against a purely political ecclesiasticism of the ruling segment and the search for a new Christocentric piety. Precisely this protest provoked not only the reaction of the political power structure—although one should not argue that Church and state acted in concert in the brutal destruction of the convent of Port-Royal, given the complex motivation for it—but also led to a politicization of Jansenism, noticeable especially in its expansion abroad in Italy (Chap. 28) and the Empire (Chaps. 23–24). It may well be called a tragedy of church history that the religious energies, engendered with such great promise in seventeenth-century France were consumed in the eighteenth century by the Jansenist controversy—a battle fought on the wrong fronts. A universal history of piety, yet to be written, which would make up for the lead of French research on this subject, will have to point out very heterogeneous currents, decisively influenced by the Baroque and Enlightenment (Chap. 29).

The history of Anglican spirituality and its remarkable connections with the French continent (Chap. 22) and German pietism (Chap. 28), which in many respects had parallels to Jansenism, shows that there was in the seventeenth and eighteenth century a sort of common search for a Christian answer to the modern world, regardless of all the denominational and especially ecclesiological differences. The different development in the Russian Orthodox Church (Chap. 13) is exemplified by the fate of Patriarch Nikon (1652–66). His church reforms after the Greek model provoked resistance within the clergy and, on the other hand, his attempts to make the Russian Church independent of the state made the tsar remove him from his office. The joint resistance of the Old Believers and the patriarchal Church against Peter the Great (1682–1725) and his policy of Europeanizing Russia failed. The persecution of the Old Believers had serious consequences especially for the monastic system in Russia. The year 1700 marked the end of the independent patriarchate.

With some few exceptions the systematic theology of the period was merely heir to previous achievements (Chaps. 6, 28). It established no contact with the intellectual movements of its time, either Christian spirituality or the Enlightenment. This was essentially the case in all the denominations. A few notable exceptions were the attempt by the Oratorian Malebranche (d. 1715) to combine Descartes with Augustinianism and the search by Protestant physicotheologists to achieve a concordance with the natural sciences. The theology of Wolff was an unproductive adaptation and the extreme rationalism in the theology of the late eighteenth century the initial step towards surrender. Except for the contemporary accentuation of moral and pastoral theology the main concentration was on historical theology, for Catholicism primarily in France (Chap. 6) and Italy (Chap. 28), for Protestantism in Germany (Chap. 28) where the church history by L. Mosheim also started the exclusion of this discipline from the field of theology. The assertion that this period marked the beginning of a golden age of historical theology is worth considering in connection with a well-known statement by Hegel even if one does not share the dogmatic objections over which that field of research had to prevail.

The fate of the Catholic Church in territories under non-Catholic rule, in England and Ireland (Chap. 12), in Russia (Chaps. 14 and 25), and in Prussia after its annexations corresponded as much as the eviction of Protestants from Salzburg (1731–32) to the conditions of a time which was still struggling to reach a state of practical toleration. The efforts towards an ecclesiastic reunification in France (Chap. 4) and in the Empire (Chap. 27) took place partly under the sign of toleration (like the latter they were threatened by the danger of indifferentism) and partly under the sign of politics. But at the same time they were a first sign of religious reason which was ultimately promoted by the Enlightenment.

The history of the missions was deliberately placed in the middle of the volume (Chaps. 15, 16, 17) since it provides an essential indication of the historical situation of the Church, within and without, during the different periods. The fact that the royal missionary patronages became increasingly problematic was an outgrowth of absolutism. In spite of its regression in the seventeenth and eighteenth century, ultimately caused by the history of the European states, the mission work received a new impetus thanks to the initiative of the religious orders, the Propaganda and the seminars of the Paris Foreign Mission Society (founded in 1660). The farsightedness of the Propaganda was manifested by its emphasis on the education of a native clergy and its efforts to depoliticize the missions. The jailing of Propaganda missionaries by the *Padroado* inquisition in Goa corresponds to the overall image of this period of established Churches. The lack of coordination with the Church, as in the relationship of the secular and regular clergy or in the undelineated juxtaposition of the Propaganda and the *Padroado* missionaries, was distressing. The differentiation of the rites issue, attempted in this volume, may contribute towards a reevaluation of judgments too hastily made.

In an attempt to characterize this century and a half of the Church in spite of the many different and contradictory elements one can perhaps call it a period of transition, from a Church which—despite the schism in the sixteenth century—existed in a society seeing itself as a *corpus christianum,* to one which was forced to reduce itself more and more unto itself. The difficulty of this process was manifest in all the vital areas of the Church, in its adherence to outmoded positions as well as its helplessness against the forces of a new age. The French Revolution which initiated the nineteenth century aggravated these problems. Contrary to the original design they will be discussed in Volume VII.

The contributions in this volume have deliberately refrained from any references to the present Church. But the scientist who makes use of them and the readers of whom we hope to have many will discover without any effort that the Church's past even if one would like to cast it off will inevitably affect the present and the future. The contributors and editors of this volume also hope to provide a contribution to overcoming the present crisis of the Church.

Hubert Jedin
Oskar Köhler
Wolfgang Müller

LIST OF ABBREVIATIONS

AAM *Abhandlungen der Bayerischen Akademie der Wissenschaften.* Phil.-hist. Klasse, Munich 1835ff.

AAS *Acta Apostolicae Sedis,* Rome 1909ff.

AAug *Analecta Augustiniana,* Rome 1905ff.

AcLinceiMem. *Atti di Accademia nazionale dei Lincei,* Rome.

AcModena *Atti e memorie della Accademia di scienze, lettere e arti,* Modena.

AcTorino *Atti di Accademia di scienze di Torino,* Turin 1865ff.

AE *Analecta ecclesiastica, presbyterorum s. Ludovici de Urbe curis edita,* Rome 1893–1911.

AElsKG *Archiv für elsässische Kirchengeschichte,* Gesellschaft für elsässische Kirchengeschichte, ed. J. Brauner, Rixheim im Oberelsaß 1926ff.; 1946ff., ed. A.M. Burg, Strasbourg

AFrH *Archivum Franciscanum Historicum,* Florence 1908ff.

AHPont *Archivum Historiae Pontificiae,* Rome 1963ff.

AHSI *Archivum historicum Societatis Iesu,* Rome 1932ff.

AHVNrh *Annalen des Historischen Vereins für den Niederrhein, insbesondere das alte Erzbistum Köln,* Cologne 1855ff.

AkathKR *Archiv für Katholisches Kirchenrecht,* (Innsbruck) Mainz 1857ff.

AKG *Archiv für Kulturgeschichte,* (Leipzig) Münster and Cologne 1903ff.

ALW *Archiv für Liturgiewissenschaft* (previously: *JLW*), Regensburg 1950ff.

AMrhKG *Archiv für mittelrheinische Kirchengeschichte,* Speyer 1949ff.

AnGr *Analecta Gregoriana cura Pontificiae Universitatis Gregorianae edita,* Rome 1930ff.

Annales E.S.C. *Annales: Économies, sociétés, civilisations,* Paris 1946ff.

Anthropos *Anthropos. Internationale Zeitschrift für Völker- und Sprachenkunde,* Mödling 1906ff.

Antonianum *Antonianum,* Rome 1926ff.

AÖG *Archiv für österreichische Geschichte,* Vienna 1865ff.

Aportes *Aportes. Revista de estudios latinoamericanos,* Paris 1966f.

APraem *Analecta Praemonstratensia,* Tongerloo 1925ff.

ArSKG *Archiv für schlesische Kirchengeschichte,* ed. K. Engelbert, I–VI, Breslau 1936–41; VIIff., Hildesheim 1496ff.

ASRomana *Archivio della Reale Scoietà Romana di Storia Patria,* Rome 1878–1934 (1935: *ADRomana*).

Astraín A. Astraín, *Historia de la Compañía de Jesús en la Asistencia de España* I–VII, Madrid 1902–25.

Augustiniana   *Augustiniana. Tijdschrift vor de studie van Sint Augustinus en de Augustijnenorde*, Louvain 1951ff.

BAE   *Biblioteca de Autores Españoles*, Madrid 1846ff.
BÉCh   *Bibliothèque de l'École des Chartes*, Paris 1839ff.
BLE   *Bulletin de littérature ecclésiastique*, Toulouse 1899ff.
BullRom   *Bullarium, Diplomatum et Privilegiorum Romanorum Pontificum*, ed. G. Tomassetti et al., Turin 1857ff.

Catholicisme   *Catholicisme. Hier—Aujourd'hui—Demain*, ed. G. Jacquemet, Paris 1948ff.
CH   *Church History*, New York and Chicago 1932ff.
Ciaconius   A. Ciaconius, *Vitae et res gestae Pontificum Romanorum et S.R.E. Cardinalium*, 2 vols., Rome 1601f., completed by F. Cabrera Morales; 1630 ibid., continued to Clement VIII by A. Victorelli; 1677 ibid., 4 vols., continued to Clement IX by A. Oldoini; 1751 ibid., 6 vols., continued to Clement XII by Guarnacci; Vol. 7 ibid., 1787.
Cîteaux   *Cîteaux. Commentarii cistercienses*, Westmalle (Belg.) 1950ff.
CivCatt   *La Civiltà Cattolica*, Rome 1850ff. (1871–87 Florence).
CollFr   *Collectanea Franciscana*, Rome 1931ff.

D   H. Denzinger and A. Schönmetzer, *Enchiridion Symbolorum, Definitionum et Declarationum de rebus fidei et morum*, Freiburg i. Br. 1967.
DHGE   *Dictionnaire d'histoire et de géographie ecclésiastiques*, ed. Baudrillart, et al. Paris 1912ff.
DSAM   *Dictionnaire de Spiritualité ascétique et mystique. Doctrine et Histoire*, ed. M. Viller, Paris 1932ff.
DThC   *Dictionnaire de théologie catholique*, ed. A. Vacant and E. Mangenot, continued by É. Amann, Paris 1930ff.
DZKR   *Deutsche Zeitschrift für Kirchenrecht*, Tübingen 1861–1917.

ED   *Euntes docete* (*Commentaria urbana*), Rome 1948ff.
ÉO   *Échos d'Orient*, Paris 1897ff.
Études   *Études*, Paris 1856ff. (until 1896: *Études religieuses*)

FDG   *Forschungen zur Deutschen Geschichte*, 26 vols., Göttingen 1860–86.
Feine *RG*   H. E. Feine, *Kirchliche Rechtsgeschichte* I: *Die katholische Kirche*, Cologne and Graz 1964.
FreibDiözArch   *Freiburger Diözesan-Archiv*, Freiburg i. Br. 1865ff.

Gebhardt-Grundmann   B. Gebhardt, *Handbuch der deutschen Geschichte*, 8th printing, ed. H. Grundmann, Stuttgart, I, 1954; II, 1955; III, 1960.
GGA   *Göttingische Gelehrte Anzeigen*, Berlin 1738ff.
Gr   *Gregorianum*, Rome 1920ff.
Grabmann   G. M. Grabmann, *Die Gerschichte der katholischen Theologie seit dem Ausgang der Väterzeit*, Freiburg i. Br. 1933.
GWU   *Geschichte in Wissenschaft und Unterricht. Zeitschrift des Verbandes der Geschichtslehrer Deutschlands*, Stuttgart 1950ff.

Heimbucher   M. Heimbucher, *Die Orden und Kongregationen der katholischen Kirche*, 3 vols., Paderborn 1907–8; 1932–34 ibid., 2 vols.

HH.ST.A. *Wien   Haus-, Hof-und Staatsarchiv Wien* (Vienna).

Hinschius   P. Hinschius, *Das Kirchenrecht der Katholiken und Protestanten in Deutschland*, 6 vols., Berlin 1869–97.

Hisp. Am. Hist. Rev.   *Hispanic American Historical Review*, Durham 1918ff.

HJ   *Historisches Jahrbuch der Görres-Gesellschaft* (Cologne 1880ff.), Munich 1950ff.

Hochland   *Hochland*, Munich 1903ff.

HPBl   *Historisch-politische Blätter für das katholische Deutschland*, ed. F. Binder and G. Jochner, 171 vols., Munich 1838–1923.

Hurter   H. Hurter, *Nomenclator literarius theologiae catholicae*, 6 vols., Innsbruck 1903–13; I, 1926, ed. F. Pangerl.

HZ   *Historische Zeitschrift*, Munich 1859ff.

IKZ   *Internationale Kirchliche Zeitschrift*, Berne 1911ff.

IPO   *Instrumentum Pacis Osnabrugense et Monasteriense.*

Irénikon   *Irénikon*, Amay-Chevetogne 1926ff.

JGO   *Jahrbücher für die Geschichte Osteuropas*, Munich 1953ff.

JKölGV   *Jahrbuch des Kölnischen Geschichtsvereins*, Cologne 1912–41, 1950ff.

JLW   *Jahrbuch für Liturgiewissenschaft*, Münster 1921–41 (now: *ALW*).

Jugie   M. Jugie, *Theologia dogmatica Christianorum orientalium ab ecclesia catholica dissidentium* I–V Paris 1926–35.

KRA   *Kirchenrechtliche Abhandlungen*, founded by U. Stutz, Stuttgart 1902ff. (so far 118 vols.).

Kyrios   *Kyrios. Vierteljahresschrift für Kirchen- und Geistesgeschichte Osteuropas*, Berlin 1960ff.

LJ   *Liturgisches Jahrbuch*, Münster 1951ff.

LThK   *Lexikon für Theologie und Kirche*, Freiburg 1957ff.

Maaß   F. Maaß, *Der Josephinismus. Quellen zu seiner Geschichte in Österreich* I–IV, Wien 1951ff. (*Fontes rerum Austriacarum* II/71–74).

MAH   *Mélanges d'archelologie et d'histoire*, Paris 1880ff.

Mansi   J. D. Mansi, *Sacrorum conciliorum nova et amplissima collectio*, 31 vols., Florence and Venice 1757–98; reprint and continuation, ed. L. Petit and J. B. Martin, 60 vols.; Paris 1899–1927.

MCom   *Miscelánea Comillesa*, Comillas/Santander 1943ff.

MF   *Miscellanea francescana*, Rome 1886ff.

MH   *Missionalia Hispanica*

Mid-America   *Mid-America. An Historical Review*, Chicago 1918ff.

MIÖG   *Mitteilungen des Instituts für österreichische Geschichtsforschung*, (Innsbruck) Graz-Cologne 1880ff.

MiscMercati *Miscellanea Giovanni Mercati*, 6 vols., Rome 1946.

Monumenta Nipponica   *Monumenta Nipponica. Studies on Japanese culture past and present*, Tokyo 1938ff.

MÖSTA   *Mitteilungen des Österreichischen Staatsarchivs*, Vienna 1948ff.

MthSt(H)   *Münchener theologische Studien*, ed F. X. Seppelt, J. Pascher, and K. Mörsdorf, Historical Section, Munich 1950ff.

MThZ   *Münchener Theologische Zeitschrift*, Munich 1950ff.

NDB	*Neue Deutsche Biographie,* Berlin 1953ff.
NZM	*Neue Zeitschrift für Missionswissenschaft,* Beckenried 1945ff.
Orbis	*Orbis. Bulletin international de documentation linguistique,* Louvain 1952ff.
OrChr	*Oriens Christianus,* (Leipzig) Wiesbaden 1901ff.
OrChrA	*Orientalia Christiana* (Analecta), Rome (1923–34: *Orientalia Christiana;* 1935ff.; *Orientalia Christiana Analecta*).
OrChrP	*Orientalia Christiana periodica,* Rome 1935ff.
OstKSt	*Ostkirchliche Studien,* Würzburg 1951ff.
Pastor	L. v. Pastor, *Geschichte der Päpste seit dem Ausgang des Mittelalters,* 16 vols., Freiburg i. Br. 1885ff.
QFIAB	*Quellen und Forschungen aus italienischen Archiven und Bibliotheken,* Rome 1897ff.
Quétif	J. Quétif and J. Echard, *Scriptores Ordinis Praedicatorum,* 2 vols., Paris 1719–21; 3 suppl. vols., 1721–23; continued by R. Coulon, Paris 1909ff.
RAM	*Revue d'ascétique et de mystique,* Toulouse 1920ff.
RET	*Revista Española de teología,* Madrid 1941ff.
Rev. Arch. Bibl. y Museos	*Revista de Archivos, Bibliotecas y Museos,* Madrid 1871ff.
RevÉAug	*Revue des Études Augustiniennes* (cont. of: *L'Année Théologique Augustinienne*), Paris 1955ff.
RevSR	*Revue des Sciences Religieuses,* Strasbourg 1921ff.
RF	*Razón y Fe,* Madrid 1901ff.
RGG	*Die Religion in Geschichte und Gegenwart,* Tübingen 1909–13; 1927–32; 1956ff.
RH	*Revue historique,* Paris 1876ff.
RHE	*Revue d'histoire ecclésiastique,* Louvain 1900ff.
RHEF	*Revue d'histoire de l'Église de France,* Paris 1910ff.
RHM	*Revue d'histoire des missions,* Paris 1924ff.
RHR	*Revue de l'histoire des religions,* Paris 1880ff.
RömHM	*Römische Historische Mitteilungen,* Graz and Cologne 1958ff.
RQ	*Römische Quartalschrift für christliche Altertumskunde und für Kirchengeschichte,* Freiburg i. Br. 1887ff.
RQH	*Revue des questions historiques,* Paris 1866f.
RSIt	*Rivista storica Italiana,* Naples 1884ff.
RSR	*Recherches de science religieuse,* Paris 1910ff.
RSTI	*Rivista di storia della chiesa in Italia,* Rome 1947ff.
Saeculum	*Saeculum. Jahrbuch für Universalgeschichte,* Freiburg i. Br. 1950ff.
SAW	*Sitzungsberichte der* (from 225, 1, 1947: *Österreichischen*) *Akademie der Wissenschaften in Wien,* Vienna 1831ff.
Schnabel G	F. Schnabel, *Deutsche Geschichte im 19. Jahrhundert* I, Freiburg i. Br. 1948; II, 1949; III, 1954; IV, 1955.
SEER	*The Slavonic and East European Review,* London 1922.
Seppelt-Schwaiger	F. X. Seppelt, *Geschichte der Päpste von den Anfängen bis zur Mitte des 20. Jahrhunderts* I, II, IV, V, Leipzig 1931–41; I, Munich 1954; II, ibid. 1955; III, ibid. 1956; IV, ibid. 1957; V, ibid. 1959.
SM	*Studien und Mitteilungen aus dem Benediktiner- und Zisterzienserorden bzw.*

zur Geschichte des Benediktinerordens und seiner Zweige, Munich 1880ff. (1911ff., n.s.).

SPM   *Sacrum Poloniae Millennium,* Rome 1954ff.

Stamer   L. Stamer, *Kirchengeschichte der Pfalz* I, Speyer 1936; II, 1949; III, 1 1955.

StdZ   *Stimmen der Zeit* (prior to 1914: *Stimmen aus Maria-Laach*), Freiburg i. Br. 1871ff.

StG   *Studia Gratiana,* ed. J. Forchielli and A. M. Stickler, I–III, Bologna 1953ff.

StL   *Staatslexikon,* ed. H. Sacher, Freiburg i. Br. 1926–32 (*StL:* ibid. 1957ff.).

StMis   *Studia Missionalia,* Rome 1943ff.

Streit   *Bibliotheca Missionum,* founded by R. Streit, continued by J. Dindinger, (Münster, Aachen) Freiburg i. Br. 1916ff. (to 1968: 26 vols.).

StudFr   *Studi francescani,* Arezzo-Florence 1903ff.

ThGl   *Theologie und Glaube,* Paderborn 1909ff.

ThLZ   *Theologische Literaturzeitung,* Leipzig 1878ff.

ThQ   *Theologische Quartalschrift,* Tübingen 1819ff.; Stuttgart 1946ff.

ThSt   *Theological Studies,* Baltimore 1940ff.

Tr   *Traditio,* New York 1943ff.

TThZ   *Trierer Theologische Zeitschrift* (to 1944: *Pastor Bonus*), Trier 1888ff.

Veit-Lenhart   L. A. Veit and L. Lenhart, *Kirche und Volksfrömmigkeit im Zeitalter des Barock,* Freiburg i. Br. 1956.

Werner   K. Werner, *Geschichte der katholischen Theologie. Seit dem Trienter Konzil bis zur Gegenwart,* Munich and Leipzig 1889 (= *Geschichte der Wissenschaften in Deutschland.* (Modern Times, Vol. 6).

WZ   *Westfälische Zeitschrift. Zeitschrift für vaterländische Geschichte,* Münster 1838ff.

Zagaglia   *Zagaglia. Rassegna di scienze, lettere ed arti,* Lecce 1959ff.

ZBLG   *Zeitschrift für Bayerische Landesgeschichte,* Munich 1928ff.

ZGObrh   *Zeitschrift für die Geschichte des Oberrheins,* Karlsruhe 1851ff.

ZHTh   *Zeitschrift für die historische Theologie,* 45 vols., Leipzig-Gotha 1832–75.

ZKG   *Zeitschrift für Kirchengeschichte,* (Gotha) Stuttgart 1876ff.

ZMR   *Zeitschrift für Missionswissenschaft und Religionswissenschaft* 34 ff., Münster 1950ff. (*Zeitschrift für Missionswissenschaft* 1–17, ibid. 1911–27; *Zeitschrift für Missionswissenschaft und Religionswissenschaft* 18–25, ibid. 1928–35; *Zeitschrift für Missionswissenschaft* 26–27, ibid. 1935–37; *Missionswissenschaft und Religionswissenschaft* 28–33, ibid. 1938–41, 1947–49).

ZRGG   *Zeitschrift für Religions- und Geistesgeschichte,* Marburg 1948ff.

ZSavRGgerm   *Zeitschrift der Savigny-Stiftung für Rechtsgeschichte,* Germanistische Abteilung, Weimar 1863ff.

ZSavRGkan   *Zeitschrift der Savigny-Stiftung für Rechtsgeschichte,* Kanonistische Abteilung, Weimar 1911ff.

ZSKG   *Zeitschrift für Schweizer Kirchengeschichte,* Fribourg 1907ff.

ZSTh   *Zeitschrift für systematische Theologie,* (Gütersloh) Berlin 1923ff.

PART ONE

The Leadership Position of France

Ecclesiastical Life in France

CHAPTER 1

Christian Renewal after 1615

French Catholicism under Louis XIII

When Henry IV was assassinated on May 14, 1610, France had again become a great Catholic nation which was not only tied closely to the Roman Catholic religion, but had even begun to put religious sentiment above national considerations. Proof of this can be perceived in the unpopularity of the war against Spain prepared by Henry IV at the time of his assassination. However obscure the background of the regicide may be, religion was a definite motivating factor in Ravaillac's crime. Spain—hitherto an obstacle in the path of French expansionism—was at this time already on the decline. Under these conditions, waging war to confirm the hegemony of France would have been politically justified. Public opinion in France was nonetheless opposed to it since the most pressing obligation of the Catholic states was considered to be an alliance against the Protestant Reformation.

Although Protestantism still occupied a powerful position, it was evident that in France the Reformation had to end in failure. The conversion of Henry IV had no doubt been a mere gesture of political opportunism by a rule indifferent to the faith. But it became obvious that no Huguenot ruler could be forced upon the kingdom. Calvinism had reached its pinnacle about the year 1571. Although its outward manifestations seemed unimpaired, it was in a process of irreversible retrogression. It became a minority party and was conscious of that fact. After the religious wars the real basis for the appeal of Protestantism was the intensive religious life of many of its members, which hardly found a counterpart in the politicized Catholicism of the Holy League. Towards the end of the reign of Henry IV, however, the Reformation had lost this advantage. Endeavors by the great Catholic spiritual leaders—Francis de Sales, Benedict of Canfield, Father Coton, Bérulle, and many others—had brought about a Catholic climate whose piety and inward orientation was equal to that of the Reformed Churches. At this time, this *milieu dévot* or *parti dévot*, as it was also called, was still a compact group firmly united by common ideals revolving around the

3

triumph of Catholicism and the defeat of Protestantism. On the other hand, the Protestants found themselves more and more hampered by becoming socially disadvantaged. Following the King's example, other conversions had taken place among the aristocracy and the upper bourgeosie—with equal lack of sincerity. Now it was obvious that being Catholic would henceforth be an indispensable prerequisite for achieving high positions. For a long time Sully was to be the last Protestant minister of France and the death of Henry IV forced him to resign, albeit not until he had calmly amassed a fortune. For quite some time France, along with the rest of Europe, was far from reaching the maturity needed for a tolerant attitude.[1] The attitude of public opinion toward the Edict of Nantes was symptomatic in this regard. No one perceived in it a laudable attempt at achieving religious peace. The Catholics considered it a concession required by necessity, a despicable and offensive infringement on the immutable rights of the true religion, while the Protestants saw it as something fundamentally too unjust and precarious to be permanent. Although the two blocs had for the time being abandoned the violence of the religious wars, beneath the surface the antagonism remained unchanged. Given another opportunity, it could break out into open warfare once again.

Materially speaking, the situation of the Church steadily improved under the reign of Henry IV. Of course not all the devastation caused by the religious wars could be repaired. Even today more than a few abbeys and parish churches are still in ruins. The possessions of the Church however had regenerated very quickly and—since their parts by definition cannot be lost—increased steadily. In a memorandum written around 1625 Richelieu estimated that one-third of the national property was in the hands of the clergy.[2] This financial aspect was preeminent in the eyes of many Catholics. This was true especially for members of high society who felt and advocated quite openly that the possessions of the Church should be used to make up for the insufficiencies of family fortune. As late as 1647, President Molé—against the express advice of Vincent de Paul—had his patently incompetent son invested as bishop of Bayeux in order to "shield him from any and all want," and he added that his son could always compensate for his incompetence by calling upon capable advisers. The same view was held by the lower class, for whom the priesthood represented the only possibility for social advancement: the father of Vincent de Paul had sold a pair of oxen to finance his son's education, and the son himself was already received by the Queen. As a matter of fact, the sees continued to be the appanage

[1] J. Leclerc, *Toleration and the Reformation,* 2 vols. (New York 1960): contains important general views of the beginnings of the seventeenth century.
[2] G. d'Avenel, *Richelieu et la monarchie absolue* (Paris 1884–90), III, 277.

of the aristocracy. Although Richelieu appointed a few bishops from among members of the upper bourgeoisie, he no doubt did so hoping they would submit to him more readily than the members of the high aristocracy. The distribution of the social origin of the bishops was not broadened appreciably until Louis XIV and even then the richest dioceses were reserved for the very prominent families. But the selection of the bishops was always made within the circle of the royal court. A cleric unknown at the court had no chance to rise to the bishopric. Many great families moreover acted as if an episcopate once possessed were a kind of inheritance which was to be retained at any price by means of a royal warrant authorizing it to be handed on from uncle to nephew. The bishopric of Reims was thus perpetuated as a regular de Guise dynasty and in the period from 1568 to 1662 four members of the Gondi family held the office of bishop of Paris. Philippe de Gondi, General of the Galleys, friend of Vincent de Paul and later on an Oratorian, developed a personal interest in this matter in order to secure for his son Paul, who later became Cardinal de Retz and who called himself "possibly the least ecclesiastical soul in the universe,"[3] the succession to the bishopric of his uncle. The nominations of bishops were made by the King and were generally decided by the *Conseil de Conscience*, but even Vincent de Paul, a member of this council from 1643 to 1652, could not prevent some scandalous appointments, such as that of Beaumanoir de Lavardin, bishop of Mans (1684), who was held to be a complete unbeliever and probably justifiably so. There were indeed very distinct differences in the quality of individual appointees. The first few bishops dedicated to reforms and a sense of duty are found under Louis XIII—yet they were exceptions. Many prelates continued their propensities and interests in contradiction with their priestly role. Numerous bishops remained in the service of the court or pursued literature, warfare or diplomacy and never actually set foot in their respective dioceses.

The condition of the parish clergy as well had hardly improved since the religious wars. The root cause for this stagnation lay in the almost total lack of education of the clergymen. In France, the pertinent regulations established by the Council of Trent remained largely unimplemented and the few timid attempts at establishing seminaries undertaken after 1610 extended to only a small number of persons. For the purpose of ordination, most bishops were satisfied with mere rudimentary knowledge and only a few demanded even as much as a few days of spiritual retreat. Since the bishops rarely resided in their dioceses, the candidates for priesthood had themselves—if possible with the written consent of the appropriate bishop—ordained by another bishop. This

---

[3] M. Allem, ed., *J. F. de Gondi, Cardinal de Retz, Mémories.* La Pléiade (Paris 1956), 3.

situation was even further aggravated by the innumerable bishops *in partibus* who were roaming the realm ordaining any and everyone. The deplorable consequences of such practices are not surprising. In 1643 an archdeacon of Bourges ascertained that many priests did not know Latin, several could hardly read and some were incapable of administering the Holy Sacraments validly and did not even know the words of absolution. Concubinage and drunkenness among the clergy were widespread and in some dioceses were looked upon as common practice. Besides their clerical duties many priests held common jobs and frequented taverns. In certain areas they frequently practiced exorcism.[4] Most of them never preached a sermon, no longer taught catechism and abandoned their churches to a state of scandalous neglect and squalor. As late as 1660, the archdeacon of Evreux, Henri-Marie Boudon, was horrified at the condition of the tabernacles and ciboria he saw. But these shortcomings were rarely ever remedied. Intervention was very difficult because bishops could make appointments in only a few parishes of their diocese since most of them were controlled by abbeys or by lay patronage. Another impediment was the canonical regulation requiring three corresponding verdicts against an accused priest before he could be prosecuted, a situation that could be indefinitely extended. Clerics who were forced to leave their locality because of extremely serious scandals usually sought to hide out in Paris, which was teeming with priests who managed to evade the police and some of whom made their livelihood in transactions which were in flagrant contradiction to their vocation.

Conditions among the members of religious orders were hardly better, although here sporadic attempts at reform had been introduced since the end of the sixteenth century and especially under Henry IV. By and by, the members of religious orders had no doubt relinquished their military habits of the time of the Holy League, but their morals had hardly improved. In fact, all orders were in need of reform, with the exception of the Carthusians, who at this time were relatively numerous and had their establishments in close proximity to the towns. They had retained their traditional obligations; their austerity impressed the masses and even led to conversions. And yet the image of the other orders should not be painted entirely black. To be sure, even now there were frequent and blatant scandals. In 1609 the parliament of Toulouse had to have the Augustinian superior Burdeu executed since he had been convicted as an accessory in the killing of the husband of his mistress, Violante du Chastel.[5] At the same time, a sister of the famous Belle

---

[4] Especially characteristic cases were investigated by J. Bernou, *La chasse aux sorciers dans le Labourd* (Agen 1897).

[5] See A. Praviel, *Violante et ses amants* (Paris 1934).

Gabrielle, mistress of Henry IV, was the abbess of the Cistercian nuns of Maubuisson. She was Angélique d'Estrées, who had twelve children by twelve different fathers. But public opinion proved less and less prepared to accept these unbelievable conditions. The court, influenced by the *parti dévot*, began to deal with these matters and civil authorities intervened in order to eliminate the most flagrant abuses. But this happened only in exceptional cases. On the whole the monasteries deteriorated into physical and moral mediocrity; they hardly even kept up the appearance of monastic seclusion, which was to them merely a distant memory, for now outsiders came and went freely and casually. In 1614 at the occasion of the investiture of Charles Faure, who later reformed the Genovevians, the canons of Saint Vincent-de-Senlis received all the participants, even the women, in the refectory, where there was dancing. The young abbess of Port-Royal, Angélique Arnauld, intent on reform, had triggered quite a scandal on 25 September 1609 on the occasion of the famous "day of the grating" when she refused even her own family admission to the convent.[6] Often the vow of poverty existed in theory only; monks and nuns usually established their own financial resources aiming thereby to alleviate the deficiencies of a life which all too often was characterized by a distressing degree of penury.

This decadence which had become more and more noticeable since the end of the Middle Ages had its foremost cause—common to both men and women—in the quality of the vocation or rather in the lack of a true vocation. The number of those entering of their own accord was very small. The family commonly made the decision to enter their children in a monastery—and usually for financial considerations. Excess children who for lack of necessary family means could not be put into suitable positions, the later-born left without an inheritance, those unable to bear arms, girls who could not be given a dowry, all of them were simply pushed off on the Church. Girls especially were sent into convents at an irresponsibly young age. In 1599, the God-fearing Attorney General Simon Marion, grandfather of the famous Mother Angélique Arnauld, without hesitation had two of his granddaughters take the veil at seven and five years of age respectively. To make his decision more palatable to them he promised to make them abbesses. He kept his promise in as much as Angélique became abbess of Port-Royal at the age of eleven.

Another practice, but one that affected monasteries only, contributed to the mediocrity of the monastic environment. This was the fairly common custom of the commendam, which originated in France in the thirteenth century and was generally applied after the Concordat of

---

[6] See L. Cognet, *La réforme de Port-Royal* (Paris 1950), 114–21.

1516. The procedure consisted of separating the clerical functions of an ecclesiastical office from the secular income connected with it. The office was granted to a titular who was barred by canon law from executing its office and who was therefore dependent upon another person who had the necessary authority. The holder of the benefice, however, kept the greater part of the income and only gave the substitute and his subordinates a barely sufficient part, the *portio congrua*. In time, the beneficiary became accustomed to curtailing it even more so that the designation ultimately came to mean a "restricted and insufficient part." This practice had rendered the enormous properties of the Church back into the hands of the monarchy. The Kings used them unscrupulously for the purpose of rewarding loyal servants and supporting artists and literati: Sully, although a Protestant, was titular of four abbeys. When Louis XIII began his reign, some of the abuses of the commendam had disappeared; the system was no longer applied to bishoprics, but only to monasteries. And yet virtually all monasteries and priories were benefices and many of their titulars were mere tonsured people less than twenty years of age. Richelieu himself continued to reward the musicians of his orchestra with abbeys and priories. Indeed, up until the Revolution most bishops supplemented the income of their bishoprics by the proceeds from one or more abbeys. Bossuet added the abbey of Saint-Lucien-lès-Beauvais to his bishopric of Meaux, and Fénelon was accused of zealotry upon his appointment to the see of Cambrai when he relinquished his abbey of Saint Valéry at Caux. Even among the most conscientious clerics there were few who did not hold benefices. Duvergier de Hauranne remarked that the modest abbey of Saint-Cyran in Poitou which he had received in 1620 was his "disgrace";[7] yet he kept it till he died. Some, like the famous Philippe de Gamaches, professor at the Sorbonne, and even J.-J. Olier, the founder of the Society of the Priests of Saint Sulpice, practiced the accumulation of benefices forbidden by canon law. In most cases the titulars kept at least two-thirds of their incomes for themselves and many attempted to increase their portion by reducing the number of monks. They were therefore not at all inclined towards initiating any sort of reform or even to tolerating one that would have resulted in lowering their income. It was a rare titular, such as Barcos, the nephew of Saint-Cyran, who withdrew to his abbey in order to reform it. Even rarer were those who, like the famous Rancé, became titular abbot of their own abbey.

Overall the situation was further impaired by unpleasant differences of opinion between the secular clergy and the orders. The latter enjoyed the privilege of exemption and therefore could almost completely

[7] See L. Cognet, "La jeunesse d'Antoine Singlin," *Chroniques de Port-Royal* (1953), 10.

evade the jurisdiction of the bishops. This had a twofold disadvantage. For one, it caused reform bishops who were becoming more numerous in the course of the century to encounter insurmountable obstacles, which frustrated their attempts at abolishing certain scandalous conditions and enabled the large abbeys, including those of nuns, brazenly to defy those bishops. As late as 1690, for example, Bossuet was embroiled in a long and dramatic conflict with the abbess of Jouarre, Henriette de Lorraine.[8] In addition, some ardent and influential congregations used their status of exemption to establish a sort of parallel clergy. They did this by attracting to their chapels a great number of visitors who—frequently members of aristocratic families—deserted their own parish churches. This held true especially for the Jesuits and Capuchins. The diocesan and provincial synods attempted to alleviate this problem by obliging the faithful to attend Mass at their parish churches on a certain number of Sundays: the Council of Bordeaux, for instance, prescribed one Sunday in three (1582).[9] But these measures had virtually no success and worse, they often led to violent incidents such as the one in the spring of 1620, when the pugnacious bishop of Poitiers, La Rocheposay, collided with the Jesuits of that town. So it is not surprising that even the best representatives of the episcopate were somewhat reluctant to oppose the orders whose good qualities they otherwise valued. One of the most prominent champions of this cause was Jean-Pierre Camus (1584–1652), bishop of Belley, who was a friend of Francis de Sales and an extremely prolific spiritual writer.[10] Again and again he polemicized against the demands of the orders and was not afraid to compose works of unusual vehemence such as his polemic *Rabat-joie du triomphe monastique* (1634). At first he was encouraged by Francis de Sales, who wrote to him on 24 August 1614: "It redounds to the honor of God that our episcopal order be recognized as such and that this moss that constitutes exemption be torn from the tree of the Church on which it has inflicted such damage, as we have seen." Later, in 1632, Saint-Cyran also joined the fray. Under the pseudonym Petrus Aurelius he emphatically defended the rights of the hierarchy in a number of pamphlets which received official character, so to speak, by being approved by the *Assemblées du Clergé*. To be sure, the situation subsequently calmed down a bit, but difficulties of this sort nonetheless surfaced throughout the *ancien régime*.

Negative aspects notwithstanding, French Catholicism had embarked on its renewal (see Chap. 5) with the beginning of the reign of

[8] See Y. Chaussy, *Jouarre et Bossuet: L'abbaye royale de Jouarre* (Paris 1961), 247–94.
[9] Text in: J. Godefroy, *Le Mercure Jésuite* (Geneva 1630–31), I, 25.
[10] See F. Boulas, *Un ami de saint François de Sales, Camus évêque de Belley* (Lyon 1878); R. Heurtevent, "Camus," *DSAM* 2, 62–73.

Louis XIII. The *milieu dévot* which had originated with the Holy League was an extremely eager and active Catholic group. Its central figure was a mystic from the highest level of society, Mme Acarie.[11] In her circle one could at times encounter a bishop in the person of Francis de Sales, more frequently such secular priests as Bérulle[12] and Gallement, or professors at the Sorbonne such as Duval,[13] Jesuits like P. Coton, father confessor to the King, Capuchin monks such as Benedict of Canfield,[14] Carthusians such as Dom Beaucousin, and ladies of high society including Mme de Sainte-Beuve or Mme de Maignelay, sister of Gondi. At first this group was primarily concerned with monastic reforms which had actually had definite results in only two convents, the Benedictine convent of Montmartre (1598) and that of the Cistercians of Port-Royal (1608). The movement subsequently encompassed other convents as well. Another effort concerned the introduction of orders from other countries, where they had already been reformed. Considerable success was achieved with the Carmelites who had been reformed in Spain by Saint Teresa: as early as 1610 the French branch of the order, founded in September 1604, had established eighteen houses and by 1630 as many as forty-six, whose members were predominantly from the aristocracy. The prioress of Paris, Madeleine de Saint-Joseph, née Fontaines-Marans, exerted an unusually strong spiritual influence upon the whole Parisian society. In 1610, through the combined efforts of Mme Acarie and Mme de Sainte-Beuve, the Ursuline order founded in 1596 in the *Comtat-Venaissin*, which had been dedicated to improving the often neglected education of young girls, was established in Paris. It developed rapidly and by the turn of the century had approximately 300 houses.[15] The male congregations fared less well with the exception of the two large orders, the Jesuits (1552) and the Capuchins (1573), introduced into France in the sixteenth century; they flourished and were able to maintain their influence in spite of all the attacks upon them. But in 1601 the *Frères de la Charité* of John of God were hard put to establish a hospital in Paris. Although the barefoot Carmelites managed to extend their order from Spain to France in 1611, they were opposed in this by the *milieu dévot*, who were afraid of their competition in directing the affairs of the Carmelites. Nevertheless Mme Acarie and her friends had an efficacious hand in a number of foundations. One of

[11] See Bruno de Jésus-Marie, *La Belle Acarie* (Paris 1942).

[12] See J. Dagens, *Bérulle et les origines de la restauration catholique* (Bruges and Paris 1952).

[13] See L. Cognet, "Duval," *DHGE* 14, 1213–16.

[14] See Optat de Veghel, *Benoît de Canfield, sa vie, sa doctrine et son influence* (Rome 1949).

[15] See Louise de Jésus, *La Vénérable Madeleine de Saint-Joseph* (Clamart 1935); Marie de Chantal Gueudré, *Histoire de l'ordre des Ursulines en France*, 3 vols. (Paris 1957–63).

the most significant was the Order of the Visitation of Holy Mary in 1610 by Francis de Sales and Jane Frances de Chantal.[16] It was initially conceived as a partially active congregation without complete claustration, but in 1618, impelled by Marquemont, archbishop of Lyon, it had to change into a contemplative order with ceremonious public vows. But this did not impede its expansion in any way: at the death of its founder (1641) the Visitation of Holy Mary had more than 80 houses. Soon the sisters of the Visitation, as had many other claustrated convents (e.g., Port-Royal), took over educational tasks. School congregations were also founded, such as the *Filles de Notre-Dame* by Jeanne de Lestonnac[17] in Bordeaux (1606), the *Soeurs de Notre-Dame de Lorraine* of Saint Peter Fourier (1618), the *Filles de la Croix*,[18] established in Paris in 1641 by Mme de Villeneuve, and many others. Later we shall talk about the congregations devoted to the nursing of the sick.

After 1610 the *milieu dévot*, despite its vitality, began to dissolve. It was gradually weakened by internal dissention and the fact that Mme Acarie, having become a Carmelite in 1614, could no longer serve as its focal point. She was, moreover, personally embroiled in the controversies concerning the leadership of the Carmelites, which Bérulle, in opposition to Duval and Mme Acarie, wanted to transfer to the French Oratory.[19] This conflict, which had initially been confined pretty much to the level of the parties involved, became public after 1618 and was intensified by the appearance of two new opponents of Bérulle: the Carmelites, who wanted to take over the direction of the whole order, and the Jesuits, who in their various apostolates feared the competition of the Oratory founded by Bérulle in 1611. All these hostilities contributed toward putting Bérulle into a difficult situation; his approach was suspect, the *milieu dévot* was undermined and its slow deterioration became inevitable.

Richelieu and the *Milieu Dévot*

At the beginning of the regency of Marie de Médicis the *milieu dévot* was highly respected. It could easily impress the not so intelligent queen, who valued the piety, probity and unselfishness of its representatives. Bérulle, who by way of his mother belonged to the Séguier family, at

[16] See E. J. Lajeunie, *Saint François de Sales,* 2 vols. (Paris 1966); H. Bremond, *Sainte Chantal* (Paris 1912).
[17] L. Entraygues, *La Bienheureuse Jeanne de Lestonnac* (Périgueux 1940).
[18] See A. de Salinis, *Mme de Villeneuve* (Paris 1918).
[19] See Mme Acarie, *Mémoire sur la fondation, le gouvernement et l'observance des Carmélites déchaussées,* 2 vols. (Rheims 1894).

the time one of the most important families of France by virtue of its position and wealth, was of course an important figure in this group. The queen's favorite, Concini, maréchal d'Ancre, willingly left all religious affairs to the *parti dévot.* He did not consider himself to have sufficient authority nor was he particularly interested in them. Because of these circumstances, Bérulle contributed considerably to advancing the career of a young cleric who had become bishop of Luçon in 1606; Armand du Plessis du Richelieu, ten years his junior and from a less distinguished family, but in whom he had discovered brilliant abilities. Ambitious and clear-sighted, Richelieu did not hesitate to seek contact with the queen mother and the *parti dévot* although later he was to turn against it. He began by flattering Bérulle and in 1612 he was one of the first to introduce the Oratory in his diocese. His widely noticed speech to the Estates-General in 1615 contained skillful encomia for Marie de Médicis, which gained him entrée to the affairs of state. In November 1616 he became minister of foreign affairs to Concini, whose assassination almost caused him to fall out of favor. That Richelieu was able to rehabilitate himself in 1619 was primarily due to the support of a member of the *parti dévot,* Sébastian Bouthilliers. Not until 1624 was he actually appointed to a first-rate position, but by that time his political ideas had fully matured and increasingly he conflicted with Bérulle and the latter's friends. In 1619, after Richelieu's brother Henry died a tragic death in a duel, Bérulle, moreover, made the somewhat naive mistake of taking Richelieu's protestations that he wanted to withdraw from politics seriously. Aggravating the relationship further was the fact that in 1621 Bérulle had a hand in Richelieu's being denied the cardinalship, which he subsequently did not receive until September 1622.

Bérulle and Richelieu indeed developed their respective political positions in totally opposite directions. Bérulle (see Chap. 5) above all else wanted the triumph of Catholicism over the Protestant heresy. Richelieu's unshakable goal was to provide the French monarchy with a firm national foundation and to insure France's hegemony in Europe— even at the price of Catholic interests. In this regard Richelieu was an heir to Philip the Fair and the French canonists. Bérulle and the *parti dévot* subordinated politics to the concerns of religion while Richelieu's position was the exact opposite. A clash between these contradictory tendencies could not be avoided for long. Gradually the supremacy of the state became Richelieu's basic argument.[20] The *parti dévot* on the other hand, reinforced by Port-Royal, demanded priority for the rights of religion over the claims of individual conscience. Richelieu's views, taking up, as they did, political ideas dating back to the Middle Ages,

---

[20] See E. Thuau, *Raison d'état et pensée politique à l'époque de Richelieu* (Paris 1966).

were without doubt reactionary, whereas those of the *parti dévot* showed the way into the eighteenth century and into the mentality of the modern era.

Before Richelieu had firmly secured his position, the contradiction between the two positions became manifest as a result of several incidents. In the conflict between the new Emperor, Ferdinand, and the Protestant Elector Palatine Friedrich V, which broke out toward the end of 1619, President Jeannin, through mediation by Bérulle and Minister Luynes, succeeded in gaining the support of the Royal Council for the Catholic faction. But the victory of the Catholics at the end of 1620 had radicalized the claims of Austria and Spain, putting France into a difficult situation. As a consequence, Richelieu was moved to criticize the policies of Luynes and of the *parti dévot* by means of several anonymous pamphlets. The controversy became even more evident on the occasion of the marriage of Henriette de France, sister of Louis XIII, to Charles I of England. Bérulle favored this marriage because through it he hoped to save what was left of Catholicism in England. Richelieu wanted it as well, but hoped to secure through it the alliance with England against Spain. But both were soon disappointed. Bérulle—even at the price of war—wanted to realize those clauses in the marriage contract which would have favored the Catholics. But Richelieu, who had scant concern for the English Catholics and was governed by ruthless realism, dropped the contractual clauses without regrets and turned towards Protestant Germany. In 1626 Richelieu disapproved of Bérulle's action at the Treaty of Madrid, in which the Valtellina problem was solved in a manner far too favorable to Spain. But Bérulle, who in 1627 had also become a cardinal, continued to exert a powerful influence on the queen mother, who had remained well-disposed towards the *parti dévot*. After the conquest of La Rochelle the latter was planning an alliance with Spain and Austria which was finally to destroy Protestantism. But in 1629 Bérulle irrevocably fell out of favor when Richelieu succeeded against Bérulle's recommendation in inducing the Royal Council to come to the aid of Charles de Nevers, Duke of Mantua, who was under siege by the Spanish at Casal. On 15 September 1629 Bérulle refused his consent to the Treaty of Susa, which in the end sanctioned an alliance against England. Just as Richelieu was about to rid himself of his adversary by dispatching him to Rome as French ambassador, Bérulle suddenly died on 2 October 1629. On the following 21 November Richelieu was appointed first minister of the state.

The death of Bérulle was a heavy blow to the *parti dévot*. Although the minister of justice, Michel de Marillac, was now the most significant person in the party, he lacked the stature that would have enabled him to take the place of the dead cardinal. A final crisis which momentarily threatened Richelieu's power ended in the *Journée des Dupes* (Day of Dupes, 12 November 1630) and the queen mother being exiled. After this, Richelieu was in a position methodically to eliminate his opponents. Marillac was arrested and died in prison on 7 August 1632; he never received a proper trial, which would have proved his innocence. His brother Louis, marshal of France, was accused of misappropriation of public funds and was beheaded on 10 May 1632.[21] But Richelieu found himself confronted by yet another opponent who was all the less vulnerable in as much as he rarely involved himself in affairs of state. He was Jean Duvergier de Hauranne (1581–1643), of Basque origin, abbot of Saint-Cyran since 1620 (see Chap. 5). He had been a brilliant university student, friend and fellow student of Cornelius Jansen from Flanders. After finishing his studies, Saint-Cyran had embarked on a career as secular cleric which had led to ties of friendship with Richelieu. In 1618, on the occasion of his ordination, Saint-Cyran had undergone a moral crisis, from which he emerged a changed person, converted to an inner life. A chance meeting around 1620 soon led to a close friendship and occasional collaboration with Bérulle. Gradually Saint-Cyran identified himself with Bérulle's point of view and began to express his position against the latter's opponents, not only the Jesuits and Carmelites, but even Richelieu himself. After the death of Bérulle the Oratory, for fear of the cardinal-minister, hardly dared eulogize their founder. Yet Saint-Cyran on 5 October circulated an impressive letter to Fr. Bourgoing, the subsequent second successor to Bérulle in the generalship of the congregation, which contained unreserved praise of the deceased. In other respects, too, Saint-Cyran's keen intelligence was widely known: Guez de Balzac called him "the oracle of the monastery of Notre-Dame," after his place of residence. Without wanting to, Saint-Cyran quickly occupied an exposed position with the *parti dévot* and became an opponent of Richelieu. During the brief period in which the party held decisive power, immediately prior to the *Journée des Dupes*, the queen mother had even designated him bishop of Bayonne. Initially, Richelieu did not dare proceed against his former friend, because he either lacked sufficient grounds or was still hoping to win him back over to his side.

Saint-Cyran, knowing himself to be in a dangerous situation, behaved most cautiously while the cardinal's anti-Spanish policies intensified and in May 1635 culminated in a declaration of war. Yet the public was aware that Saint-Cyran condemned the hostility towards a great

[21] See G. Pagès, "Autour du Grand Orage, Richelieu et Marillac, deux politiques," *RH* 179 (1937); P. de Vaissière, *Un grand proces sous Richelieu, l'affaire du Maréchal de Marillac* (Paris 1924).

Catholic nation as well as Richelieu's alliance with the Protestants of Germany. In the course of the summer of 1635 Jansen, whose connection with Saint-Cyran was well-known, published his *Mars gallicus, seu de justitia armorum et foederum regis Galliae,* a blunt and cutting pamphlet against Richelieu's foreign policy. Saint-Cyran did not approve of this far too partisan comment. But Richelieu was offended; he reacted sharply and marked Saint-Cyran the victim of his revenge. At the same time, he was afraid that his opponent might openly resist him in a delicate matter of extreme importance to him. It involved the marriage of Gaston d'Orléans, brother of the King, who on 3 January 1632 had married Marguerite of Lorraine without the crown's consent.[22] This union interfered with Richelieu's policies because he was speculating on the properties of Marguerite's brother, the duke of Lorraine. By an edict of parliament (1634), the minister had the marriage dissolved on the strange pretext that Gaston had been the victim of an abduction. To buttress his case and to soothe the King's conscience Richelieu obtained—though not without difficulty—expert opinions from the Assembly of the Clergy, from fourteen Parisian congregations, and from sixty doctoral academicians, all of whom attested to the marriage being invalid. But the Holy See continued to consider it valid. This was also Saint-Cyran's opinion and in spite of using the utmost discretion he could not conceal it, particularly because he was a friend of Condren, general of the Oratory and Gaston's confessor. Richelieu, aware of this, was at once resentful and uneasy; he feared that Saint-Cyran might publicly express himself in this matter after Condren and even Vincent de Paul had already been neutralized. Richelieu, with newspaper writers in his paid employ, knew very well of the power of the press and of public opinion, which could have been reversed by an active intervention on the part of Saint-Cyran. At this time, moreover, the minister was making public his plan to establish a French patriarchate relatively independent of the Holy See. It was obvious from the beginning that Saint-Cyran would oppose with all his force this schismatical design in which Richelieu, as he was well aware, had most of the nation against him. So Saint-Cyran unintentionally became the cardinal's foremost antagonist. Once more Richelieu attempted to win him over by arranging to have the bishopric of Bayonne offered to him in the spring of 1637. The abbot refused because he did not want to relinquish his independence, but knowing full well that this refusal would expose him to greater danger. At this point Richelieu actually thought of using force. But the intellectual authority of the abbot, his reputation for piety and integrity, and the seclusion in which he dwelt made him a difficult target. It took the incidents at Port-Royal, with which we shall soon deal, to provide the cardinal with

---

[22] See A. Degert, "Le mariage de Gaston d'Orléans," *RH* 143 (1901), 161ff.

the seemingly religious pretext he was seeking. In any event, Richelieu could now assume that the arrest of Saint-Cyran would seal the disintegration of the already weakened *parti dévot*. He could not foresee that Port-Royal would endure as the strongest bastion of resistance against absolutism.

The Reform of the Clergy

During the few years under the regency of Marie de Médicis in which the *parti dévot* enjoyed a full measure of power, its foremost aim was the reform of the secular clergy and that of the orders. This endeavor was supported and continued by Richelieu. After 1610 the efforts in behalf of monastic reform were not only sustained by the *milieu dévot*, but were indeed frequently pursued by civil authorities as well. It must be pointed out that the idea of monastic reform had a twofold significance. In some cases an outstanding religious personality at the head of a community was able to restore strict observance and to turn it into a center of spirituality simply by persuasive power and by setting an example. In other cases, the authorities intervened from the outside and when necessary applied force in order to do away with the most flagrant excesses and to bring about at least a minimum of observance of the rules. The religious significance of the reform is of course basically different in the two cases.

An amusing example of the second kind is represented by the Cistercian abbey of Maubuisson, headed, as we mentioned before, by the amorous Angélique d'Estrées. Age apparently had done nothing to moderate her since her well-known liaison with a nobleman continued to feed the chronicles already rich in scandals.[23] Finally, in 1617, the court ordered the abbot of Cîteaux, Dom Boucherat, to restore order to Maubuisson. Dom Boucherat made a canonical visitation. Consequently, on 5 February 1618, he had Mme d'Estrées arrested by royal police and interned with the *Filles répenties*. Then he sent for Mother Angélique Arnauld, abbess of Port-Royal, and three of her nuns to administer and reform the house. By 10 September 1619 the situation had improved, but now Mme d'Estrées, having escaped from the *Filles répenties*, stormed the abbey in company with a number of nobles devoted to her. Mother Angélique and the nuns loyal to her had to flee to Pontoise. It took a second expedition by the police to evict Mme d'Estrées, who had by the way managed to abscond, and to reinstall Mother Angélique. Subsequently and indeed on several occasions, the latter was in danger of being murdered. Not until the spring of 1623 was Mme

[23] See L. Cognet, *La Mère Angélique et saint François de Sales* (Paris 1951).

d'Estrées finally replaced by another abbess so that Mother Angélique could return to Port-Royal. To be sure, this was an especially romantic episode, but by no means the only one in this period.

A decisive position in the movement for monastic reform was occupied by Cardinal François de la Rochefoucauld (1558–1645).[24] He had been court prelate and, at the time of the League, a combative bishop of Clermont. In his youth he had met Saint Charles Borromeo in Italy; now he was consumed with the idea of emulating Borromeo's reformatory zeal. La Rochefoucauld had close ties to the *parti dévot* and it was probably Henri de Gondi, bishop of Paris, who had recommended him to Louis XIII in about 1620 to work on monastic reform. A brief by Gregory XV, dated 8 April 1622, assigned him to the task; this was confirmed by royal letters patent on the following 13 July, setting him to work with the utmost vigor. La Rochefoucauld, who by the way was unscrupulous in his accumulation of church benefices, had among his acquisitions of abbeys that of Sainte-Geneviève in Paris, a monastery of the Canons Regular, which made him primarily interested in the reform of this particular branch. For this purpose he collaborated with Father Charles Faure (1594–1644), a pious monk from Senlis,[25] in establishing the *Congrégation de France*, which was to integrate all the abbeys of the Canons Regular. In accomplishing his goals the cardinal was not without ruthlessness, as in the case of the venerable Alain de Solminihac,[26] bishop of Cahors, who from his abbey at Chancelade had established his own branch of the Canons Regular. La Rochefoucauld was not as successful with other chapters, especially those of Clairvaux and Cîteaux. Dom Denis Largentier, abbot of Clairvaux, joined by several abbeys, had introduced reforms in 1615. Dom Nicolas Boucherat, abbot of Cîteaux, supported the reformed chapters and permitted them to elect their own vicar general. But in May 1622 at a conference chaired by La Rochefoucauld, he acceded to the latter's suggestions by allowing the reformed chapters to form their own congregation. But the following May the chapters general rescinded this decision.[27] When Dom Largentier and Dom Boucherat died shortly after one another (1624, 1625), their places were taken by abbots antagonistic to reform. Thereupon Dom Étienne Maugier, abbot of La Charmoye, took over the leadership of the reform movement. With the support of La Rochefoucauld he initiated a movement claiming independence for the reformed chapters. The ensuing dissension split the order until the end of the century. Even

---

[24] See G. de la Rochefoucauld, *Le Cardinal de la Rochefoucauld* (Paris 1921).
[25] See L. Cognet, "Faure," *DHGE* 16, 714–19.
[26] See E. Sol, *Le Vénérable Alain de Solminihac* (Cahors 1928).
[27] See J. Canivez, "Cîteaux," *DHGE* 12 (1952), 950–97.

the constitution *In suprema* by Alexander VII, prescribing slightly more moderate statutes, could not restore harmony, but on the contrary evoked spirited resistance. Among the disputants was Armand-Jean Le Bouthillier de Rancé (1626–1700). After a checkered career as a wordly abbot he converted and in 1664 became titular abbot of his commendam La Trappe in Normandy,[28] where he embarked upon a reform of his abbey. While far exceeding the Cistercian ideal in its scope and severity, his reforms nonetheless caused an immense awareness because Rancé was known widely. But within the order it was greatly resisted by, among others, Dom Eustache de Beaufort, who had initiated the reform of his abbey of Sept-Fons in Bourbonnais in 1663.[29] The Cistercian nuns also joined the reform movement, which had been initiated in Port-Royal in 1608; by the end of the century several congregations of reformed Bernardine nuns had been founded. Among the most interesting was the one founded in 1618 at Tart in the diocese of Langres; it was suggested by Mother Jeanne de Courcelle de Pourlan and supported by Bishop Sébastien Zamet[30] and the nuns of Port-Royal. Another congregation founded by Mother de Ballon with support by Saint Francis de Sales was established in 1621 in Rumilly.

The Benedictines as well benefited from several attempts at reform emanating from Lorraine where the congregations of Saint-Vanne and Saint-Hydulphe had been formed in 1604. The reform of Saint-Vanne was transferred to France in 1613, mediated by Dom Bénard, prior of the Collège de Cluny in Paris. Several cloisters joined in, but since Lorraine at this time was part of the Empire, they had to form an autonomous congregation in 1618, the *Congrégation de Saint-Maur*; this was encouraged by Louis XIII and canonically sanctioned in 1921. In 1624 Dom Grégoire Tarrisse,[31] a superior administrator, became president of the congregation and gave it a strong centralized organization. Gradually most of the important Benedictine abbeys joined the congregation with the exception of Cluny and its chapters. In 1631 the renowned abbey of Saint-Germain des Prés in Paris emerged as the center of the Maurists.[32] In Cluny, Abbot Jacques de Veny d'Arbouze unsuccessfully attempted a reform in 1622. Richelieu, who had become

[28] See H. Bremond, *L'abbé Tempête, Armand de Rancé et la réforme de la Trappe* (Paris 1926).
[29] See B. Martelet, "Dom Eustache de Beaufort et la réforme de Sept-Fons," *Cîteaux* 14 (1963), 4, 281–92.
[30] See L. Prunel, *Sébastien Zamet, sa vie, ses œuvres* (Paris 1912).
[31] See F. Rousseau, *Un promoteur de l'érudition bénédictine, Dom Grégoire Tarrisse* (Lille 1924).
[32] Collected contributions for the Centennial of the Abbey of Saint-Germain-des-Prés in *RHEF* 43 (1957).

commendam abbot of Cluny in 1629 and wanted to unite all French Benedictines in one body,[33] attempted to fuse the Cluniacs with the Maurists into the congregation of Saint-Benoît. But Rome never agreed and when the cardinal died, the plan was abandoned. A subsequent attempt by Mazarin to combine the reformed houses of Cluny with the congregation of Saint-Vanne failed as well. Indeed, the Cluny group remained rather undistinguished, whereas the Maurists flourished. Simultaneously, instances of reforms in the Benedictine convents also increased. Highly esteemed were the reforms introduced in 1619 by Marguerite de Veny d'Arbouze in her abbey of Val-de-Grâce and continued when the abbey was transferred to Paris in 1631. She was aided by the affection of Anne of Austria and her statutes were adopted by numerous houses. Some of these reforms adapted the Benedictine traditions to contemporary forms of piety, as was the case with the Benedictine nuns of Calvary. This chapter had been founded in 1617 in Poitiers by Antoinette d'Orléans[34] with support by the famous Capuchine Father Joseph du Tremblay, who later received the sobriquet "the gray eminence." The change was even more marked in the case of the Benedictine nuns of the Holy Sacrament founded in 1653 by Mother Mechtilde in Paris.[35] The atonement of injuries done to the Holy Sacrament by the Huguenots was then a central devotional act within the *milieu dévot;* after 1647 it was also practiced by the Cistercian nuns of Port-Royal.

During the first half of the seventeenth century almost all the old established orders in fact had to submit to reform for internal reasons. For the Dominicans, Sebastian Michaelis had managed in 1608 to establish a reformed congregation for the Toulouse region; in 1613 it expanded to Paris, where it assumed the name *Congrégation de Saint-Louis*. Seven years later Father Antoine Le Quieu founded a new, even stricter reform chapter also consecrated to the Holy Sacrament.[36] The reform of the Premonstratensians started in 1617 in Lorraine and spread to France in 1623. First indications of a Carmelite reform of Touraine appeared in 1604.[37] Reform of the clergy of the orders on the whole resulted from individual and private efforts, rather than from initiatives by the state. The commission under the chairmanship of La

---

[33] Cf. P. Denis, *Le Cardinal de Richelieu et la Réforme des monastères bénédictins* (Paris 1913).

[34] See P. Petit, *Vie de la Mère Antoinette d'Orléans* (Paris 1880).

[35] M. Hervin and M. Dourlens, *Vie de Mechtilde du Saint-Sacrement* (Paris 1883).

[36] See R. L. Oechslin, *Une aventure spirituelle: Vie du Père Antoine Le Quieu* (Paris 1967).

[37] See S. M. Bouchereaux, *La réforme des Carmes en France et Jean de Saint-Samson* (Paris 1950).

Rochefoucauld, in spite of his personal effort, achieved but very limited success. Later on Richelieu had the abbeys of Cluny, Cîteaux and Pré-montré conveyed to himself in order to be in a position to intercede effectively. Yet he used them primarily for the income he derived from them. In reality, the leadership was making too much profit from the existing abuses to want to remedy them. But for all the difficulties they faced, the efforts by the reformers were not in vain. Many cloisters not only turned into places of sincere spiritual life, but also had a profound effect on the laity. Groups of friends gathered around the convents of Port-Royal, Val-de-Grâce, the Carmelites and the Visitation; at La Trappe, Rancé received the most important personages of his time. Even in houses at the periphery of reforms the most scandalous excesses were stopped; transgressions were no longer overt. Eventually the religious orders regained their dignity.

Reform of the secular clergy posed a completely different problem. From the outset, the whole *milieu dévot* agreed that it would be useless to undertake a reform of the present clergy, that it was necessary to start all over again by bringing up a new clergy. But from this point on, the proposed solutions diverged. One feasible idea was the creation of an organism whose sole function was to be the education of a clergy worthy of its duties. This had actually been prescribed by the Council of Trent when it ordered the establishment of seminaries. Yet in spite of efforts in this direction by many clerics including La Rochefoucauld, the council's decrees never became state law;[38] implementation was left instead to private initiative. So the bishops were quite late when they began to establish seminaries, which, moreover, were frequently forced to operate under very difficult conditions. Without a doubt the pioneer in this field was Adrien Bourdoise (1584–1665),[39] an impressive figure who lived outside the customary frame, passionately involved in the idea of clerical reform, a man of uncompromising severity and insufferable character whose vagaries even Vincent de Paul and Bérulle were not spared. In 1612 he formed a society for aspiring priests in Paris where he gave an education almost exclusively aimed at practical application and that was very limited intellectually.[40] Following a verbal approval in 1631, Bourdoise's seminary experiment finally received its official approval in 1643. His example was emulated: between 1622 and 1680 there appeared in twenty French towns seminary societies of this type,

---

[38] See V. Martin, *Le gallicanisme et la réforme catholique, essai sur l'introduction en France des décrets du Concile de Trente* (Paris 1919).

[39] See J. F. Darche, *Le saint abbé Bourdoise*, 2 vols. (Paris 1884); J. Harang, *Bourdoise* (Paris 1949).

[40] See P. Schoenher, *Histoire du Séminaire de Saint-Nicolas du Chardonnet*, 2 vols. (Paris 1909–11).

several of which were but short-lived. Initially Bourdoise's enterprise required true courage, for at that time even La Rochefoucauld did not dare open a seminary either in Clermont or in Senlis, the diocese he was given later on. Bourdoise's influence was to prove vital in connection with other foundings, such as the Oratory and Saint-Sulpice.

In fact, there appeared to be another solution to the reform of the parish priests: the creation of a secular clergy to be both example and complement to the existing clergy. It was this solution Bérulle approved on 10 November 1611 when he founded the Oratory of Jesus, an unpretentious congregation of secular clerics without special vows. His model was the foundation of Saint Philip Neri in Rome. Neri had designed the Oratories in the various towns as autonomous houses without an organic connection. In contrast, Bérulle had planned his French Oratory from the beginning to be a single congregation structured under the authority of a superior general whose members could change houses if required by circumstances.[41] In this respect, Bérulle's design was better adapted to the requirements of France, which had the kind of political unity totally lacking in Italy. The members of the Oratory immediately took over the various forms of parish apostleship, to which they soon added educational duties. The Oratory developed swiftly. By the time of its first plenary session in August 1631 it already had seventy-one houses. This quantitative as well as qualitative achievement proved that the Oratory fulfilled the needs of a large segment of the religious public. In spite of its liberal attitude, expansion and centralization actually gave the Oratory the posture of a large national congregation, comparable in France to the Society of Jesus. Since the latter was actively dedicated to the same areas of endeavor, conflicts between the two were unavoidable; in 1620 an open quarrel ensued. In December 1623, after an exchange of highly aggressive memoranda, Bérulla and the Jesuits brought the matter before the papal nuncio, Corsini. Yet the hostility between the two congregations did not abate and later on led a significant group of Oratory members to join the Jansenists.

The role and influence of the Oratory and the priestly spirituality promoted by Bérulle and his successors,[42] contributed significantly to raising the level of the secular clergy. Meanwhile the Oratory and its followers were occupied also with the first of the above-mentioned solutions, to create institutions which were to insure the proper education of the clergy. While Bérulle was alive, the Oratory already took over seminaries, many of which were attached to secondary schools such

---

[41] See A. George, *L'Oratoire* (Paris 1928).
[42] See M. Dupuy, *Bérulle et le sacerdoce* (Paris 1969).

as the seminary of Saint-Magloire, founded for the Paris diocese. But these institutions met with limited success in counteracting the problems within the secular clergy. Bérulle's successor at the head of the Oratory, Charles de Condren (1588–1641), an indecisive person who shunned responsibility, did not make an effort to continue the task of establishing seminaries within the Oratory although he recognized the need for them and recommended them to his students. One of them, Jean-Jacques Olier (1608–57), realized a work of fundamental significance.[43] Having become pastor of Saint-Sulpice in 1642, he established a seminary in his parsonage which soon brought forth the *Compagnie de Saint-Sulpice,* an association of secular priests. Following the model of the Oratory, it was dedicated to teaching at diocesan seminaries and directing them.[44] In Olier's lifetime four more such associations were established. Following his death numerous additional houses were either established or received into the association both in France and Canada. Before long the Sulpician seminaries were considered exemplary and their education became the prototype of clerical training. Educated in accordance with the spiritual principles of Bérulle regarding the eminence of the priesthood and its place in the hierarchy, a certain type of priest emerged from these seminaries. Pious, well educated and charitable, leading a dignified and retired life, they all came from a certain social stratum, which was to endure through the upheavals of the Revolution to the threshold of our century. However, the education and training was limited by the quality of the candidates. This improved, although a decision for the priesthood was not always in response to a true calling. The aristocracy continued to provide the recruits for the episcopate, but usually had its candidates, too, go through the seminaries. Talleyrand's *Mémoires* indicate that these clerical youths on the eve of revolution were prepared to upset the strict order of the seminaries. Among the lower levels of society, the priesthood remained as always the simplest means for social mobility. Parents would simply enter their most gifted children into the priesthood—whether the children wanted it or not. So it is easy to understand that the pseudophilosophy of the eighteenth century met with a great deal of concurrence among the rural clergy, for whom Rousseau's *Vicaire Savoyard* was by no means a mere mythical figure.

The reform movement also brought about other foundations which were concerned with clerical education. One of the most significant emanated from Vincent de Paul (1581–1660) (see Chap. 5). As a farm-

[43] See P. Pourrat, *J. J. Olier* (Paris 1932).
[44] See P. Boisard, *La Compagnie de Saint-Sulpice, trois siècles d'histoire* (n.p., 1959); not available commercially.

er's son from the area of Landes, Vincent's youth had been wanting in material things. Although his reputed stay in Tunisia must be considered a legend,[45] he nevertheless had to undergo a number of adventures before he settled in Paris at the end of 1608. After 1610 his life led him on the path to an even more demanding holiness under the influence of Bérulle. Yet he took many more years to discover his true destination. In 1618 he started to devote himself to the rural missions, but not until 1625, supported by one of the most powerful families of the *milieu dévot*, the Gondi, did he establish the *Congrégation des Prêtres de la Mission*, housed initially in the Collège des Bons Enfants and then in 1632 in Saint-Lazare, the former home for lepers and future center of the congregation. The new congregation, which initially occupied itself with the rural apostolate and later on with several foreign missions, developed so rapidly that by 1641 Vincent de Paul was able to use his priests in establishing some diocesan seminaries. At the time of his death there was a total of about a dozen houses. At the request of the archbishop, Vincent de Paul five or six times a year offered a week's contemplation at Saint-Lazare for candidates for ordainment. These retreats were highly frequented and very successful; in 1652 even Bossuet prepared for his ordination there and later returned four times to preach. In July 1633—also at Saint-Lazare—the renowned Tuesday conferences were initiated (*Conférences du Mardi*), at which gathered the foremost representatives of the Parisian clergy to instruct one another and to discuss the problems of the apostolate. The following years, the Vincentians established similar organizations in the large provincial towns. All of these institutions were objects of Vincent de Paul's constant occupation; at certain points he spent considerable time looking for the right solution to problems. This was true especially for the seminaries where the candidates for the priesthood unfortunately spent no more than a few months. This was too short a time to enable them to receive a solid education. Even at that, the results were positive as Vincent himself stated at the end of his life.

Vincent de Paul quickly freed himself from Bérulle's initial influence; this even led to some differences of opinion between the two. In addition to them, the Oratory brought forth another great founder in the area of rural mission and seminary work: Saint John Eudes (1611–80),[46] a member of the Oratory from 1623 to 1643. The sole reason for his leaving the Oratory in 1643 was the fact that he was opposed by the

[45] See A. Dodin, *Saint Vincent de Paul et la charité* (Paris 1960); L. Cognet, *Saint Vincent de Paul* (Paris 1959); P. Debongnie, "Saint Vincent de Paul était-il à Tunis en 1606–1607?" *RHE* 58 (1963), 862–64.
[46] See D. Boulay, *Vie du Vénérable Jean Eudes*, 4 vols. (Paris 1905–08); Berthelot du Chesnay, *Les missions de saint Jean Eudes* (Paris 1967).

superior general, François Bourgoing, when he established a seminary in Caen. He founded the *Congrégation de Jésus et Marie,* which assumed the direction of numerous seminaries and remained dominated by a spirituality inspired by Bérulle. At the same time there were other experiments and foundings. One of them in the south of France was the *Congrégation des Pères de la Mission* by Christophe d'Authier de Sisgaud, which to some degree was at variance with Vincent de Paul's congregation; but all of these groups were limited in their range and duration. And yet these efforts did lead to a genuine, gradually expanding reform of the prevailing mentality. After 1650 most of the dioceses established seminaries; the conditions for ordination began more and more to conform with canonical norms with the result of raising standards among the parish clergy rapidly without, however, going beyond the above-mentioned limitations (see Chap. 5).

CHAPTER 2

Origin and Development of Jansenism to 1653

Augustinianism in Louvain and Jansen

The congregations *De Auxiliis* had not resulted in a condemnation of Molina's *Concordia.* While Paul V did not want to diminish the esteem enjoyed by the Jesuits, who had rendered to him inestimable political services, he was nonetheless determined to maintain the fundamental position of the Augustinian-Thomist system of grace. This is why he allowed the Dominican Diego Álvarez (d. 1635) to publish his monumental treatise *De auxiliis divinae gratiae* (1611) as a work of quasi-official character. In order to prevent works on the same topic by the Jesuits Lessius and Suárez to be published, he had the Holy Office issue a decision (not a decree!), which was communicated to those involved and forbade them to publish anything involving the subject of grace. In spite of this, the faculty of Louvain reaffirmed its censures of the Jesuits Lessius and Hamelius. In December 1614 the Jesuit General Claudius Acquaviva, fearing that the old quarrels would be revived, directed Thomism to be taught at the colleges of the society. Yet neither Paul V nor Acquaviva succeeded. Numerous works proclaiming to be commentaries on the *Summa* of Saint Thomas circumvented the prohibition of 1611; the Jesuits on the whole continued to defend Molina. Under those circumstances, Urban VIII—elevated to the papacy in 1623—reiterated the prohibition in December of the same year and acknowledged it by formal decree on 22 May 1625. But even he could not settle the quarrels about the concept of grace.

The Louvain group then remained identified with Augustinianism; Baius, whose condemnation was considered unfair, enjoyed continued sympathy especially among such famous professors as the Franciscan Florent Conry (Conrius) (1590–1629) and Jacques Jansson (1547–1629). It was in this atmosphere that Cornelius Jansen (Jansenius) (1585–1638) developed.[1] From 1602 to 1604 and from 1607 to 1609 he was a student in Louvain, the latter two years under the tutelage of Jansson. From 1609 to 1616 he resided for the main in France, where he met and for some time shared a domicile with Jean Duvergier de Hauranne, who later was to become abbot of Saint-Cyran (see Chap. 1). After his return to Flanders he dedicated himself to a peaceful and honorable university career. From 1617 until 1624 he was president of the Sainte-Pulchérie Seminary and was then appointed representative of the university at the court of Spain, where he successfully defended the monopoly of the faculty against the Jesuits, who were applying for the privilege to award degrees. In March 1630 he was rewarded with the regius chair of Sacred Scripture and wrote commentaries on numerous books of the Bible, which avoided the touchy issue of grace. In the meantime his ideas about this problem had taken on very definite form. In the course of his studies, he had read excerpts from Augustine, but without paying any special attention to him. Only after his return to Louvain—under the influence of Jansson—did he undertake a systematic study of Augustine's works, excerpting the essential theses and compiling them into a system of thought. In 1621 he allied himself with Conrius, who influenced him in like manner.[2] At this point Jansen began to secure various political connections—in France with the help of Saint-Cyran—who were to aid him in his intention to bring about a triumph of Augustinianism over Molinism. Since 1621 he had also been planning to write a comprehensive synthesis of the Augustinian doctrine of grace. To this end, he spent the years 1623–26 in a final systematic study of the works of Augustine. Obligations at the university and his trip to Spain delayed the start of the manuscript until 1627. After this it advanced with remarkable speed; his letters to Saint-Cyran offer insight into the various stages of progress. On 27 March 1630 he was able to send him the table of contents for the first volume. In spite of interruptions by his professorial duties and the anti-Protestant polemics in 1630–31, he started on the third volume in February 1635, hoping to finish it within a year. But in August 1635 he was appointed rector of the university; on 28 October 1636, he became bishop of Ypres and was

[1] See J. Orcibal, "Jansénius," *Catholicisme* 23 (Paris 1963), 332–43; A. Vandenpeereboom, "C. Jansénius évêque d'Ypres," *Ypriana* VI (Bruges 1882).
[2] See L. Ceyssens, "Florence Conry, Hugh de Burgo, Luke Wadding and Jansenism," *Festschr. Father Luke Wadding* (Dublin 1957), 295–304.

occupied intensively with his episcopal duties. Under these circumstances he was unable to complete his great treatise. When he was about to finish it, he started worrying about its publication. With a caution understandable in a time that was aggravated by polemics, he had gone about his work with the utmost discretion. Rather than submit his writings, he decided to install a printing shop in his palace together with all the necessary materials. In April 1638 the work was finished, crowned by a dedication to Pope Urban III.[3] But he was not to see its publication. He died from the plague in God's peace on 6 May 1638, having placed his manuscript into the hands of his pupils Henri Calenus and Liber Froidmont.[4]

In spite of Jansen's precautions, the Jesuits of Flanders had some knowledge of his undertaking. Since the Jesuits looked upon a resumption of the polemics on this topic as a potential disaster, they had mobilized support for themselves especially in France and Spain and had also kept the Jesuits of Rome informed. Soon they knew that Jansen had left behind a completed work and so did their utmost to prevent its publication. Through an internuncio in Brussels, Richard Stravius, they reminded Calenus and Froidmont of the prohibition of 1611 and the decree of 1625, which forbade publications on the subject of grace. But since these decisions were never officially communicated to the University of Louvain the latter considered them of no consequence.[5] When Jesuits appealed to the Council of Brabant and the Privy Council, Calenus and Froidmont countered by pointing to the enormous sums of money already invested by the printer, Zegers, and they finally prevailed. The treatise was made public in September 1640. This huge folio of more than thirteen hundred pages in small print of two columns per page was entitled simply *Cornelii Jansenii Episcopi Yprensis Augustinus.* It was no doubt with regard to the prohibitions by the Holy See that Jansen's representatives omitted his dedication to Urban III.

This extensive book, the work of a lifetime, was indeed in itself a remarkable synthesis of the Augustinian concepts on grace and predestination. But in it Jansen proceeded from the most extreme positions advocated by Saint Augustine in his fight against the Pelagians without

[3] See L. Ceyssens, "De dedicatiebrief van C. Jansenius aan Paus Urbanus VIII," *AGAU* 66 (1947), 203–22; 67 (1948), 13–14.

[4] See C. Callewaert and Q. Nols, *Jansénius évêque d'Ypres, ses derniers moments* (Louvain 1893); L. Ceyssens, "Libert Froidmont," *BullSocAHLiège* 43 (1963), 1–46; ibid., "Hendrik Calenus pastoor van Asse," *Ascania, driemaandelijks tijdschrift voor Asse* 4 (1961), 15–50; idem, "Henri Calenus évêque manqué," *Bulletin de la Commission royale d'Histoire* 127 (1961), 33–128.

[5] See L. Ceyssens, "La publication de l'Augustinus d'après la correspondance de Henri Calenus," *Antonianum* 35 (1960), 417–48.

taking into consideration the long history of their development. What evolved was a rigid system often sharply formulated. The first volume treats the positions of the Pelagians or Semi-Pelagians. In a "Liber proemialis" introducing the second volume, Jansen investigates the correlations between philosophy and theology; he opposes the methods of Scholasticism as being too rationalistic and claims Augustine's authority in regard to the issue of grace. He then talks about the state of fallen nature from a perspective characterized by Augustinian pessimism with special emphasis on the basic depravity which emanated from sin and about the power of concupiscence, which grants man no more than the freedom of evil. In the process he also addresses the classical problem of the state of pure nature, which he solves in a negative fashion. He concludes that by creation man was elevated to a supernatural calling. The third volume, by far the most significant, examines the healing of human nature and its restitution to true freedom by virtue of the redeeming grace in Christ. Jansen stresses emphatically that grace becomes unfailingly effective without however destroying Man's freedom and that this grace is accorded to him by God totally unowed by virtue of a decree of predestination. He passes over the classical explanation of the Thomists, which goes back to the *praemotio physica;* but he rejects the notion of freedom—also Thomist—which consists of the ability to posit opposite actions. In his view, freedom is identical with the unfathomable spontaneity of nature, which he calls will. Thus he disregards the Scholastic distinction between will as instinct and will as free choice. His will seeks fulfillment and pleasure spontaneously. But a fallen nature can find its fulfillment only in the creature, in egotistical self-love and therefore turns away from God perforce. It takes the intercession of grace in order to heal it, to breathe into it an inspiration of divine love which resurrects the will in this love and inclines it to a spiritual and holy pleasure through which he puts his whole happiness in God and in the fulfillment of His demand. This is his theory of victorious pleasure through which the will unfailingly enters into harmony with God. In all this, Jansen supposedly reflected the thoughts of Saint Augustine, but actually it is evident that he was influenced by the Baianistic atmosphere of his training. The work as such obviously avoids any and all polemics, but an appendix entitled *Parallèle* vigorously attacks the Molinists and compares their teachings with those of the Pelagians.[6] Jansen strove strictly to maintain the language of Augustinianism and, like Baius, rejected the concepts of the Thomists, which otherwise would have given strong impulses to his undertaking.

---

[6] See A. de Meyer, "De Werkwijze van Jansenius en zijn Augustinus," *Mededelingen der Kon. VI. Academie van Belgie* (1946), VIII, I.

Augustinianism in France: Saint-Cyran and Port-Royal

While it was torn by the religious wars, France paid scant attention to the controversy concerning divine grace. With peace restored, the universities, above all the Sorbonne, regained their former luster; the most famous professors lectured with great clarity concerning grace, openly adhered to Thomism and revered Augustine as their teacher; Molinism was either completely or almost unknown to them. From the beginning of his career, Bérulle appeared dominated by Augustinianism, but not exclusively because in 1612 he accepted Guillaume Gibieuf into the Oratory, who at that time was a confirmed Molinist and only under Bérulle's influence turned to Augustinianism. Duvergier de Hauranne, formerly a Jesuit pupil, too, did not at first oppose the new ideas. During the busy years he spent with Jansen at his estate Camp-de-Prats near Bayonne (1611–16) he did not seem to have been occupied with the issue of grace in any intensive way. But just about the time when Jansen in Louvain discovered Augustinianism, a similar range of perception opened up to the future abbot of Saint-Cyran under the influence of Bérulle. Yet the strictly intellectual mode of Augustinianism, which Jansson had disclosed to his pupil Jansen, was not identical to the Augustinianism provided to Saint-Cyran by Bérulle. The latter was not very much interested in abstracting a coherent theory of grace and predestination from the works of the bishop of Hippo. Involved in the practice of Christian spirituality, he sought to derive from Augustine a method that would make the souls realize their total dependence on God and their personal wretchedness. Saint-Cyran moved along the same lines. Yet, disregarding the difference in their individual outlook, Jansen and Saint-Cyran united in a common defense of Augustinianism. In the autumn of 1621 Saint-Cyran spent some time with Jansen in Louvain. At this meeting they decided to enlist political support in order to effect a breakthrough of Augustinianism against the Jesuits. After their meeting they started cultivating the proper connections. With this in mind, Jansen helped introduce Bérulle's Oratory into Flanders during the following years. But these political initiatives were unsuccesful: given Richelieu's attitude, the two friends realized that they could not hope for anything from him. On 10 May 1623, they met again in Péronne and decided upon a "change of plans," namely to start waging the battle in the universities and on the intellectual level. After 1621 they had made use of a secret code, a common practice at a time when the postal service was still very uncertain. This enabled them to carry on a regular and sufficiently secure correspondence until 1635, when it was interrupted by the war. Until this time, Saint-Cyran was thus in a position to follow the progress of this great treatise, to give data and advice to his friend and even to send him a first draft of the "Liber proemialis." Unfortunately he was unable to lend him his support in editing the third volume, the most important of all, whose content he did not learn until after it was published. Only Jansen's letters were preserved, but they show clearly that he and Saint-Cyran developed in two different intellectual worlds and that Augustinianism never meant the same to the two of them.

As mentioned already, Jansen's pamphlet against Richelieu, *Mars Gallicus*, was a sore point with the cardinal, yet Richelieu did not draw upon this pamphlet for his main argument against Saint-Cyran, who was at the pinnacle of his fame by 1634. Generally considered the indisputable head of the *parti dévot*, he maintained excellent connections through his friendship with the elite of French Catholicism. But by then another event involving him was unsettling his life. Since 1620 he had been a close friend of Robert Arnauld d'Andilly, a diplomat, active at the court. The eldest child of a family whose nobility derived from being in the King's service, he was a brother of the famous Mother Angélique, abbess and reformer of the Cistercian abbey of Port-Royal, which had formerly been located in the Chevreuse Valley and in 1625 transferred to Paris. Saint-Cyran had only had occasional slight connections with Mother Angélique and her sister Mother Agnès. Meanwhile Mother Angélique had left Port-Royal for a few years. Together with the bishop of Langres, Sébastien Zamet, she had founded a new order, the *Institut du Saint-Sacrement*.[7] But Zamet, a strange and uneven personality, soon incurred the enmity especially of the archbishop of Sens, Octave de Bellegarde. The latter, intending to damage the *Institut*, provided himself with a devotional text by Mother Agnès entitled *Chapelet secret du Saint-Sacrement*.[8] He represented it as the spiritual charter of the new foundation and managed to have it critically examined by eight professors of the Sorbonne on 18 June 1633. Upon Zamet's request, Saint-Cyran agreed to defend the text, in which he recognized Bérulle's influence. He won out totally and incurred Mother Angélique's deep gratitude. This established a closer relationship between them in the course of which Mother Angélique came to admire Saint-Cyran not only as a pure intellectual, but also as a great spiritual leader.

Yet in this area Saint-Cyran had some very personal convictions inspired in part by Francis de Sales and Bérulle. He rejected the idea that Christian life could alternate constantly between a state of grace and a state of sin. So he endeavored to lead his charges to a truly new life by a method designed to trigger a psychological shock. It consisted of going

---

[7] See L. Prunel, *S. Zamet, sa vie et ses œuvres, les origines du jansénisme* (Paris 1912).
[8] See L. Cognet, "Le Chapelet secret du Saint Sacrement," *Chroniques de Port Royal* (1951), 3–14.

through the intermediate stage of penitence, yet during this period the penitent would deny himself Communion and delay receiving absolution. Only after this delay, generally lasting a few weeks, did he receive absolution and Communion. Following this he had to live in as much seclusion as possible in order to preserve the grace he had received. This method had been worked out prior to 1627, but until that time Saint-Cyran had had little opportunity to apply it. But he made the mistake of telling the nuns of Port-Royal and Saint-Sacrement about it. They were filled with enthusiasm for it, indeed all of them wanted to set out on this journey to self-renewal. But they also talked about it outside their monastic environs without considering that they were exposing Saint-Cyran to accusations of indulging in dangerous innovations and were providing Richelieu with weapons against him. Plagued by severe scruples, Mother Angélique remained without Holy Communion from Easter to Ascension Day 1635. That she did so in spite of reprimands by Saint-Cyran did not lessen his responsibility for it in the eyes of the public. But soon this affair concerning the recluses of Port-Royal took on a completely different significance. Mother Angélique had a nephew, Antoine Lemaistre, a brilliant young lawyer in whom high hopes were placed for a future in the Paris court of law. In 1634, following a sentimental disappointment, he wanted to commit suicide, but was stopped by Saint-Cyran. The sudden death of one of his aunts on 24 August 1637 brought about an enthusiastic wish for conversion. After a long probationary period, Saint-Cyran, on about 15 December 1637, permitted him to write an open letter to Chancellor Séguier in which he announced his decision henceforth to live in seclusion and penitence, but without wanting to become a priest or joining an order. It was common knowledge that Saint-Cyran was his spiritual guide and so he was accused of wanting to establish a new order, especially since other pupils of his began to join Lemaistre in his seclusion. Richelieu took this to be a budding resistance and decided to intervene severely. But before he did, he tried once again—and failed—to buy the benevolence of his erstwhile friend by offering him a bishopric in February 1637. In March 1638 Claude Séguenot, a member of the Oratory, published a translation of Saint Augustine's *De Sancta Virginitate* together with a commentary in which he violently attacked the religious orders and espoused a rigid uncompromising Augustinianism. Journalists in the pay of Richelieu designated Saint-Cyran as the actual author of the book, since his connection with the Oratory was well known. The arrest of Séguenot on 7 May was followed on 14 May by the incarceration of Saint-Cyran at the palace of Vincennes.

Public opinion initially considered Saint-Cyran guilty of aggravated heresy and Richelieu intended to compromise him by putting him on trial. But when his papers were scrutinized and his friends and pupils interrogated, the accused turned out to be completely innocent. For a while, Richelieu hoped to use the issue of attritionism against him since Saint-Cyran had always defended the need in the Sacrament of Penance for a *contritio* based on the love of God. Richelieu held this concept to be in contradiction to the decisions of the Council of Trent. But on 14 May 1640 Saint-Cyran, for whom this problem was actually of little practical importance, announced that he was prepared to draft a letter relatively favorable to attritionism. By doing so, he deprived Richelieu of his main charge. Nevertheless Saint-Cyran remained in custody without a trial. His only hope was that the unhealthy conditions of his jail at Vincennes would soon destroy his fragile health. By now the Catholic circles among the public knew what was going on and public opinion turned against the cardinal. Saint-Cyran, on the other hand, having acquired an aura of martyrdom was able to initiate from his jail a voluminous correspondence which influenced an ever more significant group of pupils. Seriously ill and threatened by blindness he was repeatedly near death. Yet he was destined to outlive Richelieu, who passed away on 4 November 1642. Saint-Cyran was able to leave his jail on 6 February 1643. But he remained in ill health and died of apoplexy on 11 October, without having resumed his activities. Yet he left a number of pupils who continued his work.

The Beginnings of the Jansenist Conflict
The Bull *In eminenti*

It was foreseeable that the publication of Jansen's *Augustinus* would ultimately result in a renewed controversy regarding the question of grace. So no one, least of all the Louvain group, was caught unprepared; in fact, everyone had carefully prepared his position ahead of time. The Jesuits started the campaign by disregarding the prohibitions (1611 and 1625) of publications on the topic of grace, in which they had originally concurred without reservations. On 22 March 1641 lectures were read at the Jesuit college of Louvain in which Jansen was accused of renewing the errors of Calvin and Baius, of reducing human freedom to nothing and of limiting salvation to the chosen few.[9] These theses met with spirited rejoinders and innumerable polemics. Henceforth the faculties were split into Jansenists and anti-Jansenists.

France, too, was a ready battlefield for renewed strife. Saint-Cyran had hoped that of his pupils his nephew Martin Barcos

---

[9] See L. Ceyssens, "Le jansénisme, considérations historiques préliminaires à sa notion: Nuove ricerche storiche sul giansenismo," *AnGr* 21 (1954), 3–32.

(1600–1678), who had studied with Jansen in Louvain, would continue his work. But Barcos quickly proved to be very unsettled in his judgment.[10] Saint-Cyran's spiritual heir turned out to be the youngest brother of Mother Angélique, Antoine Arnauld (1612–94), whom posterity accorded the sobriquet Le Grand Arnauld. Initially a student of law, he turned to theology in 1632. For a long time Saint-Cyran was disappointed by the young man's exclusively intellectual and all too worldly ambitions although he demonstrated remarkable abilities all along. At that time the short works by Augustine against the Pelagians were hardly available, but through Jansen's good offices Saint-Cyran had gotten about twenty copies of the Louvain edition of 1555.[11] He gave one of them to young Arnauld and was amazed at the quickness and depth with which the latter grasped the main points of the treatise. For the baccalaureate in theology on 14 November 1635, Saint-Cyran had him defend some clearly Augustinian theses whose content was close to that of *Augustinus*. The defense proved quite successful; it demonstrated that Augustinianism continued to have enthusiastic adherents at the Sorbonne and provoked no polemics of any kind. In December 1638 Arnauld received the subdeaconate; shortly thereafter he converted to an intensive and challenging life of the spirit under the exclusive guidance of Saint-Cyran. The latter had him continue his studies at the Sorbonne, where he was awarded his doctorate on 18 December 1641. By that time Saint-Cyran had already called on him to defend his ideas in several publications.

Since Augustinians as well as Molinists had correspondents in Louvain, several copies of *Augustinus* were sent to France when it appeared in September 1640. The following November and December six Parisian professors gave their approval for a reprint which appeared in 1641 in Paris, followed by another one in Rouen in 1643. It was in the nature of things that violent polemics ensued between the detractors and defenders of Jansen. Among the latter there were groups whose defense of Augustinianism had by then become a tradition: Oratorians, Dominicans, Carmelites and numerous professors at the Sorbonne. But several professors joined the fray on the side of the anti-Jansenists, among whom the Jesuits played an especially significant role. Foremost among Jansen's opponents was Richelieu, who had never forgiven him for his *Mars Gallicus*. Richelieu was inclined toward Molinism; in his *Instruction du Chrétien* of 1619 he had supported attritionism, whereas *Augustinus* represented a lively defense of contritionism. Yet he did

---

[10] See J. Orcibal, "Martin de Barcos abbé de Saint-Cyran et sa correspondance," *RHE* 52 (1957), 877–99.

[11] *D. Aurelii Augustini opera contra Pelagianos*, 2 vols. (Louvian 1555).

want to spare the Jesuits, several of whom were rendering him great political service at the time. Although he showed his sympathies openly, he was very late in giving the signal for the start of the battle. No doubt he was aware of the power of the Augustinian party.

By the end of 1640 Saint-Cyran, too, had in his jail a copy of *Augustinus*. But weakened by illness and in danger of going blind, he was unable to analyze the large folio systematically. Apparently he read only the table of contents and a few chapters. No doubt he derived his knowledge of the work primarily from analyses given him by Arnauld or Barcos. He had had no connection with Jansen since 1635, so he was not familiar with the final projections of the work, especially of the third volume, in which he was astonished to find an attack on attritionism. He had been unable to keep his original agreement with Jansen, namely to go over the work before it was published. Now he found it dry, harsh, incongruous with its subject matter and out of touch with the spiritual aspects of the problem. Nevertheless he acknowledged it as a well-founded presentation of the fundamentals of Augustinianism. A short time later, for the benefit of informing Arnauld d'Andilly, he expressed his own ideas about it in a small treatise *De la grâce de Jésus-Christ*.[12] The continuous development of the relationship of grace and incarnation shows him to be thematically closer to Bérulle than to Jansen. At any rate, he desired no hasty polemics and impressed this upon his pupils. He confined himself to promoting other Augustinian writings which complemented the works of Jansen. The Paris edition of *Augustinus* contained an appendix with a treatise by Conrius in which he maintained that children who die without the benefit of baptism were condemned to hell. Shortly thereafter appeared the *Pèlerin de Jéricho* by the same author, a somber depiction of the humiliation of man after his Fall. At the same time a small treatise by Jansen, *Oratorio de interioris hominis reformatione* (1627) was printed and translated into French by Arnauld d'Andilly in 1642. This prompted the Jesuits to have the anti-Jansenist theses, presented at the University of Louvain in March 1641, reprinted. Shortly before his death Richelieu initiated the altercation by ordering Isaac Habert, canon and professor at the Sorbonne, to attack Jansen in his sermons. Habert complied in sermons at Notre-Dame on 30 November, 21 December and another the following Septuagesima Sunday. This last attack was especially vehement. Thereupon the prisoner of Vincennes decided to let Jansen's defenders break their silence and charged Arnauld with a reply to Habert. Arnauld, under the direction of Saint-Cyran, then composed his extensive *Apologie pour M. Jansénius,* but the intervention by President Molés and the archbishop of

[12] Text: J. Orcibal, *Spiritualité*, 233–40.

Paris, François de Gondi, who preferred continued silence, delayed its publication until September 1644. They could not prevent the appearance meanwhile of numerous polemics. The Feuillant Pierre de Saint-Joseph attacked Jansen in his *Défense de Saint Augustin*. The Oratorian Collin du Juanet replied with *Saint Augustin enseignant par lui-même*, an interesting collection of texts indirectly justifying the *Augustinus*. At the same time Jacques Sirmond, a learned Jesuit well known as a specialist in Christian antiquity, attempted to prove that Augustine had been accused of the heresy of so-called predestinarianism. This caused a vehement controversy.

The Flemish Jesuits and the internuncio, Stravius, had reported to Rome concerning the events surrounding *Augustinus* even before its publication. But it is improbable that this affair had a strong effect on Urban VIII. He was an old man consumed by illness and scruples who occupied himself mainly with poetry and politics, concentrating his efforts on the glory of his family, the Barberini, and leaving the government to his nephew, Cardinal Francesco Barberini. The latter—since he had been unable to prevent the publication of *Augustinus*—at the very least wanted to silence those involved in the controversy. On 1 August 1641 he published through the Holy Office a decree which condemned *Augustinus* as well as the theses of the Jesuits and numerous other publications of both parties. But the council of Brabant raised several legal obstacles allowing the University of Louvain to suppress the decree, which was thus left without any practical significance. Then the Jesuits started a comprehensive campaign aimed at having the teaching of *Augustinus* explicitly condemned. Several lists of anathematizeable theses were sent to Cardinal Barberini, but the Holy Office refused to condemn them before studying the work itself. However, Barberini superseded this decision and condemned the work on the grounds that it reiterated sentences condemned by Pius V and Gregory XIII. A corresponding bull dated 6 March was proposed. It was probably authored by Francesco Albizzi, an assessor in the Holy Office who took an especially active part in this affair. But additional negotiations ensued in which the nuncio of Cologne, Fabio Chigi, took a significant part because he expected to gain from them a reputation as a peacemaker. These negotiations delayed the publication in Rome of the bull *In eminenti*[13] until 19 June 1643. The circumstances associated with its publication were very debatable. The Belgian Jesuits had received copies of the bull from their Roman brothers and published it on their own responsibility even before the nuncios had been appraised of it.

---

[13] Text: *BullRom* 15, 92; Text and French trans.: *Recueil historique des bulles*, 36–45; see L. Ceyssens, "Les origines romaines de la bulle *In eminenti*," *Jansenistica* 3, 7–110.

Antonio Bichi, internuncio in Brussels, who had succeeded Stravius in that office in July 1642 and his uncle, Fabio Chigi, nuncio in Cologne, were officially informed of the bull shortly thereafter and published it, but they amended their own text and dated it 1643. Other editions were circulated, again offering different variations. Under these conditions the Dutch public for a while even doubted the authenticity of the bull. When it was finally recognized, the text contained so many doctrinal and juridical difficulties that in Flanders it was not effectively published until 1651.[14]

In Louvain the dean of theology, Schickelius, who had been won over to anti-Jansenism, tried to have the bull accepted before its publication. But he failed because most of his colleagues considered its motives erroneous, especially the assertion that *Augustinus* had stirred up trouble in the Church.[15] In order to change the Pope's decision, the Jansenists, in the name of the University of Louvain and the Brabant states, sent two representatives, Johannes Sinnich and Cornelius de Paepe, to Rome, where they arrived on 24 October 1643.[16] But this delegation proved useless since the Holy Office, in which Albizzi ruled supreme, let it be known at once that the bull would not be revised under any circumstances. De Paepe died in Rome. Sinnich received an audience with Urban VIII in the course of which the venerable Pope acknowledged that it was his intention not to have Jansen named in the bull. This indirectly implicated Albizzi as being responsible for the actual authorship of the bull. Taken aback by this development, Albizzi had the bull confirmed by a decree of the Holy Office on 16 June 1644.[17] Urban VIII died on 29 July 1644 and was succeeded by Innocent X (Pamfili). In several briefs[18] he demanded execution of the bull, but in reality he would have preferred to have things drag on. Sinnich returned to Louvain empty-handed in September 1645. The situation in the Netherlands gradually calmed down. It was in France that this matter was to take a decisive turn.

For some obscure reasons, the nuncio of Paris, Cardinal Hieronymus Grimaldi, did not receive his copy of the bull *In eminenti* which had been dispatched on 10 June 1643; the official documents regarding this

[14] Idem, "L'impasse de la bulle *In eminenti* en les années 1646–1649." *A Praem* 31 (1955), 227–52; 32 (1956), 5–59.
[15] Idem, "L'enquête officielle faite en 1644 sur le scandale causé par l'Augustinus," *AFrH* 43 (1950), 68–160.
[16] See Sinnich's report to the Louvain faculty in L. Ceyssens, "Verslag over de eerste Jansenistiche deputatie van Leuven te Rome, *Bulletin de l'Institut historique belge de Rome* 22 (1942), 31–111.
[17] Text, *Recueil historique des bulles*, 49.
[18] See the brief to Governor Castelrodrigo, ibid., 55–58.

problem did not reach him until September. In the meantime, the Jesuits of Rouen had had the text of the bull printed, which had already been disseminated by their fellow Jesuits in Flanders. But the numerous absurdities in it at first caused even Grimaldi to consider this publication a forgery. Arnauld, advised by Saint-Cyran, now gathered all possible arguments against the authenticity of the bull. These appeared in his *Premières* and *Secondes observations sur la bulle* in August 1643 and made a strong impression on public opinion. In the fall, after the authenticity of the bull had been acknowledged conclusively, the delegates from Louvain arrived in Paris on their way to Rome and coordinated their moves with the French Jansenists. With the help of efficacious parliamentary support Jansen's followers succeeded in preventing the adoption in France both of the bull and the decree of 16 June 1644. This was at the beginning of the regency of Anne of Austria and the unsettled state of the country marked by Mazarin's rise to power provided the Jansenists with opportunities for wide-ranging action. In September 1644 Arnauld circulated his *Première apologie pour M. Jansenius;* he followed it with a second in reply to renewed attacks by Habert. At the same time Arnauld replied to a Jesuit polemic against Saint-Cyran in his *Apologie pour M. de Saint-Cyran*, the first two parts of which had been composed by Lemaistre in 1639. It touches upon several problems of the doctrine of grace. But the basic problems of doctrine in *Augustinus* were hardly referred to at that time.

This unstable period was above all affected by conflicts kindled by Arnauld's *De la Fréquente communion*. This voluminous quarto had originally been nothing more than a very brief refutation of an essay published in 1641 by the Jesuit Sesmaisons, who presented ideas regarding penance and the Eucharist which were diametrically opposed to those of Saint-Cyran. With the aid of Saint-Cyran, Arnauld's work had grown into a comprehensive defense of Saint-Cyran's theses concerning the practice of "renewals," which later were represented as a return to the discipline of the early Church. This in turn had to please the representatives of the *milieu dévot* and of the Counter-Reformation. In August 1643 the work appeared with an approbation by fifteen bishops and twenty-one professors. It triggered a spirited exchange of charge and countercharge; Father Nouet attacked it vehemently in sermons at the Jesuit professed house in Paris. Arnauld countered in 1644 by publishing a copious collection of texts translated by Lemaistre, *La tradition de l'Église sur le sujet de la pénitence et de la communion*. But governmental circles where Mazarin's anti-Jansenism was gaining ground were not well-disposed towards Arnauld. Mazarin considered himself to be in a position to initiate rapport with the Holy Sea by ordering Arnauld and Barcos personally to defend the work in Rome. Arnauld and Barcos preferred to withdraw from Mazarin's immediate sphere of influence, but the Gallican circles protested against the decision, which in the last instance remained inconsequential. Those bishops who had given their approval felt involved by the controversy and brought the matter before the Holy See through a letter of 5 April 1644. A professor of the Sorbonne who had been one of those who had given their approval also was dispatched to Rome. By the time he returned in 1646,[19] the Holy Office had examined the book thoroughly and declined to censure it. In 1647 it merely condemned—without reference to the work—one sentence from the preface written by Barcos. It speaks of Peter and Paul as two heads of the Church, but who are one.[20] Parallel to this quarrel, which actually was a mere diversion, the first attacks against the laxism of the Jesuit theory of morality in the *Théologie morale des jésuites* (coauthored by Arnauld and Hallier, a professor at the Sorbonne, whose arguments were later to be reiterated by the *Provinciales*) began.

The Five Theses and the Bull *Cum occasione*

By 1645 it became obvious that Mazarin was exercising complete control over the queen regent and was continuing Richelieu's policies, including the latter's anti-Jansenist orientation. At court several of the friends of Port-Royal grasped the situation and changed their position. Those who remained loyal to Port-Royal were considered part of the opposition and were excluded. Arnauld d'Andilly himself ended his secular career and in 1646 withdrew from court. Vincent de Paul, a member of the *Conseil de Conscience* since 1643 and formerly a friend of Saint-Cyran, to whom he was indebted for many services, no longer dared oppose his fellow councilors; in 1648 he came out against Jansenism. Several others thought it wise to do the same. Finally Port-Royal remained the last bastion of resistance, which first Mazarin and then Louis XIV sought to reduce. For several years there were mere superficial quarrels in which the Jansenists were prominently represented by Arnauld, Barcos, and the Oratorian P. Desmares, and the anti-Jansenists by Habert and the Jesuits Deschamps and Pinthereau. The latter managed to procure some of the papers confiscated in Saint-Cyran's apartments and from 1646 to 1655 he published skillfully chosen excerpts from them, supplemented by an exceedingly dishonest commentary. In this manner he provided posterity with a wealth of valuable documents. By 1649 the stage was set for a massive attack on

[19] The report written by Bourgeois was published in 1695 through the efforts of Quesnel, see A. Arnauld, *Œuvres* 18, 665–734.
[20] Text of the decree: *Recueil historique des bulles*, 59–63.

Jansen. At a meeting of the Sorbonne on 1 July 1649 the syndic Nicolas Cornet, without reference to a particular work, submitted the following seven propositions to be examined:

1. Some of God's commandments cannot be followed by the righteous with the help of those powers available to them in the present state even if they want to follow them. Neither do they have the grace which would make it possible for them to be followed.
2. In the state of fallen nature inner grace never meets resistance.
3. In the state of fallen nature merit or demerit does not require man's freedom from inner compulsion; freedom from outer constraint is sufficient.
4. The Semi-Pelagians admitted the necessity of antecedent inner grace for the individual acts, also for the beginning of faith. Their error was to maintain that human will could resist or obey this grace.
5. It is Semi-Pelagian to assert that Christ has died or shed his blood for all men.
6. The acts of disbelievers are sins.
7. The Church earlier believed that the Sacrament of Penance was not sufficient for secret sins.

Immediately a stormy and chaotic discussion ensued, in the course of which several professors asserted that the present intention was to condemn the teachings of Augustine under the name of Jansen. In spite of the opposition of seventy of the participants a commission was charged with the examination requested by Cornet. A short time later Arnauld made public his *Considérations sur l'enterprise faite par Maître Nicolas Cornet,* in which he declared the formulation of the propositions to be deliberately ambiguous. In as much as a superficial reading could make them appear to have a heretical meaning, they could—from the Augustinian viewpoint—be taken in a completely orthodox sense. In the end, an appeal based on misuse of authority filed by sixty-one professors gave President Molé an opportunity to impose on both parties a four-month armistice which was honored only in the breach. The situation at the Sorbonne was further complicated by the fact that professors belonging to a religious order were each given a vote, whereas the old rules limited this right to only two representatives of each order so that block voting in accordance with instructions by the order could be avoided. Under these conditions it was impossible to compose and publish a censure of the propositions. Recourse to the Holy See, suggested earlier by the Roman Jesuits, now appeared unavoidable. This coincided with Rome's desire not to have such an important issue left up to the Sorbonne.

Towards the end of 1650, Isaac Habert, by now bishop of Vabres, wrote to Innocent X, submitting to him the first five propositions and vaguely ascribing them to Jansen.[21] For this letter the anti-Jansenists collected the signatures of bishops and when it was sent to Rome early in 1651 there were seventy-eight, another fifteen signatures were added later. At that time the French episcopate totaled about one hundred and thirty bishops. Arnauld countered the letter by arguments similar to those used in his reply to Nicolas Cornet. The episcopate also had supporters of Jansen, among them Henri Arnauld, bishop of Angers and brother of the Great Arnauld. At the meeting of clergy from February to March 1651 several bishops protested to the nuncio against Habert's action. A little later eleven participants wrote a letter to Innocent X, an action which later gained the support of two more bishops. Saint-Amour, a professor at the Sorbonne who happened to be in Rome, was willing to represent their cause and presented the letter on 10 July 1651. In the following months other Jansenist delegates came to Rome. The anti-Jansenists, too, initially represented there by the Franciscan Mulard, sent three more emissaries in April 1652. All signs pointed to a long wait for a decision. Meanwhile the conflict again turned to less important matters. One of them involved the appearance of a *Catéchisme de la grâce* by the Jansenist Feydear; another was provoked by the teachings of Alphonse Le Moyne, an anti-Jansenist professor at the Sorbonne whom Arnauld opposed by his *Apologie pour les saints Pères*, one of his best works. Other incidents concerned the convent of Port-Royal, whose father confessor, Antoine Singlin, was prohibited from preaching in 1649. In a pamphlet by the Jesuit Brisacier, *Le jansénisme confondu* (1651) the convent also was accused of surreptitious Calvinism.

From the start, the Jansenist delegation in Rome made the mistake of demanding convocations with public discussions similar to the congregations *De Auxiliis*, while Innocent X wanted to be the sole judge in this issue. The precise details of these tiresome negotiations can be perused in Saint-Amour's *Journal*.[22] In April 1651 a commission of cardinals was formed; in September 1652 another commission, consisting of theologians, dealt with the matter. There was only one Jesuit member and it was distinguished by the remarkable manner in which the Franciscan Luke Wadding[23] defended Jansen. The two delegations

---

[21] Habert's letter can be found in *Recueil historique*, 74–77.

[22] Saint-Amour kept a diary of his negotiations; it was edited by Arnauld and published in 1662.

[23] See L. Ceyssens, "Florence Conry," cf n. 2.

were empowered to send briefs to the commission, but were not allowed official meetings with each other. They were received in audience very rarely and even then only separately. Several extremely interesting polemical writings originated at that time, especially the *Écrit à trois colonnes*[24] which was handed to the commission by Jansen's supporters on the occasion of their last audience on 19 May 1653. It is extremely significant if one is to understand Jansenist thought. For each of the five propositions it distinguishes between orthodox and heretical meaning and also lists the opposing Molinist position. In reality political factors had a decisive part in the negotiations. On the one hand, Rome did not want to change its mind and retract the bull *In eminenti*. On the other hand, the Holy See—very sensitive on the issue of Gallicanism—had been well disposed to the appeal by the anti-Jansenist bishops and was prepared to allow them to emerge victorious especially since they represented a large majority of the episcopate. After all, Mazarin, with whom good contacts were desired, had come out openly against Jansenism and in 1651 had even sent to Rome a letter signed by the young King Louis XIV. Given these conditions, another condemnation of Jansen was unavoidable and indeed it seems as though the responsible circles in Rome never thought of an alternative. Here and there certain representatives wanted orthodox Augustinianism to be excepted explicitly from the condemnation, but this was not done. The bull *Cum occasione*, dated 31 May 1653 and published on 3 June, condemned without reservations the five propositions which it ascribed to Jansen, the first four as heretical, the fifth one as erroneous.[25] This bull was a complete victory for the anti-Jansenists. In Flanders it was accepted without difficulties. The Jansenists, hit hard by the recent censures of the archbishop of Mechelen and the bishop of Ghent and much weakened by the deaths in quick succession of Calenus and Froidmont (February, October 1653, respectively), resisted but feebly. Indeed Louvain was no longer the home of the Jansenist party: it was now Paris.[26]

---

[24] The "Écrit à trois colonnes" is in the appendix of the *Journal de M. de Saint-Amour* (n. p. 1662).

[25] Text: *BullRom* 15, 720: Text and French trans.: *Recueil historique des bulles*, 79–86; see D 2001–07.

[26] L. Ceyssens, "La publication aux Pays-Bas de la seconde bulle contre Jansénius," *Augustiniana* 7 (1957), 196–240, 389–426, 576–93.

CHAPTER 3

The Jansenist Conflict to 1713

The *quaestio juris* and the *quaestio facti*
The *Provinciales*

The bull *Cum occasione* no doubt represented a victory for the anti-Jansenists, since Mazarin exerted his own efforts at having the bull accepted throughout France. An order to this effect was addressed to parliament and the clergy by means of a royal declaration dated 4 July 1653. Mazarin had the bull acknowledged in the name of the whole clergy by the twenty-eight bishops present in Paris at that time and shortly thereafter the Sorbonne was also forced to accept it. But a few bishops published it with certain reservations by means of which they sought to save orthodox Augustinianism. Port-Royal found itself in an especially difficult situation. The *Fronde* had become weaker and weaker. In the most recent disturbances the people of Port-Royal, while proving their absolute loyalty to the crown, had clearly shown their antipathy towards Mazarin, the real victor. In addition, there is no doubt that several pamphlets by the coadjutor of Paris, the future Cardinal Retz, had been edited by the men of Port-Royal. It is therefore understandable that the Jansenists at first took refuge in silence. But the clumsy triumph of their adversaries enabled them to come out into the open again. First they responded to a tasteless cartoon in an almanac which appeared in 1654. In it Jansen and his pupils are depicted throwing themselves into the arms of Calvin. Sacy replied to it with a long satirical poem *Enluminures du fameux almanach des jésuites*. In February 1654 the Jesuit Father François Annat, the King's father confessor, published a polemic with the title *Chicanes des Jansénistes* asserting that the Pope in his last bull had intended not even to spare the teachings of Saint Augustine. He also maintained that the five propositions had been taken literally from the *Augustinus*. In March Arnauld responded with three essays which represented a manifesto of the new Jansenist point of view. First he cleared up the question of the so-called *quaestio facti;* he proved that only the first proposition is contained in the *Augustinus* but in a context proving it to be orthodox. He goes on to prove that the rest of the propositions might have summarized other passages of the work, but that these, too, are de facto orthodox and reflect only Augustinian thinking. Finally, he cites propositions from the *Augustinus* which pronounce the opposite of those that were condemned. Arnauld concludes that while the propositions with a heretical meaning were justifiably condemned by Innocent X, they were in their heterodox meaning not ascribable to Jansen.

But Arnauld could not actually reach public opinion. In a conference of thirty-eight bishops of 9 March 1654, Mazarin prevailed with a text which acknowledged the condemnation of the propositions as reflecting Jansen's ideas. In a rejoinder of 29 September Innocent X issued a brief with the same objective.[1] On 15 January 1655 Mazarin forced a conference of 15 bishops to have all the clergy and female branches of orders sign a formulary condemning Jansen. But in order not to aggravate the situation, this measure was not immediately implemented. Once again the actual doctrinal issue was not resolved. The Jesuit Étienne Deschamps revived it in his voluminous treatise *De l'hérésie jansénienne* (1654). By means of a formulary, later taken up by Bossuet, he tried to prove that the five propositions were the core of *Augustinus,* but he had absolutely no success. The pamphlets then turned to the realm of politics. In his *Relation juridique* (1654) the publicist Filleau de la Chaise spread the falsehood that a meeting had taken place in 1620 at the Carthusian monastery of Bourgfontaine in the course of which Jansen, Saint-Cyran, and others had articulated a plan to introduce deism and to destroy belief in the Eucharist. At the same time the royal almoner Marandé made an effort in his *Inconvénients d'état* to represent the Jansenists as dangerous opponents of the authority of the state.

Another incident soon heated up the conflict again. On 1 February 1655 the vicar of Saint-Sulpice, Picoté, refused absolution to the duke of Liancourt because of the duke's well-known relations with Port-Royal.[2] Picoté was supported in his stand by the famous Jean-Jacques Olier, pastor of Saint-Sulpice, who was extremely hostile towards Jansenism. This incident attracted much attention and even the intercession by Vincent de Paul came to nought. Three weeks later Arnauld made the issue public through his *Lettre à une personne de condition*, which his adversaries countered with about ten pamphlets. It took Arnauld four months, until 10 July 1655, to reply to them in his *Seconde lettre à un duc et pair*, which is actually an extensive work summarizing the position of French Jansenism with a remarkable degree of clarity. He accepts without reservation the condemnation of the heresy contained in the five propositions, but he considers it preferable not to comment as to whether or not they should be attributed to Jansen. He adds that he had not discovered them in a close reading of *Augustinus*. Then he vigorously attacks the Molinist concept of *gratia sufficiens* citing Peter and his denial of the Lord as an example of a righteous person who sinned because he was lacking in grace. Arnauld's opponents immediately

---

[1] Letter and brief: *Recueil historique des bulles,* 120–131.
[2] See the duke's authentic report: "Une relation authentique du duc de Liancourt," *Documents d'Histoire* 3 (March 1912), 90–96.

sought to have him condemned because of the last two propositions concerning the *Augustinus* and Peter. Arnauld wanted to anticipate them by bringing the issue before the Holy See by a letter of 27 August. Nonetheless it was placed on the agenda of a meeting of the Sorbonne on 4 November. It took place in spite of protests by Arnauld, who asked in vain for a hearing and just as unsuccessfully multiplied his written justifications to the assembly. An initial censure was pronounced on 14 January 1655 under circumstances so contrary to the rules that sixty professors withdrew from the Sorbonne. Nevertheless Arnauld was expelled from the Sorbonne on 15 February. In his defense he was supported by a young theologian from Chartres, Pierre Nicole (1625–95), who from then on played a significant role in the quarrel over Jansenism. Unfortunately Arnauld and Nicole only spoke the language of theologians. Whereas their extraordinary level of erudition in this field assured them of a hearing among their kind, their works hardly met with a response from the general public. At this time, however, as Mazarin's position was gradually weakening, the actual problem was on the level of public opinion. Then, even before the final condemnation of Arnauld, Port-Royal found a man who was uniquely suited to help them out: Blaise Pascal (1623–62).

Up to this time the recluses of Port-Royal[3] had considered Blaise Pascal (Chap. 6) a young man of the world, occupied with the sciences, a recent convert who was friendly towards the convent in which his younger sister Jacqueline had lived as a nun since January 1652. When Arnauld, Nicole, and he were in Port-Royal des Champs in January 1656, a casual invitation by Arnauld prompted him to lend his literary ability to a polemic which was intended for society at large and not for specialists. On 23 January 1656 the *Provinciales* came into being. This first letter to a friend in the country was an enormous success and initiated a new episode in the conflict. The collaborators quickly found that they were on the right path and so another seventeen *Provinciales* were issued in the course of a little more than a year, the last one dated 24 March 1657. This campaign, being rather dangerous, forced Arnauld, Nicole, and Pascal to go into hiding in order to evade a *lettre de cachet* which would have sent them to the Bastille. The printing, too, was done in hiding and successfully evaded every police investigation. In spite of the dangerous conditions the *Provinciales*, starting with the fifth letter, were printed in 6,000 copies, at that time an unusually large circulation.[4] Attesting to the lasting nature of their success is the fact

[3] See L. Cognet, "Le jugement de Port-Royal sur Pascal," *Blaise Pascal, l'homme et l'œuvre* (Paris 1956), 11–30.
[4] See L. Parcé, "La réimpression des premieres Provinciales," *Pascal, textes du tricentaire* (Paris 1963), 142–59.

that three editions in one volume appeared between 1657 and 1659. For a long time the public was left to guess about the author; not until 1659 did the fact of Pascal's authorship gradually become known.

Pascal collaborated closely with Arnauld and Nicole; he lent the magic of his incomparable style to the documentation and arguments of the two specialists. He also made use of numerous polemic writings which had appeared earlier and whose contents were now made known to the broad public. Yet he did not meet with complete agreement at Port-Royal; Mother Angélique and Singlin considered this campaign to be irreconcilable with Christian love. With the fifth *Provinciale*—after Arnauld was defeated at the Sorbonne—Pascal counterattacked. Taking up an old polemic, he assailed the laxist morality of the Jesuit casuists. With this topic he found himself on favorable terrain. Rigorism in morality was indeed not only inherited by Port-Royal, but widespread as well among the best representatives of the clergy and among the faithful. By identifying the Jesuits with laxism, Pascal discredited the Society of Jesus to such an extent that they could never quite overcome it. The conflict thus introduced was to continue far beyond the *Provinciales*. The secular clergy took up the fight again by means of the *Écrits des Curés de Paris*, in which Pascal also collaborated. This led to a number of decrees by the Holy Office under Alexander VII (1665, 1666) and Innocent XI (1679),[5] which condemned 110 laxist propositions; 50 of them were indirectly from the *Provinciales*. Unfortunately Pascal had no congenial adversary in the opposite camp. Aside from several replies by individual anti-Jansenists, the Jesuits after the sixth letter published collaborative retorts whose main authors were probably Fathers Annat and Nouet, the latter an excellent writer in the field of spirituality, but merely an average polemicist. These retorts, discussing a boundless wealth of details from the casuist texts quoted by Pascal, were indeed mediocre. But they benefitted Pascal since they gave the impression to the public that the Jesuits were actually identifying themselves with these controversial casuistic positions. The tone of the *Provinciales* became increasingly sharper and more vehement; the last two addressed directly to Father Annat are especially caustic. But this did not prevent a Parisian Jesuit, Georges Pirot, from publishing a clumsy *Apologie des casuistes* in December 1657, which by provoking spirited disapproval further weakened the Jesuit position.

The *Provinciales* indeed had great influence on the public; this is reflected in the letters of Mme de Sévigné and the physician Guy Patin. Public opinion was also agitated by the famous miracle of the holy thorn

---

[5] Text of Alexander VII's decrees: *BullRom* 17, 387–389, 427–428; D 2021–65; Innocent XI's *BullRom* 19, 145–149, D 2101–67.

which occurred on 24 March at Port-Royal, where Pascal's niece, Marguerite Périer, was healed from a lachrymal fistula by means of a thorn from the Holy Crown. In spite of objections by the Jesuits this was generally seen as a sign in favor of Port-Royal. But none of this changed the attitude of the prominent circles. Mazarin, as well as Chancellor Séguier, irritated more than ever by the *Provinciales*, made increasing attempts to eliminate Jansenism. Innocent X, of a rather more indifferent nature, never wanted to get seriously involved in this fight. When he died on 7 January 1655 he was succeeded by the former nuncio of Cologne, Fabio Chigi, a decided anti-Jansenist who acceded to the papal throne as Alexander VII. As of the end of 1655, a new bull concerning Jansen was being prepared, but initially kept secret in order to be issued at some advantageous point in time. In the summer of 1654 the French assembly of the clergy pressured by Mazarin again ordered signing of the formulary against Jansen and by an official letter to Alexander VII, dated 2 September, requested a definitive decision in the *quaestio facti*.[6] The Holy See considered this a favorable moment: on 16 October 1656 the bull *Ad sacram*[7] was officially signed. A nuncio extraordinary, Piccolomini, took it to Paris the following January, but various negotiations delayed its official delivery to the King until 2 March 1657. Mazarin, on 17 March, forced the Assembly of the Clergy to accept. Parliament put off its acceptance for a while longer and it took a formal court day on 29 November to break its resistance (Chap. 7).

The Formulary

The bull *Ad sacram* caused a violent outbreak of emotion in France. For the Jansenists it represented another defeat and forced them into formulating a new position. Arnauld and Nicole dealt with this problem in various writings published between April and August 1657. In the *quaestio juris*, that is concerning the heresy contained in the five propositions, Arnauld came out in full agreement with the papal condemnation. But in the *quaestio facti*, that is concerning the actual presence of the five propositions in the *Augustinus*, he presented the view that the Pope was simply in error. He maintained that this was entirely possible since the Church was not infallible in nonrevealed facts. On this point he thus refused his inner concurrence and obliged himself to a mere "reverential silence." But this attitude on the part of Arnauld and Nicole did not meet with complete agreement by Port-Royal. Several

---

[6] Letter: *Recueil historique des bulles,* 136–43.
[7] Text of the bull: *BullRom* 16, 247, see D 2010–12; text and French trans.: *Recueil historique des bulles,* 144–149.

thought that in the last analysis the condemnation of the five propositions redounded upon Augustinianism as such and that it should therefore be opposed without reservation, even at the price of a schism. The major proponents of this extremist group were the bishop of Alet, Nicolas Pavillon, who was widely revered because of the holiness of his life, and the abbot of Haute-Fontaine, Guillaume Le Roy. Yet others held Arnauld's tactical comments to be absurd. Proceeding from the concept of an unalterably evil world in which it is impossible to defend the truth, they thought it better to submit to the papal condemnations and to leave to God's care the victory of His cause. Barcos, the nephew of Saint-Cyran, was a central figure of this group. But by virtue of his theological authority, Arnauld's ideas were clearly given preeminence.

For Mazarin, anti-Jansenism had actually been above all an argument intended to secure papal neutrality in the conflict with Spain. Having reached this goal he was no longer intent upon a crisis. But after his death (9 March 1661) Louis XIV personally took charge of the battle. Pursued by the specter of the *Fronde* he was determined to do away with all the sources of opposition which endangered national unity. His determination had a bearing upon both Jansenism and Protestantism. Yet on this point the King, who was not very intelligent and indeed very ignorant in religious matters, was totally in the hands of his Jesuit confessors. On 20 February 1661 the bishops of the Assembly of the Clergy had again taken up the issue of the formulary and had asked Alexander VII for his approbation.[8] On 23 April a decree by the Council of State relentlessly demanded the signing of the formulary and in doing so forced the Jansenists to take a stand. Arnauld declared himself ready to sign the formulary, but only if his distinction between the *quaestio juris* and the *quaestio facti* were appended to it. The two vicars general who were administering the Paris diocese in the absence of their archbishop, the famous Cardinal Retz, who had fled, accepted Arnauld's condition. On 8 June 1661 a pastoral letter probably edited by Pascal himself prescribed the signing with the added distinction, which satisfied the group around Arnauld. But faced with opposition by official circles they had to retract the pastoral letter on 31 October and instead to demand the signing without any reservation. Thus Port-Royal was driven to refusal.

At this point the convent and its friends had already suffered severe agitation against them. By 23 April the postulants and pupils had been removed. The spiritual leaders and confessors as well as the most prominent recluses were to be exiled by *lettres de cachet* or imprisoned, but they managed to flee, pursued by the authorities. Later, in May

[8] Text: ibid, 151–65.

1666, the police with the aid of an informant succeeded in arresting the nephew of Mother Angélique, Isaac Lemaistre de Sacy, who was subsequently jailed in the Bastille till October 1668. The nuns were prohibited from flight by their monastic confinement and were therefore in the midst of the situation. Naturally none of them had ever read the *Augustinus* and only three or four of them, such as Angélique de Saint-Jean Arnauld d'Andilly, the niece of Mother Angélique, had even had any theological education. But their reverence for Saint-Cyran absolutely convinced them of Jansen's orthodoxy. So a majority of them rejected any signing of the formulary, even a conditional one, and on this point stood in opposition to Arnauld. Mother Angélique died in August 1661; in the course of the summer passionate internal disagreements erupted at Port-Royal. The resistance was led by Angélique de Saint-Jean and Jacqueline Pascal. But when the pastoral letter by the vicars general was retracted Arnauld and the nuns again agreed in their unqualified refusal to sign. A short time later the archbishop of Paris, Retz, resigned; his successor, Pierre de Marca, died four months later without having occupied the bishopric. Thereupon Louis XIV appointed his former teacher Hardouin de Péréfixe. But in July 1662 some difficulties arose between France and the Holy See. As a result Péréfixe had to wait one and a half years for his bull of investiture and the events centered upon Port-Royal were left in abeyance. There were some who understood that compromise was preferable to the continued conflict. Among them was the bishop of Comminges, Gilbert de Choiseul, who attempted to reconcile the parties in 1663, but the respective views concerning the *quaestio facti* proved irreconcilable.

In April 1664 Péréfixe finally became archbishop of Paris. At once irascible and good natured, an average theologian, he was convinced that he could easily overcome the Jansenist resistance. On 8 June 1664 he issued a pastoral letter which acknowledged the distinction between de jure and de facto by demanding the divine faith for the *quaestio juris* and a simple "human faith" for the *quaestio facti*. But this could only half satisfy the theologians of Port-Royal, who were unwilling to go beyond the "reverential silence" in the *quaestio facti*. Nicole was entrusted with the reply and in his *Lettres sur l'hérésie imaginaire* and other pamphlets he sharply rejected the archbishop's view. Péréfixe, beside himself, took his revenge on the nuns. On 21 and 26 August, after two dramatic visits at the convent of Paris, he had twelve of them deported to other convents. Among them were Angélique de Saint-Jean and the aged Mother Agnès. In Paris and at the convent of des Champs the nuns were refused the sacraments and were placed under police supervision. The incredible moral torture brought about by such coercion on the part of the archbishop and his people finally made twelve of the nuns sign the formulary, but some of them renounced it later. Reports about these events written by the nuns immediately afterwards and smuggled outside were published. They created a great stir, for the archbishop had frequently been compromised by his intemperate disposition. Furthermore the *Apologie pour les religieuses de Port-Royal*, composed at the beginning of 1665 by Arnauld and Nicole, brought all the events before the public. Through one of the nuns who had signed, the "traitoress" Flavie Passart, Péréfixe had found out about the internal tensions at Port-Royal and wanted to make use of them with the help of the publicist Desmaret de Saint-Sorlin. But Nicole succeeded in neutralizing the latter by ridiculing his exaggerated mysticism in the *Visionnaires*. The small number of signatures he had gotten from the nuns was a serious defeat for the archbishop. In an attempt to stabilize the situation, those nuns who refused to sign were gathered at Port-Royal des Champs and guarded by a police unit, while those who had signed stayed in Paris with a special abbess, Dorothée Perdreau. But neither of these measures solved the problem.

In the meantime Alexander VII had responded to the wishes of the French clergy by issuing in February 1665 the bull *Regiminis apostolici*, which also ordered the signing of a formulary.[9] But the bull only made matters worse because four bishops published it together with a clear distinction between the *quaestio juris* and the *quaestio facti* and in doing so openly took the side of Port-Royal. Among them were Henri Arnauld and Nicolas Pavillon. The Courts of France and Rome were equally annoyed. Father Annat considered the possibility of asking the Pope to remove the four bishops, but this idea had to be given up in order not to provoke the opposition of the entire episcopate, who would not have tolerated such a measure. In January 1667 the Holy See appointed a commission to initiate a trial against the dissidents. This prompted an immediate declaration of solidarity by nineteen bishops; twenty more entered a protest against the papal action. But Clement IX, a peaceful man, who had succeeded Alexander VII as Pope, desired reconciliation (see Chap. 7). Louis XIV, having also recognized that war with Holland was unavoidable, wanted to settle the religious quarrels and reunite the kingdom. In 1668 Nuncio Bargellini was charged with the task of seeking ways to reach an agreement. The Jesuits were excluded from the negotiations in which Gondrin, archbishop of Sens, Ligny, bishop of Meaux, and Vialart, bishop of Châlons, played a decisive role. In the summer of 1668 there was reason for hope. It was agreed that the four bishops in question were to write to the Pope

[9] Text of the bull: *BullRom* 17, 336, see D 2020; text and French trans.: *Recueil historique des bulles*, 223–30.

pledging to publish the bull *Regiminis apostolici* again and to have it signed in their dioceses. The Pope on his part was to tolerate tacitly that the signing would be performed through protocols which—theoretically secret, but in reality generally known—would make the distinction between de facto and de jure. The group of people around Arnauld and Nicole who tended more towards the status of a moderate third party was completely satisfied with this agreement, but not so the extremists of the two opposing parties. A council decree of 23 October 1668 and a brief by Clement IX of 14 January 1669 gave the Clementine Peace official sanction. But the nuns of Port-Royal, still tortured by the same doubts as before, could not decide in favor. Urged by Sacy, they finally signed on 15 February 1669 and were ceremoniously admitted to receive the sacraments.

The Clementine Peace

For almost thirty years the Clementine Peace, imperfect though it was, brought to an end the doctrinal controversies and accorded Port-Royal its last quiet decade. During this period the old convent had loyal and highly placed friends; it was cared for and protected by the former heroine of the *Fronde*, the duchess de Longueville, cousin to the King. But all this could not but displease Louis XIV, who continued to see in this circle a source of opposition against his absolutism. Yet he was intent on letting nothing happen that could reignite the conflicts.

The people of Port-Royal were now in a position to turn their intellectual endeavors to peaceful areas, in which they had excelled earlier, among them the subject of spirituality. A decision was made to research the documents left by the great deceased, to emend them and make them available to the public. At the beginning of 1670, Pascal's *Pensées* appeared, followed in 1671 by two volumes of the *Considérations sur les dimanches et les fêtes,* excerpts from the notes of Saint-Cyran, whose *Lettres chrétiennes et spirituelles* was reissued in Louvain in 1679. Also published were original works such as the *Traités de Piété* by the physician of Port-Royal, M. Hamon (1617) and the *Essais de Morale* by Nicole (1671). Translations were also published, among them Teresa of Ávila (1670), John of Ávila (1673) and many others. Port-Royal strove to make biblical texts accessible to the faithful. During the last crisis in 1667 the group had published a translation from the Greek of the New Testament. Called the *Nouveau Testament de Mons*[10] after its place of origin, it owes its existence primarily to Arnauld, Nicole and Sacy.

[10] See E. Hublard, *Le Nouveau Testament de Mons, histoire d'un livre* (Mons 1914); E. Jacques, "Les sympathies jansénistes à Mons à la fin du XVIIᵉ siècle, *Annales du Cercle archéologique de Mons* 66 (1965–67) 249–309.

Although it was a precise and elegant translation, it provoked a violent polemic and was put on the Index in 1668. Sacy—while jailed at the Bastille—had started work on a translation of the Vulgate which he began publishing together with commentaries from the church Fathers. After his death in 1684 his pupils concluded the work. The liturgical translations of Port-Royal—*Heures de Port-Royal* and *Office de Saint-Sacrement* (1659) had several revised reprints. Finally the group also turned to polemicizing against the Calvinists, Arnauld and Nicole collaborating with Bossuet. It is possible that Arnauld even had a significant hand in the *Expositions de la doctrine de l'Église catholique* published by Bossuet in 1671. Nicole—although collaborating with Arnauld—was the main author of *Perpétuité de la foi de l'Église catholique touchant l'Eucharistie*, an imposing work whose first volume appeared in 1669.

In reality both sides knew that the peace thus maintained was very fragile and several incidents clearly demonstrated the true sentiments of the court. In 1675 Henri Arnauld was accused of not permitting the unqualified signing of the formulary in his diocese of Angers. For this Louis XIV reprimanded him through the Edict of Camp de Ninove (30 May 1676). The King was very annoyed in the beginning of 1677 when a memorandum authored by Nicole and signed by two bishops submitted several laxist propositions to the new Pope Innocent XI. But most of all it was the unpleasant regalia quarrel between Louis XIV and the Holy See going on since 1675, in which Arnauld unequivocally sided with the Holy See against the King.[11] When the Treaty of Nijmegen had ended the war and the duchess of Longueville died on 15 April 1679 Louis XIV decided to liquidate Port-Royal without, however, causing the doctrinal quarrels to be rekindled. On 16 May the confessors, pupils, and novices were removed from the convent, an action which condemned it to die out. Arnauld, fearing for his freedom, left the country in June 1679. Although Innocent XI had a retirement home and probably also a cardinalate offered to him, he rejected this solution because it would make it impossible for him to return to France. After a long period of indecision he took up residence in Brussels, where he died on 8 August 1694, having continued polemics against the Jesuits and later on against Malebranche and his ideas of grace. Nicole, who had gone into exile with Arnauld, received the support of the new archbishop of Paris, Harlay de Champvallon, which enabled him to return to France in 1683. But he no longer participated

---

[11] See A. Latreille, "Innocent XI pape janséniste, directeur de conscience de Louis XIV," *Cahiers d'histoire* [publications of the universities of Grenoble, Lyon, and Clermont-Ferrand], 1 (1956), 9–39.

in the conflicts with the Jesuits and because of this the party looked upon him to some extent as a turncoat.

In 1685 Arnauld received two Oratorians in Brussels who had been forced to leave France because of their Augustinian convictions. The younger of the two, Jacques-Joseph Du Guet (1649–1733), was soon forced by ill health to return home, where he began a career as a religious writer. The other, Pasquier Quesnel (1634–1719) (See Chap. 5), remained till the end a loyal companion to Arnauld. Before his arrival, Quesnel had distinguished himself by scholarly works, among them an excellent edition of the writings of Leo the Great. His personal views were determined by an Augustinianism strongly influenced by Bérulle. He was also strongly affected by the thoughts of Saint Thomas Aquinas, whose work he knew extremely well. Given these conditions, the rigid, archaizing Augustinianism of Jansen did not appeal very much to him and so it was understandable that he had earlier signed the formulary four times. Quesnel, moreover, tended towards Gallicanism and was influenced by ideas advocated by Edmond Richer at the beginning of the seventeenth century. He shared Richer's belief that within the Church the blessing of truth is not entrusted to the Pope and the bishops alone, but to the totality of the faithful who share the responsibility for it and therefore have the same right as the hierarchy to judge the doctrine. A dogmatic truth then could only become binding if the host of the faithful accepted it. Intellectually Quesnel clearly influenced Arnauld in a Thomist direction. This is apparent most of all in the last great works of the aged theologian. Quesnel was also much more the politician than Arnauld. A determined opponent of Jesuits and Molinists, he perceived that the presence of Jansenism among the leading ranks of those advocating parliamentarianism, which was traditionally opposed to royal absolutism, created a set of favorable circumstances to be used to good advantage. For this purpose Jansenism had to be changed into a firmly structured party and this was Quesnel's achievement. Clear-sighted and persistent, endowed with leadership qualities, he soon established an expansive network of Jansenist agencies all across Europe and so perfected the work started by some of his predecessors, mainly by Du Vaucel and Pontchâteau.[12] But even though Quesnel wanted the Augustinian party to be victorious, he was not willing to side with Jansenism, which he did not esteem very highly. Through his *Tradition de l'Église romaine sur la prédestination des saints et*

[12] See B. Neveu, "Un janséniste à Rome: les deux missions de M. de Pontchâteau (1677–1680)," *Annuaire de la section des Sciences religieuses de l'École pratique des Hautes-Études* 74 (1966–67), 197–202.

sur la grâce efficace, which connected incarnation and grace completely from the perspective of Bérulle and thereby at great remove from Jansen, he tried to remain aloof from the latter (1687–90).

But there still were supporters of Jansen who considered him the authentic interpreter of Saint Augustine. This view was shared by Barcos (whose manuscripts Quesnel at one time even ordered destroyed), by a significant group of theologians in Louvain who put up a desperate fight, and by a French Benedictine, Dom Gabriel Gerberon (1628–1711), whose intransigent Jansenism forced him into Dutch exile. From there he liberally criticized Arnauld and Quesnel, who on their part held him to be a dangerous muddlehead. To counter Quesnel's ideas, Gerberon had an earlier essay by Barcos, in which the latter had advocated an aggressive but awkward Augustinianism, *Exposition de la foi catholique touchant la grâce et la prédestination,* published in 1690. This untimely publication led to excited protests in Paris even by moderate Jansenists. But at the same time it offered the intransigents a point of reference. The new archbishop of Paris, Noailles, outwardly manifested Augustinianism. He felt obliged to condemn the *Exposition,* and did so in an order of 20 August 1696, whose doctrinal part, composed by Bossuet, emphatically laid a foundation for Augustinianism. Of course he distrusted everyone. Quesnel thereupon advised silence, but Gerberon and the intransigents in Paris circulated several pamphlets against the archbishop, among them the especially malicious *Histoire abrégée du jansénisme* (1697).

In 1695 when he was still bishop of Châlons, Noailles had given his approbation to Quesnel's *Le Nouveau Testament en français avec des réflexions morales sur chaque verset,* a revised edition of a much shorter work of the year 1671. On the spiritual level much of the commentary was excellent, but Quesnel's Augustinianism was often expressed in very categorical formulas and his sympathies for Richer's system were clearly discernible. Noailles was quite dismayed when a brochure entitled *Problème ecclésiastique* appeared towards the end of 1698 which posed the question of whether the Noailles who had approbated Quesnel or the Noailles who had condemned Barcos was to be believed. He found himself in a position of having contradicted himself. For a long time this piece was attributed to the Jesuits; the real author was not identified until modern times: he was Dom Hilarion Monnier, a Benedictine from Saint-Vanne who was an extreme Jansenist, but had had nothing to do with its publication.[13] The pamphlet was condemned by parliament on 10 January 1699—a reply was imperative. Noailles turned to Bossuet, who

[13] See A. Vacant, "Renseignements inédits sur l'auteur du Problème ecclésiastique, *"Revue des sciences ecclésiastiques* 61 (1890), 411–25; 62 (1891), 34–50, 131–50.

composed an *Avertissement* to appear at the beginning of a new, revised edition of the *Réflexions morales*. But meanwhile the prelates got into a squabble over the issue of quietism. Bossuet's text was not published until 1710, but Noailles made use of it in the four *Lettres d'un théologien* (1700). Although he was not immediately involved in this matter, Quesnel again played the part of a mediator. At this point the whole affair came to a halt and no one could foresee that it was destined to become the starting point for eighteenth-century Jansenism.

The Way to the Bull *Unigenitus*

Another incident soon renewed the conflict. At the beginning of 1701 the priest of Notre-Dame du Port at Clermont, Fréhel, submitted to the Sorbonne a question of conscience. It was soon common knowledge that it concerned Pascal's nephew, Louis Périer. The question: can a penitent be granted absolution when he asserts that he cannot go beyond the reverential silence in the *quaestio facti?* A well-known Jansenist, Nicolas Petitpied, drafted a positive answer which—after various negotiations—was approved by forty professors on 20 July 1701, but rejected by Bossuet. It was not published right away and indeed it should never have been published. But in July 1702 the *Cas de Conscience* and the answer were printed and promptly generated a flood of pamphlets. The Holy Office condemned the *Cas* on 12 February 1703. Noailles, who had initially been on the positive side, joined in the condemnation on 22 February. But this did not end the polemic, for not until 4 September 1704 did the Sorbonne issue the condemnation. Petitpied refused to recant and withdrew to Holland.

By that time Fénelon (see Chap. 5) had decided to enter the fray. Sympathetic to the Jesuits, who for the most part had defended him loyally on the issue of *L'Explication des Maximes des Saints sur la vie intérieure*, he had opposed Jansenism for the past ten years.[14] So when Gerberon offered to defend his ideas concerning Pure Love, he did not have to change his convictions at all.[15] On 15 February 1704 he made public a pastoral instruction[16] in which he developed ideas which placed him in the center of the conflict without being able to satisfy anybody at all. As he saw it, the condemnation of Jansen could have a bearing only on the *sensus obvius* of his book, but not on the personal intentions of its author. But concerning this *sensus obvius*, the Church could make a decision and indeed an infallible one. In fact he asserted that the Church

[14] See H. Hillenaar, *Fénelon et les jésuites* (The Hague 1967).
[15] See J. Orcibal, "La spiritualité de Dom Gabriel Gerberon, champion de Jansénius et de Fénelon," *RHEF* 43 (1957), 151–222.
[16] Fenelon, *Œuvres* 3, 573–636.

could be infallible in such dogmatic facts as were not revealed; that included Jansen's *quaestio facti* as well. This theory encountered opposition by almost all the specialists in France and by many theologians in Rome. But Fénelon defended and further defined his ideas in three more pastoral instructions in March and April 1705. At the same time he made use of his good relations with Pope Clement XI in order to achieve an unequivocal opinion from the Holy See in favor of his thesis of infallibility in nonrevealed facts. But the Holy See was not so inclined and would have preferred for Fénelon to support the thesis of the personal infallibility of the Pope defended by a majority of the Roman theologians. This led to a misunderstanding and cooled the relations between the prelate and Rome,[17] whereupon Fénelon—sorely disappointed—no longer demanded the formulary to be signed in his diocese.

In the meantime the pamphleteering of Quesnel and Gerberon had made the authorities of the Netherlands uneasy. On 30 May 1703 the two were arrested in Brussels and incarcerated at the jail of the court at Mechelin. Gerberon was extradited to the French police and never regained his freedom, but Quesnel managed to flee in a most unusual manner on 13 September. He took up residence in Amsterdam and resumed his activities. But the documents confiscated in his apartment demonstrated the power and efficacy of the Jansenist network spread over all of Europe. They led directly to the arrest of a number of party agents, among others Quesnel's correspondent in Paris, Germain Vuillarts.[18] The documents also showed the strange way in which the Jansenists adhered to the respectful silence; it did not keep them from publishing innumerable works. Louis XIV—badly informed until that time—had thought Jansenism almost extinguished; Quesnel's documents made him comprehend how much alive and how dangerous it was and also that his efforts had failed. Mme de Maintenon, who gave herself the appearance of being extremely orthodox so that the issue of quietism would be forgotten, urged him to request another bull from Rome condemning the respectful silence. But Clement XI, who understood that this measure would not be any more efficacious than the past ones, was not very enthusiastic and delayed his decision. Only when the French court kept urging him, did he issue the bull *Vineam Domini Sabaoth*.[19] While it condemned the respectful silence, it did so in such

[17] See J. Orcibal, "Fénelon et la Cour romaine," *Mélanges d'archéologie et d'histoire de l'École française de Rome* 57 (1940), 235–348.
[18] See L. Ceyssens, "Les papiers de Quesnel saisis à Bruxelles et transportés à Paris en 1703 et 1704," *RHE* 44 (1949), 508–51; ibid., "Suites romaines de la confiscation des papiers de Quesnel," *Bulletin de l'Institut historique belge de Rome* 29 (1955), 5–27.
[19] Text of the bull: *BullRom* 21, 235, see D 2390.

terms as to imply that the silence concerned the *quaestio juris*, but not the *quaestio facti*. Fénelon was disappointed that it did not contain a statement about infallibility regarding the facts. In some points, moreover, the documents contradicted Gallican principles; as a result, parliament—to Rome's chagrin—only accepted it with serious reservations. Of the numerous polemics inspired by the bull, the *Denuntiatio Bullae Clementinae* by a theologian from Louvain, De Witte, is especially important. It contained an appeal to the general council, an idea which would show an effect in the future.

Aside from this revival of the conflict the bull *Vineam Domini* had few actual results if one excepts the last nuns of Port-Royal. Death had gradually decimated their ranks and only about twenty aged nuns occupied the imposing building of Port-Royal des Champs. They were forced to sign the bull, but they added a reservation saying that they were not willing to deviate from the arrangement made for them in the Clementine Peace. Not even threats could make them submit. Finally, at the urging of Mme de Maintenon, Louis XIV in October 1709 had their community dispersed and the nuns deported by the police to several different convents. This act of force was roundly condemned by public opinion, even by people who did not consider themselves Jansenists. To prevent the deserted convent from becoming a place of pilgrimage, Louis XIV had it demolished in 1711 and had the remains of the graves thrown into a mass grave in the cemetery of Saint-Lambert. In spite of this, there were pilgrimages and the stones of the ruins became relics. The abbot Le Sesne d'Etemare and the Jansenists published the *Gémissements sur la destruction de Port-Royal*, which was well received.

The bull *Vineam Domini* was indeed a disappointment for Louis XIV. The difficulties regarding its acceptance by parliament and also by the Assembly of the Clergy showed him that Jansenism could count on substantial support, even extending into the episcopate, for whom the King had always selected candidates who were above the slightest suspicion. Among these friends of Jansenism, Noailles, who owed his see in Paris to Mme de Maintenon's favor, soon played a prominent role. Quesnel from his shelter in Amsterdam quickly reorganized his network. His arrest had made him the undisputed leader of the party, especially since the disappearance of Gerberon had destroyed integral Jansenism once and for all. Quesnel used his voluminous correspondence to extend his influence far afield. But he was ominously destined to draw future attacks by the anti-Jansenists. After some cooling, Fénelon had reestablished his close relations with Rome. He immediately resumed his polemics against Jansenism. Deviating not a whit from any of his ideas, he warned the Holy See untiringly of the seriousness of the situation. Future events proved him correct. In 1710 he attacked Quesnel. The latter, no mean polemicist himself, vigorously rejected the prelate's ideas in some blunt pamphlets. One of Quesnel's advocates turned out to be Noailles, whom Fénelon resented ever since he had opposed him on the issue of quietism. So Fénelon decided to direct his attack to Quesnel's *Réflexions morales*. This work had already been denounced in Rome by the Capuchin Timothée de la Fleche in 1703 and condemned on 13 July 1708 by the brief *Universi Dominici gregis*. But the brief contained clauses contradictory to Gallican principles and had not been accepted in France. Fénelon, unwilling to be personally involved, used two of his friends, the bishops of Luçon and La Rochelle, as straw men. Those two issued a pastoral letter whose details were furnished by Fénelon. In it they condemned the *Réflexions morales*, accusing them of reiterating the errors of Baius and Jansen. Noailles, having approved the work, thus considered himself indirectly addressed and correctly so. Both bishops had nephews at the seminary of Saint-Sulpice, the diocesan seminary of Paris. Noailles promptly dismissed them without giving a reason. On 28 April 1711 he replied to his adversaries in a sharply worded pastoral instruction. The King thereupon reprimanded Noailles and through Mme de Maintenon demanded that he retract his approbation of Quesnel's book. Noailles of course refused to do so.

Noailles's refusal resulted in a complicated web of intrigue. Gradually Mme de Maintenon turned against the former protégé. At the very least she wanted to scare him into acquiescence. She apparently succeeded in making the new confessor to the King, the Jesuit Le Tellier, go along with her, whereas his predecessor, La Chaize, had consistently thwarted her plans. With her approval, Tellier collected a file of letters by bishops demanding the condemnation of the *Réflexions morales* and then sent a sample letter ultimately intended for the King to several different dioceses. But a letter by Abbot Bochart de Saron to his uncle, the bishop of Clermont, uncovering the scheme was intercepted in the mail and made public by the Jansenists. Noailles was extremely angry and hardened his position. When the King pressed him again to disassociate himself from Quesnel he refused and it became more and more obvious that part of the episcopate was supporting him. Louis XIV, grasping that he was threatened by a schism in the hierarchy, found himself in a quandary. The only way out seemed to be to involve Rome. So on 16 November 1711 he requested a papal bull against Quesnel, assuring the Holy Office that he would be able to force it upon the episcopate and parliament if he were made privy to its contents beforehand. At this point Noailles declared himself willing to submit to the Pope's decision. But when the King's request was transmitted by the

French ambassador it encountered less enthusiasm than had been assumed. The Pope was extremely well informed and—unlike the King—had few illusions about the effect such a measure would have in France. He was also anxious to avoid the appearance of following orders by Louis XIV. The commissioners charged with examining the problem quickly recognized moreover that the subtle, unctuous text of the *Réflexions morales* offered less of a basis for attack then the *Augustinus*. But after long hesitation Clement XI gave in: on 8 September 1713, he signed the bull *Unigenitus Dei Filius* condemning 101 propositions from the *Réflexions morales* (see Chap. 9).

CHAPTER 4

Gallicanism and Protestantism

Gallicanism at the Beginning of the Seventeenth Century

In the beginning of the seventeenth century the theses offered by the majority of French theologians and canonists concerning the function and power of the Pope were clearly aimed at decreasing his importance. These "Maxims of the Parisian School," supported by the writings of such medieval luminaries as Jean Gerson, Pierre d'Ailly, Jacques Almain, and John Mair, endorsed the relatively independent authority of the bishops in their respective dioceses, but they refused to consider the Pope a universal bishop. They demanded superiority of the general council over the Pope and maintained that the council could convene even without the Pope. They concluded that the Pope was in no way omnipotent and that natural law, canon law, and even the civil law of Christian nations placed limits upon his authority. Yet the French theologians unanimously acknowledged the true primacy of the Pope, his universal authority, and his position as the center of the unity of Christians.

Of course, none of these ideas was intended to sacrifice a single one of the privileges traditionally called "Liberties of the Gallican Church." On this point their views were clearly political and identical with that of Parliament which saw itself as official guardian of these liberties, which had been codified in 1594 by Pierre Pithou, a lawyer of parliament. While this codification remained authoritative for the whole *ancien régime,* four more treatises on this topic by parliamentary jurists had appeared between 1594 and 1604, with more to come. These works clearly demonstrate to what extent French parliamentary jurists viewed themselves as heirs to the great medieval jurists whose traditions they were continuing. The eighty-three liberties listed by Pithou were unequivocally aimed at restricting the authority of the Holy See in France, limiting its interference to a minimum and at the same time expanding the King's powers relative to religious matters. Although he had no spiritual authority, the King was responsible for the well-being of the French Church, possessing the requisite authority by virtue of divine right. Yet the crown was free of any and all vassalage or state of dependence vis-à-vis the Pope. Parliamentary jurists and theologians alike appeared sensitive to a high degree on all issues concerning the person of the King, who was regarded as sacrosanct. The theological faculties repeatedly censured writings which sought to justify not only the Pope's authority to depose a ruler guilty of heresy but even theories advocating tyrannicide. This latter issue was especially sensitive because the assassinations by Jacques Clément, Jean Chatel, and Ravaillac were not yet forgotten. So it was not surprising that essays by the Jesuits Mariana (1611) and Santarelli (1625), one an apologia for regicide, the other a demand for papal authority to depose kings, provoked great excitement and censure. All of this contributed towards maintaining a state of latent tension which was skillfully manipulated until the time of the Revolution by kings and ministers intent on expanding the power of the monarchy.

The manifestations of Gallicanism, however, continued to be relatively moderate; its advocates kept a low profile by avoiding extremism. This was shown in the events surrounding the writings of Edmond Richer (1560–1631).[1] Richer, a priest from Langres who was a creative personality with an excellent education, became syndic of the theological faculty of Paris in 1608. In 1606 he had published the writings of Gerson with additional annotations and treatises designed to emphasize the latter's Gallican tendencies. In 1610 Bellarmine published his *Tractatus de potestate Summi Pontificis in rebus temporalibus adversus Gulielmum Barclaeum*, which emphatically reclaimed the rights of the Holy See. Richer replied in 1611 with a small brochure of only thirty pages, *De ecclesiastica et civili potestate libellus*, which summarized in the name of the tradition of the Parisian School his own very extreme ideas. According to him temporal and spiritual authority—each in its respective realm—are sovereign and independent. But he goes beyond that in asserting that the Church possesses spiritual authority only and must be subordinate to the King in all temporal matters and requirements. He agrees with Gerson that the Pope is merely the prime minister of the Church, whereas the Church's head is Jesus Christ. But while Gerson

[1] See E. Puyol, *Edmond Richer, étude historique et critique sur la renovation du gallicanisme au commencement du XVIIe siècle*, 2 vols. (Paris 1876).

meant to say that the Pope is Christ's deputy receiving from him the authority for the commonweal of the Church, Richer interpreted this concept in a way that conceded nothing more than an executive authority to the Pope. The actual legislative authority, the leadership, is constituted in the general council, which alone is infallible because infallibility is a property only of the whole Church, whose representatives comprise the general council. The Pope is responsible only for the *status*, that is for the implementation of the canons issued by the council, but he can not impose anything binding upon the Church without its consent. Richer, however, avoided the multitudinism advocated by Marco-Antonio de Dominis, the apostate archbishop of Spalato, who defected to the English schism. In Richer's view Christ has entrusted jurisdiction of the Church to the totality of the priestly order within which the bishops represent the Apostles and the pastors the seventy-two disciples. The Church, then, is led by an aristocracy, the bishops, who by divine right are above the priests and whose authority is binding even on the Pope. The episcopate does not constitute an order of its own since the body of the priesthood is already realized in the priests; instead it constitutes simply an office which, derived from divine right, gives them an immediate jurisdiction independent of the Holy See. In its roots Richer's theory is thus a form of episcopalism which strongly projects the rights of the clergy and the faithful even if they are subordinate to those of the bishops. By stressing the fact that the *Depositum fidei* is indivisibly entrusted to the complete Church, Richer concludes that a dogmatic statement can become obligatory only if agreed to by the total Church and that neither the Pope nor the bishops can force the acceptance of such a statement upon the Church without its agreement. To all practical extent, this makes the faithful into judges of the dogma. One of his pupils, Simon Vigor (1556–1624), a member of the grand council, paralleled Richer in several of his works, which extended the Gallicanism of his teacher to an extreme point: he denied the Pope any and all primacy and declared invalid all definitions and institutions issued or established after the fifth century.

The publication of Richer's *Libellus* created considerable excitement at the universities and in political circles. Rome immediately pronounced condemnations, but they were neither unexpected nor did they have any practical significance, because one of the infamous Gallican Liberties stipulated that the decrees of the Holy Office would not be accepted in France. But the condemnation of the work by a provincial council (March 1612) chaired by the famous Cardinal du Perron in the archbishopric of Sens, to which Paris was subordinated at that time, was quite serious. The theological faculty joined in the condemnation and—for the first time since its existence—dismissed its syndic. Richer took a stand and emphatically defended his ideas in several publications, in turn provoking numerous replies, before he finally admitted defeat. On 30 July 1622 he was prudent enough to sign a declaration submitting to the Holy See and maintaining that it had been his intention merely to "summarize the old teachings of the Parisian School." In actuality he persisted in his viewpoints; even another recantation forced on him by Richelieu on 7 December 1629 did not change that. Richer continued to attract followers. While, in 1630, France was not yet ready for his ideas, these were to reemerge in the Jansenism of the eighteenth century and take on great significance.

Richer's most determined opponent in this fight was another professor at the Sorbonne, André Duval (1564–1638).[2] His views demonstrate clearly how far those Frenchmen who—in relative terms—were most dedicated to the idea of ultramontanism were willing to go. Duval, a professor at the Sorbonne since 1597, had opposed Richer ever since the latter had published Gerson's works in 1606. A friend of the Jesuits and of Nuncio Barberini, later Pope Urban VIII, Duval in effect defended views which openly favored the rights of the Holy See, but he avoided any one-sidedness. In 1612 he replied to Richer in an elenchus sharply rejecting his adversary's *Libellus*. In addition to several other pamphlets he wrote two rather more significant works relating to this quarrel: *De suprema romani pontificis in Ecclesiam potestate* (1614) and *Tractatus de summi pontificis auctoritate* (1622), the latter opposing Simon Vigor. The ideas developed in these works are remarkably balanced, moderate and conciliatory. He determines very precisely those points actually stipulated by Christian faith and respects freedom of opinion vis-à-vis others. Regarding the superiority of the general council over the authority of the Pope he remarks that the theological faculty of Paris alone supports this view, but he presents these opposing views objectively and refrains from rendering a qualifying judgment on either position. He openly defends the personal infallibility of the Pope without, however, raising the accusation of heresy against those who deny it. With this presupposition he advocates the view that a doctrinal decision by the Pope can actually be binding on the faithful only after the universal Church has accepted it at least tacitly. This does not go as far as the theories of Bellarmine, from whom Duval candidly disassociates himself. While obliging the ruler to respect those privileges which are the Pope's, he upholds the King's independence in the temporal and political realm; Duval later concurred in the condemnation of Santarelli's

[2] See A. Dodin, "Duval," *DSAM* 3 (1957) 1857–62; L. Cognet, "Duval," *DHGE* 14 (1960), 1213–16.

book. It is obvious, then, how moderate Duval's so-called ultramon-tanism was in comparison to Rome's demands.

Richelieu and the Holy See

In 1612 Duval said of Richer and his views that the hot-tempered syndic unwittingly paved the way for the schism. As a matter of fact, from this point on some French Catholics considered a more or less total divorce from the Holy See. In the Estates General of 1614 the Third Estate proposed a basic law which was to stipulate France as being immediately dependent only on God, but du Perron wisely thwarted this undertak-ing. The attitude of numerous clerics during Marie de Médicis' regency provided Rome with a feeling of relief. After the Regent transferred the conduct of foreign affairs to Richelieu in 1617, the latter began conceal-ing his true sentiments, allowing the nuncio to think that he was squarely on the side of the Holy See and Spain. Not until 1621 when he urged the King to resist Spain did he give even a hint of his true position. Spain, as a great Catholic nation, traditionally could count on the sup-port of the Holy See. In his conflict with Spain, which even within France was opposed by the *parti dévot,* Richelieu thus had to ensure himself of Rome's neutrality by any available means. Blackmailing Rome with the issue of Gallicanism was the most effective method towards achieving this aim and the cardinal-minister made use of it unscrupulously. In the messages of gratitude written after his elevation to the cardinalate (September 1622) he praised the kindness of the King, but never once mentioned the Pope. At that time Richer's ideas found a responsive chord at the Sorbonne and Richelieu had defended the theological faculty against the ultramontanist tendencies of Cardinal de La Rochefoucauld. At the same time he engaged in several demon-strative diplomatic and military initiatives which could not but have disquieted the Holy See: an alliance with the Protestant united prov-inces, negotiations with the German Protestants, attacks on the papal fortifications in the Veltlin and ratification of a treaty very favorable to the Huguenots (5 February 1626). This makes it clear why he did not intervene in 1625 and 1626 when the Assembly of the Clergy, the Sorbonne, and Parliament, on the issue of Santarelli's book, sharply condemned ultramontanism. He managed to make a decided enemy of Urban VIII and turned the sentiments of the French *parti dévot* against himself. After June 1626, when he needed the Pope's support in the Mantua problem, he tried to reverse his policies. He kept the Sorbonne from publishing its censure of Santarelli and increased his political concessions. In France he resumed the fight against the members of the Reformed Churches.

But this was a mere episode, and Urban VIII saw through it although he, too, made a conciliatory move. At the end of 1628 Richelieu entered the war against Austria and again signed treaties with the Protestants of Germany and England. The Pope now stiffened his attitude against the minister by systematically denying him all favors he requested. In spite of Richelieu's urging he refused to elevate Father Joseph to the cardinalate (1632) and made Mazarin wait for it a long time (1641). In 1634 he prevented Richelieu's having himself named bishop of Speyer, which would have given the cardinal access to the German College of Electors. He also refused him several briefs in matters of the episcopate and the religious orders, and, most importantly, he never agreed to nullify the marriage of Gaston d'Orléans, which was essential to Richelieu's politics. After the latter declared war on Spain (26 May 1635) the situation was further aggravated. In order to defy Urban VIII, Richelieu appointed Marshal d'Estrées, who was known for his temper and crudity, ambassador to Rome. The marshal occasioned so many incidents that in 1639 his equerry, Rouvray, was murdered. Almost simultaneously the Pope, in a countermove, appointed Scotti, hardly an ideal choice, as the new nuncio to Paris. It is accurate to say that the Pope at this particular time enjoyed considerable sympathy among the French episcopate, which was up in arms about the heavy taxation imposed on the Church's possessions by Richelieu. Public opinion for the better part did not approve of this opposition to the Holy See.

This tense situation explains why Urban VIII used all means to prevent Richelieu from assuming any sort of legal or canonical authority over the Church of France. The minister, eager in every way to consolidate his power, had long wanted such authority. In 1627, during a short span in which his relations with Rome were somewhat less aggravated, he let it be known discreetly that he would be glad to accept the title of permanent papal legate to France; ultimately he unequivocally demanded the title. Although Richelieu argued the precedent of Cardinal d'Amboise, Urban VIII, convinced of the cardinal's schismatic intentions, did not relent. It was only with great reluctance that he offered him the title for the limited period of a few months after the birth of the Dauphin, but Richelieu declined.

In 1635 Richelieu began to develop a new plan. The obligation on the part of the French clergy to obtain bulls for the canonical investiture of various church benefices from the Holy See, sanctioned in the Concordat of 1516, was obviously very unpopular and led to a number of protests. What Richelieu had in mind was branding the Concordat as illegal and contradictory to the old church discipline, and returning the privilege of electing bishops to the chapters. Subsequently he planned to call a national council into session where the King was to forego his regalia, which was very oppressive to the dioceses. In return he was to be given the right to hand out benefices directly and without participation by the Holy See. The final stage provided for Richelieu to be appointed patriarch of Gallia or of the Occident, with privileges similar to those of an Eastern patriarch. This would make the French Church almost independent of Rome in all but matters of faith, and the Pope would actually retain no more than an honorary primacy. Richelieu appears to have soon made a few politicians he trusted privy to his plan. Among them Chancellor Séguier, who suggested the royal councilor Pierre de Marca, in his role as a jurist, and several newspaper writers capable of propagating the idea among the public. Richelieu was well aware of the great difficulties he faced in trying to realize his plan. He also knew how difficult it would be to win the French public over to his scheme. He hoped to win public opinion over to his side by personally initiating a mass conversion of Protestants, who would look favorably upon such an undertaking by a French patriarch. This explains his mild treatment of the defeated Calvinists whom he allowed the free exercise of their cult. Polemicists in the minister's pay were ordered to extend concessions to members of the Reformed Churches as far as possible. As a result several pastors were won over. Richelieu even thought of calling a spectacular conference of Protestants with him as their protagonist.

In order to create a basis for his plan, Richelieu again facilitated publications with Gallican tendencies. This was the case with an anonymous pamphlet, *Le Nonce du Pape français* (1637), probably written by one of the cardinal's confidants, which asked the King to end the oppression of France by papal power and to create instead an ecclesiastic authority independent of the Holy See. Public reaction was more negative than positive. Two years later, in 1639, the brothers Dupuy, two well-known scholars, published two works by order of the minister: the *Traité des droits et libertés de l'Église gallicane*, a voluminous folio, followed by *Preuves des libertés de l'Église gallicane*.[3] These works, based on ample documentation, virtually did away with everything, including the special privileges of the Pope and immunity of the clergy. The public was greatly perturbed. On the initiative of Cardinal La Rochefoucauld, who defended Rome, and Nuncio Bolognetti, eighteen bishops present in Paris severely censured the work. The cardinal-minister permitted the censure, but did not in any way suppress the books of the brothers Dupuy.

---

[3] See P. Demante, "Histoire de la publication des livres de P. Du Puy sur les libertés de l'Église gallicane," *BÉCh*, ser. 1, 5 (Paris 1843).

At that point the project of the Gallican patriarchate was beginning to be talked about, although in cryptic fashion. By January 1646 the public had become so sensitized to the subject that the tiny pamphlet *Optatus gallus de cavendo schismate*, announcing the impending schism, created an enormous emotional response. The author, whom Richelieu could not identify, was Charles Hersent, a former Oratorian. Initially the minister was very annoyed with the pamphlet. But then it probably occurred to him that the *Optatus gallus* incident, given the proper exaggerative embellishment, would alarm Rome sufficiently to form the basis for extensive extortion. So he ordered several of his favorites to reply to the *Optatus gallus*. One of the replies, whose author, the Jesuit Rabardeau, made it appear to be coming officially from Richelieu himself, represented the establishment of the patriarchate as being totally legitimate and in no way schismatic. In fact, several Jesuits openly supported Richelieu's plan. The most significant of the replies was one by Marcas, *De concordia sacerdotii et imperii* (1641), who sought to prove that the Gallican Liberties did not run counter to the rights of the Holy See.[4] Rome appeared to take the apparent schismatic intentions of Richelieu very seriously, especially when he confirmed them by various measures designed to prevent all contact between the nuncio and the episcopate. But Urban VIII was clever enough to exercise extreme restraint. In time Richelieu had to admit to himself that his plan of a patriarchate was not meeting with a favorable response from the public, especially when the war against Spain as well as his domestic policies were becoming more and more unpopular. When Richelieu died on 4 December 1642 the issue was unresolved. Urban VIII manifested his sentiments for the dead prelate by forbidding the solemn mass for the dead, customarily celebrated in Rome at the death of a cardinal.

Mazarin, although a cardinal, was hardly an ecclesiastic personality in the customary sense; he was unable to continue Richelieu's undertakings. And yet he inherited his policies, especially in regard to Spain, and thereby incurred Rome's enmity. Innocent X scorned Mazarin as much as his predecessor Urban VIII had hated Richelieu. But now the Jansenist conflict began to interfere with Gallicanism and to slightly modify the respective positions.[5] The attitude of the French government became unequivocally anti-Jansenist, a position it would maintain for some time to come. It was its anti-Jansenism that forced the French court constantly to appeal to the dogmatic authority of the Holy See. This met with some benevolence on the part of the papal court. Origi-

[4] F. Gaquère, *P. de Marca* (1594–1662). *Sa vie, ses œuvres, son gallicanisme* (Paris 1932).
[5] See L. Cognet, "Le jansénisme drame gallican," *L'Année canonique* 10 (1965), 75–83.

nally Rome had been favorably disposed towards the French *milieu dévot*, the traditional defender of papal rights, and had emphasized this attitude by refusing to condemn Arnauld's *Fréquente Communion* as requested by Mazarin. But when the *milieu dévot* turned into the Jansenist party, Rome was forced to intercede against it. While this created an area of rapprochement with the French court, Rome's reticence nonetheless remained obvious. Mazarin experienced this in the upheavals during the *Fronde* when he found himself in opposition to the famous Cardinal Retz, coadjutor of Paris, who had automatically succeeded his uncle François Gondi as archbishop after the latter's death on 3 March 1654. Upon his flight Retz sought refuge in Rome in September 1654. Innocent X welcomed him benignly; he treated him according to his station as archbishop and cardinal and denied Mazarin the right to appoint a commission of bishops for the purpose of initiating a trial against Retz. Mazarin was forced to dispatch Lionne as ambassador to Rome to negotiate this matter. After the death of Innocent X, Lionne could not prevent the election of Fabio Chigi, the former nuncio of Paris, who was not well disposed towards France. Lionne thus encountered great difficulty when he worked out an agreement regarding the temporary administration of the Parisian diocese. This dilemma was not resolved until the dismissal of Cardinal Retz in 1661. The Holy See also stubbornly refused Mazarin and young Louis XIV the extension of the Concordat of 1516 to the newly conquered areas, especially the diocese of Arras.

The Gallicanism of Louis XIV

During the last years of his life Mazarin had been determined to maintain the status quo. But under young Louis XIV this position underwent a fundamental change. Imbued with absolutist ideas, the King strove for religious as well as political unity in his realm. Moreover, he was surrounded by advisers with decidedly Gallican tendencies, among them his confessors Father Annat and Father de la Chaize,[6] who—although they were Jesuits—were shaped by the Gallican tradition. A revival of Gallican ideas can be perceived from the very beginning of the grand monarch's absolute rule. On 12 December 1661 the Flemish Jesuit Coret presented theses at Clermont College in which he defended the infallibility of the Pope in the *quaestio juris* as well as in the *quaestio facti*. In so doing he provoked a lively controversy. Louis XIV rebuked Coret and ordered him to be silent because he did not want to provide the Jansenists with additional arguments by a discussion on the Pope's

---

[6] See G. Guitton, *Le P. de la Chaize confesseur de Louis XIV,* 2 vols. (Paris 1959).

infallibility. The violent confrontation between the Corsican guards and the French soldiers which took place on 20 August 1662, not far from the Palazzo Farnese, seat of the French ambassador, apparently had no doctrinal significance, but Louis XIV used the occasion to threaten an invasion of the Papal States and to humiliate the Pope, who was ultimately forced to capitulate at the Peace of Pisa (12 February 1664). In January 1663 Gabriel Drouet de Villeneuve had meanwhile presented some theses to the Sorbonne which openly advocated papal authority, calling the Gallican Liberties simple privileges granted by the Holy See. A parliamentary decree censured three of these theses on 22 January. The Sorbonne was very indignant over this incursion into its decision-making area. Bossuet, at that time just embarking on his Parisian career, endangered his advancement by joining the opponents. On 1 March the Sorbonne capitulated. But a month later, on 4 April, another incident occurred regarding the theses of Laurent Desplantes, a Cistercian monk, who granted to the Pope total jurisdictional authority in the entire Church *in foro externo* as well as *in foro interno*. The court and parliament vehemently demonstrated their opposition and took repressive steps. On 11 May, upon the intervention of the King's minister Michel Tellier,[7] the Sorbonne signed six clauses in favor of the independence of the King and of the Gallican Liberties, rejecting both the Pope's superiority over the council and his infallibility. A year later, in April 1664, the faculty censured a work by the Carmelite friar Bonaventura Hérédie,[8] published under the pseudonym Vernant, which defended extreme Montanist theses. In February 1665 a work published under the name of Guimenius was censured as well. Authored by the Jesuit Mateo Moya, it defended the casuists and acknowledged papal infallibility.[9] This time Rome reacted: the bull *Cum ad aures* by Alexander VII (25 June 1665)[10] condemned and annulled the faculty's censure. On 29 July Attorney General Talon delivered a vehement indictment of the document in parliament, but in the end the matter was permitted to rest: on the eve of the war with England, Louis XIV did not want the additional burden of clashing with the Holy See. At the same time the Jansenist conflict reached a critical juncture and the French court had to call for the assistance of the authority of Rome

---

[7] See L. André, *Michel Le Tellier et Louvois* (Paris 1942), 448; J. Sahuc, *Un ami de Port-Royal, messire Pierre Jean François de Percin de Montgaillard* (Paris 1909), 37–43.

[8] *La défense de l'autorité de Notre Saint Père le Pape et de Messeigneurs les cardinaux, les archevêques et évêques et de l'emploi des religieux mendicants contre less erreurs de ce temps* (Metz 1658).

[9] *Amadaei Guimenii Lomarensis opusculum singularia universae fere theologiae moralis complectens* (Lyon 1664).

[10] Text of the bull: J. Boileau, *Recueil*, 92–96.

several times. This explains the relative quiet lasting until the Clementine Peace (1668) and beyond.

Yet Louis XIV continued his efforts towards religious unity in his realm and to insist upon extending the Concordat of 1516 to all the areas subject to him, to bishoprics as well as abbeys. This presupposed a broadening of the right of regalia, the spiritual regalia which enabled the King to fill the benefices of a bishop while the bishopric was vacant, and the secular regalia enabling the King to gain possession of the income of vacant bishoprics. An edict of 10 February 1673 made this extension official and a declaration of 2 April 1675 recognized the measure. It applied to approximately sixty dioceses, for the most part in the southern provinces, which had been exempt from the regalia. Almost all bishops submitted, although in some cases with covert resistance. Only two resisted openly: Nicolas Pavillon, bishop of Alet, and François Étienne Caulet, bishop of Pamiers. Both of them had already demonstrated their independence on the issue of the formulary. Thus Jansenism unequivocally manifested its opposition to Gallicanism. In their instructions Pavillon and Caulet expressly rejected the sovereign rights and submitted the matter to the Assembly of the Clergy of 1675. They simultaneously excommunicated the prebendaries named on the title of the regalia.[11] To be sure, Pavillon and Caulet presided over tiny, out-of-the way dioceses, but were venerated as examples of the episcopate because of their virtue. Louis XIV hesitated to engage in open conflict with them because he knew that part of the public would not concur in it. Not until the middle of 1677 did he decide to intervene by having the council of state annul the instructions of the two rebellious bishops, who promptly turned to the Holy See for support. Innocent XI, elected in 1676, had immediately proved his zeal for ecclesiastic reform by abolishing nepotism and by defending his rights against the princes. It could be assumed that he favored the opponents of the regalia, but he had not as yet spoken out on this point. On 30 July 1677 Pavillon sent a letter to Innocent XI by way of one of the recluses of Port-Royal, Pontchâteau.[12] The latter was supported by the Roman Jansenists and could easily have convinced the Pope to side with the anti-regalists.[13] Unfortunately Pavillon died shortly thereafter (18 December 1677) and the regalia were immediately extended to his diocese. The burden of

[11] L. Bertrand, *Bibliothèque sulpicienne ou histoire littéraire de la Compagnie de Saint-Sulpice*, 3 vols. (Paris 1900), III, 42–57.

[12] See B. Neveu, *Sébastien Joseph du Cambout de Pontchâteau (1634–1690) et ses missions à Rome* (Paris 1969).

[13] See A. Latreille, "Innocent XI, pape janséniste, directeur de conscience de Louis XIV," *Cahiers d'Histoire publiés par les universités de Grenoble, Lyon et Clermont-Ferrand* 1 (1956), 9–39.

the fight was now on Caulet, who had been condemned by his metropolitan, the archbishop of Toulouse, and had turned to the Pope on 26 October 1677. In a highly laudatory brief of 2 March 1678, Innocent XI sided with the prelate against the King. Certain of Rome's support, Caulet now opposed the King in ever more vehement fashion. In 1679 this resulted in the confiscation of his benefices. There followed two additional briefs, of 20 December 1679 and 17 July 1680, which praised the bishop even more than the first one had. But Caulet died on 7 August 1680 without having received the last brief. Meanwhile the foreign minister, Arnauld de Pomponne, a nephew of the Great Arnauld, who had exercised a moderating influence on the King, had fallen out of favor[14] and the King stiffened his attitude. But several incidents in connection with church appointments in which Innocent XI annulled decisions of Louis XIV made it clear that the Pope, too, was not willing to give in (see Chap. 8).

But the matter of Pamiers was by no means ended by Caulet's death: the chapter elected a new chapter vicar who continued the resistance and was supported in it by Rome. Next, Louis XIV tried to intimidate Innocent XI by furnishing proof that he had public opinion and the clergy well in hand. He ordered publication of the treatise *De l'autorité légitime des rois en matière de régale* (1682) by the reporter on petitions in the council of state, Le Vayer de Boutigny, who vigorously defended the regalia. At the same time the plenary Assembly of the Clergy of 1680 and another assembly at the beginning of 1681 assured the King of their loyalty. But Louis XIV was resolved to escalate his intimidation. On 31 October 1681 he convoked a special plenary assembly, attempting to lend to it the significance of a genuine national council. The deputies were carefully selected and demonstrated total deference to the royal power. Bossuet played a significant part in this assembly, but in reality he was a mere instrument in the hands of the archbishop of Paris, François Harlay de Champvallon, a figure of dubious morality who nonetheless had the King's ear. On 3 February 1682 the assembly officially accepted the extension of the right of regalia; on 19 March it published the four articles of the famous Declaration of the French Clergy (*Declaratio cleri gallicani*). This document asserted the independence of civil authority in secular matters and the council's superiority over the Pope. His authority was thereby limited to the Church canons; his decisions, even in matters of faith, were to be subject to concurrence by the total Church. On 23 March a royal decree ordered the *Declaratio* to be included in the curriculum of all universities and seminaries. But this incurred strong opposition from the clergy and the public. Innocent

[14] C. Gérin, "La disgrâce de M. de Pomponne," *RQH* 23 (1878), 170.

XI openly showed his bitterness, but the Roman commission charged with examining the four articles could not agree upon the qualification to be imposed upon it. Innocent XI therefore chose not to take any official measures. He merely refused to issue the bulls for canonical investiture to those new bishops who had participated in the assembly of 1682. As a consequence France had thirty-five vacant bishoprics in January 1688.

Around this time the conflict between France and Rome reached another climax. To restore orderly conditions to the city of Rome, Innocent XI had revoked the quartering privileges of houses located in close proximity to the embassies in 1677 (see Chap. 8). But Louis XIV had refused to yield to this measure. So the bull *Cum alias* of 12 May 1687 excommunicated those who acted contrary to the decree. On 16 November 1687 the new French ambassador, Marquis de Lavardin, entered Rome at the head of 100 armed men. In spite of having been excommunicated, he had the sacraments administered to himself in full view of the public at the church of San Luigi dei Francesi. As a result the church was interdicted. At the beginning of January 1688 Innocent XI secretly informed Louis XIV that he and his ministers had been excommunicated.[15] The King immediately took several countermeasures. On 22 February 1688 General Harlay, speaking before parliament, appealed the decision to a general council; the following day the Solicitor General Talon delivered a violent indictment against Innocent XI in which he renewed the prior appeal and stated that the newly appointed bishops would simply forego the papal bulls of investiture. A decree to this effect was approved by parliament and posted in Rome on 8 February by Lavardin. At the same time Louis XIV openly prepared the occupation of the papal possessions of Avignon and Comtat-Venaissin. Innocent XI expressed his indignation, but did not pronounce an official condemnation of the action because he felt that even in Rome a number of cardinals would not support his unyielding stance. Next, Louis XIV, wanting to bring about the election of an elector-bishop in Cologne who was well inclined towards France, attempted to establish improved rapport with the Holy See by using the services of a secret agent. But Innocent XI rejected these overtures. On 16 September Louis XIV occupied Avignon and Comtat-Venaissin. On 27 September he formally renewed his appeal to the general council and had it recognized by several clerical bodies, among them the various theological faculties. Finally, he not only had the papal nuncio, Ranuzzi, unlawfully jailed, but he also forbade the bishops and Jesuits any and all correspondence with Rome. The actions of Louis XIV against Rome

[15] See M. Dubruel, "L'excommunication de Louis XIV," *Études* 137 (1913), 608–35.

were actually supported by many Jesuits, among them Father de la Chaize, the King's confessor. Since 1675 the *Conseil de conscience* which had to decide religious matters had consisted merely of La Chaize and Harlay who, by the way, were agreed in only one thing, namely to calm down the King regarding his differences of opinion with the Holy See. The general public liked Innocent XI and was not well inclined towards the King's intransigent position, but through forged documents, skillfully propagated by the King's minister, Colbert de Croissy, in the summer of 1688, public opinion was modified somewhat on this point. But the majority of the Jansenist party remained loyal to the Pope. This in turn gave the necessary argument to La Chaize that prompted him to accuse Innocent XI himself of Jansenism.[16] The situation was now in danger of entering a period of stagnation, when suddenly it was fundamentally altered by an unforeseen event: the conquest of England in November–December 1688 by William of Orange. Faced with this new danger, Louis XIV attempted rapprochement with Rome and recalled Lavardin. But Innocent XI, without even referring to his previous statements, remained silent, made no official decisions, and continued to keep the King's excommunication secret. The Pope died on 12 August 1689 without having issued a single act against the regalia, against the Declaration of the French Clergy 1682 or the appeal to the general council of 1688, and, lastly, without having had an idea that his patience had paved the way for Jansenism in the eighteenth century.

During the pontificate of the very conciliatory Innocent XII (1692) the aim was mutual pacification. An agreement was achieved in September 1693. The conflict regarding the regalia, which was destined never to be resolved, was simply ignored. A letter from Louis XIV to the Pope said that all possible steps had been taken to prevent the execution of the edict of 1682 concerning the Four Articles. In the future, relations between Rome and France achieved a relatively peaceful "modus vivendi" lasting for the remainder of the *ancien régime*. Yet the ideas involved in the dispute went their own way (on the subject of the State Church see Chaps. 17 and 23).

Protestantism in Seventeenth-Century France

After the death of Henry IV, Catholics as well as Protestants considered the regime established by the Edict of Nantes a mere armistice in a continuing state of opposition. Hardly anyone perceived in it the basis for mutual toleration. At this time the Huguenot party knew themselves

---

[16] See J. Bruckner, "Le P. de la Chaize dans les conflits de Louis XIV avec Innocent XI," *Études* 160 (1919), 304–23.

to be a minority, but they did not give up. The regency of Marie de Médicis was not well disposed towards them, indeed it brought men of the Catholic Counter Reformation to power. The renewal of Catholic spirituality deprived the Huguenots of the esteem they enjoyed because of the deep personal piety of many of them. From this point on, conversions from Protestantism to Catholicism increased while those in the other direction decreased. The Huguenots were therefore firmly resolved to make full use of the guaranties given them by the Edict of Nantes and indeed even to broaden them. Accordingly the assembly of La Rochelle in May 1621 established a military structure for the whole of France in which the country was divided into eight districts. While the plan did not come to full fruition, it nonetheless formed the basis for the Protestant rebellions of 1622 and 1626. But the Huguenots encountered resistance on the part of Richelieu, who had his own ideas in this matter. He was not about to tolerate the creation of a state within the state by the Reformed religion nor that it maintain connections with foreign powers. So he decided to subjugate La Rochelle, the bastion of the Calvinists, which was considered to be impervious to attack. The city surrendered after a terrible siege of eleven months. Although Bérulle and the *parti dévot* tried to talk Richelieu into exterminating all vestiges of heresy, the cardinal refused to follow up his victory. The Peace of Alais (28 June 1629) granted to the Calvinists the free exercise of their religion and equality in the service of the King, but it deprived them of their military guarantees. In this way Richelieu was not only hoping to keep his connections with Germany's Protestants intact, but perhaps—as has been mentioned—even to become the promoter of a general return to the faith by the Protestants. This would have put him in a very strong position with the Holy See. Mazarin, on the other hand, preferred to let the matter rest, especially since the Protestants had been clever enough to render proof of their very deep loyalty during the upheavals of the *Fronde*.

Intolerance was the rule on both sides. There was not a single Assembly of the Clergy that did not remind the King to work towards the destruction of heresy; in every one of these assemblies complaints were voiced about the "unholy freedom of conscience" granted to the Reformed Church. The Protestant congregations, numerically inferior in most areas, had to suffer manifold insults from the Catholics almost everywhere, but wherever they themselves were in the majority they in turn harassed the minority loyal to Rome. Protestants and Catholics lived in a sort of mutual fear of each other which frequently led to indelible hatred. It was only within the educated and moneyed classes that friendly relationships could at times exist.

The beginning of the absolute reign of Louis XIV brought about certain changes. In the very limited intellectual horizon of the King, whose ignorance in religious matters was well known at court, the political unity of the kingdom had to be followed by religious unity as well. The cohesion and power of the Protestant community appeared dangerous to him, especially since this active, diligent, and enterprising minority[17] possessed a significant part of the national wealth. He therefore more or less confessed to a desire to weaken it if not to disband it altogether. Initially he thought that he would reach his goals by means of an intellectual controversy and by withdrawing royal favor from them. After 1660 the learned disputes on Christian dogma gained added intensity. Bossuet stood out through his keen perspicacity and his irenic spirit. It was probably in collaboration with Arnauld that he created a masterful work, *Exposition de la foi catholique* (1671), in which Roman dogma was rid of its incidental elements and the difficult issues were presented with remarkable skill. As mentioned above, the people of Port-Royal played a significant role; the very aspect of their inward Christianity, oriented along biblical and liturgical lines, brought them closer to the Protestants. These disputes also led to positive results, the most manifest being the public abjuration by Turenne (23 October 1668), which was the culmination of a long intellectual development. There was in fact no dearth of Reformed who desired reunification and a return to the oneness of the Church. And so there were several common attempts along those lines. From 1660 to 1662 Marshall Fabert negotiated with the pastor of Sedan, Le Blanc de Beaulieu. Around 1665 Bossuet received instructions from a kind of semiofficial conference formed around the royal minister Le Tellier and the royal confessor Father Annat, with the participation of Turenne, to negotiate with the well-known Pastor Ferry. After the Peace of Aachen (2 May 1668) Turenne, who by now had converted, conceived a comprehensive plan which envisioned winning over at least fifty absolutely reliable pastors and convening a conference with them. The positive outcome of such a conference could not but have an impact on the very spirit of the Reformed. He also planned the revocation of the Edict of Nantes for some point in the future when the conversion of the majority of Protestants would have made the edict academic. Nuncio Bargellini was toying with similar ideas. Turenne appears actually to have been successful with some of the pastors, but he encountered the firm resistance of the intransigent faction of Calvinists who did their utmost to nip the plan in the bud. The war against

---

[17] About the relationship between Protestantism and the development of modern economy cf. the classic analysis by Max Weber, "Die protestantische Ethik und der Geist des Kapitalismus," *Archiv für Sozialwissenschaft und Sozialethik* 20/21 (1904–05).

Holland and the death of Turenne put a final stop to it. So the "cabal of the mediators between the religions"—as it was called then—proved unavailing.

There were moral and religious, but also material and financial reasons for that failure. Indeed it took money to aid the newly converted and especially the pastors, who were frequently abandoned to misery by their return to the Roman Church. Earlier, the only money available had been in the form of private donations, above all from the famous *Compagnie du Saint-Sacrement*, known to be extremely hostile to the Calvinists. Aside from these, very limited contributions had been solicited from the Assemblies of the Clergy. Turenne had finally managed to interest Louis XIV in this problem. At this point the former first secretary of Superintendent Fouquet, Paul Pellison-Fontanier, set to work. He succeeded in persuading the King to create a cash fund, soon known as the "conversion fund" (November 1677), to which was allotted a part of the income from regalia benefices. Famous Protestants such as Jurieu, Bayle and Spanheim raised accusations of corruption, but Innocent XI, Bossuet, Fénelon, Arnauld, and Bourdaloue approved of Pellison's methods. The view prevailed, at any rate, that the application of money could make the use of force unnecessary and that at least the children of converts would become good Catholics. Pellison was also interested in the distribution of Bibles and liturgical texts to the newly converted. His achievements were significant, but more so among the common folk than among the wealthy families.

Meanwhile the Catholic public in France was strongly affected by events in England and the resumption of the persecutions of "Papists." The execution of five Jesuits in London on 30 June 1679 triggered violent emotions, and now the attitude began to prevail that the civil authorities in France were much too tolerant of the heretics. It appeared to Louis XIV that the occasion was ripe for violent measures. Actually such measures had been used since the beginning of his reign: while the Peace of Saint-Germain had been favorable to the Reformed, a new declaration of 1669 applied a much more restrictive and oppressive interpretation to the Edict of Nantes. From 1660 to 1679 there were a mere twelve official acts against the Huguenots; in the six years from 1679 to 1685 there were eighty-five. Not only were all churches, opened after 1598, destroyed, but also those which were in any way found to be in violation of existing laws. In addition, harsh restrictions were imposed on the ministry of pastors. Gradually the Protestants were excluded from the majority of public offices and a large number of professions. But the most effective method was one conceived by the provincial governor of Montauban, Foucault: soldiers were forcibly quartered with the Reformed; their actions were equivalent to those in occupied territories. This was the origin of the infamous *dragonnades* which aroused indignation throughout Europe. Actual responsibility for them must be borne by Minister Louvois and the provincial governor of the Poitou, Marillac. Of course this method effected many conversions and even now some families started emigrating abroad. In 1683 riots took place in Vivarais and in the Dauphiné, but they were bloodily put down.

Neither Father de la Chaize, the King's confessor, nor Mme de Maintenon, however, appear to bear the responsibility—generally ascribed to them—for the way these methods developed.[18] It is certain that the King's motives were religious in only a few of the cases; for the most part they were political in nature. The events in Holland caused him to impute republican sympathies to the Reformed. He was also convinced that his fame would rest on the completion of the work he had initiated: the restoration of the religious unity of the kingdom. Lastly, he hoped that this would make him appear to be the great defender of Catholicism in the eyes of Innocent XI and thus put the latter in a difficult situation regarding Gallicanism. These motives led him to use violent measures which actually did not correspond to his character. When it was noticed in the summer of 1685 that the number of new converts, having reached several hundred thousand, represented a financial problem because they enjoyed freedom from taxation, Louis XIV thought the time had come for a final decision. On 14 October, against the advice of some of those around him, he published the Edict of Fontainebleu. It revoked the Edict of Nantes and prohibited the public exercise of the Reformed religion. With few exceptions, the most famous being that of Vauban, French and even foreign public opinion accepted this act enthusiastically. Innocent XI, who gauged the motives of Louis XIV correctly, was among the most reticent. He waited for a full year before he had a Te Deum celebrated in gratitude. But the revocation also had more serious consequences, both religious and political. The ensuing emigration by the Protestants unbalanced the economy of the realm. The abominable persecution following on the heels of the revocation is a blemish on French Catholicism. The forced conversions prepared the soil for the spread of religious relativism and indifferentism in the eighteenth century (Chap. 18).

The King, moreover, was forced to acknowledge that the revocation was for the most part a failure, for in spite of everything a strong Protestant resistance was kept alive, especially in areas with a traditionally Calvinist majority. Bloody proof of this was furnished by the Camisard rebellion of 1702 in the Cévennes. Painful and dangerous, the

---

[18] See C. Pascal, *La révocation de l'Édit de Nantes et Mme de Maintenon* (Paris 1885).

condition of the Protestants remained a constant source of unrest for the remainder of the *ancien régime*. It was beyond doubt one of the causes of the Revolution.

CHAPTER 5

Spirituality in Seventeenth-Century France

Major Trends in Seventeenth-Century Spirituality

The French *milieu dévot*, which made its appearance after the religious wars and brought about a true renewal of Catholicism, exhibited very clear directions within its spirituality.[1] Despite the chaotic conditions, French spiritual literature was abundant during the whole of the sixteenth and the first third of the seventeenth century, but it consisted almost totally of translations.[2] The foremost were the great authors of Rhenish-Flemish mysticism, Tauler, Suso, Harphius, Ruysbroeck, Louis de Blois and the *Perle Evangélique*; Spaniards such as Louis of Granada and above all John of Ávila; later on Saint Teresa[3] and John of the Cross also played a significant role; the Italians are represented by the *Combat spirituel* of Saint Catherine of Genoa. These mystics, who combined Platonic theories with the mysticism of Nordic spirituality, were strongly influenced by the writings of Pseudo-Dionysius, excellently translated by the Feuillant friar Dom Goulu into French. The foundations were laid for a spiritual forum characterized by a mysticism whose ultimate fulfillment of the inner life was an immediate union with the divine essence, surpassing all created means and even the humanity of Christ. The growing influence of this "abstract school" was favored by the impassioned predilection of this period for mysticism. The period is rich with mystics who enjoyed great esteem. While some of them, such as Mme Acarie[4] and later the blessed Carmelite Marie de l'Incarnation (1566–1618) belonged to the noblest Parisian society, there were others like Marie Teysonnier (Marie de Valence) (1570–1648) and Marie des Vallées (1590–1656), the Saint of Coutances, who came from the

---

[1] See Louis Cognet, *Les origines de la spiritualité française aux XVIIᵉ siècle* (Paris 1949).
[2] Bibliographical selection: J. Dagens, *Bibliographie chronologique de la littérature de piété et de ses sources, 1501–1610* (Paris 1952).
[3] See P. Sérouet, *De la vie dévote à la vie mystique* (Paris 1958); A. Vermeylen, *Sainte Thérèse en France au XVIIᵉ siècle* (Louvain 1958).
[4] See Bruno de Jésus-Marie, *La Belle Acarie* (Paris 1942).

poorer classes.[5] Their mystical experiences were interpreted by those around them in a very abstract sense.

To complete the picture, it should be mentioned that parallel to the mystical trend there was also a propensity for the diabolic. It originated in the Middle Ages and persisted throughout the seventeenth century, at times leading to tragic incidents.[6] The cases of demoniacal possession produced lively curiosity; immense numbers of people hurried to witness these events. In most cases the person accused of being possessed ended up at the stake after a questionable trial. Incidents of this kind can be found throughout the century. Among the best-known cases we might mention those of Elizabeth of Ranfaing at Nancy[7] and of the Ursuline nuns of Loudun (1632–40), whose principals were Prioress Jeanne des Anges and the Jesuit Jean-Joseph Surin (1600–1665), an admirable spiritual author, who had, however, been mentally ill for many years.[8] Public exorcisms degenerated into horrific mass hysteria. But Richelieu, who was personally interested, encouraged them because he hoped they would provide him with decisive arguments against the Protestants. Only towards the end of the century did persecutions of witches and devil trials abate.

The themes of the abstract school were summarized in the work of a Capuchin friar of English origin, Benedict of Canfield (1562–1610). In 1609, almost at the end of his long career as master of novices and guardian, Canfield published his *Règle de perfection*. But the first version was so abstract and contained so many Platonic audacities that his superiors forced him to publish an amended edition in 1610.[9] Of merely mediocre stylistic quality, the work nevertheless went through twenty-five printings in the seventeenth century and had a profound influence. Under the guidance of Dom Beaucousin, prior of the Paris Carthusians, young Bérulle composed a *Bref discours de l'abnégation intérieure* (1597) which was actually no more than a very abstract adaptation of a small Italian work, but it enjoyed lasting success. On the other hand, the monumental *Palais d'amour divin* (1602) by the Capuchin friar Laurent de Paris (1563–1631)[10] as well as the *Sentiers de l'amour divin* (1623) by

[5] See E. Dermenghem, *La vie admirable et les révélations de Marie des Vallées* (Paris 1926).

[6] Valuable bibliographical data in the special issue of *Études carmélitaines*, "Satan" (Paris 1948).

[7] See E. Delcambre and J. Lhermitte, *Un cas énigmatique de possession en Lorraine au XVIIᵉ siécle: Elisabeth de Ranfaing* (Nancy 1956).

[8] Notable edition of letters: J. J. Surin, *Correspondance*, ed. by M. de Certeau (Paris 1966); cf. L. Cognet, "A propos des lettres du P. Surin," *RSR* 56, 2 (1968), 269–82.

[9] See J. Orcibal, "La 'Règle de Perfection' de Benoît de Canfield a-t-elle été interpolée?" *Divinitas* 11 (1967), 845–74.

[10] See C. Dubois-Quinard, *Laurent de Paris, une doctrine du pur amour en France au début du XVIIᵉ siècle* (Rome 1959).

yet another Capuchin, Constantin de Barbanson (1582–1631),[11] manifesting similar tendencies, were soon forgotten. Although Platonic mysticism slowly became unfashionable after 1630, it did have advocates even into the time of Fénelon. Between the years 1654 and 1659 the work of a blind Carmelite, John of Saint-Samson (1571–1636), a great mystic, appeared posthumously. His writings took up the most extreme themes of Ruysbroeck and Henry of Herp. Also inspired by this kind of mysticism, although on a lesser plane, were François Malaval of Marseilles (1627–1719),[12] also blind, in his *Pratique facile pour élever l'âme à la contemplation* (1664), and the Premonstratensian Epiphanius Louys, abbot of Étival (d. 1682), in his *Conférences mystiques* (1676).

In the reign of Henry IV other spiritual tendencies began to appear which were no less fruitful. In his *Introduction à la vie dévote* (1609) Francis de Sales strove to make Christian perfection attainable for simple Christians all over the world. To this end his *Traité de l'amour de Dieu* (1616) develops an extraordinarily well-balanced concept of Christian mysticism centered around charitable love and a very optimistic view of the possibilities of man, a concept placing him in close proximity to humanism. By leading the soul to a devotion to God in "holy indifference" he points the way for most of the representatives of the classical period of spirituality to follow, each in his own way. Numerous printings of his *Introduction*—almost one a year in the course of the century—were spreading the Salesian view of piety. But although the influence of Francis de Sales was almost worldwide, he yet had no actual disciple or successor, since this designation could not be granted unequivocally even to his friend, the very prolific Jean-Pierre Camus (1584–1652), who authored more than two hundred works and became the founder of the religious novel.[13]

The founder of a true school of spirituality is encountered in the person of Pierre de Bérulle (1575–1629), appointed cardinal in 1627, whose political activities we have already discussed (Chap. 1). Proceeding from the abstract school he brought about a truly Copernican change in the field of spirituality by recognizing the preeminent significance for the inner life of the secret of Jesus' incarnation and by subsequently concentrating his piety on the person of the Incarnate Word. His ideas were first put down in a number of small devotionals which remained unpublished for a long time. It was only when forced to

[11] See Théotime de Bois-le-Duc, "Le P. Constantin de Barbanson et le préquiétisme," *CollFr* 10 (1940), 338–82.

[12] See. J. Bremond, "Le quiétisme de Malaval," *RAM* 31 (1955), 399–418.

[13] See L. Lafuma, *Les histoires dévotes de Jean-Pierre Camus* (Paris 1940); J. Dagens, "Camus, écrivain dévot," *Studi francesi* (1958).

defend his position that he gave definitive shape to his ideas in the twelve volumes of *Discours de l'état et des grandeurs de Jésus* (1623),[14] which he composed with the help of his friend Saint-Cyran. His influence was maintained through the Oratory and the Carmelites and even though—as we shall demonstrate later—his was not the only impulse for the Christological piety of the seventeenth century, it has remained the most significant one. Some of Bérulle's pupils remained loyal to their master's ideas, such as Saint-Cyran and above all the Oratorian François Bourgoing (1585–1662).[15] The many reprints of the latter's *Vérités et excellences de Notre-Seigneur Jésus-Christ* (1636) made Bérulle's system accessible to a wide public in the form of devotionals. Guilleaume Gibieuf (1580–1650)[16] who had published Bérulle's collected works in 1644 was the first to come out with a treatise of Platonic orientation, *De libertate Dei et creaturae*. But in his *La vie et grandeurs de la très sainte Vierge Marie* (1637) he initiated the Mariological orientation of Bérullism. Other successors gave their own imprint to Bérulle's ideas. Foremost among those was Charles de Condren (1588–1641), Bérulle's successor in the Oratory, an intellectually curious spirit, but hostile to the written word, whose influence was felt above all by way of the spoken word. In Condren's ideas the themes of vanity of the human creature and of sacrifice through destruction gain extraordinary significance and lend strangely pessimistic and negating characteristics to him.[17] Similar perspectives formulated with rare literary talent determine the work of one of Condren's pupils, Jean-Jacques Olier (1608–57), founder of Saint-Sulpice, whose *Journée chrétienne* (1657) enjoyed rare success. Saint John Eudes (1601–80), also an Oratorian until he founded his own *Congrégation de Jésus et Marie* (1643), was at first under the profound influence of Bérulle and later under the more mystically oriented influence of Marie des Vallées. In its simplicity, his first great work, *La Vie et la royaume de Jésus dans les âmes chrétiennes* (1637), is essentially obligated to Bérulle. He was among the initiators of the devotion to the Sacred Heart of Mary and the Sacred Heart of Jesus, which he later developed in a Christocentric atmosphere.[18] Thus, among

---

[14] See L. Cognet, "Bérulle et la théologie de l'Incarnation," *XVIIᵉ siècle* 29 (1955), 330–52.

[15] See M. Leherpeur, "Le P. François Bourgoing," *L'Oratoire de France* 28 (1937), 286–99; 31 (1938), 241–56; 34 (1939), 125–38.

[16] See R. Notonier, "Le P. Guillaume Gibieuf," *Oratoriana* (1960–61); L. Cognet, "Gibieuf," *DSAM* 6 (1965), 356–63.

[17] See B. Kiesler, *Die Struktur des Theozentrismus bei Pierre de Bérulle und Charles de Condren* (Berlin 1934).

[18] See L. Cognet, "Le Cœur de Jésus et la Trinité d'après saint Jean Eudes," *Le Cœur du Seigneur* (Paris 1955), 180–91.

the authors of the classical period, the efforts of Bérulle's successors gradually led to a theological wealth of piety under the imprint of the devotion to Christ, a piety resting soundly on biblical and patristic foundations.

A special position in this development is occupied by the French Jesuits. But their spirituality was in no way uniform. Especially at the beginning of the century, many of their members arrived at the *humanisme dévot* through their predilection for aesthetic literature. They weakened, at times to a dangerous extent, the traditional demands of Christianity. This holds true for Louis Richeome (1544–1625) as well as Étienne Binet (1569–1639), who otherwise manifested some very beautiful, profoundly religious perceptions. But in Pierre Coton (1564–1626), the compliant confessor of Henry IV, we encounter a rival of Francis de Sales. His *Intérieure occupation d'une âme dévote* (1608) also attempts to make piety accessible to the members of the court, but with less psychological penetration. In the person of Louis Lallemant (1588–1635) we meet a true mystic who in his capacity as instructor of the tertiaries put his stamp on a whole generation of Jesuits.[19] He wrote nothing himself, but with the help of lecture notes from his pupils, Father Champion later compiled a *Doctrine spirituelle* (1694) which appears to reflect his teachings faithfully. Lallemant skillfully combined the most essential themes of Ignatian mysticism with those stemming from Rhenish-Flemish mysticism. The significance he gives to the unity of man with Christ puts him close to Bérulle, whom he admired without, however, being influenced by him. The same Christocentrism is found in one of Lallemant's contemporaries, who, in contrast to the latter, was an extremely prolific author: Jean-Baptiste de Saint-Jure (1588–1657). It is apparent primarily in his first work, which is also his best, *De la connaissance et de l'amour du fils de Dieu Notre-Seigneur Jésus-Christ* (1634), in which he demonstrates his profound knowledge of the literature of mysticism. Lallemant, too, had numerous successors who were true to his inspiration. Among them are Surin, in his unsettled way, and the very sympathetic group of Breton Jesuits consisting of Jean Rigoleuc (1595–1638), Vincent Huby (1608–93), and Julien Maunoir (1606–83), who excelled in the area of popular missions. The work of François Guilloré (1615–84), especially his interesting *Secrets de la vie spirituelle qui en découvrent les illusions* (1673), accentuates the mystical aspect. Unfortunately, its value is impaired by its ponderous style.[20]

[19] See J. Jiménex, "Précisions biographiques sur le P. L. Lallemant," *AHSI* 33 (1964), 269–331; idem, "En torno a la formación de la Doctrine spirituelle del P. Lallemant," *AHSI* 32 (1963), 225–92.

[20] See A. Klaas, "La doctrine spirituelle du P. François Guilloré," *RAM* 24 (1948), 143–55 (Source for numerous other articles).

The Great Christian Works

Although the French *milieu catholique* was characterized by a spirituality rooted in mysticism, it nonetheless grew into a center of practical activities and efficacious undertakings. We have already mentioned its popular mission work and the reform of the secular clergy and that of the religious orders, but it also initiated numerous other works. Vincent de Paul (see Chap. 1) became a symbol of Christian charity. There was hardly a single sort of distress that escaped his attention. Starting in 1618, he turned his attention to the miserable condition of the galley slaves, touching the imagination of the people to such an extent that legend had him take the place of a manacled galley slave. As we know, abject poverty and begging were two of the great festering sores of the seventeenth century and Vincent de Paul quickly became involved in these problems. In 1624 he found a helper of extraordinary ability in the person of Louise de Marillac (1591–1660). Born out of wedlock to Louis de Marillac, she married Antoine le Gras in 1613 and was widowed in 1625. In September 1621 Vincent de Paul had established a *Confrérie de la Charité* in Mâcon to help the poor. With the participation of the aristocracy, similar institutions were founded in other towns. But it was difficult to create close ties between the individual fraternities. In 1628 this task was entrusted to Louise de Marillac. A year later she was asked to organize the charitable fraternities in Paris and in 1634 she was given the very important charge of helping the sick of the Hôtel-Dieu. The most noble ladies of Paris participated in this work, especially the duchess of Aiguillon, a niece of Richelieu. But of equal importance was the formation of a group of helpers of the poor for such tasks as were closed to the ladies of the aristocracy by the conventions of the times. This came about, to a very modest extent, as early as 1630, but did not take on final form until the courageous Louise de Marillac became its focal point in November 1633. This was the beginning of the *Filles de la Charité*, whose formation was promoted vigorously by Vincent de Paul. Soon after, they were practicing the apostolate of charitable love.

In the wake of Vincent de Paul's foundings, other similar ones occurred which were, however, of lesser and generally mere local significance.[21] In 1638 through the *Dames de Charité* Vincent de Paul was able—initially on a very modest basis—to establish a charity for foundlings. Although it continued to grow, it never reached the level required to solve this painful problem; in the seventeenth century there were three to four hundred foundlings in and around Paris every year who were sold at eight *sols* to one *livre pièce* to beggars and carnival people.

---

[21] See M. d'Escola, *Misère et charité au Grand Siècle* (Paris 1942).

Yet another broad field of endeavor for Vincent de Paul's charitable love was to ameliorate the sufferings of war. In the almost total absence of logistics for supplying the troops, they existed at the expense of the populace. In the process, the mercenaries committed wholesale murder, arson, pillage, and plunder, and left in their wake fields which were devastated for a long time to come. In 1639 Vincent de Paul became involved in the sad fate of Lorraine, the Picardie, and the Champagne, which were destroyed by the Thirty Years' War. Even though he had gone over to the anti-Jansenist side—albeit more from opportunism than conviction—he yet dared turn to Charles Maignart de Bernières (1616–62), a friend of Port-Royal.[22] In order to arouse the public to this problem, twenty-nine *Relations* were distributed from 1650 to 1655 describing the plight of the respective provinces. In this way, abundant alms were collected and distributed on the spot to refugees.

In all his charitable works Vincent de Paul frequently received support from a secret association of piety and brotherly love, the *Compagnie du Saint-Sacrement*. It had been founded in 1630 by Henry de Lévis, Duke of Ventadour, with the concurrence of Louis XIV, but without official approbation.[23] It developed very rapidly and soon counted some of the most illustrious names of France among its members. Among those who were especially active in its overall administration were Gaston de Renty and above all Jean de Bernières-Louvigny (1602–59). The latter was an interesting personality, a mystic and author of religious texts, of which *Le Chrétien intérieur* (1660/77) enjoyed great success.[24] Beyond that, Bernières founded a house for spiritual exercises, called *Hermitage,* which radiated its effect through all of Normandy. We should also mention René Le Voyer d'Argenson, a productive religious author,[25] and the Marquis de Salignac, an uncle of Fénelon. The *Compagnie du Saint-Sacrement* placed a high value upon maintaining its lay character and its independence; it accepted no members of religious orders and very few priests, one of whom was Bossuet. Spread across France and having at its disposal a far-flung network of connections by virtue of the high social standing of its members, it played an important role on the

[22] See A. Féron, *La vie et les œuvres de C. Maignart de Bernières, 1616–1662* (Rouen 1930).
[23] See A. Rébelliau, "Un épisode de l'histoire religieuse au XVIIᵉ siècle, la Compagnie du Saint-Sacrement," *Revue de Deux-mondes* 16 (1903), 49–82; F. Bégouen, *Une société secrète émule de la Compagnie du Saint-Sacrement, l'Aa de Toulouse aux XVIIᵉ et XVIIIᵉ siècles* (Paris 1913).
[24] See M. Souriau, *Deux mystiques normands, G. de Renty et J. de Bernières* (Paris 1913); R. Heurtevent, *L'œuvre spirituelle de Jean de Bernières* (Paris 1938).
[25] See M. de Certeau, "Politique et mystique, René d'Argenson, 1596–1651," *RAM* 153 (1963), 1–37.

religious as well as the political level. The *Compagnie du Saint-Sacrement* frequently had large financial resources; it was in a position to support numerous charitable works and often put funds at Vincent de Paul's disposal. The national and foreign missions, especially those of Canada, owe much to the *Compagnie*. A number of its members made great sacrifices for the poor, the sick, the prisoners, and the galley slaves without regard for their own well-being. At times the activities of the *Compagnie* were viewed with some reticence if not hostility. Its fight against the practice of dueling—although supported in governmental circles—met with vehement criticism from among the aristocracy. Mazarin disliked the *Compagnie*'s political perspectives, which were exclusively Catholic-oriented; some of its members, moreover, had repeatedly demanded his dismissal from the Queen. Its virtually omnipresent system of police surveillance, used to prevent the laws of the Church from being violated, was ill-received, as was its intercession to have the most important posts filled with good Christians and to exclude men who were suspected of free thought. And finally the *Compagnie* showed itself to be utterly merciless in the fight against the Protestants. It did not hesitate to use any means at its disposal to close the churches and schools of the Reformed faith. It even went so far as to have Calvinist tradesmen barred from working. But more than anything else it attacked the Jansenists, who in turn swore bitter revenge. In 1660 a well-known Jansenist, Charles du Four, abbot of Annay, published two pamphlets about the *Hermitage* of Caen, which was known to be an affiliate of the *Compagnie*, and mentioned the latter by name. When Mazarin made skillful use of the situation, the *Compagnie du Saint-Sacrement* understood the implications: in the summer of 1660 it announced its disbandment and destroyed the larger part of its archives. On 13 December a decree prohibited all associations which had not been authorized by royal letters patent. Only a few groups in the provinces continued their activities until 1664, but more or less secretly. As late as 1664, Molière attacked the *Compagnie* in his *Tartuffe*.[26] Other secret associations were formed later which appear basically to have been a continuation of the *Compagnie du Saint-Sacrement*.

Among the apostles who were supported by the *Compagnie* was the venerable nun Marie of the Incarnation (1599–1672)—not to be mistaken for the Carmelite by the same name. Born Marie Guyard, she married Claude Martin in 1617 and was widowed two years later. Leading an intensely mystical life, she joined the Ursulines in 1630, became a friend and confidante of Bernières and in 1639 went to Canada, where she completely immersed herself in her apostolic work.

---

[26] See M. Émard, *Tartuffe, sa vie, son milieu et la comédie de Molière* (Paris 1932).

In this period she arrived at the most exalted stages of mystical union. Her spiritual experiences are preserved in two admirable autobiographical reports. Her voluminous correspondence with numerous people in France is an extraordinarily rich source and a valuable contribution to the history of Canada. Bossuet considered Marie of the Incarnation the "Teresa of France"; in her capacity as a religious writer she is without a doubt comparable to the great Carmelite. Moreover she bears witness to the rich development of French mysticism in the middle of the seventeenth century.

The *milieu catholique*, being dedicated above all to the task of education, continued the initiatives of the early sixteenth century. The Society of Jesus, with its long tradition in this form of the apostolate, remained the leader in this field. Their colleges enjoyed continued esteem; they were frequented by the aristocracy and granted royal favor. Mazarin had his nephew educated the Clermont College, which assumed the name Louis le Grand in 1682 when it had an enrollment of two thousand pupils, four hundred of them in residence.[27] The college Henry IV in La Flèche and that at Rennes were even more prominent.[28] Since the society concentrated heavily on the teaching of Latin literature, it trained many excellent humanists[29] and some eminent specialists, the most famous being Dominique Bouhours (1628–1702). But then the Jesuits encountered serious competition in the form of the Oratory.[30] Initially Bérulle had not intended the establishment of a college, but in 1616 he changed his mind and founded one in Dieppe, which was soon followed by others. The Académie royale, founded in 1639 in Juilly, was among the most famous of them.[31] The Oratorian colleges usually had fewer students than the Jesuit ones, although in 1642 Dieppe reached an enrollment of twelve hundred. But an experiment in a dual emphasis on Greek and Latin was not entirely successful. Mathematics and physics, on the other hand, were given a prominent position in the curriculum. On the whole the pedagogical methods of the Oratorians were both more liberal and more modern. Their colleges, too, were well attended by the most prominent society. In the framework of education we should also mention the "schools" of Port-Royal, not for the size of their enrollment but for their historical significance. In the brief span of their existence from 1646 to 1660 they only educated one

[27] See G. Dupont-Ferrier, *Du Collège de Clermont à Louis-le-Grand,* 3 vols. (Paris 1921).
[28] See G. de La Rochemonteix, *Le Collège Henri IV de La Flèche,* 4 vols. (Le Mans 1889).
[29] See F. de Dainville, *Naissance de l'humanisme moderne* (Paris 1940).
[30] See P. Lallemand, *Essai sur l'histoire de l'éducation dans l'ancien Oratoire de France* (Paris 1887).
[31] See C. Hamel, *Histoire de l'abbaye et du collège de Juilly* (Paris 1868).

hundred pupils,[32] the most famous of whom was Racine.[33] Of all the Port-Royal "recluses" it was Claude Lancelot[34] who was most consistently involved with them. He created a number of "methods" for these schools, among them the famous *Jardins des Racines grecqes* (1657), which advanced the state of pedagogy considerably. We have already mentioned the activities of the Ursulines and the Sisters of the Visitation in the field of girls' education. Their education never received the same high level of attention as that of boys. Even the intellectual level of the flexible and admittedly intelligent program designed by Fénelon in his famous *Traité de l'éducation des filles* (1687) remained quite modest. Thus the school for girls from needy aristocratic families founded by Mme de Maintenon in the former abbey of Saint-Cyr in 1686,[35] to which she devoted constant personal care, was far from turning out learned women. In spite of these lacunae, the education of the higher classes had reached an excellent level by the end of the seventeenth century.

This did not hold true for the lower classes. To be sure, parish schools and charitable schools had been established almost everywhere, but these had encountered great difficulties both in general and in the training of teachers; for these reasons their achievements were not more than mediocre. This explains the fundamental importance of a small number of teachers sponsored in 1684 by the former prebendary of Reims, John Baptist de la Salle (1651–1719), who were given a definitive organization in Vaugirard (1694): the Brothers of the Christian Schools (*Frères des Écoles chrétiennes*). This new foundation initially encountered great difficulties but finally blossomed until it corresponded perfectly to its task of providing an elementary education in its various forms. In the course of the seventeenth century it led to similar efficacious, albeit more limited experiments of this sort. But in the countryside the problem stayed largely unsolved, as demonstrated by the continuing high number of illiterates.

Christian Life

The efforts by involved Catholics showed rapid achievements in the realm of religious practices, piety, and Christian life. Along with the increasing renewal of the clergy the parishes were once again turning

---

[32] See L. Cognet, "Les Petites-Écoles de Port-Royal," *Cahiers de l'Association internationale des études françaises* 3–5 (1953), 20–29.

[33] See J. Orcibal, "L'enfance de Racine," *Revue d'Histoire littéraire de la France* 51 (1951), 2–16.

[34] See L. Cognet, *Claude Lancelot Solitaire de Port-Royal* (Paris 1950).

[35] See T. Lavallée, *Mme de Maintenon et al Maison royale de Saint-Cyr* (Paris 1862).

into genuinely spiritual places. Sermons were given regularly; the clergy had recourse to solid materials in sermon books readily at their disposal. Sermons by such famous practitioners as the Oratorian Le Jeune, Sénault, and later Bossuet, Bourdaloue, Massilon, Mascaron, Fléchier, and many others were not only published as religious reading, but were to serve as examples to the clergy and to inspire them. The great number of such works appearing throughout the century cannot even be estimated.[36] Catechism classes were revived; many dioceses published catechisms, some of which enjoyed great success,[37] as for instance the *Catéchisme des trois Henris* (entitled after the first names of the editing bishops) used in the dioceses of Angers, Luçon and La Rochelle. This revival made possible a steady increase in devotional literature. As a matter of fact, the production in this area is overwhelming; it includes works designed for a relatively well-educated audience as well as for the more simple readers. Jesuits, the Oratory, and Port-Royal were competing to outdo each other in productivity; to the present day it has not been possible to compile an exhaustive bibliography. In the process there came about a variety of literary genres, of which three were favored: works of meditation, moral treatises concerning the duties of daily life, and the hagiographies. While the saints occupied the first place among the latter, they satisfied a mere part of the demand. The seventeenth century loved religious biographies, and whenever a personality revered in some fashion died, a historian surfaced, so that there was never a dearth of such books.

The seventeenth century was above all a privileged period for devotions. While they were not any more popular than in the Middle Ages, they now found followers among the educated and were propagated by the great representatives of spirituality and by famous theologians. In first place was the worship of Mary, a symbol of which may have been the gesture by Louis XIII on 15 August 1638 to dedicate his kingdom to the Most Blessed Virgin, an act that horrified the Protestant ambassadors.[38] Although thologians repeatedly protested abuses in the worship of Mary, especially towards the end of the century,[39] they received no support among the general populace. We have already mentioned the devout worship of the Sacrament of the Altar, with its intention of expiating the insults by the Calvinists. The group around Bérulle now

---

[36] See E. Griselle, *Bourdaloue, Histoire critique de sa prédication* (Lille 1901); J. Lebarq, *Histoire critique de la prédication de Bossuet* (Paris 1888).

[37] See J. C. Dhôtel, *Les origines du catéchisme modern d'aprés les premiers manuels imprimés en France* (Paris 1967).

[38] See C. Flachaire, *La dévotion à la Vierge dans la littérature catholique au commencement du XVIIᵉ siècle* (Paris 1957).

[39] See P. Hoffer, *La dévotion à Marie au déclin du XVIIᵉ siècle* (Paris 1938).

developed a loving worship of Jesus' infancy. This was inspired primarily by a young Carmelite from Beaune, Marguerite Parigot, whose convent name was Marguerite of the Blessed Sacrament (1619–48). In 1636 she founded a devout association called the *Famille du saint Enfant-Jésus*.[40] The Oratory and the Carmelites took over the propagation of the worship of the Infancy of Jesus, aided energetically by Mme Guyon later on.[41] While devotion to the Sacred Heart has earlier origins, it nonetheless created special forms of expression in the seventeenth century. They were initiated by Saint John Eudes, who was the first to establish that liturgical cult around 1670. But the decisive role in this was played by a member of the Sisters of the Visitation, Saint Margaret Mary Alacoque (1647–90).[42] Completely self-taught and of modest education, she was but a mediocre author whose writings moreover were destroyed upon her death by her mother superior. Yet she conveyed very touching private revelations which were in part made known to the public before her death by the *Retraite spirituelle* (1684), the posthumous work of her spiritual guide, the Jesuit Claude de la Colombière (1641–82). But this new type of piety encountered strong resistance and did not spread until the following century.

The liturgical efforts of the seventeenth century must be viewed from a threefold perspective. First, new liturgical texts were created. At this time the bishops had extensive authority in this matter. To be sure, a detailed history in this regard has not yet been written, but it is certain that numerous dioceses had their own breviaries or missals. In 1680 Harlay de Champvallon had texts stricken from the Parisian breviary concerning episodes of legendary origin; also an attempt was made to reintroduce a uniform character to the divine service. This effort was made in many other dioceses as well. There was also an attempt to provide the liturgical books with thorough and accurate theological commentaries, modeled after the famous *Instructions du Rituel d'Alet* (1667), requested by Pavillon from the group of Port-Royal and edited by Barcos, the nephew of Saint-Cyran. In spite of their Jansenist origin they were approved by thirty bishops; although they did provoke a polemic they were even adopted by dioceses which were headed by anti-Jansenist prelates. Finally, a third problem had to be solved: the liturgical text had to be made accessible to those of the faithful who did not understand Latin. This presented an obstacle of a very special kind.

---

[40] See E. Deberre, *Histoire de la vénérable Marguerite du Saint-Sacrement* (Paris 1907).
[41] See I. Noye, "Enfance de Jésus," *DSAM* 4 (1959), 652–82.
[42] See A. Hamon, *Histoire de la dévotion au Sacré-Cœur*, 5 vols. (Paris 1923–40); P. Blanchard, *Sainte Marguerite-Marie, expérience et doctrine* (Paris 1961).

Many Catholics feared that the translation of liturgical texts into French might favor the Calvinist spirit, since this was precisely one of the main demands of the Reformed Church. On the other hand, there was also the conviction that the use of Latin provided a necessary element of mystery to the ceremonies which would be lost by translating, especially the Canon of the Mass. Yet in the period 1587 to 1660 at least five separate translations of the Ordinary were printed. Port-Royal had played a significant role in these efforts with its *Office de l'Église et de la Vierge en latin et en français* (1650), generally referred to as *Heures de Port-Royal*, which enjoyed great success with its many printings. It was followed by the *Office du Saint-Sacrement* (1659) and the *Piété des chrétiens envers les morts* (1665). But a violent controversy was triggered by the translation of the complete missal in 1660 by Jacques de Voisin (d. 1685), an erudite and by no means Jansenist theologian who was victimized in part by political considerations. Voisin's work was censured immediately after it appeared by the Assembly of the Clergy and by the Sorbonne. It was also condemned in a brief by Alexander VII dated 12 January 1661. But this brief, which never came up for passage in parliament, had limited success, since it did not keep Voisin from publishing in 1662 a translation of the Office of Holy Week. Among the defenders of Voisin was Arnauld. But the most important work of this kind was that of one of the confessors at Port-Royal, Nicolas Le Tourneux (1640–86). At his death he left behind a manuscript in the process of being published, *Année chrétienne*. Completed by his friend Ernest Ruth d'Ans,[43] it constitutes a remarkable spiritual explication of the liturgical texts. In addition he wrote a translation of the Roman breviary, also published after his death. The Jansenist origin of these works led to several incidents and in 1695 *Année chrétienne* was placed on the Index. But Le Tourneux's work was taken up again in the eighteenth century and led to a renewal of liturgical devotion in France.

Translation of the books of the Bible posed similar problems. Reading the Holy Scriptures in French was one of the chief demands of the Reformed Church and this created among the Catholics a certain emotional prejudice towards any such translations. Consequently the number of French translations available to the Catholics for most of the seventeenth century was very small.[44] Foremost among them were those by Deville (1613), Frizon (1621), Pierre de Besse (1631), and Corbin (1643), all of which followed the old Louvain translation very closely. But they were hardly known to the public.

[43] See X. Janne d'Othée, *Ernest Ruth d'Ans, secrétaire du grand Arnauld* (Verviers 1949).
[44] See D. Lortsch, *Histoire de la bible en France* (Paris 1910); J. Baroni, *La Contre-Réforme devant la bible* (Lausanne 1943).

Only the New Testament which appeared frequently in separate printings, improved through a few supplementary translations, achieved a broader distribution. The situation changed somewhat after 1660 when several translations such as the New Testament by the Oratorian Amelote (1667) and of the Bible by Desmarets de Saint-Sorlin (1669) reached the general public. The Jansenists played a significant role in this field of endeavor with the so-called Mons New Testament (1667) and, above all, with the Bible annotated by Sacy whose thirty-two volumes appeared from 1672 to 1696. Predictably, the translations of Port-Royal caused several polemics in which Arnauld took an effective part. But these attacks did not make them any less appreciated. Moreover, as mentioned earlier, translations of the Bible and liturgy were frequently needed for use by new converts from Protestantism.

A significant part of Christian life was the development of religious art. Characterized by a profound inwardness in the very sobriety of its form it slipped into a decorative phase after 1668.[45] This development is especially noticeable in religious painting where the initial tendency is incorporated: in the work of Simon Vouet (1590–1649), Georges de la Tour (1593–1657), Eustache Le Sueur (1617–55), and Philippe de Champaigne (1602–74). The later phase is represented by Pierre Mignard (1610–95) and Charles Le Brun (1619–90). In the field of architecture the difference in inspiration is to a certain extent obscured by the continuity in planning. At first a strong Roman influence can be perceived: even Bernini was asked for designs. A great religious zeal produced a boom that resulted in more than thirty churches being built in the first half of the century. Several among them excel by virtue of their truly authentic religious character, such as Port-Royal of Paris, Val-de-Grâce, and the chapel of the Sorbonne. After 1660 church architecture became an instrument to the glory of the King, as represented by the Hôtel des Invalides and also by the chapel of Versailles, both of which attest in their own way to the change in the artistic climate.

From Cartesianism to Quietism

The far-reaching religious transformation in France after 1660 came from a profound change of mentality in which Cartesian rationalism was able to gain ground. There was a simultaneous development towards psychological and moral analysis and introspection. The tendency in regard to the inner life was towards seeking one's own identity within a

---

[45] See C. Mauricheau-Beaupré, *L'art au XVIIe siècle*, 2 vols. (Paris 1947).

clear consciousness, within clearly formulated thoughts; all obscure elements and those that could not be articulated were viewed with distrust. Mystical experience gradually disappeared from the perspective of consciousness; its dynamic and fundamental role in Christian life was being forgotten. In its place a spiritual psychologism and moralism were introduced into devotional literature. Yet this current did produce some valuable works which were based on a dogmatic fundament indebted to Bérulle's Christocentricity.

One of the most prominent representatives of this movement was the Jansenist Pierre Nicole (1625–95), the longtime collaborator of Arnauld. In 1672 he began publishing his famous *Essais de morale,* a sequence of small treatises and commentaries on the Bible which enjoyed great popularity until the Revolution. Two other Jansenists were competing with him. One was the Oratorian Pasquier Quesnel (1624–1719), whose religious and political role has already been discussed. He was also a remarkable religious author. It should be remembered that his *Réflexions morales* (1693), long before they became the immediate cause of the bull *Unigenitus*, served as the basis for meditation to many of the faithful, even among non-Jansenists. His many other devotional writings, especially his frequently reprinted *Prières chrétiennes* (1687), demonstrate a remarkable talent for dealing exhaustively with topics of Bérulle's theology. Quesnel's literary abilities almost equaled those of Jacques-Joseph Du Guet (1649–1733), a former Oratorian as well, who was deeply engaged in the disputes over Jansenism.[46] Du Guet was an admirable author who deserves to be counted among the greatest. Unfortunately the very enormity of the body of his works, which exceeds one hundred printed volumes, as well as the all too undifferentiated uniformity of his very perfection detract from his work. But it should yet be possible to reawaken an interest in some of his most successful works, such as the *Traité de la prière publique* and the ten volumes of his *Lettres de morale et de piété* (1707–53). He advanced the art of psychological analysis farther than did Quesnel and showed rare powers of differentiation. Quesnel and Du Guet followed in Nicole's footsteps and ensured the continuity into the eighteenth century. But they should not obscure the other authors of like tendencies. A special place is occupied by the doctor of Port-Royal, Jean Hamon (1618–87), who left behind a voluminous body of writings, part of which was not published until much later.[47] His poetic and colorful style, above all in his *Lettres et opuscules* (1734) and his treatise *De la solitude* (1734), distinguish them

[46] P. Chételat, *Étude sur Du Guet* (Paris 1877).
[47] See L. Cognet, "Hamon," *DSAM* 7 (1968), 64–71.

from the somewhat drab language of the rest of the works from Port-Royal. Finally, we should call attention to the third superior general of Saint-Sulpice, Louis Tronson (1622–1700), whose famous *Examens particuliers* (1690) made an imprint on the development of conscience and on introspection for innumerable generations of priests. They have been read in most of the religious orders up until our day.

The development of psychologism in spirituality gradually led to a distrust of mysticism and created a climate favorable to the outbreak of a crisis. This process crystallized around a woman, Jeanne-Marie Bouvier de la Motte (1648–1717), married to Jacques Guyon du Chesnoy[48] and widowed since 1676. She was a devout person given to a somewhat exaggerated mysticism who used her considerable fortune and the freedom of her widowed state in order to dedicate herself to a spiritual apostolate which led her, together with her spiritual guide, the Barnabite François La Combe (1643–1715), to Savoy, Turin, and Grenoble.[49] Having returned to Paris in 1686, she was embroiled in a financial controversy in 1688 caused by the greed of Harlay de Champvallon and leading to the incarceration of Father La Combe. Mme Guyon was released upon the intervention of Mme de Maintenon. The latter introduced her into the royal residence of Saint-Cyr, where in October 1688 she met Fénelon. After a little hesitation he recognized her spiritual gifts and entered into a close relationship with her. By this time Mme Guyon had already written a lot, but published very little. Only her *Moyen court et très facile pour l'oraison* (1685) had been fairly successful. The rest of her writings were published very much later, between 1712 and 1720, by the pietistic pastor Pierre Poiret, one of her ardent admirers. Not very original, but also not without talent and skill, Mme Guyon's writings present the classical teachings of the great tradition of Christian mysticism. But at times her expression lacks precision, which explains why her books occasionally caused some disquiet.[50]

Fénelon, too, had been introduced at Saint-Cyr by Mme de Maintenon. Under his and Mme Guyon's leadership the spirituality there was influenced in a clearly mystical direction. But the trial in Rome against Molinos (1687; Chap. 8) had aroused public opinion even in France and resulted in an attitude hostile to mysticism. Given the maliciousness of the court, where Mme de Maintenon was hated, this was enough to accuse her of spreading quietism at Saint-Cyr. Mme de Maintenon tried to counteract the accusation by removing Fénelon and Mme Guyon

---

[48] See ibid., "Guyon," *DSAM* 6 (1967), 1306–38.
[49] See G. Boffito, *Scrittori Barnabiti* II (Florence 1933–34), 305–11.
[50] See L. Cognet, "La spiritualité de Mme Guyon," *XVIIᵉ siècle* 12–14 (1952), 269–75.

from Saint-Cyr in the spring of 1693. She also prevailed in having Mme Guyon's writings examined by Bossuet, who was by no means a specialist in matters of mysticism. In fact these were almost totally foreign to him. This did not prevent him from rendering an unequivocally negative judgment in March 1694. Above all he reproached Mme Guyon for her views on the passive state, which in his opinion was incompatible both with the practice of the prayer of supplication and the exercise of Christian virtues. Thereupon Mme Guyon demanded a more precise examination. This led to the discussions of Issy from July 1694 to 10 March 1695 in which Bossuet, Noailles, and Tronson conferred, with none of them actually being competent in this matter. Fénelon, having been appointed archbishop of Cambrai in February 1695, succeeded in having a protocol composed which contained thirty-four paragraphs relating to the inner life. This brought the conferences to a hardly satisfactory conclusion.

Next Bossuet wrote a long pastoral instruction on this topic largely designed to prove Mme Guyon wrong for which he hoped to obtain Fénelon's concurrence and, with it, the latter's disassociation from Mme Guyon. But Fénelon rejected any sort of condemnation of her. He had received significant ideas from her and maintained an unswerving devotion towards her, proof of an admirable degree of loyalty. In July 1696 Fénelon received Bossuet's manuscript and returned it to him with a categorical rejection. Yet he perceived that the time had come for him to clarify his own position. In the summer of 1696 he used a stay in Cambrai to compose his *Explication des Maximes des Saints sur la vie intérieure*, a compact systematization of his mystical spirituality centered around his ideas of pure love and completely unselfish Christian charity. Bossuet, having been appraised of the existence of the work, tried to prevent its publication. But Fénelon's friends thereupon hurried the printing along so that the *Maximes* were published at the beginning of February 1697, more than a month before Bossuet's *Instruction sur les états d'oraison*, a work very much lacking in matters of spirituality which nonetheless attacked Mme Guyon violently. Next, Bossuet started agitating public opinion and prejudicing the King against Fénelon, whom he openly accused of quietism. But Fénelon succeeded in securing the King's permission to put the matter before the Holy See.

In France, Fénelon and Bossuet exchanged numerous polemics and the conflict was joined by many other experts. On 15 September 1697 Fénelon defined his ideas extremely well in a remarkable pastoral instruction which received the support of numerous theologians. By April 1698 Bossuet realized that he would not win this fight on the level of doctrine. Urged on by part of those around him and blinded by vengefulness, he then engaged in a contemptible campaign of defamation. In

June 1698 he published his *Relation sur le quiétisme* which completely avoided the basic problems and was nothing but a long persiflage. Moreover, he included many slanderous innuendos regarding the relationship between Fénelon and Mme Guyon, making use, with incredible indiscretion, of even the most confidential communications. This tactic turned out to be very effective and Fénelon's beautiful *Réponse à la relation* (August 1698) was unable to save the situation.

Innocent XII, who scorned Bossuet because of the latter's Gallicanism, did not conceal his sympathy for Fénelon because of the latter's recognition of papal prerogatives. Convinced of the archbishop's profound orthodoxy and of his loyalty to the authentic mystical tradition, he tried his best, including the use of procrastination, to avoid having to condemn Fénelon.[51] But Bossuet's propagation in Rome of the *Relation sur le quiétisme* was most injurious to Fénelon's reputation. Yet Innocent XII would probably not have given in had it not been for the personal persistent interference on the part of Louis XIV, who was completely on the side of Bossuet. The disfavor aimed at Fénelon, his family, and friends clearly showed the King's attitude; barely disguised threats reached all the way to the Vatican. It was well known that, given the Pope's advanced age, a conclave was not far off and that the cardinals feared a negative attitude on the part of France. So they pressured Innocent XII in order to obtain a condemnation in principle and the Pope regretfully gave in. But Cardinal Albano, secretary of briefs and the future Clement XI, succeeded in defying Bossuet even by means of this condemnation. The brief *Cum alias*,[52] dated 12 March 1699, was simply a brief, whereas Bossuet had expected a formal bull. Furthermore, it contained the proviso "motu proprio," which usually caused the French parliament to reject it. Twenty-three sentences from the *Maximes* were condemned as a whole, but without any individual qualifications. The term "heretical" did not occur in the brief. Fénelon accepted the condemnation without reservation in a pastoral letter of 9 April, and on this occasion Innocent XII sent him a letter of unusual praise. A little later, in October, in order to demonstrate his sympathy he announced his intention to elevate Fénelon to a cardinalship, an honor which he persistently refused Bossuet. But Fénelon's friends kept him from it because they feared the wrath of Louis XIV. For the rest of his life Fénelon was banished from the court to his diocese of Cambrai; yet he continued to maintain his deep affection for Mme Guyon, who had been incarcerated in December 1695 under most obscure circumstances. It was only in March 1703 that she was freed and exiled to

[51] See J. Orcibal, *Le procès des Maximes des Saints devant le Saint-Office* (Rome 1968).
[52] Text: *BullRom* 20, 870b.

Blois. From here she was able secretly to correspond with Fénelon, who in turn sent his nephews and selected pupils to her. Mme Guyon subsequently had a strong influence on the milieu of Protestant Pietism, especially in England.[53] But the foresight of Innocent XII was proved correct: the condemnation of Fénelon damaged Christian mysticism on the whole and caused it to enter a period of regression for more than a century.

[53] A. de la Gorce, "Mme Guyon à Blois," *Études* 310 (1961), 182–96.

CHAPTER 6

Christian Thought in Seventeenth-Century France

Systematic and Scholastic Theology

Catholic renewal, initiated at the beginning of the seventeenth century, was manifested less in the realm of thought than in the area of Christian life and spirituality. The men of the Counter Reformation did not occupy themselves with a renewal of theological methods. Patristics and history became objects of detailed studies only inasmuch as they were forced upon them by the exigency of polemics with the Reformed Churches. But it was not their intention to continue the efforts of the great Christian humanists of the Renaissance in these areas. The famous theological faculties and above all the Sorbonne remained bastions of traditional speculative theology. Here the situation of the prominent Parisian professors was characteristic. Their teachings were almost exclusively Thomistic, their lectures nothing but commentaries on the *Summa theologica*. This does not mean, however, that they were actually based upon a genuine Thomism. Rather they were frequently influenced by the deteriorating Scholasticism of the waning Middle Ages.

We see this reflected in the case of the well-known Philippe de Gamaches (1568–1625), professor at the Sorbonne, whose honor it was to count Bérulle and Condren among his pupils and who doubtlessly strongly influenced Bérulle. Although he, together with Duval, was among the first to occupy one of the chairs for positive theology established by Henry IV in 1598, his method remained absolutely Scholastic. His numerous quotes from the Fathers were intended as proof or illustration, but not as a return to the thought of Christian antiquity. Vestiges of nominalism as well as a strong Augustinian influence are occasionally discernible in his work. His competitor Nicolas Isambert

(1565–1642), who published a voluminous commentary on the *Summa* in 1639, represented a much more consistent Thomism, although he did not universally accept the concept of absolute predestination independent of previous merit. Aside from the Sorbonne professors many Jesuits could be mentioned who under the cover of Saint Thomas Aquinas introduced ideas of the new theology of Molina and Lessius.

Within the same framework were others representing even more independent thoughts. This holds true for André Duval, whose role in the Gallican conflict we have mentioned before. His commentary on the *prima pars* of the *Summa* is still unpublished in the Bibliothèque Nationale in Paris; that on the *secunda pars* was published by him in 1636. Duval, a follower of the abstract school, approved of Canfield's theses. He had read Ruysbroeck and Henry of Herp and was preoccupied with Platonic ideas. All these influences are reflected in his commentary on Saint Thomas Aquinas as well. He is therefore an informative witness for the Platonic tendencies in spirituality and theology especially up to 1630; its presence up to Bérulle has already been mentioned. It was in the latter's circle that a strange theological study appeared which did not claim the auspices of Saint Thomas Aquinas and furthermore made no bones about its Platonic origin: *De libertate Dei et creaturae* by the Oratorian Guilleaume Gibieuf, whose Marian spirituality has been mentioned earlier.[1] Gibieuf's complex system posits the highest idea of freedom in God and its perfect realization in Jesus Christ, the God-Man. Therefore, man's freedom increases the more it approximates that of Christ and becomes incapable of sin. Gibieuf rejects both the Thomist idea of *praedeterminatio physica* as well as the Molinist idea of the *scientia media*. His thoughts are clearly inspired by Ruysbroeck and Henry of Herp. This work provoked a violent controversy in which the Jesuit Theophile Raynaud pointed out the Rhenish-Flemish origins of his opponent. Gibieuf's presentation breaks with Scholastic tradition by virtue of its continuous structure, but his primarily deductive method is absolutely ahistoric. His work was unique in its way, since Platonism in theology as well as in spirituality was retreating after 1630. The only treatise which could be connected with Gibieuf's work is *De Sancto Sacerdotio* (1631) by the Oratorian Paul Métézeau (1583–1632), who develops a hierarchic, Platonic, and dionysian theology of the priesthood.[2]

After this period the teaching at the theological faculties more and

---

[1] See G. Marafini, *Agli albori del Giansenismo, Guglielmo Gibieuf e il suo pensiero intorno alla libertà* (Rome 1947); J. Orcibal, "Néoplatonisme et jansénisme, du *De libertate* du P. Gibieuf à l'*Augustinus*: 'Nuove ricerche storiche sul giansenismo,' " *AnGr* 71 (Rome 1954), 33–57.

[2] I. Noye, *Sacerdoce et sainteté d'après le P. Métézeau: La Tradition sacerdotale* (Le Puy 1962), 169–89.

more lost contact with reality, towards an abstract speculation out of step with the spiritual tendencies of the time. The rejection of Cartesianism by official circles—a topic to be dealt with later—may serve as an example. A characteristic work in this regard is the *Opera theologica* of Martin Grandin (1604–91), who was famous for his piety and erudition. Published posthumously in 1710 by his former pupil and compilator Charles du Plessis d'Argentré, it is a more or less mediocre commentary on a few articles of the *Summa*, devoid of any originality. Henceforth the teaching duties at the Sorbonne, instead of being a source of true intellectual education, appeared to even the best of minds as no more than a condition for achieving university degrees. It is a significant fact that even Bossuet did not keep his notes of the lectures he attended at the Collège de Navarre. Some minds were aware of this stagnation and, in an attempt to renew the theology from within, strove for a synthesis with spirituality, yet still by traditional methods. One of them was Louis Bail (1610–69), who wanted to create a comprehensive work on spiritual theology on a Scholastic basis, his *Théologie affective ou saint Thomas en méditations,* which appeared in four parts from 1638 to 1650. This work is not without merit, but has a certain ponderousness about it. Besides, it is not entirely free of commonplaces. In this field Bail is far behind the Dominican Guillaume de Contenson (1641–74), the author of the *Theologia mentis et cordis* (1668–87). Left incomplete, it was concluded by his fellow Dominican Massoulié. The *speculationes,* a presentation of the dogma with a heavy Scholastic imprint, are followed by the *reflexiones,* subtly differentiated spiritual discussions which—while at times going rather far afield—do contain some very beautiful pages. Unfortunately these spiritual reflections are not always connected in a natural fashion with the theological part. Consequently the work does not show the necessary unity; its speculative tendency is weakened by its methodology.[3]

Moral theology was no doubt in a more critical situation. Theologians frequently developed problems of moral theology following the respective *quaestiones* of Saint Thomas's *Summa,* but in a purely speculative and theoretical fashion. No one intended to create the basis for an individual theological moral philosophy. At the same time an ever more distinct predilection for casuistry was developing. To a certain extent this development was even demanded by the need to reform the clergy as well as by the necessity to educate sufficiently well-instructed confessors. Instruction in the *casus conscientiae* was included in all the curricula

---

[3] See A. Bozaudun, *Une gloire dominicaine, histoire du T.R.P. de Contenson* (Montauban 1863).

of clerical education. In this area the Jesuits, the great guides of souls, are undeniable masters. Yet the Society of Jesus scarcely produced any famous casuists in France; the most prominent authors in this field were foreigners. In passing, one could mention Étienne Bauny (1564–1649) who taught at Clermont College from 1618 to 1625. He is primarily known as the author of a French handbook for priests who could not read Latin sufficiently well, the *Somme des péchés qui se commettent en tous états* (Paris 1634). This casuistry is nothing more than a collection of guidelines for the treatment of specific cases, but the fundamental problems of morality are not at all mentioned. Probabilism, without any theoretical justification, is applied as the basic principle. The method of casuistry soon crossed over into the field of controversialism and in so doing became one of the most controversial topics of seventeenth-century religious thought, mainly for political reasons. The major cause lay in the old enmity between the university and the Jesuits. A regulation, issued in 1618 and jealously upheld, obliged the candidates for a baccalaureate degree to study for three years with the professors of the theological faculty and not to have any other teachers of theology. This excluded the Jesuit pupils from the baccalaureate. The Jesuits were most reluctant to submit to this humiliating regulation; towards the end of 1642 they attacked it, causing another round of polemics. In order to discredit the Jesuits, partisans of the university published a pamphlet in August 1643 entitled *Théologie morale des jésuites extraite fidèlement de leurs livres*, a collection of clearly laxist solutions from the pens of Jesuit casuists. This pamphlet was written by Doctor François Hallier and the young Antoine Arnauld, who was then at the beginning of his career. Although the controversy was belayed quickly, the public remained sensitive to this issue. Thus the ground remained fertile for the great talent of Pascal, who resumed the battle in 1656 with his fifth *Provinciale*. At this point the issue of laxist casuistry interfered with the Jansenist conflict and furnished a veritable arsenal of arguments against the Jesuits which were used again and again. But it should be noted that no one actually unfolded the problem by starting with its root causes. Neither Pascal nor Nicole in his annotations, added to his Latin translation of the *Provinciales* (1658), nor the Jesuit Georges Pirot (1599–1669) in his *Apologie pour les casuistes* (1657) posed the question of the actual value of probabilism in its fundamental principles. Henceforth Jesuits and laxism, and Jansenism and rigorism were firmly identified with each other in the eyes of the general public. Not even the example of a rigorist Jesuit such as Bordaloue could change that. The moralism of the spiritual authors of the waning seventeenth century is of a purely psychological and empirical nature. Not until the *Traité de morale* (1683) of Malebranche do we encounter an essay on Christian moral philosophy, but it was conceived in an atmosphere dominated entirely by Descartes.

The Development of Historical Theology

Various causes contributed to the fact that Scholasticism gradually became archaic and unfashionable. The anti-Protestant controversies played a significant role in this development. We should recall that the Reformed, especially the Calvinists, refused to recognize medieval theology, viewing it as the application of totally heathen logic to the realities of the revelation. So their own weapons had to be used against them: the Scriptures and the Fathers. From 1575 on, the *Bibliotheca patrum* of Marguerin de la Bigne (1546–90) offered a valuable source to the controversialists. In 1644 it was reprinted in seventeen folios. After 1600, scientific editions of authors from Christian antiquity multiplied, and numerous formerly unpublished works were made accessible. Work in this field encompassed the entire century and reached a high level of scientific precision, especially in the great editions of the Benedictines of Saint-Maur. Initially this abundant material was used primarily for polemics; the *Discours de controverse* by Bérulle (1609) is a good example of that sort of use. But soon the scientific investigation of that period became an independent science, disregarding polemical prejudice and seeking fulfillment in the interest in Christian antiquity, an interest which spread from the Italian Counter Reformation to the French *milieu dévot*.

Some famous specialists excelled in this field, the Jesuit Jacques Sirmond (1559–1651) for instance, who during his long life was able to engage in extensive editorial activities, above all the *Concilia antiqua Galliae* (1629). There was also his fellow Jesuit Théophile Raynaud (1582–1663), whose polemics against Gibieuf have already been mentioned. He gave us an excellent edition of Anselm of Canterbury (1630). Among the Dominicans we should mention François Combéfis (1605–79), a specialist in Greek patristics who published a remarkable edition of the writings of Maximus Confessor (1675). It was also his somewhat dangerous merit to prove that the acts of the Sixth Ecumenical Council concerning the condemnation of Pope Honorius were in no way a falsification. The Oratorians made their contribution in the person of Jean Morin (1591–1659), whom we shall meet again in his capacity as exegete, but who was also an admirable expert in oriental liturgical texts. The two volumes of *Supplementum operum sancti Augustini* (1654), edited by his fellow Oratorian Jérôme Vignier (1606–61), also known as an exegete, are unfortunately full of errors into which he was led by his anti-Jansenist zeal.[4]

Among the French scholarly groups the reformed Benedictines of Saint-Maur (Maurists) whose center was the Benedictine abbey of Saint-Germain-des-Prés occupied a special place. The initial impulse came from their first superior, Dom Grégoire Tarrisse,[5] but the actual organizer of their scholarly work was Dom Luc d'Achéry (1609–85), the founder of the marvelous library of Saint-Germain who placed at the disposal of his fellow monks tools which were unique at that time.[6] His work was continued by the famous Dom Jean Mabillon (1632–1707) a milestone of whose prodigious production was his edition of the writings of Bernard of Clairvaux (1667).[7] Aside from him there were others, no less famous, such as Dom Bernard de Montfaucon (1655–1742), Dom Thomas Blampin (1640–1710), who directed the edition of the works of Saint Augustine, and many more. The work of the Maurists continued until the Revolution and comprised the majority of the patristic literature. Even today their folios represent a prime example of scholarship. Their untiring efforts extended into all other areas of the holy sciences. Yet prior to them, other learned circles had exercised a similar influence, such as the one formed around the brothers Dupuy, where Bossuet developed his critical thinking and scholarship.[8] The role of this circle in the issue of Gallicanism has already been mentioned.

Another product of these editorial activities were the comprehensive syntheses of patristic theology. Several names already mentioned in connection with their editorial work excelled in this field as well. These endeavors were dominated, however, by the mighty figure of the Jesuit Denis Petau (1583–1652), whose *Dogmata theologica* (1644–50) represented a theretofore unsurpassed monument of patristic work of extraordinary informational and analytical exactness.[9] In the person of Louis Thomassin (1619–95) he had a competitor from the ranks of the Oratorians, but Thomassin's comprehensive *Dogmata theologica* (1680–84), written in a more personal vein, was inferior to Petau's in its lack of objectivity. He also authored a number of historical and dog-

---

[4] See E. Havet, "Les decouvertes de Jérôme Vignier," *BÉCh* 46 (Paris 1885); L. Saltet, "Un mystificateur janséniste," *BLE* 43 (1942), 75 ff.

[5] See F. Rousseau, *Dom Grégoire Tarrisse, premier supérieur général de la Congrégation de Saint-Maur* (Paris 1924).

[6] See M. Laurain, "Les travaux d'érudition des Mauristes, origine et évolution," *RHEF* 43 (1957), 231–72.

[7] See H. Leclercq, *Mabillon*, 2 vols. (Paris 1953–57).

[8] See I. Uri, *Un cercle savant au XVIIᵉ siècle* (Paris 1886).

[9] See J. C. Vital-Chatellain, *Le P. Denis Petau d'Orléans, jésuite, sa vie et ses œuvres* (Paris 1884).

matic treatises in French.[10] Petau's work quite unintentionally sealed the disrepute into which Scholasticism had fallen even before the century had reached its midpoint. Jansen had already criticized its methods in his *Augustinus* and Saint-Cyran faulted Saint Thomas for having lived in a century in which philosophy and human judgment were overvalued.

An analogous development can be traced in the field of exegesis. The tradition of spiritual, moral, and even allegorical exegesis no doubt continued to be widespread. They were used primarily by the people of Port-Royal, and especially in Sacy's Bible and in the *Explications sur le Nouveau Testament* (1683) by his secretary Nicolas Fontaine (1625–1709); both of them joined the patristic tradition and particularly that of Augustine. Bossuet too can be added on the basis of his *Apocalypse avec une explication* (1689). A parallel, albeit less significant tradition, was that of scientific exegesis. It originated in the humanistic endeavors of the Renaissance and was represented by the Jesuit Johannes Maldonatus in Paris. In 1645 this form of exegesis had led to the publication of the beautiful polyglot Bible by the lawyer Guillaume Le Jay. Also in this line was the work of the Oratorian Jean Morin, a convert to Judaism and a great scholar of rabbinical literature who demonstrated its importance for the interpretation of Holy Scripture. But he also expressed the daring idea that the Masoretic interpreters had falsified the Hebrew text. He offered this theory in his *Exercitationes ecclesiasticae* (1631) about the Samaritan Pentateuch and in his *Exercitationes biblicae* (1633), which provoked spirited polemics. But the actual founder of biblical criticism was another Oratorian, Richard Simon (1638–1712), an unsavory character but intellectually a genius of comprehensive education. Initially he tried to achieve a clear and satisfactory definition of the infallibility of the Bible and thus to demonstrate that the normal methods of historical criticism could be applied to the Holy Scriptures.[11] In 1678 he attempted to present his ideas in his *Histoire critique du Vieux Testament*. But Bossuet, warned through an indiscretion, managed to get a table of contents of the book and promptly intervened. He had the work confiscated and all copies destroyed. The Oratorians thought their congregation endangered by Simon and expelled him on 21 May 1678. He then became parish priest at Bolleville in the diocese of Rouen. His ideas were indeed too far ahead of his time, and all the world opposed him; Bossuet, the Great Arnauld, and Protestants such as Vossius and

[10] See P. Clair, *Louis Thomassin, étude biographique et bibliographique* (Paris 1964).

[11] See J. Steinmann, *Richard Simon et les origines de l'exégèse biblique* (Paris 1960); P. Auvray, "Richard Simon d'après des documents inédits," *Oratoriana* 1 (1960), 46–68; idem, "Richard Simon après 1678," 6 (1962), 55–69; idem, "Richard Simon, Bossuet et l'abbé Bibnon," 14 (1968), 89–103; idem, "Richard Simon et Jean Leclercq," 15 (1969), 26–42.

Jurieu. Yet he persisted in his views. The *Histoire critique du texte du Vieux Testament* was reprinted in Holland in 1680 and 1685. In 1689 Simon published a *Histoire critique du texte du Nouveau Testament*, followed by several similar works and finally by a translation of the New Testament in 1702 which led to another incident with Bossuet. The latter continued the fight, but died without having completed his *Défense de la tradition des Saints Pères*, in which he wanted to refute the exegetical methods of Richard Simon and to justify the traditional principles. Simon was in fact not emulated because his ideas were considered too daring in those days. A contemporary of that pioneer of genius was another Oratorian, Bernard Lamy (1640–1715), a well-educated and skilled exegete and friend of Malebranche.[12]

The development of scholarship was attended by that of historiography, which now ceased being a literary composition in favor of becoming a genuine science. This movement had already been indicated since the beginning of the century by the historian Eudes de Mézeray, brother of Saint John Eudes, but its actual development did not start until 1630. In the field of church history Baronius had some competitors in France since all the great specialists in historical theology were interested in it as well. Jean Morin, Petau, and Thomassin created significant works in this field, but the true French Baronius was an Oratorian, Charles Lecointe (1611–81), whose *Annales ecclesiastici Francorum* appeared in eight folios from 1665 to 83. Lecointe wisely avoided including the first two centuries so he would not have to dispute the legends which traced back the origins of many French dioceses to the apostles. But in this connection the Bollandists served as an example in France inasmuch as numerous specialists now tried to examine the historical truth of the lives of local saints. In this regard a professor of the Sorbonne, Jean de Launoy (1603–78), developed a deterrent reputation which gained him the sobriquet "Nest robber of the Saints." He had the courage to attack the legends of Provence about Saint Lazarus and Saint Magdalen (1641), those of the city of Paris concerning Saint Dionysius (1641) and the ones of the Carmelites about Simon Stock and the scapular. As a consequence he found himself exposed to intense polemics. Others nonetheless followed in his footsteps, mainly the Benedictines of Saint-Maur, who excelled in this sort of research, contributing an extraordinary number of works. By virtue of the quality as well as quantity of his work Mabillon occupied the most prominent position among them. He authored the *Acta sanctorum ordinis sancti Benedicti* (1668–1701; in collaboration with Dom Thierry Ruinart) and

---

[12] F. Girbal, *Bernard Lamy, étude biographique et bibliographique* (Paris 1964); B. Lamy, *Entretiens sur les Sciences*, ed. by F. Girbal and P. Clair (Paris 1966).

the *Annales ordinis sancti Benedicti* (1703–13). In his famous work *De re diplomatica* (1681) he determined the basic rules applying to works in the field of historiography. Many of the successors and pupils of Mabillon gained prominence in the difficult area of local and regional history. Later on, Dom Denys de Sainte-Marthe (1650–1725) took over the task of reediting and completing the *Gallia christiana*. These works gained a considerable reputation throughout Europe for their comprehensiveness and quality. Louis XIV expressly requested to have Mabillon introduced to him. Port-Royal, too, contributed one of its finest representatives in this field in the person of one of its last pupils, Sébastien Le Nain de Tillemont (1637–98).[13] While he was not blessed with a long career, his enormous energy enabled him to complete a monumental number of works. In addition to the six volumes of the *Histoire des empereurs* (1690–1738), there are the sixteen volumes of his *Mémoires pour servir à l'histoire ecclésiastique des six premiers siècles* (1693–1712). All of his work is characterized by a profound scholarship and an unusual scientific rigor. In addition, Tillemont, whose kindness was inexhaustible, furnished the documentation for numerous other works. Sacy, who had agreed before his death to write a history of Saint Louis for the Dauphin (the son of Louis XIV), had received some admirable treatises from Tillemont which manifest an unusually profound knowledge of the Middle Ages. These manuscripts remained unpublished until the nineteenth century.[14] Tillemont, who was very sympathetic to the Maurists, left to them his complete documentation on Augustine, from which the Benedictines compiled a history of the life of Saint Augustine and added it to volume twelve of his works (1700). Additionally, he collaborated on the patristic biographies of the Jansenist Godefroy Hermant (1617–90), who wrote the lives of Saints Athanasius (1671), Basilius, Gregory of Nazianzus (1674), and Ambrose (1678). Lastly, a valuable work by another Oratorian, Jacques Lelong (1665–1721), should be mentioned: the *Bibliothèque historique de la France* (1719), which represents an indispensable source even today.

Cartesianism and Religious Thought

One of the main reasons for the decline of Scholasticism in the seventeenth century was the success of Cartesian philosophy. In order to comprehend its full significance, the presence of a latitudinarian, skepti-

[13] See B. Neveu, *Un historien à l'école de Port-Royal, Sébastien Le Nain de Tillemont* (The Hague 1966).
[14] *Vie de saint Louis roi de France, par Lenain de Tillemont*, ed. by J. de Gaulle, 6 vols. (Paris 1847–51).

cal, and even at times atheistic current in France has to be taken into consideration. Its origins go back to the sixteenth century and possibly even farther;[15] it invokes Jean Bodin,[16] Montaigne,[17] and Pierre Charron.[18] For the first thirty years of the seventeenth century this intellectual current attracted a large part of high society. The circle of Gaston d'Orléans and of the famous lady of the demimonde, Ninon de Lenclos,[19] was characterized by latitudinarianism. In these circles were poets such as Théophile de Viau,[20] Saint-Amant, Tristan, and even Cyrano de Bergerac. They were joined by philosophers as well, one of them being François de la Mothe le Vayer (1588–1672), the teacher of Monsieur, brother of Louis XIV. In his treatise *De la vertu des païens* (1640), de la Mothe le Vayer represents the view that Christianity is superfluous if not pernicious, since pagans can possess the same virtues as Christians. Another prominent member of this group is Pierre Gassendi (1592–1655), canon of Digne and professor of mathematics at the Royal Bourbon College, a splendid scholar who advocated Epicureanism.[21] Around them gathered the *libertins érudits,* the learned latitudinarians who were also encountered in scholarly circles and even in the famous cabinet of the brothers Dupuy. Latitudinarianism persisted throughout the century. Temporarily forced into retreat and anonymity when Louis XIV was under the influence of Mme de Maintenon, it made itself felt more strongly than ever after 1717.

René Descartes (see Chap. 18) was himself in no way a latitudinarian. His Christian education was profound, his faith serious, and his astonishing ties with Thomism are of greater significance for deciphering his personal thought than generally assumed.[22] It is understandable that he was encouraged by Bérulle at the beginning of his career. When he structured his essay on the rational mastery of all reality by following a method of systematic doubt, Descartes had no anti-Christian intentions. He limited himself to pursuing the old dream of a comprehensive explanation of material as well as intellectual reality by means of a single

---

[15] See F. Lachèvre, *Le libertinage au XVIIe siècle* (Paris 1920).

[16] See R. Chauviré, *J. Bodin auteur de la République* (Paris 1928).

[17] See P. Villey, *Montaigne et la postérité* (Paris 1925).

[18] See J. Sabrié, *De l'humanisme au rationalisme, Pierre Charron* (Paris 1913).

[19] See E. Magne, *Ninon de Lenclos* (Paris 1925).

[20] See A. Adam, *Théophile de Viau et la libre-pensée française en 1620* (Paris 1935).

[21] See B. Rochot, *Les travaux de Gassendi sur Epicure et l'atomisme, 1619–1658* (Paris 1944); R. Pintard, *La Mothe le Vayer, Gassendi, Guy Patin, études de bibliographie et de critique* (Paris 1943).

[22] See H. Gouhier, *Les premières pensées de Descartes, contribution à l'histoire de l'anti-Renaissance* (Paris 1958); C. Serrurier, *Descartes, l'homme et le penseur* (Paris and Amsterdam 1951).

principle. But the *Discours de la Méthode* (1637) represents in every respect a turning point in Western thought. His search for evidence, aimed for by the application of sharp and clear logic, created a new way of thinking. This gradually crossed over into the religious realm and left behind the cumbersome synthetic dialectics of Scholasticism, but by its systematic application of doubt it also furnished arguments for the skepticism of the latitudinarians. The success of Cartesianism was extraordinary. To be sure, its success was most prevalent in the social salons, but even the best of minds were affected by it. It is very interesting to see for instance how widespread Cartesianism was even in Port-Royal circles.[23] Arnauld and Nicole adhered to it without, however, renouncing Augustinianism and Thomism. In dealing with this problem they made an extremely valuable contribution with their famous *Logique de Port-Royal* (1662), which probably owed a great deal to Pascal.[24] In Port-Royal as well as in secular circles Cartesianism was of great interest for the sciences, especially mathematics and physics. This interest spread to the intellectuals among the clergy. It is very illuminating that a pious and modest confessor of Port-Royal such as Antoine de Rebours from Auvergne (1595–1661) had in his library a unique collection of scientific works.[25] Philosophic-scientific circles were formed in Paris. One of the most famous was the one around Marin Mersenne (1588–1648), the founder of a successful academy frequented by some of the greatest scholars of their time, among them Roberval. One of its first members was the father of Pascal, Étienne Pascal.[26]

Pascal (Chap. 3) also owed much to Cartesianism, although he turned against it after his conversion. Pascal's is an interesting case inasmuch as he is at the origin of a new Christian philosophy. But we should not forget that he did not at all aspire to be a philosopher and that his interests were not in this area. He wanted to be an apologist and defend the Christian religion against the latitudinarians, whom he had gotten to know better than anybody else during his secular period.[27] In this regard he joined a long tradition,[28] as had the Jesuit François Garasse[29] and

---

[23] See G. Lewis, *Augustinisme et cartésianisme à Port-Royal: Descartes et le cartésianisme hollandais* (Paris and Amsterdam 1950), 131–82.

[24] See P. Clair and F. Girbal, eds., *La logique ou l'art de penser* (Paris 1965).

[25] See L. Cognet, *Antoine de Rebours, confesseur de Port-Royal, ami de la famille Pascal: Clermont, ville de Pascal* (Clermont 1962), 219–29.

[26] See R. Lenoble, *Mersenne ou la naissance du mécanisme* (Paris 1943).

[27] See J. Mesnard, "Introduction à l'étude de Pascal mondain," *Annales Universitatis Saraviensis* 3 (1954), 76–94.

[28] See Julien-Eymard d'Angers, *Pascal et ses précurseurs* (Paris 1954).

[29] See J. Lecler, "Un adversaire des libertins au début de XVIIe siècle, le P. Garasse," *Études* 209 (1931), 570–72.

the Capuchin Yves de Paris.[30] But these pre-Pascal polemics missed their target because they were too ponderous and inept. On the day after the miracle of the Holy Thorn (24 March 1656) Pascal had jotted down some notes concerning the value of miracles. But not until 1657 did he resolve to oppose the latitudinarians and to collect notes with a view towards an apologia. His project had caused some disquiet at Port-Royal since he was considered a mere amateur in the field of theology. Moreover, Port-Royal, while skilled in controversies with the Protestants, had no experience in polemics against the latitudinarians. So Pascal was asked to give a lecture which was to detail his plan. For this conference Pascal took an initial inventory of his notes. Fortunately this compilation is pre-served and provides insight into Pascal's way of thinking at the time of this presentation, probably around June 1658. Pascal's sickness and subsequent early death kept him from completing his work, which, by the way, was not given very great importance by Port-Royal. In honor of his memory, Pascal's sister Gilberte and his friend, the duke of Roannez, insisted on compiling the *Pensées* from the surviving papers. These appeared in 1670, but only in a partial edition whose text was much changed. Not until 1844 was the precise and complete wording of Pascal's manuscripts made accessi-ble to the readers. But the edition of Port-Royal had sufficed to call the public's attention to Pascal's method, his rich view of man and the world, and the profundity of his analysis of the *conditio humana* and *christiana*. But it was merely a limited success: in his manner of humiliating man's intellect vis-à-vis a God unfathomable to the in-tellect but able to be experienced by the heart, Pascal opposed the rationalism of Descartes, which nonetheless won out. Few people in the eighteenth century understood the *Pensées*. We know that Vol-taire used them as the butt of his ridicule.

Only those who attempted a synthesis between Cartesianism and Christianity managed to reach public opinion. They deserve praise be-cause this undertaking was not without danger. In fact the official circles soon initiated a reaction against the further spread of Descartes's ideas. This resulted in a fight replete with complex and unpleasant episodes, reaching a climax on 1 September 1671 when, after the Mass of the Holy Ghost, the resolutions against Descartes's philosophy were read at the Sorbonne. The dean, Morel, explained that this condemnation con-cerned especially those who denied the *materia prima* and the *formae substantiales*. The public derided the Sorbonne's insistence upon this

---

[30] See Julien-Eymard d'Angers (C. Chesneau), *Le P. Yves de Paris et son temps, 1590–1670*, 2 vols. (Paris 1946).

sort of archaic Scholasticism and Boileau mocked it in his *Arrêt bur-lesque*. But the majority of the congregations thought it wiser to prohibit any and all teaching smacking of Cartesianism in their schools. This prohibition was enforced even with measures insulting to some professors. Lamy, whose exegeses have been mentioned before, was summoned to the philosophical faculty of Angers in 1673 and charged with teaching the traditional philosophy of Aristotle and Saint Thomas Aquinas. In his lectures he expressed some clearly pro-Cartesian theses and was promptly exiled to Grenoble on the heels of some dubious incident. Yet he held on to his Cartesian views.

Understanding these conditions makes it easier to appreciate what the courage of Nicolas Malebranche (1638–1715), also an Oratorian, meant in such an atmosphere. To fully comprehend him we need an appreciation of what he really was: an admirable religious author who expressed himself through his metaphysics.[31] He was also an apologist, but one who proceeded from his heart, who wanted to lend to religion a metaphysical and logical coherence able to convince both the intellect and the heart in this century of Enlightenment. His daring identification of *ratio* with the word of God combined Descartes's method with the original Augustinian principles, and that is the meaning of the synthesis for which he strove. A Cartesian by deep conviction, he proceeded to contemplate the religious universe of Augustinianism. In his *Recherche de la vérité* (1674) Malebranche presented his basic ideas precisely at the time of the incidents at Angers. His opponents immediately gave voice. From this point on, the mild-mannered and peaceable Malebranche showed himself to be the kind of powerful polemicist he was to remain till the end of his life. In subsequent editions of his work he countered every attack. His other works raised the expression of his thought to ever higher levels, probably reaching a climax in the *Méditations chrétiennes et métaphysiques* (1683). In contrast to the apologias of Pascal, those of Malebranche merged beautifully with the spirit of the century. This accounts for their great success, as demonstrated by the many reprints of his works. But his apologias also embroiled him in lively polemics with the representatives of the old school. Furthermore, his *Traité de la nature et de la grâce* (1680) involved him in a lengthy controversy with the Great Arnauld in which both gave as well as they took. The system by means of which Malebranche wanted to synthesize the mechanism of Descartes with the Augustinian concepts of the *praedestinatio* and the *gratia efficax* was daring and new. But it did contain numerous weak points, which was why Malebranche encountered such a dangerous adversary in the person of the Great Arnauld and why

[31] See A. Robinet, *Système et existence dans l'œuvre de Malebranche* (Paris 1965).

this dispute ended in a draw. Malebranche was quite conscious of that. Long after Arnauld's death in 1712 he was still planning a summary of all his responses to Arnauld. Bossuet was quite hostile to Malebranche's views. In 1684 he charged the young Fénelon, with whom he was on friendly terms at the time, to compose a *Réfutation du système du P. Malebranche*. Fénelon obeyed, but in reading the manuscript Bossuet recognized that these all too youthful comments merely scratched the surface of a difficult problem. Fénelon's work was not published. In spite of the resistance from various parties, the reputation of Malebranche grew more and more. In all of Europe those who knew the problems involved—foremost among them Leibniz—considered it an honor to have maintained connections with Malebranche[32] (see Chap. 18).

For posterity the fame of Malebranche has overshadowed less prominent Cartesians who were making similar efforts at that time. Yet several of them are of interest even today. We have already named Lamy, but we should also mention the Oratorian Nicolas Poisson (1637–1710), the author of the rare book *Commentaires ou remarques sur la méthode de M. Descartes* (Vendôme 1671), which played an important role in the history of Cartesianism. Clerselier suggested that he also write a biography of the great philosopher. We should not forget the very interesting Géraud de Cordemoy (1626–84),[33] who enjoyed the esteem of both Malebranche and Leibniz. But these are only the privileged representatives of a movement the detailed history of which has not yet been written. It was a movement which—no doubt unintentionally— paved the way for the rationalism of the eighteenth century.

[32] See A. Robinet, *Malebranche et Leibniz, relations personnelles* (Paris 1955).
[33] See G. de Cordemoy, *Œuvres philosophiques, avec une étude bio-bibliographique*, ed. by P. Clair and F. Girbal (Paris 1968).

The Papacy in the Period of French Hegemony

Introduction

The Peace of Westphalia, which ended the Wars of Religion in Europe (with the exception of England) and determined the configuration of the confessional map of Europe up to the first half of the present century, also meant a turning point in the position of the papacy. It had to resign itself to the factual situation. The protest of Innocent X charging the accords with contravening or injuring the rights of the Church have frequently encumbered the Church by the implication that the Pope, by his protest, wanted to undermine the making of peace in favor of continuing the war. Yet it amounted to nothing more than a formal legal reservation which, furthermore, was published with considerable delay in the brief *Zelus Domus Dei*, antedated by almost two years, so that the protest really had no practical effect.

The outcome of the Thirty Years' War meant a strengthening of the power of the state in ecclesiastical matters as well and led to the gradually expanding principle of the established Church, which, although developing differently in the various countries, had in common the diminution of the influence of Rome. In the following period the papacy increasingly lost esteem and the power to influence events. This can be demonstrated by the diminishing participation of the Holy See in the peace negotiations of the time. Whereas it took an active part in the Peace Conference of Münster in the person of its legate Chigi, the representative of the Pope was seldom listened to by the end of the century. In the eighteenth century decisions between the powers were generally made without the Pope and at times even against him.

As far as the Catholic powers were concerned, the papacy became in this period an object of their politics rather than those politics being determined to any degree by the Pope. In any given case he was caught within the existing and continuing field of tension based upon the constant opposition between France and the Habsburgs on the one hand, and between France and England on the other. The only area in which the Pope retained a certain initiative of his own was leadership in repelling the continuing Turkish threat.

For the most part the papal elections turned into political power plays between groups of cardinals in sympathy either with France or the Emperor. It was only in rare cases that the "Third Party" of independents—after the conclave of 1655 they were called the *squadrone volante* because of their political neutrality and their mobility resulting from it—could make a decision. As the result of political pressure on the papal elections it was not altogether rare that a compromise had to be sought and that sometimes there were elections which would have been unthinkable without the massive intervention of the various powers. In general it held true that no candidate could be elected against the express will of the French King. Yet this did not always mean invoking the *ius exclusival,* since the two-thirds' majority required by the rules of papal elections did create the possibility of a blocking minority. The fact that papal elections of this period generally took a very long time was due—aside from the slowness of communication and the difficulties encountered in traveling—precisely to those political interventions.

The appointments of cardinals as well were jealously watched by the various governments so that none of the individual powers would in any way be favored. There still remained the unwritten "right" of Catholic sovereigns to suggest to the Pope a number of candidates for the cardinalate in order to have, by virtue of these "Cardinals of the Crown," a special representation of their own interests within the College of Cardinals primarily for the event of a papal election. The nepotism of the previous period was not entirely overcome, even if some Popes kept themselves either partially or totally aloof from this traditional form of governing and family welfare.

The position of the papacy in the field of dogma and church discipline was aggravated and even endangered by tensions that appeared at midcentury which, spreading rapidly, were destined to lead to internal divisions. The ideas of Gallicanism and the Jansenist movement continued to be in opposition to each other into the next century. Thus it could happen that a comment by the Holy See against one was almost interpreted as partisanship in favor of the other party. No doubt the Church lost a good deal of initiative and strength by these continuing dogmatic disputes which no longer were of concern merely to theological experts, but encroached on the life of the Church itself (Chaps. 2–4).

The intellectual movement known as the Enlightenment also had its beginnings around this time. Rome was late in recognizing its importance and even then underestimated it because the Holy See's attention was riveted too much upon the negative effects and especially upon the attack on the belief in revealed religion. This necessarily widened the gulf between the leadership of the Church, arrested in traditional ways of thinking, and the new intellectual current emanating from England and France and influencing the whole Western world, a movement that soon went beyond the narrow circle of scholars to lead to a generally accepted new attitude towards life and the intellect even within the bourgeoisie. Its basic concerns, such as the demand for critical examination instead of a mere faith in authority, or its idea of tolerance and a practical humanity were viewed with distrust and rejection even when they were pronounced with the best of intentions by the foremost moderate representatives of the Enlightenment, such as Leibniz. The fact that the Church offered nothing but a rigid rejection of this challenge directed energetically against the traditional forms of church life contributed to both Church and papacy being viewed more and more as outmoded. More so than in other countries, where certain concerns of the new intellectual current were gradually accepted by ecclesiastical circles, resulting in something like a Catholic Enlightenment being formed, the above reaction could not but have its effect in Italy and primarily in the Papal States. It was here that the influence of Rome was most immediate and developments which were possible elsewhere could only take place with great difficulty or not at all (Chap. 18).

The simple faithful remained relatively untouched by the Enlightenment; they preserved their faith. A clear indicator of this was the noticeably high participation of the faithful in the popular missions which experienced a new flowering in this period especially in Italy. Above all it was the two Segneri, Paolo (1624–94) and his nephew Paolo the Younger (1673–1713), who developed their own exemplary missionary style with impressive elements of a baroque, sometimes perhaps exaggerated piety (with penitential processions, public flagellation, and dramatic religious plays). Aside from the religious benefits of this novel pastoral method, contemporaries especially recognized its social success, consisting of settling family and blood feuds as well as economic injustices. Of similar importance was the Capuchin Francesco Maria Casini (1648–1719), who preached at the papal court for fourteen years. In his sermons before the Pope he criticized the failings of the clergy and the administration of the Papal States with surprising frankness.

CHAPTER 7

The Popes from Alexander VII to Clement X

Alexander VII (1655–67)

After the death of Innocent X, Cardinal Mazarin, who conducted French policies, wanted to push through the election of Giulio Sacchetti. The latter had been considered as far back as 1644 but had been excluded by Spain and since then been called Cardinal Trentatre because of the insufficient thirty-three votes he consistently received over a period of time. But Sacchetti personally intervened with Mazarin in favor of the candidacy of Fabio Chigi, which he had earlier opposed. Because of his actions at the Peace Conference of Münster (Westphalia) he was initially not agreeable to France.[1] But with Mazarin's concurrence Chigi was elected on 7 April 1655 after a conclave of eighty days. He chose his name in memory of his countryman Alexander III.

The newly elected Pope was born into a Siena family who had been generous patrons of the arts two generations earlier in Rome (Farnesina, chapels in Santa Maria della Pace and Santa Maria del Popolo). After twelve years as nuncio on the Rhine his predecessor appointed him Secretary of State in 1651 and cardinal in the following year. But towards the end of the pontificate of Innocent X he lost influence because of Olympia Maidalchini's intrigues against him. Alexander VII, impressed by his personal experience of the extant abuses, was initially resolved to end the practice of nepotism completely. But later on he gave in to the entreaties of diplomats and even some well-known cardinals who urged him to call his relatives to the papal court and entrust them with governmental positions. The safeguards designed to prevent abuses subsequently proved insufficient.

From the very beginning of Alexander's pontificate, his relationship with France, the supreme Catholic power, was tense. Added to the fact that Chigi was not Mazarin's actual choice, his papal government was also encumbered by problems he inherited from his predecessor. Among them was that of Cardinal de Retz (Jean-François Paul de Gondi), who had been arrested in France as an enemy of Mazarin. In August 1654 he was able to escape and make his way to Rome via Spain by the end of the year. In spite of all the efforts by the Pope to arrive at a satisfactory solution of this case, the presence of de Retz in Rome could not fail to have a deleterious effect on the relationship with France. In addition, the negotiations concerning the appointments of bishops in the newly acquired areas of France, which were not covered by the Concordat of 1516, had stagnated under Innocent X. Lastly, Mazarin did not like the Pope's efforts to promote peace between France and Spain.

---

[1] P. Richard's criticism is very sharp and probably not without exaggeration: "Il est indéniable que Chigi a travaillé au congrès contre la France, et mis tout en œuvre pour faire échouer ses vues et ses prétentions. C'était peu répondre à un programme de médiation, et justifier par avance l'animosité dont le poursuivirent plus tard les hommes d'État français, Mazarin en tête. . . ." But even he admits: "Ce qui justifie l'attitude du nonce médiateur, c'est que les Français abandonnaient l'Église pour les protestants, ce que lui, agent de la papauté, ne pouvait, ne devait pas admettre." (DHGE 2, 235 f.).

Therefore Rome was excluded as the site of a peace conference. In March 1656 the French ambassador at the Holy See was recalled. The negotiations, which resulted in the Treaty of the Pyrenees (1659) and the uniting of the dynasties of France and Spain through the marriage of Louis XIV to the infanta Maria Teresa, the daughter of King Philip IV, took place to the deliberate exclusion of the Pope. In the peace treaty the two powers even obliged themselves to support the claims of the Este family to the coastal town of Comacchio and those of the Farnese family to Castro which ran counter to the interests of the Holy See.

After the death of Mazarin (9 March 1661), tension between France and Rome increased. The twenty-two-year-old Louis XIV, convinced of his dignity and power and raised in the spirit of Gallican ideas, sought to prevail in his ecclesiastic policies. Sending the duke of Créqui as ambassador to Rome in June 1662, although welcomed by Alexander VII as a sign of support of the papal defensive policy against the Turks (see below), was designed at the same time to demonstrate the hegemony of France. Then problems of ceremony led to displeasure. The new ambassador, moreover, claimed immunity for the buildings bordering on the Palazzo Farnese. The demand of this extended "quartering privilege" was initially rejected. After several fights between the ambassador's retinue and the papal soldiers from Corsica billeted near the Ponte Sisto, the Corsicans got carried away and fired upon the Farnese Palace on 20 August 1662, putting Créqui himself in danger of his life, and then molested the duchess and her companions, who were returning to the palace just then. In spite of immediate measures by the papal administration and an offer by the Pope to make amends, Créqui retired to Florence. The incident offered to French policy makers a good opportunity to exact some special concessions in matters of ecclesiastical policy and so they escalated their demands. Avignon was occupied and military actions against the Papal States were prepared. It was under this kind of pressure that the Treaty of Pisa was concluded on 12 February 1664. Alexander VII was compelled to accept the humiliating conditions which included, among others, the erection of a memorial pyramid bearing a confession of guilt which was not removed until more than four years later (31 May 1668). On the issue of bishops' appointments the Pope had to comply fully with the wishes of the French King. Only then did Louis XIV return Avignon (May 1665); in order to give another signal for the decrease of tension he recalled the duke of Créqui in May 1665 and put in his place the duke de Chaulnes.

The Pope's attitude towards France was also conditioned by the Turkish threat. The island of Crete, belonging to Venice, was especially vulnerable. A diversionary attack against the Dardanelles in June 1657, conducted with papal support, failed and resulted in the loss of several islands in the Ionian Sea. In 1660 after the Battle of Clausenburg the Turks conquered Grosswardein. When Emperor Leopold I appealed to him for aid, the Pope attempted to establish a defensive league. But the success of his efforts depended entirely on France. The negotiations conducted by the duke de Créqui were interrupted by the incident involving the Corsican soldiers. It was feared that the Turks would attack Vienna as early as 1664. Surprisingly, Louis XIV sent a contingent of seven thousand men in the summer of 1664 with whose help the Turks were decisively defeated near the Cistercian convent of Sankt Gotthard on the Gyor River (1 August 1664). Yet the victory was not exploited. The Emperor was eager to conclude the Peace of Eisenburg because he could neither be sure of continued aid from the Empire nor of support from France. The next military objective of the Turks was again Candia. In the last months of his life Alexander VII again sent an urgent appeal to Louis XIV and the other Catholic princes asking for military aid for the Signoria of Venice. The Pope on his own part authorized a great sum of financial aid and had the papal galleys prepared. The total expenditures in connection with the papal fleet in defense against the Turks during the pontificate of Alexander VII are estimated at more than one and a half million scudi.

In his appointments to cardinalates, Alexander VII kept to the traditional practice of giving primary consideration to Italians. Out of a total of thirty-eight appointments with six promotions, foreigners were appointed only twice—two Spaniards and Germans each and one Frenchman. The conspicuous favoring of Sienese was taken note of even then; the great number of reservations *in petto,* a total of seventeen, is surprising. The reason for that was the lack of adequate remuneration for the appointees. But the appointments were nonetheless pronounced in order to complete the traditional membership of seventy in the College of Cardinals and thereby to forestall the demands by Catholic powers for crown cardinals. The most prominent among the appointees were the Jesuit Pallavicino, a friend of the Pope's and well known through his history of the Council of Trent; the bishop of Regensburg, Franz Wilhelm zu Wartenberg, who had worked with Chigi at the Peace Conference of Münster; and Gregorio Barbarigo, bishop of Bergamo and later of Padua, who came close to being elected Pope in subsequent conclaves.

The condemnation of laxist propositions by the Holy Office in 1665 and 1666 (D 2021–65) are thematically related to the continuing Jansenist disputes. The decrees were triggered by censures on the part of the universities of Louvain and Paris, some of whose wording was included verbatim in the Roman condemnations. Even though probabilism was not rejected as a system, this first detailed condemnation of "laxist" propositions represented a considerable success for the opponents of the Jesuit order, which was accused of lax morality.

A great stir was caused when Queen Christina of Sweden, daughter and successor of Gustavus Adolphus, renounced her throne and converted to Catholicism. The assertion that her conversion was without actual religious conviction and merely an escape from her dynastic responsibility is undoubtedly without fact. We need not dwell on the questions whether or to what extent her decisive motives were a compelling insight in matters of faith, or a certain aversion for the rigidity of the kind of orthodox Protestantism in Scandinavia at that time and the desire for greater intellectual freedom.[2] After renouncing the throne on 6 June 1654, Christina secretly pronounced the Catholic confession of faith on Christmas Day that year in Brussels. On 2 November 1655 she reiterated it publicly in Innsbruck. Shortly before Christmas she entered Rome with great ceremony. It was characteristic of the situation that the Pope exhorted the cardinals to make sure that the royal convert could not take offense at their behavior. He told them how his own work in Germany had taught him how scrupulously the northerners watched the Romans. Impulsive spending, political gaffes—especially her attempts to attain the crown of Naples—lack of sensitivity, and her scornful criticism of the customs of Roman piety led to friction. Yet Alexander VII was never lacking in benevolence and helpfulness towards the former queen. The tension decreased after Cardinal Azzolini gained influence about 1660 and managed to eliminate the undependable elements from Christina's retinue. Aside from two stays in France and two trips to Sweden in connection with her appanage, the former queen remained in Rome. Her apartments—initially in Mazarin's palace on the Quirinal and later in the Palazzo Riario on the right bank of the Tiber—became a center of the cultural life of Rome.

Rome's culture was considerably enhanced by the extension of the University of Rome. New chairs were established, among them that of church history, together with an appropriate library called the Biblioteca Alessandrina after its founder. But most prominent were the construction projects in the Vatican initiated by the Pope and executed by Bernini. The *Cathedra Petri*,[3] a simple oaken armchair decorated with small antique tablets of ivory and used in the Middle Ages in the

---

[2] See S. Stolpe, *Königin Christine von Schweden* (Frankfurt 1962); *Queen Christina of Sweden: Documents and Studies*, ed. by M. von Platen (Stockholm 1966); C. Weibull, *Christina of Sweden* (Göteborg 1966); G. Masson, *Queen Christina* (London 1968).

[3] See D. Balboni, *La Cattedra di San Pietro* (Vatican City 1967); for an initial tentative report of the results of the examination which was made by a commission appointed by Paul VI in 1968/69, see *L'Osservatore Romano* no. 275 of 28 November 1968, p. 3.

liturgy on Saint Peter's Day (22 February) was to be the focal point in the apse of Saint Peter's, which was empty at that time. Bernini's design of four bronze statues of the great church Fathers carrying the *Cathedra* enclosed in bronze was approved by the Pope, who personally supervised all the work. Construction of Saint Peter's Square was started at the same time, again planned and executed by Bernini. According to the original design as shown on a medallion coined on 28 August 1657 on the occasion of the laying of the cornerstone, the space between the two half-arches of the colonnades was to be closed by a continuation separated only by two relatively narrow entrances. By the end of Alexander VII's pontificate only part of the construction work was finished. The Pope also had Bernini build new stairs to the Scala Regia and to the Sistine Chapel; this Scala Regia was finished in 1666. Four years later the equestrian statue of Constantine the Great, created by Bernini and completed during Alexander's VII lifetime, was placed in the vestibule.

Clement IX (1667–69)

On 20 June 1667 Cardinal Giulio Rospigliosi was elected Pope after a remarkably brief conclave of only eighteen days. As nuncio at Madrid he had obtained Spain's goodwill, but—unknown to Spain—he was also in the favor of Louis XIV. Also active in his behalf were the cardinals of the *squadrone volante*, who were primarily credited with the outcome of the election. The new Pope had been secretary of state under his predecessor and was famous for his humanistic education and poetic talent. A number of his dramas, based in part on Spanish models, were successfully performed at the time. His choice of the name Clement was prompted by the meaning of the word rather than its connection with an earlier bearer of the name, as was often the case. One of the few medallions of his brief pontificate is inscribed "Aliis non sibi clemens." A short pontificate was expected from the start because of his frail health.

The pontificate of Clement IX was troubled by two major problem areas. One was the continuing tensions in France caused by the Jansenist movement and the Pope's efforts to allay them. This was to be achieved by the so-called Clementine Peace (Chap. 3), but in the last analysis the Pope's efforts remained unsuccessful. The other was the danger posed by the Turks. The island of Crete was again their prime objective. They had already conquered the larger part of the island and were preparing to attack the capital of Candia (Megalo Castro), still in the hands of the Venetians. Just like his predecessor, Clement IX attempted to bring about joint aid by the Western powers. He tried to bring an end to the war between Louis XIV and Spain (War of Devolution) which broke out in May 1667 when France invaded the Spanish Netherlands. But the Pope's suggestions and the entreaties of various nuncios extraordinary sent to all the capitals were hardly successful. But the political constellation resulting from the alliance between Holland, England, and Sweden made the French King condescend to a negotiated peace. He kept his conquests in the Netherlands, but had to return the occupied Franche-Comté. The fact of the papal mediation was emphasized in the peace treaty of Aachen (2 May 1668). Finally, the removal of the humiliating pyramid erected in Rome in 1664 was intended to seal the reconciliation between France and the Holy See. The peace treaty also increased hopes of joint aid for the island of Crete. But the assurances given by the Western powers were only partly kept and were insufficient to boot. Even the French expeditionary corps, numerically small in the summer of 1668 but significantly increased the following year, was unable to change the outcome. Naval superiority was not exploited and so the fortress of Candia was forced to surrender on 6 September 1669.

Clement X (1670–76)

A few days before he died on 9 December 1669, Clement IX had appointed seven cardinals, bringing the complement of the college back up to the traditional seventy. The subsequent conclave, lasting more than four months, proved difficult. Among the sources informing us in detail of the events and negotiations, the voluminous correspondence between Queen Christina and Cardinal Azzolini is especially interesting. The French rejected two possible candidates (D'Elce and Odescalchi), while the Spanish opposed two others (Vidoni and Brancaccio), virtually eliminating any chance of those four being elected. Vidoni was the candidate promoted by Queen Christina and Azzoli. The long duration of the conclave provoked great displeasure and gave rise to many satires. The representatives of the Catholic powers probably exerted greater influence on this papal election than on any previous one. Upon mediation by Venice, Spain and France finally agreed that one of the cardinals appointed by Pope Clement IX before his death should be elected. The choice was the oldest of that group, the eighty-year-old Cardinal Altieri. The election took place on 29 April 1670. Resisting for some time, Altieri finally gave in to the urgings of the cardinals and accepted the election as Pope Clement X. The advanced age of the newly elected Pope resulted in the cardinal-nephew Paluzzi-Altieri gaining in importance while the secretary of state lost influence. While Clement X personally urged thriftiness, he could not prevent his nephew from enriching himself by means of his position.

The pontificate of Clement X was largely determined by the increasing danger posed by Turkey. In 1672 the objective was Poland, which was weakened by internal disorder. The Pope sought to have the Emperor and the Catholic princes of Germany coalesce into a defensive alliance and even appealed—probably following a suggestion by Queen Christina—to the King of Sweden, Charles IX, who refused, however, to enter into any direct negotiations with the Pope. Conversely, Russia now sought Western support against the Turks and after thirteen years of war concluded an alliance with Poland. With financial support from the Pope and a personal contribution from Cardinal Odescalchi, John Sobieski had formed his own army in 1673. He advanced against the Turks and defeated them decisively at the Dniester (11 November). On the eve of the battle the Polish King, Michael Wiśniowiecki, had succumbed to an illness. In lengthy negotiations concerning the succession to the throne, the Pope and his nuncio, Buonvisi, insisted on a Catholic candidate. But the candidacy of the papal nephew, Gaspare Altieri, suggested by Rome in the course of the negotiations, was rejected as totally impossible by the nuncio. But more dangerous by far were the applicants from the house of Brandenburg. Finally, on 20 May 1674, John Sobieski was elected king. The following summer he again succeeded against the Turks in the defense of the city of Lemberg.

While the Pope made every effort to form a defensive alliance against the Turks, Louis XIV prepared for a war of conquest against Holland, which had permitted itself to become politically isolated. This war was propagated by France as a holy war for the restoration of the Catholic religion. Initially the Pope in fact believed this professed goal. Briefs of praise and Te Deums in Rome upon the victories of the French army demonstrate how effective that propaganda was. The military aid given to the Dutch by Emperor Leopold I was disapproved of as a weakening of the unified front against the Turks. The intervention of Spain was also condemned by the Pope. After about the summer of 1674 Clement X perceived that he had been deceived regarding the actual aims of the war against Holland. In addition, Louis XIV tried to frustrate the Pope's peace negotiations at every turn. Nevertheless three nuncios extraordinary were sent to the western capitals of Paris, Vienna, and Madrid in October 1675 in order to prepare for peace negotiations. At the same time a papal representative was designated for the actual peace conference, although no place or time had been considered yet. The instruction composed for this purpose is important since it clarifies the developments since the time of the Peace of Westphalia.[4] At that time Chigi had strictly to hew to the traditional rule of dealing only with the Catholic powers and not having anything to do with the apostates. But now the papal representative was permitted to establish communication with the Protestants as well. He was instructed not to offend them by pedantic considerations and to make concessions for the sake of peace in Europe. Yet for the time being these preparations did not lead to anything.

More than his predecessors the aged Pope was hard pressed by the Catholic powers to accede to appointments to the cardinalate. In addition to fifteen Italians, Clement X appointed a mere five cardinals of other nationalities: two French, one German, Spanish, and English. France especially exerted constant pressure. Louis XIV above all wanted to have the bishop of Laon, César D'Estrées, promoted to cardinal. So the King sent him to Rome as an ambassador extraordinary to enable him personally to pursue his appointment. D'Estrées was indeed appointed *in petto* on 24 August 1671, but he was not satisfied with that. Even before the appointment was published the brother of the new cardinal arrived in Rome as the new ambassador of France. By order of Louis XIV, César also remained at the Curia. Now both brothers pursued the appointment of additional favorites of the French King to cardinalates. On 21 May 1675 their strenuous efforts led to a serious incident. In a papal audience the duke D'Estrées addressed himself to the subject of appointments still outstanding. In the process he vehemently reproached Cardinal Altieri, the papal nepotist. When the Pope wanted to signal the end of the audience by means of his bell, the ambassador obstructed him by grabbing his hand. When Clement X made another attempt to end the audience, D'Estrées would not leave. After a third signal of the bell the Pope tried to get up and was pushed back into his chair by D'Estrées. A few days later the Pope appointed six new cardinals, his last ones, among whom there was not a single Frenchman.

[4] The most important part of the instruction in *QFIAB* 15 (1913), 366 f., n. 3.

CHAPTER 8

Innocent XI

After having met with the determined resistance of France at the previous conclave, Cardinal Odescalchi's election came as a complete surprise. At the beginning of the present conclave his candidacy had been openly promoted by the nephew of the late pope, Cardinal Altieri, with whom Louis XIV and his ambassador to Rome were totally at variance. Furthermore, Altieri acted in concert with the Spanish cardinals, also opponents of France. When D'Estrées threatened to invoke the *ius exclusivae* if the election were to take place before the arrival of the French cardinals, the number of votes for Odescalchi decreased markedly. But in the meantime the French ambassador had asked Louis XIV to approve the election of the candidate originally rejected by him. Cardinals Chigi and Rospigliosi, both in the King's favor, supported this action by emphatically recommending Odescalchi to Louis XIV. The King concurred and he was elected unanimously on 21 September 1676, after having received a mere eight votes on the previous day.

The new Pope chose his name in memory of the one who had appointed him cardinal in 1645 when he was a mere thirty-four years of age. He came from a wealthy mercantile family in Como and made a name for himself in the administration of the Papal States under Urban VIII and Innocent X. His charity, extreme conscientiousness, and austere piety were widely acknowledged. Before he accepted the election he insisted that all cardinals sign the fourteen articles of reform suggested by him during the conclave.[1] Always intent upon safeguarding and defending the rights of the Church, he was not very open to the advice of others and at times persisted all too rigidly in his own views. Moreover, he had never spent any time abroad, so that his knowledge of the political situation was insufficient. While he was an excellent administrator with a special skill in financial matters, he was lacking in knowledge of human nature and even in theological education.

Innocent XI refrained from any kind of nepotism. Frugal by nature, he put the financial affairs of the Papal States in order. But in his strict, sometimes overly pedantic instructions concerning any sort of luxury and the reform of public order he several times went so far as to prohibit all carnivals, consequently becoming the butt of ridicule by the Romans.

The pontificate of Innocent XI bears the stamp of two problem areas.

---

[1] The text of the articles of reform is published in Bojani I, 31–37.

In addition to his efforts in the defense against the Turks (see below), the tense relationship between the Holy See and France was a major problem. It emanated from the unrestricted right of regalia claimed by the French King. Ever since the Middle Ages the King had had the right to make appointments to ecclesiastical livings in certain vacant dioceses (spiritual regalia) and to receive the revenues of bishoprics (temporal regalia). Since Louis XIII, care had been taken not to use these revenues for improper purposes. The second council of Louvain (1274) had forbidden further extension of this right. In so doing it appeared to recognize implicitly or at least to condone it. After several earlier attempts to extend the right of regalia to other dioceses, Louis XIV—considering it a true right of the crown—decreed in 1673 and 1675 that it was to apply to all areas subject to the French crown. Clement X, informed of the decree by his nuncio, did not make any response. Almost all the French bishops, in part influenced by the papal silence which could be construed as acquiescence, submitted to the royal decree. Only Bishop Pavillon of Alet and Bishop Caulet of Pamiers resisted. Not getting any support from their metropolitan, they appealed to the Pope. The fact that Innocent XI accepted the bishops' appeal was in accord with his conviction not to permit any encroachment upon the rights of the Church. But under the circumstances it was a somewhat dangerous assertion of principle in a matter of secondary importance. As a consequence the Pope was viewed as a friend of the Jansenist party. This was incorrect yet understandable in view of the personality of the two appellants, who were well known from the Jansenist conflict. The situation vis-à-vis France, already tense, was unnecessarily aggravated by this incident. In two briefs of March 1678 and January 1679 the Pope admonished the King not to follow the bad advice which was misleading him into an extension of the right of regalia and with it into a violation of the rights of the Church, but instead to keep in mind the salvation of his soul. A third brief, sent in March 1680, was more to the point. It warned the King of the wrath of Heaven which could manifest itself in making him die without a successor. But Louis XIV, having been struck by the idea of a national council, decided upon a noncommittal answer. At the Curia, the King's confessor, de la Chaize, and his fellow Jesuit Maimbourg were wrongly given the major portion of the blame for the King's inflexibility. In the meantime, the French Assembly of the Clergy of 1680 had taken the King's part. Louis XIV, wanting to gain time, suggested negotiations. After a lengthy delay, Cardinal d'Estrées, who was to conduct them, arrived in Rome in the spring of 1681. But Innocent XI had already given a sharp allocution against France in a consistory on 13 January 1681. At that time the so-called "Small Assembly" of the French clergy under the direction of the archbishop of

Paris, Harlay, and the archbishop of Reims, Le Tellier, supported the King's position concerning the right of regalia and suggested convening a national council or an extraordinary Assembly of the Clergy. Aside from their original function as a "tax parliament" which decided the contributions of the French Church to the King (*don gratuit*), these periodic assemblies since their inception had also dealt with other ecclesiastical matters.[2] In general they involved efforts genuinely serving the reform and the promotion of church life even though the self-consciousness of the Gallican Church appears always to have been involved, intent on safeguarding its special privileges and position. Depending on the importance of these assemblies, the King and his government increasingly tried to influence their composition, either by means of recommendations or by exerting pressure upon the elective body of the individual church provinces. Such measures were also employed in the preparation of the assembly of October 1681. Again under the direction of Harlay and Le Tellier, it turned into an obedient tool of the government. The assembly agreed with the King that regalia was an exclusive right of the crown. In a general way the assembly noted that the ruler was independent of the authority of the Church in all purely temporal matters. The codification of additional articles designated as "Gallican Liberties" required lengthy discussion. In the end they were formulated by Bossuet, who was trying to avoid a more radical version. The King then decreed that they be included as binding doctrine.

The news of the assembly's conclusions arrived in Rome during the negotiations between the Pope and Cardinal d'Estrées, which were immediately interrupted. In his brief of 11 April 1682, Innocent XI sharply rebuked the assembly while sparing the King as much as possible. The Pope's chagrin was primarily directed at de la Chaize, the King's confessor, but the latter's influence was overestimated and his personal attitude misunderstood.[3] Indeed, Louis XIV suspended the assembly on 9 May and dismissed it at the end of June in order to bring about a resumption of the interrupted negotiations in Rome. Since the threat of Turkey had become more and more acute, Innocent XI was prepared for a moratorium. As an outward sign of détente he was to send a nuncio extraordinary to France upon the birth of the first son of the Dauphin. Although it was not the birth of a crown prince, the nuncio was to present the diapers blessed by the Pope as a special sign of goodwill.

---

[2] See P. Blet, *Le Clergé de France et la Monarchie: Étude sur les Assemblées Générales du Clergé de 1615 à 1666* (Rome 1959).
[3] See G. Guitton, *Le Père de la Chaize, Confesseur de Louis XIV* (Paris 1959); P. Blet, "Jésuites Gallicans au XVIIᵉ siècle," *AHSI* 29 (1960), 55–84.

But the most important reason for the nuncio's mission was to get the support of Louis XIV for the war against the Turks and to pave the way for a reconciliation between France and the Emperor. The gravest impediment was the issue of the vacant sees. Innocent XI steadfastly refused to confer canonical investiture upon the new bishops nominated by the King if they had participated in the Assembly of the Clergy of 1681/82 and had not disavowed the four Gallican articles.

Louis XIV was convinced that his measures against the Huguenots, resulting in the revocation of the Edict of Nantes in 1685, would meet with the Pope's approval and he therefore expected Rome's cooperation on the issue of the regalia. But Innocent XI maintained his reserve for two reasons: the actions against the Huguenots were prompted by Gallicanism, and the Pope expressly disapproved of the violent methods applied against them.

During this conflict between the Pope and France another one arose in Rome. It had to do with the quartering privilege claimed by the ambassadors to the Holy See. Their demands for concomitant immunity from police supervision and for extensive freedom from customs duty, which led to trade and business transactions on a large scale, stretched the quartering franchise to troublesome proportions. From the very beginning of his pontificate Innocent XI was determined to put an end to those abuses. Spain declared its willingness to forego the quartering privilege if the other powers would follow suit. But no agreement could be reached. So the Pope let it be known that he would receive no new ambassador unless he would surrender the franchise in advance. Venice was first to give in. After a lengthy period of resistance Spain followed suit in 1682. After the death of the French ambassador d'Estrées (30 January 1687), the Pope informed France that the new ambassador would only be received if he acceded to the conditions laid down by him. Subsequent proposals for settling the issue were rejected by Innocent XI. In November the new ambassador de Lavardin entered Rome at the head of a large retinue. Since he was considered subject to the sanctions of the bull *In Coena Domini*, he was not granted the papal audience he had requested. At the same time the French King was informed by the nuncio that the censure of the bull applied to him as well. The conflict broke into the open on 24 December 1687 when de Lavardin attended midnight Mass at the French national church of San Luigi dei Francesi. He was ushered to the seat of honor according to his rank of ambassador and given the sacraments. The Pope thereupon put the church under the interdict.

The tension was increased by the issue of the appointment of a coadjutor of Cologne. After the sudden death of the elector of Cologne, Maximilian von Wittelsbach, the election of a successor had to be endorsed. Both candidates, Cardinal Wilhelm von Fürstenberg, Bishop of Strasbourg, nominee of Louis XIV, and the seventeen-year-old Clement of Bavaria, the Emperor's nominee, needed the Pope's dispensation. The election was inconclusive. In spite of threats from Louis XIV, the Pope appointed the Bavarian. This led to the outbreak of the war between France and the Emperor in September 1688. Attempts at mediation on the part of James II of England failed. In April 1689 de Lavardin was recalled from Rome without having been received in audience by the Pope. The following May Nuncio Ranuzzi left Paris, having been under police supervision since October 1688.

The conflict with France had a bearing on simultaneous efforts by the Pope to establish a defense against the Turks. These constitute the foremost achievements of his pontificate, as is rightfully pointed out on his tomb in Saint Peter's.

At about the beginning of Innocent XI's pontificate, Kara Mustafa had become grand vizier and had taken over the direction of the Turkish government. This increased the danger of a renewed offensive. In order to counter this danger and to make sure of an effective defense the Pope engaged in mediation to end the war between France and the Emperor. For this purpose he sent a legate to the peace negotiations at Protestant Nijmegen. This was the first time since the schism that a papal representative set foot on Dutch soil. But his authority displeased France since it was the custom that only the Emperor was mentioned by name while the other rulers were mentioned collectively. Because of these problems of protocol the legate, Bevilacqua, could not sign the peace treaties and the papal mediation was not mentioned at all. The peace terms were especially unfavorable for Catholics living in Protestant areas. By doing nothing to advance the cause of the Catholic religion Louis XIV disappointed the Pope's expectations.

The advent of peace did not further the Pope's main goal of bringing about a defensive and offensive alliance against the Turks. In the east his efforts were thwarted by the distrust prevailing between Russia and Poland. This was aggravated by the initial Francophile policy of King Sobieski, who—disregarding the Pope's admonitions—supported the Hungarians revolting against Emperor Leopold I by letting them recruit troops in Poland. In return Louis XIV stated his readiness to try to have his ambassador in Constantinople ensure that Poland would not be attacked by Turkey. If such an attack were to take place, he promised to come to Poland's aid. At the Imperial Diet of 1680 renewed attempts to form a league with the Emperor failed; in the following year the French influence once again managed to prevent a resolution by the Polish Diet in favor of an alliance against the Turks. Yet Innocent XI did not tire in pursuing his plans of a great offensive. He envisioned French naval operations in support of a land-based attack by the Emperor and Poland. This was basically the same plan suggested fifteen years before to Louis XIV by the young Leibniz.[4] Actually Louis XIV informed the Holy See that he would help Poland and Venice if they were attacked, but that the Emperor would not be able to count on his aid. This assurance of benevolent neutrality in the eventuality of an attack upon the Emperor coupled with Thököly's revolt in Hungary confirmed Kara Mustafa in his intentions against Austria. But now this direct threat had the effect of reversing Polish policy, leading to a defensive alliance with the Emperor (April 1683). The Pope expended approximately one and a half million guilders in subsidies, about two-thirds of which went to the Emperor. By 14 July Vienna, defended by Rüdiger von Starhemberg, was completely surrounded. The Emperor and his court had shortly before fled to the west. The siege was prolonged by the unswerving courage of the numerically weak garrison of Vienna and by tactical mistakes on the part of the Turks. At the very last moment a relief force consisting of Austrian, Polish, and Bavarian troops under the nominal command of Sobieski approached and on 12 September 1683 forced the Turks to retreat. Vienna owed its liberation above all to the efforts of Innocent XI.

In spite of the allied victories at Ofen and the conquest of Gran in October of the same year, the alliance was endangered by a renewed rapprochement between Sobieski and the Hungarian rebels and by Louis XIV's attempts at joining Poland to France in a closer relationship. But the Pope managed to maintain the alliance. In 1684 it was joined by Venice after diplomatic relations, terminated five years prior because of the quartering franchise, were reestablished between the Serenissima and the Holy See. The powers of the "Holy League" pledged to use their troops only against the Turks, to update war plans annually, and not to negotiate without the agreement of the other allies. Again the expansionist policies of France impaired the effectiveness of the league. In May 1684 Genoa, refusing to bow to the wishes of France, was destroyed by a French fleet and Luxemburg was conquered by French troops. Therefore the military operations of the league could not begin until late in 1684 and, with the unsuccessful siege of Ofen, showed scant success. Primarily owing to the Pope's urgent appeals, a peace treaty and subsequent alliance against the Turks were concluded between Poland and Russia. The successes of the following years were primarily due to the Austrian and imperial troops, whereas Sobieski was inactive. But the Emperor's offensive against the Turks was stopped in

[4] A. Foucher de Careil, ed., "Projet d'expédition d'Égypte présenté à Louis XIV," Œuvres de Leibniz V (Paris 1864).

1688 by the beginning of the third French war of conquest. In addition to the significant financial aid—the Emperor alone had been paid approximately five million guilders by the apostolic treasury—it was the untiring efforts of the Pope which had brought about the alliance against the Turks and at least to some extent had kept it together.

Innocent XI was extremely strict in his direction of the Church. He tried to restore church discipline especially among the clergy and the orders, but in the process he sometimes dissipated his energy in details. His conscientiousness, almost bordering on scrupulousness, was also manifest in the promotion of cardinals. During his pontificate he decided on only two appointments. The first one, numbering sixteen, was comprised of Italians only (1681), which led to a protest by France. The second promotion again consisted of sixteen Italians, but also of an additional eleven foreigners. Among the latter there were four Germans, but among them the bishop of Strasbourg, Egon von Fürstenberg, who was on the side of Louis XIV.

Innocent XI's position within the Church was marked by his firm opposition against any form of Gallicanism. Opponents of Gallicanism met with ready understanding on the part of the Pope and with support that was not always wise from a tactical viewpoint. This explains why many of the Pope's decisions and actions were viewed as partisanship in favor of the Jansenist movement, since it was precisely the Jansenists who took an especially strong stand against the Gallicanism of the King. In addition, the manifest religious severity of Jansenism and its stress on church discipline corresponded with the Pope's personal views. The moral system of probabilism offered by the Jesuits, who were certainly the most confirmed enemies of Jansenism, nonetheless represented a dangerous move towards laxism. Even at the beginning of his pontificate a small group of French bishops, among them Pavillon of Alet, urged the Pope to condemn certain moral propositions. Their agents in Rome, starting with Possion and continuing with the abbot of Pontchâteau and Louis de Vaucel, were able to wield considerable influence. At the same time, the University of Louvain attempted to effect a similar condemnation. This took place in 1679 by means of a decree of the Holy Office (D 2101–67). Within the Jesuit order, Tyrsus González de Santalla tried to push back probabilism; in 1680 he received papal approbation for his system of probabiliorism (D 2176–77). The fact that he was elected general of the order in 1689 was a result of the benevolence of Innocent XI, who clearly let it be known to the General Congregation of the order on the occasion of an audience whom he wished to have at the head of the Society of Jesus.

Ever since the middle of the century a quietistic current had spread primarily in Italy. Beginning with an intensification of the religious life of the individual and stressing the practice of contemplative prayer, the movement led to the sole emphasis on the efficacy of grace to the total exclusion of personal deeds, amounting finally to a complete passivity of the individual. The Spanish priest Miguel Molinos became the focal point of a large circle in Rome where he was joined by important laymen as well as by many clerics, among them Cardinal Odescalchi. More than his book *Guía espiritual*, which first appeared in Rome in 1675 and could be interpreted in a harmless fashion, it was his guidance of souls through an active correspondence by which he made his influence felt. When the Roman Inquisition dealt with him, it tracked down approximately twelve thousand such letters, from which it compiled the quietistic doctrines. Jesuits were the first to offer reservations against Molinos and his doctrine. In 1680 Paolo Segneri published a treatise concerning contemplative prayer which was forbidden by the Inquisition. In the meantime more reservations against Molinos's doctrine arose. In 1682 the Holy Office had Cardinal Hieronymus Casanate compose an instruction for confessors (D 2181–92) whose actual publication can not be ascertained. In 1685 Molinos was arrested by the Inquisition and his writings were confiscated. Innocent XI had earlier had high esteem for Molinos. As late as 1686 he had elevated Pier Matteo Petrucci, who had held similar views, to the cardinalate. So he waited for some time before granting his permission for a formal trial, which was concluded in 1687. Of an original 263 propositions 68 were condemned (D 2201–68). Thirteen of these were taken from the defense which Molinos submitted to the Inquisition. (D 2241–53). Molinos was condemned to life in prison and died in 1696. After an investigation against Cardinal Petrucci the latter had to recant in front of the Pope. But Innocent XI advocated mild treatment. As a consequence Petrucci retained all his rights as a cardinal and as bishop of Jesi.

When Queen Christina of Sweden died on 19 April 1689, the Pope ordered a formal funeral in Saint Peter's, which was attended by all cardinals. Shortly thereafter his condition deteriorated. For years he had suffered from painful illnesses to which he succumbed in the Quirinal on 12 August.

Soon after his death the Romans began to venerate Innocent XI as a saint, but not until 1956 was he canonized by Pius XII.[5] The procedure, initiated by Clement XI, was delayed primarily by the opposition of the French government, which was apparently unable to forget the Pope's struggle with Louis XIV which had endured through almost his whole pontificate.

[5] A balanced overview of the entire pontificate is provided in the address by Pius XII at the beatification (*AAS* 48 [1950], 762–78), written by Father Robert Leiber, S.J., who also revised the major portion about Innocent XI by Pastor.

CHAPTER 9

The Popes from Alexander VIII to Clement XI

Alexander VIII (1689–91)

The conclave took place during a war which enveloped the larger part of Europe. The Emperor and the King of France were represented by ambassadors extraordinary attempting to exert their influence upon the papal election. But before the monarchs' wishes were made known, the majority of the cardinals had already decided upon Pietro Ottoboni from Venice. France concurred in his candidacy after Ottoboni's nephew had given assurances that canonical investiture would be conferred on the French bishops who had participated in the Assembly of 1681/82 and that Lavardin would be received as ambassador. The new Pope chose his name in memory of Alexander VII, to whom he felt especially obliged. Although he was eighty years of age, he performed his work with unusual energy. His personal life-style was diametrically opposed to that of his predecessor, which ensured him of the immediate goodwill of the Romans. It was disastrous, however, that he permitted the practice of nepotism to be revived. His barely twenty-year-old grandnephew Pietro, in addition to being appointed cardinal and reigning nephew, was invested with large benefices. Other family members as well were beneficiaries of the Pope's largesse, who is credited with the pronouncement: "Let us make haste as much as possible, for the clock has struck the twenty-third hour."

Alexander VIII also differed from his predecessor Innocent XI in his attitude towards the great powers. Relations with the German Empire cooled off noticeably. Financial aid granted Leopold I for the Turkish Wars was decreased considerably, not in the least because Venice, worried about its own interests in the Levant, looked with a jaundiced eye upon Austria's great military successes. On the other hand, the Pope sought improved relations with France, which had a growing number of uninvested bishops. The consistory of February 1690 was designed as a sign of rapprochement. Disregarding serious reasons to the contrary as well as protests by the Emperor, the Pope fulfilled a longstanding wish of Louis XIV by appointing to the cardinalate the bishop of Beauvais, Toussaint de Forbin-Janson, who had participated in the assembly of 1682. When the third consistory of Alexander VIII passed in November 1690 without the Pope appointing any of the Emperor's nominees, Vienna threatened to break off diplomatic relations. The ambassador was indeed recalled, but additional resolves were not translated into action because of the Pope's serious illness.

But attempts by the King of France to represent his war as a war in defense of Catholicism and to have it approved as such by the Pope were unsuccessful. Since Louis XIV, largely under the influence of the newly appointed Cardinal Forbin-Janson, who was leading the negotiations in Rome, proved to be unyielding on the issue of the Gallican articles, Alexander VIII, already on his deathbed, decided to publish the decree prepared under Innocent XI which nullified the four Gallican Liberties. (D 2281–85).

By condemning propositions which manifested a tendency towards laxism, Innocent XI gave support—albeit unintentionally—to the opponents of the Jesuit order and to the friends of the Jansenist party. Under Alexander VIII contrary propositions, excerpted primarily from writings published in Belgium, were condemned. These propositions, originally ninety-six in number, had been submitted to Rome in 1682; the examination was finished in 1686, but no actual decree was issued. In the end, thirty-one propositions were condemned in 1690 (D 2301–32).

Alexander VIII fell ill in January 1691. On 30 January, in the presence of ten cardinals he ordered the publication of the above-mentioned decree against the Gallican articles and dictated a personal letter to Louis XIV. On 1 February he died at the age of eighty-one.

Innocent XII (1691–1700)

The conclave beginning on 12 February 1691 lasted exactly five months. The front-runner was Gregorio Barbarigo. But Vienna considered him too submissive to France because of his connections with Venice. As a consequence the imperial government sought to prevent his election, yet without making use of a formal *exclusivae*. Since the French group also failed to support Barbarigo's election—which was promoted by the *Zelanti*, the apolitical party of the College of Cardinals—although Barbarigo was personally agreeable to Louis XIV, his candidacy failed. After many futile attempts at a compromise, agreement finally centered on Antonio Pignatelli, who received the votes of various blocks and finally those of the French as well. The seventy-five-year-old aristocratic cardinal from the south of Italy had been nuncio in Poland and Vienna; he had been raised to the cardinalate rather late, in 1681, by Innocent XI. His choice of name was intended to be an expression of gratitude for his predecessor. In his mode of governing, his care for the poor, and the simplicity of his personal

life-style, he indeed resembled Innocent XI. The most important reform document of his papacy was the bull against nepotism (22 June
1692). After some initial resistance by a good many cardinals, this bull,
which for all practical purposes put an end to the practice of nepotism in
papal history, was signed by all cardinals.[1] Innocent XII also restricted
the sale of ecclesiastical offices at the Curia. To make up for the resulting
financial loss he applied thrift to the running of the papal court, and, most
importantly, he enlarged the harbors of Civitavecchia and Netuno in order
to promote trade. Yet many of his reform measures were impeded by his
excessive attention to details.

A compromise was reached with Louis XIV after the latter was forced
to be more conciliatory by the formation of the Grand Alliance. As an
initial step, the new bishops, appointed by the King since 1682, who
had not participated in the Assembly of the Clergy of that year, were
granted papal approbation. In return, Louis XIV promised to revoke
the decree prescribing the four articles of 1682 as doctrine. The participants of the assembly signed a declaration of obedience. Although clad
in provisos, it nonetheless amounted to a recognizable repudiation of
their original resolutions. In return the King kept his promise and revoked the decree concerning the Declaration of the French Clergy.
Thereupon the bishops in question were granted canonical institution.
By the end of 1693 the French hierarchy was restored. Yet the King's
right of regalia remained intact in spite of the Pope's protestations. But
this act of rapprochement between Rome and France was viewed with
distrust by the Emperor. Initially the Pope, following Innocent XI's
policy in this regard, gave liberal support to the Emperor in the defense
against the Turks. But gradually relations between them became more
and more strained, due in part to the unwise behavior of the imperial
ambassadors in Rome, Liechtenstein and Martinitz. This tension was
skillfully exploited by the French ambassador, Cardinal Forbin-Janson.

The death of Sobieski in 1696 reignited the struggle for the Polish
succession. Ostensibly maintaining neutrality, the Holy See nonetheless
made efforts to have a Catholic King elected. The candidacy of the
French Prince Conti, understandably rejected by Austria, Russia, and
Prussia, was successfully contested by Friedrich August, elector of
Saxony, who had declared his willingness to convert to Catholicism in
the event of his election. Innocent XII was initially somewhat reticent
about the new Polish King. Only when the latter had consolidated his rule
did the Pope have his letter of recognition and congratulation transmitted.

Innocent XII, having increased his efforts since 1696 towards bringing about an end to the European war of Louis XIV against the Grand

[1] Text of the bull in *BullRom* (ed. by Taur.) 20, 441–46.

128

Coalition, welcomed the Peace of Rijswijk (1697) although the Holy See had not been officially represented at the congress. He especially liked the so-called Rijswijk Clause, a stipulation keeping the Catholic religion intact in all places made subject to Protestant rule by the terms of the peace. Originally suggested by the Count Palatine Johann Wilhelm von Neuburg, the clause was included in the negotiations and put through at the last minute by the representatives of Louis XIV, to whom it had been expressly recommended by the Pope.

At the end of his pontificate the Pope had to deal with the issue of the Spanish succession. The heir designated by the childless Spanish King, Charles II, died suddenly on 6 February 1699. He had been the Bavarian electoral prince Joseph Ferdinand, grandson of Charles II's sister, who was the wife of Emperor Leopold I. The Spanish King wanted a successor from the Austrian dynasty, but the Council of State under the direction of Cardinal Portocarrero preferred the French dynasty. Innocent XII, whose advice the Spanish King had requested, approved the decision of a commission of cardinals in favor of the French solution. The demise of the Pope (27 September 1700) preceded that of Charles II by a mere few weeks.

Clement XI (1700–1721)

The death of Charles II led to protracted political manipulations and finally to the election of Cardinal Gian Francesco Albani, nominated by the *Zelanti*. Albani accepted the unanimous election only after several days of consideration and after soliciting formal opinions by several theologians. He chose the name Clement XI after the saint of the day (23 November). Appointed by Alexander VIII, he had become probably the most powerful of the cardinals during the pontificates of Alexander and the latter's successor. He had received his ordination late (in September 1700) and was consecrated a week after his election to the papacy. Since he was only fifty-one years old, he could count on a long pontificate.

From the very beginning the new pontificate was affected by the danger of renewed warfare in Europe. While King Philip V of the French dynasty was recognized by most of the European powers and the Pope as well, Leopold I formally protested the testament of Charles II of Spain. By recognizing the royal title, arbitrarily assumed by the elector of Brandenburg, the Emperor was able to ensure himself of Prussia's support. He also obtained the support of the two naval powers England and Holland, who felt themselves endangered by France's expansionist policies. Clement XI was immediately involved in the conflict by his very proximity to the Kingdom of

Naples, which he considered a papal lien. His claim was disputed by both the opposing sides. At first he tried to avoid a decision in order to gain time. But the Emperor considered the Pope to be a partisan of France primarily because of his quick recognition of Philip V as King of Spain and because of his protest in April 1701 against the assumption of the royal title by the elector of Brandenburg. The Pope's attempt to keep Italy out of the war and to form a defensive league of the Italian states for the purpose of protecting his own neutrality failed. After Mantua surrendered to the French troops without a battle (5 April 1701), Italy became a theater of war with parts of the Papal States under occupation. At the end of 1701 the Emperor requested free passage to Naples for his troops, which was denied. Both belligerents violated the neutrality of the Papal States in northern Italy. France's skillful propaganda, representing the Emperor's alliance with the Protestant powers as a danger to the Church and to France and simultaneously picturing Spain as the sole protector of Catholicism, achieved some success with the Pope, especially since his efforts to achieve peace were brusquely rejected by the Court of Vienna. When Joseph I succeeded his father Leopold I on 5 May 1705, tensions between the Pope and the Emperor worsened. During the following year the military situation clearly changed in favor of the Emperor. In September, after Prince Eugene's victory at Turin the French troops had to vacate all of northern Italy. In spite of protests by the Pope the imperial army occupied some of the legations. In May 1707 the Pope was forced to grant free passage to Naples for the imperial troops. Within a few weeks almost all of the kingdom was in their hands. Contrary to papal claims, Parma and Piacenza were taxed as imperial liens. A bull of 27 July 1707 pronouncing excommunication against those abuses achieved nothing. Since Clement XI still adhered to Philip V as the rightful King of Spain, the Austrian pretender, Charles III, ordered a freeze on all revenues of the Church in Lombardy and Naples (April 1708), which caused many members of the Curia to lose a considerable part of their income. Next, the imperial troops invaded the Papal States without a declaration of war and occupied the Comacchio, important for its production of salt (situated between Ravenna and Ferrara on the coast). In autumn 1708, hoping for help from Louis XIV, the Pope decided to oppose the Emperor by force of arms. But left to his own devices, Clement XI was unable to stop the attacking imperial army. On 15 January 1709 he had to accept the Emperor's harsh conditions: disarmament of the papal troops, recognition of Charles III as King of Spain, recognition of the Emperor's precedence over the King of France, a peaceful solution of the territorial issues concerning Parma, Piacenza, and Comacchio. In return he received a promise that the prohibition against the transfer of money would be revoked and compensation would be paid for the damages caused by the occupation of the Papal States.

Although Philip V had encroached on church rights several times, the actual break occurred upon papal recognition of his rival Charles. The defeat of Louis XIV at Malplaquet and Spain's breaking off of diplomatic relations with Rome resulted in a definitive recognition of Charles III on 10 October 1709. Clement XI refused canonical investiture to the bishops appointed by Philip V after the latter had closed the nunciature in Madrid. In the end the Pope suggested mediation by Louis XIV. Yet the development towards an established Church in Spain continued. Conversely, Charles III, residing in Barcelona, demanded a nuncio proper, who arrived in 1711. The negotiations concerning the return of Comacchio and the encroachment on church rights in Naples conducted in Rome since 1710 were protracted. They were concluded after a year with an agreement stipulating the return of that coastal town. The unexpected death of the Emperor on 17 April 1711 of smallpox and that of the French Dauphin, who had succumbed to the same disease three days earlier, caused a complete turnabout in the issue of the Spanish succession. The dead Emperor left only daughters, so that his brother Charles was the logical choice to succeed him in Austria. In the face of French machinations, the Pope held fast to Charles's candidacy. But his nephew Albani, whom he dispatched to the imperial election in Frankfurt as his personal envoy, was kept from exerting any and all influence and was treated curtly on every occasion. England was immutably opposed to a union of Spain and the Empire under one monarch: Philip V was to remain King of Spain while Austria was to be compensated by the Spanish possessions in Italy and the Habsburg Netherlands.

At the peace congress starting in Utrecht in January 1712, the papal representative Passionei—since he was devoid of any diplomatic rank he could only act as a common agent of the Pope—had a twofold charge: to prevent the revocation of the Rijswijk Clause and see to it that the feudal rights of the Pope over Parma, Piacenza, and Sicily (the latter was to be given to the duke of Savoy) were upheld. But he could, in fact, achieve very little. The territorial alterations turned out to be damaging to the Church. France recognized the Protestant succession in England and withdrew its support of the pretender James III of the house of Stuart, hitherto staunchly supported by the Pope; Sicily was promised to the duke of Savoy without consultation with the Pope. Personal efforts by the Pope to influence Louis XIV notwithstanding, the Rijswijk Clause—while not formally revoked—was in effect weakened. However, in the parallel peace treaty concluded in Rastatt between the Emperor and the King of France (March 1714) the clause was included. But since the estates of the realm had not participated in the negotiations, a new congress had to be convoked. This took place in Baden, Switzerland, where the Protestant estates again worked towards a revocation of that clause. Passionei, back in his role as papal agent, was again charged with upholding the rights of the Church, with the Rijswijk Clause still being promoted by the Pope. The imperial peace concluded in September 1714 indeed corresponded to that of Rastatt, so that the efforts of the Holy See can be considered partially successful.

Passionei had to protest against those stipulations that were unfavorable to the Catholic Church: the recognition in toto of the Peace of Westphalia, the recognition of the Protestant electoral status of Hanover and of the Prussian royal title, and the ceding of Catholic territories to Protestant princes. In the consistory of 21 January 1715, in which he talked about the three peace treaties, Clement XI had his protest publicly reiterated.

While the Northern War, which lasted beyond the War of the Spanish Succession, did not directly affect the papacy and the Church, the end of the European war renewed the Turkish threat. Initial preparations by the Holy See centered around Venice. Following the example of Pius V, Pope Clement XI tried to bring about a defensive alliance against the Turkish naval threat. Yet the Emperor, distrustful of the French, was unwilling to engage in a military operation on such a large scale. As a consequence the Turkish fleet achieved a series of great successes in the summer of 1715. Venice lost the entire Peloponnesos; an attack upon Italy itself was greatly feared. Urged by the Pope, Philip V of Spain had Clement XI transmit formal guarantees to the Emperor at the end of 1715 that the imperial possessions in Italy would not be endangered for the duration of the Turkish war. This declaration was influenced more than anything by the abbot Giulio Alberoni, a native of Piacenza and envoy of the duke of Parma in Madrid who had promoted the second marriage of Philip V with Elizabeth Farnese. With great financial aid and upon constant urging by the Pope, the Emperor concluded an alliance with Venice in April 1716. The offensive in Hungary was initiated in the summer of that year. The subsequent victory by Prince Eugene at Peterwardein and the successful defense of Corfu against the Turks were a welcome prelude to the operations.

In order to interest Spain in taking an active part in the war against Turkey and on the condition of completely restoring the nunciature in Madrid, the ambitious Alberoni, who had created for himself a superlative position of power, was appointed cardinal.[2] The Spanish fleet,

---

[2] The more recent research has for the most part exonerated Alberoni; cf. A. Arata, *Il processo del card. Alberoni* (Piacenza 1923); P. Castagnoli, *Il card. G. Alberoni* (Piacenza

largely equipped by means of financial aid from the Pope, was now expected to intervene in the naval war against the Turks so that the continental military operations of the Emperor, which had led to the conquest of Belgrade in August, could be supported. Instead Spain had conceived a plan to attack the Italian possessions of the Empire in order to establish a secundogeniture. Four days after Alberoni found out about his elevation to the cardinalate the Spanish fleet sailed from its harbor and—in violation of the peace—took Sardinia from the Emperor. The Pope, who had given a moral guarantee for the security of the imperial possessions in Italy was assigned part of the blame for this outrageous betrayal and even accused of complicity in it. When the Pope took certain measures against Spain they were called insufficient by Vienna; the Emperor insisted on a complete break with Spain. The situation was further aggravated by the fact that the nuncio at Madrid, Aldrovandi, obviously permitted himself to be influenced by the Spanish government. By invading papal territories and making unacceptable demands Madrid increased the tensions to the point of a complete break of diplomatic relations with Rome. In 1718, while the Spanish fleet was busy conquering Sicily, the Emperor, France, England, and Holland formed a quadruple alliance for the purpose of reordering Italy. When Spain rejected the suggestions of the alliance, the Spanish fleet was destroyed by the English fleet. Intent on taking care of his own interests, King Philip disavowed Alberoni, blaming him for his own political failures. The Emperor acquired Sicily; Sardinia went to Savoy. Don Carlos, son of Philip V and Elizabeth Farnese, was to assume the succession in Parma and Piacenza. The traditional feudal rights of the Holy See in these territories were disregarded. The trial against Alberoni, initiated by Clement XI and promoted strongly by Philip V for political reasons, was concluded under Clement's successor, Innocent XIII, on the whole in favor of the cardinal, who had even participated in the conclave of 1721. His office and rank were completely restored to him.

In addition to the difficulties caused by the wars, the long pontificate of Clement XI was also troubled by a series of natural catastrophes such as floodings of the Tiber river, epidemics, and earthquakes. These and other problems prevented him from taking far-reaching measures. The penal institution for juveniles, San Michele in Rome, established in 1703, was a pioneering effort in the modern penal system.

Clement XI has been criticized for his timid and indecisive character

and Rome 1929); R. Quazza, *Dizionario Biografico Italiano* I, 662–68; G. F. Rossi, *La bibliografia Alberoniana di Mons. Antonio Arata* (Piacenza 1964).

and his inability to lend needed emphasis to important decisions.[3] But the lack of success of his pontificate in the area of politics and the Church was surely caused above all by the unfavorable state of affairs confronting the Pope. He never quite recovered from a serious illness in the beginning of 1710. In the winter of 1720 his health further deteriorated. He personally dictated to his nephew the inscription for the simple grave already prepared for him. During the following months his condition was precarious. He died on 19 March 1721 after a pontificate lasting over twenty years.

[3] Pastor XV, 385.

The End of the Denominational Era in Europe—
Progress and Stagnation of the World Mission

CHAPTER 10

Reconstruction and Constitution of the Church of the Empire

The Peace of Westphalia had ended the Thirty Years' War, but it had not been able to bring peace to the Empire. Throughout a series of wars lasting into the first third of the eighteenth century and barely interrupted by a few years of peace, the ecclesiastical states within the "constituted anarchy" of the Empire were helpless pawns of the great powers. Again and again afflicted by military campaigns and the aftermath of war, repeatedly threatened by secularization and manipulation at European peace conferences, their reconstruction was also seriously impeded by their own constitution as electoral states, by joint dominion with the cathedral chapters, a lack of continuity, and the dual function of ecclesiastical princes.

In the period of 1500 to 1720, the archbishopric of Trier, for example, had to suffer a total of one hundred years of war, pestilence, and occupation.[1] The small bishopric of Worms, almost completely surrounded by the Protestant Palatinate, its cathedral used as a garrison church by the Swedes, is another case in point. Only after the Catholic house of Neuburg succeeded the house of Pfalz-Simmern in the Palatinate could Prince-Bishop Franz Ludwig von Pfalz-Neuburg begin to overcome the terrible destruction of the Orléans War and to restore church life under the protection of the controversial Rijswijk Clause. The Turkish threat,[2] reflected even in motifs and figures of popular piety, was not banished until the Treaty of Passarowitz (1718). Only the peace treaties of Utrecht, Rastatt, Baden (1713/14), and Aachen (1748) were preludes to lengthier periods of peace. Lamentations were heard across the land uniformly decrying, in the typical hyperbole of the

---

[1] G. Reitz, *Die Größe des geistlichen und ritterschaftlichen Grundbesitzes in ehemaligen Kur-Trier* (Koblenz 1919), 43.

[2] H. Watzl, ed., *Flucht und Zuflucht. Das Tagebuch des Priesters Balthasar Kleinschroth aus dem Türkenjahr 1683* (Graz and Cologne 1956); L. A. Veit and L. Lenhart, *Kirche und Volksfrömmigkeit im Zeitalter des Barock* (Freiburg i. Brsg. 1956), 64ff.

baroque, the pervasive wretchedness, the misery of the war in the west, the threat of the Turks in the east, joined by woeful tales of pestilence, famine, and the decay of morals.[3] Even if one were inclined to take the tendentiousness and exaggeration of the contemporary accounts into consideration and not view conditions as being totally hopeless, the political and economic reconstruction, beset by constant reverses, was yet an impressive achievement. The same holds true for the renewal and deepening of religion and church life, which were palpably expressed in the sacred art under the rule of the various dynasties, those of Wittelsbach, Habsburg, Pfalz-Neuburg, and Schönborn.

The ecclesiastical territories of the Empire, militarily and politically impotent and reduced to relying on the law, had been afflicted most grievously during the Thirty Years' War. Hardly a prince-bishop was able to do what the zealous Archbishop Paris Lodron of Salzburg (1619–53) had accomplished: preserved his land from war and its aftermath, founded the university, the Collegium Marianum (1645), the Rupertinum (1653), and finished construction of the cathedral.[4] Neutrality had neither spared the prince-bishopric of Liège under Ferdinand of Bavaria[5] nor the bishopric of Basel, although the migration after the war into more depopulated areas of the Empire,[6] as for instance from Liège to Seligenstadt, might have created the opposite impression. Even in those areas of the Catholic Church of the Empire which had never

---

[3] Regarding the misery of war from 1703 to 1713 the Luxemburg Carmelite Father Pacificus a Cruce remarks: "Now all is subjected to war and in a bad state; the Netherlands have been further lowered by war; Alsace has become a place of misery; the Rhine a river of pain; Italy is a battleground. . . . War and misery are everywhere! . . ." quoted from E. Donckel, "P. Pacificus a Cruce, Ordinis Fratrum B.M.V. de Monte Carmelo. Sein Leben—Sein Predigtwerk," *Festschrift für Alois Thomas* (Trier 1967), 106, n. 43.—A little later a contemporary of his complains about the conditions in the bishopric of Speyer: "There was no trace left of the *disciplina ecclesiastica*, no sinful excess so great that it was not also seen among the clergy. The teachings of Christ have proved to be unknown in many places." Cited from O. B. Roegele, "Damian Hugo von Schönborn und die Anfänge des Bruchsaler Priesterseminars," *FreibDiözArch* 71 (1951), 10.
[4] F. Martin, *Salzburgs Fürsten in der Barockzeit (1557–1812)* (Salzburg 1966), 85–105.
[5] P. Harsin, "Les origines diplomatiques de la neutralité liégeoise," *Revue belge de philologie et d'histoire* 5 (1926), 423–52.
[6] Regarding loss of population and war damages, see G. Franz, *Der Dreißigjährige Krieg und das deutsche Volk* (Stuttgart 1961); J. Schmidlin, *Kirchliche Zustände und Schicksale des deutschen Katholizismus während des Dreißigjährigen Krieges nach den bischöflichen Romberichten* (Freiburg i. Brsg. 1940); A. Rothbauer, "Der Dreißigjährige Krieg im Spiegel der ältesten Langenloiser Matrik, *Jahrbuch für Landeskunde von Niederösterreich* n.s. 35 (1964), 357–63; H. Steinberg, *Der Dreißigjährige Krieg und der Kampf um die Vorherrschaft in Europa 1600–60* (Göttingen 1967), is not very convincing in his attempt to correct the "traditional" image of the terrible catastrophe of the Thirty Years' War and to deemphasize its destructive effects on culture and morals.

directly suffered pillage and destruction, the war had increased prewar indebtedness, severed traditional ties, created misery for many refugees, and affected living conditions. By 1659 the bishopric of Brixen was so deeply in debt that the annates and taxes to Tyrol could not be paid and the major portion of its revenues had to be applied to the amortization of interest. A report by Prince-Bishop Karl Emanuel shows that in 1653 economic conditions in the prince-bishopric of Trent were hardly better.[7]

Compared to the bishoprics on the periphery of the Church of the Empire west and south of the Danube, political, economic, religious, and moral conditions around the middle of the seventeenth century were even worse in the so-called "priests' alley" on the Rhine and Main, as well as in those bishoprics of northern Germany which had remained Catholic. In most of the ecclesiastical territories whole regions had to be almost completely recolonized, numerous deserted villages and decayed towns rebuilt, exorbitant debts repaid, monetary confusion and infringements by secular masters on the assets and prerogatives of churches and clerics had to be checked. "Reports received by us of visitations undertaken at war's end show a disconsolate picture of the destruction of churches, of the inferior condition of the sparse number of clerics, of the dissolution and ruin of all church life, of the moral degeneration and the wild superstition of the populace."[8]

In 1647 upon the accession of Johann Philipp von Schönborn in Mainz, the so-called primary see with its second residence of Aschaffenburg had vacancies in 77 of 105 parishes. The archbishopric on the left bank of the Rhine including Mainz, which was left half-destroyed after the Swedish occupation, remained in French hands until 1650. In the archbishopric of Bamberg "the population was decimated by atrocities, famine, and pestilence. The survivors were quite impoverished as a consequence of repeated tributes."[9] In the prince-bishopric of Münster, religious and moral conditions were more precarious than the economic ones. Church discipline had deteriorated, strange cults had been introduced, and when Bishop Christoph Bernhard von Galen entered office, a large part of the clergy lived in concubinage.[10] The report to Rome by Bishop Johann Franz Vogt von Altensumerau and Praßberg of Constance, the largest diocese of the Catholic Church of the Empire,

---

[7] I. P. Dengel, "Berichte von Bischöfen über den Stand ihrer Diözesen (Relationes status ecclesiarum). Als Beitrag zur Kirchengeschichte Österreichs im 16. und 17. Jh.," *Forschungen und Mitteilungen zur Geschichte Tyrols und Vorarlbergs* 6 (1907), 323–26, 337–40.

[8] F. X. Seppelt, *Geschichte des Bistums Breslau* (Breslau 1929), 71.

[9] J. Kist, *Fürst und Erzbistum Bamberg* (Bamberg 1962), 103.

[10] W. Kohl, *Christoph Bernhard von Galen: Politische Geschichte des Fürstbistums Münster 1650–78* (Münster 1964), 26–32.

counted only six hundred occupied parishes among more than a thousand. In 1654 the bishopric of Regensburg had more than three hundred vacant parishes. Conditions were not much better in most of the remaining prince-bishoprics. In addition to the well-known aftermath of the war, the political, economic, and religious reconstruction was often impeded by foreign occupation troops, raids, and considerable reparations.[11]

Wherever reliable sources are available, they demonstrate that the indebtedness of many prince-bishoprics dating back to the late Middle Ages could not be reduced substantially even in the most affluent arch-dioceses. Among the reasons were the financial burdens of war, monetary deterioration, wrong financial policies, excessive expenditures for households, construction projects, and maintaining the relatives of the reigning princes.[12] During the seventeenth and eighteenth centuries the following prince-bishoprics were considered either quite poor or highly indebted: Chur, Constance, Regensburg, Paderborn, Hildesheim, in part also Worms, Speyer, Trier, and Freising. The cumulation of bishoprics has to be seen from economic viewpoints as well. Those bishoprics which were economically healthy and therefore relatively rich were desirable political objects for princes and knights of the Empire. In the period mentioned, these included the archbishopric of Mainz with annual revenues of approximately 1.5 to 1.7 million imperial talers (around 1790), the archbishopric of Cologne, the bishoprics of Münster, Strasbourg, Würzburg, Augsburg, and also Bamberg after it was reconstructed by Bishop Philipp Valentin Voit von Rieneck. The revenues of Bishop Wilhelm Egon von Fürstenberg (1740) from the prince-bishopric of Strasbourg, the abbeys of Saint Arnulf in Metz, Saint Michel and other benefices are estimated at 600,000 to 700,000 *livres* annually, those of Elector-Archbishop Max Franz of Cologne at more than one million imperial talers.

Yet the justifiable criticism of the financial policies[13] of many an

[11] The prince-abbeys of Murbach and Luders, for example, had to pay an immense sum in reparations. This had a negative effect until the eighteenth century; A. Gatrio, *Die Abtei Murbach im Elsaß* II (Strasbourg 1895), 553.

[12] The Mainz elector-archbishop Friedrich Karl von Ostein reported to Maria Theresa on 20 March 1763 that the Seven Years' War had "left behind nothing but beggars. Chapters and convents are totally prostrate regarding their revenues. Indeed, there is no hamlet in my entire archbishopric so small that it does not have debts as much and often manifold as is its worth." According to a calculation by the Mainz electorate of 16 October 1763, losses and damages by the French, imperial, Prussian, and allied troops, including the expenditures for the Mainz contingent of the Imperial Army, amounted to 20, 156, 447 guilders and 21 crowns. (*Haus-, Hof- und Staatsarchiv Wien* MOG, 25 A, [n.d.], 20).

[13] The policies of expenditures, revenues, and debts of the ecclesiastical princes have not yet been examined closely. Only two pertinent investigations regarding the eighteenth

ecclesiastical prince should not obscure their merits in the promotion of the arts, especially architecture—as by the Schönborns[14]—painting, the music of the baroque and Rococo, but also of science, and their charitable efforts, all of which can more than hold their own in comparison with the more powerful secular territories. The absence of standing armies, the primary instrument of power in modern absolutist states, and the close connection between the military and the exchequer tended to hold back the ecclesiastical territories in their public organization and as a political factor. At the same time it provided them with the possibility to solve by means of older forms of governing the basic question of the affairs of any state, to bring about in a faster and simpler way and in correspondence with the natural order a relationship between the individual and society, between man and the state, not least under the aspect of future salvation in the hereafter. The lack of political format, destined to become a fateful issue in the areas governed by crosier and miter, could not but provoke criticism on the part of the Enlightenment; yet it was nonetheless a positive force since it promised relatively more freedom and a certain worldly happiness according to the proverb "Under the crosier one can rest assured." On the eve of secularization, Friedrich Carl von Moser wrote: "The often scorned *Pfaffengasse* [priests' alley] constitutes a Pyrenees of sorts of inestimable value to the German people and worthy of their eternal gratitude. Thanks to it the power of monarchs was prevented from enchaining all and everything, as it did in France and Spain, leaving these Alps intact." He continues by saying that only the ecclesiastical princes "deserve the name of public administrators in the true sense of the word because bad and damaging actions are not let pass, as in the case of secular sovereigns, since the eyes of the chapter are on and around them."[15]

The ecclesiastical princes could not expect significant help from Rome or from the nunciatures in Cologne, Vienna, and Lucerne for the task of

---

century can be mentioned: H. Maas, *Verwaltungs- und Wirtschaftsgeschichte des Bistums Speyer während der Regierung des Fürstbischofs Franz Christoph von Hutten (1743–1770)* (diss., Göttingen 1931); O. Schneider, "Die Finanzpolitik des Kurfürsten Clemens Wenzeslaus von Trier," *Finanzwissenschaftliche Forschungsarbeiten* n.s. 19 (Berlin 1958).
[14] M. V. Freeden, *Würzburgs Residenz und Fürstenhof zur Schönbornzeit* (Würzburg 1949); idem, *Kunst und Künstler am Hofe des Kurfürsten Lothar Franz von Schönborn* (Würzburg 1949); J. F. Albert, *Vom Mäzenatentum der Schönborn* (Würzburg 1949); M. Braubach, "Politik und Kultur an den geistlichen Fürstenhöfen Westfalens gegen Ende des alten Reiches," *WZ* 105 (1955), 65–82; also in: *Bonner historische Forschungen* 33 (1969), 546–62; "Kurfürst Clemens August, Landesherr und Mäzen des 18. Jahrhunderts," *Katalog der Ausstellung in Schloß Augustusburg zu Brühl 1961* (Cologne 1961).
[15] F. C. v. Moser, *Über die Regierung der geistlichen Staaten in Deutschland* (Frankfurt and Leipzig 1787), 163.

religious reconstruction. There is scant reference to actions by the nunciatures on behalf of reforms, unlike the case in the waning sixteenth century and the first two decades of the seventeenth century.[16] As a matter of fact, some bishops pushed through reforms against the resistance of certain nuncios. In the case of Cologne, hardly more than the central part (the bishoprics of Cologne and Liège) were left of the vast jurisdictional area which the nuncio of Cologne, Sanfelice, casting his eyes towards Metz, Toul, and Verdun, warned against giving up. Even in 1670 the *Uditore Fini* claimed all of it in his instruction: ". . . si estende questa Nunziatura per tutto quel tratto di paese, che bagna il Rheno, cominciando da Basilea fino alle sue bocche dell'Oceano Britannico."[17] But even in the part that was left, opposition against the jurisdiction and the existence of the nunciature assumed dangerous proportions.[18]

The latent existential crisis or the threatening "total ruin" of some prince-bishoprics could not be averted by either the nunciatures or by the steadily weakening papacy. They could be averted only by the Emperor and the Empire and by the policies of the Wittelsbachs and the Habsburgs, of the Pfalz-Neuburgs, and the great chapter families such as the Eltz and Schönborns, the von der Leyens, Dalbergs, Stadions, Metternichs, Walderdorffs, and their relatives among the knights of the Empire. After a fashion, these efforts were fairly successful in the first century after the Peace of Westphalia, but less so after the middle of the eighteenth century. Much to their credit was the securing of ecclesiastical properties and the re-Catholization in the Upper Palatinate, Silesia, Jülich and Berg, in the diaspora areas of the Catholic Church of the Empire. But the political results of the conversion of princes have usually been overestimated.[19]

---

[16] A. Franzen, "Die Finalrelation des Kölner Nuntius Sanfelice vom Jahre 1659," *RQ* 50 (1955), 69–88 idem, "Französische Politik und Kurkölns Beziehungen zu Frankreich unter Erzbischof Max Heinrich (1650–1688), *RQ* 52 (1957), 169–210; H. Raab, "Die Finalrelation des Kölner Nuntius Fabrizio Paolucci," *RQ* 55 (1960), 129–50; idem, "Die Relation des Kölner Nuntius Gaetano de' Cavalieri von 1732," *RQ* 58 (1963), 71–88; idem, "Die Instruktion für den Kölner Nuntius Jacopo Oddi," *RQ* 62 (1967), 36–69; A. Levinson, "Nuntiaturberichte vom Kaiserhofe Leopolds I. (1657–1669)," *AÖG* 103 (1913), 547–831; R. Scotti, *Helvetia sacra. Relatione de Vescovati, Abbatie, et altre dignità subordinate alla Nuntiatura helvetica* (Macerata 1642); K. Haid, "Aus der Aktenmappe des Monsignore Francesco Boccapaduglio, Nuntius in der Schweiz," *ZSKG* 38 (1944), 121–53.

[17] L. Just, "Die Kölner Nuntiatur nach einer Information des Uditore Fini von 1670," *AHVNrh* 155/56 (1954), 314.

[18] See Chap. 23: "Episcopalism in the Church of the Empire."

[19] Concerning Johann Ludwig von Nassau-Hadamar, who converted to Catholicism in Vienna in 1628 and as a widower and father of a large number of children, some of

The renewal of church life, initiated in force after 1648, received a late start in comparison with the Romance countries. It can only be fully understood if its special constitutional aspects and the difficulties arising from them are taken into account.[20]

According to the constitution of the Empire, the bishops were not only dignitaries of the hierarchy and successors of the apostles, but as holders of ecclesiastical territories granted as fiefs of the Empire they were also pillars of the Empire, full members with a vote in the imperial diet, princes with the sovereignty granted them by the Peace of Westphalia, albeit a sovereignty which few of them were able to claim for lack of concrete power. This duality of ecclesiastical and secular functions of the prince-bishops and prince-abbots had a positive potential for Church reform. But it also represented a temptation which in a courtly world of absolutism frequently surpassed their strength and permitted the worldly prince in them to win out over the bishop. Forgoing the pomp and circumstance, as was often demanded by contemporary critics, or the demand for a more profound scientific education on the part of prince-bishops[21] only scratched the surface of the problem.

A Church of the Empire in the sense of an association comprising all bishoprics under an ecclesiastical head empowered to lead and direct

---

whom were already placed in German chapters, applied in 1650 for the prince-bishopric of Münster, see K. Wolf, "Johann Ludwig, Graf von Nassau-Hadamar," *Nassauische Lebensbilder* II (Wiesbaden 1943), 109–23; W. Kohl, "Nassauische Absichten auf das Bistum Münster," *Westfalen* 36 (1958), 92–102; concerning Ernst von Hessen-Rheinfels, who promoted re-Catholicization in St. Goar, Bad Schwalbach, Rotenburg/Fulda, see H. Raab, *Landgraf Ernst von Hessen-Rheinfels (1623–93)* (St. Goar 1964). The conversion of Duke Alexander Heinrich von Holstein (1649), Duke Friedrich von Hanover (1651), Count Palatine Christian August von Sulzbach, Elector Friedrich August I of Saxony, the dukes of Württemberg, etc. had little or no consequence from the standpoint of denominational politics.

[20] It is self-evident that space does not permit us to write the history of the counter-reformational and reformational efforts of the seventeenth and early eighteenth century in the Church of the Empire, although in spite of a number of monographs this field has remained largely unexplored.

[21] In his "Speculum pro Episcopo et simul Principi saeculari" Landgrave Ernst von Hessen-Rheinfels expressed the view that a bishop should be allowed the exercise of ecclesiastical and temporal power only "propter duritiem cordis, that is, according to the present state of the world." No bishop was to be implicated, like Christoph Bernhard von Galen of Münster and the Popes Julius II and Innocent X "in war and matters of war." Thorough knowledge of theology, academic titles, and experience in the ministry should be demanded of every candidate for the office of bishop. Membership in a certain estate should not exclude him from being eligible for election.—According to the prince-abbot Bernhard Frank von Disentis eighty years later, "an uneducated bishop is a speechless herald" (L. Schmid, *Bernhard Frank von Frankenberg, Fürstabt von Disentis 1742–63* [Chur 1958], 53.).

never existed. As far as its unity was concerned, the Church of the Empire could not be compared with the *Ecclesia Gallicana*. But after the canonical and historical foundation of episcopalism, initially in imitation of Gallicanism, had made some progress, it proudly put its own freedoms—Prince-Abbot Martin Gerbert even spoke of a "national freedom of the German Church"—on a higher footing than those of the Gallican Church, which were considered basically to give expression only to the dominance of the King over the Church. In its legal aspects the Church was initially and exclusively based on the Concordat of Vienna (1448),[22] including, most importantly, its stipulations regarding the filling of bishoprics in the Empire, the granting of benefices, and the financial tribute to the Roman Curia. In the late seventeenth century, following the ambiguous Cologne election of 1688 and the efforts of G. W. Leibniz, there was an attempt to revive the Concordat of Worms and to deduce from it the right of the Emperor to decide conflicting elections.[23] The episcopal church law of the Empire stressed the redis-covered *Concordata Principum* of 1447 and specifically the Mainz Ac-ceptation of 1439 in order to use them in an attempt to modify the Concordat of Vienna.[24] The reform councils of Constance and Basel viewed as foundations of the Church of the Empire the pertinent stipu-lations of the Peace of Augsburg, the Peace of Westphalia, the Em-peror's election capitulation, and the Rijswijk Clause, in addition to the more significant peace treaties of the seventeenth and eighteenth cen-turies. In neither of these centuries did the Church of the Empire effect a new concordat satisfying the demands of the time.

The church province of Mainz and the idea of a *Primas Germaniae* was brought up as an age-old unifying tie between the bishoprics of the Empire. When Magdeburg joined the Reformation, the archbishops of Salzburg not only claimed the title of *Primas Germaniae*, but were able to maintain their claim with the support of the Emperor and even have it recognized by the Imperial Chancellery in 1750. Yet it had never really amounted to more than an honorary title when the elector-archbishops of Mainz raised their claim to it. This held true even though Mainz, with some justification, was considered the *Metropolis Germaniae* until the fall of the Empire, "increasingly in the sense that involved legal and constitutional aspects of the Empire, decreasingly in the sense of ecclesiastical primacy, and hardly at all in the sense of territorial power."[25]

[22] H. Raab, *Die Concordata Nationis Germanicae in der kanonistischen Diskussion des 17. bis 19. Jh. Ein Beitrag der episkopalistischen Theorie in Deutschland* (Wiesbaden 1956).
[23] P. Kopfermann, *Das Wiener Konkordat im deutschen Staatsrecht* (Berlin 1908).
[24] See Chap. 23: "Episcopalism in the Church of the Empire from the Middle of the Seventeenth to the End of the Eighteenth Century."
[25] J. Bärmann, *Moguntiae Metropolis Germaniae* (Mainz 1965), 23.

It was in his capacity as elector-archchancellor of the Empire that the archbishop of Mainz occupied the most respected position among the ecclesiastical princes.[26] The prince-bishops of Eichstätt assumed the title of a *Sanctae Moguntinae Sedis Cancellarius* whose task it was to watch over the inviolateness of the Empire and the rights of its Catholic Church. But in spite of the occasional use of the title of primate and some attempts to make themselves the spokesmen representing the interests of the Church of the Empire, their ecclesiastical authority was no greater than that of the other three archbishops.

The extent and borders of the Church of the Empire have never been precisely defined; nor do they correspond to Wessenberg's later definition of the "German Church" under a German primate.[27] They are best determined according to the area affected by the Concordat of Vienna (1448) combined with the basic law of the Empire calling for the free election of bishops. Fluidity and obscurity of its borders, overlapping authority, strange legal conditions, as in the case of the prince-abbeys of Sankt Gallen and Murbach-Luders, the Salzburg bishoprics proper, the abbeys *nullius dioecesis*[28] and the quasi-bishoprics, the alternation of Osnabrück and the denominationally mixed cathedral chapters and benefices all lent a special character to the Church of the Empire and made many a reform difficult. Not counting the elevation of Fulda and Corvey to bishoprics in the second half of the eighteenth century, the number of bishoprics remained constant during the 150 years following the Peace of Westphalia. Neither strength nor will were sufficient to establish Counter Reformation bishoprics, although Joseph II was not the first to perceive the necessity for reordering the organization of the bishoprics, which was almost a thousand years old at that time. Landgrave Ernst von Hessen-Rheinfels (1623–93) demanded that the Empire be restructured into 150 archdioceses and dioceses with each of them having no more than 200 parishes and annual revenues of 4000 talers. Even individual corrections in the administrative structure could not be effected without considerable difficulty. Thus the centuries-old issue between Salzburg and Passau[29] concerning exemption was not decided until 1728, in favor of Passau.

For all practical purposes, the Catholic Church of the Empire ended at the borders of the Emperor's patrimonial dominions, yet it also overlap-

---

[26] H. Mathy, "Über das Mainzer Erzkanzleramt in der Neuzeit Stand und Aufgaben der Forschung," *Geschichtliche Landeskunde* II (1965), 109–49.

[27] I. H. von Wessenberg, *Betrachtungen über die Verhältnisse der katholischen Kirche im Umfange des deutschen Bundes* (1818).

[28] Hofmeister, "Gefreite Abteien und Prälaturen," *ZSavRGkan* 50 (1964), 176ff.

[29] E. M. Eder, *Beiträge zum Passauer Exemtionsstreit*, (diss., Vienna 1962).

ped the borders of Switzerland and France. In spite of some corresponding details, its situation in the Bavarian sphere of influence cannot simply be compared with that of the Rhenish ecclesiastical electorates. In the
Austrian hereditary lands the Church was to a large extent an established Church; despite their extensive property holdings, the bishops
were merely members of the provincial diets. With the exception of
aristocratic clerics of the Empire who played a significant role in Vienna
or Prague (as did the vice-chancellor of the Empire, Walderdorff, and
Archbishops Manderscheid and Salm-Salm), and the bishops of Brixen,
Trent, Seckau, and Lavant, the clergy of the hereditary lands, unless
they simultaneously occupied a seat in the cathedral chapters of Passau,
Salzburg, Regensburg or in imperial chapters, simply could not have
very strong feelings regarding their ties to the diocesan structure of
Germany. Since the turn of the eighteenth century, moreover, the
Habsburg emperors started to carve an Austrian monarchy from the
Empire and increasingly to consider themselves heads of an established
Church.

And yet if one looks for a head of the Church of the Empire, able to
exert influence upon it, it would most likely be the Emperor, the *Advocatus ecclesiae*.[30] The seat of German Kings and Emperors in the choir
stall of many a cathedral, to be sure, had become a sort of venerable
legacy. The office of an archchancellor of the empress, occupied by the
prince-abbot of Fulda, or that of the archmarshall, claimed by the
prince-abbot of Kempten was endowed with a very modest influence.
But these various offices and the artistic aspects of "Imperial Halls," the
historiography and architecture of the *Germania sacra* demonstrate its
"amphibious constitution."[31] In spite of the denominational split, the
Empire remained Catholic, albeit semiecclesiastic in its claims and its
mission. It was not only political self-preservation that prompted a bond
with the Empire, generally stronger than in most of the secular territories. Only within the framework of the Empire were these many
Caesaropapal states of varying size able to develop a political and cultural life or eventually realize their lack of political power relative to the
rise of the modern absolutist states.[32]

[30] L. Glier, *Die Advocatia ecclesiae Romanae imperatoris in der Zeit von 1519 bis 1648* (diss.,
Erlangen 1897); R. Müller, *Die rechtlichen Wandlungen der Advocatia Ecclesiae des römischen Kaisers deutscher Nation* (diss., Erlangen 1895).
[31] This apt expression was first found in N. Lieb, "Die Stiftsanlagen des Barocks in
Altbayern und Schwaben," *SM* 29 (1968), 120: "From the standpoint of creativity in
architecture, the synthesis of a monastery and an immediate ecclesiastical state can be
compared to the combination of bishop's church and royal church in the Gothic
cathedral."—G. Iller, *Die Malereien des Kaisersaales zu Fulda* (1939).
[32] Joseph von Eichendorff, "Über die Folgen der Aufhebung de Landeshoheit der Bischöfe und Klöster in Deutschland," *Sämtliche Werke,* ed. by W. Kosch and A. Sauer, X

The basic laws of the Empire, especially the stipulations of the Peace of Westphalia and the electoral capitulation obliged the Emperor to secure the status quo of the Church of the Empire,[33] to maintain the *Concordata Nationis Germanicae*, and to stop the complaints against the Roman Curia.[34] Since the thirteenth century the German Kings and Emperors had exercised the privilege of "First Entreaties" (*Jus primariarum precum*)[35] even without a papal indulgence and under Joseph I held fast to it in the face of a violent dispute with Rome. They granted so-called panis letters "which ordered a religious chapter or congregation that upheld or was still upholding the custom of a common table to provide for a certain person's livelihood for life either in agricultural products or money."[36]

Although basically respecting the electoral freedom of the cathedral chapters, the Emperor was nonetheless able to influence the filling of bishoprics and through this the policies of ecclesiastical territories by dispatching electoral ambassadors, or by means of recommendations, tokens of favor to Austrian canons or those loyal to the Empire, that is by political and financial means. The presence of imperial election commissioners at the decisive preliminary negotiations, although not at the election itself, was considered legally necessary.[37] But even the right of decision in ambiguous episcopal elections and the *ius exclusivae,* for whose justification the proponents of an established Church in favor of increased advocacy invoked the Concordat of Worms and imperial cus-

---

(Regensburg 1911), 169: "[The ecclesiastic territories] as the only remains of a monstrous ancient temple maintained, in the midst of the flood of changes, a steadfast, almost mystic connection with and reference to their great past, the memory of which other states could not destroy fast enough."

[33] Ferdinand III, for example, admonished the Swiss Confederation in 1656 to leave the seminary of Sankt Gallen unmolested on the grounds of "the regalia, privileges, and jurisdiction it held in fief from the Holy Roman Empire." Emperor and Empire regarded Sankt Gallen as belonging to the Empire, that is, as not affected by the Peace of Westphalia. This was evident in their conduct during the Toggenburg War.

[34] W. Wagner, *Das Staatsrecht des Heiligen Römischen Reiches deutscher Nation. Eine Darstellung der Reichsverfassung gegen Ende des 18. Jh. nach einer Handschrift der Wiener Staatsbibliothek* (Karlsruhe 1968), 58–62.

[35] H. E. Feine, "Papst, Erste Bitten und Regierungsantritt des Kaisers seit dem Ausgang des Mittelalters," *ZSavRGkan* 20 (1931), 1–101; F. J. Heyen, "Die kaiserlichen Ersten Bitten für das Erzbistum Trier von Ferdinand I. bis Franz II. (1531–1792)," *Festschrift für Alois Thomas* (Trier 1967), 175–88.

[36] W. Wagner, *Staatsrecht*, 64.

[37] About the claim to send imperial curate delegates to the election of bishops, cf. W. Hermkes, *Das Reichsvikariat in Deutschland. Reichsvikare nach dem Tode des Kaisers von der Goldenen Bulle bis zum Ende des Reiches* (Karlsruhe 1968), as well as Chap. 24: "The Established Church."

tom, did not prevail against the resistance of the cathedral chapters and the prebendal aristocracy.

In Trent, where the Compacts of 18 September 1363 and the Note of Speyer of 1571 granted extensive concessions to the Habsburgs, and in Brixen, Passau, Eichstätt and Salzburg, whose "Eternal Statute" (1606) prohibited the election of Bavarian princes and Austrian archdukes and practically excluded all but Tyrolians and Lower Austrians, as a rule candidates from Austrian nobility and those in the service of the Emperor ascended to the see. A position unique in the Church of the Empire and indeed within the Church as a whole was occupied by Salzburg. It had the privilege of appointing, confirming, and consecrating the bishops of its own four small bishoprics of Gurk, Seckau, Chiemsee, and Lavant. Only in the case of Gurk had there been an arrangement made between King Ferdinand I and Archbishop Matthäus Lang (25 October 1535) to the effect that of three successive bishops the first two would always be appointed by the ruler.

The ecclesiastical territories on the Main and middle Rhine were for the most part ruled by prince-bishops who were patriotic and loyal to the Emperor. These cathedral chapters of knights of the Empire repeatedly and successfully demonstrated their independence to candidates nominated by the respective rulers. The knights of the Empire prevailed over proof of ancestry and immediate exclusiveness as well as over the great Catholic dynasties such as the Wittelsbachs, Habsburgs, Pfalz-Neuburgs, and Wettins. But they also prevailed over the mediate nobility who dominated the northwest German cathedral chapters but were in a much more difficult situation in trying to ward off the candidates of their princes. Their resistance was aggravated by the system of coadjutorships, which was expanded in the course of the Counter Reformation and dynastic policies to the extent of a "quasi-hereditability" in a number of states. Thus the prince-bishopric of Freising was referred to as "our parish" by the court of Munich. As a consequence of the Wittelsbach coadjutorships only two elections took place in more than two hundred years in the archbishopric of Cologne (1688 and 1763), although the election of coadjutors was never acknowledged as an actual election or postulation by the Curia, at least in theory. Yet in spite of considerable disadvantages, the coadjutorships at least had the advantage of avoiding interregna and provisional governments by cathedral chapters in the case of vacant sees and the attendant negative consequences.

The ecclesiastical territories were electoral states without any continuity in their foreign and domestic policies or in their attempts at clerical reform. To be sure, they were spared disputes and partitions of inheritance, but were not immune to dynastic rivalries, the ambitions of prebendal families, their nepotism and conflicts of interest. Interregnum and provisional governments during vacancies—not unfairly characterized as "cathedral chapter harvest"—were frequently marked by an express animosity towards the person, the family, and government of the deceased prince-bishop, as well as against his advisers, who at times were not spared personal persecution.[38] This, as well as the considerable cost of an episcopal election and the sums to be raised for annates, services, and pallium contributions, made all reforms exceedingly difficult. Many prince-bishops started their reign without financial means and consequently with little authority. In addition they were tied to the electoral capitulations acknowledged by the Peace of Westphalia,[39] which secured for the cathedral chapters joint government in the bishopric and participation in the clerical administration of it, altogether guaranteeing the estates to be constitutionally embodied in the ecclesiastical territories.[40]

Some wishes for church reforms were reflected in the electoral capitulations, among them the demand to forgo accumulations of bishoprics, a stricter observance of the residence obligation, the settlement of clerical jurisdiction, and the care of elderly and indigent clergy. Those elected were frequently obliged not to take on a coadjutor, not to seek a cardinalate or to do so only if the electoral privilege of the cathedral chapter was assured, not to admit religious orders, which could mean a diminution of episcopal jurisdiction, to root out heresy and to promote the Catholic mission. In the prince-bishoprics of Würzburg, Speyer, and Eichstätt, lengthy lawsuits ensued because of the electoral capitulations. In 1690 Prince-Bishop Johann Gottfried II von Guttenberg of Würzburg managed to be absolved from the electoral capitulation by the Pope. The prince-bishops of Eichstätt, Bamberg, and Constance tried to achieve a similar solution. In 1692 a particular congregation examined all the German electoral capitulations.

---

[38] G. Christ, "Der Wiener Hof und die Wahl Conrad Wilhelms v. Werdenau zum Fürstbischof von Würzburg 1683," *Würzburger Diözesangeschichts-Bll.* 26 (1964), 298.
[39] J. F. Abert, "Die Wahlkapitulationen der Würzburger Fürstbischöfe bis zum Ende des 17. Jh.," *Archiv des Hist. Vereins für Unterfranken u. Aschaffenburg* 46 (1969), 104ff.; J. Kremer, "Studien zur Gesch. der Trierer Wahlkapitulationen (1286–1786)," *Westdt. Zschr. ErgH* 16; G. Weigel, *Die Wahlkapitulationen der Bamberger Bischöfe 1328–1693* (Bamberg 1909); L. Bruggaier, *Die Wahlkapitulationen der Bischöfe und Reichsfürsten von Eichstätt Eine historisch-kanonistische Studie* (Freiburg i.Brsg. 1915); N. Fuchs, "Die Wahlkapitulationen der Fürstbischöfe von Regensburg 1437–1801," *Verhandlungen des Hist. Vereins für Oberpfalz und Regensburg* 101 (1960–61), 5ff.
[40] R. v. Oer, *Landständische Verfassungen in den geistlichen Fürstentümern Nordwestdeutschlands: Ständische Vertretungen in Europa in 17. und 18. Jh.*, ed. by D. Gerhard (Göttingen 1969), 94–119.

Following its suggestions, Innocent XII issued the constitution *Ecclesiae catholicae* (22 September 1695). By threatening dire penalties, it prohibited any and all agreements prior to the election and made all obligations to be contracted after the election subject to concurrence by the Holy See in order to be valid. Emperor Leopold I expressed similar sentiments concerning the invalidity of the electoral capitulations. This *Constitutio Innocentiana* was a decisive blow to the electoral capitulations of several archbishoprics, such as Würzburg, Bamberg, Cologne, and Salzburg, but in those chapters which refused to obey the papal bull and the Emperor's resolution it could not abolish them. In those places a tolerable modus vivendi was obtained which was only occasionally disturbed since the capitulars made the bishops keep to their stipulations and forgo recourse to Rome. Moreover, no prince-bishop who had to consider the consequences for his family could afford deliberately to seek a conflict over the electoral capitulation.

Social differences, reduced during the late Middle Ages, again played a more prominent role in the Church of the seventeenth century. In an unprecedented campaign of securing established positions and in the process of Catholic renewal the hierarchy and leadership of the Church of the Empire consisted exclusively of the few Catholic princely families and the prebendal nobility. Until the death of the Archdukes Leopold Wilhelm (1662) and Karl Joseph (1664), and of the Cologne elector Ferdinand (13 September 1650), who had singlehandedly accumulated five archbishoprics, one prince-abbey and one prince-priory, had never been consecrated, and yet had done well in reforms, half of the Church of the Empire seems to have been dominated by the Habsburgs and Wittelsbachs. Finally, when the archdynasty of Austria for lack of male descendants could no longer furnish candidates for the bishoprics,[41] the nobility of the hereditary lands and later on the related houses of Pfalz-Neuburg, Wettin, and Lorraine took their place.

To be sure, accumulations of bishoprics as practiced under Leopold Wilhelm of Austria and Ferdinand of Bavaria were rarely equaled after the middle of the seventeenth century. Yet for another century the northwest German *Germania Sacra* from Liège to Hildesheim remained almost exclusively an ecclesiastical secundogeniture of the Wittelsbachs

---

[41] A. Schulte (*Der Adel und die deutsche Kirche im Mittelalter* [Stuttgart 1922]) repeatedly pointed out that quite a few noble families jeopardized the continuation of their line when their sons entered the ecclesiastical estate.—H. L. Krick, *212 Stammtafeln adeliger Familien, denen geistliche Würdenträger des Bistums Passau entsprossen sind* (Schweiklberg 1924) shows 134 of 212 families as having died out; of these, however, ca. 60 through circumstances other than the entrance of male descendants into the ecclesiastical estate. Beside the Habsburgs, the Wittelsbach, Pfalz-Neuburg, and Slavata families were diminished through ecclesiastical professions.

until the death of Elector-Archbishop Clemens August of Cologne (1761). The prince-bishoprics of Freising and Regensburg were occupied almost throughout by Wittelsbachs until the passing away of Cardinal Johann Theodor of Bavaria (1763). The Thuns alone furnished four prince-bishops of Passau, the rich archdiocese of Strasbourg was in the hands of the Fürstenbergs from 1663 to 1704; until its decline it was a prebend of the princely family Rohan. The prince-bishopric of Basel came under the rule of a group of "ten families whose seats were on the left and right banks of the Rhine."[42] For three generations the history of the ecclesiastical territories on the Rhine and Main was determined by the rule of the Schönborns and their related families.[43]

Dynastic policies within the Church of the Empire undoubtedly contributed to a concentration of power, securing of ecclesiastical properties, and slowing the process of secularization. But as a means of securing a livelihood for younger sons of princes not always suited for the clerical estate they also carried with them grave dangers for the Church. Even taking into account the beneficial influence of the suffragan bishops, the accumulation of bishoprics nonetheless militated against church reform emanating from the hierarchy. Towards the end of the seventeenth century the Church of the Empire had a number of weak and theologically uneducated bishops who were more interested in politics, war, art or entertainment than in their clerical tasks. Yet the number of unconsecrated bishops did decrease. In fact, there were more excellent and truly religious bishops who came close to the ideal than is immediately apparent. Among the exemplary bishops who earned great merit in the implementation of church reforms were the following: Johann Hugo von Orsbeck, archbishop of Trier; Johann Ernst von Thun (1709), archbishop of Salzburg; Sebastian Count von Pöking (1673–88), bishop of Passau; the reformatory Franz Wilhelm von Wartenberg, bishop of Regensburg and Osnabrück (d. 1661), "one of the greatest church politicians of his century";[44] and J. F. Eckher von Kapfing (d. 1724), bishop of Freising, who was "the type of baroque prince of the Church whose intellect and soul were dedicated to the *Tridentinum*."[45]

---

[42] H. Rössler, *Deutscher Adel 1555–1740* (Darmstadt 1965), 196.

[43] Ibid. On p. 194 Rössler quotes from a report by the imperial legate to the Rhenish electoral courts, Trauttmannsdorff, of 1786, according to which the Schönborn and Stadion families were still considered as being in the top group of the nobility of electoral Mainz.

[44] G. Schwaiger, *Kardinal Franz Wilhelm von Wartenberg als Bischof von Regensburg (1649–61)* (Munich 1954), 302.

[45] B. Hubensteiner, *Die geistliche Stadt Welt und Leben des Johann Franz Eckher von Kapfing und Liechteneck, Fürstbischofs von Freising* (Munich 1954), 193.

The capitulars looked on themselves as "hereditary lords" of the archbishoprics, as "condomini et conregnantes" or as "patriae et statuum protectores" (from the 1729 electoral capitulation of the electorate of Trier). These "princes of the Papal States" (Sartorius) have often enough been harshly judged. They were taken to task for their inept mediocrity, their lack of zeal and theological education, their chasing after prebends, belligerence, and their chronic gambling and drinking (deplored by the papal nuncios almost in terms of a German national vice). They were blamed for a good part of the abuses in the Church and for the fact that they delayed or hesitated in implementing reform. It is indeed not easy to do them justice, especially if we take into account that while the chapters were similar on the whole they nonetheless differed considerably in detail regarding size, revenues, and structure. The prebendal nobility was rooted deeply in the courtly world of the baroque. There were lethargic, incompetent prebendaries, talented politicians, sophisticated cavaliers in the cathedral and collegiate chapters, but there were also unobtrusive supplicants and humble pious priests. Greed for fame and money were widespread, but so were preparedness for penitence and expiation. The prebendal nobility were not exclusively engaged in taking care of their families. While they were open to criticism concerning the "aristocratic Church of the Empire," their achievements for Church and Empire, for the arts and sciences deserve recognition. The Schönborns and Eltzes, the Stadions and Dalbergs, the von der Leyens, Breidbach-Bürresheims, Walderdorffs, Fürstenbergs, Thuns, and Firmians, to mention a few, have left their mark on inner and outer aspects of the Church. Their clerical and political decisions, their courts and church architecture, their collections and foundations represent prominent high points in the course of German history.

Efforts to strengthen the principle of exclusiveness had to do with the desire for political, economic and religious security. In the course of the seventeenth century the requirements regarding proof of ancestry were generally augmented. In 1606 the cathedral chapter of Bamberg increased its demands to include eight ancestors. The statutes of the cathedral chapter of Mainz dated 19 December 1654 required of prebendal applicants the witness of eight matriculated knights of the Empire to the effect that the former's ancestors corresponded with the traditions of the Mainz Church. Towards the end of the seventeenth century the closely connected chapters of Mainz, Bamberg, and Würzburg demanded proof of sixteen immediate ancestors of the Empire. The cathedral chapters of Eichstätt, Constance, Passau, and Regensburg were satisfied with proof of four ancestors. The farther the chapters were situated to the east and south of the Empire, the less stringent were the requirements and the less frequent the rejection of spurious ancestors. The mediate nobility of these areas did not try to compete in its requirements with those of the knights of the Empire. By increasing their demands regarding proof of ancestry in Bamberg, Würzburg, Mainz, and later on in Trier, Worms, and Speyer, the knights achieved exclusive status for their class and to a large extent also for their territories, unaffected by the resistance of the mediate nobility of the Lower Rhine and Westphalia, who were supported by Prussia and Hanover. The bishops of these dioceses—disregarding the special circumstances in Trier—were almost exclusively from families of knights of the Empire from Franconian, electoral Rhenish, and Swabian areas.

In 1526 the bishopric of Chur had gained territorial exclusiveness by means of the Articles of Ilanz, which, in fact, made the cathedral chapter and the archdiocese into an institution of triple ties. A strong Italian, Tridentine character was preserved in the cathedral chapter of Trent. Eight of twenty-four capitular prebends had been open to the French high aristocracy since 1687; in 1713 the requirements for proof of ancestry were made much less stringent. In the cathedral chapter of Liège the number of prebendal German nobles decreased steadily. In the eighteenth century the cathedral chapters of Paderborn, Hildesheim, and Münster attempted to come to an agreement regarding estates and territories of the Empire. It was their intention to no longer admit either Rhenish, Swabian, or Franconian knights of the Empire—with the exception of the cantons of Hegau, Allgäu and Bodensee—or Bohemians and Moravians. In the cathedral chapter of Cologne, where proof of sixteen ancestors had had to be demonstrated since the end of the fifteenth century, the dominance of the nobility was breached by eight pastoral prebends accessible to members of the bourgeoisie. These prebends required both ordination and the doctorate; the equality of rank between the doctoral degree and noble origin thus continued. In the cathedral chapters of Liège, Brixen, and Chur the bourgeois element was not only represented, but actually gained influence in the course of the eighteenth century. Even if one readily admits to cases of reactions against the candidacy of prebendal nobles or princes of the Empire in Stablo-Malmedy or Liège, reactions based on territorial issues or the question of mediate or immediate imperial status, the assumption of a contrast between an aristocratic Church and a rising bourgeoisie can no longer be taken for granted. This is the conclusion to be drawn if one examines the composition of the upper German chapters, the list of their abbots—with Sankt Gallen a case in point[46]—as well as the origin of the various prelates[47] and the suffragan bishops. Entering a monastery in the period of the baroque was more a matter of "social rise than a policy for securing a livelihood,"[48] for the monasteries of that period made tremendous contributions towards reforms and cultural changes, not least in the area of equalizing the differences between social classes.

The Council of Trent had aimed at strengthening the position of the bishops within the diocese, doing away with the separation of the pontificate and the secular-political office characteristic of the development of the Church of the Empire prior to the Reformation. It had also raised a demand for the abolition of the suffragan bishop, this *larva ecclesiae Dei*. To be sure, the bishops had increasingly returned to the center of diocesan life, especially since the middle of the seventeenth century, and there was hardly a diocese within the confines of the Church which could not point to at least one and in most cases several exemplary bishops in the period between the Peace of Westphalia and the Catholic Enlightenment. Yet there was no dearth of complaints concerning the position of the suffragan bishops, that German "bizarrerie, que l'Évêque in partibus n'est que pour les fonctions Épiscopales de l'ordre, et qu'il n'a que voir au gouvernement spirituel, celui qui en est chargé n'étant que Prêtre,"[49] more so if conditions in the Church of the Empire were measured against the Tridentine or early Christian ideal. "A bishop can do everything according to his plans," was the complaint of the learned and profoundly religious suffragan bishop Niels Stensen, who withdrew to his jurisdiction of the "Nordic Missions" as a protest against the controversial election of the Cologne elector Max Heinrich to the prince-bishopric of Münster. He continued: "But I am only permitted pontifical acts; therefore all those other functions, such as visitations,

---

[46] As early as 1430–36 Sankt Gallen abolished the exclusion of nonnobles. Three of its eight abbots between 1630 and 1803 came from the lowest social stratum (two were sons of poor peasants, one the son of a shoemaker); the majority of the others came from the bourgeoisie. Of more than 350 conventuals between 1648 and 1803 only seven were real nobles. The last noble conventual took his vows in 1723 (cf. J. Salzgeber, *Die Klöster Einsiedeln und St. Gallen im Barockzeitalter* [Munich 1966]).

[47] E. Krausen, "Die Zusammensetzung bayerischer Prämonstratenserkonvente," *HJ* 86 (1966), 166ff.; idem, "Die Herkunft der bayerischen Prälaten des 17. und 18. Jh." *ZBLG* 27 (1964), 259–85.

[48] J. Salzgeber, op. cit., 90.

[49] Antoine Arnauld to Landgrave Ernst von Hessen Rheinfels, 30 September 1683. *Lettres de Messire Antoine Arnauld, Docteur de la Maison et Société de Sorbonne* II (Paris and Lausanne 1775), 353.

synods, schools, and other things necessary to prepare a candidate for ordination, are out of my hands."[50]

Compared to the aristocratic ecclesiastical princes, not all of whom had been consecrated or were able to fulfill their residence obligation, the suffragan bishops were very much in the background even in the historical representations of the Church, since their work appears to have been limited primarily to pontifical acts and their lives were evidently lacking in prominent events and were too dull and colorless to merit the interest of historians. This one-sided picture of an aristocratic Church of the Empire in modern times must be rectified by an improved assessment of the role and origin of the suffragan bishops. From the Peace of Westphalia to secularization, the Mainz suffragan bishops *in partibus Rheni* were almost exclusively of bourgeois origin, most of them from rather modest circumstances. From 1600 to 1800 there was not a single aristocrat among the ten suffragans of Speyer; the seven suffragans of Basel during the same period were either bourgeois or patricians. Although the prince-bishops and the cathedral chapter of Strasbourg were exclusively members of the high nobility, the vast majority of the suffragans were from the bourgeoisie. This was also the case in Augsburg during the seventeenth century, while during the eighteenth century it was the knights of the Empire who predominated, so that in the course of two centuries the two were approximately of equal representation. In the same two centuries the tendency in favor of the aristocracy manifest in Augsburg was even more prominent in Constance in the form of a transition from graduated theologians to the barons of the baroque.

The suffragans more or less took care of the ministry in their bishoprics and undertook a great part of the reforms. Their work, insufficiently known even today, characterized an inner aspect of the Church of the Empire, which at times has been seen too much as an "aristocratic Church," as ecclesiastical principalities, as a merger of secular and clerical rule, and as the exclusive domain of Catholic princes and aristocratic families.

In the duchy of Berg and later as suffragans in Mainz and Cologne the brothers Peter and Adrian van Walenbusch dedicated all their energies to church reform and the reunification in the faith. As suffragans of Mainz, their friend, the convert Adolf Gottfried Volusius, as well as Mathias Starck and Christian Nebel continued their efforts towards intensifying the life of the Church. In northern Germany it was

---

[50] Quotation from M. Berbaum, *Niels Stensen. Von der Anatomie zur Theologie (1638–1688)* (Münster, n.d.), 100.

the extraordinarily capable Osnabrück suffragan Kaspar Münster (d. 5 February 1654), "filled with a burning zeal for reform,"[51] who worked for the implementation of the Edict of Restitution and the propagation of the faith. The larger part of his inheritance went to the Cologne Archbrothership of the Sufferings of our Lord,[52] that is for the benefit of the ministry to converts. The learned Niels Stensen was hard at work in the prince-bishopric of Münster and in the "Nordic Missions." But the attempt, welcomed by the Jansenist Antoine Arnauld as an "action agréable à Dieu," to attract Stensen as suffragan in the service of the pious Johann Hugo von Orsbeck of Trier came to naught.[53] In the diocese of Regensburg, reforms and the reconstruction of the Church were given strong impulses by Bishop Wartenberg's excellent collaborator, the titular bishop of Almira, Sebastian Denich. During the reign of the Wittelsbach prince-bishops Joseph Clemens, Clemens August, and Johann Theodor, who rarely resided there, these tasks were undertaken by the saintly suffragan bishop Gottfried Johann Freiherr Langwerth von Simmern, a convert and a distant relative of Freiherr vom Stein.[54] During his long tenure, the titular bishop of Edremit, Kaspar Zeiler (1645–81), applied his energy to the restoration of church life in the bishopric of Augsburg. The learned Thomas Henrici, titular bishop of Chrysopolis (1648 to 1660) and public advocate of the reunification of the Churches, worked in the bishopric of Basel. The Suffragan Bishops Peter Verhorst and Matthias von Eyss led the defense against Jansenism in the archdiocese of Trier. Cologne developed an active church life under the Francken-Siersdorf suffragans. Representative of many other suffragans of the seventeenth century for their achievements and reforms were the following: Johannes Brunetti and Elias Daniel von Sommerfeld in Breslau, Paul Aldringen (1592–1644), who came from a poor Luxemburg family and in his role as suffragan under Archduke Leopold Wilhelm was the actual bishop and reformer

---

[51] G. Denzler, *Die Propagandakongregation in Rom und die Kirche in Deutschland im ersten Jahrzehnt nach dem Westfälischen Frieden* (Paderborn 1969), 179.

[52] About this archbrotherhood, see L. Just, "Beiträge zur Geschichte der Kölner Nuntiatur," *QFIAB* 36 (1956), 248–320.

[53] Stensen died 12 May 1686. For almost four months before his death he had waited in vain for a decision from Rome concerning "sia in ordine alla licenza di ritornar in Italia, sia per veder cosa si possa far a Treveri, secondo le instanze dell' Eminentissimo Signor Elettore, sia di veder come posso trattenermi ne' vicariati" (G. Scherz and J. Raeder, eds., *Nicolai Stenonis epistolae et epistolae ad eum datae* II [Hafniae-Friburgi 1952], 894 f.; H. Raab, "Landgraf Ernst von Hessen-Rheinfels und der Jansenismus," *AMrhKG* 19 [1967], 48–56).

[54] H. F. Langwerth v. Simmern, *Aus Krieg und Frieden. Kulturhistorische Bilder aus einem Familienarchiv* (Wiesbaden 1906), 83–254.

of the Strasbourg diocese,[55] his successors Gabriel Haug and the Titular Bishop of Adrianople, Johann Peter Quentel (d. 1710), from the well-known Cologne family of printers, who last worked in Münster. Others who deserve mention by virtue of their political or diplomatic missions, or the promotion of science and art during the eighteenth century are the suffragan bishops Nalbach of Trier, Jacquet of Liège, Toussaint Duvernin of Strasbourg,[56] and Ungelter of Augsburg.[57] For personal achievements in the areas of historical research, canon law, reforms of church life, and a Catholic Enlightenment they were surpassed by the great bourgeois suffragans at the end of the eighteenth century, such as Johann Nikolaus von Hontheim from an old patrician family of Trier; the Mainz suffragans Ludwig Philipp Behlen, the son of a simple Eichsfeld family; and Valentin Heimes, who came from a family of vintners in the Rheingau. In company with the Worms suffragan Stephen Alexander Würdtwein, who prepared a tremendous amount of source material for the history of the Church of the Empire; Suffragan Bishop Seelmann in Speyer, his successor; the prominent canonist Philipp Anton Schmidt,[58] brother of the "historiographer of the Germans"; and, lastly, Dalberg's suffragan Kolborn,[59] they left the imprint of their names upon the final attempts at a reform of the Church in an episcopal sense and upon the theological and canonical discussions of the waning eighteenth century. And finally, after similar demands had been raised here and there in the chapters of Germany, Valentin Heimes attempted at the Congress of Ems to limit the privileges of the nobility within the Church of the Empire in favor of improving the quality of the ministry.

The economic condition of the parish clergy and its education immediately after the Thirty Years' War was poor throughout. Even in the following decades, ravaged by war and epidemics, it was rarely better.

[55] Aldringen's younger brother Johann Markus became canon in Salzburg and Olmütz and was bishop of Seckau from 1633 to 1664. One should really pay attention in research to "bourgeois" bishops' families. A good example is the family of the innkeeper of "The Lion," Hans Jakob Haus from Stein am Rhein near Säckingen. His two sons, Johann Christoph (1652–1725) and Johann Baptist (1672–1745) became suffragan bishops of Basel, as did their great-nephew Johann Baptist Gobel, who later became constitutional bishop of Paris.

[56] J. Gass, *Straßburger Theologen im Aufklärungszeitalter* (1766–90) (Strasbourg 1917), 183–85.

[57] F. Zoepfl, "Weihbischof Ungelter und Christoph Schmidt," *Christoph Schmid und seine Zeitgenossen*, ed. by H. Pörnbacher (Weißenhorn 1968), 43–49.

[58] W. Kratz, "Exjesuiten als Bischöfe 1773–1822," *AHSI* 6 (1937), 200.

[59] H. Raab, "Aus dem Briefwechsel des Aschaffenburger Weihbischofs J.H.K. v. Kolborn mit dem Generalvikar von Konstanz Ignaz von Wessenberg," *Aschaffenburger Jb.* 2 (1955), 98–135.

Abject poverty, hunger, and totally inadequate housing were frequent occurrences. The comment by the deacon of Bingen, Dr. Vogt, regarding the conditions at Niederheimbach pertained to the average income of many priests: "The revenues of the parish priest are such that they do not permit a priestly existence unless he were to sustain himself by means of only bread, milk, and smoked meat, without wine except in autumn, when he may drink cider until the wine is finished and sold."[60]

Greed, gambling, drunkenness, and violation of the law of celibacy in many a place were probably consequences of dire distress. The circumstances explain why many a priest assumed the glebe lands for his own use, disregarding encumbrances and the unavoidable consequences. Patronage rights and incorporation on one hand, surplice fees and oblations on the other, but also economic and spiritual anguish, the difficulties in ministering and trying to lead a pious life can no more than imply the problems of the parish clergy in the second half of the seventeenth century and the early eighteenth century until the reform efforts of the Enlightenment and the parish regulation of Joseph II.

The words of Leonhard Mayr, longtime priest of the court church in Neuburg, expressed in one of his last sermons before his death (1665), apply to many other priests of his time: "Since 1617 I have remained with you through all sorts of adversity, untoward conditions, dearth, through hunger and grief, raging pestilence, in danger of life and limb, never have I forsaken you, but have instead persevered. *Mementote!* Preserve my memory! During that time 2,857 have died; to each of them, except for pestilence, have I given the funeral rites. I have baptized 2,500 children and have had many books put in print."[61]

The parish clergy was often hopelessly overburdened. Given the severe lack of priests during the seventeenth century, the restoration of church life would have been impossible without aid not only by the orders, especially the Capuchins, Carmelites, and the Jesuits, but also by the chapter clergy. The number of monastic parishes in Bavaria and Austria was considerable. The prebendary chapter of Sankt Florian near Linz administered thirty-three parishes; Klosterneuburg near Vienna twenty-three, and in the Cologne deaconry of Zülpich thirty parishes were in the care of religious orders. But these "expositures" led to many an incompatibility for the *expositi*, their monastic establishments, and the secular clergy. On the whole, the end of the eighteenth century not only saw an increase in the number of priests but also a more profound intellectual and religious life within the clergy.

---

[60] A. L. Veit, *Kirchliche Reformbestrebungen im ehemaligen Erzstift Mainz unter Erzbischof Johann Philipp von Schönborn 1647–73* (Freiburg i. Brsg. 1910), 64.
[61] Veit-Lenhart, 217.

In the opinion of contemporary sources of the seventeenth century, seminaries appeared to be the best means to restore and improve church discipline. Given the great need for priests, it was tempting to favor exemplary conduct over theological education, thus enabling a less than ideal alternative to have its effect on the rivalries of the ministering regular clergy. The first seminary in Germany was established in 1564 by Bishop Martin von Schaumburg in Eichstätt over the opposition of his cathedral chapter. But the Swedes destroyed it in 1634 and it could not be reopened until 1710. The seminary of Breslau, founded by the cathedral chapter in 1565 almost against the wishes of its bishop, began to flourish again after the Thirty Years' War under the reign of Archduke Leopold I Wilhelm of Austria (1656–56). The diocese of Ermland had a seminary since 1567; it closed its doors between 1625 and 1637 as a result of the Swedish incursion and was given a new building in 1651. Other seminaries were opened in Würzburg (1570), Salzburg (1577/79), Basel (1606), and Dillingen (1614, for the Augsburg diocese). With the exception of Salzburg these seminaries were unable to develop steadily either because of the vagaries of war or because of financial problems. As was the case in Basel under Prince-Bishop Johann Konrad von Reinach in 1716,[62] they had to be reformed or reestablished in the second half of the seventeenth or during the eighteenth century.

In 1639 the seminary in Münster, established in 1613 and named after Suffragan Bishop Johannes Kridt (d. 9 July 1577), failed. A new seminary was founded in 1776 under Franz von Fürstenberg in the abandoned Benedictine monastery of Überwasser. On 1 December 1615, Archbishop Ferdinand opened a seminary in Cologne with a mere twelve boarding students, but it ceased to exist on 1 May of 1645 as a result of the war. Reopened in 1658/60 with a discouragingly small number of students, it had to be dissolved fifteen years later because of the catastrophic economic condition and the effects of the Dutch War. During its tenure it had produced no more than two novice priests per

---

[62] A letter from the prince-bishop of Basel elucidates the situation: "Il a passé un siècle qu'un de mes prédécesseurs put élever un bâtiment dans ma ville de Porrentrui qui devait servir de Séminaire pour le Clergé de son diocèse, mais côme les guerres ensuites en ont affligé la plus grande partie, ce dessein est demeuré sand exécution. . . . La première raison qui m'y a porté a esté la disposition de l'Église . . . et la seconde estait le dérèglement, l'ignorance et le libertinage qui commençoit à se glisser dans mon Clergé, le tout fautte d'occasion à instruire les Ecclésiastiques dans leurs ministères et à donner de vives corrections à ceux qui s'écartaient à leur devoir." (Quotation from A. Schaer, Le clergé paroissial catholique en haute Alsace sous l'Ancien régime 1648–1789 [Paris 1966], 119).

year.[63] It was not until 1738, after difficult negotiations, that the Seminarium Clementinum was founded. The situation was somewhat better in the archbishopric of Mainz, where Johann Philipp von Schönborn, the "German Solomon," having seen the Institute for a Universal Clergy of Bartholomäus Holzhauser in Gastein, put him in charge of the Mainz seminary in 1660. Holzhauser himself took over the difficult parish of Bingen; for over a century Sankt Emmeran of Mainz, the parishes of Frankfurt, Heppenheim an der Bergstrasse, and Duderstadt were domains of the Bartholomites. Under their guidance the seminary of Würzburg educated 187 seminarians in the years from 1655 to 1679.[64]

The seminary in Osnabrück, founded by the reform bishop Franz Wilhelm von Wartenberg, closed soon after the latter's death (1 September 1661) during the reign of the Protestant pseudobishop Ernst August. The one in Wartenberg's second diocese of Regensburg which he entrusted to the Bartholomites in 1650 and which was reestablished in 1665 under the direction of the Jesuits, continued in spite of considerable difficulties, but did not begin to flourish until the reign of Prince-Bishop Anton Ignaz von Fugger (1769–87).[65]

The college of clerics at the Porta Beatissimae Virginis Mariae developed into a Seminary for a Universal Clergy for the Prince-Abbey of Sankt Gallen because the college was unable to implement its own theological curriculum (1642) as a result of the war.[66]

After the deluge of the Thirty Years' War and given the total impoverishment of the ecclesiastical territories and their deep indebtedness even from the period before the war—in Constance under Prince-Bishop Jakob Fugger (1604–26) it amounted to 200,000 florins—there could be no thought of establishing new seminaries. It was not "a lack of goodwill on the part of the bishops and not a matter of resistance against

---

[63] E. Reckers, *Gesch. des Kölner Priesterseminars* (Cologne 1929), 93.

[64] M. Arneth, *Bartholomäus Holzhauser und sein Weltpriesterinstitut* (Würzburg 1959); A. Werfer and H. Wildanger, *Der ehrwürdige Bartholomäus Holzhauser und sein Weltpriesterinstitut* (Munich 1941); K. Böck, "Bartholomäus Holzhauser," *Lebensbilder aus dem bayerischen Schwaben* 5 (1956), 221–38; K. Braun, *Gesch. der Heranbildung des Klerus in der Diözese Würzburg seit ihrer Gründung bis zur Gegenwart*, 2 vols. (Mainz 1897); A. P. Brück, "Das Mainzer Priesterseminar der Bartholomisten," *AMrhKG.* 15 (1963), 33–94.

[65] G. Schwaiger, *Kardinal Franz Wilhelm von Wartenberg als Bischof von Regensburg (1649–61)* (Munich 1954), 151–71; E. Meißner, *Fürstbischof Anton Ignaz Fugger (1711–87)* (Tübingen 1969), 243f.

[66] J. Duft, *Die Glaubenssorge der Fürstäbte von St. Gallen im 17. und 18. Jh. Ein Beitrag zur Seelsorgsgeschichte der katholischen Restauration als Vorgeschichte des Bistums Sankt Gallen* (Lucerne 1944), 103ff.

the idea of seminaries as such, but primarily the question of finances which created the greatest difficulty."[67]

The papal seminaries in Fulda and Dillingen, to be sure, provided some relief and the relatively well educated monastic clergy successfully took part in the ministry. Yet the fact that many bishops had to have their theologians trained in the orders or in foreign and often backward universities was rather disadvantageous for the Church of the Empire. There was a noticeable discrepancy between the meager and sometimes very poor conditions in the training of priests and the background of monumental architecture in the ecclesiastical states; in the mediate chapters, there was a vivid contrast between many a poor village church and splendid monastic libraries.[68] The difficulties encountered by the large diocese of Chur in the education of its priests are well known. Supported by only a small prince-bishopric and scant revenues, its attempts to obtain a seminary were fruitless throughout the seventeenth century. Until the time of Napoleon it had to depend on the Jesuit college in Feldkirch, which was abolished in 1773, and on vacancies in Rome, Milan, Vienna, and Dillingen. Not until the end of the seventeenth and the first decades of the eighteenth century, when the worst aftermath of the war had been overcome by the *Germania Sacra*, were existing seminaries restored and new ones opened. This development was accompanied by a new striving for reforms especially during the reign of the Schönborns, to whom four seminaries owed either their existence or their support. Wilhelm Egon von Fürstenberg founded a seminary for the diocese of Strasbourg (1683) which enjoyed an excellent reputation up to the end of the eighteenth century. He also relocated the Catholic university of Molsheim to the episcopal seat. After all its attempts since the Salzburg Synod of 1569 had failed, the bishopric of Freising finally obtained a seminary in 1691, thanks to an unequivocal demand by Pope Innocent XI.[69]

---

[67] E. Reckers, *Kölner Priesterseminar*, 25.

[68] Some light is shed on the morals of the students of theology, for example at the University of Dillingen. Immediately before Sailer's appointment there prevailed, "especially among the students of theology, the most immoderate drunkenness, even in the dormitory, and the zeal for study had slackened." (Quotation from H. Schiel, *Johann Michael Sailer, Leben und Briefe* I [Regensburg 1948], 84).—The impressions gathered by the regent of the Würzburg seminary for priests, the future suffragan bishop Fahrmann, on a trip for "seminary, literary, architectural purposes" in 1787 are most informative. The Strasbourg Seminary made the best impression on him: "Discipline here is by far not as strict as in Besançon, yet it works fairly well. The students are cheerful and filled with respect and love toward their superiors." (Quotation from J. Gass, *Straßburger Theologen im Aufklärungszeitalter* [Strasbourg 1917], 3).

[69] B. Hubensteiner, *Die geistliche Stadt Welt und Leben des Johann Franz Eckher von Kapfing und Liechteneck, Fürstbischofs von Freising* (Munich 1954), 157.

Seminaries were founded in Königgrätz (1706) and Leitmeritz (1736). But in Speyer and Trier the training of clerics was insufficient until the turn of the eighteenth century. The boarding seminary of the Speyer cathedral chapter had perished in the tumult of the Thirty Years' War. During the warring seventeenth century there had not been enough money, and so it was not until 1723 that Prince-Bishop Damian Hugo von Schönborn was able to establish a pastoral seminary.[70] Trier did indeed have the Bantus Seminary founded in 1586/92 and, after 1667, there was the aristocratic, lavishly endowed Lambertus Seminary established by an endowment of Ferdinand von Buchholtz,[71] but it hardly produced any ministering clergymen. The strange founding of a seminary in Koblenz during the reign of Elector Franz Ludwig von Pfalz-Neuburg, who forwent consecration for dynastic and political reasons, illuminates the difficulty of the conditions at that time. In Koblenz twelve younger but not yet sufficiently educated priests were supposed to live together with eight older ones and thus further their education in theology and canon law.[72] Not until the reign of the last Trier elector-archbishop, Clemens Wenzeslaus von Sachsen, was a satisfactory solution found in the form of the *Seminarium Clementinum*. Under the influence of reform-Catholic efforts and a moderate administrative enlightenment, a considerable improvement took place in the condition of the ministering clergy. This included the establishment of houses for retired priests and a better education of recruits for the priesthood. The Bamberg seminary was reformed under Prince-Bishop Friedrich Karl von Schönborn (1729–46); his brother Damian Hugo opened the seminary of Constance (1734–35),[73] and the third great Schönborn of that generation, the elector of Trier and prince-provost of Ellwangen Franz Georg, founded the seminary on the Schönenberg. In Paderborn the Harsewinkel *Seminarium clericorum* came into being in 1776. In the waning years of the prince-bishopric of Chur, where the education of priests was endangered by the abolition of the Society of Jesus and the loss of student vacancies in Rome, Milan, Vienna, and Dillingen, Gottfried Purtscher opened a small seminary in Meran on 9 September 1800, but this was closed again by the provisions of the Peace of Preßburg after the attack on Tirol by Bavaria.

---

[70] O. B. Roegele, "Damian Hugo von Schoenborn und die Anfänge des Bruchsaler Priesterseminars," *FreibDiözArch* 71 (1951), 5–51.

[71] P. A. Reuß, *Gesch. des bischöflichen Priesterseminars zu Trier* (Trier 1890).

[72] P. Reitz, "Das zweite Koblenzer Priesterseminar von 1728," *Pastor bono* 40 (1929), 54–58.

[73] F. Hundsnurscher, *Die finanziellen Grundlagen für die Ausbildung des Weltklerus im Fürstbistum Konstanz vom Tridentinischen Konzil bis zur Säkularisation mit einem Ausblick auf die übrigen nachtridentinischen Bistümer Deutschlands*, (diss., Freiburg i. Brsg. 1968).

CHAPTER 11

Spain and Portugal to 1815

The General Intellectual Situation

The structure of the Spanish and Portuguese Church from 1650 to 1815 was determined by the rules and mentality of the *ancien régime*. It was a socially privileged Church with significant agricultural and urban assets, with an unchallenged authority over the faithful. Based on a religious foundation, it also exerted its influence on the bureaucracy of the state. The period falls into two divisions: the century from 1650 to 1750 bears a counterreformational character, while the period from 1750 to 1815 should be considered part of the Enlightenment. However, this concept demands refinement. Was the Spanish Enlightenment Catholic or antireligious? Was it an importation or did it stem from inner dynamics, although characterized by foreign elements? What relationship was there between the Spanish Enlightenment, the Encyclopedists, and the French Revolution? Was it congruent in time with the rest of Europe? These questions contain a number of stimulating problems which cannot be comprehensively or even adequately solved here, but must be mentioned briefly in order to provide a perspective towards a better understanding of this period. The three basic components of the "enlightened Spaniard" as he was represented by a good many clerics of that time were: a Catholic education, European culture and a social and economic reformative zeal.

In its origins, the Spanish Enlightenment was not antireligious. While anticlerics and disbelievers could have joined it, all the typical exponents of the Spanish Enlightenment were Catholic. The clergy especially, being most prominent in the life of the nation, were considered the great representatives of this form of the Enlightenment. The fact that the most pressing problem was socioeconomic reform, with the state as its most important instrument, was not accompanied by scorn for the supernatural order and even less by opposition to it. And if the authority of the state did usurp the rights of the Church in a pernicious and extremely destructive manner, it was an error on the part of the authority and not of the Enlightenment. Similar to the Renaissance, Enlightenment existed only in its various shadings according to the perception of those who adapted to it.

The representatives of the four generations of the Spanish Enlightenment, referred to by Vicens Vives[1] and adopted here according

[1] J. Vincens Vives, *Approximación a la Historia de España* (Barcelona 1960), 175.

to their respective generations are Feijóo (1676–1764), Flórez (1702–1783), Campomanes (1723–1802), and Jovellanos (1744–1811). The first two were prominent personalities from religious orders. Jovellanos was tonsured and, although not ordained, remained loyal to the principles of his ecclesiastical office. Campomanes, one of the great regalists of his century, was educated by his uncle, the capitular of Oviedo, and by the Dominicans of Santillana; he steadfastly avowed his Catholicism.

The Geographic, Sociographic, and Economic Situation

At this time Spain had eight Church provinces and 56 bishoprics. Only one change was brought about in the seventeenth century: the loss of the bishopric of Elna when Roussillon became French (1659). Four new dioceses were founded in the eighteenth century: Santander (1754), Tudela (1783), Ibiza, and Minorca (1795), so that the number of bishoprics was 59 by the end of the century.

At the end of the sixteenth century the population of the Iberian Peninsula totaled 9,485,000; of those 1,250,000 were in Portugal. About three-fourths, that is 6,910,000, were in Castile. According to Felipe Ruiz there were 33,087 secular clerics, 26,297 monks, and 20,369 nuns. These amounted to 11.33 per thousand of the population. These figures contradict the exaggeration in that part of the secondary literature where the number of clerics is given at 200,000. By the end of the seventeenth century the total population of Spain decreased considerably due to wars and epidemics, but by 1797 it again increased to a total of 10,541,221. According to Canga Argüelles this figure included 57,488 secular clerics, 49,365 monks, and 24,007 nuns. The number of clerics also contained those who had received minor orders. The 73,372 monks and nuns were distributed among forty-three orders. The male orders owned 2,104 houses and the female orders 976.

At the beginning of the nineteenth century the Spanish Church had 59 bishoprics and, beyond that, 648 dignities, 1,768 prebends, 216 pensions and 200 half-pensions in the cathedrals and collegiate churches. There were 64 collegiate and 16,481 parish churches.[2] The wealth of the Church at that time has been exaggerated just as much as the number of clerics. Yet it must be noted that the economic condition of the Church was good. As in society at large, there existed a significant

---

[2] *Censo de población de las provincias y partidos de la Corona de Castilla en el siglo XVI* (Madrid 1829); J. Nadal, *Historia de la población española (siglos XVI a XX)* (Barcelona 1966); Felipe Ruiz, "La población española en los tiempos modernos," *Cuadernos de Historia. Anexos de la revista Hispania* 1 (1967), 189–202; Miguel Artola, *La España del Antiguo Régimen* (Salamanca 1967); José de Canga Argüelles, *Diccionario de Hacienda* (Madrid 1833).

inequality between the higher and the lower clergy. The most important source of revenue was the *diezmo*, the tenth part of the agrarian gross income. But it fluctuated according to the harvest. In 1592 the annual income of the Church amounted to 10,400,000 ducats; by 1638 it had decreased to 7,000,000. In addition there were the simple benefices and the religious foundations. But these revenues were decreased by a number of contributions to the state or the Roman or national church administration, such as annates, bishops' subsidies, pensions, welfare funds, monthly assessments, etc. There were also the church seigniories, which were dependent on bishoprics, monasteries, or other church bodies. Most of this economic system disappeared in the nineteenth century, together with the *ancien régime*.

Portugal had three church provinces and sixteen dioceses during the eighteenth century.

The Development of Ecclesiastical Institutions

In the present state of research it is not easy to render a complete picture of the hierarchy, but some general characteristics can be pointed out.

In spite of political decadence, church discipline did not deteriorate. The lateral transfer of prelates was more frequent in the earlier years. From the point of view of the pastoral administration it was possible that this practice was commendable. The question then is whether the motive should be sought in rank or remuneration.

Towards the end of the seventeenth century there was an increase in the appointments of bishops from the ranks of religious orders. We do not know the reasons for this phenomenon. Rome did not have full confidence in the Spanish episcopate; several expressions of distrust were voiced regarding its loyalty to the disciplinary norms of the Curia. The episcopate was assumed to be subservient to the court. It was suspected of standing up more for the fulfillment of its own material interests than for the defense of church jurisdiction and the decisions of the Roman Curia. The latter therefore called the attention of the nuncios to this situation and to the existing tension between the lower clergy, organised in a large association called the *Congregación del clero de Castilla y de León*, and the residing bishops. The nuncios were recommended, whenever justified, to support the demands of the cathedral chapters against the bishops, thereby making them ever more dependent on the will and the protection of the nuncios. Was there a reason for the state secretariat to interpret the situation in this manner? No doubt there was a danger that being dependent on the King for promotion to a better paid or more prestigious position could change into a golden cage. On the other hand, there was criticism in Spain of the Curia and the nepotism of Popes and members of the Curia. The sources do not reveal that the submissiveness of the episcopate to the King or his dynastic concerns was a fundamental disadvantage for the Church. Devotion to the King had its limits; in every case we know of the bishop either accepted the royal decrees in accordance with his conscience or he freely argued his pastoral duties when these did not permit him to obey such decrees. Conversely, opposition of Spanish bishops to the Curia was frequently aimed at the latter's centralism and fiscalism or the anti-Spanish policies of Popes. In the seventeenth century Spain had neither a political and theological episcopacy, as did France, nor did the episcopate form a united front with a more or less uniform mentality for or against Rome or Madrid.[3]

In the middle of the eighteenth century the historian and enlightened reformist Gregorio Mayáns y Siscar (1699–1781) deplored the lack of interest of some bishops in culture and enlightenment and their pre-occupation with Scholasticism. Yet the research by J. Sarrailh proves that most of the bishops made great efforts in the area of charity and material improvement within their dioceses. Since they were generally of modest origins, they stayed in contact with their faithful. J. Sarrailh presents a list of such "charitable" bishops whose energy was applied to ameliorating misery and to promoting the well-being of their sees. He also points out the "economically active" bishops who promoted public buildings and established schools and houses for the poor.

Within the episcopate a group of Jansenist bishops[4] attained prominence. Though small, it was extremely active and influential: Asensio Salas and José Climent, both of them bishops of Barcelona, Felipe Bertrán of Salamanca, Antonio Tavira, also of Salamanca and later of Osma, as well as others. As bishop of Salamanca, Tavira—in the company of the bishop and the archdeacon of Cuenca and two capitulars of the chapter of San Isidoro—regularly attended the meetings of the duchess of Montijo, who had translated the Jansenist work *Instrucciones cristianas sobre el sacramento del matrimonio*, whose foreword was written by Bishop Climent.

At the end of the eighteenth century (19 November 1799) the Austrian ambassador to Madrid, Kageneck, had some disparaging things to say about the bishops of that time. According to him they had no influence on the government, in spite of their wealth, nor did they form a social body within the monarchy. Yet all the while they represented a high level of authority for the pious faithful in the provinces. He con-

---

[3] Q. Aldea, *Iglesia y Estado en siglo XVII* (Comillas [Santander] 1961), 105–08.
[4] A. Mestre, *Ilustración y Reforma de la Iglesia* (Valencia 1968), 219–29.

tinues by saying that it was the custom of the Spanish cabinet of the time not to select highly intelligent people for high offices and none at all who could pose a serious threat to the regime. Kageneck did not reproach the high clergy so much in regard to morality, but referred to the majority of the prelates as insignificant, of low estate, occasionally given to intrigues once they attained positions of leadership, and of being covetous of honor and money. He describes the Spanish episcopate at the end of the *ancien régime* thusly: "The majority of prelates who play a very small part at the court and rarely appear in the capital are very pious but also very hard-hearted."[5] No doubt this is a generalization and exaggeration; at any rate this judgment can not be applied to the whole century. The fact that the bishops were not as submissive as could be assumed was evidenced on the occasion of the regalia decree of Urquijo (5 September 1799). Of sixty-one bishops only ten agreed to it, among them the leaders of the Jansenists, Antonio Tavira, bishop of Salamanca, and Francisco Mateo Aguiriano, bishop of Calahorra (see below). Regardless of all the weakness of the system, this century had great bishops, such as Belluga, Valero, and Lorenzana.

As in other countries and times, the lower clergy, too, was deeply in need of reform and adaptation. To be sure, the demands of the Council of Trent for reforms were theoretically still in force. But a broad spectrum of the clergy—with the exception of some select groups—lagged far behind the priestly ideal. Ignorance, stinginess, and a wordly spirit were the deficiencies castigated by Cardinal Belluga, bishop of Cartagena, in his lengthy pastoral letter of 1705. In order to remove these ills, Innocent XIII, with the help of Belluga, issued the bull *Apostolici ministerii* (13 May 1723) containing twenty-six points for the reform of the clergy. This bull replaced the provincial councils, advocated by the archbishop of Toledo, Francisco Valero, and the national council, demanded by some politicians. From 1650 to 1815, as a consequence, no provincial councils were convened, the only exception being the province of Tarragona, where seventeen meetings were called, the majority of them to deal with economic matters.[6]

Preaching had declined from the classical ideal of the "Golden Era" of Spain, which boasted of so many exemplary teachers. Even Belluga deplored the foolishness of the sermons "full of exquisite voices, exuberant phrases, and hairsplitting concepts." Father Francisco Isla fought against this by means of his burlesque *Fray Gerundio de Campazas*, in which he ridiculed the severe shortcomings of contemporary sermons.

[5] R. Olaechea, *Las relaciones hispano-romanas en la segunda mitad del XVIII* II (Saragossa 1965), 586.
[6] Rafael Serra Ruiz, *El pensamiento social-politico del Cardenal Belluga* (Murcia 1963), 242–47.

This in turn brought down upon the Jesuits the wrath of other orders who felt they were the accused. But there was a sizeable school of parish missionaries who regularly traversed the peninsula. Dominicans, Franciscans and Capuchins competed in this apostolic task, but the Jesuits were the leaders. One of the most prominent parish missionaries of this period was Father Jerónimo López (1589–1658), who untiringly wandered through Catalonia, Aragon, Valencia, the Balearic Islands, Navarre, and many villages of the two Castiles. He was the author of the well-known *Acto de contrición*, a pious book of devotions with which he went through the streets delivering sermons. His pastoral successor was Father Tirso Gonzáles (1624–1705), who later became general of the Society of Jesus. Accompanied by many helpers he made 120 trips in northern Spain alone in a period of four years (1671–75), many of which lasted more than twenty days. Other great parish missionaries were the Jesuit Pedro de Calatayud (1689–1773) and the blessed Diego de Cádiz, a Capuchin. These missions were extremely fruitful; above all they revived the practice of the sacrament among the masses.

A typical form of piety in this period was the Sacred Heart devotion. It was propagated by Fathers Cardaveraz (d. 1720), Bernardo de Hoyos (d. 1735), Juan de Loyola (d. 1762), and Pedro de Calatayud. In his apostolic travels Calatayud founded congregations whose members were pledged to dedicate themselves to the Sacred Heart devotion, to confess monthly, and to receive Communion. Along with the parish missions, though without the fanfare, went retreats which gradually changed the lives of certain groups of priests and laymen.

In Portugal there were two great figures who deserve special mention, Antonio Vieira (1608–97), called "the Portuguese Demosthenes," and Manuel Bernardes, more esteemed as an author than as an orator.

The persecution of the Jesuits started in Portugal, a country most favored by the society. Under the weak King José I, his minister, the Marquis de Pombal, reigned supreme. Pombal ordered the confiscation of all Jesuit property in 1759 and a few months later their expulsion. Seventeen hundred Jesuits (aside from the nine hundred missionaries) were expelled in a most brutal fashion, deported to the Papal States, or incarcerated in dirty jail cells in their own homeland. Some twenty Jesuit schools were taken over by laymen.

The Jesuits in Spain had great influence and practically a monopoly in the educational system, having a total of 130 colleges. This was one of the causes leading to a tragedy in Spain similar to the one in Portugal. Other reasons for the expulsion were: prejudices on the part of those who had earlier felt themselves disadvantaged by the Jesuits, their assumed wealth, the close connection of the Society of Jesus with the Pope, the suspected opposition to the authority of the King (the Jesuits were said to have been responsible for the rebellion of Esquilache), theological differences of opinion, especially on the issue of probabilism, which many orders and bishops, such as Lorenzana and Armañá, condemned as laxism but without actually knowing it. In addition there was their political and social influence, and finally, the example of Portugal and France. The trial did not take place in the *Consejo* of Castile, as had been the custom, because there the majority favored the Jesuits. For this reason the famous *Consejo extraordinario* was convened, excluding all having any connection with the Jesuits. During the night of 2 and 3 April 1767, all Spanish Jesuits, approximately twenty-seven hundred, with twice that number overseas, were driven from their homeland without having been given a hearing or having been properly convicted. Fear of repression by the King suppressed all protest. The reasons for this decision remained a secret of Charles III. Through his ambassador in Rome, Moñino, he obtained from Clement XIV the brief *Dominus ac Redemptor* (21 July, 1773). When in 1769 the King questioned fifty-six bishops, forty-two of them agreed with the measures against the society, six abstained, and eight opposed them.[7]

The decree *Pro Seminariis* of the Council of Trent, stipulating the establishment of a seminary in every diocese, was at first followed conscientiously. But the difficulties encountered militated against further implementation. Among those were the large number of colleges, which absorbed the elite of the youth, and the high cost of constructing the necessary buildings. But more important than the construction costs were the direction of seminaries, the selection of applicants and the curricula, which were generally antiquated. By the end of the sixteenth century twenty seminaries were founded; in the seventeenth century eight, and in the eighteenth century seventeen, for a total of forty-five by 1816. Of the thirteen seminaries existing in Portugal by that year, five were established in the eighteenth century.

As everywhere in Europe, Scholasticism and above all theological studies at the universities slowly regressed. There was a lack of originality and realism. One was satisfied with composing the no doubt necessary *cursus* or compendium of theological or philosophical knowledge for the use in schools. But in the background of Scholasticism were the new philosophy, the Enlightenment, and the positive sciences. There were significant personalities nonetheless, such as Cardinal Alvaro Cienfuegos (d. 1737), Pedro Manso (1736), Luis de Losada, Francisco Armañá and others. The moral theologian Miguel de Molinos

---

[7] V. Rodríguez Casado, "Iglesia y Estado en el reinado de Carlos III," *Estudios Americanos* 1 (1948–49), 5–57; F. Tort, *Francisco Armanyá* (Villanueva and Geltrú 1967), 113–48.

(1628–96) gave rise to a great controversy when sixty-eight propositions of his *Spiritual Guide* (Rome 1675) were condemned as quietistic by Innocent XI.

Historical studies flourished considerably through men such as José Sáenz de Aguirre, Enrique Flórez (author of the *España sagrada*), Andrés Burriel, and Jaime Villanueva. There was a group of literary figures of great quality, such as Benito Feijóo, Francisco Isla, and the group of exiled Italian Jesuits.[8] Among the religious authors who should be mentioned were the venerable Mother Agreda (d. 1665), who was often consulted by Philip IV, and Manuel de Reguera y Álvarez de Paz, and the Portuguese Luis Brandão and Alonso de Andrade.

The authority of the Inquisition decreased considerably, as can be seen by the number of autos-da-fé held at the time: there were 782 under Philip V, 34 under Ferdinand VI and only a dozen under Charles III and Charles IV. The last condemnation by the Inquisition was pronounced in Seville on 7 November 1781.

The royal confessors, who did not limit themselves to the sacraments but freely interfered in the problems of state, enjoyed great esteem. In the council of state they had a voice and a vote just like any other member of the council.

Under the Habsburgs those positions were occupied by the Dominicans. Among the confessors of Philip IV were Antonio de Sotomayor, archbishop of Damascus and inquisitor general, and Juan de Santo Tomás, a famous Portuguese theologian. Under Charles II the position again was entrusted to the Dominicans, but Queen Mariana, following the custom of the imperial court, brought along Father Eberhard Nidhard. The Spanish Bourbons followed French custom: Philip V had as his confessor the Jesuit Daubenton. The last and probably best known of the Jesuit confessors was Francisco de Rávago, professor of theology at the Roman college and provincial of Castile.

In the course of the sixteenth century and at the beginning of the seventeenth century twenty Spanish saints were canonized, whereas the period we are discussing here lists only two: José Oriol (1650–1702) and José Pignatelli (1737–1811).

Church and State

Relations between Spain and the Holy See rested on the principle of the two authorities: the papal and the royal authority, each supreme in its realm. But the person of the Pope had an additional position: not only was he the successor of Saint Peter, but the prince of the Papal States as

---

[8] M. Batllori, *La cultura hispano-italiana de los jesuitas expulsos* (Madrid 1966).

well. In cases of doubt the Spanish politicians followed the delimitation formulated by Gabriel Pereira: if there is doubt whether a civil law violates the ecclesiastical weal, the decision of the Pope has to be adhered to. Whenever there is doubt whether it violates the political weal, the decision of the civil authorities prevails. These principles were applied in the theory of the indirect authority of the Pope in Spain under the Habsburgs, and the concepts of the great Spanish writers Vitoria, Molina, Mariana, Suárez and others were followed. Just shortly before the Bourbons took over the reign, Bossuet formulated his views of the divine origin of the monarchs' absolute power on which the Bourbons based their interference in church affairs, especially in the second half of the eighteenth century (see Chaps. 4 and 7).[9]

The legal claims of royal intervention were based—over and above his general position as a Christian prince—on the obligation to ensure observation of the decrees of the Council of Trent and, above all, on the royal patronage of Spain, from which the missions patronage over the West Indies is derived as well. The institution of the patronage in Spain was traced to the sixth canon of the twelfth Council of Toledo (681) and formulated by Philip II (1565) in the first law, section six of the first volume of the *Nueva recopilación* as follows: "Legally and on the basis of old custom, just claims as well as apostolic concessions we are patrons of all cathedral churches of these kingdoms and are entitled to appoint the archbishops and bishops, the prelates and abbots of these kingdoms even if they fall vacant in Rome." The following were the decisive steps in the development of the patronage system: The granting of universal and eternal patronage over the Kingdom of Granada, the Canary Islands and Puerto Real (from this was derived in part the royal patronage over the West Indies), which was granted by the bull *Orthodoxae Fidei* (13 December 1486) by Sixtus IV; the granting of presentation in the cathedrals and consistorial benefices for the rest of Spain by a bull of Hadrian VI (6 September 1523); the granting of the royal universal patronage over the entire national territory by virtue of the concordat of 11 January 1753. Benedict XIV reserved for himself no more than the granting of fifty-two benefices. This constituted the climax of the presentation privilege in Spain.[10]

Since the reign of Philip II, Spain and Portugal had been united under the Spanish crown. In 1640 the Portuguese rose up against Philip IV and crowned Juan IV (1640–70) King. This posed great problems for the Holy See, not just because of the diplomatic recognition of the new King, but also regarding the filling of vacant bishoprics in Portugal,

---

[9] Q. Aldea, *Iglesia y Estado en el siglo XVII,* 57–63.
[10] Ibid., 63–111.

which was the King's prerogative. The conflict lasted until the consolidation of Portuguese independence. In 1670 relations between Portugal and Rome were resumed and the bishoprics filled.

A special role was played by the *Gravamina Ecclesiae Hispanae.* In 1632 the parliamentary estates of Castile and León submitted to the King a petition listing the encumbrances of the Spanish Church by the Roman Curia and the nunciature in Madrid. The number of complaints, especially against the dataries, increased until the end of the eighteenth century. Several Spanish cardinals, such as Zapata and Gil de Albornoz, criticized the granting of marriage dispensations, the filling and authentication of church benefices, and the distribution of pensions from them. The complicated fees in the case of marriage dispensations, their high rates (two tables from the end of the seventeenth and eighteenth centuries have been preserved), and their arbitrary application led to Cardinal Zapata comparing the datary with a house of commerce. Complaints against the Apostolic Chamber in connection with the *spolia* and the revenues of vacant bishoprics did not cease until the publication of the Concordat of 1753, whose ARTICLE 20 granted these revenues to the church where they originated. The Madrid nunciature was accused of economic and jurisdictional abuses, the latter as well bearing close connection with economic factors. It was accused of charging inordinately high fees, accepting original law suits, making illegal demands for gold and silver money, issuing marriage dispensations contravening the decrees of the Council of Trent and so forth. In 1634 when repeated protests on the part of the ambassadors in Rome, especially by the ambassadors extraordinary Pimentel and Chumacero, were rejected, Madrid used the pretext of the death of Nuncio Campeggi to discontinue the activities of the Madrid nunciature for the period of one year. The so-called agreement of Nuncio Facchinetti of 1640 brought about a new table of rates, but until the Concordat of 1753 and essentially until 26 March 1771, when the Spanish *Rota* was established according to the model of the Roman *Signatura iustitiae*, the problem remained unsolved.[11]

"Regalism," that is the abuse of privileges or rights of the King in church matters, is an ambiguous concept. Regarding Spanish regalism one has to differentiate between the reign of the Habsburgs and that of the Bourbons. One must also take into consideration the dialectics of a modern state with its steadily growing administrative autonomy and the intimate ties between Church and state of earlier epochs. The inordinate extent of ecclesiastical immunity of persons as well as properties had

[11] Ibid., 115–85.

created a state within the state and triggered considerable tensions. This explains the origin of recourse to the King, the reticence of papal bulls and the laws of amortization. Yet these events are also a page in the process of secularization of modern society, manifesting itself in the usurpation of spiritual tasks and hostility towards ecclesiastical institutions.[12]

After 1700, when the first Bourbon, Philip V, had ascended the throne of Spain, monarchical absolutism following the French example was intensified by attempts to limit the independence of the Church. Regalism, more radical than ever before, was turned against the papal reservations which had developed into a sort of "regalism of the pope." One of the bishops fighting against Roman centralism was Francisco de Solis, bishop of Ávila and later of Córdoba, who in 1709 composed the famous *Dictamen sobre los abusos de la Corte Romana por lo tocante a las regalías de su M.C. y jurisdicción que reside en los obispos*. He went so far as to maintain that: "On the basis of these privileges His Majesty is permitted and even obligated to protect His kingdoms and churches from the slavery of the Roman Curia and to liberate them from it . . ." He was referring to the illegal limitation of the authority of bishops, without however going into the opposite extreme.

Philip V reacted violently against the recognition of Archduke Charles as King of Spain, a step forced upon Clement XI during the War of Sucession (1700 until 1715). He founded the *Junta Magna*, which on 25 February 1709 ordered the nuncio expelled and the nunciature closed, the *spolia* and revenues of vacant bishoprics sequestered and all relations of Spanish ecclesiastics with Rome prohibited. These were restored after the Peace of Utrecht (1713) and a provisional concordat concluded in 1717. The concordat was broken a year later when the nuncio was expelled again; only in July 1720 was he permitted to return to Madrid.

When Charles III ascended to the throne (1759) the front of the advocates of regalism hardened. The political and ecclesiastical complications brought about by the letter of exhortation of Parma, the expulsion of the Society of Jesus, the Fourth Mexican Provincial Council (1771) and the State Junta (1784), with its famous *Instrucción reservada,* were manifestations of an extreme regalism. Charles IV followed along this path until the publication of the decree of 5 September 1799. It provided that the Spanish bishops in case of a *sedes vacans* of the Holy See "would in accordance with the old church discipline make use of all their faculties for marriage dispensations and other powers," without

---

[12] Alberto de la Hera, *El Regalismo Borbónico* (Madrid 1963).

regard to the papal reservations.[13] This betrayed the extreme philosophy of the royal minister Urquijo, whom a good many people called a schismatic. But actually this event proved the words of the Austrian ambassador Kageneck right, who said that "schisms are not possible in Spain."[14]

After the eradication of the *ancien régime* by the French Revolution the vestiges of Bourbon regalism gradually died out in Spain. The rebellion of Porto in 1820 signaled the beginning of new ideas in Portugal and the start of an epoch of liberalism in both countries.

[13] J. A. Llorente, *Colección Diplomática* (Madrid 1809), 65–66. This book contains some of the letters of reply concerning the above-mentioned decree; Luis Sierra, *La reacción del episcopado español ante los decretos de matrimonios del ministro Urquijo de 1799 a 1813* (Bilbao 1964).
[14] R. Olaechea, *Las relaciones hispano-romanas en la segunda mitad del XVIII* II, 585.

CHAPTER 12

*The Condition of the Catholics in Great Britain and Ireland
in the Seventeenth and Eighteenth Centuries*

The Early Stuarts

The history of English Catholicism in the first half of the seventeenth century has already been treated briefly. What remains to be added is that English Catholicism at this time had already assumed the social structure which it was to retain until the great Irish immigration during the Industrial Revolution. The faith survived in isolated groups on the estates of individual rural aristocrats who supported the clergy and consequently demanded a certain amount of control over them. The same structure also dominated among the few Catholics of the Scottish Lowlands. On the Gaelic islands and in the Scottish Highlands, Catholicism maintained itself in stronger groups. They were efficaciously supported by Franciscan missionaries.[1] In Wales Catholicism was almost completely abolished after 1650 when Puritan preachers introduced the nonconformist tradition.

Ireland, on the other hand, had remained predominantly Catholic. Subject to the English crown but with its own parliament, the island had not developed into a homogeneous nation. At the beginning of the seventeenth century three groups can be clearly distinguished: The old Irish of Gaelic origin; the old English from before the Reformation, and

[1] C. Giblin, *Irish Franciscan Mission to Scotland 1619–1646* (Dublin 1964).

the new English who had come to Ireland since the Reformation. The latter group was Protestant, the former two were Catholic. The Tudors had subordinated their desire for religious conformity to political conquest. The old English, strongly represented in the Tudor parliaments, had seen to it that the penal laws in Ireland were never as strict as in England. In addition, the local administration was in the hands of the old English, so that the laws were not as harshly applied as the government might have wished. After about 1570 the Irish—by nature a conservative people who for religious reasons were little susceptible to Protestantism—had at their disposal a growing number of priests who had been educated on the continent according to Tridentine ideals. A considerable number of Irish seminaries had been established on the continent as early as around 1600. To be sure, the seminary priests did not gain immediate access to the old Irish, but these had suffered so deeply during the Tudor conquest that their Catholic faith had become part of their resistance against the new rulers. The old English, on the other hand, continued to keep their wealth and possessions.[2]

In the early seventeenth century the Irish Catholics fought in vain for a political agreement which was to recognize both their loyalty and their Catholicism. Just as in England, James I continued the Elizabethan penal legislation. He also promoted her policies of colonialization. Extensive settlements, especially in Ulster, brought a strong Protestant element into the country for whose economic acumen the conservative Irish Catholics were no match. The King's policies, moreover, excluded the Catholics from public service. The parliament of 1613 clearly manifested that the Catholic influence on legislation had sharply decreased.[3] Political pressure upon them was maintained; around 1640 the old English Catholics had every reason to fear that in the eyes of the administration they were merely "semisubjects"—as James I had called them—who, like the old Irish, were robbed of their political rights because of their religion and whose right of property was being questioned.

Yet in actual practice there was sufficient tolerance at this time to enable the Catholic Church to carry out a comprehensive reorganisation of its mission. From the colleges on the continent Ireland received enough priests who were trained to teach a people whose religious formation had been neglected for a long time. The Catholic episcopate, too, had been renewed. Even during the reign of Elizabeth nominations to

---

[2] A. Clarke, *The Old English in Ireland 1625–42* (London 1966); P. J. Corish, *The Origins of Catholic Nationalism* (Dublin 1968).

[3] T. W. Moody, "The Irish Parliaments under Elizabeth and James I," *Proceedings of the Royal Irish Academy* 45 (1938–40), 42–81.

the Irish bishoprics had not ceased, although there had at times been lengthy vacancies. From the ranks of the first generation of seminary priests emerged a superior group of bishops who had been appointed around 1620. They were confronted by serious problems, especially on the part of the monastic clergy, who continued to claim the right of extensive missionary authority as it had been granted to them by the Holy See at the time of Elizabeth. But in collaboration with the newly founded Roman Congregation for the Propagation of the Faith the bishops succeeded in establishing a parish system. The monastic clergy calmed down since it now became possible for them to found their own houses. By 1636 the situation had been stabilized by a series of decrees for the Irish mission issued by the Propaganda.[4]

In 1641 the old Irish took up arms in order to reconquer their rights and property. After brief hesitation the old English joined them. United in the Confederation of Kilkenny, they undertook anew an effort to regain their position as "the King's Catholic subjects." Their negotiations with the King were difficult and were further aggravated by the arrival of the papal nuncio, Rinuccini, in 1645, who demanded the restoration of Catholicism on the basis of strict counterreformational principles which did not take into account the complexity of the Irish situation. Several attempts to prevail with his views, even in the face of ecclesiastical censure, finally split the confederation and forced him to leave the country.[5] Thus weakened and divided, Ireland easily fell prey to Oliver Cromwell.

Commonwealth and Restoration

Under Cromwell's rule the two islands had a single administration in the years around 1650. This meant that the more repressive English laws were automatically extended to Ireland as well. Cromwell's concept of "freedom of conscience" condemned the Anglicanism of the High Church of Charles I and Catholicism in like measure. Paradoxically, this meant that the English Catholics were not subject to the bloody persecutions which they had feared because their sympathy had been with the royalists during the civil war. They escaped persecution because they constituted a minority and also because for a time they could successfully claim the principle of freedom of conscience.

The Irish Catholics, on the other hand, suffered a bitter fate. In addi-

---

[4] See B. Jennings, ed., "Acta Sacrae Congregationis de Propaganda Fide 1622–1650," *Archivum Hibernicum* 22 (1959), 28–139.

[5] Rinuccini followed a much stricter direction in Ireland than the papal ambassador Fabio Chigi (the future Pope Alexander VII) took at the peace conference in Münster.

tion to their being Catholics they were viewed as inferior and uneducated, criminal and politically dangerous. Cromwell had conquered the country in a brutal war of extermination. As a general rule, clergymen captured in the war were executed without a trial. Then followed a large-scale process of confiscation. The propertied Catholics were banished to the province of Connaught. A sharp distinction must be made between the continuity of Catholicism in Ireland and England.

When the war was over, a priest—according to an Elizabethan decree of 1585—was guilty of treason by his mere presence in Ireland. As a result many clergymen voluntarily went into exile. Those who stayed were persecuted relentlessly, but after 1654 the government preferred to jail the prisoners or to banish instead of executing them. Only a relatively small number of priests were able to follow their vocation—receiving help in numerous ways and assuming various disguises. Mass was usually celebrated in the open, on the "Mass rock." No doubt this was the most severe test ever faced by the Irish Catholics. Fortunately, it lasted but a short time.

The reorganization of the previous generation had been totally destroyed. Again priests exercised their office by virtue of missionary authority if indeed they had such authority at all. But around 1657 the Propaganda in Rome set up new plans for the Irish mission. By the end of 1659, two bishops had returned to Ireland. On 29 May 1660, Charles II reoccupied the throne of his father.

Following the Restoration, England, Scotland, and Ireland again had separate parliaments, which were now much more powerful than under the early Stuarts. The King, striving to safeguard his personal authority, endeavored to secure the support of his royal cousin, Louis XIV of France. The struggle between King and parliament in England was aggravated by distrust on the part of parliament of the King's benevolence towards the Catholics (Charles himself converted to Catholicism on his deathbed and his brother James, duke of York, the heir apparent, converted shortly after 1668).

In 1670 Charles signed the treaty of Dover with Louis XIV, which parliament countered a year later with an act banishing the Catholic clergy. Charles in turn issued the Declaration of Indulgence in 1672, which extended toleration to the dissenters, including Catholics. But parliament proved to be the stronger. The Test Acts of 1673 and 1678 affirmed the exclusion of Catholics from public life. Although the balance of power between King and parliament was sufficient to guarantee the Catholics enough toleration, some of the Catholic gentry and consequently their tenants and vassals left the faith. Church authority was maintained in a much reduced fashion by a canon chapter established in

1623 by Apostolic Vicar William Bishop. It represented a conservative body with Gallican tendencies in which vacancies were filled by election.

In Ireland, Charles had to accept the fact that power was held by those who had profited by the great land confiscations and now increasingly looked on themselves as the "Protestant Interest." In trying to prove their loyalty, Catholic laymen gave considerable support to a movement known as the "Remonstrance," which wanted to obtain from the Irish Church a declaration of Gallican principles. The resistance of the clergy against this demand, which to some extent can be seen as a justification of Rinuccini's ultramontanistic attitude of twenty years before, came to a head in 1666 during a synod in Dublin. But at this point it had become clear that a large majority of the dispossessed Catholics would not get their property back.

Again the Church had to rebuild its ministry. There were only two bishops remaining in the country and those who lived in exile were politically compromised by the events of the religious conflicts so that they were not permitted to return. There was indeed a real shortage of priests. For almost a decade no new bishops were appointed, but priests were ordained in considerable numbers—often with insufficient or no preparation for their vocation. Both decisions appear to have been made by Rome; no doubt they were the wrong ones.[6]

It was not until 1669 that the first bishops were appointed; by 1671 most of the sees were again occupied. The new bishops were worthy men, some of them even superior. Helped by a greater degree of toleration in the years around 1670, they started the restoration of the parish system by a series of synods and visitations. But toleration was merely relative; congregations continued to be reduced to making use of the "mass rock," although there were some modest chapels or "mass houses" the Catholics were able to establish. But in 1673 a royal proclamation ordered all members of religious orders and clerics with jurisdictional authority to be banished. While this proclamation was not implemented strictly, it did affect an episcopate already in distress. Some of the clerics, ordained in the last decade, now proved themselves unequal to their task. The reconstruction of the parish system led to renewed divergence between the secular and monastic clergy, aggravated by the fact that all the clergy were dependent on gifts by the people, since the Catholic laymen as well as the clergy had lost all their wealth and property.

The Catholics of both islands were exposed to bloody persecutions when Titus Oates instigated a conspiracy in 1678 in order to exclude

---

[6] B. Millett, *Survival and Reorganization 1650–1695* (Dublin 1968), 12–22.

the duke of York from the royal succession.[7] Oates was an unprincipled adventurer and totally untrustworthy, but because of the political hysteria of the time he was able to have an impact. On 11 October 1678 the archbishop of Dublin was arrested; he died in jail in November 1680. The trials in England began on 15 November 1678. More than twenty-five Catholics were executed and the number of those who were jailed ran into the hundreds. The last and best-known victim was the blessed Oliver Plunkett, archbishop of Armagh, who was executed at Tyburn on 1 July 1681. He was the last victim of the conspiracy as well as the last priest to be executed under the penal laws applying at that time.

The hysteria collapsed as quickly as it had arisen. In February 1685 James II followed his brother to the throne. He was an incompetent politican and ignored the fact that at most 10 percent of his English subjects were ready to accept a Catholic monarchy. The birth of a Catholic heir cost him the throne, which went to his Protestant daughter Mary and her husband William of Orange. James fled to France and later returned to Ireland to lead the resistance there.

The great Catholic majority in Ireland had enough freedom to exercise their religion. The bishops received a maintenance from the government and the congregations were established publicly. When James arrived in Ireland, he convened a parliament which promised freedom of religion and the return of confiscated property to the Catholics. But the further course of events was determined by William's victory over the Irish-Jacobite forces, which enabled the "Protestant Interest" to regain its political power.[8]

The Penal Code of the Eighteenth Century

After William's victory the laws excluding Catholics from public life in England were again noticeably tightened up. On the other hand, several laws concerning property proved to be ineffective and the Catholic landed gentry continued to be accepted on the social level. Yet in the following century there were more and more cases of apostasy among them. During the reign of James II there had been about 300,000 professed Catholics, by 1780 this figure had decreased to 70,000.

An act of parliament of 1700 replaced the death penalty decreed in 1585 with life imprisonment. William tended toward a concept of limited toleration practiced in Holland. Although the English Protestants could not quite accept this, there was, in practice, an increasing extent

---

[7] See mainly J. Lane, *Titus Oates* (London 1949).
[8] J. G. Simms, *Jacobite Ireland 1685–91* (London 1969).

of toleration; only a few priests were actually jailed. Those who were under the protection of the Catholic gentry were almost completely safe, although the price of this safety may at times have been a humiliating state of dependence. Other clerics, especially in London, had to execute their office in greater secrecy. Bishop Giffard, the vicar apostolic of the London district, was jailed several times.

The jurisdiction of the bishops had been reestablished in England during the reign of James II. In 1685 John Leyburn was appointed vicar apostolic and in 1688 the country was divided into four districts, each headed by a vicar apostolic. All four vicars were jailed during the revolution, but released afterwards. Their authority over the clergy had to be exercised very carefully, especially over those who were chaplains with the gentry and even more so with the monastic clergy who were against the restoration of the bishops' authority. In 1753 Benedict XIV made a final decision in favor of the bishops.

The only truly predominant figure among the English bishops of the eighteenth century was Richard Challoner (1691–1781), who was head of the London district for more than forty years. Reticent, strict, and very English, he had a great formative influence on Catholicism not only in England but to some extent also in Ireland. He made his influence felt through numerous written works which he composed over and above a life filled with the work of ministry. His *Garden of the Soul* (1740) *Think well on't* (1728), and *Meditations* (1753) became almost synonymous for his kind of spirituality. Challoner was also influential through his translation of the *Imitatio Christi*, the *Confessiones* of Augustine and the *Introduction à la vie dévote* of Francis de Sales. His revision of the bible translation of Douai-Reims continued to be the Holy Scripture most used in England until recently.

The Scottish Catholics were subjected to penal legislation very similar to that of England,[9] but for them it was frequently even more oppressive, since Jacobite sympathies were more widespread in Scotland. In 1653 a priest had been installed for the purpose of directing the Scottish mission and in 1694 Bishop Thomas Nicholson was appointed vicar apostolic. In 1731 two more vicariates were established, one for the Highlands and one for the Lowlands. From the remote hamlet where each bishop had his residence he directed the education of candidates for the priesthood in order to do his part for the next generation which emerged from the Scottish colleges on the continent. The Catholics of the Highlands suffered profoundly under the repression after 1745,

[9] The Act of Union (1707) united England and Scotland into the Kingdom of Great Britain with a single parliament in London.

which led to a lasting wave of emigration, particularly to the country which was given the name "New Scotland" (Nova Scotia).

The minority in Ireland, constituting the "Protestant Interest," was faced by some very complex problems. Theoretically it was obliged to work towards the extermination of Catholicism. But for all practical purposes a mass conversion was unthinkable, since this would have meant an immediate threat to the property which the "Protestant Interest" had gained by confiscation. The religious articles of the Treaty of Limerick (1691) had promised the Catholics even better conditions than had prevailed under Charles II. William wanted to respect these agreements, but after the Treaty of Rijswijk (1697) he was more inclined to give in to the Protestant parliament in Dublin.

An act of 1697 ordered all members of religious orders and clerics with jurisdictional authority banished. Those who returned were put under sentence of death. About five hundred monastic clerics were deported and only three bishops managed to stay. The secular clergy had always enjoyed a certain immunity, an outcome of the resistance on the part of the old English in the Elizabethan parliaments. The aim was to put the clergy under surveillance by means of the Registration Act of 1703 and if possible to oppress them. The act provided for the official registration of one priest for each parish; he had to perform his duties under strict control. There were no provisions at all to fill vacancies. In 1704 a total of 1089 priests registered in accordance with the Registration Act, they included three bishops and a number of priests who can be identified as monastic clerics.

The system of controls and possible extermination collapsed with the Act of Renunciation of 1709, which demanded of each priest an oath renouncing the cause of the Stuarts. Only thirty priests swore the oath. Although new laws were passed for another generation, the government had finally given up its goal of religious conformity and instead pledged itself to a policy of social and political humiliation. The Acts of Banishment and Registration were not consistently implemented. No more priests were condemned to death. To be sure, parliament passed laws, but their implementation was in the hands of an executive answerable directly to the crown. The administrative apparatus was weak, especially in remote areas, and even in Dublin it had to proceed with caution to keep the Catholic masses from rioting.

In spite of the Act of Banishment new bishops were appointed in 1707 and almost all the sees were occupied by 1720. Priests were ordained, some on the continent, others within the country, but the latter all too often were given insufficient preparation. The monastic clergy had a large number of recruits and after 1720 were able to resume a certain measure of communal life. But many of its representatives were not personally engaged and were often in unpleasant competition with the parish priests for the alms of the faithful. In spite of great difficulties the bishops wanted to reinstall a parish clergy. But because their mere presence was legally prohibited, they had to act with caution, especially in times of political tension, as for instance in 1715 or 1745. Poverty was a constant problem and sometimes it was very difficult for them to live in their dioceses for any length of time.

By 1730 a more stable parish system emerged. The conflicts between the secular and monastic clergy were lessened by a number of decisions from Rome, which were reaffirmed by Benedict XIV in 1751.[10] They placed limitations upon the monastic clergy which transcended even the rules prescribed by general canon law. On the other hand, they also limited, perhaps too rigorously, the number of priests to be ordained by any one bishop. Yet the papal decisions were motivated by well-founded grievances, based above all on numerous cases of premature ordination. Within a short time there were complaints concerning the shortage of priests to minister to the growing populace, but this situation was never very serious. The continental colleges took care of the recruits needed for the priesthood until they were closed by the French Revolution and Maynooth assumed their role in 1795.

By the middle of the century the "mass rock" was replaced everywhere by the "mass house." Only in Ulster did this process take longer, because the large-scale settlements at the beginning of the seventeenth century had created a Protestant majority there. For the most part, the parish priests had their own houses and the monastic clergy, too, were able to maintain a communal life. Each of the two groups developed its own missionary field. The offerings of the faithful guaranteed both of them a suitable subsistence. In the eighteenth century Ireland finally found peace and gradual economic improvement. Problems reemerged when England—unlike Ireland—was industrialized. Most of the Catholics remained impoverished. This was the case in all the social classes, even though a small number of the gentry had at least kept some of their estates and a middle class was able to establish a certain affluence from skills and commerce. But it required the first Relief Act of 1782 for new churches to be built. In 1800 a report of the bishops to the government made note that the average annual income of a bishop amounted to 300 pounds sterling and that of a priest to 65 pounds sterling. This constituted a modest but sufficient subsistence.

The long fight for the Mass had inculcated the latter firmly into the

---

[10] See H. Fenning, "John Kent's Report on the Irish Mission 1742," *Archivum Hibernicum* 28 (1966), 59–102.

center of religious life in Ireland. Veneration of the Most Blessed Virgin and above all the Rosary had also become deeply rooted. Catholic teachers, although outlawed, continued to teach religious instruction in cooperation with the clergy. By the late seventeenth century religious tracts in English were widely distributed; during the eighteenth century a sizeable system of publication and distribution was developed. The inventories of book dealers in the second half of the century show that the works of Richard Challoner were the most popular. Almost nothing was printed in the Irish language, but a good many devotionals were distributed by means of copies, a procedure based on a long tradition. These writings, too, were for the most part translations, occasionally from English, but most of them were translations of European works of counterreformational spirituality.

The traditional devotions also survived. The great pilgrimages expecially were kept alive, although the bishops frequently forbade them because of the danger of superstition connected with them. The government also prohibited them because it feared all gatherings of Catholic groups. Modern Irish-Catholic spirituality as it crystallized in the eighteenth century was a mixture of old and new characterized—at least in the English-speaking middle class—by a strict and fearful ethos. This is customarily ascribed to the Jansenist influence, but historically this connection cannot be demonstrated[11] and many other causes can be assumed for it. One of the predominant traits of Irish Catholicism is its traditional severity; even today the popular pilgrimage to Lough Derg is considered a genuine penance. To some extent this attitude is derived from the strict attitude of Challoner, but perhaps more so from the experience of persecution which has been deeply imprinted on Irish Catholic consciousness.

Catholic Emancipation

The Relief Acts canceling the penal laws were prompted primarily by the situation in Ireland, where the consequences of the acts were extremely important. Under the reign of George II (1727–60) suggestions were submitted on numerous occasions which aimed at the approval of a "suitable number" of priests and even some bishops, provided that they would accept a certain measure of government supervision. But these suggestions were unacceptable to parliament. The succession to the throne by George III (1760), the death of the

---

[11] See R. Clark, *Strangers and Sojourners at Port Royal* (Cambridge 1932), 210ff.; C. Giblin, "Catalogue of Material of Irish Interest in the collection *Nunziatura di Fiandra* (Vatican Archives)," *Collectanea Hibernica* 5 (1962), 73ff.

eldest son of James II (1766), and the American Declaration of Rights (1774) created a changed political climate which made it possible to alleviate the condition of the Catholics.

Derived from English tradition, the Declaration of Rights had been partisan to the politically oppressed. A more urgent problem was England's need to increase its army; to this end the Catholics of Ireland and the Scottish Highlands constituted a promising pool of recruits. To call them to arms without granting them a certain measure of political recognition was impossible. So in 1774 an oath of allegiance, couched primarily in political terms, was accepted by parliament and—after some initial hesitation—by the Catholics as well. In 1782 some concrete concessions were made. These were easier to put through in England, but an attempt to expand them to Scotland had to be given up in the face of the Protestant rebellion.

In 1782 the Gallican laity of England founded the Cisalpine Club, which suggested an oath of allegiance for England very similar to the one decreed by James I in 1607. This oath rejected papal power of removal as being "heretical" and in so doing resurrected an issue which had been largely laid to rest. More importantly, the oath withdrew from the Pope all spiritual authority which was not in accordance with the laws and constitutions of the Kingdom. The vicars apostolic resisted, whereupon parliament decided to replace that suggestion with the Irish oath of 1774.

By 1791 full religious emancipation had been achieved in England; in 1793 it was extended to Scotland. The Irish Catholics, too, obtained similar relief, wrested in a long fight from a resisting parliament by a middle class which was developing the beginnings of a Catholic democracy.

Many political deficiencies continued to exist. Their elimination was difficult as long as Ireland, with its sizeable Catholic majority, retained its own parliament. William Pitt, the English prime minister, therefore suggested a common parliament for the two islands with some governmental control of appointments in the Catholic hierarchy. After the sudden loss of all their continental seminaries the Irish bishops had accepted a subsidy from the government when Maynooth was founded in 1795; four years later, in 1799, they accepted in principle a government veto power over appointments of bishops.

The union of the parliaments took place in 1801, but George III refused to support Catholic emancipation, and for a number of years the issue of the veto dominated public and parliamentary discussion. In 1805 the Holy See approved a limited veto privilege and thereby created acceptable conditions for the leaders of the Catholic laity in England. But in Ireland the budding Catholic democracy rejected this concession; in February 1809 the Irish bishops declared the veto to be unacceptable. An opinion from Rome of 1813 and another from Pope Pius VII two years later favored the veto, yet neither of the two opinions appeared to be acceptable to Ireland. In 1813 the Irish Catholic democracy had found a talented leader in Daniel O'Connell. Political emancipation was finally granted in 1829 without creating any obligations for the Church vis-à-vis the government. In consideration of the annual subsidy the curators of Maynooth were the only ones answerable to parliament until the Irish Church Act of 1869.

CHAPTER 13

The Russian Orthodox Church

The rise of the duchy, or rather grand duchy, of Moscow to the tsardom and the close connection of the Orthodox Church of Russia with the rulers in Moscow led to the relocation of the metropolitan see of Kiev and all of Russia to the north. The dependence of the Russian branch Church upon the patriarchate of Constantinople was weakening as was attested to in a letter dated 1393 from Patriarch Antonios to Grand Duke Vasili I (1389–1425). As a result of the election at the Moscow synod (1448) of Bishop Ioanna of Riazan as metropolitan (1448–61), desired by Grand Duke Vasili II (1425–62) and certified in the synod of 1459, the Church for all practical purposes obtained its ecclesiastical independence, even though it was not released from the jurisdictional ties with Constantinople until its elevation to a patriarchate.

Moscow the Third Rome[1]

After the fall of the imperial city on the Bosporus in 1453, the metropolitans, in concert with the rulers of Moscow, expanded their inde-

---

[1] V. Malinin, *Starec Eleazarova monastyrja Filofej i ego poslanija* (Kiev 1901). N. F. Kapterev, *Charakter otnošenij Rossii k pravoslavnomu vostoky v XVI i XVII stoletijach* (Sergiev Posad 1914 = The Hague and Paris 1968), 26–102; N. Zernov, *Moscow the Third Rome* (London 1937); H. Rahner, *Vom ersten bis zum dritten Rom* (Innsbruck 1950); I. Smolitsch, *Mönchtum*, 129–34; H. Schaeder, *Moskau das Dritte Rom* (Darmstadt 1957); W. Lettenbauer, *Moskau das dritte Rom* (Munich 1961); H.-D. Döpmann, *Der Einfluß der Kirche auf die moskowitische Staatsidee* (Berlin 1967), 152–60; K. Onasch, op. cit., 30–34; M. Hellmann, "Moskau und Byzanz," *JGO* n.s. 17 (1969), 338–44. H. v. Rimscha, *Geschichte Rußlands* (Darmstadt 1970), 152–59.

pendence and gradually took over the central position, which had been occupied by Byzantium, the New, the Second Rome, for almost a millennium. The formulation of a "Third Rome" represented an easily remembered symbol for the symbiosis between the Moscow tsars and the metropolitans. In 1472 Ivan III (1462–1505) married as his second wife Sophia (Zoë), niece of the last of the Palaeologoi emperors, Constantinos XI (1448–53). He included the Byzantine double eagle in his coat of arms,[2] assumed the Greek imperial title of autocrat and the Byzantine court ceremonial. In 1492 Metropolitan Zosima (1490–95) designated: "Ivan Vasilevich, chosen by God, loyal to faith, as tsar and autocrat of all of Russia, a new Emperor Constantine for the new Constantinople-Moscow."[3] The writings of Filofei of the monastery of Saint Eleazar near Pskov at the beginning of the sixteenth century reveal the essential ideas of the Third Rome. His letter to Grand Duke Vasili III (1505–33)[4] reads: "For the Church of the Old Rome has fallen by the unbelief of Appollinarian heresy. The doors of the Second Rome, Constantine's city, were shattered by the axes of Hagar's offspring. This is now the Church of the Third, the New Rome, of your sublime realm the Holy Catholic (*sobornyi*) Apostolic Church, which at the ends of the earth shines brighter than the sun in the Orthodox Christian faith on all the earth. Know, Your Majesty, pious tsar, that all the realms of the Orthodox Christian faith together have been transferred into your singular realm. You alone are on all the earth tsar of the Christians."[5]

These utterances should not be overestimated, especially since the panegyrics on the Third Rome were accompanied by admonitions to the orthodox tsar to protect Russia's orthodoxy and the continuance of the Church. But they should not be underestimated either, as though only refugees from Serbia and Byzantium in the Russian grand duchy, the only country not ruled by the infidel, viewed it as "the refuge of orthodoxy, the hope for the liberation of the homeland."[6] Intellectual-historical, political and religious motives, ideas of Rome, New Rome,

[2] M. Hellmann disagrees, op. cit., 330–38.
[3] A. M. Ammann, op. cit., 164.
[4] V. Malinin, op. cit., appendix, 49–66a; H. Schaeder, op. cit., 206–9. Also cf. N. Andrejev, "Filofey and his epistle to Ivan Vasilyevich," *SEER* 38 (1959), 1–31.
[5] H. Schaeder, op. cit., 206–7.—A letter to Michail G. Misjur' Munechin, an official of the grand duke (cf. V. Malinin, op. cit., appendix, 37–47), states, following a similar praise of the tsar: "All Christian realms have vanished and together have merged into the One Realm of our sovereign, according to the prophetic books: That is the Russian Empire. . . . For two Romes have fallen, but the third lives, and there will not be a fourth (H. Schaeder, op. cit., 204).
[6] M. Hellmann, op. cit., 342.

and Jerusalem, Byzantine heritage, a messianic sense of mission and eschatology mingled with each other and formed a concept which was to prove historically powerful. The theory of Moscow as the Third Rome lent to the Orthodox faithful and to the tsar a strong sense of mission, which continued its effect in the Russian ideology of state and empire and was evidenced even in the first decades of the twentieth century in the newly established Moscow patriarchate.[7]

The First Moscow Patriarchate

The ecclesiastical independence existing since the middle of the fifteenth century was under the direction of the metropolitans of Moscow, who—given the symbiosis of Church and state in the grand duchy of Moscow and the growing power of the Moscow tsardom—grew ever more dependent on the state. A new ritual was published by Metropolitan Makari (1542–63) and Tsar Ivan IV (1533–84). The Synod of the Hundred Chapters (1551)[8] solved the conflict between the "Altruistic" and the "Propertied" by compromise. The former were composed of followers of starets Nil Sorski (d. 1508), who advocated a complete separation of Church and state. The latter, called "Josephites" after their founder Iosif of Volokalamsk (d. 1515), were in favor of close collaboration of Church and state and wanted to put at the state's disposal an elite troop to permeate society in the form of a tightly organized monasticism. The rule of terror by Ivan IV (starting in 1560) which gave him the sobriquet "the Terrible," rigorously interfered in the affairs of the Church. Makari's successors tried in vain to put a stop to his ruthless frenzy. Metropolitan Afanasi (1564–66) resigned; Metropolitan German (1566) was driven out; Metropolitan Philip (1566–68) was banished to a monastery and strangled in 1569.[9] Their successors Cyril III (1570–77), Antoni (1577–80), and Dionisi (1581–86) were helpless in the face of Ivan's fury; he traced his autocracy back to God and used church property for purposes of the state. The Church's dependence on the state persisted under Ivan's mentally retarded son Fedor I (1584–98) and the latter's brother-in-law, Boris Godunov, who reigned in his place and followed him as tsar (1598–1605). When Metropolitan Dionisi attempted to limit Godunov's influence, he was removed from office and replaced by Archbishop Job of Rostov (metropolitan: 1586–89, patriarch: 1589–1605). The "dismissals and appointments of hierarchs by the ruler" can be called with some justification "Russian

---

[7] Cf. H. Rahner, op. cit., 18; H. Koch, *Schriften* (incl. biblio.), 195–225.

[8] A. Herman, op. cit., 51–64.

[9] The martyr Metropolitan Filipp was canonized in 1636 as fighter for the truth; in 1652 his remains were brought to Moscow.

Gallicanism."[10] These actions did not prevent the patriarchs of the East who suffered under the supreme rule of the sultan to request and receive gifts from the Moscow tsar. Negotiations and visits made the tsar's authority within the total Orthodoxy grow. In 1585, for instance, Silvester, patriarch of Alexandria, communicated to the tsar "not to let the Holy Places be lacking in his protection."[11] At the same time he prophesied for him the inheritance of Emperor Constantine. These and other utterances prompted the government to aspire to have the autocephalic Russian Church elevated to a patriarchate in order to strengthen its position in the sense of the Orthodox symphony of state and Church. When Patriarch Joachim V of Antioch visited Moscow as a petitioner in 1586, he received—along with generous gifts of money for the other patriarchs as well—the charge to enlist their sympathies for a Moscow patriarchate. When the Serbs had obtained the restoration of their patriarchate of Peć at the insistence of Grand Vizir Mohammed Sokolović, the ecumenically minded patriarch was faced by the decision to recognize yet another autonomous patriarchate.

When Patriarch Jeremias II of Constantinople arrived in Moscow in 1588, he was forced to agree to the establishment of an independent patriarchate of Moscow and of the entire Russian tsardom (*patriarchestvo moskovskoe i vsego rossiiskago czarstviia*). The synod meeting in January 1589[12] nominated three candidates for the new office, of whom the tsar selected Metropolitan Job of Moscow, who was anointed and enthroned by Jeremias II on 26 January 1589 as the first Russian patriarch. At another synod the eparchies of Novgorod, Kazan, Sarai (Kruticy), and Rostov were elevated to metropolitanates. The ecclesiastical arrangement also included six archbishoprics and eight bishoprics whose borders were determined.

Tsar Fedor I and Boris Godunov forced Jeremias II to recognize the patriarchate by a synodal resolution of the other patriarchs. The synod in May 1590 in Constantinople[13]—in the absence of the patriarch of Alexandria, Silvester, who had died and whose successor had not yet been elected—approved the actions of Jeremias II and assigned to the Moscow patriarchate the fifth place in the ranks of the patriarchates (Constantinople, Alexandria, Antioch, Jerusalem, Moscow). The tsar was not satisfied with this order; he claimed the third place. He

[10] K. Onasch, op. cit., 57; K. Onasch, op. cit., 29: Note 11 refers to the parallel he drew to Gallicanism as "Russian Gallicanism within Byzantine Orthodoxy." His examples represent a fertile hypothesis.

[11] A. I. Muravev, *Snošenija Rossiis Vostokom do dělam cerkovynym* I (St. Petersburg 1858), 151.

[12] A. Herman, op. cit., 57–58.

[13] W. Regel, op. cit., 85–91.

further insisted that Meletios Pigas, the new patriarch of Alexandria, who had not entered his office until June 1590 and had protested the resolution, agree to this. Fedor I sent messengers to the four patriarchs with letters and gifts of money to persuade them to agree. In 1593 a synod in Constantinople finally announced the approval of all the patriarchs,[14] without, however, changing the ranking.

The establishment of the Moscow patriarchate in 1589 and its recognition by the whole of Orthodoxy did away with the special position usurped by the Russian Church since the middle of the fifteenth century and concluded its Slavonicization. The diarchy of ecclesiastical and secular rule, considered agreeable, was now represented by a tsar and patriarch who were dependent upon each other. According to the theory of the Third Rome, they stood side by side to act in concert for the salvation of the faithful entrusted to them. In point of fact, the patriarchs remained just as dependent on the tsars as had been the case with the Russian grand dukes and the Moscow metropolitans. Only under special circumstances did some of the eleven patriarchs (1589–1700) succeed in asserting themselves in the face of the tsarist autocracy and to strengthen the authority of the Church by dint of their powerful personalities.

Patriarch Job (1589–1605) was completely overshadowed by Fedor I and Boris Godunov. Following the extinction of the Riurik dynasty, there occurred the "Time of Troubles," during which the false Dmitri pretended to be a son of Ivan IV. With Polish help he conquered Moscow in 1605, deposed Job and elected Ignati, until then archbishop of Riazan, in his stead. (1605/06). After the assassination of Dmitri under the rule of Tsar Vasili IV Shuski (1606–10), Ignati had to make way for the metropolitan of Kazan, Germogen, who became patriarch from 1606 to 1612. When the Poles again advanced to Moscow in 1610, they threw Germogen into jail and reinstated Ignati as patriarch. Germogen on his part stirred up nationwide resistance against the Poles until the exterior threats and upheavals of Russia could be overcome by the election of Tsar Michail Romanov (1613–45).

The tsar's father, Fedor Romanov, who had assumed the name Filaret after he entered the monastery and who, as metropolitan of Rostov had been imprisoned by the Poles until 1618, had been designated for the office of patriarch. When he regained his freedom, he took over the highest church office in Russia (1619–33) whose affairs had been conducted by an administrator for seven years (1612–19). Until his death a constellation unique in Russian church history prevailed: father and son—both had the title of "Sublime Ruler" (*velikii gosudar*)—reigned

---

[14] A. Herman, op. cit., 40–41.

together as patriarch and tsar. The Orthodox symphony of spiritual and secular power became a reality in this rule of two tsars (*dvoeczarstvie*) in which the two forces strengthened each other and gave a strange imprint to the idea of the Third Rome. The Moscow patriarchate was stabilized by the establishment of the archbishopric of Tobolsk in Siberia (1620), the reordering of the patriarchal administration within the structure of the state (1625), and the rejection of all Western infiltrations by the Roman Catholic Church, the Uniates, and the Protestants.

The next patriarchs Ioasaf (1634–40) and Iosif (1642–52) benefited from the heritage of their predecessor Filaret, even though the reign of Tsar Alexei (1645–76), who codified extant law in 1649, brought about a noticeable tendency towards subordination of the Church under the authority of the state. The establishment of a central government office for church affairs and the prohibition of acquisition of property by the Church initiated the deterioration of church privileges. Patriarch Nikon (1652–66)[15] attempted once again to achieve a status of priority of the Church over the state. In an appendix to the *Epanagoge*, a Byzantine book of laws written between 879 and 886 in which Patriarch Photios opposed the hegemony of the Emperor in the Eastern Church, Nikon developed an ideal of church autonomy: "To the tsar are entrusted the affairs of the body, to the clergy those of the souls . . . therefore the priesthood is far higher than the tsardom."[16] His recourse to Greek models is demonstrated as well by his re-edition of the collection of canon law of the *Nomokanon* (*kormčaia kniga*)[17] and in the improvement of liturgical texts in adherence to the Greek originals by correcting the deviations which had become custom in Russia. With this work he continued the views of Grecophile Russian hierarchs who expected to raise the cultural level of the clergy and ministry by contacts with the Eastern patriarchs. Nikon, who had met the patriarch of Jerusalem, Paisios, in Moscow received texts, among others "a ritual for the execution of the liturgy in the East by a bishop."[18] They were transmitted to him by the former ecumenical patriarch Athanasios III Patellaros, who had been in Moscow in 1653–54. In 1653 the ecumenical patriarch of Constantinople, Paisios I, sent him a large volume containing the precise rules of the Greek Orthodox liturgy and descriptions of the holy implements and vestments.

---

[15] N. F. Kapterev, *Patriarch Nikon i caŕ Michajlovič*, 2 vols. (Sergiev Posad 1909–12); M. V. Zyzykin, *Patriarch Nikon*, 3 vols. (Warsaw 1931–38).

[16] A. V. Karešev, *Očerki poistorii russkoj cerkvi* II (Paris 1959), 195.

[17] A. Herman, op. cit., 23–33; H. Neubauer, op. cit., 134–35.

[18] I. Smolitsch, *Mönchtum*, 366.

With the help of these and other documents Nikon initiated his reforms. In an admonition to the Moscow clergy in 1653 he ordered the
seventeen genuflections at certain prayers reduced to four and decreed
the use of three instead of two fingers for making the sign of the cross.[19]
Even these first few reforms on the Greek model created confusion in
Moscow. The Moscow protopopes Avvakum (1621–82)[20] and Ivan
Neronov protested against the innovations and appealed to the tsar as
the protector of Orthodoxy. At the Moscow synod of 1653 Nikon had
Neronov condemned, demoted, and banished to a remote monastery;
Avvakum was sent to Siberia. At the Moscow synods of 1654, 1655,
and 1656[21] the patriarch pushed through the adaptation of the liturgy to
the Byzantine liturgy. He was supported by Serbian Patriarch Gabriel,
Patriarch Makarios of Antioch and the representative of the ecumenical
patriarch, Paisios I. Tsar Alexei acknowledged the reform resolutions,
made them law, and recognized the penalties against protesting clerics,
simultaneously trying to have them ameliorated. The close ties between
the Moscow and Constantinople patriarchs opened political perspectives. Because the Treaty of Pereiaslaw of 1654 united the larger part of
the Ukraine with Russia—since then Nikon had called himself patriarch
of Greater Russia, Russia Proper, and Byelorussia—the avenue to Constantinople appeared open. At the occasion of his stay in Moscow the
former ecumenical patriarch, Athanasios III Patellaros, had implied that
the orthodox subjects of the sultan could place themselves under the
protection of the tsar and encouraged him to "conquer Constantinople
and to install his patriarch there as ecumenical patriarch."[22] There were
distinct possibilities of the Third Rome uniting with the Second.

Nikon, allowed since 1654 to bear the title of *velikii gosudar*, like his
predecessor Filaret, was administrator of the realm during the Russo-
Polish War of 1654/55. His exaggerated self-assurance, the overem-
phasis of his position, above all the growing movement of the Old
Believers, who considered the reforms[23] as interference with the blessed

---

[19] J. Chrysostomus, *Die "Pomorskie Otvety" als Denkmal der Anschauungen der russischen
Altgläubigen gegen Ende des l. Viertels des XVIII. Jh.* (Rome 1957), 174–92; H. Koch,
Schriften, 94–103.

[20] P. Pascal, *Avvakum et les débuts du Raskol* (Paris 1963), incl. biblio.

[21] A. Herman, op. cit., 60–61.

[22] A. M. Ammann, op. cit., 270.

[23] P. Hauptmann, *Altrussischer Glaube. Der Kampf des Protopopen Avvakum gegen die Kirchenreform des 17. Jh.* (Göttingen 1963).—Ibid., 86: Enumeration of the main components of Nikon's cultural reform: Text revision of agenda, the cross made with three
fingers instead of two, three instead of two hallelujahs, orthography and pronunciation
of *Jesus* ("Jisus" instead of "Isus"), reduction of liturgical bows to the ground, changes in
the creed of Nicaea-Constantinople, five prosphorae instead of seven, reversal of direction of procession.

Russian tradition and consequently took up a fight against the state and the Church causing a schism (*raskol*)[24] within the Russian Orthodox Church unsolved to the present day, all these contributed to a break between him and the tsar in 1658. Nikon threatened his resignation, whereupon Alexei took away his title of *velikii gosudar* and convoked a bishops' synod in 1660 which was to issue a declaration that the patriarch had resigned his office voluntarily. When this attempt failed, Greek theologians were called in and expert opinions were requested from the four former patriarchs. At the great Moscow synod of 1666/67,[25] in which the patriarchs Paisios of Alexandria and Makarios of Antioch as well as numerous monks and Greek princes of the Church participated, Nikon was dismissed for refusing the opinion of the united Orthodox patriarchs, for restructuring valid canon law, and resigning unjustifiably. He had to retreat to a monastery as a simple monk and spend the last fifteen years of his life there (d. 1682). Nikon's attempt to upgrade the office of the patriarch had failed; the tsar had had his way. At the end of January 1667 the synod submitted a list of three possible candidates for a successor, of whom Alexei chose Ioasaf, the aged abbot of the Monastery of the Trinity near Moscow, to be the next patriarch. The fall of Nikon affirmed the priority of the secular ruler in church matters.

The last four patriarchs who were more or less appointed directly by the government could not stop this development. Ioasaf II (1667–72) followed the tsar's wishes in every way. To be sure, at the end of the great synod he advocated the rights of the Church and obtained an amelioration of the limitations put upon the ecclesiastical court jurisdiction in 1649, but had to recognize that the reform of the liturgy implemented by Nikon had actually been advised by the tsar. According to the records of Paisios Ligarides, a member of the Jerusalem patriarchate,[26] the position of the tsar within the Church was solved by a compromise according to which "neither of the two powers were to interfere in the affairs of the other. In secular matters the tsar was to prevail, the patriarch was to have priority in spiritual ones."[27] The resolutions of the synod honored the tsar as a new Constantine, Zealot of the faith, Defender of the true faith, Judge and Avenger for the Old

[24] V. V. Andreev, *Raskol i ego značenie v narodnoj russkoj istorii* (St. Petersburg 1870=Osnabrück 1965); J. Chrysostomus, op. cit., 1–34; V. Pleyer, *Das russische Altgläubigentum* (Munich 1960); P. Hauptmann, op. cit.

[25] A. Herman, op. cit., 63–64; cf. H. Neubauer, op. cit., 142–98, about the deposition of Nikon and its consequences.

[26] N. F. Kapterev, *Patriarch Nikon* II, 227–50.

[27] H. Neubauer, op. cit., 176.

Believers and the disobedient.[28] The Old Believers rejected their being condemned as a partisan and uncanonical act. The brotherhood of the Solovecki monastery on the Caspian Sea reasoned for their views in several petitions: it was convinced that the end of the world was immediately impending, since tsar and hierarchs had fallen from the old faith and had betrayed the charge of the Third Rome, while the members of the synod had interpreted the idea of the Third Rome according to their own opinions. The brotherhood did not accept the Archimandrite Iosif appointed by Patriarch Ioasaf II and elected its own superiors. The monks defended themselves passionately and resisted the troops called out against them from 1670 to 1676, when their monastery was finally stormed.[29]

After only seven months in office Patriarch Pitirim (1672–73) was followed by Ioakim (1674–90). Next to promoting strict monastic and Church discipline and rejecting all Western influences, he considered the implementation of the decisions of the 1666/67 synod one of his main tasks. This was shown at the bishops synod of 1675[30] and even more so at the synod of 1682,[31] which continued the development of liturgical reform and declared anew that the punishment of the Old Believers was a duty of the state. One of the first victims was the Protopope Avvakum, who ended at the stake in 1682. A religious conference at the beginning of the reign of Tsarina Sophia (1682–89), who took over the regency for her minor brothers Ivan V and Peter I after the death of Tsar Fedor II (1676–82), ended with draconic measures and the execution of the main speakers for the Old Believers. A ukase of 7 April 1685 ordered their prosecution and conviction as rebels and enemies of the state. In the following years thousands of them were executed; many evaded their persecutors by self-immolation. They rejected the actions of the state and the Church as being dictated by the Anti-Christ, idealized the past of the Russian Church, and as itinerant priests proselytized for their views. Two groups were now formed, those with priests (*popovcy*) and those without (*bezpopovcy*). The suppression of the *raskol* had serious consequences for Russian monkdom. Many monasteries which had hitherto been centers of religious life and literary production, now ceased to fulfill that function. Most of the monks, because they had joined the Old Believers and rejected the reforms decreed by the patriarchal Church and later on also by the government, were suspected to be enemies of the state.

[28] Ibid., 177–78.
[29] I. Smolitsch, *Mönchtum*, 374–81.
[30] A. Herman, op. cit., 64.
[31] Ibid., 64–65.

The synod of 1682 was also occupied with the moral and educational reform of the secular and monastic clergy. New bishoprics were established and the organization of the metropolitanates was tightened. In 1685 the metropolitanate of Kiev was incorporated in the patriarchate; in 1686 Patriarch Dionysios of Constantinople released it from his jurisdiction. This incorporation aggravated the tensions within the Russian Church because the academy founded by the Ukrainian metropolitan Peter Mogila (1633–47) in Kiev was prepared to engage in a discourse with Catholicism and the Counter Reformation. It also required a knowledge of Latin in addition to Greek and gained influence beyond its borders of the Ukraine in the second half of the seventeenth century. One of its pupils, Simeon of Polock (1629–80), who had been tutor of the princes in Moscow and had opened a Latin school, and his friend, the monastic priest Silvester Medvedev, spread the many-faceted intellectualism cultivated in Kiev to Moscow.[32] The fight between the conservative forces and those of the "Latinists" who were supported by the government came to a head during negotiations concerning the establishment of a university in Moscow.[33] Although a Slavic-Greek-Latin academy was founded in Moscow in 1687, Patriarch Ioakim prevailed at the Moscow Synod of 1689/90: the followers of the Ukrainian movement were demoted; Medvedev was convicted, laicized, and executed.[34]

The relative uniformity of Russian church life at the beginning of the patriarchate gave way to noticeable differentiations at the end of the seventeenth century.[35] Although publications on canon law, liturgy, and hagiography predominated, the revision of the liturgical books represented a new scientific contribution. The interior disputes with Ukrainian and Greek theologians led to a loosening of traditional ties. Baroque culture flowing from the Ukraine to Russia enriched church literature, architecture, painting, and music. The icon painter Simeon Ushakov (1626–86) made use of typically baroque emblematics, the icons show traces of individual portraiture. In architecture the traditional elements combined with Greek ideas and influences of the baroque. Polyphony was added to the customary homophonous singing. The Russian Church, then, received many impulses during the time of the first patriarchate, but these were rejected by the influential conservative circles that determined matters.

One of them was Patriarch Adrian (1690–1700). He tried once again

---

[32] A. M. Ammann, op. cit., 346–55.
[33] H. Neubauer, op. cit., 204–21.
[34] A. Herman, op. cit., 65.
[35] *Jugie* I, 558–78; K. Onasch, op. cit., 77–87.

to protect the privileges of the Church, but did not have the strength to prevail against Tsar Peter I,[36] who, together with his debilitated half-brother Ivan V (1689–96) and after the latter's death, ruled and restructured the realm as autocrat (1696–1725). Just as his predecessor Ioakim, Adrian was so steeped in tradition that the tsar's predilection for foreigners and his European trip (1697–98) were totally inconceivable to him. When Peter I returned from abroad in 1698 and ruthlessly proceeded against the revolt of the Streltsi, Adrian, paralyzed since 1696, asked him in vain to apply mercy; henceforth tsar and patriarch communicated only in writing. The patriarchal Church and the Old Believers were united in rejecting the new customs introduced by the tsar, as for instance the wearing of European clothes and shaving of beards. Peter I did not refrain from parodying and scorning church ceremonies. His church policies[37] were an integrated part of his desire, shaped by rationalism and the philosophy of early Enlightenment, to reform the realm. His reforms were aimed at the commonweal (*vsenarodnaia polza*)—albeit interpreted by him in an arbitrary fashion—and for this he made use of the Church as well. While he took into account the ties of his people with the Orthodox faith, he nonetheless considered the Church no more than an institution for moral education, which he wanted to implement by legal norms instead of religious commandments. During his travels through Catholic and Protestant countries he had become familiar with the dependence of the Churches upon secular authority. He was determined to subordinate the Church to the state in Russia as well.

The Dissolution of the Patriarchate and the Establishment of the Holy Synod

The death of Patriarch Adrian on 16 October 1700 meant the end of the autonomous patriarchal administration. Peter I arbitrarily interfered in church affairs. He did not allow the election of a new patriarch. Two months later he simply appointed Stefan Javorski (1658–1722),[38] metropolitan of Riazan, to the position of administrator and regent of the patriarchate. He was given the supervision of ecclesiastical matters, the right of nomination to fill vacant bishoprics—they amounted to a total of

[36] R. Wittram, *Peter I. Czar und Kaiser. Zur Gesch. Peters des Großen in seiner Zeit,* 2 vols. (Göttingen, 1964).

[37] H. Koch, *Die russische Orthodoxie im Petrinischen Zeitalter* (Breslau 1929); R. Stupperich, *Staatsgedanke und Religionspolitik Peters des Großen* (Königsberg/Pr.-Berlin 1936); R. Wittram, "Peters des Großen Verhältnis zur Religion und den Kirchen," *HZ* 173 (1952), 261–96; I. Smolitsch, *Geschichte,* 57–75.

[38] J. Šerech, "Stefan Yavorsky and the Conflict of Ideologies in the Age of Peter the Great," *SEER* 30 (1951–52), 40–62.

twenty-three—and the surveillance of opponents of the Church, especially the Old Believers, whereas the overseeing of church properties was handed to the Office of Monasteries (1701–20); church judicature was considerably curtailed. The tsar thought that Stefan Javorski, a former professor of the Kiev academy who had occupied himself with polemical theology and had lectured at the Moscow Academy in 1697/98, would be open to his plans.

Initially they collaborated in the mission to the pagans and Mohammedans[39] and in the struggle against the Old Believers. In 1703 Stefan Javorski had dealt with them in an essay, "The Signs of the Appearance of the Antichrist and the End of the World."[40] But he was soon chagrined by several significant measures of the tsar's. The latter confiscated monastic revenues to finance his army; he practiced tolerance towards the Protestants, granting them freedom of conscience and autonomous rights when he annexed the Baltic provinces; he appointed Pastor Barthold Vagetius superintendent of the Lutheran congregations in Russia, and, finally, he subordinated the Office of Monasteries to the "Reigning Senate" created in 1711, which became the supreme supervisory office, usurping all administrative and judicial functions. In 1712 Javorski used a sermon to take a stand against the church policies of Peter I and his marriage to Katharina (Catherine) Skravronka, later Tsarina Catherine I: "You stormy sea of man's transgressions of the law, why do you break and devastate the shores? The shores are God's law; since its creation it has consisted in not coveting the wife of one's neighbor and in not leaving one's own . . ."[41] In 1689 the tsar had separated from Evdoxia Lopuxina, mother of Tsarevich Alexei, and decreed that she enter a convent. In the same sermon, Stefan Javorski also expressed his sympathies for the heir to the throne who did not agree with his father's methods of governing. As a consequence Javorski was prohibited from giving sermons for the period of three years. His polemics against the Protestant circles of Moscow and the army surgeon Dimitri Tverentinov, who represented Calvinistic views, led to a summons before the Senate. When the physician Foma Ivanov, a follower of the surgeon, hacked apart some icons, the patriarchal regent had a bishops' synod in 1714 sentence him to death at the stake. The tsar, outraged by this action, forced Stefan Javorski into humiliating apologies. Henceforth the latter did not dare express his opinions freely. But he put them down in his "Rock of Faith, Dedicated to the

[39] J. Glazik, *Die russisch-orthodoxe Heidenmission seit Peter dem Großen* (Münster 1954); idem, *Die Islammission der russisch-orthodoxen Kirche* (Münster 1959).
[40] I. Smolitsch, *Geschichte*, 80.
[41] Ibid., 87.

Sons of the Holy Orthodox-Catholic Eastern Church for their Strengthening and Spiritual Edification, but as Support and Betterment for Those who Perceive it as a Stumbling Block."[42] In this manuscript dedicated to Tsarevich Alexei he maintained that the Church was superposed over the state: "Tsars are the guardians of the laws of God and of the Church, but they are not legislators; it is not theirs to determine what should be part of the faith."[43]

When the conflict between the tsar and his son caused a trial in 1718 against Alexei and his followers, the investigation extended to ecclesiastic dignitaries, who were made answerable for the widespread opposition and an alleged conspiracy. Stefan Javorski advocated a pardon, but was unable to avert the death penalty. The opposition between the patriarchal regent and Peter I, whose founding of Saint Petersburg (1703) had created a symbol for the Russia changed by him, had become unbridgeable. Church life was paralyzed more and more each year by the incursions of the autocrat. In 1714 he prohibited the building of new churches for ten years in favor of the construction of Saint Petersburg, elevated in 1712 to be the capital. In 1716 the Senate ordered the bishops to bind themselves by oath to deal mildly with the opponents of the Church, to employ clerics and sacristans only when needed, and not to interfere in secular affairs. In 1717 the tsar demanded of all confessors that they tell him personally all news of attempts directed against the state. In 1718 he ordered Feofan Prokopovich (1681–1736)[44] to draft a "Description and Evaluation of an Ecclesiastical College," intending to direct the central authority of the Church according to his ideas and to incorporate it in the total administration of the state.

Feofan Prokopovich was one of the most important Russian theologians of the first half of the eighteenth century. Although he referred to certain basic ideas of Protestantism and tenets of the Enlightenment, he tried to combine the Byzantine heritage and Moscow tradition with the demands of his time. After his studies at the Kiev Academy he had temporarily become a Basilian monk and successfully passed a course in Catholic Scholastic philosophy at the Greek College of Saint Athanasius (1698–1701). On his way back through Switzerland and Germany he had met Calvinist and Lutheran theologians. In 1704 he became an Orthodox monastic priest and soon rose to the position of professor

[42] K. Onasch, op. cit., 100.
[43] R. Stupperich, Staatsgedanke, 51–52.
[44] R. Stupperich, "Feofan Prokopovič in der neuren Lit." Festschrift für Margarete Woltner zum 70. Geburtstag, P. Brang et al., eds. (Heidelberg 1967), 284–93; H.-J. Härtel, Byzantinisches Erbe und Orthodoxie bei Feofan Prokopovič (Würzburg 1970, incl. biblio.).

(1706) and then rector (1711) in the academy. In 1716 the tsar, who had known him personally since 1706, called him to Saint Petersburg as his adviser and in spite of reservations on the part of the patriarchal regent succeeded in having him appointed bishop of Pskov in 1718.

After his sermon concerning the power and honor of the tsar on 6 April 1718, the basic ideas of which he deepened in 1722 in his essay "The Right of the Monarchic Will," the collaboration between him and the tsar became closer. Its product was the *Spiritual Regulations (duxovnyi reglament)*, which made the Russian Church a part of the order of the state and placed at its head the Holy Synod as a state institution.[45] The text drafted by Feofan Prokopovich in 1720 was corrected by Peter I and submitted to the Senate for its information and for all bishops to sign. It regulated church supervision, church education, the order of Mass, appointment to church offices, the ecclesiastical court and the administration of church property. The tsar's manifesto of 25 January 1721[46] made the council form of government of the Church stipulated in the regulations its basic law and decreed that the Ecclesiastical College could not do anything without his approval. In the first meeting of 14 February 1721 Feofan Prokopovich gave the opening speech based on John 15:16, stressing the decisive role of the monarchic will. At this meeting the designation "Ecclesiastical College" was changed into "Most Holy Governing Synod." It was composed of eleven members who received princely salaries. Saint Petersburg was designated as the seat of this office. Peter I appointed Archbishop Stefan Javorski first president and Bishop Feofan Prokopovich second president. When Javorski, who could not stop this development and whose protests were disregarded, died in 1722, the tsar did not appoint another president but transferred the authority to Prokopovich as vice-president. In April 1722 the Holy Synod issued supplements to the regulations concerning the monastic system. Men could not be vested as monks anymore until the age of thirty; women were prohibited from being vested until the age of fifty to sixty.

On 11 May 1722, Peter I—to whom the Senate had given the title of Emperor (*imperator*) and the sobriquet "the Great" (*Velikii*) in 1721— installed within the Holy Synod the office of a chief procurator corresponding to the procurator general in the Senate. Subordinate to the will of the tsar, who simultaneously made him head of the chancery of the synod, he was to have full supervision of the synod "as Our eyes and administrator of the business of the state."[47] J. V. Boltin,

---

[45] I. Smolitsch, *Geschichte*, 99–132.

[46] Mansi XXXVII, 1–99; A. Herman, op. cit., 80–83; I. Smolitsch, *Geschichte*, 103–05.

[47] R. Stupperich, *Staatsgedanke*, 86.

colonel of the dragoons, was the first chief procurator (1722–25). His successors were elevated to the rank of ministers in the nineteenth century and became key figures of the Russian established Church. Under the direction of its vice-president, the Holy Synod attempted to return the Old Believers to the Church by means of words of exhortation; it took steps to reform the monastic system and to make it useful to the state, to improve the education of the people, and to raise the level of knowledge of the clergy. Feofan Prokopovich composed a "First Instruction for Boys,"[48] a catechism for children which had to be read to all the congregations four times a year. He also expanded the Alexander Nevski Monastery in Saint Petersburg into a model seminary.

It was not easy for the members of the Holy Synod to explain to the Orthodox clergy within and without Russia its role as a bishops' synod, able to invoke Orthodox traditions, and its functions as an organ of the state. The Holy Synod had the legislative, executive, and judicial power within the church government which had earlier rested with the Moscow patriarchate. It tried to calm the bishops with the following message: "The synod has the honor, authority, and power of the patriarchs, if not more so, because it is a council (sobor)."[49] The petitions of the liturgy henceforth mentioned the Holy Synod instead of the patriarchs. The commemoration of the other patriarchs was to cease, lest it create the impression that the Holy Synod was below them. When Stefan Javorski raised an objection, he was outvoted. The tsar took it upon himself to inform Patriarch Jeremias III of Constantinople of the new church order in Russia and asked him in turn to communicate it to the other three patriarchs of the East. But in his devoutly phrased letter of 30 September 1721 he did not mention the content of the regulations, which he designated merely as "Instruction." He also kept silent concerning the incorporation of the Holy Synod into the collegiate system of state administration and the subordination of the Church to the supervision of the state. Furthermore, he changed the text of the manifesto of 25 January 1721 in several places.[50] In 1723 the patriarchs of Constantinople, Alexandria, and Antioch recognized the "Most Holy Governing Synod" as "Holy Brother in Christ,"[51] only Patriarch Chrysanthos Notara of Jerusalem refused his approval. Aside from the one-sided information they had received, the decisive factor in obtaining

---

[48] Ibid., 92–93. Cf. the list of works by Feofan Prokopovič, H. J. Härtel, loc. cit., 13–14.
[49] I. Smolitsch, *Geschichte*, 124.
[50] Ibid., 107–8; R. Wittram, *Peter I. Czar und Kaiser* II, 192–93.
[51] Kartašev II, 363–67.

their recognition was the patriarchs' dependence on Russian subsidies because they were under Turkish domination.

The uncanonical installment of the Holy Synod meant the complete dissolution of the Moscow patriarchate. The Russian Orthodox Church became the Orthodox Church in Russia. To be sure, it continued to be connected with the other Eastern Churches in its teachings, the celebration of its liturgy and sacraments, but received a new structure in its relation between Church and state by virtue of the abolition of the earlier dual rule of tsar and patriarch and its subordination to the state. The decrees of the Holy Synod were published in the name of the tsar, by order of His Imperial Majesty. The harmonious collaboration between state and Church aligned for centuries according to the symphonious Byzantine model was part of history. Dostoevski's acerbic judgment that "the Church has been in a state of paralysis since Peter the Great,"[52] is exaggerated. But in the history of the Russian Church the establishment of the Holy Synod meant the beginning of the dictatorship of the established Church (*gosudarstvennaia czerkovnost*).

The Russian Established Church under the Holy Synod

The Holy Synod was the instrument by which the state subjugated the Church in the eighteenth century. Its members, reduced to four in 1730 and fluctuating between three and eight in the following decades, possessed the legislative, administrative and judicial power. The administrative offices of the Holy Synod prepared all decisions for the conferences usually taking place twice a year. The directives of the ruler were decisive in everything; the chief procurators appointed by them merely received orders.

Under Catherine I (1725–27) the Holy Synod was placed under the "Supreme Secret Council" established in 1726. Archbishop Feodosi Janovski of Novgorod, having shortly before criticized the tsarina's church policies, was demoted and banished to a monastery on the Caspian Sea as an ordinary monk. Feofan Prokopovich, promoted to archbishop of Novgorod in 1725, had to fight for his leadership position in the Holy Synod during the reign of Peter II (1727–30), the son of Tsarevitch Alexei, because the great families protecting the young tsar again declared Moscow the capital of Russia and permitted discussion of a possible restoration of the patriarchate stimulated by some princes of the Church. In 1728 Archbishop Lopatinski of Tver published the "Rock of Faith" written by Stefan Javorski, in which the basic attitude of Feofan

---

[52] F. M. Dostojevskij, *Dnevnik pisatelja. Sobranie sočinenij* V (St. Petersburg 1885), 356.

Prokopovich was suspected as Lutheranism. The first edition was quickly out of print; the second was sent to all bishops and abbots in 1729.

After the death of Peter II, under the reign of Anna Ivanovna (1730–40), a niece of Peter the Great, Archbishop Prokopovich again obtained dictatorial powers. He removed from the Holy Synod three members who had been supporters of the nun Evdoxia Lopuxina, the first wife of Peter I, for the succession to the throne. He also proceeded against all people who had favored the dissemination of the "Rock of Faith." The Metropolitans Georgi Dashkov and Ignati Smola were stripped of their ecclesiastical office and dispatched to separate monasteries as ordinary monks; Archbishop Lopatinski was divested of his bishopric after a three-year pretrial arrest (1738) and taken to the fortress of Vyborg. Feofan Prokopovich cast suspicion on his adversaries as enemies of the state; he packed the Holy Synod, by now subordinated to the cabinet of ministers, with men whom he trusted and intensified the dependence of the Church upon the state. He punished bishops and abbots if they resisted government regulations, such as total obedience to monastic legislation. When he died in 1736, the arbitrary rule of the tsarina and her favorite, Duke Ernst Johann von Biron, interfered even more in church matters. In 1737 all church officers between the ages of fifteen and forty with the exception of priests and deacons were drafted into the army. Conscription even reached into the monasteries. These and other measures, making it problematical to enter a monastery, reduced the number of monks and nuns from approximately twenty-five thousand to hardly fourteen thousand.[53] In 1738 the Holy Synod had to hand the College of Economics over to the jurisdiction of the Senate, with the result that all church property revenues flowed into the state exchequer. The tsarina ostensibly represented herself as a benefactress of the total Orthodox Church. In 1732 she established a budget for gifts of charity, granting the patriarch of Constantinople an annual 1000 and the other patriarchs 100 rubles each. Other beneficiaries were the Balkan Slavs, the Athos Monasteries, and the Georgians.

After the short interregnum of the minor Prince Ivan VI and the regent Anna Leopoldovna (1740–41) the oppressed situation of the Church improved temporarily at the beginning of the reign of Tsarina Elizabeth (1741–61), a daughter of Peter the Great. She granted freedom to several bishops and returned the administration of the prop-

[53] I. Smolitsch, *Mönchtum*, 389: there were 7,829 monks and 6,543 nuns around 1740.—The number of monastics receded even more in the second half of the eighteenth century; cf. I. Smolitsch, *Geschichte*, 713: in 1764 to 7,659 monks and 4,733 nuns, in 1796 to 4,160 monks and 1,671 nuns.

erties of the Church and monasteries to the Holy Synod. Basically she continued the church policies of her father. The chief procurator, Prince Shakovskoi (1742–53), and his successors made sure that the interests of the state were safeguarded; they prepared for the secularization of all church property. The mission among the Mohammedans of the Volga region, suppressed under Anna Ivanovna, was now promoted by the state. For the period 1743 to 1747 the "Office for the Newly Baptized" registered 217,258 baptisms, from 1748 to 1760 another 192,606,[54] which could only be brought about by forcible measures. Thus mosques in places cohabited by Christians and Mohammedans were destroyed. In the province of Kazan 418 of 536 Islamic places of worship were leveled, in the province of Tobolsk 98 of 133, in Astrakhan 29 of 40.[55] In Siberia conversion to Christianity was promoted with the promise of economic favors. The increase in the number of souls by almost a half million may have strengthened the self-assurance of some bishops, to be sure, but the necessary expansion of the church organization—in 1753 there were thirty bishoprics with about 18,000 parishes—was limited to mere outward appearances. The edition of the Holy Scripture, a revision of the 1581 edition in Church Slavonic of the Ostrog Bible after the Greek original text, which was published by the Holy Synod in 1751, and the exhortations of some princes of the Church against the incursions of ideas of the Enlightenment were unable to stop the process of the Church being pushed more and more from public life. Moscow University and its branches, founded in 1755 (see Chap. 18), did not include a theological faculty.

Over the following decades the Church lost the last vestiges of its autonomy. The infantile Peter III and his ambitious wife Catherine II (née princess of Anhalt-Zerbst), who pushed him aside and usurped the throne, continued the subjugation of the Church under the yoke of the state. Peter III, the son of Tsarina Anna and Duke Karl-Friedrich of Holstein-Gottorp, reigned for only half a year (1761–62). He did not have the slighest understanding of the special character of the Orthodox Church. The president of the Holy Synod, Archbishop Dimitri Seshchenov of Novgorod, was expected to remove all icons except those of the Redeemer and the Blessed Virgin, to abolish the monasteries, and make the clergy adopt the dress of Protestant ministers. Complete control by the state over all church property was introduced by the reinstatement of the governmental College of Economics and the inventorying of all monastic estates.

[54] J. Glazik, *Heidenmission*, 79.
[55] J. Glazik, *Islammission*, 87.

To be sure, Catherine II (1762–96) designated herself "Orthodox Empress," but was guided mainly by the spirit of the French Encyclopedists, with whom she corresponded. She deliberately and stubbornly completed the church policies of Peter I.[56] Even prior to her coming to power she had jotted down the following maxim: "Respecter la religion, mais ne la faire entrer pour rien dans les affaires d'État."[57] Once empress she called herself "chef de l'église grecque" or "chef de son église."[58] At times she referred to the bishops as "people being part of the administration of the state, subject to the will of the monarch as well as to the Gospel."[59] Chief procurators, such as J. J. Melessino (1763–68), who suggested the abolition of fasting, abbreviation of the Mass, and facilitation of divorces, and P. P. Shehebyshchev (1768–74), an avowed atheist, gradually made the Holy Synod comply with the wishes and demands of the tsarina.

At the very beginning of her reign Catherine II appointed a commission to deliberate the problem of the Church properties. The result was the secularization law of 26 February 1764, which ordered all properties to be transferred to the Office of Economics. Four hundred eighteen monasteries were dissolved; the budget for all bishoprics, churches, and monasteries, whose number was further decreased in the following years, provided for three different income scales. At first the process of secularization included only the monastic institutions of Greater Russia; after the special status of the Ukraine was phased out in 1786 and 1788, it was extended to the southwestern territories as well. Aside from a very few other clerics only one prince of the Church, Metropolitan Arseni Masejevich of Rostov (1742–63), who had earlier proved his courage by a paper opposing the wrongs done to Stefan Javorski, dared protest publicly against the nationalization of church property. When he prophesied the destruction of Church and piety in two petitions to the Holy Synod, whose members he characterized as "mute dogs" who "look on without barking,"[60] he was tried by a synodal court in 1763, stripped of his consecration as bishop and priest, and banished to a remote monastery. Shortly thereafter he also lost his monastic status and was condemned to life in prison at the fortress of Reval, where he died in 1772.

The established Orthodox Church bowed to the will of the Tsarina in all matters. This was manifest in the preparation of a new legal code

[56] I. Smolitsch, *Geschichte*, 247–72, 346–56.

[57] Ibid., 251.

[58] Ibid., 252.

[59] A. M. Ammann, op. cit., 405.

[60] I. Smolitsch, *Geschichte*, 264.

and the expansion of the system of higher education. The religious academy in Moscow, being refused any connection with the university, and the seminaries were so meagerly supported that the Church was reduced more and more to the liturgical realm. All the while Catherine II represented herself as guardian of the Orthodox faith. In the peace treaty with Turkey in 1774 she obtained protectionary rights over the Orthodox faithful in the principalities of Moldavia and Walachia. The "Greek Project,"[61] a plan to restore the Byzantine Empire under a Russian secundogeniture, pursued visions of even greater scope, which could not, however, be realized.

In the second half of the eighteenth century the Church—in a condition of total dependence on the state since Peter I—was endangered from within by the advances of rationalism, the Enlightenment and Freemasonry. Some princes of the Church sought to avert the infiltration by means of compromise, such as the Moscow metropolitan Platon Levshin (1773–1812). He went back to the works of Feofan Prokopovich, whose views were prevailing at the Moscow Academy, and himself published sermons and catechetical works. The number of bishops and monks who deliberately concentrated on the religious core of their tasks was small. One of them was Bishop Tixon of Voronezh (1763–67), who withdrew to the monastery of Zadonsk and, as a hermit and religious writer, radiated great influence.[62] Another was Metropolitan Gavril Petrov of Saint Petersburg (1770–1801), who oversaw the printing of the Church Slavonic translation of the *Philokalia* (*dobrotoliubie*). The translator Paisi Velichkovski (1722–94)[63] renewed the "altruistic" current of monasticism, represented by Nil Sorski around 1500, and revived the institution of monastic elders (*staretsy*), which led the Russian monasteries out of the crisis of the closing eighteenth century. Such personalities of high profile were exceptions in the Orthodox Church of Russia at the time of Catherine II. The condition of the Church was characterized by the process of secularization, through which it had lost the major part of its self-support for its charitable and social tasks. The schism of the Old Believers continued. The government tried to move those who followed official church dogma to recognize the established Church and was prepared to tolerate separate customs for its concession. But it also took harsh measures when it deported twenty thousand Old Believers who had settled on the Dnepr island of Vjatka to Siberia. The "priestless" Old Believers split up in

[61] E. Hösch, "Das sogenannte 'griechische Projekt' Katharinas II.," *JGO* n.s. 12 (1964), 168–206.
[62] I. Kologriwow, *Das andere Rußland* (Munich 1958), 288–326.
[63] Ibid., 326–39.

numerous groups. New sects were formed, such as the Chilysty, Skoptsy, Milk-Drinkers (*molokany*) and Dukobors, who separated from the established Church and—although they were small in numbers—were troublesome to the Holy Synod.

Paul I (1796–1801) considered the Church an ally in his fight against the consequences of the French Revolution. He called the welfare of its servants "one of the main duties of the imperial rule"[64] and made the expansion of church schools possible so that four Church academies and forty-six seminaries were in existence at the end of the eighteenth century, but he considered the clerics civil servants, as had his mother Catherine II. He was the first to award medals to the bishops, thereby tying the already pliant ecclesiastic princes even more firmly to the state. Even as heir apparent he had a religiously embellished concept of an autocrat feared and honored by his subjects "because he is the image of the Most High."[65] In the law of succession drafted in 1797 he had himself designated "Head of the Church."[66] He chaired the Holy Synod and claimed supreme supervision of the established Church; he appointed and transfered bishops according to whim. The designation of the tsar as "Head of the Church" was the culmination of the development of centuries and sealed the state's domination of the Orthodox Church of Russia.

Protestants and Catholics in Russia

The population of Russia at the time of Peter the Great is estimated at approximately 14 million,[67] most of whom were of the Orthodox faith. The attitude of the patriarchal Church towards the Lutheran congregations which had formed in the course of the seventeenth century was negative. When the number of Protestant immigrants grew considerably at the beginning of the eighteenth century, especially after the Edict of Solicitation and Toleration by Peter I (16 April 1702) and the annexation of the Baltic provinces, the state issued special regulations for them.[68] In 1721 the Holy Synod was given control over all congrega-

---

[64] I. Smolitsch, *Geschichte*, 274.

[65] Ibid., 142.

[66] Ibid., 142–44.

[67] Ibid., 9. By 1762 the population increased to 19 million and reached ca. 41 million in 1812.

[68] J. C. Grot, op. cit. I–III; R. Stupperich, ed., *Kirchenordnungen der evangelisch-lutherischen Kirche in Rußland* (Ulm 1959); G. Langer, "Zuständigkeitsabgrenzungen für die christlichen Kirchen Rußlands in der Gesetzgebung des 17. bis zum Anfang des 19. Jh." *ZSavRGkan* 46 (1960), 452–470; E. Amburger, *Geschichte des Protestantismus in Rußland* (Stuttgart 1961, incl. biblio.); I. Smolitsch, *Geschichte*, 129–32.

tions. In addition to ministering to the Orthodox it became responsible for the administrative and judicial problems of the Lutherans, Calvinists, Catholics, and Jews as well. The individual Protestant congregations were dependent upon themselves and had no higher administrative office. Only the church organizations in Livonia, Estonia, and Finland had their own central administration which represented their interests to the state. The congregations had to announce the election of their clergy and the prepositors to the Holy Synod for confirmation. The prepositors had to affirm their loyalty to the tsar by oath. In turn they took the oath from all pastors and submitted pertinent documentation with their signatures. The Holy Synod had to give its approval for the opening of new churches and the establishment of church schools. The College of the Judiciary, founded in 1718, and its department for Livonian and Estonian affairs extended its authority to include supervisory power over the Protestant Church. In spite of ostensible recognition the Protestants had to obey the repeated prohibition against proselytizing (1702, 1723, and 1735).[69] Special advantages were promised to those who converted to the Orthodox faith. In her manifesto of 22 July 1763, Catherine II solicited new settlers from Germany and western Europe for the Volga regions. She promised them free exercise of their religion, but prohibited clerics of non-Orthodox Christian faiths from attempting to convert Russian subjects to their faith.

While the Protestants in Russia—in spite of subordination to the Holy Synod and subsequent limitations—were tolerated by the government and in part furthered, the situation of the Catholics of the Latin and Uniate Rite was oppressive.[70] Following the split between the Western and Eastern half of Christianity in the Middle Ages, an anti-Catholic prejudice had developed in Russia; it became even more pronounced after the Unions of Florence and Brest, which rejected the papacy and condemned Roman efforts at union as interference in the rights of the Orthodox Church. The repeated conquests of Moscow at the beginning of the seventeenth century were connected with the Catholic Counter Reformation and strengthened the distrust of every-

---

[69] G. Langer, op. cit., 460, 462, 466.
[70] J. C. Grot I–II; A. Theiner, *Die Neuesten Zustände der Katholischen Kirche beider Ritus in Polen und Rußland seit Katharina II. bis auf unsere Tage* (Augsburg 1841); D. Tolstoy, *Le catholicisme romain en Russie*, 2 vols. (Paris 1863–64); R. Ryšavy, "Die Reformatenmission in Rußland," *AFrH* 27 (1934), 179–224; A. V. Florovský, *Čeští Jesuité na Rusi* (Prague 1941); A. M. Ammann, op. cit., 373–75, 409–10, 441–47, 457–63; J. Reinhold, *Die St. Petersburger Missionspräfektur der Reformaten im 18. Jh.* (Florence 1963); B. Stasiewski, "Die kirchliche Organisation der deutschen katholischen Siedler in Rußland," *Festschr. für Margarete Woltner zum 70. Geburtstag* (Heidelberg 1967), 270–83.

thing Catholic. The Jesuits who had come to Moscow in the retinue of foreign legations in 1684 were expelled in 1689.[71] Although they returned after a few years as legation priests of Emperor Leopold I, their ministry was severely limited to Catholic immigrants; they were again expelled in 1719.[72] Their place was taken by Capuchins and Reformists, who were given scant possibilities to function and were, moreover, suspected of espionage.

Peter I, who—after his visit to the Sorbonne in 1717—had ordered an opinion from Feofan Prokopovich and Stefan Javorski regarding prospects of a union between the Russian and Catholic Churches, kept up a good personal relationship with several Catholics in his service, among them Vice-Admiral Matvei Zmaevich and the architect Carlo Bartolomeo Rastelli. But he showed a clear dislike for the Uniate Catholics whom he encountered during his campaigns in White Russia and Lithuania. He was angered by the fact that of the four Orthodox bishops in the southeast of Poland-Lithuania three (of Przemyśl, Lemberg, and Tuck) had joined the Union of Brest (1691 and 1702). In 1706 he had the Uniate, formerly Orthodox Bishop Dionysius Zabrokricki of Łuck forcibly taken to Russia, where he died in jail in 1715. Shortly before this incident, in 1705, there had been a verbal dispute between Peter I and some Basilian monks which ended with five monks being beaten to death.

When the Catholics, along with all other non-Orthodox Christians, were placed under the authority of the Holy Synod in 1721, there were mainly German, French, Italian, and Polish immigrants involved. The suppression of the Orthodox in Poland-Lithuania in the first half of the eighteenth century increased anti-Catholic sentiment in Russia. In 1746 and 1760 Tsarina Elizabeth allowed the Austrian auxiliary troops freedom of their religion only because she had to. In 1747 the Capuchins on mission work in Astrakhan were expelled. As a result of the settlement manifesto of 1763 about six thousand German Catholics came to the Volga region of Saratov. They were permitted to build churches, but monasteries and conversion among members of other Christian faiths were forbidden to them.[73] Disputes among Catholics in Saint Petersburg who were of different nationalities and subsequent appeals to the government led to the establishment of the Livonian department of the College of the Judiciary as their office of appeal. It drafted a set of regulations for the Catholic congregations which was published in 1769. It put the Catholics under state supervision and granted the laity a decisive influence in the election of the clerics.

[71] A. V. Florovský, op. cit., 149–67.
[72] Ibid., 320–27.
[73] R. Ryšavy, op. cit., 185.

After the Counter Reformation had prevailed in Poland-Lithuania and Catholicism as the national religion had relegated the other Christian faiths to a minor role,[74] Catherine II contrived to have her favorite, August Poniatowski, placed on the Polish throne (1764–95). Through her ambassador Nikolai Vasilevich Count Repnin she repeatedly interfered in the ecclesiastic affairs of her neighbor to prevent reforms initiated by prominent clerics. In 1767 she had the Bishops Kajetan Sołtyk of Crakow and Józef Andrzej Załuski of Kiev arrested and deported to Russia because they resisted her demands. The Polish partitions (1772, 1793, and 1795) caused large segments of the Catholic population to come under Russian rule. The tsarina found a willing helper in the person of the former Calvinist Stanisław Siestrencewicz-Bohusz (1731–1826),[75] who through her protection rose from suffragan bishop in Vilna to metropolitan of Mogilev, an archbishopric created by her. The new archbishopric to which all Catholic parishes were attached had to follow the *Regulations* of 1769. Only the Jesuits were able to preserve a certain amount of independence after their order was officially dissolved by Clement XIV (1773), because they willingly placed themselves at the disposal of the new rule in the capacity of teachers. The protest by Nuncios Giovanni Andrea Archetti and Lorenzo Litta notwithstanding, all Catholic church property in the areas occupied by Russia were secularized.

Catherine II proceeded ruthlessly against the Uniate Catholics.[76] With the exception of the archbishopric of Polock all Uniate bishoprics were dissolved. Moral force and police measures recombined the Uniates with the Orthodox. Those who dared protest were convicted as rebels. When the Uniate metropolitan of Kiev, Feodosi Rostovski, traveled to Saint Petersburg in order to protest, he was not allowed to return. The bishops of Chelm and Vladimir and the coadjutor of Łuck tried in vain to obtain help from the Curia. The Basilian order was secularized, its monasteries and property confiscated. The church policies of Catherine II cost the Uniate Church 8 million faithful, 9,316 parishes, and 145 Basilian monasteries from 1773 to 1796. In the region of Polock, too, government pressure became unmistakable. In a pastoral letter of 3 November 1795, Archbishop Heraklius Lisowsky had to announce that no one was allowed to put obstacles in the path of those who wished to convert to the Orthodox faith.

---

[74] B. Stasiewski, *Reformation und Gegenreformation in Polen* (North Rhine-Westphalia 1960); idem, "Tausend Jahre polnischer Kirchengeschichte," *Kirche im Osten* 10 (1967), 48–67, especially 55.

[75] A. A. Brumanis, *Aux origines de la hiérarchie latine en Russie Mgr Stanislas Siestrzencewicz-Bohusz* (Louvain 1968).

[76] J. Madey, *Kirche zwischen Ost und West* (Munich 1969), 100–10.

Under Paul I there was at first some amelioration. The former Warsaw nuncio, Lorenzo Litta, participating as papal legate in the crowning of the tsar in 1797, submitted a memorandum concerning the desperate situation of the Uniate Catholics and the wishes of the Pope for improving the relationship between the two rites in Russia. The tsar did not accede to any negotiations, but he did revoke the dependence of the Catholics on the Department of Livonian and Estonian Affairs, decreed at the beginning of his reign, and instead subordinated them to a special department of the College of the Judiciary. Of his own accord he ordered six suffragan bishoprics to be incorporated in the archbishopric of Mogilev, recognized the Uniate archbishopric of Polock, and reestablished the dissolved Uniate bishoprics of Łuck and Brest in order to calm the unrest that had broken out in Wolhynia and White Russia. In November 1798 he issued a *reglament* for the Catholic Church of the Latin and Uniate Rites. After expelling Lorenzo Litta he appointed Archbishop Stanisław Siestrencewicz-Bohusz as head of the Catholic Church in Russia. A ministerial instruction explained the decree by saying that the complete "outward aspect" of the Church was claimed by the state and only the "religious aspect" was part of the Pope's supremacy.[77]

Parallel to the development in western, central, and southern Europe, where the system of established Churches had to a large extent prevailed, the absolute claim of the state's leadership over the Church had become a reality in eastern Europe as well. Neither the Orthodox Church nor other Christian faiths could avoid this development.

[77] A. M. Ammann, loc. cit., 461.

CHAPTER 14

The Autonomous and the Uniate Churches in the East

After the conquest of Constantinople by the Turks in 1453 the Ottoman Empire reached the zenith of its power under Selim I (1512–20) with its expansion to Syria and Egypt and under Suleiman I (1522–66) with advances into southeastern Europe, the Mediterranean, and Asia, which made its sphere extend from Algeria and Tunisia to the Persian Gulf. In the seventeenth century a gradual decline set in brought about by interior crises as well as pressure from the Republic of Venice, the Habsburgs, Poland-Lithuania and the rise of Russia. The Sultans succeeded in spreading the Islamic faith to the Bulkans and in consolidating it in their empire, which spanned three continents.[1] The Koran was considered binding not only as a religious code but it also shaped the empire's political and cultural life. The "infidels" who did not embrace the faith of Mohammed were *reaya* ("grazing herd") and had to pay a head and property tax to the sultan. They had limited rights and were merely tolerated. The Moslems as representatives of the ruling religion designated the heretical religious communities as *millet.* This concept goes back to the Koran designating the Jews (Abraham's *millet*). In Turkish the word underwent a secular change coming to mean "nation." Thus the Orthodox Christians were combined in the *rum millet,* the Monophysite Christians in the *ermeti milleti,* which also included the Armenians, Copts, and Jacobites. A religious head (*millet bashi*) was responsible for the independent administration of these various bodies; he was directly under the sultan. The ecumenical patriarch, whose title the Greeks freely translated as "Ethnarch," was the most prominent. He could stabilize his ecclesiastical power by adaptation to the sultanate. The interests of the small groups of Catholics of the different Uniate rites and the even smaller ones of the Latin Rite, especially in the Holy Land, were represented by the Pope, French diplomats, and after the seventeenth century also by the German Emperor. Some Orthodox Churches were financially and politically supported by the Russian government. These factors contributed to the fact that the Ottoman Empire, imbued with the Islamic faith, guaranteed certain rights to individual Christian communities. But to a large extent the Eastern Churches, whether separated from or connected with Rome, were exposed to the caprice of the sultans and their officials. Consequently there were a great many defections from Christianity to Islam.

The Autonomous Eastern Churches

The constituents of the autonomous Eastern Churches were the four Eastern patriarchates of Christian antiquity,[2] the patriarchates in Bulgaria and Serbia, established in the Middle Ages, the Moscow patriarch-

---

[1] G. Vismara, *Bisanzio e l'Islam, per la storia dei trattati tra cristianità orientale e le potenze musulmane* (Milan 1950); T. Papadopoulos, *Studies and Documents Relating to the Greek Church and People under Turkish Domination* (Brussels 1952); B. Homsy, *Les capitulations et la protection des chrétiens au Proche-Orient aux XVIe, et XVIIe, et XVIIIe siècles* (Harissa 1956); A. Bombaci, "Das osmanische Reich," *Historia Mundi* VII (Berne 1957), 439–85; A. Fattal, *Le statut légal des nonmusulmans en pays d'Islam* (Beirut 1958); W. E. D. Allen, *Problems of Turkish Power in the XVIth Century* (London 1963); A. J. Arberry, loc. cit. II, 1–362; *Atlas zur Kirchengesch.* (Freiburg 1970), maps 72 and 96A.
[2] W. de Vries, *Die Patriarchate des Ostens, bestimmende Faktoren bei ihrer Entstehung: I patriarcati orientali nel primo millenio* (Rome 1968), 13–36.

ate (founded in 1589),[3] the Orthodox Churches on Cyprus and Mount Sinai, the Eastern national Churches of the Orthodox Georgians, the Nestorians, and the Monophysites; among the latter we have to differentiate between the Churches of the Jacobites, the Christians of St. Thomas, the Copts, Ethiopians and Armenians.

The Orthodox Churches

Of the four Eastern patriarchates the youngest, Constantinople, achieved a leading position around the middle of the fifth century, a position it was able to maintain into the modern period. The appointment of Patriarch Gennadios Scholarios by Sultan Mehmed II in 1454 changed the harmonious balance, which had existed for a millennium between the Emperors and the patriarchal Church in Byzantium, into a state of dependence dictated by the state. Each newly elected patriarch had to request recognition by the sultan, for which he had to pay considerable sums of money. From the end of the fifteenth century on he also had to pay annual taxes, a large part of which he could only cover by selling ecclesiastical offices. In each case the official written recognition returned to the patriarch stipulated his authority. As the responsible head of the Orthodox population the patriarch was granted judicial and police powers on the basis of the *millet* system. By virtue of his political function as ethnarch he was considered governor of the sultan with the rank of a pasha. The disadvantages of such close ties to the Porte were evident in the fact that the patriarch's position was very insecure. Of the 162 "Archbishops of Constantinople, the New Rome, and Ecumenical Patriarchs" (their official title since 588) reigning at the time of the Ottomans, only 22 died in office.[4] Many of them—especially in the seventeenth century—were dismissed by the sultan and reinstalled,[5] some were executed at his order. As a result their average time in office between 1453 and 1821, the beginning of the Greek war of liberation, was only two and a half years. In the period from 1625 to 1700 the patriarchate was filled fifty times; in the eighteenth century there were 48 patriarchs in the course of seventy-three years.

After the Hagia Sophia was changed into a mosque, the patriarchs designated the monastery of Pammakaristos as their patriarchal church and relocated their see to the buildings of the monastery (1456–1586). Because the environs were inhabited almost exclusively by Turks they

[3] See Chap. 13.
[4] F. W. Fernau, op. cit., 73.
[5] Patriarch Cyril Lucaris even seven times: 1612, 1621–23, 1623–30, 1630–33, 1633–34, 1634–35, 1637–38. After his last dismissal he was strangled by Turkish soldiers on his way to the fortress of Rumeli Hisāri.

found a temporary abode in the palace of the prince of Walachia. Around 1600 they located their see in the *Phanar,* the Greek part of the city, where they raised the Church of Saint George to the status of patriarchal church. The *Phanar* was comparable to the Vatican. The great synods were convened in the *Phanar;* all matters were decided in the presence of as many archbishops and bishops as possible and the synods were frequently attended by the other Orthodox patriarchs or their representatives. The laymen involved in the administration of the Church rose to become the influential segment of the so-called *Phanariots,* who strengthened the Ottoman government in Moldavia and Walachia and strove for the Hellenization of the Orthodox Church on the Balkan peninsula.

The move to independence on the part of the Russian Patriarchal Church under Patriarch Jeremias II (1589), the Union of Brest (1595/96), the actions of the Curia to win over the Orthodox faithful, evidenced by the founding in Rome of colleges for the Eastern Churches, the appearance of Jesuits and Capuchins in Constantinople and other places forced the Orthodox Churches to counter Roman propaganda for the union and her mission policies. In the period of renewal within the Catholic Church and the time of the Counter Reformation, the Protestants had sought contacts with the Orthodox Church.[6] The scholarly Ecumenical Patriarch Cyril Lucaris (1624–38, with four brief interruptions),[7] who had been present at the Synod of Brest (1596) as representative of the patriarch of Alexandria and who had also been patriarch of Alexandria (1602–20), took from the works of Calvin arguments for use in his fight against Rome. He hoped that the creation of a united front of Orthodox and Calvinists would bring about a union in the true faith. His relationship with Cornelius Haga, the Dutch ambassador to Constantinople (1621–39), and with Antoine Léger, predicant at the Dutch embassy (1628–36), deepened his knowledge of Protestant confessional writings. He wanted to reform the Orthodox Church and to this end composed a *Confessio fidei,* which was published in Geneva first in Latin (1629) and then in a Greek translation (1633); in addition, one English and four French translations appeared simultaneously.[8] In this creed Cyril Lucaris relinquished important dogmas of the Eastern Church; he embraced the doctrine of the *sola scriptura,*

---

[6] E. Benz, *Wittenberg und Byzanz. Zur Begegnung und Auseinandersetzung der Reformation mit der östlich-orthodoxen Kirche* (Marburg 1949).
[7] R. Belmont, "Le patriache Cyrille Lukaris et l'union des églises," *Irénikon* 15 (1938), 342–63, 535–53; G. A. Hadjiantoniou, *Protestant Patriarch. The Life of Cyril Lucaris (1572–1638), Patriarch of Constantinople* (London 1961); G. Hering, *Ökumenisches Patriarchat und europäische Politik 1620–1638* (Wiesbaden 1968; biblio.)
[8] G. Hering, op. cit., 188; also cf. Jugie I, 505–7.

denied the real presence of Christ in the Eucharist, expressed regret at the veneration of icons, and called the invocation of the saints idolatry. The opposition against Cyril Lucaris was led by Metropolitan Contares of Berhoia, who took the former's place several times as Patriarch Cyril II (1633, 1635–36, 1638–39).[9] Contares was supported by the Vatican, as well as by French and imperial diplomats. The accusation that Cyril Lucaris had initiated treasonous connections with the tsar led to his fall; he was condemned to death. Three months later, on 24 September 1638,[10] his *Confessio fidei* was rejected by a large synod in Constantinople in which patriarchs of Constantinople, Alexandria and Jerusalem, twenty-one metropolitans and twenty-four other clerics took part. In 1640 Metropolitan Petrus Mogilas of Kiev drafted a *Confessio orthodoxa* which argued against the Calvinist views of Cyril Lucaris and represented the Orthodox point of view. Translated by the Greek theologian Meletios Sygiros from Latin into Greek, it was accepted by all the Eastern patriarchs at the Synod of Jassy in 1642 and the Synod of Constantinople in 1643.[11] The initial attempts by Cyril Lucaris to renew the Orthodox Church, to cleanse it of alleged falsifications by "papist innovations," and to bring about an approach to Protestantism had failed. The reorganization of the patriarchate of Constantinople, the establishment of a printing shop, and the translation of the New Testament into the Greek vernacular were stopped in their initial stages; only the planned educational reform of the priests was developed further at a later time. He failed in his attempt to involve the *Phanar* in the complicated maneuverings of European diplomacy along with the Sublime Porte, the Vatican, and the Catholic and Protestant powers in order to influence the presence and future development of Christianity. The ecumenical patriarchate remained in a state of dependence on the sultanate. Cyril II Contares was dismissed in 1639, arrested, deported to North Africa, and strangled in 1640.

Under supervision by the government, the subsequent patriarchs made efforts to preserve their jurisdictional sphere and to consolidate it in present-day Albania, Yugoslavia, Bulgaria, Rumania, and Greece. By 1700 they were at the head of sixty-three metropolitans, eighteen exempt archbishops, and seventy bishops. Whereas the Slavic languages dominated the Balkans in the sixteenth century, the new upper class promoted Greek. Initially the Greek-speaking families furnished the higher ecclesiastical dignitaries, but after the seventeeth century the bishops were almost exclusively Greek. The *Phanar,* meanwhile, aimed at eliminating the autonomy of the Balkan Orthodox Churches. In 1766

[9] G. Hering, op. cit., 427.

[10] Mansi XXXIV, 1719–21.

[11] Ibid., XXXIV, 1629–38; Jugie I, 508–9; G. Hering, op. cit., n. 103.

the Serbian patriarchate of Ipek was abolished; in 1767 the autocephaly of the Bulgarian archbishopric of Achrida was dissolved by Sultan Mustafa III and incorporated in the ecumenical patriarchate and Hellenized by it. The Turkish designation of its dominion in Europe as Rumeli, Land of the Rum (Greeks), appeared justified. Patriarch Samuel Khanzeris (1763–68, 1773–74), a Phanariotic parvenue whose brother, the governor of Walachia, was recalled and executed by the Sultan for extortion, attempted to lessen the influence of the Sublime Porte on the election or appointment of the patriarchs by forming a college of councilors. But he could not keep the rival Greek families from increasing the dependence of the patriarchate upon the sultan by calling upon him as a referee in their fight for political and ecclesiastical positions.

The dependence of the ecumenical patriarchs on the government of the Ottoman Empire merely guaranteed outward security. The life of the Church was unable to develop. The threat of the death penalty for conversion to Christianity, the ban against building new churches, the apostasy of Orthodox faithful to Islam were dangerous implications. In the face of these, the patriarchs made efforts to improve the education of the priests; Cyril Lucaris (1627), Samuel Khanzeris (1767), Gregorios V (1798), and others set up printing shops. But the Orthodox heritage of the forefathers was primarily preserved by the monasteries. The monks and recluses on Mount Athos,[12] whose privileges were not touched by the Turks and were, in fact, expanded with the help of the Russian Tsars and Emperors, formed a religious center which was supported by the whole Orthodox Church. Their abbots did not shy away from traveling to the West asking for money, as did Abakum Andriani, abbot of Iberon, at the beginning of the eighteenth century.[13] The Athonias School near the monastery of Vatopädi had been planned as an academy; its director, Eugenios Bulgaris (1753–57), made a name for himself as editor of Greek authors and as a controvertist, but because of the resistance of numerous monks against all higher education the school did not flourish.

The patriarchs of the four Eastern sees had the title "Father and Shepherd, Pope and Patriarch of the Great City of Alexandria of Lybia, Pentapolis, Ethiopia, Father of Fathers, Shepherd of Shepherds, Bishop of Bishops, Thirteenth Apostle and Judge of the World." But even at the end of the sixth century the glory of the Alexandrian Church of Christian antiquity faded when most of the faithful joined a form of

---

[12] *Le millénaire du Mont Athos 963–1963, études et mélanges,* 2 vols. (Chevetogne 1964); P. Huber, *Athos. Leben, Glaube, Kunst* (Zurich 1969).

[13] H. de Greeve, "Neue Quellen zur ersten Reise des Athosabtes Abakum Andriani in Westeuropa," *OstKSt* 16 (1967), 325–33.

Monophysitism under its own Coptic patriarch. Copts and Melchites (from the Syrian *malko*), as the Orthodox followers of the Byzantine Emperor were called, were equally oppressed by the Arabs. The dependence on Byzantium of the Melchite Orthodox patriarch of Alexandria, whose following was further decreased by anti-Christian government measures, brought with it the displacement of the stately old Alexandrian liturgy by the Byzantine liturgy. From 1209 to 1316 the patriarchs resided in Constantinople; they were represented in Alexandria by a deputy. After the fall of the imperial city many Greeks fled to Alexandria. Following the conquest of Egypt by Sultan Selim I, Patriarch Joachim Pany (1487–1567) established good relations with the Turkish rulers, but under his successors the patriarchate deteriorated into total dependence on the Sublime Porte and the ecumenical patriarch. Initially the patriarchs took up residence in Constantinople while an archimandrite ministered to the faithful, who were reduced to a mere five thousand in the eighteenth century. Several patriarchs of Alexandria played a fairly important role in the *Phanar*. Among them were Meletios I Pegas (1590–1601), who administered the ecumenical patriarchate in 1597/98; the already mentioned Cyril Lucaris (1602–20); Gerasimos Startaliotes (1620–1639), who founded the first Greek schools in Cairo and Alexandria and maintained connections with the Moscow patriarchate and the Anglican Church; Paisios (1657–77) who took part in the Moscow Synod of 1666 against Nikon; and, lastly, Samuel Kapasulis (1710–23).

At the time of the Arab rule and the Ottoman Empire, the patriarchs of Antioch also depended strongly on the patriarch of Constantinople. At the end of the thirteenth century they relocated their residence to Damascus, the capital of the Arab caliphate. After the conquest of Syria by Sultan Selim I in 1516 they had to submit to the Turks, whose taxation added greatly to the debt of the patriarchate. Patriarchs Joachim V (1584–87) and Makarios III (1647–72) made trips to Russia for the purpose of soliciting gifts of money. In the course of the seventeenth century, Jesuits and Franciscans achieved some success in their efforts regarding union. In 1683 Archbishop Euthymios of Sydan and Tyre embraced Catholicism. He initiated the establishment of an independent Uniate Melchite patriarchate (1724), which was joined by many Orthodox faithful. In 1718 Archbishop Euthymios was excommunicated by Ecumenical Patriarch Jeremias III and then arrested by the Sultan, but Louis XIV brought about his release. From 1724 to 1851 the *Phanar* made sure that only Greeks would hold the office of patriarch. Among the Arabic-speaking people they competed for influence with the Monophysites and the Uniate Catholics.

The island of Cyprus, originally under the patriarchate of Antioch,[14] preserved its autocephaly, recognized by the Council of Ephesus, for over a thousand years throughout all political and ecclesiastic disorders into the sixteenth century. When the Turks occupied the island in 1571, they introduced the *millet* system and appointed the archbishop as ethnarch of all the Greeks living there. They suffered greatly under the oppressive new rule, especially in the seventeenth century. The Synod of Leukosia (1668) under Archbishop Nikephoros condemned the Calvinist views of Patriarch Cyril Lucaris. Being isolated, the archbishops again reestablished a connection with the patriarchs of Antioch, from whom they received the Holy Myron in 1860.

After 1543 the patriarchate of Jerusalem, too, was occupied exclusively by Greeks. After Selim I incorporated Palestine into the Ottoman Empire, they were politically and ecclesiastically under the influence of Constantinople. Since they were leading the "Brotherhood of the Holy Sepulchre," the sultan granted them full jurisdiction over the holy places in Jerusalem and Bethlehem; this was contested by several other Christian communities. Patriarch Germanos Peloponnesios (1534–79) and many of his successors made frequent trips to the centers of Orthodox Christendom collecting funds for the places of pilgrimage. In addition, the ecumenical patriarchs and the ecclesiastical princes of Moldavia and Walachia also extended their efforts towards the preservation of those places. Some patriarchs made serious efforts to gain possession of the holy places. Among them were Patriarchs Theophanes III (1608–44), Paisios (1645–60), Nektarios (1660–69), and Dositheos II (1669–1707),[15] who enjoyed great esteem among the whole Orthodox Church. He established a Greek press with which to counter the propaganda of the Roman and Uniate Catholics. At a synod in Bethlehem-Jerusalem in 1672[16] he had the rejection of the *Confessio fidei* by Cyril Lucaris reasserted; the rejection was seconded by a synod in Constantinople the same year.[17] The struggle over the holy places was continued by Patriarchs Chrysanthos (1707–31) and Parthenios (1737–66). They succeeded in regaining possession of the places of pilgrimage, administered since 1689 by the Franciscans. At the beginning of the seventeenth century the patriarchate comprised six metropolitans, seven archbishops, and one bishop. Most of them lived in Jerusalem, four in their small eparchies, and one in the monastery on

---

[14] Hippolytos, "Die Autokephale Apostolische Orthodoxe Kirche Cyperns," *Ekklesia* X 117–29.
[15] A. Palmieri, *Dositeo, Patriarca greco di Gerusalemme* (Florence 1909).
[16] Mansi XXXIV, 1651–1776; Jugie I, 509–10.
[17] Mansi XXXIV, 1777–90.

Mount Sinai. The patriarchal school established in 1736 intensified its activities under Patriarch Anthimos (1788–1808).

Closely connected to the patriarchate of Jerusalem was the small Orthodox church on Mount Sinai. It was led by an archbishop who at the same time was abbot of the Monastery of Saint Catherine.[18] Its monks received letters of safe passage from Sultan Selim I and his successors. The monastic buildings adjacent to the church and protected by a wall against attacks by the Bedouins contained a famous library with valuable Greek, Georgian, and Slavic manuscripts, as well as a pinacotheca with old icons. Its abbot-archbishop cultivated good relations with the patriarchs of Alexandria and Jerusalem and with the Orthodox Greeks on the island of Crete. The monks of Mount Sinai built a school in Herakleion on Crete among whose graduates were Alexandrian Patriarch Meletios Pegas and the painter Domenicos Theotokopoulos (1548–1614), known as El Greco. Because the patriarchs of Alexandria and Antioch contested each other's jurisdiction over the archbishopric of Sinai, the Synod of Constantinople declared the church autocephalic in 1575; this ruling was recognized by all Eastern patriarchs in 1782. Each abbot of Sinai was consecrated as bishop by the patriarch of Jerusalem.

While the Church on Mount Sinai in the south of the Ottoman Empire gained its independence, the Bulgarian and Serbian Churches on the Balkan Peninsula lost theirs. Since the early Middle Ages the Byzantine Church had achieved great successes in its mission there. During the periods of 927 to 1018 and 1235 to 1393 the Orthodox Bulgarians had their own patriarchate with the residence in Achrida and Trnovo respectively. After the conquest of Bulgaria by the Turks in 1393 they were placed under the archbishopric of Achrida, which became ever more dependent on the ecumenical patriarchate in the centuries which followed.[19] Bulgarian rebellions (1595 and 1688) against the Turkish rule heightened the tensions between the monasteries adhering to the national traditions and the upper clergy installed by the *Phanar*. By order of Sultan Mustafa III the archbishopric was incorporated into the patriarchate of Constantinople in 1767; the books in Church Slavonic were removed and replaced by Greek ones. The Bulgarian language was suppressed by the Greek hegemony; the church administration was completely in the hands of Greeks. The same sort of

---

[18] H. L. Rabino, *Le monastère de Saint-Catherine du Mont Sinai* (Cairo 1938).
[19] I. Snĕgarov, *Istorija na ochridskata archiepiskopija-patriarsija ot padeneto i pod turcitĕ do nejnoto uništoženie 1394–1767* (Sofia 1931); A. P. Péchayre, "L archevêché d'Ochrida de 1394 à 1767," *ÉO* 35 (1936), 183–204, 280–323; S. Zankow, "Die Bulgarische Orthodoxe Kirche in Gesch. und Gegenwart," *IKZ* 48 (1958), 189–208.

development took place in the principalities of Moldavia and Walachia, where the Rumanian liturgical language began spreading after 1648, but the Greek influence nonetheless remained decisive after the eighteenth century.

The Serbian Church also lost its independence. In 1219 it had been granted its own archbishopric and in 1351 its own patriarchate in Peć (Ipek); in 1459 it was placed under the jurisdiction of the archbishopric of Achrida. In 1557 Grand Vizier Mehmed Sokolović, a Serb converted to Islam, reinstated the patriarchate and appointed his brother, the monk Makarios, patriarch of Ipek. For the next two centuries Serbs and Greeks fought for this office, which the sultan gave to those who offered the most for it.[20] From 1690 to 1765 a total of fourteen patriarchs succeeded one another, continually increasing the debt of the patriarchate from one decade to the next. The emigration in 1690 of thirty thousand Serbian families led by their patriarch Arsenije III into areas taken from the Turks by the Habsburgs and the emigration of a similar number under their patriarch Arsenije IV caused the *Phanar* to intensify its efforts to place only dependable Greeks in the patriarchates and the bishoprics. In 1766 Patriarch Samuel Khanzeris of Constantinople finally induced Sultan Mustafa III to abolish the Serbian patriarchate. It was combined with the metropolitanate of Prizren and incorporated in the ecumenical patriarchate. Several Serbian hierarchs turned to Tsarina Catherine II for help, but were unable to obtain relief. All bishoprics were subsequently filled by Greeks. The only exception was the metropolitan of Cetinje in Montenegro, whose princes had wrung some degree of independence from the Ottoman rule and established close connections with Russia. He managed to avoid the incorporation, and as a result the Orthodox Church of Montenegro became autocephalic.

The abolition of the national Serbian and Bulgarian Churches in 1766 and 1767 placed all Christian subjects of the sultanate in Europe under one uniform ecclesiastical administration. The ecumenical patriarch promoted the use of Greek for the Mass in every part of the patriarchate; he had Greek schools established and consolidated his position throughout the Ottoman Empire.

Only one numerically strong autocephalic Orthodox Church re-

[20] N. Djordjević, *Die Selbständigkeit der Serbischen Kirche* (diss., Berne 1922); A. Hudal, *Die serbisch-orthodoxe Nationalkirche* (Graz and Leipzig 1922), 21–38; L. Hadrovics, *Le peuple serbe et son église sous la domination turque* (Paris 1947); C. Jelavich, "Some aspects of Serbian Religious Development in the eighteenth Century," *CH* 23 (1954), 144–52; V. Pospischil, *Der Patriarch in der Serbisch-Orthodoxen Kirche* (Vienna 1966), 32–45.
[21] M. Tamarati, *L'Église Géorgienne* (Rome 1910); M. Tarchnišvili, "Die Entstehung und Entwicklung der kirchlichen Autokephalie Georgiens," *Kyrios* 5 (1940–41), 177–93; C. Toumanoff, "Introduction to Christian Caucasian History," *Tr* 15 (1959), 1–104.

mained, the Greater Church of Georgia,[21] which had separated from the patriarchate in the early Middle Ages and formed a catholicate at the end of the seventh century. The Byzantine rule in the eleventh century produced an accommodation with the Church of the Byzantine Empire for which the adoption of the Byzantine liturgy in the Georgian language was symbolic. After the collapse of political independence in the late Middle Ages, Turks and Persians fought for Georgia, the larger part of which came under Persian supremacy. But the majority of the population remained Orthodox and resisted the Islamization by their rulers, although defections to Turkish tribes near Batum and on the coast of the Black Sea did occur and a so-called third faith, a mixture of Christian, Islamic, and heathen ideas, started spreading. The catholicos was dependent on the benevolence of the Persian governor. When Catholicos Jesse became susceptible to overtures by the Capuchin and Theatine friars regarding union, he was dismissed by a synod in 1755. King Erekle II of East Georgia (1744–98) sought closer connections with Orthodox Russia in order to decrease his dependence on Persia. His treaty with Catherine II (1783) initiated the eventual annexation by Russia. In 1801 Tsar Alexander I declared western Georgia and in 1803 all of Georgia to be Russian provinces. Catholicos Antonios II had to abdicate and go to Russia. The catholicate was dissolved and the Georgian Church was entrusted to a Russian exarch (1817) who had his residence in Tiflis. The construction of Russian monasteries in Georgia was intended to add to the number of the Russian Orthodox faithful.

The Oriental National Churches of the Nestorians and Monophysites

The Nestorian Church,[22] whose missionary work had spread its faith to Persia, Turkestan, Tibet, Mongolia, China, and to the Malabar Coast in India during the Middle Ages, was confined by the Mongols, especially Timur Lane (1360–1405), to the mountain regions of Northern Kurdistan and Persian Azerbaijan on Lake Urmia.[23] The Nestorian catholicos, i.e., patriarch, who had resided in Baghdad from 750 to 1258 moved his see to the monastery of Rabban Hurmuz near Mosul. Since the middle of the fifteenth century it had become customary to have nephew follow uncle in the catholicate. But after the death of Patriarch Simon VII bar Mamma, part of the clergy and laity refused to recognize his

[22] *Atlas zur Kirchengesch.* (Freiburg 1970), map 27.
[23] A. R. Vine, *The Nestorian Churches* (London 1937); B. Spuler, "Die nestorianische Kirche," *Hdb. der Orientalistik*, Abt. 1, VIII/2 (Leiden and Cologne 1961), 120–69; P. Kawerau, "Die nestorianischen Patriarchate in der neueren Zeit," *ZKG* 67 (1955/56), 119–31; A. S. Atiya, op. cit., 237–302.

nephew Simon VIII Denha (1551–59) and instead elected John Sulaga, abbot of the monastery of Rabban Hurmuz. But the latter could not be consecrated for lack of an authorized Nestorian metropolitan. So John reestablished ties to the Curia, which had been fashioned by the Nestorians in the high and late Middle Ages. He went to Rome, embraced the primacy and the Catholic creed, was consecrated bishop in 1553 and proclaimed patriarch of the Chaldeans by Pope Julius III. When he returned home, he was arrested by the Turks, rulers of the land of the Euphrates and Tigris since 1534. He died a prisoner in 1555. In 1672 Simon XIII Denha separated from that Uniate patriarchate with its seat in Diarbekr west of the upper Tigris and founded his own, the so-called Mountain Nestorian patriarchate, with the residence in Kotschannes in Kurdistan. The old Nestorian patriarchate also remained; its faithful— in contrast to the Uniate Chaldeans—were called Assyrians. Defections by Uniate patriarchs to Nestorianism and back increased the confusion among the Nestorians (comprised of about forty thousand families).

Among the Monophysite communities there were the Churches of the Jacobites of western Syria, the Christians of Saint Thomas, the Copts, Ethiopians and Armenians.

The Jacobite Syrian Church,[24] having flourished in the twelfth and thirteenth centuries, was divided in the late Middle Ages and split into four rival centers which suffered under the oppression of the Mongol Timur Lane. In 1495 Ignatius XII Noah (1483–1509) was able to re- unite the patriarchate. But his successors, who had resided in Amida since 1555 and in Aleppo since the seventeenth century, had a mere twenty bishoprics under their jurisdiction; the number of faithful was estimated at fifty thousand families in 1583. The majority of them inhabited Tur-Abdin in the Izla Mountains, where their survivors are living even now. The existence of the Church was further weakened by successful efforts at union during the second half of the seventeenth century. Yet the Church experienced some growth when it was joined by Uniate Nestorians in South India during the patriarchate of Ignatius XXIII (1662–86). But the lack of seminaries for priests and monks prevented development of the Jacobite Syrian Church in the eighteenth century.

The Nestorian faithful in South India were called *Surjani* (Syrians) because of the language of their cult. They called themselves Christians of Saint Thomas after the Apostle Thomas.[25] Their bishops were ap-

---

[24] P. Kawerau, *Die jakobitische Kirche im Zeitalter der syrischen Renaissance* (Berlin 1955); B. Spuler, "Die westsyrische (monophysitische/jakobitische) Kirche," *Hdb. der Orientalistik,* Abt. 1, VIII/2 (1961), 170–216; A. S. Atiya, op. cit., 167–235.
[25] E. Tisserant, *Eastern Christianity in India. A History of the Syro-Malabar Church from the Earliest Time to the Present Day* (London, New York and Toronto 1957); B. Spuler,

pointed by the Nestorian catholicos. The union effected under Portuguese rule in the sixteenth century and the decisions of the Synod of Diamper (Urdiamperur) near Cochin in 1599 met with considerable resistance. Archdeacon Thomas Palakomot, having protested unsuccessfully in Rome (1637) against the destruction of most of the Nestorian liturgical books and also against the Latinization of his Church, established contacts with the Nestorian, Jacobite, and Coptic patriarchs, asking them to furnish a bishop. In 1653 twelve priests declared him their Metropolitan Mar Thomas I by the laying on of hands. He is assumed to have been legally consecrated ex post facto by the Jacobite Bishop Mar Gregorios of Jerusalem. In an open letter he asserted the correctness of the Syrian faith and rite as opposed to the Catholic Church. The majority of the approximately two hundred thousand Christians of Saint Thomas joined him; only a small percentage remained obedient to the Portuguese Roman Catholic Archbishop Franciscus Garcia (1641–59).[26] Mar Thomas I started the line of metropolitans of the Christians of Saint Thomas who subordinated themselves to the western Syrian patriarchate. Mar Thomas II (1670–86) and Mar Thomas IV (1688–93) were able to offset Nestorian attempts at reconversion and solidify the Monophysite Church organization with support by the western Syrian patriarchs. Their struggle for autonomy progressed during the eighteenth century, but so did efforts at union by the Jesuits and Carmelites. By 1770 their Church comprised about fifty thousand faithful in thirty-two parishes under Metropolitan Mar Thomas VI, who assumed the name Mar Dionysios I (1765–1808) after his consecration in 1772.[27] That same year a congregation in the north of the Christian area which did not recognize the dependence on the western Syrian patriarchate defected and declared itself the autonomous Church of Annur. The fact that a considerable segment of the original Nestorian Christians of Saint Thomas changed to Monophysitism proves that the latter had more charisma than the Nestorian Church of the seventeenth century. Metropolitan Mar Dionysios I, who came from an aristocratic Catholic family but had been educated by his Monophysite uncle Mar Thomas V, repeatedly negotiated union

---

"Die Thomas-Christen in Süd-Indien," *Hdb. der Orientalistik*, Abt. 1, VIII/2 (1961), 226–39; P. J. Podipara, *Die Thomas-Christen* (Würzburg 1966); N. J. Thomas, *Die Syrisch-Orthodoxe Kirche der Südindischen Thomas-Christen* (Würzburg 1967); A. S. Atiya, op. cit., 357–88.

[26] K. Werth, *Das Schisma der Thomaschristen unter Erzbischof Franciscus Garzia* (Limburg a.d. Lahn 1937).

[27] J. Kollaparambil, "Mar Dionysius the Great of Malabar, for the One True Fold," *OrChrP* 30 (1964), 148–92.

with the vicar apostolic of Malabar. In 1799 he reembraced Catholicism, but reverted to Monophysitism after another six months.

The Coptic Church of Egypt, consisting of six million Christians in the early Middle Ages, called *kibt* (Copts) by their Arabian conquerors, lost in importance in the further course of the Middle Ages because of internal conflicts and anti-Christian measures by their Islamic rulers, especially the Mamelukes. By about 1400 they were a mere tenth in an Arab population embracing Islam. Under Turkish rule from 1517 to 1798,[28] which installed Mameluke governors in Cairo, the patriarchs residing in Cairo were unable to stop the deterioration of theological education and the decline in the number of their faithful. These were estimated at a mere one hundred fifty thousand around 1700. Most of their once flourishing monasteries had been either dissolved or had disintegrated. The Turkish government prevented contacts with other Monophysite Churches, such as the Egyptian Church, all of which were prosecuted as being dangerous to the state. In the second half of the eighteenth century the Coptic Church was indebted to the politically influential and wealthy Gauhari family for generous gifts. Ibrahim Gauhari had old Coptic manuscripts copied and given to several churches restored by him. Under Marcus VIII (1796–1809) the Coptic patriarchate showed the first signs of a renewal which was to continue throughout the nineteenth century. He relocated his residence to the property deeded to the Church by Ibrahim Gauhari in Ezbikije, a suburb of Cairo, where he rebuilt the old monastery church of Saint Mark, which had been burned in street fighting with the French in 1798.

The established Monophysite Church of Ethiopia[29] was dependent on the Coptic patriarch, who delegated to it a metropolitan as its *abuna* (our father). One of his tasks was to anoint the king (*negus*). The most prominent position next to him was occupied by the abbot of the monastery of Dabra Libanos; in his capacity as court confessor he was given the title of *etschege* (the one standing next to the assistant of the throne) in the fifteenth century. He was the one who supervised all monastic property. The Church's ties to its mother Church were not

---

[28] R. Strothmann, *Die Koptische Kirche in der Neuzeit* (Tübingen 1932); M. Cramer, *Das christlich-koptische Ägypten einst und heute* (Wiesbaden 1959); S. Chauleur, *Histoire des Coptes d'Égypte* (Paris 1960); B. Spuler, "Die koptische Kirche," *Hdb. der Orientalistik,* Abt. 1, VIII/2 (1961), 269–308; A. S. Atiya, op. cit., 99–101; A. J. Arberry, op. cit. II, 423–53.

[29] H. M. Hyatt, *The Church of Abyssinia* (London 1928); B. Spuler, "Die äthiopische Kirche," *Hdb. der Orientalistik,* Abt. 1, VIII/2 (1961), 309–24; E. Hammerschmidt, *Äthiopien. Christliches Reich zwischen gestern und morgen* (Wiesbaden 1967); A. S. Atiya, op. cit., 146–66; op. cit., 454–81.

very close because of the spreading of the Islamic faith in Egypt and Nubia. Black tribes advancing from the periphery into the interior of the country increased its isolation. When new attacks by Islamic princes took place at the beginning of the sixteenth century and the Ottomans of Massaua in Eritrea threatened to shake the state structure of Ethiopia in 1527, Negus Lebna Denghel (1508–40) sought help from the Pope and the King of Portugal, who in turn was seeking bases in order to secure naval passage around Africa to his possessions in India. With the help of the Portuguese the negus and his successors managed to vanquish the fanatical Islamic invader Ahmad ibn Ibrahim al Ghazi, who had destroyed many churches and monasteries. The Jesuits who had come into the country with the Portuguese were later expelled by Negus Claudius (1540–59). Half a century later Negus Atnas Sagas (Za Denghel) was converted to Catholicism by the Jesuit priest Pedro Páez (1569–1622) just before he died. Páez also persuaded the former's successor, Malak Sagad III (Susenyos) (1607–32), to conclude a union. The abuna's protests against the union and against the patriarch of Ethiopia, Alonso Mendes, who had been designated by King Philip IV of Spain and recognized by Pope Urban VIII, and the rebellions against the Latinization of the Ethiopian Church by the Portuguese forced the negus to abdicate. His successor, Fasiladas (Basilides) (1632–67), canceled the union and imposed the death penalty on Catholic clerics who entered the country. The stirrings of union in the Ethiopian Church were reflected in various writings of the period in the colloquial language of Amharic. After its ties with the Coptic Church were restored (1632), translations of theological and legal works from the Arabic (of which there had been earlier evidence) increased, but ended in the eighteenth century as a result of civil wars and wars with the Hamitic nomads. In the seventeenth century the issue, discussed as early as the Middle Ages in rival monastic schools, of whether Jesus Christ received his divine nature at birth or later at the baptism on the Jordan (*unctio*, anointment) created the two parties of the Uniates and Unctionists. Around 1740 a third group maintained that Jesus was "anointed," "anointment" and "the anointed" in one. These and other Christological disputes extended into the nineteenth century. In the process there was no lack of mutual accusations of the Arian, the Nestorian, and the Cryptocatholic heresies. There were turbulent disputations and temporary predominance of one or the other current of thought, leading to victory by the abuna, a provincial prince, or the negus, often after bloody battles. But the basic Monophysite concept proved stronger in the end than all the quarrels concerning the interpretation of the one nature of Christ, and the unity of the Ethiopian Church remained intact.

In the Middle Ages the Monophysite Armenian Church,[30] also called Gregorian (after its founder Gregory the Enlightener), had broken up into several jurisdictions. This had been caused by the migrations and subsequent divisions of the Armenian people. In addition to the catholicate of Wagharchapat, or Aghtamar in its original homeland, a patriarchate with residence in Sis in the kingdom of Lesser Armenia had come into existence during the second half of the thirteenth century. It ministered to the Armenians in Cilicia, northern Syria and on the island of Cyprus. Since 1311 there had also been a patriarchate of Jerusalem. In 1441 several bishops, having quarreled with the patriarch of Sis, who had been raised from the office of catholicos, founded a new catholicate at the monastery of Etchmiadzin at Mount Ararat. In 1463 Sultan Mehmed II had the patriarchate of Constantinople established for the Armenians in the Ottoman Empire. Without clarifying the canonical aspects, the catholicos of Etchmiadzin came to be the most influential ecclesiastical shepherd of the Armenians for the next few centuries. In the middle of the seventeenth century he was recognized by the sultanate as the supreme Armenian ecclesiastic, although the patriarch of Constantinople retained his special civil position. Caught between the expansionary struggles of the Ottoman and Persian rulers, the Armenians repeatedly suffered persecutions which caused part of them to emigrate to the Holy Land, Poland-Lithuania, and India. The Persians forced those Armenians living on the western periphery of their realm to leave their settlements, assigning them new ones in Iran. Shah Abbas I (1587–1628) carried the catholicos off to his capital of Isfahan. The new Catholicos Moses III (1629–32), elected during his predecessor's imprisonment, had come from a reformed monastic order and renewed church life. Some of his predecessors as well as successors, such as Stephan V (1545–64) and Nahapet (1691–1705), were prepared for union with Rome. While pertinent negotiations were successful in the patriarchate of Sis, they were suppressed in the patriarchate of Constantinople by Patriarch John Golod (1715–41). In the second half of the eighteenth century the supreme shepherds of Etchmiadzin established ties with the Russian Empire, which was expanding into the Caucasus. In 1797 northern Armenia and in 1828/29 the largest part of Greater Armenia were annexed by Russia. After 1800 the catholicate was under Russian influence.

---

[30] F. Tournebize, *Histoire politique et religieuse de l'Arménie* (Paris 1910); M. Ormanian, *The Church of Armenia* (London 1955); B. Spuler, "Die armenische Kirche," *Hdb. der Orientalistik,* Abt. 1, VIII/2 (1961), 240–68; J. Mécérian, *Histoire et institutions de l'Église arménienne* (Beirut 1965); A. K. Sanjian, *The Armenian Communities in Syria under Ottoman Dominion* (London 1965).

During the first few decades of the nineteenth century all autonomous Orthodox, Nestorian, and Monophysite Churches suffered greatly under the strong pressure of their Turkish, Persian, and Russian rulers. This restricted their development and limited their work to the liturgical realm. The number of their faithful decreased, but in spite of all the oppressions those who remained loyal to their faith preserved the heritage of their fathers, the properties of their faith, and their liturgies, the essentials of which had their origin as far back as Christian antiquity. Their perseverance in the midst of trials and tribulation gives witness to their Christian history.

The Uniate Churches

The union of Rome with the Greeks, signed at the Council of Florence in 1439 and in 1442–45 joined by the Armenians, Copts, Syrian Jacobites, and groups of Nestorians and Maronites living on Cyprus, was but of short duration. The further the Ottomans advanced west and south, the more quickly the ties between the Apostolic See and the Uniate Churches in the Near East, the islands of the eastern Mediterranean and the Balkan peninsula were cut. The Popes had no means by which to counter these reverses. Their expectation that military victory over the Turks fighting under the banner of their prophet might pave the way for reunification of the separated halves of Eastern and Western Christendom proved illusory. They tried in the sixteenth and seventeenth century to bring about coalitions against the Turks, and at times were successful, as evidenced by the defense of Vienna in 1689. But their becoming part of the development of the Western world was manifested in the modern-day unions organized by them. To be sure, these unions bore a different stamp from the *communio* of all partial Churches in existence during the first millenium. In the West a uniformly and well-organized Church had been developed under the direction of Popes who had scant understanding of the autonomous administration of the Eastern Churches which had developed since Christian antiquity. In addition, many members of religious orders urged Latin spirituality upon the Uniate Churches and, further, the Greek (1576) and Maronite Colleges (1584) founded in Rome for the education of Uniate clerics were based (among other things) upon Scholastic theology. The Congregation for the Propagation of the Faith gave orders initially to win individual believers over to the Catholic Church but at first to have them remain in their mother Church. The intention was to gain influence slowly and—given a vacancy—to get a patriarch or catholicos appointed who would embrace Catholicism. One such instance was the elevation of Michael Garweh to the patriarchate of Antioch after the death of George III in 1783.[31]

For several reasons the unions—with the exception of the one concluded with the Maronites in 1515—lasted but a short time or proved to be durable only after several tries. The Popes paid close attention to keeping the privileges granted the Uniate Churches and safeguarding their Armenian, Byzantine, Chaldaic, Coptic, Maronite, and Syrian rites. But several Western rulers formulated plans to effect a union while pursuing their own motives, as for instance the Kings of France in the Near East, the German Emperors in Siebenbürgen (Hungary), and the Kings of Poland-Lithuania with their magnates in the Ukraine.

The unions were generally considered an intermediate step between Latin Christendom and an Eastern Christendom which was to be eschewed. In the course of the centuries the influences of Latin liturgy and Roman canon law became more and more noticeable in the life of the Uniate Churches. The blend of Eastern features and Latin traditions, sharply criticized as "Uniatism" by Eastern theologians, militated against the development of many unions in eastern and southern Europe, in the Near East, in northeastern Africa, and the Indies.

The union with the Ruthenians and Ukrainians in Poland-Lithuania, concluded in Rome (1595) and accepted at the synod in Brest (1596), was slow to permeate all segments of the population.[32] It lacked the support of the authoritative circle of the magnates, who were either Orthodox or Roman Catholic. Polish theologians considered union as a transitional phenomenon and therefore extended their efforts towards a reduction in the separate customs granted to the Uniate rites and towards a gradual Latinization of their cult. In 1620 when the Orthodox Church reestablished its metropolitanate of Kiev, which flourished quickly under the leadership of Archbishop Petrus Mogilas (1633–45), several Uniate bishops returned to it. The piecemeal defections from the union could not be stopped until the reign of King Jan III Sobieski (1674–96), when the Uniate Basilians formed a new congregation and several Orthodox eparchs switched to the union. The Synod of Samosc (1720),[33] convened by Archbishop Leo II Kiszka (1714–28), was presided over by the papal nuncio Girolamo Grimaldi. Its significance for

---

[31] W. de Vries, *Rom,* 245 and 356.

[32] A. M. Ammann, *Abriß der ostslawischen Kirchengeschichte* (Wien 1950), 199–215, 299–336, 415–447; A. G. Welykyj, ed., *Documenta Pontificum Romanorum historiam Ucrainae illustrantia (1075–1953),* 2 vols. (Rome 1953–54); G. Lužnickij, *Ukrainska cerkva miž schodom i zachodom* (Philadelphia 1954); W. de Vries, *Rom.* 102–7; J. Krajcar, "The Ruthenian Patriarchate. Some remarks on the project for its establishment in the 17th century," *OrChrP* 30 (1964), 65–84.

[33] J. Bilanych, *Synodus Zamostiana an. 1720* (Rome 1960); J. Madey, op. cit., 78–84.

the Uniate Ukrainians has been compared to that of the Council of Trent for the Latin Church. It wanted to eliminate abuses, elevate education and discipline among the clergy and populace and harmonize the Orthodox tradition with the demands of the time. Its decisions—in contrast to those of the Synod of Brest—demonstrated a certain amount of adaptation to the Latin Rite and the customs of the Roman Church. This synod gave to the Byzantine-Ukrainian Rite its special form, which has remained the most widespread non-Latin Rite of the Catholic Church to the present day. After just a few decades of undisturbed development, witnessed by the church architecture of Lemberg, Polock, and other towns, the Polish partitions and the westward expansion of Russia initiated strong political pressure against the Uniate rites within the Russian sphere of influence, forcing them to return to the Orthodox Church.[34] Only in Galicia, which had come under Austria, could they continue to develop their Churches.

In 1646, in accordance with the example of the Union of Brest, the Union of Užhorod[35] was concluded with the Ruthenians who had settled in Podcarpathia (Carpathian Ukrainians) who belonged to the Orthodox bishopric of Mukačevo, established in the second half of the sixteenth century. From 1633 to 1711 that area was the domain of the Princes Rakoczy, who enlisted sympathies for the spread of Calvinism. This prompted the bishops of Mukačevo to seek ties with the Catholic Church. Bishop Basilios Tarasovič (1633–51) negotiated union with the Latin bishop of Erlau, George Lippay (1637–42), who rose to become bishop of Gran and primate of Hungary (1642–66), as well as with Emperor Ferdinand III and the apostolic nuncio Gasparo Mattei. In 1642 he embraced the Catholic faith in Vienna, but was prevented by Prince George I Rakoczy (1630–48) from returning to his see. Although he reverted to the Orthodox Church, he did recommend shortly before his death (1651) the election of a successor who would be sympathetic to the union. In 1646, meanwhile, the union had been announced by the bishop of Erlau, George Jakušič. It was embraced by 63 of 650 priests and spread further by Bishop Petrus Partheneus Petrovič (1651–66). Upon his death a serious crisis set in when— in addition to the successor elected by the Uniate Church—the Emperor and Princess Sophie Rakoczy each appointed another successor. This confusion was not ended until the appointment of the vicar apostolic of Mukačevo, John Joseph Camillis (1689–1706), a Greek born in Chios and edu-

---

[34] See Chap. 13.
[35] M. Lacko, *Unio Užhorodensis Ruthenorum Carpaticorum cum Ecclesia Catholica* (Rome 1955); idem, "Die Užhoroder Union," *OstKSt* 8 (1959), 3–30; idem, "Die Union von Užhorod 1646," W. de Vries, *Rom*, 114–131.

cated at the Greek college in Rome. He convened several synods, published a catechism and consolidated the union, which had 420 member parishes by 1693. During the first several decades of the eighteenth century the Latin bishops of Erlau managed to have the Uniate bishops of Mukačevo made subordinate to them. The Uniate clergy protested in vain against the restrictions placed upon their bishops. Not until 1771 did Pope Clement XIV alleviate the tense situation by issuing his bull *Eximia regalium* and granting personal jurisdictional rights to their bishops. The Uniate bishopric was comprised of 839 churches and 675 parishes; in 1776 it became a suffragan bishopric of the archbishopric of Gran.

Similar to Podcarpathia, Calvinist rulers also had great influence in Siebenbürgen. When the region came under imperial supremacy and was placed under the Hungarian crown, the danger of domination by both Magyars and Calvinists was a growing threat. The Orthodox Bishop Theophilos Szeremy of Alba Julia detailed a plan for union on the occasion of a Rumanian synod in 1697. The members of the synod were favorably inclined, but demanded complete safeguards of their Orthodox rites and customs as well as equality with the Catholic clergy. The union was accepted under Bishop Atanas Anghel (1697–1713) at the Synods of Alba in 1698 and 1700[36] after the Emperor granted to the Uniate Church the same rights as were enjoyed by the Catholics. In 1701 the imperial court named Atanas bishop of the Rumanian nation in Siebenbürgen. Cardinal Leopold Karl Kollonics, archbishop of Gran, conditionally reconsecrated him, an action which was sharply protested by the Orthodox theologians and bishops. Yet the Uniate Bishop Atanas was joined by almost all the Orthodox Rumanians, about half a million. In 1721 Pope Innocent XIII established the bishopric of Fagaras for the Uniates, which was joined with the archbishopric of Gran by Emperor Charles VI. In spite of the difficulties created by the Calvinists and the emissaries of the Orthodox patriarch of Ipek the Uniate bishops were able to consolidate the union. In the town of Blaj the Uniate Bishop Peter Paul Aron (1752–64) founded a college led by Basilian monks and a press which published liturgical books and brochures for religious instruction. The union was further promulgated by his successors, such as Athanasios Rednik (1764–72) and Gregor Major (1773–82), with support by Empress Maria Theresa and many clerics who had studied in Rome.

The families who had emigrated from Bosnia to Croatia in 1573 were

---

[36] G. Patacsi, "Die unionfeindlichen Bewegungen der orthodoxen Rumänen Siebenbürgens in den Jahren 1726–29," *OrChrP* 26 (1960), 349–400; W. de Vries, *Rom,* 132–80, 394–423.

served by the Orthodox bishop who resided at the monastery of Saint Michael in Marca. In 1611 Bishop Simeon Vratanja embraced Catholicism before Cardinal Robert Bellarmin, but was able to persuade only a part of the monks of the Marca monastery and of the Orthodox Serbians to join the Union.[37] Subsequent tensions with the Latin archbishop of Zagreb (who considered the Uniate bishop a subordinate auxiliary bishop), efforts by the patriarch of Ipek to rejoin the Uniates with the Orthodox Church, the existence of a Uniate vicariate for Syrmia (1688–1706), whose ordinary resided at the Monastery of Hopovo, and the sacking and destruction of the monastery of Marca by members of the Orthodox Rite (1739) prompted Bishop Gabriel Palkovič (1751–59), who saw his bishopric endangered from within and without, to relocate it to Pribic. In 1777 Pope Pius VI issued the bull *Charitas illa*, creating the diocese of Kreutz for the Uniate Church of Byzantine Rite as part of the archbishopric of Gran.

The majority of Greeks who had fled from Albania to southern Italy and Sicily, the so-called Italo-Albanians (Italo-Greeks) succumbed to a process of Latinization. After they had achieved the opening of seminaries for the education of their own priests at Piana in Sicily (1716), at Ullano in Calabria (1732), and at Palermo (1736), Pope Benedict XIV acknowledged in his constitution *Etsi pastoralis* (1742) the validity of the Greco-Albanian customs, but he stressed the *praestantia* of the Latin Rite. The Italo-Greeks were given an auxiliary bishop in Calabria (1735) and in Sicily (1784). Of the numerous Greek monasteries in Italy only Grottaferrata near Rome and Piana in Sicily preserved the Byzantine Rite although there, too, mixed forms of the liturgy were practiced along with the Latin liturgy.

In addition to the unions of different national groups of Orthodox Christians in eastern Europe, southern Europe, and Italy mentioned so far, there were the Monophysites who had emigrated from Greater Armenia to Poland-Lithuania and had an Armenian bishopric in Lemberg. Bishop Nikolaus Torosowič (1627–81) joined Rome in 1630. While he did become archbishop of the Uniate Armenians for Poland and Walachia with his residence in Lemberg (in 1635),[38] it was his coadjutor and successor Vatan Hunanian (1686–1715) who definitively broke with the catholicate of Etchmiadzin and stabilized the union. The

---

[37] J. Šimrak, *De relationibus Slavorum meridionalium cum Sancta Romana Sede Apostolica saeculis XVII–XVIII* I (Zagreb 1926); G. Hoffman, "Urkunden zur Union des Bischofs Vratanja," *OrChrA* 8 (1927), 290–98; M. Lacko, "Die Union in Kroatien 1611," W. de Vries, *Rom,* 108–11.

[38] G. Petrowicz, *L'Unione degli armeni di Polonia con la Santa Sede 1626–86* (Rome 1950).

Polish partitions caused the archbishopric to be split into a Russian and an Austrian part.

Efforts by zealous religious prompted some individual Armenian bishops in Constantinople, Etchmiadzin, and Sis to agree to the union. But the Dominicans in Transcaucasia, the Mechitarists[39] called into existence in 1701 by Mechithar of Sebaste (1676–1749), and the missionary order of the Armenian Antonites founded in Lebanon during the eighteenth century, had only limited success. In Syria the Catholics attempted to fill the vacant patriarchal see of Sis with one of their own in 1737. The Monophysite Armenians elected Michael, the Catholics elected Archbishop Abraham Ardzivian of Aleppo as successor.[40] The latter received recognition of his office and the pallium as Catholicos Abraham Peter I (1740–69) by Pope Benedict XIV in 1742. But his intention to relocate his residence to Constantinople was thwarted by the protest of the Monophysite Armenians. So he resided at the monastery of Krim in Lebanon and his successors in nearby Bzommar. They were responsible for the Uniate Armenians in Cilicia, Palestine, Mesopotamia, and Egypt. The members of the Uniate rites in the north and west of Asia Minor, in Constantinople, and the European part of Turkey were given their own vicar-bishop, who was subordinate to the Latin vicar apostolic of Constantinople.

While efforts towards union were initially unsuccessful among the Orthodox Georgians, they showed promise among the Orthodox Melchites, but could not come to fruition because of the rivalry among Uniate dignitaries during the eighteenth century. Although Capuchins, Carmelites, and Jesuits in Syria enlisted some bishops and patriarchs for the union, a widespread movement did not occur until the appointment of Archbishop Euthymios of Sidon and Tyre (1683–1723), administrator of all Catholic Melchites in the patriarchate of Antioch since 1701, and the engagement of the missionary congregation of the Most Holy Redeemer, founded by him in accordance with the rules followed by the Basilian order. After the death of the Melchite Patriarch Athanasios (1724), who embraced Catholicism on his deathbed, the Catholic minority elected as his successor Seraphim Tanas, a nephew of Euthymios, who assumed the name of Cyril VI (1724–59). At the same time the opponents of the union elected a nephew of Athanasios as Patriarch Jeremias III. The latter had Cyril and his followers excommunicated at a

---

[39] P. Krüger, "Die armenischen Mechitharisten und ihre Bedeutung," *OstKSt* 16 (1967), 3–14.

[40] M. Terzian, *Le Patriarcat de Cilicie et les Arméniens catholiques 1740–1812* (Beirut 1955).

synod in Alexandria in 1728. Having been forced to leave Damascus, Cyril VI took up residence in Sidon. He initiated the line of Uniate Melchite patriarchs of Antioch whose jurisdiction was broadened in 1772 to include all Catholics of the Byzantine Rite within the confines of the patriarchates of Jerusalem and Alexandria.

After Capuchins and Jesuits had enlisted some individual Jacobites for the Church, Bishop Andreas Akidjian of Aleppo was elevated to the vacant Monophysite patriarchate (1662–77).[41] As a result of mediation by the French consul he was recognized as patriarch of the Syrian nation by the sultan. His successor Ignatius Petrus IV (1677–1702) was repeatedly persecuted for his adherence to the union, alleged to be an agent of France, and finally driven out. Many Uniate western Syrians left Monophysitism, part of them going over to the Maronites. Their number diminished in the course of the eighteenth century so that by 1768 no more than 150 Uniate families were counted in Aleppo and 50 in Damascus. Not until 1783 were they given a new patriarch in the person of Ignatius Michael Garweh (1783–1800). His election in Mardin in 1781 by four of the six Jacobite bishops was recognized neither by his opponents nor by the Turks. He was forced to make way for the Jacobite Patriarch Matthias and withdrew to the monastery of Scharfeh in Lebanon. In 1783 the Pope recognized him as the Syrian patriarch of Antioch whose line can be traced up to the present.

Since the Nestorians of eastern Syria had been split into several jurisdictional areas, the Chaldeans who had joined the union also formed several centers. The patriarchate of the Chaldeans in Diarbekr, created in the middle of the sixteenth century under John Sulaqa, came to an end by the return to Nestorianism of Simon XIII (1662–1700). Archbishop Joseph of Amida (Diarbekr), who had become Catholic in 1672, was elevated to the patriarchate as Joseph I (1681–96).[42] He ministered to about one thousand faithful. His successor Joseph II (1696–1713) called himself patriarch of Babylon and the nation of the Chaldeans. The Dominicans succeeded in recruiting for the union the nephew of the Nestorian patriarch, Elias XII Denha (d. 1778), who resided in the monastery of Rabban Hurmuz near Mosul. He was elected patriarch and then appointed metropolitan of Mosul and administrator of the patriarchate of Babylon. The rivalry between the two Chaldean patriarchates of Diarbekr and Mosul, which latter was com-

---

[41] W. de Fries, "Dreihundert Jahre syrisch-katholische Kirche," *OstKSt* 5 (1956), 137–57.

[42] A. Lampart, *Ein Märtyrer der Union mit Rom. Joseph I. 1681–96. Patriarch der Chaldäer* (Einsiedeln 1966).

prised of a mere few thousand faithful, ended in 1834 with the enthronement of John Hormez as patriarch of Babylon.

The Maronite Church of Lebanon[43] had been firmly tied to Rome since the Fifth Lateran Council. The embassy of the Jesuit Giambattista Eliano (1578 and 1580) introduced an increased Latinization of the Antioch Rite which was protested in vain by several monks and bishops. In 1584 Pope Gregory XIII created the Maronite college in Rome which produced a number of important priests and scholars, the members of the Assemani family (as-Simani) being especially prominent among the latter. In 1606 the Gregorian calendar was introduced among the Maronites. Patriarch Stephanus Ad-Duwaihi (1670–1704), who had been educated in Rome, had valuable help from the order of Saint Anthony of Saint Isaias in developing his Church. The disputes created by the elections of dual patriarchs and the rejection of increasing Latinization were to be resolved in 1736 at the Synod of Kesrowan. In the presence of the papal legate Joseph Simon Assemani,[44] the decisions of the Council of Trent and the *Catechismus Romanus,* which appeared in Arabic in 1786, were accepted. Latin vestments were prescribed for celebrating the Eucharist. In 1741 Pope Benedict XIV accepted the decisions of the synod. The following year he divided the patriarchate into eight dioceses, giving them the titles of old Syrian metropolitanates. Five Maronite monks were in sharp disagreement with the negotiations of the synod and the papal utterances. Not until the second half of the eighteenth century under Patriarch Joseph Estephan (1766–92) could unity be reestablished in the Maronite Church. The seminary founded by Estephan in Ain-Warka (1789) continued the activities of the Armenian college in Rome after it was dissolved in the tumult of the French Revolution. The Synod of Bkerke in 1790 contributed significantly to consolidating the Maronite Church.

Among the Monophysite Copts the contacts with Patriarch John XVI (1676–1718), initiated by Jesuits and reformed Franciscans, were unsuccessful.[45] The assistant to the patriarch of Cairo, the Coptic Bishop

[43] J. B. Chabot, *Les listes patriarcales de l'Église Maronite* (Paris 1938); B. Spuler, "Die Maroniten," *Hdb. der Orientalistik,* Abt. 1, VIII/2 (1961), 217–25; P. Dib, *L'Église Maronite,* 2 vols. (Beirut 1962); A. S. Atiya, op. cit., 389–423.

[44] P. Mahfoud, *Joseph Simon Assimani et la célébration du concil libanais maronite de 1736* (Rome 1965).

[45] J. P. Trossen, *Les relations du patriarche copte Jean XVI avec Rome 1676–1718* (Luxemburg 1948); A. Colombo, *Le origini della gerarchia della chiesa copta cattolica nel secolo XVIII* (Rome 1953); G. Giambernardini, *I primi copti cattolici* (Cairo 1958); G. D'Albano, *Historia della missione francescana in alto-Egitto-Fungi-Etiopia 1686–1720* (Cairo 1961).

Athanasios of Jerusalem, who had embraced Catholicism in 1739, was given the leadership of the approximately two thousand Uniate Copts by Pope Benedict XIV in 1741. But since he was unwilling to terminate his connection with the Coptic Church, the Propaganda named Justus Maraghi vicar general (1744–49). He was followed in that office by prefects of the reformed Franciscans. In 1761 the former Coptic Archbishop Antonius Fulaifil became the first vicar apostolic in Cairo. He was unable to achieve much progress because the bishops and priests who were prepared to join the union insisted on conditional reconsecration.

After the initial successes in Ethiopia achieved by Portuguese missionaries in the seventeenth century collapsed, the union was unable to establish firm roots.[46] Capuchins and Franciscans who dared enter the country of the negus were either driven out or died a martyr's death. Efforts by the Franciscan Theodor Krump, in his capacity as royal physician (1701–02), to enlist the negus and etschege for the union came to nought. Father Liberat Weiss and his friends were condemned and stoned to death in 1716. Bohemian Franciscans were expelled from the country in 1752 after a brief sojourn. The native Bishop Tobias George Ghebragzer, consecrated in Rome in 1788, fled to Cairo in 1797.

The successful union concluded in the sixteenth century with the Christians of Saint Thomas in India was weakened by the creation of the Jacobite Church under Mar Thomas I in the middle of the seventeenth century. Those Thomas Christians who had remained Catholic were under a vicar apostolic directly subordinate to the Propaganda; at the same time they were under the Portuguese *padroado*, which in turn was under the influence of the Jesuits. The vicar apostolic, Mar Alexander Parampil (1663–94), was successfully supported by Carmelites who became his successors. The partition into two jurisdictional areas brought with it all sorts of difficulties which were overcome only when the Jesuit order was dissolved in 1773 and the Carmelite order started furnishing the majority of apostolic administrators.

In spite of the tensions from without and within to which the unions, concluded from the sixteenth to the eighteenth century, were exposed, the Apostolic See was able to unite both large and small religious communities with Rome. Reverses were inevitable and many unions were limited to small numbers of faithful. Yet the eastern border of the Catholic Church, rigid since the Middle Ages, became fluid. Several ethnic groups of eastern and southern Slavs, of Maronites, Thomas Christians, and others were joined to the Roman center of the Church.

[46] T. Somigli, *Etiopia francescana nei documenti dei secoli XVII e XVIII*, 2 vols. (Quaracchi 1928–48); G. Manfredi, "I minori osservanti riformati nella prefettura dell'Alto Egitto-Etiopia 1697–1792," *Studia orientalia christiana* 3 (Cairo 1958), 83–182.

CHAPTER 15

The Propagation of the Faith in America

The Waning of the Missionary Spirit and the Decline of the Missions

The manifest diminution of the missionary spirit in the seventeenth and eighteenth century contrasted with manifold, often heroic incidents of missionary activity. This fact alone shows clearly that the history of the propagation of faith in America did not follow a simple and transparent line of development, but was instead of a rather complex nature. The gradual flagging of the missionary spirit with its logical consequences goes back to events of the sixteenth century, which must be described briefly if one is to understand and judge fairly the course of the seventeenth and eighteenth century.

A decisive factor was the long struggle between Pius V (d. 1572) and Philip II (d. 1598) for the growing and potentially immense Church in the New World. Philip II demanded the establishment of an "Indian Patriarchate" which was to exist and be considered as a more or less autonomous Church parallel to the Roman Church. The patriarch was to be appointed by the King and reside in Madrid. This demand was emphatically rejected by Pius V, as was the moderated form of a "royal vicariate" for the overseas territories, which was also opposed in 1634 and 1643 by the newly founded Congregation for the Propagation of the Faith.[1] Pius V, on his part, sought ways in which to realize the papal claims and the papal influence in Spanish America. Upon the suggestion and with the collaboration of the Jesuit general Francis Borgia, he formed a congregation of cardinals in 1568 for the ecclesiastic and religious affairs in the overseas territories which—while its structure and goals already corresponded to those of the Congregation of Propaganda to be organized in 1622—could neither be an effective instrument nor a permanent one.[2] Subsequently Pius V strove in vain to foil the machinations of the Spanish crown, first by dispatching a nuncio and then, with the help of papal visitors composed in the main of Spanish or Hispanophile Jesuits, by at least providing himself with precise knowledge concerning the situation in the American lands.[3]

---

[1] P. de Leturia, S.J., "El Regio Vicariato de Indias y los comienzos de la Congregación de Propaganda," *Relaciones* I, 101–52.

[2] L. Lopetegui, S.J., "San Francisco de Borja y el plan misional de San Pio V. Primeros pasos de una Congregación de Propaganda Fide," *AHSI* 11 (1942), 1–26.

[3] P. Borges, "La Nunciatura Indiana. Un intento de intervención directa en Indias bajo

After the Pope had exhausted all means of subordinating the American Church to papal supremacy, he tried to make the powerful personalities of the New World responsive to the interests of the Church by means of personal letters and briefs.[4] But Pius V could hardly foresee that as of the end of 1568 all his efforts would be in vain. That year an event took place which—as we know today—assumed an essential, indeed decisive significance for the development of the Church in America: the Great Junta of Madrid in 1568.[5]

The *Junta Magna*, which in addition to selected members of the Council of Castile included all the members of the Council of the Indies and other prominent personalities, was to reach two goals which Philip II had in mind: (1) to expand the right of patronage to such an extent that any influence of Rome would be excluded for all times (Up to that point the patronage had been restricted more or less to the outer organization of the Church, the establishment and borders of the dioceses, the appointment of the bishops and other ecclesiastical dignitaries. From now on the system was to be extended to include not only every representative of the clergy, secular and regular, but also the internal affairs of the Church.); (2) to supplant the Indian Church coming into existence by achieving a breakthrough for a Church which would bear the Spanish imprint.

The implementation of the decisions of the *Junta Magna* was entrusted to the newly appointed viceroy of Peru, Francisco de Toledo,[6]

Felipe II., 1566–88," *MH* 19 (1962), 169–227; idem, "La Santa Sede y América en el siglo XVI," *Estudios Americanos* 21 (Seville 1961), 141–68 (mentions for the period of 1513–70 fourteen letters from America expressing an urgent desire for a vicar apostolic); A. de Egaña, S.J., *La teoría del Regio Vicariato español de Indias* (Rome 1958); J. Wicki, "Nuovi documenti attorno ai piani missionari di Pio V nel 1568," *AHSI* 57 (1968), 408–17 (publishes the list of the appointed groups of visitors).

[4] M. Monica, *La gran controversia del siglo XVI acerca del dominio Español sobre America* (Madrid 1952), 249 f., for example the brief of Pius V to Francisco de Toledo; see also Card. Grente, *Le pape des grande combats. Saint Pie V.* (Paris 1956), 189ff., 199ff.

[5] M. Monica, op. cit., 197–240; P. de Letuira, S.J., "Misiones hispanoamericanas según la Junta de 1568," *Relaciones* I, 205–31. For an evaluation of the Junta and its impact the following aspects appear important as well. Las Casas, the courageous pioneer in a fight for freedom of the Indians, had died in 1566. The proponents of his ideas in Spain, especially the professors in Salamanca, had no political influence. Philip II, moreover, thwarted them by appointing his confessor, Father Diego de Chaves, to the position of theologian. R. Richard summarized briefly in 1966: "C'est surtout à partir de Philippe II et davantage à partir de l'installation des Bourbons sur le Trône d'Espagne en 1700, que les progrès de l'esprit régaliste ont fait du patronage un instrument d'asservissements pour l'Église des Indes" ("La 'Conquête spirituelle du Mexique revue après trente ans," *La Découverte de l'Amérique. Esquisse d'une synthèse* [Paris 1968], 231).

[6] R. Levillier, *Don Francisco de Toledo, Virrey del Perú, Supremo organizador del Perú, su vida, su obra (1515–82),* 4 vols. (Madrid 1929–40).

who not only participated in several of the junta's meetings, but was also furnished a set of secret instructions. It was quite certainly a skillful move by Philip II that he selected a personal friend of the Jesuit general Francis Borgia to execute his plans while simultaneously acceding to the latter's repeated requests to permit the first large-scale expedition of twenty-four Jesuits to South America, a prelude to the missionary activities in Spanish America by that order.[7] It can be assumed that Philip II gave his viceroy some valuable instructions regarding missionary work, but most probably of such nature that he, i.e., the government, became the actual guarantor of the conversion of the Indians; the previous secular and regular missionaries turned into mere executive organs.[8]

As was the case for all Spanish laws overseas, it took some considerable time of compromises and transitional solutions until the patronage right was implemented down to its very last ramifications. In the course of the seventeenth and eighteenth century the King and the Council of the Indies received crucial help from theologians as well as jurists. As early as 1600 the Franciscan Miguel Agia, missionary in Guatemala, published his fundamental work on the necessity and importance of the secular arm for missionary work.[9] This work was concretely applied in three expert opinions on the forced labor of the Indians (1604).[10] Among the Augustinians it was the bishop of Santiago de Chile, Gaspar de Villaroel, who traced the line from the right of patronage to regalism in his comprehensive *Govierno Eclesiástico Pacífico*, which first appeared in 1656 and was reprinted in 1738. Actually his work was intended to reduce the tensions between Church and state in America.[11] An extreme partisan of regalism towards the end of the eighteenth century was the Carmelite José Antonio de San Alberto, bishop of Tucumán

---

[7] Preceded a few years earlier by the more modest mission in Florida, see F. Zubillaga, *La Florida. La misión jesuítica (1566–72)* (Rome 1941). The first Jesuit expeditions to Mexico took place in 1572.

[8] Even the Jesuits who maintained ties of friendship with the viceroy were made to feel this. In 1577, filling a need for the ministry, they built a branch in the mission town of Potosí with the viceroy's permission. By the latter's order they had to relinquish it (A. de Egaña, *Monumenta Peruana* II, 476–84, 542–54, 558–69; R. Vargas Ugarte, op. cit. I, 141).

[9] Streit I, 116.

[10] Ibid., 125. See the review of the critical edition (Seville 1947), *Hisp. Am. Hist. Rev.* (1947), 300–304.

[11] Streit, 233f., 421; A. J. González Zumariaga, *Problemas del patronato indiano a través del "Govierno Eclesiástico Pacífico" de Fr. Gaspar de Villaroel* (Vitoria 1961); J. López Ortiz, *El regalismo indiano en el Govierno eclesiástico pacífico de Don Fr. Gaspar de Villaroel. Real Academia de Jurisprudencia y Legislación* (Madrid 1947). (G. de Villaroel was born in 1587 in Quito and died in 1665 as bishop of Buenos Aires.)

(Córdoba) and later archbishop of La Plata. With his legalistically oriented pastoral letter of 1786 he published a *Catecismo real*, as the work was called.[12] The scholarly Jesuit Pedro Murillo Velarde compiled the regalist canon law in the more than one thousand pages of his two-volume work *Cursus Juris Canonici Hispani et Indici* in 1743.[13] His fellow Jesuit Diego de Avedaño had taken a more reticent stance in his *Encyclopädie für die Missionspastoral und für das Missions- und Kolonialrecht Thesaurus Indicus* (Antwerp 1668).[14]

But in the final analysis neither theologians nor canonists exerted the decisive influence regarding the extension of the right of patronage; the most prominent part was played by the counsels for the crown. Among them were Pedro Fresso in Lima,[15] A. J. Álvarez de Abreu,[16] A. J. Ribadeneyra y Barrientos in Mexico,[17] and, most prominently, Juan de Solórzano Pereira (1575–1655). He was professor in Salamanca, official of the Curia in Lima, and after his return to Spain a member of the Council of the Indies. The first volume of his *De Indiarum Jure* appeared in 1629, the second in 1639.[18] They are a consistent continuation and development of the basic ideas of Ginés de Sepúlveda, the great adversary of Bartolomé de Las Casas. For more than two centuries this work determined the relations between the state and the Church in accordance with Spanish state law. To be sure, it was condemned and put on the Index by Rome in 1642.[19] But since the Council of the Indies did

---

[12] The actual title was "Instrucción donde per lecciones, preguntas y respuestas se enseñan a los niños y niñas las obligaciones mas principales que un vasallo debe a su rey y señor." R. Esquerra, "La crítica sobre América en el siglo XVIII," *Revista de Indias* 22 (1962), 246ff.

[13] Streit I, 439.

[14] Ibid., 268f., with voluminous supplements from 1675 (ibid., 283) and 1686 (ibid., 307f.). See P. de Leturia, "Misioneros extranjeros en Indias según Diego de Avendaño," *Relaciones* I, 453–67 and A. de Egaña, "El P. Diego de Avendaño y la tesis teocrática 'Papa, dominus orbis'," *AHS* XVIII (1949), 195–225.

[15] *De regio patronatu indiano 1671, 1679*; Streit I, 287f. The work was placed on the Index in 1688.

[16] *Victima real legal* (Madrid 1726); Streit I, 379.

[17] *Manuel Compendio de el regio Patronato Indiano* (Madrid 1755); Streit I, 470.

[18] Streit I, 191, 262. The Spanish edition appeared in 1648 under the title *Política Indiana* (ibid., 217f.); its fourth edition appeared in 1776 and a third edition in Latin came out in 1777 (ibid., 529f.). See F. J. de Ayala, "Ideas Canónicas de Juan de Solárzano. El Tratado *De Indiarum Jure* y su inclusión en el Índice," *Anuario de Estudios Americanos* 4 (Seville 1947), 579–614; A. de Egaña, "La función misionera del poder civil según Juan de Solárzano Pereira (1575–1654)," *StMis* 6 (Rome 1951), 69–113; idem., *La teoría del Regio Vicariato Español* (Rome 1958), 106–73.

[19] P. de Leturia, "Antonio Lelio de Fermo y la condenación del *De Indiarum Jure* de Solórzano Pereira," *Relaciones* I, 335–408.

not recognize Rome's decision, it had no validity in Spain and America.[20]

Theory and practice gradually led to extensive legislation which more and more constricted the activities of the Church. The final codification (1791) in the *Recopilación de Leyes de los Reynos de las Indias*[21] represented the finishing touch, predetermined as early as 1771 by the fourth provincial council of Mexico in accordance with the precise instructions of the Council of the Indies.[22]

Regalism or state absolutism proved to be one of the most serious obstacles to the missionary development of the American Church in the seventeenth and eighteenth century. Except for the papal bulls of investiture and some few privileges, all the influence of Rome was practically eliminated. This had a paralyzing and demoralizing effect on the total missionary effort.[23] Just how negative its effect on individual missions was can be gleaned from unpublished documents—unpublished because mention of such matters was not allowed in print—concerning the life of the Apostle of California, Junípero Serra.[24] For this reason his biography, written by his long-time companion and successor Francesco Palou (1787), speaks only of the positive aspects concerning the coop-

[20] In fact there would hardly have been a person in Spanish America who knew of the condemnation by Rome. The work was used as a basic handbook by the temporal and ecclesiastic authorities.

[21] Especially in bk. I, Chap. 8, "Del Patronazgo Real de Las Indias." See F. J. de Ayala, "Iglesia y Estado en las Leyes de Indias," *Estudios Americanos* 1 (1948/49), 417–60; R. Gomez Hoyo, *La Iglesia de América en las Leyes de Indias* (Madrid 1961).

[22] M. Giménez Fernández, "Estudios para la Historia del Regalismo Español, I: El Concilio IV Provincial Mejicano," *Anales de la Universidad Hispalense* I and II (Seville 1939).

[23] G. Desdevises du Dezert, "L'Église espagnole des Indes à la fin du XVIIIᵉ Siécle," *Revue Hispanique* 39 (1917), 112–293. Basing his claims on numerous documents from the Indias-Archives, the author proves that all provincial synods were predetermined down to the smallest details by royal instructions (see 115–20), further, how complicated the appointment of parish priests by the local authorities was (172ff.), that the visitors of the orders were appointed by the Council of the Indies in Spain (221), and so forth. See also Alluto de la Hera, *El Regalismo Borbónico en su proyección indiana* (Madrid 1963).

[24] M. Geiger, *The Life and Times of Fray Junípero Serra OFM*, 2 vols. (Washington 1959). Volume II, 329ff. gives an example of the bureaucracy making the mission work more difficult. It took four years for the authorization by Rome for conducting confirmations to make its way through the various authorities in Spain and Mexico and another three years for the subordinate authorities to recognize the signatures and seals. The authorization granted in 1774 and limited to ten years could, in the end, be used by Serra for all of three years.

eration of Church and state and of the necessity for military protection of the missions in Mexico as well as California.[25]

Not only was the application of the principle of regalism most injurious to the interests of the Church, but the brutal prevention of establishing an Indian Church turned an already bad situation into a catastrophe, because it was an Indian Church and not one after the Spanish model that was envisioned by the missionaries, especially the Franciscans, soon after the beginning of evangelization,[26] even if neither the goal nor the means were as yet fully recognized.[27]

That the *Junta Magna* of 1568 prevented the Indian Church from coming into being can be shown by several negative features which were clearly recognizable as the result of its decisions. Principal among them is the suppression of all publications relative to the propagation of the faith which stressed the great abilities and good qualities of the Indians. Of the Franciscan writings we mention *Motolinia* (Toribio de Benavente), *Historia de los Indios de la Nueva España*, a basic source, first published 1858 by its discoverer, the Mexican historian J. García Icazbalceta,[28] the *Historia Eclesiástica Indiana* by Gerónimo de Mendieta (also discovered by Icazbalceta; published in 1870),[29] and last but not least the life's work of the scholar Bernardino de Sahagún. Only one of his many works was published during his lifetime, the *Psalmodia christiana* (Mexico 1583). The manuscripts of his other works, his comprehensive *Historia general de las cosas de Nueva España* included, were confiscated and sent to Spain for examination only to disappear in government archives, where they were newly discovered in the nineteenth century.[30]

Whereas Bartolomé de Las Casas was able to have a number of his writings printed in 1552, among them the virulent *Brevísima Relación de la destrucción de las Indias*, his other works, especially the lengthy *Historia General de las Indias*, were not published until the ninteenth and

---

[25] See especially the English translations with the valuable notes by M. Geiger, *Palou's Life of Fray Junipero Serra* (Washington 1955).—Without this nationalistic direction Palou would hardly have received the required state and Church imprimatur.

[26] R. Ricard, "La Conquête spirituelle." The impressive lists (pp. 345–52) of the works written in Indian languages alone clearly show this direction; P. Borges, *Métodos*.

[27] J. L. Phelan, *The Millenial Kingdom of the Franciscans in the New World. A Study of the Writings of Gerónimo de Mendieta (1525–1604)* (Berkeley and Los Angeles 1956), which stresses the eschatological utopian characteristics in the work of the Mexican Franciscans.

[28] Streit III, 581.

[29] Ibid. III, 605–7.

[30] Ibid. II, 216–22.

twentieth century.[31] His fellow religious, Diego Durán, did not fare any better with his *Historia de la Indias de la Nueva España,* which was completed in 1581.[32] Conditions in other countries, especially Peru and Colombia, were no different from those in Mexico.

The lifework of the Franciscan Pedro Aguado, the first chronicler of Colombia, which did not become well known until the twentieth century, was illuminated by the Colombian historian Juan Friede by means of a comparison of handwritings. In the process he sifted out the principles of government censorship (those of the Church had to be obtained beforehand in each case).[33] They were: (1) everything that diminished the good reputation of the *conquista* or the *conquistadores* had to be suppressed; (2) in treating the missions, all mention of conflicts, especially those with government offices, had to be left out; (3) the Indians had to be represented as a low human race without culture.[34] Authors, including chroniclers of the religious orders, who wanted to obtain the requisite imprimature had to follow these unwritten yet painstakingly enforced rules.

The discrimination against the Indians, carried out according to J. Friede by government censorship, shows clearly that it was aimed against an essential element in the creation of an Indian Church: the education of indigenous clergy.[35] Indeed the Council of Mexico had already prohibited the ordination of Indians in 1555, but in a more general context (in connection with the Muslims [*moros*], mestizos, and mulattos),[36] but at the Third Council of Lima in 1567/68 the prohibition already referred exclusively to the newly converted Indians.[37]

Judging from the text of the council, precluding priesthood for the Indians appeared to have been a temporary measure (*hoc tempore*). In point of fact it was to last until the eighteenth century. The Franciscans

---

[31] Ibid. II, 27–32.

[32] Ibid. II, 226.

[33] "La Censura Española del Siglo XVI y los libros de Historia de América," *Revista de Historia de América* 47 (Mexico City 1959), 45–94.

[34] Aguado described the prominent tribe of the Muiscas Indians and according to the table of contents planned twenty chapters for that part (op. cit., 88–90), all of which were eliminated by censorship for the reasons stated.

[35] J. Specker, "Der einheimische Klerus in Spanisch-Amerika im 16. Jh. Mit besonderer Berücksichtigung der Konzilien und Synoden," in J. Beckmann, *Der Einheimische Klerus in Gesch. und Gegenwart (Festschr. L. Kilger)* (Beckenried 1950), 73–97; A. Pott, "Das Weihehindernis für Indianer im 3. Konzil von Lima," *NZM* 12 (1956), 108–18.

[36] J. Specker, op. cit., 78f.

[37] "Sentit sancta Synodus, et ita servandum statuit, hos noviter ad fidem conversos, hoc tempore non debere ordine initiari. . . ." R. Vargas Ugarte, *Concilios Limenses (1551–1772)* I (Lima 1951), 192.

found this out in their college of Tlaltelolco (Mexico), which had been established by Bishop Zumárraga in 1536 primarily for the education of a native clergy. The various parties, those among the laity, the secular and the regular clergy—even among the Franciscans—who were hostile to the Indians continued to hold the upper hand and after the 1560s the formerly flourishing school was merely vegetating.[38] The same experience was had by the Jesuits working in the country since 1572. Under the spiritual leadership of Juan de Tobar, who was born in Mexico, they tried to get permission from the Jesuit general to establish a college for the education of Indian priests. After fifteen years of trying, their plan was categorically rejected.[39] The final decision by General Claudius Acquaviva had been indicated earlier by the guidelines of the junta of 1568.[40]

In this connection the efforts of the Propaganda, i.e., of its first secretary Francesco Ingoli, are deeply moving. In letters and petitions to popes, cardinals, and generals of the orders he gave the most cogent arguments for the ordination of Indian priests in America, but the power of the Council of the Indies could not be broken even by the Popes.[41]

---

[38] R. Ricard, *La Conquête spirituelle*, 260–84.

[39] In addition to various references in the *Monumenta Mexicana* (I–IV) and in F. J. Alegre, op. cit., see also the summary study by J. Lafaye, "Une lettre inédite de XVIe siècle, relative aux collèges indiens de la Compagnie de Jésus en Nouvelle-Espagne," *Annales de la Faculté des lettres et Sciences humaines d'Aix*, t. 38 (2d fasc.) (Gap 1964), 9–21, (19–21 contains the letter from Father Pedro Díaz to the general of the Society of Jesus, dated 21 June 1592).

[40] Father Juan de Tobar already demonstrated clear insight when he wrote: "se perdieron las mejores ocasiones que jamás tendremos moralmente hablando" (E. J. Alegre, op. cit. I, 546).—The education of a native clergy in Paraguay was therefore principally out of the question.

[41] J. Metzler, "Francesco Ingoli und die Indianerweihen," *NZM* 25 (1969), 262–72. Ingoli's perspicacity is shown by his summary of 1638 to the general of the Augustinian order: "If the Spanish regulars do not consecrate any Indians, the Church in both Indies will always be a small child and will never grow inwardly strong." (op. cit.). R. Ricard, who adduces these facts in a lecture of 1966 in the process of clarifying some details of his classical work of 1933 (*La "Conquête spirituelle du Mexique" revue après trente ans: La Découverte de l'Amérique. Esquisse d'une synthèse* [Paris 1968], 236), attempts to muster some understanding for his attitude against a native clergy. As its motive he cites the total strangeness of the Indian races and cultures to the Spaniards and also a certain fear of a "Luther" who might emerge from an "Indian Church." There was the distinct possibility that such reasons carried a certain weight in small circles, but decisive for the crown were political and economic reasons. As Ricard, too, sees clearly (p. 235f.), a native Church was rejected because ecclesiastical independence brought with it the danger of political independence and because the Spanish conqueror caste and its successors scorned all physical labor to such an extent that they thought they could not exist without slaves or the slave labor of the Indians. These connec-

In his ideas of regalism Philip II was by no means guided by anti-Church sentiments. He was deeply convinced of the divine mission which he thought to have been given especially for the formation of the American Church. The bishops nominated by him were all well educated, pious and apostolic men, as were the visitors of the orders. The building of churches and monasteries, of hospitals and schools was supported. Beyond that he tried to promote everywhere the veneration and reverence for the Holy See and the Popes. Thus we witness the paradox that reverence for the Pope was nowhere greater than in the American territories, where practically all papal influence was eliminated.[42] It was well known that his opponent, Pius V, had the implementation of the Council of Trent close to his heart. So in order to keep him from making demands regarding the American Church, Philip II in a letter of 12 July 1564 had ordered the implementation of the Tridentine rules. Consequently, Archbishop Alonso de Montúfar as early as 1565 convened the Second Council of Mexico, which was to promulgate, adapt, and reacknowledge the Council of Trent. The Third Council of Lima in 1567/68 served the same purpose for South America.[43]

While the Council of Trent was a blessing for the European Church, it was a double-edged sword for the budding Indian Church. Quite aside from the fact that—as a result of the actions of Charles V and Philip II—America, in spite of the efforts by individual bishops, was not represented in Trent and its problems were nowhere discussed,[44] the centralist tendencies beginning at this point could not but have an impeding and in the long run seriously damaging effect.[45] The greatest damage was probably in discontinuing the already initiated organic growth of an Indian Church; the original main ideas concerning missionary work were discarded with noticeable haste. The first generation of missionaries had in mind the example of the original Church; the dogma of

---

tions were clearly seen by Las Casas and Mendieta. On this topic, see R. Konetzke, "Einige Grundzüge der geschichtlichen Besonderheit Lateinamerikas in der westlichen Hemisphäre," *HZ* 204 (Munich 1957), especially p. 29ff. regarding unwillingness to work.

[42] Thus A. Ybot Leon in the chapter about the patriarchate in India, which according to the intentions of the Spanish rulers was to weaken the papacy outwardly as well, used illustrations of the twelve Popes from Leo X to Pius VI (op. cit. II, 1–23).

[43] J. Specker, *Die Missionsmethode*, 36f. The widespread acceptance of the Tridentine regulations led to the great councils of Lima (1583) and Mexico City (1585).

[44] P. de Leturia, "Perchè la nascente chiesa ispano-americana non fu rappresentata a Trento?" *Relaciones* I, 495–509; F. Mateos, "Ecos de América en Trento," *Revista de Indias* VI (1945), 559–605.

[45] Regarding the impact of the Tridentine regulations in America see R. Lebroc, "Proyección tridentina en América," *MH* 26 (1969), 129–207.

the Church as the mystical body of Christ was impressed very quickly on their Christians.[46] The message was deeply rooted in the Holy Scripture and the doctrines of the Fathers.[47] That the dogma was adapted especially to the intellectual capacity of the Indians, is supported by the expression Theologia Indiana.[48] In the sixteenth century this referred to the instructional books and tracts in the native languages. After the sixteenth century this intellectual attitude receded more and more, making way for a purely European-Spanish direction, for instance by translating European catechisms (like the one by Bellarmine) and relegating the Holy Scripture and the Fathers to a position of lesser importance.[49]

In the exterior realm it was primarily the execution of the Tridentine rules concerning the ministry of regulars and their relationship to the bishops which had appalling consequences, especially since both sides, bishops as well as the orders, were somehow right. On the side of the bishops were the regulations of the Council of Trent, at whose inception, however, no one had thought of missionary conditions. On the side of the mendicant orders were experience in missionary practice and the

---

[46] In addition to the *Doctrina* of Pedro de Córdoba we should mention especially the works of the first bishop of Mexico, Juan de Zumárraga. See J. Beckmann, "Die Erziehung der Christen zum kirchlichen Denken in der jungen Kirche Mexikos," *Novella Ecclesiae Germina* (Nijmegen 1963), 45–60; P. Borges, *Métodos*, 31–44.

[47] J. Specker, "Die Einschätzung der Heiligen Schrift in den spanisch-amerikanischen Missionen," in Beckmann, *Die Heilige Schrift in den Katholischen Missionen* (Beckenried 1966), 37–71. On the church Fathers see for instance A. Etchegaray, "Saint Augustin et le contenu de la catechèse prétridentine en Amérique latine," *RevÉAug* 11 (Paris 1965), 277–90.

[48] The name given a few small volumes in an Indian language of Guatemala by Dom. de Vico, a companion of B. de Las Casas. Streit II, 325: the Franciscan Franc. Maldonado also named his religious treatise in three languages of Guatemala (thirteen volumes by the time of his death) "teología indiana muy útil a los ministros evangélicos de aquellas provincias, y muy provechosa a los neófitos" (Beristain de Souza, *Bibliotheca Americana Septentrionalis* III: *Mexiko* [1947], 178). One of the finest examples of subtle and tactful adaptation are the translations into the Aztec language of the sermons by the first Franciscans in Mexico preserved by Sahagún (W. Lehmann and K. Kutscher, *Sterbende Götter und christliche Heilsbotschaft. Wechselreden indianischer Vornehmer und spanischer Glaubensboten in Mexiko 1524* [Stuttgart 1949]).

[49] The history of the Inquisition, too, has to be viewed in this context. Initially individual inquisitors were appointed as organs of the Spanish Inquisition for certain countries and periods. But toward the end of the sixteenth century independent, full-fledged tribunals were established in Lima (1569), Mexico (1571), and Cartagena (1610). They watched over the faith and morality not only of the Spaniards but also the Indians, who were made subject to the Inquisition in Mexico as early as 1573. See the various sources and histories by J. Toribio Medina. Brazil did not have its own Inquisition; instead the Portuguese crown appointed inquisitors for individual cases. Regarding Mexico see Lopetegui-Zubillaga, *Historia*, 438–47.

immense distances of the sees.[50] It was self-evident that the increase in the number of secular clerics would place the regular Spanish ministry in their hands. But the conditions were different in the often remote and extensive *doctrinas* (missionary stations) of the Indians. Their creation and expansion throughout was the work of the mendicant orders, who were executing their priestly functions on the basis of a papal bull of Hadrian VI (1522) known by its abbreviation *Omnimoda*.[51] These privileges were reaffirmed again and again by successive Popes, such as Pius V in 1567.

When efforts by the bishops resulted in an increase in the number of secular clerics in the second half of the sixteenth century, and the positions in the cathedral chapters and parishes heretofore administered by missionaries were occupied by them, the secular clergy pushed more and more into the well-established *doctrinas* of the Indians. The transfer of the *doctrinas* had already begun in the sixteenth century. In spite of resistance by some orders the change initially took place without resulting in great damage, especially since knowledge of the native language and suitability for serving in the *doctrinas* were required of the secular clerics as well. Only after the great councils of Lima and Mexico was the extent of the transfer of *doctrinas* to the secular clergy increased and the earlier missionaries with all their experience and linguistic ability were shunted into the large religious houses in the cities. The great disadvantages of this practice began to have a real effect in the seventeenth century. The most fatal actions in this connections were probably those of Bishop Juan de Palafox y Mendoza (1600–59), bishop of Puebla and visitor general of Mexico since 1639 (in 1642 he was viceroy of Mexico until the arrival of the newly appointed viceroy; he rejected the archbishopric of Mexico and returned to Spain in 1646, where he died as bishop of Osma). Barely having arrived in Mexico, he already submitted to the King an indictment against the Franciscans charging them with usurpation of jurisdiction. The same year he issued his first pastoral letter to the clergy of Puebla, in which he stressed the right of ministry on the part of the secular clergy for the total ministry. In 1642 the Dominican Luis de Orduna sent a defense to the King. But because of the bishop's authority all the *doctrinas* of the Franciscans were soon transferred to secular clerics. Other bishops in Mexico and South America followed this example. By these actions Palafox had inflicted upon the American Church what was perhaps the worst possible irreparable damage.[52] This becomes clear if one takes into account the fact that the

---

[50] J. Specker, *Die Missionsmethode*, 25–29; P. Borges, *Métodos passim*.
[51] P. Torres, *La Bula "Omnimoda" de Adriano VI* (9. 5. 1522) (Madrid 1946).
[52] F. Sánchez-Castañer, *Don Juan de Palafox, Virrey de Nueva España* (Sarragosa 1964),

mendicant orders, especially the Franciscans, maintained in their *doctrinas*, frequently serving more than twenty thousand Indians, relatively small religious houses with only three to five priests. Only one of these, the *doctrinero*, was paid from government funds, while the others, as auxiliary staff, depended upon the Indians for their livelihood. While the secular priests did use the religious houses as their parish houses, they had no auxiliary staff available to them.[53]

The conflicts between the bishops and the Jesuits, resounding worldwide, were concerned with jurisdictional issues, but were primarily centered around the issue of the tithe which the bishop demanded form the missions' property.[54]

In view of the Tridentine reforms and state absolutism, Palafox acted correctly. Privately he had great respect for the Indians and their abilities;[55] he provided a thorough education for the clergy by establishing the first Tridentine seminary in the New World, combining with it the first public library in Mexico.[56] But Palafox overestimated his secular clergy, to whom he respectfully referred in his first pastoral letter as "Venerable Congregación de San Pedro";[57] they could not take the place of the missionaries of the mendicant orders in the *doctrinas,* especially in the barely accessible ones. Many a parish was soon dissolved as such or rarely visited by a priest, and the unadorned but attractive religious and parish houses fell into ruin.[58]

67–72 (Las doctrinas o Parroquias rurales); idem, comprehensive introduction to the new edition of the works of *Juan de Palafox y Mendoza, Tratados Mejicanos*, 2 vols. (Madrid 1968); L. Lopetegui and F. Zubillaga, *Historia*, 729–32.

[53] Individual statistics of the year 1565 already show this phenomenon (instead of two to three Franciscans, more than three Augustinians, five to six Dominicans, and so forth they merely indicate "1 clérigo") (P. Borges, *Métodos*, 532–34).

[54] The most detailed presentation of the Jesuit point of view is found in Astrain V, 356–411; C. E. P. Simmens ("Palafox and his Critics. Reappraising a Controversy," *Hisp. Am. Hist. Rev.* [1966], 394–408) tries to defend the measures taken by the bishop of Puebla against the members of orders, especially the Jesuits. He believes that the expulsion of the Jesuits would have been avoided if the bishop had been able to prevail with his reform ideas. Concerning the large land holdings of the orders, especially the Jesuits, see F. Chevalier, *La formation des grandes domaines au Mexique* (Paris 1952).

[55] He wrote the *Virtudes del Indio* (1650), a small treatise which went through several editions; Streit II, 515.

[56] This is the Seminario Palafoxiano and the Bibliotheca Palafoxiana in Puebla (J. Specker, "Die 'Bibliotheca Palafoxiana' in Puebla," *ED* 21 [Rome 1968] [Festschrift Rommerskirchen], 487–509).

[57] Streit II, 472.—For the genesis and significance of this appellation see R. Ricard, "El habito de San Pedro," *Bulletin Hispanique* 59 (1957), 304–8.

[58] Various illustrations in G. Kubler, *Mexican Architecture of the Sixteenth Century*, 2 vols. (New Haven 1948).

The problem can be illustrated by the following figures: in the sixteenth century 63.16 percent of the appointed bishops were from religious orders, in the seventeenth century it was still 50.81 percent, but in the eighteenth century it was only 24.25 percent.[59] The development reached a climax of sorts under Bishop Palafox even though it did not actually prevail in the more remote areas. Yet as late as 1722 the nuncio in Madrid received an instruction from Rome for the archbishop of Mexico concerning the transfer of Indian parishes to secular clerics.[60]

The above figures are not intended to represent a value judgment. Among both types of clerics there were superior missionaries. Among the bishops of the secular clergy we should mention the contemporary of Bishop Palafox, Alonso de la Peña Montenegro (1596–1687, bishop of Quito).[61] He, too, looked after his rights vis-à-vis the regulars, the Franciscans and the Jesuits,[62] but without onesidedness and imprudence. His *Itinerario para parochos de Indios* (Madrid 1668)[63] had an enduring influence throughout the Spanish colonial period. Its tenor is a sense of missionary responsibility and great respect for the Indians, although a strong canonistic-casuistic direction and a narrow application of the Tridentine regulations for the Indian mission are also noticeable.

In the initial stages of missionary work by the secular clergy the lack of linguistic knowledge had an important negative effect. But this was improved by the establishment of teaching chairs for the study of native languages at the large universities of Mexico and Lima and later on in Guatemala and other places; missionaries of the secular clergy produced some outstanding linguistic experts.[64] It was precisely their knowledge of languages and their solidarity with the people which enabled them to participate in extraordinary measure in missionary work and to serve the bishops as visitors or interpreters.[65] Some also fought paganism in their role as writers. In connection with Peru we should mention the works of the mestizo priest Dr. Francisco de Ávila, as well as those of Hernando de Avendaño, Pablo José de Arriaga,[66] and Juan Pérez Bocanegro.[67]

The displacement of the regular clergy gave rise to many a quarrel,

[59] A. Ybot León, *La Iglesia* II, 168.

[60] A. de Egaña, *La teoría del Regio Vicariato Español* (Rome 1958), 302 f.

[61] M. Bandin Hermo, *El Obispo de Quito Don Alonso de la Peña Montenegro* (Madrid 1951).

[62] Ibid., 189–96: relationship to the Franciscans; 197–222: relationship to the Jesuits.

[63] Streit I, 271 f. The work had five editions, the last one as late as 1771.

[64] C. Bayle, *El Clero Secular y la Evangelización de América* (Madrid 1950), 197–220.

[65] Ibid., 223–291, and the introduction to the "Crónicas peruanas de interés indígena," *Biblioteca de Autores Españoles* 209 (Madrid 1968); L. Millones, "Introducción al estudio de las idolatrías. Análises del proceso de aculturación religiosa en la área andina," *Aportes* (Paris 1967), 47–82.

[66] The Spanish works of these three authors in a new edition are contained in Vol. 209 of the *Biblioteca de Autores Españoles*. For Francisco de Ávila, see H. Trimborn and Klelm

especially on the issue of language. The Hispanicizing decrees of the Council of the Indies, applied to the Indian settlements as well, were for the most part without effect because no financial means were allocated for their execution, but especially because the priests in the Indian parishes, both the regular and the secular priests, but above all the mestizos, resisted the decrees most strenuously. Most deleterious was the decision by the archbishop of Mexico, Antonio de Lorenzana (d. 1804 as cardinal-archbishop of Toledo), in a pastoral letter to require the acquisition of Spanish for the benefit of the Indians and the elevation of religious life in Mexico.[68]

The character of Portuguese Brazil was completely different from that of the Spanish territories.[69] The Spanish had occupied and settled whole countries, whereas the Portuguese for a long time limited themselves to individual coastal areas. They did not advance into the interior of the country until the seventeenth century and then only did so gradually. The establishment of bishoprics reflects both the colonial and the ecclesiastical expansion. After 1551 Bahia was the only bishopric for over a century. In 1676 it was joined by Rio de Janeiro, Olinda-Recife, and Maranhão; in 1745 by São Paulo and Marianna (Minas Gerais); in 1781 by Goiaz and Cuiabá. Missionary work, too, had initially limited itself to the coastal areas, where Franciscans and Dominicans, Jesuits and Capuchins, but also Benedictines and Carmelites were active in the seventeenth and eighteenth century. In order to

---

Antje, *Francisco de Ávila* (Berlin 1967); concerning Arriaga and the entire problem, see J. Specker, "Das Weiterleben des Heidentums in den peruanischen Missionen des 17. Jh.," *Jb für Gesch. von Staat, Wirtschaft und Gesellschaft Lateinamerikas* 3 (Cologne 1966), 118–40; C. Bayle, "Los Clérigos y la extirpación de la idolatría en los neófitos americanos," *MH* 1 (1944), 53–94.—The battle against the enduring paganism was of course also waged by the missionaries of the orders. For the sixteenth century, see P. Borges, *Métodos*, 247–306; L. Clark Keating, *The Extirpation of Idolatry in Peru* (Lexington 1968).

[67] *Ritual, formular e institución de cura para administrar a los naturales de este reino* (Lima 1631). Bishop Peña Montenegro also deals with this question comprehensively in his *Itinerario para parochos de Indios* 6k. II, tract IV (1754), 219–35. In all these works of the Peruvian secular clerics we should not ignore the antipathy, often strong, against the regular clergy. In addition to the documentation for the continuing existence of paganism, which reasonable Indian missionaries never denied, they should also document the deficient missionary work of the regular clergy.

[68] R. Konetzke, "Die Bedeutung der Sprachenfrage in der Kolonisation Amerikas," *Jb. für Gesch. von Staat, Wirtschaft und Gesellschaft Lateinamerikas* 1 (Cologne 1964), 72–116; R. Ricard, "Le problème de l'enseignement du castillan aux Indiens d'Amérique durant la période coloniale," *Bulletin de la Faculté des Lettres de Strasbourg* 39 (1961), 281–96.

[69] R. Richard, "La Dualité de la civilisation hispanique et l'histoire religieuse du Portugal," *RH* 216 (1956), 1–17; idem, "Comparison of Evangelization in Portuguese and Spanish America," *The Americas* 14 (Washington 1957/58), 444–53.

ameliorate the conflicts between the individual orders there was a rough jurisdictional division of certain areas between the Jesuits, Franciscans, Capuchins, and Carmelites. In the larger monasteries and colleges of the coastal areas the orders also educated native priests, sons of Portuguese settlers, mestizos, and some few Negroes (but no Indians), all of whom demonstrated a higher degree of adaptability and linguistic ability than the European missionaries.[70]

Aside from the effects of patronage, injurious in Brazil as well,[71] missionary work there was hampered in the seventeenth century by the Dutch occupation in the north and the French occupation in the south. But the greatest disaster was slavery. The Dutch occupation (with its center in Pernambuco) united all forces in the country, governmental and ecclesiastical, Portuguese and native, in a common defense. Yet the prevailing attitude towards slavery became a significantly divisive element in missionary work. The Franciscans sought to protect the Indian villages (*Aldeias*) which they served against the Portuguese slaveholders, whereas the Jesuits under the leadership of the most eloquent Antonio Vieira (d. 1697) pursued their fight against slavery in Brazil as well as in Portugal primarily in the public forum. Neither order achieved any lasting success. In 1640 the Jesuits were even driven out of São Paulo. They were not allowed to return until 1653, and then only after they promised not to oppose the slave expeditions of the Paulists or *Bandeirantes* inasmuch as the latter were concentrating on the Indians in the reductions of Guairá, which belonged to the Jesuit province of Paraguay. A royal edict of 1758 tried to put a definitive end to Indian slavery although the enslavement of Negroes continued until the end of the nineteenth century.

[70] An example of the increasing number of native-born priests is given by the statistics in S. Leite, *Suma Histórica de Companhia de Jesus no Brasil (1549–1760)* (Lisbon 1965), 257. This shows the Brazilian province in 1757 to have had 210 native-born among a total of 474 members, whereas the vice-province of Maranhão had only 13 Brazilians among 155 members. For the history of the Jesuits in Brazil, see S. Leite, *Historia da Companhia de Jesus no Brasil,* 10 vols. (Lisbon 1938–50); for the Franciscans, see V. Willeke, O.F.M., "Franziskanermission in Brasilien 1500–1966, *NZM* 1967 ff; for the Capuchins, see Metodio da Nembro, O.F.M. Cap., *Storia dell'attivitá missionaria dei Missioni Cappuccini nel Brasile (1538?–1889)* (Rome 1958); for an overview see A. L. Farinha, *A expansão de fé na Africa e no Brasil* (Lisbon 1942), 419–542. A comprehensive history of the mission in Brazil is lacking.

[71] B. Biermann, O.P., "Die Sklaverei in Maranhão—Brasilien im 17. Jh. Ein unveröffentlichtes Dokument aus der Tätigkeit des P. Ant. Vieira," *NZM* 13 (1957), 103–18; 217–25; G. Freyre, *Casa-Grande e senzala,* 2 vols. (Rio de Janeiro 1954), Eng.: *The Masters and the Slaves* (New York 1946), French: *Maîtres et Esclaves* (Paris 1952). Regarding the unceasing efforts of the missionaries for the human rights of the Indians, see M. Kiemen, O.F.M., *The Indian Policy of Portugal in the Amazonas Region 1619–1693* (Washington 1954).

Under these conditions it is not surprising that the first synod in Brazil was not convened until 1707. On this occasion Archbishop Sebastian da Vida published the first constitutions of the archdiocese of Bahia after he had become personally familiar with the church situation in the country through laborious visitations.[72] The second synod of Brazil did not take place until 1888. The great significance of the *Constitutiones* of 1707 lies in the fact that for the first time the total religious life of Brazil, down to the last details, was dealt with and regulated in 1,318 paragraphs, giving thought to the Indians and Negroes in the appropriate places with the intention of securing their religious life.[73] The constitutions were printed in Lisbon (1719) and Coimbra (1720), but in 1750 Marquis de Pombal began his activities, which were to be equally disastrous for Brazil.

The Revival of the Missionary Spirit and the Expansion of the Missions

The extant religious missions in America again and again produced prominent men in the course of the seventeenth and eighteenth century, so that the orders cannot be said to have been decaying.[74] The original missionary spirit was revived by new foundations and orientations.

THE FRANCISCANS

The rejection of an Indian Church by Philip II and the Council of the Indies damaged the Franciscan mission more than others, as did the gradual transfer of the already established *doctrinas* to the secular clergy. To be sure, the Franciscans retained a number of *doctrinas,* even in Mexico, after the actions of such prelates as Bishop Palafox.[75] Propagation of the faith among the remaining pagan Indians was both started and continued, albeit with great sacrifices. But it took Antonio Llinás to bring about a true reorientation.[76] Born in Mallorca in 1635, he joined

---

[72] O. Schulte O.F.M., *De primis Archidiocesis Bahiae constitutionibus anno 1707 promulgatis* (Rome 1962).

[73] Ibid., 140–66.

[74] The best overview of all the orders is probably A. Ybot León, *Iglesia* II, for the Franciscans: 243–510; Dominicans: 511–631; Mercedarians: 632–88; Augustinian Hermits: 689–794; Augustinian Recollects: 795–840; Jesuits: 841–994; Capuchins: 995–1028, with an abundant bibliography for each section.

[75] According to a report in 1691 by the archbishop of Mexico 147 parishes and *doctrinas* were served by regular clerics and only 79 by secular clerics (L. Lemmens, op. cit., 226).

[76] E. R. Paxos, *De Patre Antonio Llinás Collegiorum Missionarum in Hispania et America Fundatore 1635–93* (Vich 1936); he is treated in detail by the chronicler F. de Espinosa, O.F.M., *Crónica de los Colegios de Propaganda Fide de la Nueva España*, ed. by Lino G. Cañedo (Washington 1964), books II–III, 233–443. A good summary is found in D.

the Franciscan order of strict observance and went to Mexico in 1664. After he worked as a lecturer in philosophy and theology for ten years, he became guardian in Valladolid in 1674. He did his duty and pursued music as a hobby. But the stricter observance of the rules of the order and devotion to apostolic work (popular missions) led to his being elected in 1679 as representative to the upcoming chapter general. At the beginning of 1680 he arrived in Spain and used his time until the chapter of Toledo to prepare his lifework, the foundation of mission colleges. For soon after he began his apostolic work, Llinás recognized that the required apostolic manpower could no longer be obtained from the large monasteries in the cities of Mexico, most of which had been in existence for more than one hundred years. In 1682 the general of his order agreed to the statutes of these mission colleges and designated the monastery of the Holy Cross in Querétaro, Mexico, for the planned new foundation; he allowed Llinas to recruit twenty-four missionaries in the Spanish provinces. Innocent XI approved the statutes through a brief of 8 May 1682, the Congregation for the Propagation of the Faith did so by decree of 15 June 1682. The Holy Office also assigned the necessary faculties for the apostolic work.[77]

The constitutions of the mission colleges, probably authored by the general of the order, José Ximénez Samaniego,[78] but derived from Llinas's experiences, were based on the perception that true apostolic work is only possible in conjunction with the strictest observance.[79] The monastery of the Holy Cross in Querétaro, the cradle of the mission colleges, was already a monastery of recollection (recolección) and strict observance.[80] As were later mission colleges, it was released from the provincial structure and placed directly under the commissioners of the order in Mexico. The college was to be an institution for training in the missionary parish work and in the languages of the natives. It was planned to enable the missionaries to retreat there for longer or shorter periods of time for the purpose of contemplation. The rule for the new Indian missions was that the missionaries would only work there until the Indians were truly converted and could be left to the care of the

---

Saiz Diez O.F.M., "Los Colegios de Propaganda Fide en Hispanoamérica," MH 25 (1968), 257–318; 26 (1969), 5–113.

[77] The three documents were ratified by the Council of the Indies and approved in 1683 (see R. Pazos, op. cit., 72).

[78] V. Añibarro, O.F.M., "El P. José Ximénez Samaniego Ministro General O.F.M. y Obispo de Placencia," Archivo Ibero-Americano 3 (Madrid 1943), especially 292–309.

[79] F. de Espinosa, Crónica in the introduction by P. L. G. Cañedo, XXVff.

[80] M. B. McCloskey, The Formative Years of the Missionary College of Santa Cruz of Queretaro 1683–1733 (Washington 1955).

secular clerics.[81] Because of the disputes between the native Spanish regulars and the Creoles, the mission colleges sought to refill their ranks with new recruits from Spain, although in principle Creoles and members of other provinces in the country were not excluded.[82] This attitude with its attendant consequences prompted the founder of the college of Querétaro to return to Spain at the end of 1684 in order to save the endangered foundation.[83] The superiors both of the order and the Church renewed their approbation. But Llinás did not go back to Mexico because he was entrusted with a new challenge in Spain which he had not foreseen, but nonetheless accepted with pleasure: the founding of similar mission colleges in Spain, which were to secure a rising generation, grown up and already schooled in the missionary spirit of the overseas colleges. The colleges in Spain were also to take over the task of popular mission there.[84] Their title, *Colegios de Propaganda Fide*, is surprising and can be traced to the recognition of the foundation in Querétaro by the Propaganda. They were accorded great esteem but no more. The mission colleges were also subject to the Spanish right of patronage. When Llinás was negotiating in Rome in 1685/86, the Spanish ambassador received a letter from the Council of the Indies requesting him to make sure that no patronage rights were violated. It stipulated that Llinás was not to confer about the conversion of the Indians because the King himself, contrary to opinions in Rome, had manifested the greatest concern for the missionary work. All documents written in Rome prior to and at this time were to be submitted again to the Council of the Indies for their appraisal.[85]

---

[81] By means of this regulation the general attempted to prevent conflicts with the secular clergy. Thus the college of San Fernando in Mexico handed the flourishing mission in the Sierra Gorda over to the secular clergy (see M. Geiger, *Palou's Life of Fray Junípero Serra* (Washington 1955), 35 f.). The basis was the mutual esteem as expressed in the fraternal accord between the secular clergy of Queretaro and the College of the Holy Cross (see F. de Espinosa, *Crónica,* 217–21 [Hermanidad ejemplar que hizo la muy ilustre y venerable congregacion de Nra. Sra. de Guadelupe con el colegio, a chapter which is exemplary for the new spirit of the colleges]).

[82] For Queretaro, Father Lino Gómez Cañedo lists the following figures for the period of 1683–1750: 142 priests and 14 lay brothers who were from Spain, 58 priests and 36 brothers from among the Creoles who were accepted into the novitiate, and 11 priests and 4 brothers who transferred into the mission college from other provinces (F. de Espinosa, *Crónica*, XXVIII).

[83] R. Pazos, op. cit., 104ff.

[84] The care applied to the selection process for the mission college is shown by the regulations left for his successors by Father M. Mingo de la Concepción, who represented the mission college of Tarija (Bolivia) in Spain (P. Borges, "Trámites para la organización de las Expediciones misioneras a América [1780]," *Archivo Ibero-Americano* 26 [Madrid 1966], 405–72).

[85] R. Pazos, op. cit., 112f.

The most important mission colleges were founded in Mexico. The monastery of the Holy Cross continued to be the parent monastery, as it were. The missionaries initially worked in the pagan enclaves of the country, among the Otomis near Querétaro, the Tlaxcaltecs near Puebla, the Coles and Lacadones in the Verapaz, and among the Licques Indians of Honduras. To these were soon added the Talamanca mission in the southeast of Costa Rica and missionary work in what is now Texas. The mission in the Verapaz and among other Indian tribes of Guatemala prompted the establishment of the second mission college of the "Crucified Christ" in the city of Guatemala. Another foundation, "Our Dear Lady of Guadalupe" in Zacatecas, received royal acknowledgment in 1704. Emanating from Zacatecas, the southern stretch of land in the Gulf of Mexico known as Nuevo Santander was successfully missionized.[86] In 1733 the college of San Fernando was founded in the capital; it was confirmed by the King in 1733. Since the Discalced also opened a similar mission college (1733), designed to take over the mission in the barely accessible mountains of Zimapán, Mexico now had five colleges for the propagation of the faith.

Mexico also became the point of departure for the establishment of other colleges in South America. In Ocopa in the south of the archbishopric of Lima the Colegio di Santa Rosa was founded (1724). From 1779 to 1783 it was charged with the mission on the island of Chiloé and later on some additional ones, among them those of the expelled Jesuits.[87] In Colombia the colleges of Popayán (founded 1747 in Quito and relocated 1749 in Popayán) and Cali (1756) were set up. In Tarija (Bolivia) the local college took over the mission among the Chiriguanos in the Chaco, stagnant for over two hundred years. Their apostle was the venerable Franciscus del Pilar, who, living among them as helper and servant of all from 1765 until his death in 1803, gradually overcame their resistance. By 1810 the mission comprised twenty-two stations with 16,425 Christians.[88] In 1756 the college of Chillán (Chile) was founded; after 1767 it was in a position to take over the majority of

---

[86] F. de Lejarza, O.F.M., *Conquista espiritual del Nuevo Santander* (Madrid 1947). Here, too, the missionaries established twenty-three Indian villages (see pp. 187–295). Following the expulsion of the Jesuits the missionaries of Zacatecas were able to take over the Jesuit missions among the Tarahumara Indians as well (J. A. Alcocer, O.F.M., *Bosquejo de la historia del Colegio de Nuestra Señora de Guadalupe y sus misiones. Año de 1788* [Mexico City 1958]; A. M. Carreño, "The Missionary Influence of the College of Zacatecas," *The Americas* 7 (Washington 1950/51), 297–320).

[87] O. Maas, O.F.M., *Las Órdenes religiosas* (contains a number of informative documents especially about the activities of this college).

[88] L. Lemmens, op. cit., 319–23. Another Bolivian college was established at the end of the eighteenth century in Tarate.

the missions of the expelled Jesuits.[89] The last college to be founded in the eighteenth century was San Carlos on the Paraná (1784); it was designed especially for the conversion of the Indians in the southern Chaco and in Paraguay.[90] The historian of the Franciscan order justifiably speaks of "that glorious new epoch of the eighteenth century which begins with the entrance of the apostolic colleges into the vineyard of the Lord."[91] The new missionary spirituality is especially well reflected in the life of two men.

One of the founders of the Mexican colleges was Antonio Margil (1657–1726). He spent forty-three years in Central America and not only founded the colleges of Guatemala and Zacatecas, but to a large extent put his stamp on the spirit of the colleges. He worked as a missionary in all the areas of Central America, to Talamancas in Costa Rica, and on the other side up to Texas, where he spent the period from 1716 to 1722. After his sermons got him a firm foothold somewhere, he hurried on, leaving his successors to consolidate his achievements.[92] The apostle of California, Junípero Serra (1713–84), belonged to the mission college of San Fernando in Mexico. In 1750 he left the professorship of his native university (Palma de Mallorca) and at first worked among the Indians of the Sierra Gorda and after 1767 as superior of the Franciscan mission in California, initially in Baja California, where the Franciscans of the colleges took over the missions of the expelled Jesuits. Finally, he pioneered the mission in present-day California, where even now a number of Franciscan names are a reminder of the modest beginnings of Indian missions. In a constant fight with regalism, dominant even in California, Serra succeeded in establishing a chain of missionary stations all the way to San Francisco. The state of California has placed a statue of its actual colonizer in the capital in Washington.[93]

---

[89] L. Lemmens, op. cit., 312–16. In 1777 this college initiated the founding of a college for Indian priests the first three of whom were ordained in 1794 (ibid., 313). It was closed in 1811 when the new national government proved to be even more opposed to the Indians than the former Spanish rule.

[90] Ibid., 332. In his history Lemmens makes additional references to smaller colleges as well.

[91] Ibid., 239. F. de Espinosa, *Crónica de los Colegios*, 783–88 (contains a good summary of the first sixty years of the colleges in Mexico and their actual missionary work).

[92] The first account of his life is by his contemporary F. de Espinosa, *El pelegrino Septentrional Atlante . . .* (Valencia 1742); Streit III, 130; critical biography by Rios and Leutenegger, *Life of Fray A. Margil OFM* (Washington 1959).

[93] First biography by his countryman and successor F. Palóu, *Relación Histórica* (Mexico City 1787) (English translation with critical commentary by M. Geiger [Washington 1955]); *The Writings of J. S.*, trans. and ed. by A. Tibesar, 3 vols. (Washington 1955–56); standard biography by M. Geiger, O.F.M., *The Life and Time of Fr. J. S.*, 2 vols. (Washington 1959).

By the middle of the eighteenth century and the expulsion of the Spanish by the Americans the mission colleges had—with few exceptions—taken the place of the earlier missionaries of the Franciscan provinces in the newly opened missions in the north, and in the states of New Mexico, Texas, Arizona, and California (later annexed by the United States). The spirit of these colleges could only be broken by force,[94] in Mexico by their abolition in 1827, somewhat later in other countries. Just a few of them continued on into modern days, incorporated in the reorganized Franciscan provinces.

THE JESUITS

A new impetus to the missionary spirit was expected from the Society of Jesus, which arrived in America relatively late. But government and Church alike wanted the Jesuits above all to serve the Spaniards, or rather the Creoles, especially in the field of education, where they indeed earned their greatest merits, indirectly of benefit to the Indian mission as well. Subaltern officials and the secular clergy were educated in their schools.[95] The dispatch of the Jesuits to America met with great opposition in Spain and indeed even within their own order.[96] Thus the Jesuits only gradually grew into their role as Indian missionaries. Even in the vice-kingdom of Peru, where they had arrived in 1568 and where the propagation of the faith had developed most intensively, it was not until 1576 that the provincial chapter of Cuzco took over the large missionary center of Juli on Lake Titicaca, sending the first missionaries there in the same year.[97] Yet at the colleges of Lima and Cuzco the Jesuits had already worked successfully among the Indians in those areas. The refusal to take over their own *doctrinas* or Indian parishes was

[94] An abundance of details in the two volumes of O. Maas, op. cit.—Approximately eighty years after the establishment of the college of Querétaro the Capuchin Father Franc. de Ajofrín praised its apostolic spirit (B. de Carrocera, "Noticias Misionales de Méjico en los años 1763–1767." *MH* 11 [1954], 221ff.). The same spirit was still widespread in Spain as noted by a report of the Comisario Collector for the year 1811 (F. de Lejarza, "Las Levas misioneras en el siglo XIX," *MH* 13 [1956], 179–90).

[95] The Jesuits substantially elevated the education and social status of the secular clergy so that together they represented the third party (in addition to the bishops and the mendicant orders) (See R. C. Padden, "The Ordenanza del Patronasgo 1574. An Interpretative Essay," *The Americas* 12 [Washington 1955/56], 333–54, esp. 353f.).

[96] Astraín II, 284ff.; F. Mateos, "Antecedentes de la entrada de los jesuitos españoles en las Misiones de América (1538–63)," *MH* 1 (1944), 109–66.

[97] A. Echánovo, "Origen y evolución de la idea jesuítica de 'Reducciones' en las Misiones del Virreinato del Perú," *MH* 12 (1955), 95–144; *MH* 13 (1956), 497–540; A. de Egaña, *Monumenta Peruana* II (Rome 1958), see Index p. 875. But even later on complaints reached Rome which prompted General Claudio Acquaviva to issue his encyclical to the missions (dated 15 June 1584), which Egaña calls the "Carta Magna Misional" of the order (ibid. III, Doc. 100).

probably based on the fear that this would tie them too closely to the civil and ecclesiastic authorities.[98]

In the following period Juli not only became a model of Jesuit missionary work on Lake Titicaca, but a universal center of Peru. The missions of the Maynas (on the upper Amazon in eastern Ecuador), among the Moxos (in present-day Bolivia), and especially in Paraguay had their roots there. The Chiquitos mission in Bolivia, too, was indirectly connected with Juli.[99]

This expansion of the Jesuit colleges and missions in South America resulted in the formation of more and more provinces.[100] What gave these areas, especially the missions among the Indians during the seventeenth and eighteenth century, their very own character was the steady increase of non-Spanish missionaries. Jesuits from countries under Spanish dominion, such as Italians, Flemish, and Walloons were the first to be admitted.[101] Then, towards the end of the seventeenth century, subjects of the Habsburg lands received permission to travel abroad (1678),[102] and finally others as well, such as Germans and Swiss. The major portion of the non-Spanish missionaries went to the reductions in Paraguay. According to A. Huonder, the province of Paraguay, separated from Peru in 1606, included about one hundred twenty-five German-speaking missionaries, most of them in the reductions.[103] The reason for this was not only the fact that the foreign Jesuits in faraway Paraguay were at greater remove from supervision of Spanish officials, but also that their labor and skills were highly esteemed. They excelled as prominent architects and musicians, as for instance the Austrian Anton Sepp von Reinegg or the Swiss Martin Schmid;[104] as ethnologists like

---

[98] In 1576 the eminent mission theoretician José de Acosta was the provincial of the Peruvian province. The decision for the taking over of the *doctrinas* can probably be attributed to him (L. Kilger, "Die Peru-Relation des José de Acosta 1576 und seine Missionstheorie," *NZM* 1 [1945], 24–38).

[99] In July, for instance, there was a rule that after twenty days of work in the *doctrinas* the missionaries had to return to the religious house for eight days of spiritual renewal and communal life (A. Echánovo, "Origen y evolución . . . ," *MH* 12 [1955], 117f.).

[100] Details in Streit II and III and in the supplementary volumes XXIV–XXVI; E. Cardozo, *Historiografía Paraguaya* (Mexico City 1959).

[101] P. Delattre and E. Lamalle, "Jésuites wallons, flamands, français, missionaires du Paraguay 1608–1767, "*AHSI* 16 (Rome 1947), 98–176.

[102] F. A. Plattner, "Die Groß-Expedition von Jesuiten deutscher Zunge," *NZM* 1 (1945), 169–83. These were the expeditions of 1680.

[103] *Deutsche Jesuitenmissionare des 17. und 18. Jh.* (Freiburg 1899), 139–51; A. Blankenburg, "German Missionary Writers in Paraguay," *Mid-America* 29 (Chicago 1947), 34–68, 122–31.

[104] F. A. Plattner, *Ein Reisläufer Gottes. Das abenteuerliche Leben eines Schweizer Jesuiten P. Martin Schmid aus Baar* (1694—1772) (Lucerne 1944); idem, *Genie im Urwald. Das*

Martin Dobritzhoffer, whose work on the Abipones is highly respected even today, or the Silesian Florian Paucke, whose observations were published only recently.[105] Very much in demand were the German and Flemish brothers who were highly skilled in the trades but were also working as artists and apothecaries. All of this was of great use to the reductions, but caused growing antipathy among the Spanish population in the surrounding countryside.[106] Immense herds of mules and cows provoked the envy of the urban Spaniards.[107] The major export articles were Paraguay tea, the production rights of which was granted to the Indians by a royal cedula on 1645,[108] and woven goods.[109] The tragic outcome of the courageous fight against the slave hunters of São Paulo, leading, in the end, to Portugal's claiming a number of reductions in the present Brazilian state of Paraná contributed significantly to the decline of the large-scale "Indian State" of the Jesuits. The order by the Jesuit general to obey in every way the regulations of the Portuguese and finally the cession to Portugal of seven reductions, together with all their territory (stipulated by the Treaty of Madrid in 1750), had a disastrous effect. The missionaries were forced to abandon their Indians when the latter, deprived of help from the fathers and the other reductions, were defeated in battle by a Portuguese-Spanish alliance. This completely undermined the Indians' confidence in their missionaries. The Jesuits, frequently with great ceremony, had assumed the legal protection over the Indians because they knew all too well that their Christians were sold without mercy on the slave markets of Brazil, especially since they were more valuable to the sellers than other Indians by virtue of their skills in agriculture and the crafts. In 1768 when the Jesuits, together

---

Werk des Auslandschweizers M. Schmid (Zurich 1959); idem, *Deutsche Meister des Barock in Südamerika im 17. und 18. Jh.* (Freiburg 1960).

[105] Zwettler Codex 420 of P. Florian Paucke. *Jesuiten-Mission in Paraguay* I (Vienna 1959); II (ibid. 1966); H. Hoffmann, "Der Indianermissionar Florian Paucke SJ aus Winzig in Schlesien," *Beiträge z. schles. Kirchengeschichte. Gedenkschrift für Kurt Engelbert* (Cologne and Vienna 1969), 376–81.

[106] See especially M. Mörner, *The Political and Economic Activities of the Jesuits in the La Plata Region* (Stockholm 1953); pp. 6–21 have a thorough introduction to the published and unpublished sources especially of the reductions; pp. 229–41 contain an excellent bibliography.

[107] Even in 1680 there were thirty-five hundred mules sold from Cordoba to Peru (M. Mörner, op. cit., 167). In addition to the mules the college of Buenos Aires, where the superiors of Paraguay province resided, regularly exported approx. twenty thousand other animals (ibid.).

[108] M. Mörner, op. cit., 100. See 150f. regarding the planting of yerba, as the tea was called commercially, its expansion and the resulting decrease of its price on the world market.

[109] M. Mörner, op. cit., 163.

with about one hundred thousand Indians, were driven out of their remaining thirty reductions, there was no resistance on the part of the Indians.[110]

Closely connected with these events was probably the downfall of the social utopias which had initially been nurtured by older Jesuits and then taken root among the Indians, leading to some syncretistic movements among them.[111] In the end, this undermined the vitality of the Indians of Paraguay and the surrounding reductions. Adding the totally paternalistic attitude of the missionaries, which had after all prevailed for 150 years,[112] one can understand in historical terms the extent of the tragedy inherent in the downfall of such an idealistic undertaking. But one must also know that the missionaries of other orders, especially the Franciscans, were no more successful. By 1802 the thirty former Jesuit reductions contained a mere 30,116 inhabitants. A large number had retreated into the forests.

The arrival of the Jesuits in the vast areas of New Granada (Colombia) and Venezuela occurred relatively late and they had few missions there. But early on they built a large college in the port city of Cartagena, the point of entry for vast areas of South America and at the same time the largest place of reshipment in the slave trade. At least two names should be mentioned among the missionaries of this college as an example of the apostolate among the black slaves. Alonso de Sandoval (1571–1652) was not only the actual organizer of this ministry, but also the first and only theoretician of the Negro mission in America. In 1627 a Spanish-language version of his work appeared in Seville.[113] The thirty-two chapters of the first part of his *De Instauranda Aethiopum salute* dealt with Africa and its cultures, primarily those between the islands of Cape Verde and Angola, from where most of the slaves were coming. The second part describes the miserable conditions of the Negro slaves; the third part treats the qualities and methods required for this special

---

[110] R. Lacombe, "Problème et mystère des Jésuites du Paraguay," *Sciences Ecclésiastiques* 17 (Montreal 1965), 89–109, 283–95. The most informative treatment of the war and its background is provided in G. Kratz, S.J., *El Tratado Hispano-Portugues de Límites de 1750 y sus consecuencias. Estudio sobre la abolición de la Compañia de Jesús* (Rome 1954).

[111] M. Humbert, "Indiens et Jésuites au Paraguay. Rencontre de deux messianismes," *Archives de Sociologie des Religions* 27 (Paris 1969), 119–33.

[112] idem, *La vie quotidienne du Paraguay sous les Jésuites* (Paris 1967).

[113] Streit I, 188. The Spanish title is *Naturaleza, Policia sagrada i profana, Costumbres, Ritos, Disciplina—Catechismo Evangélico de todos Etíopes*. The work was probably supposed to have had the Latin title *De instauranda Aethiopum salute*. This is indicated in the preface. A second printing (Madrid 1647) comprised only the first three books (Streit I, 217). A reprint of the Seville edition appeared in 1956 in Bogotá under the title *De instauranda Aethiopum salute. El mundo de la esclavitud negra en América*.

kind of ministry;[114] the fourth part gives the reasons which call for Jesuits above all to dedicate themselves to this task.[115] Sandoval's pupil and successor, the Catalan Pedro Claver (1581–1659), sought to ameliorate the social conditions of his charges as much as possible. He secured the privilege for Negroes of attending Mass in the college church of the Jesuits. He defended them before the courts and the Inquisition. By taking on the role of "slave of the slaves" day after day he was protesting the practice of slavery.[116]

The Jesuits did not come to the vice-kingdom of Mexico until 1572. Here, too, their principal service was initially to the white population. By and by colleges were built in Mexico, Puebla, Oaxaca, and Valladolid, the great novitiate of Tapozotlán, the seminary of San Ildofonso in Mexico, and the residences in Guadalajara, Pátzcuaro and Vera Cruz. For some time there was no actual Indian mission, a fact which was deplored in contemporary documents by those Jesuits who were eager to missionize. An order by the Jesuit General Acquaviva was required to initiate Indian missionary work of more sizeable proportions;[117] this started in 1584 in the northwestern part of the country. The work not only comprised the Tarahumara Indians,[118] but also the tribes of Sonora and the Pimeria Alta and spread from there across the area of present-day Arizona to Southern California. The most prominent figure among these Jesuit missionaries was a native of Trent, Eusebio Francisco Kino (1645–1711),[119] trained in that southern German province not only to

---

[114] See also the hardly known instructions of the archbishop of Seville, Pedro de Castro y Quiñones, of 1614 for the conversion and ministry of the Negro slaves (Ed. 1956, 463–75).

[115] In spite of the zeal for the religious care of Negro slaves there is not a single chapter challenging the principle of Negro slavery either because the author as a product of his time did not consider it a problem or because censorship did not allow it. Unfortunately, a critical appraisal of Sandoval's work is still lacking, as is a general treatment of the religiomissionary problems of the Negro slaves in the Americas.

[116] For the numerous biographies, see Streit II, III, XXIV, XXVI. The last critical biography was written by A. Valtierra, S.J., *El santo que libertó una raza* (Bogotá 1959), Eng.: *Peter Claver Saint of the Slaves* (London 1960).

[117] F. Zubillaga, op. cit. III (1585–90) (Rome 1968). Even in 1589 reports indicate that of a total of 180 Jesuits no more than 12 or 13 were in the Indian mission (p. 384).

[118] P. Master Dunne, S.J., *Early Jesuit Mission in Tarahumara* (Berkely 1948).

[119] The best biography is by the American scholar of the "border mission," H. E. Bolton, *Rim of Christendom. A Biography of Eusebio Francisco Kino, Pacific Coast Pioneer* (New York 1936, 1960). The most important source for his lifework is the *Favores Celestiales*, written in 1699–1710 in the nature of a biography, ed. with critical commentary by H. E. Bolton, *Kino's Historical Memoir* (Rome 1954) (letters by Kino to the generals of the Society of Jesus); idem, *Kino writes to the Duchess* (Rome 1965), Span. (Madrid 1964) (letters to the great patroness, the duchess of Aveiro); idem., *Kino's Plan to the*

become one of the greatest missionaries, but also a superior explorer and cartographer. The world owes him the first precise knowledge of California.[120] But Father Kino was foremost a missionary and organizer of the far-flung northeastern missions, architect and builder of mission stations and churches. He was so modest about his mission theory that it was not discovered until very recently; it has yet to be evaluated.[121] His greatest worry was the dearth of suitable missionaries; his requests for additional missionaries, especially from German-speaking countries, were fulfilled. H. E. Bolton remarked that more and more "black robes" with non-Spanish names emerge from the annual reports of Pimeria Alta, Sonora, and California during the eighteenth century.[122] Yet the shortage persisted. In his annual report to the general of 1 December 1751 the Swiss provincial Johann Anton Balthasar mentioned that of the 624 members of the Mexican province there were only 111 missionaries available for the territories of the northwest and California.[123]

Contrary to Hispanic America, the Jesuit mission in Brazil (after 1503) and Maranhão (after 1627) was more limited in its development, though not for lack of manpower. The Portuguese homeland allowed neither the establishment of a university nor of a press. Industries whose development the Jesuits had aided were restricted or prohibited altogether lest the colonies become too strong. The predominant Jesuit of the seventeenth century was Antonio Vieira (1608–97), whom we have mentioned before.[124] His parents had brought him

Development of Pimeria Alta, Arizona and Upper California (Tucson, Arizona 1961) (the great justification to the viceroy of Mexico [1703]).

[120] E. J. Burrus, *La obra cartográfica de la provincia mexicana de la Compañía de Jesús (1567–1967)*, 2 vols. (Madrid 1967), especially I, 15–26 (lists thirty-one maps of areas explored and mapped by Kino; ten of them are published in Vol. 2).

[121] E. F. Kino, S.J., *Vida del P. Francesco J. Saeta SJ Sangre Misionera en Sonora*, ed. by E. J. Burrus (Mexico 1961). The eighth book of this bibliography is entitled: "Dictámenes de Misionero Apostólico del Venerable Padre Francisco Javier Saeta, sacados de sus cartas y de su religiosa conversación," 159–83.

[122] *Rim of Christendom*, 594.—For the first two areas he names: Benz, Fraidenegg, Gerstner, Gratzhoffer (= Kratzhoffer), Hoffenrichter, Hlava, Keller, Klever, Kolub, Kürtzel, Middendorff, Miner, Mentwich, Och, Pauer, Rhuen, Sedelmayr, Segesser, Slerag, Steb, Stiger, Wazer and Weiß; for California: Baegert, Bischoff, Consag, Ducrue, Gasteiger, Gordon, Helen, Link, Neymayr, Retz, Tempis, Teursch and Wagner. Concerning the missions in California see P. M. Dunne, *Black Robes in Lower California* (Berkeley 1968).

[123] Ms. in the archive Al Gesù "Fondo Jesuitico," 630 C.

[124] R. Ricard, *Antonio Vieira et les missions du Brésil septentrional au XVIIᵉ siècle* (Louvain 1927) (also in *Études et documents* [Louvain 1930], 189–203); C. R. Boxer, *A Great Luso-Brazilian figure: Padre Ant. Vieira* (Paris 1960); M. Haubert, *L'Église et la défense des "sauvages": Le Père Ant. Vieira au Brésil* (Brussels 1964). These new works list the collections of sources, his writings, and fifteen volumes of his sermons.

to Brazil as a little boy; in 1623 he joined the Society of Jesus. Having worked as Portuguese legate in various countries, he returned to Brazil as a missionary in 1652. Because of his fair and humane partisanship for the Indians he and the other Jesuits of the college of Belem were deported to Portugal by the colonists. Some individual doctrines in his prophetic, utopian works, primarily in his *Esperanças de Portugal, Quinto Imperio do Mundo* and the *Historio de futuro,* resulted in his being jailed by the Inquisition after a trial lasting four years. A change of government brought about his release in 1669.[125] Vieira viewed the widely expanded system of patronage as the instrument willed by God for the final realm of the Messiah, the fifth realm of the eschatology coinciding with the universal rule of Portugal.[126] While he was in Rome to justify himself from 1669 to 1675, he was removed from the jurisdiction of the Portuguese Inquisition, but he rejected all ecclesiastical offices offered to him. After twenty years of banishment he returned to the Maranhão mission, where he died at the age of eighty-nine at the college of Bahia. The strength of the Society of Jesus in Brazil now seemed to be spent. The discovery of the gold mines of Minas Gerais and the coffee plantations of São Paulo no longer offered the same possibilities for missionizing as before. In 1759 the Jesuits were expelled by Pombal.

After an auspicious start, the wars between the Iroquois and Hurons and the killing of the Jesuits working among them (1642–49) brought an end to the mission in the French colonies. Only after 1665, when Carignan secured Canada for the French, was missionary work able to be resumed in earnest. The Jesuits joined in it until the Peace of Paris in 1763, which relinquished Canada to England. During these 100 years they furnished 320 missionaries, most of them for the five Indian villages built after the fashion of Paraguay.[127] As a result of an agreement between the Jesuits and the French Capuchins (1632), the latter worked in Nova Scotia while the Sulpicians, the Paris Missionaries, and the

---

[125] The trial is treated in the 2-volume work of Hernani Cidade, *Ant. Vieira, Defesa Perante o Tribunal do Santo Ofício* (Bahia 1957).

[126] R. Ricard, "'Prophecy and Messianism in the Works of Antonio Vieira," *The Americas* 17 (April 1961), 357–68.

[127] For sources and literature see Streit II and III. F. B. Steck, O.F.M., *Marquette Legends* (New York 1960) (Attempts to prove that Marquette was not the discoverer of the Mississippi, but two of his younger fellow religious who used the great reputation of the older man to issue the reports under his name); also C. de Rochemonteix, *Les Jésuites et la Nouvelle France au XVIIIᵉ siècle,* 2 vols. (Paris 1906); S. Delacroix, op. cit. II, 281–99.—C. C. O'Neill, *Church and State in French Louisiana* (New Haven 1966).

Recollect Franciscans supported the work of the Jesuits in Canada proper.

During the Indian Wars a number of Catholic Indians had been pushed south and southeast. This occasioned the great explorations of the Jesuits, foremost the ones by Jacques Marquette (1637–75), who reached the Mississippi in 1673 and worked among the Illinois and Miami Indians. Other Frenchmen, such as de la Salle, among whose companions was the Franciscan Louis Hennepin (d. 1701), succeeded in exploring the entire stream to its estuary. The Jesuits restricted their mission work to the Indian tribes in the northern areas with whom they were familiar, while others, especially those of the Foreign Missions of Paris, were active farther in the south. None of these groups was truly successful. In spite of all efforts Louisiana was not given its own church organization; it was under the jurisdiction of Quebec until the eighteenth century.

OTHER ORDERS

The Dominicans were the first missionaries of Peru; from there they spread all over South America. The two saints of this order in Peru can be considered as programmatic symbols: Rosa of Lima (1586–1617), a Creole, member of the Third Order and example of a contemplative, mystical life,[128] and Martín de Porras (or Porres, 1569–1639), a mulatto from Lima trained in the art of healing, a Dominican brother who gave himself in charitable love to all, regardless of class or race.[129]

The Dominicans also maintained the Indian missions established in the sixteenth century and further expanded them during the next two centuries. They achieved special merit in the promotion of higher education. In addition to the state universities in Lima and Mexico City founded in the sixteenth century, they operated the University of Santo Domingo from 1538 into the eighteenth century. In 1620 they initiated a *studium generale* in Guatemala which was expanded into a full-fledged university as the Real y Pontificia Universidad de San Carlos, recognized in 1676. Following this, two more universities were founded: the Universities of Santiago de Chile (1685) and Quito (1688). The seventeenth century also marked the beginning of a most quarrelsome competition with the Jesuits, who were able to base their claim on papal briefs similar to those of the Dominicans. As a result, places such as

---

[128] The first biography appeared in 1654 (Streit II, 536), a second one in 1659 (ibid., 550); further biographies appeared almost annually in all sorts of languages.

[129] Sanctification in 1962. More recent biographies by Vargas Ugarte (Buenos Aires 1949), John Jordan (Dublin 1957), and E. Romero (Lima 1959).

Bogotá, Quito, and Santiago de Chile soon had a Dominican and a Jesuit university. The Dominican monastery of San Juan de Letrán in Cuba was expanded into a university in the eighteenth century, as was their Colegio Seminario of Caracas.[130] In some fashion all these institutions were in the service of the Indian mission because the secular as well as the regular clergy received their education and their training in the native languages there.

The humanistic aspect of missionary work in the sixteenth century was primarily represented by the Augustinian Hermits. Alonso de la Vera Cruz was the first professor of theology in the New World (University of Mexico); even his first lectures in 1553/54 dealt with the Indian problem in the spirit of Las Casas and with the weapons of a theologian schooled in Salamanca.[131] The fact that succeeding generations of Augustinian Hermits of the seventeenth century were filled by his spirit is demonstrated by the chronicles of Fray Antonio de la Calancha[132] and Francisco Romero. The latter, a Creole Augustinian from Peru and itinerant missionary of South America, wrote the very moving *Llanto Sagrado de la América Meridional,* printed in Milan in 1693. It was a fearless indictment of the Spanish policy of exploitation of the Indians and was immediately confiscated by the Inquisition.[133] In spite of their efforts Romero and the missionaries recruited by him did not succeed in converting the Tames Indians in the province of Popayán in present-day Colombia.[134] At the beginning of the seventeenth century the wilderness of Raquira became the site of the first hermitage, Our Lady de la Candelaria, founded by the reform movement of the Barefoot Augustinians (Recollects). It became the focus of renewed missionary zeal and religious renewal for Colombia, Venezuela, Central America, and later on for Peru and Mexico. But the Philippines ultimately were to become the most fertile missionary field for them.[135]

[130] R. Konetzke, "Spanische Universitätsgründungen in Amerika und ihre Motive," *Jb. für Gesch. von Staat, Wirtschaft und Gesellschaft Lateinamerikas* 5 (Cologne 1968), 111–59.

[131] E. J. Burrus, "Las Casas and Veracruz: their Defense of the American Indians Compared," *NZM* 22 (1966), 201–12; idem, *The Writings of Alonso de la Vera Cruz* II: *The Defense of the Indians: Their Rights. Latin Text and English Translation* (Rome and St. Louis 1968).

[132] *Cronica Moralizada del Orden de San Augustín en el Perú* I (Barcelona 1639), II (Lima 1653).

[133] For the long title of the Milan edition see Streit II, 655.

[134] J. Metzler, "Das Missionsunternehmen des Francisco Romero O.E.S.A. Ende des 17. Jh.," *NZM* 21 (1965), 1–17.

[135] In addition to A. Ybot León, op. cit. II, 795ff., see especially J. A. Salazar, *Los Estudios eclesiásticos superiores en el Nuevo Reino de Granada 1563–1810* (Madrid 1946), 123ff. and the *Bullarium Ordinis Recollectorum S. Augustini* I (Rome 1954), II (1961).

The last Spanish missionaries in the Americas of the seventeenth century, the Capuchins, initially went to what is now Venezuela. The Council of the Indies had been unwilling to admit yet another order to America. But the lay brother Francisco de Pamplona, formerly General Don Tiburcio de Redín (with excellent connections to Philip IV), prevailed in having missionary work initiated first in Darien and then in Venezuela proper (1650).[136] The first Capuchins did not establish large monasteries nor did they accept novices from the ranks of the Creoles. Thus they maintained closer ties with their Spanish homeland provinces than the other orders.[137] They also sought to implement a new method of missionary style. From the north they advanced to the yet unconverted Indians, establishing small houses and gradually moving farther and farther south and southeast. Thanks to their unobtrusive method they were able to survive the tumult of the times.[138]

It is a striking fact that the participation of the nuns in the task of conversion in America has either been omitted or at best just cursorily described.[139] Remarks by early writers permit us to conclude that the problem of women's education was indeed tackled, since Bishop Juan de Zumárraga, to whom Queen Isabella had sent help in the persons of tertiaries (*Beatas*) in 1531 and 1535. Towards the end of the seventeenth century there were twenty-two convents in the city of Mexico alone and ten in Puebla.[140] All of these convents counted among their pupils Spanish, Creole, and Indian girls.[141] Such convents were also founded exclusively for Indian girls, daughters of caciques, among them

[136] The first biography was written by the Capuchin chronicler Mateo de Anguiano, *Vida y virtudes del Capuchino Español, el Venerable Servo de Dios Fray Francisco de Pamplona* (Madrid 1686); a modern critical one by L. de Aspurz (Madrid 1951); see also B. de Carocera, "F. Francisco de Pamplona, organisador de Misiones y conductor de Misioneros," *MH* 9 (1952), 5–51.
[137] For the American Capuchin mission see Froilán de Rionegro, *Relaciones de las Misiones de los PP. Capuchinos en las Provincias españoles hoy República de Venezuela (1650–1817)*, 2 vols. (Seville 1918). Additional sources and literature in A. Ybot-León. op. cit., 1021ff.
[138] Information about the ethnological and linguistic works of the Capuchin friars provided in their journal *Venezuela Misionero* I (Caracas 1938)ff.
[139] I am not aware of any comprehensive work on this topic although reference is made to it in individual sources and in monographs about several convents.
[140] F. Chevalier, *La formation des grands domaines au Mexique* (Paris 1952), 330f.
[141] Ibid., 331. About the convents of Mexico City see the monograph by J. Muriel, *Conventos de monjas en la Nueva España* (Mexico City 1946). At the beginning of the seventeenth century Lima had six convents. B. Cobo, S.J., *Fundación de Lima*, ed. by F. Mateos (Madrid 1956), 428–33; of special interest is the chapter on the Carmelite nuns, "Del colegio de Nuestra Señora del Carmen," 434–36; it also maintained a girls' school and a girls' orphanage. For the educational work of a Dominican convent in Oaxaca, see J. Muriel, "Notas para la Historia de la educación de la mujer durante el Virreynato," *Estudios de Historia Novohispaña* II (1968), 25–33.

the convent of Corpus Christi in Mexico (1724).[142] Emanating from
here, the Indian convents of Cosamalsapán (1737) and Oaxaca (1782)
were established with the particular aim of avoiding tensions among the
races. Indian women had never been denied admittance to the orders.[143]
The provincial synod of Charcas (Sucre, Bolivia) of 1629 indeed
stressed that all sisters would enjoy equal rights in the convents. It
emphasized that half-castes were to be accepted among the officiating
nuns, "cum apud Deum fides non genus in pretio sit."[144] In the more
distant provinces missionaries probably followed the example of the
Beatas of the sixteenth century, founding *Beaterios* with the daughers of
Indians. Two such convents are mentioned by the Capuchin friar
Francisco de Ajofrín in his memoirs concerning his mendicant travels in Mexico.[145] The chronicler of the Dominican province of
Guatemala reports that Benito de Villacañas founded such *Beaterios*
in Guatemala and San Juan Sueatepequez and wrote the life of
Christ and of Saint Catherine of Siena in the language of the sisters, that is, in Cacchiquel.[146] Only a thorough study will be able to
show the extent of the contribution to the cultural life of the individual countries made by the convents. At this time it is enough to
mention the poetess, dramatist, and essayist Sister Juana Inéz de la
Cruz (1648–95), a Creole and Carmelite nun, still recognized

---

[142] J. Muriel, *Las indias caciques de Corpus Christi* (Mexico City 1963); in addition to a
thorough introduction this work contains eight biographies of Indian sisters.

[143] F. de Lejarza, O.F.M., "Expansión de la Clarisas en América y Extremo Oriente,"
Archivo Ibero-Americano 14 (1954), 446f., 450f. Another convent was dedicated in the
province of Michoacán (Valladolid) in 1743. The dedicatory sermon was given by the
secular priest Juan Wallo Anguita. It was published under the title: *Oración panegírico de
la dedicación del convento de indias capuchinas de Valladolid de Michoacán* (Mexico City
1743). Beristain de Sousa, *Bibliografía Hisp. Am. Sept.* I (Mexico City 1947), 144.

[144] *MH* 21 (1964), 120.—That Negresses were accepted is shown by a remark of the
Franciscan chronicler Diego de Córdova Salinas, *Crónica Franciscana de las Provincias del
Perú*, ed. by L. G. Cañedo (Washington 1957), 950. He speaks of a Negress who
entered the Clarisse convent of Cuzco together with her daughter when they were freed
from slavery.—Poor Indian women who did not have the required dowry often came as
servants to their Creole mistresses, whom they continued to serve in the convent and in
whose cells they usually lived. (See the reference in J. de Palafox y Mendoza, *Virtudes
del Indio* [Madrid 1893], 58).

[145] B. de Carrocera, O.F.M.Cap., "Noticias Misionales de Méjico en los años 1763 à
1767," *MH* 11 (1954), 218 (Xalapa), 227 in Salvatierra. About the *Beaterios* of the
Indian sisters in the sixteenth century, see esp. G. de Mendieta O.F.M., *Historia
Eclesiástica Indiana* (Mexico City 1870), 420–24.

[146] F. Ximénez O.P., *Historia de la Provincia de San Vicente de Chiapa y Guatemala* II
(Guatemala 1930), 49. The Calle de las Beatas Indias in Guatemala is mentioned on p.
282.

throughout the tumultuous history of her native land as "the most important author ever born in Mexico."[147]

The alleviation of misery and disease was the goal not only of all the religious orders but also of the native societies, such as the numerous brotherhoods, founded for Spaniards, Indians, and Negroes. Social aid in all of Brazil was taken over primarily by the brotherhood of the *Misericordia,* whose model dates back to 1498 in Lisbon. The Hospitalers of Saint John of God, active in Mexico since 1603, especially excelled in the nursing of the sick. From Mexico they spread out to the Central and South American countries, establishing their hospitals and gaining the recognition of all levels of the populace in the service of lepers and those sick with the plague. In Mexico alone sixteen of their number died during the plague of 1736.[148] Long before this, in 1594, Clement VIII had granted the privileges of hospitalers to a society in Mexico founded by Bernardino Álvarez. They were named Hippolites, after the first hospital they built in Mexico dedicated to Saint Hippolyte. After the first vow dedicating themselves to the care of all the sick, they also took the vow of obedience and after 1700 also that of celibacy.[149]

The order of the Bethlemites, originated in Guatemala, maintained its own character. It went back to Pedro de San José Betancur (1616–67), who initially undertook the education of children, but then included the care of convalescents, especially of strangers and transients. After Betancur's early death his helpers continued his work. They founded an order of lay brothers which was recognized by the Pope in 1672 and spread surprisingly fast to Mexico and South America. Towards the end of the eighteenth century the order deteriorated and was dissolved in 1820. At this time it still operated ten hospitals in the Mexican and twenty-two in the Peruvian provinces.[150] A similar foundation for women, started by Maria Anna del Galdo in Guatemala (1688), did not grow very much and was also discontinued in 1820.[151]

Every one of these hospitaler orders had physicians trained in the native country. The fact that racial discrimination had no place in

---

[147] Most recent collected works in Mexico City 1969.—In a monograph R. Ricard shows the poetess combined Spanish-Creole and native Indian elements into a natural unity: "Sur 'El Divino' Narciso de Sor Joana Iñés de la Cruz," *Mélanges de la Casa de Velasquez* 5 (Paris 1969), 309–29.

[148] L. Lopetegui and F. Zubillaga, *Historia*, 736–38.

[149] Ibid., 736; Heimbucher I, 607f.

[150] J. Specker, "Der Spiritualorden der Bethlehemiten in Lateinamerika (1667–1820)," *Das Laien-Apostolat in den Missionen (Festschr. Joh. Beckmann)* (Schöneck/Beckenried 1960), 181–99.

[151] Heimbucher I, 609.

the treatment of the sick constitutes a great part of its missionary importance.

The Enlightenment and Its Consequences

A fair evaluation of the Enlightenment in Latin America is a difficult undertaking even now. The intellectual history of Spain and Portugal of the eighteenth century as a period of obscurantism and Scholastic rigidity has received scant attention up to the most recent past. This holds true even more so in regard to America, little of whose intellectual life in the colonial period is known in Europe. As a consequence, historical research has shown little interest in the cultural phenomena in which the missionaries had a significant part.[152] The first generation of missionaries in Mexico, such as the Bishops Juan de Zumárraga and Vasco de Quiroga, were guided by contemporary humanists: Zumárraga by Erasmus,[153] Quiroga by Thomas More.[154] This intellectual attitude continued to be the determinant, especially for the missionary work. Two institutions were always connected with European intellectual life: the libraries, especially those of the monasteries, and the universities.

Although there are only a few monographs and precious few particulars or even inventories of books from the earliest times, references in letters, chronicles, and books relating to libraries[155] manifest two facts: 1. their collections were comprehensive; theological works most surely predominated, but there was no dearth of works from classical and modern literature; 2. new European publications, even from distant or

[152] "The history of rationalism and Enlightenment in Brazil has remained almost totally uninvestigated; their impact on the religious life of Brazil cannot yet be estimated" (R. Konetzke, "Forschungsproblem zur Gesch. der Religionen und ihrer Bedeutung in den Kolonisationen Amerikas," *Saeculum* 10 [1959], 95).—This remark to some degree is true also for Spanish America, for which there is no comprehensive work either. The thorough treatise by J. Sarrailh, *L'Espagne éclairée de la seconde moitié du XVIIIᵉ siècle* (Paris 1954) is limited to Spain, but does permit some conclusions regarding the New World.

[153] M. Bataillon, *Erasmo y España*, 2 vols. (Mexico City and Buenos Aires 1950), esp. the last chapter of Vol. 2 concerning the influence of Erasmus in Mexico; this chapter is missing in the French edition.

[154] S. Zavala, *La "Utopia" de Tomás More en la Nueva España* (Mexico City 1937); newly edited with supplementary studies in *Recuerdo de Vasco de Quiroga* (Mexico City 1965).

[155] F. Fernández de Castillo, *Libros y Libreros del siglo XVI* (Mexico City 1914) (mostly booklists compiled by officials of the Inquisition on the arrival of ships in Veracruz). The Argentinian Jesuit and historian G. Furlong refers to such a work ironically: "A los pobres de espíritu que creen y propagan que el Nuevo Mundo no llegaban sino novenas y trisagios, les recomendamos nuestra monografía sobre las *Bibliotecas Argentinas durante la Dominación Hispánica* (Buenos Aires 1944)" (*Nacimiento y desarrollo de la Filosofía en el Río de la Plata 1536–1810* [Buenos Aires 1952], 52).

Protestant cities, reached the Spanish American countries relatively quickly.[156]

The universities were decisive elements of intellectual life. Towards the end of the colonial period there were twenty-three universities in Spanish America. Seven of them were comprehensive state universities, probably with a faculty of theology, but—just as in Spain—operated by secular and regular priests. In addition to the state universities there were sixteen other ones, recognized by the state, with only faculties of philosophy and theology. Fourteen of these were led by the various orders, two of them by bishops. The preponderance of higher education was undeniably in the hands of the state universities, in which laymen had the major influence.[157]

Libraries and universities prepared the way for the advance of new ideas and the advance of the Enlightenment with its positive and negative elements. The Jesuit college of Saint Paul in Lima contained the collected works of Isaac Newton, as well as histories and publications of the Académie des sciences and the Prussian Academy in Berlin. The major works of one of the most important forerunners of positive Enlightenment, the Benedictine Benito Gerónimo Feijóo y Montenegro (d. 1764), the *Teatro crítico universal* in eight volumes and the *Cartas Eruditas* in six volumes were to be found not only in the college libraries but also in the private libraries of the professors.[158] Even works by the English deists were widely represented in the libraries. But the French deists Bayle, Voltaire, Rousseau, and the Encyclopedists were not available in the overseas territories until the Spanish minister Count

---

[156] See for example J. Beckmann, "Alte Basler Drucke im Dienste der Christianisierung Mexikos," *ZSKG* 59 (1965), 107–12. In arguing that the activities of the Inquisition militated against the exchange of ideas with the European centers of culture, the great difference between theory and practice is often overlooked. There were, to be sure, very strict regulations for the export and import of suspect or even heretical books. But the findings of M. Defourneaux (*L'inquisition espagnole et les livres français au XVIIIᵉ siècle* [Paris 1963]) regarding the eighteenth century are valid for the seventeenth and sixteenth centuries as well: for periods of years and, indeed, decades the book dealers of Seville were not at all checked by the officials of the Inquisition. The lists published by F. Fernández de Castillo (op. cit.) are representative for the import; again and again there is a notation that so and so many crates of books were destined for members of the orders who were exempt from the controls of the Inquisition. The remainder, rather superficially catalogued, was probably only for sale by the bookdealers.

[157] Of 150,000 academic degrees awarded between 1550 and 1821 the number awarded by the University of Mexico alone amounted to 39,367 (J. T. Lanning, "The Church and the Enlightenment in the Universities," *The Americas* 15 [1958/59], 334).

[158] L. Martín, *The Intellectual Conquest of Peru, The Jesuit College of San Pablo* (New York 1968), 93–96. The works of Feiyóo in Spanish and Latin were present in all libraries "from Mexico City to Tucumán" (G. Furlong, op. cit., 64).

de Aranda ordered their importation.[159] The Latin works of the German philosopher Christian Wolff could be found in several libraries of Latin America.[160] (see Chap. 18)

These books were eagerly studied everywhere and used in lectures at the universities and colleges. Wherever the well-educated Creoles, even missionaries at remote stations, manifested familiarity with the intellectual currents of Europe, they owed it to the education they had received at the universities or at their monasteries.[161] The two examples of the Jesuit universities of Quito and Córdoba demonstrate the reception of modern European intellectualism. The Swiss Jesuit Jean Magnin in Quito was probably the first to deal systematically with René Descartes after 1746.[162] The English Jesuit Falkner, a pupil of Newton, introduced experiments in the natural sciences in Córdoba and closely followed Christian Wolff in his philosophy lectures.[163] His fellow Jesuit Domingo Muriel before him had incorporated modern philosophy in his lectures. In 1749 one of his students wrote about him: "In order to further the understanding of the old scholastic philosophy he added a precise knowledge of the modern."[164] Richard Konetzke justifiably countered the wrong impressions by saying "that rationalism and the Enlightenment were propagated early and quickly in Spanish America, where contemporary European currents were almost immediately experienced . . . it was precisely the priests, monks, and prebendaries who were the forerunners of the Enlightenment in Spanish America . . ., modern ideas were promulgated especially by the Jesuits . . ."[165] Thus the ideas of the Enlightenment were able to be promulgated on all the cultural

---

[159] G. Furlong, op. cit., 47.

[160] G. Furlong, op. cit., index, 751.

[161] Although the individual orders had the upper levels of philosophy and theology taught by their own members, the latter nonetheless had to earn their required degrees for teaching at the universities.

[162] He had translated a work about Descartes from French into Latin, a manuscript of 262 pages, which is kept at the National Library of Quito. J. Beckmann, "La première Traversée de la Colombie par un missionaire suisse (1725). Le Père Jean Magnin SJ," *Annales Fribourgeoises* 46 (1964), 33–65.—G. Furlong, *Filosofía,* gives the subtitle "Cartesianismo" to the second part, which treats mainly the philosophy after the expulsion of the Jesuits to the end of the eighteenth century (223–483).

[163] G. Furlong, op. cit., 177f.

[164] "Añadiendo a la comprensión de la antigua filosofía escolástica, el conocimiento puntal de la moderna" (G. Furlong, op. cit., 178).

[165] Research topic 95. The reaction of the individual orders to the Enlightenment was not alike. The Franciscans everywhere had explicit orders to follow "modern" currents and in a good many places, esp. in Guatemala, were members of the leading circles. The Dominicans did not have a uniform direction. Depending on conditions and pressure they either defended the old Scholastic methods or took over the new ones (J. T. Lanning, op. cit., 343ff.).

levels of the individual American countries through the universities, colleges, and seminaries. Initially they had a positive effect. The level of studies was raised everywhere and expanded; a fresh wind blew through the institutions of learning, which had become somewhat rigid.[166] Research centers in the natural sciences were established, as were associations of scholars. There was a first wave of periodicals, but it died out after a few years even in the large countries such as Mexico and Peru. In all these movements the clergy furnished the initial contributors; the episcopate promoted participation or at least did not oppose it. The Inquisition generously granted permission for the reading of proscribed books or overlooked violations of the Index.[167] Overall, the Enlightenment in Latin America was able to develop more freely than was initially the case in Europe.

Initially the intellectual elements of the Enlightenment had less of a negative impact than the abuses of regalism (Chap. 11), whose anti-Roman tendencies were strengthened by the skillful promotion of Gallican and Febronian ideas.[168] Most fatal—especially overseas—was the implicit acceptance of decisions by the state in religious matters, which became more and more a matter of course. Two events had far-reaching consequences. The expulsion of the Jesuits, initiated in 1759/60 by the Marquis de Pombal both in Portugal and the colonies, was followed by the Spanish colonies in 1767. It was executed smoothly but mercilessly, ending in 1768 in the deportation of the missionaries from the reductions of Paraguay. In regard to Brazil and the Spanish colonies various reasons were advanced to justify the expulsion of the Jesuits. The main one was that the Jesuits because of their inner structure could not be made an integral part of the regalist framework of enlightened absolutism.[169] Just how seriously the re-

---

[166] In the somewhat modest San Carlos University of Guatemala the number of baccalaureate examinations in philosophy was 108 during the first quarter of the eighteenth century; it was 538 in the last quarter; the corresponding figures for philosophy were 22 and 79 resp. The licentiates and doctorates in theology at the University of Mexico increased from 107 to 184 (J. T. Lanning, op. cit., 339).

[167] K. Schmitt, "The Clergy and the Enlightenment in Latin America," *The Americas* 15 (1958/59), 381–91.

[168] It is typical that the works of the French Oratorian Fleury, of Bernhard Zeger van Espen, professor at Louvain, and of the suffragan bishop of Trier, Hontheim (=Febronius) were prohibited by the Roman Index but not by the Spanish one (N. M. Farris, op. cit., 102).

[169] M. Mörner, *The Expulsion of the Jesuits from Latin America* (New York 1965), a collection of opinions by prominent historians of all persuasions; idem, "The Expulsion of the Jesuits from Spain and Spanish America 1767 in the Light of 18th Century Regalism," *The Americas* 23 (1966/67), 156–64. A more recent French Americanist, P. Chaunu, expresses the opinion of historians which prevails today: "Il est incontestable que l'acte de l'expulsion des Jésuites de 1767 a porté un coup extrêmement dur à

galist attitude, especially of some bishops, obstructed a realistic view of the issue is demonstrated by the pastoral letter of the bishop of Puebla, Fabián y Fuero, dated 28 October 1767, which referred to the expulsion of the Jesuits as part of the "rightful use of privileges which God accorded to the King along with the crown."[170] The other equally portentous event was the provincial synods of 1771, invoked by the Spanish King. A detailed list of points to be negotiated, the *tomo regio,* had been given beforehand to the members of the synods by the Council of the Indies. Archbishop Francesco Antonio de Loranzana presided over the synod of Mexico; those of Lima and La Plata took place in 1772. Loranzana submitted decrees drafted by him and the bishop of Puebla, Fabián y Fuero, and then simply called for a vote, precluding any discussion. In order to prove their loyalty to the representative of the viceroy they added two provisions which threatened the penalty of excommunication for any form of resistance to a royal decree or any insult to the King.[171] When the bishop of Durango, José Vicente Díaz Bravo, called this procedure tyrannical, he was put on trial, deprived of his bishopric, and sent to Madrid to defend himself. He died on the journey to Spain.[172] Loranzana and his colleague from Puebla, on the other hand, were promoted, the former to the office of archbishop of Toledo (1789) and to the cardinalate, the latter was elevated to the bishopric of Valencia.[173] These regalist synods were never recognized by Rome and even Loranzana did not dare submit the *acta* to Rome.

The negative elements of the Enlightenment as an intellectual movement were noticeably slow to develop in America. They were, moreover, of a different nature from those in Europe (Chap. 18). Eighteenth-century America appeared not at all to be a carbon copy of European mentality. Even in the transition to the nineteenth century, America represented the most diverse views encompassing the entire

---

l'œuvre de l'Espagne dans le nouveau monde. Sur ce point, adversaires et amis sont définitivement d'accord: puisque, dans leur œuvre civilisatrice, dans l'aide qu'ils apportèrent à la colonisation, les milliers des Jésuites expulsés n'ont pu être remplacés" (*RH* 214 [1955], 159). The same is stated for the Portuguese territories by C. R. Boxer: "Whatever the failings of the Jesuits, the fact remains that they were the best educators, teachers, and missionaries in the Portuguese colonial world. Their sudden and drastic removal left gaps which were not filled for centuries, if indeed they have all been filled at the present day" (*Four Centuries of Portuguese Expansion, 1415–1825. A Succinct Survey* [Johannesburg 1963], 84).

[170] N. M. Farriss, op. cit., 52.
[171] Ibid., 32–38.
[172] Ibid., 26f.
[173] Ibid., 35.

spectrum from strict spirituality to rationalistic thought. G. Furlong has called this period in Argentina that of "Eclecticismo."[174] An actually anticlerical, radically nationalistic current appeared later when the university chairs were occupied by Creoles who had received their education in Coimbra (dominated by Pombal),[175] or at French universities, and to a lesser extent in Spain. Yet at the turn of the nineteenth century political freedom was the one element which unified all the different currents.

The paradoxical aspect of the Spanish movement of liberty and independence lies in the fact that it was triggered primarily by the enlightened absolutism of the mother country and especially by the often farsighted and just rules for reform. Although many a utopian concept may have been connected with them,[176] the improvement of conditions, especially for the Indians, and the elimination of the vestiges of slavery and forced labor were based precisely on these rules.[177] The above-mentioned role of the Creoles in the context of the Enlightenment is very ambivalent, for the ideals of freedom valid for all mankind contradicted their traditional economic and political world. While they did claim these freedoms for themselves, they denied them to the Indians. From this Creole element emerged the Spanish-speaking clergy who were in the front lines in the wars of independence.[178]

The victims of these conflicts were the Indians. The Spanish had oppressed and exploited them, but for all that they had at least created a paternalistic relationship which was sought to be further improved by

[174] G. Furlong, op. cit., 487–717.

[175] A typical example is the life of José Joaquino de Cunha de Azeredo Coutinho (1742–1821), born in Rio de Janeiro, who studied theology in Coimbra, became bishop of Pernambuco in 1794, and founded the seminary of Olinda in the spirit of Coimbra. He was later promoted to bishop of Braganza and Miranda (E. Bradford Burns, "The Role of Azeredo Coutinho in the Enlightenment of Brasil," *Hisp. Am. Hist. Rev.* [May 1964], 145–60).

[176] The count of Aranda seriously planned the partition of Spanish America into three kingdoms for the three sons of Charles III, who was then to assume the title of Emperor (J. Sairrailh, *L'Espagne éclairée* [Paris 1954], 58).

[177] Count Aranda wrote: "I do not understand why there should be a distinction, not only between the Creoles and natives of Spain, but also regarding the Indians; only the suitability of the individual should be taken into account." R. Konetzke adds the remark: "These Spanish statesmen of the second half of the eighteenth century can not be accused of European arrogance towards the overseas possessions nor of racial prejudice towards the native populations" (Staat und Gesellschaft in Hispano-Amerika am Vorabend der Unabhängigkeit," *Saeculum* 12 [1961], 165).

[178] In the appendix for Mexico N. M. Farris lists all those priests named in the sources who were called "subversive," "insurgent," "conspirator," "collaborator," etc. The list contains the names of approximately 250 secular and 160 regular clerics from the various orders (op. cit., 254–65).

the enlightened monarchs and their ministers. Although the Indians for the most part had fought on the side of the Creoles against the Spaniards, they were soon ignored by the victors and indeed considered as nonexistent.[179] Their particular problems have remained unsolved even today, as have those of the mestizos, Negroes, and mulattos. From this point of view, Richard Konetzke has characterized the movement for independence as a "reaction against historical progress. In this regard the era of the waning Spanish colonial rule was at any rate more modern than the subsequent epoch of independent states during the nineteenth century."[180]

[179] This gradual state of "no longer existing" is reflected in the decrease of language studies in new states and especially the abolition of chairs for native languages at the state universities.

[180] "Staat und Gesellschaft," op. cit., 164.

CHAPTER 16

The Propagation of the Faith in Africa

Whereas the Church in America comprised large but defined areas and paganism was pushed to the peripheries or hard-to-approach regions, only a few coastal areas of Africa, aside from the Congo and Angola, could be missionized, most of them only temporarily.

The north of Africa can not be included in the actual missionary area, at least not in the narrow sense because there the Islamic and Christian faith had been opposing each other in implacable enmity ever since the Middle Ages. And yet the land belt from Morocco to Tunisia developed a Christian idealism and heroism often superior to that in the actual missionary countries. Free exercise of religion and with it missionary activity were ensured by treaties.[1] Franciscans, Mercedarians, and Trinitarians had been working there since the Middle Ages. The treaties and their own religious rules prescribed their primary task to be the ministry to Christian merchants and the ransom of Christian slaves. As the great distress in connection with the Berbers surfaced, Vincent de Paul's first letters of 1643 demonstrate that the ministry to Christian slaves and the actual missionary task, initially consisting of returning the renegades to the fold, had become his main concern. He therefore purchased—through the great missionary benefactress, the duchess

[1] For a survey of these treaties see T. Grentrup, *Jus Missionarium* (Steyl 1925), 361–69; Streit XV, 74–79.

d'Aiguillon—the French consulate in Algiers. After 1646 he had its affairs conducted by his fellow religious, the Lazarists. Under their protection others were able to pursue their ministry.[2] The mission of the Lazarists was able to be maintained with growing skill until Tunisia and Algeria were conquered by France.

Catholic missionary work among actual followers of Islam was not permitted. Yet again and again there were conversions by Muslims to Christianity, most of which could be kept secret. But individual cases, often those occurring abroad in Italy and Spain, were divulged and frequently resulted in persecution of the Christians and the death of missionaries in the respective North African countries.[3] The Franciscans were especially well prepared for this apostolic task because of their excellent knowledge of Arabic.[4]

Aside from the often orphaned dioceses of Spanish and Portuguese enclaves in western North Africa,[5] the missions had been under the authority of the Propaganda since the middle of the seventeenth century. This was not so for West and East Africa. All of West Africa was under the two bishoprics of the Cape Verde Islands and São Tomé, established in 1534; East Africa was under the bishopric of Goa, established separately from Funchal at that time. As early as the sixteenth century Portuguese missionaries (Jesuits, Augustinians, and Dominicans) had started missionizing in the various West African countries. Along the coast of Guinea, in the arch stretching from present-day Portuguese Guinea to Nigeria, and especially in their initial area, Sierra Leone, and the final extension, the old Kingdom of Benin, they had achieved some successes, albeit of varying duration. But towards the end of the century and increasingly during the seventeenth century the weakening of the military impetus of the Portuguese also impaired the missionary thrust. The English and Dutch now obtained secure footholds in these territories. The Dutch effort was crowned by the occupation of Luanda in Angola (1640) and São Tomé (1641). Although the Dutch were driven out again (1645), a coastal area of about four hundred kilometers contained more than thirty fortresses manned by dif-

---

[2] Among the most prominent representatives was Jean Le Vacher, who started working in Tunisia and Algeria. In 1650 he was appointed vicar apostolic and in 1677 French consul. He was shot by Muslims in 1683; Streit, XVI, 728–33.

[3] One of the most significant conversions was that of the young Moroccan Sidi Muhammad ben Muhammad el Hadji ed Dilai (1654), who went on to become a Jesuit priest. He received the call for the mission in India, but died before his departure in Lisbon (J. Henninger, NZM 10 [1954], 207; Streit XVI, 653 f.).

[4] A. Kleinhans, *Historia Studii Linguae Arabicae et Colegii Missionum OFM in Conventu ad S. Petrum in Monte Aureo Romae erecti* (Karachi 1930).

[5] A. Lopez, O.F.M., *Obispos en el África Septentrional desde el siglo XIII* (Tangier 1941).

ferent nations, Portuguese, Spanish, French, Dutch, Danish, Swedish and Prussian, who, succeeding each other, sought to acquire the profitable slave trade.

In these territories the Propaganda succeeded in breaking through the rigid barriers of the Portuguese system of the *Padroado*. After repeated reconnaissance, Capuchin monks from Brittany were sent to the west coast in 1634, especially to Benin. But all their attempts failed. In 1651 when the provincial of Brittany reported about it, he noted only that nine Breton Capuchins had already died on the coast of Guinea. They were followed by the Spanish Capuchins, who—with great sacrifice and scant success—again and again pursued missionary work in Sierra Leone and Benin until about 1700.[6] In present-day Dahomey, at the time the Kingdom of Arda, a group of Spanish Capuchins started missionizing in 1660, but in spite of repeated efforts they failed.[7] In the eighteenth century French Dominicans tried to renew the mission in Guinea. Gottfried Loyer was appointed apostolic prefect by the Propaganda, but the difficulties encountered were so great that they retreated to France.[8]

The main concentration of Portuguese missionary work in the sixteenth century took place in the large reaches of the Congo and in Angola. But there, too, Christianity regressed after some initial successes because of a shortage of missionaries. The Congo Kings attempted to establish direct contact with Rome by means of their own embassies in order to extend their political independence to the religious realm as well and to obtain non-Portuguese missionaries through the Pope and the Propaganda. Thanks to the untiring efforts by the Capuchin friar Francisco de Pamplona, the former Spanish General Tiburcio de Redín,[9] resistance by the Spanish and Portuguese was gradually overcome. In

[6] L. Kilger, O.S.B., "Die Missionen in Oberguinea und Ostafrika nach den ersten Propaganda-Materialien 1622–1670," *ZMR* 20 (1930), 297–311; idem, "Die Missionsversuche in Benin," *ZMR* 22 (1932) 305–19. At about the same time, various attempts to found missions in Oeri or Overo (present-day Owerri in Nigeria) were made.

[7] H. Labouret and P. Rivet, *Le Royaume d'Arda et son Evangélisation au XVIIIe siècle* (Paris 1929; facsimile of the Arda-Catechism of 1658); B. de Carrocera, O.F.M. Cap., "Misión Capuchina al Reino de Arda," *MH* 6 (Madrid 1949), 523–46.

[8] G. Loyer, O.P., *Relation du Voyage du Royaume d'Issing . . .* (Paris 1714); J. Schmidlin, "Die Afrikamission nach Fortiguerra (1707)," *ZMR* 16 (1926), 125.

[9] L. de Aspurz, *Redín, soldado y misionero 1597–1651* (Madrid 1951); idem, "Un momento de contacto entre el Consejo de Indias y la Congregación de Propaganda Fide (1644–51)," *MH* 8 (1951), 505–24; B. de Carrocera, "Fray Francisco de Pamplona, organizador de Misiones y conductor de Misioneros," *MH* 9 (1952), 5–51; F. Bontinck, "Répercussion du conflit entre le Saint Siège et le 'Padroado' sur l'évangélisation de l'Ancien Royaume du Congo," *AHPont* 4 (1966), 197–218.

1645 the first group of missionaries, seven Spanish and five Italian Capuchin friars, were sent to the court of King Garcia II of the Congo.[10] Subsequent expeditions came to the Congo aboard Spanish ships. But after the defeat of the Dutch by the Portuguese in 1648 the Portuguese influence was strengthened. The Spanish missionaries had to leave the country and the Italians were forced to travel on Portuguese passports via Lisbon, which was always connected with lengthy negotiations.

A first significant success by Capuchin missionaries was the return to the faith of Queen Anna Nzinga of Matamba. Although baptized in Luanda in 1622, she had defected. After she was reaccepted in the Church in 1656, she zealously tried to propagate Christianity at her court and in her realm. With the help of the Capuchins she built churches and towns and sought to Christianize the life of her subjects by means of education and upbringing.[11] Her sister, who succeeded her in 1663, continued to support and consolidate the work of the missionaries. After paganism won out briefly, the Capuchins again managed after 1684 to strengthen Christianity in Matamba. But towards the end of the century domestic wars and unsafe routes forced the Capuchins to shift their attention more and more to the Kingdom of Congo and to Angola, with their center in Luanda.

From the start the Propaganda had elevated the Capuchin mission to the level of an apostolic prefecture, although to some extent subordinated to the bishops of Congo and Angola. The latter had been residing in Luanda beginning in the seventeenth century. Unfortunately this jurisdictional structure again and again gave rise to disputes and quarrels within as a consequence of claims of patronage and opposition to the secular clergy.[12]

Just how serious the Italian Capuchins were about their missionary work in the Congo and Angola is shown by their linguistic works, such as grammars, dictionaries, and catechisms,[13] their many different questions to the Propaganda, and, above all, their handbook on missionary

---

[10] Jean-François de Rome, O.F.M.Cap., *La fondation de la mission des Capucins au Royaume du Congo* (1648), ed. by F. Bontinck (Louvain 1964).

[11] F. M. Gioia, *La maravigliosa conversione alla Santa Fe della regina Singa e del suo regno di Matamba* (Naples 1669).

[12] L. Jadin, "Le clergé séculier et les Capucins du Congo et d'Angola aux XVIᵉ et XVIIᵉ siècles," *Bulletin de l'Institut hist. Belge de Rome* 36 (Rome and Brussels 1964), 185–483. Only in 1726 was a balanced jurisdictional agreement between Portugal and the Propaganda worked out which was valid until the missions treaty of 1940; the text is in A. Brasio, *Spiritana Monumenta Historica. Series Africana* I/1 (Pittsburgh and Louvain 1966), 16–20.

[13] B. de Carrocera, "Los Capuchinos españoles en el Congo y el primer Diccionario congolés," *MH* 2 (Madrid 1949), 209–30.

273

behavior and work in the eighteenth century.[14] Using new sources, L. Kilger, an expert in African missionary history, demonstrated a mere few decades ago how groundless the oft-repeated accusations of precipitous baptism were.[15]

We should add the fact that for 150 years the missionary work of the Capuchins had to proceed under continually unfavorable conditions. The tropical climate often killed the missionaries within a very short time after their arrival; at times they suffered a violent death, as did their fellow brother Georg von Geel (d. 1652).[16] The Spanish chronicler Father Mateo de Anguiano presents an impressive list of 230 names for the period of 1645 to 1705.[17] By the end of the Capuchin mission in the Congo approximately 400 members of the order lost their lives in the service of this fruitless mission.[18] Toward the end of the eighteenth century, French secular priests attempted to missionize a part of the Congo, an area generally lacking in priests.[19] For them the Propaganda established the apostolic prefecture of Loango, where nine priests and six lay assistants were active from 1766 to 1776.[20]

---

[14] *Pratique missionnaire de PP. Capucins italien* (Louvain 1931). A compilation of rules in missionary methodology from 1747 by the missions' prefect Fr. Giacinto da Bologna. This work with its trenchant observations and critical appraisal of customs and usages was not the only one of its kind, as demonstrated by the as yet unpublished "Avvertimenti salutevoli alli apostolici Missionari nè Regni del Congo, Angola e circunvicini" by P. Giovanni di Roma of 1681 (see *NZM* 24 [1968], 210).

[15] L. Kilger, "Die Taufpraxis in der alten Kapuzinermission im Kongo und in Angola," *NZM* 5 (1949), 30–40, 203–16 (Schriftenreihe *NZM* 7) (Schöneck/Beckenried 1949). But all the efforts by the missionaries, whose number was always small, could not prevent the formation towards the end of the seventeenth century of the syncretistic sect of the Antonites. Essentially a precursor of the movements of religious fanatics in modern day Africa, it was named after a Christian Negress who asserted that she was possessed by Saint Anthony (L. Jadin, "Le Congo et la secte des Antoniens 1694–1718," *Bulletin de l'Institut hist. Belge de Rome* 33 [Brussels and Rome 1961], 411–615.

[16] P. Hildebrand, *Le Martyr Georges de Geel et les débuts de la Mission du Congo (1645–52)* (Antwerp 1940).

[17] *Misiones Capuchinas en África* I (Madrid 1950), 468–79.

[18] L. Jadin, *L'Afrique et Rome,* 53. For the slow extinction of the old Congo-Angola Mission, see L. Jadin, *Les Missionnaires du Congo à la fin du XVIIIᵉ siècle* (Lisbon 1961); for the period of 1746 to 1761, see J. Cuvelier, "Le Vén. André de Burgio," *CollFr* 22 (1952), 85–115. They show a high rate of decline in the number of missionaries.

[19] In 1669 the Jesuits had already relinquished their college in San Salvador, the capital of the Congo kingdom; the Capuchins started their work in neighboring Matamba and were subsequently unable to furnish more than a few missionaries for the Congo.

[20] J. Cuvelier, *Documents sur une Mission Française au Kakongo 1766–76* (Brussels 1953), 14 f. For earlier missionary attempts of the Flemish Franciscans, see L. Jadin, "Rivalités luso-néerlandaises au Sohio, Congo 1600–75, "*Bulletin de l'Institut hist. Belge de Rome* 37 (Brussels and Rome 1966), 137–360.

The greatest impediment not only to the Capuchin mission but to all the missions in West Africa was the slave trade, gaining ground from the seventeenth century on, in which nearly all the countries of Europe were participating.[21] A fatal flaw was the fact that missionaries, too, were caught up in the ideas of their time: they treated the slaves benignly, but did not question slavery as a social institution. Jesuits as well as Capuchins were slaveholders, the so called *esclaves de l'église.* Secular priests, in the absence of pay from Portugal, frequently ensured their livelihood by participating in the slave trade. Others participated without any qualms at all, including some from São Tomé.[22] Farsighted methods in missionary work, as on the issue of the native clergy, did not make up for this tacit approval of slavery.[23]

In South Africa neither the care of souls nor mission work was possible. Only after the conquest of the cape by the English did the situation appear to improve. But the Treaty of Amiens in 1802 ceded the Cape of Good Hope back to the Dutch, who were now more open to the question of ministry for their Catholic soldiers and inhabitants. In 1804 Jan Lansink became apostolic prefect; he started his work with two

---

[21] The great worldwide significance of the African slave trade is highlighted in C. R. Boxer, *Salvador de Sá and the Struggle for Brazil and Angola 1602–86* (London 1952). For the slave trade as an impediment to the mission see C. P. Groves, op. cit. I, 160–64; R. M. Wiltgen, S.V.D., *Gold Coast Mission History 1471–1880* (Techny 1956), 93–105.

[22] Around 1760 the Jesuit college in Luanda, for instance, had more than one thousand slaves on its various properties (*DHGE* 15, 426); J. Cuvelier and L. Jadin, *L'ancien Congo d'après les archives romaines, 1518–1640* (Brussels 1954) (in various documents, esp. 85–92, there is a summary of the slave trade and the participation of the missionaries). Among the Capuchin missionaries the Spanish seem to have been opposed the most to the slave trade. According to the information provided by the chronicler of the order, Mateo de Anguiano, this is shown not only by their petitions to the King of Portugal and the Pope, but even more so by the fact that they were expelled from the Congo and the West-African territories precisely "for damaging Portuguese trade" (= slave trade) (*Misiones Capuchinas en Africa* II [1957], 199f.; pp. 131–46 contain a detailed description of the slave trade). Of course there were individual missionaries and bishops who spoke for the slaves and attacked especially the slave expeditions which violated contemporary law. But only the newly baptized Queen Nzinga addressed the Propaganda by letter in 1660 asking for a decree which would forbid the sale of baptized Negroes as slaves (Mateo de Anguiano, op. cit. II, XIII).

[23] L. Kilger, "Der erste einheimische Ordenspriester in der alten Kongo-Mission," *NZM* 14 (1958), 50–52; B. de Carrocera, "Los capuchinos españoles en el Congo y sus trabajos en pro la formación del clero indígena," *España Misionera* 2 (Madrid 1945), 183–206.—The extent to which Portuguese circles as well were convinced of the necessity for a native clergy is shown by the Portuguese polyhistor Manuel Severino de Feria (d. 1655), who emphasized in a memorandum of 1622 that a true success in the christianization of Guinea could only be achieved by educating a black clergy (J. Faro, "Manuel Severino de Feria e a evangelização da Guiné," *Boletim Cultural de Guiné Portuguesa* 14 [Bissau 1959], 459–97).

secular priests. But in 1806 when the English permanently reconquered the cape, the Dutch priests were expelled.[24]

In the eastern half of Africa three missionary areas can be clearly marked: in the southeast there was Mozambique and the bordering land of the Monomotapa (Rhodesia), Mombasa with its immense Jesus Fortress securing the Portuguese maritime route to India, and in the northeast there was Ethiopia.

Following the failure of the Jesuit mission in the sixteenth century, the Dominicans had resumed missionary work in southeast Africa in 1577. In 1607 they were again followed by the Jesuits. The lack of clearly defined borders between the missions of the two orders led to many a dispute. After the Dominicans succeeded in converting the Monomotapa and his sons in 1629, all the missionary work in the realm of the "Golden Emperor" gradually passed to them. The Jesuits engaged in the conversion of the ethnic tribes on the Lower Zambezi. In 1612 Mozambique and its surrounding lands was elevated to the status of a free prelature, which it retained into the twentieth century. A report to the Propaganda in the 1730s indicated eleven mission stations staffed by eleven secular priests, one Augustinian, twenty-five Dominicans and eighteen Jesuits.[25] The Dominicans, mostly Goanese, were foremost in striving to educate many good native clerics. Two of their African members were known as lecturers of theology in Goa, Father Manuel around 1670 and Father Constantino de Rosario around 1712.[26]

As a result of wars and political power struggles the realm of the Monomotapa and with it the Dominican mission collapsed. The order subsequently restricted itself to Mozambique. The Jesuit mission on the Zambezi was able to develop until its expulsion by Pombal in 1759. At that time the Jesuits were replaced by Franciscan and Dominican missionaries. Aside from some secular priests only Dominicans appear to have been active in Mozambique as of the end of the eighteenth century,[27] until the abolition of all religious orders in the Portuguese territories in 1835 paralyzed the missions for a number of decades.[28]

[24] J. Rommerskirchen, *Die Afrikamission um das Jahr 1805: 50 Jahre katholische Missionswissenschaft* (Münster 1961), 157 f.
[25] L. Kilger, "Die Mission in Oberguinea und in Ostafrika nach den ersten Propaganda-Materialien (1622–70)," *ZMR* 20 (1930), 307.
[26] L. Jadin, *L'Afrique et Rome* (Louvain 1965), 62.
[27] J. Rommerskirchen, *Die Afrikamission um das Jahr 1805,* 154.
[28] For a complete overview of the mission in Southeast Africa, see esp. Harald v. Sicard, *Karangafolkets äldsta Missions-Historia* (Stockholm 1943); also P. Schebesta, *Portugals Conquistamission in Südostafrika. Missionsgeschichte Sambesiens und des Monomotapareiches (1560–1920)* (St. Augustin 1966), 54–292; F. Hoppe, *Portugiesisch-Ostafrika in der Zeit des Marquês de Pombal (1750–77)* (Berlin 1965).

The decisive achievement of the Portuguese in the eastern half of Africa was the rolling back and weakening of Islam beyond Mombasa. The two decades of Portuguese dominance on the east coast of Africa is described by L. Kilger as follows: "The Portuguese policy concerning Islam managed successfully to hold down the Mohammedans in the south and kept them from obtaining a sizeable and dominating position in the north."[29] In 1592 Mombasa with its fortress became the seat of the Portuguese governor; at this time the Portuguese Hermits of Saint Augustine began their missionary work. In 1630 Jussuf ben Hassani, a Christian prince educated by the Augustinians in Goa, became ruler of Mombasa. In his initial zeal he violently turned upon his former brothers in faith. But he soon recognized that this was not the way to make his government popular. So he promptly reembraced Islam, took the Portuguese fortress in a surprise attack, and created a horrible bloodbath among the Christians, both Portuguese and natives. But in 1631 Mombasa was reoccupied by the Portuguese and the missionary work of the Augustinians could be resumed with growing success. Portuguese rule and the mission lasted until 1729, at which point both had become severely weakened and had to make way for the stronger Islam. From their sizeable seminary in Mombasa the Augustinians were able to expand their work southward to the islands of Pemba and Zanzibar. They achieved few conversions among the Muslims, but they were more successful among the Negro population.[30]

From its stronghold in Goa, Portugal had decisively resisted the advance of Islam in remote Ethiopia and through the heroic fight of its *Fidalgos* (1541 and after) saved it for Christianity. The rest of the troop settled there under the ministry of the Jesuits, who were unceasingly working for the union of the Ethiopian Church with Rome (which came to pass in 1622). The same year, the Jesuit Pêro Pais, one of the great

---

[29] "Christliche Islam-Mission und Islam-Politik in Ostafrika," *ZMR* 7 (1917), 16–36. This appraisal is supported by the German colonial historian J. Strandes, *Die Portugiesen-Zeit in Deutsch- und Englisch-Ostafrika* (Berlin 1899), 314. According to him the Portuguese deserve thanks for having prevented the Turkish-Muslim rule from gaining a foothold in East Africa and India (L. Kilger, op. cit., 36). The excellent treatise by Justus Strandes is supplemented by new sources in C. R. Boxer and C. de Azevedo, *A Fortaleza de Jesus e os Portugueses em Mombaça* (Lisbon 1960).

[30] The most important source for the Augustinian mission is the "Manual Eremitico da Congregação da India Oriental . . . pelo Fr. Manuel da Ave Maria" of 1817, published by A. da Silva Rego in "Documentoção para a Historia das Missões do Padroado Português do Oriente," *India* 11 (Lisbon 1955), 95–833; Manuel da Purificação, "Memorias da Congregação Agostiniana na India Oriental," *India* 12 (Lisbon 1958), 3–98; A. Hartmann, "The Augustinians in the Land of the Swahili," *AAug* 25 (Rome 1962), 326–39.

missionaries and promoters of the union, died.[31] In 1625 the new patriarch appointed by Rome arrived in the Ethiopian highland. But the union was of short duration. In 1632 a change in government and the Latinizing tendencies of the Jesuits brought the Monophysite form of Christianity back to power. The patriarch and the rest of the Jesuits were expelled from the country; those arriving later were murdered in 1638. After this failure the newly founded Propaganda took over the mission in Ethiopia. Unfortunately the congregation was prone to make mistakes from the beginning. It permitted itself to be convinced by the fraudulent Zaga Christos that the cancellation of the union in his homeland was based solely on dislike for the Jesuits; he did not rest until the mission work was transferred to the Franciscans. They took over the new task joyfully and enthusiastically, but were soon disappointed in their expectations.[32]

French Capuchins also attempted to advance to Ethiopia from Egypt, as did Jesuits from Goa via Mombasa and smaller places along the Red Sea. But even the smallest of successes had to be paid for with great danger and suffering: in 1638 the two Capuchin friars Agathangelus de Vendôme and Cassian Vaz were murdered, as were the Franciscans Francisco de Mistrella and Ludovico de Laurenzana (1668), and Liberatus Weiss and his companions of the same order (1716).[33]

In 1788 the Propaganda tried a new tactic in having the Ethiopian priest Tobias George Ghebragzer consecrated bishop and sending him and others of his countrymen back to Ethiopia. But after a short sojourn he was subjected to severe sufferings, for never before had an Ethiopian been bishop of his country. The patriarch of Alexandria excommunicated him. For several years he had to flee for his life. He died in Cairo in 1801.[34]

Cairo should have become the center and gateway of the Ethiopian mission, but circumstances turned it more and more into a point of departure for the Coptic mission in Lower Egypt, which is to be treated in another connection. Striking out from Egypt, Franciscans tried to

---

[31] This Spanish Jesuit Pedro Páez wrote the *Historia Ethiopiae,* which was edited by Beccari in Vols. II and III of his collection of sources (1905–06). A critical Portuguese edition was done by Lopez Teixeira, *Pêtro Pais, Historia da Etiopia* I–III (Oorto 1945–46).

[32] T. Somigli de Detole, *Etiopia Francescana* (1928–48); J. Dindinger, "Bemerkungen zu den ersten Missionsversuchen der Franziskaner in Äthiopien," *Antonianum* 20 (Rome 1945), 97–126.

[33] See the bio-bibliographical data on the individual missionaries in Streit XVI, 219–21, 627; XVII, 137–38.

[34] N. Kowalsky, "Tobias Georg Ghebragzer. Ein "schwarzer" Bischof im 18. Jh.," *NZM* 15 (1959), 198–204.

establish a mission in Central Sudan (Boznu) at the beginning of the eighteenth century. It failed because of the great difficulties in getting there.[35]

Many efforts were made by the Propaganda to missionize the large island of Madagascar. Following unsuccessful attempts by Portuguese Dominicans in the sixteenth century and by Jesuits at the beginning of the seventeenth century, the Italian Jesuit Cristoforo Borri submitted to the Propaganda a memorandum concerning the establishment of a mission on the island, one that allowed it to serve as a center for expanded mission in the newly discovered lands of the South Seas. The Propaganda actually did establish an apostolic prefecture for the Discalced Carmelites in 1640. But because the French had gained a foothold on the island at the same time, the sending of Italian Carmelites had to be canceled and the offer by Saint Vincent de Paul to transfer this new mission to the Lazarists had to be accepted.[36] The first two Lazarists arrived on Madagascar in 1648. The murderous coastal climate claimed many victims, whom the homeland again and again sought to replace until in 1674 the French mission station was removed and with it the backbone of the missionary effort.[37]

In the seventeenth and eighteenth century the French had also occupied and settled the islands of Mauritius and Réunion. When the Lazarists were charged with an apostolate, they hoped to renew from there the old mission on Madagascar. They made some attempts to this end, but none of them succeeded.[38]

[35] J. Schmidlin, "Die ersten Madagaskarmissionen im Lichte der Propagandamaterialien," *ZMR* 12 (1922), 193–205.
[37] Streit XVI, 421 ff., 547 ff., about the first linguistic works and the first catechism of the Vincentians.
[38] J. Rommerskirchen, *Die Afrikamission um das Jahr 1815: 50 Jahre katholische Missionswissenschaft* (Münster 1961), 154–57; F. Combaluzier, "François-Marie Halnat (1760 bis 1808)," *NZM* 10 (1954), 208–23, 264–78; 11 (1955), 42–55.

CHAPTER 17

The Propagation of the Faith in Asia

While the activities of the Church were able to develop within a relatively uniform framework in America, the Asian continent was full of contrasts. There were the Islamic realms of the west with that of the Moguls extending deeply into the Hindu territories, the Hindu and

Buddhist states, and, finally, China, which had put a Confucian stamp on its peripheral tributaries. Following the Portuguese, who had obtained strategic footholds in Asia since the end of the fifteenth century, the Spanish—after several attempts—managed to get to the area of the Spice Islands and, in 1565, to the Philippines. Their conquest of Portugal gave them nominal rule over the Portuguese overseas territories from 1580 to 1640 as well. Following the overthrow by the new ruling house of the Braganza in 1640, Rome, under pressure from Spain, was unable to appoint Portuguese bishops. Not until 1670 did a papal nuncio resume residence in Lisbon. The improvement in the relations between Rome and Portugal was also repeated in the vast colonial territories. In 1600, East Indies companies were founded both in England and Holland. The Dutch, anti-Catholic and uninterested in missionary work, displaced the Portuguese from their dominant position in the commerce with Japan and conquered the fortress of Malacca in 1641. This gave them a key position regarding Indonesia and the vast coastal areas of Indochina, which they ultimately lost to the Danes and the English. The French East Indies company, founded in 1664, first settled in Surat and then in Pondicherry (1674).

These often bloody conflicts between the European powers, who were frequently allied with indigenous forces, more and more impeded the missionary work. Additional obstacles were raised within the ecclesiastical ranks, especially by the collision between the Congregation for the Propagation of the Faith, established in 1622 and called the Propaganda for short, and the Portuguese system of the *Padroado.* The latter was of such importance for the entire missionary history of the seventeenth and eighteenth century that it merits description before we treat the missions in the individual countries.

The Propaganda and the Portuguese *Padroado*

The Popes and the Propaganda reluctantly accepted the established church system in America because those territories were actually ruled by Spain and Portugal and had become true colonies, whereas the commercial colonization was satisfied with individual bases.

The Propaganda held the view that these bases and the hinterland dominated by Portugal should be subject to the *Padroado,* but not those countries independent of Portugal. But the latter insisted on a universal system of the *Padroado.* It took a long time and many reversals for both the Propaganda and Portugal slowly to recast these sharp differences into a bearable modus vivendi. Until this happened, the mission in the Portuguese areas and those under the jurisdiction of the Propaganda suffered greatly.[1] The extent to which collaboration between the missionaries of the Propaganda and the *Padroado* was impaired was demonstrated by the modest activities of the Franciscans, most of them Italian, in the northern Chinese province of Hopei during the eighteenth century. Neither the orders from Rome nor those from the bishops, in fact not even bloody persecution were able to enforce harmony in the preaching of the faith.[2]

The first and most enduring success of the Propaganda was brought about by the dispatch of the first vicars apostolic to East Asia.[3] The idea for this undertaking came from a missionary of the *Padroado,* the Jesuit Alexandre de Rhodes (1591–1660) of Avignon.[4] As a result of the persecutions in Japan he and his companions from the Japanese provinces had established a flourishing community of Christians in Tongking. Its backbone was the *domus dei,* with carefully trained catechists. Adapting to local conditions, these religious communes put their very own stamp on the entire mission of the East Indies for centuries.[5] To be sure, de Rhodes had written a catechism for the purpose of training his catechists,[6] but priests and bishops who could ordain them were sorely lacking. In 1649 he arrived in Rome and was instructed to look for suitable candidates himself. After unsuccessful efforts in Italy he went to Paris in 1653, where he met the future vicars apostolic in a community of young priests (*Les Bons Amis*) led by his fellow Jesuits. But in 1654, probably at the instigation of Portugal, he had to take on another task; he died in 1660 as superior of the mission in Ispahan. While de Rhodes was awakening a missionary spirit in France, Rome hesitated. Not until July 1658 were two members of the *Bons Amis* consecrated

[1] A. Jann, op. cit.; B. J. Wenzel, *Portugal und der Heilige Stuhl* (Lisbon 1958); A. da Silva Rêgo, *O Padroado Português do Oriente. Esboço Historico* (Lisbon 1940) (French; Lisbon 1957); J. Wicki, "Il patronato portoghese d'Oriente," *CivCatt* III (1955), 527–29.

[2] G. Mensaert, O.F.M., "Les Franciscains au service de la Propagande dans la Province de Pékin 1705–1784," *AFrH* 51 (1958), 161–200, 273–311.

[3] H. Chappoulie, op. cit.; A. Launay, *Histoire générale*, I (Paris 1912); idem, *Mémorial;* G. Goyau, *Les prêtres des Missions étrangères* (Paris 1925); L. Baudiment, *François Pallu, principal fondateur de la Société des Missions Étrangères (1626–84)* (Paris 1934).

[4] H. Chappoulie, op. cit. I, 3–41, 102–13; A. Launay, *Histoire de la Mission du Tonkin* (Paris 1927).

[5] N. Kowalsky, "Die Anfänge der 'Domus Dei' in Tongking und Cochinchina," in: J. Specker and W. Bühlmann, *Das Laienapostolat in den Missionen (Festschr. Beckmann)* (Beckenried 1961), 155–60.

[6] *Catechismus pro ius qui volunt suscipere Baptismum* (Rome [press of the Propaganda] 1651), new ed. with Vietnamese text, introduction and commentary by A. Marillier, CC. Larre and Pham Dink (Saigon 1961); a French translation by H. Chappoulie, op. cit. II, 147–261.

bishops and vicars apostolic: François Pallu (1626–84) and Pierre Lambert de la Motte (1624–79). A third, Ignatius Cotolendi, died en route in 1662. The bishops and their companions from the newly founded missionary seminary of Paris had to take the difficult overland route through Syria, Persia and northern India.[7] In 1662 and 1664, respectively, they arrived in Ajuthia, the capital of Siam, but a war forced them to stay there. So they established the center of their East Asian mission in Ajuthia, combining it with a central seminary for the training of a native clergy.[8]

The arrival of the first vicars apostolic in Siam definitely represented not only the most significant measure by the Propaganda in the entire course of missionary history, but the most important one for the young Church of the Far East overall.[9] Most important was the advance of Rome into the hitherto Portuguese jurisdictional sphere. The achievement was of course not reached by the mere dispatch of vicars apostolic. Initially the vicars did not even have the necessary papal jurisdiction for Siam. This was finally granted to Louis Laneau (1637–96) in 1673. But foreign jurisdiction in Portuguese territory was so unusual that the missionaries hardly paid attention to it except for the difficulties created by the Inquisition emanating from Goa and by the bishops appointed after 1670. This prompted Pallu to go to Rome, where he convinced the Propaganda to take firm steps. These included corresponding briefs by Clement IX (1669). But the latter's successor, Clement X, had his mind changed by the Portuguese ambassador, until the vicars apostolic remonstrated anew. In 1673 briefs were issued to the inquisition and to the cathedral chapter of Goa, withdrawing from them all jurisdiction outside the Portuguese territories.[10] In 1677 the Propaganda ordered all Jesuit missionaries to swear an oath of obedience to the vicars apostolic. In 1678 the oath was extended to include all missionaries in the Far East. In 1680 this was reaffirmed by another decree. Portugal consequently demanded from all missionaries departing from Lisbon an oath of

---

[7] See the detailed travelogue by Pallu from his diaries and letters in L. Baudiment, op. cit., 99–161.

[8] P. Destombes, M.E.P., *Collège Général de la Societé des Missions Étrangères* (Paris 1934).

[9] The new element regarding the vicars apostolic appointed in 1659 was that they were given full jurisdiction for large territories and were, at the same time, titular bishops. Prior to this their only function had been to represent a bishop who was in some way prevented from exercising his office. The change was intended for a brief transitional period but instead it endured for more than 300 years (N. Kowalsky, "Zur Entwicklungsgeschichte der apostolischen Vikare," *NZM* 13 [1957], 217–86).

[10] H. Chappoulie, op. cit. I, 233ff.

loyalty to the *Padroado* which encompassed the political interests of Portugal as well.[11] Thus one oath was pitted against another.

While this affair was settled relatively soon in East India—probably because of the bloody persecutions and the vastness of the countries— the China mission erupted in a storm of protest. Pallu came to China as vicar apostolic of Fukien and administrator of China in January 1684 and immediately published the decree of 1680. At the same time he transmitted an order by the Jesuit General to the missionaries of the *Padroado*. As a result all but one Spanish missionary took the oath. But Spanish Franciscans, Dominicans and Augustinians had heretofore obeyed only their superiors in Manila, and therefore resisted the oath.[12] The Jesuits, sent to Siam and China under Louis XIV, were prohibited by the state from taking the oath. Closure of the seminary of the Parisian Missionaries and the recall of the vicars apostolic were imminent. But compromises and jurisdictional reordering indirectly invalidated the Roman oath. Yet Lisbon insisted on an oath to the *Padroado*. As a result the situation was severely aggravated throughout the eighteenth century. Given this attitude by Portugal, which stiffened even more after its newly won independence (1640), the missionaries were forced to seek new routes by which to get to the Far East. Jesuits had earlier contemplated a land route to China via Russia and had sought to acquire precise knowledge of it by means of expeditions.[13] Unfortunately all their efforts were in vain. The Propaganda recommended the land route via Persia and Mesopotamia and strongly requested avoidance of all Portuguese territories.[14] For his first trip Pallu had already reconsidered the land route through Russia. For his last trip he actually attempted to get permission for it from the Russian Tsar through the good offices of the French King.[15] Towards the end of the seventeenth century the

[11] Delacroix, op. cit. II, 190f.

[12] A. van de Wyngaert, "Mgr. Fr. Pallu et Mgr. Bernardino della Chiesa, Le Serment de fidélité aux Vicaires Apostoliques, 1680–88," *AFrH* 31 (1938), 17–47; O. Maas, "Zum Konflikt der spanischen Missionare mit den französischen Bischöfen in der Chinamission des 17. Jh.," *Spanische Forschungen der Görres-Gesellschaft* III (Münster 1930), 185–95.

[13] B. Zimmel, "Bemühungen um den Landweg nach China. Die Expedition P. Aimé Cherauds S.J. nach Chorassan 1659," *NZM* 25 (1968), 102–8 (with references to earlier efforts).

[14] Instruction of 1659 (H. Chappoulie, op. cit. I, 394). A possibility to get to East Asia through America, considered earlier, had to be abandoned as utopian (J. Schmidlin, "Projekt eines nordamerikanischen Missionsweges nach China in der Frühzeit der Propaganda," *ZMR* 15 [1925], 147–49).

[15] L. Baudiment, *Pallu*, 88, 360f.—It is surprising that missionaries even before were not so much blaming Russia but Lisbon for failing to gain an overland route to China. The French sinologist P. Pelliot states emphatically that all efforts for an overland route foundered on the resistance of Portugal, which was intent on securing Macao as a

Portuguese rule to effect entry exclusively through Macao became meaningless because the English and French were only too glad to transport the missionaries on their vessels.

More difficult than opening up land routes was the problem concerning new missionaries. The cardinals of the Propaganda were perhaps privately convinced that those missionaries operating under the *Padroado,* at least those outside the Portuguese territories, would agree to go under the jurisdiction of the French bishops. But the large religious orders, foremost among them the Jesuits, who were doing the major portion of the missionary work in the provinces of the vicars apostolic, had no intention of exchanging the *Padroado,* which had proved its excellence for over 150 years, for an unproven new institution.

As early as 1658 the vicars apostolic—in addition to Pallu and Lambert de la Motte, there was the first vicar apostolic of Quebec, de Laval—had sent a petition to the Propaganda which mentioned for the first time the establishment of a seminary. They maintained that the education of a native clergy in Canada, China, and Tongking required helpers who had to be prepared in their own seminaries. The secretary of the Propaganda noted on the margin; "Will be heeded!" But the plan was actually realized by the procurators of the missionary bishops. In 1663 they founded the seminary in the Rue du Bac, where it continues today. In the same year it received royal sanction as the Séminaire pour la conversion des Infidèles dans les pays étrangers. Recognition by Rome followed in 1664.[16]

The second religious community to place its members at the disposal of the Propaganda was the Capuchin order. Their first vicar apostolic was the famous "grey eminence" of Cardinal Richelieu, Father Joseph Leclerc du Tremblay or Father Joseph of Paris. Missionaries for Canada, Brazil, and the French bases in India (Surat, Madras) also came from the French provinces.[17] Members of the

---

gateway for the Catholic missionaries (*T'oung Pao* 26 [Leiden 1929], 192f.). In 1707, in fact, Peter the Great had let Clement XI know that he would permit the Catholic missionaries to use the route through Russia (*AFrH* 27 [1934], 181).

[16] J. Guennou, M.E.P., *Les Missions Étrangères* (Paris 1963), 67 (the author also treats the pertinent French background, esp. the Compagnie du Saint-Sacrement); idem, "Le troisième centenaire du Séminaire des Missions Étrangères de Paris," *NZM* 19 (1963), 290–99.

[17] G. ce Vaumas, *L'éveil missionaire de la France* (Lyon 1942); idem, *Lettres et Documents du Père Joseph de Paris concernant les Missions Étrangères (1619–38)* (Lyon 1942); idem, "L'activité missionnaire du P. Joseph de Paris," *RHM* 15 (Paris 1938), 336–59; O. M. Jouve, "Le Père Joseph Leclerc du Tremblay, Capucin, et les Missions de la Nouvelle France (1632–33)," *RHM* 16 (Paris 1939), 206–32; G. Goyau, "Le Père Joseph et les Missions Capucines," *L'Église en Marche* V (Paris 1936), 63–93.

Italian province of the Carmelite order also entered the service of the Propaganda. The initial impetus owed a lot to certain of its members. They had had a mission in Persia since the beginning of the seventeenth century and had spread from there to various countries of Indochina and finally also to India. Leandro de la Anunciación—a native Spaniard to be sure—succeeded in founding a first branch in Goa, followed by a second one in 1630 which was actually a missionary seminary. Its graduates soon became missionaries for those parts of India occupied by the English.[18] The Italian province of the Franciscans also gave missionaries to the Propaganda who were primarily active in China. In 1687 the first Italian arrival, Bernardino della Chiesa, was consecrated bishop by Pallu. In the following period the Italian Franciscans were especially active in the northern provinces of China.

The Propaganda itself, especially its first secretary Francesco Ingoli, preferred secular priests, especially for the office of vicar apostolic. The congregation founded in 1646 in Naples as the *Congregazione delle Apostoliche Missioni* developed well, but domestic and foreign political events thwarted all missionary work.[19] In 1639 when the Augustinian Recollects (or Barefoot Augustinians), a reformed branch of Augustinian Hermits with origins in Spain, placed their experience in the Philippines at the disposal of the Propaganda for service in China, the latter did not accept the offer;[20] only members of the Italian province could now and then work in China.[21] On the other hand the Italian association of the Congregation of Secular Clergy of the Battistini, recognized in 1753 by Benedict XIV, was readily used for the China mission. Among the ranks of the religious orders the Propaganda also employed the Italian Barnabites for the mission in Burma.[22]

The conflict caused by the complexity of the organizational structure of the missions was demonstrated by a papal visitation in Cochinchina conducted by the French Mgr. E. F. des Achards de la Beaume (d. 1741), who heightened the confusion rather than eliminating it.[23] To some extent these difficulties were the fault of the Propaganda itself. All

---

[18] Florencio del Niño Jesús, *La Orden de Santa Teresa, la fundación de la Propaganda Fide y la Misiones Carmelitas* (Madrid 1923), 91ff.

[19] J. Metzler, "Das erste Weltpriesterinstitut im Dienste der Propaganda," *NZM* 17 (1961), 161–74.

[20] This is shown esp. in *Bullarium Ordinis Recollectorum S. Augustini* II (1623–83) (Rome 1961).

[21] J. Beckmann, "Zur Missionstätigkeit der italienischen Unbeschuhten Augustiner im Fernen Osten," *NZM* 22 (1961), 62–65.

[22] L. Gallo, *Storia del Cristianesimo nell'Impero Barmano*, 3 vols. (Milan 1862).

[23] Streit VI (Aachen 1931), 454.

the missionaries of the *Padroado* were obedient to the superiors of their respective orders, yet the Propaganda immediately wanted to remove them from their traditional structure and subordinate them directly to the Propaganda.[24] Furthermore, the Propaganda was largely lacking in understanding of the ideals and way of life of the regular clergy.[25] In the course of the seventeenth and eighteenth century there was a growing necessity to separate the missionary dioceses by religious orders and congregations and to appoint separate vicars apostolic for the Franciscans, Dominicans, and Parisian missionaries.

A decisive element for judging the work of the Propaganda in the Far East was the new spirit manifest in the principal documents and in the work of its missionaries. Ever new formulations emphasize the purely religious character of the mission, placing the spreading of the Gospel at the center of all endeavors.[26] This basic character of the mission was most emphatically demonstrated in the instruction of 1659 to the newly appointed vicars apostolic.[27] In part one, regarding the selection of their missionaries, the departing bishops are exhorted above all to pay attention to the spiritual and religious qualities and the character of the candidates over and above their physical condition. Part two deals with the travel route. The third and most thorough part contains the basic missionary program: "Do not demand of those peoples that they change their ceremonies, customs, and habits if these do not quite obviously contradict religion and decency, for what could be sillier than to want to import France, Spain, Italy, or any other country into China? Not these but the faith is what you shall bring to them, which neither rejects nor fights against any peoples' customs and traditions, but rather seeks to keep them inviolate."[28] Commercial and political activities were forbid-

---

[24] As a result the home provinces and monasteries showed little interest in the fate of their brothers in the Propaganda. When the Capuchins, for instance, complained to the Propaganda that they could not live in accordance with the rules of their order, the congregation asked the mission prefect, Father Joseph de Paris, to remove them "de peur qu'ils se fissent turcs" (G. de Vaumas, *L'éveil Missionnaire de la France* [Lyons 1942], 121).

[25] This is manifest from many letters from missionaries kept in the archive of the Propaganda which have not yet been closely examined.

[26] K. Pieper, "Ein Blick in die missionsmethodischen Erlasse der Propaganda," *ZMR* 12 (1922), 31–51; J. Beckmann, "Der religiöse Charakter von Mission und Missionar nach den Bestimmungen der Propaganda-Kongregation," *Kath. Missionsjahrbuch der Schweiz* (1946), 13–23.

[27] A critical edition *Instructio Vicariorum Apostolicorum ad Regna Sinarum Tunchini et Cocincinae profiscentium 1659* by H. Chappoulie, op. cit. I, 392–402; see also the commentary in L. Baudiment, *Pallu* 61ff.

[28] H. Chappoulie, op. cit. I, 400.

den to the missions; the training of an indigenous clergy was demanded. The confrontation of this instruction with the practice in the missions in Siam resulted in the *Instructiones ad munera apostolica rite obeunda*[29] in ten chapters and several practical appendices.

The goals and means of the mission were attuned to each other. The very important eleven articles concerning the catechumate were the first systematic and probably deliberate renewal of an institution going back to Christian antiquity. It represented the first fundamental break with the medieval missionary method. The guiding thought of conversion was no longer embodied in the principle of working down from the top, that is, the conversion of the masses by their political leaders as the Jesuits in East Asia aspired, but rather in the reverse procedure of working up to the top, that is through the conversion of the masses and the establishment of Christian communities.[30] Very important was the third chapter *De recto mediorum humanorum usu*,[31] a declaration of war against the missionaries of the *Padroado* and—probably not intended for them at the time—against the Jesuits as well, who provided, after all, the greater number and the most prominent of the missionaries of the *Padroado*.[32] The fight was concentrated against the close connection between the mission and the politics of Portugal, the world power, and the involvement of missionaries in commerce. The number of Jesuit missionaries alone departing via Lisbon and supported by Portugal made any blunt solution of the problem impossible.[33] The Propaganda, moreover, did not take into account the immense sacrifices that Portugal, small as it was, had made for the total missionary effort from Goa to

[29] This work was first printed in 1669 by the press of the Propaganda (Streit I, 275). The instructions were reedited again and again; since 1840 they have been entitled *Monita ad Missionarios*. The following is based on the Hong Kong edition of 1893.

[30] The chapter "De regimine cuiuscumque particularis Ecclesiae, maxime ubi Sacerdos deficit," op. cit., 130–35, probably contributed in a decisive way to the fact that the congregations founded by the Paris Missionaries were able to save themselves even in the bloodiest persecutions.

[31] Op. cit., 21–35.

[32] A thorough investigation of the *Monita ad Missionarios* is still lacking.—Pallu and his companions assuredly were not basically opposed to the Jesuits. They had gone through the ascetic school of P. Bagot in Paris; the Jesuit de Rhodes had selected them; two of Pallu's brothers were Jesuits and the Jesuit General Paul Oliva even saved the new undertaking from being abolished by Louis XIV. Initially Pallu considered harmonious collaboration with the Jesuits completely natural. For individual references see esp. H. Chappoulie, op. cit. I (index).

[33] J. Wicki, S.J., *Liste der Jesuiten-Indienfahrer 1541–1758: Aufsätze zur portugiesischen Kulturgeschichte* VII (Münster 1967), 252–450. In 1541–1658 the number of Jesuits departing from Lisbon was 1,047. In the period 1658–1758 it was 1,073.

Japan even though after 1600 it was no longer capable of protecting its bases or its missionaries.[34] The dogged obstinacy of Portugal's claim for power vis-à-vis the mission was experienced not only by individual members of the Parisian Missionaries who were caught and were languishing in the jails of the Inquisition in Goa, but also by the papal legate Maillard de Tournon (d. 1710), who was deported by the Chinese to Macao after an unsuccessful missionary effort and held in jail by the Portuguese until his death.[35]

Even Pallu was not free from the same political ambitions of which he accused the missionaries of the *Padroado*. He advised the French East Asia Company and, more than that, tried to influence the royal minister Colbert towards bringing the power of France to bear in India and East India.[36] In this way he helped initiate the policy which in 1685/86 led to an exchange of ambassadors between France and Siam and, a 100 years later—with the help of the vicar apostolic of Cochinchina, Mgr. Pierre Pigneaux de Béhaine (d. 1799)—resulted in France obtaining a firm foothold in East India.[37] The first problem to arise was the participation by the missionaries in commerce, involving primarily the Jesuit mission in Japan, in part because of the extremely high costs of operation and in part because of insufficient subsidies from Portugal and other sources in Europe. The visitant of the Far East, A. Valignano, in opposition to the general of the order, Claudio Acquaviva (d. 1615), took the stand that the mission could only be maintained through participation in the commerce between Macao and Japan.[38] After the collapse of the Japanese

---

[34] B. Biermann, O.P., "Das Spanisch-portugiesische Patronat als Laienhilfe für die Missionen," *Das Laienapostolat in den Missionen (Festschr. Beckmann)* (Beckenried 1961), 161–79.

[35] The main task of Cardinal de Tournon was not to end the rites quarrel but to establish a direct relationship between Rome and Peking (on the basis of a nunciature). This would have ended the Portuguese influence in Peking (F.-A. Pouleau, "Maillard de Tournon," *AHSI* 31 [1962], 264–323).

[36] H. Chappoulie, op. cit. I, 278–82.

[37] G. Taboulet, *La geste française en Indochine* I (Paris 1955) (161–239 about Mgr. Pigneaux de Béhaine).

[38] A. Valignano, *Sumario de las Cosas de Japón* (1583), ed. by J. R. Álvarez-Taladriz (Tokyo 1954), 334–39 and the editor's introduction, 41–50.—According to the unpublished dissertation by L. Bourdon, "La Compagnie de Jésus et le Japon" (Paris), Pierre Chaunu quoted the expenditures of the Japan mission for 1579 at 6,000 cruzados; by 1582 they increased to 12,000. From 1581 to 1582 the mission needed 8,650 cruzados for subsistence for the personnel, for buildings, presents, etc. and 2,100 for necessary purchases in India and Europe. Of this, the Portuguese exchequer paid 4,000. In addition there were the gifts by certain benefactors (such as Pius V) and the revenues from the port of Nagasaki, granted to the Jesuits, and their possessions in Macao and Bazain. The silk trade brought in 4,000 cruzados and the remainder was taken in by private trade of individual missionaries (P. Chaunu, "Une grande puissance économique et

mission the missionaries who had been expelled or newly designated for Japan were sent to East India, where participation in the trade was probably upheld as a sort of traditional privilege. At any rate, the report of the vicars apostolic in Ajuthia was followed by the pointed brief of Clement IX *Sollicitudo Pastoralis officii* (17 June 1669), which reiterated all prior regulations and prohibitions of trade by the missionaries.[39] The *Instructiones* of the Paris Missionaries, who fought against commerce, were published in the same year.[40] The fact that the Jesuits—in spite of all the prohibitions and claims by their superiors—did not stop their involvement in commerce is shown by an inquiry of 23 June 1797 by Ángel de la Fuente, administrator of the assets of the suppressed Society of Jesus in the Philippines. He wanted to know what was to happen to the 254,320 pesos, invested by the Jesuits in the trade between China and Mexico. In 1775 this sum had been 306,341; by 1793 it had grown to 393,454 pesos.[41]

The reorientation of the mission relinquishing the principle of "working down from the top" required a different missionary method.[42] This involved the formation of individual parishes with catechists, priests, sisters, and a native episcopate. These aspects will be treated in detail as we deal with the respective countries. In general it can be said that the method of proceeding from the princely courts, advocated especially by the Jesuits of the *Padroado,* in the final analysis was ineffectual. The Propaganda, for its part, had to postpone its lofty program of a native Church led by indigenous bishops because the foundation of individual parishes initially claimed all the available energy.

The position of the Propaganda, or rather of its missionaries, on the

---

financière: les débuts de la Compagnie de Jésus au Japon [1547–83]," *Annales—Economies. Sociétés. Civilisations* V [Paris 1950], 198–212).

[39] The connections are shown by the fact that the regulation was emphasized to apply also to the Society of Jesus and even if the trade was the only means to maintain the mission (T. Grentrup, "Das kirchliche Handelsverbot für Missionare," *ZMR* 15 [1925], 257–68).

[40] "De illicita et indigna Viro Apostolico negotiatione" (*Monita,* op. cit., 23–25). At the same time the generals of the Society of Jesus had renewed the prohibition of trade (J. Humbert, "Some Answers of the Generals of the Society of Jesus to the Province of Goa," *AHSI* 36 [1967], 72–103).

[41] P. S. Lietz, *Calendar of Philippine Documents in the Ayer Collection of the Newberry Library* (Chicago 1956), Doc. 256, p. 129.—The author explains that the Jesuits (in the Philippines) invested their assets one third each in trade with Mexico, with China and Indonesia, and as a reserve, idem, Doc., 257, p. 130.

[42] The chapter by H. Bernard-Maître, "La Rencontre du Padroado et du Patronat: l'affrontment des méthodes," Delacroix, op. cit. II, 323–36, and its thesis of the tabula rasa on the part of the Spanish and a progressive method of accommodation among the *Padroado* missionaries (i.e., Jesuits) is historically untenable.

issue of Chinese and Malabar Rites is also connected to the new methodological direction.[43] The third chapter of the *Monita ad Missionarios*[44] clearly shows the position of the Paris Missionaries, although at the time of its writing this issue was not at all contemplated, since it was hardly known to exist beyond a small circle.

Development and Decline of the Missions in the Asian Countries

The development of the Propaganda missions in Asia brought about an expansion of their territories into those of the *Padroado*. Initially both sides employed every means at their disposal to hold fast to their respective right to propagate the faith. Not until the eighteenth century did this attitude give way to an implicitly recognized, sometimes geographically separated coexistence, the form of which differed from one country to the other.

INDIA

Throughout the seventeenth and eighteenth century India was the heart of the Portuguese rule and with it of the mission. The city of Goa was still wealthy and powerful, the seat of the viceroy and of the great convents and monasteries of the various religious orders. From here spread the impulse for the missions and ministry in all the countries from East Africa to Japan. The archbishop of Goa was the highest ecclesiastical authority in all these territories. Thus the fact that the bishoprics were vacant for decades in the hard years of political and jurisdictional crises had a fatal effect. Portugal had achieved its political independence in 1640. Yet for the next thirty years Spain was still powerful enough to prevent any direct connection between Portugal and Rome. Only after 1670 was it possible to appoint new bishops for India.

Until the middle of the eighteenth century the Jesuit college was the backbone of the mission in all the *Padroado* countries. The Jesuit press operating since 1556 was the only one to continue printing the necessary books in the various languages.[45] After 1572 the strongest mendicant order in Goa were the Augustinian Hermits, who trained their own

---

[43] Sources and literature esp. in Streit V, VI, VII (with supplements in Vols. XII–XIV). More recent literature in *DHGE* XII, 741 and *LThK* VIII, 1324.—In the dispute over the rites and in other decisions it has to be noted that the Propaganda Congregation had no theologians of its own; instead all decisions were made by the Holy Office (J. Metzler, "Controversia tra Propaganda e S. Officio circa una commissione teologica [1622–1658]," *Annales Pont. Univ. Urbaniana* [Rome 1968–69], 47–62).

[44] De recto mediorum humanorum usu (op. cit., 21–35).

[45] "Impresa em Goa." *Boletim do Instituto Vasco da Gama* (Bastora and Goa 1956). Memorial vol. for the four hundredth anniversary.

missionaries for work in the Muslim areas from Africa through Indochina all the way to Bengal. It was from them that the viceroys
preferred to select their ambassadors to the courts of the Mongolian
rulers.[46]

The five councils of Goa (1567, 1575, 1585, 1592, 1606) were concerned most with adapting the Tridentine reforms to the native conditions.[47] Yet in Goa especially the actual conditions were behind the
stated ideals, most of all in the social sector. Slavery, as at the time of
Francis Xavier,[48] was still a wide-spread practice in the seventeenth and
eighteenth century. It was calculated that an average Portuguese civil
servant needed fifteen to twenty male and female slaves. Even the one
convent in India, the Augustinian convent of Saint Monica (founded in
1606), was granted 120 female servants and slaves by no less than royal
order. Black male and female slaves were highly regarded because of
their capacity for work.[49] We know—not only from numerous prohibitions by various offices in the homeland, but also from actual
reports—that the male orders were keeping slaves.[50] The slaves, as
well as Indians and Brahmins, were refused Communion, though
not as a matter of principle, but yet in practice. The Italian Theatine Father Antonio Ardizone Spinola was the first to give a sermon
against this discriminatory practice. It was entitled: "Sigh of the
Christian Brahmins and Canarins and many other castes and peoples
because they never in all their life . . . are allowed to commune."[51]

Equally fatal was the effect of the Inquisition, active in Goa from

[46] A. da Silva Rêgo, "Documentação," *India* XI, IX–XIII stresses the importance of the
Augustinians for the missions of the East and publishes the *Manual Eremitico da Congregação da India,* which was finished by Manuel da Ave-Maria in 1815, pp. 95–833.

[47] J. Wicki, S.J., "Die ältere katholische Mission in der Begegnung mit Indien," *Saeculum*
VI (1955), 345–67, (335–60: the Goan councils and India); idem, "Die unmittelbaren
Auswirkungen des Konzils von Trient auf Indien (ca. 1565–85)," *AHPont* I (1963),
241–63.

[48] G. Schurhammer, *Franz Xaver, sein Leben und seine Zeit* II/1 (Freiburg i. Brsg. 1964,
Index).

[49] L. Kilger, "Das erste Frauenkloster in Portugiesich-Indien. St. Monika 1606–1834,"
NZM 7 (1951), 119–23, esp. 121ff.

[50] When a Portuguese religious or nobleman traveled, he had himself carried by
blacks in a sedan (A. Zerlik, *P. Xav. Ernbert Fridelli S.J., China-missionar und
Kartograph* [Linz 1962], 13).—The fact that Propaganda missionaries held identical
views is attested to by a letter from Pallu to Paris (20 Dec. 1683) in which he
ennumerates the persons for whom he had to care, "sans compter un grand nombre
d'esclaves" (*Lettres de Mgr. Pallu,* ed. by A. Launay, I [Angoulême 1914], 378).

[51] R. Cantel, "Le Père Ardizone Spinola et son 'Cordal Triplicado de Amor a Jesus
Sacramentado'," *Mélanges Marcel Bataillon-Bulletin Hispanique* 54 (Bordeaux 1962),
347–57. Subsequent sermons on the same topic in 1645, 1646, 1647, 1648.

1560 to 1812, which decreed penalties ranging from flogging to public burning at the stake. As in America the Inquisition was above all the highest office for the safeguarding of patronage rights. Several missionaries of the Propaganda became rather familiar with the inside of the Goan jails of the Inquisition.[52] Of great help to the Christian congregations was the *Pai dos Christãos*. The office of this "Father of the Christians" was usually entrusted to such missionaries who were able to work in the field of social welfare and against the exploitation of the new Christians, especially in the vicinity of Goa and other bases.[53]

The area around Goa was apportioned to the three major orders who were initially working in India: the province of Bardez went to the Franciscans, a number of islands off the coast of Goa to the Dominicans, and the peninsula of Salsette to the Jesuits. From the seventeenth century on the Goan clergy gained more and more importance. It is among the merits of the *Padroado* that it stressed from the very beginning the education of a native clergy.[54] To be sure, the Portuguese in India had their own racial prejudices;[55] in the early period only members of the Brahmin caste were ordained in the priesthood. Up until the eighteenth century Indians were accepted into religious orders only in individual cases.[56] Yet a great number of secular priests were educated at the Jesuit College of Saint Paul in Goa, in the Franciscan seminaries in Reis Magos (Bardez) and Kranganore, in the Thomas Academy of the Dominicans in Goa, and later at the archdiocesan seminary of Goa and at the Great Seminary of Rachol.[57] Not only were these clerics suitably trained to take over the parishes founded by the individual orders, but they also

---

[52] A. Baião, *A Inquisição de Goa,* 2 vols. (Coimbra 1930–49).—See also the discourse in A. D'Costa, S.J., *The Christianisation of Goa Islands* (Bombay 1965), 193–200, who proves that the Inquisition did not extort forced conversion from the missionaries.

[53] J. Wicki, S.J., *O Livro do "Pai dos Cristãos"* (Lisbon 1969).

[54] C. Merces de Melo, *The Recruitment and Formation of the Native Clergy in India* (Lisbon 1955) 65–205; J. Wicki, S.J., "Der einheimische Klerus in Indien (16. Jh.)," in J. Beckmann, *Der einheimische Klerus in Gesch. und Gegenwart (Festschr. Kilger)* (Schöneck/Beckenried 1950), 17–72.

[55] C. R. Boxer, *Race Relations in the Portuguese Empire 1415–1825* (Oxford 1963), 57–85.

[56] A. Meersman, "The Question of Admitting Indians to the Franciscan Order," *NZM* 13 (1957), 29–34; J. Wicki, S.J., "Pedro Luis, Brahmane und erster indischer Jesuit," *NZM* 5 (1950), 115–26.

[57] The annual report of 1646 by the provincial mentions that the colleges of Goa, Rachol, and Bassein also taught the Brahmans Latin, philosophy, morals, and speculative theology, paid for by the Society of Jesus, until they were ordained (M. de Melo, *The Recruitment,* 183f.).

performed capably as missionaries in the countries of the *Padroado*.[58] It was Goan priests who saved the Christian congregations in the areas which were lost by Portugal in the course of the centuries. Thus one of them wrote: "Although these priests had to do without the help of the Jesuits since 1760, forego the help of all the other orders since 1834, and since the middle of the nineteenth century were deserted by a government formerly sympathetic to the mission, the Goan clergy, especially since the eighteenth century, has worked with great dedication towards maintaining the congregations founded and built up by the missionaries of the *Padroado*."[59] Contrary to the widely held opinion that the *Padroado,* or rather the state exchequer, paid the expenditures of the congregations, it is a fact that these were also born by the faithful themselves. A certain basic asset were the lands of the suppressed Hindu temples.[60] Numerous brotherhoods in almost all the congregations paid for other expenditures, such as the celebration of religious high holidays.[61] These brotherhoods, invariably led by laymen, were an important element of Christian life.

In Ceylon it was the establishment of the Oratory of the Holy Cross in Goa[62] which gave the clergy a special apostolic impulse and saved the Ceylonese Church. Its moving spirit was Joseph Vaz (1651–1711), "the Apostle of Ceylon."[63] He came to Ceylon in 1687 disguised as a beggar. After 1696 he was supported by other priests of the Oratory of Goa, which alone had carried the burden of that hard-pressed Church for 150 years.[64] In its main features the organization of this mission can be traced back to Father J. Vaz.[65] In very perilous times the Kingdom of Kandy, which was independent of Holland, offered refuge. Here too originated the major portion of the Catholic Singhalese literature.

---

[58] In faraway Ethiopia the Goan B. da Silva worked from 1598 to 1613 (Streit XV, 621, 637f.; XVI, 2); and in Madagascar three Goan Oratorians tried to found a mission in 1726 (*AHSI* 41 [1962], 244).

[59] F. Coutinho, *Le régime paroissial* 24/25. See also p. 282.

[60] A. D'Costa, S. J., "Demolition of the Temples in the Islands of Goa and the Disposal of the Temple Lands," *NZM* 18 (1962), 161–76.

[61] F. Coutinho, op. cit. 130–38.

[62] M. da Costa Nuñes, *Documentação para a historia da congregação do Oratorio de Santa Cruz del Clero natural de Goa* I (1681–1727) (Lisbon 1966).

[63] S. G. Perera, *Life of the Venerable Father Joseph Vaz, Apostle of Ceylon* (Galle 1953).

[64] When the Dutch had conquered the Portuguese territories of Ceylon (1638–58) they prohibited all Catholic cults and ordered forced Calvinization (19 Sept. 1658) (R. Boudens, O.M.I., "Negombo. Un centre de résistance catholique à Ceylon sous l'occupation hollandaise [1658–1796]," *NZM* 11 [1955], 81–91; idem, *The Catholic Church in Ceylon under Dutch Rule* [Rome 1957]).

[65] Ibid., 89–115; see 173–88 for the method of the Oratorians.

Father Vaz himself acquired an excellent knowledge of the language, but he persuaded his younger fellow Oratorian Jacome Gonçalvez (d. 1742) to dedicate himself to the apostolate of the book.[66] That the missionary spirit of the Oratorians stayed alive was witnessed by the Capuchin Marco della Tomba, who was traveling through. In 1783 he reported of fourteen Oratorians who attended to 90,000 Catholics in 400 parishes of varying size.[67] In 1796 the Dutch were driven out by the English, but the Catholics did not get full religious freedom until 1806. Later on the Oratorians had to be replaced by European missionaries of the Propaganda.[68]

The intervention of the Propaganda in India came to pass through an individual case. In 1625 the young Brahmin Matthaeus de Castro arrived in Rome and was ordained for the priesthood five years later.[69] In 1633 he was sent back to India as a *missionarius apostolicus.* But his faculties were recognized neither by the secular nor by the ecclesiastical authorities. So he traveled to Rome a second time and was appointed vicar apostolic of Bijapur[70] and consecrated bishop in 1637. Before entering into his office he was to accompany the newly appointed Bishop Francesco Antonio de S. Felice Frasella to Japan.[71] But since the latter was not longer able to travel there, de Castro began his work as vicar apostolic. But his unwise actions and efforts to have the Dominican, Augustinian, Franciscan, and Jesuit congregations taken over by the Brahmin priests ordained by him caused Lisbon to institute harsh measures which de Castro was able to evade only by flight to Rome (1644). After an interlude as vicar apostolic in Ethiopia he returned to India in 1653. But in the meantime the sultan there had established good relations with the Portugese so that the Portuguese Jesuits were able to resume their work and de Castro found his see occupied. At this time he wrote the pamphlet *The Brahmin Mirror,* attacking the Portuguese and the Jesuits. In 1658 he again traveled to Rome but received no cooper-

---

[66] R. Boudens, *Catholic Church* (Index); Streit VI, 217–19 (list of his works in Singhalese, Tamil, and Portuguese); E. Peiris, O.M.I., *Singhalese Christian Literature of the XVIIth and XVIIIth Centuries* (Colombo, n. d.).

[67] R. Boudens, *Catholic Church,* 169f.

[68] Because of resistance by the Dutch and the native population the Oratorians could not consider the training of a native clergy until the second half of the eighteenth century; even then they were unsuccessful (see R. Boudens, *Catholic Church,* 186–88).

[69] T. Ghesquière, *Mathieu de Castro, Premier Vicaire Apostolique aux Indes* (Louvain 1937); J. Metzler, "Der Brahmanenspiegel des Matthäus de Castro," NZM 23 (1967), 252–65.

[70] Bijapur was a Muslim sultanate east of Goa, inaccessible to the archbishop of Goa.

[71] A. Meersman, "A Few Notes Concerning Archbishop Franc. Ant. Frascella O.F.M. Conv. in Goa 1640–1653," MF 59 (1959), 346–51.

ation this time. He died in 1677 at the College of the Propaganda. His successor, Custodio de Pinho (d. 1697), a Brahmin as well, did live in peace with the representatives of the *Padroado,* but he was unable to repair the damage his predecessor had done.[72] It was to no avail that Rome appointed him apostolic visitant for Malabar, where the Italian Carmelites had taken the place of the Jesuits in 1656.[73]

In 1669 the vicariate of Bijapur was enlarged by the Muslim state Golconda in the east and in 1697 by the complete realm of the grand mogul; as a result the mission see comprised ninety percent of the Indian subcontinent. But the establishment of a native hierarchy, envisioned by the secretary F. Ingoli at the time of de Castro's appointment, was stopped abruptly in 1696 by the appointment of the papal nephew Petrus Palma-Pignatelli as vicar apostolic by Innocent XIII. This action delayed the envisioned development by centuries. Palma-Pignatelli had worked as a missionary in Malabar; in 1701 (five years after his appointment), he died at Surat.[74] His successors continued to be selected from the Carmelite order.

Goa had not reacted strenuously against the appointment of Indian vicars apostolic except in de Castro's case. But then ensued the real conflict between the *Padroado* and the Propaganda in which the latter did not realize that Portugal's influence in Asia was still quite strong. The Portuguese bishops claimed territories of the Propaganda and in 1709 the viceroy of Goa expelled the Carmelites, active in Goa since 1620.[75]

In 1661 when the marriage contract between Charles II of England and Catherine of Braganza ceded (yet) unimportant Bombay to England, the Portuguese Franciscans were able to continue their missionary work in full freedom. But in 1730 they were finally expelled and replaced by Italian Carmelites.[76] From 1789 to 1791 Goa again exercised jurisdiction over Bombay with the result that the Carmelites now had to leave. This was followed by the disastrous compromise of the

---

[72] G. Radaelli, "Mons. Custodio de Pinho e la sua opera Missionaria," *Pensiero Missionario* (1942), 23–37; idem, "Le Missioni Cattoliche di Mogul, Golconda e Idalcan alla metà del secolo XVII," *Pensiero Missionario* (1941), 214–26.

[73] Idem, "Un Visitatore Apostolico indigeno nel Malabar," *Pensiero Missionario* (1942), 122–35.—Mgr. de Pinho had been consecrated bishop by the vicar apostolic of the Comorin Coast, the Brahman Thomas de Castro, who was a cousin of M. de Castro.

[74] Ambrosius a S. Theresia, *Hierarchia Carmelitana* III, 101–8.

[75] The Carmelites had been well prepared at the mission college in Rome (see L. Kilger, "Eine alte Hochschule missionarischer Fachbildung," *ZMR* 5 [1915], 207–24).

[76] A. Meersman, *The Franciscans in Bombay* (Bangalore 1957), 81–102; J. H. Gense, *The Church at the Gateway of India 1720–1960* (Bombay 1960), 32–69.

double jurisdiction by which the parishes were divided among the *Padroado* and the Propaganda missionaries. This also happened in several parts of British India[77] and was especially disadvantageous for the so-called Christians of Saint Thomas of the Malabar Coast. In these congregations of the Eastern Rite, which had been afflicted by earlier schisms and were unwilling to acquiesce to Latinization, Propaganda and *Padroado* bishops had worked side by side since 1704.[78] According to a report by the Carmelite missionary Paulinus a S. Bartholomeo, who worked on the Malabar Coast,[79] there were at that time eighty-four Uniate and thirty-two non-Uniate congregations. The former were split up among the bishops of Kranganore (twenty congregations) and the vicars apostolic in Verapoly (sixty-four congregations).[80]

In the Jesuit literature the Malabar mission not only comprised the actual Malabar Coast, but the total area of the earlier Malabar province established in 1610. Part of it was Madura, probably the most flourishing mission of the entire seventeenth and eighteenth century.[81] Located outside the Portuguese territory, it was affected by the wars of native princes, Muslims, and Hindus, and additionally by the terror of native despots. The Portuguese Jesuit João de Britto (1647–93) died a martyr there and was canonized in 1947.[82] The missionaries of this mission founded by Father Nobili were foremost in creating values which are still alive today by making use of Indian doctrines of wisdom and the native languages for the propagation of the faith.

The so-called Malabar Rites in India had a considerable bearing on the missionary method of Roberto Nobili and his successors. But protest against certain customs arose from the ranks of his own brethren, the Portuguese Jesuits. In 1623 Gregory XV had approved Nobili's

[77] Concerning the legal position of the Catholics in English territories, see M. Arputhasamy, *L'Église catholique dans l'Inde. Étude Historico-juridique* (diss., Fribourg 1948).
[78] K. Werth, *Das Schisma der Thomas-Christen unter Erzbischof Franciscus Garzia* (Limburg 1937); E. Tisserant and E. R. Hambye, *Eastern Christianity in India* (London 1957), esp. 69–97; Placid J. Podipara, *Die Thomas-Christen* (Würzburg 1966).
[79] Concerning his works: Ambrosius a S. Theresia, *Bio-Bibliographia Missionaria omnis Carmelitarum Discalceatorum* (Rome 1940; Index); L. Wetzel, *Der österreichische Karmelit Paulinus a S. Bartholomaeo, Persönlichkeit und Werk* (Vienna 1936); Streit VI, 187–91.
[80] See E. Tisserant and E. R. Hambye, op. cit., 97; P. Placid, an Indian Carmelite writes: "In perusing the documents and works of the sixteenth, seventeenth and eighteenth century one is quite surprised to see how the Thomas Christians became victims of the conflicts between Franciscans and Jesuits, between Jesuits and Carmelites, between the dioceses of Cochin and Angamale (Cranganore), and between the jurisdiction of the *Padroado* and the Propaganda" (op. cit., 137).
[81] D. Ferroli, *The Jesuits in Malabar* II (Bangalore 1951).
[82] The first and fundamental biography was written by his brother Pereyra de Britto (Coimbra 1722).

practices. But these concessions were seriously questioned by the missionaries of the Propaganda, especially by the Capuchin Father M. de Tours. Since Mgr. Maillard de Tournon had been appointed apostolic legate for East Asia and China in 1701, he was charged with clarifying the issue of Indian customs on the spot. In July 1704 Tournon issued a decree in Pondicherry which prohibited the Malabar Rites. This was protested above all by the archbishop of Goa, so that the legate's decree was not given papal recognition until 1734 and then again in 1739. The final condemnation of these and the Chinese Rites came from Benedict XIV in his bull *Omnium sollicitudo* of 1744. Modernization and secularization prompted the Propaganda to issue a decree in 1940 concerning the toleration of these rites.[83]

Among the great successors of Nobili were the Italian G. C. Beschi (1680–1747)[84] and the German E. Hanxleden (1681–1732).[85] G. Constancio Beschi worked for about twenty years in the area of Travancore, dominated by the Danes, where a German Lutheran mission had also established itself under Ziegenbalg. Circumstances and the order of his superior Dom Madeira made him the first controvertist theologian in the Tamil language.[86] In his annual report on the Madura mission to which Tanjore belonged as well, Beschi wrote that every priest attended to from five to twenty thousand Christians.[87] The missionaries always held fast to Nobili's guidelines: among the Brahmins and the higher castes the missionaries worked as *Sannyasei;* the pariahs had their own padres. The dispute over the Malabar Rites, rekindled around 1700 in distant Madras—in Travancore itself the tolerated rites were fought by the Lutherans as idolatry—actually had little influence on the missions because the last condemnation by Benedict XIV of 1744 was hardly known prior to the expulsion of the Jesuits by Pombal.

Portuguese Franciscans who had been active in some areas since the sixteenth century were also working in the Tamil-speaking part of the Jesuit province of Malabar. After the expulsion of the Jesuits they were

---

[83] *AAS* 32 (1940), 379.

[84] For a list of his works, see esp. Streit VI, 30–41; M. Ledrus, *Beschi* (Louvain 1931); D. Ferroli, op. cit., 298–314.

[85] D. Ferroli, op. cit., 315–32; A. Huonder, *Deutsche Jesuiten-Missionare* (Freiburg i. Brsg. 1899), 175. For the complete Christian literature in Tamil see Devanesan Rayarigam, *Christliche Literatur in der Tamilsprache* (Gütersloh 1961) (reviewed by A. Lehmann in *ThLZ* [1962], 306f.).

[86] The Danes were more tolerant than the Calvinist Dutch so that Catholic missionary work could be continued in their territories (A. Meersman, "The Catholic Church in Tranquebar and Tangore During the Formative Years of the Lutheran Mission," *Indian Church History Review* 1 [1967], 93–112 [about Beschi see 110–12]).

[87] A. Meersman, op. cit., 111.

able to take over their stations.[88] In contrast to other countries, the collaboration between the mendicant orders, Jesuits, and the secular priests of the *Padroado*—except for some minor disputes—was rather more harmonious in India.

The missions in the vast realm of the grand mogul were also part of the Malabar province of the Jesuits. Those missions had had a promising start under the rulers Akbar and Jahangir, but in the seventeenth and eighteenth century they had to be confined to ministering to the already converted Christians and those who migrated there. Among the most important Jesuit missionaries the following deserve special mention: the Germans Heinrich Roth (1620–88), author of the first Sanskrit grammar,[89] and Andreas Strobl (1703–70), who worked at the Muslim courts of northern India as a distinguished natural scientist, and the Tyrolian Joseph Tieffenthaler (1710–85), probably the most important geographer of India.[90]

The Portuguese Franciscans who organized two large expeditions to northern India had no lasting successes.[91] The Carmelites of the Italian province who started missionary work in Persia in 1607 and from there advanced to the northern Indian province of Sind were forced to confine themselves to the ministry of Portuguese and other Christians in the large port of Tatta, where they had arrived in 1672.[92] The same was true for the Augustinian Hermits who also gained a foothold in Tatta in 1624 in order to hold on to the important Portuguese bases for the jurisdiction of the archbishop of Goa and for the *Padroado*.[93]

Even in Tibet the interests of the *Padroado* and the Propaganda collided. The Portuguese missionary Antonio d'Andrade managed to settle in Tsaparang in 1624, but six years later wars within the country forced the missionaries to leave Tibet.[94] In 1704 the Propaganda transferred

---

[88] A. Meersman, *The Franciscans in Tamilnad* (Schöneck/Beckenried 1962).

[89] A. Camps, "Fr. Heinrich Roth SJ (1620–68) and the History of his Sanscrit Manuscripts," *ZMR* 53 (1969), 185–95.

[90] Concerning the cultural and scientific achievements of the India Missionaries see A. Ballini, "Il contributo delle Missioni alle conoscenza delle lingue e della cultura dell'India," *Le Missioni Cattoliche e la Cultura dell'Oriente* (Rome 1943), 233–60; L. Ambruzzi, S.J., "Il contributo dei Missionari cattolici alla conoscenza delle religioni, dei costumi e della geografia dell'India," *Le Missioni Cattoliche e la Cultura dell'Oriente* (Rome 1943), 261–92.

[91] A. Camps, "Franciscan Missions to the Mogul Court," *NZM* 15 (1959), 259–70.

[92] E. Berden, "The Carmel in Sind" *NZM* 11 (1955), 169–78, 241–50.

[93] J. Beckmann, "Die Augustiner-Eremiten in Sind," *NZM* 13 (1957), 191.

[94] G. Toscano, *La Prima Missione Cattolica nel Tibet* (Hong Kong 1951). The reports by Father d'Andrades are backed by Tibetan historical sources; A. H. Francke, "Die Jesuitenmission in Tsaparang im Lichte der tibetanischen Urkunden," *ZMR* 15 (1925), 269–76.

the mission to the Capuchin friars of Piceno. They arrived in Lhasa in 1707, but were forced to return to Bengal in 1712.[95] In the meantime Ippolito Desideri had been selected for the Tibet mission by the Jesuit provincial of Goa. He arrived in Lhasa in 1716, where he encountered the new Capuchin mission, but he did not believe that he was entitled to transfer his charge to them. In 1718 Rome consequently was required to entrust the Tibet mission to the Capuchins for a second time. Father Desideri thereupon left Lhasa and returned to Rome in order to render his report (d. 1733).[96]

The beginnings of the Capuchin mission in Lhasa were modest, but thanks to their linguistic and religious knowledge the missionaries—especially under their prefect Francisco Orazio Oliverio della Penna di Billi (d. 1745)—were able to establish a peaceful relationship with the Mongols.[97] Yet in 1742 the Capuchins had to retreat before the persecution instigated by the leaders of the Lama. They withdrew to Nepal until 1771, when they were driven out from there as well. They continued their hard work in Hindustan.[98]

The East Coast of India around the vast Gulf of Bengal was part of the diocese of São Tomé, Mylapore. This was the area in which the conflicts between the European powers were to be decided in favor of England.

These territories remained free from ecclesiastical conflicts: the Capuchins, missionaries of the Propaganda, received jurisdiction only for the French settlements, initially in Madras and later in Pondicherry; missionary work among the natives remained the prerogative of the *Padroado* missionaries. Bengal was a traditional missionary field of the Augustinian Hermits and the Portuguese Jesuits. In the neighboring provinces, especially in distant Carnate, the French Jesuits operated their own mission. They had their own superior and enjoyed a certain amount of independence. During the eighteenth century

---

[95] L. Petech, *I Missionari Italiani nei Tibet et nel Nepal. I Cappuccini Marchigiani* I–IV (Rome 1953).

[96] L. Petech, op. cit.; *Ippolito Desideri S J*, V, VI (Rome 1954–55); G. Castellani, "Un trattato di Missionologia del sec. XVIII," *CivCatt*, 1933, III, 127–40; *DHGE* XIV, 1503–5.

[97] A. Jann, "Zur Kulturarbeit der katholischen Kirche in Innerasien. Die missionarische und literarische Tätigkeit des Apostolischen Präfekten von Tibet, P. Franz. Horatius Oliverius della Penna di Billi 1712–45," *Studien aus dem Gebiet von Kirche und Kultur* (*Festschr. Gustav Schnaürer*) (Paderborn 1930), 128–207; Streit VI, 96–100.

[98] Abundant source material for this period in A. Jann, *Monumenta Anastasiana* I (Lucerne 1939), 970–1152.—Perhaps the largest obstacle was the abject poverty of the missionaries. For this reason the missionaries in Mexico were permitted to conduct a collection for the mission from 1763 to 1767 (see F. de Aljofrén, *Diario del Viaje . . . a la América Septentrional en el siglo XVIII*, 2 vols. [Madrid 1958–59]).

their mission was conducted by an average of 20 Jesuits, whose activities were not affected by Pombal's anti-Jesuit policy. In 1776, after the abolition of the Society of Jesus, their mission was entrusted to the Paris Missionaries.[99] The English victory and the effects of the Revolution on Pondicherry, which had stayed French, impeded the mission. One of their most significant representatives was Jean Antoine Dubois (1766–1848), whose somewhat pessimistic work about Indian customs and traditions determined the European attitude towards India during the nineteenth century.[100]

Burma, respectively the Kingdoms of Ava and Pegu were also part of the diocese of Meliapur. Portuguese Franciscans had worked there and especially in Pegu since the sixteenth century.[101] In 1721 when the missionaries of the Propaganda (Barnabites) arrived there, they met with heavy resistance, which they tried to avoid by confining their work to the Kingdom of Ava. Pegu always remained the preferred domain of the Franciscans. In 1766 Giovanni M. Percoto was named vicar apostolic of Ava and bishop of Maxula. The West owes him the first Buddhist manuscripts in Pali (on palm leaves). In various manuscripts and works not published until the nineteenth century he proved himself to be an expert on Burmese Buddhism.[102]

Far distant from India, yet part of Portuguese India, there was a number of Christian centers in Indonesia. After the conquest of Malacca (1640) by the Dutch, Macassar (on the island of Celebes) briefly became the center of the *Padroado* mission in Indonesia. But in the treaty of Batavia of 1660 the Dutch managed to force the ruler, Sultan Hassan Udin, to deport all Portuguese and their followers, i.e., Catholics.[103] But with heavy sacrifices the Dominicans were able to save

[99] A. Launay, *Histoire des Missions de l'Inde* I (Paris 1898); J. Lafrenz, *Précis de l'Histoire de la Mission de Pondichéry* (Pondicherry 1953). From 1736 to 1741 the Capuchin Norbert de Bar-le-Duc (1697–1769) worked in Pondicherry. His works on the conflict over the Malabar Rites poisoned the atmosphere in the mission; he also made it impossible for the first European sisters, the French Ursulines, to work in India. They had settled in Pondicherry in 1738 (J. Lafrenz, op. cit., 4f.).

[100] The English East India Company published the manuscript in London in 1817 (Streit VIII, 27f.).

[101] A. Meersman, "The Franciscans in the Burmese Kingdoms of Ava and Pegu 1557–1818," *AFrH* 31 (1938), 356–86.

[102] P. Anatriello, "I Cattolici ed il Buddismo Birmano," *NZM* 22 (1966), 260–69.

[103] B. Biermann, O.P., "Frei Luis de Andrade und die Solormission," *ZMR* 43 (1959), 176–87, 261–75 (on Makassar 274f.). For the sojourn of the Franciscans in Makassar, see A. Meersman, O.F.M., *The Franciscans in the Indonesian Archipelago* (Louvain and Paris 1967), 115–22.

their Solor mission into the nineteenth century.[104] Always weak, they nonetheless managed to uphold the remainders of Catholic congregations in neighboring Flores as well.[105] Again and again the Franciscans, too, sent individual missionaries to Indonesia; some of them using disguises were able to get to Malacca to minister to the native Christians.[106] North of Sumatra a new field of mission even offered itself to them. There the much feared Atjehr (or Achin) were reconciled with the Portuguese so that the Portuguese Franciscans could work there again from 1688 to 1775.[107]

INDOCHINA

In 1664, two years after their arrival in Ajuthia, the capital of Siam, the missionaries of the Paris Seminary established a seminary for the education of a native clergy which was to become the central seminary for all of East India and southern China. It was destroyed during the invasion by the Burmese in 1769, but found a new home near Pondicherry where it fell victim to the French Revolution a few decades later. In 1808 it was opened again in English-owned Pulo-Penang.[108] Beyond this the new missionaries also developed a direct apostolic activity in Siam. For 100 years the Dominicans had had a monastery and church in the Portuguese quarter for the ministry to the Portuguese. The Jesuits, driven from Japan by persecutions, found a new sphere of activity in the Japanese quarter and the Paris Missionaries found theirs in the Chinese quarter. The first vicar apostolic, Louis Laneau (1674–96), transferred his residence to Bangkok and through Goa and Rome he prevailed in having all regular clerics subordinated to his jurisdiction. But in spite of his excellent knowledge of the language[109] he and his missionaries did not succeed in gaining ground among the Buddhist population of the Thai, good relations between France and Siam notwithstanding. The opening of a mission in Burma failed as well and in 1693 the first two

---

[104] B. Biermann, "Die alten Dominikanermissionen auf den Solorinseln," *ZMR* 14 (1924), 12–48, 269–73.

[105] Idem, "Lieder der Florinesen," *NZM* 10 (1954), 141–45.

[106] A. Meersman, op. cit., 184ff.

[107] Ibid., 123–44.

[108] A. Launay, *Histoire de la Mission de Siam 1662–1811* (Paris 1920); idem, *Documents Historiques,* 2 vols. (Paris 1920); H. Chappouli, op. cit. I, 131ff.; T. Destombes, *Le Collège Général de la Societé des Missions Étrangères de Paris* (Hong Kong 1934); G. Cassac, "Les Missions d'Indochine après l'arrivée des Vicaires Apostoliques (1658–1799)," *Delacroix II, 213–26*; H. Bernard-Maître, *Pour la compréhension de l'Indochine et de l'Occident* (Paris, n. d.).

[109] A. Launay, *Memorial,* 356–59. Laneau was the first to translate the Gospels into the Thai language.

missionaries of the Seminary of Paris were murdered. Yet by the formation of a native clergy Laneau had created a tranquil and secure center.

Lambert de la Motte, the first vicar apostolic to Cochinchina,[110] whose
mission also included neighboring Cambodia, briefly worked there on
two separate occasions. In 1671/72 he got as far as the port of Faifo,
where he conducted a synod with three of his missionaries and several
catechists. In spite of its modest character this synod was to form the
legal basis for the mission of the Propaganda. In 1675/76 he worked as a
ship's chaplain on a French ship. Francis Pérez (1687–1728) later
worked there as vicar apostolic. In spite of violent persecutions, especially in 1698 and 1700, he succeeded—probably because he was a
native and quite independent—in unifying the missionaries under the
jurisdiction of the Propaganda. Later on there ensued some serious
dissension, primarily between the Spanish Franciscans from the Philippines and the French missionaries. Two Roman visitations in 1740 and
1744 failed. In 1750 all missionaries and their Christians were afflicted
by a general persecution[111] from which the congregations had great
difficulty recovering. For the most part they were attended by Chinese
and native priests.

In 1666 by order of Mgr. Pallu the first missionary of the Paris
Seminary, François Deydier (1637–93), pushed up into the vast
areas of the north, to Tongking,[112] supported after 1670 by his
colleague Jacques de Bourges (1630–1714). When Pallu suggested
dividing the area into two vicariates apostolic, the latter became
vicar apostolic of West Tongking in 1679; in the same year he
consecrated his colleague François Deydier bishop of East Tongking.
At this time the two vicariates already contained three hundred
thousand Christians. Although the Tongkinese Church had been
founded by Alfonso de Rhodes and the Jesuits driven out of Japan
(missionaries of the Portuguese *Padroado*), Tongking became the area
where the Paris Missionaries could execute the principles and the
program of the Propaganda. Moreover, Tongking represented the
first sizeable sphere of activity for the native clergy, part of whom
had been trained locally (mostly on fishing boats because of the
persecutions), the rest in Siam. The future vicar apostolic, Louis
Néez (1680–1764), who during fifty-two years of active missionary

[110] A. Launay, *Histoire de la Mission de Cochinchine* (1658–1823), 3 vols. (Paris 1923–
25).
[111] The two bishops and seven of the Paris Missionaries, two Italian Dominicans and a
priest from Nepal, nine Spanish Franciscans from the Philippines and eight Jesuits of
the *Padroado*, five Portuguese and three Germans were caught. Only Johannes Koffler,
S.J., was able to remain (as a physician at the royal court of Hué).
[112] A. Launay, *Histoire de la Mission du Tonkin. Documents Historiques* I (Paris 1927).

work got to know most of them personally, wrote biographical sketches of fifty-three of them, stressing their personal merits during the times of persecution.[113] In 1694 Mgr. de Bourges nominated one of them to be his successor as bishop and vicar apostolic. Along with the education of a native clergy, the organization of catechists and of the first congregation of native sisters, the Lovers of the Cross, who worked for the education of women and girls, proceeded apace. Around 1765 West Tongking alone included twenty branches with twenty to thirty sisters each.[114] But during the seventeenth and eighteenth century periods of toleration and tranquility were rare[115] and bloody persecutions frequent. Nonetheless, there were disagreements between the missionaries of different nationalities and religious orders, although the common goal prevented serious conflicts. An initial fundamental solution appeared to have been found in the transfer of the vicariate of East Tongking to the Spanish Dominicans of the Philippines (1679), who had been working in the country since 1675. But in addition to the Dominicans there were also some Italian Discalced Augustinians working there who disputed parts of the Dominican territory. But in 1757 these Augustinians were recalled by the Propaganda and their station handed over to the Spanish. In different places of West and East Tongking there were Jesuit missionaries of the *Padroado* who went over the heads of the vicars apostolic of both regions. This attitude hardened when after decades of a *sedes vacans* a bishop was finally residing again in Macao in 1692 who as the next *Padroado* bishop also claimed jurisdiction in Tongking. The strong ties of the missionaries to their congregations, strengthened in times of persecution, made any delineation of territories impossible. As a result there were constant conflicts via Rome or Lisbon until the abolition of the Society of Jesus.

CHINA

Thanks to the influential position of the Cologne Jesuit J. A. Schall von Bell (1592–1666) under both the Ming and Manchu dynasties (the latter since 1644) the tumultuous domestic politics at first had no damaging effects for Christianity in China. But the persecutions of 1664 came upon the young Church like a whirlwind. Father Schall, already beyond the age of seventy, was removed from his governmental positions and

---

[113] *Documents sur le Clergé tonkinois au XVIIIᵉ siècle,* ed . by A. Launay (Paris 1925).
[114] N. Kowalsky, *Stand der katholischen Missionen 1765* (1957), 26.
[115] About the scientific works, see Streit VI, XI and G. Dindinger, "Il contributo dei Missionari cattolici alla conoscenza del Siam e dell' Indochina," *Le Missioni cattoliche e la cultura dell'Oriente* (Rome 1943), 293–338.

condemned to death. His penalty was later reduced to imprisonment.[116] All churches were destroyed and twenty-five missionaries of the Jesuit and mendicant orders taken off to be imprisoned in Canton.

The Belgian Jesuit Ferdinand Verbiest (1623–88)[117] and two of his brethren were not banished to Canton. Thanks to his knowledge of astronomy, which he had displayed as a coworker of Father Schall, he became the savior of the mission. Called upon again to work in the mathematical institute of the court, he became its director in 1670. One of his first acts was to obtain the release of Father Schall so that the latter could die in freedom in 1666. After the Manchu ruler Kangshi ascended to the throne in 1667,[118] Verbiest gained his confidence and became his teacher of mathematics and astronomy. In 1671 the missionaries imprisoned in Canton were able to return to Peking.[119] Verbiest became interpreter for the court's relations with foreign ambassadors, a position held by Catholic missionaries into the nineteenth century. Appointed vice-provincial in 1677, he employed all the means at his disposal to increase the number of missionaries. This included letters to the Jesuit general and the Pope, but, most importantly, an appeal of 15 August 1678 to his brethren in Europe.[120] This appeal, supported by Philipp Couplet (1624–92), was most successful in France. Not only did many Jesuits there enlist for duty in China, but Louis XIV also assumed the cost of travel and subsistence for the missionaries. On 7 February 1688, ten days after the death of Verbiest, the first five French Jesuits arrived in Peking.[121]

The French Jesuits gave a great impetus to the Chinese mission. The Manchu ruler maintained good relations with them, above all with Father J. Bouvet (1656–1730), who became his ambassador to Louis

---

[116] A. Vath, S.J., *Joh. A. Schall v. Bell* (Cologne 1933), 295 ff.; about the Jesuit missionaries in China, L. Pfister, S.J., op. cit.

[117] H. Josson and L. Willaert, *Correspondance de Ferdinand Verbiest de la Comp. de Jésus (1623–88)* (Brussels 1938).

[118] L. Wei Tsing-sing, "Louis XIV et K'and-Hi. L'épopée des missionaires français du Grand Siècle en Chine," *NZM* 19 (1963), 93–109, 182–204.

[119] Verbiest's letter to Innocent XI (1678) praises the missionary importance of astronomy (*Correspondance*, op. cit., 227–28).—H. Bernard-Maître, S.J., *La science européene au tribunal astronomique de Pékin* (Paris 1952).

[120] *Correspondance*, 230–53. On the success of this appeal by Ferd. von Fürstenberg, bishop of Münster and Paderborn (1682), see O. Maas, "Die Stiftung Ferd. von Fürstenbergs zum Besten der ostasiatischen Missionen," *ThGl* 25 (1933), 701–10.

[121] P. Bornet, "La Mission Française à Pékin (1688–1775). Notes sur son origine et son personnel," *Bull. Cath. de Pékin* 25 (1938) 555–63, 609–16; C. de Rochemonteix, *Jos. Amoit et les derniers survivants de la Mission Française à Pékin* (Paris 1915).

XIV and his biographer.[122] He gave a piece of property near his palace to the French for a church and missionary station where a sizeable library was installed.[123] The French Jesuits became the most eager promoters of Chinese culture in Europe, especially by means of the seventeen-volume *Lettres Édifiantes et Curieuses,* published from 1702 to 1726,[124] and the voluminous folios about China by J. B. du Halde.[125] These works played an important role in the criticism of followers of the Enlightenment concerning the Christian belief in revealed religion and religious history.[126]

The French Jesuits were not about to submit to the laws of the *Padroado.* Louis XIV demanded categorically that his missionaries were not to be placed under the authority of foreign, non-French superiors, which was in contradiction to the basic rules of the order. This brought about tedious negotiations between the general of the order, Tirso González, and Louis XIV, respectively his father confessor de la Chaise. The French Jesuits were given their own superior, but legally they remained part of the vice-province of China.[127] Even on the issue of the rites they were not uniformly among the Ricci front.

While the persecutions in China were followed by a quiet reconstruction of the missions, King Pedro II of Portugal attempted to call everything into question again. He prevailed with Pope Alexander VIII (1689–91) in the establishment of two new bishoprics of the *Padroado,* Nanking and Peking, which were approved by the Pope in 1690 as though no vicariates apostolic existed there. Portugal sought to weaken the objections of the Propaganda by suggesting the two vicars apostolic for these bishoprics. But the Propaganda could not be satisfied with this. The next Pope, Innocent XII (1691–1700), tried to make up for the overly compliant action of his predecessor. By a brief of 15 October 1696 he confined the Portuguese bishoprics of Macao, Nanking, and Peking to two provinces each; vicariates apostolic were to be estab-

---

[122] J. C. Gatty, *Voiage du Siam du P. Bouvet* (Leiden 1963), esp. the introduction and bibliography of his works; L. Wei Tsing-sing, op. cit., 185–87. Bouvet published the *Histoire de l'Empereur de la Chine 1699* in Paris.

[123] See esp. the introduction by H. Verhaeren, C.M., *Catalogue of the Pei-tang Library* (Peking 1949), I–XXVII. A photomechanical reprint appeared in Paris in 1969.

[124] A. Rétif, "Brève histoire des Lettres édifiantes et curieuses," *NZM* 7 (1951), 37–50.

[125] *Description géographique, historique, chronologique, politique et physique de l'Empire de la Chine* (Paris 1735).—See also A. Brou, S.J., "Les Jésuites sinologues de Pékin et leurs éditeurs à Paris," *RHM* 11 (1934), 551–66.

[126] B. Guy, *The French Image of China before and after Voltaire* (Geneva 1963). See chapter 19 of this volume.

[127] G. Guitton, S.J., *Le Père de la Chaise, confesseur de Louis XIV,* 2 vols. (Paris 1959).

lished in the rest of the provinces. In the course of time some vicariates were converted into administrative regions. For almost 100 years the three *Padroado* bishoprics existed side by side with the three vicariates apostolic of Fukien, Szechwan, and Shansi.[128]

The lines of the bishoprics and vicariates had been precisely adapted to the geography of the Chinese provinces, but were disregarded in personnel matters. Thus the Spanish Franciscans of the Philippines were working in the areas of the *Padroado* as well as those of the vicars apostolic. By and by the mission fields were divided by orders. Well into the nineteenth century Peking had four stations and churches, two of the Jesuits of the *Padroado,* one of the French Jesuits, and one of the Propaganda missionaries. From the end of the seventeenth century on the jurisdiction of the whole China mission was as follows: The missionaries of the *Padroado,* mostly Jesuits, attended to a broad strip stretching from Macao beyond Peking via Nanking.[129] The Dominicans of the Rosary Province of the Philippines worked in the coastal provinces, first in collaboration with the Paris Missionaries and later by themselves. From the beginning of the eighteenth century they were also in charge of the vicariate of Fukien, to which the provinces of Kiangsi and Chekiang were joined in 1718.[130] The Paris Missionaries concentrated more and more on the vast provinces of western China, consisting of the provinces of Kweichow, Kwangsi, and Yünnan.[131] A prepared missionary field in the northwest, long since abandoned by the Jesuits, was encountered by the Italian Franciscans. This was the vicariate of Shansi, together with Shensi and Kansu, joined in 1792 by the double province of Hukuang (Hunan and Hupei).[132]

The missionaries' differences of nationality and order did not prevent the uniformity of their efforts. An exception were the missionaries in Peking who were in the service of the Chinese Emperor. Both *Padroado* and Propaganda missionaries worked as painters and musicians, physicians and engineers, but especially as astronomers and mathematicians.

---

[128] P. d'Elia, "L'Istituzione della Gerarchia Episcopale e dell'Internunziatura in Cina," *StMis* II (1946), 1–31; J. Beckmann, "Die hierarchische Neuordnung in China," *NZM* 3 (1947), 9–24.

[129] The best information about this is still contained in L. Pfister, also the surveys by J. Dehergne mentioned in n. 158.

[130] J. M. González, O.P., *Historia de la Misiones Dominicanas de China,* 5 vols. (Madrid 1964–67).

[131] A. Launay, *Histoire des Missions de Chine. Mission du Se Tchoan,* 2 vols. (Paris 1920); idem, *Mission du Kouy-Tchéou,* 3 vols. (Vannes and Paris 1907); idem, *Mission du Kouangsi* (Paris 1903); idem, *Missions du Kouang-Tong* (Paris 1907).

[132] *Sinica Franciscana,* ed. by A. von den Wyngaert, G. Mensaert, F. Margiotti and S. Rossa, vols. II–VII (Karachi and Rome 1933–65).

Even during the cruelest persecutions of the eighteenth century they were protected, but their spiritual activities were more and more confined to the ministry of Christians in the capital, while the mission stations in the countryside were left to other missionaries and native priests who waited in vain for the help of their Peking brethren, who in reality no longer had any influence. Even Emperor K'anghsi, who as late as 1692 had issued a decree of toleration for Christianity, in 1717 reacted favorably to a memorandum from his ministries which was radically hostile to Christians. This was the prelude to the local persecutions in the provinces, which became ever more widespread and cruel under the Emperors Yung Cheng (1722–35) and Ch'ien Lung (1735–96). Just how serious the situation in the middle of the eighteenth century was, even in Peking, is shown by a letter of 1753 from the Jesuit Antonio Gaubil (1689–1759) to the general of the order: "The Emperor is still tolerating a certain amount of religious freedom in Peking, but all Chinese and Tartars (i.e., Manchus) know full well that he hates the Christian name and know his resolve not to tolerate missionaries in the provinces and not to permit any Mandarin to become a Christian. . . . The Emperor thinks that he has done enough for us by elevating four of us to the rank of Mandarin. . . ."[133]

But not all the Peking missionaries showed such discernment. During the hard periods of persecution in the provinces most of them were living as on an island, aggravating their lives by quarrels connected with national rights and canon law. The most disastrous of them was the so-called Peking Schism.[134] After the death of Bishop Polykarp de Souza (d. 1757), until then the only bishop able to reside in Peking, disagreements ensued among the Peking missionaries concerning the administration of the bishopric by the neighboring Bishop Gottfried von Laimbeckhoven (1787) of Nanking. The quarrel was aggravated by the appointment and consecration of the Italian Augustinian Salusti in 1780. His successor Alexander de Gouvea, who arrived in Peking in 1785, was able to eliminate the schisms and realize the last eighteenth century revival of Catholicism in Peking.[135]

[133] In C. de Rochemonteix, *Jos. Amiot* (Paris 1915), 35.
[134] R. Primon, O.S.M., "L'atteggiamento della Congregazione di Propaganda Fide nello scisma di Pechino," *Missionswissenschaftliche Studien* (*Festgabe Dindinger*) (Aachen 1951), 315–31; G. Mensaert, O.F.M., "Nouveaux documents sur le soi-disant Schisme de Pékin," (*Festgabe Dindinger*), 332–46.
[135] J. Beckmann, "Bischof Alexander de Gouvea von Peking (1771–1808) im Lichte seiner Bibliothek" (*Festschr. Rommerskirchen*) in *ED* 21 (1968), 457–79. In a report to the Propaganda the new bishop writes in 1785: "Pekini omnia erant calumniae, rixae, murmurationes et charitatis fraternae violationes," and then he complains that the missionary activities of his priests had been reduced to zero. "Non loquor de omnibus, sed de maxima parte" (C. de Rochemonteix, *Jos. Amiot* [Paris 1915], 542–47).

While the situation of the Peking Church was in many ways serious, the provincial congregations were ailing badly yet always fighting heroically. The persecutions began in the province of Fukien in 1723. The harsh decree of the local viceroy against the Christians was immediately approved by the Emperor and consequently applied in the other provinces as well. In short order about thirty banished missionaries arrived in Canton. When several of them managed to return to their missions in secret, all banished missionaries were later transported to Macao. The individual congregations were affected even more severely by the laws of persecution.[136] Most of them were left for decades without a resident priest. Among the missionaries who returned from Canton the blessed Pedro Martyr Sanz and four of his brethren who accompanied him were condemned to death.[137] In 1784/85 all of China was involved in the persecution of Christians. On 27 August 1784 four new Franciscan missionaries designated for the Shansi/Shensi mission were arrested. Because a dangerous Muslim revolt had broken out in the western border region, the prisoners were immediately suspected of collusion with the enemy (popular view considered Islam and Christianity one and the same religion). To be sure, the trial in Peking clearly established their innocence, but the case had grave consequences. The Peking authorities were surprised that in spite of all imperial prohibitions there were still so many Christians in the country. Forty priests were finally caught and transported to Peking; seven Europeans among them died of the extreme exertion. The rest of the Europeans were deported to Macao, while the native priests and Christians were condemned to banishment beyond the Great Wall.[138] The matter of Christianity and the missionaries henceforth became the responsibility of the subordinate authorities, who were outdoing themselves in tracking down Christians.[139] And yet new missionaries were able again and again

[136] According to a "Catalogus omnium missionariorum qui Sinarum imperium ad haec usque tempora ad praedicandum Jesu Xi Evangelium ingressi sunt" written shortly before the persecution (*Revue de l'Extrême-Orient* 2 [Paris 1883], 58–71), there were eighty-eight churches and mission stations in the provinces. In addition there were sixty missionaries in the four churches and residences of Peking.
[137] J. M. González, O.P., *Misiones Dominicanes en China (1700–1750)* (Madrid 1952).
[138] B. Willeke, O.F.M., *Imperial Government and Catholic Mission in China During the Years 1784–85* (New York 1948).
[139] After the persecution the procurator of the Propaganda, J. B. Marchini, reported on 10 December 1785 that the following missionaries were still at their posts: Bishop Gottfried von Laimbeckhoven (Nanking) with one European and one Chinese priest; the vicar apostolic of Szechwan, Mgr. Pottier, with three European and six Chinese priests; in Fukien four Spanish Dominicans and three Chinese priests; in Shantung one Spanish Franciscan; in Kwangsi and Kwantung one native priest each; in Shansi three native priests; in the Peking outer missions seven Chinese priests. In addition there was

to reach their stations by covert routes. Naturally the persecutions resulted in considerable attrition in the Christian communities. The China mission was burdened by the problem of apostates for a number of decades. But many missionaries and Christians of this era manifested great heroism.[140] The causes of the persecution are manifold. The one of 1784/85 shows clearly that Christians and Muslims were considered as potential allies of foreign or domestic opponents of the regime. The fact that K'anghsi admonished his successor Yung Cheng to tolerate the missionaries in his service in Peking, but never in the provinces, demonstrated the limits of even that Emperor's attitude. A special problem was posed by the Mandarins. Many of them intensely disliked having foreigners on equal footing with them or, worse yet, having them as their superiors. In addition, most missionaries misunderstood Buddhism and Taoism. Their attacks on Buddhist and Taoist superstitions frequently affected the Confucian circles of the Mandarins as well because syncretism had taken place among them long ago.[141] The missionaries in Peking and to a larger extent their defenders in Europe pointed to the papal condemnation of the Chinese Rites as the main cause. A connection cannot be denied. Yet the issue of the rites and their significance requires a more subtle treatment.

The issue of the rites refers to the often violent quarrels regarding the sanction of Chinese ceremonies and observances for use by the Christians. Closely connected with this were the proclamation and obligation of the positive commandments of the Church.[142] Four stages in this issue can be identified in China.

Thanks to the authority of the mission's founder, Matteo Ricci (d.

Bishop A. de Gouvea in Peking with sixteen European missionaries (Propaganda Archives, Rome, *Scritture riferite nei Congressi* 38, fol. 255/56).

[140] We need only mention the Austrian Jesuit Gottfried von Laimbeckhoven, who was appointed bishop of Nanking in 1752, but could not enter his bishopric until 1768 because of the fear of his Christians. Until his death in 1787 he had no fixed residence, being forced to wander constantly. After the abolition of his order Portugal did not pay him a salary for a period of years. He nonetheless felt bound to his oath as a *Padroado* bishop, which, in turn, brought him into conflict with the Roman authorities (J. Krahl, S.J., *China Missions in Crisis. Bishop Laimbeckhoven and His Times 1738–87* [Rome 1964]).

[141] The Dominican Domingo Fern. Navarrete wrote about this phenomenon after his sojourn in China (1658–69) and added that he had heard of a Christian in Peking who also wanted to merge Christianity with these three religions (J. S. Cummins, *The Travels and Controversies of Friar Domingo de Navarrete (1618–86)* II [London 1962], 249 [see also I, LXIX]).

[142] Concerning these peripheral questions, see X. Bürkler, *Die Sonn- und Festtagsfeier in der katholischen China-Mission* (Rome and Immensee 1942); idem, Die Fasten- und Abstinenzpraxis in der chinesischen Mission," *NZM* 1 (1945), 258–71.

1610), the Jesuits initially proceeded in concert.[143] The problems within the ranks did not surface until after his death. His successor, N. Langobardi (d. 1654), took the stance that the heretofore tolerated rites and terminology were not permitted. He probably knew that Ricci's predecessor, Michele Ruggieri (d. 1607) did not have in mind an adaptation to the Confucian ideas of the well educated, but rather to the religious forces residing within the people in the form of Buddhism and Taoism.[144] The firm rejection of accommodation by the missionaries of Japan probably affirmed him in his own position.[145] Just how serious a question this was within the orders is shown by the fact that by 1665 seventy-four conferences on the issue had taken place. While Ricci and his followers, as it appears, referred to the original Confucianism, his opponents were convinced that they should consider the doctrines of the commentaries published at that time. The arrival of the Spanish mendicant orders from the Philippines in the midst of the negotiations broadened the conflict. To come to their own conclusions, the latter proceeded from the conditions as they actually were. But since they could not arrive at an understanding with the Jesuits, who were positively inclined towards the rites, they sent the Dominican J. B. de Morales to Rome, which decided the disputed issues in their favor in 1645. Shortly thereafter when the Jesuit Martin Martini of Triest (d. 1661) presented the purely private character of the rites to the Roman authorities, they were permitted by Alexander VII in 1656. For the time being there were two views which were diametrically opposed to each other. The conferences by the missionaries interned in Canton (1664–70), the efforts by the Spanish Dominican D. E. Navarrete (d. 1688),[146] and even the letter to Philipp V (1647) and Pope Innocent X (1649) by the otherwise respected and influential bishop of Puebla in Mexico, Juan de Palafox y Mendoza, were unable to change the matter in favor of the mendicant orders.[147] In addition to the objective differences there

---

[143] Among the more recent historians of the Society of Jesus H. Bernard-Maître esp. tried to prove that Matteo Ricci considered permission, while not certain, yet at least probable. Except for a brief reference in his *Storia* there is nothing at all regarding the problem of the rites. The most recent presentation of the Jesuit point of view is G. H. Dunne, *Generation of Giants* (Notre Dame 1962) (opposing viewpoints: B. Biermann, O.P., in *ZMR* 46 [1962], 296–302; B. H. Willeke, O.F.M., in *NZM* 22 [2966], 144–46).

[144] J. Shih, S.J., *Le Père Ruggieri et le problème de l'évangélisation en Chine* (Rome 1964).

[145] G. Schurhammer, S.J., *Das kirchliche Sprachproblem in der japanischen Jesuitenmission des 16. und 17. Jh.* (Tokyo 1928).

[146] J. S. Cummins, *The Travels and Controversies of Friar Domingo de Navarrete 1618–88,* 2 vols. (London 1962).

[147] Idem, "Palafox, China and the Chinese Rites Controversy," *Revista de Historia de América* 51 (Mexico City 1961), 395–427.

were also the political ones between Portugal and Spain. The arrival of the Paris Missionaries (1684) changed the situation. The Portuguese and Spanish combined to oppose the vicars apostolic. Pallu's successor, Charles Maigrot (1652–1730), decided against the rites in his letter of 1693. He was not only vicar apostolic of Fukien, but had also been appointed apostolic administrator for all of China by Pallu prior to the latter's death. After years of negotiations which escalated the disputes, which up to then had been pursued objectively, Clement XI condemned the Chinese rites (1704). Within China Maigrot's pastoral letter had split the missionary community into two camps: The Propaganda missionaries joined by the Spanish missionaries from the Philippines and, on the opposite side, the *Padroado* missionaries, most of them Jesuits. But in 1687 the French Jesuits, the "mathématiciens du Roi" (Louis XIV), had also come to China. They were not inclined to accede to the claims of the *Padroado*. They produced the men who, later on, were called the figurists or symbolists and who embarked on a third path. They searched the Chinese classics, especially the Tao Te Ching, for prophetic images and sayings which anticipated certain teachings of Christianity. They also thought that they were best able to render the Christian name of God by the ambiguous "Tao." Yet neither the superiors in China nor in Europe agreed with their ideas.[148]

The issue of the rites was one reason, though not the most important one, for dispatching the first papal legate to China, Maillard de Tournon. On 31 December 1705 he had an audience with Emperor K'anghsi—an extraordinary achievement considering Chinese circumstances—but he could not bring about the establishment of direct relations between Rome and Peking which would shunt aside the *Padroado*.[149] When the legate's health became precarious, Chinese custom forced him to leave the capital in August 1706. He was therefore unable to execute the second part of his task, the visitation of the Chinese mission. On top of it all, his departure from Peking was followed by a sharp reversal of the Emperor's formerly favorable attitude. In 1707 de Tournon published the decision of Clement XI of 1704 against the rites in a pastoral letter. Twenty-two Jesuit missionaries and the Spanish Augustinian de Benavente[150] appealed to Rome, but they made the mistake of submitting this church matter to Emperor K'anghsi

---

[148] J. Beckmann, "Die katholischen Missionare und der Taoismus vom 16. Jh. bis zur Gegenwart," *NZM* 26 (1970), 1–17.

[149] F.-A. Rouleau, S.J., "Maillard de Tournon. Papal Legate at the Court of Peking," *AHSI* 31 (1962), 264–323.

[150] An Augustinian in Colombia wrote a Latin work against this appeal; it appeared in Bogota in 1712 (see *NZM* 15 [1959], 180).

as well, who decided in their favor.[151] Upon the publication of his pastoral letter the legate was banished to Canton, where he founded the procuration of the Propaganda for the Chinese and East Indian missions which for about 150 years formed the backbone of the Propaganda mission in East Asia.[152] By his efforts he achieved the subordination in principle of all missionaries under the jurisdiction of the *Padroado* bishops, respectively vicars apostolic.[153] After an appeal by the proponents of the rites the Pope upon further examination issued the brief of 1715, reiterating the decree of 1704. Another legate, A. Mezzabarba (1719–21), was as unsuccessful as his predecessor. Besides, he had created new problems by his *Permissiones* of 1721. His orders caused Rome to reexamine the whole issue. By his bull *Ex quo singulari* (1742) Benedict XIV definitively rejected the rites.[154] Because of the persecutions by the Chinese authorities the papal bull did not meet with any substantial resistance. But towards the end of the century the issue of the rites briefly flared up again between the two vicars apostolic of the seminary of the Paris Mission, Pigneaux de Béhaine of Cochinchina and de Saint-Martin of Szechwan in western China. This time the issue was focused on certain rites of Chinese funerals, held to be permissible by the former and forbidden by the latter.[155] Because both the times and the meaning of the rites had changed, they were permitted with certain conditions and stipulations in 1939.[156]

A historian will find it difficult to render a balanced judgment on the issue of the rites in China. Both sides had in common their goodwill and the goal of building a Chinese Church. Any judgment is made more difficult by the fact that the persecutions prevented the two theories from being evaluated in actual missionary practice.[157]

---

[151] The vicars apostolic Maigrot and Mezzafalce were expelled; the Lazarist Appiani, who was accompanying the legate, was arrested and imprisoned for twenty years.

[152] S. De Munter, O.F.M., *De S. Congr. de Prop. Fide Procurae Cantonensis Primordiis* (Rome 1957).

[153] Later on the legate was himself imprisoned until his death by the Portuguese in Macao. The Pope approved of his behavior and elevated him to the cardinalate in 1707.

[154] The disputes in Europe were aggravated in 1700 by the actually justified intervention of the Sorbonne; Charles Maigrot was a doctor of theology of the University of Paris (J. Davy, "La condamnation en Sorbonne des Nouveaux Mémoires sur la Chine du P. Le Compte," *RSR* 54 [Paris 1950], 366–97).

[155] The correspondence of the two bishops in A. Launay, *Histoire des Missions de Chine, Mission du Se-tchoan* II (Paris 1920), Appendix, 21–82.

[156] *AAS* 32 (1940), 24 ff.

[157] The difficulty of an appraisal of the rites problem even for an objective historian is shown in the contribution of H. Bernard-Maître, "La correspondance Becker-Brucker sur la question des rites chinois (1885–1907)," *RSR* 54 (Paris 1966), 417–25. J. Brucker, S.J., had written the article about the rites in *DThC* on which Pastor and most

Persecutions and even the conflict of the rites led to a substantial reorientation of the missionary method in China. As of the end of the seventeenth century the main stress of missionary work was undeniably placed on the individual congregations in the provinces.[158] Knowledge of the languages, something all the orders tried to achieve, was a condition for fruitful missionary work. The first Chinese grammar was published by the Spanish Dominican Francisco Varo (1627–87) in 1703.[159] It was surpassed by the Jesuit de Prémare's *Notitia Linguae Sinicae,* completed in 1728 in Canton.[160] The first comprehensive Chinese-Latin lexicon was written by the Italian Franciscan Basilio Brollo de Gemona (1648–1719), who had been vicar apostolic of Shensi since 1700.[161] The missionaries were also pioneers in the research of Chinese dialects.[162]

Aside from the rites issue, all the missionaries were in agreement regarding their outward adaptation to the Chinese way of life and thought. All of them were satisfied with Chinese food; they clothed themselves and lived in the Chinese manner.[163] The most profound understanding was manifest in their deep respect for the social structure, the community spirit, and the spirit of the greater family. An example of true Sinicism of the Catholic form of prayer were the forms of the chanted public prayers alive all over China. As far as we know, the form of private prayer in the European manner did not develop in China.[164]

---

of the other historians based their work. Father Émile Becker was superior of the China mission in the province of Hopei; in reference to the rites problem he wrote: "Quand on veut justifier la Compagnie dans la question des rites chinois, il ne faut pas chercher à rejeter sur les autres tous les torts" (op. cit., 419).

[158] The individual investigations by J. Dehergne, S.J., of the status of the missions around 1700 provide an extremely valuable overview (see *AHSI* 22 [1953], 314–38; 24 [1955], 251–94; 28 [1959], 289–330; 30 [1961], 307–66; 36 [1967], 32–71, 221–46; idem, "La mission de Pékin à la veille de la condamnation des rites," *NZM* 9 [1953], 91–108).

[159] J. M. González, O.P., "Semblanzas Misioneras: P. Francisco Varo OP," *MH* 12 (Madrid 1954), 145–91.

[160] De Prémare sent the manuscript to his "friend" Fourmont in Paris, who had just written his own grammar, that is he had translated the one by P. Varo from the Spanish; so the manuscript disappeared. It was published in Malacca in 1831 by Protestant missionaries (1666–1736) (Streit V, 958).

[161] Streit V, 874 f.; *Sinica Franciscana* VI, 789–802.

[162] Yang Fu-mien, S.J., "The Catholic Missionary Contribution to the Study of Chinese Dialects," *Orbis* 9 (Louvain 1960), 158–85.

[163] The first doubts concerning the suitability of a Chinese diet for Europeans appeared in the nineteenth century; they were increasingly affirmed.

[164] For the text of the prayers, see Paul Brunner, S.J., *L'Eucholog de la Mission de Chine* (Münster 1964). The rich Mass proclamation of the Alsatian Jesuit R. Hinderer (1669–1744) was sung by the Christians (P. Brunner, S.J., "La Messe Chinoise du Père Hinderer," *NZM* 15 [1959], 271–84).

With the exception of Macao there was no possibility of establishing true convents in China. So the Dominican missionaries went back to the form of the *Beata* popular in Spain. The Chinese virgins, while taking their vows, continued to live with their families, where they taught the women and children and during the times of persecution became the true pillars of the faith within the greater families.[165] The Paris Missionaries introduced this institution in their missions in Szechwan. In 1744 the vicar apostolic de Martillac published the first rules of conduct for them in a pastoral letter. Later on these rules were adapted to changing conditions, especially by the blessed Jean-Martin Moyë (1730–93), who implemented this institution outside the family as well. The synod of Szechwan of 1803 extended it to include all of China. One of the most beautiful documents of a natural and generous adaptation are the so-called *Ordonnances de la Sainte Église,* which originated during the persecutions after 1644 and served as guidelines for parishes deprived of their priests.[166] The *Ordonnances* also instructed the catechists and Christians how to propagate the faith without polemics running counter to accepted Chinese views.[167]

One of the consequences of the persecutions from 1664 to 1670 was that probably all the missionaries accepted the need for a native clergy. After the return to their stations they were able to see what the first Chinese priest, the Dominican Lo Wen-tsao (1617–91),[168] had done to save the congregations. But differences of opinion arose in regard to their education. By his brief *Romanae Sedis Antistes* of 27 June 1615 Paul V had allowed the use of Chinese as a liturgical language. During the persecutions Ludovico Buglio had started the necessary translation, but his Jesuit superiors in Macao had not released the brief for purposes of practical missionary work.[169] So the missionaries of the order and later on the missionaries of the Paris Seminary sought to apply papal permission. Yet as time went on they encountered less and less understanding for their wishes in Rome. Initially their efforts led to a compromise. As early as 1659 the vicars apostolic received permission to ordain Chinese

---

[165] B. Biermann, O.P., *Die Anfänge der neueren Dominikanermission in China* (Münster 1927), 163–65.

[166] H. Verhaeren, C.M., "Ordonnances de la Sainte Église," *Monumenta Serica* 4 (Peking 1939–46), 451–77 (Chinese text with French trans.)

[167] Op. cit., 456 f. We should mention the areas of Christian art, the liturgical vestments and the churches (as late as 1936 I was permitted to visit the church in Shanghai built by Father Brancati in 1640, which had the shape of a Chinese temple) (S. Schüller, *Die Gesch. der christlichen Kunst in China* [Berlin 1940]).

[168] J. M. González, O.P., *El primer Obispo Chino* (Villalva 1967).

[169] J. Jennes, "A propos de la liturgie chinoise. Le Bref Romanae Sedis Antistes de Paul V (1615)," *NZM* 2 (1964), 241–54; for a treatment of the entire problem, see F. Bontinck, *La lutte autour de la liturgie chinoise au XVIe et XVIIIe siècles* (Louvain 1962).

natives, as long as they could read Latin, even if they did not understand it. In accordance with that, the first Chinese bishop, the above-mentioned Lo Wen-tsao, ordained the first Chinese priests in China on 1 August 1688.[170]

It was strictly an expedient, for all the orders tried to give their Chinese clerics a thorough education in Latin, the Jesuits in Macao, the Dominicans in Manila, and the Paris Missionaries in their Seminary General in Siam. There the German Lazarist Johannes Müllener (1673–1742), vicar apostolic of Szechwan since 1715, had personally trained men for the priesthood and was able to ordain four of them before he died.[171] The Propaganda missionary Mateo Pipa (1682–1746) even tried to educate seminarians in the imperial city of Peking, but defamations forced him to give up his undertaking. Yet as one of few European missionaries he received permission to take his Chinese students to Europe in 1723. In Naples he founded a college, the congregation for secular priests of the Holy Family. Since the missionaries of the Propaganda, especially those of the vicariate of Shensi, regularly sent over candidates who were already trained, more and more new missionaries could be sent from Naples to China.[172] However, the perils of the trip and the disadvantages of a lengthy and alienating sojourn abroad prompted the missionaries to educate native priests in China. The blessed J. M. Moyë, one of the most eager champions of this idea, was the first to take on this task, which he later transferred to his fellow religious, Thomas Hamel (1745–1812). The latter continued this work for thirty-five years in the hard-to-approach border region between Szechwan and Yünnan. Before he died, he graduated twenty priests from his seminary.[173] All of these Chinese priests pursued their apostolic work during the periods of persecution in the eighteenth century.[174] The diary (not intended for publication) of one of them, Andreas Li (1692–1775), for a long time the only priest of the province of Szechwan, offers an intimate insight into the details

---

[170] J. Beckmann, *Die lateinische Bildung des chinesischen Klerus im 17. und 18. Jh.;* J. Beckmann, *Der einheimische Klerus in Gesch. und Gegenwart (Festschr. L. Kilger)* (Schöneck/Beckenried 1950), 163–87.

[171] J. v. den Brandt. op. cit., 17.

[172] M. Ripa, *Storia della Fondazione della Congregazione et del Collegio dei Cinesi,* 3 vols. (Naples 1832). Until the closing of the college by the Italian government in 1869 it had graduated 106 Chinese priests (*Elenchus Alumnorum, Decreta et Documenta quae spectant ad Collegium S. Familiae Neapolis* [Shanghai 1917], 1–10).

[173] A. Launay, *Mémorial,* 307.

[174] X. Bürkler, "Die Bewährungsgeschichte des chinesischen Klerus im 17. und 18. Jh.," in: J. Beckmann, *Der einheimische Klerus in Gesch. und Gegenwart (Festschr. Kilger)* (Schöneck/Beckenried 1950), 119–42.

of the work and problems of the Chinese clergy.[175] He refused the rank of bishop, which his European brethren intended for him to have. In view of this attitude during a period of persecution the Propaganda seriously considered the consecration of bishops from the ranks of the Chinese priests,[176] even though the larger circles were lacking the necessary sympathy for this plan.

In 1762, in the midst of persecutions and quarrels within the missionary community, Pombal's order to arrest the Jesuits arrived; twenty-four fathers and brothers were taken to Lisbon. In the interior of China it was the actual papal abolition of the order in 1773 that had a disastrous effect after it arrived in 1775 and was announced by Bishop von Laimbeckhoven in his role as bishop of Nanking and administrator of Peking. The few Jesuits in the interior were able to continue their work because the power of Portugal could not reach them there. In Peking this measure caused a schism. After almost ten years of negotiations the Portuguese and French Lazarists were finally willing to continue the work of the Jesuits.[177] The advances on the part of the French and the Spanish to establish a French patronage bishopric in Mukden (Manchuria)[178] and a Spanish one in Fukien[179] were rejected by Rome. On 29 April 1785 when the first French Lazarists arrived in Peking with the new bishop of Peking, A. de Gouvea, the latter succeeded in allaying the schism. The new superior of the French Lazarists and of the *Peitang,* Joseph Raux (1754–1801), was not only a superior mathematician (in 1795 he was appointed mandarin of the mathematical institute), but he also had a well-balanced personality. Thus he was able to win over the French Jesuits while opposing all attempts for autonomy of the French mission.

It was during the last decades of the eighteenth century that the Korean Church originated. After some initial fleeting contacts and a few

---

[175] *Journal d'André Ly, 1746–1763,* ed. by A. Launay (Paris 1906). The diary containing almost seven hundred pages consists of the annual reports.

[176] J. Beckmann, "Beratungen der Propaganda-Kongregation über die Weihe chinesischer Bischöfe (1787–1819)," *Missionswissenschaft und Religionswissenschaft* 3 (Münster 1940), 199–217.

[177] H. Cordier, "La suppression de la Compagnie de Jésus et la Mission de Pékin," *T'oung Pao* 17 (Leiden 1916), 217–347, 561–623; *Mémoires de la Congrégation de la Mission. La Chine* II (Paris 1912); C. de Rochemonteix, *Jos. Amoit* (Paris 1915), 258ff., 379ff.

[178] C. de Rochemonteix, op. cit., 437–53. Memorandum by Jos. Amiot of 1 October 1774; this was supported by another by the Count de Vergennes in Paris of 1 March 1779 (text in the Propaganda Archives, Rome, *Scritture riferite nei Congressi,* Vol. 36, fol. 35ff.).

[179] J. Beckmann, "Ein spanischer Versuch zur Errichtung von Patronatsbistümern in China und Hinterindien (1778–82)," *ZMR* 27 (1937), 164–72.

conversions in the course of the Japanese wars of conquest of the 16th century,[180] Christian ideas were spread in Korea by means of religious literature created by the Peking missionaries in the seventeenth and eighteenth century. It is certain that the first Korean baptized in the Church of the *Peitang* in 1784 already knew of the necessity for baptism; he became the first apostle of the as yet priestless Church of his country. The Korean embassies to Peking were a way to create firmer ties with the young lay Church. But not until 1793 did Bishop de Gouvea, to whom the Propaganda had expressly given the direction of the Korean Church, succeed in sending one of his Chinese priests to Korea; he was executed in 1801 as a victim of persecution. As early as 1791 persecutions had flared up here and there; cases of martyrdom show that the Church was firmly anchored. In his report to the Propaganda of 1797 Bishop de Gouvea spoke of four thousand Korean Christians.[181]

JAPAN

Most accounts of missionary history end the presentation of the Kirishitan period with a note on the persecutions. The actual time of suffering by the Japanese Christians, however, did not start until Japan was completely sealed off from the outside.[182] Yet by no means did the efforts by Christendom to aid the Japanese Church stop. After the peasant revolt of 1637/38, initially a social act of desperation on the part of the exploited populace, the Christians had to pay a high tribute in blood. Thirty thousand men, women, and children were executed. The most stringent regulations forbade any and all connections with other countries, including the Philippines and Macao. In 1640 when Macao, hit hard by the prohibition of trade, tried to change the minds of the Japanese by sending its own delegation of ambassadors, the four ambassadors and fifty-seven of the ship's crew were executed. Thirteen were allowed to return to Macao in order to spread the word of the horrible deed.[183] Deshima, a small island off Nagasaki, which had served as a residence for Portuguese merchants, was assigned to the Dutch in 1640; from there they barely managed to maintain their trade monopoly with Japan until 1854.[184] The closing off to the outside world, applying of

---

[180] J. Laures, "Koreas erste Berührung mit dem Christentum," *ZMR* (1956), 177–89, 282–87.

[181] A. Choi, *L'Érection du premier Vicariat Apostolique et les origines du catholicisme en Corée* (Schöneck/Beckenried 1961), 1–60.

[182] Arimichi Ebisawa, "The Jesuits and their Cultural Activities in the Far East," *Cahiers de l'Histoire Mondiale* 5 (Neuchâtel 1959), 345–74.

[183] C. R. Boxer, *The Great Ship from Amacon, Annals of Macao and the old Japan Trade, 1555–1640* (Lisbon 1959), 163ff., 331ff.

[184] It is not true that the Dutch also demanded "stepping on the pictures."

course also to Japanese who wanted to travel abroad, was accompanied by ruthless actions against the native Christians. In 1640 the "Office of Inquisition for Christian Affairs" was established in Edo (i.e., Tokyo) with its own buildings, jails, trial procedures, and judges. Approximately two thousand trials against Christians were conducted under its first inquisitor, Inoue Masashige (1585–1661).[185] The surveillance of Christians was closely tied to the social system of the "Five Families," which were answerable for one another.[186] Especially artful was the procedure of the E-Fumi.[187] Usually around New Year's all inhabitants of the island of Kyushu, but also those of other areas, had to step on a Christian picture or a cross, an act which was carefully recorded by the authorities in the form of a protocol. Even foreign merchants, with the exception of the Dutch, were forced to undergo this test upon landing on Japanese shores. This procedure was not abolished until 1857. In addition there were official rewards for the denunciation of Christians the amounts of which were scaled in accordance with the stature of the accused within the Church.[188] The uncovered Christians were taken to the jail of the inquisition in Edo, most of them to be tortured most horribly. During the *tsurushi* those tortured were hung by their feet above a deep hole; the slightest movement was considered a sign of apostasy. In 1633 the Jesuit provincial Cristovão Ferreira broke under this torture. He married and became a spy and interpreter for the Japanese inquisition.[189] But the apostates did not have it easy; for generations they and their descendants were subject to humiliating special rules. When the persecution reached its climax (about 1680–1700), all visible signs of Christianity had disappeared, but the Japanese authorities knew their countrymen well: the uncovering of the Old Christians of Nagasaki in the nineteenth century attested to the presence of a

---

[185] For the official accounts of his activities, his guidelines for the conduct of trials, etc., see *Kirishito-Ki;* German by G. Voss and H. Cielsik, *Kirishito-Ki und Sayoyo-roku. Japanische Dokumente zur Missiongeschichte des 17. Jh.* (Tokyo 1940); H. Cieslik, "Das Christen-Verbot in Japan unter dem Tokugawa-Regime," *NZM* 6 (1950), 175–92, 256–72; 7 (1951), 24–36.

[186] H. Cielsik, "Die Fünferschaft im Dienste der Christenüberwachung," *Monumenta Nipponica* 7 (Tokyo 1951), 102–55.

[187] M. Marega, "E-Fumi," *Monumenta Nipponica* 2 (Tokyo 1939), 281–86; idem, "Memorie cristiane della Regione di Oita," *Annali Lateranensi* 3 (1939), 9–59.

[188] Details in H. Cieslik in *NZM* 6 (1950), 188f.

[189] Ibid., 259; Ferreira died in 1650; it can probably not be ascertained whether he died a repentant martyr as rumored in India. There were also local persecutions of Christians where they were killed on the spot: Cieslik lists a number of such cases of martyrdom involving hundreds of Christians from 1657 to 1680 on the island of Kyushu (ibid., 262).

Christian underground. Missionaries kept arriving, such as the second Rubino group of four fathers, one brother, and five catechists, who were caught immediately upon landing. Although the inquisitor Inoue later told the Dutch that they had apostatized during the *tsurushi,* this was not likely because none of them was freed, as Ferreira had been. All of them, in fact, died in prison.

The former missionaries of Macao, especially, tried to help the Japanese Christians by means of literature, but the authorities quickly composed lists of banned books.[190] Even at the end of the century it was decreed: "Whoever secretly introduces Christian writings or articles into Japan, will be executed without exception."[191] Yet again and again European ideas, especially in the fields of the natural sciences and medicine, but also in religion, infiltrated Japanese writings. At about this time there were lively discussions by Buddhist and other parties about Christianity.[192] Some learned Japanese who no longer wanted to be apart from European sciences published their work under a Dutch name, under the tolerated "Dutch Flag." They even managed to designate Jesuit works imported from China as works by Dutch scientists.[193]

As soon as it was established, the Propaganda paid close attention to the Japanese mission, especially after the Dominican Diego Collado arrived in Rome in 1622. The long negotiations resulted in the bull *Ex debito Pastoralis officii* (1633), which assured missionaries of all orders free access to Japan by any and all routes.[194] The lack of familiarity with conditions in Japan and the efforts by Rome to exclude Japan from the Portuguese *Padroado* led to difficulties and delays in the appointment of new bishops.[195] But the Propaganda did not neglect the Japan mission; it sought information from the missionaries in China.[196] A remarkable

---

[190] Such lists also form the basis of the works by H. Bernard, "Traductions chinoises d'ouvrages européens au Japon durant la période de fermeture (1614–1853)." *Monumenta Nipponica* 3 (1949), 40–60.

[191] H. Cieslik in *NZM* 6 (1950), 185.

[192] J. van Hecken, "Le problème du dialogue chrétien avec les Bouddhistes du Japon," *NZM* 23 (1967), 3ff.; H. Cieslik, "Nambanzi-Romane der Tokugawa-Zeit," *Monumenta Nipponica* 6 (1943), 13–51. These anti-Christian novels, some of which were not printed until the Meiji period, especially demonstrated the fact that Christian views among the people remained alive for centuries.

[193] Cf. Arimichi Ebisawa, op. cit., esp. 369ff.

[194] L. M. Pedot, *La S. C. de Propaganda Fide e le Missioni del Giappone (1622–1838)* (Vicenza 1946); Text of the bull in L. Magnino, *Pontificia Nipponica* I (Rome 1947), 160–64.

[195] H. Cieslik, "Zur Gesch. der kirchlichen Hierarchie in der alten Japanmission," *NZM* 18 (1962), 42–58, 81–107, 177–95 (esp. 188–95); also L. M. Pedot, op. cit., 163–221.

[196] L. M. Pedot, op. cit., 314–41.

undertaking was that of the Italian secular priest Giovanni B. Sidotti (1668–1715), who arrived in Manila in 1704 and four years later made a covert landing on the Japanese coast. After three days he was caught and taken to the inquisition's jail in Edo, where he died in 1715 what was probably a martyr's death.[197] During his imprisonment he encountered the Japanese philosopher and statesman Arai Hakuseki (1657–1725), who interrogated him for three years. In the process Hakuseki obtained excellent insight into the Christian religion, which he put down in two works. Although he rejected Christianity as an absurdity, his was one of the best presentations written in Japanese. It was helped by the fact that he was a confirmed Confucian who did not hide his rejection of Buddhism and Shintoism. Thus, through him Sidotti influenced the educated Japanese well into the nineteenth century.[198]

The continued spread of persecutions after the 1720s prompted many Japanese Christians to flee abroad, as long as flight was still possible. This is how the Japanese Christian congregations in the large port and mercantile city of Faifo originated. In this Japanese quarter the expelled missionaries found a new field of action.[199] Another refuge was Ajuthia, the capital of Siam, where the Japanese merchants already had a base. Here, too, the Jesuits took care of the Christians and converted others.[200] Manila also became a haven for many Christians from the missions of the Spanish mendicant orders. Japanese seminarians and religious were able to receive their ordination either in Macao or Manila and some of them were able to return to their native land as missionaries.[201] Yet the congregations abroad did not endure, since the Japanese were assimilated more and more by their host countries. But the interest in Japan stayed alive among the missionaries. Even in distant Mexico a Japanese grammar was printed as late as 1738 in the unshakable hope that it would serve new missionaries in Japan.[202]

---

[197] A bio-bibliographical sketch in Streit VI, 403–5; for the years in Edo, see R. Tassinari, "The End of Padre Sidotti. Some New Discoveries," *Monumenta Nipponica* 5 (1942), 246–53.

[198] Furukawa Tetsushi, "The Growth of Anti-Religious Rationalism and the Development of the Scientific Method in Japan," *Cahiers de l'Histoire Mondiale* 7 (1963), 739–55.

[199] H. Chappoulie, op. cit. I, 170, 180.

[200] H. Cieslik, "Die erste Jesuitenmission in Siam 1626–30," *NZM* 26 (1970).

[201] H. Cieslik, "Das Schicksal der letzten Japan-Missionare im 17. Jh.," *NZM* 13 (1957), 9–28, 119–38; idem, "The Training of a Japanese Clergy in the Seventeenth Century," *Studies in Japanese Culture* (Tokyo 1963), 41–73.

[202] J. Laures, *Kirishitan Bunko* (Tokyo 1957), 125–26.

THE PHILIPPINES AND THE SOUTH SEAS

Concerning the Philippine Church in the seventeenth and eighteenth century there is abundant source material[203] which has hardly been evaluated.[204] And yet these two centuries were of decisive importance for the Christianization of the Philippines. After 1595 Manila and its suffragan bishoprics of Nueva Segovia, Nueva Cáceres and Cebú were an archbishopric. Five orders had organized their own provinces: the Augustinian Hermits, the Jesuits, Dominicans, Franciscans, and the Augustinian Recollects. As far back as 1594 Philip II had divided that vast island realm among the various orders. The most important islands were conquered by the Spanish almost without bloodshed; the natives joined the Christian faith without resistance. To be sure, violent acts by the Spanish, who initially thought they could continue their American methods of colonialization on the Philippines, here and there led to bloody revolt and the assassination of missionaries, but by and large the islands enjoyed a tranquil political and religious development.

By the end of the seventeenth century the Islamic faith, whose missionaries were active mostly on Mindanao, but also on Luzon among the Malay tribes at the time of the arrival of the Spaniards, had been pushed back. As a consequence Islam made no additional progress towards the east. This was made possible only through the Christianization of the Philippine populace and the tight organization of their congregations. In the cities these formed around the core of the Spanish population; in the more sizeable villages they were centered around the churches and monasteries. The attempt at enslaving the Filipinos, a continuation of the method in South America, was quickly turned back by the government and the Church. The country was poor; the colonists subsisted mainly on the trade between China and Mexico. A population on such a low level did not have a particular attraction for the missionaries either. The first generation considered the Philippines to be no more than a transit station on the way to China.[205] In fact the mendicant orders

[203] Streit V, 237–361 for the seventeenth century and VI, 239–400 for the eighteenth century. The most important collection of sources, *The Philippine Island,* by Blair-Robertson, comprises fifty-five vols. of documents, mostly trans. from the Spanish (Cleveland 1903–9). The collection by Torres y Lanzas, *Catálogo de los documentos relativos a las islas Filipinas* (Barcelona 1925–36) totaled nine vols.

[204] E. g., the four-volume work by S. Delacroix II. The most recent Catholic history of the mission by A. Mulders (1960) also deals very briefly with the beginnings in the sixteenth and seventeenth century (221–23), continuing with the history of the nineteenth century (387–88). Only K. S. Latourette, Vol. III, 307–21 continues to the end of the eighteenth century.

[205] J. Beckmann, *China im Blickfeld der mexikanischen Bettelorden im 16. Jh.* (Schöneck/Beckenried 1964), 46–65.

always maintained missions there, as they did in China, East India, and previously in Japan, whereas the Jesuits were prohibited by their superiors from any sort of activity in the provinces of their brethren of the Portuguese *Padroado*.[206] In the course of the seventeenth century the direction of the missionary effort seems to have changed, concentrating as it did on the Philippines. More and more reinforcements arrived from Mexico and Spain. Missionizing the population in the environs of the bases on the major islands was concluded around 1650. It was then expanded to the less accessible islands. The Augustinian Hermits, carrying the main burden of mission and ministry, had to request protection by royal laws from having their reinforcements, destined for the Philippines, intercepted in Mexico.[207] When local superiors in Spain put up increasing numbers of obstacles, the Philippine province of the Name of Jesus founded the Real Colegio Seminario of Valladolid (1743), which is still a replacement center even today.[208]

This uninterrupted supply of missionaries demands deep respect[209] inasmuch as the work outside the urban centers required extreme physical exertion.[210] It was there that a realistic counterweight to the China rapture was created which can compare even with the martyrdom in Japan.[211]

The tranquility of the development of the Philippine Church was disturbed by disputes between the bishops and the regular clergy.[212] In 1567 upon the request of Philipp II, Pope Pius V made an exception for the mission countries with their vast distances and small number of bishops. He granted permission to the orders to pursue their ministry independently of all episcopal authority. But in 1585 the Spanish king, first for the Council of Mexico and then for all Spanish dominions, ruled that the orders be subject to episcopal visitation. This led to many a conflict in the Philippines. For all practical purposes the bishops throughout the seventeenth and eighteenth century had to give in on

---

[206] Some Jesuits even considered this prohibition the cause of many a case of depression of younger missionaries and of their untimely death (H. de la Costa, op. cit., 244–45).

[207] J. Beckmann in *NZM* 23 (1967), 148.

[208] M. Merino, op. cit., XVIII–XX.

[209] The number of Augustinian Hermits until about the eighteenth century would have been over fifteen hundred according to the necrology compiled by M. Merino for the occasion of the four hundredth Anniversary of the Christianization of the Philippines (op. cit.). Until their abolition the number of Jesuits was on the average one hundred fifty in the course of the eighteenth century (H. de la Costa, op. cit., 553).

[210] A vivid picture is provided by J. Schmitz, *Die Abra-Mission auf Nordluzón, Philippinen (1598–1955)* (St. Augustin 1964).

[211] Cases of martyrdom were exceptions in the Philippines.

[212] H. de la Costa, "Episcopal Jurisdiction in the Philippines During the Spanish Regime," in G. H. Anderson, op. cit., 44–64.

this issue, especially since the privations during travel did not make the visitations very attractive. Archbishop Felipe Pardo (1611–89) there-fore attempted to prevail in his privileges in Manila against the opposi-tion of the secular authorities as well as the Jesuits.[213] But the latter enjoyed enough political support to make the archbishop lose the ensu-ing lawsuits.[214] A closely related issue was the authority to be granted the secular clergy to whom the organized parishes were to be trans-ferred according to an order of Philip III (1603). But almost all the Spanish secular priests were living in the cities, occupying the positions of the cathedral chapters, so that every time there was the merest threat of a conflict with the bishop, the orders threatened to remove all their members from the mission stations. This invariably forced the bishop to give in. The idea of a native clergy was as yet rejected, even by Arch-bishop Pardo, although he changed his mind shortly before his death in 1689.[215] It does appear that while Pallu was being held by the Philip-pine authorities in 1672 he first formulated a plan for training a native clergy.[216] In 1680 high ranking civil servants sent a pertinent letter to Madrid. In 1702 Philip V ordered the establishment of a seminary for eight seminarians. Two years later Sidotti arrived in Manila and with the help of the citizens there founded the seminary, but large enough for seventy-two seminarians. It was demolished by order of the King and replaced by one for eight seminarians, as had been ordered. This aroused a spirit of opposition in Manila. Although its seminary was not built until 1772, Dominicans and Jesuits, in the spirit of sincere compe-tition, must have admitted Filipinos to the study of theology before that. At any rate, around the middle of the century there was already a relatively strong native clergy in existence who were not limited to auxiliary service, as Philip V had ordered.

This sign of opposition[217] can be seen as well in connection with the attempted Hispanization of the islands, demanded again and again by Madrid. The state wanted to suppress the native languages by any means. Yet with the exception of Manila no country did as little as the Philippines in cultivating the Spanish language. The missionaries everywhere were propagating the faith in the native languages and the

---

[213] H. de la Costa, *The Jesuits,* esp. 489–502 and passim; F. Fernandez, op. cit., 189–93.
[214] In the anti-Jesuit disputes this trial was given widespread attention in Europe. See the work about him published in Lugano in 1760 (Streit VI, 308).
[215] J. S. Cummins, "Archbishop Felipo Padro's 'Last Will,' " G. H. Anderson, op. cit., 105–12.
[216] H. de la Costa, "The Development of the Native Clergy in the Philippines," in G. H. Anderson, op. cit., 65–104.
[217] H. de la Costa, *The Development,* 86ff.

orders, in fact, demanded of them the requisite linguistic skills.[218] Paradoxically, Spain owed its great success in the Philippines precisely to the opposition of the lower level provincial bureaucrats and to the missionaries.[219] Not only did the latter create the linguistic basis, such as grammars and dictionaries, needed for research in the most important languages of the Philippines,[220] but an abundant Christian literature as well.[221]

The tranquil development of the Philippine Church was suddenly interrupted by the expulsion of the Jesuits by Charles III in 1767. It involved 148 Jesuits, six colleges, nine residences and three missions.[222] But since the Society of Jesus did not have a dominant part in the ministry there, their expulsion could be compensated for more quickly in the Philippines than in other countries. But the state absolutism which manifested itself in this matter was fraught with serious consequences.[223]

Because their general had forbidden the Jesuits to work in the territories of the Portuguese *Padroado,* they looked for other missionary fields in the Pacific, foremost on the Mariana and Caroline Islands. The founder of the first permanent mission on Guam was Diego Luis Sanvitore (1627–72), who was murdered by an apostate a few years later. In the ensuing revolts of the natives in 1674–76 and 1684/85 twelve more Jesuit missionaries were killed. Yet the main islands were already predominantly Christian around 1740. The Mariana and Caroline Islands gradually turned into way stations and were no longer attended by missionaries on a regular basis.[224]

As early as the turn of the seventeenth century Franciscans from Peru who had come to the South Seas with the discoverer Pedro Fernando de Quirós explored the Solomon Islands and the New Hebrides.

---

[218] The Augustinian Recollects even planned the establishment of a monastery in Salamanca for the study of the major language, Tagalog. The plan was approved by the Propaganda in 1626, but probably disallowed by Madrid (see *Bullarium Ordinis Recollectorum S. Augustini* II [Rome 1961], 77, 78, 82).

[219] J. L. Phelan, *The Hispanization of the Philippines. Spanish Aims and Filipino Responses 1565–1700* (Madison 1959).

[220] J. L. Phelan, op. cit., 51f.; idem, "Philippine Linguistics and Spanish Missionaries 1565–1700," *Mid-America* 37 (Chicago 1955), 153–70; N. Cushner, "A Note on Jesuits, Linguistics and the Philippine Missions," *NZM* 19 (1963), 116–21.

[221] The references in the volumes of Streit alone provide abundant material for a history of this Christian literature yet to be written.

[222] N. Cushner, *Philippine Jesuits in Exile. The Journal of Francisco Puig SJ 1768–1770* (Rome 1964).

[223] K. S. Latourette, *History* III, 313.

[224] E. J. Burrus, "Jesuits and Terra Australis," *NZM* 22 (1966) 89–97; idem, "Sanvitores" Grammar and Catechism in the Mariana (or Chamorro) Language (1668)," *Anthropos* 49 (Fribourg 1954), 934–60; Streit XXI, 1–82.

But their plans for a mission became illusory after the untimely death of de Quirós.[225] Later attempts by Juan de Silva (1617–94) were also unsuccessful, as was an expedition to Tahiti in 1774/75, inasmuch as it did not result in a permanent mission station there. But successes are not a measure of Christian missionary spirit.

[225] C. Kelly, *La Austrialia del Espíritu Santo,* 2 vols. (Cambridge 1966).

PART TWO

The Established Church and the Enlightenment

Concepts

CHAPTER 18

*Foundations and Forms of the Established Church
in the Bourbon States of the Seventeenth and Eighteenth Centuries*

The decline of papal power from the middle of the seventeenth century, contrasted with the intellectual and spiritual flowering of baroque Catholicism and the development of royal absolutism, is manifested not only by the European peace congresses,[1] the unsuccessful protests against the Prussian demand for the royal title (1701), and the establishment of the house of Hanover as the ninth electorate (1707). The papal elections and the use of the *ius exclusivae* by Catholic powers[2] demonstrate even more clearly the deterioration of the international esteem in which the papacy had been held previously[3] and the growing strength of the concept of the established Church. To be sure, the papal elections during the seventeenth and eighteenth century almost invariably fell on deserving candidates. Yet they were aged and in many cases because of age and illness they were unable to respond to the demands of their office.

The interests of the state and the ambitions of absolutist rule over the Church turned almost every conclave into a battleground mainly between France on one side and Spain and Austria on the other, with all

---

[1] J. Müller, *Das Friedenswerk der Kirche* (1927) (inadequate). Except in Pastor XIV–XVI, the role of the Popes in the European congresses after 1648 and the peace nunciatures is only treated in monographs, e.g., A. v. Reumont, "Mons. Agostino Franciotti und der Aachener Friede von 1668," *Zschr. des Aachener Geschichtsvereins* 5 (1883), 53–74; C. Terlinden, "La diplomatie pontificale et la paix d'Aix-la-Chapelle de 1668," *Bulletin de l'Institut Historique Belge de Rome* 27 (1952), 249–68; S. v. Lengefeld, *Graf Domenico Passionei, päpstlicher Legat in der Schweiz 1714–16* (Zurich 1900) (needs to be supplemented); G. V. Vella, *Il Passionei e la politica di Clemente IX, 1708–16* (Rome 1953); I. P. Dengel, *Die politische und kirchliche Tätigkeit des Monsignor Josef Garampi in Deutschland 1761–63. Geheime Sendung zum geplanten Friedenskongreß in Augsburg und Visitation des Reichsstiftes Salem* (Rome 1905).

[2] E. H. Feine, *RG,* 575f., with biblio.

[3] "The conditions under Benedict XIII reduced the Pope to an object of ridicule by the European governments, as clearly indicated by the reports of ambassadors" (Seppelt-Schwaiger V, 424).

parties seeking preliminary decisions reflecting their ambitions for an established and national Church. Until the middle of the eighteenth century each succeeding pontificate endured growing pressure from Spain, France, Austria, and the Bourbon secundogenitures of Italy. In addition, the militarily helpless, irreparably indebted Papal States, which could no longer fulfill their original purpose of ensuring freedom of action for the head of the Church, inescapably enmeshed the Popes in the tumult of the Italian policies of the great powers. Rigid adherence to outdated legal claims, such as feudal supremacy over the Kingdom of the Two Sicilies and the duchy of Parma-Piacenza challenged those states which were in the process of integrating to take ever harsher countermeasures against palpal church supremacy, *pirateria beneficiale,* nunciatures, and ecclesiastical jurisdiction.

The desire to influence the papal elections had grown in proportion to Italy's having become the battleground of the European powers and the growing conviction that the inviolability of the Papal States appeared better safeguarded by an Italian prince than by the head of Christianity. The *ius exclusivae* of the Kings of Spain, France, and the German Emperor, applied more and more frequently since the middle of the seventeenth century and based on legalities of the established Church, was "in reality a demand of the voters not to give their vote to a certain candidate in the interest of peace between the state and the Church"[4] and to exclude that candidate legally.

At the very beginning of the conclave following the death of Urban VIII (d. 29 July 1644) Spain eliminated the candidate of the Barberini party, Cardinal Giulio Sacchetti, by means of the *ius exclusivae*. It repeated this action against the same candidate in the conclave of 1655. In 1644, however, Mazarin's veto against Cardinal Giambattista Pamfili arrived too late to forestall his election (Innocent X, 1644–55). At the next election in 1655 Mazarin also failed in his opposition to Fabio Chigi (Alexander VII, 1655–67). The election of Giulio Rospigliosi was by no means owing to the protection of Louis XIV alone, even though it was later represented in this manner by the French. The Spanish, not knowing of France's sympathy for him, had also supported Rospigliosi. Finally, the latter had also impressed the *Squadrone volante* as the most suitable candidate. Clement IX, whose election, then, had not been clouded by any exclusion, was granted the privilege of having a part in ending the war between Spain and France and bringing about the Peace of Aachen (2 May 1668). By doing so, he was able to attenuate the humiliation of the papacy by the Peace of Pisa (1664) and to weaken the French concept of an established Church.[5]

[4] Wahrmund, *Die kaiserliche Exklusive im Konklave Innozenz' XIII.,* 15.

[5] Regarding the intention of Franz Egon von Fürstenberg to play the role of a peace

The conclave upon his death was again characterized by opposition between Spain and France and a heretofore unprecedented influence by the ambassadors. The French ambassador Chaulnes formally applied the *ius exclusivae* to Cardinal d'Elce, whereas the Spanish ambassador Astorga presented the reservations of his queen-regent against Cardinal Vidoni and caused the candidacy of Cardinal Brancaccio to run aground on the *ius exclusivae*. The mediation of Venice finally steered the election to the eighty-year-old, kind, but insignificant Emilio Altieri (29 April 1670, Clement X, 1670–76). His successor, Innocent XI (Benedetto Odescalchi) was not elected until the approval of Louis XIV had been delivered to the entrance of the conclave on 20 September 1676. Although the War of the Spanish Succession prompted great efforts in connection with the election of Alexander VIII (1689–91), neither Louis XIV nor Leopold I was able to exert any decisive influence this time. The next lengthy conclave (12 February–12 July 1691) was again dominated by opposition between the French and the Spanish-Austrian parties. The promising candidacy of Gregorio Barbarigo, who was later canonized, failed by virtue of the fact that Emperor Leopold I, while foregoing formal exclusion, called his election undesirable, the Spanish ambassador conspired against it, and Louis XIV resisted it out of consideration for his allies. Cardinal Antonio Pignatelli (Innocent XII, 1691–1700), who was elected in the end, was a compromise candidate already seventy-five years of age.

The Spanish succession—Charles II, the last of the Habsburgs on the Spanish throne had died little more than a month after Innocent XII (d. 27 September 1700)—and the prospect that because of the dead Pope's partisanship for the French succession, the feudal claim over the Kingdom of the two Sicilies, and the helpless military condition of the Papal States the Apostolic See would be involved in that European conflict overshadowed the conclave (9 October to 20 November 1700). In this conclave the *Zelanti* were finally able to prevail with their candidate, Gian Francesco Albani (Clement XI,[6] 1700–1721). On 2 April 1721 during the scrutiny prior to reaching a two-third's majority, Cardinal Althan announced the imperial exclusion preventing the election of the

---

mediator in Aachen, see A. Franzen, "Französische Politik und Kurkölns Beziehungen zu Frankreich unter Erzbischof Max Heinrich (1650–88) in römischer Sicht," *RQ* 52 (1957), 200.

[6] "Clement XI was the last Pope who represented the lofty ideas and principles of Gregory VII in all respects with the energy and firmness of his great predecessor. A noble, dignified personality with the most sensitive conscience and full of the fear of God, imbued with the desire to restore the peace between Church and state, he personally pursued that peace for fully twenty years with the greatest sacrifices, but never came to enjoy it" (F. J. Sentis, *Monarchia Sicula,* 157f.).

candidate of the nepotist party, Fabrizio Paolucci.[7] After the Emperor and France had reached an understanding, Cardinal Conti (Innocent XIII, 1721–24) was elected. Nine years later the candidate of the *Zelanti*, Lorenzo Imperiali, foundered on the protest of the Bourbon courts and Paolucci on the exclusion of the previous conclave. The papal election of 1730 also marked the first appearance of the Savoy Party. The last public exclusion was issued by France on 24 June 1758 against Cardinal Cavalchini because of his position in the canonization of Bellarmine and on the issue of the constitution *Unigenitus*.

The *ius exclusivae* was to serve the fulfillment of aims regarding the established Church and the attainment of other long-range goals. For the common disputes with the Church either the already existing institutions of the pre-Tridentine established Church were further developed or new means created. The confinement of the nunciatures to a position of mere diplomatic representation of the Papal States,[8] put into effect by the established Churches in an alliance with episcopalism, was complemented by the institution of the *Agenzie*,[9] developed in Spain and France and taken over in 1714–17 by Charles VI first for his Dutch and Italian possessions and then for the hereditary lands and the Empire as well. In 1759 the ordinariates of the Habsburg monarchy were ordered to make use of the Roman *Agenzie;* after 1767 all business with Rome, with the exception of the *forum internum*, had to go exclusively through this state institution. More than anything else the established Church made use of the *Appellatio tanquam ab abusu* and of the *placet* in its disputes with the hierarchy.

The *Appellatio ab abusu*, also called *Recursus ab abusu, Recursus ad principem, Appel comme d'abus,* or *Recurso de fuerza,* is the appeal to state authority against an alleged misuse of church authority, especially in connection with jurisprudence and administration.[10] Even in its initial

---

[7] For Paolucci, who had been nuncio in Cologne from 1696 to 1698 and cardinal secretary under Clement XI, see H. Raab, "Die Finalrelation des Kölner Nuntius Fabrizio Paolucci," *RQ* 55 (1960), 129–50; L. Jadin, *L'Europe au début du XVIIIe siècle. Correspondance du Baron Karg de Bebenbourg, Chancellier du Prince-Évêque de Liège Joseph Clément de Bavière, Archevêque Électeur de Cologne avec le Cardinal Paolucci, Secrétaire d'État (1700–19)* (Brussels and Rome 1968).—Wahrmund (*Die kaiserliche Exklusive im Konklave Innozenz' XIII.,* 23) views the exclusion of Paolucci perhaps as the "somewhat rash step of a cardinal less experienced in the practice of the elections in Rome."
[8] See Chap. 23; K. Walf, *Die Entwicklung des päpstlichen Gesandtschaftswesens in dem Abschnitt zwischen Dekretalenrecht und Wiener Konkordat (1159 bis 1815)* (Munich 1966), 219f.
[9] R. Blaas, "Die k. k. Agenzie für geistliche Angelegenheiten," *MOESTA* 7 (1954), 47–98; H. Herrmann, "Die Römische Agenzie für kirchliche Angelegenheiten Deutschlands und Österreichs," *RömHM* 11 (1968), 188.
[10] E. Eichmann, *Der Recursus ab abusu nach deutschem Recht* (Breslau 1903); P. G. Caron, *L'appello per abuso* (Milan 1954).

stages this institution, which grew from various roots in Spain, France, and in the medieval communities and principalities of Italy, signaled the claim of absolute rule over the Church. If possible all jurisdiction competing with that of the state was to be eliminated. In conjunction with the Pragmatic Sanction of Bourges (1438), the *Appel comme d'abus* had been expanded, acknowledged by Leo X in the Concordat of 1516, and legalized in the *Ordonnance* of Villers Cotterêts of 1539. In the course of the seventeenth and eighteenth century the *Recursus ab abusu,* although condemned since 1581 by the bull *In Coena Domini* and censured by the Church, was developed in all Catholic states "as a weapon of territorialism against the hierocratic system."[11] In Lorraine, where the conflict regarding the Code Léopold (1701–10) was almost exclusively focused on the *Recursus ab abusu,*[12] it represented a means of defense on the part of national autonomy. The *Recursus ab abusu* was intended to express the territorial sovereignty of the state and to complete the development initiated by the *Privilegium de nonevocando,* with state control of church jurisdiction. But it was also intended to delineate the respective competencies of the state and the Church. While it was primarily an instrument of the established Church, it also contributed towards putting into disuse the Pope's recourse to a general council.

The sharpest weapon of the established Church, "the main guarantee of the rights of the state,"[13] was the *placet* (also called the *Placetum regium, Exequatur, Jus retentionis,* and, in Lorraine, *Pareatis*). It was first formulated in England; after the tumult of obedience ensuing from the Great Western Schism it was used as a prescriptive right by the sovereign princes. It represents the right on the part of the sovereign or those offices charged by him—as the Inquisition tribunal in Spain—to examine with a view towards the interests of the state certain church decrees, especially by foreign superiors, to permit their publication and execution or to prohibit them under certain penalties, of which those ordered by Philip II in 1569 were especially harsh (they included banishment and even the death penalty). Within the concept of the established Church the *placet* was part of the *Jura circa sacra* and of the sovereignty of the state. It was based on council resolutions, the Catholic view of the state, the responsibilities of the sovereign prince, and, during the eighteenth century, increasingly on natural law. The state has the *placet* vis-à-vis the Church, but not the other way around because the Church is in the state, whereas the state is not within the Church. In the seventeenth and eighteenth century the *placet* was

[11] E. Eichmann, op. cit., 58.
[12] L. Just, *Clemens XI. und der Code Léopold (1702–10). Die kuriale Politik im Kampf mit dem lothringischen Staatskirchentum* (Frankfurt a. M. 1935).
[13] E. Friedberg, *Die Gränzen zwischen Staat und Kirche,* 799.

applied against papal and episcopal decrees of disciplinary as well as dogmatic content, even though Philip IV (10 June 1659), emphasizing that it was unnecessary in connection with instructional announcements, at that time prohibited such innovative application in the Netherlands. The greater duchy of Tuscany, as well as Spain, France, Venice, Naples, and Vienna, denied the *Exequatur* for the bull *Auctorem Fidei* (28 August 1794) of Pius VI condemning the Synod of Pistoia.

The *placet* had the purpose of maintaining law and order in the state, preventing intervention or abuse by the Roman Curia in the affairs either of the state or the competent bishops. Ever since Innocent VIII and his Bull *In Coena Domini* the *placet* was censured, but not until the middle of the nineteenth century was the *ius, quod vocant* "exequatur" actually condemned.[14] An ordinance of 1475 by Louis XI had ordered the *placet* for papal edicts as part of the Gallican Liberties. An inspection *placet* had existed in Lorraine since 1484. Recommended by Cardinal Ximenes and emphatically prescribed for all Catholics by Ferdinand (1509), it was one of the fundaments of the Spanish concept of the established Church. It became a model via the Netherlands and Northern Italy for the Habsburg established Church, which increased its application even under Leopold I.

A treatise published in 1712 by the well-known Louvain canonist van Espen took on special importance for the theoretical justification of the *placet*.[15] Van Espen viewed the *placet* not as a means of limiting the independence of the Church, but rather as a means of the authorities, who were instituted by God, of maintaining both ecclesiastical and political order. Van Espen's views were of enduring influence on the Josephinist study of canon law. During the last few years of Charles VI the glare of public attention focused on the discussion regarding the appointment to the chair of canon law at the University of Innsbruck, which was to be taken away from the Jesuits and conferred on Paul Josef Rieger. As admitted by the government, the crux of the matter was to protect the students from the very injurious principles aimed at the predominance of the clergy and instead to teach them "the true doctrine as reflected in Covarruvias, Van Espen *et similibus*."[16]

In an unsuccesful effort Innocent X and Clement XI tried to counter the *placet* by the bull *Nova semper* of 9 November 1714. The fight with

---

[14] *Litt. Apost. Ad Apostolicae,* 22. 8. 1851; Syllabus 8. 12. 1864, par. 6, ART. 41.

[15] E. Von Espen, *Tractatus de promulgatione legum ecclesiasticarum ac speciatim bullarum et rescriptorum Curiae Romanae ubi et de placito regeo, quod ante earum publicationem et executionem in provinciis requiritur* (1712); see also L. Willaert, "Le Placet royal aux Pays-Bas," *Revue belge de philologie et d'histoire* 32 (1954), 466–506, 1075–1117.

[16] G. Mraz, *Geschichte der Theologischen Fakultät der Universität Innsbruck von ihrer Gründung bis zum Jahre 1740* (Innsbruck 1968), 193.

the established Church, which had grown in strength since the Counter Reformation and had displayed ever stronger aspirations in the course of the seventeenth and eighteenth century, is reflected in the history of *In Coena Domini,* in the form of its text as well as in the measures by the various sovereign princes. Its publication in Spain had led to serious conflicts even under Charles V and Philip II. In 1763 a new prohibition was issued in Spain. In retaliation to the papal monitory, *In Coena Domini* was suppressed in 1768 in Parma, Venice, Naples, Spain, Austrian Lombardy, and Bohemia. After 1770 it was no longer announced. The established Church also ignored the Roman *Index librorum prohibitorum.* Under the principle of advocation the *Ius proscribendi libros perniciosos* was claimed for the state, which then could refuse the request of the Church for intervention and could even act against the wishes of the Church. The Church was forced to suffer its most infamous defeats of the eighteenth century in this arena in the form of repeated failure to proscribe Hontheim's ("Febronius") *De statu ecclesiae* and Osterwald's *Wider die geistliche Immunität in zeitlichen Dingen,* and, finally, it had to tolerate the abolition of the Apostolic Book Commissariat in Frankfurt am Main.[17]

The established church system, promoted by the Church during the Counter Reformation for the sake of self-preservation and reform, differed in the structure attained during the seventeenth and eighteenth century from the pre-Tridentine form by its consistent systematism and doctrinarianism. It flourished in the absolutist Catholic states, in Spain and France, the Bourbon states of Italy, in the Spanish Netherlands, Lorraine, the Republic of Venice, several Catholic cantons of Switzerland, in the Electorate of Bavaria, and in Austria.[18] In regard to canon law the established Church was a complex system whose bent for episcopacy, national Church, and opposition to the Curia differed from one state to the other. Gallicanism, deeply rooted in French history and closely related to the growing strength of a national kingdom, the weakness of the papacy during the Avignon exile and the Great Western Schism, was firmly placed on a course of maintaining the national unity of the Church in the time following the Reformation. Its goal in counteraction to papalism was the reform of the church constitution in the episcopal or Richerian sense, but above all it aimed at the predominance of the state over the Church. Its claim was based on the Pragmatic

---

[17] The end of the apostolic book commission, connected with the imperial one by personal union, came about on 28 February 1780 when Emperor Joseph II appointed the Reformed book dealer Johann Konrad Deinet to take the place of the deceased Worms suffragan bishop Franz Xaver Anton v. Scheben (H. Raab, "Apostolische Bücherkommissare in Frankfurt a. M.," *HJ* 87 [1967], 326–54).

[18] See Chap. 24.

Sanction of Bourges (1438) and, after its abolition by the Concordat of 1516, on the latter's stipulations which granted the King the right of appointment to almost all bishoprics and abbeys and, with it, factual dominance over the Church of France. The introduction of the *placet* for papal decrees (1475), the *Appel comme d'abus* (1539), and the writings of Pierre Pithou, Dupuy, de Marca, and Richer[19] around the turn of the sixteenth century strengthened the system of the established Church and the concept of the so-called Gallican Liberties, which according to Pithou's authoritative interpretation merely paraphrased the rule of the King over the Church in France.

Following the quarrel over the quartering privilege and the Peace of Pisa (1664), which humiliated the papacy, the issue of Gallicanism reached its climax in the regalia dispute and the *Declaratio cleri gallicani* of 19 March 1682. Next, Louis XIV treated the regalia right as an essential right to the crown. He extended the right of nomination according to the Concordat of 1516 to all the bishoprics and abbeys; he also claimed the ecclesiastical regalia, which enabled him to fill all the benefices of a bishopric while the latter was vacant. When Innocent XI demanded the revocation of the edict, the Assembly of the Clergy under the influence of the King and with decisive participation by Bossuet, who had been appointed bishop of Meaux, decided to accept the expanded regalia right and the *Declaratio cleri gallicani de potestate ecclesiastica*. According to these four Gallican articles (19 March 1682), which constituted a revival of the Pragmatic Sanction of Bourges, the authority of the Pope did not extend to civic and temporal matters (John 18:36; Luke 20:25, Rom. 13:1f.). According to divine order, kings and princes are not subject to ecclesiastical authority in temporal matters. Thus they can neither be directly deposed by it, nor indirectly by releasing their subjects from their oath of loyalty. In spiritual matters as well the authority of the Apostolic See was limited in France by the decrees of the Council of Constance concerning the superiority of the council. These decrees had been approved by the Apostolic See, acknowledged by their application throughout the Church, and most scrupulously observed, especially by the Gallican Church. The exercise of papal power was regulated by the *canones*, the statutes of the church Fathers, tradition, and the prescriptive law of France and the Gallican Church. In matters of faith the Pope was most favored, but his judgment was subject to change unless the total Church agreed to it.

The four articles were published as state law and taught at the universities. Not until 1690 was a declaration of nullification pronounced by Alexander VIII. The tensions with Rome concerning the regalia right

[19] See Chap. 4.

and the *Declaratio* were aggravated by the quarrel about the quartering privilege, but a schism was avoided. Innocent XII reached a compromise (1693) by which Louis XIV forewent the implementation of the four articles in exchange for toleration of his regalia right and recognition of the bishops appointed by him. But well into the nineteenth century the established church law continued to be determined largely by the *Declaratio cleri gallicani.* In 1749 an amortization law against the acquisition of property by the Church was passed; in 1762 the Society of Jesus in the French province was dissolved by application of the *Appel comme d'abus.*

The Spanish established Church was tightly structured. Owning a disproportionate part of the real property and national income, it was totally in the hands of the state. Its rise and fall proceeded in tandem with the political development. The King had nomination right for all bishoprics and—as under the weak Habsburgs in the seventeenth century and the Bourbons of the eighteenth century—many an unworthy person was appointed. The princely income of many bishops was in glaring disproportion to the condition of the ministering clergy, to the poverty of the lower classes, and the meager theological education among large segments of the regular and secular clergy. Attempts at reform by the Jesuit Eberhard Nidhard (d. 1681 as a cardinal), whom Queen-Regent Anna Maria had appointed grand inquisitor and member of the Secret Council of State, were doomed to failure. The consolidation of absolutism under Philip V also began to have its effects on the relationship with the Church. When Clement XI recognized the Habsburg pretender to the crown, Charles III (1709), the results were the cessation of diplomatic relations with Rome, the closing of the nunciature in Madrid, the suspension of the temporalities, and—as a countermeasure—refusal by the Pope to confirm the bishops appointed by Philip V. In 1713 Melchior Raphael de Macanaz, treasurer of the Council of Castile, summarized the doctrines and demands of the regalists: abolition of the bull *In Coena Domini,* abolition of the Pope's supremacy over the kings, and universal patronage over all church benefices. The concordats of 1717 and 1732 could not allay all the disputes; they actually pleased neither party. The concordat, concluded in dire straights by Benedict XIV, gave to the Spanish King the universal patronage he demanded, with the exception of fifty-two benefices, besides "creating an almost total change in the discipline of the Spanish Church."[20] And yet new conflicts were created under Charles III when

---

[20] P. A. Kirsch, "Das durch Benedikt XIV. im Jahre 1753 mit Spanien geschlossene Konkordat," *AkathKR* 80 (1900), 320.

P. R. Conde de Campomanes (1723–1892) intensified the *placet* (1761) and expelled the Jesuits.

On the basis of the privilege *Quia propter prudentiam tuam*, granted Count Roger by Urban II (5 July 1098), the kings of the Two Sicilies ever since the end of the Middle Ages had claimed the title and rights of a *legatus natus papae* or a *legatus a latere* and with them all those rights not expressly reserved for the Pope. Ever since the sixteenth century this legatine power was characteristically called *Monarchia Sicula*. Ferdinand I, "the Catholic" (d. 1516), possessing the ecclesiastical jurisdiction as well, had himself called *Monarca*. The *Monarchia Sicula* involved the claim of the right of visitation of dioceses and monasteries, the right of decision in the election of church superiors, the right of excommunication and absolution even of cases in the papal reserve, the penal right for bishops, nuncios, and cardinals, and the right of demoting secular and regular clerics. When Philipp II failed to obtain a confirmation of the *Monarchia Sicula* from Rome, he appointed Nicolaus Stizzia to the position of the first permanent judge of the "Monarchy" (*Judex Monarchiae Siculae*) on 13 July 1579. In so doing he created "a central authority which systematically combined the highest ecclesiastical jurisdiction in one hand."[21] The trials before the tribunal of the "Monarchy" were not permitted to be advocated by the Pope nor brought to Rome by way of recourse.

The constant conflicts with the *Monarchia Sicula*, the latter being motivated by rigorous principles of an established Church and extreme "schismatic principles,"[22] reached a climax under Pope Clement XI during the Spanish War of Succession and the disputes connected with the efforts by Joseph I and Charles VI towards an established Church. The cause, insignificant on the surface, was the filling of the episcopal see of the Lipari Islands, on which occasion a small tax was levied. This appeared to Bishop Tedeschi, the secretary of the Congregation of Rites, a violation of ecclesiastical immunity in the sense of the bull *Coena Domini*.[23] So he reacted by excommunicating the responsible civil servants, whereupon the judge of the "Monarchy" pronounced absolution. When the dispute went to the Congregation of Immunities in Rome by way of recourse, it quickly became part of the fierce quarrel between Clement XI and Philip V.

By recognizing the Habsburg pretender Charles III as "Catholic King of Spain" (10 October 1709) Clement XI had gained some concessions

---

[21] F. J. Sentis, op. cit., 130.

[22] Ibid., 139.

[23] K. Pfaff, "Beiträge zur Gesch. der Abendmahlsbulle 51," Censure of encumbering ecclesiastical persons and institutions without papal permission.

in the Emperor's Italian policy, but at the same time he had to suffer harsh retaliatory measures by Philip V: Nuncio Zondadari was expelled from Madrid, all relations with Rome were prohibited, all revenues of the Holy See in Spain were frozen, ecclesiastical immunity and jurisdiction came under attack. On 11 October 1711, Clement XI declared all decrees directed against church immunity and jurisdiction null and void, and their originators to be subject to church censure. In addition he refused to confirm the bishops nominated by Philip V.

This immediate quarrel intensified the conflict over the *Monarchia Sicula*. A decree by the Congregation of Immunities (26 January 1712) and a brief by Clement XI (12 June 1712) declared the absolution by the judge of the "Monarchy" of those involved in the excommunication as being invalid and reconfirmed their excommunication. The response was given in the form of an edict by the viceroy: all papal decrees and edicts were null and void because they violated municipal laws, privileges, customs, and the regalia of the realm. The battle was then propelled to its climax by excommunications and local interdicts by one side, countered on the other side by absolution from Church censure by delegates of the "Judge of the Monarchy," suspension of temporalities, and the expulsion of the bishops of Catania, Girgenti, and the archbishop of Messina.

Disregarding the feudal claims of the Pope, the Peace of Utrecht (1713) demanded the transfer of Sicily from Spain to Duke Victor Amadeus II of Savoy. Additionally, the already tense relations between the Curia and Piedmont were aggravated to the extreme by exceedingly harsh measures in Sicily. As a consequence Clement XI on 20 February 1715 annulled the *Monarchia Sicula* by his bull *Romanus Pontifex*, predated by exactly one year.

The annulment received attention only because of an appeal by the procurator of the treasury prompting Philip V of Spain to insist on his rights by means of a formal protest. Less than three years later the establishment of the Quadruple Alliance (2 August 1718) gave Sicily to Austria in exchange for Sardinia. After difficult negotiations Emperor Charles VI agreed to return Comacchio to the Papal States (1725), a process in which Prosper Lambertini, the future Pope Benedict XIV, collaborated. This opened the door to a compromise regarding the *Monarchia Sicula*. Benedict XIII—while not expressly revoking the absolution bull—insisted in his bull *Fideli* (ratified 30 August 1728; in Vienna: 10 November 1728) that the *causae vere maiores* remain in the province of the Roman Curia or a special papal delegation in Sicily, that, furthermore, the title "Judge of the Royal Monarchy" be changed to *iudex ecclesiasticus delegatus*. The King received the privilege to appoint as the highest juridical office a *Iudex delegatus in partibus*.

The Vienna Treaty (3 October 1735)—again in complete disregard of the papal feudal rights—gave Naples and Sicily to Don Carlos as a Spanish-Bourbon secundogeniture. Under his rule (which he assumed after the death of his half-brother), but even more so under his minor son Ferdinand IV, the minister of state and chairman of the council of regents, Bernardo Tanucci,[24] articulated the claims of dominance of an enlightened absolutist state by means of passionate attacks on the Church, harsh reforms, and endless harrassment. The excommunication of the duke of Parma by Clement XIII (30 January 1768) furnished the pretense for reprisals by the Bourbon family alliance against the "ridiculous and scandalous pretentiousness" of the Roman Curia. These reprisals included the occupation of the papal enclaves of Benevento and Pontecorvo. Only after the abolition of the Society of Jesus, which Clement XIII was still rejecting at that time, were these territories returned (1774).

In implementing his church reforms, many of which were not without inner justification, Tanucci invoked the *Monarchia Sicula* and the presuppositions created by the unfortunate Pietro Giannone (1676–1748),[25] whose *Istoria civile del Regno di Napoli* (4 vols., 1723) has been called "the bible of anticurialism."[26] He also invoked kindred spirits among Jansenists and enlightened Freemasons. An Italian translation of Mesenguy's *Exposition de la doctrine chrétienne* appeared between 1758 and 1760.[27] The Enlightenment, regalism of the Spanish variety, Jansenist and Freemasonic influences under Tanucci were meshed into a system whose anticlericalism continued well beyond his fall, brought about by Maria Carolina (1776).

Even the enfeoffment of the Kingdom of the Two Sicilies (10 May 1738) granted by Clement XII did not improve the tense relations between Rome and Naples. Nor did the concordat[28] concluded by Benedict XIV after difficult negotiations (2 June 1741) lead to a modus vivendi, but instead to ever new conflicts in spite of the fact that the Pope—much to the chagrin of several cardinals—made substantial concessions. Agreement concerning the controversial "Tribunal of the Monarchy" was reached by which a court consisting of three clerics and

---

[24] Most recent monograph: R. Mincuzzi, *Bernardo Tanucci, ministro di Ferdinando di Borbone 1759–76* (Bari 1967).

[25] L. Marini, *Pietro Giannone e il giannonesimo a Napoli nel Settecento* (Bari 1950).

[26] G. Schnürer, *Katholische Kirche und Kultur im 18. Jh.* (Paderborn 1941), 13.

[27] E. Passerin d'Entrèves, "La riforma "giansenista" della Chiesa e la lotta anticuriale in Italia nella seconda metà del Settecento," *RSIt* 71 (1959), 210: according to the author there was a close "collaborazione fra riformatori . . . giansenisti e filogiansenisti e campioni della lotta anticuriale."

[28] A. Mercati, *Raccolta di Concordati*, 338–64.

two laymen appointed by the King was to execute church jurisdiction on a higher level as well. Rome made concessions in the matter of personal, local, and property immunity; the right of sanctuary was circumscribed; foreigners were excluded from holding benefices in the kingdom and a few smaller bishoprics were abolished. In exchange the *placet* was to be eliminated and the *Recursus ad principem* modified.

But soon the interpretation of the concordat and the unchanged establishmentarian, anticlerical course set by Tanucci in Naples resulted in endless new disputes. Tanucci, who made the Church responsible for the economic miseries of the kingdom, disregarded the Benedictine concordat; he reduced the number of monasteries, restored the amortization regulations, eliminated the spolia right, and claimed for himself the power of appointment to all bishoprics and the awarding of all benefices. The unscrupulous expansion of the *placet,* which had been founded in "international law and the peaceful spirit of religion," to include even the *forum internum*, the confinement of the Church to the sacraments and liturgy, and, finally, the expulsion of the Jesuits from the realm (1769) were expressions of that harsh establishmentarianism and radical anticlericalism for which Tanucci formulated the recipe regarding relations with Rome: "Raise the stick high! Keep your mouth shut! That is the way to tame that Roman tiger."[29]

Tanucci's fall meant the end of the reforms, but not the end of anticlericalism and vexatious oppression of the Church. In 1778 all connections between the monasteries and Rome were interrupted. The *placet* was refused for all briefs and dispensations if the royal permission for recourse to Rome, the so-called *Liceat scribere*, was not obtained first. In point of fact, this procedure cut off all communication with the head of the Church. The claim of a royal presentation right in all bishoprics led to thirty vacant sees in 1784 in Naples alone; in 1798 there were more than sixty.[30] In 1787 the King of the Two Sicilies formally refused to recognize papal feudal rights by refusing the presentation of the White Horse (*Chinea*), customary sign of vassalage since the time of Charles of Anjou, and payment of the usual seven thousand gold ducats, invoking international law and historical grounds. The papal protest ceremoniously pronounced in Saint Peter's on 29 June 1788 fell on deaf ears.

During the second half of the seventeenth century and in the eighteenth century as well, anticlerical policies and strict establishmentarianism continued to flourish in the Republic of Venice even after the worst of the conflicts over Paolo Sarpi was overcome. In 1754 the republic demanded government permission for all communication of its

[29] From Tanucci to Galiani, dated 30 April 1768. Quoted in Pastor XVI, I, 875.
[30] F. J. Sentis, 195.

subjects with Rome, as well as for the execution of papal bulls and decrees. Gifts to the dead hand were forbidden, monasteries were closed, and the religious orders were placed under the authority of the bishops, who were not permitted to leave their dioceses without government permission.

Establishmentarianism assumed even harsher forms in Parma under Guglielmo Du Tillot and after the excommunication of the duke (30 January 1768), but after the fall of the prime minister the latter's successor reverted to a more moderate course (1771). In Sardinia the *Appel comme d'abus* remained in effect even after the concordats of 1727 and 1742; it was further expanded by additional regulations in 1770 and 1771. The right of sanctuary was modified, but the bishop was enabled to invoke the aid of the temporal authorities against the clergy. Establishmentarianism in Tuscany was not developed until the rule of the dukes of Lorraine. Francis I transferred the book censorship to the temporal authorities; he issued an amortization law and closed several monasteries and convents. The canonical reforms of his son Leopold, for which Pompeo Nero and Giulio Rucellai had paved the way, with some few modifications were basically identical to those in Austrian Lombardy, the Kingdom of the Two Sicilies, Parma, and Piacenza, but Leopold's aims went far beyond theirs and the establishmentarianism of Josephinism. The formative development of the Habsburg establishmentarianism, starting with the consolidation of imperial power and the integration of the state under Leopold I, Joseph I—the conflict involving Comacchio and the recuperation policy in Italy—and under Charles VI was influenced by the model of Venice, the Spanish Netherlands, and Lorraine.

CHAPTER 19

The Enlightenment

Concept

The epoch of intellectual history called "La crise de la conscience européenne,"[1] "Lumières" (French), "Enlightenment" (English), "Illuminismo" (Italian) indicated not so much a tendency towards crisis but rather its distant origin: the metaphysics of light[2] left to the formative

[1] P. Hazard, *Krise* (1939).
[2] L. Oeing-Hanhoff, "Licht, II Philosophisch," *LThK* VI (1961), 1024.

Western world by Augustine. The designation "Aufklärung" (C. W. Wieland), applied since the middle of the eighteenth century to the intellectual progress taking place, corresponds to the older French "éclaircissement."[3] But the Augustinian "illuminatio" of God within man was now conceived to mean man's self-illumination in the light of autonomous reason. This authorization of the human intellect which had its prehistory in the power asserted by Thomism that enables man in the knowledge of creation to rise to an analogous knowledge of God, except that rationality (according to Scholastic philosophy) is to be combined with the belief in revealed religion, now sought its reason within itself. The rationalism of Enlightenment is historically inconceivable without the philosophy of Scholasticism.[4] By the same token, the anti-institutionalism of Enlightenment, initially aimed at the constituted Church and accepting for the time being the absolutist state, which in turn took its ideological foundation from the rational law of nature, but then ended in the Revolution, had its roots, through its ties with the religious inwardness of Pietism,[5] in the Christian concept of the uniqueness and freedom of the individual person. Rationalism and anti-institutionalism, which was in the process of emancipation from its own tradition, furnished the conditions for the universal concept of Enlightenment of the one humanity. But for its part the latter is inconceivable without the Passion and Salvation of Christ, which in its original form was universal ("Jews and Gentiles" in Rom. 11:25; 1:16; 10:12), but then again historically particular (*gesta Dei per Francos*). But even if Enlightenment can be viewed as the result of centuries of "diastasis" of medieval history (Mayer-Pfannholz),[6] the diastasis between the ecclesiastical and political realm, between inwardness and institution, freedom and authority, the world and God, it is precisely because of the result of that diastasis that it constituted a crisis of the European intellect. This crisis is institutionally characterized by the fact that the Church now "lost its position of leadership" and that Christianity, from which Enlightenment stemmed, was "publicly put on trial"[7]—with different degrees of intensity, to be sure, varying in accordance with the people and countries involved—without the accuser being able to be distinguished from the accused even before the end of the epoch had been determined. In looking at the characteristics of this crisis, not only

[3] Regarding the concept of the period of Enlightenment, absolutism, and baroque, see F. Wagner, *Handbuch,* 2–5 (incl. biblio.).

[4] "The deepest roots of Enlightenment reach back to the Middle Ages." (F. Valjavec, op. cit., 16).

[5] See below, p. 537.

[6] A. Mayer-Pfannholz, "Phasen des Mittelalters," *Hochland* 36 (1938/39), 188.

[7] P. Hazard, *Vernunft,* 25.

its origin in the tradition of Western thought,[8] but also its complexity, indeed its inner contradictoriness must be taken into account. Skepticism was not only turned on the dogmas of Christian faith; it was the innermost element of man's reason itself and this reason could therefore be celebrated enthusiastically, be subjected to criticism and—although only on the periphery at first—be cynically discredited. Against the certainty of Cartesian consciousness and its "innate ideas" the psychological empiricism of J. Locke was raised, for whom the soul is a blank page. He was to have a profound influence on Montesquieu, Voltaire, Rousseau and others, finally ending in sensualism. Hume attacked Locke's deism as a new dogma and criticized the concept of "natural religion," which was to be the dome over all the revealed religions, as an empty construct. In its place he posited, in terms of psychology, the religious need, rooted in fear and hope, as only one of the many other needs. Theology, more substantially than in the course of the English Enlightenment, continued to be an ever present partner in the dialogue of the German philosophy of Enlightenment from Leibniz to Kant, albeit a partner separated by a critical line of demarcation. This clearly supports for the overall context of Europe the fact that in the aspirations towards Enlightenment "Christianity was the infinite object of toil for the centuries constituting the modern age."[9] And if one is not deceived by the acid quality of the language, this partnership was also felt in French Enlightenment, in the person of Pierre Bayle, son of a pastor, whose relationship with Calvinism is controversial, and in the anticlerical hatred of Voltaire's "Ecrasez l'Infame." If one considers the Enlightenment in its totality without arbitrarily separating the great personalities from the multiplicators, who had a profound effect on the broad segment of the educated, including those people who, while they could not read, had themselves read to, then the scope of the En-

---

[8] This element is usually given scant attention in the Catholic literature on the Enlightenment. The undifferentiated negative cliché of "indifferentism, rationalism, agnosticism, naturalism, materialism" (Funk-Bihlmeyer III [1934], 217f.; more subtle in the seventeenth ed. [1961], 249 ed. by H. Tüchle) regularly appears together with the positive cliché "humanization of the law, the fight against superstition esp. the belief in witchcraft, interest in pedagogy, bourgeois tolerance" (the latter with some qualifications); see also A. Schwarz, "Aufklärung," *LThK* I (1957), 1058 with the additional remark that the positive, to be sure, refers "only to watered-down Christian ideals."

[9] H. Freyer, *Weltgeschichte Europas* (Stuttgart 1954), 527.—"Too credulous and too sceptical" is the appraisal of the Enlightenment by C. L. Becker (op. cit., 30f. He continues: "There is more of Christian philosophy in the writings of the 'Philosophes' than has yet been dreamt in our histories." Critical of this "brilliant" piece of work, A. Cobban (op. cit., 228) stresses that "the Enlightenment is correctly identified as the source of the current conflict in ethical values and the consequent pessimism."

lightenment reached from an "insipid striving for bliss to the sublime mysticism of Spinoza and Malebranche."[10]

Next to the concept of philosophy as the "universal process of philosophizing," which intended to bring about a new order,[11] the natural sciences were a determining element of this epoch. Their observations and experiments provided an ever growing consciousness of man's sovereignty. Although the mathematics and physics of Newton created a lasting understanding, whereas the biology of the seventeenth and eighteenth century in the aggregate is no more than historically significant, an epochal turn of events made all of nature including man the object of empirical research. Its results confronted the traditional theory of creation, a confrontation not lightly undertaken by the prominent natural scientists.[12]

This endogenous process of the European Enlightenment corresponds with the criticism prompted by reaction to world exploration, a criticism of Western traditions, of Christianity (or at least its practice in Europe), brought about by comparison with the high cultures of Asia or primitive peoples of America. Its significance—at the time unintended yet innate—lies in the fact that it was above all the reports by missionaries from Asia, especially China, and from America which caused a "cultural crisis," just as Saint Francis Xavier had done before, intending at first to raise up a Tacitean mirror to their native countries. But the result was that precisely those men who had stepped out into the world for the sake of Christian faith and its propagation unintentionally laid the foundation for doubting the complex claim of Christianity's absolute nature through criticism which had actually been intended for only that form of the claim representing an identification of *christianitas* with Western culture.[13] Thus the Christian faith proved to be an "enlightenment" inasmuch as it questioned its own historical embodiment and with it the whole Eurocentric view of the historical world. Just as the doctrine of creation became a problem vis-à-vis empirical knowledge of nature, so did the doctrine of salvation become problematic for the experience of a universal history, notwithstanding the lack of clear factual knowledge.

---

[10] F. Wagner, *Handbuch,* 129.—"Not only was there in some of the intellectual leaders a great aspiration to demonstrate that the universe ran like a piece of clockwork, but this was itself initially a religious aspiration" (H. Butterfield, *Origins,* 119).

[11] E. Cassirer, op. cit., Foreword, X.

[12] In the bibliography to Chap. 6 see esp. E. J. Dijksterhuis, H. Butterfield, H. Lange, E. Ungerer; in Chap. 7: O. Zöckler, W. Philipp, P. Althaus, R. S. Westfall, and the individual scholars of the period.

[13] See above, p. 305.

The "rationalism" of the Enlightenment represents radicalization of Western rationality as well as misunderstanding of the secret which man will always be; "naturalism" is both discovery of the world and the loss of its total dimension in the abbreviation of materialistic interpretation; the detheologization of natural law in a line from Grotius to Pufendorf and Thomasius is at once the foundation of the tolerant state as well as its becoming an absolute concept as the *primum principium* of political and social life; in actuality "indifferentism" is both nihilistic skepticism and the tolerance which was indicated intellectually and politically after the dissolution of medieval universalism (which had its own problems) and was reaching for a new universality of truth. The Enlightenment can only be understood in the light of this ambivalence, which is especially noticeable in its mixed relationship with the idea of progress which had taken the place of the promise represented by the traditional belief in salvation.

The altercation with tradition was reflected also in the system of education. The old institutions, the universities and the ecclesiastic and municipal schools for a long time were averse to the Enlightenment. Its major influence emanated from the academies and scientific associations, followed by the private tutors of the aristocratic families and the salons. Almost all the proponents of the Enlightenment were occupied with pedagogical questions. The most prominent pedagogues of this period were John Amos Comenius (1592–1670 [Amsterdam]) with his *Orbis sensualium pictus* (1654) and his *Didactica magna* (1672)[14] and J.-J. Rousseau (see below). Reaching the broad masses of the people with the spirit of the Enlightenment, however, is a long process which— moved from within by a "second Enlightenment"—has lasted into our century. The communications media played an important part in this.[15]

If the Enlightenment is considered solely in its historical context, it is not easy to determine its beginning. It is different from humanism inasmuch as the latter—in spite of its strong pagan features—is yet part of criticism and reform within the Church;[16] where it initiated seculari-zation, it tended generally to avoid the theological realm. This can be seen most clearly in the development of its attitude towards history. Regional areas are subjects of humanistic historiography; it takes them out of the medieval horizon of Christian salvation, applies its criticism to

---

[14] K. Schaller, *Die Pädagogik des J. A. Comenius* (Heidelberg 1962).—See chap. biblio.
[15] C. Ledré, *Histoire de la Presse* (Paris 1958).—See biblio. under the heading of individual countries.
[16] Humanism and the Reformation "merely reduced the decisive importance of tradition" (F. Valjavec, op. cit., 9). The "destruction of universalism" in the vast political-economic spaces of absolutism was first described by F. Wagner (*Europa im Zeitalter des Absolutismus* [Munich 1948], 3f.) as the end of the Middle Ages.

its proper objects, but—contrary to Voltaire—it leaves the *Historia Divina* unscathed. It can hardly be said that "only a return to life on a Christian basis" after humanism led to overcoming the "static thinking of antiquity" (which was not all that static).[17] This much of it is indeed valid, namely, that the radical argument between the Enlightenment and the Christian faith received both from this argument and from the secular reinterpretation of Christian eschatology those dynamics which characterized the new age. The Enlightenment was by the knowledge of itself distinguished from the Renaissance and humanism. Because of this the dispute between the "Ancients" and the "Moderns" conducted in French literature since the seventeenth century inclined progressively towards the side of emancipation from antiquity (Fontenelle [1657–1757] spoke of the "absurdities" of Greek mythology;[18] Voltaire criticized the "blind adoration of antiquity,[19] although the art of antiquity at the same time remained the absolute model for the Neoplatonism of A. Shaftesbury [1671–1713]). Criticism of antiquity and of the relationship between humanism and antiquity is part of the Enlightenment's criticism of tradition on the whole. Benedetto Croce viewed the intellectual consciouness of the time by saying that it not only emerged from the "darkness" of the Middle Ages, but also from the "dawn" of humanism and the Renaissance into the full light of reason.[20] The changed relationship with the Christian faith is the most essential element of the connection as well as of the difference between humanism and the Enlightenment—not only in the context of church history.

The Enlightenment within the Political and Social Conditions of Individual Countries

The course of the Enlightenment proceeded in several phases, in intellectual climates which differed according to the countries involved. The individual proponents of the Enlightenment also occupied opposing positions; their personal relationship to each other could change from affinity to pronounced hostility. Regardless of the way in which the Enlightenment was a consequence of processes in the history of Western ideas, it was conditioned in the totality of history by the extremely rapid consumption of religious views during the religious wars for the

[17] H. Lange, *Physik* I, 166.
[18] Quoted in P. Hazard, *Vernunft,* 79.
[19] *L'Histoire du Parlement de Paris,* cap. 50.
[20] B. Croce, *Theorie,* 208; E. Cassirer, on the other hand, emphasizes that the Enlightenment, regardless of loosening its traditional ties, "relishes a return to intellectual motives and problems of antiquity" (op. cit., 314).

purpose of undergirding positions of political power. This consumption was aggravated by the indifference of purely political acts of tolerance, in the bottleneck of establishmentarian censorship of French absolutism as much as in the abolition of precensorship and the supervision of book imports in England (1695). In the context of social history the consumption took place mainly in the rise of an educated bourgeoisie,[21] which relegated the orthodox clergy to backwardness. Even though it was isolated from the common folk, it yet claimed a monopoly in education.

In England[22] the religious opposition of the Puritans and the parliamentary opposition established an alliance against the Anglican absolutism of James I (1603–25). This was followed by the "Holy War" of Oliver Cromwell, to which not only Charles I (1649) fell victim but also the Presbyterians of parliament. Yet during the Restoration under Charles II (1660–85) religious engagement of the public had remained so strong that religious statements were among the most important arguments in the fight for seats in parliament. But in this body the "genuine Protestantism was defended by those who unscrupulously fulfilled the Test Act (1673; prescribing the Anglican Communion and the oath of supremacy of the Anglican Church for all occupants of government offices), because they were for the most part freethinkers."[23] After the Glorious Revolution the Toleration Act of 1689, while still stipulating the Anglican faith to be that of the realm and at least for the time being not barring nonconformists from holding state office, provided an arena[24] in which the Enlightenment could develop in a more or less unfettered way, especially after the succession of George I (1714) from the Lutheran house of Hanover. The Royal Society[25] had been founded in 1662; ten years later it counted Isaac Newton as its most prominent member among such others as the founder of scientific chemistry, Robert Boyle, the mathematician John Wallis, the physicist, astronomer, and architect Christopher Wren, and others. The Royal

---

[21] E. Labrousse, "Voies nouvelles vers une histoire de la bourgeoisie occidentale aux XVIIIe et XIXe siècles (1700–1850)," *Relazioni del X Congresso Int. di Scienze Storiche* IV (Florence 1955), 365–96; O. Brunner, " 'Bürgertum' und 'Feudalwelt' in der europ. Sozialgeschichte," *Gesch. in Wiss. u. Unterricht* 7 (1956), 599–614.

[22] C. R. Cragg, *From Puritanism to the Age of Reason 1660 to 1700* (Cambridge 1950, 1966); L. Stephen, *English Literature and Society in the 18th Century* (London 1904, 1963); H. M. Carre, *Phases of Thought in England* (Oxford 1949); W. K. L. Clarke, *18th Century Piety* (London 1944).

[23] K. Kluxen in F. Wagner, *Handbuch*, 319.

[24] R. B. Barlow, *Citizenship and Conscience. A Study in the Theory and Practice of Religious Toleration in England during the 18th Century* (Philadelphia 1963).

[25] M. Purver, *The Royal Society. Concept and Creation* (London 1967); M. Ornstein, *The Role of the Scientific Societies in the 17th Century* (Chicago 1928).

Society was a model for the founding of academies everywhere; they were progressive institutions compared to the universities. In 1709 the *Tatler* appeared, followed in 1711 by the *Spectator,* the model for the daily and weekly papers which spread the great intellectual movement for the benefit of the progressively minded reader. Following the *London Gazette,* which appeared at irregular intervals (1665), the *Daily Courant* appeared (1712), on which the leading intellectuals of England were collaborating.[26]

In the *Discourse on Freethinking* (London 1713) Anthony Collins (1676–1729) for the first time generally applied the term "freethinker" to fellow deists (formerly used for John Toland specifically), whereas in France "libres penseurs" primarily denoted atheists such as Helvetius and Holbach. It was also in England that Freemasonry originated, that "self-demonstration of a European society which was freeing itself from the ties of the estates, from political forms of authority, and from church dogmata."[27] In the course of the seventeenth century the associations of church stonemasons that also had technicians and natural scientists as honorary members had grown into intellectual groups, into lodges. The association of the Greater Lodge of England (1717), whose constitution was drafted in 1723 by the Anglican cleric James Anderson at Saint Paul's in London, was a signal for similar foundings in almost all the European countries, albeit with different intellectual tendencies which indeed led to some divisions.[28] English Freemasonry was dedicated to the moralistic ideal of "Men of Honor and Honesty," to be enhanced by deistic piety.

Such was the political and social context which permitted England to be the first country in which the Enlightenment developed, although with a certain degree of dispassionate moderation. The movement was able, moreover, to benefit from the footing of centuries of empiricism

---

[26] K. K. Weed and R. P. Bond, *Studies of British Newspapers and Periodicals from their Beginning to 1800. A Bibliography* (Chapel Hill 1946); F. S. Siebert, *Freedom of the Press in England. 1476–1776; the Rise and Decline of Government Controls* (Urbana, Ill. 1952); J. Frank, *The Beginnings of the English Newspapers, 1620–1660* (Cambridge, Mass. 1961).

[27] F. Wagner, *Handbuch,* 123.

[28] J. Anderson, *The Constitutions of the Free-Masons* (London 1723; reproduction, Twickenham 1952); G. Martin, *Manuel d'Histoire de la Franc-Maçonnerie française* (Paris 1934); H. Boos, *Gesch. der Freimaurerei. Ein Beitrag zur Kultur- und Literaturgeschichte des 18. Jh.* (Aarau 1906; reprint 1967); B. Fay, *La Franc-Maçonnerie et la révolution intellectuelle du XVIII\u1d49 Siècle* (Paris 1935, 1942); R. F. Gould, *The History of Freemasonry,* 6 vols. (London 1884–87; revised ed. by H. Poole, 4 vols., London 1951); G. Serbanesco, *Histoire de la Franc-Maçonnerie universelle,* 6 vols. (Paris 1963ff.), Vol. I; P. Naudon, *La Franc-Maçonnerie* (Paris 1963); idem, *La Franc-Maçonnerie et le divin* (Paris 1960). See biblio. under individual countries.

as an intellectual trait of the nation. In his *Novum organum scientiarum sive indicia vera de interpretatione naturae* (1620) Francis Bacon (1561–1626)[29] had tried to refute atheism by means of a sharp separation of *theologia naturalis* and *theologia revelata*. He offered a theory of empiric-inductive science founded on philosophy as one who, much like a bee, not only (empirically) gathers, but also (interpretatively) alters. The *Philosophiae naturalis principia mathematica* (1687) of Isaac Newton (1643–1727), insisting on an absolutely inductive method, is as different from Bacon as it is from Cartesianism. In his introduction Newton defined the method according to which the "force of gravity" is deduced from "celestial phenomena" by means of mathematical postulates and maintained that "the other phenomena of nature should be deduced from mathematical principles" as well. As an author of theological works on the Old Testament, the discoverer of calculus was "ever intent on investigating the total intellectual structure of the empirical world, which permitted an inference of the Christian God of creation."[30] From the first to the third edition of his *Principia,* to be sure, he exhibited a tendency towards a theory of an absolute absence of presuppositions in natural science. Around the middle of the seventeenth century the physician William Harvey (1578–1657), who had studied in Padua and become professor of anatomy in London in 1615, gained fame as the discoverer of the circulatory system, for which he was censured by the Sorbonne. In his *Exercitationes de generatione animalium* (London and Amsterdam, 1651) he applied the causal-inductive method. To be sure, he formulated his theory "ovum esse primordium commune omnibus animalibus" without ever having seen a mammalian egg. The turn of the century brought the English form of empirical criticism, systematic empiricism. In his *Essay Concerning Human Understanding* (1690) John Locke (1632–1704),[31] not one of the most profound, yet one of the most successful intellectuals of his time, especially in his political writings, turned the subject of who investigates nature into the object of his

[29] *The Works,* coll. and ed. by J. Spedding, R. L. Ellis and D. D. Heath, 14 vols. (London 1858–74; reprint, Stuttgart 1963).—Lit. in P. Hassfeld, "Francis Bacon und die naturwissenschaftl. Begriffe seiner Zeit" (unpubl. diss., Bonn 1951).

[30] F. Wagner, *Handbuch,* 137; idem, "Kirchengeschichte und Profanhistorie im Spiegel Newtons und seiner Zeit," *Saeculum* 17 (1966), 193–204; F. Dessauer, *Weltfahrt der Erkenntnis. Leben und Werk Isaac Newtons* (Zurich 1945); *Isaac Newton. Theological Manuscripts,* selected and ed. with an introduction by H. McLachlan (Liverpool 1950); L. T. More, *Isaac Newton, A Biography* (London and New York 1934); F. E. Manuel, *Isaac Newton as Historian* (Harvard 1963); A. Koyré, *Newtonian Studies* (London 1965); M. C. Jakob, "John Toland and the Newtonian Ideology," *Journal of the Warburg Institute* 32 (1969), 307–31.

[31] *The Works of John Locke,* a new ed., corrected, 10 vols. (London 1823; reprint, Aalen 1963); M. W. Cranston, *John Locke. A Biography* (London 1957).

concern. This empiricism rather than the "innate ideas" of Descartes henceforth dominated the period (even though George Berkeley [1685–1753], continuing in Locke's footsteps, considered human perceptions as being arranged by God [*Treatise Concerning the Principles of Human Understanding* (1710)]). Locke's substantiation of deism in the *Letters Concerning Toleration* (1689/92) were no less important than his influence on political theory (contract, separation of powers). In the *Letters* Locke attempted to imbed historical revelation and the proof of its reasonableness in the general system of rationality (*The Reasonableness of Christianity* [1695]). The doctrine of "Natural Religion" had already been offered by Herbert of Cherbury (1582–1648) under the title *De veritate, prout distinguitur a revelatione, a verosimili, a possibili et falso* (1624). John Toland (1670–1722), initially raised in the Catholic faith, who influenced such materialists as Holbach, drew more radical conclusions than Locke from the rationalization of revealed religion. In his publicly burned essay *Christianity not mysterious* (1696; reprint 1969) he maintained that faith did not contradict reason, but conversely did not contain anything beyond that either. Matthew Tindal (1656–1733) on the other hand interpreted the Gospel as a restoration of natural religion (Republication of the Religion of Nature) in his *Christianity as old as the Creation* (1730). In addition to his psychological writings (*Enquiry Concerning Human Understanding* [1758]), those on moral philosophy (*Enquiry Concerning the Principles of Morals,* [1751]), and political science (*Political Discourses,* [1752]) David Hume (1711–76), probably the most important figure of the English Enlightenment, was also an incisive critic of natural religion and deism. His *Natural History of Religion* (1755) and *Dialogues Concerning Natural Religion* (posthumously; 1779) influenced Rousseau, J. G. Herder, and especially Kant. According to Hume, man is determined not by his perceptions, part of which is natural religion, but by his behavioral modes (in the case of religion, by fear and hope), which should be analyzed by psychology. The theologians, he maintained, are intent on proving the greatest paradox; instead, man should admit that "the whole of the world is an enigma, an unfathomable mystery" (*History of Religion,* sec. XV).[32] In his important early work *A Treatise of Human Nature* Hume prophetically related all sciences to the doctrine of man, from which a "complete system" was to be developed (Introduction). A work by the Socinian J. Priestley (1733–1804),[33] *A Comparison of the Institutes of Moses with those of the Hindoos and other Ancient Nations* (1799), is characterized by one of the

[32] Quoted in Cassirer, op. cit., 244f.—D. Hume: *The Philosophical Works,* ed. by H. Green and T. H. Grose, 4 vols. (1882–86; reprint, Aalen 1964).—Lit. in F. H. Heinemann, *David Hume. The man and his Science of Man* (Paris 1940).
[33] A. Holt, *A Life of Joseph Priestley* (London 1931).

most important elements of the Enlightenment: the knowledge of non-Christian religions, promoted most of all by Christian missionaries. His *History of the Corruption of Christianity* (1782), a theme also of the pietist J. G. Arnold, is an example of the kind of criticism to which Christian morality, too, was subjected. Sociological and political theories—although characteristic for all of the Enlightenment and its rationalization of natural law—are yet a special feature of the English variant. Whereas an individual and social catalogue of virtues could be derived from the psychology of the liberal David Hume, H. Bolingbroke (1678–1751),[34] politically a Tory (in 1714 he was forced to flee to France), but intellectually an extreme freethinker, replaced the moral idea with his sensualism, of influence also on Voltaire. His ideas were followed by Bernard de Mandeville (1670–1733), born the son of French parents in Holland, who developed the thesis that egoism is the only real social principle (*The Table of the Bees* [1714]). Next Adam Ferguson (1723–1816)[35] attempted to elevate sensualism into a sociohistorical concept. In it, history, brought about by the human species, becomes the essential differentiation from the animal world (*Essay on the History of Civil Society* [1766]). Egoism was viewed as the central principle of social life regardless of the fact that T. Hobbes (1588–1679)[36] developed a theory of absolutism (*Leviathan sive de materia, forma et potestate civitatis ecclesiasticae et civilis* [1651]; *De homine* [1658]) from the formula "Homo homini lupus" or that Adam Smith (1723–1790) a century later offered a theory of liberalism (*Inquiry into the Nature and Causes of the Wealth of Nations* [1776]).

In France[37] the politically motivated confessional toleration under

---

[34] C. A. Petrie, *Bolingbroke* (London 1937).

[35] W. C. Lehmann, *A. Ferguson and the Beginnings of Modern Sociology* (New York 1930).

[36] *Opera philosophica quae latine scripsit omnia,* 5 vols. (1839–45; reprint, Aalen 1961);—*English Works,* ed. by W. Molesworth, 11 vols. (1839–45; reprint, Aalen 1966); *Leviathan,* ed. with intro. by M. Oakeshott (Oxford 1957)—Lit. in F. C. Hood, *The Divine Politics of Thomas Hobbes. An Interpretation of Leviathan* (Oxford 1964); M. M. Goldsmith, *Hobbes's Science of Politics* (New York 1966).

[37] P. Sagnac, "La Révolution des idées et des mœurs et le déclin de l'Ancien Régime (1715–1788)," *La formation de la societé française moderne* 2 (Paris 1946); B. Benichou, *Morales du Grand siècle* (Paris 1948); L. G. Crocker, *An Age of Crisis. Man and World in the Eighteenth Century French Thought* (Baltimore 1959); H. Kirkinen, *Les origines et la conception moderne de l'homme-machine. Le problème de l'âme en France à la fin de règne de Louis XIV sur l'histoire des idées* (Helsinki 1960); P. Gay, *The Party of Humanity. Essays in the French Enlightenment* (New York 1964); L. G. Crocker, "Recent Interpretations of the French Enlightenment," *Cahiers d'histoire mondiale* (1964), 426–56; R. R. Palmer, *Catholics and Unbelievers in 18th Century France* (Princeton 1939); C. Le Bras, *Introduction à l'histoire de la pratique religieuse en France,* 2 vols. (Paris 1942–45); idem, *Études de sociologie religieuse,* 2 vols. (Paris 1955–56); R. L. Bach, *Die Entwicklung der frz. Ge-*

Henry IV (Edict of Nantes [1598]) had created a climate in which, parallel to Catholic renewal in the first half of the seventeenth century, an attitude ranging from indifference in matters of Church and religion all the way to atheism was able to flourish as well. Indifference was indirectly promoted by the conflict with Jansenism, whose political persecution (aside from that by the Church) finally led to its own politicization, just as its religious spiritualism gradually converged with the Enlightenment. But the most important element was the radical move initiated by Richelieu to make the Church into a function of the state whether it be an antipapal move (Declaration of the Gallican Liberties [1682]) or—following an understanding with the Curia—consisted of granting the bishops special privileges vis-á-vis parliament and the lower clergy (Edict of 1695). The revocation of the Edict of Nantes (1685), an outgrowth of establishmentarianism and the authoritative attitude of Louis XIV, had a considerable impact within France when it prompted the emigration of about half a million Huguenots. It was especially important within the European intellectual context, for in addition to the lodges of the Freemasons these refugees represented an "adhesive of European consciousness." Furthermore, their younger, elitist generation, outgrowing their church ties, "replaced the parish congregation with an international republic of letters" (F. Wagner).[38] Aside from the religious nonconformists of France, the Calvinists and Jansenists, who were fighting among themselves, the rationalists as well became increasingly suspect to the absolutist state. While the state had founded the Académie des Sciences in Paris (Colbert in 1666), it also maintained the strictest control over the system of publication and the press within the framework of its mercantile policies. On the other hand, the bourgeoisie,[39] experiencing a powerful rise under Louis XIV, was both bearer and audience of the intellectual movement. During the political and economic decline and in spite of continuing censorship after the death of Louis XIV[40] the Enlightenment was able to develop strongly

---

schichtsauffassung im 18. Jh. (diss., Freiburg i. Brsg. 1932); H. Vyverberg, *Historical Pessimism in the French Enlightenment* (Harvard 1958); G. Snyders, *La pédagogie en France aux XVIIᵉ et XVIIIᵉ siècles* (Paris 1965).

[38] F. Wagner, *Handbuch,* 118, 120; idem, "Die Hugenotten—ein europäisches Schicksal," *Der deutsche Hugenott* 27 (1963), 103–16; E. Haase, *Einführung in die Literatur des Refuge. Der Beitrag der frz. Protestanten zur Entwicklung analytischer Denkformen am Ende des 17. Jh.* (Berlin 1959).

[39] B. Groethuysen, *Die Entstehung der bürgerlichen Welt- und Lebensanschauung in Frankreich,* 2 vols. (Halle 1927–30); C. Moraze, *La France bourgeoise. XVIIIᵉ–XXᵉ siècles* (Paris 1946).

[40] D. T. Pottinger, *The French Book Trade in the Ancien Régime. 1500–1791* (Cambridge 1958).

and even to deviate into extremes. The literary circles and salons, whose members had equal rights of membership after the middle of the century, were the centers of the movement. But the most significant propagator was the *Encyclopedia,* initiated by Jean-Lérond d'Alembert (1717–83); he was named Jean le Pond after the church where he had been abandoned as an illegitimate baby;[41] his intellectual guide was Denis Diderot (1713–84) who was the son of a smith and had studied with the Jesuits.[42] His *Pensées philosophiques* (Paris 1746), publicly burned as anti-Christian, was crowned by the *Promenade d'un sceptique* and a materialistic philosophy of nature. The *Encyclopedia*[43] documented the second half of the century of France by the different positions of its authors, the predominance of empiric sciences, and in its history (1751–72: twenty-four volumes, by 1780: seven supplementary volumes); it was initially granted imprimatur by the Sorbonne, prohibited in vain in 1752, and indexed by Clement XIII. About a decade before the Revolution, almost a century after England, the censorship laws were practically overcome. In 1771 the *Journal de Paris* began to appear. Together with the literary salons the lodges of the Freemasons[44] were the social foundation of the Enlightenment; the Scottish current was conservative, the merger of many lodges forming the *Grand Orient de France* (1773) was a radical and emphatically anticlerical move. In 1738 and 1751 papal prohibitions were issued against it.

Twenty years after the death of René Descartes (1596–1650),[45] his philosophy was banned in France. Its method of doubt was considered as absolute skepticism; there was fear that it was dissolving the authority of the state and society. The Jesuit pupil Descartes (1606–14 at the college of La Flèche), who all his life considered himself to be a devout Catholic, but for the most part was forced to live outside of France, had questioned daily experience as well as general concepts. In this process of critical thinking he had found "clear and explicit" certainty only in

[41] R. Grimsley, *Jean d'Alembert, 1717–83* (Oxford 1963).

[42] A. M. Wilson, *Diderot. The Testing Years 1713–1759* (New York 1957); J. Proust, *Diderot et l' "Encyclopédie"* (Paris 1963); L. G. Crocker, *Diderot. The Embattled Philosopher* (New York 1966); P. Altari, *Voltaire, Diderot e il Partito filosofico* (1965).

[43] F. Venturi, *Le origini dell'Enciclopedia* (Turin 1963); J. Proust, *L'Encyclopédie* (Paris 1965).

[44] D. Ligou, *La Franc-Maçonnerie française au XVIIIe siècle: L'Information historique* (Paris 1955); G.-H. Luquet, *La Franc-Maçonnerie et l'Église en France au XVIIIe siècle* (n. p., 1955); for the connection between Freemasons and the French Revolution, see E. Weis in F. Wagner, *Handbuch,* 297, n. 29–33.

[45] *Œuvres complètes,* ed. by C. Adam and P. Tannéry, 12 vols. (Paris 1897–1910); *Prinzipien der Philosophie,* trans. by A. Buchenau (Leipzig 1922).—Lit. in R. Lefèvre, *La vocation de Descartes* (Paris 1956); idem, *L'humanisme de Descartes* (Paris 1957).

the *res cognitans* itself. Equally clear to him was the concept of God: as He is perfection, human *cognatio* possesses but one aspect of Him (his major works: *Meditationes de prima philosophia* [1641]; *Principia philosophiae* [1644]). To speak of Descartes's emancipation of philosophy from theology is valid only in a limited sense by virtue of the fact that only by means of the theological implication of the truth of God can the *res extensa* of divisible matter of physical things be called certain, representing of course a single geometric mechanism. Yet within this mechanism Descartes's *Discours de la méthode* (1637) qualitatively equates the universal saving nature of God's help in the execution of the natural laws, initially created for the chaos, with the act of creation itself. Here is a profound difference from the physicist Pierre Gassendi (1592–1655), who, contrary to both Aristotelian and Cartesian philosophy, viewed all processes in nature as being caused by forces contained in the atoms.[46] The philosophy of Descartes can be interpreted as an endeavor to overtake the emancipation—triggered by Galileo's[47] interpretation of the Copernican view of the world—not only from theology but also from traditional philosophy in an attempt to "trace mathematics back to philosophy"[48] and to do so by means of logic and its direction from the general to the specific. This led to the anti-Cartesian reaction of the empirically oriented eighteenth century. Based on Descartes, the Oratorian Nicole Malebranche (1638–1715)[49] attempted to go back to Augustinian metaphysics of light. In his concept of "Vision en Dieu," merely stimulated by sensual experience, in which all ideas are directly seen (as distinguished from Descartes's "innate ideas") he sees in God the sole *causa activa seu efficiens,* which makes use of human action as the *causes occasionelles* (*Recherche de la verité* [1674]). This was of great influence on Leibniz. But these attempts to obtain in an era of autonomous reason and mathematical-scientific thought a new central position for theology were rejected alike by the Sorbonne, the traditional theologians (especially the Jesuits), and in part by the Jansenists, as well as by the intellectuals of the Enlightenment, whose philosopher was not Descartes but Locke. In the person of Pierre Bayle (1647–

[46] J. S. Spink, *French Free-Thought from Gassendi to Voltaire* (London 1960).
[47] Whereas Gassendi knew how to defend Galileo's views of the universe without leaving himself vulnerable to censorship, Descartes in his treatise on the method left the possibility of error open. The fact that Galileo determined his fate by treating his question as a theological one as well "instead of relegating it to the theologians" became the problem of the Enlightenment, which no longer thought such relegation possible.
[48] H. Lange, *Physik* I, 193.
[49] G. Sebba, *Nicolas Malebranche, 1638–1715. A preliminary Bibliography* (Athens, Georgia 1959); G. Stieler, *Leibniz und Malebranche und das Theodiceeproblem* (Darmstadt 1930). See Cognet above.

1706)[50]—son of a Huguenot pastor, attended the Jesuit school at Toulouse in 1669, a Catholic for a period of seventeen months, and after 1681 professor of philosophy in Rotterdam—France produced the man who largely determined the intellectual climate of the century. He did so by his unsparing and exceedingly effective criticism of tradition, by the categorical separation of faith and knowledge, by his criticism of the moral discrimination of atheists, but also by his skepticism towards reason (which he considered stronger in the discovery of errors than in positive cognition). He was opposed to Leibniz, Descartes, and Spinoza, yet also cognizant enough of the consequences of the "Pyrrhonisme" to hold fast to the natural idea of reasonableness as the basis for an autonomous moral law. His *Dictionnaire historique et critique* (1697) often adds to insignificant keywords lengthy footnotes which contain the actual substance of the work. But while Bayle could unequivocally state that he would rather be godless than an idolator, the aristocratic Montesquieu (1698–1755)[51] in his *Esprit des lois* (1748) considered the various religions from the point of view of their usefulness to the state. In his conservative criticism of absolutism he held religion to function as the only existing limitation upon those who disregard human laws. This work, which first appeared anonymously in Geneva, exercised great influence by its many editions and translations, representing as it does a biological (climate) and sociological comparative constitutional doctrine. But there exists for him an original ground of being to which the laws are connected, since the absurdity of blind fate would not have been able to produce intelligent beings. Montesquieu rendered one of the most characteristic judgments of Voltaire (1694–1778; son of a notary)[52]: Just as monks did for the glory of their order, so did Voltaire

[50] E. Beyreuther, "Zinzendorf und Pierre Bayle," *Herrnhuter Hefte* 8 (Hamburg 1955); J.-P. Jossua, "P. Bayle précurseur des théologies modernes . . . ," *RevSR* 39, 2 (1965), 113–57.

[51] *Œuvres complètes,* ed. by A. Masson, 3 vols. (Paris 1950–55); German trans. of *Esprit des lois* by E. Forsthoff, with an important intro., 2 vols. (Tübingen 1951).—Lit. in J. Mailhol "Die Methode des Kulturkritikers u. Geschichtsdenkers Montesquieu" (unpubl. diss., Mainz 1955); M. Göhring, *Montesquieu. Historismus und moderner Verfassungsstaat* (Wiesbaden 1956); R. Shackleton, *Montesquieu. A Critical Biography* (London 1961, with biblio.).

[52] *Œuvres complètes de Voltaire,* Nouvelle éd., 52 vols., ed. by A. Beuchot and L. Moland (Paris 1877–85); *Voltaire. Correspondance,* ed. by T. Besterman, 2 vols. (Paris 1964–65).—Lit. in W. Kaegi, *Voltaire u. der Zerfall des Geschichtsbildes: Historische Meditationen* (Zurich 1942); R. Naves, ed., *Voltaire. Dialogues et anecdotes philosophiques* (Paris 1955, with biblio.); J. H. Brumfitt, *Voltaire Historian* (London 1958); A. Noyes, *Voltaire* (Paris 1936, German: Munich 1958; attempts to show the Christian Voltaire); R. P. Pomeau, *La religion de Voltaire* (Paris 1956); W. Weischedel, *Voltaire: Große Geschichtsdenker. Ein Zyklus Tübinger Vorlesungen von K. A. Fink u. a.,* ed. by K. Stadelmann (Tübingen and

write history for the glory of "his monastery," but bad history. Voltaire's partisanship for his "monastery" of restless spirits is the pendant of his fanatical hatred of the Catholic Church (*Sermon des Cinquantes* [1761], *Le philosophe ignorant* [1766], *Profession de foi des Théistes* [1768], and *Dieu et les hommes*[1769]). His life and voluminous literary work cannot be reduced to a formula. The deist philosophy he received from England is meager, but the *Eléments de la philosophie de Newton* (1738)[53] were deadlier for Cartesianism in France than its prohibition by the established Church. Like all those in France who called themselves "philosophes" Voltaire is the prototype of the *écrivain* who was equally able to write the cynical epic *La pucelle d'Orléans* (1739) as well as the profoundly moving *Poème sur le désastre de Lisbonne"* (1755). Following is a brief biographical sketch: from 1704 to 1710 he was at the Jesuit college Louis-le-Grand; in 1717 he spent eleven months in the Bastille; as an eminent writer he was received into aristocratic society, this permitted his secret return from banishment in England (1726–28). A successful financial speculator, member of the Academie in 1746, intellectual vagabond after 1750, he spent his final twenty years in Fernay near Geneva. From there he exerted his intellectual influence on all of Europe by means of his voluminous correspondence, aside from the *Encyclopedia* the most important factor in the propagation of the thought of the Enlightenment. His *Candide ou l'optimisme* (1759) documented in exemplary fashion the ever-present possibility of a sudden shift into pessimism. The *Essai sur les mœurs et l'esprit de nations* (1756)[54] gained fame through its added introduction entitled "Philosophie de l'histoire." It represents a fundamental attack on the interpretation of world history according to the details of the Christian Gospel. Next to Bayle, Montesquieu, and Voltaire—his life in many respects is comparable to Voltaire's but a complete opposite in the course of his intellect—Jean-Jacques Rousseau (1712–78),[55] the son of a watchmaker from a Huguenot family who had emigrated to Geneva, was the most signifi-

---

Stuttgart 1949); H. T. Mason, *Pierre Bayle et Voltaire* (London 1963); R. A. Brooks, *Voltaire and Leibniz* (Geneva 1964); *Studies on Voltaire and the 18th Century,* ed. by T. Besterman (Geneva 1955).

[53] P. Brunet, *L'introduction des théories de Newton en France au XVIIIe siècle. Avant 1738* (Paris 1931), treats the reception of Newton to that point.

[54] Vol. 11 of the ed. by A. Beuchot and L. Moland.

[55] Jean Jacques Rousseau, *Œuvres complètes,* ed. by B. Gagnebin and M. Raymond (Paris 1959–64).—Lit. in E. Hirsch, "Rousseaus Geschichtsphilosophie," *Rechtsidee u. Staatsgedanke. Festgabe für Julius Binder* (Berlin 1930); F. C. Green, *Jean-Jacques Rousseau. A Critical Study of his Life and Writings* (Cambridge 1955); M. Rang, *Rousseaus Lehre vom Menschen* (Göttingen 1959); F. Jost, *Jean-Jacques Rousseau suisse,* 2 vols. (Freiburg i. Ue. 1961); O. Vossler, *Rousseaus Freiheitslehre* (Göttingen 1963).

cant figure of the French Enlightenment. Under the guidance of the convert Mme von Warens in Annecy (Savoy), who later became his lover, he converted to Catholicism in 1728. But neither his conversion nor his return to the Reformed Church in Geneva (1754) were among the essential inner stations of his life to which his literary work corresponds. All self-stylization aside, his "Inspiration of Vincennes" (conceived in 1749 on his way to visit Diderot in jail) described in the *Confessions* ("en remontant aux traces de mon etre sensible," finished in 1770) may be ascribed the significance of a turning point. As it says in the *Confessions,* it is solely the institutions which make man evil. Following the criticism of culture represented by his *Discours sur les sciences et les arts* (1750), criticism of its institutions was also the thesis of the second discourse ("Sur l'origine et les fondements de l'inégalité parmi les hommes") in 1754. It was this radical inwardness, this resolute anti-institutionalism with its pietistic extension in J. G. Arnold which— aside from determining Rousseau's pedagogy of self-development (*Émile ou sur l'éducation* [1762]; burned as atheistic)—produced the immediate revolutionary impact of Rousseau. The *Contrat sociale* (1762) in one of its possible interpretations did not become truly significant until the French Revolution. There were individual reasons for Rousseau's disassociating himself in 1758 from Diderot, who had influenced him so strongly, for opposing Voltaire, and becoming alienated from D. Hume, with whom he had gone to England in 1765. What these actions demonstrate is the transition from an Enlightenment of reason to an Enlightenment of the "heart," which loses none of its explosive power in the course of nineteenth century intellectual and social history. Rousseau's temporary intellectual companion Diderot, at least initially, had moral reservations against atheism, as did Voltaire. These were not shared by the physician Julien Offroy de La Mettrie (1709–51),[56] who viewed human intellectual powers as pure bodily functions (*Histoire naturelle de l'âme* [1745]). In the Netherlands, where he went after the condemnation of this work, he published the radically materialist, atheist essay *L'homme machine* (Leiden 1748), in which he transferred the mechanism of the physical world, asserted by Descartes, to man as an intellectual being. The same anthropology was advocated by Claude Helvetius (1715–71)[57], son of a Dutch doctor, in his *De l'esprit* (1758), which was placed on the Index by the Sorbonne. Differing from Hel-

[56] G.-F. Tuloup, *Julien Offroy de la Mettrie. Un précurseur méconnu* (Paris 1938).
[57] J. Cumming, *Helvetius: his Life and Place in the History of Educational Thought* (London 1955).

vetius, Étienne Condillac (1715–80)[58] in his sensualism based on J. Locke (*Traité des sensation* [1754]) does not touch on the immorality of an immaterial soul nor on the issue of deist faith. As many of the writers of the Enlightenment, he was still worried about securing the moral bases of society. The extreme representative of materialist atheism in France was P. H. D. von Holbach (1723–89).[59] Raised in France as the son of a wealthy upstart from the Palatinate, his vulgarly materialist *Système de la nature* (1770) also appeared in a German translation (1783). His pamphlet *Les Prêtres démasqués* (1768) was rejected even by the likes of Diderot as tasteless. Voltaire, Rousseau, and Georges-Louis de Buffon (1707–88), the famous author of the *Histoire naturelle* (1749–88: thirty-six volumes; 1804: a total of forty-four volumes), withdrew from the circle which Holbach attracted around himself. In contrast to the materialism of the literary figures the important natural scientists of the eighteenth century for the most part were reluctant to accept generalizations—regardless of the radical manner by which they delimited their empirical methods from theology and metaphysics. This was also true of G.-L. de Buffon,[60] intendant of the royal gardens in Paris since 1739, to whom Louis XIV dedicated a bust with the inscription "Majestati naturae par ingenium." He held fast to the "infinite distinction" between man and "the most perfect animal"; for him the "unnoticeable degrees" of gradation in nature were "suddenly rendered invalid" by virtue of the difference between the thinking and the material being.[61] His original theory of the constancy of species, which—it was long felt—could not be abandoned in view of the doctrine of creation, was corrected by de Buffon after 1753. This theory was even more decisively polemicized against by de Buffon's friend and protége Jean-Baptiste de Lamarck (1744–1829),[62] who offered an initial theory of evolution (*Philosophie zoologique,* 2 vols. [Paris 1809]; *Histoire naturelle des Animaux sans vertèbres,* 7 vols. [1815–22]). But avowed atheism is

[58] R. Bizzarri, *Condillac* (Brescia 1945).

[59] P. Naville, *Paul Thiry d'Holbach et la philosophie scientifique au XVIIIe siècle* (Paris 1943); V. W. Topazio, *D'Holbach's Moral Philosophy* (Geneva 1956).

[60] Georges Louis Leclerc Buffon, *Œuvres complètes,* ed. by H. R. Duthilloeul, 12 vols. (Paris 1822); G. L. L. Buffon, *Œuvres complètes avec la nomenclature Linnéenne et la classification de Cuvier, par M. Florens,* 12 vols. (Paris 1853–55).—Lit. in L. Roule, *L'histoire de la nature vivante d'après l'œuvre des grands naturalistes français,* 6 vols. (Paris 1924–32), Vol. I on Buffon; O. Fellows, *Buffon's Place in the Enlightenment* in T. Besterman, ed., *Studies on Voltaire and the 18th Century* (Geneva 1955ff.); E. Genet-Varcin and J. Roger, *Bibliographie de Buffon* (Paris 1955).

[61] G. L. L. de Buffon, *Histoire naturelle de l'homme* (Paris 1749) II, 8.

[62] L. Roule, *L'histoire . . .* IV; G. Wiehler, "Lamarck," *Der Biologe* 9 (1940).

encountered more among the literati than the truly scholarly natural scientists. The idea of progress,[63] just as atheism, was in its enthusiastic form of expression mainly a phenomenon of the French Enlightenment. But it was also a case where the French Enlightenment retained an amount of skepticism towards that faith, as was nowhere more clearly expressed than with Voltaire. Robert-Jacques Turgot (1727–81)[64] who initially studied theology and then turned to economics—he was finance minister from 1774 to 1776—in 1750 read two essays at the Sorbonne entitled "Sur les progrès successifs de l'esprit humain" (not published until 1809). In them he established a correspondence between the historical development of production stages and global commerce on the one hand, and the development of moral forces towards a moderation of customs and habits and a peaceful rapprochement of nations on the other, which includes the influence of Christianity. A friend of Turgot's was the Girondist Antoine de Condorcet (1743–94).[65] His *Esquisse d'un tableau historique des progrès de l'esprit humain,* written in 1794 when he faced death at the hands of the Revolution, in such a situation could not fail to go beyond the question of perfectivizing the satisfaction of basic needs, posing the question which fundamentally contradicts the belief in progress, the question of individual death, which cannot be extinguished by any collective perfectibility of mankind. The answer lies in the hope for a time in which individual life expectancy has been expanded far enough so that man slowly looses his energies and desire for life and, while not becoming immortal, dies satiated by life. To be sure, in such a meditation, eye to eye with one's own violent death, the possibility of the "unusual coincidence" cannot be excluded.

In 1621 after the Synod of Dordrecht (1619) the Remonstrant Hugo Grotius was forced to flee to France and was banished again upon his return in 1632 from the Republic of the United Netherlands, which had been founded in 1588 following the battle against religious and political oppression. In his Dutch refuge Descartes had met with the opposition of the Calvinists, just as he had met with the opposition of the Sorbonne

---

[63] C. Frankel, *The Faith of Reason; the Idea of Progress in the French Enlightenment* (New York 1948); M. Ghio. *L'Idea di progresso nell'illuminismo francese e tedesco* (Turin 1962); G. Iggers, "Der Fortschrittsgedanke noch einmal kritisch betrachtet," *Saeculum* 16 (1965), 409–22.

[64] *Œuvres de Turgot et documents le concernant,* ed. by G. Schelle, 5 vols. (Paris 1913–23); F. Alenguy, *Turgot (1727–1781). Homme privé, homme d'État* (Paris 1942); P. Jolly, *Turgot* (Paris 1944); C.-J. Gignoux, *Turgot* (Paris 1946).

[65] *Œuvres de Condorcet,* ed. by A. Condorcet O'Conor and M. F. Arago, 12 vols. (Paris 1847–49); E. Kohn-Bramstedt, "Condorcet u. das Geschichtsbild der späten Aufklärung," *AKG* 20 (1930) 52f.; A. Cento, *Condorcet e l'idea di progesso* (Florence 1956); J. Bouissounouse, *Condorcet. Le philosophe dans la révolution* (Paris 1962).

and the Jesuits in France. But in 1638 Galilei's main work, the *Discorsi e dimonstrazioni,* was able to appear in Leiden. For the Trinitarians, expelled from Poland in 1658, the federation became the same refuge which it later became for the Huguenots. It was celebrated by Pierre Bayle, who had been in Rotterdam since 1681, where he met with John Locke[66] as "l'arche des fugitifs." There Bayle founded the *Nouvelles de la République des Lettres,* a journal read by modern intellectuals all over Europe (Amsterdam 1684–89 in six volumes; edited by Bayle himself until February 1687). But in 1693 he was forced to relinquish his chair of philosophy. Yet the Netherlands, led by an urban bourgeoisie with their avant-garde gazettes in Leiden and Utrecht,[67] their presses, whose names appear in the best-known works of the Enlightenment, and with its book trade became an intellectual market place. The botanical collections in Leiden, as well, became an attraction for critical spirits such as Carl v. Linné.

The philosopher Baruch (Benedictus in his own Latinization) de Spinoza (1632–77),[68] of Portuguese Jewish parentage, is only geographically Dutch. Ceremoniously expelled from the synagogue in 1656, he lived in lonely poverty in The Hague from 1670 on as a grinder of optical instruments. In his philosophy—the main work being his *Ethica ordine geometrico demonstrata,* published posthumously in 1677—he takes up the basic problem of Cartesian dualism, asserting the *res cogitans* and the *res extensa* is being the two recognizeable ones under the attributes of the *deus omnium rerum causa immanens, non transiens* of the *natura naturans.* This philosophy was rejected by Leibniz and did not have a full impact until the post-Kantian philosophy of monism in Germany, even though it had had some influence on G. E. Lessing and J. G. Herder.

In the German Empire and its countries[69] the principles of the Reli-

[66] P. Dibon, ed., *Pierre Bayle le philosophe de Rotterdam* (Amsterdam and Paris 1959); according to Ivo Schöffer in F. Wagner, *Handbuch,* 654, n. 3, the lit. on the Huguenots in the Netherlands is very outdated.

[67] E. Hatin, *Les gazettes de Hollande et la presse clandestine aux XVIIe et XVIIIe siècles* (Paris 1865).

[68] K. Fischer, *Geschichte der neueren Philosophie 2: Spinozas Leben, Werke und Lehre* (Heidelberg 1946); L. Strauss, *Die Religionsphilosophie Spinozas als Grundlage seiner Bibelwissenschaft* (Berlin 1930); P. Vernière, *Spinoza et la pensée française avant la Révolution,* 2 vols. (Paris 1954); H. M. Wolff, *Spinozas Ethik. Eine kritische Einführung* (Berne 1958); G. Friedmann, *Leibniz et Spinoza* (Paris 1962); A. S. Oko, *The Spinoza Bibliography* (Boston 1964).

[69] F. Brüggemann, ed., *Das Weltbild der deutschen Aufklärung. Philosophische Grundlagen und literarische Auswirkung* (Leipzig 1930); E. Ermatinger, "Deutsche Kultur im Zeitalter der Aufklärung," *Hdb. der Kulturgeschichte,* ed. by H. Kindermann, Abt. 1 (Potsdam 1934–35); H. M. Wolff, *Die Weltanschauung der deutschen Aufklärung in geschichtlicher Entwicklung* (Berne 1949); H. Schöffler, *Deutscher Geist im 18. Jh. Essays zur Geistes-*

gious Peace of Augsburg concerning the determination of 1624 as the fixed year had been modified in 1648 inasmuch as a change of denominations occurring between 1624 and 1648 was tolerated, although with some exceptions. The formation of larger territories had resulted in a mixing of denominations (the Reformed Churches were also recognized); in individual cases the immigration of new elements of population had been promoted (especially through the admittance of Huguenots); the "enlightened absolutism," theoretically based on Pufendorf's and Thomasius's doctrine of natural law, had developed (although at different times) in the various countries. But in spite of some modern features in government, conditions had on the whole remained conservative in comparison to western Europe. A primary reason for this is the fact that even under the enlightened regimes the bourgeoisie did not play as prominent a role by far as it did in England and France. Additionally the Reformation had continued to constitute a much more serious religious and theological problem in the Empire than in western Europe. This also contributed to the fact that church historiography, as presented elsewhere in this volume, was a specific medium for the process of Enlightenment in western Europe. Corresponding in its mathematical spirit to the Enlightenment, the worldly age of the baroque, in addition to its music and architecture, also created religious monuments of exceptional splendor in the German countries and Italy. Because of the chronological lag of the German Enlightenment compared with that of western Europe, arising from historical conditions, the intellectual movement in Germany was confronted with the extremes of the late Western Enlightenment and especially the terrorist phase of the French Revolution, and thus became susceptible to restorative ideas. Romanticism subsequently created revolutionary elements of its own kind.

Important centers of German Enlightenment were the universities of Halle (1694), part of Brandenburg since 1680, and Göttingen (1737),[70] whose Hanoverian rulers became kings of England in 1714, a factor which influenced the political and historical sciences taught there. Among those founded in Germany on the model of the Berlin Academy

---

und Religionsgeschichte (Göttingen 1956); W. Krauss, *Studien zur deutschen und französischen Aufklärung* (Berlin 1963); F. Valjavec, *Der Josephinismus. Zur geistigen Entwicklung Österreichs im 18. und 19. Jh.* (Munich 1945); E. Winter, "Der Josefinismus und seine Geschichte. Beiträge zur Geistesgesch. Österreichs 1740–1848," *Prager Studien . . . zur Geistes- und Gesinnungsgeschichte Ostmitteleuropas* (Brünn and Munich 1943).
[70] K. Hunger, *Die Bedeutung der Universität Göttingen für die Geschichtsforschung am Ausgang des 18. Jh.* (diss., Leipzig 1933); G. v. Selle, *Die Georg-August-Universität zu Göttingen. 1737–1937* (Göttingen 1937).

(1700) whose establishment was assisted by Leibniz, the Göttingen Academy was one of the most important ones (1751).[71] In 1732 the *Göttingische Zeitungen von Gelehrten Sachen* started to appear; as the *Göttingische Gelehrte Anzeigen* it became the leading voice of liberal science in Germany. Among the numerous "Moralische Wochenschriften" in Germany, appealing especially to women eager for education, *Die vernünftigen Tadlerinnen* (from 1725) by J. C. Gottsched (1700–1766), based on Wolff's philosophy of rationalism, was very successful. Its competition was the *Discourse der Mahlern* (from 1721), edited by the Swiss J. J. Bodmer (1698–1783) and J. J. Breitinger (1701–76), which was critical of Gottsched's rationalistic poetry. In 1773 the *Teutsche Merkur,* edited by C. M. Wieland (1733–1813), appeared as an organ of confirmed Enlightenment.[72] Following the *Lexicon universale* (1697) of J. J. Hofmann of Basel, the *Große Vollständige Universallexikon aller Wissenschaften und Künste* (1732–50) represented the new status of general education and the difference in spirit from the French *Encyclopedia.* But the most prominent propagandist of German Enlightenment was the Berlin publisher Friedrich Nicolai, editor from 1765 of the journal *Allgemeine deutsche Bibliothek* (106 volumes). Starting in 1761 he also edited the *Briefe, die neueste Literatur betreffend,* one of whose contributors was G. E. Lessing. In 1788 Nicolai published his *Öffentliche Erklärung über seine geheime Verbindung mit dem Illuminatenorden.* This order had been established in 1776 by the Ingolstadt professor, A. Weishaupt and suppressed in 1783.

Along with Descartes and Spinoza, Gottfried Wilhelm Leibniz (1646–1716)[73] was the most important philosopher of the pre-Kantian

[71] A. Kraus, *Vernunft u. Geschichte–Die Bedeutung der deutschen Akademien für die Entwicklung der Geschichtswissenschaft im späten 18. Jh.* (Freiburg i. Brsg. 1963).

[72] L. Salomon, *Geschichte des deutschen Zeitungswesens,* 3 vols. (Oldenburg 1900–1906), Vol. I; J. Kirchner, *Die Grundlagen des dt. Zeitschriftenwesens mit einer Gesamtbibliographie der dt. Zeitschriften* (Leipzig 1931); idem, *Das dt. Zeitschriftenwesen, seine Geschichte und seine Probleme,* 2 parts (1958–62), Part 1; F. Hertz, *The Development of the German Public Mind,* 2 vols., II: *The Age of Enlightenment* (London and New York 1957), D. Freiberg, *Der Wiener literarische Journalismus im 18. Jh.* (unpubl. diss., Vienna 1954).

[73] Leibniz, *Sämtl. Schriften u. Briefe,* ed. by the Preuß. Akad. d. Wiss., 40 vols. (Darmstadt 1924ff.); Leibniz, *Philosophische Werke,* ed. by A. Buchenau and E. Cassirer (*Philos. Bibliothek* [Leipzig 1924ff.]); "Apokatastasis panton," see M. Ettlinger.—Lit.: W. Dilthey, "Leibniz und sein Zeitalter," *Ges. Schriften* III (Stuttgart and Göttingen 1959), 1–80; M. Ettlinger, *Leibniz als Geschichtsphilosoph* (Munich 1921); W. Conze, *Leibniz als Historiker* (Berlin 1951); J. O. Fleckenstein, *G. W. Leibniz. Barock und Universalismus* (Thun and Munich 1958); H. H. Holz, *Leibniz* (*Urban-Bücher* 34 [Stuttgart 1958]); R. Wisser, "Leibniz u. Vico" (unpubl. diss., Mainz 1954); W. H. Barber, *Leibniz in France, from Arnauld to Voltaire; a Study in French Reactions to Leibnizianism* (Oxford 1955).

period. After serving the elector of Mainz from 1666 to 1673, he traveled to Paris and London for three years, subsequently serving as librarian and privy councilor at the court of Hanover. A scientist and mathematician, he wrote a criticism of the anti-Cartesian empiricism of Locke (*Nouveaux essais sur l'entendement humain,* posthumously [1765]). In his *Monadologie* (1714) he attempted to overcome both Descartes's dualism and Spinoza's monism by positing the universe as joined in the form of monads in "prästabilierter Harmonie" (predetermined harmony), but independent of each other and immaterial. Since they are nonconstructed units they can only "come about and perish all at once," that is they can only be created by creation and perish by destruction.[74] They are ordered according to Cartesian "distinctness and clarity"—man on an intermediate level is unclear regarding his senses and therefore only conditionally clear regarding his reason—in ascending order to God as the uncreated "central monad." While God is called "inventor and master builder" for the "works of nature," He manifests himself "on the other hand as king and father of substances endowed with intellect whose souls are formed according to His image."[75] In his *Essai de Théodicée sur la bonté de Dieu, la liberté de l'homme et l'origine du mal* (Amsterdam 1710) against Bayle, Leibniz addressed one of the major problems of the whole epoch, the question of the origin of evil in the world, to a greater extent than Shaftesbury, Pope, Rousseau, and, in his own way, Voltaire had done. In it he states that the world is of necessity imperfect because it is necessarily limited. Just as Leibniz's monadology and theodicy at important junctures function theologically, so is his position on history determined by religion. His confidence in the progress of humanity in the sense of an infinite process in the last analysis is founded in his faith in a divine universal design: "It is not in keeping with divine harmony to err frequently in the same manner."[76] Regardless of the rationalism of his philosophical theology, his differentiation of the two kinds of truth, the *vérités de fait* and the *vérités de raison,* prevents a rationalization of faith as that of Toland and Tindal. In contrast to historical pyrrhonism the *vérités de fait* are actual truths, part of which are the doctrinal truths of revelation. Christian Wolff (1679–1754), a protégé of Leibniz's at the University of Halle (1706), did not reach the latter's profundity. As a reaction to psychologism Wolff took up elements of "Scholasticism which had until then been pushed into the background."[77] Because of a speech about Chinese moral philoso-

---

[74] E. Cassirer II, 435.
[75] Ibid. II, 63.
[76] Fragment "Apokatastasis panton" (1715); see n. 3.
[77] M. Wundt, op. cit., 124.

phy he got into a conflict with the orthodox segment; as a result of their agitation he was banished from Halle by Friedrich Wilhelm I in 1723. Friedrich II permitted him to return from Marburg seventeen years later. Because of this conflict, and even more so because of his conciliatory attitude (which fit in with the German intellectual climate) Wolff obtained great influence, which extended even to Russia (*Vernünftige Gedanken von Gott, der Welt und der Seele des Menschen, auch allen Dingen überhaupt* [1719]). Among his colleagues in Halle who had found refuge there was the lawyer Christian Thomasius (1655–1728),[78] whose theory of natural law continued the process of rationalization started by Hugo Grotius by separating the legal duties from the inner moral ones. His teacher, Samuel Pufendorf (1632–94), the first German to be appointed professor of natural and international law in Heidelberg,[79] had already established the separation from theology in his major work *De Jure Naturae et Gentium* (1672). To be sure, he defined the *primum principium* as constituting the divine will, but in practice as the absolute state: it is "the pinnacle of human achievement if one, supported by the totality of the powers of the state, can say that one recognizes none higher."[80] But in his doctrine of duty he demonstrated a conservative attitude. Yet in the German domains theological issues retained their priority. The fact that Leibniz's philosophy, oriented towards theology, continued to dominate that geographic area until the arrival of Kant is manifest even in Gotthold Ephraim Lessing's (1729–81)[81] essay *Das Christentum der Vernunft* (1753). But Lessing, the son of a Lutheran pastor, a considerable part of whose literary work was occupied by the issue of the Christian doctrine of revelation, was at the intersection of differing intellectual currents. He was impressed by P. Bayle, for a time by Voltaire, but also by the philosophy of Spinoza. Although he applied as a criterion the correspondence with "Natural Religion" in his work *Über die Entstehung der geoffenbarten Religionen* (1755), he differed from French deism by adhering to the historic necessity of true and false positive religions. These were ideas which he expanded in a more profound fashion in his *Erziehung des Menschengeschlechts* (1780). It is here—more so than in his polemic with the Hamburg pastor J. M. Göze, caused by Lessing's edition of the radically rationalist *Wolfenbütteler Fragmente eines Ungenannten* (by the orientalist H. S. Reimarus [d. 1768]; 1774–78)—that Lessing's specific relationship with Christianity

---

[78] E. Wolf, *Große Rechtsdenker der deutschen Geistesgeschichte* (Tübingen 1963), 371–423 (with biblio.).
[79] Ibid., 311–70 (with biblio.); H. Rabe, *Naturrecht u. Kirche bei Samuel von Pufendorf* (Tübingen 1958); H. Welzel, *Die Naturrechtslehre Samuel Pufendorfs* (Berlin 1958).
[80] *De Jure Nat. et Gent.* II, 2, par. 4.
[81] A. v. Arx, *Lessing und die geschichtliche Welt* (Frauenfeld 1944).

is expressed. For him it was not a matter of finding an abstract rational concept for the truth of revelation. Instead he traces the education of mankind as an analogy of Christian salvation through the stages of the revelation (warning against its untimely abandonment) to the God-given *ratio* which is a category of the future, the "new eternal Gospel"[82] which Lessing invokes with reference to Joachim von Fiore. Just as Lessing's "Natural Religion" differs from the indifference of late French Enlightenment, so does his concept of tolerance: the model for his drama *Nathan der Weise* was the philosopher Moses Mendelssohn (1728–86),[83] who had remained true to his Jewish faith. Enlightenment as history, as in the *Erziehung des Menschengeschlechts,* was a lifelong topic of Johann Gottfried Herder (1744–1803),[84] a church official in Bücke-burg from 1771 to 1776. But he sounds more like a Christian in the *Älteste Urkunde des Menschengeschlechts* (1774), where he investigates the difference between the biblical and the general manifestation of God in nature, and in his *Auch eine Philosophie der Geschichte zur Bildung der Menschheit* (1774), a combination of philosophy and theology (a second part, which he planned under the title *Religion, Christus, Ende der Welt mit einer glorreichen seligen Entwicklung,* did not come about). But only in his *Ideen zur Philosophie der Geschichte der Menschheit* (1784–91) does the Christian religiosity recede behind a concept of universal nature initiating Romanticism. As F. Meinecke stressed, Jesus is now designated as the teacher of "the most genuine humanitarianism." Yet for Herder's total undertaking the words of Kant in his critique of the *Ideen* apply: ". . . a sagacity skillful in the finding of analogies . . . combined with the skill to captivate one through feelings and perceptions for a subject always kept at a mysterious distance."[85] Immanuel Kant (1724–1804),[86] whose critique of metaphysics and the bases of percep-

[82] *Erziehung des Menschengeschlechtes,* par. 86.—Thus Lessing overcomes the opposites of reason and history, one of the main problems of his epoch ("Die Form der Zeitlichkeit als solche ist kein Gegensatz zum Sein" [E. Cassirer, op. cit., 256]).

[83] Lessing is the best example for Cassirer's remark (op. cit., 218f.) that tolerance was indifferentism only among the small minds; but among the great minds it was the pathos of truth which should be divorced from all merely partial orthodoxy.

[84] *Sämtliche Werke,* ed. by B. Suphan, 33 vols. (Berlin 1877–1913).—Lit.: T. Litt, *Die Befreiung des geschichtl. Bewußtseins durch J. G. Herder* (Leipzig 1943); A. Gillies, *Herder. Der Mensch und sein Werk* (German; Hamburg 1949); D. W. Joens, "Begriff und Problem der histor. Zeit bei J. G. Herder," *Göteborgs Universitets Arskrift* 62.5 (1956); *J. G. Herder, Mensch und Geschichte. Sein Werk im Grundriß,* ed. by W. A. Koch (Stuttgart 1957).

[85] Insel-Edition 1, 243.

[86] In addition to the ed. by the Berliner Akademie: *Philos. Bibliothek,* ed. by K. Vorlän-der et al., 10 vols. (Leipzig 1903ff.); ed. by E. Cassirer, 11 vols. (Berlin 1912–22); ed. by W. Weischedel, 6 vols. (Frankfurt 1956ff.).—Lit.: T. Litt, *Kant und Herder als Deuter der*

tion was prompted by the Enlightenment, overcame the latter by attempting to fathom it. He raised it to a universal principle with his famous definition: "Enlightenment is the emergence of man from a state of minority of his own making." (1784). In his essay *Mutmaßlicher Anfang der Menschengeschichte* (1786) he applied Lessing's method of interpretation to Genesis 2–4, without Herder's application of feeling, but also without the historical sense with which Lessing lets the revelation pass in his *Erziehung des Menschengeschlechts*. By interpreting the transgression of God's command as the "first attempt at a free choice," which was connected with "the discharge from the maternal womb of nature," Kant defined man in his historical relevance more thoroughly than Voltaire and Herder. By his fall from grace man exits "from the era . . . of peace into that of work and discord, as the prelude to joining in society"; but the goal, the use of reason—as it is expressed in his essay *Idee zu einer allgemeinen Geschichte in weltbürgerlicher Absicht* (1784)—is not reached within the individual, but rather against the individual of the species, in the "antagonism of unsocial sociability of man," which causes the birth from history of "Enlightenment as a great possession." Here the detheologization of history is radical. But at the same time Kant's *Idee zu einer allgemeinen Geschichte . . .* seeks to forestall a concept of history as "a purposeless aggregate of human actions." This is not only an historiographical problem, one that was discussed explicitly by the Göttingen historian August Ludwig Schlözer (1735–1809),[87] who had had a falling out with Herder. More so than the moral work *Die Religion innerhalb der Grenzen der bloßen Vernunft* (1793)—suppressed by order of the Prussian council as a "disparagement of Christianity"— the two above-mentioned works from 1784 and 1786 manifest the critique of religious tradition, whose Western themes nonetheless continued to be the guiding ideas in the great works of Kant: soul, world, God—immortality, freedom, God (G. Söhngen).

If anything, the Enlightenment in Switzerland was even more conservative than in the territories of the Empire. Here the differences in the intellectual climate of the cities played a considerable role; the German-speaking part of Switzerland was more practical than speculative.[88] The first masonic lodges were established in the French part of

---

geistigen Welt (Heidelberg 1949); G. Söhngen, *Die Theologie im "Streit der Fakultäten": Die Einheit in der Theologie* (Munich 1952).

[87] T. Benz, *Die Anthropologie in der Geschichtsschreibung des 18. Jh. An Hand einer Auswahl* (Wuppertal and Elberfeld 1932).

[88] P. Wernle, *Der schweizerische Protestantismus im 18. Jh.*, 3 vols. (Tübingen 1923–25; also deals with the Enlightenment); H. Hubschmid, *Gott, Mensch u. Welt in der schweizerischen Aufklärung* (Affoltern 1950); E. Fueter, *Geschichte der exakten Wis-*

Switzerland, in Geneva and Lausanne, then in Basel and Zurich, whereas Bern suppressed the order. In all of these cities (except for Berne) academies were founded. The fact that members from both denominations could belong to the *Helvetische Gesellschaft* (1761)[89] was a first step beyond the long-lasting Swiss confessionalism. Among the most important figures of modern science in Switzerland were the brothers Jakob (1654–1705) and Johann Bernoulli (1667–1748), both of them mathematicians in Basel. Jakob Bernoulli, initially a pastor and widely traveled in France, the Netherlands, and England brought up again the suppressed Copernican system, but in the spirit of Newton he considered the mathematical laws a natural manifestation of God. Jean-Alphonse Turretini (1671–1733) can be seen as representative of the French part of Switzerland. He was a theologian and naturalist in Geneva who represented a moderate orthodox Enlightenment based on ethics. The Berne patrician Albrecht von Haller (1709–77), who had studied medicine in Tübingen and Leiden, became a pupil of Johann Bernoulli. He described his naturalist observations as poetic impressions (as in the didactic poem "The Alps"), but got into difficulties with his research in anatomy. In 1738 he became a professor at the University of Göttingen and, having attracted considerable fame, returned to his native city in 1753. He was a preformationist who considered the germ cell to contain the whole animal in miniature (*Elementa physiologiae corporis humani,* 8 vols. [Berne 1757–66]) and polemicized against La Mettrie's "godless opinion" of the soul (*De partibus corporis humani, sensibilibus et irritabilibus*). The Genevan Charles Bonnet (1720–93) was able to combine Locke's empiricism with the theory of preformation. He was widely criticized for his *Palingénésie philosophique* (1769), which attempted to combine the belief in revealed religion with Voltaire's empiricism. For his research concerning the reproduction of plant lice he was appointed a corresponding member of the Paris Academy at the age of twenty. He developed a theory of the stages of nature according to their organizational perfection, excluding not even the angles (*Idée d'une échelle des êtres naturels* [1745]) and believed in the possibility of "constant progress of all species towards a higher state of

---

senschaften in der schweizerischen Aufklärung, 1680–1780 (Aarau 1941); R. Feller, *Geschichte Berns* III (Berne 1955) 575f.; M. Wehrli, *Das geistige Zürich im 18. Jh.* (Zurich 1943); P. Kälin, *Die Aufklärung in Uri, Schwyz und Unterwalden im 18 Jh.* (Schwyz 1945); L. Weber, *Pädagogik der Aufklärungszeit* (Frauenfeld 1941), treats esp. J. Locke and Rousseau; contains a separate chapter on the Enlightenment in Switzerland (52–103).
[89] H. Nabholz, *Die Helvetische Gesellschaft 1761–1848* (Zurich 1961).

perfection."[90] The naturalist and historian Isaac Iselin (1728–82)[91] worked in the tradition of Basel humanism; in 1747 he lived in Göttingen, in 1752 in Paris, where he met J.-J. Rousseau, whose criticism of culture he rejected. Raised with the philosophy of Christian Wolff and deeply impressed by the *Esprit des lois,* he advanced a utilitarian ethic. After an illness in his thirties he changed his attitude towards Enlightenment: Voltaire now appeared to him to be "a witty poisoner of the human heart." In 1764 after a long period of preparation his *Geschichte der Menschheit* appeared.

French Enlightenment extended to the southern European countries, but its influence within society was limited, but least so in Portugal[92] under the rule of Pombal (1699–1782; prime minister after 1756). In Spain[93] under Charles III (1759–88) the reading of works by Montesquieu, Voltaire, and Rousseau became proof of a progressive mind; authors of the English Enlightenment were translated. Enlightenment in Italy[94] came from the same sources, but there it was Jansenism which represented the actual critical element. The native modernistic literature in the southern European countries ran the gamut from critical Catholic reform to a moderate Enlightenment (with the exception of Portugal). The Italian physician and physiologist Mariello Malpighi (1628–94, in 1691 appointed as his personal physician by Innocent XII) was epoch-making in the biological developmental theory; he investigated the egg of a chicken and of a silkworm microscopically and advanced the hypothesis of the universal unity of developmental laws in flora and fauna. At the same time he maintained that since "the essence

[90] *Palingénésie* III, 3; R. Savioz, *La philosophie de Charles Bonnet* (Paris 1948).

[91] U. Im Hof, *I. Iselin, Sein Leben und die Entwicklung seines Denkens bis zur Abfassung der "Geschichte der Menschheit" von 1764* (Basel 1947); idem, *I. Iselin u. die Spätaufklärung* (Basel and Munich 1967).

[92] H. Juretschke, "Die Aufklärung und innere Entwicklung in Spanien und Portugal von 1700–1808," *Historia Mundi* IX (Berne and Munich 1960), 135–57.

[93] O. V. Quiroz-Martínez, *La introducción de la filosofía moderna en España; el eclecticismo español de los siglos XVII y XVIII* (Mexico City 1949); R. Ceñal, "Cartesianismo en España," *Revista Universidad de Oviedeo* (1945), 5–17; P. Mérimée, *L'influence française en Espagne au XVIIIe siècle* (Paris 1936); L. Rodríguez, "La recepción e influjo de la Filosofía de Locke en España," *Revista de Filosofía* 14 (1944), 359–81; M. Defourneaux, *L'inquisition espagnole et les livres français au XVIIIe siècle* (Paris 1963).

[94] C. Ottaviano, *L'unità del pensiero cartesiano e il Cartesianismo in Italia* (Padua 1943); H. Bedarida and P. Hazard, *L'influence française en Italie au XVIIIe siècle* (Paris 1934); E. Godignola, *Illuministi, giansenisti, giacobini nell'Italia del settecento* (Florence 1947); M. Fubini, ed., *La cultura illuministica in Italia* (Turin 1957); F. Catalano, *Illuministi e Giacobini del Nettecento italiano* (Milan 1959); F. Venturi, "Le siècle des lumières en Italie," *Cahiers d'Histoire mondiales* 8 (Paris 1960); A. Noyer-Weidner, *Die Aufklärung in Oberitalien* (Munich 1957); E. W. Cochrane, *Tradition and Enlightenment in the Tuscan Academies 1690–1800* (Rome 1961); idem, "French Literature and the Italian Tradition in 18th Century Tuscany," *J. of the History of Ideas* 22 (Lancaster, Pa. 1962).

of things is hidden," one would have to "go through the whole range of phenomena" empirically (*Anatome plantarum*, 2 vols. [London 1675–79])[95] A solitary figure within his century, misunderstood even by many of his late discoverers, was the highly gifted historian Gianbattista Vico (1670–1744),[96] an unappreciated professor of rhetoric in his native Naples. In his *Scienza nuovo* (1725, revised 1744)—contrary to the geometric ideas of Cartesianism, but tying in with Augustine—he attempted to discover the one "ideal, eternal history, in accordance with which the course of all the histories of all peoples passes chronologically." Whereas man cannot recognize the order of nature in which God rules "freely and unimpeded," he can recognize the world of history which he himself made. But since man, "intending the opposite," was led to a just society only by providence, the object of the "New Science" must be a "rational theology of divine providence in history."[97]

The Scandinavian countries reacted to Enlightenment primarily in a receptive manner. Stockholm had the reputation of being a refuge (although not always an auspicious one) for great foreigners or a place where their work would come to fruition, as it was for Descartes and Pufendorf respectively. The son of a Swedish country pastor, the physician Carl von Linné (1707–78),[98] who during his studies in Uppsala was asked to assist the theologian Olaf Celsius in compiling a work about biblical plants, represented his country prominently in the history of natural sciences, although many of his works appeared in the Netherlands, where he had investigated the botanical collections in Leiden. He attempted to discover a natural system of organisms in which their "rational order" would be visible. For purposes of the flora he chose—although not exclusively—the reproductive organs as a principle of classification. The sentence which has become a classic in the constancy of the species is found as thesis 157 of the *Fundamenta botanica* (1736): "Species tot sunt, quot diversas formas ab initio produxit infinitum Ens,

[95] M. Cardini, *La vita e l'opera di Marcello Malpighi* (Rome 1927).

[96] *Opera*, ed. by B. Croce, G. Gentile and F. Nicolini, 11 vols. (Bari 1911–41); *Scienza nuova*, (1744).—Lit.: B. Croce, *La filosofia di G. Vico* (Bari 1911, 1953), R. Stadelmann, "Die Geschichtsphilosophie G. B. Vicos," *Geistige Welt, Vjschr. für Kultur- u. Geisteswiss.* (Munich 1947; best work about Vico's Christianity); E. de Negri, "Theologien des Historismus [Vico u. Hegel]," *Roman. Forschungen* 62 (1950), 277–93; G. B. Vico, *La Scienza nuova e opere scelte*, ed. by N. Abbagnano (Turin 1952); H. J. Daus, *Selbstverständnis und Menschenbild in den Selbstdarstellungen G. B. Vicos u. P. Giannones; ein Beitrag zur Gesch. der italienischen Autobiographie* (Geneva 1962); B. Croce, *Bibliografia vichiana* (Naples 1904); idem, *Bibliografia vichiana, accresciuta e rielaborata da F. Nicolini*, 2 vols. (Naples 1947–48).

[97] See *Scienza nuova* 44.

[98] K. Hagberg, *Carl Linnaeus* (Stockholm 1939); E. Malmeström, "Die relig. Entwicklung und die Weltanschauung C. von Linnés," *ZSTh* 19 (1943), 31–58.

quae formae produxere plures et sibi semper similes." Like Buffon before him, Linné later abandoned this theory and considered the generation of new species possible. Characteristic of the enlightened optimism is the transference of absolutistic notions to nature where God has "police supervision" and the animals have the duty "to maintain the balance among the plants . . . so that the perfection of the creator can shine in its full glory everywhere" (*Politia naturae* [Uppsala 1760]).

The history of the Enlightenment in eastern Europe was similar to that in northern and southern Europe. As a consequence of the political history in Poland, French Enlightenment—especially that of Rousseau—did not have a noticeable influence there until the end of the eighteenth century. The Enlightenment was received both sooner and more extensively—yet also in an adapted form—in Russia,[99] where it also became an element in its native literature. In a country without a bourgeoisie this was a process initiated from above. The Academy of Sciences in Petersburg[100] was built in the spirit of Peter the Great (1689–1725), but for a long time it had to rely on a foreign faculty. A significant role was played by the Western doctrine of natural law, which was, however, subject to certain limits because of the Russian concept of sacred rule. Suvalov, minister of state to Elizabeth (1741–62), the daughter of Peter the Great, who founded the first Russian university in Moscow (1755), commissioned Voltaire to write the *Histoire de l'empire de Russie sous Pierre le Grand* (1759–63). Under her rule M. V. Lomonosov (1711–65)[101] was appointed professor of the academy at Petersburg. A follower of the philosophy of Christian Wolff, which had generally spread in Russia, he combined an unorthodox religiosity with an optimistic rationalism. Princess Sophie Auguste von Anhalt-Zerbst, who became Tsarina Catherine II (1762–96), opened her court to the influence of French Enlightenment. Under her rule it was possible to publish the five-volume *History of Russia from its most Ancient Times,* written by V. N. Tatiscev from 1686 to 1705. Its theological and philosophical interspersions represented anti-Church criticism as well as the principles of a "Natural Religion." Catherine read Pierre Bayle and Montesquieu, corresponded with Voltaire, Diderot, d'Alembert, and

[99] R. Wittram, *Peter I., Czar und Kaiser, Zur Geschichte Peters des Großen in seiner Zeit* II (Göttingen 1964); H. Jablonowski, "Die geistige Bewegung in Rußland in der 2. Hälfte des 18. Jh.," *Collana di Ricerche Slavistiche* 2 (1962); A. S. Vucinich, *Science in Russian Culture* I: *A history to 1860* (Stanford, Calif. 1963); M. Raeff, *Origins of the Russian Intelligentsia, the 18th Century Nobility* (New York 1966); E. Haumant, *La culture francaise en Russie, 1700–1900* (Paris 1910).
[100] E. Amburger, *Beiträge zur Geschichte der deutsch-russ. kulturellen Beziehungen* (Giessen 1961).
[101] M. V. Lomonosov, A. L. V. Schlözer and P. S. Pallas, *Deutsch-russ. Wissenschaftsbeziehungen im 18. Jh.,* ed. by E. Winter et al. (Berlin 1962).

permitted masonic lodges. To be sure, the effects of this sort of literature were limited. But the elements carried into the educated aristocracy by French tutors by means of the French language—the latter having been made the European educational medium by the Enlightenment—can be traced throughout the modern history of Russia.

Creation and Natural Law—The History of Salvation and the World of History

As far as the Enlightenment was concerned, the objectionable theses of the Christian faith were identical with those to which the classical opponents of Christianity and those involved in present-day theological discussion have objected: original sin, the incarnation, and the resurrection. The deist concept of God cannot be reduced to a simple formula. It was characterized by two elements of intellectual history: the perception of a universal law in the natural world and the experience of plurality in the world of history, either recognizable in its laws (the *ricorso* of Vico or the variously perceived progress) or unrecognizable in its context (as in Pierre Bayle), a world no longer identifiable with the world of Christian salvation. The concept of a *providentia divina,* although often used as an empty moralistic formula—especially during the late Enlightenment—continued to pose a problem, preventing a monistic idea of the world among the significant thinkers such as Descartes, Newton, Leibniz, or Vico. Regardless of the various interpretations of the concept of "soul," the idea of the difference between man and the world was adhered to, except by the representatives of a radical materialism. Although the variations of customs, laws and morality, conditioned by nature or history, were stressed (as by Montesquieu), the uniformity of humanity was not questioned, but was rather to be reconceived beyond the level of historical differences.

The two typical forms which furnished the battleground for the fundamental conflict between tradition and the present were represented within the movement of the Enlightenment: harmonizing the opposites and controversy, both on a high and low level. The Anglican bishop J. Butler gained fame with his conciliatory essay *The Analogy of Religion, Natural and Revealed, to the Constitution and Course of Nature* (1736).[102] A classical representative of a decisive separation of the two realms was Pierre Bayle, whose Calvinist tradition has been underestimated heretofore. He demanded a resolution of the *difficultés de la raison*

---

[102] J. L. Murphy, "The Influence of Bishop Butler on Religious Thought," *ThSt* 24 (1963), 361–401.

solely by means of *raison*. But to the Christians he said—and there is no reason to interpret his words as scoffing: "C'est aux Métaphysiciens à examiner s'il y a un Dieu et s'il est infaillible; mais les Chrétiens, en tant que chrétiens, doivent supposer que c'est une chose déja jugée." And, not so far from Pascal's position, he writes about Jesus ("Il a voulu que son Évangile choquât"), religion, and pagan aphorisms in Paulinian terms.[103] Bayle's harsh "all or nothing" was for those who wanted to save the Trinitarian faith, but abandon original sin. Yet attempts at reducing the nature of the conflict to a superficial and harmless level should be distinguished from the true intellectual effort in this period to preserve the continuity of tradition while trying to resolve the crisis. These efforts revolved around two main problems.

The laws of mathematics and physics could be conceived as the work of the *factor coeli et terrae,* the master builder of the world. Just as Leibniz emphatically considered himself a "Christian mathematician," so did Newton call the "omnipotent" God the one who "guides all things and knows all things which are or can be created."[104] But the problem—while not in the case of Newton himself—consisted of describing the divine will in mathematical terms, from which resulted in the perception of the eighteenth century the absolutely regular course of the world in accordance with theoretical principles and without the need for the continued presence of God once it was set in motion. The topic is broached when Newton mentions God's "unlimited, uniform sensorium," in which God moves the bodies and in so doing is able "to create and recreate the parts of the universe."[105] He posits his sensorium, namely absolute space, in terms of physics, whereas Leibniz ascribes the latter to the "seat" of God. From then on the dilemma was created between the laws of the world—open to *ratio*—and the mystery of the world. This was a dilemma which G. Berkeley in his *Analyst* (1734) would only name but not solve when, in his polemic against the astronomer Edmond Halley (1656–1742; discoverer of the autonomous motion of the fixed stars) and in disagreement with the principles of calculus, he posed the question whether such findings were more plausible than the "religious mysteries and the articles of faith." The course of rationalism was indeed unstoppable; it was a distant path to the rediscovery of the mystery. But the issue concerning God had yet another aspect for mathematicians and physical scientists such as New-

---

[103] In *Eclaircissement* on the article "Pyrrhonisme": *DHGE.*
[104] See H. Lange, *Physik* II, 212, according to Dampier, op. cit., 210: "Er lenkt alle Dinge und kennt alle Dinge, die sind oder geschaffen werden können . . . . , der, an allen Orten gegenwärtig, leichter imstande ist . . ."
[105] Ibid., 210.

ton and Leibniz. The *factor coeli et terrae* is also a recognition of the *pater omnipotens,* the God of history who led Israel out of Egypt. The importance of Newton's essays on the Bible, long excluded from his biographies as mere eccentricity, is now recognized.[106] Leibniz's writings concerning biblical language and history as well as his fragment on the history of theology are more than the work of a "polyhistor."

Historiographers completely disregarded Newton's theological writings. Other theologically motivated theories on the problems of biology in the course of the seventeenth and eighteenth century take on the appearance merely of burdensome elements retarding the course of research if one regards them solely in the perspective of modern biological insight. But seen in the historical perspective they represent an admirable effort in the conflict between empirical research and religious interpretation.[107] Two main theories were involved, that of the preformation of the living being in the germ cell and that of the constancy of species. Jan Swammerdam (1637–80), cofounder with Malpighi of microscopic anatomy, attempted by means of insects and parts of their bodies to prove the thesis that all parts are preformed in miniature in the germ cell. Except for Caspar Friedrich Wolff (1733–94), who did not accept "the idea which is inherent in the uterus"[108] and whose epigenetic theory had already been implied by W. Harvey, the preformation theory was generally accepted. It was given a religious foundation by A. von Haller and C. Bonnet, whose *Paligenesis* was translated by Lavater with the title *Philosophische Untersuchung der Beweise für das Christentum* (Zurich 1771). The thesis of all succeeding generations also being contained in the germ cell was comprised in Leibniz's theory of the pre-

---

[106] F. Wagner in *Saeculum* 17 (1966), 202f.

[107] Unreflected naivety, prevalent even at the beginning of our century, leads F. Dannemann (op. cit. III, 3) to maintain that the empirical method alone is able to "distinguish between truth and error," whereas the Church's "religion with its eye toward the hereafter," lacking empirical means, adheres to its antiscientific authority. This remark certainly addresses a historical factor. But the problem is more subtle. E. Ungerer (op. cit. I/1, 6) remarks that while the "opposite world views" in the history of natural sciences appear to us now like "temporary diversions," they should nonetheless be respected because "the 'existential' view" too, has its rights. While O. Zöckler (op. cit. II, 3) is too intent on placating the opponents when he speaks of the "intimate relations between theology and science," W. Philipp (*Zeitalter der Aufklärung,* p. LIX) uses the example of Newton to demonstrate "that in this case the religious impulse carried the research," a fact which was insufficiently appreciated if one registered with great astonishment no more than "the 'religious returns' among the heroes of progress and Enlightenment." It is perhaps exaggerated, but not unfounded, if he maintains that "the investigation of the intellectual and theological history of the period of Enlightenment is in its infancy" (ibid., p. XI).—See F. Wagner, *Saeculum* 17 (1966), 193–204.

[108] *Theoria generationis* (1759), quoted in "Ostwalds Klassikern der exakten Wissenschaften" Nr. 84 (Leipzig 1896), vol. II, 84.

formed germ cells existing continuously since creation. The idea of extreme constancy of the species because their propagation is "vera continuatio," as formulated by the early Linné in his *Philosophia botanica* (1751), is based on the theory of the initial perfection of creation. This was accepted in principle by Descartes, although he added the proviso that it would improve the understanding of this matter if "the gradual genesis from the seed were observed."[109] Linné himself modified the theory of the constancy of the species. His contemporary opponent, G.-L. Buffon, called Linné's classification an invented construct and considered "the nature of the species" to be constant, "just as old and constant as nature," even if there are variabilities resulting from climatic effects, but all of them within the "idea of an initial plan." In opposition to the "rash" classification by Linné, which postulates the "omnipotence of nature, capable of extracting" all organized beings from a single one, he emphatically invokes the Book of Genesis.[110] But Buffon, too, arrived at a point where he modified his thesis. Lamarck considered the constancy of the species for the duration of many generations merely a rare special case. If all organisms are products of nature, their gradual subsequent origin begins with the simplest organizations without a goal being involved—this was in contradiction to Leibniz's image of the world. What appears to us as a goal "is in reality only a necessity."[111] An opponent of his was Erasmus Darwin (1731–1802). In his *Zoonomia* (1794) he combined the change of species with the faith in the creation by the assumption of a "first great cause" which gave to changeability the direction towards perfection. Joseph Gottlieb Koelreuter (1733–1806) represented a caesura inasmuch as he violated the taboo of "unnatural propagation" by attempting crossbreeding.[112]

With all the consequences resulting from the total scientism, progressively applied to the world view (including present-day space travel), the issue of the human being was a decisive one. The fact that much existed in the world prior to the arrival of man, as Descartes emphasized,[113] could be reconciled with the report of the creation. But has the world been created with a view towards man? Leibniz gave an

[109] *Principia* III, 45.
[110] *Œuvres complètes* (ed. by Florens, see n. 60) II, 412–16.
[111] *Philosophie zoologique,* 2 vols. (Paris 1809), Vol. I, 217; *Hist. nat. des animaux sans vertèbres* (Paris 1815–22) I, 323.—But as Dijkerhous (op. cit., 551) stresses, this "necessity" is not conceived according to the literary model of the Enlightenment as that of a clockwork because the classical natural sciences did not pose the question of beginning and purpose.
[112] J. G. Koelreuter, *Vorläufige Nachrichten von einigen das Geschlecht der Pflanzen betreffenden Versuchen . . .* (Leipzig 1761–66).
[113] *Principia* III, 3.

affirmative answer to this question, albeit with some provisos. On his "échelle des êtres naturels," C. Bonnet (1745) placed man at the top because his organization was the highest; above him were the angels. But like most of the natural scientists he too underwent a change in his world view, even though he continued to adhere to the "fins" of creation. Still concealed, but nonetheless efficacious, was the documentation of the sort of masochism which prompted man, who was just then reaching for his godlike humanity, to kick himself from the throne of creation by pronouncing an unreflected evolutionism deriving man from the fishes, as proved by the scales on his skin.[114] For Holbach's materialistic anthropology the question of the origin of man was essentially irrelevant; La Mettrie introduced a temporary parting from philosophy by remarking that "an unlimited number of experiences and observations . . . can be found in the annals of medical scientists who were philosophers, but nowhere among the philosophers who were not medical scientists."

Perhaps the discussion of Kant's critique of divine proof on the part of New Scholasticism permitted the problem "creation and natural law" to gain inordinate prominence in the development of Enlightenment vis-à-vis the other process, which touches more profoundly on the Christian faith because the latter is essentially a historical faith: the "Enlightenment" of the Christian history of salvation. The exact formulation of that which happened there comes from Voltaire. In his polemic against Bossuet he called it ridiculous "to attempt to prove that the God of all nations of the earth and of all creatures of other stars did not occupy himself with the revolutions of Asia and that only with a view upon the small Jewish nation did he send so many conquerers, one after the other, in order to humiliate that nation and then again to lift it up . . . , and that this small stubborn and rebellious horde were the center and the object of world revolutions."[115] This points up two aspects: the denial of the specific history of salvation explodes the medieval congruence of world history and the history of salvation; at the same time it poses the question of a universal view of history to include all cultures. We must hasten to add that the same Voltaire for whom "true history is the history of progress of the human intellect" expressed the profound skepticism of his age towards history: "Les temps passés sont comme s'ils n'avaient jamais eté. Il faut toujours partir du point où l'on est

---

[114] B. de Maillet (1656–1738), French consul general in Egypt in his work: *Telliamed, ou entretiens d'un philosophe Indien avec un Missionnaire François, sur la diminution de la mer, la formation de la terre, l'origine de l'homme* . . . , 2 vols. (Amsterdam 1748, The Hague 1755; Engl. trans., London 1750); "Telliamed" is an anagram of Maillet.

[115] *Essai sur les mœurs* . . . , op. cit. (n. 54), XI, 158.

. . ."[116] No matter the point of time in the present, which latter can be celebrated and also scorned: these words by Voltaire mark with brilliant trenchancy what would be called the "loss of history" in the twentieth century, the break with tradition. The words of Pierre Bayle: "A historian as such is like Melchizedek without a father, without a mother, and without parentage,"[117] cited most often as testimony for the approaching objectivity of historicism, should rather be viewed as witness of precisely that break. Origin and future designated by Christian salvation has been lost. But all of these and other similar utterances must be kept in mind in order not to have the relationship between the Enlightenment and history (containing the problem of salvation) blocked by the scolding of it by the Romanticists. The latter were first refuted by W. Dilthey when he said: "Enlightenment . . . has brought about a new perception of history. . . . The view of the solidarity and the progress of the human race in these works spread its light across all peoples and eras."[118] In view of the enduring Eurocentricity of the Enlightenment these words cannot be accepted without reservation. B. Croce's remark, on the other hand, according to which the Asian cultures had served Enlightenment only for the purpose of "expressing its love of tolerance or rather of religious indifference" without their representatives having taken the "historic realities" seriously,[119] requires an added remark: while Orientalistics in the strict sense belongs to a later time, the idea of viewing all nations and ages from the perspective of the human race is indeed a fruit of the Enlightenment. The fact that the problem of the presentation of universal history was one involving the subject matter itself if it was to be more than a mere aggregate was demonstrated with astonishing farsightedness by August Wilhelm Schlözer of Göttingen in his *Vorstellung einer Universalhistorie* (1772). He obviously refers to Bayle in demanding of a universal history that it should spread "without a fatherland" across all geographic areas. With reference to Voltaire he demands that it not have a predilection for "the people of God, nor Greeks and Romans," but rather be occupied with everything, "be it on the Hwang Ho and Nile, as well as on the Tiber and Vistula." The criterion of selection, he maintains, could not be gleaned from "special histories" but only with a view towards its "influence in the whole or in large parts of the world," thence a world history will order the "special histories" into a "lucid whole." In view of the fact that a universal connection of events appears only with the advent of moder-

---

[116] E. Cassirer, op. cit., 224.
[119] Art. "Usson", note F in *DHGE*.
[118] W. Dilthey, *18. Jahrhundert*, 209.
[119] B. Croce, *Theorie*, 216.

nity, "the universal history will connect nations who formerly had no connection or no visible one and will create a system by means of which the multiplicity can be comprehended all at once." But, contrary to J. G. Herder, this is not to be a system of philosophers but of historians. What is to be demonstrated is the way in which man, "this mighty sub-God," recreated the earth into his dwelling, this man who, to be sure, "is kept on a long chain" by the highest of beings.[120] Schlözer did not write this world history, but—except for the rational-theological concept of Vico—he formulated the problems it entailed as hardly another. In this way he was a creature of the Enlightenment, which, after all, only created the designs for a universal history, but no world history deserving that name. Yet the Enlightenment recognized that such a history could no longer be comprehended in a state of identity with the history of salvation, which was Vico's main problem. No doubt this is also reflected in the Enlightenment's doctrine of the state, in the rationalization of international law from Grotius to Thomasius, in the rationalization of administration and politics. In addition, the question should be brought up as to what distinguishes the sacred foundation of the absolutist kingdom from the sacredness of the medieval ruler to the point when finally "the theocratic charge is viewed in a more and more conventional manner."[121]

The causes of this profound change in the relationship to history were contained partly in the endogenous process of European Enlightenment and partly in the concrete experience of the world outside of Europe. In the process the two elements intensified each other. The strongest impression was made by the reports of missionaries since the late sixteenth century, upon which the Augustinian Juan Gonzales de Mendoza relied in his description of China. Foremost among them were the reports of Jesuits, those of Matteo Ricci (1552–1610), followed by the *Nouveaux mémories sur l'état présent de la Chine* (1696) by Louis Le Comte,[122] who reflected on the relativity of traditional customs. They also included the *Description . . . de la Chine et de la Tartarie chinoise* (1735) by Father Du Halde. The other authentic and fictional travelogues cannot be explicitly mentioned here.[123] The fact that François de la Mothe Le Vayer (1588–1672; tutor of Louis XIV), in his essay *De la vertu de payens* (1642) was tempted to exclaim "Sancte Confuci, ora pro nobis," not only antici-

---

[120] A. W. Schlözer, *Vorstellung einer Universalhistorie,* 2 parts (Göttingen 1772–73), pt. 1, 28, 20, 34, 32, 10, 38.
[121] F. Wagner, *Handbuch,* 87.
[122] J. Davy, "La condamnation en Sorbonne des 'Nouveaux . . . ,'" *RSR* 37 (1950), 366–97.
[123] W. Franke, *China und das Abendland* (Göttingen 1962, -Kleine Vandenhoeck-Reihe 146–48).

pated Arnold Toynbee's syncretistic litany, but it also demonstrates the profound impression made by this figure who was instrumental in bringing about the China rapture enduring until the end of the eighteenth century, parallel to which criticism of Chinese absolutism also grew stronger and stronger as a vehicle of criticism of European absolutism. The fascinating aspects of China were its sophisticated culture without a religious doctrine of revelation, the moral philosophy on a purely natural, societal fundament, and the high culture based on it. With an astonishing intuition Leibniz in his *Novissima Sinica historiam nostri temporis illustratura* (1697) called China "orientalis quaedam Europa," endorsing in that way the only high culture which had a global opportunity like that of Europe. In accord with his harmonizing way of thinking he expressed the idea that China send missionaries of natural theology to the corrupt Europeans, while the Christians should dispatch missionaries of revealed theology to China. Following the erroneous opinion that Chinese philosophy originated long before Greek philosophy, he condemned as unwise the prejudice that "nous autres nouveaux vénus après eux, et sortis a peine de la barbarie" condemn Chinese philosophy because it does not correspond with Scholastic concepts.[124]

Perhaps more profound yet than the ideas of the high culture of China was the effect of the encounter with the primitives of America[125] on European historical consciousness, primarily because the enduring topic of the "noble savage," originating in the sixteenth century, was a means of cultural criticism. Here, too, missionary reports played a large part. In his *General History of the Antilles* (1654, enlarged in 1667) the Dominican Du Tertre does not tire to contrast the natural morality and simplicity of the people falsely called "savages" with the evils of European civilization. Programatic by virtue of their title are the two volumes *Moeurs des Sauvages Amériquains comparées aux Moeurs des Prémiers temps* (1724) by the Jesuit Lafiteau, in which the Iroquois and Hurons of Canada are described as witnesses of original manifestation and as counterwitnesses of Bayle's assertion of atheism among the primitives. While the missionary reports only indirectly resulted in criticism of the Christian tradition, it was different in the case of Baron de La Hontan, who had served with the French army in Canada, had gone over to the Indians, and returned in 1715. Protected by the mantle of a fictitious

---

[124] *Leibniz to de Remond,* ed. by Dutens, vol. IV/1, 171; see A. Hilckmann, "Leibniz und die Pluralität der Kulturen," *Saeculum* 18 (1967), 317–21; U. Aurich, "China im Spiegel der dt. Lit. des 18. Jh.," *Germanist. Studien* 169 (1935); A. H. Powbotham, "China in the *Esprit des lois,*" *Comparative Literature* 2, 4 (1950), 354–359; D. F. Flach, "The Sinophilism of Christian Wolff," *Journal of the History of Ideas* 14, 4 (1953), 561–74.

[125] G. Chinard, *L'Amérique et le rêve exotique dans la littérature française au dix-septième et au dix-huitième siècle* (Paris 1913, 1934).

polemic with an Indian, his *Travels, Memories and Dialogues* (1703) attacked the Christian faith head on by awarding victory to the "natural religion" of the primitive. Enlightenment itself attacked the legend of the "noble savage," Voltaire with sarcastic scorn, Kant based on his principle of societal antagonism. Rousseau's "homme naturel" is not the primitive who is already a representative of a developing society, but the ideal construct of man prior to history. This going beyond all history back to the "beginning," from which vantage point one hoped to arrive at a critical judgment of history as a whole and win the future, was the revolutionary element. Whether it was a case of praising the "noble savage" in his heavenly countryside and his "natural religion," which was superior to revelation, or a case of outdoing each other in imagining the beginnings of mankind in animalistic ways, the origins of the history of mankind became a problem which the Bible no longer appeared to solve.

This loss of an answer in terms of salvation history to the question concerning the origin and the future, the latter either pessimistically conceived or optimistically envisioned as progress, constitutes the general historical situation of the Enlightenment. Its attempts to find new answers is only judged fairly if one views this situation not as an unavoidable but as a logical result of Western history and if one reflects upon the reasons why the Church "lost its leadership."

Church Life under the Influence of the Established Church and the Enlightenment

CHAPTER 20

Jansenism in Eighteenth-Century France

The Bull *Unigenitus*

On Friday, 8 September 1713, Clement XI signed the bull *Unigenitus Dei Filius*, which condemned 101 theses from the *Réflexions morales sur le Nouveau Testament* by Pasquier Quesnel.[1] This was the first official condemnation of Quesnel, who was generally considered the head of the Jansenist party after the death of Arnauld; the brief of 1708 had not been accepted, although it could have been assumed that this document, requested by the King, would meet with strong sympathy. In spite of the initiatives undertaken by the Holy See, France was not immediately informed of the text of the bull; on 9 September it was simply handed to Cardinal de La Trémoille and not made public until 11 September. Louis XIV received it on 24 September at Fontainebleau and immediately expressed his extreme satisfaction because with it he believed to have found the argument necessary for the liquidation of Jansenism. According to Gallican prescriptive law the bull, in order to become legal, had to be provided with letters patent, accepted by the bishops and registered by the chambers of parliament. The text was therefore carefully designed not to affect the sensitivities of Gallicanism. But difficulties arose from another side. The 101 articles selected for condemnation from a list of 155 were to be arranged in such a way as to furnish a sort of summary of the Jansenist doctrine. But a number of these articles could be authenticated by means of patristic texts; some of them in fact seemed to be nothing but quotes from the most esteemed of the Fathers. Furthermore, several of them on first perusal appeared to express the traditional Augustinian doctrines, especially those of unmerited predestination and efficacious grace. Obviously an interpretive effort was needed to glean from them a heretic meaning. The fact that Quesnel was the author was beyond doubt: the

[1] Text: *BullRom* XXI, 568 ff.

Latin translation was a faithful rendition of theses from the *Réflexions morales*. In contrast to what had happened in Jansen's case, the *quaestio facti* caused no problems here. But in the eyes of many readers the bull seemed to go beyond Quesnel and actually to condemn Augustinianism, to which many of the theologians and the faithful continued to adhere passionately, considering it one of the cornerstones of Christian thought. For them the bull was totally erroneous regarding the *quaestio facti*. One should also not disregard the fact that at this time the personal infallibility of the Pope was advocated by hardly any of the French theologians and that there was no agreement that this privilege even extended to so simple a bull. Thus the circumstances were quite different from those at the time of the Jansenist conflict.

Louis XIV at first did not conceive of any difficulties in getting the bull accepted. Accustomed for a long time to absolute subservience, he did not take into account that he had aged, that the end of his reign had become predictable, and his opponents now dared act much more openly. It can be assumed as almost certain that he had assured Clement XI that the bull would be accepted without prior discussion. Initial events seemed to prove him right. By means of a pastoral letter dated 28 September the vacillating archbishop of Paris, Noailles, retracted his approbation of the *Réflexions morales,* but without expressly recognizing the bull. On 27 and 28 September it was submitted to a group of parliamentarians, and Procurator General Daguesseau determined the central aspect of the debate by declaring that for him the bull was proof of the fallibility of the Popes. The parliamentarians did recognize that the bull contained nothing contradictory to the Gallican Liberties, yet they demanded provincial synods to be convened which were to accept the bull prior to its registration. At this point Louis XIV and Le Tellier, his confessor and advisor, recognized that their plan was more difficult than they had expected. Since the solution involving the provincial synods appeared to be all too difficult, the court decided to have the bull accepted by a special synod which was to be convened as quickly as possible and include all bishops present in Paris and those who could be summoned without delay. A letter of 5 October convened this synod for the sixteenth of the month. On that day twenty-nine prelates gathered at the episcopal see in Paris under the chairmanship of Noailles; during the following few weeks they were joined by another twenty prelates. The motion for an immediate acceptance of the bull was at once rejected in spite of the efforts of a small minority because the bishops were claiming the right of an examination of the papal decision. A commission of six members under the direction of Cardinal de Rohan was entrusted with an examination of the bull. In the process, Msgr. Bissy, bishop of Meaux, quickly assumed a significant position because of the confidence he enjoyed on the part of the King and Le Tellier. Clement XI predictably felt insulted; through his nuncio he complained about the fact that his decision was not to be subjected to judgment by the bishops.

By the court's request one of the first actions of the commission around 4 November was the dissemination of a French translation of the bull.[2] But this proved to be a mistake since it prompted the formation of a spirited opposition movement within the clergy and the public. The deliberations by the committee were protracted. By the end of December it finally became quite clear that a majority of the assembly were resisting the King's pressure, refusing simple acceptance. As a condition for any acceptance at all they demanded explanations which would preserve the Augustinian doctrine. Arguments for and against the bull were circulated; memoranda composed by Quesnel himself were sent to the commission.[3] In the course of January 1714 Clermont-Tonnerre, bishop of Langres, with the collaboration of Rohan suggested acceptance of an annotated version of the bull by means of an episcopal pastoral instruction. At first Noailles seemed to be agreeable, but then his friends moved him to revert to his earlier decision. On 12 January eight bishops, among them Noailles's brother, gathered about him and declared their intention not to take part in the meeting scheduled for the fifteenth. But the King, informed of their decision, ordered them to attend, so that the assembly finally included all forty-nine prelates present in Paris. The sessions were lengthy and stormy. On 1 February Noailles and the eight opponents declared their unwillingness to take any action until the Pope had been requested to furnish explanations which they considered indispensable for the preservation of the inviolate doctrine. The assembly dissolved on 5 February after forty bishops had accepted the constitution and the nine opponents had rejected it. Louis XIV denied them permission to send a collective letter to the Pope. On 8 February Noailles was ordered not to appear at court; the other eight were told by secret letter to return to their dioceses. From this point on the split in the episcopate became common knowledge.

Yet the King considered the acceptance by forty bishops sufficient to have the bull registered in parliament. The letters patent were issued without delay despite the heated opposition of numerous members of parliament who rejected the formulation "we are making it the bishops' duty to accept the bull." But the King insisted on precisely this wording because it was intended to enable him to proceed harshly against the

---

[2] Text: C. du Plessis d'Argentré, *Collectio judiciorum de novis erroribus* (Paris 1728), 3 vols., 3/II, 462 ff.

[3] List and Analysis: Louail-Cadry I, 80–105.

opponents. The registration took place during a session of parliament on 15 February where several members refused to take part; Daguesseau and Pucelle especially were marked in their opposition. The resistance in parliament aggravated the King to such an extent that he burst into veritable fits of anger at Versailles in the presence of Daguesseau and the advocate general, Joly de Fleury.[4] In the meantime the declaration of acceptance had been sent to Rome and Clement XI thanked the forty bishops involved in a brief full of praise. But the Gallican public was shocked by the significance which the brief ascribed to this act of submission to the Holy See. On 28 February Noailles reacted by circulating a pastoral instruction dated 25 February in which he forbade the clergy in his diocese to accept the bull, pending further instruction. Several other opponents followed his example. The King thereupon decided to force the Sorbonne into accepting the bull. It was submitted at a regular meeting on 1 March and accepted over the violent opposition of Dr. Witasse in a vote which took place under very dubious circumstances. A number of professors protested; five of them were exiled by secret letter.[5] Shortly thereafter the pastoral instruction, composed by the assembly and edited by Bissy, the bishop of Meaux, was sent to the entire episcopate. During the following months the bull was published in 112 of the 126 dioceses of France. No doubt this constituted a large majority, but not the unanimity which the King desired.

The most grievous problem was that those bishops who had accepted the bull were in fact not supported by any sizeable part of their clergy. A number of priests refused to read the pastoral instruction of their bishop from the pulpit or did so only with reservations. The same split occurred in the orders and monasteries. The opposing bishops, for their part, issued pastoral letters expressing the desire for a papal explanation of the bull. Yet most of them accepted a temporary condemnation of Quesnel's works in their dioceses with the notable exception of Jean Soanen, bishop of Senez, a former Oratorian who was soon to occupy a central position within the Jansenist resistance. At any rate, the debate was now conducted before the public and prompted the appearance of an incredible number of works of any and all format, ranging from brief brochures to voluminous folios: in 1714 alone the contemporary catalogues listed more than 180 titles. This large volume of writing actually made use of only a very limited number of basic arguments. Those favorable to the bull, a small minority by far, stressed that submission was due the King as well as the Pope and strove to demonstrate

---

[4] See "Fragment inédit des mémoires du chancelier Daguesseau," ed. by A. Gazier in *Bulletin philologique et historique* (1918).
[5] See (Witasse), *Relation des délibérations de la Faculté de Théologie de Paris au sujet de l'acceptation de la bulle Unigenitus* (n. p., 1714).

the identity of Quesnel's Augustianism with that of Jansenism. This was the basic idea especially of a memoir ("où l'on prouve que les évêques de France doivent accepter la Constitution par voie de soumission et d'obéissance") which was widely circulated in the form of a manuscript. No doubt for good reason it was ascribed to a professor of the Sorbonne, Honoré Tournély (1658–1729), at the time a highly esteemed personality. On the side of the opposition, too, the fight was conducted on two levels. The primary intent was to present the basic orthodoxy of Quesnel, his absolute conformity with the Fathers, and, most of all, with Augustine. The most important of those works is *Les Hexaples ou les six colonnes sur la Constitution Unigenitus* (Amsterdam 1714), in which the 101 condemned theses are juxtaposed with the Holy Gospel and tradition and are justified by other passages from the works of Quesnel and by additional long treatises. All the great theologians of the Jansenist party contributed to it. The work, originally comprising one quarto, was enlarged with each succeeding edition until in 1721 it reached the very respectable extent of six volumes. In addition to these, the same group of collaborators published a four-volume *Histoire du livre des Réflexions morales* which, while partisan, was admirably well documented, thus representing an important source. Beyond this, the opponents had to justify their position vis-à-vis a formal decision by the Pope in a question which no longer, as in the case of Jansen, concerned the *quaestio facti*, but the *quaestio juris*. Characteristic in this regard was the treatise by the Oratorian Vivien de la Borde (1680–1748) entitled *Du témoignage de la vérité dans l'Église* (1714). Its author wanted to show that within the Church it is the totality of the faithful and clergy and not only the Holy See and the hierarchy who are the custodians of the truth of revelation. It follows from this that the bishops and the Pope can err; it can even happen that the majority of the bishops can be in error. In such a case, it is the reaction of the Christian conscience on the part of the faithful which is the sign of the truth. The author does not hesitate to push his principles to the very extreme by asking all his readers to consider themselves judges of the doctrine by the same right as the hierarchy. By encouraging them into unfettered examination he manifests the motive force of E. Richer, whose influence on Quesnel we have already pointed out. The Jansenist literature of this period generally manifested an increasing receptivity to Richer's ideas, accentuated by the demands of the lower clergy, who were hard put to bear the absolutism of the episcopate. This literature shows the first designs of political Jansenism and its agreement with Gallicanism.

Louis XIV and the people around him did not grasp the seriousness of the problem. The animosity against the bull was to them merely the sort of resistance which had to be broken. Moreover, a brief by Clement

385

XI of 8 May 1714 recalled to the King in a veiled fashion the obligations which he had contracted.[6] But to find the right methods was not
easy. Since it was evident that the Holy See would never give the
explanations demanded by the opposition, Cardinals d'Estrées and de
Polignac attempted to act as mediators in order to induce the King to
accept the following solution: In a pastoral instruction Noailles was to
give his own explanation and under this condition to accept the bull. In
the course of the summer of 1714 a hesitant Noailles appeared to tend
towards this suggestion, but then Rohan and Bissey managed to interfere in the negotiations and to insert clauses which Noailles held to be
unacceptable. The result was a renewed split by the end of October.
Irritated by the delays, the Pope at times seems to have mentioned his
inclination to let the French bishops lacerate each other without inter-
vening. But at this point the intervention of Fénelon became decisive.
The latter's anti-Jansenist sentiments had become stronger than ever,
especially since he now saw an opportunity to take revenge on Noailles.
For the purpose of publishing the bull *Unigenitus* in the French part of
his diocese of Cambrai he had used—with some modifications—the
model of the pastoral instruction stipulated by the February assembly.
For the Flemish area he composed a separate pastoral letter, dated 29
June, which represented an emphatic defense of the bull. In the course
of the summer he also published his voluminous "Instruction pastorale
en forme de dialogue sur le système de Jansénius." As of 1709 the
relationship between Fénelon and the Holy See had improved. Fénelon
thus was a suitable mediator; it is certain that Le Tellier more than once
asked for his advice. After all, it was well known that Fénelon had had a
part in the dispatch of the brief of 8 May 1714. In October 1714, after
the negotiations had failed to produce an agreement, Louis XIV decided to proceed against Noailles although this was difficult to do without arousing the opposition of his colleagues in the episcopate. Around
25 October a system advocated by Fénelon was adopted: the convocation of a national council which was to condemn the opponents and
pronounce their removal from office. This plan was not without a certain
amount of danger. On the one hand, even the weight of the King's
authority could not ensure the assembled bishops to be prepared to
accept such injurious measures against their colleagues in the episcopate. On the other hand, it was certain that Rome—distrustful of national councils, especially in the Gallican Church—would not be particularly eager to agree to the scheme. But Fénelon was not to be
deterred by these obstacles. He was more than ever convinced that
forcible measures were needed, because any attempts at conciliation

[6] Text: Louail-Cadry I, 238.

with Noailles would be to the advantage of Jansenism. Also he was now mentioned as possible president of the proposed future council, which would give him far-reaching possibilities to proceed against Noailles and the other opponents. In addition, the esteem that he was held in by the Pope and the Curia had reached its high point; shortly before Christmas 1714 Clement XI openly alluded to his intention to appoint Fénelon to the cardinalate in the very near future. At this point Fénelon decided to make use of his influence by sending the Holy See two memoranda concerning the necessity for a national council and for promulgating the bull in every single church.[7] At the same time Louis XIV dispatched his minister of state, Amelot, to Rome, where he was to negotiate this matter. The King had a great deal of confidence that Fénelon's intervention in this undertaking would be crowned by success. The archbishop of Cambrai for his part was quite ready to do everything in his power when his untimely death on 6 January 1715 robbed both the Pope and the King of an irreplaceable mediator.

Given this situation, Amelot's negotiations in Rome took a difficult turn. Renewed attempts in Paris to reach a compromise failed and Bissy, the bishop of Meaux, was appointed cardinal at the request of the King (June 1715). In July 1715 the King announced that the council would be convened even without the agreement of the Pope. Parliament stayed in the background; several memoranda favoring the opponents mentioned the possibility of an appeal to the general council, an idea which soon began to spread. Shortly thereafter the King made known his intention to have parliament pass a formal resolution excluding the opponents from the future council. But this idea encountered resistance on the part of several parliamentary councilors, especially Procurator General Daguesseau and the advocate general Joly de Fleury. In order to have his way the King prepared for a formal trial proceeding in parliament. But neither in Rome nor in Paris had any final decision been made when Louis XIV died on 1 September 1715. The idea of a national council died with him.

In his memoranda to Rome and his correspondence with Le Tellier Fénelon again and again had stressed the fact that for the most part public opinion, in spite of an outward show of submission prompted by fear of the authorities, in reality adhered to Jansenism. Events following the death of Louis XIV proved him right. The regent, Philipp of Orleans, who was almost wholly without faith in religious matters, initially went against the policies of the deceased King and deliberately favored the Jansenists, especially since there were many personal enemies of his among those who had accepted the bull. After he had the

---

[7] Fénelon, *Œuvres complètes,* 10 vols. (Paris 1851), VIII, 269–81.

testament of Louis XIV (which only granted him the chairmanship of the council of regents) declared invalid and had himself appointed sole regent of the realm, he rewarded parliament by creating six councils charged with conducting public affairs in which the parliamentary councilors were to occupy an important position. One of them was the *Conseil de Conscience*, whose function had been severely limited under Louis XIV. Now it was enlarged and Noailles was made its president. The archbishop of Paris once again was an important personality at court; Daguesseau and Pucelle, well known for their opposition to the bull, were also invited to court, whereas Bissy and Rohan were excluded. Le Tellier was exiled, first to Amiens and then to La Flèche. At the beginning of October Clement XI expressed his dissatisfaction in a brief. The majority of persons exiled or jailed because of their advocacy of Jansenism regained their freedom. For a while recalling Quesnel to France was even contemplated, but in a communication by Pouillon several of his friends advised him "not to accede to the urgings to relinquish a state which derived to his glory."[8] The old man elected to remain in his seclusion. In his first appointments to bishoprics the regent favored persons who openly showed their Jansenist sympathies, as in the case of Bossuet's nephew, Jacques Bénigne, who was appointed bishop of Troyes, a person of more than dubious morality who used the fame of his uncle as a cover. Clement XI refused his bulls of investiture for the regent's candidates. But an Assembly of the Clergy, convened on 25 May 1715, had not been interrupted by the death of Louis XIV. One of its most marked decisions was the condemnation of the *Hexaples* (15 October) and of the *Témoignage de la vérité* (29 October), which permits the conclusion that these two works were considered the two most important ones in opposition to the bull. The regent promptly forbade publication of these censures.[9] But this did not represent any progress in the issue of the original condemnation either.

During this time, public opinion considered the pro-Jansenist attitude of the regent a veritable liberation. Numerous people and bodies of people now retracted their original acceptance of the bull, pointing to the pressure to which they had submitted. This was the case with the Sorbonne when it elected a syndic in the person of Ravechet, who openly favored Jansenism. The result was a number of stormy sessions, characterized by acrimonious disputes with the acceptants among the bishops. Yet the Sorbonne did not expressly retract its acceptance of the bull. But other theological faculties did so, among them those of Nantes (2 January 1716) and Rheims (1 July 1716). Yet the problem of the

[8] J. Tans, *Quesnel,* 491.
[9] Text: Louail-Cadry I, 458.

opposing bishops was not removed. Initially the regent hoped to solve the issue in a way to which Noailles had agreed in principle: an acceptance of the bull in connection with a pastoral instruction which was to give a more explicit explanation compared to that of 1714. In December 1715, eighteen bishops from among the acceptants signed a letter to the regent asking him to request explanations from the Pope. A second, more satisfactory letter increased the number of signatories to thirty-two.[10] The rest of the original acceptants adhered to their decision in spite of the regent's requests, to whom it would have been useful to have a majority of the episcopate demand an explanation. Shortly thereafter Clement XI let it be known that he would not give any explanation until the bull was accepted unanimously; in May 1716 he sent a brief with threats against the opponents, which was rejected by the regent. At this point a different plan was formulated. Since the fall of 1715 the opposing bishops, with the concurrence of the regent, had gathered around Noailles in Paris. They had agreed to compose a "corps de difficultés" containing their objections to the bull, and a "corps de doctrine" which was to present their opinions regarding the controversial points. Yet agreement on this was also not easily achieved; from this point on four of the bishops seceded from the group as protagonists of extreme resistance against a bull which they considered irreparably bad. These were Jean Soanen, bishop of Senez; Colbert de Croissy, bishop of Montpellier; Pierre de la Broue, bishop of Mirepoix; and Pierre de Langle, bishop of Boulogne. The documents were finally published in May 1716, albeit not without difficulties. What remained was to induce Rome to accept this solution. The regent decided to entrust the negotiations to a man whom he trusted completely, the Abbé Chevalier, vicar general of Bissy, who tended somewhat towards Jansenism. The Abbé's sympathies became obvious when he chose de la Borde, author of the *Témoignage de la vérité*, as his traveling companion. This could not have a convincing effect on Clement XI. Provided with instructions by Noailles, Chevalier set out on 14 May.

The negotiations were difficult from the start. Chevalier was not received by the Pope; not until 25 June did he even receive an audience with Secretary of State Paolucci, which was hardly encouraging. On 26 June Clement XI convened a general congregation of cardinals present in Rome, which was extremely unusual. In a speech lasting two and a half hours he presented the background of the bull and announced the dispatch of two briefs which were to demand of Noailles and the opponents to accept the bull within two months. Then he asked the cardinals how they would proceed against the opponents. The Pope did agree to

[10] Ibid., 490–97.

have Chevalier meet separately with the cardinals and since he did not want to receive him in audience he appointed two cardinals who were to hear Chevalier and give him an account. The letters of Chevalier show that he was laboring under some illusions concerning his talks with the cardinals. These submitted their opinions around the middle of July; on the whole they were strongly against Noailles and the opponents. The more moderate cardinals were satisfied to request one more attempt at reconciliation before proceeding harshly. Chevalier meanwhile continued his negotiations until the middle of August. At that point Clement XI told the representative of France, Cardinal de la Trémóille, that he did not intend to give any explanations of the bull *Unigenitus* because he assumed that they would not be any better received than the bull itself. Although Chevalier remained in Rome until the fall of 1717, his mission had actually failed. Rome and Paris agreed on another negotiator, the Jesuit Pierre-François Lafitau, whose service was rewarded with the bishopric of Sisteron in 1719. At the time he was living in Rome and in September 1716 he spent about three weeks in Paris, without an official title. He, too, was to pass on the "corps de difficultés" and the "corps de doctrine" compiled by Noailles and the other opponents and to effect their acceptance. These documents were dispatched to him shortly after his departure for Rome. But Lafitau could achieve no more than Chevalier. He was not received by Clement XI either. The latter, in fact, hardened his position. On 6 December 1716 a courier extraordinary arrived in Paris carrying a letter from the Sacred College to Noailles exhorting him to accept the constitution. He also delivered a papal brief for the regent demanding that he proceed against Jansenism and a brief for the acceptants encouraging them to reject any and all compromises and to announce measures against the opponents, and, lastly, a brief for the Sorbonne canceling its privileges.[11]

The regent and his advisers were disappointed and confused by this renewed opening of hostilities. Noailles, on the other hand, sensing support from the court, had more and more stiffened his resistance. On 17 August 1716 he had announced to the Jesuits of his diocese that he would not renew their right of sermon and confession, with the exception of the five Jesuits active at the court. But before his authority had run out Cardinal de Rohan, grand almoner of France, had appointed a Jesuit, de la Ferté, Advent preacher at the court. Consequently the Jesuit assumed himself to be fully authorized to begin his sermons on All Saints' Day, according to custom and with the concurrence of the

[11] Text of the briefs: *Suite de la relation des délibérations de la Faculté de Théologie de Paris*, 3 vols. (n.p., 1718), II, 1–39.

regent. But Noailles, incited by part of his clergy, obtained a revision from the regent and then revoked all privileges from the Jesuits. There was growing agitation on the part of the lower clergy manifesting violent opposition to the bull. Noailles felt overwhelmed by the letters and expressions of solidarity heaped upon him by his priests.[12] Publications for and against the bull continued to appear with great rapidity in 1716, although not quite as numerous as in the preceeding year. Those concerned with the disputes of the Sorbonne constituted a large number, but all of them evidenced the rise of Richer's ideas. In such an atmosphere it is understandable that new papal statements met with a negative reception. The regent refused to accept the brief addressed to him and forbade the letter by the cardinals to Noailles. On 9 December in a letter written by Maupéou, representative general of the clergy, he forbade the acceptants among the bishops to accept the brief addressed to them. Finally, a decree of parliament dated 16 December, followed by numerous provincial parliaments, prohibited the acceptance of the brief against the Sorbonne. Going back to Gallican positions once again made it possible to completely neutralize the Roman intervention.

Although an Assembly of the Clergy was planned for 20 November, the regent preferred to cancel it in view of the unsettled circumstances and instead to permit only partial conferences conducted on a private level. These again dealt with the issue of a "corps de doctrine" as a precondition for accepting the bull. In spite of conciliatory efforts by the regent the positions of the opposing parties proved to be farther apart than ever, especially since Colbert and Soanen heatedly announced that they were prepared to resist to the utmost. At this time the Sorbonne managed to clarify its position in an extraordinary assembly on 12 January 1717. It declared the bull to be unacceptable and assured Noailles of its alliance. All the while the negotiations were continued. On 1 February 1717 Daguesseau became chancellor and minister of justice. His great authority in this area enabled him to support his regent's efforts at conciliation. Noailles did not cease to vacillate, creating ever more difficulties. In spite of a warning from the papal state secretary Paolucci, Rohan and the other acceptants appeared to be ready for some concessions, which met with some positive inclination by the regent. A final meeting on 26 February 1717, while not reaching a definitive goal, did show some progress. For a while it appeared as if agreement was near, but then one incident was to put everything in doubt again.

---

[12] Texts of the letters to Noailles, collected: *Témoignage de MM. les curés de Paris*, (n. p., 1717) and: *Cri de la foi* I.

The Appellation

With the convening of new conferences in November 1716 an extremist group within the ranks of the opponents gradually had a significant impact. The initiative leading to its formation appears to have come from Jean Soanen (1646–1740). An Oratorian from the Auvergne, he had started his brilliant career as court chaplain. Jansenist correspondents accused him of being ambitious and having obtained his modest bishopric of Senez (1695) merely by virtue of his complacency towards de la Chaise. He was pious and charitable and an excellent bishop[13] who did not enter the controversy until the bull *Unigenitus* was published. A solid theologian and confirmed Augustinian, he expressed his opposition from the start. Gradually he became convinced that any attempt at reaching a compromise was dangerous. The death of Louis XIV increased his hopes and prompted him to spend some time in Paris in order to follow further developments there. Noailles's indecisiveness began to irritate him to the point of creating friction between them. In the fall of 1714 he appears to have decided upon a method designed to exclude any possibility of compromise: an appeal to a general council. In his radical opposition to the bull he had found support in the person of Colbert de Croissy (1667–1738), son of the minister to Louis XIV, bishop of Montpellier since 1696. He was a member of a powerful and wealthy family, no doubt accustomed a little too much to pomp and luxury. Yet he was an upright bishop who did his duty faithfully. Early on he had had some problems with the Jesuits in his diocese, but had not involved himself officially in the Jansenist issue until he started to express his opinions in 1713. At that point he did not hesitate to join Soanen in the latter's emphatic opposition.[14]

In November 1716 Soanen and Colbert decided to appeal to the general council. We do not know just what prevented them from going ahead with it at that time. In the course of the following weeks Soanen and Colbert gained two more allies for their appeal: Pierre de Langle (1644–1724), bishop of Boulogne, and Pierre de la Broue (1643–1720), bishop of Mirepoix, both of them virtuous and highly respected prelates. But in this issue they only played a subordinate role. Consultations between these four bishops were kept secret and nothing seems to have been divulged to the general public. It is certain that Noailles was informed and that he encouraged the appellants, but was unwilling to compromise himself. After several corrections demanded by La Broue the appellation document written by the theologian Boursier was signed

---

[13] See M. Laurent, "Jean Soanen évêque de Senez devant le concile d'Embrun," *Revue d'Auvergne* (Clermont 1968), 82, n. 2, 95–112.

[14] See V. Durand, *Le jansénisme au XVIIIᵉ siècle et Joachim Colbert* (Toulouse 1907).

in the presence of a notary from Paris, Chouvenot, on 1 March 1717.[15] Most of the text had been taken from the "corps de difficultés" of the opponents. What was left was to negotiate the canonical significance of the appellation. The four bishops considered the theological faculty to be the most suitable organ for the implementation of their plan. Ravechet, the syndic, had been won over and the faculty had been alienated by a very recent *lettre de cachet* from the regent which demanded that the act of 12 January containing a pronouncement against the bull be eliminated from the register. Ravechet was taken into confidence, but the vast majority of the public was totally surprised on the morning of 5 March 1717 when the four bishops requested to be admitted to the extraordinary session of the faculty about to begin. La Broue read a preamble and Soanen read the appeals document, which was then deposited in the chancellery of the Sorbonne. Of the 110 professors present 97 immediately voted for the appeal. At the beginning of the session one of the professors left in order to notify Rohan and the regent, who immediately had Noailles informed of the proceedings. On the very next day the archbishop expressed his sympathy for the four bishops by having their appeal registered with his office. After this the matter entered a new phase.

One of the initial effects of the appeal consisted of the regent switching to the anti-Jansenist side. On the evening of 5 March a council of which Rohan and Bissy were members decided to banish the four bishops to their dioceses, to exile the syndic Ravechet by means of a *lettre de cachet*, and to throw the notary Chouvenot into the Bastille, where he remained from 15 to 24 March. Ravechet died on his way into exile in Rennes on 24 April 1717 and was celebrated as a martyr by the entire party. But it was too late to stop the movement. Almost two years of policies sympathetic to Jansenism were bearing fruit and the regent was soon to become aware of it. News of the appeal spread rapidly, causing enthusiasm among many of the clergy. It is very difficult to get a precise idea of the situation because the contemporary literature did not give an objective account of it and we have no accurate statistics. It appears that those priests who favored the appeal were especially numerous around the universities and among the urban clergy. Montempuys, the rector of the University of Paris, on 6 March started to get other universities to join in the appeal, but the regent forebade discussion of the matter, though without success. Shortly thereafter the theological faculties of Nantes and Rheims joined the appeal. After their return to their dioceses the four bishops immediately published pastoral letters containing their appeal. In the course of a few

---

[15] Text: Louail-Cadry I, 764–70.

months fourteen colleagues in the episcopate joined them. On 3 April 1717 Noailles also signed the appeals document, but to the chagrin of the other appellants kept the fact secret for a long time. In fact, several among them did not divulge their position until much later. This was especially true for the bishop of Auzerre, Charles de Caylus, who had signed his appellation on 14 May 1717, but did not make it known until 4 October 1718 in a pastoral letter. Later he nonetheless assumed a very important position within the Jansenist party. Among the lower clergy, too, the appellations increased. It is impossible to make a listing; given the present state of documentation even a numerical estimate will perforce be inaccurate since some kept their appellation secret, others retracted it very quickly. On the other hand, the united support of numerous parishes must be qualified by the fact that genuine unanimity was never really achieved. Based on the very well-documented collective work edited by the Jansenist Nivelle, *La Constitution Unigenitus déférrée à l'Église universelle* (Cologne 1757), it can be assumed that the number of appellants ranged between 3,000 and 4,000, while the total number of clerics in France was approximately 100,000. But these numbers again have to be interpreted by taking into account that, on the one hand, there were appellations based on mere favor which—if one is to believe the acceptants—were even bought with money; on the other hand, many of the nonappellants accepted the bull against their will because they did not dare expose themselves; yet in their hearts they were on the side of the appellants. In addition, there were appellants among the nuns and laymen. On the whole the number of appellants formed a relatively small minority, but one that was very active and enjoyed the sympathy of a broad segment of the public. The action by the four bishops was highly effective since it placed the problem on safe ground, given the prevailing Gallican atmosphere.

It could, in fact, invoke a well-known precedent: the appellation by Louis XIV to the council against Innocent XI (January 1688), which has already been mentioned. This appellation, while not having the desired results, had not been condemned by the Pope. On 22 June 1716 in a speech to a general assembly of the university its rector, Montempuys, had recalled that in 1688 Procurator General Harlay had requested only one second to the appellation, namely that of the university.[16] Thus the precedent had not been forgotten. Parliament on the whole considered the appellation canonically unimpeachable. The regent was of like opinion and in an audience of 10 March 1717 he told Noailles and the opponents so. His only complaint was that the appellation had been undertaken without his knowledge. Several of the acceptants among the

[16] Ibid., 726.

bishops confirmed the canonicity of the appellation. Memoranda on this issue were circulated in the form of brochures. The acceptants on their part merely countered that the appellation was null and void and could not be supported because the bull had already been implicitly accepted by the whole Church. Thus the Gallican principles which had formed the clergy for more than thirty years gave the appellants a solid base for their undertaking. Under these conditions the publication of the appeal changed the situation and led the whole issue into a new phase. It is now understandable why there were seven bishops among the appellants who had initially accepted the bull; this was the case, among others, with Caylus, who had published the bull in his diocese on 28 March 1714. Furthermore, it should be stated that all the appellant bishops had been appointed by Louis XIV, who was intent on keeping clerics sympathetic to Jansenism out of the episcopate; further, that all of them had signed the formulary against Jansenism, that almost all of them continued to demand its signing in their dioceses, and that some of them even asserted that Quesnel's book renewed the errors of Jansenism: this fact reveals the extent to which the issue of Jansenism was perceived as being independent from the issue of the bull *Unigenitus*. Lastly, the appellation in its broad spectrum reveals the influence of Richerism, which had gradually permeated the lower clergy and even the faithful, who now frequently considered themselves judges of the doctrine. In this regard a reading of the appeals document is important. Here, too, the events of 1688 represent a precedent because Louis XIV had ordered Harlay to obtain the consent of the Parisian clergy. In the ensuing period of time the theoretical positions had been formulated. Publications openly inspired by Richer were now multiplying. We have already mentioned the *Témoignage de la vérité* by de la Borde. In June 1716 Nicolas Le Gros, canon of Rheims, who had been exiled because of his Jansenist position and returned after the death of Louis XIV, published his treatise *Du renversement des libertés de l'Église gallicane* (1716), which was an immediate success. This work is more moderate than that of de la Borde. But it is based on the principle that within the Church the authority of the body of the faithful is fitting and the members of the hierarchy are only its delegates. He designates the priests as successors of the seventy-two disciples of Christ and demands a special position for them. Lastly, he concedes validity to the judgment of the bishops only inasmuch as it expresses that of their flock and especially that of the body of the priests. Thus a sort of church democracy began to take shape which was destined to develop further throughout the century. As a consequence the Church of France was placed in a state of war, since all its dioceses were divided into appellants and acceptants and the bishop's authority was generally disregarded by the followers of the party opposed to him. For many years French Catholicism was split because of a number of conflicts which had a debilitating effect, although this was not being admitted. The regent recognized it, however, and tried to prevent appellation by priests and laymen, but it was too late for such a reaction.

Pursuant to the desire of the four bishops, the appellation temporarily blocked all attempts at conciliation. The disquiet it had caused in Rome was partly ameliorated by the news that the regent had joined the party of the anti-Jansenists. Yet Rome and Paris alike were unclear about the method to be applied now. On 21 April Clement XI sent a personal letter dated 25 March to Noailles, couched in paternal and imploring terms.[17] It had no effect on Noailles, who—as was known—had signed the appellation on 3 April and confidentially began to talk about it now. By the end of May even Rome was informed. The regent sent the Duke de La Feuillade to Rome in order to renew negotiations. To the bishops he sent an encyclical prohibiting appellations "without need and as long as the negotiations are under way." Around 6 July Noailles answered the letters by the cardinals and the Pope, warning against forcible and severe methods which could not but embitter the people and lead to unrest. These letters reached Rome on 23 July, spreading great disappointment. At about this time the regent made desperate attempts to regain control of the situation. On 7 October he issued a royal decree ordering both parties to be silent on the matter. In fact, he distrusted all parties involved, including Clement XI, who found out about this on 19 October and was injured by the fact that both appellants and acceptants were put on the same level with each other. Next, the regent had an outline of the doctrine, written by one of the acceptants, sent to the Pope in an attempt to obtain approbation by the Holy See and in the hope that this would induce Noailles and his party to accept the bull. But on 9 November Clement sent a severely negative answer. Meantime, in order to again disrupt the search for a compromise, the appellants had printed and circulated Noailles's appeals document, a copy of which had probably been found among the papers of the deceased bishop of Lectoure. Noailles, although angered, emphatically refused to deny his text, ignoring pressure by the court. At the beginning of December the regent pushed through parliament several decrees which suppressed Noailles's appellation and condemned a publication running counter to the royal decree. Some success in Rome gave rise to the hope that an agreement could yet be reached. But again the regent encountered an unbending attitude on the part of the appellants and unwillingness by Nuncio Bentivoglio, who was hostile to any compromise. Once

[17] Text: Dorsanne I, 337.

more the regent tried to demonstrate his preparedness to Rome by dismissing Daguesseau and replacing him as chancellor with Voyer d'Argenson, lieutenant general of the police, who was known as a friend of the Jesuits. But even this had no positive results: France ignored the order of silence and Rome initiated forcible measures.

On 8 March an inquisition decree surfaced condemning the appellation of the four bishops and that of Noailles. Parliament countered by condemning that decree on 28 March. Now the regent tried another way of putting pressure on the Holy See. Since the Pope had stubbornly refused to issue bulls of investiture for the bishops appointed by the regent, the latter convened a commission at the beginning of May which was to find a solution to this problem. Saint Simon, one of the members, solicited pertinent memoranda from experts, among them several of the great Jansenist theologians: Du Guet, Petitpied, Boursier, and Le Gros.[18] The majority of answers demanded the right of the chapters in the election of their bishop, some with the proviso that it had to take place upon nomination by the King. The person elected could thus be consecrated independently of any bull from Rome. These recommendations were favorably received in France and discussed publicly. The Holy See was informed about this by the nuncio. In the regency council mention was made of appealing to a general council the name of the French nation. In an attempt to intimidate Rome the regent mentioned in a letter the possibility of return to the old customs. This time Clement XI gave way; on 15 May 1718 the bulls of investiture arrived in Paris. But the regent seems not to have intended to reintroduce the right to appoint bishops, he merely wanted to scare Rome. But the idea went its own way and was soon to be realized in the Dutch Church. The dispatch of the bulls did not defuse the tense situation in Rome. Clement XI appeared less and less inclined towards a compromise. Correspondence from Rome in the summer of 1718 more and more frequently alluded to new forcible measures. In Paris one bishops' conference was followed by another, all of them gradually running out. But in them a new personality played an ever more significant part. This was Jean-Joseph Languet de Gergy (1677–1753), appointed to the bishopric of Soissons in 1715. He was consecrated by virtue of the recently arrived bull and was to become archbishop of Sens in 1730. Because the situation continued to stagnate, Clement XI intended to decide the matter by publishing the *Pastoralis officii* (8 September 1718), a letter addressed to all the faithful which excommunicated all those who did not accept the bull, yet did not make mention of the appellation. Pre-

---

[18] Their views are contained in L. T. Hérissant, *Avis aux princes catholiques*, 2 vols. (n. p., 1768).

dictably, the opponents hardened their position. On 24 November Noailles officially published his appeals document,[19] causing another wave of approval. On 3 October he issued another pastoral letter protesting the *Pastoralis officii*. This met with the approval of the majority of his clergy, while within the dioceses tension and unrest were on the increase. Also on 3 October the parliament in Paris issued an appellation decree against the *Pastoralis officii*; it was immediately followed by the provincial parliaments. In practical terms this deprived the excommunication of any actual effect and consequence.

In the meantime a new personality had come upon the scene on the side of the regent: Abbé Dubois, who fancied himself the Richelieu of his time. The acceptants held a large majority, so he thought it best to bet on them and to influence the regent accordingly. On the other hand he was hoping to be rewarded with a cardinalate, for which Rome made him wait until the following pontificate in July 1721. But Dubois completely failed to master the events. In the course of the summer of 1718 Bissy and the bishop of Nîmes Laparisière, an acceptant, published a collection of pastoral letters by French and foreign bishops favoring the constitution under the title *Témoignage de l'Église universelle en faveur de la bulle Unigenitus*. On 14 January 1719 Noailles countered with a pastoral instruction couched in extremely sharp terms. In Rome, as in Paris, it was recognized more and more that Noailles would never accept the bull. In the course of 1718 Languet de Gergy had become prominent by the publication of his blunt *Avertissements de Msgr. l'évêque de Soissons à ceux qui dans son diocèse se sont déclarés appelants de la Constitution*, which had brought him heated answers by Guillaume Dagoumer and Nicolas Petitpied. De Gergy was also the one who used a pastoral letter of 2 February and another one of 25 March 1719 to reply both to Noailles and to a pastoral letter by the appellant bishop of Angoulême. Bissy also answered by a pastoral letter of 22 February. In his own pastoral instruction of January, Noailles seemed to make some concessions that were disquieting to the rest of the appellants. The latter clarified the matter on 25 May 1719 in a pastoral letter by Langle, who published the appellation of the four bishops against the *Pastoralis officii*. To complicate matters further, the accepting archbishop of Rheims, the hotheaded Mailly, published a letter dated 14 May to all cardinals, archbishops, and bishops energetically advocating the cause of the bull. This letter was rejected by parliament on 22 June. Shortly before that, on 5 June, another royal decree tried to impose quiet on both parties for one year. Neither in Rome nor in Paris was it received any better than the one before and it had just as little effect. It could also not prevent

[19] Text: Louail-Cadry II, 149–56.

parliament from proceeding severely against de Gergy in the following few weeks.

While he engaged in intrigues in Rome by means of Lafitau and at the same time tried to secure for himself the archbishopric of Cambrai and the cardinalate, Dubois was also concerned with achieving religious peace. From his retreat in Fresnes, Daguesseau, still out of favor, took an active part in the religious issues but moderated his position. In three memoranda he authored in December 1719 and January 1720 he considered the appellation a failure because the number of appellants was too small. The memoranda indicated that he had returned to the idea of an interpretation of the bull by a "corps de doctrine." A new text, written under the watchful eye of the regent by one of Noailles's theologians, the Abbé Couet, was submitted to Noailles, Rohan, and Bissy in January 1719. The latter two had demanded of Noailles that he retract his appellation and his instruction of January 1719; the prelate seemed ready to give in. In March thirty-eight bishops present in Paris were prepared to sign the "Explications sur la bulle Unigenitus." Mailly, too, accepted the signing after de Gergy had intervened with him. Emissaries of the regent were to obtain the signature of the other bishops in the provinces. By 10 May 1720 a total of ninety-four prelates had approved the agreement. Approval by Noailles, which would have brought around a large number of the opponents, was counted upon. But in the meantime the safeguards to ensure secrecy had been broken and the public had been informed. Among the ranks of the priests and the laity violent opposition was aroused against any compromise at all and the four bishops, joined by Caylus, sharply criticized Noailles's "apostacy." The Pope, on the other hand, appeared little inclined towards a compromise which he viewed as an impairment of the rights of the Holy See. A letter of Noailles to his priests explaining his actions was condemned sharply in his diocese. In a parallel action many of the acceptants accused Languet de Gergy of having weakened. In addition to that, parliament, which had been exiled to Pontoise as a result of the Law affair, refused to register a royal declaration of 4 August sanctioning the agreement, in spite of the fact that Daguesseau, who had returned to the chancellorship a few weeks prior and had changed his position, exerted all his influence. Having delayed his acceptance all summer long, Noailles finally gave in and published a pastoral letter on 19 November containing his acceptance coupled with explanations. At that time parliament also joined a compromise and was recalled to Paris on 16 December. Then the Sorbonne submitted. Dubois and the regent thought they had won the day. La Broue had died on 20 September, but not before he and the three other bishops had signed a reappeal document on 12 September, authored by Laurent Boursier, which sharply admonished Noailles.[20] It was published by the three other bishops almost simultaneously with Noailles's pastoral letter and his acceptance. A decree by the regency council of 31 December prohibited the reappeal document. In the meantime a reappeal document for the lower clergy dated 19 November had appeared.[21] It contained the signatures of a large number of appellants, about fifteen hundred. But this number was far below that of the appellations of 1717, so the court was not visibly moved by it. Shortly thereafter a handwritten list of appellants was circulated and printed in 1721; this put the reappellants within the grasp of the authorities. At the head of this list was Abbé Jacques de Bidal d'Asfeld, a friend of Du Guet, who had to appear before a police lieutenant and was exiled to Villeneuve-le-Roi. At that point the three reappealing bishops wrote to the regent explaining their position. None of their colleagues from the episcopate followed suit. Languet redoubled his polemics. The death of Clement XI caused a moment's confusion, but soon it was clear that his successor, Innocent XIII, would continue somewhat the same policy. The confused polemics which filled his brief pontificate of three years hardly changed the elements of the problem. Initiated on 9 June by a letter to the Pope, signed by seven appealing bishops,[22] these conflicts provoked a large number of publications in which Languet de Gergy was in the forefront of the acceptants, while Colbert and Caylus played an ever more significant role on the side of the appellants. Bissy joined the fray with a sharply worded lengthy pastoral instruction of 17 June 1722 which provoked an answer in much the same tone by the six appellants in February 1723.[23] Dubois and the regent tried to control the situation by reintroducing the signing of the formulary against Jansenism as a condition for obtaining benefices and university titles; this custom had been discontinued in many faculties and dioceses. The result of this measure, implemented on 11 July 1722, was renewed unrest, especially in the university circles. The majority of the appellants obeyed because for them the issue of Jansenism was quite apart from that of the bull. But Colbert signaled the connection by prescribing the signing in conjunction with the distinction between the *quaesto juris* and the *quaesto facti* and the words of Clement IX concerning the keeping of the peace. In doing so he became involved in a long and embarrassing affair which we shall discuss later. The year 1723 was characterized by profound changes among the main actors on the stage. On 15 February Louis XV was declared of age; Dubois died on 10 August; the regent on 2 December. A little later, on 7 March 1724,

[20] Text: Colbert, *Œuvres* I, 265.
[21] Text: Louail-Cadry II, 518.
[22] Text: Colbert I, 303–54.
[23] Ibid., I 381–580.

Innocent XIII also died. At the same time a new protagonist appeared in the person of André de Fleury, bishop of Fréjus and former teacher of the King, who had enjoyed the latter's complete trust.

The new Pope, Benedict XIII, a former Dominican friar, was very open to the doctrines of Augustine and Thomas, but could not simply cancel the problem caused by the bull. But he issued the brief *Demissa preces* of 6 November 1724,[24] addressed to the Dominican general, which expressed his great sympathy for Augustinianism and Thomism and gave renewed hope to the opponents of the bull. But Noailles, in spite of the Pope's conciliatory stance, persistently refused to retract his appellation. At the beginning of January, following a very disappointing series of correspondence with Rome, he sent to Rome a collection of twelve doctrinal articles, characterized strongly by Augustinianism (which were probably edited by Boursier), and asked for their approbation by the Holy See.[25] Some of these articles openly seemed to favor Jansenism and the Roman authorities were scarcely inclined to accept them. In France, Rohan and Bissy, supported by Fleury, took a position against negotiations which they thought could cause acceptants to leave the fold, and the bishops of Saintes and Marseille condemned the twelve articles by pastoral letter. By an encyclical dated 20 June 1725 Colbert finally let the opponents know that in his opinion the twelve articles would not make the bull any more acceptable. Under these conditions there was no use in continuing the negotiations. A short time later, in June 1726, the duke of Bourbon fell from favor and was replaced by Fleury, who occupied this post until 1743. Smooth and agile, but of steely persistence, Fleury was firmly resolved to weaken the Jansenist opposition. With support by the moderates and those inclined towards reconciliation he did not hesitate to proceed severely against the extremists; more and more he resorted to the weapon of the *lettre de cachet,* a policy that proved effective in the end.

First he had to make an example of one of the appellant bishops in order to frighten the others. The most rebellious among them was without a doubt Colbert, who strove for the signing of the formulary after 1722. On 21 September 1724, a decree of the council of state had even deprived him of his temporal revenues. But Colbert had strong support. The aged Du Guet had a letter printed which he had written to the bishop on 25 July 1724 and which strongly influenced public opinion. On 13 February 1725, by the way, this letter and the publications of Colbert regarding the same topic were condemned by the Holy Office. The Assembly of the Clergy of 1726 demanded the convening of pro-

---

[24] See Louail-Cadry IV, 165–67.
[25] See Colbert I, 635; Louail-Cadry IV, 341.

vincial councils to counteract the unrest and, in this regard, joined forces with Fleury. But the latter did not dare attack Colbert, who was protected by the power of his family. On the other hand, the utterly defenseless Soanen, bishop of the tiny diocese of Senez, was a suitable victim. Soanen himself furnished the weapons for his adversaries. Towards the end of 1727—believing that he had only a short while to live—he made public a pastoral instruction dated 28 August 1726 which was to represent his spiritual testament. In it he emphatically took the part of Colbert and, unraveling the whole background of the bull, he violently attacked its acceptants. This seemed a sufficient pretext. By 24 May 1727, all the bishops of the province of Embrun, to which the diocese of Senez belonged had *lettres de cachet* delivered to them. Their metropolitan was Pierre Guérin de Tencin (1680–1758), formerly a close collaborator of Dubois and the latter's representative in Rome, a prelate of more than dubious morality. Tencin convened a provincial council for 16 August 1727, which Soanen attended. This council was characterized by complex and stormy episodes where irregularities abounded. On 18 August Soanen had rejected the jurisdictional competence of his judges, whose partisanship and hostility were beyond doubt, but an appeal based on misuse of power filed by Soanen on 26 August was ignored. On 27 August he protested against the irregularity of his trial in an encyclical to all the bishops. The judgment was dated 20 September and pronounced two days later. Soanen was dismissed from all his functions as bishop and priest, pending retraction of his pastoral instruction. Shortly thereafter he was exiled by *lettre de cachet* to the abbey of La Chaise-Dieu. He left Embrun on 13 October and arrived at the abbey ten days later. In spite of his advanced age he lived there for another thirteen years; he died on 25 December 1740 at the age of ninety-three, revered by the entire Jansenist party as a saint and martyr. All the while he had conducted a voluminous correspondence and taken an active part in most of the affairs that concerned public opinion. After his death even the smallest objects which he had used were preserved as relics. The council of Embrun, called by the opponents "the Synod of Robbers," did not have quite the effect hoped for by Fleury. To be sure, the Holy See approved it by brief of 17 December 1727, and it induced about ten opponents to switch sides. But the unrest it caused was lasting and violent. On 28 October 1727, twelve bishops, among them Noailles, Colbert, and Caylus, sent a letter of protest to the King authored by Petitpied, which was returned to them on 15 March 1728, together with a legal opinion which was disquieting to some of the signers. Boursier collected and published a *Consultation de 50 avocats* which asserted the invalidity of the council of Embrun. This was protested on the part of the acceptants by a *Lettre de 26 évêques au rois* (4 May 1728), which in turn provoked a polemic by the lower clergy calling attention to its rights. Since Soanen had demanded a general council beyond the provincial one, petitions were circulating in the dioceses for his appeal; they contained no less than two thousand signatures. Innumerable polemics appeared; the portrait of Soanen, the "Prisoner of Jesus," was distributed in copper etchings; a number of his followers managed to visit him at La Chaise-Dieu. The conflicts which were tearing the diocese of Senez apart were passionately commented on. In the end the total result was uncertain. The procedure was not repeated even though there was a plan afoot to convene a provincial council at Narbonne for the purpose of condemning Colbert, who had emphatically defended Soanen.

One of Fleury's major goals continued to be the neutralization of Noailles. At the end of 1726 the rumor surfaced that Noailles would give in to pressure by the minister and publish a pastoral letter containing an unqualified acceptance. It prompted a large number of the Parisian clergy to rise up against it. On 3 February 1727, a letter to Noailles, edited by Petitpied, appeared in which thirty parish priests who considered themselves successors of the seventy-two disciples refused to follow Noailles in any act of submission. Furthermore, they demanded that a general synod of the diocese be convened. The movement was lead by Goy, the appellant priest of Sainte-Marguerite, and Feu, appellant priest of Saint-Gervais. A decree of 14 June prohibited this letter, but in the "Très humbles remontrances des curés de Paris" of 5 September Petitpied again brought up this topic. In the meantime—as we have mentioned—the affair of Embrun had led Noailles back to the opposition. After he signed the letter of the twelve bishops, he also signed (on 7 May 1728) a document opposing the registration of the papal brief which had approved the council of Embrun. But soon the situation changed. By this time Noailles was visibly weakened by age and his ideas became increasingly unclear. Towards the end of February 1718 sickness had deprived him of his most valued adviser, who had always encouraged him to resist: Antoine Dorsanne, official of Paris and author of a *Journal* which was published posthumously in 1753. Fleury, on the other hand, found allies among those around the cardinal in the persons of the chancellor Daguesseau and especially the archbishop's niece, wife of the Maréchal de Grammont. They obtained Noailles's signature on a document revoking his stand against registration of the papal brief of 7 May. On 19 July he also signed a letter to Benedict XIII assuring him of his submission and absolute obedience.[26] At this point several appellants appear to have regained some influence over him inducing him to sign a declaration (22 August; the original version was sent to Soanen) in

[26] Text: Dorsanne II, 463–66, also for the following documents.

which Noailles revoked the document of 19 May and in advance repealed any public document accepting the bull which might be wrung from him in the future. On 24 September, furthermore, he signed another document protesting in advance against any forced dismissal from his archbishopric. This did not prevent a pastoral letter by Noailles, dated 11 October and containing an unqualified acceptance of the bull *Unigenitus*, from being posted in Paris on 24 October. As a countermeasure the appellants had the revocation act of 22 August posted as well. The Duke de Noailles, nephew of the archbishop, managed to induce him to write a letter to Fleury in which he revoked this act of the twenty-second. But a few weeks later, on 17 December, he reaffirmed it. In addition he signed another declaration on 26 February 1729 in which he revoked his pastoral letter of 11 October; the manuscript of that declaration was also sent to Soanen. The death of the unfortunate cardinal on 4 May 1729 finally put an end to these embarrassing conflicts revolving around an old man whose weakness and instability had been cruelly exploited.

The Defeat of Jansenism

The death of Noailles represented a turning point in the history of Jansenism. It marked the disappearance of the most important man of the party, whose personal deficiencies had nonetheless been clad with the aura of the cardinalate. More deaths and desertions from the ranks of the appellants followed, soon leaving a mere four. Aside from Soanen, who was exiled to his faraway mountains and deprived of all his authority, there were Colbert in Montpellier (d. 1738), Bossuet in Troyes (d. 1743), and Caylus in Auxerre, who survived the others until 1754. Although Jansenism, to the extent that it was inspired by Quesnel, developed more and more in the direction of parochialism by according a growing importance to the parish priests and the lower clergy, it found no leader. There was nothing that could make up for the lack of leadership, properly provided by a bishop; none of the three remaining appellant bishops were able to fill that role. Nor did anyone take the place of Quesnel, who died on 2 December 1719 in Amsterdam at the age of eighty-five. In spite of some internal disagreements the Jansenist party did preserve a real cohesion, but in the future it was an army without a general.

Noailles's successor was Charles-Gaspard de Vintimille du Luc, until then archbishop of Aix. He was moderate yet an acceptant by conviction, fully in agreement with Fleury's opinions. Henceforth *Unigenitus* posed no more problems regarding compromise. The French court and the Holy See agreed in their demand of an unreserved acceptance.

Vintimille was firmly resolved to break all Jansenist resistance in his diocese of Paris, even though it initially appeared that he underestimated the difficulties of such an undertaking and the impossibility of destroying an opposition which, to some extent, was to endure until the Revolution. Within a few days of taking office, on 6 September 1729 he obtained approval of the bull from twenty-five canons of Notre-Dame, but met with resistance among the lower clergy. This did not keep him from enforcing the signing of the bull by a pastoral instruction of 29 September. At the beginning of November a *lettre de cachet* declared the appellant professors to be dismissed from the Sorbonne, depriving it of a number of famous theologians; the remaining faculty was characterized by Pucelle as a "rump." Other opponents were eliminated posthaste by *lettre de cachet*, especially those among the parish clergy. On 29 October all confessors and priests were ordered to appear within four months at the episcopal see in order to have their ecclesiastical authority renewed. This enabled Vintimille to refuse that authority to about thirty appellants among approximately eleven hundred priests. The others had to accept the bull.

It was probably by request of Vintimille that Fleury initiated even harsher measures. A royal declaration of 24 May 1730 elevated the bull *Unigenitus* to the level of a state law; it again ordered the signing of the formulary of Alexander VII and declared the benefices of those who did not sign it as "vacant and available for reappointment by full legal power."[27] The weight of economic and financial sanctions of this declaration brought about the desired effect. Since church life in the *ancien régime* was founded on the system of benefices, such a measure put the Jansenists outside the pale of the existing order. But the text of the declaration, recognizing a papal act as state law, clearly manifested an ultramontane inspiration. Owing to Fleury's skill, it demonstrated a new posture, through which France and Rome found a modus vivendi which for a long time eliminated this perilous problem from the relationship between the two courts. It was in the nature of things that the most spirited resistance to this scheme came from parliamentary circles. In fact, the parliaments in their opposition took the place of the clergy, who, due to their very insecure position, could hardly express their opinion anymore. This explains the growing connection between Jansenism and parliamentarianism, a connection which cannot but seem paradoxical because a growing number of parliamentarians left the faith and turned to the Enlightenment instead. Parliament refused to register the declaration of 24 March. It took a formal trial proceeding to change its mind on 3 April 1730. The declarations of the ecclesiastical councilors

[27] See Cerveau, *Nécrologe* V, 270–79.

concerning this topic were substantially inspired by E. Richer, they strongly advocated the demands of the parish priests. Applying the same principles a short time later, parliament supported three parish priests of the diocese of Orléans against their bishop, Fleuriau d'Armenonville. This explains why the Assembly of the Clergy in 1730 complained about the rebelliousness of the lower clergy and the transgressions by parliament. The growing importance of parliamentarians led to the Jansenist theologians placing more and more stress on an argument taken over from Quesnel and de la Borde: the validity of lay witness. Innumerable polemics continued to develop this argument and defended it against attacks by the proponents of the bull.

When Daguesseau and Joly de Fleury submitted the royal declaration to parliament, they assumed that it would be a purely theoretical matter without any practical application. But in fact this declaration opened the floodgates for persecution of the Jansenists. The *Nouvelles ecclésiastiques*, numerous polemics, and an incredible number of archival documents testify to numerous unpleasant incidents concerning priests, laymen, parishes, and whole congregations. By means of the simple *lettres de cachet*, which dispensed with all due process, a large number of opponents were sent into jail or exile. Since there are no statistics available, it is impossible to list accurate figures, but it can be assumed as certain that practically all dioceses and orders were affected, including the women's congregations, the Benedictines and the Oratorians, the Carmelites and the Sisters of the Visitation, and even the Carthusians. In the fall of 1725 about thirty Carthusians and fifteen Cistercians of Orval thought it wise to leave France and seek refuge in Holland. In order to reduce the extent of resistance, the powers that be unscrupulously resorted to forcible measures: several houses were closed and their members either deported or dispersed. Several episodes, such as the ones involving the Sisters of the Visitation of Castellane, who sympathised with Soanen, the Carmelite nuns of the Rue Saint-Jacques in Paris, and the abbey of Saint-Polycarpe in the diocese of Narbonne agitated public opinion to a great extent. It all contributed to the creation of a martyrdom mentality in Jansenist circles. But the measures were effective; by and by the various congregations officially accepted the bull, albeit generally without enthusiasm. The Dominicans had done so in 1728; the Benedictines and Doctrinarians followed suit in 1744, the Genovevians in 1745, and the Oratorians a year later in 1746. But it must be added that the acceptance was never general and that a good many members of religious families more or less admittedly continued to be sympathetic towards Jansenism. This was true especially in the case of the Oratorians and the Benedictines of Saint-Maur, many of whom remained loyal to the Jansenist party. The dioceses of the appellant bishops continued to represent a natural refuge for those who managed to escape exile or jail: Montpellier, Troyes, and Auxerre took in many refugees; others sought asylum in Holland. Others were accepted into communities covertly under an assumed name. Numerous laymen placed themselves, their homes, and fortunes in the service of those persecuted. After the death of Nicole in 1695 his inheritance had been handed over to the Oratorian Fouquet and the Abbot d'Eau. It laid the foundation for a fund providing assistance to persecuted clerics, and in the course of the eighteenth century it was augmented by numerous private gifts.

Vintimille's tenure in office also abounded in parliamentary conflicts. The first dispute ensued when a council decree suppressed a memorandum by forty lawyers from Paris in favor of opposing priests from Orléans. At first the other lawyers reacted heatedly, but calmed down when Daguesseau intervened and ameliorated some of the harshness. But the forty lawyers were called to task by some of the bishops, among them Vintimille. They were about to formulate a reply when another council decree again put them in the wrong. Thereupon they went on strike. In retaliation ten of them were exiled, but the others did not give in and so the ten had to be recalled from exile in November 1731. The highly complex and more or less emotional hostilities continued and parliament had to suffer a *lettre de cachet* forbidding any discussion of matters pertaining to the bull. By publishing a pastoral letter on 27 April 1732, abruptly suppressing the party organ *Nouvelles ecclésiastiques* Vintimille initiated a new phase in the conflict. As many as twenty-one priests in Paris refused to disseminate the pastoral letter; in other parishes some of the faithful left the church while it was read. A royal declaration of 10 May 1732 forbade the parliament from dealing with this affair. The ecclesiastical councilor Pucelle and another by the name of Titon protested loudly and were promptly arrested. A strike suppressed by royal decree provoked new incidents and 158 officials of the magistrate were dismissed on 20 June. When parliament remonstrated, the dismissals were retracted by the court. The remonstrations by parliament were very serious and on 8 August the court replied with a harsh statement which could only be registered after a formal trial on 1 September. This led to renewed protests resulting in 140 parliamentarians being exiled. But now the public was so enraged that the government had to give in, admonish Vintimille, and forgo proceedings against twenty-one protesting priests. This is a good example of the way in which ecclesiastical matters were again taken up by parliament.

Thereafter Vintimille avoided any additional problems. He shunned conflicts with priests who were undeterred and continued in their appeals; he even maintained friendly relations with some of them. He extended authorizations for hearing confession or renewed them in the case of opponents and asked well-known Jansenists for their services. When he died in 1746 he had succeeded relatively well in keeping peace in his immediate environs. The church policy of Fleury has been subject to various kinds of judgment. It could be considered brutal and repressive and it is certain that he did everything he could to diminish the ranks of the appellants. The forty-thousand *lettres de cachet* supposedly issued under his government as asserted by some historians demand closer examination. Without doubt he was interested in a peaceful settlement of the problem. His appointments placed moderate bishops at the head of dioceses. He avoided chicanery towards those prelates who were suspected of Jansenist sympathies. In 1735, for example, the bishop of the small diocese of Saint-Papoul, Jean-Charles de Ségur, submitted his resignation after he published a pastoral letter explaining his scruples and acknowledging the appellation of 1717. The pastoral letter was suppressed by council decree, but the prelate was left unscathed. He died peacefully at the parish house of Saint-Gervais in Paris, whose appellant priest François Feu gave the eulogy. Fleury died in 1743; his successor in the Ministry of Culture was the Theatine Jean-François Boyer, who had become Bishop of Mirepoix in 1730 and tutor of the Dauphin in 1736. Boyer proved to be much more unyielding than Fleury, often brutal. Although he was the black sheep of the Jansenists, as explained in the many articles about him in the *Nouvelles ecclésiastiques*, he was not even respected by the enemies of Jansenism. His death in 1755 was generally felt to be a liberation.

Boyer had to undergo the last embarrassing affair of the Jansenist conflict, that of the certificate of confession. A preliminary sign was the fact that some of the acceptants among the bishops were refusing the last rites to notoriously obstinate appellants. Towards the end of 1739 the bishop of Laon, La Fare, issued a pastoral instruction forbidding the priests either to administer the sacraments to appellants or to give them ecclesiastical burial. In 1746 the bishop of Amiens, La Motte, issued a proclamation containing similar rules. This affair reached its climax with the intervention of the archbishop of Paris, Christophe de Beaumont, the uncompromising successor of Vintimille. He resumed the fight against Jansenism and ordered his priests who were ministering to the dying to demand from them a certificate of confession, written by a regularly approved priest, in which the dying would accept the bull *Unigenitus*. The most astonishing aspect was that this measure was applied without reservation even in the case of poor and totally uneducated people. One of the first incidents (on 17 February 1749) involved the Jansenist theologian Boursier, whom the priest of Saint-Nicolas du Chardonnet, Garnot, gave the last rites and a formal burial with the complete rites of the church without having demanded a recantation. Garnot was exiled to Senlis. On 21 June 1749, the former rector of the university, Charles Coffin, died without the last rites because he refused to show the required certificate of confession, though he did receive a church burial in Saint-Eustache. During the following months several more incidents occurred and the problem spread to other dioceses in the provinces whose bishops had issued similar rules. Parliament, of course, repeatedly intervened in favor of the opponents and its relationship with the court became so critical that it was exiled from May 1753 until September 1754.

At this point Louis XV resolved to put an end to this conflict which weakened royal authority and could even call into question the very institutions themselves. Upon the return of parliament he issued a declaration, written on 2 September and registered on 5 September, which imposed silence on both parties.[28] This important declaration marked the beginning of yet a new phase because the King, especially as of 1756, was bent on having it respected. In order to set an example, several bishops who violated it—among them Beaumont himself—were temporarily exiled. Then, too, the Holy See was at this time occupied by a well-educated and moderate man, Benedict XIV. The divided Assembly of the Clergy of 1755 turned to him and in reply received the brief *Ex omnibus* (16 October 1755), which approved the silencing and treated the matter of the certificate of confession in an acceptable manner. Boyer died in 1755; his successors, Cardinal de La Rochefoucauld and after him Jarente de la Bruyère were intent on pacification and succeeded in having the order of silence respected. More and more bishops concurred in their views. This attitude, combined with the progressive deterioration of the Jansenist party, altered the elements of the problem.

The scene of events also changed. Although the Society of Jesus had played a relatively subordinate role in the context of political Jansenism, it incurred violent hostility, not only from the Jansenists but also from several acceptants among the bishops. Several incidents occurred in quick succession. The first one revolved around a work by the Jesuit Jean Pichon, which appeared in 1745 under the title *L'esprit de Jésus-Christ et de l'Église sur la fréquente communion*. In it Pichon resurrected a problem treated a century before in the famous work by Arnauld. He attacked any delay of absolution, advocated communion immediately following confession of even the most grievous sins, and—according to a formula of P. Sirmond attacked by Pascal in his *Provinciales*—reduced the love of God to the fact of not hating God in any way. In 1747 the

---

[28] Ibid., 363.

Nouvelles ecclésiastiques sat in judgment over Pichon's book. Then several pastoral instructions condemned the work, the first few of which were issued by bishops who were either known to be Jansenists or who sympathized with them: Caylus; Rastignac, bishop of Tours; Fitz-James, bishop of Soissons. Languet de Gergy pronounced a prohibition. Then Beaumont had to publish a recantation by Pichon in the diocese of Paris, dated 24 January 1748. But he was unable to avert condemnation of Pichon; during the next few months twenty-seven additional bishops censured the book. In August 1748 Pichon was exiled to Mauriac by *lettre de cachet*. On 11 December 1748, his book was condemned by the Holy Office. Parallel to the Pichon affair another one had erupted which was to reach its climax just a little later. In 1738 Isaac-Joseph Berruyer, a Jesuit, published the first part of a voluminous *Histoire du peuple de Dieu* which presented the passion and salvation of Christ in the form of a novel. It was condemned by Colbert, enabling Daguesseau to resist publication of the following volumes. The eight volumes of the second part did not appear until June 1753. They were not approved by the Jesuit superiors, a fact which incurred for them the reproach of duplicity. The ensuing scandal was of considerable proportions. In December 1753 the work was condemned by twenty-seven bishops. But Berruyer defended himself; a condemnation issued by Benedict XIV on 16 February 1758 did not keep him from publishing the remaining five volumes of the third part, which were condemned on 2 December 1758. Numerous polemics against Berruyer appeared, the most significant of which was written by a former theologian of Colbert's, Jean-Baptiste Gaultier. His *Lettres théologiques* also attacked another Jesuit, Jean Hardouin, who—although he had died in 1729—was considered to be the source of Berruyer's ideas. On 1 August 1759, Fitz-James joined the fray with a pastoral instruction of several thousand pages, composed by a well-known Jansenist theologian, Étienne Gourlin, and containing a severe refutation of Hardouin and Berruyer. It was followed by other censures, including one by the Sorbonne.

All this created an atmosphere favoring further attacks against the Society of Jesus, whose reputation had been declining—even in Rome—since the end of the seventeenth century and which was now coming under attack from almost all sides. At a time when political power was increasingly based on a growing nationalist sentiment, the society was accused of being allied with a foreign power, the temporal power of the papacy. Conversely, contemporary philosophy saw the society as the strongest barrier against the deism of Voltaire. Henceforth even the slightest incidents were pounced upon. In 1756 a regrettable financial affair involving a Jesuit, de la Valette, furnished the desired pretext. The parliaments went on the attack against the society, a decree of 8 August 1761, the first of several others, declared its constitution irreconcilable with the laws of the realm. After several cases involving promissory notes the King gave in to the pressure exerted by Mme de Pompadour and his minister Choiseul: a decree of 18 November 1764 banned the Society of Jesus in France. A similar campaign had been carried out in a number of European countries and led to the brief *Dominus ac Redemptor* by Clement XIV (see also Chap. 30), by which he abolished the Jesuit order. These measures were celebrated as victories by the Jansenists, who were unable to see that it was a triumph of skepticism and not of Saint Augustine. On both sides of the issue the conflict led to a great number of publications, the most interesting of which is still the *Annales de la Société des soi-disant jésuites,* an ambitious work which was probably financed by Choiseul himself and compiled by the Jansenist Gazaignes. It remained unfinished but its completed five volumes (1764–71) contain a wealth of valuable details.

These polemics involving the Society of Jesus refrained from resuming the Jansenist issue because the court was firmly resolved to enforce the law of silence and to avoid any rekindling of the conflict. Proof of that was an incident involving the appellant François-Philippe Mésenguy (1677–1763), who—out of modesty—had remained a mere acolyte and whose views had forced him in 1728 to resign his function as superior at the Collège de Dormans-Beauvais. Mésenguy was a respected theologian; without regard to his views Vintimille had employed him to improve the second edition of the *Bréviaire de Paris* in 1736 and had entrusted him with the editing of the *Missel de Paris* two years later. In 1744 Mésenguy had published his lectures under the title *Exposition de la doctrine chrétienne.*[29] The *Exposition* had been mentioned in 1752 by the *Dictionnaire des livres jansénistes* by the Jesuit Patouillet, but its being placed on the Index in 1757 was based exclusively on its Gallican tendencies. One year later the book was translated into Italian and this translation was considered Jansenist. As a consequence it was condemned by Clement XIII in his brief *Dum inter gravissima* (1761). But the courts of France, Spain, Naples, Vienna, and the Republic of Venice refused to accept the brief. Louis XIV forbade the nuncio to promulgate it in any way in France and Choiseul sent a severe official protest to the Pope. Even Rome now understood that it was better not to permit the matter to be revived. The pontificate of Clement XIV was ready to let things rest. Pius VI on the occasion of his trip to Vienna on 20 April 1782 publicly announced to the bishops of Hungary that the bull *Unigenitus* should be spoken of in historical terms and not in dogma-

---

[29] Mésenguy himself composed a "Mémoire justificatif" about this affair which was published shortly after his death (n. p., 1763).

tic ones, "historice, non dogmatice." Several years later, with the advent of the French Revolution, the political aspect of the problem was to enter a completely new phase.

In the meantime political Jansenism—as opposed to the religious Jansenism of the seventeenth century, which had been limited to France and Louvain—had gained considerable ground. In the Netherlands, where the Jansenist group enjoyed firm support, the situation quickly came to a head. The eight dioceses had accepted the bull *Unigenitus* almost immediately after it had been issued. Prior to that the faculty of the University of Louvain had accepted it, although not without spirited resistance by part of its members. In 1716 Thomas-Philippe d'Alsace de Bossu, hostile to Jansenism, became archbishop of Mechelen. On 17 October 1718, he issued a pastoral letter which excommunicated the opponents of the bull. The other seven dioceses, as well as the Louvain faculty, followed suit. Supported by officialdom, the archbishop initiated a number of forcible measures against the opponents. Towards the end of 1727 the famous canonist Zeger-Bernard Van Espen (1646–1728) had to flee to Holland, where he died six months later.[30] In the meantime Van Espen's advice had contributed considerably towards the creation of a schism in the Dutch Church.[31] Since the end of the sixteenth century the Church had been governed by vicars apostolic with the title "in partibus infidelium." Jean de Néercassel, vicar apostolic of Utrecht, had been a close friend of Arnauld's and had facilitated the Jansenist infiltration into Holland. His successor in 1688 was Pierre Codde, archbishop of Sebaste, who had flatly refused to sign the formulary. He was cited to Rome, but even there he adhered to his position and was banished for it (May 1702). The chapters of Utrecht and Harlem stood up for him; the latter quickly gave in, but Utrecht, followed by a large number of its faithful, stood fast in its opposition to the Holy See and refused to recognize the vicars apostolic who succeeded Pierre Codde. Several French prelates were willing to ordain priests who had been issued letters dimissory by the chapter acting as administrator of the archbishopric, but the regent prohibited the bishops from continuing this practice. Thereupon the chapter of Utrecht and its faithful who had joined in the appellation of the bull *Unigenitus* consulted several canonists, among them Van Espen, who had always supported the legiti-

---

[30] See G. Dupac de Bellegarde, *Mémoires historiques sur l'affair de la bulle Unigenitus dans les Pays-Bas,* 4 vols. (Brussels 1755); G. Leclerc, "Zeger Bernard van Espen (1646–1728), un canoniste janséniste," *Miscellanea jansenistica offerts à Lucien Ceyssens* (Herverlee and Louvain 1963), 174–200.

[31] See G. Dupac de Bellegarde, *Histoire abrégée de l'Église d'Utrecht* (Utrecht 1755); B. Van Bilsen, *Het schisma van Utrecht* (Utrecht and Brussels 1949); J. Tans and M. Kok, *Rome - Utrecht* (Hilversum and Antwerp 1966).

macy of the rights of the chapter. The majority of the replies reaffirmed the chapter's right to elect its bishop and to have him consecrated. A priest of the foreign mission, Dominikus Varlet, consecrated bishop "in partibus" of Babylon, was willing to act as consecrator upon the request of the Dutch chapter but was suspended for so doing (1720). He took up residence in the United Provinces and on 15 October 1724 he consecrated Cornelius Steenoven, the elected candidate of the Utrecht chapter, who in turn consecrated the first three of his successors. Furthermore, the archbishopric of Utrecht created suffragan seats in Harlem (1742) and Deventer (1758), ensuring the continuity of apostolic succession. Although supported by the Dutch government, the Church of Utrecht suffered a rapid decrease in its membership: around 1750 it had less than ten thousand members, contrasted to the total of two hundred thousand Catholics in Holland. Several attempts at rapprochement with Rome were undertaken, but all of them foundered upon the steadfast refusal by the chapter to recognize the bull *Unigenitus*. Throughout the eighteenth century the Church of Holland served as a refuge for numerous appellants; even today their archives, enriched by many documents from France, constitute one of the most important sources regarding the history of Jansenism. The French immigrants, several of whom, such as Leclerc and Le Sesne d'Étemare, were widely acknowledged theologians, contributed to maintaining an undeniable intellectual vitality in the Utrecht schism in spite of its numerical minority. The Jansenist infiltration in Ireland, England, Germany, Austria, and Spain was of minor importance, but not so in Italy. There the problem took on a special aspect, which is to be examined later (Chap. 26).

Jansenism and the Religious Mentality
of the Eighteenth Century

When the conflict involving the bull *Unigenitus* broke out, Jansenism included a large number of first-rate theologians in its ranks. Several of them by their age were still part of seventeenth-century Jansenism. Pasquier Quesnel, who, as we have seen, occupied a place of extraordinary importance, possessed an amazing vitality belying his eighty years. The incredible number of memoranda, polemics, and replies which he authored until shortly before his death on 2 December 1719 in Amsterdam is astonishing. But this wealth of literature did not augment his system. He continued to represent a moderate Augustinianism as coined by Bérulle. Richer's ideas, advocated by him, combined with the fact that the army of appellants was composed primarily of priests and faithful, led him to accord increasing value to the rights of the lower clergy and laity without, however, going as far as the almost Protestant exaggerations of de la Borde. While he did, in fact, remain a revered figure within the Jansenist group, he was surpassed by some of the younger of his allies, over whom he no longer had the uncontested authority he did during the period between 1690 and 1710. Not so in the case of Jacques-Joseph du Guet (1649–1733), his younger companion who had accompanied him to his refuge with Arnauld in 1685 but was forced to return to France soon afterwards.[32] Although thereafter he lived in cautious seclusion, his voluminous correspondence with numerous friends even outside the Jansenist circle had proved his extraordinary intellectual and literary abilities and had obtained for him a position of high respect expressed by the sobriquet "the Seer," given to him by his friends. Although he had at first shown little inclination for writing, he had two small treatises printed in 1717 (*Traité de la prière publique* and *Traité des saints mystères*) which enjoyed great success and made his name as an author. He also continued his career as a moralist, especially in the ten volumes of his *Lettres de Morale et de piété*, several of which had been printed in 1707 without his permission and which he edited himself after 1718. The last few volumes appeared posthumously. He was a gracious and shy person who eschewed public appearances. For that reason he refused to take on a prominent role of leadership in the controversy involving the bull. But he was frequently asked for advice; he checked and corrected numerous writings of his friends. Himself an appellant and reappellant, he had advised the four bishops at the time of the appellation. But the number of polemics published by him is small, the most important one being his letter to Colbert of 25 July 1724 concerning the signing of the formulary which he had printed the following November. His actual theological work is limited to a small volume entitled *Dissertation théologique* (1727) which deals primarily with baptism and the Eucharist. In addition there are the two volumes published posthumously of the *Conférences ecclésiastiques* (1742), actually a work of his youth. Written around 1678 it demonstrates the influence of Richer's doctrine as advocated by Quesnel. But in general, Du Guet's ideas, dominated by Augustinianism, are sharp, penetrating, very subtle and solid, his morality determined by a relatively moderate rigorism. Innumerable reprints throughout the eighteenth century popularized this admirable, talented author who deserves better than the oblivion which has been his fate.

François-Laurent Boursier (1679–1748), professor at the Sorbonne, was a much stronger and more aggressive personality. Highly respected as a theologian by his peers, he made a name for himself in 1713 by his

[32] P. Chételat, *Étude sur Du Guet* (Paris 1877).

414

book *De l'action de Dieu sur les créatures, traité dans lequel on prouve la prémotion physique par le raisonnement*, a powerful defense of Augustinian-Thomistic ideas. Malebranche, who felt himself and his *Traité de la nature et de la grâce* attacked, considered the work worthy of an answer and replied in his *Réflexion sur la prémotion physique* (1715). Unfortunately, the ensuing polemic claimed all of Boursier's strength, so that he did not find time to realize his plan for a comprehensive work concerning the *gratia efficax*. As a confidant of Noailles and the appellants he composed a respectable number of texts for them, including the appeals documents of 1717, 1719, and 1720 and several of Soanen's pastoral instructions. He also achieved merit as the central figure in the negotiations, initiated with Jubé, the priest of Asnières, and eighteen other professors, which were to bring about a rapprochement with the Russian Orthodox Church.[33] His exclusion from the Sorbonne (1730) was predictable and his death in the parish house of Saint-Nicolas du Chardonnet, as mentioned above, provoked an incident. An important theologian with a comprehensive patristic as well as Scholastic education, courageous and unselfish, Boursier enjoyed an undisputed authority within the Jansenist party and his intervention was usually decisive. Comparable to him was another professor of the Sorbonne, Nicolas Petitpied (1665–1747), who had expressed his views on the issue of conscience at the beginning of the century and for that reason was forced to flee to Holland. He was a highly respected canonist; in 1718 Saint-Simon had him return to France in order to ask his advice in the matter of the bulls of renewal rejected by Rome. On 1 June 1719, he was readmitted to the Sorbonne. The anti-Jansenist reaction forced him to go into hiding and then again to flee to Utrecht in 1728. As a moderate yet unyielding spirit, he objected to the deviations of the Jansenists and their acts of violence against the hierarchy and because of that was accused of weakness. But his sterling character ensured him of high esteem even on the part of his adversaries and in 1734 the court permitted him to return to France. But his esteem within the party gradually decreased, his intervention against several polemics met with heated criticism. Soanen was the only one who kept him in his confidence and Bossuet of Troyes asked him until the end to write his pastoral instructions for him. His work is considerable: it comprises more than eighty titles, but is submerged totally in his polemics. There are three major works: two volumes entitled *Oboedientiae credulae vana religio* (1708), defending the *silentium respectuosum*; the five volumes of his *Réponses aux avertissements de M. l'évêque de Soissons* (1719–24), a

---

[33] The documents of this affair are compiled in: *Histoire et analyse du livre de l'action de Dieu*, 3 vols. (n. p., 1753), III.

powerful refutation of Languet de Gergy; and the posthumously published *Examen pacifique de l'acceptation de la bulle*. The lucid and prolific intelligence of Petitpied's was able to contribute new and unassailable arguments on a number of ever-recurring problems and many of his writings deserve to be read even today. Along the same lines, albeit of a lesser intellect, the deacon (who also had licentiate from Sorbonne) Jacques Fouillou (1670–1736) deserves mention. He was also prominent in the issue of conscience and joined Quesnel in Holland in 1705. He did not return to France until 1720, where he helped formulate Boursier's *Prémotion physique* and furnished a significant contribution to the famous *Hexaples* concerning the bull *Unigenitus*. But his major work is the three volumes of his *Justification du silence respectueux* (1707). Jean-Baptiste Louail (d. 1724), prior of Auzay, is best known as the author of the first part of the *Histoire du livre de Réflexions morales*, which has already been discussed. The main author of the remainder of the work is Jean-Baptiste Cadry (1680–1756), former teacher of theology at the cathedral chapter of Laon, who also wrote numerous polemics of lesser interest.

In the person of Nicolas Le Gros (1675–1751), doctor of theology and canon of Rheims, forced by his quarrels with Bishop Mailly in 1714 to take refuge with Quesnel, we encounter a personality of a different spirit. He returned from his exile after less than a year to resume the fight. In 1716 he brought out the best known of his works, *Du renversement des libertés de l'Église gallicane dans l'affaire de la Constitution Unigenitus*. In it he advocates a very traditional Gallicanism, modified by a few theses of Richer's concerning the rights of the parish priests, whom he calls shepherds just like the bishops. The latter are therefore obliged to act in concert with their priests and to listen to their advice. But he also upholds the rights of the hierarchy. Although he accords to the Christian people the right to elect their bishops and priests, he nonetheless stipulates that this election does not give them the power of consecration or jurisdiction, which they must receive from God through the mediation of the established hierarchy. This starting point leads him to a very subtle theory combining Gallicanism and the position of Richer with great success. An appellant and reappellant, he barely managed to evade a *lettre de cachet* and, following a sojourn in Rome and England, he once again returned to Holland. He joined the Church of Utrecht, to which he was of great service in the years between 1726 and his death. He was one of the first to create close connections between the French Jansenist faction and the Dutch schism. While in Holland he worked on a comprehensive volume, part of which is dedicated to a commentary on the Holy Gospel applying the mode of allegorical exegesis favored in Jansenist circles. Around 1745 the Utrecht Church had a somewhat more burdensome guest in the person of Pierre Leclerc (1706 until approx. 1781), subdeacon of the diocese of Rouen, a strange and in some respects eccentric figure with an obscure past. In 1756 he published two slim volumes under the title *Renversement de la religion et des lois divine et humaines par toutes les bulles et brefs donnés depuis près de 200 ans contre Baius, Jansénius, les cinq propositions, pour le formulaire et contre le P. Quesnel.* In it he develops an exaggerated presbyterianism by equating priests with bishops and insulting the Pope and the hierarchy. The same ideas are repeated in other works in which he called himself another Gilles de Wittes, former priest of Mechelen who also had strong Presbyterian tendencies. He found followers in the Church of Utrecht and created disciples for himself, but for the Jansenist faction both of France and Holland he was a disappointment. In September 1763 the archbishop of Utrecht convened a provincial council in which the parish priests had the same vote as the bishops; this council was strongly protested by Leclerc. Although he published a few more tracts marked by extraordinary vehemence, all traces of him were eventually lost.

In spite of his excesses the personality of Pierre Leclerc manifested the problem of the propagation of Richer's ideas within the Jansenist faction. In the meantime a canonist who possessed the requisite erudition which Leclerc was lacking had given voice to the most daring demands of the lower clergy. This was Nicolas Travers, (1674–1750), a prolific writer and local historian. He became known in 1734 by virtue of his work *Consultation sur la juridiction et approbation nécessaires pour confessor,* followed in 1744 by the *Pouvoirs légitimes du second ordre dans l'administration des sacrements et le gouvernement de l'Église.* He denies the bishops any and all priority of *jura divina,* regarding them as of purely human origin; he also denies them any special power of ordination and advocates that all functions reserved for the bishops can also be delegated to simple priests. From this he draws the conclusion that all priests by virtue of their own ordination receive the power of ordination and of jurisdiction and consequently have no need for an authorization by the local ordinary to hear confessions and to grant absolution validly and licitly. Travers's ideas produced mixed reactions among the Jansenists; they were virtually put on the Index; the *Nouvelles ecclésiastiques* speaks of the work with contempt and no necrology of the Jansenist party even mentions it. But it is possible that his ideas spread and were actually practiced by some Jansenist priests; at least they are emphatically accused of this by their opponents. Similar theses, but based on a wealth of extraordinary erudition, are found in the large body of works of a lay canonist, the lawyer Guilleaume-Nicolas Maultrot (1714–1803). A specialist in curial law, he tried to prove in a series of twenty-nine volumes the most daring positions of Richer's and the right of the parish priests to jurisdiction on the basis of their ordination. During the second half of the eighteenth century Maultrot met with a relatively favorable response in Jansenist circles and was supported by another renowned lawyer and canonist, Adrien Le Paige.

Among the last great theologians of Jansenism at least three deserve mention. First among them is Jean-Baptiste Le Sesne de Ménilles d'Étemare (1682–1770). He became a cleric at the suggestion of Du Guet and was ordained in 1709. He read one of his first Masses at Port-Royal, shortly before the expulsion of the nuns. Part of his superabundant work is as yet unpublished, a significant part, as we shall see later, is occupied with allegorical exegesis. He took an active part in all the controversies and maintained an intensive correspondence with the entire Jansenist group. In order to retain his independence, he carefully avoided all official titles and functions. He loved to travel, spent time in Rome, England, and frequently visited Holland, where he took up residence in 1754 and died in 1770. In Rhynwick he founded a sort of French seminary under the auspices of the Church of Utrecht, to which he had close ties, leaving to it an admirable collection of documents. D'Étemare was an important spirit with a profound and comprehensive education whose work, though extremely interesting, is never even marred by his allegorical exegesis. Another theologian worth mentioning was a friend of D'Étemare's, Jean-Baptiste Raymond de Beccarie de Pavie de Fourquevaux (1693–1767), a former officer whose modesty prompted him to remain a mere acolyte. The regular correspondence which he maintained with D'Étemare represents an extremely fertile source of information deserving publication. As a confirmed appellant he published several polemics, the most interesting of which is the *Catéchisme historique et dogmatique*. Its first two volumes appeared in 1729; a new edition of 1758 enlarged the work to five volumes. It is a historic presentation of the controversies surrounding the bull *Unigenitus*. Because of its admirable documentation it is in many aspects a valuable source for us. But the horizon of Fourquevaux's presentation is very narrow. Such cannot be said of the third theologian to be mentioned in this context: Pierre-Étienne Gourlin (1695–1775), bachelor of theology, vicar at Saint-Benoît, appellant, and victim of the interdict by Vintimille, which forced him to spend his life in seclusion. He authored several very important polemical works, the best of which is the comprehensive *Mémoire justificatif* (1742; for the appellation of the priests of Sens against Languet de Gergy). He put his pen in the service of several bishops, among others the previously mentioned author of Fitz-James's pastoral instruction against Berruyer. He also left a considerable number of theological treatises in manuscript form; unfortunately, not all of them have been published. But two of the most important ones did appear: *Tractatus theologicus de gratia Christi salvatoris* (1781) and *De Jansenio et de Jansenismo* (1790). At a time when no one was occupied with Jansenism anymore and even Augustinianism had fallen into the background, these two works witness an unusual erudition and a thinking of rare profundity. In the France of this epoch Gourlin is probably the last heir of the great theological tradition. One must acknowledge also that the Jansenist group was at that time the only one in which theological thought remained truly active. Independently of the great controversies, this group was also involved in several other interesting theological disputes. The first of them—concerning the relationships between the *timor servilis* and the *fiducia filialis*—was caused in 1728 by the appearance of Fourquevaux's *Traité de la confiance chrétienne,* attacked by Petitpied in 1734 in nine successive letters but defended by D'Étemare, who in turn was disputed by his fellow member of the Oratory, Mariette. Other controversialists entered the fray until Boursier, in his *Lettre sur l'espérance et la confiance chrétiennes,* finally put an end to the conflict in notable fashion (1739). Petitpied and Boursier also were the protagonists in a controversy concerning the theological virtues (1742–46) in the course of which Boursier wrote a very interesting *Dissertation sur les vertus théologales* (1744) which was primarily directed against a new treatise by his fellow Oratorian Mariette. Unfortunately, all the great minds of Jansenism had already passed away by 1778 when a last great doctrinal controversy broke out involving the *Traité du sacrifice de Jésus-Christ* by Abbé François Plowden, a cleric of English origin who sympathized with the Jansenists. He viewed the essence of the sacrifice of the Mass not in the destructive change of the offering, but in the presentation of a sacrifice made once and for all. The entire Jansenist contingent entered this controversy; the publications in this context deserve a careful investigation.

After 1730 the Jansenist party was irrevocably condemned and it was aware of it. A minority from the start, it now watched its substance gradually melt away without a chance to renew itself. Even the diligence of its members could not deceive anyone about the impending fateful end. The mentality of the group changed progressively: it assumed the attitude of a clan withdrawn unto itself, embittered, full of resentment, belligerent, narrow-minded, suspicious; the tenor of Jansenist polemics became more and more unpleasant. The most significant document in this regard was the famous *Nouvelles ecclésiastiques*. During the Council of Embrun (1727) the party had planned establishment of an informational journal which was to replace the hand-copied *Nouvelles ecclésiastiques* which had appeared in the seventeenth century. This plan seems to have originated primarily with D'Étemare and two very wealthy Jansenist clerics, Jean-Baptiste and Alexis Desessarts. Du Guet, whose advice had been solicited, responded positively. The editorship was initially entrusted to a deacon, Boucher, and to a chaplain of Bicêtre, de Troya, but the latter was incarcerated a short while later. A few months later Boucher, who continued to collaborate on the journal, handed its direction over to a priest of the diocese of Tours whose Jansenist membership had forced him into exile, Jacques Fontaine de la Roche (1688–1771). The latter quickly demonstrated an extraordinary organizational talent; he built up a network of information and distribution of such perfection that he was able to thwart investigation by the police throughout the century. The first issue of the *Nouvelles* appeared on 23 February 1728. But the authors also published a fascicle reviewing the sequence of events since the issuance of the bull. In the face of all sorts of difficulties Fontaine succeeded in maintaining the weekly appearance of the publication almost without interruption. D'Étemare, the brothers Desessarts, and Fourquevaux were regular contributors, especially noted for the reviews and the doctrinal articles. After the death of Fontaine, his responsibilities were taken over by Marc-Claude Guénin de Saint-Marc, supported by a group which included Gourlin and Maultrot. After 1794 the *Nouvelles* was continued in Utrecht by a refugee priest, Jean-Baptiste-Sylvain Mouton, who reduced it to two issues a month. The last one appeared on 24 May 1803; Mouton died on the following 13 June. The basic tone of the *Nouvelle* is one of incredible vehemence. Everything coming from the appellants is heaped with praise; the slightest utterances by an acceptant or a Jesuit is mercilessly criticized. Reading the journal is simply unpleasant, yet one must acknowledge the extraordinary accuracy of the information used in it. This makes it for us an extremely valuable source. Predictably the *Nouvelles* was subject to repeated condemnations, among them a decree of parliament of February 1731, a pastoral letter by Noailles of April 1732, and a decree by the Holy Office of April 1740. Starting in 1734 the Jesuits tried to counter the *Nouvelles* by their own *Suppléments*, which was by no means any more objective and had to be discontinued in 1748. The *Nouvelles* also reflected the controversies which split the Jansenist milieu. Its vehement tone caused them to be condemned by some of the most famous Jansenist theologians. Du Guet was a case in point: he condemned the *Nouvelles* in a letter (dated 9 February 1732) to a young fellow Oratorian of the Collège de Juilly, Pinel. At the instigation of a niece of Du Guet's, Mme Mol, who was hostile to the Jansenists, this letter was publicized. This resulted in a long series of polemics between D'Étemare and Le Gros. This was also the case with a letter by Petitpied made public in 1735. As a countermove Fontaine welcomed the touching approbations of Soanen and gave them all the desired publicity he could. In addition to the *Nouvelles* there was a wealth of published material the majority of which were pamphlets of the most regrettable satire, some of which, however, are publications of valuable documents, especially the irreplaceable *Journal* by Dorsanne (1753) and the *Anecdotes ou mémoires secrets sur la Constitution Unigenitus* by a member of the Academy, Joseph Bourgoin de Villefore (1744).

On the whole the spirituality of the Jansenist milieu of the eighteenth century continues to be of the intellectual, psychological, and rational kind. The doctrinal reliability of the works it created could not, however, hide the progressive withering coming about as a consequence of its break with the living sources of inner experience. The literary production is more than abundant. Jérôme Besoigne (1686–1763) and René Cerveau (1700–1780), best known as historians, published a considerable number of devotional books. Yet more frequent were reprints or editions of hitherto unpublished works of the seventeenth century. The fourteen volumes of the *Essais de morale* by Nicole came out in incredibly quick succession and were even incorporated in non-Jansenist libraries. In addition, there were the *Instructions chrétienne* by Singlin (1744); about twenty works by the doctor of Port-Royal, Jean Hamon, among them some previously unpublished ones; the interesting *Lettres chrétiennes et spirituelles* by Saint-Cyran, which had also been previously unpublished (1744); the *Exercices de piété* of Port-Royal (1787), and many others. Naturally the Jansenists were emphatically antimystical, manifest in the irony with which the *Nouvelles* announced the publication in 1752 of the admirable *Instructions spirituelles en forme de dialogue* by de Caussade. But the main target of the Jansenists was the devotion to the Sacred Heart of Jesus.[34] Strangely enough, the people of Port-Royal had frequently talked of the Heart of Jesus devotion in their devotional literature. But in 1729 when Languet de Gergy published a voluminous *Vie de la Vénerable Mère Marguerite Alacoque*, the *Nouvelles* published a malicious review in January 1730 in which the Heart of Jesus, however, was hardly mentioned. Not until 1758 did its opposition to this devotion become apparent. It became more virulent in 1765 when a brief by Clement XIII officially recognized the devotion to the Sacred Heart of Jesus. Thereupon the *Nouvelles* increased the number of articles rejecting the devotion. In 1781 the most vehement polemicist in the person of Marc-Antoine Raynaud, the priest of Vaux (1717–96), joined the battle, heaping insults and sarcasm upon those whom he called "cordicoles."

The Jansenist faction, nonetheless, must also have been aware of the fascination of the miraculous and irrational. Ever since the famous Mira-

---

[34] See L. Cognet, "Les jansénistes et le Sacré-Cœur," *Le cœur*, *Études carmélitaines* (Paris 1950), 234–53.

cle of the Sacred Thorn in 1656 most of their representatives were forced to accept the idea that God manifests himself in favor of His cause by means of miracles. Yet miraculous events within the group of appellants did not occur until relatively late. On 31 May 1725, Anne Charlier, the wife of Lafosse was suddenly healed of a chronic uterine bleeding during a sacramental procession in which the appellant priest of Sainte-Marguerite, Jean-Baptiste Goy, was carrying the Blessed Sacrament. Noailles recognized the reality of the miracle in a pastoral letter and the parish of Sainte-Marguerite introduced a service commemorating the event. The appellants, of course, viewed that event as a sign in their favor and hastened to publicize it. They increased the publicity in 1727 when suddenly miracles began to happen at the grave of a well-known appellant, Gérard Rousse, canon of Avenay in the diocese of Rheims. These constant references by the appellants led to a heated polemic between Languet de Gergy and Colbert which at least had one positive result: In a printed letter of 5 February 1727, Colbert published Pascal's thoughts concerning miracles. These were previously unpublished fragments of his unfinished letter about the Miracle of the Sacred Thorn, copies of which were circulating in the Jansenist faction. But the most spectacular events occurred in Paris in the small cemetery surrounding the church of Saint-Médard at the grave of an appellant and reappellant, François de Paris (1680–1727), the eldest son of a rich parliamentary councilor, who had modestly remained a mere deacon. He had lived and worked in seclusion and written a few commentaries on the Holy Gospel and several devotional works. The occasionally frightening asceticism of his way of life and his inexhaustible charity towards the poor had made him famous; his personal holiness cannot be doubted. His funeral on 3 May 1727 was triumphal and there was talk of miracles reputed to have happened at that occasion. Noailles finally ordered an investigation which was interrupted by his death and the unwillingness of his successor to resume it. But the masses continued to come and pray at the grave of François de Paris. Again and again miracles were said to have occurred. But on 3 November 1730, the sensational healing of a certain Anne Lefranc occurred, which was doubted and declared false by a pastoral letter of Vintimille dated 15 July 1731. Additional miracles created great excitement among the public, which now veritably flooded the small cemetery of Saint-Médard.

A short time later another episode began.[35] On 21 July 1731, a poor and almost totally paralyzed servant woman by the name of Aimée Pivert was healed at the deacon's grave and immediately afflicted by

[35] See P. F. Mathieu, *Histoire des miraculés et des convulsionnaires de Saint-Médard* (Paris 1864).

violent nervous seizures. During the next few weeks the phenomenon reoccurred with other patients. At the beginning of September a cleric, the Abbé de Bescherand, was seized at each of his visits at the cemetery, his reactions evident to all. This phenomenon proved to be more and more contagious, turning the cemetery into a scene of extraordinary mass hysteria in the course of autumn 1732; soon the discussions of the onlookers degenerated into brawls. Several interventions by the police led to a royal decree on 27 January 1732 ordering the cemetery to be closed and placed under police surveillance. But the convulsions did not cease.[36] They merely assumed a different character. Until then they had been a healing process, but now they turned into a prophetic manifestation. Several people, as a general rule members of the highest society and among them even a brother of Voltaire,[37] had strange meetings at their homes around a crucifix or some Jansenist relic, most often one of Deacon de Paris. Following a period of prayer an individual participant, especially gifted in this manner, fell into a trance and began to prophecy in favor of the appellants while the rest of those present reverently collected and wrote down his words. Among these were some privileged beings, such as the famous Sister Holda, who were given warlike names and considered genuine oracles. The wealth of manuscripts with her prophesies contains, among a lot of verbiage, some beautiful pages.[38] Several participants fulfilled prophetic deeds, others regressed into a childlike state. All of the participants, of course, viewed the phenomenon as a divine sign in favor of the appellation. Then various phenomena of yet another kind occurred. At the end of 1732 several among them in a trance asked the others to beat them or wound them in order to give them relief. This practice spread rapidly and became customary among the convulsionaries. Truly sadistic meetings ensued. A distinction was made between the "small assistance"—beatings with whips, sticks, or wooden trestles—and the "large assistance" or "murderous assistance," for which nails, daggers and swords were used. There were women whose breasts or extremities were pierced, others who were crucified for several hours. What had started as acts of penance became the miraculous manifestation of insensitivity, invulnerability, and sudden healing of injuries. The participants wrote exceedingly accurate reports, many of which were left to us but are hard to judge so long after the events. In many cases fraud or hysteria are easy

[36] See P. Gagnol, *Le jansénisme convulsionnaire et l'affaire de la Planchette d'après les archives de la Bastille* (Paris 1911).

[37] See A. Gazier, "Le frère de Voltaire," *Revue des Deux-Mondes*, 1 April 1906.

[38] Interesting texts by Marie-Anne Fronteau, called Sœur Holda, have been summarized by L. Silvy: *Extraits d'un recueil de discours de piété sur nos derniers temps*, 5 vols. (Paris 1822).

to distinguish, but in some cases one seems in fact to be confronted by strange and extraordinary phenomena which are hard to understand. In all of this the participants, of course, saw miracles in favor of Jansenism. It is, on the other hand, quite certain that this system of "assistance" which gradually spread over a large part of France made possible a number of moral aberrations and sexual excesses. The abominations happening among the pupils of a certain Abbé Causse, called Brother Augustin, and among those of a certain Vaillant created a tremendous scandal.

The authorities tried to restrict the convulsionaries to their homes. Then a royal decree of 17 February spoke against them and their meetings were prosecuted by the police. From 1732 on there were innumerable arrests; the questionnaires kept in the archives of the Bastille furnish a number of interesting details in this matter. Yet the meetings of the convulsionaries continued into the nineteenth century. Such an unsettling phenomenon predictably led to heated conflicts within the Jansenist party, where the positions differed considerably. There were avowed opponents of both the convulsionaries and their assistance. The best known among them was no doubt Du Guet, who died in 1733 and witnessed only the beginnings of it. But his niece, Mme Mol, continued the fight in his name, followed by a number of the great theologians of the party: Fouillou, Boursier, Petitpied, and Gourlin. The expert opinion against the convulsions signed by thirty doctors on 7 February 1735 includes many Jansenists. The most vehement opponent no doubt was Debonnaire, who thundered against the convulsions in a number of pamphlets. By all accord, the one who showed the most common sense was the physician Pierre Hécquet. In his book *Naturalisme des convulsions* (1733) he characterized them as either fraud or sickness. Most characteristic is the case of the bishop of Auxerre, Caylus, who at first recognized the miracles of the deacon François de Paris, but then emphatically turned against the movement of the convulsionaries. The attitude of the Jansenist opponents in this matter naturally furnished a welcome issue to the defenders of the bull, especially to the Benedictine Dom Lataste. Others, while they approved the convulsions as a prophetic manifestation, condemned the so-called assistance as most immoral. This was the position of Colbert, Soanen, D'Étemare, and the *Nouvelles ecclésiastiques*. But there were also some passionate advocates of the so-called assistance, as well as of the convulsions, whose leader apparently was the parliamentary councilor Louis Carré de Montgeron (1686–1754), an atheist who had converted at the grave of F. de Paris on 7 September 1731. As a manifestation of his conviction he wrote a comprehensive work, lavishly illustrated by Restout, *La vérité des miracles opérés à l'intercession de M. de Paris* (1737). He was daring enough to go to Versailles and submit the first volume to the King, whereupon he was interned for the rest of his life. Yet he was able to have the remaining two volumes of his work, which were dedicated to a passionate defense of the convulsions and the assistance, published as well. This strange personality attracted followers such as the brothers Desessarts, the Oratorians Pierre Boyer and Julien de Gennes. The wealth of literature produced by this controversy, which dragged on until the Revolution, is astonishing.

The bull *Unigenitus* posed a difficult problem for the Jansenist party. They considered it totally erroneous in the area of the faith, but were forced to admit that the majority of the Church had recognized it. What then was the state of the promise of infallibility which Christ had given to his Church? The main features of the answer to this question were outlined even prior to 1720, they took on a clear form after 1730: this almost general apostasy of the Church is the sign that the end of time is drawing nigh. This was presaged in the Holy Gospel and the appellants are the small remainder of the steadfast mentioned by the prophesies. This is the cause for the strange eschatological mentality in the Jansenist faction, the expectation of the impending and victorious return of Jesus Christ. Many theologians of the group sought their justification in the Holy Gospel, interpreting it according to the principles of a very specific allegorical exegesis practiced neither by the great theologians of the seventeenth century nor by Quesnel, but whose initial features can be encountered in Pascal. Du Guet's system, which can be called figurism, consists of viewing everything that has happened to the Jewish people as an allegory, a figure of that which is fated for the Church. By this perspective he arrived at the conviction that the end of time had to be preceded by a general conversion of Israel. It is possible that he even managed to convert Bossuet to his ideas around 1682.[39] The exegetic principles of Du Guet's, however, were not published until later, in his *Régles de l'intelligence des Saintes Écritures* (1716), on which his friend D'Asfeld had collaborated. This slim volume also contains an (important) appendix concerning the conversion of the Jews. In the course of his long career Du Guet applied his method to lengthy commentaries on a part of the Bible. For the most part they were not published until the end of his life or after his death. The entire work comprises about fifty volumes, but the text has been emendated several times. These commentaries, whose spiritual aspects often result in some admirable perspectives, enjoyed success even outside of the Jansenist milieu. But in the meantime Du Guet had been passed by his pupils. On 8 April

---

[39] See A. F. Vaucher, *Une célébrité oubliée, le P. Manuel de Lacunza y Diaz* (Collonges-sous-Salève 1941); idem, *Lacunziana* I (Collonges-sous-Salève 1949).

1722, D'Étemare had been present at a conversation about this topic between Du Guet and Charles de Sévigné, son of the famous Marquise de Sévigné, and this talk which converted him to figurism had opened up broad perspectives for him. He followed Du Guet's system to its outer limits and arrived at a point where he viewed the entire Holy Gospel as a chain of symbols concerning the Church, the future of the Jewish people, and the end of time. In it he thought to have found proof that the apostasy of almost the entire Church had to be followed immediately by the conversion of the Jews. In 1723 he started developing his views in several works, primarily in his *Tradition sur la conversion des Juifs* (1724). Du Guet, who held these ideas to be exaggerated, was irritated and criticized them in his conferences. Yet D'Étemare had become popular and found many followers, among them Le Gros, Fourquevaux, and many others. The expectation of the conversion of the Jews to the Christian faith and that of the arrival of Elijah as a sign of the end of time played a significant role in the Jansenist milieu. The convulsionaries spoke of it in their prophesies and the famous/infamous Vaillant called himself Elijah. The apocalypse offered the ideal subject matter for such commentaries, but these were generally so audacious that no one dared to publish them. Those of D'Étemare did not appear until the nineteenth century (1866), those of Le Gros have remained unpublished. D'Étemare clearly expressed the idea that the locusts are identical with the Society of Jesus and Le Gros thought that Babylon represents the Christian and corrupt Rome. In addition, D'Étemare advocated the idea of a "millenium," a spiritual reign of Christ on earth prior to the end of the world. Some of the exegetes attempted by means of calculations, whose perspicacity, however, was again and again deceived, to determine the date of the conversion of the Jews. Today we are hard put to imagine the strange climate of this eschatological expectation which brought about such an incredible volume of writing.

One last feature characterized the Jansenist faction, one that stemmed from its mentality as a minority: its hero cult. Initially its heroes were essentially the great men of Port-Royal, the nuns and friends of Port-Royal. Then towards the end of the century the famous appellants became objects of veneration. Some Jansenists remembered them during Mass on the same level with the canonized saints. Their relics developed into a veritable cult; even the smallest vestiges of bone or clothing were kept in valuable reliquaries. But this veneration is interesting to us primarily because of the preservation and publication of important documents which fortunately were left to us and represent an irreplaceable source. The Church of Utrecht has a collection of documents of incredible abundance the most important part of which is kept at the seminary of Amersfoort, which has possession of it today. Another collection was compiled by Françoise-Marguerite de Joncoux (1668–1715), a loyal friend of the last nuns of Port-Royal, who managed with the help of a Lieutenant Voyer d'Argenson to save the documents confiscated at the destruction of the convent. She also collected a wealth of other items or had them copied. Mlle de Joncoux, who had received an extraordinarily thorough theological education, took an active part in the controversies and in 1699 originated the idea of publishing the *Provinciales,* in which she translated Nicole's Latin annotations into French. During the eighteenth century her work went through fifteen reprints. At her death her collection was left to the Abbey Saint-Germain-des-Pres and is now in the National Library. Another much larger and more complete collection was compiled by Marie-Scholastique de Ménilles de Thémericourt (1671–1745), who had been a pupil at Port-Royal and had close ties to the nuns and their friends. About 1715 she undertook a systematic listing of all historical documents relating to the dissolved convent. She was supported in her task by some devoted friends, such as Mme de Bourdun, the mother of D'Étemare. She could only collect a few of the original documents, but employed several professional copiers who copied and carefully compared all documents which she was able to borrow. Then she put them together into various methodically arranged collections which she then annotated. She also inspired several publications. Later on she added her manuscripts to the rich collection of documents relating to the controversies which was compiled by Adrien Le Paige; the entire collection remained in the possession of the Society of Port-Royal. Several other holdings have been transferred to public libraries without any sizeable losses.

These archives were able to satisfy the needs of Jansenist circles for veneration because they placed at their disposal the works of their heroes and the recollection of the authors of memoirs. According to the custom of the times these publications changed the text to some extent, leaving out what could be troublesome or superfluous; yet they are very informative. A close determination of the conditions under which these editions originated is quite difficult. Some of the collaborators can be identified, such as Michel Tronchay (1666–1733), the former secretary of Tillemont; Claude Goujet (1697–1767), literary figure, historian, and contributor of the *Nouvelles*; Favret de Fontette and Barbeau de la Bruyère. Pierre Leclerc was responsible for the *Vies intéressantes et édifiantes des religieuses de Port-Royal* (1750–52), the *Vies des amis de Port-Royal* (1751), and the curious *Recueil de pièces sur le formulaire* (1754). The production was especially intensive around the middle of the century; thereafter there were hardly any more new editions, proof that interest was gradually lessening. Instead there appeared the *Lettres* of Mother Angélique (1742), the "memoirs" about her written by various nuns, which have become known under the title *Mémoires d'Utrecht* (1742), numerous devotionals by her niece Angélique de Saint-Jean, and the famous *Recueil d'Utrecht*, containing voluminous documentation about Pascal (1740). The great memoirists of Port-Royal were presented to the public: Lancelot and Fontaine in 1738, Thomas du Fosse in 1739. There were several attempts at historical synthesis which, although tendentious in favor of the Jansenists, are nonetheless interesting. The best work is the *Histoire générale de Port-Royal* (1757) by the Benedictine monk Dom Clémencet. Also deserving mention are the somewhat anecdotal work by Jérôme Besoigne *Histoire de l'abbaye de Port-Royal* (1752) and the strange *Mémoires historiques* (1759) by Pierre Guilbert, both full of theretofore unpublished but unfortunately unfinished writings. In 1737 Fouillou published the *Lettres* of Arnauld, but later on this work was relegated to less importance by the monumental edition of the *Œuvres complètes* of Arnauld in forty-three volumes, edited by Dupac de Bellegarde, Larrière, and Hautefage (1775–83) and printed in Lausanne with historically valuable introductions. This remarkable work, no doubt the most important one produced in this field during the eighteenth century, which far surpassed similar ones dedicated to Fénelon and Bossuet, is a testimonial to the collapse of Jansenism.

CHAPTER 21

Spirituality and Its Development in Eighteenth Century-France

Christian Life

In eighteenth-century France the religious energies were for the most part consumed by the Jansenist conflict and its aftereffects. This led to impoverishment in other areas as well. Embroiled in daily battles which left room for only the most immediate questions, even the best minds were unable to recognize that the actual danger was lurking in the growing influence of deist philosophy. On 18 November 1751, a collaborator of the *Encyclopedia,* Abbé Jean Martin de Prades (1720–82), submitted to the Sorbonne several theses inspired by philosophic deism which the syndic Dugard naively found to be "full of nice sentiments in favor of religion." Although parliament reacted soon after, it was only against a contumacious thesis regarding the inequality of the classes. The Jansenist Étienne Gourlin was the only one to attack the problem perspicaciously, making the bull *Unigenitus* responsible for this pervasive blindness. This explains to a great extent the weakness of Catholic apologetics in the century of the Enlightenment.[1]

Spiritual life itself was impoverished because of the crisis of quietism, which for a long time discredited all mystical elements, cutting off Christian piety from its living sources of inner experience. Henceforth psychologizing moralism, whose gradual advance we have already examined, was to triumph. Several authors who were actually part of the seventeenth century had their widest dissemination in the eighteenth century. As mentioned above, this was the case with the great Jansenist moralists: Nicole, Du Guet, and Quesnel; Jean-Jacques Boileau (1649–1735) who sympathized with the Jansenists but was clever enough never to expose himself unduly, also belongs to this group. He was the author of several very conventional devotional books, but above all he was appreciated as a spiritual guide. After his death two volumes of *Lettres sur différents sujets de morale et de piété* (1737–47) were published which really deserve our interest. They are the source for the famous story of the chasm which Pascal constantly thought he saw on his left side.[2] Lastly, it should be remembered that Bossuet also did not become famous as a religious author until the eighteenth century, since his great works in that field *Élévations sur les mystères* (1727), *Méditations sur l'Évangile* (1731), and the *Lettres et opuscules* (1748) were not published until then.

The Jansenist tradition was continued by numerous authors the majority of whom have deservedly been relegated to oblivion. One of the most interesting authors among them was no doubt Paul Collard (1698–1775), superior of the small seminary of Troyes at the time when Bossuet's nephew was bishop there. He was a keen spiritual guide, dedicated to a rigorism that made no concession, author of the posthumously published *Lettres spirituelles* (1784) in which he developed a severe spirituality raised to extremes. Similar qualities are encountered in the historians Jérôme Besoigne (1686–1763) and René Cerveau (1700–1780), who also wrote devotional literature. Their works are doctrinally sound and their devotion to the incarnate word places them among the successors of Bérulle. But their style is dry and artificial, their psychology insufficient and conventional, which makes them hardly worth reading. Similar qualities can be ascertained in several of their non-Jansenist contemporaries.

This situation attests to an undeniable deterioration of the intellectual level while that of Christian practice was maintained—or so it

---

[1] See F. Bouillier, "L'abbé de Prades," *Revue politique et littéraire,* 11 October 1884; A. Gazier, *Mélanges d'histoire et de littérature* (Paris 1903).

[2] See A. Durengues, *Monsieur Boileau de l'Archevêché* (Agen 1907).

appears—throughout the century. There were villages even in 1788 whose number of inhabitants was determined by attendance at the Easter Communion and where this number was destined to sink almost to zero in 1804, after the concordat. The congregations, especially the contemplative ones, attracted fewer and fewer members; the nadir appears to have been reached around 1765, at the time when the government took up the problem by means of the famous *Commission des Réguliers*.[3] Later on the houses again attracted a greater number of recruits and this increase continued until the Revolution.[4] In this climate new foundations were rare, yet where they were undertaken they were invariably dedicated to teaching or the care of the sick. But the charitable organizations of the laity remained active; the secret "A.A." associations (*Associatio amicorum*) were formed everywhere. The work of the popular missions was continued, ensuring a periodic renewal of parish life. Religious zeal stayed alive to the extent that it made possible the Catholic resistance during the Revolution and the subsequent renewal.[5]

In addition, we have to call attention to the liturgical efforts in eighteenth-century France. The best example was the initiative by Vintimille, the archbishop of Paris, who provided for his diocese a new missal (1736) and a new breviary (1738), which latter enjoyed a great success. The missal was the work of Mésenguy, an appellant and reappellant; the breviary had been adapted by the Oratorian Vigier, who was sympathetic to the Jansenists. Both books contained admirable Latin poetry in the form of hymns, prose texts, and sequences, among them the older creations of the canon of Saint-Victor, Santeul, and the very beautiful ones by the rector of the university, Charles Coffin (1676–1749), as well as hymns by other authors. The breviary offered a new order of psalter which made its weekly recital possible since the excessively long psalms had been shortened. As we know this was the model for the breviary of Pius X. Although both the missal and the breviary were very controversial, they made their way and were adopted or imitated by many other dioceses.

The Continuance of Mysticism

It would be wrong to assume that the crisis of quietism extinguished mysticism; it merely pushed it to the periphery and almost made it into a secret movement. A detailed examination of the documents shows, for

---

[3] See P. Chevallier, *Loménic de Brienne et l'ordre monastique 1766–1789,* 2 vols. (Paris 1959).

[4] See B. Plongeron, *Les réguliers de Paris et les serments révolutionnaires* (Paris 1963).

[5] See P. Mouly, *L'association secrète denommée Aa* (Montgeron, n. d.).

SPIRITUALITY IN 18TH-CENTURY FRANCE

instance, that the number of nuns in the convents who received the grace of mysticism stayed exactly as high as in the preceding century. But whereas it had once been surrounded by an interested environment and almost invariably attracted a biographer, they were now enveloped by silence and secrecy, penetrated only by a few of the initiated. This was true for the Marseille Sister of the Visitation Anne-Madeleine de Rémusat,[6] a champion of the Sacred Heart of Jesus devotion. Her spiritual guide was the Jesuit Claude-François Milley (1668–1720), who died as the result of his caring for the plague-stricken. He did not publish anything during his lifetime, but his very beautiful spiritual correspondence appeared in print not too long ago.[7] To his charges he preached unreserved surrender of the self, disassociation from all temporal ties, the secluded life in God and pure love; thus he continued the great seventeenth-century mystical tradition of the Society. No doubt he was also influenced by Guillore and Surin. In his proximity—although not on his level of teaching and coherence—was Claude Judde (1661–1735), whose *Œuvres spirituelle* was published posthumously in 1781;[8] he, too, is part of the tradition begun by Lallemant and Surin.

Other congregations furnished just as interesting a contribution. The *Avis sur différents états de l'oraison mentale* by the Dominican Jean-Baptiste Rousseau (d. 1756), which came out after the quietistic crisis, courageously fights for the legitimacy, indeed the necessity of contemplative prayer, manifesting the influence of the great Rhenish-Flemish mystical tradition down to Saint Theresa and Saint John of the Cross. This little but very valuable work unfortunately seems to have remained almost unnoticed. The Pauline Jean-Baptiste-Élie Avrillon (1652–1729), on the other hand, was a well-known preacher, famous spiritual guide, and author of numerous works. His mysticism is primarily characterized by the emphasis on the affective elements of spirituality, but he often speaks openly, if with some reservation, about the passive stages and the unifying life. His most characteristic work in this regard is the *Année affective ou sentiments de l'amour de Dieu sur le Cantique des Cantiques* (1707).

The best religious author of the eighteenth century no doubt was the Jesuit Jean-Pierre de Caussade (1675–1751), who seems to have owed much to the Sisters of the Visitation of Nancy, with whom he resided from 1729 to 1731 and again from 1733 to 1739.[9] He published only

[6] See G. van den Berghe, *Anne-Madeleine de Rémusat* (Paris 1877).
[7] See J. Bremond, *Le courant mystique au XVIIIᵉ siècle, l'abandon dans les lettres du P. Milley* (Paris 1943).
[8] See R. Daeschler, "Le P. Judde et la 'tradition mystique,'" *RAM* 11 (1930), 17–36.
[9] See Madeleine Huillet d'Istria, *Le P. de Caussade et la querelle du Pur amour* (Paris 1964).

one work, the *Instruction spirituelle en forme de dialogues sur les divers états d'oraison suivant la doctrine de M. Bossuet* (Perpignan 1741).[10] In it he undertakes the difficult task of demonstrating that Fénelon and Bossuet concurred in the essential points and that Bossuet was basically a defender of mysticism. To prove his point he referred to a text entitled "Manière courte et facile pour faire l'oraison en foi et de simple présence de Dieu" which had been ascribed to Bossuet by the Sisters of the Visitation of Meaux and which de Caussade published in an appendix. Ironically, it appears that this originally anonymous little work was actually by Mme Guyon. Although de Caussade's argumentation is not totally convincing, his essays on contemplative prayer and the unifying life are most interesting. His correspondents and the Sisters of the Visitation had gathered several collections of his letters on the topic of spiritual guidance. In the nineteenth century Ramière compiled from them the book *L'abandon à la Providence divine* (1861), which gained posthumous fame for Caussade, acknowledged by numerous reprints and a critical edition which appeared quite recently.[11] Caussade shows himself to be heir to the great authentically mystical Ignatian tradition as well as to Salesian influences. It is easily noticeable that he is also indebted to Surin and the Jesuits of the seventeenth century; moreover, Fénelon remains in many aspects his major stimulus. Just like the latter, Caussade wanted to lead man to pure faith and pure love, to guide him in holy indifference to a total devotion to God and to introduce him to contemplation beyond all conceptual and didactic ways. Caussade's remarkable literary talent ranks him among the foremost of the religious authors, a position granted him by our time, whereas in his own time he was scarcely known beyond the circle of his charges.

Aside from him—albeit on a slightly lower level—a few others should be mentioned. The Capuchin friar Ambroise de Lombez (1708–87) was the author of a small *Traité de la paix intérieure* (1757). Reprinted frequently even today, it manifests a very subtle and well-balanced moralism with a discreet mystical quality. The Jesuit Guilleaume Berthier (1704–82) was a defender of the great mystics, especially John of the Cross and Jean de Bernières in his treatises collected under the title *Réflexions spirituelles* (1790). The work of yet another Jesuit of this period, Barthélémy Baudrand, (1701–87), which demonstrates a great wealth of spiritual themes, looses by its prolixity. But towards the end of the century we encounter a truly great author in the Jesuit Jean-Nicolas Grou (1731–1803), who was also influenced by the Sisters of

---

[10] Reedited by H. Bremond under the title: *Bossuet maître d'oraison* (Paris 1931).
[11] J. P. de Caussade, *Lettres spirituelles,* ed. by M. Olphe-Gaillard, 2 vols. (Paris 1961–64); *L'abandon à la Providence divine,* ed. by M. Olphe-Gaillard (Paris 1966).

the Visitation. In England, where he was forced to seek refuge in 1792, he composed the major part of his voluminous work, which was not published until the nineteenth century and is read even now. It presents to us in an admirable form a profound mystically oriented doctrine of the inner life. This context also requires mention of Pierre-Joseph Picot de Clorivière (1735–1820) who, although active in the subsequent period, played a significant part in the reconstruction of the Society of Jesus.[12]

Popular Devotions

We have already mentioned that devotions continued to be popular among the people in the seventeenth century, but the educated public took a critical stance towards them, demanding moderation and theological distinctions. Some aspects of the devotion to Mary, especially, were questioned. But the spirited controversy provoked in 1673 by Widenfeld's *Monita salutaria* and continued in 1693 by the pamphlet *De la vraie dévotion à la Sainte Vierge et du culte qui lui est dû* by the Jansenist sympathizer Andrien Baillet barely reached into the eighteenth century. It was simply a case of special caution being applied on this point. But it was precisely this epoch that witnessed the work of Saint Louis-Marie Grignion de Montfort (1673–1716),[13] whom posterity has considered one of the great apostles of the devotion to Mary. Yet the question arises of whether (at least to some extent) this might not be a case of optical illusion. His work has been handed down to us under very unsure circumstances. His career, short but checkered, was primarily occupied with his missionary work, in which the devotion to Mary played a significant although not exclusive role. This is the case in the only work he ever published, the *Lettres aux amis de la Croix. L'amour de la Sagesse éternelle,* which he left in manuscript form and the accurate text of which was not published until 1929, is certainly the best of his writings. In it the influence of Suso is combined with that of the Bérulle school, which he received during his education at Saint-Sulpice. But the significance of his *Traité de la vraie dévotion à la Sainte Vierge,* now his best-known work, should not be exaggerated. To be sure, the idea of Marian servitude advocated by him is highly interesting, yet it resumes—in a very personal form—a practice reaching back into the sixteenth century and used by Bérulle. But one must question to what extent Montfort actually disseminated it beyond just a small circle of the

[12] See P. de Clorivière, *Prière et oraison,* ed. by A. Rayez (Paris 1961).
[13] See Saint Louis-Marie Grignion de Montfort, *Œuvres complètes,* ed. by M. Gendrot et al. (Paris 1966).

initiated. It is certain that the manuscript of the *Vraie devotion* was forgotten after the death of its author. Rediscovered in 1842, it was published a year later and did not find an echo until the nineteenth century. Although the doctrine presented in the pamphlet cannot be faulted, some of its formulations would hardly have permitted its publication in the eighteenth century.

The spread of the Sacred Heart devotion within the framework treated here was in fact one of the most significant elements characterizing the eighteenth century. Although it prevailed in the end, it was preceeded by lengthy controversies. We have seen that at the end of the preceding century this devotion had assumed two forms: that of Saint John Eudes, the more theologically oriented form, and the more emotional one of Saint Margaret Mary Alacoque, whose central idea was penance. This latter form was able to prevail very quickly, propagated by the Sisters of the Visitation and the Society of Jesus, who then accorded a central position to the revelations of Saint Margaret Mary and emphasized the painful and human aspect, as symbolized by the human heart of Jesus. These traits appeared very clearly even in the first of the significant works dedicated to this topic, that of the Jesuit Jean Croiset (1656–1738). Published in Louvain, it was very successful, but it was also resisted to the same extent, especially from within the ranks of the Jesuits. In 1704 it was finally placed on the Index. In the meantime another Jesuit, François Froment (1649–1702) had published his *Véritable dévotion au Sacré-Cœur* (1699), in which the theological reasoning is more thoroughly worked out. But the decisive work was written by Joseph de Gallifet (1663–1749), who occupied an especially influential position by virtue of his office as assistant to the Jesuit general in Rome. In 1726 he submitted to the Congregation of Rites a very important memorandum "De cultu sacrosancti Cordis," in which he developed the theological reasons for the devotion, perhaps insisting too much on the heart as the seat of the emotions and on the revelations of Margaret Mary. Prosper Lambertini, the future Pope Benedict XIV, took a stand against him and on 12 July 1727 the congregation gave him a negative reply, reiterated in 1729, concerning the introduction of the celebration of this feast. This did not discourage Gallifet; in 1733 he had a French translation of his work published under the title *L'excellence de la dévotion au Cœur adorable de Jésus-Christ* in which the major part of Margaret Mary's autobiography appeared for the first time.

At about this point a rather important episode occurred in this connection. In 1729 Languet de Gergy, bishop of Soissons and late archbishop of Sens, had published his *Vie de la Vénérable Mère Marguerite Alacoque*. Although at this time the work was attributed to the Jesuits, to whom Languet had merely lent his name, the latter does seem to have been the actual author who had edited the documents placed at his disposal by the convent of Paray-le-Monial. By the criteria of his time the work was not bad. But Languet was then one of the celebrities of anti-Jansenism and the book inevitably provoked the opposition of that group which had earlier been indifferent to the Sacred Heart devotion. This hostility, which we have already mentioned earlier, became especially virulent after 1765. But in view of the progressive weakening of the Jansenist party at that time its opposition had no more than a limited effect, presenting no obstacle to the continued development of the devotion, which was able to spread almost everywhere.[14]

On 26 January 1765 a brief by Clement XIII finally approved a Mass and an office for the Sacred Heart of Jesus for Poland and the Roman archfraternity. This made possible the liturgical devotion wherever there was a desire to introduce it. In 1748 an altar had been dedicated to the Sacred Heart of Jesus at the church of Saint-Sulpice in Paris. On 22 June 1767 a pastoral letter by the archbishop of Paris, Christophe de Beaumont, ordered the feast of the Sacred Heart to be celebrated in his diocese, and several other dioceses followed suit. The polemic now reached its climax. Disregarding it, Fumel, the bishop of Lodève, published a pamphlet *Le cult de l'amour divin ou la dévotion au Sacré-Cœur de Jésus* which was violently attacked by the Jansenists. Yet the confraternities dedicated to the Sacred Heart multiplied almost everywhere and attracted followers even among that segment of the aristocracy who remained tied to the traditional religion. This astonishing growth explains the fact that devotion to the Sacred Heart continued to flourish unimpaired even during the Revolution.

[14] See L. Cognet, "Les jansénistes et le Sacré-Cœur," *Le Cœur, Études carmélitaines* (Paris 1950), 234–53.

CHAPTER 22

Anglican Spirituality in the Eighteenth Century

The Anglican spirituality of the seventeenth century produced fruitful and manifold impulses. They reflect the essence of a profound but highly intellectual piety tied strictly to the Gospel, best exemplified by Bishop Lancelot Andrewes (1555–1626).[1] His *Preces privatae* is an admirable collection of poetry compiled from biblical texts and written

[1] See P. A. Welsby, *Lancelot Andrewes* (London 1958).

almost exclusively in Greek. Newman, a great admirer of this work, published its well-known translation in a series of pamphlets by the Oxford movement. Other authors express this sort of piety by poetry of a tender mystical lyricism. This is the case with John Donne (1572–1631), a passionate and complex figure, and more so with the admirable Henry Vaughan (1622–95), some of whose poems, as for example "The Night," remind us of John of the Cross.[2] Yet other poets anticipated pietism, especially the strange Nicholas Ferrar and the Puritan Thomas Goodwin (1600–1680), whose work *The Heart of Christ in Heaven towards Sinners on Earth* (1642) was a precursor to the Sacred Heart devotion.[3] The Platonizing tendency, well developed especially among the educated circles of Oxford, brought forth interesting and curious works, especially those of Henry More. He was under the influence of the esoteric mysticism of Jakob Böhme, who enjoyed great esteem in seventeenth-century England; Charles I had a personal interest in him and had his works translated. One of the most interesting works from the Puritan circles is that of John Bunyan (1628–88), a tinker who became a popular preacher. He achieved lasting fame through his treatise *Grace abounding to the Chief of Sinners* (1666), but even more so through his *Pilgrim's Progress* (1678),[4] expressing a spirituality which—while intellectually meager—is pragmatic and soulful. Even more interesting—by virtue of his position at the periphery of the official Churches—is the case of the founder of the Quaker movement, George Fox (1624–91).[5] His intriguing diary offers a beautiful itinerary of his calling; his numerous spiritual treatises develop an illumination theory sharply opposed to all institutional Churches, but especially to Catholicism.[6] His protégé, William Penn (1644–1719), the founder of the Quaker state of Pennsylvania, was much more tolerant. In his famous treatise *No Cross, no Crown* (1669) he defends the Quaker view of life and does not hesitate to quote an excerpt from the biography of the Baron de Renty by the Jesuit Saint-Jure as proof of his thesis that the soul must concentrate on a point in the sea of destruction.

This quote raises the question of the influence of continental spirituality on Anglicanism. An examination of the total picture shows that this influence was very significant even in the seventeenth century and that it deepened even more during the following centuries. The English public was very much interested in the religious controversies which

---

[2] See F. E. Huntchinson, *Henry Vaughan, a Life and Interpretation* (Oxford 1947).

[3] See M. Kyne, "Goodwin," *DSAM* 6 (1966), 601.

[4] See A. Talon, *John Bunyan, l'homme et l'œuvre* (Paris 1948).

[5] See P. Held, *Der Quäker George Fox, sein Leben, Wirken, Kämpfen, Leiden, Siegen* (Basel 1953).

[6] See P. Janelle, "Fox," *DSAM* 5 (1963), 770–79.

were stirring up France and frequently interpreted them in an antipapal sense. In general their sympathies were with Port-Royal and the Jansenists, who were viewed as the least corrupted among the Roman Catholics. Numerous texts of Jansenist origin were quickly translated into English, among them the *Provinciales* (1657) and the *Pensées* (1704) by Pascal. In 1669 Theophile Gale published *The True Idea of Jansenism;* based on his stay in France, his work is remarkably well informed and perspicacious. But some other representatives of French spirituality were also highly respected. The Puritan J. Alleine invoked De Renty, just as Penn had. The famous historian G. Burnet (1643–1715), a bishop with latitudinarian tendencies, did likewise. R. Roach, who had at first been a member of the sect of the Philadelphians, inspired by Böhme, and had then become a millenarian, expressed his admiration for the mystics from Francis de Sales to Fénelon (1725).

At the very beginning of the eighteenth century the influence of Fénelon and Mme Guyon in England was indeed very considerable.[7] There was also a noticeable influence of a much less convincing mystic, Antoinette Bourignon (1616–80), who was officially a Catholic but joined a variation of illuminatism, similar to that of the Quakers. While English publicists ironically compared the Quakers with the quietists of the continent, the Quakers themselves devoutly invoked Fénelon, Mme Guyon, and Antoinette Bourignon. Between 1727 and 1738 one of them, Josiah Martin, published translations of Fénelon and Mme Guyon, while Nathanael Hooke, a Catholic sympathizer and friend of Pope's, translated the *Vie de Fénelon* by Ramsay. Personal ties were soon formed. Numerous members of the English aristocracy visited Fénelon at Cambrai, where he had been banished, and Mme Guyon, exiled to Blois after she was set free. Both of them had a profound influence on the Protestant segment of England, especially on the followers of James II in Scotland, where several of their friends were arrested and executed during the rebellion of 1715. The most prominent personality of the Protestant group was André Michel Ramsay (1686–1743), who converted to Catholicism when he was with Fénelon and became secretary to Mme Guyon until her death.[8] A well-known physician from London, John Keith served as a focus for the whole group where all the correspondence converged. Through him Mme Guyon sent a copy of her autobiography to England. This entire group also had great appreciation for Pierre Poiret (1646–1719), a pietist pastor of Calvinist origin, editor

[7] See J. Orcibal, "L'influence spirituelle de Fénelon dans les pays anglo-saxons au XVIIIe siècle," *XVIIe siècle* 12–14 (1951/52), 276–87.
[8] See A. Chérel, *Histoire de l'idée de tolérance: un aventurier religieux au XVIIIe siècle, A. M. Ramsay* (Paris 1926); G. D. Henderson, *Chevalier Ramsay* (London 1952).

of the works of Mme Guyon, Antoinette Bourignon, and of many other mystical texts. Their admiration was, by the way, quite eclectic, extending as it did to Francis de Sales, Pascal, Renty, Olier, Surin, Laurent de la Résurrection, a fellow Carmelite well liked by Fénelon, as well as to a simple Breton servant woman, Armelle Nicolas (1606–71), called the Bonne Armelle.[9]

The Episcopalian milieu of Scotland was in fact strongly influenced by the mysticism of the continent since a command of French was widespread among the educated. Robert Leighton, originally Presbyterian and then Archbishop of Glasgow, had lived on the continent for a long time and maintained close ties with the Jansenists; like them he favored Augustinianism and had a certain preference for the early Church. In regard to spiritualism his most sincere sympathies were reserved for Francis de Sales, in whom he sought the idea of a preeminent inner religion beyond all dogmatic controversies. His pupil Henry Scongal, before his untimely death at a very young age, was able to publish a small volume oriented along those lines, *The Life of God in the Soul of Man,* whose many reprints attested to its success. Two of his friends, James and George Garden, Episcopalians and pastors in Aberdeen, continued his work. In 1699 James attacked the intransigent dogmatism of the Presbyterians in his *Theologia comparativa,* published by Poiret in a translation. George was initially a pupil of Antoinette Bourignon, but her strange ways worried him a bit and around 1710 when he discovered his ideal in Mme Guyon he embraced the latter's cause with great zeal.

Similar influences were at work in the circle of those clerics who had refused to swear the oath of loyalty to William of Orange after the revolution of 1688. Spiritually and liturgically they formed a very interesting group, asserting themselves until the very beginning of the eighteenth century. They had close ties with French Gallicanism and Bossuet. In 1712 and 1718 efforts were made toward reunion. The pious bishop of Bath and Wells, Thomas Ken, who had a reputation for saintliness, sought his ideal in the Jansenist Nicolas Pavillon and was inspired by Pascal and Saint-Cyran. A member of the group, Francis Lee, translated Fénelon's pastoral letter concerning the love of God in 1715. Thus their ritualistic tendency by no means kept them from making the personal inner life the foremost goal of their efforts.

Among those who had refused the oath of loyalty, William Law (1686–1781) was an interesting personality and a great author. His convictions had forced him to leave Cambridge and he withdrew to the house of the historian Gibbon as tutor of the latter's family. As an

---

[9] See Le Gouvello, *Armelle Nicolas dite la Bonne Armelle* (Paris 1913).

438

author of devotional literature he was strongly influenced by Francis de Sales. While God must be the only object of human activity, he asserted that the Christian can arrive at holiness under all conditions. An expert in German religious thought, he was also influenced by Tauler and the *Theologia teutsch*. This concept of Christian perfection, at once challenging and elastic, is expressed in his two best works, *Treatise of Christian Perfection* (1726) and *Serious Call to a Holy Life* (1728), both of which—though especially the latter—are classics of the Anglican spiritual literature. Around 1733 he made the acquaintance of George Cheyne, a fashionable physician who took a passionate interest in mysticism. He was a friend of Pope's and pupil of the brothers Garden, as well as of the French eccentric Saint-Georges de Marsay. Under Cheyne's influence Law discovered Böhme, whom he learned to admire and through whom he arrived at a unique esoteric position. On the other hand, he severely criticized Antoinette Bourignon and Marsay; yet he consistently respected Fénelon and Mme Guyon.[10] Among Law's friends, John Heylin should be mentioned. He was a teacher at the cathedral school of Westminster Abbey and had lived in France for some time. In 1724 Heylin published *Devotional Tracts concerning the Presence of God and other Religious Subjects,* which includes texts by Fénelon, Mme Guyon, and, above all, Laurent de la Résurrection. In 1721 Heylin also published a translation of the homilies of the pseudo-Macarius, which had a strong influence on Wesley, who was one of his friends. Lastly, we cannot leave the topic of the High Church without making mention of Joseph Butler (1692–1752), bishop of Bristol and later of Durham, author of a work entitled *The Analogy of Religion Natural and Revealed* (1736), remarkable by virtue of its view of conscience and the supernatural which greatly influenced Newman during the latter's youth.

John Wesley (1703–91) and Methodism

Of all the religious currents which were shaping England in the eighteenth century Methodism possessed the greatest vitality. Its founder's family was of Puritan origin; his parents, Samuel and Susanna Wesley, however, had staunchly adhered to the High Church and faithfully kept to its principles in their small parish of Epworth. The parents gave their large progeny of nineteen children an example of piety and learning. Samuel was enthusiastic about the early Church and occupied himself with the works of Bossuet and Arnauld; Susanna had memorized almost the entire translation of Pascal's *Pensées* by Kenneth

---

[10] See M. Grainger, *William Law and the Life of the Spirit* (London 1948); A. W. Hopkinson, *About William Law* (London 1948).

(1704). The example set by his family could not but influence Wesley strongly; he belonged to the High Church until 1737. Later on he reproached himself for indifference in his spiritual life until 1725. At this point he experienced his first conversion, in which he also involved his brother Charles, who appears to have played a prominent role in the subsequent events. This first experience, which prompted Wesley to devote himself entirely to God, was influenced by reading the *Imitation* by Jeremy Taylor and the works of Scongal and Law. As we know, the latter two were very much steeped in the mystics of the continent. Wesley now sought to go back to the sources. Around 1730 he read Francis de Sales, Pascal, Quesnel, and Fénelon. At this time he was also influenced by Heylin in a clearly mystical sense. In 1732 he had the opportunity of making the acquaintance of William Law, but as a person the latter disappointed him.[11] On the other hand, he was still fascinated by the vision of the original Church. He now read *Les mœurs des chrétiens* by the confirmed Gallican historian Claude Fleury (1640–1723), who was a friend of Fénelon's and Bossuet's. At about this time he also read Tillemont and in 1733 he even sought the acquaintance of the latter's translator, Thomas Deacon. Together with his brother and some other fellow students he founded a student society in Oxford, the "Holy Club," where he lectured about his ideas. At that time he discovered the work *Vie de Renty* by Saint-Jure, who was also revered by his father. Its discovery was followed by that of Tauler, Mme Guyon, and Molinos.

In point of fact, Wesley, during the years 1731–36, underwent a severe inner crisis and sought help from the Catholic mystics. Towards the end of this crisis he took part in a missionary expedition to Georgia. But the meager success of this mission caused him great disappointment and affected him profoundly. In the course of this mission he met the Moravian Brethren, pupils of Zinzendorf, who was a strange mystic of illuminism. After his return to England a short time later Wesley initiated personal ties with Zinzendorf. For a time the Lutheran-inspired Moravian Brethren caused him to give primary importance to the idea of justification solely on the basis of faith and the idea that the justification of man is solely the justice of Christ imputed to him.[12] At the occasion of a conference of the Moravian Brethren on 24 May 1738 Wesley heard a reading of Luther's introduction to the letter to the Romans. This became a decisive element, causing his second, his "evangelical" conversion. He felt his heart "strangely warmed" and received the inner conviction that Christ had forgiven his sins and saved him from the law of sin and death. After a short sojourn in Germany,

[11] See J. B. Green, *John Wesley and William Law* (London 1948).
[12] See J. E. Rattenbury, *The Conversion of the Wesleys* (London 1937).

where he visited the communities of the Moravian Brethren, Wesley, supported by his brother Charles and some of his pupils, began to pronounce his ideas by means of open-air or field preaching. To this task he dedicated himself until his death with a courage and stamina that shrank from nothing. He gave about forty thousand sermons, and we also have a considerable number of hymns composed by his brother Charles for those camp meetings. But John Wesley did not want to be a "dissenter" at all. What he actually wanted was to give people a personal religious life within the framework of the established Church and he consistently refused to give up those ties which connected him with official Anglicanism. He was accused of "enthusiasm," meaning an irrational illuminism, and for that reason he encountered strenuous resistance, especially on the part of Joseph Butler. But Wesley did not change his position. He knew how to organize and sweep along his listeners so that soon he had strong groups of followers. He divided them into classes of twelve faithful each who were under the direction of a leader who was responsible for their spiritual progress. These firm and clearly delineated structures impressed public opinion; hence the name "Methodism," initially given to them somewhat scoffingly. As a matter of fact, the activities of Wesley and his group had the effect generally of raising the social and human level of his followers, having a positive and beneficial influence on English society.

Early on Wesley apparently started to keep a diary whose entries as of 1735 have come down to us, still partly unpublished. Aside from being a fascinating document concerning his travels and sermons, it also offers us a spiritual experience of rare quality, some points of which, however, remain obscure. It is, for example, not easy to find out why Wesley in 1736, towards the end of his crisis, turned against the same mystics from whom he had sought help and solace before. He reproaches them for their excessive desire to isolate the Christian in solitude and for their attempt to reinterpret the inner trials as constituting grace while he saw in it nothing but a sign of God's anger. His brother Charles, although his confidant, did not follow him in this. As we shall see, Wesley later on changed his position without, however, expressly revoking it and included the mystics in his anthologies. At any rate, it is certain that his experience of 24 May 1728 was not the last of his spiritual trials; his state of depression lasted for several months until he regained his inner peace. Several commentators think that this is proof enough for questioning the actual significance of that experience. But the value which Wesley himself gave to it contradicts this interpretation. There can be no doubt that the analysis of his own case led him to put his "evangelical" experience on a much less sentimental level than some of his successors did and to put it manifestly in the area of a moral decision.

Thus Wesley arrived at very complex points of view regarding certain Protestant positions. He had always been an opponent of the Calvinist idea of predestination and on this point he soon contradicted his pupil Whitefield. But to the extent in which he became aware that conversion had to be translated into a challenge within practical life he rejected the Lutheran idea of justification solely through faith and without good works. No doubt he held the opinion that Christ is the sole savior and that man is saved only by believing in Him. On this point he completely shared the Christocentricity of the Moravian Brethren, but without accepting its sentimental and pious aspects. More and more he arrived at the conviction that faith could be given valid expression only through works. Luther's commentary on the letter to the Galatians and his reflection on the letter of James which Luther called an "epistle of straw" seemed blasphemous to him. At the same time he began to reject the idea of imputed justice as absurd. On this point he was contradicted by the Moravian Brethren and Zinzendorf; he conferred with the latter on 3 September 1741, but their talk was disappointing because each persisted in his position. Shortly thereafter Wesley encountered similar resistance from some of the members of his own movement.

Yet his ideas continued to develop in this direction. More and more he arrived at the conviction that justification had to be connected with a progressive sanctification through man, a sanctification achieved through his own efforts under divine grace, leading man to a genuine moral progress. In his eyes, faith acted through love and love was developed through deeds. Factually he drew away farther and farther from the positions of Protestantism while approaching traditional Catholic ethics; from this he unhesitatingly drew the moral consequences necessary for the actual ministry. Once he did this, he encountered the problem of creating the instruments and aids for his faithful which they needed on this path towards perfection. For this purpose he published the fifty volumes of his *Christian Library* (1750–56), a collection of spiritual anthologies to which more volumes of the same genre were added later on.[13] Its very eclectic selection is highly significant. Naturally the English and among them the Anglicans are most prominently represented, but there are also many Puritans whose seriousness and Christocentrism Wesley appreciated. There are some German Pietists, especially Arndt. The Spanish are represented by John of Ávila, Gregor López and Molinos. Because of their exclusively mystical orientation, Wesley did not include Saint Teresa and Saint John of the

[13] See J. Orcibal, "Les spirituels français et espagnols chez John Wesley et ses contemporains," *RHR* (1951), 50–109; idem, "L'originalité théologique de John Wesley et les spiritualités du continent," *RH* (1959), 51–80.

Cross. The French are heavily represented with Laurent de la Résurrection, Fénelon, Mme Guyon, Antoinette Bourignon, Saint-Cyran, Pascal, Du Guet, De Renty, and Armelle Nicolas. In his selection Wesley seems to have been inspired by similar anthologies of Pierre Poiret, although he limited the proportion of mystics.

In such a perspective the spirituality of John Wesley, without loosing its elasticity, gradually reassumed the moral and even pragmatic shadings which were given a rare communicative value by virtue of his eloquence. Of course he encountered the spirited resistance not only of the Calvinists, who accused him of giving man the possibility of saving himself by his own power, but also that of the established Church, which he stirred from its lethargy by reminding it emphatically of the urgency of its apostolic task. But it must also be admitted that he developed, especially towards the end of his life, a certain indifferentism towards the strictly dogmatic aspects by moderating their severities and lessening their significance. This point of departure, to be sure, enabled him to create an attractive, albeit fragile, synthesis between the Protestant doctrine of grace and the Catholic ethic of sanctification. The respectable spread of Methodism after Wesley's death attests to the vitality of the spiritual enthusiasm he created. But the Calvinist orientation of many of his disciples shows how difficult it was to maintain that doctrinal balance for which Wesley had hoped.[14]

---

[14] See H. Lindeström, *John Wesley and Sanctification* (Uppsala 1946); C. G. Cell, *John Wesley's Theology* (Cokesbury 1950).

CHAPTER 23

Episcopalism in the Church of the Empire from the Middle of the Seventeenth to the End of the Eighteenth Century

Practical Episcopalism from the End of the Seventeenth to the Beginning of the Eighteenth Century

The roots of the seventeenth and eighteenth-century episcopalism of the Church of the Empire extend back to the late Middle Ages.[1] Spanning the Council of Trent and the Reformation, it tied in with the

---

[1] L. Mergentheim, "Die Wurzeln des deutschen Febronianismus," *HPBI* 139 (1907), 180–92; H. Raab, *Die Concordata Nationis Germanicae* (Wiesbaden 1956); A. Werminghoff, *Nationalkirchliche Bestrebungen* (Stuttgart 1910); F. Vigener, "Gallikanismus und episkopalistische Strömungen," *HZ* 111 (1913), 495–581.

reaction against papal claims in the late Middle Ages, with the church reform movement of the fourteenth and fifteenth centuries, the Councils of Constance and Basel and the prereformational *gravamina*. As a practical episcopalism it initially based its claims concerning beneficiary rights, episcopal jurisdiction, and payments to the Curia on the Concordat of Vienna of 1448. Using the controversial clause "In aliis autem" (buttressed by historical research) as its point of departure, episcopalism next extended the basis of its claim to the Princes Concordats of 1447, which were acknowledged in the above clause and were much more advantageous to the Church of the Empire. Finally it advanced as a rationale the Mainz Acceptation of 1439, comparable to the Pragmatic Sanction of Bourges, the basic law of the Gallican Church. After 1762 the episcopalism of the Church of the Empire viewed as its basic law and program the Basel Decrees accepted in Mainz.[2] The attempt to reform the Church's constitution in favor of episcopalism, simultaneously changing the ecclesiastical principalities into modern, enlightened absolutist states on a Catholic foundation was shaky from the start. It was to be brought about by reviving the decrees of the Council of Basel; in some places there was even talk of overcoming the religious schism. This attempt, however, was immediately countered by more than three hundred years of ecclesiastical and imperial history; it was full of inner contradictions and doomed to failure by the empirichistoric method it was based on.

The Council of Trent had created decisively positive as well as negative conditions for the revival of episcopalism a century after its last sessions. The less the ecclesiastical territories were threatened in their existence and the more the prince-bishops concentrated on their ecclesiastical and political tasks,[3] the more frequent were the quarrels with the papal nuncios in Cologne, Vienna, Lucerne, and with the Roman Curia about violations of the Vienna Concordat, the archiepiscopal indults for the papal months, quinquennial faculties, the jurisdiction of the nunciatures, annates, confirmation fees, pallium payments, exemptions, and decimations.[4]

---

[2] H. F. Hürten, "Die Mainzer Akzeptation," (unpubl. diss., Münster 1955); H. Raab, *Concordata,* 125 ff.

[3] The archbishop of Salzburg, Wolf Dietrich, had already prepared the theory that he was a prince of the Empire holding the archdiocese as a vassal of the Emperor. As a prince, he asserted, he was not subject to the authority of the Pope and would furthermore remain a prince even if he resigned as bishop (F. Martin, *Salzburgs Fürsten in der Barockzeit* [Salzburg 1966], 36).

[4] W. Michel, *Das Wiener Konkordat vom Jahre 1448 und die nachfolgenden Gravamina des Primarklerus der Mainzer Kirchenprovinz* (diss., Heidelberg 1929); L. Mergentheim, *Die Quinquennalfakultäten pro foro externo* (Stuttgart 1908); A. Franzen, "Eine Krise der deutschen Kirche im 17. Jh.?" *RQ* 49 (1954), 56–111.

In the first decades after the Treaty of Westphalia, leadership of the opposition in the Church of the Empire was represented by the elector-archbishops of Mainz and Cologne, Johann Philipp von Schönborn[5] and Max Heinrich von Bayern. In his capacity as lord chancellor of the Empire, Johann Philipp considered it his foremost task to watch over the liberties and rights of the German nation. As archbishop of the *Metropolis Germaniae,* concerned with the reform of the higher and lower clergy, he complained in 1648 about the diminution of his ordinary rights by the Cologne nunciature. He was confirmed in his hostility to the nunciature by his political and Gallican views as well as by the unionist intentions and anti-Roman sentiments on the part of several of his advisers, especially the convert Johann Christian von Boineburg.[6] For the Cologne elector Max Heinrich, whose heated disputes with Johann Philipp concerning the right of coronation had been resolved in the so-called Coronation Tractate of 1657,[7] there were several causes for the outbreak of tensions with Rome in 1659. Among them were theological and canonical misgivings regarding the direct interference of the nuncios, especially those of Cologne and Liège, with their idea of the special rights of a "born legate of the Holy See"; the influence of his favorite, Franz Egon von Fürstenberg, who was oriented towards the Gallican model; and, most importantly, the Wittelsbach church policy.

In this regard it should be stressed that nine years earlier, in 1650, the election of the very pious, yet weak Max Heinrich in Münster had been rejected by Christoph Bernhard von Galen because Max Heinrich "was too much a cleric to be a good ruler and general as demanded by the times."[8] When his brother Albrecht Sigismund planned to resign,[9] he sought to succeed him in the bishopric of Freising, although he already held the Cologne electorate and the prince-bishoprics of Hildesheim

---

[5] G. Mentz, *Johann Philipp v. Schönborn. Kurfürst von Mainz, Bischof von Würzburg u. Worms 1605–73* (Jena 1899) 172 f.; re. Johann Philipp see also *LThK* IX (1964), 451 and biblio.

[6] *NDB* 2 (1955), 424 f.; St. v. Dunin Borkowski, "Aus der Briefmappe eines berühmten Konvertiten des 17. Jh.," *StdZ* 105 (1923), 132–47. The following quote from a letter by Boineburg to Hermann Conring (23 January 1659) is characteristic: "Let the Romans hate us, as long as they fear us."

[7] G. Mentz, *Johann Philipp* II, 20 f.; A. M. Reitzel, *Das Mainzer Krönungsrecht und die politische Problematik* (Mainz 1963); G. Wallner, *Der Krönungsstreit zwischen Kurköln und Kurmainz* (1653—57) (diss., Mainz 1967).

[8] W. Kohl, *Christoph Bernhard von Galen. Politische Geschichte des Fürstbistums Münster 1650–1678* (Münster 1964), 3.

[9] Albrecht Sigismund had been elected coadjutor of Freising at the age of sixteen; he was religious and without blemish. Upon entering his office he applied for dispensation from consecration (H. E. Feine, *Die Besetzung der Reichsbistümer vom Westfälischen Frieden bis zur Säkularisation* [Stuttgart 1921; reprint, Amsterdam 1964], 35, 38f.).

and Liège; as far as political power was concerned Freising was insignificant. With some justification it was later designated as "our parish" by the elector Max Emanuel.[10] With only two interruptions, the Wittelsbach dynasty ruled the prince-bishopric from the middle of the sixteenth to the middle of the eighteenth century. But it was an "arcanum" of Freising politics in no case ever to separate from the Emperor and the Empire. One of the goals of the Wittelsbach church policy had always been to unite Freising in a personal union with either the old Bavarian bishopric of Regensburg or the ecclesiastic secundogeniture in the northwest German *Germania Sacra,* founded by Duke Ernst. In addition to Max Heinrich, the other candidates for Freising were Cardinal Friedrich of Hesse,[11] Franz Egon von Fürstenberg, and the prince-bishop of Osnabrück and Regensburg, Franz Wilhelm von Wartenberg, progeny of the marriage of Duke Ferdinand of Bavaria to a commoner.

But Pope Alexander VII refused to accept Albrecht Sigismund's resignation unless the Holy See were granted the unreserved right to the new appointment; he withdrew the election rights from the Freising chapter and ordered the nuncio to thwart the election of the Cologne elector.[12] These differences, stemming from the policies of the Wittelsbach imperial Church were intensified by the failure of Max Heinrich's designs on Paderborn, because of the quarrels covering the quinquennial faculties and the archiepiscopal indults to fill the benefices becoming vacant during the papal months. In the fall of 1660—probably on the advice of his minister Franz Egon von Fürstenberg, who was hostile to Rome—Max Heinrich suggested the convocation of a national council to counter the presumptiousness of the Holy See and the abuses in the Church of the Empire.

According to the Vienna nuncio, this was to be accompanied by the reunion project, the so-called "Mainz Plan," propagated in September 1660 by Frankfurt.[13] Its goal was said to be the reunion of the Church into a national Church achieved by means of far-reaching concessions to the Protestants. One year later, in November 1661, the Cologne nuncio, Marco Gallio, declared that he had heard of a plan of an intended union between the three ecclesiastical electors in order to "realize an absolute power of disposition over all church benefices, independent of Rome."[14]

[10] B. Hubensteiner, *Vom Geist des Barock. Kultur und Frömmigkeit im alten Bayern* (Munich 1967), 37.
[11] F. Noack, "Kardinal Friedrich von Hessen. Großprior in Heitersheim," *ZGObRh* 80 (1928), 341–86.
[12] A. Franzen, *Krise der deutschen Kirche,* 87 f.; A. A. Levinson, "Nuntiaturberichte vom Kaiserhofe Leopolds I.," *AÖG* 103 (1913), 667ff.
[13] See Chap. 27 : "Attempts at Church Reunion."
[14] A. Franzen, *Krise der deutschen Kirche,* 103.

At the Imperial Diet in Regensburg violent attacks against Rome were to be expected. According to testimony by the Salzburg archbishop Guidobald von Thun, the elector-archbishop of Cologne intended "di costituire un patriarca in Germania e di costituire o almeno d'introdurre nel clero dell'imperio la prattica e lo stilo della chiesa Gallicana."[15] The compromise, achieved by conciliatory action of the Pope, was of short duration. In 1665 the Diet and the Supreme Court in Speyer unequivocally opposed the practice of appeals to the Pope and the nuncios in trials concerned with temporal matters.

A first climax in the opposition by the Church of the Empire is the *gravamina* of the three Rhenish elector-archbishops in 1673.[16] Max Heinrich, elector-archbishop of Cologne and prince-bishop of Liège and Hildesheim; Lothar Friedrich von Metternich, elector-archbishop of Mainz and prince-bishop of Speyer and Worms; and Karl Kaspar von der Leyen, elector-archbishop of Trier formally protested the violations of the Vienna Concordat concerning the freedom of episcopal elections, the annates, and the right of appointing beneficiaries. They demanded that the Curia respect the indults granted the archbishops when the Vienna Concordat was accepted and, further, that the German Church not be placed at a disadvantage compared to the French and Spanish Church.

Nor was there any lack of complaints in the future about violations of the concordat and interferences by the nuncios in the ordinary episcopal jurisdiction. When Archduke Joseph was elected Roman King (1690), the electorate of Trier moved to renew the formulation of *gravamina* against the Holy See. The pertinent article of the electoral capitula-

---

[15] Caraffa, Regensburg, 26 Dec. 1663 quoted in A. Levinson, *Nuntiaturberichte,* 763.—G. Mentz (*Johann Philipp,* 184) mentions demands to convoke a combined German-French council towards resisting the presumptions of the Holy See.

[16] The *Gravamina* of 1673 in Gärtner, *Corp. jur.* II (1799), 322f.; F. J. Buß, *Urkundliche Gesch. des National- und Territorialkirchentums in der kath. Kirche Deutschlands* (Schaffhausen 1851), 702–10; H. Raab, *Concordata,* 67; concerning Lothar Friedrich, successor of Johann Philipp von Schönborn, elected with the help of the French, see M. Braubach, "Politische Hintergründe der Mainzer Koadjutorwahl von 1670," *RhVjBl.* 15/16 (1951), 313–38; also in M. Braubach, *Diplomatie und geistiges Leben im 17. u. 18 Jh.* (Bonn 1969), 43–77; on Max Heinrich, see A. Franzen, *Krise der deutschen Kirche* (with biblio.) and M. Braubach, *Kurkölnische Miniaturen* (Münster 1954), 1–24; concerning Karl Kaspar von der Leyen, see P. Pillorget, "La France et l'Électorat de Trèves au temps de Charles Gaspard de la Leyen (1652–76)," *Revue d'histoire diplom.* 78 (1964).—It is noteworthy that none of the elector-archbishops advocated the same political line. The archbishop of Trier was one of the most reliable followers of the Emperor. Metternich was expected to fix Mainz more firmly into the French system. Max Heinrich was weak and unreliable; under Fürstenberg's influence he tended towards France.

tion,[17] which had bound even Ferdinand III in 1654 to remove jurisdiction in temporal matters from the nunciatures and the Roman Curia and to insist on the observance of the concordat, had been discussed again and again. At the election of Charles VI in 1711 that article was reformulated as ARTICLE XIV, remaining valid until the time of Leopold II. A "language quite corresponding"[18] to the Punctation of Ems in 1786 appeared in a complaint by the *Corpus Evangelicorum* as early as 1703, when it intervened in the quarrel that began in 1699 between the Roman Curia and the cathedral chapter of Münster concerning the appointment to the provostship. Similar conflicts ensued between the Curia and the cathedral chapters of Worms and Constance.[19] The episcopal attitude of the Mainz chapter during the waning seventeenth century, hostile to the nunciatures, is sufficiently characterized by the remarks of the Cologne nuncio Buonvisi: "Non essendoci niuno provisto dalla Santa Sede, non vi è chi voglia havere corrispondenza col Nuntio."[20] Elector-Archbishop Lothar Franz von Schönborn resolutely opposed all attempts on the part of the Cologne nunciature to communicate officially with Mainz or Bamberg, since "neither the archbishopric of Mainz nor the local bishopric (Bamberg) are located within the boundaries of his legation, but are both *ab omni nuntiatura* free and directly subject to the Holy See."[21]

For a time it might have seemed as though Lothar Franz von Schön-

---

[17] F. Hartung, "Die Wahlkapitulationen der deutschen Kaiser und Könige," *HZ* 107 (1911), 306–44; idem, *Volk und Staat in der deutschen Gesch.* (Leipzig 1940); G. Kleinheyer (*Die kaiserliche Wahlkapitulation. Gesch. Wesen und Funktionen* [Karlsruhe 1968]; does not deal with this problem.

[18] *Mainzer Monatsschrift von geistlichen Sachen* IV (1788), 420–23; H. Raab, *Concordata,* 68; F. Keinemann, *Das Domkapitel zu Münster im 18. Jh.* (Münster 1967), 85ff.

[19] K. Wild, *Lothar Franz von Schönborn. Bischof von Bamberg u. Erzbischof von Mainz 1693–1729* (Heidelberg 1904), 154.—For the provision by the Swiss A. S. Reding which led to a lengthy conflict between the bishop and the cathedral chapter of Constance on one side and the Roman Curia, the nunciature of Lucerne, and the Helvetic Confederation on the other, see R. Reinhardt, *Die Beziehungen von Hochstift und Diözese Konstanz zu Habsburg-Österreich in der Neuzeit* (Wiesbaden 1966) 75f. The German party urged a settlement in Mainz where the "customs" of the German Church were well known and sought to obtain "as a matter of principle the imperial court or at least an ecclesiastic trial court in Germany as the place of venue for all disputes concerning aristocratic origin in the Church of the Empire." Emperor Leopold, in order to protect the imperial-Austrian position in the Lake Constance area against the influence of France and the Helvetic Confederation, emphatically took the part of the cathedral chapter.

[20] Buonvisi to Paluzzo-Altieri, Cologne, 2 Nov. 1670. F. Diaz, ed., *Francesco Buonvisi. Nuntiatura a Colonia* I (Rome 1959), 86.

[21] H. Weber, "Die Privilegien des alten Bistums Bamberg," *HJ* 20 (1899), 40, 634; A. Veit, "Die Kölner Nuntiatur und der Mainzer Hof," *HPBl* 167 (1921), 208–16.

born[22]—after his uncle Johann Philipp the second prominent lord chancellor of the Empire from that family which for three generations determined the episcopal history of Germany—would place himself at the head of the aspirations for a national Church. The relationship between the Rhenish archbishops and the Cologne nunciature deteriorated "to the outer limits of tolerance"[23] as a result of the proscription of Elector Joseph Clemens von Bayern, the most recent armed conflict between the Emperor and the Pope involving Comacchio, the execution of the controversial *preces primariae.* and, finally, the *Privilegium illiminatum de non appellando* granted to the electorate of Trier. As the executor of "First Prayers" and uncle of the imperial vice chancellor Friedrich Karl von Schönborn,[24] who with Joseph I was held responsible for the latter's anti-Roman policy (dictated by specific Habsburg interests), Lothar Franz was made to feel Rome's irritation at his coadjutor election in Bamberg and the demanded recantation. He found himself in a very delicate situation between the Emperor and the Pope. Yet in spite of his episcopal antipathy towards Rome and his patriotism for the Empire he did not permit himself to be made a tool of Josephinist church policy. This emerging dilemma of episcopal Germany caught between the Pope and the Emperor, or rather between Rome and Vienna, was at the same time aggravated by differences with the Catholic lay princes, as in the case of Elector Palatine Karl Philipp (from 1731 to 1734),[25] who managed—against the resistance of the prince-bishops—to shift their oppressive tax burdens onto the Church, thanks to papal indults. Practical episcopalism, even before it was provided with a sufficient theoretical foundation, was confronted at the beginning of the eighteenth century with the same constellation of forces which had frustrated it earlier in the fifteenth century.

The Canonical and Theological Foundation of Episcopalism in the Church of the Empire

The political-ecclesiastical opposition within the Church of the Empire against Rome, notwithstanding its severity in the first third of the

---

[22] See *LThK* IX (1964), 452; H. Reifenberg, "Lothar Franz von Schönborn und die Liturgie im Bistum Bamberg," *103. Bericht des Histor. Vereins für die Pflege der Gesch. des ehemaligen Fürstbistums Bamberg* (Bamberg 1967), 419–66.

[23] K. Walf, *Entwicklung des päpstlichen Gesandtschaftswesens.* 151.

[24] H. Hantsch, *Reichsvizekanzler Friedrich Karl von Schönborn:* M. Braubach, "Friedrich Karl von Schönborn und Prinz Eugen," *Festgabe für H. Hantsch* (Graz, Vienna and Cologne 1965), 111–31; also M. Braubach, *Diplomatie und geistiges Leben im 17. und 18. Jh.* (Bonn 1969), 301–20.

[25] H. Duchhardt, *Philipp Karl von Eltz. Kurfürst von Mainz, Erzkanzler des Reiches (1732–1743)* (Mainz 1969), 119f.

eighteenth century, lacked a real theological and canonical foundation; it was only peripherally touched by the Enlightenment and not at all by theological rationalism. Only occasionally did such opposition arise because of the striving by ecclesiastical principalities for an order corresponding to their dual function within Church and Empire. Since the "evolution of Austria from the Empire" and the strengthening of the established Church within the monarchy the opposition could only occasionally rely on the Emperor as the *Advocatus Ecclesiae,* as the *Vindex canonum.* Aside from such occasions as the rejection of Gregory VII's "Offizium," the false "Hildebrandism," and "ultramontane"[26] principles practiced too openly, an appreciable reaction among the faithful occurred only during the conflict involving the Munich nunciature or the Udligenschwyl dispute. The episcopalism of the Church of the Empire can only vaguely be compared with Gallicanism. Even in its most radical utterances it never put in doubt the unity of the Church; it never strove for a German national Church, but merely for the securing of its rights and liberties.

Efforts towards a justification of practical episcopalism based upon canon law and theology did not start until the end of the seventeenth century under the impact of the conflicts between Louis XIV and Innocent XI, the growing particular differences with the nuncios and Rome and with the acceptance of Gallican and Jansenist ideas and those concerning an enlightened established Church.[27] One of the pioneers of German church freedoms, the Protestant canonist Johannes Schilter, was indebted to Petrus de Marca in his work *De libertate ecclesiarum Germaniae,*[28] written one year after the *Declaratio Cleri Gallicani.* It

---

[26] H. Raab, "Zur Gesch. und Bedeutung des Schlagwortes 'ultramontan' im 18. und im frühen 19. Hh.," *HJ* 81 (1962), 159–73.

[27] For Bossuet's influence on Febronius, see J. Kuntziger, op. cit., 30, 40f. As yet a history of the reception of Bossuet in the Church of the Empire is lacking. Some references in this connection in H. Raab, *Concordata,* 64, 157. In the announcement of Bossuet's defense in the *Mainzer Monatsschrift* IV (1788), 496f., we find the following: ". . . daß dieses treffliche Buch an recht vielen Orten seine gesunden und wahren Grundsätze verbreite, curialistische Maßnahmen und den gesamten Isidorischen Sauerteig verbannen helfe."—On Jansenism in Germany, see the following work, which, while very much in need of updating, is still of primary importance: W. Deinhardt, *Der Jansenismus in deutschen Landen* (Munich 1929); also L. Just, "Die Bekämpfung des Jansenismus in der Erzdiözese Köln unter Josef Clemens (1703)," *AHVNrh* 136 (1940), 131–38; idem, "Der Trierer Weihbishchof Johann Mathias v. Eyss im Kampf gegen den Jansenismus (1714–1729)," *AMrhKG* 11 (1959), 160–89; H. Tüchle, "Die Bulle Unigenitus und die süddeutschen Prämonstratenser," *HJ* 74 (1955), 342–50; H. Raab, "Landgraf Ernst von Hessen-Rheinfels und der Jansenismus," *AMrhKG* 19 (1967), 41–60.

[28] J. Schilter, *De libertate ecclesiarum Germaniae libri* VII (Jena 1683); H. Raab, *Concordata,* 71ff. and Chap. 27 of this volume.

contains the germ of Febronianism, intending to prepare the way for a reunification of the denominations by means of a reduction of the papal primacy of jurisdiction and the abandonment of the doctrine of papal infallibility. By its glorification of the medieval imperial power it reinforced the anti-Roman tendencies in the Church of the Empire. Episcopal, established Church, and Jansenist ideas were assimilated into the Church of the Empire from the theories of Zeger-Bernard Van Espen,[29] who published his pioneering *Jus ecclesiasticum* in 1700. The decisive stimuli for the canon law of the Empire and the theoretical justification of German episcopalism in the second third of the eighteenth century emanated from the Schönborn sphere of influence, even though the later Mainz suffragan bishop Schnernauer, during the years of feud between Cardinal Damian Hugo von Schönborn and his metropolitan, developed ideas which almost anticipated the Koblenz and Ems Punctations.

Among the professors at the seminary and university at Würzburg, where the former vice-chancellor Friedrich Karl von Schönborn had been rector since 1734, was a former pupil of Lambertini's, Johann Kaspar Barthel.[30] He was celebrated by his contemporaries as the prince of canonists and oracle of his century. In accordance with the charge by his bishop and ruler he taught a canon law which, adapted to the special German conditions, was at variance from what was taught in Rome. As the future Würzburg suffragan bishop Gregor Zirkel wrote in 1794, Barthel taught "the German Church to feel its rights and independence."[31] He contradicted the Jesuits and the Roman Curia with "German frankness," transplanted principles of French canonists to Germany, exposed Roman policies from history and thus created as many opponents to Rome as he had listeners. Barthel rejected an absolute form of governance by the Church for theological, historical and ecclesiopolitical reasons. According to him the doctrine of papal primacy should distinguish between *essentialia,* based on divine right, and *accessoria,* acquired by prescriptive right and historical development ("Olim non erat sic"). Papal primacy has not been granted "in destructionem sed in aedificationem ecclesiae" and could be limited in the interest of harmony between *imperium* and *sacerdotium.* The independence, coexistence, and orientation of ecclesiastical and temporal power

---

[29] G. Leclerc, *Zeger-Bernard van Espen (1648–1728) et l'autorité ecclésiastique. Contribution à l'histoire des théories gallicanes et du jansénisme* (Zurich 1964).

[30] H. Raab, "Johann Kaspar Barthels Stellung in der Diskussion um die Concordata Nationis Germanicae," *Heropolis jubilans* (Würzburg 1953), 599–616; idem, *Die Concordata Nationis Germanicae,* 79–96; idem, *Neller und Febronius.*

[31] A. F. Ludwig, *Weihbischof Zirkel von Würzburg in seiner Stellung zur theologischen Aufklärung und zur kirchlichen Restauration* I (Paderborn 1904), 91.

towards a common goal makes it difficult, says Barthel, to delimit the authority and rights of the two since from the fulfillment of a common divine mandate grows the "quasi confusio" of ecclesiastical and temporal laws; from necessary mutual subordination arises the obligation to create harmony between Church and state.

The episcopalism of the Barthel school,[32] following the lines of the Schönborn sphere of influence, spread from Würzburg to the ecclesiastical states on the Main and Middle Rhine and from there to Bonn, Cologne, Salzburg, and to almost all the Catholic universities. Georg Christoph Neller,[33] the most prominent pupil of Barthel, was called to the chair for canon law at the University of Trier by Franz Georg von Schönborn.[34] His appointment, opposed by the Jesuits, had important consequences. It established the connection between the Franconian Enlightenment and the political and canonical views of the Church arising from the border situation of the archdiocese and from the differences with the Austrian Netherlands and France promoted by the spread of Jansenist ideas and those of the established Church. Such views were represented at the court of Ehrenbreitstein by the convert Jakob Georg von Spangenberg and his friend, the former officialis and later suffragan bishop Johann Nikolaus von Hontheim, especially after the negotiations involving the election stipulations of Emperor Charles VII (1742). Neller's tenure in Trier, his friendship and collaboration with Hontheim marked the turning point from episcopalism to Febronianism. His *Principia juris ecclesiastici ad statum Germaniae accommodata,* compiled substantially from Gallican authors and published anonymously in Frankfurt in 1746, made his name as a scholar. In it he

[32] Students of Barthel from Franconia included the brothers Georg Christoph and Georg Franz Neller, their nephew Georg Philipp Leuxner, who was destined to succeed his uncle in Trier, and the ecclesiastical advisor of Archbishop Hieronymus von Colloredo and Salzburg's representative to the Ems Congress, Johann Michael Bönicke, the canonist and future suffragan bishop of Speyer, Philipp Anton Schmidt, his brother Michael Ignaz, "the historian of the Germans," as well as the canonists Johann Nepomuk Endres and Johann Josef Sündermahler. Franz Carl Joseph von Hillesheim (1731–1803), who played a prominent role in Cologne as an advocate of the episcopal interests, also studied under Barthel. Neller went on to become "the father of learning" in Trier. Most of the Rhenish episcopalians of the second half of the eighteenth century came from his school.

[33] H. Raab, *Neller u. Febronius,* 185–206.

[34] *NDB* V (1961), 370–71; *LThK* IX (1964), 453; E. H. Fischer, *Ellwangen, Augsburg, Rom. Die Exemtion des Ellwanger Stifts und seine Exemtionspolitik unter Fürstpropst Franz Georg von Schönborn in den Jahren 1732–1749: Ellwangen 764–1964* [1964], 423) stresses that Franz Georg tied "his see of Ellwangen closely to the Holy See through his wise and purposeful exemption policy."

sharply attacked the traditional constitutional doctrine of the Jesuit canonical position and intensified the episcopal theses. Spangenberg's wish—it is probable that Neller had already made Hontheim's acquaintance at that time—for a canonist who could differentiate between the original power of the Pope in church matters and the mere presumptions of the Curia appeared to be fulfilled by Neller's appointment. In his more than thirty years of teaching, in numerous publications Neller was largely responsible for the breakthrough of episcopal canon law in the Empire. As a friend and collaborator of Hontheim he occupies a superior place in the history of Febronianism.

Febronius and Febronianism

According to corresponding testimony by Hontheim and Spangenberg, the immediate impetus for the genesis of Febronianism[35] was furnished during the negotiations for the election of Emperor Charles VII by the discussion of ARTICLE XIV of the imperial electoral capitulation concerning the German concordats, the *Gravamina contra Curiam Romanam,* and the demand by the electorate of Trier to abolish the jurisdiction of the nunciatures in Germany. Based on his study of the *gravamina* and the reform councils, Spangenberg suggested that a future work summarize the rights and liberties of the Church of the Empire after the model of the Gallicans Pithou, Dupuy, de Marca, as well as the Protestant canonist Johannes Schilter and that it create better conditions for surmounting the "Calamitas Imperii," for the reunification of the denominations, by a far-reaching reduction of papal claims. The erudite, personally irreproachable suffragan bishop Hontheim,[36] who followed in the tradition of Van Espen's school, encountered these

[35] L. Just, *Zur Entstehungsgeschichte des Febronius;* idem, "Die römische Kurie und das Reich unter Karl VII. (1742–45)," *HJ* 52 (1932).

[36] A Hontheim biography is lacking. One-sided but still essential: O. Mejer, *Febronius;* also L. Just, *Hontheim. Ein Gedenkblatt;* H. Raab, *Neller u. Febronius;* L. Rechenmacher, *Episkopalismus;* F. Stümper, *Kirchenrechtl. Ideen des Febronius;* E. Reifart, *Kirchenstaat Trier;* H. Petersen, *Febronianismus und Nationalkirche.* Influenced by the church policy and "völkisch"-biological views of the National Socialist period, the author poses the question whether Febronius strove for a national Church in which the "national law of life" would find expression and all "alien intellectual claim of leadership is eliminated." But he concludes sadly that "Hontheim was lacking the fundament of a national world view ["völkische Weltanschauung"], which alone would have been capable of overcoming the universalistic exaggerations of the papal system" (154). The extent of agreement with Petersen, Mejer, and Zillich that a "national feeling" was the motive force behind Febronius' and the entire current of episcopalism is yet to be investigated. The designations "national feeling" and also "national Church" appear to me to be misapplied. Hontheim and the episcopals of the eighteenth century advocated "liberties" of the Church of the Empire. Imperial patriotism and anti-Roman sentiments were indeed among their impulses but not a "national feeling" or "völkische Weltanschauung."

problems in the course of his two decades of ministry in a large diocese. Through historical research, efforts to reform both the Church and the universities, but above all through scholarly collaboration with his friend Neller he hit upon possible solutions. Considerations for the Dutch and French part of the archbishopric of Trier required a modus vivendi with those governments which were oriented towards an established Church. Schönborn episcopalism had to be defended against Roman claims based upon ecclesiastical and political considerations. Religious and ecclesiastical reforms and political practice in the Church began to orient themselves after the ideal of the *Ecclesia primitiva*—the ex-Jesuit F. X. Feller called it "a whim of souls with a mania for innovation"—and to demand the restoration of a historically transfigured church constitution which had been spoiled by pseudo-Isidorianism and "Hildebrandism." Their demands were addressed one-sidedly to Rome, so that the transformation of ecclesiastical territories into enlightened absolutist states was not made impossible. These aims and a delimitation of the rights of the prince-bishops and the Pope, better corresponding to the interests of the Church of the Empire, were to be achieved, at least in part, by a work written under the pseudonym Justinus Febronius, *De statu ecclesiase et legitima potestate Romani Pontificis liber singularis ad reuniendos dissidentes in religione christanos compositus*[37] (Frankfurt 1763; reprints and supplements 1765–70; expanded to five volumes in 1770–74). The means to the goal were to be the revival of the *Concordata Nationis Germanica integra,* of the Mainz Acceptation of 1439, and the decrees of the reform Council of Basel. Reviving an idealized pre-Hildebrandian or pseudo-Isidorian church constitution was to provide the stimulus for a religious and ecclesiastical reform in connection with a moderate Enlightenment.[38] By means of the empirical-historical method, based on the Gallicans, Van Espen, and the Würzburg school of canonists, Febronius used the well-known distinction between the *jura essentialia, quae tendeunt ad unitatis ecclesiae*

---

[37] The original title of the work was: "Symbola quam(!) ad reuniendos in Religione dissidentes Christianos . . . in qua primario agitur de genuino statu et forma regiminis Ecclesiastici nec non legitima potestate Rom. Pontificis" (L. Just, *Entstehung des Febronius,* 377).—Originally it was planned, probably under the influence of Spangenberg, to have it printed in Göttingen, but then, just like Neller's first work, it appeared with Eßlinger in Frankfurt, most likely because Eßlinger's discretion was sufficiently well known to the Trier episcopals ever since the dispute involving Neller's *Principia.* Another reason was that Hontheim's friend Krufft knew that his old acquaintance Damian Friedrich Dumeiz there could supervise the printing.

[38] We should add a reminder that in 1748 Hontheim newly edited the *Brevarium Trevirense* and in 1767, following the Strasbourg example, edited a new *rituale* for the archdiocese. He also strove for improving university studies.

conservationem and the *jura accessoria* in order to relegate the papal primacy to a preeminence of honor after the model of the first eight Christian centuries. According to him, the Pope is not entitled to a jurisdiction competing with that of the bishops since the latter are not his *vicarii* but are reigning as successors of the apostles by the authority of divine right. With the help of the Holy Spirit only the Church and the General Council as representation of the *Corpus ecclesiasticum* are infallible. The Pope is the *centrum unitatis* only insofar as the representation of a federalist system permits. As is evident by the title Febronius borrowed from Pufendorf, the *Analogia Ecclesiae cum Imperio* was the godfather of his doctrine of the *status mixtus* of the Church constitution. Febronius also considers a reduction of papal rights and supervision of all undertakings of the Roman Curia necessary in the interest of the state. In spite of a basic recognition of independence, coexistence, and submission to a common final goal his ideas of the relationship between Church and state amount to a superiority of the state. It passes into Josephinism by virtue of concessions to the temporal princes—according to divine right they are the born defenders of the Church—and in view of the doctrine of the *Jus circa sacra* (*jus advocatiae, jus cavendi*). The corresponding theory of a *Jus circa civilia* is characteristically lacking.

In spite of the fact that his work was a compilation and contained innate contradictions, Febronius exercised a very strong influence on the ecclesiastical and intellectual history of the eighteenth and early nineteenth century. Beginning in 1774, under the influence of undercurrents of Enlightenment and Jansenism, Febronianism was either increasingly opposed by elements of an established Church, or accepted in a radicalized form, but it was also rejected by many moderate episcopalists, such as Abbot Martin II Gerbert.

An intense battle involving countless attacks and counterattacks by such as the brothers Ballerini, Johann Gottfried Kauffmann, Tomaso Maria Mamachi, Ladislaus Sappel, and Francesco Antonio Zaccaria was waged against Febronius. It took place on the literary and scholarly level, but beginning around 1770 it was also conducted for and against a revocation by the aged author. Not until April 1764 did the elective nuncio Niccolò Oddi with the help of the Frankfurt canon Damian Friedrich Dumeiz manage to identify Suffragan Bishop Hontheim as the author.[39] Prior to that several others had been suspected of the author-

---

[39] The question whether Neller coauthored or contributed to the Febronius, posed by the famous Salzburg episcopal Gregorius Zallwein as early as 1763, has not been clarified in detail but can generally be answered in the affirmative. Father Ferdinand Söhr, confessor of Clemens Wenzeslaus of Saxony, elector of Trier, affirmed on 27

ship, among them Barthel, Neller,[40] the enlightened Mainz lawyer Johann Baptist Horix, the future suffragan bishop Ludwig Philipp Behlen, and the canonist Benedikt Oberhauser from Fulda.[41] Hontheim's persistent denial of his authorship was facilitated by the compiled nature of the work of Febronius, the fact that his collaborator Neller was also suspected, and the benevolent attitude of the imperial court and a considerable segment of the episcopate. This denial cannot be explained sufficiently by weakness of character, being of two minds, or Jansenist insincerity. Finally, in 1778 a heavy-hearted Hontheim, upon the urging of his elector-archbishop Clemens Wenzeslaus and the "Counsel of Conscience" of the Alsatian Franz Heinrich Beck, agreed to a formal revocation.[42] On the advice of his friends and under the pressure of the discussions provoked by his revocation, and especially

---

October 1768 in a letter to the secretary of the cologne nuncio Caprara "che il maledetto Febronio è veramenta opere del Neller, e che il Suffraganeo non ha fatto altro che mettere la materia in buon stile, e ha di più avute l'imprudenza di mandare il manuscritto come suo allo stampatore." Other affirmations were similar.—A comparison between Neller's *Principia,* some of his older dissertations, and Febronius leaves no doubt that entire passages of the latter are Neller's ideas, so that he can be called a collaborator even if he did disavow Febronius under pressure by his opponents and even offered to disprove it. On this see H. Raab, *Neller und Febronius,* 200f.

[40] W. A. Mühl, *Die Aufklärung an der Universität Fulda mit besonderer Berücksichtigung der philosophischen und juristischen Fakultät (1734–1805)* (Fulda 1961), 46–49.

[41] H. Raab, "Damian Friedrich Dumeiz und Kardinal Oddi. Zur Entdeckung des Febronius und zur Aufklärung im Erzstift Mainz und in der Reichsstadt Frankfurt," *AMrhKG* 10 (1958), 217–40; A. Bach, *Goethes Dechant Dumeiz, Ein rheinischer Prälat der Aufklärungszeit* (Heidelberg 1964); corrected and supplemented by H. Raab, "Zur Geschichte der Aufklärung im Rhein-Main-Gebiet," *HJ* 88 (1968), 423–33, 442–43.

[42] L. Just, *Widerruf des Febronius;* concerning early attempts to clear up the Febronius affair, see H. Raab, *Franz Eustach von Hornstein,* 124–29 (plans of Giacomelli, Maillot de la Treille, and Suffragan Bishop Scheben).—The group of Hontheim's opponents ranged from the Worms suffragan bishop and book commissioner Franz Xaver Anton v. Scheben (see H. Raab, "Apostolische Bücherkommissare in Frankfurt am Main," *HJ* 87 [1967], 345–51), the Alsatian Beck, Suffragan Bishop Jean Marie Cuchot d'Herbain, appointed coadjutor to the encumbered Hontheim, the chancellor of the episcopal University of Strasbourg, François Philippe Louis, the Mannheim court librarian Maillot de la Treille, to Jean Pey, whose *Traité de l'autorité des deux puissances* had been called by Prince-Abbot Martin Gerbert of Sankt Blasien an iron wall against the flood of Febronian ideas, and the nuncios Carlo Bellisoni and Guiseppe Garampi. Noticeable among Hontheim's opponents were the Alsatian theologians. Alsace, measurably affected by neither Jansenism nor Gallicanism, began to prepare a restoration of the Church as early as the eighteenth century.—The Febronius affair was actually reignited in connection with Johann Lorenz Isenbiehl's attempt concerning the prophesy of Emmanuel. Hontheim's expert opinion about Isenbiehl provoked the demand for his recantation. See also F. R. Reichert, "Johann Gertz (1744–1824)," *AMrhKG,* 16 (1966), 96f.; P. Fuchs, "Der Pfalzbesuch des Kölner Nuntius Bellisomi von 1778 und die Affäre Seelmann in der Korrespondenz des Kurplfälzischen Gesandten in Rom," *AMrhKG* 20 (1968), 170f.

the press campaign involving the voluntary nature and sincerity of his utterances, Hontheim substantially attenuated his retraction by his *Commentarius in suam retractationem,*[43] (based on the Gallican theses of 1682) and by his correspondence. His ambiguous and somewhat insincere conduct, whose motives have not been clarified yet, but even more so the clumsy steps taken by the Roman Curia abetted the efforts to make him into a martyr for the freedom of the German Church against "ultramontane" positions, intrigues by the Curia, and ecclesiastical obscurantism. The assumption that Hontheim "revoked his revocation prior to his death (2 September 1790)" was countered even by his contemporaries by means of his correspondence with Prince-Abbot Martin Gerbert of Sankt Blasien and the testimony of the Luxemburg ex-Jesuit Jardin, who called attention to Hontheim's "true Catholic and apostolic-Roman' faith."[44] Yet the history of his revocation remains obscure on many points and requires additional clarification and complement.

Although the traditional constitutional doctrine was defended skillfully by Joseph Kleiner, Johann Mathias Carrich, Hartzheim, Eusebius Amort, Kauffmann, and others, the progression of the "Catholic revolution of ideas"[45] led to an ever-growing spread of episcopalism-Febronianism at the German universities and prince-episcopal sees. Even in 1758 Johann Baptist Horix in Mainz had called attention to the acceptance of the Basel Decrees of 1439. The interest he aroused gave a new impetus to the opposition of the Church against Rome. In 1763 the document of acceptance appeared in print for the first time and immediately became the charter of German episcopalism. The future suffragan bishops Behlen and Würdtwein supported the Mainz policies with their historical and canonical writings. In Salzburg the famous canonist Gregorius Zallwein[46] advocated a quasimonarchical church constitu-

---

[43] *Justini Febroni ICti commentarius in suam retractionem Pio VI Pont. Max. Kalend. Novemb. a. 1778 submissam* (Frankfurt a. M., Eßlinger 1781).

[44] In connection with the Isenbiehl affair Hontheim explained to his elector-archbishop Clemens Wenzeslaus of Trier (9 April 1778) that he was "prepared to give my blood and life for the Roman Catholic Church . . . yet I make a great distinction between the Roman Church and the exaggerated demands of the Roman court, which have caused many bad things, have impugned the holy religion in the eyes of our enemies, and are making it impossible to bring about this much-desired union, hoped for also in the imperial constitution."

[45] L. T. Spittler (*Sämtl. Werke* VIII [1835], 473) dates the beginnings of the "Catholic revolution of ideas" with the publication of Febronius's book and the Mainz acceptation of the dual election of Liège of 1763.

[46] His major work: *Principia juris ecclesiastici universalis et particularis Germaniae,* 4 vols. (Augsburg 1763); H. Raab, *Concordata,* 117f.; M. Spindler, *Electoralis Academiae Scientiarum Boicae Primordia* (Munich 1959); passim.

tion; he called for the liberties of the Church of the Empire, which he called preferable by far to the *Libertés de l'Église Gallicane,* and the special privileges of the Salzburg archbishop. The legal proceedings between the disputatious dean August von Limburg-Styrum and his cathedral chapter of Speyer (1763–64) threatened to escalate into a frontal attack of German episcopalism on the appellations, the nunciatures, and all interferences into episcopal jurisdiction, especially after the Palatinate and the archbishop of Mainz joined the action. Yet the Palatine monition during the negotiations for the electoral capitulation of Joseph II failed, as did the Trier petition of 1742 requesting limitation of the jurisdiction of the nunciatures. Febronian positions and those of the established Church merged in a work by Joseph Anton Felix Balthasar, *De Helvetiorum juribus circa sacra,* which had grown from a decimation conflict of the Republic of Lucerne with the Curia. The book was fought by the bishop of Constance and put on the Index by Rome on 1 February 1769. It nonetheless formed the basis for "the entire system of the modern-day established Church of Lucerne, starting with the monastic reform at the end of the eighteenth century to the articles of the Baden Conference," indeed, all the way to the battle against the Vatican decrees of 1870/72.[47]

The Coblenz *Gravamina* of 1769

Among the high points of episcopal aspirations in the Church of the Empire was the compilation of the Coblenz *gravamina*. It came about under the influence of publications concerning the concordats, the canonical works of the episcopalists of Würzburg, Trier, Mainz, and Cologne, and the influence of the enlightened ministers of state in the ecclesiastical electorates. On the one hand, these *gravamina* were the result of enlightened-absolutist concepts[48] which were making an ad-

---

[47] The appraisal of J. Schwendimann quoted in B. Laube, *Joseph Anton Balthasar* (Basel 1956), 87. Also U. Im Hof, *Isaak Iselin* (Bern 1967), 191f.

[48] In this connection the written justification of the Mainz minister of state Groschlag for Pergen in the spring of 1769 is revealing (K. J. Krüger, *Groschlag,* 128); H. W. Jung (*Anselm Franz von Bentzel,* 15) states the view that in electoral Mainz "claims of the absolutist state were raised under the mantle of suggestions for ecclesiopolitical reforms." The economic aspect is stressed in the little-noticed article by H. Illich, "Maßnahmen der Mainzer Erzbischöfe gegen kirchlichen Gütererwerb 1462–1792. Ein Beitrag zur Geschichte der Aufklärungszeit," *Mainzer Zeitschrift* 34 (1939), 53–82; E. Hegel (*Febronianismus,* 156) stresses the "deep religious worry of the German archbishops" in this undertaking; Emmerich Joseph, regardless of the other motives he may have had, stated his conviction that it was his duty to restore episcopal authority vis-à-vis the incursions of Rome to the state to which it was entitled according to the will of the donor of the Church.

vance at the ecclesiastical courts in the years of peace after Hubertus-burg. These concepts were aimed at reordering the relationship between Church and state primarily for political and economic reasons. On the other hand, these *gravamina* represented a reaction on the part of epis-copalism within the Empire to the constant disputes with the nuncia-tures and the papal refusal for the retention of the prince-bishoprics of Regensburg and Freising by Clemens Wenzeslaus of Saxony, who had been elected elector-archbishop in Trier and had succeeded the de-ceased prince-bishop Joseph von Hessen-Darmstadt as coadjutor in Augsburg. In this connection the Apostolic See had claimed the right to fill the two vacant Bavarian bishoprics, ignoring their right to an election as guaranteed by canon, concordat, and the law of the Empire.[49] When Clement XIII, under pressure of the Church of the Empire, finally granted an election to the two cathedral chapters, it was interpreted as an attack on the freedom of the German Church.[50] In March 1769 it was countered by the electorate of Mainz with a request to all ecclesi-astical princes for a confidential exchange of ideas directed against the ultramontane claims of rulership. In Mainz, during the disputes of the Speyer cathedral dean Damian August Philipp von Limburg-Styrum with his chapter and because of the exemption of the new bishopric of Fulda, the position, by tradition scarcely friendly to Rome and definitely hostile to the nunciature, had hardened. The reformative, moderately enlightened elector-archbishop Emmerich Joseph von Breidbach-Bürresheim,[51] embroiled in a violent fight with Rome over the annates,

[49] H. Raab, *Clemens Wenzeslaus von Sachsen,* 286ff.—In Mainz J. Baptist v. Horix, who must be regarded as a protégé of the enlightened minister of state Friedrich v. Stadion, characteristically was asked to investigate the Regensburg-Freising problem. Horix, "Betrachtungen, welche zur Erörterung der Frage dienen, ob den Domkapiteln in Teutschland das Recht zustehe, in die Stelle des zu einen sonstigen Bisthum gewählten oder postulierten Bischofs einen anderen zu wählen (1769)," *Concordata Nationis Ger-manicae integra* III, 83–109.—In 1769 the Regensburg cathedral chapter elected Anton Ignaz Fugger as bishop, who in turn appointed Clemens Wenzeslaus coadjutor for the prince-priory of Ellwangen. On Fugger see E. E. Meissner, *Fürstbischof Anton Ignaz Fugger (1711–87)* (Tübingen 1969).

[50] In this connection see also the imperial rescript to the cathedral chapter of Re-gensburg, Vienna, 30 September 1768. The Emperor as "highest guardian and protec-tor of the German Churches" rejects the Roman claim "to reserve unto the Papal See for its own appointment and disposition without canonical election the bishoprics falling vacant in such cases" (J. B. Horix, *Concordata Nationis Germ.* III [1773], 110–13).

[51] On 3 July 1763 the Cologne nuncio Lucini reported to Cardinal-Minister Torregiani: "La di lui famiglia è di massime contrarie alla giurisdizione Apostolica in questi parti." On 8 March 1768 the French ambassador Entraiques attested to the archbishop's at-titude against the nunciature: "Il ne reconnait en rien la jurisdiction du Nonce, il employe tous les moyens légaux pour prevenir les appels en Cour de Rome."—A biography of Emmerich Joseph has not yet been written. For now see L. A. Veit,

taxes, and confirmation fees for Worms and Mainz, on the advice of his minister Groschlag and his official and later suffragan bishop Ludwig Philipp Behlen,[52] strove to unite the ecclesiastical princes in a concerted action against Roman presumptions and to become the "Patriarca in Germania."[53]

Two other canonical conflicts drove the Cologne elector-archbishop Max Friedrich von Königsegg-Rothenfels to the side of Mainz. Max Friedrich, whose vicar general Johann Philipp von Horn-Goldschmidt and the latter's adviser Franz C. J. von Hillesheim held Febronian views, was enmeshed in an argument with the Cologne nunciature over the visitation of the Augustinian house of Saint Michael at Weidenbach[54] and with the Curia in Rome because of the intended closing of the Benedictine seminary of Überwasser[55] in favor of a university in Münster. In spite of a basic agreement, Cologne and even more so Münster, where Fürstenberg emphasized that he was not a Febronian,[56] were not terribly enthused about the far-reaching plans by Mainz and caused the pertinent suggestions to be attenuated. The Mainz initiative also met with misgivings on the part of the prince-bishops of Hildesheim, Paderborn, and Würzburg-Bamberg. They were worried that a realization of the Febronian program would bring no advantages to the bishops but

---

"Emmerich Joseph v. Breidbach-Bürresheim und die Verminderung der Feiertage," *Festschr. für Sebastian Merkle* (1922), 348–69; H. Illich, op. cit.; H. Raab, "Die Breidbach-Bürresheim in der Germania-Sacra," *Mainzer Almanach* (1961), 91–106; idem, *Clemens Wenzeslaus,* passim.

[52] According to the French ambassador in Mainz, Groschlag was "le premier auteur d'un nouveau sisteme ecclésiastique" (Entraiques to Choiseul, Mainz, 12 Dec. 1768).—On Behlen see H. Raab, "Der Mainzer Weihbischof Ludwig Philipp Behlen (1714–77)," *Mainzer Almanach* (1968), 59–79.

[53] This was the appraisal of the nuncio Caprara in his final relation about the aims of the Mainz archbishops, held "da tempo immemorabile." On 18 February 1770, Caprara reported about Emmerich Joseph that the latter "acknowledges totally the system of Febronius. Foremost he is intent upon his own rights as German primate. But he does not enjoy the full trust of his ecclesiastical brothers." (A. Schnütgen, *Ein Kölner Nuntius,* 751); see also H. Becher, *Der deutsche Primas* (Colmar, n. d. [1944]).

[54] C. Löffler, "Das Fraterhaus Weidenbach in Köln," *AHVNrh* 102 (1918), 174ff.; E. Hegel, *Febronianismus,* 147–286; A. Schnütgen, *Kölner Nuntiatur,* 207–41; H. Hinsen, *Kaspar Anton von Belderbusch und der Einbruch der Aufklärung in Kurköln* (diss., Bonn 1952), 140ff.

[55] R. Schulze, *Das adelige Frauen-(Kanonissen-)Stift der hl. Maria (1043/1773) und die Pfarre Liebfrauen-Überwasser zu Münster/Westfalen. Ihre Verhältnisse und Schicksale* (Münster 1952).

[56] In this connection we refer to Fürstenberg's statement in a letter to Friedrich Heinrich Jacobi of 20 June 1779: "We have never been Febronians or anti-Febronians. We are, briefly stated, orthodox without any distinction as to party." (A. Hanschmidt, *Fürstenberg,* 199).

would merely expand the metropolitan rights and, in the end, exchange dependence on Rome for an increased dependence on the German archbishops. The initiative for a union and concerted action by the ecclesiastical princes, initially the Rhenish electors, was clearly started in Mainz. It raised the threat of a national council, an assembly of the Catholic princes and dignitaries of the Imperial Diet after the model of 1523, and a new concordat. For the extreme case it toyed with the idea "that perhaps even a separation of the harmony and concurrence between Church and state might have to ensue and the rights granted to the sovereigns immediately by the grace of God prevail."[57]

On 27 January 1769, after toilsome negotiations an eight-point preliminary convention[58] between Mainz and Cologne was signed, obligating the two parties to list the "old original" episcopal rights, not to withdraw unilaterally from the concerted action, and to induce the Emperor and the elector-archbishop of Trier to join them. To be sure, considerable efforts and the diplomatic skill of the Mainz minister C. W. von Groschlag were initially required to obtain the support of Suffragan Bishop Hontheim for the plans of Mainz and, towards the end of 1769, with his help to overcome the reservations of Elector-Archbishop Clemens Wenzeslaus, which had been caused by political considerations and his innate caution. Clemens Wenzeslaus appears to have borne a grudge against the Mainz group around Emmerich Joseph, who had opposed him at the election of Trier by nominating the brother of Elector Ernst von Breidbach-Bürresheim and had thwarted his designs on the bishopric of Worms. But above all it had been his persistent designs on the foremost electoral bishopric of the Empire and for the establishment of a Wettin episcopal realm extending from Trier via Liège, Cologne, and Münster to Paderborn and Hildesheim which prompted him to use extreme caution towards Rome, the Cologne nunciature, and the Imperial court. Neither in Rome nor in Vienna did he want to see the Wettin church policy damaged by Febronian-metropolitan actions.[59]

A firm union of the three ecclesiastical princes had not yet been effected and the misgivings of the suffragans of Cologne and Mainz[60]

---

[57] From Bentzel's memorandum of 30 Oct. 1788 (H. W. Jung, *Anselm Franz von Bentzel*, 15).

[58] Preliminary convention reprinted in M. Höhler, *Arnoldis Tagebuch*, 317–20.

[59] H. Raab, *Clemens Wenzeslaus*, 307ff.

[60] Nuncio Caprara reported to the cardinal-minister on 18 February 1770 that "they (the suffragan bishops of Mainz) see no chance to obtain the advantages promised by the Febronian system. In case of its implementation they fear that they will remain in the same state of dependence, free of the Roman yoke, but encumbered by a new Mainz yoke" (A. Schnütgen, *Ein Kölner Nuntius*, 751).

concerning the archiepiscopal enterprise not yet overcome when the Mainz lawyer Deel, the Cologne ecclesiastical councilor Hillesheim,[61] and the sixty-eight-year-old Trier suffragan bishop Hontheim met in conference to put the finishing touches on the complaints against Rome and to agree on the manner of asking the Emperor, the *defensor ecclesiae,* to support their plan. In the opinion of Mainz the aid of the Emperor and a firm union of the three ecclesiastical electors were indispensable conditions for the realization of their Febronian ideas.

Within a short time, on 13 December 1769, Deel, Hillesheim, and Hontheim, who had already been agreed on the most important issues as a result of lengthy preliminary negotiations, concurred in thirty-one *gravamina* and the text of a letter which was to submit the complaints to the Emperor.[62] Under "Imperial protection" the German Churches were to regain "their hereditary freedom so that they would not be behind the churches of other countries" in order that the German church system could be reordered according to the requirements of a modern state.[63] The frailties of the church constitution and the disregard of the *gravamina* by Rome were generally considered as "one of the main causes of the weakness and debility of the Catholic lands of the Empire." The Coblenz desiderata invoked the Councils of Constance and Basel, the Mainz Acceptation of 1439, the *Concordata Nationis Germanicae,* and especially the concordats with Eugene IV (1447). All of the accepted Basel decrees "in favorem atque utilitatem Ecclesiarum Germaniae promanare possunt" would have to be executed. Episcopal authority, "the freedom of the German Church,"[64] was to be restored to its original extent, the reforms executed in a manner corresponding to

[61] Franz Carl Joseph v. Hillesheim, born in Cologne on 11 April 1731, studied in Würzburg under Johann Kaspar Barthel and became rector of the University of Cologne (1760–66). In the preparation of the Coblenz *gravamina* he played an important yet so far insufficiently determined role. He soon turned away from Febronianism and opposed Isenbiehl. He died in 1803 at his retreat in Niehl near Cologne (see A. Stelzmann, *Hillesheim*); H. H. Kurth *Das kölnische Domkapitel im 18. Jh.* (diss., Bonn 1953).

[62] M. Höhler, *Arnoldis Tagebuch,* 25–30, 253–65; older printings in Le Bret, *Magazin* VIII (1783), 1–21; Gärtner, *Corpus jur. eccl. cath.* (Salzburg 1799), II, 330–46; abundant material also in *Deutsche Blätter für Protestanten und Katholiken* 1 (1839), 38ff.: "Die Koblenzer Artikel vom Jahre 1769 nebst historischen Anmerkungen, derselben," *Deutsche Blätter für Protestanten und Katholiken* 6 (Heidelberg 1840) 1–40; also "Gutachten der churfürstlich-erzbischöflichen Rechtsgelehrten und Staatsmänner über die Rechtmäßigkeit und Ausführbarkeit der Koblenzer Artkel vom Jahre 1769."

[63] M. Höhler, *Arnoldis Tagebuch,* 253f.

[64] The concept of "Freedom of the German Church"—as is stated in the cover letter under that title by Clemens Wenzeslaus and Max Friedrich to Joseph II—"does not mean an independence which is opposed to the general structure of the hierarchical constitution. The aim of sincere conviction and of the efforts in the here and now is the

the demands of the time. The initial *gravamina* were concerned with the abuses in awarding benefices. Henceforth the archiepiscopal indult to fill the benefices of the papal months was no longer to be limited to five years but extended to life or abolished.[65] The higher nonpontifical dignities at the cathedral and collegiate churches were no longer to be subject to papal reservation but to be bestowed by the ordinary collators. The reservations of the extravagants, *execrabilis* and *ad regimen* were to cease and all chancery rules,[66] with the exception of *de idiomate, de viginti, de triennali possessione,* were to become invalid within the Church of the Empire. The annates and monastic exemptions were to be abolished. The episcopal informatory process was to be followed according to the Tridentine decrees and the "vassal oath" of the bishops, customary since Gregory VII, was to be replaced by its original form. Papal orders and decrees by Roman congregations were not to be published without prior knowledge and concurrence of the ordinaries. The power "to bind and loose" of the bishops in their sees was to be unrestricted. In legal proceedings the successive appeals were to be strictly observed; the nunciatures were to be abolished. The accepted Basel Decrees, acknowledged by the *Concordata Nationis Germanicae,* were to be the basic laws of the Church of the Empire.

Attempts to strengthen the union of the Rhenish archbishops by effecting participation by the archbishop of Salzburg, Cardinal-Bishop Franz Konrad Kasimir von Rodt of Constance and Cardinal-Bishop Franz Christoph von Hutten in Speyer failed. In Vienna, where the Coblenz *gravamina* were not submitted until July 1770, the desired support did not materialize, just as the Mainz ambassador J. G. von Brée had correctly predicted[67]; "to the immense detriment of the Ger-

---

maintenance of the Church and its original and inalienable rights and the justified redress of the well-based complaints of a whole nation" (M. Höhler, *Arnoldis Tagebuch,* 266; E. Hegel, *Febronianismus,* 156–57).

[65] A special aspect of the desideratum for electoral Trier is stressed by the reference of the viciarate general of Mainz to the great cost of registering the indults with the French parliaments. "It is therefore indicated to ask that it (the indult) be granted the respective archbishop for his lifetime" (E. Reifart, *Der Kurstaat Trier und das Staatskirchentum* [diss., Freiburg 1950], 84).

[66] L. Jackowski, "Die päpstlichen Kanzleiregeln und ihre Bedeutung für Deutschland," *AkathKR* 90 (1910), 1–47, 147–235, 432–63.

[67] On 8 October 1769, von Brée on the basis of thirty years of experience had warned against false hopes for the help of the Emperor. The court of Vienna, he said, would espouse the cause of the *gravamina* of the German Churches only if it would obtain advantages for itself from the Pope (decimation, a Turkish tax, etc.); Vienna, he continued, was very satisfied with Clement XIV, who "does everything he can to please the potentates of Europe" (M. Höhler, *Arnoldis Tagebuch,* 339–41); see E. Hegel, *Febronianismus,* 187–88 regarding the negative attitude of the Emperor.

man Church and the German Nation," as Hontheim's friend and biographer Krufft thought. Joseph II let the archiepiscopal initiative come to nothing, not because a "movement away from Rome" would have meant at the same time "a movement away from the Empire,"[68] but—this is evidently the motivation of Vice-Chancellor Colloredo—because a realization of the episcopal reform program would have strengthened those forces which were resisting the territorial established Churches and would have consolidated the position of the ecclesiastical princes in the Empire vis-à-vis the Emperor as well. In order not to endanger his own plans for an established Church, Joseph II did not want to burden himself with the complaints of the German archbishops against Rome. No doubt his delaying tactics, dictated by long-range political goals and the negative attitude of the Mainz ambassador to Vienna, Friedrich Karl von Erthal, towards the action of the Rhenish archbishops contributed to its failure.[69] The reaction in Vienna had the effect of causing Clemens Wenzeslaus to distance himself from the three ecclesiastical electors out of consideration for the Wettin church policies. Suggestions by the Mainz archbishop concerning a second meeting in Coblenz and a congress in Frankfurt for the end of August 1771 or for the dispatch of a common negotiator to Vienna foundered on the conflicts of interest between the Rhenish electoral courts.[70] The large-scale attempt to turn episcopal ideas and concepts into reality came to naught. The enlightened episcopal movement steadily gained ground as a result of the monastic regulations (30 July 1771), the amortization law (6 June 1772), the school and university reforms, and, lastly, the substantial elimination of the cathedral chapter from participation in the government until the death of Emmerich Joseph (1774). During the interregnum and the first few years of the reign of Friedrich Karl von Erthal this prompted a countermovement.

---

[68] E. Hegel, *Febronianismus*, 157.

[69] In the following two decades Erthal's views changed completely. In 1774 as candidate of the "anti-Emmerich" group, i. e., a rather conservative segment in the cathedral chapter, he was elected elector-archbishop of Mainz and soon continued the policies of his predecessor Emmerich Joseph. At the time of the Congress of Ems and the dispute over the Munich nunciature he and his suffragan bishops Valentin Heimes and Stephan Alexander Würdtwein became the spokesmen of the Church of the Empire opposition against Rome.

[70] The complex reason for the behavior of the Trier elector given by M. Höhler (*Arnoldis Tagebuch*, 46,) is not convincing. H. Schotte (*Emser Kongress*, 90) uses the argument of the ecclesiopolitical caution prevailing in Trier at that time. O. Mejer (*Zur römisch-deutschen Frage* I [1871], 38) emphasizes that temporal and not ecclesiastical considerations had prevailed. E. Reifart (op. cit., 71) blames "temporal political expedience" for Clemens Wenzeslaus's turning away from the League of Rhenish Electors.

The Nunciature Dispute and the Congress of Ems

It was not long before an anti-Roman current regained the upper hand. Stephan Alexander Würdtwein, Franz Anton Dürr, Johann Georg Schör, and Johann Jung[71] broadcast their episcopal views in numerous theses and in most of the journals. Not only the elector-archbishop of Mainz, but also the ecclesiastical electors in Coblenz and Bonn persistently tried to apply Febronian principles in cases of marriage dispensations, disputes concerning benefices, visitations, on the issue of the archiepiscopal "first prayers," and ecclesiastical jurisdiction.[72] The number of conflicts between the Church and Rome increased steadily and some of the south German prince-bishops had to wage hard-fought defensive battles against the Bavarian established church system.[73] The last great conflict of the Church of the Empire with Rome and the movement representing an established Church broke out when the Palatine-Bavarian Elector Karl Theodor tried to bring about an adaptation of the church organization of southern Germany to political borders and the replacement of prince-bishoprics by provincial ones. Eighteen nonresident bishops and archbishops were responsible for the Palatine-Bavarian territories, combined since 1777. Each of them resided outside the borders of these territories and, by means of his own territory, which was subject to the Emperor only, possessed a last independent ecclesiastical and political sphere vis-à-vis the absolutist claims of powerful temporal neighbors.

For a period of about two hundred years, the aspirations for the establishment of Bavarian provincial bishoprics had to some extent been compensated by the Wittelsbach secundogenitures, especially in the old Bavarian bishoprics of Freising and Regensburg. When Cardinal Johann Theodor died in 1763[74] the dynasty was no longer able to present proper candidates for the episcopal see and the rule over the prince-bishoprics and the Church in Bavaria had to be put on a different basis, corresponding more to the enlightened absolutist political concept of the state. An added reason was the fact that the elections were getting very hard to arrange for eligible aristocrats who could be as-

---

[71] H. Raab, *Concordata,* 143ff.; A. P. Brück, *Die Mainzer theologische Fakultät im 18. Jh.* (Wiesbaden 1961); F. G. Dreyfus, *Sociétés et mentalités à Mayence dans la seconde moitié du dix-huitième siècle* (Paris 1968), 403–41.
[72] H. Raab, "Die Finalrelation des Kölner Nuntius Carlo Bellisomi (1785–86), *RQ* 51 (1956), 70–124.
[73] G. Pfeilschifter, *Salzburger Kongreß;* K. O. v. Aretin, *Heiliges Römisches Reich* I, 379.
[74] H. Raab, *Clemens Wenzeslaus,* 130–33, 135–49, 160–66, 216–22; Reinhardt, *Hochstift Konstanz,* 103–6, 127–30f.

sumed to put up little or no resistance against the Bavarian established Church. This was clearly shown by the example of the related Clemens Wenzeslaus of the Wettin dynasty in Freising, Regensburg (1763, 1768), and Augsburg (1765). To be sure, the plan for a Munich provincial bishopric (1780–83), aimed against the aristocratic liberties of the Church of the Empire, failed. But an alliance of expedience against the common enemy represented by episcopalism, strengthened by personal meetings between Elector Karl Theodor and Pope Pius VI, produced the compromise of establishing a nunciature in Munich (7 June 1784). The new nunciature, consistent neither with the constitution of the Empire nor with tradition, was obviously intended to strengthen papal authority in the *Germania Sacra,* to meet the Bavarian established Church halfway, and to form a counterweight against Josephinism. The new nuncio Cesare Zoglio,[75] who also was to occupy the see of a provincial archdiocese, was equipped with extraordinary powers. This would enable the forces of the established Church to encompass the far-flung Palatine-Bavarian territories like a pincer and push back the episcopal movement. On the other hand it inevitably challenged the episcopate of the Empire to ward off the "curial pretensions" and the territorial established Church.

The battle of the nunciatures, smouldering for a long time with varying intensity, broke into the open even before the new nuncio arrived in Munich when the immediately affected metropolitans of Salzburg and Mainz and the Freising prince-bishop Ludwig Joseph von Welden[76] raised formal complaints. The major participant in the second phase was Elector-Archbishop Max Franz of Cologne, the brother of Joseph II,[77] whose request for the installation of *Judices in partibus* had been rejected by Rome. He now found his episcopal rights transgressed not only by the Cologne nunciature, but in addition by the Munich nunciature, responsible for the Palatine-Bavarian territories of his see. But the main defense by the Church of the Empire had to be directed against the territorial established Church. If Karl Theodor were emulated by others, "the day would come when the prince-bishops and their dioceses would be limited to their territories and lose the reason for their existence."[78] In their fight against the two fronts of Rome and the established Church, conducted against the background of the growing

[75] B. Zittel, *Vertretung des Heiligen Stuhls in München,* 419f.

[76] Information on Welden in J. Angermeier, *Das Bistum Freising im Nuntiaturstreit* (1921); see also H. Raab, *Clemens Wenzeslaus* (Index).

[77] G. J. Jansen, *Kurfürst-Erzbischof Max Franz von Köln und die episkopalistischen Bestrebungen seiner Zeit;* M. Braubach, *Maria Theresias jüngster Sohn Max Franz.*

[78] K. O. v. Aretin, *Heiliges Römisches Reich* I, 385.

threat of secularization, the German archbishops, while basically encouraged by Emperor Joseph II, were only insufficiently supported by him. The change in the endangered *Nunziatura ad tractum Rheni* by the transfer of the moderate titular Archbishop Carlo Bellisomi to Lisbon and the subsequent appointment of the merely twenty-eight-year-old Bartolomeo Pacca,[79] who was unfamiliar with the German situation, increased the tensions.

At a conference of the representatives of the four German archbishops in Bad Ems (July–August 1786), convened after lengthy preliminary negotiations and characterized by considerable differences of opinions, a twenty-two-point reform program for the Church of the Empire was formulated which constituted a declaration of war against the nunciatures.[80] The Ems Punctation (25 August 1786) took up where the *gravamina* of 1673 of the Rhenish archbishops, the Coblenz desiderata of 1769, Febronius and the *Massime moguntine,* going beyond Febronius, left off.[81] The independence of the episcopal from the Roman authority was most strenuously emphasized in Ems.[82] Additional demands included: the cancellation of the exemptions and the quinquennial faculties, the complete abolition of the nunciatures, but at least

---

[79] *LThK* VII (1962), 1329.

[80] Text in M. Höhler, *Arnoldis Tagebuch,* 171–83. The significance of the concurrent synod of Pistoia for the Church of the Empire is pointed out in F. G. Dreyfus, op. cit., 435; comparisons are contained in A. Wandruszka, "Ems und Pistoia: Spiegel der Geschichte," *Festgabe für M. Braubach* (Münster 1964), 627–34.—The most striking figure among the archbishops' delegation was the Mainz suffragan bishop Valentin Heimes. His rigidity and radical program repeatedly jeopardized the whole congress. For Heimes, see H. Raab, *Jb. für das Bistum Mainz* 7 (Mainz 1955/57), 172–89; A. Bach, *RhVjBl* 27 (1962), 97–116; idem. *Germ.-Histor. Studien* (Bonn 1964), 475–92; idem, *Aus Geothes rheinischem Lebensraum* (Neuss 1968), 329–49. The representative of Salzburg, Johann Michael Bönike, stayed in the background completely. The delegate of the electorate of Trier was the skillful vicar general Beck. He was supported by the ecclesiastical councilor Arnoldi, whose diary is one of the most important sources for the course of the conference. Electoral Cologne was represented by the administrator of the vicariate Tautphäus, a moderate, and the lector of the elector, Karl Joseph v. Wreden, who was the actual representative of Cologne although he was not officially active at the conference (H. Raab, "Briefe von K. J. v. Wreden an Stephan Alexander Würdtwein [1785–1787]," *AHVNrh,* 153–54, 170–200).

[81] Regarding the intentions of Mainz the French ambassador O'Kelli reported: "L'électeur de Mayence en proposant le congrès d'Ems avait le projet de séparer l'Église germanique du Saint-Siège et d'établir un concile national permanent qu'il aurait dirigé plus particulièrement que la Diète" (F. G. Dreyfus, op. cit., 435).

[82] "Christus . . . hat den Aposteln und ihren Nachfolgern, den Bischöfen, eine *unbeschränkte* Gewalt zu binden und zu lösen für alle jene Fälle gegeben, wo es die Notwendig- oder Nutzbarkeit ihrer Kirchen oder der zu denselben angehörigen Gläubigen immer befördern mag" (ART. I) (M. Höhler, op. cit., 172).

of their competing jurisdiction,[83] the right of the bishops to dispose of charitable contributions,[84] the episcopal *placet* for Roman bulls and briefs, and the conduct of ecclesiastical legal proceedings by native judges. The prereformational demand to reduce the annates and pallia was renewed. No longer was the Vienna Concordat (1448), but rather the Mainz Acceptation (1439) and the *Concordata Principum* (1447) to be the basis for the constitution of the Church of the Empire. Lastly, the Emperor was asked to restore the archiepiscopal rights and "to bring about the council at least on a national level which had been promised [in the German concordats] by His most high intercession to take place within two years at the most for the purpose of definitively removing all of these complaints" and in the case of insurmountable obstacles to effect redress by constitutional means.[85]

The difficulties militating against the Ems program, in spite of the positive consent of a part of the educated public, and the weakness of the archiepiscopal position in its fight against the alliance of expedience between Rome and Munich were soon evident. Emperor Joseph II had indeed declared inadmissible "the exercise of jurisdiction in ecclesiastical matters" by the nunciatures[86] and had also annulled an encyclical by Pacca. Yet he could not make up his mind about the far-reaching political plans for his Church which his brother Leopold had advised. These called for "throwing off the selfish and despotic yoke of the Roman court in Germany forever by encouraging and supporting with all one's might the German bishops, by abolishing the nunciatures in Germany forever, and convincing the bishops and ecclesiastical princes to convene and to form a national council."[87] The distrust and, finally, the resistance of the suffragan bishops against an expansion of the metropolitan authority and the power of the ecclesiastical electors assumed the character of an anti-Ems movement, especially when Prince-Bishop August von Limburg-Styrum of Speyer began to exert his efforts and when an assembly in Waghäusel or Bruchsal was suggested. The union of the four archbishops dissolved rather quickly. The Mainz electorate was pried from the ranks of the opponents of the nunciatures through Prussia, with which it was joined in the Alliance of Princes and in connection

---

[83] ". . . ebenso hören d) die Nuntiziaturen in Zukunft völlig auf. Die Nuntien können nichts anders als päpstliche Gesandte sein und dörfen . . . keine actus jurisdictionis voluntariae oder contentiosae mehr ausüben" (ART. IV) (M. Höhler, op. cit., 174).
[84] ART. III (M. Höhler, op. cit., 174).
[85] ART. XXII (M. Höhler, op. cit., 183); G. J. Jansen, op. cit., 68: Cologne and Trier prevailed over the objection of Mainz regarding the two-year deadline.
[86] Rescript of Joseph II, dated 12 Oct. 1785 (M. Höhler, op. cit., 277).
[87] Leopold to Joseph, 5 Dec. 1786 (A. v. Arneth, *Joseph II. und Leopold von Toscana. Ihr Briefwechsel* II [1869], 48f.).

with the election of Karl Theodor von Dalberg to the position of coadjutor of Elector-Archbishop Friedrich Karl. In view of its desire for a special ecclesiastical position for its northwest German possessions, Prussia was not interested in strengthening the metropolitans' power.[88] Consequently, it recognized the jurisdiction of the Cologne nunciature. Theological, canonical, and personal doubts, but especially considerations of his second bishopric of Augsburg (which extended onto Bavarian territory), as well as growing difficulties in the French parts of his archbishopric of Trier induced Clemens Wenzeslaus to disavow the Ems program. The early death of Joseph II prevented a hearing of the nunciature dispute in the Imperial Diet. Max Franz of Cologne almost single-handedly continued the fight against the nunciatures and the established Church. The only concrete result of all the efforts was the inclusion in ARTICLE XIV of the Imperial Electoral Capitulation of 1790 of a stipulation aimed at abolishing the jurisdiction of the nunciatures in ecclesiastical courts.[89] The Ems Punctation thus remained "the mere declaration of a feud against Rome, not followed by the feud itself" (Werminghoff). Under the threat of the impending French Revolution, the events in the Netherlands and their impact in western Germany the archbishops' opposition to Rome and the modern established Church collapsed. But far into the nineteenth century, when the established Church had long turned against its erstwhile ally, the papal central authority, and when the Church prepared to fight the late absolutist state for a modicum of freedom, the ideas of Ems stayed alive, to be called up again by many a government in their conflicts with Rome, even though they misunderstood the historical connections.

---

[88] According to Dreyfus: "Les princes protestants, à leur tête le roi de Prusse, défendaient le Saint-Père, car ils craignaient que tout ce que le Saint-Siège perdrait en Allemagne ne fut gagné par l'Empereur" (F. G. Dreyfus, op. cit., 435).

[89] F. W. Becker, *Die Kaiserwahl Leopolds II. 1790. Eine Untersuchung zur Geschichte des alten Reiches und der Nachwirkungen des Fürstenbundes* (diss., Bonn 1943).

CHAPTER 24

The Established Church and the Enlightenment in the Temporal Territories of the Empire—Theresianism and Josephinism

The eighteenth-century upheaval regarding the respective rights within the system of the established Church is inadequately described as a usurpation of the ecclesiastical realm or as an absolutist abuse by the ruling princes with the goal of making the state omnipotent. Neither is it sufficiently characterized as an outgrowth of enlightened absolutism, dominated by the concept of the "welfare state." As the reductions in the number of monastic establishments and the case of Josephinist charity demonstrate, the induced participation of the Church in the service of the enlightened welfare state had a special importance for the realization of the rationalistic postulate of "the greatest possible happiness of all." But this also involved the fulfillment of partly neglected yet genuine demands of Christian morality, the state as the guardian of public morality, and the creation of a Church, reformed in the Jansenist-enlightened sense, eliminating baroque abuses in the interest of a better order in this world and salvation in the hereafter.

In the Empire the problem of "state versus Church" emerged to a lesser extent as one between the Pope as the supreme head of the totality of the Church and the Emperor as the protector of the Church of the Empire. Instead it was a dispute between the larger territories rising to the status of modern states on one side and the bishops, nunciatures, and the Roman Curia on the other. As a consequence of ecclesiastical and temporal rule being combined in one person, the fact that in these cases there could be no integration into a modern state, and, lastly, because of a lack in self-reform, the ecclesiastical principalities experienced the problem more as an "internal affair," as an episcopal opposition[1] to the nunciatures and the Roman Curia or as moderate administrative enlightenment on the well-known battlefields of monastic reform, reduction on the religious feast days, amortization laws, matrimonial legislation, and the field of education.[2]

In the Catholic temporal territories the relationship between Church and state in the matter of their respective rights hardly differed from that of the Protestant states. The necessity for reforms in many areas was widely recognized here too. The realization that if the nascent

---

[1] See above, pp. 443ff.

[2] Among the abundant literature concerning these problems, see L. A. Veit, "Emmerich Joseph von Breidbach-Bürresheim und die Verminderung der Feiertage," *Festschr. für Sebastian Merkle* (1922), 348–69; H. Illich, "Maßnahmen der Mainzer Erzbischöfe gegen kirchlichen Gütererwerb 1462–1792. Ein Beitrag zur Gesch. der Aufklärungszeit," *Mainzer Zschr.* 34 (1939), 53–82; H. W. Jung, *Anselm Franz von Bentzel im Dienst der Kurfürsten von Mainz* (Wiesbaden 1966); J. Mack, *Die Reform- und Aufklärungsbestrebungen im Erzstift Salzburg unter Hieronymus von Colloredo* (Munich 1912); M. Schmidt, *Die Aufklärung im Fürstbistum Passau* (Munich 1933); M. Braubach, *Maria Theresias jüngster Sohn Max Franz, letzter Kurfürst von Köln und Bischof von Münster*; K. J. Krüger, *Carl Willibald Frh. von Groschlag* (diss., Munich 1967, Cologne 1970); R. Reinhardt, *Die Beziehungen von Hochstift und Diözese Konstanz zu Habsburg-Österreich in der Neuzeit. Zugleich ein Beitrag zur archivalischen Erforschung des Problems "Kirche und Staat"* (Wiesbaden 1966).

enlightened welfare state wanted to fulfill its comprehensive tasks it needed an enlarged material basis and therefore had to break with the traditional preferences and privileges of the Church was not limited to enlightened enemies of the Church. The amalgamation of the ecclesiastical and the temporal had reached a highpoint in the late seventeenth century. The rise to absolutist principalities had taken place thanks to extensive support to the Church inspired by the Counter Reformation. But even in the period of the Enlightenment, especially in the years of economic distress and reconstruction following the Austrian War of Succession and the Seven Years' War, the Church with its possessions and revenues continued to represent a potential reservoir of state power. By way of ecclesiastical secundogenitures it offered the Catholic dynasties a possibility of providing for their sons, of increasing their prestige and power, and promoting their foreign and domestic policies. By means of cathedral chapters and religious establishments it secured for the feudal aristocracy and the knights of the Empire a sphere of freedom against the absolutist principalities. To the chagrin of the enlightened and the reform-minded, the territory, the rise to statehood, the jurisdictions, finances, and the economy everywhere were permeated by the Church. This made it advisable for the Catholic princes who at the time of the Enlightenment were still considering themselves as protectors of both tables of law to find better ways to control the Church, both in the interest of the state and for the sake of needed reforms in the Church. The respective limits were to be redetermined based on rational law and a deepened understanding of each other's nature and tasks.

When the Catholic states began to consolidate and to take on new tasks it was but a small step from protection of the Church (*ius advocatiae, sive protectionis*) to protectorate or tutelage by means of Enlightenment. In many respects this step could appear to be almost one of self-defense by the princes against exaggerated ideas and oppressive power of the Church.[3] Dispensation from taxes and local immunity were issues well suited to promote the idea of the Church as a state within the state. The assets of the mortmain, the great number of mendicant houses, the many feast days, processionals, and pilgrimages could be represented as weakening the economic and financial strength of the territory, this in turn being responsible for the political weakness of the Catholic states. Furthermore, it could be attacked as being inconsistent with genuine piety.

There is no doubt that the growth of the established Church—especially since the middle of the eighteenth century—and its distinct

---

[3] R. Reinhardt, *Verhältnis von Kirche und Staat*, 173.

Austrian variety inadequately called Josephinism intended to reduce ecclesiastical power and ultimately achieve state supremacy over the Church. Yet this movement was neither inimical to the Church, nor was it innately synonymous with Enlightenment. Max III Joseph of Bavaria went relatively far in his sympathy with the Enlightenment; Joseph II wanted to assign it no more than a certain precisely limited sphere; and Karl Theodor, who implemented his system of an established Church in league with Rome, fought against Enlightenment in a variety of ways. A good many regulations of the established Church in the second half of the eighteenth century in ecclesiastical as well as temporal states were intended to remove abuses in the Church and to effect a church reform whose aim, dictated by the selfish interests of the state, by Jansenist, episcopal, and reform Catholic currents, was an approximation of the ideal of the *Ecclesia primitiva*.

Josephinism differs sharply from the old established church movement which reaches back into the late Middle Ages and reassumes a more prominent role as of the sixteenth century. It is "a 'harmonizing' of disparate elements of tension—disharmonious within itself"—and came about "through the mutual permeation of all movements and tendencies at work during the reign of Maria Theresa which did not unreservedly support baroque Catholicism."[4]

Theresianism and Josephinism

A fairly accurate conceptual determination of Josephinism encounters considerable difficulties because of the variety of the Habsburg territories, their rulers, and most influential personalities, and because of the interaction of disparate phases of its development. E. Winter, restricting himself to Bohemia and Moravia with their Protestant tendencies, provokingly calls Josephinism a reform Catholicism and the result of bourgeois ideas in the nascent national state. Making the unyielding established church system seem less offensive, he interprets Josephinism as "an attempt of a basic reform of the Roman Catholic Church in favor of the original Church."[5] In a narrow jurisdictional

---

[4] P. F. Barton, *Ignatius Aurelius Fessler. Vom Barockkatholizismus zur Erweckungsbewegung* (Vienna, Graz and Cologne 1969), 36. On the origins of Josephinism, see also P. Bernard, *The Origins of Josephinism: Two Studies* (Colorado Springs 1964).

[5] E. Winter, *Der Josephinismus u. seine Geschichte* (Brünn, Munich and Vienna 1943), VII; idem, *Der Josephinismus. Die Gesch. des österreichischen Reformkatholizismus* (Berlin 1962), 7. In opposition to Winter, cf. Sissulak, *Das Christentum des Josephinismus*, 89; Maaß I, p. XIX.

approach, F. Maaß calls it an enlightened Austrian established Church.[6] Not church reform, he continues, but omnipotence of the state was the ultimate goal of Josephinism. Valjavec, on the other hand, views it in its totality as an intellectual, spiritual, political, and economic phenomenon, determining Austria's history less in the eighteenth century than in the nineteenth century, whose mode of expression during the reign of Joseph II was not even its most typical. Josephinism, he maintains, was the result of attempts to harmonize the political, eccelesiastical, and cultural perceptions of the prior period and the spirit of the Enlightenment.[7] Kann minimizes the significance of the church reforms, but stresses the totalitarian features and the national component of Josephinism.[8] According to Rieser "the liquidation of the sphere of power of the Church within the state" represented the means of achieving the ultimate goal, "the omnipotence of the state."[9] Josephinism is also interpreted as a "latent decline from a revealed religion to a natural religion."[10] Reinhardt avers that Josephinism was not pointed in the direction of the future but instead represented "a reactionary force." It strove for dominance over a Church which had long before been emancipated, at least in its claims and doctrine. According to Reinhardt it attempted to glue together certain areas which had fallen apart.[11]

The immediate prior history of Josephinism, among whose pioneers the "ultra-Catholic"[12] Ferdinand II is also included, was the established church system of Maria Theresa. She was the impulsive, ambitious daughter of the pious, intolerant Charles VI, who had promoted re-Catholization in Silesia, warded off renascent heresy in Carinthia and Styria, but steered the hard Bourbon course of an established Church against the Roman Curia. Maria Theresa was part of the tradition of a crumbling Habsburg baroque piety and anticurial concepts[13] of which even Jesuits at the Vienna court of the seventeenth century were not entirely free. There were hardly any typical features of that baroque piety present in her husband, Franz Stephan of Lorraine, who appears to

---

[6] Maaß I, 71–73; F. Maaß, *Frühjosephinismus*, 8.

[7] Valjavec, *Der Josephinismus*, 7.

[8] Kann, *Kanzel und Katheder*, 136.

[9] H. Rieser, *Der Geist des Josephinismus und sein Fortleben* (Vienna 1963), 81.

[10] Ibid., 77.

[11] R. Reinhardt, *Verhältnis von Kirche und Staat*, 178.

[12] A. v. Luschin, *Grundriß der österreichischen Reichsgeschichte* (1918), 264; H. v. Srbik, *Wallensteins Ende* (Salzburg 1952), 116.

[13] F. Maaß (*Frühjosephinismus*, 13) stresses that she "had no profound theological knowledge and, moreover, had received an antipapal historical instruction in her youth."—On the "Pietas Austriaca," see A. Coreth (Vienna 1959).

have been the religiously and intellectually dominant part of that marriage.[14] During her widowhood after 1765 Maria Theresa herself was not closed to the ascetic way of Jansenism nor to reform Catholic tendencies. Privy Councilor Heinke, one of the most prominent representatives of Josephinism, showed the way towards harmonizing orthodox piety with the new enlightened established Church: "God alone entrusted the prince with his power; with it the right to protect religion and Church is inseparably connected, to the extent that he may never divest himself of this responsibility, for not without cause has God given him that right. But he protects the sanctuary of the Lord best if he redresses that which in itself can cause incurable wounds to be inflicted on the saving faith and in fact has done so."

The intensified consolidation of the Austrian established Church, which under Maria Theresa and Joseph II professed to be as ecclesiastical as before, can be attributed in part to the economic and political distress following the Austrian War of Succession and the Silesian Wars. Their contemporaries considered the cofounders of Theresianism to be the "Great Four" in Vienna: the impetuous personal physician to the Empress, Gerard von Swieten, moved by Jansenist ideas and hatred for the Jesuits, although a very religious man who in his capacity as censor released the book of Febronius and initiated university reforms; the Jansenist-leaning confessor of the Empress, Ignaz Müller, provost of the Augustinian prebendaries of Sankt Dorothea; the jurist Karl Anton von Martini, who made a name for himself as an opponent of torture; and, lastly, Ambros von Stock, prebendary of Sankt Stephan and future suffragan bishop. But the actual driving force behind the Theresian reforms and creator of the established church system based on the tenets of rationalistic law was Count Wenzel Anton von Kaunitz-Tietberg, prince of the Empire after 1764, who was a free thinker like Voltaire and a dispassionate proponent of power politics. He was supported by Privy Councilor Franz Joseph von Heinke. Kaunitz's program to transform the territories of the Habsburg monarchy into an absolutist modern state with the Church in its service contained the basic features of Theresianism and Josephinism, whose most radical manifestations he nonetheless eschewed. But the suggestion to replace the designation "Josephinism" by "Kaunitzianism"[15] is prompted by an overestimation of his influence and the erroneous assumption that this established church system can be reduced to one great personality.

[14] A. Wandruszka, "Die Religiosität Franz Stephans von Lothringen. Ein Beitrag zur Gesch. der "Pietas Austriaca" und zur Vorgeschichte des Josephinismus in Österreich," *Mitteilungen des österreichischen Staatsarchivs* 12 (1959), 172.
[15] Ellemunter, *Antonio Eugenio Visconti und die Anfänge des Josephinismus,* 179.

As a field of experimentation for the new system Kaunitz chose the Austrian Lombardy. In 1765 the *Giunta Economale* was established in Milan as the highest authority in ecclesiastical matters. The Milan governor Count Karl von Firmian was already familiar with Catholic reform concepts through his sojourn at the knights' academy of Ettal and his connections with the Salzburg Muratori circle. When difficulties with Clement XIII ensued over the appointments to the sees of Como and Mantua, the *placet* was introduced in Lombardy after the Spanish, Venetian, and Sicilian model. Next to be solved were the issues of church property, the taxation of the clergy, ecclesiastical censorship, and limiting the authority of monastic superiors. The suppression of small orders, which had been variously desired by the monks themselves, began in 1769 after compromises with the Pope. The excommunication on 30 January 1768 of Duke Ferdinand of Parma, the future son-in-law of the Empress, gave impetus to the Habsburg aspirations for an established Church. Having charged an imperial commission with the supervision of all ecclesiastical institutions in 1750, Maria Theresa radically restricted the assets of the mortmain by means of an amortization law in 1771. Regulations forbidding the taking of solemn vows before the age of twenty-four and others regarding termination, the presence of regulars outside their monastic institutions, and the abolition of monastic jails were to serve the reform of the regular clergy. Under the influence of reform Catholic and enlightened ideas, Maria Theresa then proceeded against the use of exorcism and processions. According to the canonist P. J. von Riegger, who was highly esteemed by the Empress, the reduction of church holidays, executed with the concurrence of the Pope, was an excellent means of promoting religiosity, reducing idleness, and creating due respect for useful activities and deserved scorn for useless ones.

Maria Theresa basically claimed all *Iura circa sacra*, so that the Theresian established Church differed from Josephinism merely in subtle distinctions and a stronger influence of the Enlightenment. We can no longer call Maria Theresa's attitude consistent with the traditional Catholicism of the Church; we should rather consider her the "mother of Josephinism."[16] As supreme protector and guardian of the Church, supported by Kaunitz, Joseph von Sonnenfels, Marc Anton Wittola, and Abbot Rautenstrauch (who submitted a curriculum for philosophical and theological studies), Joseph II—even during his coregency—had demanded complete subjugation of the Church under his enlightened system of an established Church. During his own reign he tried to effect this by measures which were frequently despotic and

[16] F. Maaß, *Vorbereitung und Anfänge des Josephinismus*, 297.

petty.[17] In the course of one decade more than six thousand decrees were issued in order to eliminate any voice by the Church in mixed matters, to restrict the Church to the administration of the sacraments, to intrachurch matters, and a service function in the enlightened welfare state. According to Sonnenfels the Church was a police institution, obliged to serve the aims of the state to the point where enlightenment of the people permits its replacement by the temporal police. The suppression of the Society of Jesus, pronounced by Clement XIII under pressure from the Bourbon courts (21 July 1773), was celebrated as a triumph of Enlightenment. "General seminaries" (1783) under the direction of Abbot Rautenstrauch were to educate a new sort of parish priest corresponding to the ideal of the "pastor bonus." The entire church assets were considered by Joseph II as "a patrimony for the benefit of spiritual welfare and human nature of which the clerical individuals and establishments are beneficiaries only to the extent of their needs appropriate to their station, while the secure disposition of the surplus for the above designation is a matter for the ruler as supreme guardian of the Church and the *canones*."

The evaluation of Josephinism has often been decisively influenced by its hostility to monasticism and the orders; even today this is one of the determining factors. But a one-sided picture must perforce emerge if the antimonastic attitude of the baroque is contrasted with the promonastic tendency of the Enlightenment. This is also the case if the monastic reductions are justified only by the abuses which were certainly present but tendentiously exaggerated by the contemporary printed media. The decree of 29 November 1781 initiated the abolition of all houses of contemplative orders which did not fulfill charitable, pedagogical, or ministerial tasks because—according to the influential opinion of Kaunitz—they "were incapable of promoting the best in their fellow men and were consequently useless for bourgeois society." The reductions were subsequently extended to noncontemplative orders as well. This resulted in immeasurable loss of cultural assets, considerable damage to learning, and a rather large financial loss. The confiscated assets were to be transferred to a "Religious Fund" for ecclesiastical, charitable, and educational purposes. But this did not always happen. Monastic reductions and parish regulation were closely connected with the financial aspects involved.[18] But it is debatable whether the injurious effects of the reductions on the ministry and

[17] Regulations for the service prescribed the number of candles and the length of sermons. No church was to contain more than three altars. This pedantic intervention gave Joseph II the sobriquet of "Brother Sacristan."
[18] G. Winner, *Die Klosteraufhebungen in Niederösterreich und Wien* (Vienna and Munich 1967), 147.

religious life could be made up for by the establishment of new parishes from the religious fund and the intensification of parish ministry as demanded by Jansenists and reform Catholics since the parish priests had to assume an increasing number of administrative tasks including the role of "health and veterinary police."[19] In regard to fiscal policy, which was one of the main motives for the abolition of the monastic houses, the profit does not seem to have fulfilled expectations. Also abolished in 1783 were the numerous brotherhoods, closely connected with the system of guilds, whose customs and personal religiosity were called "superstitious and fanatical" and not consistent with Catholic reform concepts. They were to be merged into a single charitable association with "all ecclesiastical privileges, indulgences, and favors" whose task it was to ameliorate existing social miseries.

The diocesan regulation by Joseph II stemmed from an old demand by the established Church to make the diocesan borders coincide with those of the territories; it was also prompted by economic and religious motives. The organization of the bishoprics in the hereditary lands, no doubt in need of reform, was to be made independent of nonresident foreign ordinaries; Austria was to be lifted out of the Empire in this regard with a concomitant practical reorganization of the indigenous sees. The new delineation of their borders was another step towards the subjugation of the Church, yet also a reform measure which held out the promise—at least to the native episcopate—of an intensification of the ministry and "the greatest possible independence from Rome and in some individual cases an expansion of the diocese."[20] To the affected prince-bishops the reordering of the dioceses could not but represent an attack on the constitution of the Church of the Empire, a violation of their "liberty"; it called for political consequences. The restructuring ran counter to the law of the Empire, all tradition, and amounted to toppling the constitution of the Church. It met with resistance in Rome. The reaction of the affected bishops ran the gamut from weak remonstrances to energetic protests (which were echoed in the Imperial Diet) to entreaties to the League of German Princes. The Mainz metropolitan and archchancellor Friedrich Karl von Erthal, in his capacity as "first archbishop and primate of the German Church," was considering joint action by the episcopate of the Empire "in order to maintain the con-

---

[19] Ibid., 70.
[20] Aretin, *Heiliges Römisches Reich* I, 138; ibid., 139: "Joseph was encouraged by his own episcopate, who were hoping that the energetic Emperor would protect them against Rome: they were convinced that the imperial reforms would be a blessing for the ministry." Kušej (26) emphasizes that "regarding the Austrian clergy and especially that of Austria proper, the reform project held no risk for Joseph II."

stitutions of the Empire and the Church, so intimately interwoven in their time-honored state."

Right after the beginning of his independent reign Joseph II initiated the reordering of the dioceses in Tyrol and Upper and Lower Austria. Following the death of Bishop Leopold Ernst Cardinal von Firmian (13 February 1783), he separated the Austrian part from the diocese of Passau, dividing it between the newly created bishopric of Linz and the former bishopric of Wiener Neustadt, which latter was transferred to Sankt Pölten. The issue was not brought up in the Imperial Diet because the cathedral chapter, consisting mainly of members of the Austrian nobility, shrank from such a step and the new prince-bishop, Count von Auersperg, was satisfied with the return of his confiscated Passau properties. In 1786 the archbishop of Salzburg, Colloredo, was forced by Joseph II to forego his diocesan rights in Styria and Carinthia, but Salzburg did retain its diocesan rights in Tyrol and the metropolitan, confirmation, and consecration rights for the enlarged sees of Seckau, Lavant, Gurk and the newly established but short-lived bishopric of Leoben. It retained the nomination right for only the three first-named bishoprics; the right of appointment was reserved for the Emperor, who was endowing Leoben.[21] The death of the Regensburg prince-bishop Anton Ignaz von Fugger in 1787[22] was exploited by Joseph II "according to the old recipe";[23] during the *sedes vacans* he separated the district of Eger from the archdiocese of Regensburg and incorporated it into the archbishopric of Prague (1787). The newly elected prince-bishop of Regensburg, Max Prokop von Törring-Tettenbach, solicited the help of the archchancellor in Mainz and of Rome protesting the separation of the Eger district, since it was a pledged imperial fief and had never belonged to the crown of Bohemia. In 1789 Joseph II finally acquiesced to the appointment of an episcopal commissioner for that district. His death in 1790 delayed the final separation of Eger until after the decline of the Empire (1807–18). Hardly a stir was caused by the separation of the districts of Freising located in Styria, and of those diocesean parts of Liège which extended into the Austrian Netherlands. A realignment of the borders of Trier did not occur for political considerations, although here, too, Joseph II severely curtailed the rights of his relative, Arch-

---

[21] Austria thus had the advantage "unlike any other states, of having four independent bishops and bishoprics of its own who were dependent on the Salzburg metropolitan in accordance with the wishes and intentions of the state instead of Rome in regard to any required changes of the bishoprics, translation of the residences, certification, and consecration of the bishops, as well as all other hierarchical matters" (Kušej, 175ff.; Seidenschnur, 280).

[22] E. Meissner, *Fürstbischof Anton Ignaz Fugger (1711–87)* (Tübingen 1969), 268.

[23] Aretin I, 145.

bishop Clemens Wenzeslaus. The strange suggestion of adapting the Silesian bishopric to the territorial borders—the Austrian part of the Breslau diocese was to be separated in exchange for Prague and Olmütz foregoing their Prussian parts—foundered on the refusal of Prussia. Efforts to realign the diocesan borders of Augsburg, Chur, and Constance also failed. Nor were plans realized to create a territorial bishopric of Bregenz[24] or to elevate the prince-abbey of Sankt Blasien to the status of a bishopric for Lower Austria. But the Austrian parts of the Venetian dioceses of Udine and Pola were separated and the diocesan borders in Bohemia, Moravia, and Galicia were realigned.

The bishops of the newly established dioceses were "in a certain sense civil servants and closely tied to the Josephinist concept of the state and the established Church" (Hugo Hantsch). Even today the cross on the chest of the vestment of the prebendaries of Linz and Sankt Pölten recalls the origin of these dioceses in the established Church. The diocesan realignment by Joseph II severed the last ties between Austria and the Empire. The reputation of the Emperor in the ecclesiastical territories, indeed in all of Catholic Europe, was damaged to such an extent that King Peter III of Portugal instituted in his realm "public hours of prayer for the Emperor blinded by the devil."[25]

Maria Theresa rejected the free exercise of religion for religious and political reasons, viewing the Catholic Church as a unifying element in the *Monarchia Austriaca*. In the second half of the century, under the influence of the Enlightenment, as well as for political and economic considerations, various German territories developed religious toleration on a legal basis which no longer took into account the existing law of the Empire.[26]

The Patent of Toleration (13 October 1781) by Joseph II, shaped by the ideas of the constitutional expert Martini[27] and Privy Councilor

---

[24] G. Karlinger and C. Holböck, *Die Vorarlberger Bistumsfrage. Geschichtliche Entwicklung und kirchenrechtliche Bedeutung* (Cologne 1963). See also F. Dörrer, *Bistrumsfragen Tirols nach der Grenzziehung von 1918* (Innsburck 1955); idem, "Der Wandel der Diözesaneinteilung Tirols und Vorarlbergs," *Tiroler Heimt, Jb. f. Gesch, und Volkskunde* 17 (1953), 41–74.

[25] Aretin I, 147.

[26] *IPO*, ART. VII, par. 2. One of the violations of imperial law was the toleration legislation in Austria which recognized the non-Uniate Greeks as a tolerated religious community. On toleration legislation by Joseph II, see the most recent work by C. H. O'Brien, *Ideas of Religious Toleration at the Time of Joseph II. A Study of the Enlightenment among Catholics in Austria* (Philadelphia 1969).

[27] Karl Anton Freiherr von Martini, who, unlike Christian August Freiherr von Beck, was not among the teachers of Joseph II, advocated a freedom of conscience beyond the intervention of the prince, but also a difference between the true and reigning religion on the one hand and the false and merely tolerated religion on the other. Beck with his

Beck, granted to the Augsburg and Helvetian Lutherans and members of the Reformed Churches as well as to the non-Uniate Greeks the right to private exercise of their religion and certain civil rights which amounted to a limited equality with the Catholics.[28] To the extent that non-Catholics already had the right of public exercise of their religion, they were not affected. The preferential position of the Roman Catholic Church—which in principle was the only one permitted to have public religious exercise—was also not to be affected by the patent. Non-Catholic churches were not to have spires, bell ringing, or access from the main street; surplice fees were to be reserved for the appropriate parish priest. Beyond the sanctioned denominations, no sects or deists were tolerated, but the emancipation of the Jews was initiated in spite of the Emperor's antipathy to them.[29]

Over the objections of the Curia and the nunciatures,[30] the toleration patent of Joseph II was soon emulated in the ecclesiastical territories of the Empire: in the archbishopric of Salzburg under the enlightened Hieronymus Colloredo, in Cologne under the youngest brother of the Emperor, Max Franz, and in Trier under Clemens Wenzeslaus of Saxony. These initiatives did not restrict the dominant position of the Catholic Church nor did they pave the way for religious indifference.

In the end, the hectic, often ruthless reforms, the petty interventions in the life of the Church and popular religious customs, the "intolerable tutelage" (H. Tüchle) of the Church by the state discredited Josephinism as a reform movement. While it stopped many an abuse and introduced welcome innovations, it also shook the fundaments of the living faith in a manner which threatened the state as well.

The objections by the Curia and the Vienna nuncios Giuseppe Garampi and G. B. Caprara against the Josephinist established church system were ineffective. The "apostolic" trip by Pius VI to Vienna (1782) brought about insignificant concessions, made out of courtesy rather than as a result of having come to an understanding about the

---

natural and international law is on the side of toleration without, however, giving any details on the legal structure of toleration.

[28] G. Frank, *Das Toleranz-Patent Kaiser Josephs II.* (Vienna 1882), 37; G. Mecenseffy, *Gesch. des Protestantismus in Österreich* (Graz 1956), 208.

[29] As of 2 January 1782, the personal customs duty for foreign Jews was abolished and on 29 March 1788 the regulations governing their mode of dress in Galicia were revoked. Furthermore, the Jews were granted the right to learn a trade, to study at the university and to establish factories. Letters patent prescribed the male and female names henceforth permitted "for use by the Jewish nation."

[30] H. Stevens, *Toleranzbestrebungen im Rheinland während der Zeit der Aufklärung* (diss., Bonn 1938); H. Raab, "Die Finalrelation des Kölner Nuntius Carlo Bellisomi," *RQ* 51 (1956), 88f., 114f.

essential problems. Emperor and Pope at first talked in a conciliatory but nonbinding fashion about the Patent of Toleration, the cancellation of the bulls *In coena Domini* and *Unigenitus*, and finally, accompanied by growing alienation, about almost all the political issues concerning the Church. An open break was avoided only by the Emperor's sudden but precisely calculated return visit to Rome in December 1783. One other result of this visit was the concordat of 20 January 1784 concerning the right of appointment for the duchies of Milan and Mantua, which had hitherto been exercised by the Holy See.

The archbishop of Vienna, Cardinal Christoph Anton Migazzi, headed the generally weak opposition against Josephinism in the hereditary lands. In Hungary, where "the desire was for an aristocratic monarchy instead of an enlightened despotism,"[31] the primate, Cardinal Joseph Batthyány, was a consistent opponent of the established Church. The rather inglorious campaign against the Turks was followed by open resistance in that kingdom and Joseph II, except for the Patent of Toleration, revoked his reform measures. From within the Empire the archbishops of Cologne and Trier registered their misgivings concerning a good many of the reforms.[32] But the most vehement opposition to Josephinism and the centralist bureaucratic system was encountered among the clergy of the Austrian Netherlands, at their head the archbishop of Mechelen, Count Johann Heinrich Ferdinand von Frackenberg, and among the cities and estates of that province. When Joseph II revoked the *Joyeuse Entrée*, the Austrian rule, except for the area around Luxemburg, collapsed in the Brabant revolution.[33]

The "deterioration in the psyche, body, and morale of the solitary and embittered Emperor"[34] and the accession of his more deliberate brother Leopold II initiated an amelioration of the Josephinist system, although Leopold was no less in favor of the established Church. The alleviation signaled by the restoration of some bishoprics and monastic establishments and the change of the order of worship, however, should not be taken as a dismantling of the established Church but rather as a contribution towards making peace. After all, Leopold's program regarding the established Church in the end went far beyond that of his brother. Because of the resistance by the bureaucracy, which continued to be dominated by the Josephinist spirit, there could be no retrenchment for

[31] H. L. Mikoletzky, *Österreich. Das große 18. Jh. Von Leopold I. bis Leopold II.* (Vienna 1967), 367.

[32] G. Mohnike, "Briefwechsel zwischen Kaiser Joseph II. und Clemens Wenzel, Churfürsten von Trier," *ZHTh* 4 (Leipzig 1834), 241–90.

[33] H. Stradal, "Die brabantische Revolution des Jahres 1789 aus Wiener Sicht," *Anciens Pays et Assemblées d'État* 47 (Brussels 1968), 273–317.

[34] A. Wandruszka, *Leopold II.* II, 97.

some time yet. Even after 1815 when the Vienna Romanticism and ecclesiastical restoration around Friedrich Schlegel, Adam Müller, Zacharias Werner, and Clemens Maria Hofbauer signaled a movement against the Enlightenment and Josephinism, it never went beyond the starting point. Ideologically and politically radicalized after the July Revolution and then becoming gradually weaker and weaker, Josephinism represented a decisive force in the history of Austria until 1859.[35] Its aftereffects are still present in many areas.

The Established Church in Electoral Bavaria

The transition from the firmly traditional church sovereignty of the *Bavaria Sacra,* often rigorously maintained at the time of the Counter Reformation and denominational absolutism, to an enlightened established Church was initiated around the middle of the eighteenth century. Elector Max III Joseph (1745–77), to be sure, went "before his public as its Catholic ruler on many days of the year,"[36] just like his predecessors had done, adhering to the exclusivity of Catholicism in his land. Yet in theory and practice the established church system became stricter under his rule and more irritating to the orthodox believers. Enlightenment enveloped the Catholic territories of the Empire somewhat later than the Protestant ones; rationalism did so to a lesser degree. The older aspirations concerning the rights of the established Church were not completely transformed by the Enlightenment. They were merely given a new direction and a justification, misunderstood as a loss of religious substance, but instead derived from rationalistic law, to a lesser extent from history, but foremost from the concept of the all-encompassing enlightened welfare state.

At the core of Bavarian church policies from the sixteenth to the nineteenth century was the issue of separating the Bavarian lands from the old diocesan and metropolitan arrangement guaranteed by the constitution of the Empire. The secularization project under Charles VII, which could have decided the issue all at once and opened the road to a rearrangement, could not be realized.[37] All attempts to establish indigenous territorial bishoprics also failed.

A measured sort of Enlightenment fashioned by Barthel's Würzburg school of canonists and the concepts of Christian Wolff (1679–1754) and Christian Thomasius (1655–1728) was started under the influence

---

[35] E. Winter, *Romantismus, Restauration und Frühliberalismus im österreichischen Vormärz* (Vienna 1968).
[36] Rall, *Kurbayern*, 255.
[37] See below, pp. 493f.

of Johann Adam von Ickstatt (1702–66).[38] He was called to Munich as tutor to the future elector Max III Joseph in 1741 and five years later took over the first chair for jurisprudence and the office of director of the Bavarian university of Ingolstadt. Ickstatt's pupil Johann Georg von Lori, like his teacher a firm opponent of the Jesuits,[39] continued the development and laid the foundation for the "Churbayerische Akademie."[40] The reform, aimed at a consolidation of the established Church and a new foundation for the *Tura circa sacra*, whose urgency was caused largely by the economic and political distress after the Austrian War of Succession and during the Seven Years' War, goes back less to Ickstatt's teacher Wolff than to Pufendorf, Thomasius,[41] and the church law of the Würzburg school of canonists, getting support also from the older laws of the Bavarian established Church. In 1750, the privy council regulation, along the lines of the territorial Church policies of the eighteenth century which viewed the Church as a state institution, called it the duty of the sovereign "to undertake to augment the glory of God, to propagate the true Catholic religion, and to prevent all superstition, heresy, and injurious error."

The actual initiator of pertinent measures which began in 1761 and no longer were based on privileges and concordats but on local law was Peter von Osterwald (1717–77),[42] a convert from Weilburg, pupil of

[38] A. Kluckhohn, *Der Freiherr von Ickstatt und das Unterrichtswesen in Bayern unter dem Churfürsten Maximilian Joseph* (Munich 1869); M. Spindler, *Electoralis Academiae Primordia* (Munich 1959), index; L. Hammermayer, *Gründungs- und Frühgeschichte der Bayerischen Akademie* (Kallmünz 1959), index.

[39] R. v. Dülmen, "Antijesuitismus und Aufklärung in Deutschland," *HJ* 89 (1969), 52–80.—On the anti-Jesuit attitude and Enlightenment among the clergy of the Church of the Empire, esp. the canonists of the Barthel school, see H. Raab, "Georg Christoph Neller und Febronius," *AMrhKG* 11 (1959), 186ff.

[40] L. Hammermayer, *Gründungs- und Frühgeschichte*, 44f.; M. A. v. Bergmann, *De Ducum Boioariae Jure regio praesertim succedendi in Nobilium Patriae feuda activa gentilitia exstinctis Masculis* (Munich 1754), a student of Lori, he based the automony of the Bavarian Church on history, tracing it to the Agilolfingians.

[41] Habenschaden, *Die Kirchenpolitik Bayerns unter Kurfürst Karl Theodor*, 335, n. 3; in contrast to Pfeilschifter-Baumeister, who stresses the influence of Wolff, he traces "all the reforms of the established Church, implemented under the influence of Ickstatt" back to Pufendorf and Thomasius. In regard to the genesis of the reform movement, Rall (260) also refers to the "orientation with the doctrine of English natural law."

[42] H. Raab, *LThK* VII (1962), 1284; Pfeilschifter-Baumeister, 101ff.; Osterwald, for the rest of his life, maintained "something of the typical severity of a convert." For him "the exclusively Catholic state remained the central axiom of his ideas regarding the canon law of the established Church. Josephinian toleration or that of the Montgelas epoch is totally alien to Osterwald's system of reforms" (Pfeilschifter-Baumeister, 103). J. Gebele, *Peter von Osterwald, ein Beitrag zur Gesch. der Aufklärung unter Kurfürst Max III. Joseph* (Munich 1891); Rall, *Kurbayern*, passim; M. Spindler, op. cit., esp. 521; L. Hammermayer, op. cit., passim.

Wolff, and temporal director of the Ecclesiastical Council as of 1761. His programmatic work *Veremund von Lochsteins Gründe sowohl für als wider die geistliche Immunität in zeitlichen Dingen* (Strasbourg 1766)[43] emanated from the disputes with the Bavarian monasteries about the decimations and was built on the writings of Van Espen, Giannone, Grotius, and Pufendorf. In it he rejects as presumptions not only the principle of immunity, hitherto claimed by the ecclesiastical authorities, but also the curialist theory of the relationship between Church and state as a "monstrous doctrine" and as "the language of all violators of royal sovereignty." Contradicting the existing view of the personal and real immunity of the clergy, which lifts it from the subject structure of the state, Osterwald points out that such immunity and the clergy's subordination under another sovereign power contradicts the sovereignty of the state. Ecclesiastical immunity in temporal matters, he continues, is a state privilege and therefore subject to immediate restriction or recall. Local immunity (the right of asylum) must be abolished. All mixed matters, merely annexed to the *spiritualia*, such as weddings, charitable bequests, exemptions of the clergy, and *spiritualia* not directly required for the blessedness of man (for instance, pilgrimages, processions, etc.) are by their nature essentially within the province of the state.

Osterwald's goal was the replacement of the numerous arrangements—often unclear in their stipulations and varying in their basic tenor—made with the prince-bishops in the last 150 years by a single uniform concordat. He strove for the extension of state sovereignty over the Church and the realization of a moderately enlightened welfare state. Osterwald's theses offered the state possibilities for far-reaching interventions even in the actual ecclesiastical realm, but on the other hand rejected any interference by the Church in temporal affairs. As a result, the Bavarian government taxed the clergy "for the needs of the land" on the basis of sovereign right (1769, 1770), creating difficulties with its own clergy. This problem as well as financial considerations soon prompted the government to seek papal decimation approvals which were quickly granted on 21 September 1771.

The amortization law of 13 October 1764 was a result of economic considerations. After previous amortization laws proved ineffective, (1672, 1704, 1730), the fight against the mortmain (with its origins in the late Middle Ages) was to be pursued more energetically in

---

[43] When the Freising prince-bishop Clemens Wenzeslaus of Saxony suppressed Osterwald's book, which had reached four printings by 1770, the elector issued a mandate against the prince-bishop (28 August 1766).

Bavaria.[44] The reorganization of the Ecclesiastical Council (1768) which restored the influence of the laity to its status prior to the concordat of 1583 improved the possibilities for putting the territorialist ideas into practice. The first monastic mandate (29 September 1768) demanded precise numerical details about the houses and submission of the letters of endowment. The founding of brotherhoods was made subject to government approval on 9 December 1768; those already in existence had to submit painstaking reports concerning their origin and founder, statutes, activities, and assets (1769). The mandate of indigenousness of 20 December 1768 excluded foreigners and nonnatives from all benefices.[45]

The reform mandates of the next few years invoked the protectionary power over Church and religion entrusted by God to the elector. On 16 February 1769, a governmental book censorship, independent of ecclesiastical censorship, was installed."The especially urgent need for a reform of the ecclesiastical right of betrothal"[46] led to the sponsalia mandate of 1769, which contained strict regulations: betrothals were henceforth to be made only in the presence of two witnesses and, in the case of young or indigent persons, only with the permission of parents, guardians, or the state; disputes involving betrothals were to be subject to temporal justice. The mandates in monastic matters, partly justified and aimed at the condition of "first investiture" were hastened by discovery and disclosures of abuses and the monachal tendency of Enlightenment. A mandate for the reform of religious orders in 1769 prohibited the taking of solemn vows before the age of twenty-one, largely limited the penal authority of the superiors, and abolished monastic incarceration. For certain cases it permitted the *Recursus ad principem,* applied since the end of the sixteenth century against excesses of ecclesiastical authority, and generally forbade collections by religious. In 1763 after the prohibition of visitations and election supervision by nonresident prelates in Bavaria, a law of 30 December 1769 aimed at a total separation of the Bavarian monasteries and convents from foreign superiors and provinces. If there were more than three institutions of the same order within Bavaria, an independent Bavarian province was to be established. The number of foreigners in monastic com-

---

[44] M. Doeberl, "Der Ursprung der Amortisations gesetzgebung in Bayern," *Forschungen zur Gesch. Bayerns* 10 (1902).—For a comparison we refer to the legislation on amortization in electoral Mainz going back to Adolf II of Nassau (1462); see the thorough treatise by H. Illich.

[45] On the difference stemming from the civil rights mandate between Bavaria and Austria, see Pfeilschifter-Baumeister, 120f.

[46] Pfeilschifter-Baumeister, 125.

munities was to be no more than one sixth of the regulars; only natives were to be entitled to the passive franchise. The episcopal elections in Freising, Regensburg, Passau, and Chiemsee were to include the presence of Bavarian election commissioners in addition to the imperial ones and the rights of the former at the elections were to be substantially expanded. On 3 April 1770, the occasionally practiced *placet* was prescribed for all ecclesiastical regulations and the practice of recourse was expanded. The congress of delegates of the Bavarian bishops in Salzburg (1770–71) represented an episcopal-Febronian reaction to this enlightened-territorial church program which culminated in the establishment of one or several territorial bishoprics.[47] The suggestions, formulated in the main by the dean of the Salzburg cathedral chapter and later bishop of Chiemsee, Count Ferdinand Christoph zu Zeil, foundered on the difficult legal situation, the lack of unanimity among the Bavarian episcopate, and on the fact that the Bavarian government came to an understanding with the Curia. Zeil managed to bring about a conciliatory agreement concerning the election of prelates (1774), but the negotiations for a uniform concordat were at an impasse when the elector died in 1777. As could be ascertained a year earlier at the talks regarding the establishment of a nunciature in Munich, the goals of an established Church in Bavaria were intended to be achieved in concert with Rome and in the face of the imperial episcopate.

Elector Max III Joseph was succeeded by the sensitive Karl Theodor (1742/77–99), who united the Palatine Electorate and Bavaria under his rule after the Wilhelminian line of the Wittelsbachs became extinct. While he vacillated "between the Enlightenment and its opposite and in 1790 once again from one pole to the other,"[48] the Bavarian established Church was not only basically maintained but further developed by means of individual regulations which extended the sovereign protection of the Church into a sort of church administration[49] and ended in the "complete muzzling of the Church" (Schwaiger). When the Ecclesiastical Council was reconstituted, the *Recursus ab abusu* was expanded, regulated by law, and the *placet* was again enjoined. In 1781 the court ordered the founding of an independent Bavarian branch of the Knights of Malta; its partial secularization was designed to provide for the court's protégés. This course was abandoned in favor of tapping the considerable assets of the suppressed Society of Jesus. The initial plan

---

[47] L. Hammermayer (M. Spindler, ed., *Handbuch der bayerischen Geschichte* II [Munich 1966], 1096) calls the congress of Salzburg "the most dangerous attack of the episcopal Church of the Empire against Bavarian territorialism."

[48] Rall, *Kurbayern*, 256.

[49] Ibid., 270.

triggered a quickly collapsing reaction by the Bavarian prelates but no objection by Rome. In spite of his measures towards an established Church, Karl Theodor remained on good terms with the Curia. These were consolidated by his personal meeting with Pius VI in Munich and stood the test of opposition by the imperial Church on the occasion of the Munich nunciature conflict.[50] Karl Theodor did not achieve his ultimate goal, the separation of Bavaria from the Church of the Empire and the establishment of one or more territorial bishoprics, a goal inherited from the Wittelsbach political tradition.[51] But he was able to obtain from Pius VI the compromise solution of a permanent nunciature in Munich (1785) and, in an alliance of expedience with Rome, to substantially subjugate the *Bavaria Sacra.*[52] By the brief *Convenit provide* (1789) Rome agreed to the founding of a court diocese after the model of Sardinia and Naples, restricted to the newly organized collegiate see of Our Lady and the court churches, but exempt from ties with the Freising diocese and the Salzburg metropolitanate. The connection between the court diocese and the presidium of the Ecclesiastical Council confirmed the political intentions of the Bavarian government in relation to the episcopate. It was—as the most immediately affected bishop of Freising had already been forced to realize when the electoral capitulation was changed by the cathedral chapter—a revolutionary intervention in the thousand-year-old German church constitution and an initial, albeit modest, beginning in the reorganization of the Bavarian episcopate.

The tensions between the Munich court bishopric and the Freising ordinariate partly explain the intervention by Karl Theodor in the Freising episcopal election, conducted during the interregnum of 1790 and vehemently attacked by the episcopal media. In contradiction to the statutes of the cathedral chapter, by applying his rights as the Palatine imperial vicar[53] and by effectively setting aside the right of free election

---

[50] See above, p. 465.

[51] Habenschaden, *Die Kirchenpolitik Bayerns,* 339.

[52] See above, pp. 465–69. The passive role of the prince-bishop of Regensburg is referred to by E. Meissner, *Fürstbischof Anton Ignaz Fugger (1711–1787)* (Tübingen 1969), 225f. Fugger saw "the main danger to the jurisdiction of the ordinaries in the claims of the four archbishops at the Congress of Ems" and less so in the rights of the Munich nuncio.

[53] W. Hermkes, *Das Reichsvikariat in Deutschland. Reichsvikare nach dem Tode des Kaisers von der Goldenen Bulle bis zum Ende des Reiches* (Karlsruhe 1968), 110 ff.; also J. R. v. Roth, *Von dem anmaßlichen Rechte eines Reichsverwesers, Reichsvikariatskommissarien zu den teutschen Bischofswahlen zu schicken* (1780); idem, *Einige staatsrechtliche Betrachtungen ueber die in den zwischen Kurmainz und Kurpfalz gewechselten Staatsschriften aufgestellten Grundsaetze, die kurpfaelzischen Reichsvikariats und kurmainzischen Erzkanzlariats-Gerechtsamen, waehrenden Zwischenreiche betreffend* (1790).

Karl Theodor prevailed with his candidate, the prince-provost of Berchtesgaden, Joseph Conrad von Schroffenberg, known as an opponent of episcopalism. Against the protests of the cathedral chapters and the Mainz elector Friedrich Karl von Erthal (in the latter's capacity as lord chancellor and "first bishop of the German Church"), he dispatched vicariate commissioners to the episcopal elections in Regensburg and Eichstätt. Although his candidate prevailed only in Regensburg—again it was Schroffenberg, who agreed in 1795 to the annexation of his chapter of Berchtesgaden by Bavaria, which was the equivalent of secularization—and he failed to obtain the right to first prayers during the imperial vicariate,[54] Karl Theodor had nonetheless succeeded in these episcopal elections "to prevail with a principle which opened new possibilities for the Bavarian established Church in future interregnums."[55]

The rights of Bavarian election commissioners regarding elections in native monasteries, consolidated under Max III Joseph, were again expanded by a decree dated 5 February 1791 for the purpose of "maintaining canonical freedom."[56] The attacks against the monasteries came to a head in 1793 with the regulation regarding investiture and profession examinations. A reform-Catholic tendency for stopping abuses appears to have determined the reduction of processions and pilgrimages, the prohibition of passion plays, and the attenuated application of regulations concerning holidays. The decimations, approved by Pius VI in 1787 and 1798 for the purpose of alleviating the state of emergency, can be taken as a result of the alliance between Rome and the Bavarian established church system. Their implementation, prepared with the help of the nuncio Ziucci for the latter's personal advantage, demonstrate the absolute sovereignty of the state in taxation. It consolidated the state's dominance over a Church already under the shadow of secularization and raised the specter of an even more oppressive estab-

---

[54] On the right of first petition claimed also by electoral Saxony, see the ref. by H. Bauer, *Das Recht der ersten Bitte bei den deutschen Königen bis auf Karl IV.* (Stuttgart 1919), 128. On the claims by the Palatine electorate, see L. Jadin, *L'Europe au début du XVIIIᵉ siècle. Correspondance du Baron Karg de Bebenbourg, Chancellier du Prince-Évêque de Liège, Joseph Clément de Bavière, Archevêque Électeur de Cologne, avec le Cardinal Paolucci* I (Rome and Brussels 1968), 476, 486.

[55] Aretin I, 420.

[56] M. Doeberl, *Entwicklungsgeschichte Bayerns* II (Munich 1928), 363; B. Walcher, *Beiträge zur Gesch. der bayerischen Abtswahlen mit besonderer Berücksichtigung der Benediktinerklöster* (1930), 26.—On the dispatch of Bavarian election commissioners to the elections of bishops, see H. Raab, *Clemens Wenzeslaus* I (Freiburg i. Brsg. 1962), 355–59. It was justified by the "Landsasserey, mit welcher diese Bischöfe (Freising, Regensburg, Eichstätt, Passau) denen Hertzögen seit den ältesten Zeiten bis weit in das 14. Jh. hinein zugetan waren."

lished church system for a future already threatened by political unrest and wars. The secularization of 1803 eliminated the ecclesiastical states, which—as irritating foreign bodies in the Bavarian territory—had been the actual opponents of the established Church and opened the way for the reorganization of the Church, an object of aspirations since the sixteenth century.

CHAPTER 25

State and Church in Poland-Lithuania to the End of the Republic of the Aristocracy

After the Counter Reformation in Poland-Lithuania had prevailed under Sigismund III (1587–1632) and Ladislas IV (1632–48), the Roman Curia expected the Polish kings to support its diplomacy in eastern Europe and consequently involved them in the coalition against the Turks and its efforts to persuade the Orthodox into union with Rome. In 1648 when the Jesuit John Casimir was elected king, Pope Innocent X granted him dispensation from his vows and laicized him. The King temporarily succeeded in pacifying his country, which had been ravaged by Swedish, Russian, and Turkish invasions, and by Cossack rebellions. The heroic defense of the Pauline monastery on the Jasna Góra near Częstochowa in 1655 turned this place of pilgrimage to Mary into a Polish national shrine. In 1656 the King declared the Virgin Mary Queen of Poland (*Regina Poloniae*). The contest by the French and Habsburg courts for influence in Poland, as well as domestic and foreign difficulties prompted him to abdicate. Successes against the Turks could not be achieved until the reign of John Sobieski (1674–96), who was instrumental in lifting the siege of Vienna by the Turks in 1683, regaining for Poland the designation of "The Outer Wall of the Occident" (*antemurale christianitatis*). But Sobieski was unable to prevail when the nobles continued to insist on their privileges. As a consequence the Polish-Lithuanian state suffered greatly under the unrestrained liberties exercised by the nobility and the disastrous veto right of any delegate to the Sejm (diet) (*liberum veto*).

During the interregnum Primate Cardinal Radziejowski solicited votes for the French candidate, Prince François Louis Conti, while the nobility were in favor of the Wettin elector Friedrich August the Strong. Prior to the election the latter secretly converted to Catholicism[1] and

---

[1] P. Hildebrand, *Die polnische Königswahl von 1697 und die Konversion Augusts I. des Starken* (Rome 1907).

when elected called himself Augustus II (1697–1733). The rival King Stanislas Leszczyński,[2] supported by Sweden and later on by his father-in-law Louis XIV, was able to maintain himself only during the Northern War (1704–09) and the Polish War of Succession (1733–35). After the death of Augustus II, Emperor Charles VI and Tsarina Anna Ivanovna made sure that the son of the dead King succeeded him to the throne as Augustus III.

The Counter Reformation had excessively enlarged the power of Catholicism. The Protestants were oppressed; they were not allowed to build any new churches after 1717; in 1724 after the Protestant population stormed the Jesuit school in Thorn, the mayor and nine other Protestants were executed. The Uniates, treated as second-class Catholics even in the seventeenth century, were forced to accept certain rites and customs of the Roman Catholic established Church.[3] The rights of the Orthodox were also restricted. The kings of Prussia and the tsars gave protection to the Protestants and Orthodox respectively. As early as the reign of the Saxon kings the Russians intervened repeatedly in Polish affairs; their troops were stationed on Polish soil after 1717 in order to break any opposition to Russian interests. After the death of Augustus III, Catherine II[4] helped her favorite, Stanisłas Augustus Poniatowski, to ascend to the Polish throne (1764–95).[5] Aside from the supremacy and discord of the Polish nobility it was the expansionist tendencies of the neighboring great powers that brought about the disintegration of Poland at the end of the eighteenth century.[6]

The Catholic patriotic opposition, founded in 1768 by Bishop Adam Stanisłas Krašinski of Kamieniec as the Confederation of Bar, was unable to stem the tide of Russian power; the rebels were crushed by the Russians after four years of fighting. The first partition, decreed by Russia, Austria, and Prussia in 1772, cost Poland about 30 percent of its territory and almost half its population. Well-known clerics participated in attempts to stabilize the domestic conditions by means of reforms. They included the Piarist Stanisłas Konarski (1700–1773),[7] famous as a preacher and politician, Bishop Adam Stanisłas Naruszevicz of Łuck (1733–96), recognized as the founder of modern Polish historiography,

---

[2] J. Staszewski, *Stosunki Augusta II z kuria rzymska w latach 1704–06* (Torun 1965).
[3] See Chap. 14 above, p. 223.
[4] See Chap. 13 above, p. 206.
[5] K. Zernack, "Stanislaus August Poniatowski," *JGO* n.s. 15 (1967), 391–92.
[6] Lord Eversley, *The Partitions of Poland* (London 1915); H. H. Kaplan, *The First Partition of Poland* (New York and London 1962).
[7] W. Konopczyński, *Stanisław Konarski* (Warsaw 1926); M. Plezia, *Dookola reformy szkolnej St. Konarskiego* (Lublin 1953); Ł. Kurdybacha, *Działalnosé pedagogiczna Stanisława Konarskiego* (Wroclaw and Warsaw 1957).

and the prebend Hugo Kołłatej (1750–1812), who reestablished the Cracow academy. They also participated in formulating the constitution of 3 May 1791, which recognized Catholicism as the state religion but also guaranteed the free exercise of religion for all dissidents. The efforts of inner renewal came to an abrupt end through the second partition of Poland by Russia and Prussia and through the third partition, wherein the three neighboring countries occupied the remainder of the country. The name of Poland was removed from all maps. Nuncio Lorenzo Litta (1793–95) protested in vain against the dismemberment of Poland-Lithuania, of which Russia had seized 465,000, Prussia 145,000, and Austria 115,000 square kilometers.

The Church was substantially weakened by confiscations and secularization. Its organization with its two church provinces of Gnesen and Lemberg was enmeshed in political disputes. The religious orders which had shaped Polish Catholicism under the successive influence of Spain and France lost many of their establishments. In spite of the threat represented by Orthodox Russia, the Josephinist established Church of Austria, and Protestant Prussia during the following decades, membership in the Catholic Church was a factor which united the majority of Poles across the borders of their partitioned country.

CHAPTER 26

The Decline of the Church of the Empire in the Great Secularization

The suspension of the Restitution Edict, the imperial offer to Brandenburg of 1 February 1647 to satisfy its compensatory claims by means of secularizations meant the beginning of the end for the ecclesiastical states and thereby the initiation of the dissolution of the Empire, concluded a century and a half later with the total secularization of 1803. Secularization, the deterioration of the Empire, and the rise of modern, absolutist German principalities in the seventeenth and eighteenth century were intertwined in a very complex process. This is demonstrated by the printed media, the political theory of the state, the peace negotiations of Osnabrück and Münster, Nijmegen, Rijswijk, and Baden, and by the secularization projects between 1648 and 1789. The Peace of Westphalia acknowledged the secularizations as a means of restitution after the standard year of 1624, as compensation and reparation. In assigning ecclesiastical principalities to temporal territories it took into account the actual denominational status and the political necessities, even to the extent of the compromise of a partial secularization of the prince-bishopric of Osnabrück by means of an alternation principle between a Catholic bishop and a prince of the Guelfs ("pseudobishop"). While the surviving ecclesiastical dignitaries of the Imperial Diet and holders of benefices did have certain guaranties by virtue of the standard year and day as well as the Imperial electoral capitulation, there were a number of secularization projects and actual secularizations of church assets by the various principalities during the seventeenth and eighteenth century. According to Pufendorf the most serious political omission by the Empire was not to go ahead with a total secularization at the Peace of Westphalia after the Swedish or Danish model. The course of church history in the period between that peace treaty and the imperial delegates' final recess was decisively determined by a number of elements: aspirations for secularization initially on the part of Protestant princes, the fear of secularization, the desire by the Church of the Empire to secure its existence by deferring to the dynastic church policies of the Habsburgs, Wittelsbachs, Lorrainers, and Wettins, and, finally, the accumulation of benefices by the eligible nobility.

In the seventeenth and eighteenth century the secularizations in their various stages of development have to be considered as a fight for the continued existence or the dissolution of the Empire, for Catholic or Protestant hegemony, and as preliminaries of the total secularization of 1803. They emanated from those territories and dynasties who thought themselves disadvantaged in the great give-and-take of administrative realignment and compensation of the Peace of Westphalia and who felt they could raise claims for ecclesiastical properties either on the basis of their being intermingled with ecclesiastical states or because of certain stipulations of the peace agreements. Among the prime objects for secularization were the archbishopric of Hildesheim, a Catholic island in the midst of the Protestant territory of the Guelfs and rendered helpless by the Quedlinburg Recession; the archbishopric of Osnabrück, partially secularized by the disastrous alternation principle; and, lastly, the small archbishopric of Worms, situated as it was in the tense area between the electorates of Mainz and the Palatinate. These ecclesiastical states were saved from secularization in the seventeenth and eighteenth century only by personal union with more powerful imperial bishoprics (such as the electorates of Cologne, Mainz, and Trier) and by the church policies of the great Catholic dynasties, who exploited the territorial and political disputes between the Protestant princes.

The plans for secularization in the seventeenth century are permeated with vaguely formulated intentions of conversion and negotiations for church reunion, especially in the cases of Ernst August von Braunschweig-Lüneburg, first in his capacity as "pseudobishop" of Osnabrück and then as duke of Hanover, and the elector Karl Ludwig of the Palatinate. The dynastic policies vis-à-vis the Church of the Empire with the expectation of consolidating ecclesiastical secundogenitures in general delayed plans for secularization in the Catholic part of the Empire. On the other hand, there were reformers of the Church and the Empire, such as Antoine Arnauld or the learned Landgrave Ernst von Hessen-Rheinfels, a convert to Catholicism who intended to establish a total of sixty new German bishoprics from secularized properties of the Church of the Empire, create an electorate reserved for the Emperor, and make an offer to the Protestant princes for a reunion with a reformed Catholic Church.

None of the revolutionary plans for reform amounting to a complete secularization—probably at the expense of the Church—were realized. A greater danger for the ecclesiastical states was the desire for expansion and administrative realignment of the temporal territories combined with inner reforms. According to the well-known words of Ranke, Prussia was not the only state founded on the principle of secularization since the time of the Great Elector. As the ecclesiastical states were gradually reduced to the status of a political sop, as manifested in the negotiations of the Nijmegen Peace, in the Austrian War of Succession, and the third Silesian War, the will on the part of the Catholic Emperor and that of the papacy as well to defend "God's inheritance" in the Empire steadily slackened. Plans to revoke the secularizations in connection with a territorial reorganization of the Empire as proffered by Nuncio Bevilacqua at the peace negotiations of Nijmegen and by Passionei at Baden came to nought because of the weak position of the Catholic powers relative to the prevailing interests and alliances.

Fears of secularization of the *Germania Sacra* were repeatedly used in the eighteenth century as weapons of Wittelbach and Hapsburg politics in the context of the Church of the Empire, especially so by Maria Theresa in her fight against the Wittelsbach Emperor Charles VII, at the episcopal elections around the middle of the century, and during the Seven Years' War against Frederick the Great for Silesia and hegemony in the Empire. At the time of the Austrian War of Succession and during the crisis of the Empire when there was a possibility of a Swabian kingdom for Charles VII and a southern German buffer state between Austria and France, Berlin promoted a secularization project. It intended to use the southern German archbishoprics of Freising, Regensburg, Salzburg, and Eichstätt as imperial reserves for the formation of a household force for the Wittelsbach Emperor Charles VII, to expand Prussia by the addition of the ecclesiastical territories of Breslau-Neiße and Münster, and, lastly, to compensate Austria with the prince-bishopric of Passau. A weak Charles VII, who had not given a clear negative reply to that tempting secularization project advocated by his Prussian ally, tried the traditional path of imperial church politics. He had in mind securing for his brother Johann Theodor—in addition to the archbishoprics of Regensburg and Freising—the prince-bishoprics of Eichstätt, Speyer, Worms, Liège, Trier, and the prince-diocese of Ellwangen. Such a second Wittelsbach episcopal realm would have created the required additional power for his dynasty by a partial, "Catholic" secularization.

Maria Theresa, at odds with Prussia and Bavaria, employed all the means at her disposal to oppose this secularization project and to discredit the powerless and landless Wittelsbach Emperor in the Catholic part of the Empire. That part of the country was dissatisfied not only with the church policies of the *Defensor ecclesiae*, but also with the attitude toward the ecclesiastical princes of the Francophile Pope Benedict XIV, who distrusted the pragmatic powers. Episcopal Germany felt the growing discomfort of Rome over the consolidation of crosier and sword, of bishopric and sovereign power. But in the interest of the Church it was unwilling to give up this consolidation, since the will and the power to protect the ecclesiastical states seemed to decrease in direct proportion to the growing authoritarian demeanor of the prince-bishops towards the nunciatures and the Roman church offices, and the more they tried to realize episcopal concepts regarding the church constitution and to execute the transition from a late medieval territory to a modern absolutist state.

By the end of 1743 the most acute danger to the ecclesiastical states had passed, even though the following year Wilhelm VIII of Hesse-Kassel staked his claim to the secularization of the prince-bishopric of Paderborn and the abbeys of Fulda and Corvey and although there was a possibility that the secularization project of the Westphalian ecclesiastic territories in favor of a new electorate of Hesse-Kassel might surface again. Plans for secularization entered a new phase with the beginning of the Seven Years' War, which Ranke thought had been a religious war, "not explicitly so, but by its nature and perceived as such by everyone."[1] An end to the alternation principle in the archdiocese of Osnabrück, the secularization of Paderborn, Hildesheim, and Münster in favor of England-Hanover, of Erfurt and Eichsfeld (at that time part of the Mainz electorate) in favor of Hesse-Kassel, Hanover, or other Protestant states played a very prominent role in the projects of Frederick the Great until 1759. Combined with other intended changes they would have enabled Prussia and Hanover "to tear Northern Germany from the

---

[1] L. v. Ranke, *Zur Gesch. von Österreich und Preußen zwischen den Friedensschlüssen von Aachen und Hubertusburg* (Leipzig 1875), 316.

Holy Roman Empire and to create independent realms."[2] In the last few years of the Seven Years' War, following the death of Elector-Archbishop Clemens August (d. 6 February 1761), the vacant archdioceses of the Wittelsbach ecclesiastical secundogenitures in the northwestern part of Germany were ideal objects for administrative realignment and compensation, not only for Prussia, England-Hanover, and Hesse-Kassel, but for a number of Catholic powers as well in order to heal the wounds of the allied electorate of Saxony and by the election of Clemens Wenzeslaus to provide for the Catholic Wettin dynasty an episcopal realm in northwestern Germany. For the northwestern German *Germania Sacra* the worst was in the end averted less by the efforts of the Emperor, the Catholic princes of the diet, or France than by the emerging differences between Prussia and England-Hanover and Holland's policy regarding the prince-bishopric of Münster. A Wettin ecclesiastical secundogeniture which would have been established at the expense of the eligible nobility was prevented by the elections *ex gremio* in Cologne, Münster, Hildesheim, and Paderborn. But in Osnabrück the election of the barely six-month-old Frederick of York, whose governmental affairs were conducted by two councilors appointed by his father, George III of England, was a step towards correcting the Peace of Westphalia.

The discrepancy between the aspirations and the capabilities in the militarily powerless ecclesiastical states, dependent for better or for worse on the Empire, and between the aspirations and obligations of the imperial and also the papal policies became more and more manifest during the second third of the eighteenth century. For the states under the crosier and infula the three peaceful decades between the Peace of Hubertusburg and the outbreak of the Wars of Revolution were neither tired and stifling nor were they the halcyon days that they were called by contemporary sources and historical presentations. Indeed, the vast majority of the ecclesiastical territories were flourishing to a greater or lesser degree under a moderate enlightenment, and respectable scholarly activities developed at many Catholic universities and monastic institutions which did not have to shrink from a comparison with developments in the Protestant parts of the Empire; perhaps no other period can better claim the old proverb that life under the crosier was good. Yet this blossoming in the bishoprics and abbeys and the eudaemonia of the Catholic Enlightenment was frequently achieved at the expense of the basic religious-ecclesiastical ideas. At the same time, the belletrists, hostile to the Church, and the enlightened advocates of the rights of the

---

[2] G. Volz, "Friedrichs des Großen Plan einer Losreißung Polens von Deutschland," *HZ* 122 (1920), 272.

state raised more and more probing questions regarding the justification for being of the ecclesiastical states and authority over the Church assets.

It is difficult to determine with any precision the significance of the publicity campaign of the cathedral canon Philipp Anton von Bibra of Fulda, the writings of Baron K. von Moser, Schnaubert, and Weiße for the preparation of secularization. The veritable flood of paper was certainly not quite as harmless to the existence of the ecclesiastical states as even some contemporary episcopal censors, such as Turin in Mainz, or later historians have occasionally assumed. It was actually more a signal for the attack of secularization and—inasmuch as it came from within the ecclesiastical states themselves—an expression of a growing "feeling of impending doom" (F. Schlegel). The signs of an inner readiness for secularization on the part of ecclesiastical institutions and territories increased, as shown by the transformation of abbeys and convents into secular institutions for nobles or institutes for secular priests, by the suppression of monastic establishments even by ecclesiastical princes with or without papal permission, and, lastly, by the growing severity of the amortization laws. The application for secularization by the prince-bishop of Trent, Peter Vigil von Thun, in 1781/82 lends credence to the fact that a secure pension could be more tempting to an ecclesiastical prince than the rule over a small, scarcely profitable territory, pressed by powerful neighbors. No doubt the tendency towards secularization was also promoted by the old rivalry between the secular and the regular clergy, by comparisons between the economic backwardness of Catholic states and the prosperity of Protestant ones, as well as by strong immanent forces within the Catholic reform movement, the concepts of Muratori, the Jansenists, and Catholic advocates of Catholic enlightenment.

After the expulsion of the Society of Jesus from the Bourbon states and its suppression in 1773 its assets were claimed by the respective states and used in accordance with the enlightened doctrines of state law which held that it was within the competency of the state to dispose of the church property in a manner most useful for the commonweal. Fiscal policies and the argument of the commonweal played a decisive role in secularizations, not least in the abolition of monastic establishments for the purpose of reform or the creation of new Catholic universities (for instance Mainz and Münster). But it is quite telling that in the process of monastic secularization in the Electorate of Mainz the state of Hesse-Darmstadt seized part of the monastic property with the justification that it was a case of ownerless property and retained it despite a vehement literary battle and a lawsuit by Mainz. Next to fiscal policy it was for reasons of ecclesiastical reform, especially parish regulation, that the Josephinist "Klostersturm" took place in 1781, to which more than seven hundred monastic houses fell victim in Austria. Disciplinary problems or economic abuses were rarely the reason for the abolitions. The loss of cultural assets was immeasurable, the damage to learning considerable, but most serious were the negative effects on the ministry and religious life, which were certainly not made up for by the reforms actually achieved.

In connection with the Bavarian succession on the one hand and the Josephinist established church system reaching over into the Church of the Empire on the other, the ecclesiastical territories were not only confronted by "northern despotism" (Franz v. Fürstenberg) but by the Catholic power of Austria as well. In addition to the northwestern German archbishoprics, those of Fulda, Bamberg (for Saxony), and Würzburg also played a part in the exchange and compensation projects of the time; there was even talk of a secularization of Cologne in favor of Prussia and fears for the continued existence of the other two Rhenish archbishoprics were not without foundation. As the state minister of Münster, Franz von Fürstenberg, remarked bitterly in April 1778: "The most convenient thing would be to abolish a few bishoprics and justify it by saying that the property of the Church could never be put to a better use than to prevent bloodshed."[3] Plans to realize the concept of a third, neutral Germany in addition to the great powers Prussia and Austria failed. They were to secure the continued existence of the ecclesiastical principalities within the framework of an interdenominational union to include the princes of the Imperial Diet. Efforts to unite the episcopate on the basis of the old constitution of the Church of the Empire in order to counter the territorial claims of princely proponents of their respective established Churches and their plans for secularization were also unsuccessful. These efforts met with the resistance not only of Austria, whose policy regarding the Empire rested largely on the ecclesiastical princes and—after the issue of the Bavarian succession— was predicated on the unavoidability of secularizations. They were also resisted by Prussia, which was "prone to conquest," and by Bavaria with its established Church.

The danger of members of the Imperial Diet being affected by secularization surfaced when Archduke Max Franz was elected prince-bishop of Münster, again when Joseph II made a surprise attack on the prince bishopric of Passau following the death of Bishop Leopold Ernst von Firmian (d. 11 March 1783), and when the Emperor spawned the fantastic plan to transfer the archbishopric of Salzburg to Liège, but to secularize that prince-bishopric together with the chapter of Berchtes-

---

[3] Quoted from A. Hanschmidt, *Franz v. Fürstenberg als Staatsmann. Die Politik des münsterschen Ministers 1762–80* (Münster 1969), 211.

gaden in favor of Austria. This project, originating as it did with the Emperor, the *Defensor ecclesiae,* five years before the outbreak of the French Revolution, and plans discussed in the electorate of Bavaria and executed in the form of "cold secularizations"[4] made abundantly clear just what the situation of the ecclesiastical states would be if the decaying Empire were to fall apart because of the egotistical interests of the states or if a European conflict were to place the "conquering" states in a position where they could cut equivalents from the last remaining patches of the ecclesiastical "robe of the old Empire" (J. J. Moser).

After the warning signals of the late eighteenth century the strongest impulses for a comprehensive secularization emanated from the French Revolution. A proposal by Talleyrand was followed on 2 November by a decree nationalizing all church property. The Civil Constitution of 12 July 1790 shattered the hierarchical order of the old France. More than fifty bishoprics, all church offices without ministry, all religious orders and congregations were abolished; in 1792 papal Avignon and Venaissin and in 1798 and 1808 the Papal States were secularized.

The attitude of the ecclesiastical princes towards the French Revolution, by no means negative at first, although it was determined by totally varying motives and differing views, became noticeably more negative after the issuance of a Civil Constitution. The ecclesiastical princes of the western German border areas were involved in their first conflict with revolutionary France when the manorial and ecclesiastical rights of princes of the Empire were abolished in Alsace. The Civil Constitution eliminated the dependence of the dioceses of Metz, Toul, Verdun, Nancy, and Saint-Dié on the archbishopric of Trier, that of Strasbourg on Mainz, and revoked the jurisdiction of the bishop of Speyer in the Alsatian part of his see; in addition, it transferred the deanery of Carignan to the newly established bishopric of Sedan. The demand by the imperial bishops[5] for the restoration of the imperial and ecclesiastical status quo in Alsace, Lorraine, and in the *Terra Gallica* belonging to the bishopric of Trier had no tangible results; neither did the call for help to Russia as a guarantor of the Peace of Westphalia nor the condemnation of the Civil Constitution by Pope Pius VI. Leopold II was unwilling to make

---

[4] The concept of "cold secularization" in H. Liermann, *Deutsches Evangelisches Kirchenrecht* (Stuttgart 1933), 214.—On secularizations and their plans in Bavaria, see G. Pfeilschifter-Baumeister, *Der Salzburger Kongreß und seine Auswirkung 1770–77* (Paderborn 1929), passim; L. Hammermayer, "Das Ende des alten Bayern," M. Spindler, ed., *Hdb. der Bayerischen Gesch.* II (Munich 1966), 1101 f.

[5] Raised most emphatically by the prince-bishop of Speyer, August von Limburg-Styrum, of whom Madam von Condenhoven in Mainz mockingly remarked that he harbored within himself the counterrevolution (J. Wille, *August Graf von Limburg-Stirum, Fürstbischof von Speier* [Heidelberg 1913], 93).

the violation of the rights of German princes and bishops by revolutionary France the cause for an intervention. He especially warned the Rhenish elector-archbishops not to take any intemperate steps in connection with their emigration policies.

The direct confrontation with France was overshadowed by the rebellion in the Austrian Netherlands, arising from opposition of the estates and ecclesiastical circles to the policies of Joseph II and the resistance of the estates against the prince-bishop of Liège, Konstantin Franz von Hoensbroech. The electors of Cologne, Trier, and Mainz, together with the neighboring estates of the Empire had to pay with a defeat for their attempt, ordered by the supreme court of the Empire, to return the Liège prince-bishop to the fold. Only after the Liège issue had widened into a real crisis for the Empire and an agreement between the two great powers had been laboriously achieved did Austria take over the imperial execution and restore the original status in Liège by force of arms.

It was under the impact of the events on the western border of the Empire and individual cases of unrest in certain German territories that the governments started to dismantle enlightened reforms and to disavow Febronianism and the Congress of Ems. This point also marked the transition from a moderate Catholic enlightenment to an ecclesiastical restoration, from indifferentism to a more profound religiosity.[6] Flight onto the harassed ship of Saint Peter seems to have been the only way out of "punishment by temporal potentates."

The relationship of several ecclesiastical states (Speyer, Mainz, Trier) with revolutionary France was complicated by their policy regarding the royalist-aristocratic and ecclesiastical emigrants. Worms or Mainz, Coblenz or Schönbornslust might have appeared to the royal and aristocratic emigrants like a small foreign Versailles, a Versailles *in partibus,* with its favorites and mistresses. While these emigrants—in spite of their political and military activities—did not pose a danger to France as long as they were not supported by the European powers, unwise and provocative policies which went beyond their merely being tolerated by their host countries offered sufficient grounds to the Girondists for counterprovocation and warnings to the ecclesiastical states. Clearly distinct from the aristocratic emigrants, who were often seen as an economic burden and an offense to the religious population, were the

[6] It would be totally wrong to interpret the Catholic restoration as a mere relapse vis-à-vis the enlightenment of the Church. The extent of the infusion of intellectual elements from the Enlightenment, esp. the moderate ecclesiastical enlightenment, into the church renewal of the early nineteenth century should be demonstrated by the example of such as Sailer, Fürstenberg, Stolberg, Dießach, Beroldingen, and others. Their respective biographies each raise the question concerning the relationship between Enlightenment and church renewal in different ways.

ecclesiastical emigrants. Through their generally exemplary religious work and their ministry they enjoyed a hospitable reception by the population and the ecclesiasts. The emigration initially flowed into the parts of the archdioceses of Basel and Strasbourg on the right bank of the Rhine, then into the electorates of Trier and Mainz, Switzerland, and the extreme southwest of the Empire to Constance, Feldkirch, to the right-bank ecclesiastical principalities, to Bavaria and Austria. Their religious activities during the last few years of the Empire and during the Napoleonic period deserves to be investigated in more detail than has been done so far.

On 20 April 1792, opposed by the group around Robespierre, the Girondists prevailed on Louis XVI to declare war against the King of Hungary and Bohemia to defend France against alleged unjust attacks, to maintain freedom, and to demonstrate the will to expand its power. The Austro-Prussian campaign, in which the ecclesiastical electors did not take part, did not, however, result in the restoration of the status of 1789 or 1782 as had been hoped within the Church of the Empire. Instead the cannonade of Valmy on 20 September 1792 led to the occupation a few days later of the episcopal residences of Speyer and Mainz, the archdiocese of Liège, the left-bank territories of the rivers Erft and Roer. The archdiocese of Basel was declared the Raurachian Republic and united with France as the Departement Mont-Terrible. Church property in all the conquered territories was to be confiscated; an oath on the Civil Constitution was to effect apostasy to the schismatic national Church. After the declaration of war by the Empire (22 March 1793) the Austrian Netherlands and the left-bank ecclesiastical territories of the middle Rhine were reconquered. Yet the disunity of the allies, a general aversion to the war, and especially the political-military disinterest of Prussia prompted the proposal by the lord chancellor, the elector-archbishop of Mainz, at the Imperial Diet in Regensburg on 24 October 1794 that the Empire should attempt to make peace with France.

In the meantime new plans for secularization were discussed in Vienna and Berlin. Prussia, the "natural opponent of the ecclesiastical states" (H. von Treitschke), raised a demand for the secularization of several prince-bishoprics to satisfy its cost of the war, since this was "sufficiently justified by history" and moreover "would not create any actual disadvantage nor dissatisfaction." Reports by agents said that even Rome was not entirely against these secularizations. By virtue of the separate peace of Basel (5 April 1795) and the secret supplemental agreements (5 August 1795) Prussia received assurances for right-bank compensations (parts of the archdiocese of Münster and Reckling-hausen), with the proviso for adding other stipulations should they become suitable, in exchange for the commitment of strict neutrality. The Prussian example was followed by Hesse-Kassel (28 August 1795), whose dynasty was related to the Hohenzollern, Württemberg (7 August 1796), Baden (22 August 1796), and Bavaria (7 September 1796). The fact that the principle of compensation by means of secularizations was intended even then to be considerably expanded and not limited to fiefs of the Empire is shown by the secret treaty between Prussia and France in favor of the hereditary governor of the Netherlands, a brother-in-law of the Prussian King. He was to be compensated by the prince-bishoprics of Würzburg and Bamberg in exchange for the commitment that these areas were to go to Prussia when the house of Orange became extinct.

Military successes by Austria in the southern German theater of war did not change the development presaged by these treaties since Napoleon, by advancing through northern Italy into the heart of the Austrian hereditary lands, was able to force Austria to accept the armistice of Leoben (18 April 1797) and the subsequent Peace of Campoformio (17 November 1797). The agreements of Campoformio went well beyond the contradictory ones of Leoben concerning the recognition of the constitutional borders of France and the integrity of the Empire: Francis II as King of Hungary and Bohemia promised to take an active part in the cession of the left-bank areas from Basel to the Nette-Roer line. This agreement would not have ceded the Cologne electorate and the Prussian duchies of Cleves and Gelderland to France and Prussian compensations on the right bank of the Rhine would have been prevented. All the ecclesiastical states west of the line of Basel-Andernach-Venlo went to France and were secularized (Speyer, Worms, Mainz, Trier, Stablo-Malmedy, Liège, Prüm, etc.). The archdiocese of Salzburg was to compensate Austria for its loss of the Netherlands and northern Italy and in exchange for the Prussian territorial gains in Poland. While Austria had not basically been an opponent of secularization since the period of Josephinism, it did want to prevent a large-scale liquidation of ecclesiastical states. According to the stipulations of Campoformio, therefore, the ecclesiastical electors were to be assured of compensation on the right bank for their left-bank losses. Detailed arrangements were to be worked out at a congress in agreement with the French republic.

In spite of the formal announcement asserting the integrity of the Empire and contrary to the misgivings held by some of the estates (especially the Saxon electorate and Würzburg) the imperial delegates in Rastatt, yielding to pressure from France, accepted the principle of indemnification by means of secularization as the basis for peace. Thereupon "the legates of the knights of the Empire in savage greed crowded upon the plenipotentiaries of the Directorate in order to obtain by favor of the enemy of the Empire a rich piece from the territories of their ecclesiastical compatriots" (Treitschke). Partial secularization would have sufficed for compensation, but the tendency, only temporarily slowed down by the victories of the second coalition, was in the direction of total secularization. Since the Austrian withdrawal from Mainz there was a growing fear of total secularization in the ecclesiastical territories on the right bank of the Rhine not only because the appropriation of ecclesiastical property was fiscally expedient given the expenditures for the war, but also because the Pope, already on his way into French imprisonment, had helped bring about a situation in Bavaria "which could not but trigger directly the process of secularization."[7]

Following the military defeats in the second war of the coalition (Marengo, Hohenlinden) the Peace of Lunéville (7 March 1801; 16 March 1801) forced the Empire to cede the left-bank areas and—implying a secularization of the ecclesiastical states—to compensate the dispossessed hereditary princes "from the womb of the Empire" (dans le sein de l'Empire). In regard to these compensations, which were to be born by the Empire in its totality (collectivement), the indefinite guidelines of the Congress of Rastatt were invoked. The four ceded Rhenish départements were declared part of the French Republic by law of 9 March 1801; the Napoleonic concordat (15 July 1801; 8 April 1802) signaled the end of the Church of the Empire in the left-bank territories. In conjunction with the ratification bull Ecclesia Christi (15 August 1801) Pope Pius VII asked all the bishops of France and those in the ceded areas of the Empire to resign. In the subsequent new circumscription Mainz and Trier lost their position as metropolitanates; Cologne did not even retain its see; the départements of the Roer and the Rhine-Mosel were combined into a new bishopric with its residence in Aachen. Together with the newly circumscribed bishoprics of Ghent, Liège, Mainz, Namur and Tournai it formed the archdiocese of Mechelen. With some exceptions, the total secularization of the entire ecclesiastical property and the abolition of the monastic institutions were decreed (9 June 1802) in order to put the left-bank territories of the Church of the Empire on an equal footing with the rest of France. In many cases the right-bank real properties and taxed revenues of the abolished left-bank sees were immediately confiscated (for instance in Hesse-Darmstadt and Hesse-Kassel) and transferred to the respective territories even prior to ratification by the Imperial delegates' final recess.

Rome had recognized the secularization in France as well as in the

---

[7] L. Hammermayer in M. Spindler, ed., Hdb. der Bayerischen Gesch. II, 1102.

ceded left-bank areas in the concordat of 1801. It had also substantially agreed in advance to the secularization in the Empire even though other promulgations designed for the German Church were to create a different impression. Severing the left-bank parts of dioceses, abolishing the left-bank bishoprics, and realigning these areas as implemented by Caprara practically brought the Church of the Empire to ruin. The papal bull *Qui Christi Domini,* which expressly excepted the remainder of the archdioceses and sees outside the French rule from recircumscription and guaranteed them the maintenance of their ecclesiastical status quo, had no effect. The fact that France sought to have the bishops of the abolished sees of Basel and Liège transferred to vacant right-bank sees in order to avoid having to pay their pensions—Franz Xaver von Neveu, bishop of Basel, personally tried for a future new Baden bishopric—puts a characteristic light on the waning days of the Church of the Empire, as does the strange reserve of Rome when Archduke Anton Viktor was elected bishop of Münster.

Since the imperial delegation was totally unable to solve the issue of compensation, the role of arbitration—implied but not expressly mentioned in the treaty of Lunéville—devolved upon France. It created the foreign policy conditions for a territorial reorganization and disintegration of the Empire by peace treaties with England (1802) and an understanding with Russia (1801), which had claimed the right of participation as a guarantor of the Westphalian peace. On 23 November 1802, the design for compensation, submitted by the arbitrating powers France and Russia, was accepted by the imperial delegation with a few changes. The imperial decree by the ratification commission (27 April 1803), brought about by a Russian threat, elevated the final recess to the status of a binding basic law of the Empire. This sealed the fate of the ecclesiastical states by shifting the burden of compensation on them and by sanctioning the secularizations. In fact, the secularization, more trenchant in its effects than the Reformation and the Peace of Westphalia, "shook the last vestiges of imperial authority, which rested on the ecclesiastical states, whose rise, after all, had given birth to the Holy Roman Empire and from whose existence it could not be separated."[8] Henceforth the union of crosier and sword was prevented, the interlacing of Church and Empire severed, and the constitution of the German Church shattered, or rather changed to a provisional arrangement.

There was an almost total absence of resistance to the secularization on the part both of Rome and the ecclesiastical princes, either from helplessness or political considerations, from indifference or curial an-

---

[8] D. Schäfer, *Deutsche Gesch.* II (Jena 1916), 271.

tipathy against the Church of the Empire. Rome was neither able nor willing to prevent the secularization; it merely wanted to see it limited. It condemned secularization as unjust and an act of violence, but did not consider it a misfortune for the Church and at times even emphasized its beneficial effects. In many cases, even ecclesiastics did not shrink from making demands for compensation from church assets and secularization. Elector-Archbishop Clemens Wenzeslaus of Trier had designs on the prince-bishopric of Constance and the prince-abbey of Kempten; the Mainz elector Friedrich Karl von Erthal demanded the prince-bishopric of Fulda as compensation; Dalberg professed himself basically in agreement with the secularization; Wessenberg advocated a partial secularization; the Knights of Malta tried to enrich themselves by means of ecclesiastical property. The bitter remark by von Lang was probably not far off the mark: "The bishops were inclined to surrender the assets of the monasteries; the archbishops thought it not amiss if only the bishoprics were affected and used to provide some consolation for the ecclesiastical electors in the form of a small expansion . . . ; among the latter, Mainz wanted to say yes in God's name if only it was assured that Mainz would remain as a German partriarch and primate, for who would want to have the dear German fatherland exist without an *Archicancellarius Imperii per Germaniam.*"

Among the stipulations of the Imperial delegates' final recess we have to distinguish between: 1. the political secularization or that of estates of the Empire, which consisted of awarding ecclesiastical compensatory territories as sovereign states to new temporal sovereigns and was based on the supreme liegedom of the Emperor, benefiting primarily the states of medium size; 2. secularization in right of one's property (paragraphs 34–36), which granted "all properties of the cathedral chapters and their dignitaries together with the episcopal domains, all properties of the endowed sees, abbeys and monastic establishments . . . to the free and full disposition of the respective sovereign for the benefit of expenditures for church services, educational institutions, and others of public benefit, as well as for the alleviation of their finances . . . with the firm proviso of certain and constant provision of the cathedral churches . . . and pensions for the suspended clergy."

The Imperial delegates' final recess secularized on the right bank of the Rhine all imperially immediate ecclesiastical territories (two ecclesiastical electoral states, one prince-archbishopric, nineteen prince-bishoprics, numerous abbeys of the Empire), with the exception of the territories of the Knights of Malta and those of the Knights of the Teutonic Order (abolished in 1809), as well as the state of the lord chancellor under K. T. von Dalberg, which was newly created from the

504

remainders of ecclesiastical territories. It represented an enclave primarily in the expanded Bavarian state and was essentially incorporated in the Kingdom of Bavaria after the ratification of the Peace of Paris. The Imperial delegates' final recess transferred the Mainz archiepiscopal see to Regensburg, combining in this way the dignities of an elector, lord chancellor, metropolitan-archbishop, and primate of Germany. More than two hundred monastic institutions were secularized. In the Habsburg realm, which was in the incipient stage of an ecclesiopolitical restoration under Francis II, those monastic institutions which had avoided secularization in 1781 were not affected.

Also not affected was the old diocesan organization until "another decision is made on the basis of imperial law" (par. 62). Bishops and cathedral chapters were to be awarded pensions, the exercise of ecclesiastical office not to be obstructed, the existing exercise of religion "protected against all sorts of abolition and injury" (par. 63). Yet the denominational status quo guarantee was restricted by the proviso that the sovereign had the privilege to tolerate hitherto not admitted denominations in his land and to grant their followers "the full enjoyment of civil rights."

The compensatory transactions of secularization were, from an overall point of view, political instead of lawful ones, even though they were clad in the mantle of the basic law of the Empire by the Imperial delegates' final recess. "Few among the upheavals of state in modern history appear as ugly, as common, as low as this revolt of the princes of 1803" (Treitschke). Even such princes who had not suffered any territorial losses on the left bank of the Rhine, such as the archduke of Tuscany, the duke of Modena, and the hereditary governor of the Netherlands were awarded compensations by secularization. Secularized ecclesiastical territories and property also went the Helvetian Federation, the imperial city of Frankfurt, and others. Frequently the loss bore no relationship to the compensation. Prussia, for example, received five times the compensation of its loss, Hesse-Darmstadt eight times, and Baden ten times.

An immediate political consequence of the secularization was that the ratio of Catholics to Protestants in the Imperial Diet shifted at the expense of the Catholics and that a decisive step was taken towards the removal of Austria from the Empire. The future political development was presaged by the territorial expansion of Prussia, Bavaria, Württemberg, Baden, and the two Hesses. Secularization placed the majority of those ecclesiastical states which were almost entirely Catholic under rulers of another denomination. The Protestant powers and the non-Catholic segment of the population were provided a numerical, political, and economic superiority and the foundation was laid for the typical diaspora situation of the Catholic population. The transition to parity was not without great tension and harsh disputes.

As a revolt of the princes and an attempt at state reform, secularization resulted in the elimination of the Church of the Empire, the end of the Empire itself, and of the German Middle Ages. The surviving temporal territories, now enlarged, strove to adapt their church organization to their state borders either by joining the secularized areas to already existing state bishoprics or by establishing their own state or "national bishoprics." According to the Imperial delegates' final recess a reorganization of the dioceses was to be undertaken by imperial law, but before the necessary foundation could be laid on the basis of law and concordats, the Empire ceased to exist as a result of Napoleon's dictum and the resignation of the imperial crown by Francis II. The reordering of the German church organization was then—if not put in doubt—at least pushed into a distant future and placed in the hands of the individual territories, whose late-absolutist, bureaucratic established church systems welcomed the fact that sees and cathedral chapters were now orphaned.

Prior to secularization the centers of the church administration had been situated in the imperially immediate, prince-episcopal areas. The established Churches of the temporal governments faced a final barrier in the sovereign independence of the imperial episcopate. At a time of vacant sees, following the secularization of the ecclesiastical states, the absolutist states were enabled to prevail in their claims vis-à-vis a powerless and disowned Church which was thoroughly shaken in its organization. The fifteen years between the Peace of Lunéville and the beginning of the vast circumscriptions were a period of more recent German church history, which had neither concordats nor bishops. By 1811 the German Church had all of nine bishops left, including those not in residence or living in exile; five of them were well into their seventies, Dalberg at the age of sixty-seven was one of the youngest. "How long," was the question Suffragan Bishop Kolborn asked in a letter to Wessenberg at the beginning of 1811, "can we wait without being totally bereft of bishops?" The cathedral chapters, largely deprived of their revenues, were dispersed here and there. Many capitulars had withdrawn to the quietude and obscurity of private life, demoralized and humiliated by the events. A regeneration of the chapters, whose members were all advanced in years, could not take place because the sustentation and pension obligation of the states extended only to those ecclesiastics who had been suspended from positions recognized by imperial law, but not to their successors. The German Church was threatened by anarchy. The vagaries of the times had uprooted the leadership of those nobles who were eligible for ecclesiastical office and had dispersed them in every direction. The feeling of humiliation, the distrust by Rome of advocates of Enlightenment and Febronianism, fear and the prospect of a dark future led to passivity and resignation. Those who were eager to get into the consistories and to seize the administration of the remainders of dioceses usually bowed, dumb and obsequious, to the established church system.[9] For a considerable part of the regular clergy the transfer to collective monasteries ("Krepierinstitute") was not a good solution. The vacant sees, the negligent search, at times determined by the sovereign's desire for splendor, for one's own, if possible a "cheap" bishop—to quote the words of a minister of Nassau-Weilburg—the usurpation of episcopal rights, the expansion of the rights of sovereignty not only *circa sacra* but *in sacra* were elements, according to the mild-mannered bishop of Augsburg, Clemens Wenzeslaus, which constituted a fatal danger for the Church. It was largely due to the efforts of Prince-Primate von Dalberg that this danger was averted.

The closing of Catholic universities, schools, and orders had an extremely negative effect on the intellectual life of the Catholic population. The education of future clerics and an orderly ministry were put in doubt; the closings marked the downfall of episcopal culture in southern Germany and the beginning of the decline of Catholic education and culture. Henceforth the patronage by the ecclesiastically eligible nobility was lacking, as was the possibility for social, economic, and intellectual rise which entering the large monastic institutions and rich abbeys had offered the Catholic segment of the population.[10] A most regrettable concomitant phenomenon was the cheap sale of works of art, libraries, manuscripts, and archives, the use for other purposes and the profanation of ecclesiastical structures. In Cologne more than fifty churches and chapels were torn down; some of the most precious li-

---

[9] Even I. H. v. Wessenberg, whose weakness regarding the established Church is well known, speaks of the "servility" into which a dependent clergy is tempted.

[10] The learned Roman Zirngibl of Sankt Emmeram in Regensburg complains: "Es hat ein französischer, preußisch-russischer Wink alle Stifter und Klöster Deutschlands zu Boden gestürzt. Die Kinder der gemeinen Älteren haben nur mehr allein eine Aussicht zum Soldatenstand. Die gründliche Litteratur wird sich nach und nach verliehren, die nach den evangelischen Grundsätzen aufgeklärte Priester, und mit denselben die positive Religion wird abnehmen und am Ende wird aus unserm Vaterlande ein militärischer Staat nach dem Modell der altpreußischen und heßischen Staaten werden" (A. Kraus, *Die Briefe Roman Zirngibls von St. Emmeram in Regensburg* [Regensburg 1965], 104).— On the aspect of economic and social elevation, in addition to the works by E. Krausen, see J. Salzgeber, O.S.B., *Die Klöster Einsiedeln und St. Gallen im Barockzeitalter. Historisch-soziologische Studie* (Münster 1967).

brary holdings in Trier were used for heating purposes,[11] the tradition of rich artistic work, of respectable scholarly achievement among the Catholics was suddenly interrupted. The economic loss due to secularization was considerable. Redistribution of wealth—while it had been initiated before—reached a climax with the sale of church property.

In the period between secularization and its laboriously achieved legal position and relative freedom, the Church "instead of the scepter of lost sovereignty bore the cane of impotence and the crown of thorns of servitude" (J. Görres). But the loss of almost a thousand years of ballast, of feudal abuses, aristocratic exclusivity of the cathedral chapters and the episcopate,[12] of nepotism, at times abundant, and of Frebronianism, connected with the favored position of the Church of the Empire, were beneficial to the Church. Fruitful impulses and forces from the very roots of religion and Church were freed in the bitter years following the secularization. The soil was prepared for the alliance of "Church and nation." Not only under the Napoleonic bishops, the zealous Colmar in Mainz, Mannay in Trier, Berdolet in Aachen, did new life begin to flourish in the Church, but even in the pseudo-constitutional states of the Rhenish Confederation as well. Within the powerless, impoverished Church, oppressed by the established church system, the concept of church unity and papal authority took on added strength. The new generation of clerics "had no home other than the Church" (Treitschkse). The fight against episcopalism, Febronianism, established Church, and Wessenbergianism assumed a more determined character. The ecclesiastical space was tightened, as it were, and filled up from within by an atmosphere of struggle; it was quite frugal in comparison with the old Church of the Empire. "As a consequence of secularization the Church was more modern than the state which gave it lodging." In the nineteenth century it "was able to become the champion of an extraterritorial sphere of freedom, not intent on successes of the day vis-à-vis the omnipotence of the state."[13]

---

[11] H. Raab, "Clemens Wenzeslaus und seine Zeit (1739–1812)," I: *Dynastie, Kirche und Reich im 18. Jh.* (Freiburg 1962), 14 f.; "Die Tatsache, daß die Säkularisation letztlich einen segensreichen geistig-religiösen Erneuerungsprozeß innerhalb der katholischen Kirche des 19. Jh. einleitet, wiegt jene (kulturellen) Verluste nicht auf" (S. Reicke, *RGG* V [1961],1286).

[12] The number of bourgeois suffragan bishops was considerable. The image of an aristocratic Church of the Empire should be treated in a more discriminating and less distorted manner.

[13] W. H. Stuck, "Zur Säkularisation im Lande Nassau," *Hess Jb. für Landesgesch*. 13 (1963), 309.

CHAPTER 27

Attempts at Church Reunion

The outcome of the Thirty Years' War, which had, at least in part, been conducted as a religious war, and the stipulations of the Peace of Westphalia had all but dashed the expectation of a restoration of religious unity in the Empire.[1] The irritant of a split Christianity had grown apace with the consolidation of denominational consciousness and denominational territories. But at the same time it had become less objectionable, since it denoted the triumph of politics in the widest sense over theology, the victory of state authority, and a beginning awareness in the German territories which indicated a shift from goals in the hereafter to the task in this world. The withdrawal from specifically religioecclesiastical tasks in the early absolutist territories began as a process of general secularization; in the leading segments of the population it started as a renunciation of the theological spirit of strife and disputatiousness, as indifferentism and skepticism in which rationalist and materialist ideas gained ground. Friedrich von Logau expressed the sentiments of his generation in his well-known distich: "Lutheranism, Papism, and Calvinism, these faiths, all three of them, are here; yet there is doubt where Christianity could be."[2] The bitter words of the "Augsburg confusion" made the rounds. The different religious parties had to learn to coexist peacefully within the Empire, a laborious process full of quarrels and hatred among territories of different denominations. The political and military impotence in the face of the enemies of Christianity to the east and those of the Empire to the north and west, the *calamitas imperii,* was to some extent held to be a consequence of the denominational strife. For that reason plans for religious reunion on the one hand and reform in the Empire on the other had had some relationship with each other since the seventeenth century. This was also the case in the opposition of the Church of the Empire to Rome as well as in Pietism and Enlightenment. Motives of patriotism for the Empire, episcopalism, Pietism, and Enlightenment played concomitant and successive roles in the history of reunion projects, as did indifferentism, credulity, theological ignorance, and material and political interests.

[1] *IPO* ART. V, par. 14: "Si vero, quod Deus prohibeat, de religionis dissidiis conveniri non possit, nihilominus haec conventio perpetua sit et pax duratura."
[2] F. v. Logau, *Sämtliche Sinngedichte*, ed. by G. Eitner (Tübingen 1872), 246.

"All dogmatic questions," admitted the philosophical wife of the bishop of Osnabrück, Sophie of the Palatinate, "touch my heart but little." To her, religion is love of God and one's neighbor, everything else is "a bunch of priestish squabbling, up to the princes to settle."[3] Reasonable people are not bothered by it. Yet Sophie, like her religiously indifferent brother, Elector Karl Ludwig, who built the Concordia church in Mannheim and wanted to tolerate "all sorts of religions" in the Palatine electorate, discussed the possibility of conversion with her sister Louise Hollandine, the abbess of Maubuisson, and showed a massive material and political interest in reunion transactions.[4]

Indifferentism, rationalism, and materialism on the one hand, religiosity (deepened by the dire straights of the Thirty Years' War), eschatological and pietistic currents, religioecclesiastic and political motives on the other are all in league with one another in the irenical efforts and those aimed at reunion. Tolerance became the political motto of state in the denominationally mixed territories and in the flourishing mercantilist thinking. The idea of the authority of the state began to surmount denominational limits and prejudice. The connection between the schism and the decline of the Empire, the question of religious reunion, reform of the Empire, and a European structure of peace were acute topics for discussion.

A bridge for reunion were those "in between things" (Latin chant, liturgical vestments, crucifixes, auricular confession, the hours), continued in the Lutheran Church and, above all, the Catholic canon law, to

---

[3] E. Bodemann, "Briefe der Kurfürstin Sophie von Hannover an die Raugräfinnen und Raugrafen zu Pfalz," *Publicationen aus den preuss. Staatsarchiven* 37 (Leipzig 1888), 91; about Sophie von der Pfalz, see P. Hiltebrandt, *Die kirchlichen Reunionsverhandlungen,* passim and M. Knoop, *Kurfürstin Sophie von Hannover* (Hildesheim 1964).

[4] The family of the "Winter King," Elector Palatine Friedrich, was totally divided in their religion and partly for that reason involved in the talks concerning the respective religions. The oldest son, Elector Karl Ludwig, and his sister Elizabeth, prince-abbess of Herford, a friend of Descartes, Labadie, and William Penn, was Reformed in name only; privately she was completely indifferent and not at all disinclined towards a conversion, given the right sort of gain (secularization of the archbishoprics of Worms and Speyer). Karl Ludwig's sister, Louise Hollandine, had turned Catholic and become abbess of the convent of Maubisson near Paris, where Mme de Brinon promoted the correspondence between Leibniz and Bossuet. Sophie, the "philosophic" daughter of the Winter King, wife of the "Pseudo-Bishop" Ernst August of Osnabrück was Lutheran in name but prepared to convert if given the right advantages. "I hope all Christians will soon be one," she wrote to Countess Louise. Two younger brothers, Eduard, who married Anne of Gonzaga in 1645, and Gustav Adolf had converted to Catholicism. Anne of Gonzaga was able to have her daughter Benedicta Henriette marry the Catholic convert Duke Johann Friedrich of Hanover (1668) and mediate the marriage between Elisabeth Charlotte of the Palatinate (Liselotte) and Duke Philipp of Orléans. Liselotte converted after the marriage contract was signed in 1671.

which the Protestant cathedral and collegiate chapters adhered "with admirable tenacity."[5] Numerous historical relics also pointed to a reunion. These included the existence of mixed chapters in Strasbourg, Lübeck, Osnabrück; the observance of celibacy in Protestant institutions, the alternation in the archdiocese of Osnabrück and the effects of the Volmar list in the parish of Goldenstedt, where the pastor was Catholic, the sexton Protestant, and where the Protestants attended Catholic Mass in which songs from the Lutheran hymnal were sung.

After the Peace of Westphalia the different currents tending towards reunification all converged at the court of the senior ecclesiastical elector, the lord chancellor and *Primas Germaniae* in Mainz. Johann Philipp von Schönborn, the "German Solomon," his suffragan bishop Peter van Walenburch, and his minister of state Johann Christian von Boineburg, who defended the rights of the *Natio Germanica* against the Roman Curia, together with other irenicists and reunionists worked on reunion projects and promoted the reduction of denominational differences. Yet the so-called Mainz Plan for Reunion of 1660 is not likely to have originated with either the elector, Boineburg, or Leibniz;[6] it is probably the product of Landgrave Ernst von Hessen-Rheinfels. As an intellectual broker of his time, a friend of Boineburg and the brothers Adrian and Peter van Walenburch from their Düsseldorf period, this prince was a member of the innermost circle of reunion politicians. By means of his worldwide correspondence, especially with Georg Calixt, Leibniz, Spener, Antoine Arnauld, Johannes Neercassel, the administrator of the Utrecht diocese, the reunionist dukes of the Guelfs, the nuncios in Cologne, and through numerous writings of his own he supported the efforts for reunion in his time.[7]

In connection with his own conversion Landgrave Ernst, who had become familiar with the mediation theology of Georg Witzel in Vienna, brought together the theologians Eberhard Happel, Peter Haberkorn, Balthasar Menser, a fellow student of Boineburg's, and the famous Capuchin friar Valerian Magni for a religious discussion in

---

[5] H. Nottarp, *Zur "Communicatio in sacris cum haereticis"* (Halle 1933), 116; also idem, *Das katholische Kirchenwesen in der Grafschaft Ravensberg im 17. u. 18. Jh.* (Paderborn 1961).

[6] A. P. Brück, "Der Mainzer 'Unionsplan' aus dem Jahre 1660," *Jb. für das Bistum Mainz* 8 (1960), 148–62.

[7] A contribution to reunion was to be the "Christlich Catholische zu S. Goar uebliche Gesang-Buch" edited by Ernst.—In the *Pia vota et recta desideria* the petition has a central role: "Dass alle sowohl Orientalische, als auch den Protestierenden Secten zugethane Christen Menschen sich wieder zur Einigkeit der Catholischen Apostolischen Römischen Kirche begeben, und durch bessern Unterricht ihren Irrthumb erkennen."

December 1651 at his castle Rheinfels above Sankt Goar.[8] In 1652 he set up a like discussion in Kassel between his confessor, the Jesuit Johannes Rosenthal, and Johannes Crocius, and a year later between Rosenthal and Haberkorn in Gießen. Although these three discussions had no tangible results other than unpleasant literary feuds for the landgrave and a campaign by the Jesuits against Valerian Magni because of his pronouncement at Rheinfels that the infallibility of the Pope as *ex solo sancto textu* could not be proved, the reunion of a split Christianity continued to be his primary and most important desire.

The connection with Erasmian spirit and the Mainz efforts is manifest in the *Motiva Conversionis Ernesti Landgravii* by the brothers Adrian and Peter van Walenburch, and, more so, in the best-known work by the landgrave of Hesse-Rheinfels himself, the *Discrete Catholische.*[9] According to his own testimony he wrote this work for all the Catholics and Protestants "whose hearts are sincerely touched by the grievous split in Christendom." Leibniz became familiar with the *Discrete Catholische* in his Mainz period and received important suggestions from it for his own efforts towards reunion. He thought the book contained an exhortation to the Protestants that they were obliged to seek reunification with the Catholic Church with all their strength, but also a challenge to the Catholics to smooth the path for reunion by eliminating the abuses and by bringing about a true reform.

For Landgrave Ernst, his Mainz friends, and for his "more than dear Leibniz," for whose conversion he was hoping, the conditions for a reunion were *discretio,* the wise differentiation in the sense of due proportion, combined with the elimination of abuses, the *consensus quinquesaecularis,* and especially the discreet view of papal primacy. "The wisdom of Solomon, the patience of Job," he says, tolerance, brotherly love and God's help in a "desperate matter" were required to bring it about. With the help of church reform and reunion a new and better order would be established in Europe—a first step being the establishment of a European court of arbitration in Lucerne—and peace would be secured within Christianity. His opinion regarding the plans of the bishop of Tina, Christoph de Rojas y Spinola, showed that Landgrave Ernst was sophisticated enough and sufficiently well versed in the history of reunionist endeavors to have the right estimate of their chances for success.

After Mainz under the reign of Johann Philipp von Schönborn the courts of Braunschweig-Lüneburg were the most fertile and receptive soil

---

[8] Most recent: G. Denzler, *Die Propagandakongregation in Rom und die Kirche in Deutschland im ersten Jahrzehnt nach dem Westfälischen Frieden* (Paderborn 1969), 185–212.
[9] H. Raab, *Der "Discrete Catholische,"* 175–98.

for reunion in the last third of the seventeenth century. This had primarily political as well as denominational, personal, and ideological reasons. Duke Johann Friedrich of Hanover (d. 1679), who had converted to the Catholic Church in Rome in 1650, had close connections to the reunionist *aula laboriosa* of the Mainz elector Johann Philipp. Leibniz's entering the service of the duke of Hanover was due in some measure to the assistance of Landgrave Ernst von Hessen-Rheinfels. The latter, moreover, supported the Catholic succession in Hanover, so that Rome's hopes raised by the princely conversion would not again be dashed in this case, "di vedere un giorno ritornato al grembo della chiesa quella numerosissima e noblissima Natione."[10]

The expectation that negotiations in Hanover would lead to reunion proved to be unfounded when the Catholic Duke Johann Friedrich was succeeded by his denominationally indifferent brother Ernst August, who was interested solely in expanding his power. When he was still pseudo-bishop of Osnabrück and then again as duke of Hanover after 1679 he repeatedly made vaguely formulated offers for his or his sons' conversion to Catholicism in exchange for the secularization of Hildesheim and the cancellation of the alternation in the diocese of Osnabrück in favor of his house. The Hanover negotiations of 1683 played a particular role in the reunion attempted by the bishop of Tina, Christoph de Rojas y Spinola. This reunion was supported by Emperor Leopold primarily for political reasons and encouraged by Clement X and Innocent XI. While the danger posed by the Turks in the east grew to alarming proportions and more and more territories were lost by reunions in the west, discussions took place in Hanover between Spinola, Walter Molanus, the abbot of Loccum, the younger Calixt, and Theodor Mayer. But a firm programmatic draft could not be obtained. Among the concessions from the Lutheran side were: celibacy for the pastors, provided the existing marriages were recognized, infallibility of the councils, recognition of the Pope as the visible head of the Church, the presence of Christ in the Eucharist and submission to a future universal council. Additional demands raised by Molanus in 1683, the resistance of the French party in Rome, who feared that reunion would strengthen the Empire, and, lastly, the fact that the "sacred cause" was subordinated to the power politics of the Guelfs led to the failure of Spinola's efforts. As Landgrave Ernst wrote in a letter to Spener and in his memoranda to Duke Anton Ulrich von Wolfenbüttel and to Leibniz, the two parties were *"in principiis et suppositis* too far apart from each

[10] Ernst von Hessen-Rheinfels to the Pope, 13 February 1665; H. Raab, "De negotio Hannoveriano Religionis," 404.

other," separated by political interests, for theological issues according to the opinion of the court of Hanover were mere insignificant details.

Attempts by Spinola to eliminate the denominational tensions in Hungary failed as well,[11] nor did the union negotiated by his successor at Wiener Neustadt, Bishop Franz Anton von Buchheim, Leibniz and Molanus in 1686 come about. In the meantime Rome's reticence became more and more manifest. The political situation, influenced by the expulsion of the Huguenots, the religious clause in the Peace of Rijswijk (1697), and the expectation of a Hanoverian succession in England were unfavorable to a reunion.[12]

There was no notable reaction to the *Friedreiche Gedanken über die Religionsvereinigung in Teutschland* (1679) by Johann Friedrich Ignaz Karg von Bebenburg, the future supreme chancellor of the Cologne electorate and abbot of Saint-Michel au Péril de la Mer (in the diocese of Avranches).[13] Irenics and polemics were merged in the *Via pacis* (1686) by the Capuchin friar Dionysius of Werl.[14] *Libertas ecclesiae Germanicae* and reunion in the faith by restoration of the "original" pre-Hildebrandian church constitution were the goals of the Protestant canonist Johannes Schilter in his seven books about the freedom of the German Church modeled on the *Declaratio Cleri Gallicani*. According to testimony by the Trier minister of state J. G. von Spangenberg, friend

[11] Upon Spinola's death Molanus wrote the poem: "In Te renatos vidimus pios Fratres / Doctosque Walenburgicos, decora aeterna / Germaniae nomenque dulce Cassandri, / Et quotquot uspiam fuere fautores / Concordiae sacrae Deoque dilectae" (H. Weidemann, *Molanus* II, 173).

[12] S. J. T. Miller and J. P. Spielman, *Cristobal Rojas y Spinola,* 79: "If all Christian princes or at least as many as supported Rojas in 1683 had for a few years remained loyal to the idea of church unity and especially if Louis XIV had subordinated his dynastic selfishness, his devious foreign policy, his insatiable addiction to glory and his brutal treatment of the Huguenots to the welfare of the Christian world, an irenical climate would most probably have been created which would have led to the restoration of unity between Rome and large groups of German Protestants."

[13] *Friedreiche Gedanken über die Religions Vereinigung in Teutschland aus dem Worte Gottes, Conciliis, Patribus, Kirchenhistorie zusammengetragen* (Würzburg 1679). The book was dedicated to Prince-Bishop Peter Philipp von Dernbach.—A biographical sketch of Karg (1648–1719), who was engaged to a considerable extent in controversial political activities and at the very least sympathized with Jansenism, is contained in M. Braubach, *Kurkölnische Miniaturen* (Münster 1954), 78–104; L. Jadin, *L'Europe au début du XVIIIe siècle. Correspondance du Baron Karg de Bebenbourg, Chancelier du Prince-Évêque de Liège Joseph Clément de Bavière, Archevêque Électeur de Cologne avec le Cardinal Paolucci, Secrétaire d'État (1700–1719),* 2 vols. (Brussels and Rome 1968).

[14] Dionysius aus Werl, *Via pacis inter homines per Germaniam in fide dissidens . . .* (Hildesii Saxonum 1686).—A. Jacobs, *Die Rheinischen Kapuziner 1611–1725. Ein Beitrag zur Geschichte der katholischen Reform* (Münster i. W. 1933), 68ff.

and collaborator of Hontheim, and by Marshal B. F. von Zurlauben, the Febronian ideas were gleaned at least in part from Schilter's work.[15]

The sermons by the Jesuit Jean Dez in Strasbourg and his book *La réunion des Protestants de Strasbourg à l'Église Romaine,* translated into German by the convert Ulrich Obrecht, attempted to demonstrate that there was no obstacle to reunification and that the *Confessio Augustana* contained nothing un-Catholic. The suggestions for a reunion by the Königsberg professor Praetorius and especially his recognition of the papal primacy which he pronounced in the preface of his *Tuba pacis* (1685) after his conversion to the Catholic Church encountered opposition in Protestant Germany.[16] The Helmstedt theologian Johann Fabricius, as did Praetorius, lost his chair at the university because he was made responsible for the expert opinion written in 1707 in connection with the conversion of Elisabeth Christine von Braunschweig-Wolfenbüttel and her marriage to Archduke Karl, the future Emperor. The Helmstedt theological faculty had stated: "We are convinced that the Catholics are the same as the Protestants and that the quarrels among them amount only to words. The basis of religion is also found in the Roman Catholic Church; one can be orthodox there, live right, die well and obtain salvation. Princess von Wolfenbüttel therefore can accept the Catholic religion for the purpose of promoting the intended marriage."[17] As the "abbot of Königslutter," Fabricius continued to work for the idea of a religious reunification. In 1704 he published a *Via ad pacem ecclesiasticam;* invoking Cassander, Witzel and Bossuet he presented the differences between the Catholics, Lutherans and Reformed as minor.

Bossuet's *Exposition de la doctrine chrétienne* (1671), which was to have the function of reclaiming the Huguenots (see Chap. 4), gave an impulse to controversial theology. Seven years later, in 1678, he started his correspondence with Leibniz. It was interrupted for a while and then

---

[15] J. Schilter, *De libertate ecclesiarum Germaniae libri* VII (Jena 1683); cf. H. Raab, *Die Concordata Nationis Germanicae in der kanonistischen Diskussion des 17.–19. Jh.* (Wiesbaden 1957); idem, "Ad reuniendos dissidentes," 129ff.; Zurlauben to Martin Gerbert, 19 February 1779; "Je sais de bonne source, que M. de Hontheim avoit puisé ses opinions 'febroniennes' dans l'ouvrage de Schilter sur 'la puissance ecclésiastique d'Allemagne' " (G. Pfeilschifter, *Korrespondenz* II, 411).

[16] In this connection see also the translation edited and annotated by the severely denominational Anton Josef Binterim (1779–1855): *Des Matthäus Prätorius aus preußisch Memel, der lutherischen Gemeinde zu Nibbudz Predigers Aufruf zur Vereinigung an alle in Glaubenssachen im Occident von einander abweichende Kirchen* (Aachen 1822).

[17] C. W. Hering, op. cit. II, 303; M. P. Fleischer, op. cit., 53; Maximilian Prechtl, abbot of Michelfeld, see n. 40 below.

resumed through Duchess Sophie of Hanover, her sister Louise Hollandine, abbess of Maubuisson, the latter's secretary Mme de Brinon, and the duchess's niece Benedicta Henrietta, who had withdrawn to Maubuisson following the death of her husband, Johann Friedrich, duke of Hanover. Parallel to Leibniz's exchange of ideas with Bossuet was his correspondence with the convert and court historiographer of Louis XIV, Pellison, and—through mediation by Ernst von Hessen-Rheinfels—with the great Jansenist Antoine Arnauld. Pellison's *Réflexions sur les différends en matière de religion,* Bossuet's monumental *Histoire des variations des Églises protestantes* (1688), and Arnauld's zealous unionism marked a promising point of departure for religious discussion. But the difficulties bound to be encountered were sufficiently characterized by the ambivalence in the behavior of the most important among the discussants.

Leibniz wanted religious unity as a condition for a European union based on Christianity first, and only then have the dogmatic issues solved by a lawful council, similar to Basel. Bossuet suggested the reverse way. The Council of Trent could not but enter into the center of the discussion: Leibniz considered it the most serious obstacle to a reunion, for Bossuet it was a position which he could not surrender. In vain Leibniz invoked patriotic motives, the Gallican provisos, the refusal by Catherine de Medici and Henry IV to recognize the council. He also argued that there existed a widespread tendency in the Church of the Empire, especially in the archdiocese of Mainz, either to ignore or even to reexamine and reject the Council of Trent. Leibniz's efforts failed because of resistance on the part of Bossuet, who in defending the Council of Trent was also defending the infallibility of the Church.

The traditional line of denominational power struggles apparently reemerged more strongly during the waning seventeenth and early eighteenth century: under William of Orange in England, with the persecution of the Huguenots in France, the Palatine religious quarrel and the "acts of revenge" by the Protestant territories in the Empire,[18] the counterreformational actions of the Habsburgs in Silesia, and, finally, the Toggenburg tumults and the second war of Villmerg in Switzerland. By their ambivalent nature these events demonstrate on the one hand a revival of denominational differences and on the other a tendency towards pacification, tolerance, and equality. But a dismantling of denominationalism by means of enlightenment and tolerance alone could

---

[18] H. Schmidt, *Kurfürst Karl Philipp von der Pfalz als Reichsfürst* (Mannheim 1963), 114ff.; M. Schwaab, "Die Wiederherstellung des Katholizismus in der Kurpfalz im 17. und 18. Jh.," *ZGObrh* 114 (1966), 147–205.

not revitalize the overall efforts, which had become noticeably weaker since the failure of the discussions between Leibniz and Bossuet.

On the Catholic side some hopes were connected with the conversion of Protestant princes, as in the case of Hontheim-Febronius and the Benedictine Karl von Piesport, who evinced great interest in the reunion with the Eastern Churches around the middle of the century and who was substantially involved in the Fulda plan for reunification.

In his anniversary bull of 5 May 1749, Pope Benedict XIV reiterated his desire for the reunification of Christendom. Cardinal Angelo Maria Quirini discussed Cardinal Reginald Pole's ideas for reunion with Johann Georg Schellhorn; with Johann Rudolf Kiesling he discussed Cardinal Contarini's doctrine of justification. When Johann Joseph von Trautson became archbishop of Vienna he took steps to bring the denominations closer together.

Attempts to overcome the "unnatural separation" of the Small Church after the Council of Utrecht in 1763 climaxed in the efforts by the acolyte Gabriel Dupac de Bellegarde (1717–89)[19] at the courts of the German prince-bishops, the court of Vienna, and in Rome. Dupac de Bellegarde, in the canonical tradition of van Espen—he published Espen's biography in 1767—was profoundly influenced by Antoine Arnauld. He reintroduced the transfigured concept of the *Ecclesia primitiva,* combined with a strong anti-Roman sentiment, to the episcopalists of the Church of the Empire, to the reformists and reunionists. He was able to call on the support of the most prominent Würzburg canonist, Johann Kaspar Barthel, and the Fulda Benedictine Karl von Piesport; his efforts were applauded by the reformists in Mainz, Passau, Laibach, and the Jansenists-Josephinists de Haen, Wittola and van Swieten in Vienna.

Whether or to what extent the Utrecht views had any influence on the reunification ideas of the *Febronius* can not yet be said with any degree of assurance. It would be natural to assume such influence from Hont-

---

[19] E. Winter, *Der Josephinismus und seine Geschichte. Beiträge zur Geistesgeschichte Österreichs 1740–1848* (Vienna 1943), 112ff.; W. Deinhardt, *Der Jansenismus in deutschen Landen* (Munich 1929), 84f.; V. Rodolico, *Gli amici e i tempi di Scipione di Ricci* (Florence 1920), 54–113; G. Leclerc, *Zeger-Berhard van Espen (1646–1728) et l'autorité ecclésiastique* (Zurich 1964); A. Ellemunter, *Antonio Eugenio Visconti* (Graz and Cologne 1963), 173f.; L. Ceyssens, "L'affaire du Séminaire de Liège d'après l'historien janséniste G. du Pac de Bellegarde," *Annales de la Commission communale de l'histoire de Liège* 3 (1947), 603–762; F. Kenninck, "Les idées religieuses en Autriche de 1767 à 1789. Correspondance du Dr. Wittola avec le Comte Dupac de Bellegarde," *Revue internationale de Théologie* 6 (1898), 308ff., 584ff.; M. Vaussard, "L'epistolaria di G. M. Pujati con canonico Dupac de Bellegarde," *Studi Veneziani* 7 (1965), 443–88.

heim's course of study, from the older Jansenist connections between the archdiocese of Trier and the Netherlands, and in view of the rather strong propaganda by the Utrecht Church, but proof of it is hard to obtain because of the fact that the most important arguments for re-union were very widespread and the worldwide correspondence of Dupac has not yet been adequately investigated. At any rate, the Ut-recht cleric followed the Febronian disputes and the revocation affair with great interest and was persistently identified with Febronianism and its consequences by his contemporaries.

When Febronius's *De statu ecclesiae* was finally published, reunifica-tion, the exclusive, dominating concern in the original concept, was pushed into the background by the problems involving the rights of the Church of the Empire. Reunification was to be achieved by the elimina-tion of the *gravamina* and the reduction of the papal primacy within the limits drawn by the original church constitution and newly cir-cumscribed by the Councils of Constance and Basel and the *Concordata Nationis Germanicae.* Aside from the Utrecht influences, Hontheim's ideas for reunion can be explained from two roots: the tradition of the Church of the Empire and imperial patriotism as well as the personal impulses he received from his friend and collaborator, the convert Jakob Georg von Spangenberg.[20] Even after his conversion to the Catholic Church Spangenberg's ideas were still largely determined by the late medieval-pietistic Christ mysticism, by Pietism and the Church of the Bohemian Brothers, whose episcopal head was his youngest brother August Gottlieb, and by his very personal form of piety. The Swabian Pietist Moser characterized him as God's very own creature from child-hood on; the Viennese privy councillor Adolf von Krufft called him the only confidant of the Febronian secrets. The experience of Spangen-berg's own life and his patriotism for the Empire must have made him feel very painfully the abuses of the church constitution and the *Calamitas Imperii,* prompting his desire for a reconciliation of denomi-national differences and yet—two decades after the appearance of the *Febronius*—reject the Fulda plan for reunion.

---

[20] G. Reichel, *August Gottlieb Spangenberg, Bischof der Brüderkirche* (Tübingen 1908).— In his instruction for Lucini in March 1760 Nuncio Oddi characterized him as "di grandissima abilità, condotta e politica ed allievo del defonto Elettore di Treveri (Franz Georg von Schönborn) da cui ha succhiato tutte le massime. Questo è uomo difficile, per ottenersi la menoma cosa che riquardi la corte di Roma"; L. Just, "Die westdeutschen Höfe um die Mitte des 18. Jahrhunderts im Blick der Kölner Nun-tiatur," *AHVNrh* 135 (1939), 64; R. Reichert, "Johann Gertz (1744–1824). Ein katholischer Bibelwissenschaftler der Aufklärungszeit im Spiegel seiner Bibliothek," *AMrhKG* 18 (1966), 98; H. Faas, "J. G. von Spangenberg," *Kurtrierisches Jb.* 8 (1968), 153–65.

No doubt Febronius—as the Protestant opponents of his ideas such as Walch, Bahrdt, C. G. Hofmann, and also the Heidelberg Jesuit J. Kleiner explained to him[21]—did not sufficiently recognize the divisive elements of the denominations and exaggerated the common ones out of anti-Roman sentiments and a confirmed patriotism for the Empire. His "Romantic" attitude, strengthened by his intensive historical studies, hoped that the problems of his own time could be solved through the contrast of a past historical epoch of idealized early Christian and medieval conditions. But even "if the Roman Church were to be given the shape which Febronius wants so laboriously to give it and in the process the Roman-Catholic doctrine and its pure source, the tradition so highly praised by Febronius, were to remain unchanged,"[22] the unification of the divided Christians would be impossible. The suggestions by Febronius were not judged quite so negatively by Abbot Jerusalem and Friedrich Karl von Moser. The latter publicised Spangenberg's credo and the reunion projects of 1614 and 1640 in his *Patriotisches Archiv* and defended Hontheim's honest desire for reunion. "Yet his suggestions for a union will remain mere dreams so long as he cannot demonstrate to the fiscally minded religious Protestant princes that they will gain something in the process. A lottery of 100 abbeys would much sooner meet with their applause."[23]

Whether the plan for reunion was only of secondary importance to Febronius or whether—according to testimony by Martin Gerber—"he was convinced that everything possible had to be sacrificed to peace and Christian unity"[24] has not yet been determined. Febronius's idea of striving for reunion on the basis of a purified canon law and a reformed church constitution was encountered at the court of the Mainz electorate in 1771, contained in the theses of the barrister Betzel,[25] the canonist Benedikt Oberhauser from Fulda,[26] in the writings of Ulrich

---

[21] H. Raab, "Ad reuniendos dissidentes," 136f.

[22] *GGA* 1765, 531; see also C. W. F. Walch, "Geschichte des von Justino Febroni herausgegebenen Buches und der darüber entstandenen Streitigkeiten," *Neueste Religionsgeschichte* I (Lemgo 1771), 189–90.—Negative appraisal also by Christoph Birkmann, senior at Sankt Egidien near Nuremberg. P. Schattenmann, *Georg Adam Michel, Generalsuperintendent in Oettingen und sein gelehrter Briefwechsel* (Nuremberg 1962), 69f.

[23] F. K. v. Moser, *Patriotisches Archiv* VI (1787), 361–89; VII (1787), 193–372; *von der Kirchenvereinigung. Ein Bedenken des Herrn Abts Jerusalem. Mit einem Vorbericht* (n. p., 1772), 42.

[24] Gerbert to Petrus Böhm in Fulda, 6 March 1780 (G. Pfeilschifter, *Korrespondenz* II, 500).

[25] H. Raab, "Ad reuniendos dissidentes," 138.

[26] Oberhauser, an extreme episcopalist who had himself celebrated as "malleus Ultramontanorum" on his headstone, was, however, "not prepared, as were some Fulda

Mayr from Kaisheim, and in the programmatic essay on reunion by Beda Mayr from Donauwörth.[27] The elector of Trier, Clemens Wenzeslaus, repeatedly demonstrating his concern for the elimination of the Utrecht schism in his talks with the Cologne nuncios, nonetheless condemned Mayr's "scrittura scandalose sul pretesto della reunione coi Protestanti" in his capacity as bishop of Augsburg. Yet shortly thereafter in his famous pastoral letter of 1780, coauthored by Johann Michael Sailer, he called the return of those "separated from the faith into the one sheeps' pen of Christ" one of the most pressing concerns.[28] But in this pastoral letter he is far from paving the way for reunion by dogmatic compromise or invoking Febronian or Jansenist ideas. "The doctrine of the Church has always been one and the same," and the Pope as Christ's deputy has always been charged with the unity of the Church and the purity of the doctrine. At the same time, the religious journals of the ex-Jesuit Hermann Goldhagen and the schoolteacher Johann Kaspar Mülle of Mainz, and also the enlightened journal of the Benedictine monks of Banz had reservations regarding reunification. Heretofore they had invariably published favorable and detailed reports about the literature of reunion, but now they joined Martin Gerbert of Sankt Blasien in the conclusion that a reunification of the Churches would be possible only by a return to the Catholic Church. All three parts were to be either Catholic or eternally separated.[29]

Among the numerous more or less successful attempts at reunion in the last third of the eighteenth century the Fulda Plan was the best known and also the strangest one. In 1768 the correspondence concerning a particular case of conversion to the Catholic Church between the Fulda Benedictine Karl von Piesport and Rudolph Wedekind, a professor in Göttingen and parish priest at the Church of Our Lady, suggested an association "to unite the warring factions of the faith."[30] Although Piesport as an episcopalist was ready "in good conscience" to give in on the issue of papal infallibility and almost implored Wedekind to "Let us conciliate; let us compromise," the latter suggested breaking

---

Benedictines two decades later, to make even seeming concessions at the expense of the true elements of faith" (W. A. Mühl, *Die Aufklärung an der Universität Fulda mit besonderer Berücksichtigung der philosophischen und juristischen Fakultät* [1734–1805] [Fulda 1961], 49). The same holds true for the Salzburg canonist Gregor Zallwein, a leading episcopalist of the Church of the Empire.

[27] J. Hörmann, *Beda Mayr*; J. Beumer, *Auf dem Wege zur christlichen Einheit*, 203f.

[28] The Augsburg pastoral letter was translated into French, Italian, and Latin. In 1843 it appeared again under the title *Beweise der wahren Kirche* (Regensburg).

[29] W. Forster, "Die kirchliche Aufklärung bei den Benediktinern der Abtei Banz im Spiegel ihrer von 1772–1798 herausgegebenen Zeitschrift," *SM* 64 (1952), 184f.

[30] Piespont to Wedekind, 1768 (Mühl, *Aufklärung in Fulda,* 70, n. 41).

off this fruitless exchange because "Doctrine, rationality and church history have to take precedence over the Pope and the council."[31]

But a decade later the climate for discussions had become more favorable by virtue of the general mood for tolerance and the threat of the Enlightenment, which was hostile to revealed religion. The efforts to bring about reunion were no doubt partly prompted by the ferment of a "negative" union, recognizeable by the growing fear of additional schisms threatened by the abused "Protestant principle," and by growing admiration for the strength of the resistance and unity of the Catholic Church. As indicated in the introduction by a Benedictine monk from Fulda to *Aurelius Augustinus, Von der Nutzbarkeit des Glaubens* (1771), a future ideological front is discernible. A generation later Adam Müller, Carl Ludwig von Haller, and after them Ludwig von Gerlach and Carl Maria von Radowitz tried to establish this front by means of a reunion of faithful Catholics and Protestants or at least by drawing them closer together for the defense of "the most sacred properties" against revolution and radicalism.

In 1778/79 the plan for the formation of a private association emerged from the collaboration between five Benedictine monks in Fulda under the direction of Petrus Böhm and Johann Rudolph Piderit, professor at the Carolinum at Kassel. The association was to contribute to the reunion of the divided denominations. According to the statutes drawn up by Piderit,[32] a committee of twelve members—six Catholic, three Calvinist, and three Lutheran theologians—in an atmosphere of "sincerity and Christian love" were to discuss the truths of the faith, formulate the differences, and investigate the possiblities for restoring harmony.

Reservations were soon announced by Johann Schmitt, a professor of theology at Mainz. The influential Kasimir Haeffelin in Mannheim reacted negatively. His friend, the abbot and librarian Maillot de la Treille, an opponent of Febronianism who used his good connections with the ultramontanes in Alsace to firm up the ecclesiastical defense from Strasbourg to Trier against the innovations of his time, raised the alarm with nuncio Garampi in Vienna. As a result of the negative reaction by the courts of Mannheim and Mainz, the solicitation of the association in Trier, Coblenz, Cologne, and Erfurt were unsuccessful. Even

---

[31] Wedekind to Piespont, 11 November 1768 (H. Raab, "Ad reuniendos dissidentes," 134).

[32] *Einleitung und Entwurf zum Versuch einer zwischen den streitigen Theilen im Römischen Reich vorzunehmenden Religionsvereinigung von verschiedenen Katholischen und Evangelischen Personen, welche sich zu dieser Absicht in eine Gesellschaft verabredet haben* (Frankfurt and Leipzig 1781).

Spangenberg, who had provided the strongest impulses to Hontheim's reunion efforts, rejected the plan; the theologian Johann Gertz from Trier had growing doubts concerning the efficacy of such a heterogeneous association[33] and terminated his participation in January 1782. It was alleged that Stephan Alexander Würdtwein, later suffragan bishop of Worms, was recruited to take the place of the Mainz theologian Schmitt. The prince-abbot of Sankt Blasien, Martin II Gerbert, refused his participation,[34] and the enlightened Abbot Stefan Rautenstrauch from Braunau distanced himself when a negative review appeared in the Vienna *Realzeitung* and Emperor Joseph II, Kaunitz, and Cardinal Herzan did not react to the reunion project. There was hardly any need for the papal letter to Prince-Bishop Heinrich VIII of Bibra to make the efforts by the Benedictines of Fulda founder. Disregarding the instructions of their bishop, they maintained the connections with their Protestant partners. But the Lutherans and Calvinists were unable to agree on a common dogma and as a consequence news of the "Fulda Plan" stopped appearing after the fall of 1782.

In the last third of the eighteenth century a positive attitude towards reunion was furthered by the promotion of tolerance on the part of the Enlightenment and by its concept of an understanding and forgiving humanity. The differences between the denominations were to be reduced to the simple basic tenets of a natural religion with the help of an increasingly secularized education. In his *Betrachtungen über das Universum*[35] Karl Theodor von Dalberg posed the question whether the time had not come to get closer to "the original Church," to the union of the "different religious parties." Christoph von Schmidt wanted to see the controversial sermons, which had been forbidden according to the Josephinist model, in the archdioceses of Cologne and Trier replaced by "union sermons" in order to "convince the Christian people that we are one in all the essentials of Christianity."[36]

The interdenominational irenic efforts towards the end of the eighteenth century received strong impulses from the ex-Jesuit Benedikt Stattler. In his *Demonstratio catholica,* edited and published several times by his pupil Johann Michael Sailer, but primarily in his *Plan* (1781)[37] he emphatically advocated reunion; not "in the heat of disputation" but only "in love" could this goal "of common longing" be

[33] R. Reichert, *Johann Gertz,* 98f.

[34] G. Pfeilschifter, *Korrespondenz* II, 483f., 500f., 506f.; G. Richter, *Wiedervereinigung,* 27f.

[35] C. T. v. Dalberg, *Betrachtungen über das Universum* (Erfurt 1777).

[36] C. v. Schmid, *Erinnerungen aus meinem Leben* I, 6.

[37] B. Stattler, *Plan zu der allein möglichen Vereinigung der Protestanten mit der katholischen Kirche und von den Grenzen dieser Möglichkeiten* (Munich and Augsburg 1781); F. X.

achieved. Only dogma was to be obligatory, theories were to be voluntarily accepted. But Stattler did set one condition for Protestants in the case of a reunion: "humble submission under the unerring judgment of the Church in every matter of faith." Stattler's *Kanones der Union* were condemned in Rome, but the procedure and publication of the condemnation were delayed until 1796 because the bishop of Eichstätt took Stattler's part.

With Stattler's pupil Johann Michael Sailer (1751–1832) and his followers in Dillingen and Augsburg, in Switzerland and northern Germany the irenic mood reached a climax.[38] Sailer saw the way to unify the Church in emulating Christ's comprehensive self-sacrificing love. The Romantic philosopher Franz von Baader interpreted the denominational splits as a mere transitional stage on the way to a higher unity, introducing an idea into the interdenominational discussions that was pursued by Sebastian Drey and by Joseph Görres until well into the latter's Strasbourg period. Johann Nikolaus Friedrich Bauer (d. 1813) attempted to take a step in the direction of reunion with the help of "sovereign reform authority." He established a theological faculty at the University of Heidelberg consisting of nine professors of all three denominations, but in 1807 the Catholic faculty members left to join the University of Freiburg.[39] Enlightened and irenic concepts merged in the desire for reunion of Prince-Primate Karl Theodor von Dalberg, his vicar general from Constance, Ignaz Heinrich von Wessenberg, and their friends.

Political and nationalist motives played a role in the attempt by the archbishop of Besançon to glorify the coronation of Napoleon by a reunion of the denominations. The extent to which such motives were connected with the desire for reunification in Germany at the beginning of the nineteenth century, a desire fed by the Enlightenment and older roots, is shown not only by the passionate discussion of the writings of Claude Le Coz and Beaufort of the reception of the history of reunion attempts written by Mathieu Tabaraud (1808), but also by the contribution of the last abbot of Michelfeld, Maximilian Prechtl.[40] "From his

---

Haimerl, "Die irenische Beeinflussung Johann Michael Sailers durch Benedikt Stattler," *Jb. des Historischen Vereins Dillingen* 52 (1950), 78–94; H. Graßl, *Aufbruch zur Romantik. Bayerns Beitrag zur deutschen Geistesgeschichte 1765–1785* (Munich 1968), 84ff.

[38] F. W. Kantzenbach, *Johann Michael Sailer und der ökumenische Gedanke* (Nuremberg 1955).

[39] G. A. Benrath, "Drei theologische Fakultäten in Heidelberg (1805–1807) und Karl Friedrichs Unionspolitik," *Neue Heidelberger Jahrbücher* n.s. 1952/53, 85–97.

[40] M. Prechtl, *Friedensworte an die katholische und protestantische Kirche für ihre Wiedervereinigung* (Sulzbach 1810); idem, *Gutachten der Helmstedter Universität bei der einer*

personal conviction that the religious upheaval of the sixteenth century was either the immediate or secondary cause of most of the political and ecclesiastical storms, including the most recent secularization," he attempted to establish " in the religious unification of Germany the best, albeit not the only means and main conditions for forceful resistance against the nascent universal Napoleonic rule." Among the irenic efforts in the conservative Prussian camp, in the Christian Germanic circles, and elsewhere the striving for denominational unity was henceforth most intimately connected with the striving for national unity. The historian and conservative politician Heinrich Leo saw the fusion of religious reunification and national unity in the nineteenth century more distinctly than Radowitz and Diepenbrock had: "Whoever wants a German state must first have a unified strong German Church again— this has been taught by six centuries of history."[41]

---

protestantischen Prinzessin angenommenen Annahme der katholischen Religion, beleuchtet von dem Verfasser der Friedensworte (Salzburg 1815); idem, Friedensbenehmen zwischen Bossuet, Leibnitz und Molan für die Wiedervereinigung der Katholiken und Protestanten (Sulzbach 1815); cf. H. Raab, "Ad reuniendos dissidentes," 145.

[41] H.-J. Schoeps, Das andere Preußen. Konservative Gestalten und Probleme im Zeitalter Friedrich Wilhelms IV. (Honnef 1957), 199; E. Hannay, Der Gedanke der Wiedervereinigung der Konfessionen in den Anfängen der konservativen Bewegung (Düsseldorf 1936).

CHAPTER 28

Ecclesiastical Learning in the Eighteenth Century— Theology of Enlightenment and Pietism

Catholic Theology

In the history of theology the period from the middle of the seventeenth to the middle of the eighteenth century marks the decline of Scholasticism; Grabmann speaks of an epigonal period. While the achievements of earlier generations were diligently collected and promulgated in compendia and textbooks, hardly anything new was added. And yet in a broad context this period was not without its own characteristics. Even the fact that moral theology was separated from dogmatics points towards growth. The theology of the period was strongly influenced by the requirements of practical ministry. Linked to medieval confessional handbooks and not without the influence of canonist

524

tendencies, it constructed a case theory which was intended to facilitate the decisions in actual cases. To be sure, the realization of Christian faith is substantially depersonalized by this and one might well regret that such phenomena as laxism, the moral dispute over probabilism, and probabiliorism emerged. Yet behind all of it was a forceful attempt to cope with everyday problems. Moreover, the possiblity of development in the area of ethical norms is visible. Parallel to all this was the great genesis of historical research which laid foundations especially in the field of Catholic theology. Since all the facts were important to them the historiographers of the baroque compiled an immense mass of materials, but they also devised methods in the science of history which are still alive. And, lastly, the Enlightenment stimulated new branches of theological science, such as scriptural science, religious science, pastoral theology with its subcategories, liturgics, catechetics, and homiletics. It is not hard to see a common element behind all these phenomena: theological speculation decreased, but actual church life was more decisively included in theological cognition. The entire situation, moreover, opened possibilities for theological points of departure which were no longer limited to the foundations derived from antiquity or the ideas of the Middle Ages.

Speculative theology was not, of course, totally extinguished; many a name is still deserving of mention. But none can be compared with the great theologians of the Middle Ages or the Spaniards of the late sixteenth or early seventeenth century. There was still a confrontation of the old theological schools. Thomism was represented by the Benedictines of Salzburg, among them Paul Mezger (1637–1702) and Ludwig Babenstuber (1660–1715), by Dominicans such as Cardinal Vincenzo Ludovico Gotti (1664–1742), Hyacinth Drouin (1680–1740), and Bernardo Maria de Rossi (1687–1775). Among the Jesuits we must mention especially the Spanish Cardinal Álvaro Cienfuegos (1657–1739) because of his special doctrine of the sacrifice of the Mass. From 1766 to 1777 four members of the Society of Jesus, professors of the University of Würzburg, wrote a remarkable *Theologia Wirceburgensis,* with reference to positive-theological and speculative elements. Its concerns were presented almost simultaneously and in similar fashion by the Spanish Jesuit J. B. Genér (1711–81). A theology resembling Augustinianism was offered by August Reding (1625–92) of Salzburg, who later became abbot of Einsiedeln; Enrico Noris and Giovanni Laurenzio Berti (1696–1766) were the main representatives of the younger Augustinian school. The Franciscan Claude Frasien (1620–1711), as much as he based his ideas on Aristotle, was a Scotist. The Capuchin theologians generally went back to Bonaventure. Interest in Raymond Lull was also revived: Ivo Salzinger (1669–1728) suggested a new edition of his works (1721–42).[1] The most important Lullist of the century, Antonio Raymundo Pascual y Flexas (1708–91), spent some time in Mainz before continuing on to Palma di Mallorca, where he worked for some decades. From the large field of controversial theology we should single out the *Ecclesiologia* (1677) by the convert Johannes Scheffler, who also created an immortal body of religious poetry under the name of Angelus Silesius. The first apologia in German was published (1787–89) by Beda Mayr, *Verteidigung der natürlichen, christlichen und katholischen Religion nach den Bedürfnissen unserer Zeit.* The title alone demonstrates that an apologia could no longer be fulfilled merely in the fight of the denominations.

There were times when a question of moral theology excited the seventeenth century: when there was serious doubt concerning the existence of a moral law, probabilism offered the possibility of a free decision if there were probable reasons for it. A stricter view demanded *more* probable reasons (probabiliorism, tutiorism); a milder view admitted weak reasons (laxism). The systematic foundation of probabilism goes back to Bartholomaeus de Medina (1577). His views were frequently represented by Dominicans and Jesuits. De Medina and all the variations of laxism were opposed by the Jansenists, especially by Blaise Pascal (see Chaps. 3 and 6). In 1665 and 1666 Alexander VII condemned laxism, as did Innocent XI in 1679 (see Chap. 3); Alexander VIII opposed tutiorism in 1690.

Practical need alone would have prompted the growth of works in the new field of moral theology; among the many authors there were some whose works were reprinted a number of times. Unfortunately, we must limit ourselves to a mere few of them.[2] These were the moral theologies of Martin Bonacina (1624) and the Jesuit Paul Laymann (1625); the *Resolutiones morales* by the Theatine friar Antonio Diana (1629–59) offered approximately six thousand cases of law and conscience; later editions were categorized either systematically or alphabetically to facilitate their use. The Cistercian Juan Caramuel y Lobkowitz (1641) and the Jesuit Ambrosio de Escobar Mendoza (1644 and 1652) published extreme laxist views in their moral theologies and were attacked by Pascal (see Chaps. 3 and 6). The Jesuit Hermann Busenbaum's *Medulla theologiae moralis* (1645) was entirely practice-oriented, while the widely disseminated work of the Franciscan Anaklet Reiffenstuel (1692), the "classicist of practical theology," paid strict attention to the separation of law and morals. The most respected moral theologian was Alphonsus Liguori (1696–1787), whose influence en-

---

[1] On Lullism in Mainz, see A. T. Brück in *Jb. des Bistums Mainz* 4 (1949), 314–38.
[2] On the French moralists, see Chap. 6 above.

dured for a century and a half. His harmonizing *Theologia moralis* (1748) was based on Busenbaum; he was an equiprobabilist, entirely fulfilled by the idea of God's mercy; his *Homo apostolicus* (1757) is constructed primarily by the casuistic method.

The great period of emotional mysticism had passed and none had an effect like Teresa of Ávila or John of the Cross. Yet this century of religiosity, moved by various baroque forms in which a comprehensive mode of Pietism crystallized among the Protestant believers, was not without examples of a profoundly religious life and ascetic discipline. John Eudes (1601–80) and Jean Jacques Olier (1608–57) have already been mentioned (Chap. 1). The ascetic writings of the Cistercian Cardinal John Bona (1609–80), such as *De sacrificio missae* (1658) and *Cursus vitae spiritualis* (1674) were widely disseminated (Bona was also an important scholar of liturgics). Saint Louis Marie Grignion de Montfort (1673–1716), one of the great missionaries who had a broad impact, wrote the *Traité de la vraie dévotion à la Sainte Vierge*, his most profound and best known ascetic work. The writings of the Jesuit Jean-Pierre Caussade (1675–1751), such as the *Instructions spirituelles* (1741), have met with renewed interest in the twentieth century. Dominik Schramm's (1723–97) *Institutiones theologiae mysticae* (1774) attempted a bridge to Enlightenment.

The severe change in the intellectual life of the period which we designate as the "Enlightenment" (see Chap. 18)[3] could, of course, not remain without impact on the concepts of systematic theology. After 1740 Cartesian ideas and those of Leibniz, presented in the rationalistic form of Christian Wolff, whose philosophy predominated among the Protestant thinkers of the time until the arrival of Kant, were frequently though eclectically used among the Catholics as well and had to be confronted with traditional speculative theology. This was undertaken rather radically by Ulrich Weiß (1713–63) in his *Liber de emendatione intellectus humani* (1747). The Augustinian friar Eusebius Amort (1692–1775),[4] a prolific author, who was also interested in natural sciences, worked in a historicocritical manner. Using the Scriptures intensively, he combined tradition with the new and applied a simplified Scholastic method to his work. As a moral theologian he was an equiprobabilist akin to Alphonsus Liguori. As late as 1768 Simpert Schwarz-

---

[3] The appraisal of Catholic enlightenment in Germany has taken a noticeably positive turn, along with a more precise and differentiated evaluation, at the beginning of the twentieth century through the work of Sebastian Merkle; see S. Merkle, *Ausgewählte Reden und Aufsätze* (Würzburg 1965), esp. 361–441.

[4] G. Rückert, *Eusebius Amort und das bayer. Geistesleben im 18. Jh.* (Munich 1956); O. Schaffner, *Eusebius Amort 1692–1775 als Moraltheologe* (Paderborn 1962).

hueber (1727–95)[5] wrote his Thomist *Ethica;* in his *Praktisch-katholisches Religionshandbuch für nachdenkende Christen* (1784–85) he also tried to combine the old and the new, though less fortuitously than Amort. The writings of the Ingolstadt Jesuit Benedikt Stattler (1728–97),[6] the teacher of Johann Michael Sailer, are characterized by an impressive universal conception. His *Demonstratio evangelica* (1770) and *Demonstratio catholica* (1775), although stylistically ponderous, should be mentioned for their strict methodology if for no other reason. In 1788 he wrote an *Anti-Kant.* In the end he was subjected to church censorship and received little attention until recently, when he evoked renewed esteem. Engelbert Klüpfel (1733–1811), a dogmatist in Freiburg, was a pioneer in historical theology and not a rationalist in his *Institutiones theologiae dogmaticae* (1789). But there were some confirmed rationalists, such as Lorenz Isenbiehl (1744–1818; exegete and author of *Neuer Versuch über die Weissagung von Emmanuel* [1788]) and Felix Anton Blau (1754–98; a dogmatist), both of them professors in Mainz, and Franz Berg (1753–1821), a confirmed skeptic in spite of his anti-Kantian position.

By combining Kant's categorical imperative and the biblical commandment of love, Sebastian Mutschelle (1749–1800) tried to establish a new speculative moral theology. After the condemnation of Jakob Danzer (1743–96) because of his *Anleitung zur christlichen Moral* (1787), the University of Salzburg was dominated once more by Scholasticism. The exegete Thaddäus Anton Dereser (1757–1827)[7] had a broad impact with his *Erbauungsbuch für alle Christen auf alle Tage des Kirchenjahres* (1792). In 1813 the liturgist Vitus Anton Winter (1754–1814)[8] published a *Deutsches kath. ausübendes Ritual* which manifested the rationalist spirit of the time more than any other contemporary work. But there were also some effective opponents of rationalism, among them Hermann Goldhagen (1718–94), with his *Religions journal* (1776–94; edited by the professors of Mainz), and Franz Oberthür (1745–1831),[9] who was an opponent of Scholasticism but nonetheless in favor of a biblical theology. Gregor Zirkel (1762–1817), suffragan

[5] A. Teleman, *Der Benediktiner Simpert Schwarzhueber 1727–1795, Prof. in Salzburg, als Moraltheologe. Seine Beziehungen zur Moraltheologie des Protestanten Gottfried Leß, zum Salzburger Moraltheologen Jakob Dauser und Ignaz von Fellani* (Regensburg 1961).

[6] F. Scholz, *Benedikt Stattler und die Grundzüge seiner Sittlichkeitslehre* (Freiburg i. Brsg. 1957).

[7] E. Hegel, "Thaddäus Anton Dereser und sein Verhältnis zum Karmeliterorden," *JKölGV* 36/37 (1961–62), 157–72.

[8] A. Vierbach, *Die liturgischen Anschauungen des Vitus Anton Winter* (Munich 1929).

[9] O. Volk et al., *Professor Franz Oberthür. Persönlichkeit und Wrk* (Neustadt a. d. Aisch 1966).

bishop of Würzburg after 1812, who was initially a Kantian, became a representative of a positive Catholicism. *Das Wichtigste für Eltern, Lehrer und Seelsorger* (1786) by Aegidius Jais (1750–1822)[10] was the best example of sex education in the period of Enlightenment. Together with Johann Michael Sailer, Jais was instrumental in overcoming the rationalism of that period.

The departure into new fields of theological learning towards an overall consolidation of church history[11] started at the turn of the seventeenth century. It was the Maurist congregation in France whose ranks provided the most prominent personalities in the field of historical research, foremost among them Mabillon (see Chap. 6). During the eighteenth century church history continued to flourish in France. Whereas the *Selecta historiae ecclesiasticae capita* (1676–86) by the Dominican Alexander Natalis,[12] the first comprehensive church history of the modern era, was still written in a polemical and apologetical fashion, the frequently translated *Histoire ecclésiastique* (1691–1720) by the secular priest Claude Fleury (1640–1723) was influenced by Mabillon and Tillemont, showing close attention to the sources and a pleasant style. Although it had a broad effect, it also provoked criticism because of its Gallican tendencies. While these church histories were written, work continued on the sources. The Jesuit Philippe Labbé (1607–67) edited the *Sacrosancta Concilia* (1671–72), providing it with valuable annotations. He was followed by his fellow monk Jean Hardouin (1646–1729), whose *Conciliorum collectio regia maxima* (1714–15) represented a more reliable edition than that of Mansi. Jacques Goar (1601–53) was among the first to establish Byzantinistics, a field to which Charles Dufresne Sieur Du Cange (1610–88) also dedicated himself. An indispensable contribution to the field of church history is Du Cange's *Glossarium ad scriptores mediae et infimae latinitatis* (1678). In 1715–16 the cleric Eusèbe Renaudot (1648–1720) published his *Liturgiarum Orientalium Collectio*. Especially prominent among the Maurists were Gabriel Gerberon (1628–1711), who suggested the controversial edition of Saint Augustine; and Achery's and Mabillon's pupil Edmond Martène (1654–1739) with his *Commentar zur Regel des heiligen Benedikt* (1690) and his work in liturgics. In the field of exegesis there were Augustin Calmet's (1672–1757) *Dictionaire historique . . . de la Bible* (1719) and Pierre Sabatier's (1683–1742) fundamental work on the *Vetus Latina, Bibliorum sacrorum versiones antiquae* (1743–49). In the

---

[10] H. Dussler, "P. Aegidius Jais von Benediktbeuren 1750–1822," *SM* 69 (1958), 214–35.

[11] For the historical view, see Chap. 19.

[12] A. Hänggi, *Der Kirchenhistoriker Natalis Alexander* (Fribourg 1955).

area of patristics Pierre Coustant (1654–1721) published an edition of Hilarius (1693); Remy Ceillier (1688–1761)[13] created a comprehensive *Histoire générale des auteurs sacrés et ecclésiastiques* (1729–63).

In the Netherlands Daniel Papebroch (1628–1714) persisted in his work on the *Acta sanctorum* of Johannes Bollandus, which differentiated between the older and newer sources. Papebroch established a methodology for hagiography and very strict rules for paleography, too strict in fact to be maintained. The Augustinian Hermit Christian Lupus (1612–81) of Louvain occupied himself with the provincial councils in his *Synodorum Generalium ac Provincialism decreta et canones* (1665). The Maurists had a profound influence on the scholarly efforts of the Benedictines in southern Germany. The first great mediator was Bernhard Pez[14] (1683–1735) of Melk, who had the help of his brother Hieronymus (1685–1762). His fundamental works are *Bibliotheca Benedictino-Mauriana* (1716) and *Bibliotheca ascetica antiquo-nova* (1721–29). Historically more important were the efforts of the abbot of Göttweig, Gottfried Bessel (1672–1749); his prodromus on the *Chronicon Gottwicense* (1732) represents a first general German diplomatics. In collaboration with Pez and Bessel, Magnoald Ziegelbauer (1689–1750)[15] of Zwiefalten worked on a source edition for the history of the Benedictine order. Anselm Desing (1699–1772), later the abbot of Ensdorf, worked in the spirit of the Maurists at the University of Salzburg, where Frobenius Forster (1709–1791) was one of his colleagues. As the abbot of Sankt Emmeram in Regensburg, Forster led this monastery to a high scholarly level; his edition of Alcuin (1777) won acclaim throughout Europe. Marquart Herrgott (1694–1762) visited the Maurists for personal instruction; after his *Vetus disciplina Monastica* (1726) he directed his efforts to the history of the archdynasty of Austria. Through him Sankt Blasien became a center of historical studies. Martin Gerbert (1720–93), abbot after 1764, became the most prominent of this group of Benedictines from the Black Forest through his works in liturgics and the history of music; his efforts are indispensable even today: *Iter alemannicum* (1765), *De cantu et musica sacra* (1774), *Monumenta veteris liturgicae Alemanniae* (1777–79) and *Scriptores ecclesiastici de musica sacra* (1784). His most important undertaking was to organize the edition of a *Germania sacra*. With it he continued the

[13] J. Villerot-Reboul, "Dom Remi Ceillier et le prieur de Flavigny-sur-Moselle 1733–61," *AE* (1959), 5e sér., X, 161–72.

[14] H. Hantsch, "Bernhard Pez und Abt Berthold Dietmayr," *MIÖG* 71 (1963), 128–39; G. Heer, "Bernhard Pez von Melk OSB (1683–1735) in seinen Beziehungen zu den Schweizer Klöstern," *Festschr. Vasella* (Fribourg 1964), 403–55.

[15] I. Stricher, "Les rétractions du mariologue bénédictin Dom Magnoald Ziegelbauer," *EThL* 35 (1959), 59–76.

effort of the Vienna Jesuit Markus Hansiz (1683–1766; *Germania sacra* [1727–58]), which had also been pursued by the Cologne Jesuit Joseph Hartzheim (1694–1762) in the field of the councils by his edition of the *Concilia Germaniae* (1759–63). The eight volumes of the Sankt Blasien *Germania sacra* appeared from 1790 to 1803;[16] this promising endeavor was abruptly ended by secularization. In the geographical area of the Rhine we should mention Johann Friedrich Schannat (1683–39) from Luxemburg, who maintained close connections with the Maurists and provided preliminary work for the *Concilia Germaniae,* and, lastly, Stephan Alexander Würdtwein (1722–96),[17] who furnished access to an abundance of source material in his two series of *Subsidia diplomatica.*

The new discipline of pastoral theology, at first also called practical theology—pastoral theology taking over some practical fields hitherto served by moral theology—was not founded extensively on actual theological ideas. Instead it was shaped by the image of man and the world on the basis of common sense using the Bible and the Fathers "for useful remarks concerning the unselfish execution of the office of a minister." It was lacking a pneumatic concept of the Church. Sailer was the one who finally resorted to biblical foundations, seeking genuine Christocentricity. In fact, the first pastoral theologies (by F. C. Pitroff [1778], Franz Giftschütz [1785], Carl Schwarzel [1799], Dominik Gollowitz [1803], A. Reichenberger, and M. Fingerlos [1805]) were devoid of actual theology. Even the basic idea of a shepherd confronted by a herd he is to lead was inadequate, especially so if the minister was considered merely as a "servant of religion" and the pastoral as a description of the duties of his office. The weaknesses in this initial attempt were not overcome until the Tübingen school developed its more genuine concept of the Church (Anton Graf, 1841).

The individual disciplines in the pastoral field did not arrive at a truly scientific theology either. The oldest, liturgics, had been blessed with an abundance of sources since the seventeenth century, but did not evaluate them correspondingly. Catechetics, which proceeded radically against the existing method of memorization in Christology, was not provided with a theological foundation until the work of Johann Joseph Augustin Gruber (1832), in spite of the relatively good start by Johann Ignaz von Felbiger (1724–88; in 1767 he also published the first Catholic school Bible in German) and Michael Ignaz Schmidt (1736–94, *Methodus tradendi prima elementa religionis . . .* [1769]). In the field of homiletics the ex-Jesuit Ignaz Wurz (1727–84) became the most

---

[16] Another volume was printed in 1862.
[17] H. Raab, "Christian Frh. v. Eberstein und Stephan Alex. Würdtwein," *AMrhKG* (1955) 378–87.

prominent scholar in the German language with his *Anleitung zur geistlichen Beredsamkeit* (Vienna 1775); he based his approach entirely on the great French forerunners such as Bossuet, Bourdaloue, Massillon, and de la Rue. But homiletics did not become a science until the nineteenth century.

For a time the eighteenth century also promulgated the concept of pastoral medicine (M. A. Alberti, 1732 [Halle] and G. M. Matthiae, 1734 [Göttingen] among the Protestants; F. E. Cangiamilia, 1751 [Milan] among the Catholics). But towards the end of the century it was replaced by the concept of a *medicina ruralis* which provided for the training of rural clerics to help out as doctors where none were available.

Scholarship in Italy

While the great speculative minds in post-Tridentine theology were in Spain, the first steps in historical theology were taken in Italy. The challenge of the Magdeburg centurists was answered by Baronius and continued in Italy as well by Raynald and Laderchi. The Venetian Sarpi turned his attention to the most recent events; his history of the Council of Trent is a very sober account, yet full of antipapal tendencies which Pallavicino tried to counter. The first Christian archeologist worked in Bosio; Lippomani created a prodromus of the *Acta sanctorum.* Lucas Wadding (1588–1657), an Irish Franciscan who lived in Rome for forty years, created the first scholarly history of the religious orders in his *Annales* (1627–54) and the *Scriptores Ordinis Minorum* (1650). The *Italia sacra* (1644–62) by the Cistercian Ferdinando Ughelli (1594–1670), categorized by dioceses, was the first church history of its kind and a model for the *Gallia christiana* and Gerbert's *Germania sacra.* This form of historiography is an especially impressive testimony of the importance ascribed to the history of the institutions by Catholic church historiography. Cardinal Enrico Noris, an Augustinian Hermit, (1631–1704) is considered the father of the younger Augustinian school. Not only was he a historian, but he was also very much involved in the emotional issues of his time concerning the interpretation of the Augustinian doctrine of grace. Yet his *Historica Pelagiana* (1673) is a superior achievement in the history of dogmatics. The Theatine Cardinal Joseph Maria Tomasi (1649–1714) published comprehensive collections of sources in the field of patristics and the history of liturgics: the *Codices Sacramentorum* (1680), *Responsalia et Antiphonaria* (1686), *Antiqui libri Missarum* (1691), and *Institutiones theologicae antiquorum Patrum* (1709–12). The Syrian Josef Simonius Assemani (1687–1768) provided productive access to the Christian East; he made the Vatican a reservoir of Eastern sources and unlocked these treasures in his *Bib-*

liotheca Orientalis (1719–28) and the *Bibliotheca juris Orientalis* (1762–66). Equally important was his edition of Ephraim (1732–46). Ludovico Antonio Muratori (1672–1750)[18] enjoyed high esteem, and not only in the area of historiography. His publication of sources for the history of the Italian Middle Ages (*Rerum italicarum scriptores* [1723–51] and *Antiquitates italici medii aevi* [1738–43]) is as indispensable for Italy as the *Monumenta Germaniae Historica* started a hundred years later is for Germany. The brothers Pietro (1698–1769) and Girolamo (1702–81) Ballerini published the works of Leo the Great (1753–57). The learned canonist Prosper Lambertini (1675–1758), who occupied the papal throne as Benedict XIV and liked to encourage scholarly endeavors, had arrived at the themes for his two main works from his own practice: in his role as the *Promotor fidei* in the canonization procedures on *De servorum Dei beatificatione* (1734–38) and as archbishop of Bologna on *De Synodo diocesana* (1755). The versatile Scipio Maffei (1675–1755) edited the works of Hilarius. In Guiseppe Bianchini we again encounter an editor of liturgical sources: in 1735 he edited the *Sacramentarium Leonianum;* in his *Evangeliarium quadruplex* (1749) he supplemented Sabatier's work on the *Itala.* The canonist Lucius Ferraris (d. 1763) created a popular lexicon *Prompta bibliotheca canonica* (1746). The Dominican Cardinal Guiseppe Agostino Orsi (1692–1761) presented a comprehensive history of the Church for the first six centuries in his *Istoria ecclesiastica* (1747–62). Giovanni Domenico Mansi joined the ranks of the great editors; his collection of the councils in two series (1748–52 and 1759–98) is indispensable even today. The Dominican Thomas M. Mamachi (1713–92) pioneered the investigation of Christian antiquity by his *Origines et antiquitates christianae* (1749–55), but he also initiated work on the history of the orders in his *Annales Ordinis Praedicatorum* (1756). Joseph Alois (1710–82), one of the two younger Assemanis, edited the *Codex liturgicus ecclesiae universae* (1749–66), while Stefan Evodius (1711–82) and his uncle edited the Vatican manuscript catalog (1756–59). The Jesuit Francesco Antonio Zaccaria (1714–92), also well versed in archaeology, wrote a *Storia letteraria d'Italia* (1750–59), as did his fellow religious Girolamo Tiraboschi (1731–94) twenty years later with his *Storia della letteratura italiana,* which was at the same time a cultural history. We should not leave unmentioned the patient work of the high-minded prefect of the Vatican archives, Cardinal Guiseppe Garampi, whose 124 volumes of *Schedulae* are still making the treasures of these archives available. If we add Giambattista Vico (Chap. 18), who has to be considered the greatest philosophical historian of the century, we can safely say that the

---

[18] S. Bertelli, *Erudizione e storia in Ludovico Antonio Muratori* (Naples 1960).

achievements of Italy can hold their own next to the luminescence of France, which was so important for the development of the science of history. Italy excelled especially through the broad scope of its aspects.[19]

Jansenism in Italy; The Synod of Pistoia, 1786

While Italy developed much initiative of its own, especially in the area of historical theology, Jansenism—although fairly widespread in Italy—received its impulses from outside, from France and Utrecht. But only small groups of the educated were open to its ideas, often with characteristic differences in the individual cities, as in papal Rome, for instance, with its representatives of Augustinian thought expressing sharp anti-Jesuit tendencies, in Pavia (Pietro Tamburini), Genoa (Vincenzo Palmieri), Turin, Milan, Venice and Naples. Jansenism was given a special characteristic in a surprising late phase in Habsburg Tuscany, where it was combined with Gallican and regalist concepts and engaged in provocative activities. Grand Duke Peter Leopold (1765–90), the younger brother of Emperor Joseph II and his successor to the imperial throne as Leopold II (1790–1792), initiated reforms similar to those of his brother in the administration, economy, the universities, and penal law. He paid particular attention to the ecclesiastical realm, where he was assisted by the Jansenist Scipione de' Ricci. In 1780 he procured for de' Ricci the conjoined bishoprics of Prato and Pistoia so that there was now a bishop who would support the reforms vigorously. These rested on a meager theological fundament, which might have been found in Quesnel's works, disproportionately affecting the practical aspects: abolition of the Inquisition, the concentration of Mass stipends for the benefit of poor priests, the equalization of benefices, parish bankruptcy, the residence obligation for parish priests, the study in episcopal seminaries instead of monastic schools, the obligation to give sermons, education of the youth, the translation of the missal, Communion during Mass, reform of the breviary, revision of the hagiographies, a minimum age of twenty-four for profession, rejection of private Masses, of the Sacred Heart cult, indulgences, exercises, and the popular mission, but on the other hand strengthening the idea of the parish. The original Church was perceived as a model, the infallibility of the Church was to rest on the totality of the faithful and not on the papacy; the jurisdiction of the bishops was held to be derived from Jesus himself. Pertinent articles were passed on 18 September 1786 by a diocesan

---

[19] For an interpretive church history in Italy, see A. Noger-Weidner, *Die Aufklärung in Oberitalien* (Munich 1957).

synod in Pistoia. The acts of the synod were edited immediately and distributed internationally. But only three additional Tuscan priests embraced these same principles, so that the overwhelming majority of the national synod convened in Florence in 1787 reacted negatively. Resistance among the population was also strong. When the grand duke left, the reforms were quickly terminated and Ricci had to resign his bishopric in 1791. In his bull *Auctorem fidei,* dated 28 August 1794, Pius VI condemned, in varying degrees, eighty-five of the theses established at the synod. Ricci submitted in 1805. In spite of the rapid victory by the papacy over this last outgrowth of Jansenism, the significance of this movement especially for Italy is today seen in a new light: in this totally Catholic country it paved the way for the *Risorgimento,* in which many became accustomed—in spite of an anticurial attitude—to seriously seeking religious modes which seemed to be more Catholic than those proclaimed by the Curia.

Protestant Theology

After the Church was deprived of its educational function, Protestant theology and through it the universities gained a profound importance which can only be briefly discussed within the framework of this book (see especially the standard work by E. Hirsch). It was initially shaped by the old Protestant orthodoxy which in both of its currents, the Lutheran and Reformed, overcame Luther's move away from philosophy. Following Melanchthon's example, Aristotle again was made the basis for ideas; this made possible many lateral connections to Thomas and also Suárez. The directional disputes and the canonization of the reformers notwithstanding, the importance of the Holy Scripture was stressed if only through the consolidation of the concept of verbal inspiration in an attempt to elevate the Scripture as opposed to tradition. At the same time the analytical method applied since Gerhard (1582–1637) gave greater weight to systematic thought relative to the Scriptures. In addition, such concepts as federal theology (Coccius) or the theology of the Kingdom of God directed attention from the individual word of the Scripture to the total meaning of divine revelation and divine mercy. In addition there was a growing appreciation of natural theology. The security of orthodoxy was shaken by two intellectual movements: Pietism and the Enlightenment. Basic to the latter was the philosophical development in England through which the so-called deism originated. While its most prominent representatives fought against the traditional Church and its doctrine, they adhered to the unity of rationalism and revelation. But their meaning was reduced to some basic truths. By this, Herbert of Cherbury hoped for a new foundation of the faith, which by that time he viewed from an exclusively anthropological standpoint. In his moderate theological rationalism Locke still recognized the function of Jesus as the messiah and accepted verification through miracles as proof of divine revelation. To him revelation was not irrational but suprarational, sharpening the vision. Locke especially established the right of the individual to think and to act for himself. Christianity in many ways became a matter of ethics for him. An aggressive deism was advocated by John Toland, who attacked the canon of the Scripture and saw the proof of the revelation not in miracles but rather in the rational nature of its content. In this he was followed by Anthony Collins, Thomas Woolston, and the most mature of the deists, Matthew Tindal (1730), for whom revelation was the promulgation of natural religion. The deist "storm flood" (Hirsch) triggered sharp reactions. But with the best of its representatives, Samuel Clarke and Joseph Butler, these could emanate only from the basis of a rational supranaturalism. David Hume criticized the security of deism as well. But its impact was greater in France and Germany than in its place of origin (see Chap. 18).

In Germany a transitional theology (Baumgarten, Buddeus, Mosheim, et al.), adhering to the existing foundations, began to stress their moral-practical aspects. For many the philosophy presented by Wolff became an important base. Also gaining in importance was the physicotheology first pronounced by the Englishman Robert Boyle. In it the work of God within all of creation is theologically formulated—an attempt to stop the separation of the temporal world from theological thought brought about by Copernicus. Very much under the influence of the Enlightenment were the so-called neologists (Ernesti, Spalding, et al.). Faith and religion were separated from theology (Semler), the Bible and dogma distinguished from one other. The Scripture was perceived as a human-historical testimony of the revelation, important wherever it serves the promotion of spirituality. Michaelis (d. 1791) advocated an explanation of the Bible free of dogma, paving the way for a historicocritical treatment of the Bible. Christian faith was reduced to those elements considered most essential, retaining recognition of the revelation and the miracles. Denominational polemics, hitherto undertaken zealously, began to recede.

Towards the end of the eighteenth century an extreme rationalism among some of the representatives of Protestant theology gained ground. The radical biblical critic Reimarus became especially well known through G. E. Lessing's defense of him.[20] In his defense of

---

[20] Beginning in 1774 Lessing participated in the theological dispute. He considered revelation to go beyond nature; yet the Bible is not revelation, but acknowledgment of

natural religion Lessing himself dissolved the belief in the revelation and the miracles so that the dogmatic foundations were lost and the Fall and redemption as facts of salvation disappeared from view. But revelation for him goes beyond nature; the Bible does not represent revelation but instead the profession of revelation, which can be perceived ever more clearly in God's work according to the *Erziehung des Menschenge-schlechtes.* A borderline case was Bahrdt, to whom Christianity appeared as mere fraud on a large scale.

Pietism, while definitely connected with the Enlightenment, was more effective in Protestant theology and spirituality by virtue of the fact that it was located overwhelmingly within the Church. It originated with P. I. Spener (1635–1705) and his main work, the *Pia Desideria* (1675). Following its publication, the orthodoxy and church administrations were subjected to increasing criticism by advocates of an individual religion on the basis of the inner self. The fact that subjectivity enhanced in Pietism did not contradict social efficacy and instead substantially furthered it was shown by Spener's pupil A. H. Francke (1663–1727), who made Halle a center of Pietism. His "endowed institutions," among them an orphanage and school, and his involvement with the Christian mission in India and the diaspora ministry characterized his life's work. The same missionary spirit inspired N. L. Zinzendorf (1700–1760), who came from the Halle group of Pietists and founded the Herrnhut Brotherhood in 1722, an independent community, yet following the Augsburg Confession. More radical than Zinzendorf's ecclesiology (the churches as "tropes") was the historical concept of the Church of G. Arnold (see below). Eighteenth-century Pietism continued in the "revival movement." The reformed Pietism stems from seventeenth-century Puritanism and developed its own communities in the Netherlands. G. Tersteegen (1697–1769) wrote his hymns and sermons in the area of the lower Rhine.[21]

The development of Protestant church history proceeded—while not exclusively yet most vigorously—in the German domain. It placed less emphasis on creating new methods, establishing source criticism, or providing an abundance of material than the Catholic side, concentrating instead on new points of departure for the total conception. The concept of decline as a basis of church history which had governed the

---

revelation; Christianity, he maintained, is older than the Bible. His special concern was to recognize the workings of God towards the education of mankind (see Chap. 19).

[21] A. Ritschl, *Gesch. des Pietismus,* 3 vols. (Bonn 1880–86); H. Bornkamm, *Mystik, Spiritualismus und die Anfänge des Pietismus im Luthertum* (Giessen 1926); M. Beyer-Frölich, ed., *Pietismus und Rationalismus* (Leipzig 1933); O. Söhngen, ed., *Die bleibende Bedeutung des Pietismus* (Berlin 1960).

Magdeburg centurists was, of course, dominant also among the Baptists and in all of mystical spiritualism and was capable of intensification to the extent that all Churches, even the Protestant ones, resembled nothing short of the iniquitous Babel. The *Summarium* (1697) by the Old Orthodox Adam Rechenberg, too, is still characterized by the theory of decline, with the difference that it is turned into the opposite by the Reformation. The *Unpartheische Kirchen- und Ketzerhistorie* (1699) by the Pietist Gottfried Arnold achieved great importance. Carefully following the sources, this work deinstitutionalizes the history of the Church and, above all, deals with the question of Christian faith through rebirth. The shape of all givens is seen as being in constant motion. His basic ideas made it possible for the concept of history to be viewed as a history of the forming of man. In 1726 Johann Lorenz von Mosheim attempted a "pragmatic," that is an undogmatic factual presentation, of church history, taking it out of the context of theology. In accordance with enlightened concepts, Johann Salomo Semler applied the idea of progress to church history (1667–69), while the rationalistic Ludwig Spittler wrote his church history (1782) much like the history of a state, radically secularized. Highly influential works were written by the rationalist supernaturalists Johann Matthias Schöckh (1768–1812; forty-five volumes, also used extensively at Catholic universities) and Gottlieb Jakob Planck (1803–09).

The first attempts in the direction of dogmatic history led to several treatments of this topic around 1800. Other new theological disciplines owe their consolidation to the Enlightenment. Among them are the denominational studies (especially by Planck in 1796) and biblical theology, which was given an important impetus by the demand of Philipp Gabler (1787) to pay attention to the development of biblical ideas. Biblical studies overall received its earliest impulses in the field of the Old Testament (by the Oratorian Richard Simon in 1678). Regarding introductory studies we should mention Michaelis (1750). Semler's canonical history (1771–75) became one of the fundamental works in its field.

An assessment of Protestant theology in this period (which cannot be given in this framework) will have to take into consideration the fact that—platitudes aside, which exist in abundance within contemporary Catholic, conservative, and enlightened theology—an honest attempt was made to prevent Christian faith and modern rationality from being split apart.

Catholic Universities

After their auspicious start in the thirteenth century the history of the universities is usually viewed in terms of a productive revival by the spirit of humanism and a flourishing in Spain followed by a long period of sterility until another upswing occurred in the nineteenth century. The fact that in the meantime the universities underwent a development of their own is most often not taken into account. In accordance with the denominational character of the period they had been founded or revived by the princes or bishops with a clear predetermination of their purpose. Most of them were therefore caught up in the fight between the denominations, whether they were newly founded or not. This held true for the Protestant universities (the Saxon universities of Wittenberg and Leipzig, the Palatine university in Heidelberg, the one of Württemberg in Tübingen or the Swiss one in Basel, the new foundation by Philipp von Hesse in Marburg (1527), which was reformed in 1605, whereupon Hesse-Darmstadt established a Lutheran university in Gießen, and the university founded by Calvin in Geneva in 1559), as well as for the Catholic universities (the Austrian universities in Vienna and Freiburg, the Bavarian one in Ingolstadt, the Belgian university in Louvain, the episcopal ones in Trier and Mainz, and the municipal university in Cologne).

Catholic foundations and revivals were generally undertaken in such a way that the new teaching order, the Society of Jesus, (which was very effective) was not only given a large part if not all of the chairs of the theological faculty, but also those of the philosophical faculty, for it was here that the basic education of all the students took place even if they chose one of the "higher" courses of study in theology, law, or medicine. A university was often started with merely philosophy and theology and supplemented by the other two faculties only after decades or much longer. Such faculty assignments to the Jesuits had been practiced since the middle of the sixteenth century, the first in 1548 in Ingolstadt, 1551 in Vienna (initially with very few chairs and a good many more in 1623), 1561 in Trier, and the year after in Mainz. Jesuits were called to the university in Dillingen in 1563 after its establishment by the bishop of Augsburg in 1551. While Dillingen achieved an importance far beyond the borders of the bishopric, it was eventually outpaced by Ingolstadt. The university in Olmütz, founded by the bishop there in 1581, had a clear counterreformational purpose from the start, as did the Austrian university of Graz (1585), which gained significance for Carinthia and had an impact even in Belgium and Poland. From their inception both universities had Jesuit professors. For the bishop of Würzburg, Julius Echter von Mespelbrunn, who was not always in agreement with the Jesuits, there was no question as to who the professors would be when he established his university in 1582. The same choice prevailed when the universities of Paderborn (1614) and Osnabrück (1629) were founded. The latter was initially spared by the war but closed four years later when the fortunes of war turned. In 1620 the Austrian sovereign had also brought the Jesuits to the university of Freiburg in the Black Forest, granting them the philosophical faculty and half of the chairs in theology. Jesuits were installed in Prague when the sovereign power obtained jurisdiction over the university, which had been Protestant until then. Another Austrian university where the Jesuit order, aspiring to monopoly over the schools, was used as faculty opened in Innsbruck in 1669. Finally, the Jesuit school in Breslau, in existence since 1635, was given university status in 1702. In Erfurt, a university of the Mainz electorate, which had to admit Protestant faculty as well, only a single chair was reserved for the Jesuits. When the Wittelsbach Pfalz-Neuburg line took over the Palatinate in 1685, it was unable to change the Reformed denomination of the land but actively favored Catholicism. The University of Heidelberg, too, was no exception. Jesuits were represented on the faculty since 1706 and Catholic theology was taught along with the Calvinist brand. Only a few Catholic universities were without Jesuits: Cologne, which nonetheless maintained a definite conservative position, and Louvain, where the disputes involving Jansenism were especially vehement and episcopalism was represented prominently by van Espen. The episcopal university in Salzburg (1617) had a character of its own; it was given to the Benedictine order, which made its best people from the southern German monasteries available as professors for the university and, in fact, had a good many of its young monks educated there. Thomistic and canonical subjects were taught extremely well there, as was history as early as the seventeenth century. In 1734 when the abbot of Fulda founded a new university and split the faculty into equal parts between Benedictines and Jesuits, the resulting tensions showed how little the two factions had in common.

But in the meantime the intellectual climate had changed, leaving the rigid system of the Jesuits, who were still following the unchanged *ratio studiorum* of 1599, out of tune. The demand for the introduction of history, a field in whose research the Benedictine order as well as the Jesuits had excelled and which had been taught at the Protestant universities for a long time, could no longer be rejected. Since the chairs of philosophy were for the most part held by Jesuits, they had to occupy themselves with history whether they wanted to or not. Also important was the acceptance of new problems in the natural sciences and practical experimental methods. It took some time to overcome the concept that no new knowledge was possible beyond Aristotle. But finally, around the middle of the century, sufficient strides were made especially in the Jesuit order. Jesuits even became leaders in the field of astronomy. Clinging to the Aristotelian-Thomistic philosophy—although the latter

540

had already been modified to some degree by Suárez and subsequently by Gregory of Valencia—constituted the one great obstacle to Cartesian ideas and, more so, to dealing with the philosophy of Leibniz and Wolff. But by around 1740 it was abundantly clear that stubborn adherence to outmoded tradition was no longer feasible. The initial resort was to a sort of eclecticism until—another thirty years later—the modern ideas achieved dominance. And yet around the mid 1750s Bertold Hauser (Dillingen) attempted to obtain a world view by means of Scholastic principles, as did (although in a different fashion) Joseph Mangold (Ingolstadt). Benedikt Sattler, the teacher of Sailer, made the most significant effort to incorporate Leibniz and Wolff. The practice by the Society of Jesus of transferring their members in quick succession from one university, college, or seminary to another and in medieval fashion to consider the lecturing of philosophy as a mere transitional stage for one's own educational process long constituted the most serious obstacle to the development of significant scholars in any individual subject. The training of specialists, attempted in Würzburg in 1731, was initially possible in law and medicine only.

In the last few years prior to the great turn of events marked by the French Revolution German bishops succeeded in three cases in opening a university in their dioceses: when the Jesuit order was suppressed in 1773, the two faculties established by that order in 1648 were expanded into a university. In 1780 the extraordinary Vicar General Franz von Fürstenberg opened a university in Münster which was characterized by the open mind and profoundly religious spirit of its initiator. The endowment of an academy in Bonn (1777), the residence of the Cologne archbishop, which was elevated to the rank of a university in 1786, was clearly undertaken with the thought in mind of training capable civil servants, a deviation of purpose influenced by the Enlightenment.

The universities, including those in the episcopal territories, were turned more and more into territorial universities, obliged to serve the training of civil servants, an area in which the clergy serving the interests of a temporal state were also increasingly involved. The most telling sign of this situation was the Theresian-Josephinist university reform which changed them completely from freely endowed into state institutions. At that point all applicants for a parish in the Austrian territories were obliged to pass a full course of theological studies, documented in detail and followed by an examination. Josephinism extended these rules to the regular clergy as well, simultaneously abolishing formal study within the monasteries. Everyone had to study at the universities, where they were installed at the newly established general seminaries. But these did not last long (1783–90). The content of theological studies was enriched considerably. Up to that point dogmatics and, beginning in the seventeenth century, the case study of morals, controversial theology, and the Holy Scripture had been taught. The Rautenstrauch curriculum[22] of the Austrian government (1774) expanded scriptural study by introducing Oriental languages and, as new courses, church history (including patristics) and the pastoral. Canon law was of course taught only in accordance with the laws of the established Church. This curriculum with its attention to biblical, historical, and practical subjects prevailed in the entire German-speaking area and its basic structure has been retained until the present day. The method of teaching also changed. The tedious method of dictation was changed to the use of textbooks, at times even Protestant ones wherever Catholic books were not yet available. The language of instruction was generally changed from the traditional Latin to German. Here and there the strict denominationalism of the universities, which had never prevailed in Erfurt and Heidelberg, was relaxed. After 1746 there were Protestant students in Mainz (and Würzburg) and, following the Mainz university reform of 1784 by the elector Friedrich Karl von Erthal (under the curator Benzel-Sternau[23]), there were also Protestant professors there. This was the case also in Freiburg after the toleration edict of Joseph II.

This express form of a state university was strongest in the University of Halle, founded in 1694. The University of Göttingen, opened in 1737, incorporated the spirit of the future (Chap. 18). At that university it was possible to develop the ideal of a free pursuit of learning, unfettered by regulations and particular purposes, where learning was governed by the determination of truth and no longer tied to any tradition. Many impulses for a more or less radical "Enlightenment" emanated from Göttingen which had some impact on Catholic universities as well. A new spirit frequently manifested itself in journals such as the decidedly enlightened *Religions journal* (Mainz), *Der Freimütige* (Freiburg), the moderate *Journal von und für Deutschland* (Fulda), and the *Mainzer Monatsschrift*. Around 1790 Kantian philosophy was frequently advocated at universities such as Fulda, Bamberg, and Heidelberg. The terror of the Revolution provoked countermovements with measures taken against overly rationalistic professors. Best known are the Dillingen events, actions against Sailer and Zimmer; similar inci-

---

[22] J. Müller, *Der pastoraltheologisch-didaktische Ansatz in Franz Stephan Rautenstrauchs "Entwurf zur Einrichtung der theologischen Schulen"* (Vienna 1969; biblio.), Beda Franz Menzel, *Abt. Franz Stephan Rautenstrauch von Brevna-Braunau. Herkunft, Umwelt und Wirkungskreis* (Königstein/Taunus 1969).
[23] H. W. Jung, *Anselm Franz von Benzel im Dienst der Kurfürsten von Mainz* (Wiesbaden 1966).

dents occurred in Mainz and also in Freiburg. A highly respected form of open-minded university life succeeded in Würzburg under the dynamic promotion by Prince-Bishop Franz Ludwig von Erthal.

Academies

While the universities through their transformation into state institutions were ever more concentrated on the training of civil servants, (in Germany this included the clergy), new associations, the academies, were formed to promote research. Such relatively loose associations had already existed in the Italian Renaissance, the "Academies" for literature and the arts. In an endeavor to encourage serious research in the natural sciences, history, or philosophy (though not in theology), various approaches were used. Among them were lectures before an audience of experts, the pursuit of topics by the dissemination of examinations, the review of submitted works, publication of discussions and treatises, or preparing editions of historical sources on well-defined themes. One of the first of its kind was the Roman Accademia dei Lincei (1603), whose research was exemplary. In 1635 the idea was adopted by Richelieu (see Chap. 18), who turned the academies into state institutions with a national accentuation. Colbert's foundation in 1662 (Académie des Inscriptions et des Belles-Lettres) became highly significant because of its strong historical orientation and an abundance of publications, in part due to its intensive collaboration with the Maurists. This was in contrast to the provincial academies in France formed in the course of the eighteenth century; the finished works had little effective impact since they were left unprinted in their libraries. A private foundation in London (1645) which emerged in 1663 as the Royal Academy was devoted to research in the natural sciences; it published Newton's discoveries. Early on Leibniz also pursued the idea of an academy, but his goal, the establishment of the Berlin Academy, was not realized until 1700. The early examples of such state institutions were not emulated until the middle of the century: 1752 in Hanoverian Göttingen, 1753 in Erfurt, an outpost of the Mainz electorate in the middle of a Protestant environment, 1759 in Munich, the capital of electoral Bavaria, where the motive force behind the academy was the Jurist Johann Georg Lori, who was familiar with the Italian models. Another was founded in 1763 in Palatine Mannheim, whose reigning dynasty was Catholic but whose population was overwhelmingly Calvinist. Its establishment was aided substantially by the most prominent Protestant historian of his time, Schöpflin from Strasbourg. In the Habsburg domains only one academy, the one in Prague, founded privately in 1770 and recognized by the state in 1784, was able to maintain itself.[24] It was devoted primarily to topics prompted by the ever growing consolidation of Czech national consciousness, its own early history, and the Slavic language. While the pursuit of natural sciences prevailed in northern Germany, historical studies predominated in the Mannheim and Munich academies, giving them their high reputation. Mannheim, under the direction of Schöpflin's secretary and pupil, Andreas Lamey, primarily concentrated on four topics. The academy of Munich, which enjoyed substantial cooperation throughout the country, became the most efficient one after obtaining the services of the Protestant Alsatian Christian Friedrich Pfeffel (1763–68). It began the edition of the *Monumenta Boica* which, although somewhat deficient at first, achieved growing reliability in making an abundance of material available until the present day.

The historical themes were taken mostly from the Middle Ages and created a counterweight to the popular contemporary view of that period as one of darkness vis-à-vis the prevailing luminescence of the age of Enlightenment. The initially tendentious view of history caused by the general state of dependency on the sovereign was soon overcome, giving way to an impartial criticism; in this way a number of highly effective and long-enduring medieval falsifications were uncovered. Although themes in church history were not especially sought after, early sources kept in the domain of the Church were made available and thus much preliminary work on the history of church institutions was done. Most decisive were the dissemination and augmentation of the Maurist method. The universities of the eighteenth century did not teach the historical method, but the work of the academies brought about its adoption. This happened primarily in France (by the Académie des Inscriptions) and in Germany. The process of printing not only made the source material accessible but it also revealed and thereby disseminated the method applied to it. This made it possible to enlarge the principle of collaboration and the exchange of ideas beyond the immediate circle of the members of a particular academy. One may have misgivings concerning the fact that the academies did not exploit the coherent force of their collective membership for more comprehensive undertakings. Only Munich made a start in this direction. In general there was a lack of purposeful planning.

Occasional mention is made of an academy movement of the seventeenth and eighteenth century (which includes even the more loosely connected forms of scientific societies and associations of the time).

---

[24] On the academy of Olmütz (1746–51), see J. Hemmerle in *Stifter-Jahrbuch* 5 (1957), 79–101.

Such a movement existed in Switzerland.[25] One would also have to include the diverse forms of collaboration among the Benedictine monasteries that endeavored for a time to establish their own academy. Their inclusion is justified especially by such a comprehensive program as the Sankt Blasien *Germania sacra* by Martin Gerbert (after the model of the Maurists), which intended to compile an accurately documented history of the individual dioceses for all of Germany.

In Italy the Instituto delle Scienze in papal Bologna, founded in 1712, investigated the natural sciences on a level comparable to the Tuscan academies. The erudite Benedict XIV gave Rome its very efficient academies for church history (1741), for the history of ancient Rome (1744), and for the history of liturgics (1748). The academy of Madrid set an example for all of Spain (1735); it devoted itself exclusively to historical research. Its goal was a geographic-historical lexicon which actually started to appear in 1802. Next to that, its greatest undertaking was the *Espanā Sagrada*, whose first few volumes were edited by the Augustinian friar Enrique Flórez. The Madrid academy was the dominant center of diverse research activities which spread far and wide.

Education

When the printing press made it possible to extend the ability to read (and to write) it was used by the Reformation above all in the service of its demand for a personal encounter with the Holy Scripture. When the sexton was charged to assist the pastor in teaching the catechism, the seeds were planted for a broad-based establishment of schools. Early school regulations are left to us from Württemberg (1558) and electoral Saxony (1580). The idea of introducing schools everywhere was formulated in Frankfurt in 1612; mandatory attendance for all was planned in Strasbourg in 1598 and required in Anhalt (1607), Weimar (1619), Gotha (1642), Brunswick (1647), and Württemberg (1649). In rural areas it was difficult to conduct classes during the summer. Pietism not only helped in the understanding of the catechism, but also in the popularization of confirmation, customary in Hesse since Bucer, as an affirmation of baptism and preparation for Communion. In the beginning of the eighteenth century the practice of confirmation gradually prevailed (Württemberg, 1722; electoral Saxony, 1723; Denmark, 1736; Lübeck, 1817; and Hamburg, 1832), giving the school a concrete goal.

By establishing a number of schools the theologian Hermann Francke (1663–1727), a leader in the Pietist revival movement, broke through

---

[25] R. Reinhardt in *ZSKG* 61 (1967), 341–50.

the social exclusivity of the educational system; he was the first to concern himself with the training of teachers.[26] In 1774 Johann Bernhard Basedow (1724–94), a rationalist imbued with the ideas of Rousseau, founded a boarding school in Dessau (Philanthropinum) which had no church affiliation; it became an example for others.

Schools were increasingly established in the Catholic territories as well. Visitation reports of the seventeenth century reflect the efforts by the bishops to introduce them. When they wanted to have control over the employment of teachers, it was for reasons of ensuring themselves of their orthodoxy. Fénelon's *Traité de l'éducation des filles* (1687) also had a considerable impact in Germany. In the second half of the century the Catholic states also issued school regulations. This included the various prince-bishoprics and prince-abbeys, some of whom conscientiously took on the badly neglected task of teacher education (the teacher academy in Mainz, 1771; the teacher seminary of Saint Urban in Lucerne, 1777; bishopric of Fulda, 1781). A shining example was the work of the abbot J. I. von Felbiger at Sagan in Prussian Silesia in 1765 (*Plan der neuen Schuleinrichtung* [1770]), who was called to Vienna by Empress Maria Theresa in 1774. He divided the schools into three different kinds (the so-called trivial, main, and normal schools), introduced classroom instead of individual teaching, and incorporated religion as a regular subject, whereas before religious instruction had simply been done through the religious reading material (catechism) used in the general lessons. In western Germany Vicar General von Fürstenberg in Münster had Bernard Overberg appointed organizer of the Catholic elementary schools. His *Anweisung zum zweckmäßigen Schulunterricht* appeared in 1793. The great pedagogical verve of the period of Enlightenment helped create the teaching profession as such and finally brought some financial security. It also helped provide a proper education and to divorce the teacher from local authority. Still, it was natural for the school to be part of the respective denominational area, so that the teacher remained closely tied to the functions of the church service in his role as sexton and organist.

[26] Johann Baptist de la Salle founded a pedagogical seminary in Rheims as early as 1684.

CHAPTER 29

Liturgy and Popular Piety—New Religious Orders

The Liturgy

After the Council of Trent had created the prerequisites for bringing about a uniform liturgy cleansed of excesses for the entire Catholic Church, the subsequent five decades witnessed the development of the required tools; the *Breviarium Romanum* appeared in 1568, the *Missale Romanum* in 1570, the *Martyrologium Romanum* in 1584, the *Pontificale Romanum* in 1596, and the *Caerimoniale Episcoporum* in 1600. The final touch was the *Rituale Romanum* in 1614, which contained the rite of the administering of the sacraments and the sacramentals; it was not binding but rather intended as a model. This enabled the multifarious diocesan rites to be maintained along with them and made it possible to some extent to use the native language. But wherever there was no tradition with its own spontaneous forms, as in the missions, the unifying force of the centrally created liturgical materials had an effect.

In the history of liturgy the three centuries following 1614 until the reforms under Pius X proved to be the centuries of "liturgical stagnation" (Klauser). The scant "improvements," for instance, of the breviary under Urban VIII, were insignificant and pedantic. A reform prepared under Benedict XIV was not implemented. The powerful advance of historical research especially in the area of liturgics did bring about rich encounters with the forms of earlier periods, including the abundance of Eastern litugies, but had no effect on the existing ways of celebrating the official Mass, which had become rigid and inflexible with the passing of time. Regarding the breviary as well as the missal, Council of Trent had created the possibility of retaining customary forms if it could be ascertained that the tradition was more than 200 years old. But even where these conditions were met, it was not always possible to withstand the unifying forces for long; as a consequence the indigenous forms—with the exception of diocesan celebrations—were gradually abandoned.[1] In France, however, the affirmation of traditional Gallicanism was too strong for a similar development to take place. During a time of emphatic canonical Gallicanism, in fact, the right to retain the old traditional ways were expanded to the point where they were further developed under the influence of contemporary ideas. New breviaries were

---

[1] Thus Mainz had its own missal in 1698; see H. Reifenberg, *Messe und Missalien im Bistum Mainz* (Münster i. W. 1960).

created in France (Cluny, 1686; Paris, 1736 [for the secular clergy]; Saint Vanne, 1777; and, as a sort of continuation of the latter, Saint Maur, 1787). These were introduced even where the Roman liturgy had already been accepted. Their main characteristic was an intensive cultivation of Scripture reading to include especially the Fathers. They also manifested a strong tendency to moralize, which corresponded with the enlightened spirit of the period. A notable fact is that the Paris Breviary distributed the whole psalter over one week, using nine psalms for Matins, and that it restored the Sundays and ferial days to their customary place, two elements which were fully taken over by the Roman breviary reform of 1911. Western German dioceses were also quick to issue new breviaries which were not entirely closed to the ideas of the Gallican breviaries (Trier, 1748; Cologne, 1780). Martin II Gerbert immediately adopted the Saint Vanne Breviary for his diocese of Sankt Blasien.[2] But aside from the calendar of religious holidays, which steadily increased the feasts of the saints and diminished the celebration of the liturgical year, public worship on the whole stayed the same. The intensity of liturgical life appears to have run aground on the excessively fastidious consolidation of the abundantly annotated rubrics; canonistic formalism and casuistry displaced the inner life of the liturgy.

The gap between liturgy and the believers, existing since the Middle Ages, was not overcome but deepened instead. The liturgy had become a liturgy for the clergy, touching the people only inasmuch as it could serve as a spectacle. The holy Mass was no longer a participatory event; the sermon had been removed from it and the Communion had become isolated from it as a separate devotion. The Mass merely had the ceremonious function of making the Eucharistic Lord present whose real presence in the sacrament was stressed most strongly. The most formal ceremony was the Mass in front of the exposed Host, where the Eucharistic blessing was pronounced right at the beginning and repeated after the sequence and again at the end. The altar was centered on the throne of exposition above the tabernacle—the latter had been prescribed by the ritual of 1614 to replace the shrine in the wall of the chancel—and on it was the monstrance, now shaped like a sun. In front of it the clergy and the acolytes performed what amounted to a courtly service. But this baroque period knew how to turn the Mass into a celebration through the splendor of the church, in which all the skill of architecture, painting, and sculpture combined to form an all-inclusive artistic frame of lofty and joyous ceremony, intensified by the multiplicity of vestments and ever more profuse music. No matter that the words

---

[2] On the introduction of the Maurist Breviary of 1787 in Hungary (1842), see *ALW* 8 (1963), 79–84.

of the liturgy and the individual acts were no longer taken in, the awareness of a great mystery and the will for devotion were still present.

Given the great discrepancy between the official church service and a religiosity that people were able to comprehend, it is not surprising that they intensively cultivated extraliturgical forms. The suitable organization for that purpose was still the fraternity. Under different names (Rosary, Sacred Heart, Happy Death, Saint Sebastian, etc.), infused with recurrent waves of piety, they gathered their members from far afield, calling them to fraternal celebrations with impressive processions and endowing altars in their name. The number of fraternities increased greatly, as did that of the Marian congregations promoted by the Jesuits. Beginning in 1751 such congregations were also established for girls and women, whereas formerly they had been reserved for boys and men. Different from those of the baroque, the fraternities were distinguished by social standing; some were for students, others for the bourgeoisie, for priests, and so forth. Often it was the fraternities that organized the great pilgrimages which reached their climax at this time. New ones originated, especially Marian pilgrimages. In addition to the famous places of pilgrimage, visited by groups of pilgrims who sometimes walked for days to get there, many small local shrines were set up for people from the immediate environs. The popularity of the Holy House in Loreto was reflected by the many Loreto chapels, most of them outside the city entrances, which sought to copy the Italian shrine. The devotion of relics was given a great, in fact, an excessive impetus. They were collected and displayed behind glass windows or pyramids, some of them augmented to form dressed skeletal figures kept in glass coffins; they were placed on the altar, under the mensa, or carried along at processions. A great role was played by the so-called saints of the catacombs, which were bones from the Roman catacombs. In spite of an alleged authentication, they were of highly dubious origin, most of the time given a fictitious name, brought in ceremoniously, and often elevated to the position of copatron of a church.[3]

The desire for a chance to obtain indulgences had extraordinarily intensified. The contemporary mania for intoxicating themselves with large numbers led people not only to seek out as many opportunities as possible to obtain a plenary indulgence, but also partial ones for thousands and thousands of years. Membership in certain fraternities, which for their part had managed to participate in the indulgence privileges of others, provided offers of such possibilities: fastidiously compiled in calendars, they would tell the believer how many indulgences

[3] *LThK* VIII, 711.

he could obtain on a given day.[4] In addition, celebrations of indulgences were also very popular, especially at certain places of pilgrimage or monastic churches where the faithful came together in droves for the pronouncement of special indulgences, granted after receiving the sacrament of penance and Holy Communion. The intensification of the popular mission, organized at times with great baroque pomp and penitential processions which might involve the carrying of hundreds of crosses, went parallel to a sort of confessional movement which was intended to stimulate more frequent confessions. This explains the increased devotion of Saint John Nepomuk, promoted especially by the Jesuits, as a martyr to the seal of the confessional; his likeness soon adorned many streets and bridges and could be found in many churches.

There is no doubt that in many cases superstitions were mixed in with popular exercises of piety. The use of sacramentals was often falsified because of it. Many superstitions, carried over into our time, had a religious form in the period of the baroque; that age, in fact, was still given too much to such ideas. We have to remember that the madness of witchcraft was barely fading; here and there the fires of the autos-da-fé continued to burn the unfortunates accused of witchcraft, putting them to an agonizing death. Among the last burnings were those in Würzburg (1749), Endingen (1751; at the Kaiserstuhl), Kempten (1775), Glarus (1782), and Posen (1793).

The sermons of the baroque were in danger of getting lost in a welter of effects and external trappings. Their scriptural base was frequently inadequate. But not a few were imbued with religious depth, full of wisdom and popular, as those of the Capuchin friar Prokop von Templin (1609–80) in Austria; the Augustinian Hermit Abraham a Santa Clara (1644–1709), who was active primarily at the court of Vienna displaying creativity and great imagination in the use of language, as well as a pointed wit; and, lastly, the Portuguese Jesuit Antonio Vieira (1608–97), who was a most moving preacher. In 1760 the excesses of the baroque sermons were attacked by an outstanding satirist in the person of Josef de Isla (1703–81), who used his *Gerundio* novel to uncover their weaknesses to such an extent that he contributed substantially to removing them from the pulpits.

At a time when more than just a few of the faithful were able to read, literary forms could be developed which had a broad impact. Among them were, on the Protestant side, Johann Arnd's *Vier Bücher vom wahren Christentum* (1605), on the Catholic side a *Hauspostille* (1690)

---

[4] W. Müller, "Ein Gnadenkalender der Rosenkranzbruderschaft," *FreibDiözArch* 88 (1968), 359–79.

by the Premonstratensian Leonhard Goffiné (1648–1719) and the diverse writings of the Capuchin friar Martin von Cochem (1634–1712), especially his *Meßerklärung* and *Leben und Leiden Jesu Christi* (1677).[5]

The great religious strength of the century—regardless of the extent of anthropocentrism—is manifest in its works of art. The stylistic means of the fine arts were formed in Italy. As signs of a living faith in the nearness of God's grace, especially in those lands which had remained Catholic, they were used to build perfect structures which imply in many ways an extension into the supernatural. The period manifested a cheerful, confident, generous, and affirmative spirit which was able to create a great abundance of multifarious religious programs. At times they addressed a certain ethnic group, such as the Romance or the Austrian-Bavarian people. While Calvinism continued to be hostile to art and music (their churches were without paintings and for a long time without organs), the depth of Lutheran religious emotion was characterized by hymns, which are precious both in text and melody, and by immortal religious music: the passions, chorales, and cantatas of Heinrich Schütz (1585–1672), Johann Sebastian Bach (1685–1750), and the oratorios of George Frederick Handel (1685–1759). On the Catholic side we should mention the great masses and oratorios of Franz Joseph Haydn (1732–1809) and the masses by Wolfgang Amadeus Mozart (1756–91). Bach's great Mass in B-Minor, which he composed for the Catholic court of Dresden, shows the extent to which the denominations can converge in their most profound aspects. Beethoven's religious music belongs to another period.

This exuberant and varied scope of religious life was bound at some point to encounter a limiting and reducing force. Secular governments, playing an increasing role which gradually encompassed all aspects of human life, demanded a reduction in the number of holidays for economic reasons (in 1642 they had already been limited to thirty-four by Urban VIII). Spain initiated this move; under Benedict XIII it succeeded in having seventeen saints' feast days changed into half-holidays. They were still holy days of obligation, but the work prohibition was canceled. In 1748 the same ruling was applied to the Two Sicilies and in 1753 to Austria as well. Clement XIV abolished these half-holidays completely. Similar holiday limitations were requested by some archbishoprics (Würzburg [1770], Bamberg [1770], and Mainz [1763–74]) and by such states as Bavaria, Prussia (1772), and Spain (1791). These measures were generally unpopular and could often be implemented only by force after a long period of time. Wherever such canceled holy days were shifted to either the preceding or the following

---

[5] L. Signer, *Martin von Cochem, ein großer Geist des rheinischen Barock* (Wiesbaden 1963).

Sunday, the reduction caused the purpose of Sunday as the day of the Lord to be obscured.

In the changing spirit of the time the curtailment of the excessive number of feasts was only a beginning; such abundance and variety were increasingly considered unessential and annoying distractions. The striving was for unadorned simplicity, which alone permits the sublime to come to the fore. Only "noble artlessness," a "purified, genuine principle" was still in demand. The idea was to separate the essential from the "coincidental," only to declare in the same breath the latter to be dispensable, indeed to be something that needed to be removed like an obstacle or could at least be neglected without harm. The application of such a differentiation was certainly indicated since it permitted a clearer perspective of things which had in many instances become hidden. So the fight began against the many processions, the pilgrimages to all sorts of large and small places of grace, against the many fraternities, and the benedictions often suffused with superstitious expectations. The use of exorcism especially seemed outmoded; now the bishops frequently made it dependent on the permission of the ordinaries. The constant repetition of the Eucharistic blessing was felt to be an exaggeration. In contrast to the overwhelming abundance of the most varied forms of veneration of saints, piety with Christ at its center was to be reemphasized. The late stage of these enlightened ideas also brought about a deeper occupation with the Holy Scripture.

These changes, penetrating as they were, did not happen all at once; they took place in phases with considerable chronological differences. The pastoral letter by the Viennese Prince-Archbishop Trautson of 1 January 1752, whose formulations were looked upon as guidelines far beyond his diocese, appeared when the art of the baroque had just entered its last formal, albeit playful stage of the rococo. In 1768 when the monastery of Sankt Blasien burned down, Martin Gerbert decided to have d'Ixnard rebuild it in the form of a classical round temple which was admired all the way to northern Germany because of its impression of sublime peace. The measures instituted by Joseph II (1780–90) were the climax of enlightened activities in the ecclesiastical realm. Not only were they frequently copied during his lifetime, but they also served as models for the position of the established church system in the first half of the nineteenth century. The extent of conformity on the part of the ecclesiastical circles is shown by the pastoral letter of Prince-Archbishop Colloredo of Salzburg dated 29 January 1782. The Synod of Pistoia promulgated a number of good ideas (especially in the area of the liturgy) which are only now having a real impact. And yet the "modern" Mainz hymnal of 1787 caused bitter disputes. The attempt to write a ritual in German was first made by C. Schwarzel around the turn of the century and concluded with the ritual by Wessenberg in 1831. The work by the most prominent reform liturgist of the Enlightenment, Vitus Anton Winter, in Ingolstadt and Landshut is also part of the new century.

The Enlightenment definitely perceived the gap between the liturgy and the people and tried to bridge it on the one hand by curtailing the indigenous forms of popular piety and on the other by establishing a connection between the believers and the liturgical event. The strides made to include the sermon in the Mass again were notable, as were the attempts to connect the Communion with the Mass. It was tempting, of course, to make the liturgy generally accessible by translating it into the native language, that is by giving up the unintelligible Latin as the liturgical language. Generally this was dared only for the administration of the sacraments and the benedictions, or for new celebrations such as first Communion or the investiture of a parish priest, but only sporadically for the celebration of the Mass. It was not done at all under Wessenberg,[6] who held back his friends when they wanted to forge ahead on this point. At first he tried to get the people to participate by means of a sort of prayer-song Mass using many different texts for the various times of the church year (Constance Hymnal, 1812). Praying something other than indicated by the context of the Mass, for instance the traditional rosary, was considered extremely improper. Masses at side altars, customarily conducted concurrently with the main Mass, were abolished. Preference was for only one altar in the church.

The basic idea of the enlightened service was eminently ministerial: The priest who knows his flock—it was improper to leave the parish for a monastery, pilgrimage, or an outside fraternity—takes care of them in the truest sense of the word. He imparts to them the word of God according to a deliberate plan and instructs them in all that they need. The service has to be organized so that it edifies and improves the participants. It should serve to make them recognize that they are all brothers of the common Father who is in heaven. This was the true brotherhood, the only one still admitted. Under Joseph II it was called the "brotherhood of the love of one's fellow man"; under Wessenberg "of God's love and the love of one's fellow man." All mechanical aspects were to disappear from prayer and the service. The ties between shepherd and flock were to be deepened so that confessions were made only to one's own priest, who knew the individual best and was therefore the only who could instruct him properly. In accordance with Wessenberg's views, the responsibility of the minister for those en-

---

[6] See E. Keller, "Die Konstanzer Liturgiereform," *FreibDiözArch* 85 (1965); on Wessenberg's *Deutsche Vespern*, see F. Poppin ibid. 87 (1967).

trusted to him was increased considerably. Seen from this point of view, the service in the period of Enlightenment did not only consist of teaching and dry moralizing mixed with a few pious sentimentalities, as it has often been represented. To be sure, the didacticism which filled the texts of the hymns as well was overstressed. Subjectivism, with its initial growth in the baroque, became dominant and the idea of the liturgy as a service before God receded to too great a degree. There is also no doubt that in the most profound sense the initial attempts in the Enlightenment to reform the service failed because the theocentricity of the service was overlooked and the attempt to improve its form missed the reality of the cultic mysticism. The strong desire for cult was no longer accorded enough significance. Piety emanating from the world all too often got stuck in the world. But to the extent that the responsibility for one another was emphasized, God, before whom the responsibility is discharged, was again included.

New Religious Orders

The history of the religious orders of the sixteenth and beginning of the seventeenth century is strongly imbued with the idea of the apostolate. This was true even more so for the following centuries. Certain characteristic concerns gained prominence, such as the construction of seminaries for the training of secular clerics among the Oratorians, the Sulpicians, and the *Congrégation de Jésus et Marie* of John Eudes; in its own fashion the work of Vincent de Paul ran parallel to that. Vincent and his Lazarists—as did the two Jesuits Paolo Segneri (1624–94) and Paolo the Younger (1673–1713) in Italy—built the type of popular mission which stayed alive until the twentieth century, representing a very important form of the apostolate of the orders. By founding the *Filles de la Charité* with the assistance of Louise de Marillac (see Chap. 5), Vincent de Paul approached the very concrete tasks of caring for orphans, the aged, and the sick in a more efficacious fashion than had ever been done before in the history of ecclesiastical charity. Similar organizations were the *Soeurs de Notre-Dame de charité de refuge* of John Eudes (1640), from whom the congregation of Our Lady of the Love of the Good Shepherd emerged in the nineteenth century, and the *Soeurs de Saint Charles* or Borromaeans who originated in Nancy and spread primarily in Lorraine after 1652. That same year the *Filles de la Charité* also started working in Poland and as late as the eighteenth century went to other European countries and America. This social and charitable service of nuns, which enabled women to take part in superior fashion in common tasks of Christian love,[7] could be possible only by abolishing the cloistral regulations which had always been inflexible in regard to nuns. These regulations had just been reapplied more severely in order to eliminate increasing abuses. This explains the considerable difficulties initially encountered by the foundations. The order of the Elizabethan nuns which developed from the medieval Begines and spread into Italy, France, the Netherlands, and the east of the Empire during the seventeenth century were never able to overcome the requirement of reclusion. For that reason they were reduced to installing hospitals solely in their own houses. The order of the Hospitallers was not impeded by the cloistral regulations.

Overcoming this obstacle was even harder for those women's orders who were active in the third area of the apostolate, the schools. Thus the Salesians could teach only girls who lived in a boarding school. And yet there was an actual school movement among the womens's orders: the Ursulines were founded in Liège in 1622 and from there spread to Germany; in 1639 they established a house in Canadian Quebec. In 1606 a free form, forgoing reclusion and vows, was established in Dôle in the diocese of Besançon; eventually this order established houses in Switzerland and southern Germany (Freiburg, Villingen). The most spirited fight for new forms for which Mary Ward aspired when she adopted the constitution of the Society of Jesus was waged by the English Ladies. Their work on the basis of less stringent vows was not fully recognized until Benedict XIV. Other women's orders also turned to the teaching of girls: the Dominican nuns in the form of congregations or the Frauen vom Heiligen Grab who flourished in their dedication to this goal especially in the Netherlands. Among the schools for boys those of the Jesuits were the most important ones, not just in France but everywhere. But other orders, such as the Benedictine monks, also dedicated part of their energies to the schools. A specific school order were the School Brothers. The order of the Piarists, specializing in building primary and secondary schools, was now spreading far and wide. When the Jesuit order was suppressed, members of these orders often jumped into the breach and kept the schools from being closed.

The few orders newly founded in the one and a half centuries prior to the great change signaled by the French Revolution were also imbued with the idea of the apostolate. In 1640 Bartholomäus Holzhauser (1613–58) founded a priestly congregation in Tittmoning (in the arch-

---

[7] Not until the nineteenth century were similar female orders (deaconesses) established in the Lutheran Church.

diocese of Salzburg) which was dedicated to the training of clerics and to the mission. After 1655 he worked in the archdiocese of Mainz consolidating his institute of the Bartholomites. The Passionists founded by Paul of the Cross (1694–1775) in Orbetello (on the shores of the Ligurian Sea between Civitavecchia and Livorno), whose generalate has been located at the monastery of Giovanni e Paolo in Rome since 1773, while dedicated to contemplation, were nonetheless active in the popular mission as well. Paul also founded a women's branch of this order which lived a strictly contemplative life. Alphonsus Liguori (1696–1787) initially founded the contemplative women's order of the Redemptorists (1731); it was followed by the male order a year later in Scala near Amalfi. Their main purpose was the mission to the most neglected among the inhabitants of the mountains near Naples. This order, looked on with suspicion by the temporal government, first spread in the Kingdom of Naples and then in the Papal States. For a while political tensions led to a split of the order into a Neapolitan and a Papal States branch. Not until 1784 were the first non-Italians permitted to join, among them Clemens Maria Hofbauer, who paved the way for the congregation's expansion into Germany.

In the course of the eighteenth century the interest in all forms of monastic life decreased. To the enlightened spirit of the century monasticism appeared to be the essence of the obscure and fanatical, forever dominated by impenetrable darkness and defending a useless life of indolence. As an outgrowth of pointed discussion of the principle of usefulness—as seen from a purely worldly point of view—a spirit of decided hostility against monasticism arose which stifled monastic vocations. There are some important data which characterize this movement: the agitation against the Jesuit order leading to its abolition (see Chap. 29); the suppression and consolidation beginning in 1766 of 386 monastic establishments which had in many cases already shrunk drastically in size; the secularization of monasteries and convents in Austria under Joseph II involving all the contemplative orders; and the facile manner in which monastic establishments were abolished in Germany even by bishops (as in Mainz or Münster) in order to use their assets for other good causes. These events did not occur everywhere or in equal fashion; thus the attack during the French Revolution, for example, on the covents involved establishments which had in no way declined and, indeed, had preserved an excellent spirit. The case of the religious orders of men was different. For 250 years the newer orders had been dedicated to obvious usefulness, such as the ministry, the inner mission, teaching, or social and charitable work, soon emulated by most of the old orders. And should not dedication to scholarly work in accordance with the most modern of methods also be considered useful? And yet in

France and Germany the axe of secularization was applied impartially to all kinds of monastic life.

Indeed, many a demand was justifiable, e.g., that the age for profession not be too young—Joseph II raised the minimum age to twenty-four—and that the size of the dowry be restricted. The growing self-confidence of man demanded a greater sense of responsibility especially on the part of monastic institutions. But this total blow against all monastic forms of existence cannot be understood merely on the basis of the argument that improvements were necessarily based on the demands of the times. Antipathy to monastic life grew to the extent that its complete dissolution appeared imminent, a fact accepted with surprising equanimity by those affected.

The Papacy under the Increasing Pressure of the Established Church

In the course of the eighteenth century the Catholic powers—France and Austria in the wake of Portugal and Spain—lost their position of primacy in Europe and overseas. Their place was taken by non-Catholic powers, Prussia in central Europe and England, which became the primary maritime power, establishing its Empire and seeking to preserve the balance of power between the states on the European continent by means of its policy of alliances and subsidies. The general development of countries into modern states, especially in the administrative and economic sectors, was not shared by the Papal States primarily because they were lacking dynastic continuity, an absolutely necessary prerequisite for long-range policies. In the crucial first half of the century, moreover, the Papal States had been sorely and repeatedly affected by wars because they were militarily and politically too weak to maintain their proclaimed neutrality and to protect themselves against violations. The discrepancy between the temporal rule of the Pope and that of the other contemporary states was steadily growing. The Papal States became a liability rather than fulfilling their original function of ensuring the Pope of the freedom and independence required for the guidance of the total Church. As the eighteenth century progressed the Papal States reached a condition which was deplored by the eminent Cardinal Consalvi in his memoirs at the beginning of the next century: "One would have to overcome all the various kinds of resistance against changes and reforms which are necessary and make sense because certain of the existing forms have become antiquated or outmoded, demeaned by abuses, or, finally, because the times and circumstances as well as the general views were changing."[1]

In those states which were still nominally Catholic the leading personalities came under the influence of an ever more radical Enlightenment, so that they could hardly be called Catholic any more. These states developed an established Church down to the smallest details, which was distinguished from the Gallicanism of the preceding century primarily by a total absence of actual religiosity as well as by a brutal

---

[1] *Alcune brevi memorie sul mio ministero: Memorie del cardinale Consalvi*, ed. by M. Nasalli Rocca (Rome 1950), 149.

arbitrariness divorced from all tradition. The Church was considered a mere instrument of the state to be employed at the discretion of the state as a state institution without regard to its specific character and inner laws. The papacy was virtually helpless in the face of demands by this type of established Church. Confronted on the part of the Catholic powers by extortionist tactics which included the threat of schism, perhaps not always intended seriously, the papacy had to make one concession after another. The extreme helplessness of the papacy can best be seen by the example of the suppression of the Jesuit order when the Holy See had to lend itself to sanctioning and actively bringing to its conclusion the hunt against the Society of Jesus which had been started by the so-called Catholic states. Although future Popes also had to endure persecution, even expulsion from Rome and imprisonment, this case of compelled complicity in the destruction of an institution of great merit to Church and papacy whose downfall was destined to do noticeable damage to both was a singularly flagrant result of the weakness of the Holy See and its dependence on outer influences.

Also a sign of weakness and considerable indecision was that the leadership of the Church tried to delay long-overdue reforms and simply refused to heed justified desires submitted to the Holy See. Concerns reflecting the demands of the time which could have been solved without particular difficulty—issues concerning monastic law, ecclesiastical immunity, the adaptation of liturgical forms—while often coupled with other demands contradictory to the essence of the Church, were rejected out of hand as attacks on the rights of the Church. Conversely, positions were adhered to which had long been outmoded and were destined shortly to be destroyed by force. The negative attitude of the Church towards the demands of the Enlightenment continuously widened the gap between the Church and contemporary culture. By the same token, adherence to such formally valid but actually outmoded structures as the Vienna Concordat of 1448 for the German Empire or the Concordat of 1516 for France, made the Church drift farther and farther away from the real and constantly changing world round it. It was nothing short of fatal that in this period no actual initiatives were taken by the church leadership to adapt ecclesiastical forms and pastoral efforts to modern circumstances. In point of fact, the violent upheaval towards the end of the century found the Church basically unprepared.

CHAPTER 30

The Popes from Innocent XIII to Clement XII

Innocent XIII (1721–24)

During his long pontificate (1700–1721) Clement XI had appointed seventy cardinals, sixteen of whom had not survived the Pope. Within the traditional factions of the conclave beginning on 31 March 1721 the imperial cardinals could no longer rely on the support of their Spanish colleagues; the change of the dynasty now allied that group with the French faction. On the first day of the conclave, with barely half the cardinals present, the election of Paolucci, the secretary of state of Clement XI, appeared to be imminent. Since Vienna blamed him for the policies of the dead Pope, said to be friendly to the Bourbons, the imperial legate, Cardinal Althan, pronounced the formal exclusion against him. During the lengthy conclave many unsuccessful efforts were made until finally the candidacy of the French Cardinal Michel Angelo de' Conti was promoted, who raised the expectation of cooperation both with the French crown and the Emperor. On 8 May 1721, he was elected unanimously. The newly elected Pope took his name after the most famous member of his family, Innocent III, who had granted his brother the fiefdom of Poli, where Conti was born in 1655. He had been nuncio in Lisbon for ten years; in 1719 he had resigned from his diocese of Viterbo for reasons of health, so a lasting pontificate could not be expected. Although the Pope did invest the Emperor with Sicily and Naples, for which the latter had waited since the beginning of the War of the Spanish Succession, the negotiations for the already decided return of Comacchio turned out to be so prolonged that Innocent XIII did not live to see it. In the first year of his pontificate he appointed a total of three cardinals in two consistories. At the beginning of his second year his old affliction of lithiasis flared up again; several times he was not expected to live. His constant illness cast a shadow over his pontificate. He was released from his suffering on 7 March 1724. He is the only Pope in the history of the modern papacy who did not get a monument in Saint Peter's, although he was entombed there.

Benedict XIII (1724–30)

In the conclave beginning on 20 March 1724 the constellation of the factions was identical to the previous one. After several unsuccessful attempts a dark horse again was nominated in order to end the conclave which had already lasted far too long. On 29 May the Dominican Cardinal Vincenzo Maria (Pietro Francesco) Orsini was elected unanimously. But only after considerable resistance could he be persuaded to accept the election. He was the eldest son of the duke of Gravina near Bari, but had forgone his hereditary rights in order to enter the Dominican order. At the time of the election he was already seventy-five years old. Urged by his family, Clement X had appointed him cardinal at the age of twenty-three; he had been bishop of Manfredonia, Cesena, and Benevento (since 1686) in succession. His pastoral zeal and his ascetic life were praised everywhere. But he had no political experience. He chose his name in memory of the Dominican Pope Benedict XI. He was given the ordinal after some initial hesitation because Pedro de Luna, Benedict XIII at the time of the western schism and the Council of Constance, was considered an anti-Pope. In his personal life he continued to be a modest religious, refusing to move into the splendorous rooms of the Vatican. Even as Pope his main concern was the conduct of the diocese of Rome; the major part of his time was spent with consecrations of churches and altars, visits to the sick, religious instruction, and the administration of sacraments.

Given this attitude to his office, the selection of the Pope's coworkers took on extreme importance. While Benedict XIII made a fortuitous move in selecting Paolucci as secretary of state, his next appointment was to be fatal for his entire pontificate. As archbishop of Benevento, he had placed unlimited trust in Niccolò Coscia from the vicinity of Benevento. Now he gave him the kind of influential position at the papal court that in earlier times would most likely have been occupied only by a papal nephew. Greedy and unscrupulous, Coscia abused his position from the very start. In 1725, against the open disagreement of several cardinals, among them Secretary of State Paolucci, the Pope appointed him cardinal. Coscia promptly put a number of other Beneventans into influential positions. The climax was reached on 12 June 1726 after the death of Paolucci when the Pope, following a suggestion by Coscia, appointed the *Maestro di Camera,* Niccolò Maria Lercari, the new secretary of state. Lercari was totally dependent on Coscia. In spite of all the accusations raised against Coscia and incontrovertible evidence of his avarice and mismanagement, Benedict XIII held fast to his favorite as though blinded. Coscia sold vacant positions or divided the revenues with their holders. He managed to isolate the Pope to such a degree that in the end the latter was advised by no one but the group around Coscia. If the financial affairs of the Papal States got into a state of total disorder as a result of his mismanagement, the all powerful Coscia would intervene in the field of foreign policy and have himself paid princely sums for his services by the ambassadors of foreign powers.

A case in point was the bothersome issue of the *Monarchia Sicula*. It designated the full ecclesiastical jurisdiction claimed by the rules of Sicily since the sixteenth century on the basis of a privilege granted by Urban II to Roger I of Sicily. This privilege had already been formally rescinded by Clement XI, but now the imperial legate, Cardinal Cienfuegos, with the help of Coscia and the canonist Prospero Lambertini, who was soon after appointed cardinal, induced the Pope to make a decision which was most favorable to the imperial government. In the negotiations which dragged on from 1725 to 1728 the negotiators appointed by the Pope actually took the part of the imperial side. Even though a formal recognition of the *Monarchia Sicula* was avoided, the solution incorporated in the bull *Fideli* for all practical purposes granted the Sicilian ruler the jurisdiction in ecclesiastical matters, undermining the rescission by Clement XI.

The house of Savoy, like that of the Emperor, knew how to exploit the situation in Rome to its advantage. Victor Amadeus II, who had assumed the royal title in 1713, managed—again with the help of Coscia, Secretary of State Lercari, and Lambertini—to obtain recognition of his royal title along with the presentation right for the bishoprics on the island of Sardinia. Although the Pope declared emphatically that he was unwilling to surrender a single right of the Church, the legate of Savoy succeeded by means of the concordat of 1727 in obtaining a solution which was most advantageous for Piedmont. The opinion of Cardinal Lambertini that nuisances had to be endured in order to prevent worse had made an impression on the Pope. The King was granted the right of episcopal appointments and the administration of the revenues during a *sedes vacans* virtually for the whole territory. All the officials of the Holy See who had had a part in the conclusion of the concordat were generously rewarded by the Turin government. This makes it obvious how the negotiations were conducted. By appointing a number of Dominicans to the sees the King assured himself of the Pope's continued benevolence in spite of the enormous concessions the Holy See had made in the concordat.

The Pope's lack of concern for the political issues confronting the Church was contrasted by his desire to do justice to his office as supreme head of the Church. He issued numerous orders for reforms and the restoration of discipline in the Church. But all too often his regulations were burdened by minutiae and were therefore without lasting effect. The jubilee of 1725, in the course of which the Spanish Stairs, under construction for four years, were consecrated, gave the Pope reason for many ceremonial Masses. The staircase, leading from the Piazza di Spagna to the church of the Trinità dei Monti was a legacy of the former French ambassador. In opposition to the cardinals he convened a

Roman provincial council after Easter which he conducted in person. This claimed his attention for weeks to the point that all other affairs came to a halt. Benedict XIII also pursued the execution of the Tridentine resolutions concerning the establishment of diocesan seminaries; he even appointed a special congregation for seminaries. Given the Pope's nature, it is not surprising that the number of beautifications and canonizations during his pontificate was noticeably high. He also continued to be attached to his former diocese of Benevento, which he visited twice, in 1727 and 1729.

Of his twenty-nine appointments to the cardinalate, made in twelve consistories, the ones of Coscia and Lercari were disastrous because of their negative influence on the Pope, while the one of Lambertini (at the end of 1726) was to be significant. The Catholic powers pressured Benedict XIII more than any other Pope before him to have their favorites elevated to the purple. It must be mentioned, however, that he did not agree to appoint Nuncio Bichi in Portugal, where he was zealously promoted by that government.

Characteristic for the situation of the Church and the papacy was the negative reaction of the powers to the Pope's efforts to have the feast of Saint Pope Gregory VII and the appropriate readings from the breviary adopted by the entire Church. Actually a minor issue, it came to be viewed as a highly political matter because of Gregory's position in the controversy over the investiture and his stand against Emperor Henry IV. In France, Naples, Belgium, and Venice the printing and distribution of the new liturgical texts were made subject to heavy penalties because this act was considered a violation of the ecclesiastical sovereignty of the state.

Benedict XIII died on 21 February 1730 after a brief illness. In accordance with his wishes he was laid to rest in the Dominican church of Maria sopra Minerva.

Clement XII (1730–40)

The death of the Pope brought with it the immediate fall of the Beneventan group in the Curia. Coscia had to leave the Vatican on the very first day after the Pope's demise. Because the wrath of the population was directed especially against him, he was forced to flee Rome in the dead of night. A month after the start of the conclave he was permitted to return with reservations; again he had to make his way through Rome at night. In addition to the traditional factions among the papal electors there was now a Savoyard party among whom were those cardinals who had participated in the concordat of 1727. In the course of the conclave more than half of the cardinals present were at one time or another nominated as candidates. After four months, on 12 July 1730, the seventy-eight-year-old Florentine Lorenzo Corsini was elected. He had been nominated two months prior by the French faction, but at that time, being a Tuscan, he had been rejected by the imperial party, which anticipated complications upon the extinction of the Medici line. In the meantime there had been successful intercession in his behalf in Vienna. But when the imperial concurrence arrived on 7 July, the French faction demurred because it forced them to relinquish their candidate Banchieri, whom they had promoted in the interim. Moreover, they suspected some sort of imperial machination behind the suddenly resumed candidacy of Corsini. The newly elected Pope had pursued his career in Rome. His domicile in the Palazzo Pamfili on the Piazza Navona had been the center of intellectual and scholarly life in Rome. Highly esteemed, he had been close to election in the two previous conclaves, but had been excluded by the great powers. By now he was too old and his vision so impaired that he became totally blind in 1732. This left the conduct of business to the immediate circle around the Pope.

The new Pope, taking his name after Clement XI, who had appointed him to the cardinalate, immediately tried to repair the damage done during the preceding pontificate. Coscia and his group were put on trial. Having fled to Naples because he was hoping for support from the Emperor for his efforts on behalf of the *Monarchia Sicula,* Coscia was now faced by the threat of demotion and excommunication. In 1732 he decided to stand trial in order to defend himself. On 9 May 1733, he was condemned to ten years at the Castel Sant'Angelo, restitution of all unlawful gains, and payment of 100,000 scudi; his franchise was revoked for the duration of his incarceration. But at the subsequent conclave in 1740 Coscia was readmitted with full rights; Prospero Lambertini, elected at that conclave, who was heavily indebted to Coscia, canceled the remainder of his prison term.

Clement XII urged revision of the concordat with Piedmont because it had been concluded illegally. In 1731 he pronounced it invalid. After initial protests Piedmont was forced to give in and agree to renegotiate the concordat. This had not been concluded by the time the Pope died. Efforts to cure the chaotic fiscal situation proved to be extremely difficult. Although new sources of revenue were found the burden of debt carried by the Papal States kept increasing.

Initially Clement XII was able to resist pressure by the great powers, installing only Italian cardinals. The single exception was the Portuguese nuncio Bichi, whose appointment had been urged by Lisbon for more than a decade. The agreement to elevate him after Bichi tendered a formal apology for his disobedience was a special act of conciliation as well as a political necessity in order to reestablish normal relations with

Portugal. In the second half of his pontificate Clement XII had to be more accessible to the wishes of the great powers. Since Portugal insisted on the appointment of the patriarch of Lisbon to the cardinalate, the Pope also had to take the demands of the larger states into account, which he did in a promotion at the end of 1737.

The first papal condemnation of the Freemasons took place in 1738. The lodges had formed about two decades before in England and spread across the continent including Rome. The condemnation can be explained by an apprehension of indifferentism and hostility to revealed religion. It was based on incomplete and one-sided information and did not do adequate justice to the many different currents represented in Freemasonry at the time.[1]

The decade brought about a new shift of power in Italy. When Duke Antonio Farnese of Parma and Piacenza died heirless on 20 January 1731, the issue of the feudal rights over these territories resurfaced. According to the peace treaty of 1720, Don Carlos, the son of Queen Elizabeth of Spain, was to receive the inheritance of the Farnese; Spain wanted his investiture by the Pope. But the Emperor claimed the feudal rights and had the territory occupied for Don Carlos. The Pope's protest was to no avail.

When the Polish King Augustus of Saxony died on 1 February 1732, the Pope initially sided with his son Friedrich August. But France, with the support of the Polish primate, promoted the candidacy of Stanislas Leszczyński, who was promptly elected. Encircled in Danzig by Russian and Saxon troops, he was reduced to waiting for help from the French. In the meantime France, Spain, and Piedmont had agreed to use the Polish War of Succession for the purpose of exploiting the difficult situation of the Empire and depriving the Emperor of his Italian possessions. By fall of 1733 Lombardy was in the hands of Piedmont. At the beginning of 1734 the Pope had to grant permission for an army under Don Carlos which was to occupy Naples to cross his territories. By the end of 1734 the entire Kingdom of Naples including Sicily was conquered by Spanish troops. Given the military helplessness of the Papal States, the Pope had no recourse when the Spaniards recruited soldiers there and passed through his territories at will. In the meantime the Peace of Vienna between the Emperor and France stipulated that Leszczyński would forego the Polish crown and in exchange receive the duchies of Bar and Lorraine, which were to go to France after his death. Duke Francis of Lorraine was to be compensated by the Grand Duchy of Tuscany after the death of the last of the Medici. Don Carlos was assured of the Kingdom of the Two Sicilies. The Emperor retained Lombardy, with the

---

[1] See K. Algermissen: *LThK* IV, 343–48; G. Schenkel: *RGG Ù*, 1113–18.

exception of a few areas which went to Piedmont, and the duchies of Parma and Piacenza. Lastly, the Pragmatic Sanction, intended to regulate the Austrian succession, was recognized by France. This shift of power in Italy was arranged without consulting the Pope and without regard to his feudal rights. Since Spain did not accept the Peace of Vienna, the war in northern Italy continued, repeatedly affecting the Papal States. In March 1736 the population of Rome revolted against the recruitment of troops by the Spanish. As a consequence several towns of the Papal States were occupied by Spanish troops. In May 1736 Spain, followed by Naples, broke diplomatic relations with the Holy See. To restore them, the Pope was forced to make large concessions in a concordat with Spain.

Notable administrative improvements in the Papal States were the promotion of trade and industry and the regulatory work in the Romagna. It was here that Cardinal Alberoni, back in favor since 1735, was active as papal legate. He established a permanent monument for himself by his generous endowment of a college in Piacenza named after him, which combined a theological boarding institution with a philosophical and theological university.[2] But his attempt to incorporate San Marino into the Papal States failed because Clement XII decided that the annexation could not be made without the free consent of its citizens.

For the last several years of his life the blind Pope was almost constantly bedridden. He died on 6 February 1740.

[2] For a detailed account, see the unpublished dissertation by A. Mezzadri submitted to the Gregoriana in 1969: *La formazione sacerdotale al collegio Alberoni di Piacenza.*

CHAPTER 31

Benedict XIV

The conclave beginning on 19 February 1740 and lasting for exactly six months was the longest since the Western Schism. For the first time the Austrian and French interests coincided; they were opposed by the Spanish cardinals, supported by those of Naples and Tuscany. Also important was the opposition between the cardinals installed by the deceased Pope and the "old" ones, appointed by his predecessor and led by Cardinal Albani. One candidate after the other failed, often on the balance of a single vote. Four cardinals died in the course of the conclave. Finally, in about the middle of August, the crown cardinals united behind the sixty-five-year-old Prospero Lambertini, archbishop of Bologna since 1731. At the beginning of the conclave he had been able to attract a few votes, but the scrutinies of the last few days prior to the decisive agreement had not given him a single vote. Yet on 17 August he was elected unanimously. He assumed his name in memory of Benedict XIII, who had elevated him to the cardinalate. The new Pope had made an excellent reputation for himself as a canonist; his work on the beatifications and canonizations became a classic in the field. Active in the Curia since the beginning of the century, he had gained influence by virtue of his thoroughness and stamina. Benedict XIII consulted him on political issues several times. More often than not Lambertini favored a policy of conciliation with an opposing state; often enough the resulting solutions did no more than save the bare principles. Beyond his specialty of canon law he was interested in the learning of his time, especially in literature and history; he was considered an "enlightened" and modern ecclesiastical prince. Witty and liberal in his private conversations, he did not shrink from criticizing institutions and personalities of the Church. He was a generous and open man, yet not always a good judge of human character. His trust in the French ambassador to Rome (until 1742), Crown Cardinal de Tencin, reflected by his friendship and voluminous private correspondence, was certainly misplaced. The Pope frankly and without reservations entrusted his thoughts on all kinds of issues to his correspondent—among them matters of policy which required the strictest secrecy. Cardinal de Tencin, who was a dependent of his immoral sister, the mother of the Encyclopedist d'Alembert, had copies and translations of the Pope's letters made and sent to the French government.

The fifty-year-old Silvio Valenti Gonzaga, nuncio in Brussels and Madrid, became secretary of state. Like the Pope, he was open to the arts and sciences. His rural estate, later called the Villa Bonaparte at the Porta Pia, became a center for scholars and artists, including foreigners.

In attempting to solve pending issues with the Catholic powers Benedict XIV in his capacity as Pope was just as ready for large concessions as he had been as Cardinal Lambertini. First to be settled were the disputes with Naples. The Pope agreed to the establishment of a mixed court of law to include laymen which was to judge ecclesiastical issues and persons. In a secret article, moreover, the *Placetum regium* was implicitly granted. More favorable to the Church was the agreement with Piedmont, but here too most of the wishes of that government were granted. The most far-reaching concession was the concordat with Spain in 1753. After initial resistance the demand for an extension of the royal patronage, already in existence in Granada and Spanish America, to all of Spain, was in the end granted by Benedict XIV. It had been demanded by Madrid for a number of decades and rejected again by the late Pope Clement XII. In secret negotiations, with sole participation by the Pope and his secretary of state and without the nuncio, Benedict acquiesced in all the important points. A mere fifty-two benefices were left to the Holy See to fill, while the King obtained the right of appointment to approximately twelve thousand of them. To make up the financial loss to the Curia the Spanish government was prepared to pay a compensation. At that time it was already a well-known fact that the secretary of state had received a significant sum of money from Spain. This put an onus on the concordat, which was made public only after its conclusion.

Of all the political changes taking place in the year 1740 the death of Emperor Charles IV on 20 October had the greatest impact. As far as the Austrian hereditary lands were concerned, female succession had been regulated by the Pragmatic Sanction. Yet Bavaria, Spain, and Prussia raised claims to parts of the inheritance. After some delay Benedict XIV recognized the hereditary right of Maria Theresa. In view of the impending imperial election, the Pope decided upon strict neutrality, to which he adhered in the face of tremendous pressure by the great powers, primarily France, which had entered into an alliance with Prussia against Austria. Only after Karl Albert von Wittelsbach had been elected Emperor Charles VII did Benedict announce his recognition of him. In the meantime Friedrich II of Prussia had occupied Silesia and Bavaria had invaded Austria with help by the French. Spain exploited the threat to Austria by attacking its possessions in Italy. In the course of their advance, Spanish and Austrian troops, unmindful of papal protests, marched through the papal territories unimpeded and even turned them into theaters of war. In May and June 1743, battles took place in the immediate environs of Rome, where the Austrian army remained until the fall of 1744. When Charles VII died on 20 January 1745, Benedict XIV assumed the same stance of neutrality as he had found years before.

In the Peace of Aachen (1748), Parma and Piacenza were again disposed of in total disregard of the Pope's feudal rights. The protest submitted by the papal legate and repeated by Benedict XIV in person was merely noted as the dissenting point of view of the Holy See.

The years of war placed a constant financial burden on the administration of the Papal States, reflected in increased debts and diminished revenues. The Peace of Aachen, which granted Italy a period of rest lasting almost half a century, initiated a time of economic recovery. The city of Rome started to regain its stature as a center of cultural life. The engravings by Giuseppe Vasi (1747–61) and especially the *Antichità Romane* (1756) and the *Vedute di Roma* (as of 1748) by Giovanni Battista Piranesi resurrected the Rome of yesteryear. Most of the restorations undertaken during the pontificate of Benedict XIV, especially during the Holy Year 1750, among them Santa Maria Maggiore, San Croce in

Gerusalemme, and Santa Maria degli Angeli, must be considered less than felicitous because they changed the original character of the churches too much in accordance with contemporary taste.

Interested in all areas of the sciences, the Pope supported individual scholars as well as large research projects not only in the humanities, foremost among them historical studies, but also in the natural sciences. A remarkable occurrence was his agreement for calling two women to the university of Bologna, his old diocese. He maintained close ties of friendship with the greatest contemporary Italian historian, Ludovico Muratori. Ill feelings were caused when the Pope accepted Voltaire's drama *Mahomet*, handed him by Cardinal Passionei, who had close ties to that representative of French Enlightenment, and the famous hexameters composed by Voltaire for the painting of the Pope. Voltaire himself soon let it be known that Benedict had thanked him, started a correspondence with him, and sent him two gold medals. This was injurious to the Pope's public esteem.

The revision of the Index and the procedure whereby printed matter was placed on the Index constituted true progress. Subsequent practice, to be sure, did not keep pace with the more modern procedure desired by Benedict XIV. He wanted the objectionable passages—in the case of a well-known Catholic author—made known to him; if the author was prepared to improve them, the prohibition was not to be published. The author, moreover, was to have the chance to defend and justify himself.[1]

Benedict XIV was especially intent on augmenting the Vatican collections and enlarging the library. He acquired the largest private collection of books in Rome, the so called *Ottoboniana*, following the death of the last Ottoboni from the family of Pope Alexander VIII. He also planned to make the manuscript holdings of the Vatican generally accessible by means of a printed catalogue to consist of twenty volumes.

[1] In a memorial speech based on a draft by Robert Leiber, S.J., and intended for the 1958 congress for canonists, which was not given because of the prior death of the Pope, Pius XII had quoted a statement from a letter of Benedict to Cardinal de Tencin. In it he had expressed his basic thoughts concerning the prohibition of books: ". . . We would burden ourselves with guilt if we did not take the necessary measures to let justice prevail. But We are convinced that We remain guiltless before God or man in as much as he loves justice if We refuse to, or better yet if We do not engage at all in condemning a work simply upon the accusation of others and without a thorough examination both of the work itself as well as of the justification submitted by the author in his defense." It can be presumed that Pius XII at the time intended to use this quotation to initiate a basic change in the prevailing practice of censorship, but that the text of his speech was changed at this place. For in the extant text in the *Osservatore Romano* the lengthy quotation from Pope Benedict's letter is introduced by the kind of banal and unnecessary remark that can not be found in any other text by Pius XII: "Likewise he (Benedict XIV) did not want a condemnation of a book without having it examined thoroughly" (*Osservatore Romano*, 9 April 1959, no. 82, 3).

In regard to the appointment of cardinals Benedict XIV, as did his predecessors, often had to accede to the wishes of certain governments to elevate their candidates. A special case at the promotion of July 1747 was the elevation to the cardinalate of the last of the Stuarts, Duke Henry of York (d. 1807), who had joined the ecclesiastical estate after the Stuarts lost the battle of Culloden in 1746.

In questions of theology, especially in the doctrine of grace, Benedict XIV tended towards the Augustinian school. The indexing of the works of Cardinal Noris by the Spanish Inquisition was revoked by him: he succeeded in having them struck from the Spanish Index after ten years of negotiations. Prior to his election to the papacy he had once mentioned that Jansenism was merely a phantom and an invention of the Jesuits. But even though he publicly rejected complaints that he was a friend of the Jansenists and an opponent of the Jesuits, the fact remains that during his pontificate Rome became a major center of the Jesuits' opponents, whose esteem and influence were rising. Focal point and head of that group was Cardinal Passionei, who had built a popular rural retreat with a valuable library in Camaldoli near Frascati. Even at that time the efforts to have the Jesuit order suppressed, pursued by the general of the Augustinian order, Vázquez, the Spanish ambassador Roda, and several prelates of the Curia, were common knowledge.

The first blow against the society was struck in the mission territories. The controversy over the rites (see Chap. 16) with its disastrous consequences for the Asiatic missions had already lasted the entire century. The pertinent condemnations pronounced by Benedict XIV in 1742 and 1744 represented a long-expected outcome. But during his pontificate the Jesuit missions in Latin America and especially their reductions were also placed in extreme jeopardy and finally marked for extinction. At the very beginning of his office Benedict XIV had already acceded to the claims of the established church of Portugal in order to alleviate the pastoral problems caused by the long *sede* vacancies in many of the Portuguese dioceses. Also fulfilled by the Pope were other demands by Portugal, such as the special recognition of the patriarch of Lisbon and his canonists and the awarding of a special title to the King (*rex fidelissimus,* in adaptation to the title *rex christianissimus,* to which the King of France was entitled). When Joseph de Varcalho e Melho, Marquis de Pombal after 1770, who had become familiar with the administration of modern state government as a diplomat in Vienna and London, was appointed secretary of state, the attack against the Jesuits began in earnest. In order to effect economic reforms in Portugal, Pombal wanted to incorporate the Church into the mechanism of the state. His measures were directed against the orders in general. After the death of the queen mother (1754) and the earthquake in Lisbon on 1

November 1755, which gave rise to some unwise utterances by a few priests, he dropped his initial caution. The Jesuits, especially, were accused of all sorts of violations and crimes. In 1758 Pombal demanded that Benedict XIV appoint the Portuguese Cardinal Saldanha, a relative of the all-powerful secretary of state and totally dependent on him, to the office of visitor of the Jesuit order for Portugal with all the requisite authority. When the Pope gave in to this demand, the fate of the order in Portugal and its overseas possessions was sealed.

In the Austro-Venetian quarrel over the patriarchate of Aquileia the Pope was also intent on a settlement which would meet the two powers halfway. In 1418/20 when Venice had annexed Friaul and terminated the temporal rule of the patriarch over that territory, the diocese was politically partitioned. The larger part with its cathedral church was given to Austria, whereas Friaul with its actual patriarchal residence of Udine became part of Venice. Since the fifteenth century Austria had repeatedly tried to be assigned its own bishop; in 1628 it finally forbade the patriarch to exercise his functions in the Austrian part and kept its subjects from turning to the bishop in Udine. In 1748 Maria Theresa again applied for the establishment of a separate bishopric. The initial solution, the establishment of an apostolic vicariate in Görz, was rejected by the seigniory, which broke off relations with Rome in the summer of 1750 after its protests had been to no avail. Upon the suggestion of France, which had intervened as a mediator in order to keep the conflict from spreading, the patriarchate of Aquileia was abolished and the two bishoprics of Udine and Görz were established. The old cathedral of Aquileia was declared exempt and the patriarch permitted to retain the title for his person.[2]

The same conciliatory attitude which Benedict XIV manifested towards the Catholic powers and which at times prompted him to make excessive concessions was also applied to non-Catholic powers in order to improve the lot of the Catholic minorities in those countries. By means of its conquest of Silesia following the death of Charles VI, Prussia had significantly increased its Catholic population. Although the peace treaty of Breslau (1742) had assured the Catholic Church that the status quo would be maintained, the Catholics in fact became second-class citizens. According to the King's view the state was to exercise supreme supervisory power over the Protestant as well as the Catholic Church. The bishop of Breslau, Cardinal von Sinzendorf, was

---

[2] See F. Seneca, *La fine del Patriarcato Aquileiese 1748–1751* (Venice 1954); C. Gode, "Angelo Maria Querini, umanista e diplomatico per Aquileia," *RSTI* 18 (1964), 23–45; J. Rainer, "Versuche zur Errichtung neuer Bistümer in Innerösterreich unter Erzherzog Karl II. und Kaiser Ferdinand II.," *MIÖG* 68 (1960), 457–69 (background).

in no position to effectively counter the extreme steps of the established Church. He himself developed the plan for a vicariate for Prussia which was actually conceived as a "royal" rather than an "apostolic" vicariate. But Benedict XIV, whose concurrence was vigorously solicited by the Breslau cardinal, insisted that the future vicar general be lawfully installed, that is by the Pope. At the same time, Friedrich II prevailed in having the twenty-six-year-old Count Schaffgotsch, whom he liked but whose general conduct caused a lot of chagrin, accepted into the Breslau cathedral chapter. Without the count's participation and against the opposition of Rome the King appointed Schaffgotsch coadjutor to Cardinal von Sinzendorf. The Pope thereupon forbade the appointed coadjutor to be consecrated bishop. Upon Sinzendorf's death in 1747 Schaffgotsch, supported by Friedrich II's favor and skillfully feigning an inner rebirth, managed to have Benedict XIV appoint him as Sinzendorf's successor. It is probable that Benedict XIV saw through Schaffgotsch's insincerity. In connection with this affair the Pope for the first time implicitly recognized the Prussian royal title by mentioning in March 1748 the "royal person of Friedrich II." Up to that time the Curia had persistently used the earlier annoying title "Margrave of Brandenburg."

Even in his advanced years Benedict XIV displayed an astonishing stamina; after the serious illness of Secretary of State Valenti Gonzaga in 1751 until the latter's death in 1756 he did not appoint a successor but burdened himself with the major portion of the additional work. As a result his own health deteriorated; after 1756 he was feared to be on the verge of death several times. He died on 3 May 1758; according to witnesses he remarked immediately before his passing that he had been betrayed by Spain in the matter of the concordat.

In his papal history Pastor makes an unqualified positive judgment regarding the pontificate of Benedict XIV and especially concerning his political efforts.[3] Yet some serious misgivings have been raised about that position. Even Pope Pius XII in a prepared but undelivered allocution on the occasion of the two-hundredth anniversary of Benedict XIV mentions that the Pope probably manifested too much acquiescence

---

[3] "That such a man would refrain from surrendering ecclesiastical rights is understood. As a skillful canonist and theologian he could distinguish very well between essential and unessential rights, between that which had to be maintained under any circumstances and that which could be surrendered without damage and, indeed, should not be adhered to in order to avoid even greater problems. . . . The fact that he yielded as far as possible in matters which did not affect dogma could only be of benefit to the Church" (XVI/1, 437).

and weakness in the concordats with Naples, Savoy, and Spain as well as in his attitude towards Friedrich II of Prussia.[4]

[4] "Mentre, nella difficile controversia . . . per l'elezione imperiale di Carolo VII e di Francesco I . . . , il suo comportamento si dimostrò un esempio di saggezza non può dirsi senz'altro lo stesso, almeno con unanime consenso, per le conclusioni dei Concordati con le Corti di Sardegna-Piemonte, di Napoli e di Spagna, e per il grande riguardo da lui avuto verso le esigenze del Re Federico II di Prussia. Si può porre cioè il quesito, se egli sia stato troppo conciliante ed arrendevole di fronte alle veementi ed eccessive pretese delle Corti secolari. La risposta non è concorde tra gli storici, che, come già i contemporanei, si dividono in difensori e critici."

CHAPTER 32

Clement XIII and Clement XIV

Clement XIII (1758–69)

In the conclave starting on 15 May 1758 there was an initial agreement by more than two thirds of the cardinals on the candidacy of Cardinal Cavalchini when the formal exclusion was pronounced against him by the French Crown Cardinal Luynes because of Cavalchini's position in the beatification of Bellarmine (this was the last formal exclusion of the eighteenth century and the only one from the French side). On 6 July the Venetian Cardinal Carlo Rezzonico was elected. He had been elevated to the cardinalate by Clement XII in 1737 and for that reason he chose the name of Clement. Bishop of Padua since 1743, he had proved himself to be an ardent and strict ecclesiastic.

The Jesuit issue became the dominant one of his pontificate. A few weeks after the election Secretary of State Archinto, reappointed by the Pope's predecessor, died. In the person of Luigi Torrigiani, Clement XIII appointed a confirmed friend of the society to that office. But Torrigiani was unable to stop the anti-Jesuit momentum. The rapidly spreading persecution of the Jesuit order was unique in the annals of church history by virtue of its extent and effect. A parallel has been drawn between this persecution and the fragmentation of Poland, for in addition to the coincidence of the events there was also the common element of a degree of cynicism which disregarded all existing rights.[1]

[1] A. Sorel, *L'Europe et la Révolution française* I (Paris 1897), 67: "Dans tout le dix-huitième siècle, je ne vois, en matière d'intervention, qu'une ligue se former entre les couronnes . . . .: c'est la ligue de puissances du nord contre la Pologne et contre la

The attack on the order has also been viewed as an attack on the Church itself and especially on the papacy.[2] There were also a variety of additional forces, such as theological and ecclesiastical special interests in a complex combination with political, anti-Church, and enlightened tendencies. All of this finally led to the vehement demand for basic changes in the structure of the Jesuit order and, in the end, for its suppression. Certainly there were faults and abuses within the ranks of the order and many of the complaints and accusations were not without justification. Yet an objective investigation will show that the discrepancy between ideal and reality in the Jesuit order was no more serious than in other ecclesiastical communities of the time.

The attack against the order began in Portugal, where a brief of Benedict XIV, dated 1 April 1758, had appointed Cardinal Saldanha, who was totally dependent on Pombal, to the office of apostolic visitor of the order with full authority. Without an actual investigation, the Jesuits were first accused of illegal commercial transactions; next, some time after the unsuccessful assassination attempt on the King on 3 September 1758, they were accused of participation in that conspiracy. In June 1759 all the assets of the order in Portugal and its overseas territories were confiscated. In September in spite of energetic intervention by Clement XIII the members of the order were deported first from Portugal and then gradually from the overseas possessions and sent to the Papal States. Many died during transport (about 90 to 100) or were kept in Portuguese jails, often under inhuman conditions (about 180), or left the order (about 250, constituting 15 percent of the Portuguese contingent of the order).

France was the first country to follow Portugal's example. But in contrast to Portugal and the other states from which the Jesuits were destined to be expelled in subsequent years, France had a strong and in part well-organized opposition against the Jesuits, especially in the parliament. This opposition increased around the middle of the seven-

---

Suède. Quant aux puissances de l'ouest et du midi de l'Europe, je n'aperçois qu'une circonstance où elles aient poursuivi de concert un objet commun, c'est la suppression de l'ordre des Jésuites. L'incident est caractéristique: il présente comme une sorte de bas-relief où s'accusent, en quelques traits saillants, les mœurs politiques de l'époque."
[2] See Pastor XVI/1, 602: "The attack was instead mostly directed against the papacy; inasmuch as it was against the Jesuit order it was only because the latter represented a kind of outer battlement which had to be breached in order to facilitate the fight with the actual opponent"; and J. Lortz, *Geschichte der Kirche,* 339f.: "In all the great conflicts of the seventeenth century the Jesuit order was the object of the attack. The explanation for that was the strictly centralist, papal, ecclesiastical nature of this order. Quite naturally it also became the single great enemy of the anti-Church Enlightenment arising from those conflicts."

teenth century, fueled by the disputes with the Jansenist movement and literarily well documented in Pascal's *Provincial Letters.* Immediately after the middle of the century some individual cases aggravated the already serious tensions. The year 1755 marked the beginning of the affair involving Lavalette, an economist and superior of the Jesuit order on the Antilles. In order to secure the economic aspects of the mission work he operated plantations and tried to sell their products in Europe. Losses due to war and the bankruptcy of his correspondent commercial house in France led to the failure of his undertakings. Initially the French courts made Lavalette personally liable for the damages, but then in 1760 the order as a whole and its assets in France in particular were declared liable. Furthermore, Mme Pompadour, rising to the position of favorite of the King in 1756 and becoming all powerful, disliked the Jesuits because they disapproved of her position at the court. After the assassination attempt on Louis XV (15 January 1757) public opinion was aroused against the Jesuits when they were accused of complicity on the basis of their doctrine regarding tyrannicide.

Desperate attempts by the French superiors of the order, extending to a formal recognition of the four Gallican articles of 1682 and, in some cases, advocating a secession from the united order by the establishment of a separate French vicariate general,[3] were unable to avert the disaster. Although the great majority of the French episcopate had pronounced themselves in favor of the Jesuits, and in spite of several interventions by Clement XIII with the bishops and Louis XV, all assets of the order were confiscated in April 1762. The following August marked the beginning of deportation. A significant percentage, especially of the scholastics and the lay brothers among the almost three thousand French Jesuits, left the order with the agreement of their superiors. On 1 December 1764, the Society of Jesus in France was officially abolished. The previously prepared bull *Apostolicum pascendi,* which reacknowledged the order and made an unequivocal statement in favor of the Jesuits, was published on 7 January 1765 as a direct answer to the French abolition. As could be expected, this public pronouncement by Clement XIII had no practical result.

In 1759 Charles III, formerly King of Naples, ascended to the Spanish throne. Dependent on his prime minister, Tanucci, he inclined towards an expansion of the established Church and a restriction of the

---

[3] In connection with these efforts, which were also pursued by French circles outside the order, Clement XIII is said to have remarked to Ricci, the general of the order: "aut sint ut sunt, aut non sint," although it is not clear whether this meaningful formulation should be attributed to the Pope himself or perhaps rather to Cesare Giulio Cordara, who quoted it.

liberties of the Church of Rome. But Tanucci was also a confirmed opponent of the Jesuit order.[4] His influence and some skillfully manipulated changes in the first rank of government affected the heretofore friendly attitude towards the Jesuits. In a later stage of the investigation but without actual proof the "Hat Rebellion" of March 1766, caused by economic and social abuses, was blamed on the Jesuits. The death of Queen Mother Elizabeth Farnese precisely that same year caused the order to lose an influential patron. Certain ecclesiastical circles, especially the Augustine General Vázquez,[5] urged the government to take steps against the Jesuit order. Giving no reasons, a royal decree of 27 February 1767 ordered the banishment of all Jesuits from Spanish territory and the confiscation of all Jesuit assets. The rules for the implementation of the decree were issued in the strictest secrecy. On 2 April the Spanish members of the order, numbering about twenty-eight hundred, were confined and deported. In the course of the year the approximately sixteen hundred Jesuits living in the overseas possessions met the same fate. In a show of resistance to the unilateral, forcible action by Spain, the papal government denied landing rights to the Spanish ships transporting the Jesuits to its ports. They finally found refuge on Corsica. In the following year when the island had become French they were able to travel to the territories of the Papal States. The protest by the Pope with the King of Spain had no effect whatsoever.

After the actions of Spain, the expulsion of the Jesuits from the Spanish secundogenitures of Naples (20 November 1767), Parma-Piacenza (7 February 1768), as well as from the island of Malta (22 April 1768) was no more than expected.

It is not surprising that an outgrowth of these individual actions would be a united plan for the total abolition of the Jesuit order by authority of the Pope. This plan seems to have been developed almost simultaneously in both France and Portugal with affirmation by Spain being assumed. The only difficult element which also took some time to overcome was the anticipated resistance of Maria Theresa, whose support could not be enlisted. Finally in 1770 she declared her neutrality and agreed not to undertake anything in favor of the Jesuits if the other powers could obtain from the Pope the abolition of the order; furthermore, she would not withhold her concurrence in the ultimate decision of the Holy See. A pretext for this alliance was the situation in Parma. Its prime minister, Du Tillot, had repeatedly violated the rights of the

---

[4] Even though he recognized that the individual Jesuit could not be reproached: "Ottimi sacerdoti ho sempre conosciuto i particolari Gesuiti, che io ho trattato, pieni di carità, di prudenza e di tutte le virtù cristiane" (Pastor XVI/1 718 n. 1).
[5] After the expulsion Vázquez did not hide his jubilation over the goal which had finally been reached; see the passage from the letter quoted by Pastor XVI/1, 786, n. 3.

Church. In a decree of 16 January 1768 he stopped any and all cases from being submitted to foreign courts, meaning also the ecclesiastical courts in Rome. On 30 January a monitory declared those violations null and void and made their perpetrators subject to the penalties of the Church according to the Eucharistic bull *In coena Domini*. Since all the Bourbon courts felt affected by this monitory they decided to undertake a concerted action. In April 1768 the respective ambassadors demanded of Clement XIII the immediate revocation of the document under threat of reprisals. When the Pope did not give in, the papal enclaves of Benevento and Pontecorvo, Avignon and Venaissin were occupied. The stubborn refusal of the Pope did not deter the Catholic powers from making additional demands. A climax was reached in January 1769 when the ambassadors formally requested the Pope for the abolition of the Jesuit order.

The financial difficulties of the Papal States, aggravated by famine and rising prices in 1763 and 1764, continued because reforms could not be implemented against the will of the large property holders. Regarding architectural projects, only the completion of the Fontana Trevi and the Villa Albani took place in these years. In 1763, following a recommendation of Cardinal Albani, the Pope appointed Winckelmann commissioner of antiquities. Before that, the Pope, scrupulously fearful, had had a number of antique sculptures covered and the *Last Judgment* in the Sistine Chapel painted over again. Even then these measures had incurred Winckelmann's scorn, but he nonetheless accepted the Pope's offer.

Like his predecessors, Clement XIII favored Italian prelates for promotion, mostly those in the service of the Curia and a few candidates suggested by the Catholic powers. The appointment of his nephew met with general agreement since the latter kept aloof from the affairs of state. Unfortunate, although unavoidable, was the elevation of the short-term French foreign minister de Bernis, whose unedifying, totally secular way of life was well known. The most important of Clement XIII's appointments turned out to be that of Lorenzo Ganganelli, the future Pope Clement XIV, who was elevated to the purple in 1759.

Clement XIII died on 2 February 1769 of a heart attack after he celebrated Mass early in the morning and consecrated the candles of the day. His tomb in Saint Peter's, created by Canova, was not unveiled until twenty-three years after his death.

Clement XIV (1769–74)

The conclave beginning on 15 February 1769 was marked by the Jesuit issue. No election could take place until the Spanish cardinals arrived in

Rome because the French, having arrived there a month earlier, had made it clear that they would use their exclusion against anyone who might be elected prior to the arrival of the Spaniards. The Catholic powers were agreed that no friend of the Jesuits should be elected, but there were noticeable differences regarding procedure. Whereas the great powers, with Spain in the lead, demanded a formal prior assurance from any serious candidate that he would abolish the Jesuit order, the crown cardinals viewed such a step as fulfilling the fact of simony and therefore rejected such a method. The favored candidate of the powers was the archbishop of Naples, Sersale, who failed because of his excessive acquiescence to the state. On the advice of the Spanish ambassador Azpuru, the candidacy of Cardinal Ganganelli was then promoted. It is certain that he did not give a promise prior to his election to abolish the order. When asked he merely explained that in his opinion a Pope could abolish the Society of Jesus just like any other order for very important reasons and with the proper observance of wisdom and justice. He was elected unanimously on 19 May 1769.

Ganganelli, born in 1705 in Sant'Arcangelo near Rimini, had joined the Franciscan Conventuals in 1723 and exchanged his baptismal name of Giovanni Vincenzo for that of his father Lorenzo. After several years of teaching in various Italian schools of his order, he became rector of the Bonaventura college in Rome and consultant of the Inquisition in 1746. He twice rejected election to the post of general of his order, probably in order to remain eligible for higher office. In 1759 Clement XIII elevated him to the cardinalate. At that time and previous to it he had been considered a friend of the Jesuits; as cardinal he gradually removed himself from them, seeking ties instead with the ambassadors of the Bourbon powers. The reproach of ambition and calculation, raised against him by Pastor, seems not to have been completely unfounded.

During his pontificate his fellow Augustinian Bontempi became his indispensable confidant. Cardinal Pallavicini, nuncio in Madrid from 1760 to 1767 and a confirmed friend of Spain, was appointed secretary of state. The first important step taken by the new Pope was to restore normal relations with Portugal, which had been broken off in 1759. Vacant dioceses could then be filled again, although only by candidates agreeable to Pombal. A nuncio was dispatched to Lisbon, but at the same time the Pope had to appoint Pombal's brother to the cardinalate and, when he died shortly after, he was forced to elevate the favorite of the all-powerful minister. The Pope was applauded by all the enlightened circles for omitting on Maundy Thursday 1770 the customary pronouncement of the bull *In coena Domini,* an action implicitly correcting his predecessor, who had expressly referred to that bull in his monitory to Parma in 1768. In 1774 the bull was formally revoked.

From the beginning of the Pope's pontificate Spain was the motive force behind the Jesuit issue. A routine brief acknowledging the customary indulgences granted to missionaries of the Jesuit order and their faithful provoked outrage. It prompted the united powers to have the French ambassador, Cardinal Bernis, formally approach Clement XIV with a demand for the abolition of the order. The Pope, unsure because of his earlier oblique assent and fearful of being poisoned by the Jesuits, finally gave in to the urging of France, which was reinforced by the threat of breaking off diplomatic relations. In a letter to Louis XIV in September 1769 he promised to abolish the order but did not set a firm date. He made the same promise in a letter to Charles III of Spain at the end of November, at the same time asking for the King's patience.

In spite of such firm assurances the next three years were marked by a noticeable wavering on the part of the Pope vis-à-vis the Jesuits. Individual harsh steps against the order, as for instance the punishment of members without a reason, discriminatory visitations of colleges, brusque treatment of the superiors, were not sufficient to pacify the united powers. Their ambassadors incessantly pressured the Pope, not without intriguing and raising suspicions among one another. The fall of Choiseul at the end of 1770, triggered by the influence of Mme Du Barry, did not make a difference in the French policy regarding the Jesuits. The actual turn of events in this matter, called "el negocio grande," was brought about with the change of Spanish ambassadors to Rome. Azpuru, who resigned at the end of 1771 for reasons of health, was followed by José Moñino, appointed count of Florida-blanca in 1773.[6] His first audience with the Pope initiated the final phase of the fight against the Jesuit order. In answer to an attempt by the Pope to bring about a gradual attrition without the need for a formal document of abolition by forbidding the acceptance of novices in the order, the ambassador threatened the expulsion of all religious orders from Spain and, finally, the breaking off of diplomatic relations. The Spanish embassy then prepared a draft of an abolition bull which was submitted to the Pope at the beginning of 1773 and approved by him in all the essential points. The fact that Madrid was satisfied with the text need hardly be mentioned since the bull was drafted in its own embassy. The Spanish member of the Curia, Zelada, who was substantially involved in the editing of the text, was appointed cardinal soon after, on 19 April

---

[6] Since he did not die until 1819, he lived to see the restoration of the order in whose suppression he had been instrumental.

1773 and—as were other pliable collaborators, foremost among them the Pope's confidant, Bontempi—richly rewarded by Spain. The last possible obstacle was overcome in the spring of 1773 when Maria Theresa, urged by Spain, reiterated Austria's neutrality of the Jesuit issue. In June—probably 9 June—Clement XIV signed the abolition document.[7] For practical and stylistic reasons it was not composed as a bull as previously planned but in the form of a brief. The printing—as yet without a date—was provided by the Spanish ambassador, the better to ensure secrecy. In the middle of July the congregation of cardinals to be charged with the implementation of the abolition was appointed. But not until 22 July did Moñino receive permission to send copies of the brief, dated the day before, to the governments involved. On 16 August it was published in Rome and implemented the very same day.

A general historical preamble to the brief *Dominus ac Redemptor noster* presents the right of the Pope regarding the recognition as well as the abolition of religious orders. It then states the difficulties—although in a very one-sided selection of facts—which the Jesuit order had had with other orders and with temporal princes in the course of its history. This is followed by the actual decree of abolition. The voluminous document concludes with the rules of implementation.

The abolition of the Jesuit order was seen as a victory of rationalism and Clement XIV was widely celebrated for his decision. In the medal for the year 1774 he referred—although discreetly—to the abolition as a peace-making event. The enemies of the Jesuits expressed their triumph more directly in an imitation of the papal medal; in a reference to the expulsion of Adam and Eve from paradise the reverse side of the medal shows the expulsion of the Jesuits with the circular notation "I know ye not" and in reference to the psalm "This is the day which the Lord hath made: we will rejoice and be glad in it."

The various countries where any Jesuits were left implemented the abolition in different ways. Because of pressure and surveillance by the Bourbon powers the procedure was harshest in the Papal States. The general of the order, Lorenzo Ricci—and with him the more important members of the order—was held in strict incarceration at the Castel Sant'Angelo until his death. Moñino successfully opposed the release of Ricci, planned by Pius VI, the successor of Clement XIV, and also tried to prevent any alleviation of the conditions at the prison. In Austria and

---

[7] The frequently mentioned assertion that before signing the brief Clement XIV looked up the founder of the Passionists, the highly esteemed Paul of the Cross, and signed the brief only after his talk with him is probably not correct; see Gaetano dell'Addolorata, O.P., in *RSTI* 13 (1959), 102–12.

Germany the abolition was generally executed without harshness. Attention was paid that the work of former Jesuits was impaired as little as possible. Maria Theresa and other princes successfully resisted the demand intended by Clement XIV that the assets of the order, which were greatly overestimated, be placed at the disposal of the Holy See. Instead the property of the order was taken over by the respective states.

Only Friedrich II of Prussia, who in 1767 had welcomed the expulsion of the Jesuits from Spain, and Catherine II of Russia (in order to maintain the Catholic school system in Silesia or White Russia) prohibited the publication and implementation of the abolition brief. Whereas Prussia did formally abolish the order a few years later, the tsarina persisted in her policy and the competent bishop ordered the Jesuits to continue their work. The assurance by the suffragan bishop of Mogilev in 1785 that Pius VI had approved of the conduct of the White Russian ex-Jesuits in a conversation with him cannot be proved historically, but it was binding for the members of the order at that time. In 1801 Pope Pius VI formally recognized the Society of Jesus for White Russia.

The abolition of the order caused severe damage especially to the Catholic school system in Europe. The deportation from Portugal and Spain had already put a stop to the missionary work of the order. The Jesuits overwhelmingly acquiesced to the papal decision although it brought with it utter distress and persecution for many. Not a few ex-Jesuits continued to excel in the service of the Church.

In exchange for the abolition of the order the Catholic powers had promised the Pope to return the occupied exclaves of the Papal States. But Clement XIV could not prevail in his suggestion to have the territories returned prior to publicizing the abolition brief. Since Tanucci wanted to retain Benevento for Naples at any price, the restitution of the occupied areas was delayed until 1774 and was, moreover, encumbered with humiliating provisos.

In twelve promotions Clement XIV installed a total of seventeen new cardinals. At the last creation (26 April 1774) two new cardinals were installed by name, among them Braschi, the successor of Clement, and eleven *in petto*. The Pope never divulged the names of these candidates although he was put under extreme pressure to do so when he was seriously ill just before his death; according to contemporary opinion all of them were most likely from the ranks of opponents of the Jesuit order.

After the abolition of the order the Pope's fears of possible poisoning by his imagined opponents increased. The state of his health, not very stable at best, deteriorated steadily, probably aggravated by his depressions and the excitements. Death came on 21 September 1774.

Rumors of poisoning immediately spread, but are generally rejected as baseless by more recent research. At the exequies of Clement XIV the customary presentation of special achievements made no mention at all of the abolition of the Society of Jesus. Clement XIV was initially put to rest in Saint Peter's; in 1802 he was transferred to the monastic church of SS. Apostoli, where the tomb created by Canova had been ready since 1787.

BIBLIOGRAPHY

GENERAL BIBLIOGRAPHY

The fact that relatively few comprehensive presentations exist is due partly to the period of church history treated in this volume and partly to the state of historical literature. We therefore call attention to the literature listed under the various sections and chapters. The titles overlapping from the sixteenth century, cited in Volume V, will not be repeated here.

I. GENERAL HISTORY

WORLD HISTORY: F. Valjavec, *Historia Mundi* VII and VIII (Berne 1957ff.).; G. Mann and A. Nitschke, *Propyläen-Weltgeschichte* VII (Berlin 1964); H. Franke et al.; *Saeculum Weltgeschichte* V (Freiburg i. Brsg. 1970), VI (in preparation); *Cambridge Modern History* III, IV (Cambridge 1904, 1906).

EUROPE: F. Hartung, *Neuzeit. Von der Mitte des 17. Jh. bis zur Gegenwart* I: *Bis zur Französischen Revolution* (*Handbuch für den Geschichtslehrer* V, 1) (Vienna 1932, reprint Darmstadt 1965); R. M. Rayner, *European History 1648–1789* (London 1949); L. Gottschalk and D. Lach, *Europe and the Modern World* I: *The Rise of Modern Europe* (Chicago 1951); M. Crouzet, ed., *Histoire générale des civilisations* IV: R. Mousnier, *Les XVIᵉ et XVIIᵉ siècles: 1492–1715* (Paris 1961); V.: R. Mousnier, E. Labrousse, and M. Bouljoiseau, *Le XVIIIᵉ siècle. 1715–1815* (Paris 1967); F. Wagner, *Europa im Zeitalter des Absolutismus. 1648–1789* (Munich 1959); G. Ritter, ed., *Geschichte der Neuzeit* II: W. Hubatsch, *Das Zeitalter des Absolutismus, 1600–1789* (Brunswick 1965); M. Beloff, *The Age of Absolutism 1660–1815* (London 1966); T. Schieder, ed., *Handbuch der europäischen Geschichte* IV: *Europa im Zeitalter des Absolutismus und der Aufklärung* (Stuttgart 1968); F. Wagner, *Europa im Zeitalter des Absolutismus und der Aufklärung* (Stuttgart 1968); P. Chaunu, *La Civilisation de l'Europe classique. 1620–1750* (Paris 1966); D. Ogg, *Europe in the Seventeenth Century* (New York 1962); C. J. Friedrich, *The Age of the Baroque, 1610–1660* (New York 1952); F. L. Nussbaum, *The Triumph of Science and Reason, 1660–1685* (New York 1953).

FRANCE: E. Lavisse, ed., *Histoire de France . . .*: VI, 2: J. H. Mariéjol, *Henri IV, Louis XIII (1598–1643)* (Paris 1905); III, 1 and 2: E. Lavisse, *Louis XIV* (Paris 1906); VIII, 1: A. de Saint-Léger et al., *Louis XIV. La Fin Du Règne* (Paris 1908); VIII, 2: H. Carré, *Le règne de Louis XV* (Paris 1909); IX, 1: H. Carré et al., *Le règne de Louis XVI* (Paris 1910); H. Méthivier, *Le siècle de Louis XIV* (Paris 1966); H. Méthivier, *L'Ancien Régime* (Paris 1964); C. J. Burckhardt, *Richelieu and His Age* I: *His Rise to Power,* trans. and abridged, Edwin and Willa Muir; II: *Assertion of Power and Cold War;* III: *Power, Politics and the Cardinal's Death* (New York 1972); W. F. Church, *Richelieu and Reason of State* (Princeton 1972); V. Tapié, *La France de Louis XIII et de Richelieu* (Paris 1967); A. Lublinskaya, *French Absolutism. The Crucial Phase 1620–1629* (London 1968); G. Hanotaux and Duc de la Force, *Histoire du Cardinal de Richelieu,* 5 vols. (Paris 1893–1944); A. Chéruel, *Histoire de France sous le ministère de Mazarin (1651–61),* 3 vols. (Paris 1882).

SPAIN: W. Coxe, *L'Espagne sous les rois de la maison Bourbon*, 5 vols. (Paris 1827); A. Baudrillart, *Philippe V et la Cour de France*, 5 vols. (Paris 1890–1901); R. Altamira, *Historia de españa y de la civilización española* III (Barcelona 1928); A. Ballesteros y Beretta, *Historia de España* IV and V (Barcelona 1926ff.); R. Konetzke, *Geschichte des spanischen und portugiesischen Volkes* (Leipzig 1939); P. Aguado Bleye, *Manual de historia de España* II and III (Madrid 1954); A. Ballesteros y Beretta, *Geschichte Spaniens* (Munich and Berlin 1943); F. Soldevila, *Historia de España* IV–VI (Barcelona 1956ff.); R. Heer, *The Eighteenth-Century Revolution in Spain* (New Jersey 1958); L. Pfandl, *Spanische Literaturgeschichte* (Leipzig 1923); R. Konetzke, *Süd- und Mittelamerika* (*Fischer-Weltgeschichte* 22) (Frankfurt am Main 1953).

ITALY: B. Croce, *A History of Italy, 1871–1915* (New York 1963); G. Candeloro, *Storia dell'Italia moderna* I (Milan 1956); F. Valsecchi, *L'Italia nel settecento dal 1714 al 1788* (Milan 1959).

GERMAN STATES AND SWITZERLAND: O. Brandt et al., *Handbuch der deutschen Geschichte* II: L. Just, *Der aufgeklärte Absolutismus* (Constance 1956); B. Gebhardt and H. Grundmann, *Handbuch der deutschen Geschichte* II: M. Braubach, *Vom Westfälischen Frieden bis zur Französischen Revolution* (Stuttgart 1965); A. Wandruszka, *Leopold II.*, 2 vols. (Vienna 1963–65); H. Nabholz et al., *Geschichte der Schweiz* II: R. Feller, *Geschichte der Schweiz im 17. u. 18. Jh.* (1938); J. Lortz, *Reformation in Germany* (New York 1968).

GREAT BRITAIN AND IRELAND: G. N. Clark, ed., *Oxford History of England* X: G. N. Clark, *The Later Stuarts 1660–1714* (Oxford 1955); XI: B. Williams, *The Whig Supremacy 1714–1760* (Oxford 1962); XII: I. Steven Watson, *The Reign of George III 1760–1865* (Oxford 1960); W. E. H. Lecky, *History of Ireland in the Eighteenth Century*, 5 vols. (London 1892).

POLAND: H. Łowminański, *Historia Polski* I and II (Warsaw 1958–61); G. Rhode, *Kleine Geschichte Polens* (Darmstadt 1965).

RUSSIA: G. Stökl, *Russische Geschichte von den Anfängen bis zur Gegenwart* (Stuttgart 1965).

THE ENLIGHTENMENT

P. Hazard, *La crise de la conscience Européenne. 1680–1715* (Paris 1935); P. Hazard, *La pensée Européenne aux XVIIIᵉ siècle de Montesquieu à Lessing* (Paris 1946); F. Valjevec, *Geschichte der abendländischen Aufklärung* (Vienna and Munich 1961); R. Mousnier, E. Labrousse, and M. Bouloiseau, *Le XVIIIᵉ siècle. 1715–1815. L'époque des "lumières"* (Paris 1967); E. Cassirer, *The Philosophy of the Enlightenment*, trans. by F. Koelln and J. Pettegrove (Boston 1955); W. Dilthey, *Weltanschauung und Analyse des Menschen seit Renaissance und Reformation* (=*Ges. Schr.* 2) (Göttingen 1960); W. Dilthey, *Selected Writings* (New York 1976); W. Dilthey, "Das 18. Jh. u. die geschichtliche Welt," *Deutsche Rundschau* (Aug./Sept. 1901) (=*Ges. Schr.* 3) (Göttingen 1959), 209–68; F. Meinecke, *Die Entstehung des Historismus* (Munich 1936, 1946); K. Löwith, *Meaning in History* (Chicago 1949); B. Croce, *History. Its Theory and Practice*, trans. by D. Ainslie. Reprint of 1920 edition (New York 1979); H. v. Srbik, *Geist u. Geschichte vom deutschen Humanismus bis zur Gegenwart* I (Munich and Salzburg 1950), 69–166; O. Zöckler, *Geschichte der Beziehungen zwischen Theologie und Naturwissenschaft mit besonderer Rücksicht auf Schöpfungsgeschichte*, 2 vols. (Gütersloh 1877–79); W. Philipp, *Das Werden der Aufklärung in theologiegeschichtlicher Sicht* (Göttingen 1957); P. Gay, *The Enlightenment*, 2 vols. (New York 1966–69).

II. CHURCH HISTORY

1. GENERAL CHURCH HISTORY

J. H. Nichols, *History of Christianity (1650–1950)* (New York 1956); L. A. Veit, *Die Kirche im Zeitalter des Individualismus* I *(1648–1800)* (Freiburg i. Brsg. 1931); G. Schnürer, *Katholische Kirche und Kultur in der Barockzeit* (Paderborn 1937); id., *Katholische Kirche und Kultur im 18. Jh.* (Paderborn 1941); A. Fliche and V. Martin, *Histoire de l'Église* 19, Parts 1 and 2: E. Préclin and E. Jarry, *Les luttes politiques et doctrinales aux XVIIe et XVIIIe siècles* (Paris 1955–56); K. Bihlmeyer and H. Tüchle, *Church History* III: *Recent and Modern Times* (New York 1970); J. Lortz, *Geschichte der Kirche in ideengeschichtlicher Betrachtung* II (Münster 1964); J. Hajjar, *Les chrétiens uniates du Proche-Orient* (Paris 1962); K. Heussi, *Kompendium der Kirchengeschichte* (Tübingen 1960); K. D. Schmidt, *Grundriß der Kirchengeschichte* IV: *Geschichte der Kirche im Zeitalter des Individualismus und des Säkularismus* (Göttingen 1960); K. D. Schmidt and E. Wolf, *Die Kirche in ihrer Geschichte. Ein Handbuch:* 4, fasc. N, part 1: F. Heyer, *Die kath. Kirche vom Westfälischen Frieden bis zum ersten Vatikanischen Konzil* (Göttingen 1963); R. Aubert, *The Church in a Secularized Society* 5: *The Christian Centuries* (New York 1969).

2. THE PAPACY

L. v. Ranke, *The History of the Popes during the Last Four Centuries* (London 1907); L. v. Pastor, *History of the Popes from the Close of the Middle Ages* (St. Louis, Mo. 1938–61); F. X. Seppelt and G. Schwaiger, *Geschichte des Papsttums* V.: *Das Papsttum im Kampf mit Staatsabsolutismus und Aufklärung* (Munich 1959); M. Brosch, *Geschichte des Kirchenstaates* (Gotha 1882); V. Mariani, *Le chiese di Roma dal XVII al XVIII secolo* (*Roma Christiana* 5) (Bologna 1963); L. Karttunen, *Les nonciatures apostoliques permanentes de 1650 à 1800* (Geneva 1912); E. Winter, *Rußland und das Papsttum,* 2 vols. (Berlin 1960–61); W. de Vries in collaboration with O. Bârlea, J. Gill, and M. Lacko, *Rom und die Patriarchate des Ostens* (Freiburg and Munich 1963).

3. THE HISTORY OF THE CATHOLIC CHURCH IN INDIVIDUAL COUNTRIES

A. Sicard, *L'ancien clergé de France,* 3 vols. (Paris 1893–1903); P. B. Gams, *Die Kirchengeschichte von Spanien* III/2 (Regensburg 1862–79; reprint Graz 1956); V. Lafuente, *Historia eclesiástica de España* V and VI (Madrid 1875); B. N. Ward, *The Dawn of the Catholic Revival in England 1781–1803,* 2 vols. (London 1909); D. Gwynn, *The Struggle for Catholic Emancipation 1750–1829* (London 1928); P. Hughes, *The Catholic Question 1685–1929* (London 1929); R. Bagwell, *Ireland under the Stuarts,* 3 vols. (London 1909–16; reprint London 1963); E. Tomek and H. Hantsch, *Kirchengeschichte Österreichs* III: *Die Zeit der Aufklärung und des Absolutismus* (Innsbruck 1959); H. E. Feine, *Die Besetzung der Reichsbistümer vom Westfälischen Frieden bis zur Säkularisation 1648–1803* (Amsterdam 1964).

4. THE ESTABLISHED CHURCH

P. Brezzi, *Stato e Chiesa nell'Ottocento* (Turin 1964); H. Raab, *Kirche und Staat. Von der Mitte des 15. Jh. bis zur Gegenwart* (Munich 1966); V. Martin, *Les origines du gallicanisme,* 2 vols. (Paris 1939); A. G. Martimort, *Le gallicanisme de Bossuet* (Paris 1953); M. F.

Miguélez, *Jansenismo y Regalismo en España* (Madrid 1895); Q. Aldea, *Iglesia y Estado en la España del siglo XVII* (Comillas 1961); J. Saarailh, *L'Espagne éclairée de la seconde moitié du XVIIIe siècle* (Paris 1954); A. de la Hera, *El regalismo borbónico* (Madrid 1963); B. Duhr, *Pombal. Sein Charakter und seine Politik* (Freiburg 1891); C. Gérin, *Louis XIV et le Saint-Siège* (Paris 1894); J. Orcibal, *Louis XIV contre Innocent XI: les appels au futur concile de 1688 et l'opinion française* (Paris 1949).

5. CHRISTIAN SPIRITUALITY

P. Pourrat, *The Christian Spirituality* (Westminster, Md. 1953–55); J. Gautier, *La spiritualité catholique* (Paris 1953); L. Cognet, *De la Dévotion moderne à la spiritualité française* (Paris 1958); L. Cognet, *La spiritualité moderne* I: *L'essor, 1500–1650* (Paris 1966); H. Bremond, *Histoire littéraire du sentiment religieux en France,* 11 vols; (Paris 1916–33). Especially Vol. IV: *L'École de Port-Royal* (Paris 1919); L. Prunel, *La Renaissance catholique en France au XVIIIe siècle* (Paris 1921); G. Le Bras, *Introduction à l'histoire de la pratique religieuse en France,* 2 vols. (Paris 1942–45); H. Busson, *La pensée religieuse française de Charron à Pascal* (Paris 1933); H. Busson, *La religion des classiques 1660–1685* (Paris 1948); H. Gouhier, *La pensée religieuse de Descartes* (Paris 1924); É. Gilson, *La doctrine cartésienne de la liberté et la théologie* (Paris 1913); J. Mesnard, *Pascal, l'homme et l'œuvre* (Paris 1951); L. A. Veit and L. Lenhart, *Kirche und Volksfrömmigkeit im Zeitalter des Barock* (Freiburg i. Brsg. 1956); W. Trapp, *Vorgeschichte und Ursprung der liturgischen Bewegung* (Regensburg 1940); C. Schreiber, *Aufklärung und Frömmigkeit. Die katholische Predigt im deutschen Aufklärungszeitalter* (Munich 1940).

6. JANSENISM

A. Gazier, *Histoire générale du mouvement janséniste,* 2 vols. (Paris 1924); J. Orcibal, *Les origines du Jansénisme,* 3 vols. (Louvain and Paris 1947–48); L. Cognet, *Le jansénisme* (Paris 1961); L. Ceyssens, *Jansenistica,* 4 vols. (Mechlin 1950–62); C. Gazier, *Histoire du monastère de Port-Royal* (Paris 1929); C.-A. Sainte-Beuve, *Port-Royal* 3 vols. (Paris 1953–55); L. Cognet, *La réforme de Port-Royal* (Paris 1950); J. Laporte, *La doctrine de Port-Royal, la morale d'après Arnauld,* 2 vols. (Paris 1951–52); P. Jansen, *Le cardinal Mazarin et le mouvement janséniste* (Paris 1967); W. Deinhardt, *Der Jansenismus in deutschen Landen* (Munich 1929); A. C. Iemole, *Il Giansenismo in Italia prima della Rivoluzione* (Bari 1928); E. Dammig, *Il movimento giansenista a Roma* (Vatican City 1945); B. Van Kley, *The Jansenists and the Expulsion of the Jews from France 1757–1765* (New Haven 1975).

7. THE NON-ROMAN CATHOLIC CHURCHES

E. Léonard, *A History of Protestantism* (London 1965); C. M. Schröder, ed., *Klassiker des Protestantismus* V: W. Zeller, *Der Protestantismus des 17. Jh.* (Bremen 1962); VII.: W. Philipp, *Das Zeitalter der Aufklärung* (Bremen 1963); G. R. Cragg, *From Puritanism to the Age of Reason. A Study of Changes in Religious Thought within the Church of England 1600–1700* (Cambridge 1966); E. and E. Haag, *La France protestante,* 10 vols. (Paris 1846–59); J. Pannier, *L'Église réformée de France sous Louis XIII,* 2 vols. (Paris 1932); J. Viénot, *Histoire de la Réforme française de l'édit de Nantes à sa révocation,* 2 vols. (Paris 1934); A. Aymon, *Actes ecclésiastiques et civils de tous les synodes nationaux des Églises réformées de France,* 2 vols. (The Hague 1710–56); P. Wernle, *Der schweizerische Protestantismus im 18. Jh.,* 3 vols. (1923–25); M. Menéndez y Pelayo, *Historia de los Heterodoxos españoles* VI and VII (Madrid 1930–33); C. W. Towlson, *Moravian and Methodist Relationships and Influence in the Eighteenth*

Century (London 1957); L. Bouyer, *Orthodox Spirituality and Protestant and Anglican Spirituality* (London 1969); J. T. Dorosh, *The Eastern Orthodox Church, a Bibliography of Publications Printed in the Roman Alphabet with Indication of Location* (Washington, D.C. 1946); D. T. Andrews, *The Eastern Orthodox Church, a Bibliography* (New York 1953); A. M. Ammann, *Abriß der ostslawischen Kirchengeschichte* (Vienna 1950; with biblio.); W. de Vries, *Der christliche Osten in Geschichte und Gegenwart* (Würzburg 1951); D. Attwater, *The Christian Churches of the East,* 2 vols. (Milwaukee 1961–62); K. Onasch, *Grundzüge der russischen Kirchengeschichte: Die Kirche in ihrer Geschichte* III (Göttingen 1967), M 1 to M 122; J. Smolitsch, *Geschichte der russischen Kirche 1700–1917* I (1964); J. Smolitsch, *Russisches Mönchtum* (Würzburg 1953); A. S. Atiya, *A History of Eastern Christianity* (London 1968); R. Janin, *Les églises orientales et les rites orientaux* (Paris 1955); W. Kantzenbach, *Protestantisches Christentum im Zeitalter der Aufklärung* (Gütersloh 1965).

8. Attempts at Ecclesiastic Reunification

C. W. Hering, *Geschichte der kirchlichen Unionsversuche seit der Reformation bis auf unsere Zeit,* 2 vols. (Leipzig 1836–38); R. Rouse and S. C. Neill, *A History of the Ecumenical Movement 1517–1948* (Philadelphia 1954); J. Beumer, *Auf dem Wege zur christlichen Einheit. Vorläufer der ökumenischen Bewegung von den Anfängen des Humanismus bis zum Ende des 19. Jh. Ausgewählte Texte* (Bremen 1966); F. X. Kiefl, *Leibniz und die Wiedervereinigung der christlichen Kirchen* (1925).

9. Theology and the History of Theology

J. Turmel, *Histoire de la théologie positive du concile de Trente au concil du Vatican* (Paris 1906); M. Grabmann, *Die Geschichte der katholischen Theologie seit dem Ausgang der Väterzeit* (Freiburg 1933), 179–212; H. Schuster, "Die Geschichte der Pastoraltheologie," *Hdb. der Pastoraltheologie* I (Freiburg 1964), 40–92; E. Hirsch, *Geschichte der neueren evangelischen Theologie,* 5 vols. (Gütersloh 1964); W. Nigg, *Die Kirchengeschichtsschreibung* (Munich 1934); E. C. Scherer, *Geschichte und Kirchengeschichte an den deutschen Universitäten; Ihre Anfänge im Zeitalter des Humanismus und ihre Ausbildung zur selbständigen Disziplin* (Freiburg i. Brsg. 1927); L. Scheffczyk, *F. L. Stolbergs "Geschichte der Religion Jesu Christi." Die Abwendung der kath. Kirchengeschichtsschreibung von der Aufklärung* . . . (Munich 1952); P. Meinhold, *Geschichte der kirchlichen Historiographie,* 2 vols. (Freiburg and Munich 1967) (sources and presentation); A. Anwander, *Die allgemeine Religionsgeschichte im kath. Deutschland während der Aufklärung und der Romantik* (Salzburg 1932).

10. Iconography

H. Aurenhammer, *Lexikon der christlichen Ikonographie,* to date only Vol. I (Vienna 1967); E. Kirschbaum, *Lexikon der christlichen Ikonographie,* publ. Vols. I and II of *Allg. Ikonographie* (A–K) (Freiburg i. Brsg. 1969–70).

11. Universities and Academies

L. E. Du Pin, *Bibliothèque des auteurs ecclésiastiques du XVIIe siècle,* 7 vols. (Paris 1708); S. Stelling-Michaud, ed., *Les universités européennes du 14e–18e siècle* (Geneva 1967); C. Jourdain, *Histoire de l'université de Paris au XVIIe et au XVIIIe siècle,* 2 vols. (Paris 1862–66); P. Féret, *La faculté de Théologie de Paris et ses docteurs les plus célèbres, Époque moderne,* 7 vols. (Paris 1900–1916); G. Ajo and C. M. Sáinz de Zúñiga,

Historia de las Universidades hispánicas . . . III–IV (Madrid 1957–67); A. Kraus, *Vernunft und Geschichte. Die Bedeutung der Deutschen Akademien für die Entwicklung und Geschichtswissenschaft im späten 18. Jh.* (Freiburg i. Brsg. 1963); H. Hurter, *Nomenclator litterarius recentioris Theologiae catholicae,* 4 vols. (Innsbruck 1903–13).

12. MISSION

K. S. Latourette, *A History of the Expansion of Christianity* III (New York 1940); S. Delacroix, *Histoire des Missions Catholiques* II (Paris 1957).

BIBLIOGRAPHY TO INDIVIDUAL CHAPTERS

Part One
The Leadership Position of France

SECTION ONE

Ecclesiastical Life in France

1. *Christian Renewal after 1615*

SOURCES

Richelieu, *Mémoires,* ed. by Delavaud-Gaucheron, 10 vols., Société de l'Histoire de France (Paris 1908–31); Saint Vincent de Paul, *Correspondance, entretiens, documents,* ed. by P. Coste, 14 vols. (Paris 1921–25); J. F. de Gondi, *Cardinal de Retz, Mémoires,* ed. by M. Allem (Paris 1956); P. de L'Estoile, *Mémoires-Journeaux,* ed. by Brunet-Champollion, 12 vols. (Paris 1875–76); P. de Bérulle, *Correspondance,* ed. by J. Dagens, 3 vols. (Louvain and Paris 1937–39); F. Garasse, *Histoire des jésuites de Paris pendant trois années, 1624–1626,* ed. by A. Carayon (Poitiers and Paris 1864); J. Godefroy, *Le Mercure jésuite,* 2 vols. (Geneva 1630–31); R. Arnauld d'Andilly, *Mémoires* (Hamburg 1734); P. Descourveaux, *La vie de M. Bourdoise* (Paris 1714); L. Abelly, *Vie du Vénérable Serviteur de Dieu Vincent de Paul* (Paris 1664); L. Batterel, *Mémoires domestiques pour servir à l'histoire de l'Oratoire,* ed. by A. Ingold and P. Bonnardet, 5 vols. (Paris 1902–11); G. Habert, *Vie du Cardinal de Bérulle* (Paris 1646); Saint Jean Eudes, *Œuvres complètes,* 12 vols. (Vannes 1905–11).

LITERATURE

BIBLIOGRAPHIES: R. Taveneaux, "La vie religieuse en France de l'avènement d'Henri IV à la mort de Louis XIV," *Histoire et Géographie* 200 (1961), 119–30; P. Chanu, "Le XVIIe siècle religieux, réflexions préalables," *Annales: Économies, sociétés, civilisations* 22 (1967), 279–302.

MONOGRAPHS: J. H. Mariéjol, *Henri IV, Louis XIII (1598–1643), Histoire de France de Lavisse* 2, 6 (Paris 1905); J. B. Perkins, *France under Mazarin with a Review of the Administration of Richelieu,* 2 vols. (London 1887); J. Pannier, *L'Église réformée de France sous Louis XIII,* 2 vols. (Paris 1932); J. M. Prat, *Recherches historiques et critiques sur la Compagnie de Jésus en France au temps de P. Coton (1564–1626),* 5 vols. (Lyons 1876–78); F. T. Perrens, *L'Église et l'État en France sous le règne d'Henri IV et la régence de Marie de Médicis,* 2 vols. (Paris 1872); K. v. Raumer, *Heinrich IV v. Frankreich* (Iserlohn 1947); G. d'Avenel, *Richelieu et la monarchie absolue,* 4 vols. (Paris 1884–90); L. Batiffol, *Richelieu et Louis XIII* (Paris 1934); G. Hanotaux and Duc de la Force, *Histoire du Cardinal de*

Richelieu, 5 vols. (Paris 1893–1944); C. J. Burckhardt, *Richelieu* (Munich 1935); S. Skalweit, "Richelieus Machtidee," *Gesch. in Wiss. u. Unterricht* 2 (1951), 719–30; V. Tormetta, "La Politica del Mazzarino verso il Papato (1644–46)," *Archivo storico Italiano* 99 (1941) and 100 (1942); A. Sicard, *L'ancien clergé en France,* 2 vols. (Paris 1893–1903); A. Degert, *Histoire des séminaires français,* 2 vols. (Paris 1912); M. Houssaye, I: *Monsieur de Bérulle et les Carmélites de France, 1575–1611* (Paris 1872); II: *Le Père de Bérulle et l'Oratoire de Jésus, 1611–1625* (Paris 1874); III: *Le Cardinal de Bérulle et le Cardinal de Richelieu, 1625–1629* (Paris 1875); J. Dagens, *Die Beziehungen Franz' v. Sales zu Kard. Bérulle* (Erlangen 1956); P. Coste, *Le grand saint du grand siècle, Monsieur Vincent,* 3 vols. (Paris 1932); G. Fagniez, "L'opinion publique et la presse politique sous Louis XIII," *Revue d'Histoire diplomatique* (1900); L. Prunel, *La Renaissance catholique en France au XVIIe siècle* (Paris 1921); O. Schneider, *Jean Eudes—Der Prophet des Herzens Jesu* (Vienna 1947).

2. Origin and Development of Jansenism to 1653

BIBLIOGRAPHY

L. Willaert, *Bibliotheca Janseniana Belgica,* 3 vols. (Namur and Paris 1949–51); A. Maire, *Bibliographie générale des œuvres de Blaise Pascal,* 3 vols. (Paris 1925–27); A. Malvault, *Répertoire alphabétique de Port-Royal* (Paris 1902).

SOURCES

C. Jansenius, *Augustinus* (Louvain 1640, Paris 1641, Rouen 1643, Frankfurt 1964); A. Arnauld, *Œuvres,* 43 vols. (Paris and Lausanne 1775–83); F. Pinthereau, *La naissance du jansénisme découverte* (Louvain 1645); idem., *Nouvelles et anciennes reliques de l'abbeé de Saint-Cyran* (n.p., 1648); id., *Le progrès du jansénisme découvert* (Avignon 1655); id., *Reliques de l'abbé de Saint-Cyran* (Louvain 1646); *L'Histoire de Jansénius et de Saint-Cyran* (n.p., 1695); R. Rapin, *Histoire du jansénisme depuis son origine jusqu'en 1644,* ed. by Domenech (Paris 1861); R. Rapin, *Mémoires,* 3 vols. ed. by L. Aubineau (Paris 1865); G. Gerberon, *Histoire générale du jansénisme,* 3 vols. (Amsterdam 1700); H. Dumas, *Histoire des cinq propositions de Jansénius* Liège 1700); H. Robillard d'Avrigny, *Mémoires chronologiques et dogmatiques,* 4 vols. (n.p., 1723); D. de Colonia and L. Patouillet, *Dictionnaire des livres jansénistes,* 4 vols. (Antwerp 1752); Saint-Cyran, *Œuvres chrétiennes et spirituelles,* 4 vols. (Lyons 1675–79); id., *Lettres chrétiennes et spirituelles,* 2 vols. (n.p., 1744); R. Arnauld d'Andilly, *Mémoires* (Hamburg 1734); id., *Lettres* (Paris 1680); id., *Journal,* ed. by A. and E. Halphen, 6 vols. (Paris 1857–1909); C. Lancelot, *Mémoires touchant la vie de M. de Saint-Cyran,* 2 vols. (Cologne 1738); Angélique Arnauld, *Lettres,* 3 vols. (Utrecht 1742–44); Agnès Arnauld, *Lettres,* 2 vols. (Paris 1858); *Mémoires pour servir à l'histoire de Port-Royal,* 3 vols. (Utrecht 1742); G. Hermant, *Mémoires sur l'histoire ecclésiastique du XVIIe siècle,* ed. by A. Gazier, 6 vols. (Paris 1905–10); J. Bourgeois, *Relation sur la défense de la Fréquente communion* (n.p., 1695); L. Gorin de Saint-Amour, *Journal* (n.p., 1662); C. Clémencet, *Histoire générale de Port-Royal,* 10 vols. (Amsterdam 1755–57); J. Besoigne, *Histoire de l'Abbaye de Port-Royal,* 6 vols. (Cologne 1752–53); P. Guilbert, *Mémoires historiques et chronologiques sur l'Abbaye de Port-Royal,* 9 vols. (Utrecht 1755–58); *Recueil historique des bulles concernant les erreurs de ces deux derniers siècles* (Mons 1704); C. Duplessis d'Argentré. *Collectio judiciorum de novis erroribus,* 3 vols. (Paris 1728–36); L. E. Dupin, *Histoire ecclésiastique du XVIIe siècle,* 5 vols. (Paris 1714); L.

Ceyssens, *La correspondance antijanséniste de Fabio Chigi* (Rome and Brussels 1957); id., *Sources relatives au début du jansénisme et de l'antijansénisme* (Louvain 1957); id., *La première bulle contre Jansénius, sources relatives à son histoire,* 2 vols. (Rome and Brussels 1961–62); J. Orcibal, *La correspondance de Jansénius* (Louvain and Paris 1947); id., *La spiritualité de Saint-Cyran avec ses textes de piété inédits* (Paris 1962); A. Barnes, *Lettres inédites de Saint-Cyran* (Paris 1962); A. Cauchie and R. Maere, *Recueil des instructions générales aux Nonces de Flandre (1596–1635)* (Brussels 1904); L. Goldmann, *Correspondance de Martin de Barcos* (Paris 1956).

LITERATURE

Pastor XIII/2, XIV/1 and 2; A. de Meyer, *Les premières controverses jansénistes en France* (Louvain 1919); N. Abercombie, *The Origins of Jansenism* (Oxford 1936); L. Willaert, *Les origines du jansénisme dans les Pays-Bas catholiques* (Paris 1948); A. Gazier, *Histoire générale du mouvement janséniste,* 2 vols. (Paris 1922); C. Gazier, *Histoire du monastère de Port-Royal* (Paris 1929); M. Krüger, *Die Entwicklung . . . des Nonnenklosters Port-Royal im 17. Jh.* (Halle 1936); X. Le Bachelet, *Prédestination et grâce efficace, controverses dans la Compagnie de Jésus au temps d'Aquaviva* (Louvain 1931); H. de Lubac, *Surnaturel* (Paris 1946); C. van Sull, *L. Lessius de la Compagnie de Jésus* (Louvain 1930); W. Haermann, *The Doctrine of L. Lessius on Mortal Sin* (San Francisco 1947); J. Paquier, *Qu'est-ce que le jansénisme?* (Paris 1909); L. Cognet, *Le jansénisme* (Paris 1961); H. Bremond, *Histoire littéraire du sentiment religieux en France* IV: *L'École de Port-Royal* (Paris 1919); P. Schneider, *Saint-Cyran u. Augustinus im Kulturkreis von Port-Royal* (Berlin 1932); J. Orcibal, *Jean Duvergier de Hauranne, abbé de Saint-Cyran, et son temps,* 2 vols. (Paris 1947–48); id., *Saint-Cyran et le jansénisme* (Paris 1961); J. Laporte, *La doctrine de Port-Royal* I: *Saint-Cyran,* II: *Les vérités de la grâce,* 2 vols. (Paris 1923); P. Féret, *La Faculté de Théologie de Paris et ses docteurs les plus célèbres, Époque moderne,* 7 vols. (Paris 1900–1916); L. Ceyssens, *Jansenistica,* 4 vols. (Mechelen 1950–62); L. Ceyssens et al., *Miscellanea jansenistica* (Louvain 1963); R. Allier, *La cabale des dévots* (Paris 1902); H. Busson, *La pensée relieuse française de Charron à Pascal* (Paris 1933); E. Wasmuth, *Die Philosophie Pascals* (Heidelberg 1949); R. Guardini, *Christl. Bewußtsein* [on Pascal] (Munich 1954); C. Cochin, *Henry Arnauld* (Paris 1921); A. Douarche, *L'Université de Paris et les jésuites* (Paris 1888); J. Frencken, *Agnès Arnauld* (Nijmegen and Utrecht 1932); P. Varin, *La vérité sur les Arnauld complétée à l'aide de leur correspondance inédite* (Paris 1847); C.-A. Sainte Beuve, *Port-Royal,* 3 vols. (Paris 1953–55).

3. *The Jansenist Conflict to 1713*

SOURCES

E. Deschamps, *De haeresi janseniana* (Paris 1728); B. Pascal, *Œuvres,* ed. by L. Brunschvicg, F. Boutroux and F. Gazier, 14 vols. (Paris 1904–14); B. Pascal, *Les Provinçiales,* ed. by L. Cognet (Paris 1965); C. Goujet, *Vie de M. Nicole* (Liège 1767); N. de Larrière, *Vie de Messire Antoine Arnauld* (Paris and Lausanne 1783); V. Cousin, *Jacqueline Pascal* (Paris 1878); P. Thomas du Fossé, *Mémoires,* 4 vols. (Rouen 1876–79); N. Fontaine, *Mémoires,* 2 vols. (Utrecht 1736); *Recueil de plusieurs pièces pour servir à l'histoire de Port-Royal* (Utrecht 1740); P. Nicole, *Lettres sur l'hérésie imaginaire,* 2 vols. (Liège 1667); id., *Lettres et Nouvelles lettres,* 3 vols. (Paris 1755–67); id., *Apologie de M. Nicole écrite par lui-même* (Amsterdam 1734); M. Feydeau, *Mémoires inédits,* ed. by E. Jovy (Vitry-le François 1905); J. Besoigne, *Vie des quatre évêques engagés dans la cause de*

Port-Royal, 2 vols. (Cologne 1756); G. Patin, *Lettres,* ed. by J.-H. Réveillé-Parise, 3 vols. (Paris 1846); Saint-Simon, *Mémoires,* ed. by A. de Boislisle, 41 vols. (Paris 1879–1928); Sourches, *Mémoires,* 13 vols. (Paris 1882–93); L. Ceyssens, *La fin de la première période du jansénisme, sources des années 1654–1660* (Brussels and Rome 1963); Angélique de Saint-Jean Arnauld d'Andilly, *Relation de captivité,* ed. by L. Cognet (Paris 1954); *Histoire des persécutions des religieuses de Port-Royal écrites par elles-mêmes* (Villefranche 1753); *Journaux de ce qui s'est passé à Port-Royal depuis que la communauté fut transférée à Port-Royal des Champs jusqu'en 1669* (n.p., 1724); P. Quesnel, *Correspondance,* ed. by Mme A. Le Roy, 2 vols. (Paris 1900); id., *La Paix de Clément IX,* 2 vols. (Chambéry 1700); id. *Histoire de la vie et des ouvrages de M. Arnauld* (Liège 1697); J. A. G. Tans, *Pasquier Quesnel et les Pays-Bas* (Groningen and Paris 1960); A. Varet, *Relation de ce qui s'est passé dans l'affaire de la Paix de l'Église,* 2 vols. (n.p., 1706); Dom Rivet de la Grange, *Nécrologe de l'Abbaye de Port-Royal* (Amsterdam 1723); C. Le Febvre de Saint Marc *Supplément au nécrologe de Port-Royal* (n.p., 1735); Louail, Fouillou, and Joncoux, *Histoire abrégée du Jansénisme* (Cologne 1697); id., *Histoire du cas de conscience,* 8 vols. (Nancy 1705–11); J. Fouillou, *Mémoire sur la destruction de Port-Royal des Champs* (n.p., 1711); F. Guelphe, *Relation de la retraite de M. Arnauld dans les Pays-Bas en 1679* (Mons 1733); N. Pinault, *Histoire abrégée de la dernière persécution de Port-Royal,* 3 vols. (n.p., 1750); J. Racine, *Abrégé de l'histoire de Port-Royal,* ed. by A. Gazier (Paris 1908); *Recueil de pièces qui n'ont pas encore paru sur le formulaire* (Avignon 1754); *Vies intéressantes et édifiantes des religieuses de Port-Royal,* 4 vols. (n.p., 1750–52); *Histoire de la sortie du P. Quesnel des prisons de l'archevêché de Malines* (n.p., 1743); G. Vuillart, *Lettres à M. de Préfontaine,* ed. by R. Clark (Geneva and Lille 1951); Fénelon, *Œuvres complètes,* 10 vols. (Paris 1851–52); Bossuet, *Œuvres complètes,* 31 vols. (Paris 1862–66); id., *Correspondance,* ed. by C. Urbain and E. Levesque, 15 vols. (Paris 1909–25).

LITERATURE

A. Chéruel, *Histoire de France sous le ministère de Mazarin (1651–61),* 3 vols. (Paris 1882); L. E. Du Pin, *Bibliothèque des auteurs ecclésiastiques du XVIIe siècles,* 7 vols. (Paris 1708); A. Gits, *La foi ecclésiastique aux faits dogmatiques dans la théologie moderne* (Louvain 1940); J. Laporte, *La doctrine de Port-Royal, la morale d'après Arnauld,* 2 vols. (Paris 1951–52); J. Mesnard, *Pascal, l'homme et l'œuvre* (Paris 1951); id., *Pascal et les Roannez,* 2 vols. (Paris 1965); L. Goldmann, *Le Dieu caché* (Paris 1965); J. Orcibal, *Port-Royal entre le miracle et l'obéissance: Flavie Passart et Angélique de Saint-Jean* (Paris 1967); P. Jansen, *Le cardinal Mazarin et le mouvement janséniste* (Paris 1967); P. Blet, *Le clergé de France et la monarchie, étude sur les assemblées générales du clergé de 1651 à 1666,* 2 vols. (Rome 1959); J. Bourlon, *Les Asssemblées du Clergé et le jansénisme* (Paris 1909); A. Gazier, *Les dernières années du Cardinal de Retz (1655–1679)* (Paris 1875); G. Namer, *L'abbé Le Roy et ses amis, essai sur le jansénisme extrémiste intramondain* (Paris 1964); A. Le Roy, *Le gallicanisme au XVIIIe siècle, la France et Rome de 1700 à 1715* (Paris 1892); G. Delassault, *Le Maistre de Sacy et son temps* (Paris 1957); L. Cognet, *Claude Lancelot Solitaire de Port-Royal* (Paris 1951); P. Chételat, *Étude sur Du Guet* (Paris 1879); E. Dejean, *Un prélat indépendant au XVIIe siècle Nicolas Pavillon évêque d'Alet* (Paris 1909); R. Traveneaux, *Le jansénisme en Lorraine* (Paris 1960); B. Neveu, *Sébastien-Joseph du Cambout de Pontchâteau et ses missions à Rome* (Paris 1969); id., *Un historien à l'école de Port-Royal, Sébastien Le Nain de Tillemont* (The Hague 1966); A. Janssen, *Un polémiste antijanséniste, le P. Annat: Mélanges C. Moeller* (Louvain and Paris 1914); R. Clark, *Strangers and Sojourners at Port-Royal* (Cambridge 1932); P. Hoffer, *La dévotion à Marie au déclin du XVIIe siècle* (Juvisy 1938); P. Blet, *Les Assemblées du Clergé et Louis XIV de*

1670 à 1693 [Analecta Gregoriana, Cura Pontificiae Universitatis Gregorianae edita, Vol. 189. Series Facultatis Historiae Ecclesiasticae: sectio A, n. 11] (Rome 1972).

4. Gallicanism and Protestantism

GENERAL BIBLIOGRAPHY: E. Bourgeois and L. André, *Les sources de l'histoire de France,* Part 3: *le XVIIe siècle, 1610–1715,* 6 vols. (Paris 1913–24).

GALLICANISM

SOURCES: *Joannis Gersonii et cancellarii Parisiensis opera,* ed. by E. Richer, 2 vols. (Paris 1606); E. Richer, *De ecclesiastica et politica potestate libellus* (Paris 1611); id., *Histoire du Syndicat d'Edmond Richer* (n.p., 1753); S. Vigor, *Opera omnia* (Paris 1683); C. de Montchal, *Mémoires,* 2 vols. (Rotterdam 1718); P. Lemerre and A. Dorsanne, *Recueil des actes titres et mémoires concernant les affaires du Clergé de France,* 15 vols. (Paris 1716–52); A. Duranthon, *Collection des procès-verbaux des Assemblées générales du Clergé de France depuis 1560 jusqu'à présent,* 9 vols. (Paris 1767–78); P. Pithou, *Les libertés de l'Église gallicane* (Paris 1594); J. Boileau, *Recueil de diverses pièces concernant les censures de la Faculté de Théologie de Paris sur la hiérarchie de l'Église et sur la morale chrétienne* (Münster 1666); *Recueil des indults accordés au roi par les papes Alexandre VII et Clément IX pour la disposition des bénéfices consistoriaux et autres* (Paris 1670); A. Leman, *Recueil des instructions générales aux nonces ordinaires de France de 1624 à 1634* (Lille and Paris 1920); G. Hanotaux, *Recueil des instructions données aux ambassadeurs et ministres de France depuis les traités de Westphalie jusqu'à Révolution,* 2 vols. (Paris 1888–1911); J. B. Bossuet, *Correspondance,* ed. by C. Urbain and E. Levesque, 15 vols. (Paris 1909–25); id. *Œuvres complètes,* ed. by F. Lachat, 31 vols. (Paris 1863–67); J. J. Berthier, *Innocentii pp. XI epistolae ad principes,* 2 vols. (Rome 1890–95); L. E. du Pin, *Histoire ecclésiastique du XVIIe siècle,* 4 vols. (Paris 1714); G. Hermant, *Mémoires sur l'histoire ecclésiastique du XVIIe siècle,* ed. by A. Gazier, 6 vols. (Paris 1905–10); E. le Camus, *Lettres,* ed. by A. Ingold (Paris 1892) L. Legendre, *Mémoires,* ed. by M. Roux (Paris 1863); P. Pellisson, *Histoire de Louis XIV,* 3 vols. (Paris 1749); N. S. Arnauld marquis de Pomponne, *Mémoires,* ed. by J. Mavidal, 2 vols. (Paris 1868); L. Delavaud, *Le marquis de Pomponne* (Paris 1911); R. Rapin, *Mémoires,* ed. by L. Aubineau, 3 vols. (Paris 1865); L. Mention, *Documents relatifs aux rapports du clergé avec la royauté de 1682 a 1705,* 2 vols. (Paris 1893–1903).

LITERATURE: A. G. Martimort, *Le gallicanisme de Bossuet* (Paris 1953); V. Martin, *Les origines du gallicanisme,* 2 vols. (Paris 1939); id., *Le gallicanisme et la réforme catholique. Essai historique sur l'introduction en France des décrets du Concile de Trente* (Paris 1919); id., *Le gallicanisme politique et le Clergé de France* (Paris 1928); J. Orcibal, *Louis XIV contre Innocent XI: les appels au futur concile de 1688 et l'opinion française* (Paris 1949); L. Dedouvres, *Le P. Joseph de Paris, capucin,* 2 vols. (Paris 1932); A. Sicard, *L'ancien clergé de France,* 3 vols. (Paris 1893–1903); C. Gérin, *Louis XIV et le Saint-Siège* (Paris 1894); id., *Recherches historiques sur l'Assemblée du Clergé de France de 1682* (Paris 1869); M. Dubruel, *En plein conflit, la nonciature de France, la Secrétairerie d'État du Vatican, les Congrégations des affaires de France pendant la querelle de la Régale* (Paris 1927); M. d'Angelo, *Luigi XIV e la Santa Sede* (Rome 1914); F. de Bojani, *Innocent XI, sa correspondance avec ses nonces,* 3 vols. (Rome 1910–12); J. T. Loyson, *L'assemblée du Clergé de France de 1682* (Paris 1870); M. Immich, *Papst Innocenz XI.* (Berlin 1900); C. Bellet, *Histoire du Cardinal Le Camus* (Paris 1886); L. André, *M. Le Tellier et Louvois* (Paris 1942); E. Dejean, *Un prélat indépendant au XVIIe siècle, Nicolas Pavillon* (Paris 1909); M. Lauras, *Nouveaux éclaircisse-*

ments sur l'Assemblée de 1682 (Paris 1878); L. Madelin, *France et Rome* (Paris 1913); E. Michaud, *Louis XIV et Innocent XI d'apres les correspondances inédites du ministère des Affaires étrangères,* 4 vols. (Paris 1883); J. M. Vidal, *François-Étienne de Caulet, évêque de Pamiers* (Paris 1939); id., *Jean Cerle et le schisme de la régale au diocèse de Pamiers* (Paris 1938); J. Tans, *Bossuet en Hollande* (Paris 1949).

PROTESTANTISM

SOURCES: L. Pilatte, *Édits, déclarations et arrêts concernant la religion protestante réformée* (Paris 1885); A. Aymon, *Actes ecclésiastiques et civils de tous les synodes nationaux des Églises réformées de France* 2 vols. (The Hague 1710–1756); I. d'Huisseau, *La discipline des Églises réformées de France* (Orléans 1675); E. Benoist, *Histoire de l'Édit de Nantes,* 5 vols. (Delft 1693–95); P. Soulier, *Histoire du Calvinisme* (Paris 1686); P. Meynier, *De l'exécution de l'Édit de Nantes* (Pézenas 1662); P. Bernard, *Explication de l'Édit de Nantes par les autres édits de pacification et arrêts de règlement* (Paris 1666); C. Brousson, *L'état des réformés en France,* 3 vols. (Cologne 1684); J. Lefevre, *Recueil de ce qui s'est fait en France de plus considérable pour et contre les protestants depuis la révocation de l'Édit de Nantes* (Paris 1686); R. Isambert, *Recueil des édits, déclarations et arrêts du Conseil rendus au sujet des gens de la religion prétendue réformée* (Paris 1714); R. Allier, *Anthologie protestante française,* 2 vols. (Paris 1920).

LITERATURE: J. Viénot, *Histoire de la Réforme française de l'édit de Nantes à sa révocation,* 2 vols. (Paris 1934); D. Bourchenin, *Étude sur les Académies protestantes en France aux XVIe et XVIIe siècles* (Paris 1882); E. Léonard, *Histoire du protestantisme* (Paris 1950); A. Rébelliau, *Bossuet historien du protestantisme* (Paris 1909); P. Hazard, *La crise de la conscience européenne,* 2 vols. (Paris 1934); E. and E. Haag, *La France protestante,* 10 vols. (Paris 1846–59); J. Chambon, *Der franz. Protestantismus* (Munich 1948); J. Pannier, *L'Église réformée de Paris sous Louis XIII,* 2 vols. (Paris 1932); A. Paul, *L'unité chrétienne, schismes et rapprochements* (Paris 1930); L. O'Brien, *Innocent XI and the Revocation of the Edict of Nantes* (Berkeley 1930); O. Douen, *La révocation de l'Édit de Nantes à Paris,* 3 vols. (Paris 1894); id., *L'intolérance de Fénelon* (Paris 1875); J. Dedieu, *Le rôle politique des protestants français 1685–1715* (Paris 1920); R. Nürnberger, *Die Politisierung des franz. Protestantismus* (Tübingen 1948); C. Weiss, *Histoire des réfugiés français protestants de France,* 2 vols. (Paris 1853); F. Puaux and A. Sabatier, *Études sur la révocation de l'Édit de Nantes* (Paris 1886); E. Guitard, *Colbert et Seignelay contre la religion réformée* (Paris 1912); E. Léonard, *Problèmes et expériences du protestantisme français* (Paris 1940); L. Bourlon, *Les Assemblées du Clergé et le protestantisme* (Paris 1909); J. Orcibal, *Louis XIV et les protestants* (Paris 1951); id. *État présent des recherches sur la répartition géographique des Nouveaux catholiques à la fin du XVIIe siècle* (Paris 1948).

5. *Spirituality in Seventeenth-Century France*

LITERATURE

GENERAL: H. Bremond, *Histoire littéraire du sentiment religieux en France,* 11 vols. (Paris 1916–33); P. Pourrat, *La spiritualité chrétienne,* 4 vols. (Paris 1926–28); J. Gautier, *La spiritualité catholique* (Paris 1953); L. Cognet, *La spiritualité moderne,* I: *L'essor, 1500–1650* (Paris 1966); id., *De la Dévotion moderne à la spiritualité française* (Paris 1958); Daniel-Rops, *L'Église des temps classiques,* 2 vols. (Paris 1958); D. Poinsenet, *La France* *religieuse au XVII^esiècle* (Paris 1954); R. Bady, *L'homme et son "institution" de Montaigne à Bérulle* (Paris 1964).

CANFIELD: Optat de Veghel, *Benoît de Canfield, sa vie, sa doctrine et son influence* (Rome 1949); P. Renaudin, *Benoît de Canfield* (Paris 1955); J. Orcibal, *La rencontre du Carmel thérésien avec les mystiques du Nord* (Paris 1959).

FRANCIS DE SALES: V. Brasier, E. Morganti, and M. Durica, *Bibliographia salesiana* (Turin 1956); E. Lajeunie, *Saint François de Sales*, 2 vols. (Paris 1966); H. Bremond, *Sainte Chantal* (Paris 1912); E. Stopp, *Mme de Chantal* (London 1962); G. Thomas, *Sainte Chantal et la spiritualité salesienne* (Paris 1963); F. Boulas, *Un ami de s. François de Sales, Camus, évêque de Belley* (Lyons 1878); F. Eggersdorfer, *Die Aszetik des hl. Franz v. Sales* (Munich 1909); M. Müller, *Die Freundschaft des hl. Franz v. Sales mit der hl. Franziska v. Chantal* (Munich 1923); J. Martin, *Die Theologie des hl. Franz v. Sales* (Rottenburg 1934).

BÉRULLE AND HIS FOLLOWERS: A. Ingold, *Essai de bibliographie oratorienne* (Farnborough 1968); J. Dagens, *Bérulle et les origines de la restauration catholique* (Paris 1952); P. Cochois, *Bérulle et l'École française* (Paris 1963); M. Dupuy, *Bérulle, une spiritualité de l'adoration* (Paris 1964); J. Orcibal, *Le cardinal de Bérulle, évolution d'une spiritualité* (Paris 1965); R. Bellemare, *Le sens de la créature dans la doctrine de Bérulle* (Paris 1949); C. de Condren, *Lettres*, ed. by P. Auvray and A. Jouffrey (Paris 1943); J. Galy, *Le sacrifice dans l'École française de spiritualité* (Paris 1951); L. Bertrand, *Bibliothèque sulpicienne ou histoire littéraire de la Compagnie de Saint-Sulpice*, 3 vols. (Paris 1900); J. J. Olier, *Lettres*, ed. by E. Levesque, 2 vols. (Paris 1935); P. Michallon, *La communion aux mystères de Jésus-Christ selon J. J. Olier* (Lyons 1943); D. Boulay, *Vie de vénérable Jean Eudes*, 4 vols. (Paris 1905–8); C. Lebrun, *La spiritualité de saint Jean Eudes* (Paris 1932); L. Tronson, *Correspondance*, ed. by L. Bertrand, 3 vols. (Paris 1904).

VINCENT DE PAUL: Saint Vincent de Paul, *Entretiens aux missionnaires*, ed. by A. Dodin (Paris 1960); L. Cognet, *Saint Vincent de Paul* (Paris 1959); A. Dodin, *Saint Vincent de Paul et la charité* (Paris 1960); D. Poinsenet, *Sainte Louise de Marillac* (Paris 1958); H. Kühner, *Vinzenz v. Paul* (Cologne 1963).

JESUITS: A. Pottier, *Le P. Louis Lallemant et les grands spirituels de son temps*, 3 vols. (Paris 1927–29); id., *Le P. Pierre Champion* (Paris 1938); C. de Rochemonteix, *N. Caussin, confesseur de Louis XIII et le Cardinal de Richelieu* (Paris 1911); P. Guitton, *Claude de la Colombière* (Paris 1943).

BOSSUET, FÉNELON AND QUIETISM: J. Calvet, *Bossuet, l'homme et l'œuvre* (Paris 1941); J. Truchet, *La prédication de Bossuet*, 2 vols. (Paris 1960); T. Goyet, *L'humanisme de Bossuet*, 2 vols. (Paris 1965); E. Carcassonne, *État présent des travaux sur Fénelon* (Paris 1939); id., *Fénelon, l'homme et l'œuvre* (Paris 1946); F. Varillon, *Fénelon et le Pur amour* (Paris 1957); J. L. Goré, *L'itinéraire de Fénelon, humanisme et spiritualité* (Paris 1957); id., *La notion d'indifférence chez Fénelon et ses sources* (Paris 1956); H. Bremond, *Apologie pour Fénelon* (Paris 1910); B. V. Kostsull, *Fénelon* (Munich 1950); R. Schmittlein, *L'aspect politique du différend Bossuet-Fénelon* (Baden-Baden 1954); L. Cognet, *Crépuscule des Mystiques* (Paris and Tournai 1958); P. Zovatto, *La polemica Bossuet-Fénelon, introduzione critico-bibliografica* (Padua 1968); H. Hillenaar, *Fénelon et les jésuites* (The Hague 1967); A. de la Gorce, *Le vrai visage de Fénelon* (Paris 1958); J. Kraus and J. Calvet, eds. *Fénelon, Persönlichkeit und Werk* (Baden-Baden 1953).

MISCELLANEOUS: On Saint John-Baptist de la Salle see the comprehensive documents in *Cahiers lasalliens*, 30 vols. (Rome 1959–69); P. Renaudin, *Marie de l'Incarnation, essai de psychologie religieuse* (Paris 1935); R. Daeschler, *La spiritualité de Bourdaloue, grâce et vie unitive* (Louvain 1927).

6. Christian Thought in Seventeenth-Century France

BIBLIOGRAPHY

H. Hurter, *Nomenclator litterarius recentioris Theologiae catholicae,* 4 vols. (Innsbruck 1903–13); A. Maire, *Bibliographie générale des œuvres de Blaise Pascal,* 5 vols. (Paris 1925–27).

SOURCES

P. de Gamaches, *Summa theologica,* 3 vols. (Paris 1627); M. Isambert, *Disputationes in secundam secundae s. Thomae* (Paris 1648); A. Duval, *Commentarii in secundam secundae partis summae d. Thomae* (Paris 1636); M. Grandin, *Opera theologica,* 6 vols. (Paris 1710–12); R. Tassin, *Histoire littéraire de la congrégation de Saint-Maur* (Paris 1770); F. Lecerf de la Viéville, *Bibliothèque historique et critique des auteurs de la congrégation de Saint-Maur* (The Hague 1726); M. Valéry, *Correspondance inédite de Mabillon et de Montfaucon avec l'Italie,* 3 vols. (Paris 1846); J. Martène, *Histoire de la congrégation de Saint-Maur,* ed. by Charvin, 10 vols. (Ligugé 1923–54); C. Cloyseault, *Recueil des vies de quelques prêtres de l'Oratoire,* 3 vols. (Paris 1882–83); R. Simon, *Bibliothèque critique ou recueil de diverses pièces critiques,* ed. by M. de Sainjore, 4 vols. (Amsterdam 1708–10); id., *Lettres choisies,* 3 vols. (Amsterdam 1702–5); J. P. Niceron, *Mémoires pour servir à l'histoire des hommes illustres dans la république des lettres,* 43 vols. (Paris 1727–45); C. Goujet, *Bibliothèque des auteurs ecclésiastiques du XVIIe siècle pour servir de continuation à celle de M. Du Pin,* 3 vols. (Paris 1736); B. d'Argonne, *Mélanges d'histoire et de littérature,* compiled by M. de Vigneul-Marville, 3 vols. (Paris 1701); J. Lelong, *Bibliothèque historique de la France,* 5 vols. (Paris 1768–78); R. Descartes, *Œuvres,* ed. by C. Adam and P. Tannery, 11 vols. (Paris 1897–1913); id., *Correspondance,* ed. by C. Adam and G. Milhaud, 8 vols. to date (Paris 1936ff.); B. Pascal, *Pensées sur la religion et sur quelques autres sujets,* ed. by L. Lafuma, 3 vols. (Paris 1951); N. Malebranche, *Œuvres complètes,* ed. by A. Robinet et al., 20 vols. (Paris 1958–67).

LITERATURE

P. Hazard, *La crise de la conscience européenne 1680–1715,* 3 vols. (Paris 1935); H. Busson, *La pensée religieuse française de Charron à Pascal* (Paris 1933); id., *La religion des classiques 1660–1685* (Paris 1948); É. Gilson, *La doctrine cartésienne de la liberté et la théologie* (Paris 1913); J. Turmel, *Histoire de la théologie positive du concile de Trente au concile du Vatican* (Paris 1906); A. Humbert, *Les origines de la théologie moderne,* I: *La renaissance de l'antiquité chrétienne 1450–1521* (Paris 1911); C. Jourdain, *Histoire de l'université de Paris au XVIIe et au XVIIIe siècle,* 2 vols. (Paris 1862–66); A. Douarche, *L'université de Paris et les jésuites* (Paris 1888); R. Pintard, *Le libertinage érudit dans la première moitié du XVIIe siècle,* 2 vols. (Paris 1943); R. Snoeks, *L'argument de tradition dans la controverse eucharistique entre catholiques et réformés français au XVIIe siècle* (Louvain 1951); P. Mesnard, *L'essor de la philosophie politique au XVIIe siècle* (Paris 1936); F. Bouillier, *Histoire de la philosophie cartésienne,* 2 vols. (Paris and Lyons 1854); H. Gouhier, *La pensée religieuse de Descartes* (Paris 1924); id., *La philosophie religieuse de Malebranche et son expérience religieuse* (Paris 1926); J. Mesnard, *Pascal, l'homme et l'œuvre* (Paris 1951); id., *Pascal et les Roannez,* 2 vols. (Paris 1965); L. Lafuma, *Histoire des Pensées de Pascal* (Paris 1954).

SECTION TWO

The Papacy in the Period of French Hegemony

GENERAL BIBLIOGRAPHY FOR THE HISTORY OF THE POPES

F. Bartolotti, *La medaglia annuale dei Romani Pontefici da Paolo V a Paolo VI, 1605–1967* (Rimini 1967); K. J. Beloch, *Bevölkerungsgeschichte Italiens,* II. *Die Bevölkerung des Kirchenstaates, Toscanas und der Herzogtümer am Po* (Berlin 1965); M. Brosch, *Geschichte des Kirchenstaates* (Gotha 1882); *Bullarum, Privilegiorum ac Diplomatum Romanorum Pontificum amplissima collectio, opera et studio Caroli Cocquelines* VI, 4ff. (Rome 1761); *Bullarii Romani Continuatio,* ed. by A. Barberi and A. Spetia (Rome 1835ff.); *Bullarum, Diplomatum et Privilegiorum Romanorum Pontificum Taurinensis* 16ff. (Turin 1869ff.); A. Ciaconis, A. Oldoini, and M. Guarnacci, *Vitae et res gestae Pontificum Romanorum et S. R. E. Cardinalium* (Rome 1751); *Collectio Lacensis: Acta et Decreta sacrorum conciliorum recentiorum* I (Freiburg 1870); *Dizionario biografico degli Italiani* Iff. (Rome 1960); I. v. Döllinger and F. H. Reusch, *Geschichte der Moralstreitigkeiten seit dem 16. Jh.,* 2 vols. (Munich 1889; reprint Aalen 1968); A. P. Frutaz, *Le piante di Roma,* 3 vols. (Rome 1962); A. Haidacher, *Geschichte der Päpste in Bildern* (Heidelberg 1965); F. Heyer, *Die kath. Kirche vom Westfälischen Frieden bis zum ersten Vatikanischen Konzil* (= *Die Kirche in ihrer Geschichte. Ein Handbuch,* von K. D. Schmidt and E. Wolf 4, Fasc. N, part 1) (Göttingen 1963); *Hierarchia catholica medii et recentioris aevi,* ed. by P. Gauchat, Ritzler, and Sefrin, IV–VI (Münster and Padua 1935–58); C. Hollis, *The Papacy, an Illustrated History from St. Peter to Paul VI* (London 1964), contains valuable illustrations; *Istituzioni finanziarie, contabili e di controllo dello Stato Pontificio dalle origini al 1870,* ed. by the Ministero del Tesoro (Rome 1961); L. Karttunen, *Les nonciatures apostoliques permanentes de 1650 à 1800* (Geneva 1912); A. Kraus, "Secretarius und Sekretariat. Der Ursprung der Institution des Staatssekretariats und ihr Einfluß auf die Entwicklung moderner Regierungsformen in Europa," *RQ* 55 (1961), 43–84; Mansi; V. Mariani, *Le chiese di Roma dal XVII al XVIII secolo* (*Roma Christiana* 5) (Bologna 1963); L. v. Matt and H. Kühner, *Die Päpste. Eine Papstgeschichte in Bild und Wort* (Würzburg 1963), excellent collection of portraits of Popes; A. Mercati, *Raccolta di concordati* (Rome 1919); C. Mirbt, *Quellen zur Geschichte des Papsttums und des römischen Katholizismus* (Tübingen 1934) (of the new expanded edition only Vol. 1 of 2 vols has appeared); V. Monachino, ed., *La carità cristiana a Roma* (*Roma Christiana* 10) (Bologna 1967); G. Moroni, *Dizionario di erudizione storico-ecclesiastica* (Venice 1840–61); R. and F. Silezi, *500 pasquinate* (Milan 1932); Pastor XIV/1–XVI/2; H. Raab, *Kirche und Staat von der Mitte des 15. Jh. bis zur Gegenwart* (Munich 1966); L. v. Ranke, *Die römischen Päpste in den letzten vier Jahrhunderten* (*Werke,* Vols 37–39, newly edited by F. Baethgen, 1953); A. v. Reumont, *Geschichte der Stadt Rom* III (Berlin 1870); F. H. Reusch, *Der Index der verbotenen Bücher* (Bonn 1883–85); L. J. Rogier, *Siècle des Lumières, Révolutions, Restauration (1715–1848)* (Paris 1966); G. Schreiber," Das päpstliche Staatssekretariat," *HJ* 79 (1960), 175–98; F. X. Seppelt, *Geschichte des Papsttums,* V: *Das Papsttum im Kampf mit Staatsabsolutismus und Aufklärung* (Munich 1959); L. Wahrmund, *Das Ausschließungsrecht der katholischen Staaten . . . bei den Papstwahlen* (Vienna 1888); K. Walf, *Die Entwicklund des päpstlichen Gesandtschaftswesens in dem Zeitabschnitt zwischen Dekretalenrecht und Wiener Kongreß* (Munich 1966); M. Dell'Arco, *Pasquino statua parlante* (Rome 1967); R. A. Graham, *Vatican Diplomacy, A Study of Church and State on the International Plane* (Princeton, N.J. 1959).

7. *The Popes from Alexander VII to Clement X*

LITERATURE

ALEXANDER VII: *BullRom Cocq.* VI 4; VI 5; VI6, 1–161; *BullRom* (ed. by Taur.) XVI, XVII 1–511; *Hierarchia Catholica* IV, 32–35; *D,* 447–55; V. Kybal and G. Incisa della Rocchetta, *La nunziatura di Fabio Chigi (1640–51)* (Rome 1943); *La correspondance antijanséniste de Fabio Chigi, nonce à Cologne, plus tard Alexandre VII,* ed. by A. Legrand and L. Ceyssens (Rome 1957); S. Pallavicino, *La vita di Alessandro VII* (new edition) (Prato 1939–40); Ciaconius IV, 707–78; Pastor XIV/1, 301–524; Seppelt V, 322–34; P. Richard: *DHGE* II, 229–44; K. Repgen in *LThK* I, 318; M. Rosa in *Dizionario Biogr. degli Italiani* II, 205–15; L. Sandri in *Bolletino Senese di Storia Patria* 68 (1961), 3–27; F. Calley, "La physionomie spirituelle de Fabio Chigi d'après sa correspondance avec le P. Charles d'Arenberg, Fr. Mineure Capucin," *MiscMercati* V, 451–76; G. Incisa della Rocchetta, "Gli appunti autobiografici d'Alessandro VII nell'Archivio Chigi," *Mélanges Tisserant* VI, 439–57; Ae. Springhetti, "Alexander VII poeta latinus," *AHPont* 1 (1963), 265–94; B. Cialdea, *Gli Stati Italiani e la pace dei Pirenei* (Milan 1961); R. Darricau, "Louis XIV et le S. Siège. La negotiation du Traité de Pise (1664)," *Annuaire-Bulletin de la Soc. de l'Hist. de France,* 1964/75, 81–156; Darricau, "Les indultes de nomination aux bénéfices consistoriaux," *BLE* 66 (1965), 16–34, 107–31; J. Rainer, "Rom und der Türkenkrieg 1663–1664," *AcModena* 6 (1964), 174–94; A. Bastiaanse, *Teodore Ameyden (1586–1656). Un neerlandese alla corte di Roma* (The Hague 1967); R. Wittkower, *Gian Lorenzo Bernini. The Sculptor of the Roman Baroque* (London 1966); P. Marconi, *La Roma del Borromini* (Rome 1968).

CLEMENT IX: *BullRom Cocq.* VI 6, 162–369; *BullRom* (e. by Taur.) XVII, 512–839; *Hierarchia Catholica* V, 3–5; Ciaconius IV, 779–96; Pastor XIV/1, 525–610; Seppelt V, 334–43; G. Beani, *Clemente IX, Notizie storiche* (Prato 1893); R. Mols in *DHGE* XII, 1297–1313; A. Cornaro *LThK* II, 1227; G. Canevazzi, *Papa Clemente IX poeta* (Modena 1900); G. Beani, *Clemente IX e l'isola di Candia* (Pistoia 1897); C. Terlinden, *Le pape Clément IX et la guerre de Candie* (Louvain and Paris 1904).

CLEMENT X: *BullRom Cocq.* VII; *BullRom* (ed. by Taur.) XVIII; *Hierarchia catholica* V, 6–9; A. de la Houssaye, *Relation du conclave de Clément X* (Paris 1676); Pastor XIV/1, 611–65; Seppelt V, 344–46; Ciaconius V, 1–104; R. Mols in *DHGE* XII, 1313–26; A. Cornaro in *LThK* II, 1227; E. Arizio, *Memorie sulla vita di Clemente X* (Rome 1863); C. de Bildt, *Christine de Suède et le Conclave de Clément X* (Paris 1906); id., *Christine de Suède et le Cardinal Azzolini, lettres inédites* (Paris 1899).

8. *Innocent XI*

LITERATURE

BullRom Cocq. VIII; *BullRom* (ed. by Taur.) XIX; *Hierarchia Catholica* V, 10–14; *Epistolae ad principes,* ed. by J. J. Berthier (Rome 1891–95); F. de Bojani, *Innocent XI, sa correspondance avec ses nonces 1676–84* (Rome 1910–12); *D,* 456–77; S. Monti, *Bibliografia di papa I: fino al 1927,* ed. by M. Zecchinelli (Como 1957); Ciaconius V, 105–312; Pastor XIV/2, 667–1043; Seppelt V, 346–70; P. Gini in *Biblioth. Sanctorum* 7 (Rome 1966), 848–56; G. Schwaiger in *LThK* V, 693–95; M. G. Lippi, *Vita,* ed. by G. Berthier (Rome 1889); C. Miccinelli (Rome 1956); G. Papasogli (Rome 1956); A. Latreille, "Innocent XI pape janséniste, directeur de conscience de Louis XIV," *Cahiers d'histoire* 1 (Grenoble 1956), 9–39; J. Orcibal, *Louis XIV contre Innocent XI* (Paris 1949); B. Neveu, "Jacques II médiateur entre Louis XIV et Innocent XI," *MAH* 79 (1967), 699–764; P. Blet, "I. et l'Assemblée du Clergé de France de 1682. La rédaction du Bref "Paternae Charitati" *AHPont* 7 (1969); G. J. Philipps, *Das Regalienrecht in Frankreich* (Halle 1873: reprint Aalen 1967); F. Margiotta Broglio, "Il conflitto della Regalia," *AcLincei Mem.* 9 (1963), 173–292; C. H. Gérin, *Louis XIV et le S. Siège* (Paris 1894); M. Dubruel, "La cour de Rome et l'extension de la Régale," *RHEF* 9 (1923), 161–76; L. O'Brian, *Innocent XI and the Révocation of the Edict of Nantes* (Berkeley 1930); A. Latreille, "La révocation de l'Édit de Nantes," *Bull. de la Soc. de l'hist. du protestant. franç.* 103 (1957), 229–36; G. Fraknoi, *Papa I. e la liberazione dell'Ungheria del giogo ottomano* (Florence 1903); A. Levinson, "Nuntiaturberichte vom Kaiserhof Leopolds I," *AÖG* 106 (1918); V. Thein, *Papst I. und die Türkengefahr im Jahre 1683* (Breslau 1912); A. Posch, "Ein kaiserlicher Gesandtschaftsbericht aus Rom 1686," *Festschr. Eder* (Innsbruck 1959), 141–54; V.-L. Tapie, "Europe et chrétienté," *Gr* 42 (1961), 268–89; J. Stoye, *The Siege of Vienna* (London 1964); *Beatificationis et canonisationis . . . Summarium. Testimonia, Documenta, Causae cursus* (Vaticano 1943); *Nova positio super virtutibus* (Vaticano 1944); *AAS* 48 (1956), 754–59, 762–78 (Beatification).

9. *The Popes from Alexander VIII to Clement XI*

LITERATURE

ALEXANDER VIII: *BullRom Cocq.* IX, 1–101; *BullRom* (ed. by Taur.) XX, 1–167; *D,* 478–84; *Hierarchia Catholica* V, 15–17; Ciaconius V, 313–86; Pastor XIV/2, 1045–72; Seppelt V, 370–74; P. Richard in *DHGE* II, 244–51; K. Repgen in *LThK* I, 318 f.; A. Petrucci in *Dizionario Biografico degli Italiani* II, 215–219; S. v. Bischoffshausen, *Papst A. und der Wiener Hof* (Vienna 1900); J. Bignami Odler, "Les collections d'un pape juriste," *StG* 13 (Bologna 1967), 257–72; S. Tramontin, "Recenti studi su S. Gregorio Barbarigo," *Boll. Ist. Storia Venezie* 3 (1961), 331–348; S. Serena, *Gr. Barbarigo* (Padua 1963); S. La Sorsa, "Pasquinate contro i cardinali," *Zagaglia* 5 (Lecce 1963), 54–73.

INNOCENT XII: *BullRom Cocq.* IX, 102–547; *BullRom* (ed. by Taur.) XX, 168–947; *D,* 484–88; *Hierarchia Catholica* V, 18–22; Ciaconius V, 389–542; Pastor XIV/2, 1073–1166; Seppelt V, 374–81; G. Schwaiger in *LThK* V, 695; M. de Forbin, "Le cardinal de Forbin-Janson à Rome, le conclave d'I," *Rev. d'Hist. diplom.* 38 (1924), 132–213; H. Raab, "Finalrelation des Kölner Nuntius Paolucci," *RQ* 55 (1960), 129–56.

CLEMENT XI: *BullRom Cocq.* XI 1; XI 2, 1–182; *BullRom* (ed. by Taur.) XXI, 1–866; *Bullarium,* 3 parts in Vol. 1 (Rome 1723); *Clementis XI opera omnia* (Frankfurt 1729); *Epistolae et brevia selectiora,* 2 vols. (Rome 1724); *D,* 488–98; *Hierarchia Catholica* V, 22–32; L. Jadin, *L'Europe au début du XVIIIe siècle. Correspondance du Baron Karg de Bebenbourg . . . avec le card. Paolucci, secrétaire d'État (1700–1719)* (Brussels and Rome 1968); Mercati, *Raccolta,* 282–86; *De vita et rebus gestis Clementis XI* (Urbino 1727); Ciaconius VI, 1–380; Pastor XV, 1–388; Seppelt V, 382–413; F. Pometti, "Studi sul pontificato di Clemente," *ASRomana* 21 (1898), 279–484; 22 (1899), 109–79; 23 (1900), 239–76, 449–515; R. Mols in *DHGE* XII, 1326–61; A. Cornaro in *LThK* II, 1227 f.; I. Galland, "Die Papstwahl des Jahres 1700," *HJ* 3 (1882), 208–54, 355–87, 596–630; P. Roi, *La guerra di successione di Spagna negli stati dell'Alta Italia* (Rome 1931); H. Kramer, *Habsburg und Rom in den Jahren 1708–1709* (Innsbruck 1936;

reprint Rome 1967); G. V. Vella, *Il Passionei e la politica di Clemente XI* (Rome 1953); A. Caracciolo, *D. Passionei tra Roma e la repubblica delle lettere* (Rome 1968); M. Braubach, *Prinz Eugen v. Savoyen* II–III (Vienna 1964); N. Huber, *Österreich und der Hl. Stuhl vom Ende des span. Erbfolgekriegs bis zum Tode Papst Klemens'* (Graz 1967); L. Just, *Klemens XI. und der Code Leopold* (Freiburg 1935).

SECTION THREE

The End of the Denominational Era in Europe—Progress and Stagnation of the World Mission

10. *Reconstruction and Constitution of the Church of the Empire*

LITERATURE

INDIVIDUAL BISHOPRICS: J. Kist, *Fürst- und Erzbistum Bamberg. Leitfaden durch ihre Geschichte von 1007 bis 1955* (Bamberg 1958); J. Looshorn, *Die Geschichte des Bistums Bamberg,* reprint of 1886/91 edition (Bamberg 1967–68); W. Kern, *Die Finanzwirtschaft des Hochstifts Bamberg nach dem Dreißigjährigen Krieg 1648–83* (diss., Erlangen 1966); L. Vautrey, *Histoire des Évêques de Bâle,* 4 vols. (Einsiedeln 1884–86); H. R. Heyer, "Die Übersiedlung des Basler Domkapitels von seinem Exil in Freiburg i. Br. nach Arlesheim im Jahre 1678 und das Schicksal seines Archivs während der Französischen Revolution," *Basler Zschr. für Gesch. u. Altertumskunde* 67 (1967), 170–83; J. Burckle, *Les chapitres ruraux des anciens évêchés de Strasbourg et de Bâle* (Colmar 1935); G. Mayer, *Geschichte des Bistums Chur* II (Stams 1914); J. Danuser, *Die staatlichen Hoheitsrechte des Kantons Graubünden gegenüber dem Bistum Chur* (Zurich 1897); G. v. Lojewski, *Bayerns Weg nach Köln. Geschichte der bayerischen Bistumspolitik in der zweiten Hälfte des 16. Jh.* (Bonn 1962); J. Oswald, "Die baierischen Landesbistumsbestrebungen im 16. und 17. Jh.," *ZSavRGkan* 33 (1944), 224–64; F. X. Seppelt, *Geschichte des Bistums Breslau* (Breslau 1929); L. Petry, "Das Haus Neuburg und die Ausläufer der Gegenreformation in Schlesien und der Pfalz," *Veröff. des Vereins für pfälz. KG* 4 (1952), 87–106; A. A. Strnad, "Wahl und Informativprozeß Erzherzog Leopold Wilhelms von Österreich, Fürstbischof von Breslau (1656–62)," *ArSKG* 26 (1968), 153–90; K. Wolfsgruber, "Die Wahlkapitulationen der Fürstbischöfe von Brixen (1613 bis 1791)," *ZSavRGkan* 73 (1956), 248–323; B. Hubensteiner, *Die geistliche Stadt. Welt und Leben des Johann Eckher von Kapfing und Liechteneck, Fürstbischofs von Freising* (Munich 1954); J. Sax, *Geschichte des Hochstifts und der Stadt Eichstätt* (Nuremberg 1885); H. Hack, "Eine authentische Rechtsauslegung unter Papst Klemens XI. und der kirchenrechtliche Status des Stifts Fulda," *Miscellanea Fuldensia. Festgabe für Dr. A. Bolte, Bischof von Fulda* (Fulda 1966), 25–71; A. Bertram, *Geschichte des Bistums Hildesheim* III (Hildesheim and Leipzig 1925); M. Braubach, *Kurkölnische Miniaturen* (Münster 1954); P. Harsin, *Les relations extérieures de la Principauté de Liège sous Jean Louis d'Elderen et Joseph Clément de Bavière (1688–*

1718) (Liège and Paris 1927); A. Franzen, "Französische Politik und Kurkölns Beziehungen zu Frankreich unter Erzbischof Max Heinrich in französischer Sicht," *RQ* 52 (1957), 169–210; G. Mentz, *Johann Philipp von Schönborn, Kurfürst von Mainz, Bischof von Würzburg und Worms,* 2 vols. (Jena 1896–99); W. Kohl, *Christoph Bernhard von Galen. Politische Geschichte des Fürstbistums Münster 1650–78* (Münster 1964); J. Staber, *Kirchengeschichte des Bistums Regensburg* (Regensburg 1966); G. Schwaiger, *Kardinal Franz Wilhelm von Wartenberg als Bischof von Regensburg (1649–61)* (Munich 1954); F. Martin, *Salzburgs Fürsten in der Barockzeit (1587–1812)* (Salzburg 1966); A. M. Burg, "Die alte Diözese Straßburg von der bonifazischen Reform (ca 750) bis zum napoleonischen Konkordat. Ein geschichtlicher Überblick mit besonderer Berücksichtigung des elsässischen Teils," *FreibDiözArch* 86 (1966), 220–51; J. Duft, *Die Glaubenssorge der Fürstäbte von St. Gallen im 17. und 18. Jh.* (Lucerne 1944); J. Kögl, *La sovranità dei vescovi di Trento e di Bressanone. Diritti derivati al clero diocesano dalla sua soppressione* (Trent 1964); J. Marx, *Geschichte des Erzstifts Trier von den ältesten Zeiten bis zum Jahre 1816,* 5 vols. (Trier 1858–64); A. Wendehorst, "Das Bistum Würzburg. Ein Überblick von den Anfängen bis zur Säkularisation," *FreibDiözArch* 86 (1966), 9–93; H. Hack, *Der Rechtsstreit zwischen dem Fürstbischof von Würzburg und dem Fürstabt von Fulda an der Römischen Kurie um die geistliche Hoheit im Gebiet des Stifts Fulda (1688–1717)* (Fulda 1956).

THE AFTERMATH OF THE THIRTY YEARS' WAR: G. Franz, *Der Dreißigjährige Krieg und das deutsche Volk* (Stuttgart 1961); K. Kollnig, *Die Pfalz nach dem Dreißigjährigen Krieg* (Heidelberg 1949); A. P. Brück, "Aus der Schwedenzeit Aschaffenburgs 1631–34," *Aschaffenburger Jb.* 4 (1957), 719–36; H. Steinberg, *Der Dreißigjährige Krieg in Europa und der Kampf um die Vorherrschaft in Europa 1600–60* (Göttingen 1967); J. Schmidlin, *Kirchliche Zustände und Schicksale des deutschen Katholizismus während des Dreißigjährigen Krieges nach den bischöflichen Romberichten* (Freiburg 1940).

CONSTITUTION OF THE CHURCH OF THE EMPIRE AND THE ECCLESIASTICAL STATES; FILLING THE BISHOPRICS OF THE EMPIRE: Feine *RG;* L. Glier, *Die Advocatia ecclesiae Romanae imperatoris in der Zeit von 1519–1648* (diss., Erlangen 1897); H. E. Feine, *Die Besetzung der Reichsbistümer vom Westfälischen Frieden bis zur Säkularisation 1648–1803* (Amsterdam 1964); R. Reinhardt, *Die Beziehungen von Hochstift und Diözese Konstanz zu Habsburg-Österreich in der Neuzeit* (Wiesbaden 1966); H. E. Feine, "Papst, Erste Bitten und Regierungsantritt des Kaisers seit dem Ausgang des Mittelalters," *ZSavRGkan* 20 (1931), 1–101; A. H. Benna, "Preces Primariae und Reichshofkanzlei," *MÖSTA* 5 (1952); F. J. Heyen, "Die kaiserlichen Ersten Bitten für das Erzbistum Trier von Ferdinand I. bis Franz II. (1531–1792)," *Festschr. für Alois Thomas* (Trier 1967), 175–88; H. Czischke, *Die verfassungsrechtliche Lage der geistlichen Kurfürstentümer Mainz, Trier und Köln am Ende des alten Reiches* (diss., Mainz 1953); R. Reinhardt, "Zur Reichskirchenpolitik der Pfalz-Neuburger," *HJ* 84 (1964), 118–28; M. Braubach, "Lothringische Absichten auf den Kölner Kurstuhl 1712/13," *HJ* 56 (1936), 59–66; H. Raab, *Clemens Wenzeslaus von Sachsen und seine Zeit (1739–1812)* I: *Dynastie. Kirche und Reich im 18. Jh.* (Freiburg 1962).

PROBLEMS RELATED TO THE ESTATES IN THE CHURCH OF THE EMPIRE: GENERAL: A. Schulte, "Der Adel und die deutsche Kirche im Mittelalter," *KRA* 63/64 (Stuttgart 1922); A. L. Veit, "Geschichte und Recht der Stiftsmäßigkeit auf die ehemals adeligen Domstifte von Mainz, Würzburg und Bamberg," *HJ* 32 (1912), 323–58; id. *Der stiftsmäßige deutsche Adel im Bilde seiner Ahnenproben* (Freiburg 1935); E. Riedenauer, *Reichsritterschaft und Konfession: Deutscher Adel 1555–1740,* ed. by H. Rössler (Darmstadt 1965), 1–63; M. Domarus, "Der Reichsadel in den geistlichen Fürstentümern,"

Deutscher Adel, ed. by H. Rössler (Darmstadt 1965), 147–71; N. v. Preradovich, "Die soziale Herkunft der österreichischen Kirchenfürsten (1648–1918),"*Festschr. Karl Eder* (Innsbruck 1959), 223–43.

CATHEDRAL CHAPTERS: A. Haemmerle, *Die Canoniker des hohen Domstifts Augsburg bis zur Säkularisation* (n.p., 1955); J. Kist, *Das Bamberger Domkapitel 1391–1556* (Weimar 1943); G. Zimmermann, *Das Breslauer Domkapitel im Zeitalter der Reformation und Gegenreformation (1500–1600)* (Weimar 1938); K. Wolfsgruber, *Das Brixener Domkapitel in seiner persönlichen Zusammensetzung in der Neuzeit 1500–1803 = Schlern Schriften* 80 (Innsbruck 1951); C. M. Tuor, *Reihenfolge der residierenden Domherren in Chur = XXXIV. Jber. der Histor. antiquarischen Gesellschaft von Graubünden* (Chur 1905); J. Obersteiner, "Die persönliche Zusammensetzung des adligen Gurker Domkapitels und Domstiftes in der Zeit von 1620–1787," *Geschichtliche und volkskundliche Beiträge zur Heimatkunde Kärntens* CLIV (Klagenfurt 1964), 221–56; H. H. Kurth, "Das Kölnische Domkapitel im 18. Jh. Verfassung und Verwaltung, Wirtschaft und persönliche Zusammensetzung" (unpubl. diss., Bonn 1953); M. Braubach, "Kölner Domherren im 18. Jh.," *Zur Geschichte und Kunst im Erzbistum Köln. Festschr. für Wilhelm Neuss—Studien zur Kölner KG* 5 (Düsseldorf 1960), 238–58; H. H. Roth, *Das Kölner Domkapitel von 1503 bis zu seinem Erlöschen 1803 = Veröff des Köln. Geschichtsvereins* 5 (Cologne 1930); J. de Theux, *Le chapitre de Saint-Lambert à Liège,* 4 vols. (Brussels 1871–73); A. Dubois, *Le chapitre cathédrale de Saint-Lambert de Liège au XVIIe siècle* (Liège 1949); L. A. Veit, *Mainzer Domherren vom Ende des 16. bis zum Anfang des 18. Jh. in Leben, Haus und Habe* (Mainz 1924); F. Keinemann, *Das Domkapitel zu Münster im 18. Jh.* (Münster in Westphalia 1967); id., "Das Domstift Mainz und der mediate Adel. Der Streit um die Zulassung von Angehörigen der landsässigen Ritterschaften zu Mainzer Dompräbenden," *HJ* 89 (1969), 153–70; L. H. Krick, *Das ehemalige Domstift Passau und die ehemaligen Kollegiatstifte des Bistums Passau. Chronologische Reihenfolgen ihrer Mitglieder von der Gründung der Stifte bis zu ihrer Auflösung* (Passau 1922); J. Oswald, *Das alte Passauer Domkapitel* (Munich 1933); H. Wagner and H. Klein, *Salzburgs Domherren 1300–1514* (Salzburg 1952); J. Riedl, "Salzburgs Domherren 1514–1806," *Mitt. der Ges. für Salzburg. Landeskunde* 7 (1867), 122–286; O. Rommel, "Das Seckauer Domkapitel in seiner persönlichen Zusammensetzung (1218–1782)" (unpubl. diss., Vienna 1955); M. Dohna, Gräfin, *Die ständischen Verhältnisse am Domkapitel von Trier vom 16. bis zum 18. Jh.* (Trier 1960), (cf. review by P. Neu in *RhVjbl* 26 (1961), 354–59); D. Leopold, "Das Wiener Domkapitel zum hl. Stephan in seiner personellen Zusammensetzung in der Zeit von der Reformation Ferdinands I. bis zu seiner Erhebung zum Metropolitankapitel, 1554–1722" (unpubl. diss., Vienna 1947); J. Embach, "Das Wormser Domkapitel in den Jahren 1789–1802" (unpubl. diss., Mainz 1952); A. Amrhein, "Reihenfolge der Mitglieder des adeligen Domstiftes zu Würzburg, St. Kiliansbrüder genannt, von seiner Gründung bis zur Säkularisation (742–1803)," *Archiv des histor. Vereins für Unterfranken u. Aschaffenburg* 33 (1890), 3–380.

INDIVIDUAL PREBENDAL FAMILIES AND PREBENDARIES: J. Kist, "Bamberger Domherren aus dem Geschlecht von Guttenberg im Zeitalter der Gegenreformation," *Jb. für fränk. Landesforschung* 11/12 (1953), 277–82; P. Michels, *Ahnentafeln Paderborner Domherren* (Paderborn 1966); M. Domarus, "Die Grafen von Dernbach, Aufstieg und Ende eines reichsständischen Hauses," *Mainfränkisches Jb.* 16 (Würzburg 1964); H. Gerig, *Der Kölner Dompropst Christian August Herzog von Sachsen-Zeitz, Bischof von Raab. Seine diplomatische Tätigkeit am Niederrhein zu Beginn des Spanischen Erbfolgekriegs im Dienst der Politik Kaiser Leopolds I. 1701–03* (Bonn 1930); H. Nottarp, "Ein Mindener Dompropst des 18. Jh," *WZ* 103–4 (1954), 93–106, reprinted in: H. Nottarp, *Aus*

Rechtsgeschichte und Kirchenrecht. Gesammelte Abhandlungen, ed. by F. Merzbacher (Cologne and Graz 1967), 96–175; H. Rössler, *Graf Johann Philipp Stadion. Napoleons deutscher Gegenspieler,* 2 vols. (Vienna 1966); H. Budenbender, "Das Familiendrama Sickingen. Sein Verlauf und sein möglicher Zusammenhang mit Schillers Räubern," *Mitt. des Historischen Vereins der Pfalz* 61 (1963), 161–200.

THE NONARISTOCRATIC ELEMENT IN THE CHURCH OF THE EMPIRE: E. Krausen, "Die Herkunft der bayerischen Prälaten des 17. u. 18. Jh," *ZBLG* 27 (1964), 259–85; id., "Die Zusammensetzung der bayerischen Prämonstratenserkonvente," *HJ* 86 (1966), 157–66; A. Lederle, "Prälaten des 17. u. 18. Jh. aus dem Kinzigtal," *FreibDiözArch* 74 (1954), 208–14; G. Richter, "Die bürgerlichen Benediktiner der Abtei Fulda von 1627–1802," *Quellen und Abh. zur Gesch. der Abtei und Diözese Fulda* 7 (1911), 73–240; J. Salzgeber, *Die Klöster Einsiedeln und St. Gallen im Barockzeitalter. Historisch-soziologische Studie* (Münster 1966).

SUFFRAGAN BISHOPS: GENERAL ASPECTS; INDIVIDUAL DIOCESES: H. Hofmann, "Hilfsmittel zur Bestimmung der Titular- und Weihbischöfe in Bayern," *Mitt. für die Archivpflege in Bayern* 10 (1964), 6–14; A. Schröder, "Die Augsburger Weihbischöfe," *Archiv für die Gesch. des Hochstifts Augsburg* V (1919); J. Jungnitz, *Die Breslauer Weihbischöfe* (Breslau 1914); F. A. Koch, "Die Erfurter Weihbischöfe. Ein Beitrag zur thüringischen Kirchengeschichte," *Zschr. des Vereins für thüring. Gesch. und Altertumskunde* 6 (Jena 1865); F. E. v. Mering, *Die hohen Würdenträger der Erzdiözese Köln, zunächst die Weihbischöfe, Generalvikare u. Offiziale* (Cologne 1846); W. Haid, "Die Constanzer Weihbischöfe 1550–1803," *FreibDiözArch* 9 (1875), 1–24, 24–31; U. Berlière, *Les évêques auxiliaires de Liège* (Bruges 1919); A. Tibus, *Geschichtliche Nachrichten über die Weihbischöfe von Münster* (Münster 1862); J. C. Möller, *Gesch. der Weihbischöfe von Osnabrück* (Lingen 1887); J. Evelt, *Die Weihbischöfe von Paderborn* (Paderborn 1869–79); K. J. Holzer, *De proepiscopis Trevirensibus* (Coblenz 1845); J. A. J. Hansen, *Die Weihbischöfe von Trier* (Cologne 1834); J. Torsy, *Die Weihehandlungen der Kölner Weihbischöfe 1661–1680. Nach den weihbischöflichen Protokollen* (Düsseldorf 1969).

INDIVIDUAL SUFFRAGAN BISHOPS: H. Enger, "Weihbischof Adam Adami und sein Wirken im Bistum Hildesheim," *Unsere Diözese in Vergangenheit und Gegenwart* 32 (1963), 13–31; H. Wamper, *Das Leben der Brüder Adrian und Peter van Walenburch aus Rotterdam und ihr Wirken in der Erzdiözese Köln bis zum Jahre 1649. Ein Beitrag zur Geschichte der Gegenreformation* (Cologne 1968); K. Opladen, "Johann Sternenberg gen. Düsseldorf, Dechant zu Rees, Propst zu Xanten, Weihbischof von Münster (d. 1662). Ein Beitrag zur Gesch. der Gegenreformation," *AHVNrh* 157 (1955), 98–146; G. Scherz and J. Raeder, (eds.), *Nicolai Stenonis Epistolae,* 2 vols. (Copenhagen and Fribourg 1952); M. Bierbaum, *Niels Stensen. Von der Anatomie zur Theologie (1638–86)* (Münster in Westphalia, n.d.); J. Köhne, "Die Tätigkeit des Weihbischofs Nicolaus Steno im Bistum Paderborn," *ThGl* 34 (1942); J. Torsy, "Die Dienstreisen des Kölner Weihbischofs Paulus Aussemius 1677–79," *Festschr. Wilhelm Neuss* (Düsseldorf 1960), 164–82; G. Schwaiger, "Römische Briefe des Regensburger Weihbischofs Sebastian Denich (1654/55)," *ZKG* 73 (1962), 299–326; M. Barth, "Der Straßburger Weihbischof Paul Graf Aldringen 1627–44," *AElsKG* 7 (1932) 363–374; id., "Peter Creagh, Erzbischof von Dublin und Primas von Irland, als Weihbischof von Straßburg 1694–1705," *AElsKG* 8 (1933), 269–86; L. Lenhart, "Zwei Mainzer Weihbischöfe des 17. Jh. als ehemalige Heppenheimer Pfarrer. Adolf Gottfried Volusius (1676–79) und Mathias Starck (1679–1708)," *1200 Jahre Heppenheim a. d. Bergstraße* (1955), 129–49; H. Raab, "Der Informativprozeß des Stiftskanonikers Johann Jakob Senft anläßlich seiner

Ernennung zum Weihbischof von Erfurt 1695," *Aschaffenburger Jb.* 4 (1957), 770–76; O. v. Looz-Corswarem, "Eine Firmungsreise des Trierer Weihbischofs Otto v. Senheim (1633–62)," *Festschr. für Alois Thomas* (Trier 1967), 259–66; B. Fischer, "Pontifikalhandlungen der beiden Speyerer Weihbischöfe Johann Philipp Burckhardt (d. 1698) und Peter Kornel von Beywegh (d. 1744) im Raume des heutigen Bistums Trier in den Jahren 1685–87 und 1708–10. Nach ihrem bisher unveröffentlichten Weihetagebuch in der Bibliothek des Priesterseminars St. Peter im Schwarzwald," *AMrhKG* 5 (1953), 311–24; L. Just, "Der Trierer Weihbischof Johann Mathias v. Eyss im Kampf gegen den Jansenismus (1714–29)," *AMrhKG* 11 (1959), 160–89; F. Schäfer, *Lothar Friedrich v. Nalbach. Sein Wirken für den Kurstaat Trier als Weihbischof 1691–1748* (Cologne 1937); H. Schmitt, "Die Aushilfe der Speyerer Weihbischöfe Johann Philipp Burckhardt u. Peter Kornel von Beywegh im Bistum Worms," *AMrhKg* 12 (1960), 237–50; id., "Der Wormser Weihbischof Johann Baptist Gegg aus Eichstätt (1716–30)," *AMrhKG* 15 (1963), 95–146; id., "Christian Albert Anton v. Merle, Weihbischof von Worms (1734–65)," *AMrhKG* 16 (1964), 200–248; R. Haaß, "Das religiös-kirchliche Leben in Köln unter dem Einfluß der Francken-Siersdorf (1724–70)," *Spiegel der Geschichte, Festschr. für Max Braubach* (Münster 1964), 581–89; A. P. Brück, "Stephan Alexander Würdtwein," *AMrhKG* 2 (1950), 193–216: H. Raab, "Valentin Heimes' Informativprozeß anläßlich seiner Ernennung zum Weihbischof von Worms (1780) und Mainz (1782)," *Jb. für das Bistum Mainz* 7 (1957), 172–89; A. Bach, "Der Mainzer Weihbischof Valentin Heimes und die 'Weinpredigt' in Goethes 'St. Rochusfest zu Bingen,' " *RhVjbl* 27 (1962), 97–116; A. F. Ludwig, *Weihbischof Zirkel von Würzburg in seiner Stellung zur theolog. Aufklärung und kirchl. Restauration,* 2 vols. (Paderborn 1904–6).

11. *Spain and Portugal to 1815*

SOURCES

P. Díaz Plaja, *La vida española en el siglo XVIII* (Barcelona 1946); G. M. Jovelannos, "Obras publicadas e inéditas," *Biblioteca de Autores Españoles,* 85–87 (Madrid 1950); J. A. Llorente, *Colección diplomática de varios papeles antiguos y modernos sobre dispensas matrimoniales y otros puntos de disciplina eclesiástica* (Madrid 1809); A. Martínez Salazar, *Colección de memorias y noticias del gobierno general y político del Consejo de Castilla* (Madrid 1764); G. Maura Gamazo, *Documentos inéditos referentes a las postrimerías de la casa de Austria,* 3 vols. (Madrid 1927–30); G. Mayáns y Síscar, *Observaciones legales, histórico-críticas sobre el Concordato de 1753* (Madrid 1847); A. Mercati, *Raccolta di Concordati* (Rome 1954); A. Muriel, "Historia del reinade de Carlos IV," *BAE* 114–115 (Madrid 1959); id., "El gobierno de Carlos III o Instrucción reservada para dirección de la Junta de Estado que creó este monarca," *BAE* 115 (Madrid 1839); Edition: *Novísima Recopilación de las leyes de España* (Madrid 1805); L. M. Portocarrero, *Sinodales de Toledo 1682* (Madrid 1682); P. Rodríguez Campomanes, *Tratado de la regalía de España* (Paris 1830); J. Tejada y Ramiro, *Colección de Cánones y de todos los concilios de la Iglesia de España y de América* VI (Madrid 1859); A. Valladares, *Seminario Erudito,* 34 vols. (important historical sources in all volumes); R. de Vélez, *Apología del altar y del trono o historia de las llamadas Cortes e impugnaciones de algunas doctrinas publicadas en la Constitución, diarios y otros escritos contra la Religión y el Estado,* 2 vols. (Madrid 1818); José Vives, "Informe del obispo Climent sobre beneficencia (text)," *Analecta Sacra Tarraconensia* 30 (1957), 159–82.

LITERATURE

A. Baudrillart, *Philippe V et la Cour de France*, 5 vols. (Paris 1890–1901); C. Corona, *Revolución y reacción en el reinado de Carlos IV* (Madrid 1957); W. Coxe, *L'Espagne sous les rois de la maison Bourbon*, 5 vols. (Paris 1827); M. Danvila, *Reinado de Carlos III*, 6 vols. (Madrid 1891); M. Defourneaux, *Pablo de Olavide ou l'afrancesado (1725–1803)* (Paris 1959); Desdevises du Desert, "Les institutions de l'Espagne au XVIIIe siècle," *Revue Hispanique* 70 (1927), 1–556 (New York-Paris edition 1928); id., *La société espagnole au XVIIIe siècle* (New York and Paris 1925); R. Konetzke, *Gesch. des spanischen und portugiesischen Volkes* (Leipzig 1939); A. Domínguez Ortiz, *La Sociedad española en el s. XVIII* (Madrid 1955); Conde de Fernán Núñez, *Vida de Carlos III*, 2 vols. (Madrid 1898); J. Fernández, "Un período de las relaciones entre Felipe V y la S. Sede (1707–17)," *Anthologica Annua* 3 (1955), 9–88; A. Ferrer del Río, *Historia del reinado de Carlos III*, 4 vols. (Madrid 1858); P. B. Gams, *Die Kirchengeschichte von Spanien*, 5 vols. (Regensburg, 1862–79; reprint Graz 1956), III/2; R. Heer, *The Eighteenth-Century Revolution in Spain* (New Jersey 1958); J. Gómez Arteche, *Reinado de Carlos IV*, 3 vols. (Madrid 1894); M. Jiménez Salas, *Historia de la Asistencia Social en España en la Edad Moderna* (Madrid 1958); V. Lafuente, *Historia eclesiástica de España*, 6 vols. (Madrid 1875), V and VI; Duque de Maura, *Vida y reinado de Carlos II* 3 vols. (Madrid 1942); M. Menéndez y Pelayo, *Historia de los Heterodoxos españoles*, 7 vols. (Madrid 1930–33), VI and VII; V. Palacio Atard, *Los españoles de la Ilustración* (Madrid 1964); L. Pastor, *Gesch. der Päpste seit dem Ausgang des MA* XIV/1–XVI/3 (Freiburg i. Brsg. 1929–32; reprint 1958ff.); V. Rodríguez Casado, "El intento español de Ilustración cristiana," *Estudios Americanos* 9 (1955), 141–69; id., *La política y los políticos en el reinado de Carlos III* (Madrid 1962); J. Sarrailh, *L'Espagne eclairée de la seconde moitié du XVIIIe siècle* (Paris 1954); Spanish edition: *La España ilustrada de la segunda mitad del s. XVIII* (Mexico 1957); L. Pfandl, *Spanische Literaturgesch.* (Leipzig 1923).

THE EPISCOPATE: J. Gómez Bravo, *Catálogo de los obispos de Córdoba y breve noticia histórica de su iglesia catedral y obispado*, 2 vols. (Córdoba 1778), II; R. de Huesca, *Teatro histórico de las iglesias del reino de Aragón* (continued by Lamberto de Zaragoza) (Pamplona and Zaragoza 1796–1807), IV and VI–IX; A. López Ferreiro, *Historia de la santa A. M. iglesia de Santiago de Compostela*, 11 vols. (Santiago 1898–1909), IX–XI; J. Martín Carramolino, *Historia de Ávila, su provincia y obispado* (Madrid 1873); T. Minguella y Arnedo, *Historia de la diócesis de Sigüenza y de sus obispos*, 3 vols. (Madrid 1910–13), III; E. Morera Llauradó, *Tarragona cristiana*, 5 vols. (Tarragona 1898–1959), IV and V; T. Muñoz y Soliva, *Noticia de todos los Ilmos. señores obispos que han regido la diócesis de Cuenca, aumentadas con los sucesos . . .* (Cuenca 1860); L. B. Nadal, *Episcopologio de Vich*, 3 vols. (Vich 1891–1904), III; V. Núñez Marqués, *Guía de la S. I. catedral del Burgo de Osma y breve historia del obispado de Osma* (Madrid 1949); E. Olmos y Canalda, *Los prelados valentinos* (Madrid 1949); D. Ortiz de Zúñiga, *Anales eclesiásticos . . . de Sevilla*, 5 vols. (Madrid 1795–96), V; M. R. Pazos, *El episcopado gallego a la luz de documentos romanos*, 3 vols. (Madrid 1946); J. M. Sanz y Artibucilla, *Historia de la fidelísima y vencedora ciudad de Tarazona*, 2 vols. (Madrid 1929–30), II; J. Solano de Figueroa, *Historia eclesiástica de la ciudad y obispado de Badajoz*, 8 vols. (Badajoz 1929–35), VIII–IX; J. A. Tapia Garrido, *Los obispos de Almería* (Almería 1968).

CHURCH AND STATE: Q. Aldea, *Iglesia y Estado en la España del siglo XVII* (Comillas 1961); J. de Covarruvias, *Máximas sobre recursos de fuerza y protección*, 2 vols. (Madrid 1829); L. Cuesta, "Jesuítas confesores de reyes y directores de la Biblioteca Nacional," *Rev. Arch., Bibl. y Museos* 69 (1961), 129–74; C. García Martín, "El Tribunal de la Rota de la Nunciatura de España," *Anthologica Annua* 8 (1960), 143–278; L. G. Alonso

Getino, "Dominicos españoles confesores de Reyes," *La Ciencia Tomista* 14 (1916), 374–451; A. de la Hera, *El regalismo borbónico* (Madrid 1963); V. Lafuente, *La retención de Bulas en España ante la Historia y el Derecho,* 2 vols. (Madrid 1865); R. S. de Lamadrid, *El Concordato español de 1753 . . .* (Jerez de la Frontera 1937); R. Olaechea, *Las relaciones hispano-romanas en la segunda mitad del XVIII,* 2 vols. (Zaragoza 1965); V. Rodríguez Casado, "Iglesia y Estado en el reinado de Carlos III," *Estudios Americanos* 1 (1948–49), 5–57; L. Sierra, *La reacción del episcopado español ante los decretos de matrimonio del ministro Urquijo de 1799 a 1813* (Bilbao 1964).

UNIVERSITIES: C. Mª. Ajo G. Sáinz de Zúñiga, *Historia de las Universidades hispánicas . . . ,* 6 vols. (Madrid 1957–67), III–VI; L. Sala Balust, *Reales reformas de los antiguos Colegios de Salamanca anteriores a las del reinado de Carlos III (1623–1770)* (Valladolid 1956); id., *Visitas y reforma de los Colegios Mayores de Salamanca en el reinado de Carlos III* (Valladolid 1958).

JESUITS: A. Astraín, *Historia de la Compañía de Jesús en la Asistencia de España,* 7 vols. (Madrid 1909–12); F. Rodrigues, *História da Companhia de Jesus na Assistência de Portugal,* 7 vols. (Porto 1931–50); M. Batllori, *La cultura hispano-italiana de los jesuítas expulsos* (Madrid 1966); C. Eguía, *Los jesuítas y el motín de Esquilache* (Madrid 1947); L. Frías, "Los jesuítas y el motín de Esquilache en la Historia de España por L. Altamira," *RF* 29 (1911), 160–74; F. Rousseau, "Expulsion des jésuites en Espagne. Demarches de Charles III pour leur secularisation," *RQH* 75 (1904), I, 113–79.

INDIVIDUALS: María de Jesús de Agreda, *Cartas de la Venerable Madre Sor—y del señor Rey Don Felipe IV,* ed. by Ozcoidi y Udave, 2 vols. (Madrid 1885–86) and *BAE* 108; P. Castagnoli, *Il cardinale Giulio Alberoni,* 3 vols. (Piacenza 1929–31); F. Tort Mitjans, *Biografía histórica de Francisco Armanyá Font OSA* (Villanueva and Geltrú 1967); C. Corona, *J. N. de Azara. Un embajador español en Roma* (Zaragoza 1948); J. Báguena, *El cardenal Belluga. Su vida y su obra* (Murcia 1935); A. Echánove, S.J., "La preparación intelectual del P. Andrés Marcos Burriel SJ (1731–50)," *Hispania Sacra;* S. de Ubrique, *Vida del Beato Diego José de Cádiz,* 2 vols. (Seville 1926); C. Gómez Rodeles, *Vida del P. Calatayud* (Madrid 1882); V. de la Fuente, "Obras escogidas del P. Fray Benito Jerónimo Feijóo y Montenegro con una noticia de su vida y juicio crítico de sus escritos," *BAE* 56; *BAE,* 141; *BAE,* 142; *BAE* 143; Francisco Mendez, O.S.A., *Noticias sobre la vida, escritos y viajes del Rmo. P. Mtro. Fr. Enrique Flórez . . .* (Madrid 1860); E. Reyero, *Misiones del P. Tirso González de Santalla* (Santiago 1913); José Francisco de Isla, "Obras escogidas, con una noticia de su vida y escritos," ed. by Don Pedro Felipe Monlau, *BAE* 15; Hans Juretschke, *Vida, obra y pensamiento de Alberto Lista* (Madrid, CSIC, 1951) (extensive biblio. 698–99); A. Mestre, *Ilustración y reforma de la Iglesia. Pensamiento político-religioso de don Gregorio Mayáns y Siscar* (Valencia 1968); J. M. March, *El restaurador de la Compañia de Jesús, beato, José Pignatelli y su tiempo,* 2 vols. (Barcelona 1935–44); C. Pérez Bustamante, *Correspondencia reservada e inédita del P. Francisco de Rávago, confesor de Fernando VI,* introductory essay by Carlos Pereyra (Madrid 1936); A. Jiménez, *Biografía del R. Padre Fray Martín Sarmiento y notas de sus obras impresas y manuscritas* (Pontevedra 1884).

PORTUGAL: Fortunato de Almeida, *Historia da Igreja em Portugal,* 8 vols. (Matosinhos 1921); B. J. Wenzel, *Portugal und der Heilige Stuhl* (Lisbon 1958); J. S. da Silva Dias, *Correntes de sentimento religioso em Portugal (séculos XVI a XVIII),* 2 vols. (Coimbra 1960); F. Rodrigues, *História da Companhia de Jesus na Assistência de Portugal,* 7 vols. (Porto 1931–50).

12. The Condition of the Catholics in Great Britain and Ireland in the Seventeenth and Eighteenth Centuries

BIBLIOGRAPHIES: For recent studies see especially *RHE; Recusant History* (Nijmegen 1958ff.); *Irish Historical Studies* (Dublin 1938ff.).

SOURCES: *Catholic Record Society,* 60 vols. (London 1904ff.) (see *A Catalogue of Fifty Volumes* published by the Catholic Record Society, 1904–57); *Archivum Hibernicum* (Journal of the Catholic Record Society of Ireland, 28 vols. (Maynooth 1912ff.); *Collectanea Hibernica,* 12 vols. (Dublin 1958ff.); J. Brady, ed., *Catholics and Catholicism in the [Irish] Eighteenth-Century Press* (Maynooth 1965).

LITERATURE: W. E. H. Lecky, *History of Ireland in the Eighteenth Century,* 5 vols. (London 1892); E. H. Burton, *The Life and Times of Bishop Challoner* (London 1909); R. Bagwell, *Ireland under the Stuarts,* 3 vols. (London 1909–16; reprint London 1963); W. Forbes-Leith, *Memoirs of Scottish Catholics during the 17th and 18th Centuries* (London 1909); B. N. Ward, *The Dawn of the Catholic Revival in England 1781–1803,* 2 vols. (London 1909); P. Guilday, *The English Catholic Refugees on the Continent 1558–1793* (London 1914); W. P. Burke, *Irish Priests in the Penal Times* (Waterford 1914; reprint Shannon 1969); D. Gwynn, *The Struggle for Catholic Emancipation 1750–1829* (London 1928); P. Hughes, *The Catholic Question 1685–1929* (London 1929); M. J. Hynes, *The Mission of Rinuccini* (Dublin 1932); B. Hemphill, *The Early Vicars Apostolic of England 1685–1750* (London 1954); M. Wall, *The Penal Laws 1691–1760* (Dublin 1961; reprint Dublin 1968); B. Millett, *The Irish Franciscans 1651–1665* (Rome 1664); id., *Survival and Reorganization 1650–1695,* and P. J. Corish, *The Origins of Catholic Nationalism* (Dublin 1968).

PERIODICALS: *Biographical Studies* (Bognor Regis [England] 1951–56, continued as *Recusant History* in 1957); *Innes Review* (Glasgow 1950ff.); *Irish Ecclesiastical Record* (Dublin 1864–1968); *Proceedings of the Irish Catholic Historical Committee* (Dublin 1955ff.); *Irish Historical Studies* (Dublin 1938ff.).

13. The Russian Orthodox Church

SOURCES: *Polnoe sobranie zakonov rossijskoj imperii. Sobranie 1,* 45 vols. (St. Petersburg 1826–30); A. Theiner, *Monuments historiques relatifs aux règnes d'Alexis Michaélowitch, Féodor III et Pierre le Grand czars de Russie* (Rome 1859); *Opisanie dokumentov i del, chranjaščichsja v archive svjatejšago pravitel' stvujaščago sinoda,* 22 vols. (St. Petersburg 1868–1914); W. Regel, ed., *Analecta byzantino-russica* (St. Petersburg 1891); A. Herman, *De fontibus iuris ecclesiastici Russorum. Commentarius historico-canonicus* (Rome 1936).

REPORTS ON THE STATE OF RESEARCH: G. Stöckl, "Russische Gesch. von der Entstehung des Kiever Reiches bis zum Ende der Wirren," *JGO* n.s. 6 (1958), 201–54, 468–88; W. Leitsch, "Russische Gesch. von der Wahl Michail Romanovs bis zur Ermordung Pauls," *JGO* n.s. 9 (1961), 541–80; 10 (1962), 215–64.

LITERATURE: J. C. Grot, *Bemerkungen über die Religionsfreiheit der Ausländer im Russischen Reiche,* 3 vols. (St. Petersburg and Leipzig 1797–98); T. V. Barsov, *Svjatejšij synod v ego prošlom* (St. Petersburg 1896); A. M. Ammann, *Abriß der ostslawischen Kirchengeschichte* (Vienna 1950; with biblio.); I. Smolitsch, *Russisches Mönchtum* (Würzburg 1953); E. Winter, *Rußland und das Papsttum,* 2 vols. (Berlin 1960–61);

H. Koch, *Kleine Schriften zur Kirchen- und Geistesgeschichte Osteuropas* (Wiesbaden 1962); H. Neubauer, *Zar und Selbstherrscher* (Wiesbaden 1964); I. Smolitsch, *Gesch. der russischen Kirche 1700–1917* (Leiden 1964; with biblio.); K. Onasch, *Grundzüge der russischen Kirchengeschichte: Die Kirche in ihrer Gesch.* III (Göttingen 1967), M1–M122.

14. The Autonomous and the Uniate Churches in the East

BIBLIOGRAPHIES

J. T. Dorosh, *The Eastern Orthodox Church, a Bibliography of Publications Printed in the Roman Alphabet with Indication of Location* (Washington, D.C. 1946); A. Salmasliam, *Bibliographie de l'Arménie* (Paris 1946); D. T. Andrews, *The Eastern Orthodox Church, a Bibliography* (New York 1953); D. Attwater, *A List of Books about the Eastern Churches* (Newport, R.I. 1960); A. S. Hernández, *Iglesias de Oriente* II: *Repertorio bibliográfico* (Santander 1963); I. Doens, "Bibliographie de la Sainte Montagne de l'Athos," *Le millénaire du Mont Athos 963–1963* II (Chevetogne 1964), 337–495. —See also the bibliographies in: *OstKSt* (1951ff.).

LITERATURE

M. Spinka, *A History of Christianity in the Balkans* (Chicago 1933); F. Heiler, *Urkirche und Ostkirche* (Munich 1937; reprint Munich 1969); *Ekklesia X: Die Orthodoxe Kirche auf dem Balkan und in Vorderasien. Die orthodoxen Patriarchate von Konstantinopel, Alexandrien, Antiochien, Jerusalem und das Erzbistum von Cypern* (Leipzig 1941); W. de Vries, *Der christliche Osten in Gesch. und Gegenwart* (Würzburg 1951); R. Janin, *Les églises orientales et les rites orientaux* (Paris 1955); D. Attwater, *The Christian Churches of the East*, 2 vols. (Milwaukee 1961–62); B. Spuler, ed., *Hdb. der Orientalistik* 1 VIII/2: *Religionsgeschichte des Orients in der Zeit der Weltreligionen* (Leiden and Cologne 1961; biblio.); A. S. Atiya, *A History of Eastern Christianity* (London 1968); A. J. Arberry, *Religion in the Middle East, Three Religions in Concord and Conflict*, 2 vols. (Cambridge 1969).

THE PATRIARCHATE OF CONSTANTINOPLE: G. M. Drabadjeglon, "Gesch. und Verfassung des Ökumenischen Patriarchats," *Ekklesia* X, 45–59; G. Every, *The Byzantine Patriarchate* (London 1947); G. Zananiri, *Histoire de l'Église byzantine* (Paris 1954); F. W. Fernau, *Patriarchen am Goldenen Horn, Gegenwart und Tradition des orthodoxen Orients* (Opladen 1967); A. T. Khoury, "Die Einstellung der Byzantinischen Kirche zur islamitischen Welt nach dem Fall von Konstantinopel," *Concilium* 3 (1967), 538–43; E. V. Ivánka, *Rhomäerreich und Gottesvolk. Das Glaubens-, Staats- und Volksbewußtsein der Byzantiner und seine Auswirkung auf die ostkirchlich-osteuropäische Geisteshaltung* (Munich 1968); S. Runciman, *The Great Church in Captivity* (Cambridge 1968).

THE PATRIARCHATES OF ALEXANDRIA, ANTIOCH, AND JERUSALEM: C. Korolewski, *Histoire des patriarcats melkites* II–III (Rome 1910–11); T. E. Dowling, *The Orthodox Greek Patriarchate of Jerusalem* (London 1913); G. Bardy, *L'Église d'Antioche* (Paris 1918); Patriarch Alexandros, "Das Patriarchat von Antiochien," *Ekklesia* X, 80–92; K. Meliaras, "Die Kirche von Jerusalem," *Ekklesia* X, 106–14; E. Michailides, "Gesch., Verfassung und Statistik des Patriarchats von Alexandrien," *Ekklesia* X, 71–79; T. Mosconas, "Das griechisch-orthodoxe Patriarchat von Alexandrien," *Kyrios* n.s. 1 (1960/61), 129–39; I. Totzke, "Die alten Patriarchate Alexandrien, Antiochien und Jerusalem," *Una Sancta* 14 (1959), 300–307; 15 (1960), 203–12.

THE UNIATE CHURCHES: B. Homsy, *Les capitulations et la protection des chrétiens au Proche-Orient* (Paris 1962); F. Heyer, "Die katholische Kirche vom Westfälischen Frieden bis zum Ersten Vatikanischen Konzil," *Die Kirche in ihrer Gesch.* IV (Göttingen 1963) fasc. N 175–95; W. de Vries in cooperation with O. Barlea, J. Gill, and M. Lacko, *Proche-Orient* (Paris 1962); F. Heyer, "Die katholische Kirche vom Westfälischen Frieden bis zum Ersten Vatikanischen Konzil," *Die Kirche in ihrer Gesch.* IV (Göttingen 1963) fasc. N 175–95; W. de Vries in cooperation with O. Barlea, J. Gill, and M. Lacko, *Rom und die Patriarchate des Ostens* (Freiburg and Munich 1963); J. Hajjar, *Die Kirche im Nahen Osten: Gesch. der Kirche* IV (Einsiedeln, Zurich and Cologne 1966), 347–90 (biblio.); J. Madey, *Kirche zwischen Ost und West* (Munich 1969).

The Propagation of the Faith and European Absolutism

GENERAL: Streit I–XXVI; Ambrosius a S. Theresias, *Bio-bibliographia Missionaria Ordinis Carm. Disc., 1584–1940* (Rome 1941); Clemente da Terzorio, *Le Missioni dei Minori Capuccini* I–IV (Rome 1913–38); K. S. Latourette, *A History of the Expansion of Christianity,* 7 vols. (New York and London 1937–45), Vols. 3–5; S. Delacroix, *Histoire Universelle des Missions Catholiques* II (Paris 1957); *Historia Missionum Ordinis Fratrum Minorum* I–III (Rome 1967–68); N. Kowalsky, *Stand der kath. Missionen um das Jahr 1765 an Hand der Übersicht des Propaganda-Sekretärs, Stefano Borgia, aus dem Jahre 1773* (Beckenried 1957); L. Lemmens, *Gesch. der Franziskanermissionen* (Münster 1929); A. Mulders, *Missionsgeschichte* (Regensburg 1960); A. da Silva Rego, *O Ultramar Português no Século XVIII* (Lisbon 1967): H.-W. Gensichen, *Missionsgeschichte der neueren Zeit* (Göttingen 1961).

15. *The Propagation of the Faith in America*

SOURCES

F. Ajofrín, O.F.M.Cap., *Diario del Viaje que por orden de la sagrada Congregación de Propaganda Fide hizo a la América Septentrional en el siglo XVIII,* 2 vols. (Madrid 1958–59); F. J. Alegre, *Historia de la Provincia de la Compañía de Jesús en la Nueva España* I–IV (Rome 1956–60); D. Basalenque, O.E.S.A., *Historia de la Provincia de San Nicolás de Tolentino de Michoacán* (Mexico City 1963); A. de Egaña, S.J., *Monumenta Peruana* I–IV (Rome 1954–66); F.J. Hernáez, S.J., *Colección de bulas y breves y otros documentos relativos a la Iglesia de América y Filipinas,* 2 vols. (Brussels 1879–95); O. Maas, O.F.M., *Las Órdenes Religiosas de España y la Colonización de America en la segunda parte del siglo XVIII,* 2 vols. (Barcelona 1918–29); F. Zubillaga, S.J., *Monumenta Mexicana* I–III (Rome 1959–68).

LITERATURE

L. de Aspurz, O.F.M.Cap., *La aportación extranjera a las Misiones Españolas del Patronato regio* (Madrid 1946); A. Astraín, S.J., *Historia de la Compañía de Jesús en la Asistencia de España* I–VII (Madrid 1902–25); P. Borges, O.F.M., *Métodos misionales en la cristianización de América* (Madrid 1960); M. Cuevas, S.J., *Historia de la Iglesia en México* I–V (El Paso 1928); A. de Egaña, S. J., *Historia de la Iglesia en la América Española. Hemisferio Sur* (Madrid 1966); N. M. Farriss, *Crown and Clergy in Colonial Mexico 1759–1821. The Crisis of Ecclesiastical Privilege* (London 1968); R. Konetzke, *Süd- und Mittelamerika* (*Fischer-Weltgeschichte* 22) (Frankfurt am Main 1965); P. de Leturia, S.J., *Relaciones entre la Santa Sede e Hispanoamérica 1493–1835* I: *Época del Real Patronato 1493–1800* (Rome and Caracas 1959); A. Ybot León, *La Iglesia y los Eclesiásticos españoles en la empresa de Indias* I (Barcelona 1954); II (Barcelona 1962); L. Lopetegui, S.J., and F. Zubillaga, S.J., *Historia de la Iglesia en la América Española. México, América Central, Antillas* (Madrid 1965); R. Ricard, *La "conquête spirituelle" du Mexique. Essai sur l'apostolat et les méthodes missionnaires des Ordres mendiants en Nouvelle Espagne de 1523/24 à 1572* (Paris 1933); G. Arcila Robledo, *La Orden Franciscana en la América Meridional* (Rome 1948); J.

Specker, S.M.B., *Die Missionsmethode in Spanisch-Amerika im 16. Jh. mit besonderer Berücksichtigung der Konzilien und Synoden* (Beckenried 1953); R. Vargas Ugarte, S.J., *Historia de la Iglesia en el Perú* I (Lima 1953); II (Burgos 1959).

16. The Propagation of the Faith in Africa

SOURCES

A. Brásio, C.Sp., *Monumenta Missionaria Africa Ocidental* 6–10 (Lisbon 1955–65); G. A. Cavazzi de Montecuccolo, *Istoria Descrittione de' tre Regni Congo, Matamba et Angola* (Milan 1690) (Port. ed.: 2 vols. [Lisbon 1965]); J. Cuvelier, ed., *Relations sur le Congo du P. Laurent de Lucques (1700–17)* (Brussels 1953); G. M. Theal, *Records of South-Eastern Africa,* 9 vols. (London 1898–1903); C. Beccari, S.J., *Rerum Aethiopicarum Scriptores Occidentales inediti,* 15 vols. (Rome 1903–17); T. Somigli di S. Detole, O.F.M., *Etiopia Franciscana,* 2 vols. (Karachi 1928–48).

LITERATURE

C. P. Groves, *The Planting of Christianity in Africa I (to 1840)* (London 1948); L. Jadin, "L'Afrique et Rome depuis l'époque des découvertes jusqu'au XVIIe siècle," *XIIe Congrès International des Sciences Historiques. Rapports,* II: *Histoire des Continents* (Louvain 1965), 33–69; J. Cuvelier, *L'ancien royaume du Congo* (Brussels 1946); Durval Piros de Lima, *O Oriente e a Africa desde a Restauração a Pombal* (Lisbon 1946); A. L. Farinha, *A expansão da Fé na Africa e no Brasil* (Lisbon 1942); J. Janin, *La Religion aux Colonies Françaises sous l'ancien régime (de 1626 à la Révolution)* (Paris 1942); Sidney R. Welch, *Portuguese and Dutch in South Africa 1641–1806* (Cape Town 1951); G. M. Theal, *History of Africa South of the Zambesi from the Settlement of the Portuguese at Sofala in Sept. 1505 to the Conquest of the Cape Colony by the British in Sept. 1795,* 3 vols. (London 1910).

17. The Propagation of the Faith in Asia

SOURCES: Streit V, VI; *Collectanea S. Congregationis de Propaganda Fide* (1622 to 1866) (Rome 1907); *Juris Pontificii de Propaganda Fide,* Pars prima I–VII (Rome 1888–97), Pars secunda I (Rome 1909).

LITERATURE: H. Chappoulie, *Aux origines d'une église. Rome et les Missions d'Indochine au XVIIe siècle,* 2 vols. (Paris 1943–48); K. S. Latourette, *Gesch. der Ausbreitung des Christentums* (Göttingen 1956); A. Jann, *Die katholischen Missionen in Indien, China und Japan. Ihre Organisation und das portugiesische Patronat vom 15. bis 18. Jh.* (Paderborn 1915); A. Launay, *Histoire générale de la Société des Missions Étrangères* I (Paris 1912); id., *Mémorial de la Société des Missions Étrangères* II (Paris 1916); A. da Silva Rêgo, *Curso de Missionologia* (Lisbon 1956–61); G. de Vaumas, *L'éveil missionnaire de la France* (Lyon 1942).

INDIA

SOURCES: *Documenta Indica,* ed. by J. Wicki, S.J., I–XI (Rome 1948–70); Paulo da Trindade, O.F.M., *Historia espiritual do Oriente,* ed. by F. Lopes, I–III (Lisbon 1962–67); A. Meersman, O.F.M., "The Chapter-Lists of the Madre de Deus Province in India," *Studia* VI (Lisbon 1960), 121–350.

LITERATURE: Ambrosius a S. Theresia, *Hierarchia Carmelitana* III: *De Praesulibus Ecclesiae Magni Mogolis seu Bombayensis* (Rome 1936); IV: *De Praesulibus Missionis Malabaricae. Pars Prior. Ecclesia Verapolitana* (Rome 1939); F. Coutinho, *Le régime paroissial des Diocèses de rite latin de l'Inde* (Louvain 1965); A. L. Farinha, *A expansão da fé no Estremo Oriente* (Lisbon 1946); D. Ferroli, S.J., *The Jesuits in Malabar* I/II (Bangalore 1939–51); P. Thomas, *Christians and Christianity in India and Pakistan* (London 1954).

CHINA

LITERATURE: Streit VI, VII, XII, XIII, XIV, 1–3; J. Beckmann, *Neuerscheinungen zur chinesischen Missionsgeschichte von 1945–1955; Monumenta Serica* XV (Tokyo 1956), 378–462; J. M. González, *Historia de las Misiones de China* V: *Bibliografías* (Madrid 1967); Toung-Li Yuan, *China in Western Literature* (New Haven 1958); K. S. Latourette, *A History of Christian Missions in China* (New York 1929); O. Ferreux, "Histoire de la Mission en Chine (1699–1950)," *Annales de la Congrégation de la Mission* 127 (Paris 1963), 3–530; J. de Moidrey, *La Hiérarchie Catholique en Chine, en Corée et au Japon (1307–1914)* (Shanghai 1914); N. Gubbels, *Trois siècles d'apostolat. Histoire du Catholicisme au Hukwang (1587–1870)* (Wuchang and Paris 1934); F. Margiotti, *Il cattolicismo nello Shansi delle origini al 1738* (Rome 1958); L. Pfister, *Notices biographiques et bibliographiques sur les Jésuites de l'ancienne Mission de Chine (1552–1773)* I, II (Shanghai 1932–34); K. Menz, *Necrologium Fratrum Minorum in Sinis* (Peking 1948); J. van den Brandt, *Les Lazaristes en Chine 1667–1935* (Peking 1936).

THE PHILIPPINES AND THE SOUTH SEAS

LITERATURE: Streit V, VI; G. H. Anderson, ed., *Studies in Philippine Church History* (Ithaca and London 1969); *IV Centenario de la Evangelización de Filipinas 1565–1965: Boletín de la Provincia de San Nicolás de Tolentino de filipinas* 55 (Marcillo, Navarra 1965) 49-303; H. de la Costa, *The Jesuits in the Philippines 1581–1768* (Cambridge, Mass. 1961); P. Fernández, *Dominicos donde nace el sol* (Barcelona 1958); M. Valentin, *Ensayo de una Síntesis de los trabajos realizados por las Corporaziones religiosas Filipinas* I (Manila 1901); M. Merino, *Augustinos Evangelizadores de Filipinas 1565–1965* (Madrid 1965).

Part Two

The Established Church and the Enlightenment

SECTION ONE

Concepts

18. Foundations and Forms of the Established Church in the Bourbon States of the Seventeenth and Eighteenth Centuries

LITERATURE

GENERAL: Hinschius; E. Friedberg, *Die Gränzen zwischen Staat und Kirche und die Garantien gegen deren Verletzung* (Tübingen 1872); E. H. Feine; G. Schnürer, *Katholische Kirche und Kultur in der Barockzeit* (Paderborn 1937); id., *Katholische Kirche und Kultur im 18. Jh.* (Paderborn, 1941); Seppelt-Schwaiger V; L. A. Veit, *Die Kirche im Zeitalter des Individualismus* I (1648–1800) (Freiburg i. Brsg. 1931); Pastor XIII–XVI; H. Raab, *Kirche und Staat. Von der Mitte des 15. Jh. bis zur Gegenwart* (Munich 1966); P. Brezzi, *Stato e Chiesa nel Ottocento* (Turin 1964); J. F. le Bret, *Gesch. der so verrufenen Bulle In Coena Domini* (Frankfurt am Main 1769); K. Pfaff, "Beiträge zur Gesch. der Abendmahlsbulle vom 16.–18. Jh," *RQ* 38 (1930), 23–76; R. Giura Longo, "La bolla in Coena Domini et le franchigie al clero meridionale," *Archivio storico per la Calabria e la Lucania* 32 (Rome 1963), 275–96; 33 (Rome 1964), 81–128; P. G. Caron, *L'Appello per abuso* (Milan 1954).

FRANCE: R. Holtzmann, *Französische Verfassungsgeschichte von der Mitte des 9. Jh. bis zur Revolution* (Munich and Berlin 1910); G. J. Phillips, *Das Regalienrecht in Frankreich* (Halle 1873; reprint Aalen 1967); V. Martin, *Les origines du gallicanisme,* 2 vols. (Paris 1939); J. Thomas, *Le concordat de 1516. Les origines, son histoire,* 3 vols. (Paris 1910); R. Folz, "Le concordat germanique et l'élection des évêques de Metz," *Annuaire de la société d'histoire et d'archéologie de la Lorraine* 40 (1931), 157–305; R. Metz, *La Monarchie française et la provision des bénéfices ecclésiastiques en Alsace de la paix de Westphalie à la fin de l'ancien Régime* (1648–1789) (Strasbourg and Paris 1947); H. G. Judge, "Church and State under Louis XIV," *History* 45 (1960), 217–33; R. Darricau, "Louis XIV et le Saint-Siège, les indultes de nominations aux bénéfices consistoriaux 1643–1670," *BLE* 65 (1965), 16–34, 107–31; id., "Louis XIV et le Saint-Siège. La négociation du Traité de Pise (1664)," *Annuaire-Bulletin de la Société de l'Histoire de France* (1964/65), 81–156; A. G. Martimort, *Le gallicanisme de Bossuet* (Paris 1953); J. Orcibal, *Louis XIV contre Innocent XI, les appels au futur concile de 1688 et l'opinion française* (Paris 1949); N. Ravitch, "The Taxing of the Clergy in 18th Century France," *CH* 33 (1964), 157–74; A. Guth, *Le don gratuit de clergé d'Alsace sous l'Ancien régime* (Strasbourg 1960); id. "Les dernières impositions royales du clergé d'Alsace," *Archives d'histoire et l'Église d'Alsace* 30 (1964), 205–72; B. Wunder, "Ludwig XIV. und die Konstanzer Bischofswahl 1689," *ZGObrh* 114 (1966), 381–91; P. Blet, *Le clergé de France et la monarchie,* 2 vols. (Paris 1959).

THE TWO SICILIES: F. J. Sentis, *Die "Monarchia Sicula." Eine historisch-canonistische Untersuchung* (Freiburg i. Brsg. 1869); E. Papa, "Politica ecclesiastica nel regno di Napoli tra il 1708 e il 1710," *Gregorianum* 36 (1955), 626–68; 37 (1956), 55–87; id., *Il regno di Napoli tra Roma e Vienna nei primi decenni del settecento* (diss. and Rome 1955); M. Schipa, *Il Regno di Napoli al tempo di Carlo Borbone* (Milan and Rome 1923); G. Falzone, *Il regno di Carlo di Borbone in Sicilia 1734–1759* (Rome 1964); R. Moscatti, *Nella Sicilia di Carlo VI. Studi storici in onore di Gioacchino II* (Florence 1958); G. Catalano, *Le ultimi vicente della Legazia apostolica di Sicilia nella controversia Liparitana alle legge quarentigie (1711–1871)* (Catania 1950); P. Onnis, "Bernardo Tanucci nel moto anticurialista del '700," *Nuova Rivista storica* 10 (1926), 328–65; id., "L'abolizione della Compagnia di Gesù nel Regno di Napoli," *Rassegna storica del Risorgimento* 15 (1938), 759–822: E. Viviani della Robbia, *Bernardo Tanucci e il suo piu importante carteggio*, 2 vols. (Florence 1942); A. Melpignano, *L'anticuralismo napoletano sotto Carlo III di Borbone* (Rome 1965); M. Rosa, "Politica concordataria, giurisdizionalismo e organizzazione ecclesiastica nel Regno di Napoli sotto Carlo di Borbone," *Critica storica* 4 (1967), 494–531; L. Spinelli, "La politica ecclesiastica di Bernardo Tanucci in tema di provista dei benefici Maggiori," *Raccolta di scritti in onore di Arturo Carlo Jemolo* I (Milan 1963), 1187–1236; R. Mincuzzi, *Bernardo Tanucci, ministro di Ferdinando di Borbone 1759–76* (Bari 1967).

TUSCANY: N. Rodolico, *Stato e Chiesa in Toscana durante la Regenza lorenese (1737–65)* (Florence 1910); F. Scaduto, *Stato e Chiese sotto Leopoldo I granduca di Toscana (1765–90)* (Florence 1885); A. Wandruszka, *Leopold II.*, 2 vols. (Vienna 1963–65); G. König, *Rom und die toskanische Kirchenpolitik (1765–90)* (diss., Cologne 1964); M. Rosa, "Giurisdizionalismo e riforma religiosa nella politica ecclesiastica leopoldina," *Rassegna storica toscana* 11 (1965), 257–300; E. Passerin d'Entrèves, "L'instruzione dei patrimoni ecclesiastici e il dissidio fra il vescovo Scipione de' Ricci e i funzionari leopoldini 1783–89," *Rassegna storica toscana* 1 (1955); id., "La riforma 'giansenista' della Chiesa e la lotta anticuriale in Italia nella seconda metà del Settecento," *RSIt* 71 (1959), 209–34.

PARMA AND PIACENZA; PIEDMONT: P. A. Kirsch, "Ein päpstliches Lehensprojekt für Parma und Piacenza unter Benedikt XIV.," *HJ* 24 (1903), 517–52; U. Benassi, "Gugliemo Du Tillot, un ministro riformatore del sec. XVIII. (1759–71)," *La politica eccles.: Arch. Stor. per le prov. Parmensi,* n.s., 24 (1924); P. C. Broglio, *Stato e Chiesa in Piemonte dal sec. XVIII al 1854* (Rome 1965); C. Caristia, "Riflessi politici del giansenismo italiano. La republica democratica in Piemonte 1798–1800," *Raccolta di scritti in onore di Arturo Carlo Jemolo* I (Milan 1963), 95–110; P. Stella, *Giurisdizionalismo e giansenismo all'Università di Torino nel secolo XVIII* (Turin 1958); id., "La bolla 'Unigenitus' e i nuovi orientamenti religiosi e politici in Piemonte sotto Vittorio Emanuele II, 1713–20," *RSTI* 15 (1961); R. Ciasca, "Contrasti giurisdizionali a Genova nel secolo XVII," *Raccolta di scritti in onore di Arturo Carlo Jemolo* I (Milan 1963), 195–213.

VENICE: B. Cechetti, *La Repubblica di Venezia e la corte di Roma nei rapporti di religione,* 2 vols. (Venice 1890); A. Battistella, *La politica ecclesiastica della Repubblica di Venezia* (Venice 1898); A. Stella, "La proprietà ecclesiastica nella Repubblica di Venezia dal sec. XV al XVII," *Nuova Rivista storica* 42 (1958), 4–30; id., *Chiesa e stato nelle relazioni dei nunzie pontifici a Venezia* (Vatican City 1964); A. M. Bettanini, *Benedetto XIV e la Repubblica di Venezia. Storia delle trattative diplomatiche per la difesa dei diritti giurisdizionali ecclesiastici* (Padua 1966).

SPAIN AND PORTUGAL: Q. Aldea, "Iglesia y Estado en la España del siglo XVII. Ideario político eclesiástico," *MCom* 36 (1961), 134–539; id., *Iglesia y Estado en la España del siglo XVII* (Comillas 1961); P. A. Kirsch, "Das durch Benedikt XIV. i. J. 1753 mit Spanien abgeschlossene Konkordat," *AkathKR* 80 (1900); R. S. Lamadrid, *El concordato español de 1753 según los documentos de su negociación* (Jerez de la Frontera 1938); B. Duhr, *Pombal. Sein Charakter und seine Politik* (Freiburg 1891); A. de la Hera, *El Regalismo Borbónico en su proyección indiana* (Madrid 1963); M. F. Miguélez, *Jansenismo y Regalismo en España* (Madrid 1895); V. Rodríguez, *Iglesia y Estado en el reinado de Carlos III = Estudios americanos* 1 (1948); R. Olachea, *Las relaciones hispano-romanas en la segunda mitad del XVIII,* 2 vols. (Zaragoza 1965).

19. *The Enlightenment*

LITERATURE

GENERAL: W. Dilthey, *Weltanschauung u. Analyse des Menschen seit Renaissance u. Reformation* [*=Ges. Schr.* 2] (Göttingen 1960); P. Hazard, *La crise de la conscience Européenne. 1680–1715* (Paris 1935); id., *La pensée Européenne aux XVIIIᵉ siècle de Montesquieu à Lessing* (Paris 1946); R. Mousnier, E. Labrousse, and M. Bouloiseau, *Le XVIIIᵉ siècle. 1715–1815. L'époque des "lumières"* (Paris 1967); R. Kosellek, *Kritik und Krise. Ein Beitrag zur Pathogenese der bürgerlichen Welt* [*=Orbis Academicus*] (Freiburg and Munich 1959); J. L. Talmon, *The Origins of Totalitarian Democracy* (New York 1960); H. Nicolson, *The Age of Reason 1700–1789* (London 1961); A. Cobban, *In Search of Humanity. The Role of the Enlightenment in Modern History* (London 1960); L. I. Brevold, *The Brave New World of Enlightenment* (Ann Arbor 1961); F. Valjavec, *Geschichte der abendländischen Aufklärung* (Vienna and Munich 1961); A. Wolf, *A History of Science, Technology and ·Philosophy in the 18th Century,* 2 vols. (New York 1961); G. Funke, *Die Aufklärung. In ausgewählten Texten dargestellt und eingeleitet* (Stuttgart 1963); P. Chaunu, *La civilisation de l'Europe classique, restituée dans son unité profonde et sa diversité* (Paris 1966); F. Wagner, ed., *Europa im Zeitalter des Absolutismus und der Aufklärung* [*=Hdb. der europäischen Geschichte* IV] (Stuttgart 1968), see especially F. Wagner, "Die Einheit der Epoche," 1–163 (space devoted to the intellectual history of individual countries varies greatly); B. Willey, *The 17th Century Background, Studies in the Thought of the Age in Relation to Poetry and Religion* (Garden City 1953); R. Mousnier, *Les XVIᵉ et XVIIᵉ Siècles. La grande mutation intellectuelle de l'humanité* (Paris 1965); B. Willey, *The 18th Century Background. Studies on the Idea of Nature in the Thought of the Period* (London 1961); *Transactions of the First International Congress on the Enlightenment,* 4 vols. (Geneva 1963) [*=Studies on Voltaire and the 18th Century,* ed. by T. Besterman, Vols. 24–27]; *Transactions of the Second International Congress on the Enlightenment,* 4 vols. (Geneva 1967) [*=Studies on Voltaire and the 18th Century,* ed. by T. Bestermann, Vols. 55–58]; W. Andreas, "Literaturberichte. Absolutismus und Aufklärung," *Geschichte in Wissenschaft und Unterricht* 5 (1954), 494–501; id., in *Geschichte in Wissenschaft und Unterricht* 9 (1958), 107–14; id. in *Geschichte in Wissenschaft und Unterricht* 16 (1965), 51–59.

PHILOSOPHY: J. Kremer, *Das Problem der Theodizee in der Philosophie und Literatur des 18. Jr.* (Berlin 1909); E. Cassirer, *Die Philosophie der Aufklärung* (1912) [*=Grundriß der philosophischen Wissenschaften*] (Tübingen 1932); S. Hampshire, ed., *The Age of*

617

Reason. The 17th Century Philosophers, Selected, with Introduction and Interpretative Commentary (Boston 1956); M. Wundt, *Die deutsche Schulphilosophie im Zeitalter der Aufklärung* (Tübingen 1945); C. L. Becker, *The Heavenly City of the 18th Century Philosophers* (New Haven 1932, 1952); see especially the chapter on "The Laws of Nature and of Nature's God," pp. 33–70.

PEDAGOGY: L. Weber, *Pädagogik der Aufklärungszeit* (Frauenfeld and Leipzig 1941); H. Weimer, *Geschichte der Pädagogik* (Berlin 1967) [=*Sammlung Göschen* 145/145a]; A. Reble, *Geschichte der Pädagogik* (Stuttgart 1962), especially 123–59.

STATE AND INTERNATIONAL LAW: F. Meinecke, *Die Idee der Staatsräson in der neueren Geschichte* (1924) [=*Werke* I] (Munich 1957), 245–400; L. Strauss and J. Cropsey, eds., *History of Political Philosophy* (Chicago 1963); G. Möbus, *Die politischen Theorien im Zeitalter der absoluten Monarchie bis zur Französischen Revolution* (Cologne 1966); T. Ramm, *Die großen Sozialisten als Rechts- und Sozialphilosophen* I,1 and I,2 (Stuttgart 1955); E. Reibstein, *Völkerrecht. Eine Geschichte seiner Ideen in Lehre und Praxis* I [=*Orbis Academicus* I,5] (Freiburg and Munich 1957), 237–609; A. Geouffre de Lapradelle, *Maîtres et doctrines du droit des gens* (Paris 1950); J. J. Chévallier, *Les grandes œuvres politiques; de Machiavel à nos jours* (Paris 1957); K. v. Raumer, *Ewiger Friede. Friedensrufe und Friedenspläne seit der Renaissance* [=*Orbis Academicus*] (Freiburg and Munich 1953); H. J. Schlochauer, *Die Idee des Ewigen Friedens. Ein Überblick über Entwicklung und Gestaltung des Friedenssicherungsgedankens auf der Grundlage einer Quellenauswahl* (Bonn 1953), 76–129.

HISTORICAL CONNECTIONS: W. Dilthey, "Das 18. Jh. u. die geschichtliche Welt," *Deutsche Rundschau* (Aug./Sept. 1901) [=*Ges. Schriften* 3] (Göttingen 1959), 209–68; B. Croce, *Theorie u. Geschichte der Historiographie u. Betrachtungen zur Philosophie der Politik* [=*Gesammelte philosophische Schriften in dt. Übertragung*, I. Reihe, 4. Bd.] (Tübingen 1930), 3–136, 188–220; F. Meinecke, *Die Entstehung des Historismus* (Munich 1936, 1946); K. Löwith, *Meaning in History* (Chicago 1949); F. Wagner, *Geschichtswissenschaft* [=*Orbis Academicus* I, 1] (Freiburg and Munich 1951, 1966), 63–140 (with biblio.); H. Gollwitzer, *Europabild u. Europagedanke. Beiträge zur deutschen Geistesgeschichte des 18. u. 19. Jh.* (Munich 1951); 54–118; H. v. Srbik, *Geist u. Geschichte vom deutschen Humanismus bis zur Gegenwart* I (Munich and Salzburg 1950), 69–166; A. Kraus, *Vernunft und Geschichte* (Freiburg i. Brsg. 1963) [Part I, "Das Jahrhundert und seine Geschichte," provides an aspect of the historical connections of the Enlightenment which goes far beyond the actual topic]; F. Günther, *Die Wissenschaft vom Menschen. Ein Beitrag zum deutschen Geistesleben im Zeitalter des Rationalismus mit besonderer Rücksicht auf die Entwicklung der deutschen Geschichtsphilosophie im 18. Jh.* (Gotha 1906); A. Schreiber, "Das Mittelalter, universalhistorisches Problem vor der Romantik," *AKG* 31 (1943), 93–120.

MATHEMATICS AND THE NATURAL SCIENCES: F. Dannemann, *Die Naturwissenschaften in ihrer Entwicklung und in ihrem Zusammenhang*, 4 vols. (Leipzig 1920–23); I: *Von den Anfängen bis zum Wiederaufleben der Wissenschaften* (403ff.); II: *Von Galilei bis zur Mitte des 18. Jh.*; III: *Das Emporblüthen der modernen Naturwissenschaften bis zur Aufstellung des Energieprinzips* (starts in the middle of the eighteenth century); W. C. Dampier, *Geschichte der Naturwissenschaft in ihrer Beziehung zu Philosophie und Weltanschauung* (Vienna and Stuttgart 1952), 179–239; A. Meier, *Die Mechanisierung des Weltbilds im 17. Jh.* [=*Forsch. zur Gesch. der Philosophie u. Pädergogik* 18] (Leipzig 1938); J. Krüger, *Das Weltbild der Naturwissenschaft im Wandel der Zeiten. Eine Geschichte der Naturforschung von den Anfängen bis zur Gegenwart* (Paderborn 1953); E. J. Dijksterhuis,

Die Mechanisierung des Weltbildes (Berlin, Göttingen and Heidelberg 1956), [pp. 319ff. to the end and especially the closing statement take religious issues into account]; H. Butterfield, *The Origins of Modern Science 1300–1800* (London 1958); R. A. Hall, *Die Geburt der naturwissenschaftlichen Methode 1630–1720 von Galilei bis Newton* (Gütersloh 1965); L. Roule, *L'histoire de la nature vivante d'après l'œuvre des grands naturalistes français,* 6 vols. (Paris 1924–32); O. Becker, *Die Grundlagen der Mathematik in geschichtl. Entwicklung* [=*Orbis Academicus* II, 6] (Freiburg and Munich 1964), 131–67; H. Weyl, *Philosophie der Mathematik und der Naturwissenschaft* [=*Hdb. der Philosophie,* newly ed. by M. Schröder] (Munich 1948); M. v. Laue, *Geschichte der Physik* (Bonn 1947); H. Lange, *Geschichte der Grundlagen der Physik,* 2 vols. [=*Orbis Academicus* II,7 and II,13] (Freiburg and Munich 1954–61), I, 165–239, II, 258–97; E. Zinner, *Astronomie. Geschichte ihrer Probleme* [=*Orbis Academicus* II,1] (Freiburg and Munich 1951); J. Anker and S. Dahl, *Werdegang der Biologie* (Leipzig 1938), 67–180; E. Ungerer, *Die Erkenntnisgrundlagen der Biologie. Ihre Geschichte und ihr gegenwärtiger Stand* [=*Hdb. der Biologie* I/1] founded by L. von Bertalanffy, ed. by F. Gessner (Constance 1965), here 26–42; E. Uhlmann, "Entwicklungsgedanke und Artbegriff in ihrer geschichtlichen Entstehung und sachlichen Beziehung," *Jenaische Zschr. für Naturwiss.* 59, M.S. 52 (Jena 1923), here 14–31; P. G. Hesse, *Der Lebensbegriff bei den Klassikern der Naturforschung. Seine Entwicklung bei 60 Denkern und Forschern bis zur Goethezeit* (Jena 1943), 30–79; E. Guyénot, *Les sciences de la vie aux XVIIe et XVIIIe siècles, L'idée d'évolution* (Paris 1941); A. Barthelmess, *Vererbungswissenschaft* [=*Orbis Academicus* II,2] (Freiburg and Munich 1952), 21–43; W. Zimmermann, *Evolution. Die Geschichte ihrer Probleme und Erkenntnisse* [=*Orbis Academicus* II,3] (Freiburg and Munich 1953), 158–336; T. Ballauff, *Die Wissenschaft vom Leben* I [=*Orbis Academicus* II,8] (Freiburg and Munich 1954), 121–343; J. Roger, *Les sciences de la vie dans la pensée français du XVIIIe siècle* (Paris 1963).

THE RELATIONSHIP BETWEEN THEOLOGY AND SCIENCE: O. Zöckler, *Geschichte der Beziehungen zwischen Theologie und Naturwissenschaft mit besonderer Rücksicht auf die Schöpfungsgeschichte,* 2 vols. (Gütersloh 1877–79); I: *Von den Anfängen der christlichen Kirchen bis auf Newton und Leibniz;* II: *Von Newton und Leibniz bis zur Gegenwart;* L. A. Veit, *Das Aufklärungsschrifttum des 18. Jh. und die deutsche Kirche. Ein Zeitbild aus der deutschen Geistesgeschichte* [=Görres-Ges. zur Pflege der Wiss. im kath. Dtl., Zweite Vereinsschrift] (Cologne 1937); W. Philipp, *Das Werden der Aufklärung in theologiegeschichtlicher Sicht* (Göttingen 1957), investigates the physicotheology of the seventeenth and early eighteenth century; concentrates expressly on the early Enlightenment; W. Philipp, ed., *Das Zeitalter der Aufklärung* [=Sammlung Dietrich 272, Series: *Klassiker des Protestantismus* VII] (Bremen 1963); the intention of this series explains the selection of personalities and textual excerpts, among them J. G. Hamann, J. K. Lavater, and M. Claudius, whereas J. Locke, D. Hume, and Voltaire, among others, are missing; id., *Das Werden der Aufklärung;* P. Althaus, *Die christliche Wahrheit. Lehrbuch der Dogmatik,* 2 vols. (Gütersloh 1947–48), a Protestant work on dogma which takes into account especially the historical problems between the natural sciences and theology; M. Scheele, *Wissen und Glauben in der Geschichtswissenschaft. Studien zum historischen Pyrrhonismus in Frankreich und Dtl.* (Heidelberg 1930); R. S. Westfall, *Science and Religion in 17th Century England* [=Yale Historical Publications, Miscellany 67] (New Haven 1958).

Church Life under the Influence of the Established Church and the Enlightenment

20. *Jansenism in Eighteenth-Century France*

BIBLIOGRAPHIES

L. Willaert, *Bibliotheca janseniana belgica,* 3 vols. (Namur and Paris 1949–51); J. Carreyre, "Les luttes du jansénisme," *RHEF* 10 (1924), 441–60; J. Dedieu, "L'agonie du jansénisme, essai de bio-bibliographie," *RHEF* 14 (1928), 161–214; V. Carrière, *Introduction aux études d'histoire ecclésiastique locale* III (Paris 1936).

SOURCES

J. Louail and J. B. Cadry, *Histoire du livre des Réflexions morales sur le Nouveau Testament et de la Constitution Unigenitus,* 4 vols. (Amsterdam 1726–34); P. F. Lafitau, *Histoire de la Constitution Unigenitus,* 2 vols. (Avignon 1737); A. Dorsanne, *Journal de M. l'abbé Dorsanne,* 2 vols. (Rome 1753); Dom V. Thuillier, *Histoire de la Constitution Unigenitus,* Bibl. Nat. Mss. F. Fr. 1731–37, partial edition of A. Ingold, *Rome et la France, la deuxième phase du jansénisme* (Paris 1901); F. Bourgoin de Villefore, *Anecdotes ou mémoires secrets sur la Constitution Unigenitus,* 3 vols. (n.p., 1730); Louis de Saint-Simon, *Mémoires,* ed. by A. de Boislisle, 41 vols. (Paris 1879–1927); Dangeau, *Journal,* ed. by Soulié-Dussieux, with a supplement by Saint-Simon, 19 vols. (Paris 1860); H. F. Daguessseau, *Œuvres,* 13 vols. (Paris 1780–89); Louis Le Gendre, *Mémoires,* ed. by M. Roux (Paris 1865); J. Buvat, *Journal de la Régence,* ed. by E. Campardon, 2 vols. (Paris 1865); N. Lenglet du Fresnoy, *Mémoires de la Régence,* 5 vols. (Amsterdam 1749); R. L. Voyer d'Argenson, *Mémoires,* ed. by Rathery, 9 vols. (Paris 1859–67); E. Barbier, *Journal du règne de Louis XV,* ed. by De la Villegille, 4 vols. (Paris 1847–49); M. Marais, *Journal et mémoires,* ed. by Lescure, 4 vols. (Paris 1863); N. de Lamoignon de Basville, *Journal historique,* ed. by H. Courteault (Paris 1910); F. de Fénelon, *Œuvres,* 10 vols. (Paris 1851–52); H. Robillard d'Avrigny, *Mémoires chronologiques et dogmatiques* (*1600–1716*), 2 vols. (Nîmes 1781); M. J. Picot, *Mémoires pour servir a l'histoire ecclésiastique pendant le XVIIIe siècle,* 7 vols. (Paris 1855–57); J. Tans, *Pasquier Quesnel et les Pays-Bas* (Quesnel's correspondence) (Groningen and Paris 1960); Mme A. Le Roy, *Un janséniste en exil, correspondance de Pasquier Quesnel,* 2 vols. (Paris 1900); R. Cerveau, *Nécrologe des plus célèbres défenseurs et confesseurs de la vérité,* 7 vols. (n.p., 1760–78); J. Soanen, *Lettres,* 7 vols. (Cologne 1750); J. B. Gautier, *La vie de Messire Jean Soanen* (Cologne 1750); C. J. Colbert de Croissy, *Œuvres,* 3 vols. (Cologne 1740); G. N. Nivelle, *Le cri de la foi* (actes d'appel), 3 vols. (n.p., 1719); id., *La Constitution Unigenitus déférée a l'Église universelle ou recueil des actes d'appel,* 3 vols. (Cologne 1757); Dettey, *Vie de M. de Caylus,* 2 vols. (Amsterdam 1765); C. G. de Caylus, *Œuvres,* 4 vols. (Cologne 1751); R. de Fourquevaux, *Catéchisme historique et dogmatique,* 5 vols. (Nancy 1750–58); *Nouvelles* *ecclésiastiques ou mémoires pour servir à l'histoire de la Constitution Unigenitus (1728–1803).*

LITERATURE

E. Préclin, *Les jansénistes du XVIIIe siècle et la Constitution civile du clergé* (Paris 1929); J. Carreyre, *Le jansénisme durant la Régence,* 3 vols. (Louvain 1929–33); J. F. Thomas, *La querelle de l'Unigenitus* (Paris 1950); E. Préclin and E. Jarry, "Les luttes politiques et doctrinales aux XVIIe et XVIIIe siècles," *Fliche-Martin* XIX/2 (Paris 1955); A. Gazier, *Histoire générale du mouvement janséniste,* 2 vols. (Paris 1924); I. Bourlon, *Les Assemblées du Clergé et le jansénisme* (Paris 1909); L. Cognet, *Le jansénisme* (Paris 1961); J. Orcibal, "Fénelon et la Cour romaine (1700–1715)," *MAH* 57 (1940), 235–348; A. Le Roy, *Le gallicanisme au XVIIIe siècle, la France et Rome de 1700 à 1715* (Paris 1892); Dom H. Leclercq, *Histoire de la Régence pendant la minorité de Louis XV,* 3 vols. (Paris 1921); L. Cahen, *Les querelles religieuses et parlementaires sous Louis XV* (Paris 1913); G. Hardy, *Le cardinal de Fleury et le mouvement janséniste* (Paris 1925); E. Bourgeois, *Le secret du Régent et la politique de Dubois* (Paris 1909); id., *Le secret de Dubois cardinal et premier ministre* (Paris 1912); E. Appolis, "La collaboration de Soanen aux Nouvelles ecclésiastiques," *RHEF* 30 (1944); H. Blanc, *Le merveilleux dans le jansénisme* (Paris 1865). For an extensive survey of recent works on Jansenism see W. H. Williams, "Jansenism Revisited," *CHR* LXII, no. 4 (1977), 573–82 and B. Van Kley, *The Jansenists and the Expulsion of the Jesuits from France, 1757-1-65* (New Haven 1975).

21. *Spirituality and Its Development in Eighteenth-Century France*

LITERATURE

GENERAL: P. Pourrat, *La spiritualité chrétienne,* 4 vols. (Paris 1926–28); L. Cognet, *De la Dévotion moderne à la spiritualité français* (Paris 1958); J. Le Brun, "Le Grand Siècle de la spiritualité française et ses lendemains," *Histoire spirituelle de la France* (Paris 1964), 227–86; G. Le Bras, *Introduction à l'histoire de la pratique religieuse en France,* 2 vols. (Paris 1942–45); J. de Guibert, *La spiritualité de la Compagnie de Jésus, esquisse historique* (Rome 1953); H. du Manoir et al., *Maria,* 6 vols. (Paris 1949–61); A. Hamon, *Histoire de la dévotion au Sacré-Cœur,* 5 vols. (Paris 1923–40); *Cor Jesu* (selected anthology), 2 vols. (Rome 1959).

22. *Anglican Spirituality in the Eighteenth Century*

LITERATURE

GENERAL: L. Bouyer, *La spiritualité orthodoxe et la spiritualité protestante et anglicane* (Paris 1965; E.T.: *History of Christian Spirituality* III, *Orthodox Spirituality and Protestant and Anglican Spirituality* [New York 1969]); R. W. Church, *Masters of English Theology* (London 1877); E. J. Watkin, *Poets and Mystics* (London 1953); G. D. Henderson, *Mystics of the North-East* (Aberdeen 1934); R. Knox, *Enthusiasm* (London 1951); C. W. Towlson, *Moravian and Methodist, Relationship and Influence in the Eighteenth Century* (London 1957); U. Lee, *The Historical Backgrounds of the Early Methodist Enthusiasm* (New York 1931); R. Green, *Antimethodist Publications* (London

1902); W. R. Inge, *Studies of the English Mystics* (London 1906); A. de la Gorce, *Wesley maître d'un peuple* (Paris 1940); M. Schmidt, *John Wesley* (Zurich and Frankfurt 1953).

23. Episcopalism in the Church of the Empire from the Middle of the Seventeenth Century to the End of the Eighteenth

LITERATURE

A. v. Roskovány, *Romanus Pontifex tamquam Primas ecclesiae et princeps civilis,* 16 vols. (Neutra and Komorn 1867ff.); A. Werminghoff, *Nationalkirchliche Bestrebungen im deutschen Mittelalter* (Stuttgart 1910); B. Gebhardt, *Die Gravamina der deutschen Nation gegen den römischen Hof* (Breslau 1895); K. Hofmann, "Die kirchenrechtliche Bedeutung des Konzils von Trient," G. Schreiber, ed. *Das Weltkonzil von Trient* I, 281–96; L. Mergentheim, "Die Wurzeln des deutschen Febronianismus," *HPBl* 139 (1907), 180–92; id., *Die Quinquennalfakultäten pro foro externo. Ihre Entstehung und Einführung in den deutschen Bistümern* [=*KRA* 52–55] (Stuttgart 1908); F. Vigener, "Gallikanismus und episkopalistische Strömungen im deutschen Katholizismus zwischen Tridentinum und Vatikanum," *HZ* 111 (1913), 495–581; id., *Bischofsamt und Papstgewalt. Zur Diskussion um Universalepiskopat und Unfehlbarkeit des Papstes im deutschen Katholizismus zwischen Tridentinum und Vatikanum* (Göttingen 1964); H. Jedin, "Die Reichskirche der Schönbornzeit," *TThZ* 65 (1956), 202–16; H. Hantsch, *Reichsvizekanzler Friedrich Karl von Schönborn (1674–1746). Einige Kapitel zur politischen Geschichte Kaiser Josefs I. und Karls VI.* (Augsburg 1929); A. Rösch, "Das Kirchenrecht im Zeitalter der Aufklärung," *AkathKR* 83 (1903), 446–82, 620–52; 84 (1904), 56–82, 244–62, 465–526; 85 (1905), 29–63; P. Muschard, "Das Kirchenrecht bei den deutschen Benediktinern und Zisterziensern des 18. Jh.," *SM,* NF 16 (47) (1929), 255–315, 477–596; id., "Die kanonistischen Schulen des deutschen Katholizismus im 18. Jh. außerhalb des Benediktinerordens," *ThQ* 112 (1931), 350–400; P. Kopfermann, *Das Wormser Konkordat im deutschen Staatsrecht* (diss., Berlin 1908); H. F. Hürten, "Die Mainzer Akzeptation" (unpubl. diss., Münster 1955); id., "Die Mainzer Akzeptation," *AMrhKG* 11 (1959), 42–75; H. Raab, "Johann Kaspar Barthels Stellung in der Diskussion um die Concordata Nationis Germanicae. Ein Beitrag zur Würzburger Kanonistik im 18. Jh." *Herbiopolis jubilans* (1952), 599–616; id., *Die Concordata Nationis Germanicae in der kanonistischen Diskussion des 17. bis 19. Jh. Ein Beitrag zur Geschichte der episkopalistischen Theorie in Deutschland* (Wiesbaden 1956); J. Hemmerle, "Wessobrunn und seine geistige Stellung im 18. Jh.," *SM* 64 (1952), 13–71; E. Plassmann, *Staatskirchenrechtliche Grundgedanken der deutschen Kanonisten an der Wende vom 18. zum 19. Jh.* (Freiburg 1968); H. Raab, "Kirche und Staat im Urteil deutscher Kanonisten 1780–1830," *ZSKG* 63 (1969), 188–202.

HONTHEIM—FEBRONIUS—FEBRONIANISM

SOURCES: J. N. v. Hontheim and J. W. v. Hontheim, *Dissertatio juridica inauguralis de jurisprudentia naturali et summo imperio* (Trier 1724); J. N. v. Hontheim, *Historia Trevirensis diplomatica et pragmatica . . . ,* 3 vols. (Augsburg and Würzburg 1750); id., *Prodromus historiae Trevirensis diplomaticae et pragmaticae . . . ,* 2 vols. (Augsburg 1757); id., *De statu Ecclesiae et legitima potestate Romani Pontificis liber singularis, ad reuniendos dissidentes in religione christianos compositus* (Boullion [Frankfurt] 1763); id., *Editio altera; priore emendatior, et multo auctior* 5 in 4 vols. (Frankfurt and Leipzig 1765–74); *Justini Febronii Buch von dem Zustand der Kirche und der rechtmässigen*

Gewalt des Römischen Papstes, die in der Religion widriggesinnten Christen zu vereinigen (Wardingen 1764); J. N. v. Hontheim, *Justinus Febronius abbreviatus et emendatus id est, de statu Ecclesiae Tractatus ex Sacra Scriptura, traditione, et melioris novae Catholicis scriptoribus adornatus ab auctore in compendium redactus* (Cologne and Frankfurt 1777); id., *Justini Febronii Commentarius in suam retractationem Pio VI. Pont. Max. Kalendis Novemb. An. 1778 submissam* (Frankfurt 1781); L. Just, "Justini Febronii epistola ad T. Mamachium," *QFIAB* 22 (1930/31), 256–88; (N. Vogt), *Briefwechsel zwischen weiland Ihrer Durchlaucht, dem Herren Kurfürsten von Trier, Clemens Wenzeslaus und dem Herrn Weihbischof Niklas von Hontheim über das Buch Justini Febronii de statu Ecclesiae et legitima Romani Pontificis potestate* (Frankfurt am Main 1813); *Einiges über Justinus Febronius und seine Meinungen* (Frankfurt and Leipzig 1779); L. Just, *Der Widerruf des Febronius in der Korrespondenz des Abbé Franz Heinrich Beck mit dem Wiener Nuntius Giuseppe Garampi* (Wiesbaden 1960).

LITERATURE: The articles on Febronianism and Hontheim in *DThC* V, 2 (Paris 1939), 2115–24; *StL* III (1959), 233–35; *LThK* V (1960) 479–80; *Evangelisches Staatslexikon*, 499–500; Feine, *RG* (1964); W. Wyttenbach-Baur, "Febronius," J. S. Ersch and J. G. Gruber, *Allgemeine Enzyklopädie der Wissenschaften und Künste*, 2d Section (Volume H–N), Part 10 (Leipzig 1833), 382–90; C. W. F. Walch, *Neueste Religions Geschichte* I (Lemgo 1771), 145–98; VI, 175; VII, 193ff., 453ff.; VII, 529ff.; G. Leclerc, *Zeger Bernard van Espen (1648–1728) et l'authorité ecclésiastique. Contribution à l'histoire des théories gallicanes et du jansénisme* (Zurich 1964); O. Mejer, *Febronius. Weihbischof Johann Nicolaus von Hontheim und sein Widerruf* (Tübingen 1885); L. Just, *Das Erzbistum Trier und die luxemburgische Kirchenpolitik von Philipp II. bis Joseph II.* (Leipzig 1931); id., "Zur Entstehungsgeschichte des Febronius," *Jb. für das Bistum Mainz* 5 (1950), 369–82; id., "Hontheim. Ein Gedenkblatt zum 250. Geburtstag," *AMrhKG* 4 (1952), 204–16; F. Kenninck, *Les idées religieuses en Autriche de 1767 à 1787. Correspondance du Dr. Wittola avec le Comte Dupac de Bellegarde = Revue internationale de Théologie* 6 (Berne 1898); H. Keussen, "Weihbischof Hontheim und die Universität Köln," *Trierer Zschr.* 5 (1930); J. Kuntziger, *Fébronius et le Febronianisme = Mémoires de l'Académie royale des sciences, des lettres et des beaux-arts de Bruxelles* 44 (Brussels 1891); L. Rechenmacher, *Der Episkopalismus des 18. Jh. in Deutschland und seine Lehren über das Verhältnis von Kirche und Staat* (Würzburg 1908); F. Stümper, *Die kirchenrechtlichen Ideen des Febronius* (Aschaffenburg 1908); H. Petersen, "Febronianismus und Nationalkirche" (unpubl. diss., Strasbourg 1942); E. Reifart, "Der Kirchenstaat Trier und das Staatskirchentum. Ein Beitrag zur Geschichte der Säkularisation" (unpubl. diss., Freiburg 1950); H. Raab, "Damian Friedrich Dumeiz und Kardinal Oddi. Zur Endtdeckung des Febronius und zur Aufklärung im Erzstift Mainz und in der Reichsstadt Frankfurt," *AMrhKG* 10 (1958), 217–40; id., "Neller und Febronius," *AMrhKG* 11 (1959), 185–206; id., *Clemens Wenzeslaus von Sachsen und seine Zeit (1739–1812)* I: *Dynastie, Kirche und Reich im 18. Jh.* (Freiburg 1962) (Vol. II, which is more extensively about Hontheim, will be published soon); id., "Der Augsburger Domdekan und Kurtrierische Konferenzminister Franz Eustach von Hohenstein. Ein Beitrag zum Problem der 'katholischen Aufklärung' und zum Kampf um Febronius," *HJ* 83 (1964), 113–34; P. Fuchs, "Der Pfalzbesuch des Kölner Nuntius Bellisomi und die Affäre Seelmann in der Korrespondenz des Kurpfälzischen Gesandten in Rom, Tommaso Marchese Antici," *AMrhKG* 20 (1968), 167–226; V. Conzemius, "Le testament de Mgr. de Hontheim," *T'Hémecht* 11 (1958) 4, 85–99; F. R. Reichert, "Johann Gertz (1744–1824). Ein katholischer Bibelwissenschaftler der Aufklärungszeit im Spiegel seiner Bibliothek," *AMrhKG* 18 (1966), 41–104.

EFFECTS OF FEBRONIANISM: G. Pfeilschifter, *Korrespondenz des Fürstabtes Martin II. Gerbert von St. Blasien,* 2 vols. (Karlsruhe 1931–43); W. Müller, *Briefe u. Akten des Fürstabtes Martin II. Gerbert von St. Blasien,* 2 vols. (Karlsruhe 1957–62); A. Cloer, "Fürstabt Martin Gerbert und der Streit um die Verfassung der römisch-katholischen Kirche in der zweiten Hälfte des 18. Jh." (unpubl. diss., Münster 1949); H. Raab, "Der Mainzer Weihbischof Ludwig Philipp Behlen (1714–77)," *Mainzer Almanach* (1968), 59–79; id., "Valentin Heimes' Informativprozesse anläßlich seiner Ernennung zum Weihbischof von Worms (1780) und Mainz (1782)," *Jb. für das Bistum Mainz* 7 (1957); A. Bach, "Der Mainzer Weihbischof Valentin Heimes und die 'Weinpredigt' in Goethes 'St. Rochusfest zu Bingen,'" *RhVjBl* 27 (1962), 97–116; A. P. Brück, "Stephan Alexander Würdtwein, eine Lebensskizze," AMrhKG 2 (1950), 193–216; H. Sturmberger, "Studien zur Gesch. der Aufklärung in Kremsmünster," *MIÖG* 53 (1939), 423–80; B. Laube, *Joseph Anton Balthasar* (Basel 1956); J. Friedrich, "Beiträge zur Kirchengeschichte des 18. Jh. Aus dem handschriftlichen Nachlaß des regul. Chorherrn Eusebius Amort" =*AAM* 13, II (Munich 1876), 1–142; M. Braubach, *Die erste Bonner Hochschule* (Bonn 1965); H. Becker, "Der nassauische Kirchen- und Oberschulrat Dr. Johannes Ludwig Koch (1772 bis 1853). Ein Exponent der episkopalistisch-staatskirchlichen und antizölibatären Bewegung," *AMrhKG* 15 (1963), 147–79; A. Müller, *Febronius der Neue oder Grundlagen für die Reformangelegenheiten der deutschen Kirchenverfassung im Geiste der Baseler Beschlüssse, der Fürstenkonkordate, der Emser Punktationen und der Frankfurter Grundzüge* (Karlsruhe 1838); C. Radlspeck, *Die nationalkirchliche Idee I. H. v. Wessenbergs im Urteil der Flugschriftenliteratur 1803–21. Ein Beitrag zur Geistesgeschichte und Restauration* (diss., Kallmünz 1930); H. Raab, "Aus dem Briefwechsel des Aschaffenburger Weihbischofs Joseph Hieronymus Karl von Kolborn mit dem Generalvikar von Konstanz Ignaz Heinrich von Wessenberg," *Aschaffenburger Jb.* 2 (1955), 98–133.

THE COBLENZ GRAVAMINA (1769)

SOURCES: M. Höhler, ed., *Des kurtrierischen Geistlichen Rats Heinrich Aloys Arnoldi Tagebuch über die zu Ems gehaltene Zusammenkunft der vier Erzbischöflichen deutschen Herrn Deputierten, die Beschwerde der deutschen Nation gegen den Römischen stuhl und sonstige Gerechtsame betreffend 1786* (Mainz 1915); B. Pacca, *Memorie storiche sul soggiorno del Cardinale Pacca in Germania 1785–94* (Rome 1832); G. Eilers, "Der Kardinal B. Pacca und der Nuntiaturstreit," *Deutsche Bl. für Protestanten u. Katholiken* 5 (Heidelberg 1840); "Mittheilungen aus dem Erzbischöflich-Trier'schen Geheimen Kabinetts-Archiv zur Charakteristik teutscher geistlicher Fürsten zum päpstlichen Stuhl," *Deutsche Bl. für Protestanten u. Katholiken* 6 (Heidelberg 1840), 69–107.

LITERATURE: H. Nottarp, "Der Koblenzer Kongreß von 1769 und Arnoldis Tagebuch vom Emser Kongrß," *ThGl* 7 (1915), 812–21; I. P. Dengel, *Die politische und kirchliche Tätigkeit des Monsignore Josef Garampi in Deutschland (1761–63)* (Rome 1905); L. Just, "Die westdeutschen Höfe um die Mitte des 18. Jh. im Blick der Kölner Nuntiatur," *AHVNrh* 134 (1939), 50–91; A. Schnütgen, "Ein Kölner Nuntius der Aufklärungszeit und die rheinischen Kurfürsten und Bischöfe. Nach vatikanischen Nuntiaturakten von 1770," *Ehrengabe der deutschen Wissenschaft,* ed. by F. Feßler (Freiburg i. Brsg. 1920), 743–66; id., "Aus der Kölner Nuntiatur um den Regierungsantritt von Clemens Wenzeslaus in Trier," *AHVNrh* 142/143 (1943), 207–41; C. Löffler, "Das Fraterhaus Weidenbach in Köln," *AHVNrh* 102 (1918), 125ff.; E. Hegel, "Febronianismus und Aufklärung im Erzbistum Köln," *AHVNrh* 142/143 (1943), 146–206; H. Raab, *Die Concordata Nationis Germanicae* (Wiesbaden 1956); id., "Die Finalrelation des Kölner Nuntius Giovanni Battista Caprara," *RQ* 50 (1955), 207–29; id., "Die Finalrelation des

Kölner Nuntius Carlo Bellisomi 1785–86," *RQ* 51 (1956), 70–124; H.-W. Jung, *Anselm Franz von Bentzel im Dienste der Kurfürsten von Mainz* (Wiesbaden 1966); K. J. Krüger, *Karl Friedrich Willibald von Groschlag (1729–99). Ein Beitrag zur Kurmainzer Politik und zur Aufklärung im Rhein- Main-Gebiet* (diss., Munich 1967); A. Stelzmann, "Franz Carl J. von Hillesheim. Ein Beitrag zur rheinischen Geistesgeschichte des 18. Jh.," *AHVNrh* 149/150 (1950/51), 181–232; A. Schulte, "Ein englischer Gesandter am Rhein. Georg Cressener als Bevollmächtigter Gesandter an den Höfen der geistlichen Kurfürsten und beim Niederrheinisch-Westfälischen Kreis (1763–1781)" (unpubl. diss., Bonn 1954); K. O. v. Aretin, *Heiliges Römisches Reich 1776–1806. Reichsverfassung und Souveränität*, Part I (Wiesbaden 1967); id., "Die Konfessionen als politische Kräfte am Ausgang des alten Reiches," *Festschrift Lortz* II, 181–84; A. Hanschmidt, *Franz von Fürstenberg als Staatsmann. Die Politik des münsterschen Ministers 1762–80* (Münster 1969).

SALZBURG CONGRESS: G. Pfeilschifter-Baumeister, *Der Salzburger Kongreß und seine Auswirkung 1770–77. Der Kampf des bayr. Episkopats gegen die staatskirchenrechtliche Aufklärung unter Kurfürst Max III. Joseph 1745–77. Verhandlungen zu einem ersten bayr. Einheitskonkordat* (Paderborn 1929); J. W. Weber, *Die Kirchenrechtswissenschaft in Bayern im Zeitalter der Aufklärung* (diss. Würzburg 1904).

CONGRESS OF EMS: *Sanctissimi Domini nostri PII Papae Sexti Responsio ad Metropolitanos Mogunt., Trevir., Colonien. et Salisburgensem super Nuntiaturis Apostolicis* (Rome 1789) (The authors are: Cardinals Garampi and Zaccaria; the materials were furnished by, among others, the Cologne nuncio B. Pacca; the *Responsio* was edited by Cardinal Campanelli); *Brief Sr. Päpstlichen Heiligkeit Pius VI. an den Erzbischof von Köln als ein Nachtrag eben seiner Heiligkeit an die Metropoliten von Maynz, Trier, Köln und Salzburg mit der Widerlegung der Vredensischen Bemerkungen* (Düsseldorf 1790); among the contemporary literature about the congress (cf. Habenschaden, *Publizistik* [see below] and Raab, *Concordata*), we merely mention the following: F. X. Feller, *Coup d'œil oder Blick auf den Congress, der im Jahr 1786 von den vier Abgeordneten der vier Metropolitan Deutschlands zu Ems gehalten wurde*, 2 vols. (Düsseldorf 1789); K. J. Wreden, *Gesch. der Appellationen von geistlichen Gerichtshöfen zur Erläuterung des Art. XXII des Embser Kongresses* (1788); id., *Kurze Beleuchtung der Fakultäten päpstlicher Nunzien in Deutschland, Zur Erläuterung des in der Nunziatursache erlassenen kaiserlichen Hofdekrets und Art. IV des Embser Kongresses* (Cologne 1789); E. v. Münch, *Geschichte des Emser Kongresses und seiner Punktate, sowie der damit zusammenhängenden Nuntiatur-und Dispensstreitigkeiten, Reformen und Fortschritte der teutschen katholischen Kirche zu Ende des 18. Jh.* (Karlsruhe 1840) (tendentious but informative for the continuing effect of the Ems program); A. Coulin, "Der Emser Kongreß des Jahres 1786. Ein Beitrag zur Gesch. des Kirchenrechts der Aufklärungszeit," *DZKR*, 3d ser., XXV (Tübingen 1916–17), 1–79; H. Schotte, "Zur Gesch. des Emser Kongresses," *HJ* 35 (1914), 86–109, 319–48, 781–820; F. X. Münch, "Der Kölner Stadtpfarrer Peter Anth (Theodolph Joseph van den Elsken). Ein Beitrag zur Kölner Kirchengeschichte an der Wende des 18. u. 19. Jh.," *AHVNrh* 82 (1907), 92–118; 84 (1909), 181–208; H. Raab, "Briefe von Karl Joseph Wreden an Stephan Alexander Würdtwein 1785–87," *AHVNrh* 153/154 (1953), 170–200; A. Wandruszka, "Ems und Pistoia," *Festschr. Max Braubach* (Bonn 1964), 627–34.

THE CONFLICT OVER THE NUNCIATURES: H. Raab, "Nuntiaturstreit," *LThK* VII (1962), 1072–73; K. Walf, *Die Entwicklung des päpstlichen Gesandtschaftswesens in dem Zeitabschnitt zwischen Dekretalenrecht und Wiener Kongreß (1159–1815)* (Munich 1966); see also: H. Raab, "Sieben Jahrhunderte päpstlichen Gesandtschaftswesens," *HJ* 89 (1969), 409–19; L. Just, "Die Erforschung der päpstlichen Nuntiaturen. Stand und

Aufgaben, besonders in Deutschland," *QFIAB* 24 (1933), 244–77; id., "Die Quellen zur Geschichte der Kölner Nuntiatur in Archiv und Bibliothek des Vatikans," *QFIAB* 29 (1938/39), 249–96; L. E. Halkin, *Les archives des nonciatures* (Brussels and Rome 1968); A. Veit, "Die Kölner Nuntiatur und der Mainzer Hof," *HPBl* 157 (1921), 208–16; M. Stigloher, *Die Errichtung der päpstlichen Nuntiatur in München und der Emser Kongreß* (Regensburg 1867); F. Endres, "Die Errichtung der Münchener Nuntiatur und der Nuntiaturstreit bis zum Emser Kongress," *Beitr. zur bayer. KG* 14/15 (Erlangen 1908–9); K. Habenschaden, *Der Münchener Nuntiaturstreit in der Publizistik* (Munich 1933); id., "Die Kirchenpolitik Bayerns unter Kurfürst Karl Theodor und ihr Verhältnis zum Emser Kongreß," *ZSavRGkan* 28 (1939), 333–417; B. Zittel, "Die Vertretung des Heiligen Stuhles in München 1785–1934," *Der Mönch im Wappen. Aus Geschichte und Gegenwart des katholischen München* (Munich 1960), 419–94; G. Schwaiger, *Die altbayerischen Bistümer Freising, Passau und Regensburg zwischen Säkularisation und Konkordat 1803–1817* (Munich 1959); A. Wandruszka, *Leopold II., Erzherzog von Österreich, Großherzog von Toskana, König von Ungarn und Böhmen, Römischer Kaiser,* 2 vols. (Vienna and Munich 1963–65); F. W. Becker, "Die Kaiserwahl Leopolds II. 1790. Eine Untersuchung zur Gesch. des alten Reiches und der Nachwirkung des Fürstenbundes" (unpubl. diss., Bonn 1943); G. J. Jansen, *Kurfürst Erzbischof Max Franz von Köln und die episkopalistischen Bestrebungen seiner Zeit. Nuntiaturstreit und Emser Kongreß* (Essen 1933); M. Braubach, *Maria Theresias jüngster Sohn Max Franz, Letzter Kurfürst von Köln und Fürstbischof von Münster* (Vienna 1961); K. Schottenloher," Der bayerische Gesandte Kasimir Haeffelin in Malta, Rom und Neapel, 1796–1827," *ZBLG* 5 (1932), 380–415; L. Litzenburger, "Der bischöfliche Informativprozeß des Münchener Hofbibliothekars C. Haeffelin," *RQ* 50 (1955), 230–47; J. Angermeier, *Das Bistum Freising im Nuntiaturstreit* (Munich 1921); A. Hoffmann, *Beda Aschenbrenner, letzter Abt von Oberaltaich* (diss., Munich 1964); R. v. Dülmen, *Propst Franziskus Töpsl (1711–96) und das Augustinerchorherrenstift Polling* (Kallmünz 1967); J. Mack, *Die Reformen und Aufklärungsbestrebungen Erzbischof Colloredos* (diss., Munich 1912); J. Schöttel, *Kirchliche Reformen des Salzburger Erzbischofs Hieronymus von Colloredo im Zeitalter der Aufklärung* (Passau 1939); H. Schlapp, *Dionys Reichsgraf von Rost, Reichsgraf und Bischof von Chur 1777–1793. Ein Beitrag zur Geschichte des Bistums Chur im Zeitalter des Josephinismus* = 93. *Jahresbericht der Histor.-Antiquar. Gesellschaft von Graubünden* (Chur 1965).

24. The Established Church and the Enlightenment in the Temporal Territories of the Empire—Theresianism and Josephinism

LITERATURE

GENERAL: L. A. Veit, *Die Kirche im Zeitalter des Individualismus* (Freiburg 1931); Seppelt-Schwaiger V (1959); E. Préclin and E. Jarry in *Fliche-Martin* XIX/1 (1956); F. Heyer, *Die katholische Kirche:* K. D. Schmidt and E. Wolf, *Die Kirche in ihrer Geschichte;* H. E. Feine, *Kirchliche Rechtsgeschichte* (Weimar 1955) (supplementary: H. F. Schmid: *MIÖG* 63 [1955], 67–79); W. M. Plöchl, *Geschichte des Kirchenrechts* III (Vienna and Munich 1959); H. Conrad, *Deutsche Rechtsgeschichte, Neuzeit bis 1806* (Karlsruhe 1966); K. u. M. Uhlirz, *Handbuch der Geschichte Österreich-Ungarns* II; H. Hantsch, *Die Geschichte Österreichs* II (Graz and Vienna 1954); J. Wodka, *Kirche in Österreich. Wegweiser durch ihre Geschichte* (Vienna 1959); M. Spindler, *Handbuch der bayerischen Geschichte* II (Munich 1969), 1090ff.; H. Raab, *Kirche und Staat von der Mitte des 15. Jahrhunderts bis zur Gegenwart* (Munich 1966); H. Conrad, "Religionsbann, Toleranz und Parität am Ende des Alten Reiches," *RQ* 56 (1961), 167–99; R. Reinhardt, "Bemerkungen zum geschichtlichen Verhältnis von Kirche und Staat," *Theologie im Wandel. Festschrift zum 150 jährigen Bestehen der katholisch-theologischen Fakultät an der Universität Tübingen 1817–1967* (Munich and Freiburg 1967), 155–78; E. Zöllner, "Bemerkungen zum Problem der Beziehungen zwischen Aufklärung und Josephinismus," *Österrreich und Europa.* Festgabe für Hugo Hantsch (Graz Vienna and Cologne 1965), 203–19; K. Schlaich, "Der rationale Territorialismus. Die Kirche unter dem staatsrechtlichen Absolutismus um die Wende vom 17. zum 18. Jahrhundert," *ZSavRGkan* 54 (1968), 269–340; P. Muschard, "Das Kirchenrecht bei den deutschen Benediktinern und Zisterziensern des 18. Jahrhunderts," *SM* n.s. 16 (1929), 225–315, 477–596; id., "Die kanonistischen Schulen des deutschen Katholizismus im 18. Jahrhundert außerhalb des Benediktinerordens," *ThQ* 112 (1931), 350–400.

AUSTRIA UNTIL 1740: I. Höss, "Die konfessionelle Lage in Brandenburg-Preußen und Österreich im Zeitalter des Absolutismus," *GWU* 15 (1964); R. A. Kann, *Kanzel und Katheder. Studien zur österreichischen Geistesgeschichte vom Spätbarock zur Frühromantik* (Vienna, Freiburg and Basel 1962); F. Wessely, "Beitrag zur Kirchenpolitik unter Kaiser Josef I." (unpublished research paper prepared by the Österreichisches Institut für Geschichtsforschung, Vienna 1925); H. Künnel, *Staat und Kirche in den Jahren 1700–1740. Ein Beitrag zur Geschichte des Staatskirchentums in Österreich* (diss., Vienna 1951); N. Miko, "Kirche und Staat im alten Österreich," *Linzer prakt. Quartalschrift* 104 (1956), 42–60; J. Sattek, *Der niederösterreichische Klosterrat. Ein Beitrag zur Geschichte des Staatskirchentums in Österreich im 16. und 17. Jahrhundert* (diss., Vienna 1949); S. Santoli, "Wirtschaftliche Grundlagen des Josephinismus," *ÖAKR* 17 (1962), 213–33; H. Kramer, *Habsburg und Rom in den Jahren 1708–1709* (Innsbruck 1936); N. Huber, *Österreich und der Heilige Stuhl vom Ende des spanischen Erbfolgekrieges bis zum Tode Klemens' XI. (1714–1721)* (Graz, Vienna and Cologne 1967).

JOSEPHINISM; MARIA THERESA; JOSEPH II; LEOPOLD II; LATE JOSEPHINISM: A Coreth, *Pietas Austriaca. Ursprung und Entwicklung barocker Frömmigkeit in Österreich* (Vienna 1957); P. Meinhold, *Maria Theresia* (Wiesbaden, 1957); O. Wormser, *Marie-Thérèse impératrice* (Paris 1960); F. Walter, *Die Theresianische Staatsreform von 1749* (Vienna 1958); id., "Die religiöse Stellung Maria Theresias," *ThPQ* 105 (1957), 34–47; A. Wandruszka, "Maria Theresia und der oesterreichische Staatsgedanke," *MIÖG* 76 (1968), 174–88; R. Reinhardt, "Zur Kirchenreform unter Maria Theresia," *ZKG* 77 (1966); A. Wandruszka, "Die Religiosität Franz Stephans von Lothringen. Ein Beitrag zur Geschichte der 'Pietas Austriaca' und zur Vorgeschichte des Josephinismus in Österreich," *MÖSTA* 12 (1959); J. Mössner, *Sonn- und Feiertage in Österreich, Preußen und Bayern im Zeitalter der Aufklärung* (1915); H. Benedikt, "Der Josephinismus vor Joseph II," *Österreich und Europa. Festgabe für Hugo Hantsch* (Graz, Vienna and Cologne 1965), 183–201; P. Bernard, *The Origins of Josephinism. Two Studies* (Colorado Springs 1964); F. Maaß, *Der Frühjosephinismus* (Vienna 1969); id., *Der Josephinismus. Quellen zu seiner Geschichte in Österreich 1760–1850,* 5 vols. (Vienna 1951–61); F. Valjavec, *Der Josephinismus* (Munich 1945); id., "Die josephinischen Wurzeln des österreichischen Konservativismus," *Ausgewählte Aufsätze,* ed. by K. A. Fischer and M. Bernath (Munich 1963), 323–30; id., "Der Josephinismus als politische und weltanschauliche Strömung," *Ausgewählte Aufsätze,* 307–22; F. Walter, *Die Geschichte der österreichischen Zentralverwaltung,* Parts 1 and 2 (Vienna 1950–56); E. Winter, *Der Josefinismus. Die Geschichte des österreichischen Reformkatholizismus 1740–1748* (Berlin 1962) (revised version of: E. Winter, *Der Josefinismus* [1943]); id., *Romantismus, Restauration und Frühliberalismus im österreichischen Vormärz* (Vienna 1968); H. Rieser, *Der Geist des*

Josephinismus und sein Fortleben. Der Kampf der Kirche um ihre Freiheit (Vienna 1963); E. Schenner, *Der Postjosephinismus und die frühfranziskische Reaktion* (diss., Vienna 1949); G. Holzknecht, *Herkunft und Ursprung der Reformideen Kaiser Josefs* (Innsbruck 1914); H. Franz, *Studien zur kirchlichen Reform Josephs II.* (Freiburg 1908); H. v. Voltelini, "Die naturrechtlichen Lehren und die Reformen des 18. Jahrhunderts," *HZ* 105 (1910), 65–104; F. Fejtö, *Joseph II. Kaiser und Revolutionäre* (Stuttgart 1956); P. Bernard, *Joseph II* (New York 1968); E. Winter, *Josef II. Von den geistigen Quellen und letzten Beweggründen seiner Reformideen* (Vienna 1946); H. Conrad, "Recht und Verfassung des Reiches in der Zeit Maria Theresias. Aus den Erziehungsvorträgen für den Erzherzog Joseph," *HJ* 82 (1962), 163–86; id., *Recht und Verfassung des Reiches in der Zeit Maria Theresias. Die Vorträge zum Unterricht des Erzherzogs Joseph in Natur- und Völkerrecht sowie im Deutschen Staats-und Lehnrecht* (Cologne and Opladen 1964); E. Zlabinger, *Lodovico Antonio Muratori und Österreich* (Innsbruck 1970); A Novotny, *Staatskanzler Kaunitz als geistige Persönlichkeit* (Vienna 1947); F. Maaß, "Die Stellungnahme des Fürsten Kaunitz zur staatlichen Festsetzung der Altersgrenze für die Ablegung der Ordensgelübde in Österreich im Jahre 1770/71," *MIÖG* 58 (1950), 656–67; W. Högl, "Bartenstein als Erzieher Josephs II." (unpubl. diss., Vienna 1959); E. Winter, "Kaiser Joseph II. und der Kardinalprotektor der deutschen Reichskirche, F. Herzan Reichsgraf v. Harras," *Prager Festgabe für Theodor Mayer* (Freilassing and Salzburg 1953), 148–55; F. Klein-Bruckschwaiger, "Franz Anton von Martini in der Zeit des späten Naturrechts," *Festschr. f. Karl Haff*, ed. by K. Bussmann and N. Grass (Innsbruck 1950), 120–29; H. Conrad, "Joseph von Sonnenfels (1733–1817). Zum 150. Todestag eines Vorkämpfers gegen die Folter," *Juristen-Jahrbuch* 8 (1967/68) (Cologne 1968), 1–16; H. Lentze, "Joseph von Spergs und der Josephinismus," *MÖSTA* supplementary Vol. III (1951), 392–412; F. Pascher, *Joseph Freiherr von Sperges auf Palens und Reisdorf* (diss., Vienna 1965). F. Dörrer, "Der Schriftverkehr zwischen dem päpstlichen Staatssekretariat und der apostolischen Nuntiatur Wien in der zweiten Hälfte des 18. Jahrhunderts," *Römische historische Mitteilungen* 4 (1960/61), 63–246; id., "Römische Stimmen zum Frühjosephinismus," *MIÖG* 63 (1965), 460–83; A. Ellemunter, *Antonio Eugenio Visconti und die Anfänge des Josephinismus* (Graz and Cologne 1963); H. Schlitter, *Die Reise des Papstes Pius VI. nach Wien und sein Aufenthalt daselbst* (Vienna 1892); G. Soranzo, *Peregrinus Apostolicus. Lo spirito pubblico e il viaggio di Pio VI a Vienna* (Milan 1937); M. C. Goodwin, *The Papal Conflict with Josephism* (New York 1938); L. Just, "Zur kirchenpolitischen Lage in Österreich bei Regierungsantritt Franz' II.," *QFIAB* 23 (1931/32), 242–66; F. Sissulak, "Das Christentum des Josefinismus. Die josefinische Pastoraltheologie in dogmatischer Sicht," *ZKTh* 71 (1949), 54–88; E. Glas, *Studien über den Einfluß Josephs II. auf die deutschen Bischofswahlen* (diss., Vienna 1949); J. A. K. Haas, "De Roermondse bisschopbenoemingen in de eerste helft van de Oostenrijkse periode, 1717–1749," *Archief voor de geschiedenis van de katholieke kerk in Nederland* 11 (1969); G. de Schepper, *La réorganisation des paroisses et la suppression des couvents dans les Pays-Bas autrichiens sous le régne de Joseph II* (Louvain and Brussels 1942); G. Winner, *Die Klosteraufhebungen in Niederösterriech und Wien* (Vienna and Munich 1967); N. Grass, "Österreichische Kanonistenschulen aus drei Jahrhunderten," *ZSavRGkan* 85 (1955), 290–411; J. Müller, "Zu den theologiegeschichtlichen Grundlagen der Studienreform Rautenstrauchs," *ThQ* 146 (1966), 62–97; F. Wehrl, "Der 'Neue Geist.' Eine Untersuchung der Geistesrichtungen des Klerus in Wien von 1750–1790," *MÖSTA* 20 (1967), 36–114; R. Reinhardt, *Die Beziehungen von Hochstift und Diözese Konstanz zu Habsburg-Österreich in der Neuzeit. Gleichzeitig ein Beitrag zur archivalischen Erforschung des Problems "Staat und Kirche"* (Wiesbaden 1966); F. Geier, *Die Durchführung der kirchlichen Reformen Josephs II. im vorderösterreichischen Breisgau* (Stuttgart 1905); J. R.

Kušej, *Joseph II. und die äußere Kirchenverfassung Innerösterreichs* (Stuttgart 1908); F. Dörrer, *Zur sog. Pfarregulierung Josephs II. in Deutschtirol* (diss., Innsbruck 1950); id., "Der Wandel der Diözesaneinteilung Tirols und Vorarlbergs," *Tiroler Heimat. Jahrbuch für Geschichte und Volkskunde* 17 (1953), 41–74; H. Kröll, "Beiträge zur Geschichte der Aufhebung der Gesellschaft Jesu in Wien und in Niederösterreich" (unpubl. diss., Vienna 1964); A. Wandruszka, *Leopold II. Erzherzog von Österreich, Großherzog von Toskana, König von Ungarn und Böhmen, Römischer Kaiser*, 2 vols. (Vienna and Munich 1963–65); id., "Geheimprotestantismus, Josephinismus und Volksliturgie in Österreich," *Zeitschrift für Kirchengeschichte* 78 (1967), 94–101; H. Ferihumer, "Kaiser Leopold II. und der Episkopat der Erbländer. Die Rolle des Linzer Bischofs J. G. Gall," *Festschrift K. Eder* (Innsbruck 1959), 181–96; A. Ernstberger, *Zur Wiederherstellung des Jesuitenordens. Vorschläge an Kaiser Franz II. 1794, 1799, 1800* = Sb. Bayer, Akad. der Wissenschaften, Phil.-Hist. Klasse, Fasz. 7 (Munich 1962); E. Weinzierl-Fischer, *Der Toleranzbegriff in der österreichischen Kirchenpolitik. XIIᵉ Congrès international des sciences historiques. Rapports* I (Vienna 1965), 135–50; D. Appelt, *Die Idee der Toleranz unter Kaiser Josef II.* (diss., Vienna 1950); C. H. O'Brien, *Ideas of Religious Toleration at the Time of Joseph II. A Study of the Enlightenment among Catholics in Austria* (Philadelphia 1969); H. Conrad, "Staatliche Theorie und kirchliche Dogmatik im Ringen um die Ehegesetzgebung Josephs II," *Wahrheit und Verkündigung, Michael Schmaus zum 70. Geburtstag* (Paderborn 1967), 1171–90; J. Mühlsteiger, *Der Geist des josephinischen Eherechts* (Vienna 1967); B. Primetshofer, *Rechtsgeschichte der gemischten Ehen in Oesterreich und Ungarn (1781–1841). Ein Beitrag zur Geschichte der Beziehungen zwischen Kirche und Recht* (Vienna 1967); D. Schwab, *Grundlagen und Gestalt der staatlichen Ehegesetzgebung in der Neuzeit bis zum Beginn des 19. Jahrhunderts* (Bielefeld 1967); F. Maaß, "Der Wiener Nuntius Severoli und der Spätjosephinismus," *MIÖG* 63 (1955), 484–99; E. Plaßmann, *Staatskirchenrechtliche Grundgedanken der deutschen Kanonisten an der Wende vom 18. zum 19. Jahrhundert* (Freiburg 1968); H. Raab, "Kirche und Staat im Urteil deutscher Kanonisten 1780–1830," *ZSKG* 63 (1969), 188–202; K. Reitbauer, *Erzbischof Johann Josef Trautson* (diss., Graz 1955); V. Einspieler, *Johann Karl Graf von Herberstein, Bischof von Laibach. Sein Leben, Wirken und seine Stellung in der Geschichte des Josephinismus* (diss., Vienna 1951); E. Hosp, *Bischof Gregorius Thomas Ziegler. Ein Vorkämpfer gegen den Josephinismus* (Linz a. D. 1956); C. Wolfsgruber, *Christian Anton Kardinal Migazzi* (Saulgau 1890); J. Obersteiner, *Die Bischöfe von Gurk (1072–1822)* (Klagenfurt 1969); H. Ferihumer, *Die kirchliche Gliederung des Landes ob der Enns im Zeitalter Kaiser Josefs II.* (Linz 1952); J. B. Lehner, "Beiträge zur Kirchengeschichte des Egerlands," *Jahresbericht zur Erforschung der Regensburger Diözesangeschichte* 13 (1939), 79–211; G. Prichan, "Über die Beziehungen Österreichs zur katholischen Kirche in Schlesien," *Jahrbuch des Vereins für Geschichte der Deutschen in Böhmen* 1 (1926); W. Sponner, *Kirchenpolitik im Banat von 1717–1778* (diss., Vienna 1941); G. Prokoptschuk, *Die österreichische Kirchenpolitik in der Westukraine unter der Regierung Maria Theresias von 1772–1780* (diss., Munich 1942); J. Tomko, *Die Errichtung der Diözesen Zips, Neusohl und Rosenau (1776) und das königliche Patronatsrecht in Ungarn* = *Kirche und Recht* 8 (Freiburg, Vienna and Basel 1968).

BAVARIA: M. Spindler, *Handbuch der bayer. Geschichte* II (Munich 1969); M. Doeberl, "Der Ursprung der Amortisationsgesetzgebung in Bayern. Ein Beitrag zur Kulturgeschichte des 17. und 18. Jahrhunderts," *Forschungen zur Geschichte Bayerns* X (Munich 1902), 186–262; H. Rall, *Kurbayern in der letzten Epoche der alten Reichsverfassung (1745–1801)* (Munich 1951); P. Krinner, *Die Quellen des bayerischen Staatskirchenrechts in der Zeit von 1583 bis 1799* (diss., Würzburg 1907); J. Weber, *Die Kirchenrechts-wissenschaft in Bayern im Zeitalter der Aufklärung* (Würzburg 1907); K. Habenscha-den, "Die Kirchenpolitik Bayerns unter Kurfürst Karl Theodor," *ZSavRGkan* 28 (1939), 333–417; H. Lazik, *Die Entwicklung der geistlichen Gerichtsbarkeit im Kurfür-stentum Bayern* (diss., Munich 1953); G. Pfeilschifter-Baumeister, *Der Salzburger Kongreß und seine Auswirkungen 1770–1777* (Paderborn 1929); W. Fichtl, "Das bayerische Bücherzensurkollegium (1769–1797)" (unpubl. diss., Munich 1941); B. Wacher, *Beiträge zur Geschichte der bayerischen Abtswahlen mit besonderer Berücksichti-gung der Benediktinerklöster* (Munich 1930); E. Krausen, "Am Vorabend der Säkulari-sation. Die Abtwahl vom 1. Oktober 1801 im Kloster Raitenhaslach," *HJ* 80 (1961), 160–73; G. Schwaiger, *Die altbayerischen Bistümer Freising, Passau und Regensburg zwischen Säkularisation und Konkordat (1803–1817)* (Munich 1959); H. Raab, *Cle-mens Wenzeslaus von Sachsen und seine Zeit. Dynastie, Kirche und Reich im 18. Jahrhun-dert* (Freiburg 1962); E. M. Eder, "Beiträge zum Passauer Exemtionsstreit" (unpubl. diss., Vienna 1962); A. Leidl, *Kardinal Leopold Ernst von Firmian (1708–83)* (Munich 1968); E. Meissner, *Fürstbischof Anton Ignaz Fugger (1711–1787)* (Tübingen 1969); G. Schwaiger, "Pius VI. in München (1782)," *MThZ* (1959), 122–36.

LORRAINE AND OTHER TERRITORIES: P. le Sourd, *La Lorraine, le Barrois, les Trois-Évêchés dans l'histoire de la France et, demain, de l'Europe* (Paris 1966); E. Dursy, *Das Staatskirchenrecht in Elsaß-Lothringen* (Strasbourg 1876); R. Folz, *Le concordat germani-que et l'élection des évêques de Metz* (Metz 1931); L. Just. *Clemens XI. und der Code Léopold (1701–1710). Die kuriale Politik im Kampf mit dem lothringischen Staatskir-chentum zu Beginn des 18. Jahrhunderts* (Frankfurt am Main 1935); id., "Das Staatskirchentum der Herzöge von Lothringen-Bar von 1445–1633," *AMrhKG* 5 (1953), 223–66; J. Krisinger, "Die Religionspolitik des Kurfürsten Johann Wilhelm von der Pfalz," *Düsseldorfer Jahrbuch* 47 (1955); H. Tüchle, *Die Kirchenpolitik des Herzogs Karl Alexander von Württemberg (1733–1737)* (Würzburg 1937); H. Krez-dorn, "Das Kirchenpatronat über katholische Pfarreien in Hohenzollern. Geschichte und Rechtsentwicklung," *Hohenzollerische Jahreshefte* 16 (1956), 5–109; W. Thoma, *Die Kirchenpolitik der Grafen von Fürstenberg im Zeitalter der Glaubenskämpfe (1520–1660)* (Münster 1963).

25. *State and Church in Poland-Lithuania to the End of the Republic of the Aristocracy*

LITERATURE

A. Theiner, *Vetera Monumenta Poloniae et Lithuaniae gentiumque finitorum historiam illustrantia* IV (Rome 1864); K. Völker, *Kirchengeschichte Polens* (Berlin and Leipzig 1930); A Klawek, *Zarys dziejów teologii katolickiej w Polsce* (Crakow 1948); A. M. Ammann, *Abriß der ostslawischen Kirchengeschichte* (Vienna 1950); *The Cambridge History of Poland,* ed. by W. F. Reddaway, J. H. Penson, O. Halecki, and R. Dyboski, 2 vols. (Cambridge 1950–51); Z. Szostkiewicz, "Katalog biskupów obrz. łac. przedrozbioro-wej Polski," *Sacrum Poloniae Millennium* I (Rome 1954), 391–608; J. Umiński, *Historia Kościoła,* ed. by W. Urban, II (Oppeln 1960); K. Górski, *Od religijności do mistyki, zarys dziejów życia wewnętrznego w Polsce* I (Lublin 1962); G. Rhode, *Kleine Geschichte Polens* (Darmstadt 1965); J. Tazbir, *Historia kościoła katolickiego w Polsce 1460–1795* (Warsaw 1966); *History of Poland* (Warsaw 1968); B. Stasiewski, "Tausend Jahre polnischer Kirchengeschichte," *Kirche im Osten* 10 (1967), 48–67; *Le millénaire du catholicisme en Pologne* (Lublin 1969).

26. The Decline of the Church of the Empire in the Great Secularization

SOURCES

Protokoll der außerordentlichen Reichsdeputation zu Regensburg, 6 vols. (2 vols. of protocols, 4 vols. of supplements) (Regensburg 1803); A. C. Gaspari, *Der Deputations-Rezeß mit histor., geograph. und statist. Erläuterungen und einer Vergleichungstafel,* 2 vols. (Hamburg 1803); id., *Der französisch-russische Entschädigungsplan mit histor., geograph. und statist. Erläuterungen* (Hamburg 1802); T. v. Traitteur, *Der deutschen Reichsstände Verlust auf dem linken Rheinufer und der Besitzungen der katholischen Geistlichkeit auf dem rechten, nach Größe, Bevölkerung und Einkünften geschätzt* (Mannheim 1799); G. F. Martens, *Recueil des principaux traités . . . conclus par les puissances de l'Europe . . . depuis 1761 jusqu'à present,* 8 vols. (Göttingen 1817–35); C. W. v. Lancizolle, *Übersicht der deutschen Reichsstandschafts- u. Territorial-Verhältnisse vor dem frz. Religionskriege, der seitdem eingetretenen Veränderungen und der gegenwärtigen Bestandtheile des deutschen Bundes und der deutschen Bundesstaaten* (Berlin 1830); A. Mercati, *Raccolta di Concordati su materie ecclesiastiche tra la Santa Sede e le Autorità Civili* (Rome 1954); A. v. Vivenot and H. v. Zeissberg, *Quellen zur Gesch. der deutschen Kaiserpolitik Österreichs während der frz. Revolutionskriege 1789–1801,* 2 vols. (Vienna 1873–74); H. Granier, *Preußen und die kathol. Kirche seit 1640* 8 and 9 (1797–1803, 1803–7) (Leipzig 1902); J. Hansen, *Quellen zur Geschichte des Rheinlandes im Zeitalter der Frz. Revolution, 1780–1801* 1–4 (Bonn 1931–38); E. R. Huber, *Dokumente zur deutschen Verfassungsgeschichte* I (Stuttgart 1961); K. O. v. Aretin, *Heiliges Römisches Reich 1776 bis 1806* II (selection of official documents) (Wiesbaden 1967); R. Freiin v. Oer, *Die Säkularisation 1803* (Göttingen 1970); U. Engelmann, ed., *Das Tagebuch von Ignaz Speckle, Abt von St. Peter im Schwarzwald,* 2 vols. (Stuttgart 1966); A Kraus, ed., *Die Briefe Roman Zirngibls von St. Emmeram in Regensburg* (Regensburg 1965).

LITERATURE

ON THE HISTORY OF SECULARIZATION TO THE END OF THE EIGHTEENTH CENTURY: Pastor XIV–XVI, 3; P. Volk, "Die kirchlichen Fragen auf dem Westfälischen Frieden," *Pax optima rerum,* ed. by E. Hövel (Münster 1948), 99–138; P. Hiltebrandt, *Die kirchlichen Reunionsverhandlungen in der zweiten Hälfte des 17. Jh.* (Rome 1922); A. M. Trivellini, *Il cardinale Francesco Buonvisi, nunzio a Vienna (1675–89)* (Florence 1958); F. Díaz, *Francesco Buonvisi. Nunziatura a Colonia (1670–72),* 2 vols. (Rome 1959); T. Vollbehr, "Der Ursprung der Säkularisationsprojekte in den Jahren 1742/43," *FDG* 26 (1886); W. v. Hofmann, "Das Säkularisationsprojekt von 1743, Kaiser Karl VII. und die röm. Kurie," *Festschr. S. Riezler* (1913); L. Just, "Die römische Kurie und das Reich unter Kaiser Karl VII.," *HJ* 52 (1932); I. P. Dengel, *Die politische und kirchliche Tätigkeit des Monsignor Josef Garampi in Deutschland, 1761–63* (Rome 1905); Maaß; A. Ellemunter, *Antonio Eugenio Visconti und die Anfänge des Josephinismus* (Graz and Cologne 1963); L. P. Behlen, *Diss. de causis secularisationum illegitimis et legitimis* (Mainz 1746); P. v. Osterwald, *Veremund von Lochsteins Gründe sowohl für als wider die geistliche Immunität in zeitlichen Dingen* (Strasbourg 1766); A. Desing, *Staatsfrage: Sind die Güter und Einkünfte der Geistlichkeit dem Staate schädlich oder nicht?* 2 parts (Munich 1768); A Molitor, *Theologische Abhandlung von der Macht der Kirche über die Kirchengüter* (Freysing 1768); B. Wöhrmüller, "Literarische Sturmzeichen von der Säkularisation," *SM* n.s. 14 (1927); H. Raab, *Clemens Wenzeslaus von Sachsen und seine Zeit* I: *Dynastie, Kirche und Reich im 18. Jh.* (Freiburg 1962); G. Winner, *Die Klosteraufhebungen in Niederösterreich und Wien* (Vienna and Munich 1967); H. v. Voltelini, "Ein Antrag des Bischofs von Trient auf

Säkularisierung und Einverleibung seines Fürstentums in die Grafschaft Tirol vom Jahre 1781/82," *Veröff. des Museum Ferdinandeum* 16, Jg. 1936 (1938); P. Wende, *Die geistlichen Staaten und ihre Auflösung im Urteil der zeitgenöss. Publizistik* (Lübeck and Hamburg 1966).

THE FRENCH REVOLUTION AND ITS EFFECT ON THE CHURCH OF THE EMPIRE

A) PREREVOLUTIONARY UNREST; THE EXECUTION AGAINST LIÈGE: P. Harsin, *La révolution liègeoise de 1789* (Brussels 1954); J. Kühn, *Wie Lüttich dem Reich verlorenging. Rückblick auf die Reichsexekution 1790/91* (1914); E. Schulte, *Der Krieg Münsters gegen Lüttich, 1789–92 = Quellen und Forschungen zur Gesch. der Stadt Münster* 3 (1927); P. Strothotte, *Die Exekution gegen Lüttich 1789–92. Ein Beitrag zur Gesch. des Heiligen Römischen Reiches deutscher Nation* (Bonn 1936); H. Stradal, "Die brabantische Revolution des Jahres 1789 aus Wiener Sicht," *Anciens Pays et Assemblées d'États* 47 (1968), 273–317; A Sprunck, "Die Lage in den österreichischen Niederlanden 1790 nach den Berichten der Statthalterin Marie Christine an die Wiener Regierung," *Mitteilungen des österreichischen Staatsarchivs* 11 (1958); K. Julku, *Die revolutionäre Bewegung im Rheinland am Ende des 18. Jh.* (Helsinki 1965); L. Vautrey, *Histoire des évêques de Bâle* II (Einsiedeln 1886); J. Rebetez, *Les relations de l'Évêché de Bâle avec la France au XVIIIᵉ siècle* (St-Maurice 1943); M. Braubach, "Bischof Gobel, Kurfürst Max Franz von Köln und das Bistum Basel," *HJ* 60 (1940), 300–311; R. Bohlender, *Dom und Bistum Speyer. Eine Bibliographie* (Speyer 1962); L. Litzenburger, "Stadt und Bistum Speyer im frz. Revolutionsradius im Jahre 1794," *RQ* 52 (1957), 240–49; L. Vezin, *Die Politik des Mainzer Kurfürsten Friedrich Karl v. Erthal 1789–92* (Bonn 1932); F. G. Dreyfus, *Sociétés et mentalités à Mayence dans la seconde moitié du 18ᵉ siècle* (Paris 1968); H. Telöken, *Kurtrierische Politik zur Zeit der Französischen Revolution* (unpubl. diss., Bonn 1951); E. Zenz, "Die kirchenpolitischen Beziehungen zwischen dem Erzstift Trier und Frankreich nach Ausbruch der Französischen Revolution," *AMrhKG* 4 (1952); W. Lüdtke, "Kurtrier und die revolutionären Unruhen in den Jahren 1789–1790," *Trierer Zsch.* 5 (1930); M. Braubach, "Die kath. Universitäten Deutschlands und die Frz. Revolution," *HJ* 49 (1929); id., *Maria Theresias jüngster Sohn Max Franz. Letzter Kurfürst von Köln und Fürstbischof von Münster* (Vienna and Munich 1961); H. Flurschütz, *Die Verwaltung des Hochstifts Würzburg unter Franz Ludwig v. Erthal (1779–95)* (Würzburg 1965).

B) THE REVOLUTION AND ITS EFFECT: K. T. Heigel, *Deutsche Gesch. vom Tode Friedrichs d. Gr. bis zur Auflösung des alten Reiches,* 2 vols. (Stuttgart 2nd Berlin 1911); B. Gebhardt, *Handbuch der deutschen Geschichte* III: *Von der Französischen Revolution bis zum Ersten Weltkrieg,* ed. by H. Grundmann (Stuttgart 1969); K. v. Raumer, *Deutschland um 1800 = Hdb. der deutschen Gesch.,* ed. by L. Just (n.d.); F. Schnabel, *Deutsche Geschichte im 19. Jahrhundert,* 4 vols. (Freiburg i. Brsg. 1949–59); E. R. Huber, *Deutsche Verfassungsgeschichte* I (Berlin, Cologne and Mainz 1957); Seppelt-Schwaiger V; A. Latreille, *L'église catholique et la Révolution Française,* 2 vols. (Paris 1946–50); J. Droz, *L'Allemagne et la Révolution française* (Paris 1949); K. D. Erdmann, *Volkssouveränität und Kirche 1789–91. Studien über das Verhältnis von Staat und Kirche in Frankreich vom Zusammentritt der Generalstände bis zum Schisma* (Cologne 1949); S. S. Biro, *The Germany Policy of Revolutionary France,* 2 vols. (Cambridge, Mass. 1957); A. Ernstberger, *Österreich und Preußen von Basel bis Campoformio 1795–97* (Reichenberg 1932); A. Wandruszka, *Leopold II. Erzherzog von Österreich, Großherzog von Toskana, König von Ungarn und Böhmen, Römischer Kaiser,* 2 vols. (1963–65).

Emigration: W. Wühr, *Die Emigranten der Frz. Revolution im bayerischen und fränkischen Kreis* (Munich 1938); id., "Emigranten der Frz. Revolution im Kurfürstentum Mainz," *Aschaffenburger Jb.* 2 (1955); id., "Emigranten der Frz. Revolution im Erzstift Salzburg," *Mitt. der Gesellschaft für Salzburgische Landeskunde* 79 (1939), 33–64; A. Gain, *Liste des émigrés, deportés, condamnés pour cause révolutionnaire du départment de la Moselle,* 2 vols. (1925–29); M. Barth, "Seminaristen und Benediktiner des Elsaß als Flüchtlinge im Kloster Ettenheimmünster während der Frz. Revolution," *Freib. Diöz. Arch.* 71 (1951); J. Vidalenc, *Les émigrés français 1789–1825* (Caen 1963); P. de Vaissière, *A Coblence ou les Émigrés français dans les pays Rhénans de 1789 à 1792* (Paris 1924); F. Baldensperger, *Le mouvement des idées dans l'émigration française,* 2 vols. (Paris 1924); M. Pawlik, "Emigranten der frz. Revolution in Österreich (1789–1814)," *MIÖG* 77 (1969), 78–127.

The Regions on the Left Bank of the Rhine: A. Quiquerrez, *Histoire de la révolution dans l'évêché de Bâle en 1791* (Porrentruy 1881); R. Reuss, *La constitution civile du clergé et la crise religieuse en Alsace* (1790–95), 2 vols. (Strasbourg 1922–23); L. Stamer, *Kirchengeschichte der Pfalz* IV (Speyer 1964); E. Isele, *Die Säkularisation des Bistums Konstanz und die Reorganisation des Bistums Basel* (Basel and Freiburg 1932); L. A. Veit, *Der Zusammenbruch des Mainzer Erzstuhls infolge der frz. Revolution* (Mainz 1927); R. Usinger, *Das Bistum Mainz unter frz. Herrschaft* (Mainz 1912); R. Werner, *Die Nationalgüter im Department Donnersberg* (Heidelberg 1922); J. Marx, *Gesch. des Erzstifts Trier* V (Trier 1867); A Eismann, *Umschreibung der Diözese Trier und ihrer Pfarreien 1802–21* (Saarbrücken 1941); G. Groß, *Trierer Giestesleben unter dem Einfluß von Aufklärung und Romantik (1750–1850)* (Trier 1956); M. Höhler, *Gesch. des Bistums Limburg* (Limburg 1908); G. Kliesing, *Die Säkularisation in den kurköln. Ämtern Bonn. Brühl, Lechenich und Zülpich in der Zeit der frz. Fremdherrschaft* (Bonn 1933); W. Klompen, *Die Säkularisation im Arrondissement Krefeld 1794–1814* (Kempen 1962); H. Mosler, "Die Zisterzienserabtei Kamp in ihrem letzten Jahrhundert," *AHVNrh* 170 (1968), 22–119.

THE IMPERIAL DELEGATES FINAL RECESS AND THE GREAT SECULARIZATION OF 1803: I. Rinieri, *Le secolarizzazione degli stati ecclesiastici in Germania* (Rome 1906); H. Bastgen, *Dalberg und Napoleons Kirchenpolitik in Deutschland* (Paderborn 1917); id., "Die Ursachen der Säkularisation der Bistümer und Domkapitel von Trient und Brixen und ihr Verhältnis zur Grafschaft Tirol," *HJ* 34 (1913); id., *Bayern und der Heilige Stuhl in der ersten Hälfte des 19. Jh.,* 2 vols. (Munich 1940); E. Bauernfeind, *Die Säkularisationsperiode im Hochstift Eichstätt bis zum endgültigen Übergang an Bayern 1790–1806* (1927); J. A. Bornewasser, *Kirche und Staat in Fulda unter Wilhelm Friedrich von Oranien 1802–06* (Nijmegen 1956); E. Buchholtz, *Die Einwirkungen des Reichsdeputationshauptschlusses zu Regensburg im Jahre 1803 und die Bulle "Impensa Romanorum Pontificum" auf das Bistum Osnabrück* (Osnabrück 1930); E. Deuerlein, *Die reichsständische Säkularisation des Hochstifts Würzburg* (Würzburg 1958); H. H. Dunkhase, *Das Fürstentum Krautheim. Eine Staatsgründung um Jagst und Tauber 1802–1806 (1839)* (Nuremberg 1968); N. Enneking, *Das Hochstift Fulda unter seinem letzten Fürstbischof Adalbert III. von Harstall 1788–1802* (Fulda 1935); W. Engel, "Aus den letzten Tagen des Hochstifts Würzburg," *Mainfränk. Hefte* 6 (1954); M. Erzberger, *Die Säkularisation in Württemberg von 1802 bis 1810* (Stuttgart 1902); E. Fleig, "K. T. v. Dalberg und die Säkularisation des Fürstbistums Konstanz," *Freib. Diöz. Arch.* 29 (1928); M. Fleischhauer, *Das geistliche Fürstentum Konstanz beim Übergang an Baden* (Heidelberg 1934); D. Froitzheim, *Das Staatskirchenrecht im ehemaligen Großherzogtum Berg* (Amsterdam 1967); E. G. Gerhard, *Gesch. der Säku larisation in Frankfurt a. M.* (Paderborn 1935); L. Günther, *Der Übergang des Fürstbistums Würzburg an Bayern* (Leipzig 1910); L. Hammermayer, "Die europäischen Mächte und die Bewahrung von Abtei und Seminar der Schotten in Regensburg (1802/03)," *Verhandlungen d. Histor. Vereins f. Oberpfalz u. Regensburg* 106 (1966), 291–306; L. Hoffmann, *Die Säkularisation Salzburgs* (diss., Vienna 1943); P. Hofmeister, "Die Reorganisation des Malteserordens nach 1798," *AkathKR* 137 (1968), 463–523; R. Haderstorfer, *Die Säkularisation der oberbayerischen Klöster Baumburg und Seeon* (Stuttgart 1967); E. Isele, *Die Säkularisation des Bistums Konstanz und die Reorganisation des Bistums Basel* (Basel and Freiburg 1933); F. Köppel, "Dahlberg und die Säkularisation des Bistums Konstanz," *ZGObrh* 102 (1954); L. Körholz, *Die Säkularisation und Organisation in den preußischen Entschädigungsländern Essen, Werden und Elten 1802–06* (Münster 1907); F. Keinemann, *Das Domkapitel zu Münster im 18. Jh.* (Münster 1967); A Meier, *Abt Pankraz Vorster und die Aufhebung der Fürstabtei St. Gallen* (Fribourg 1954); R. Morsey, "Wirtschaftliche und soziale Auswirkungen der Säkularisation in Deutschland," *Festgabe für K. v. Raumer* (Münster 1968), 361–83; W. G. Neukam, "Der Übergang des Hochstifts Bamberg an die Krone Bayern 1802/03," *Bayern-Staat und Kirche, Land und Reich. Wilh. Winkler zum Gedächtnis* (Munich 1961); H. Raab, "K. T. v. Dalberg. Das Ende der Reichskirche und das Ringen um den Wiederaufbau des kirchlichen Lebens 1802—15," *AmrhKG* 18 (1966), 27–39; H. Reich, *Die Säkularisation des rechtsrheinischen Teiles des Hochstifts Speyer* (Bottrop 1935); H. Reichert, *Studien zur Säkularisation in Hessen-Darmstadt* (Mainz 1927); E. Ringelmann, *Die Säkularisation des Hochstifts und des Domkapitels Passau* (Passau 1939); E. Probst, "Würzburg—vom Hochstift zum Rheinbundstaat," *Mainfränk. Jb. für Gesch. und Kunst* 9 (1957), 70–102; J. C. Nattermann, *Das Ende des alten Kölner Domstiftes* (Cologne 1953); R. Reinhardt, *Die Beziehungen von Hochstift und Diözese Konstanz zu Habsburg-Österreich* (Wiesbaden 1966); P. Ruf, *Säkularisation und Bayerische Staatsbibliothek* (Wiesbaden 1962); H. W. Schlaich, "Das Ende der Regensburger Reichsstifte St. Emmeram, Ober- und Niedermünster," *Vhh. des Hist. Vereins für Oberpfalz* 97 (1956), 163–376; A Scharnagl, "Zur Gesch. des Reichsdeputationshauptschlusses vom Jahre 1803," *HJ* 70 (1950); A. M. Schegelmann, *Gesch. der Säkularisation im rechtsrhein. Bayern,* 3 vols. (Regensburg 1903–8); A. Schlittmeier, *Die wirtschaftl. Auswirkungen der Säkularisation in Niederbayern, untersucht am Beispiel der Abtei Niederaltaich und seiner Propsteien Rinchnach und St. Oswald* (diss. Munich 1962); G. Schwaiger, *Die altbayerischen Bistümer Freising, Passau und Regensburg zwischen Säkularisation und Konkordat* (Munich 1959); id., "Das dalbergische Fürstentum Regensburg 1803–1810," *Zeitschrift für bayr. Landesgeschichte* 23 (1960), 42–65; id., "Die Kirchenpläne des Fürstprimas K. T. von Dalberg," *Münchener Theol. Zeitschrift* 9 (1958), 186–204; id., "Das Ende der Reichskirche und seine unmittelbaren Folgen," *SM* 79 (1968), 136–48; W. Steffen, "Rheingrenze und territoriale Entschädigungsfrage in der preuß. Politik der Jahre 1795–1798," *Westfäl Forschungen* 6 (1943/52), 149–81; P. E. Stellwag, *Beiträge zur Gesch. der Abtei Münster Schwarzach a. M. um die Zeit ihrer Auflösung 1803* (diss., Würzburg 1946); G. Seith, "Die rechtsrhein. Gebiete des Bistums Basel und ihr Übergang an Baden" (unpubl. diss., Freiburg i. Brsg. 1951); W. H. Struck, "Zur Säkularisation im Lande Nassau," *Hess Jb. für Landsgesch.* 18 (1963); M. Schöne, *Das Herzogtum Westfalen unter hessen-darmstädtischer Herrschaft 1802–16* (Olpe 1966); F. Täubl, *Der Deutsche Orden im Zeitalter Napoleons* (Bonn 1966); H. Tremel, *Die säkularisierten Klosterwaldungen in Altbayern* (1924); L. A. Veit, "Die Säkularisierung in Nassau-Usingen," *ZGOwrh* 80 (1928); B. Wagner, *Die Säkularisation der Klöster im Gebiet der heutigen Stadt Passau, 1802–03* (Passau 1935); A. Wendehorst, "Der

Untergang der alten Abteikirche Münsterschwarzach 1803/04," *Mainfränk. Hefte* 17 (Würzburg 1953); B. Wenisch, "Der Kampf um den Bestand des Erzbistums Salzburg, 1743–1825," *Mitt. der Gesellschaft für Salzburgische Landeskunde* 106 (1966), 303–46; A. Schneider, *Der Gewinn des bayerischen Staates von den säkularisierten landständischen Klöstern in Altbayern* (Munich 1970).

27. Attempts at Church Reunion

LITERATURE

J. Beumer, *Auf dem Wege zur christlichen Einheit. Vorläufer der ökumenischen Bewegung von den Anfängen des Humanismus bis zum Ende des 19. Jh. Ausgewählte Texte* (Bremen 1966); C. W. Hering, *Geschichte der kirchlichen Unionsversuche seit der Reformation bis auf unsere Zeit,* 2 vols. (Leipzig 1836–38); L. Cardauns, *Zur Geschichte der kirchlichen Unions- und Reformbestregbungen von 1538–1542* (Rome 1910); T. Schieder, "Kirchenspaltungen und Kirchenunionspläne," *Wissenschaft in Geschichte und Unterricht* 3 (1952), 591–605; G. Menge, *Versuche zur Wiedervereinigung Deutschlands im Glauben* (Steyl 1921); H. Weidemann, *Gerard Wolter Molanus, Abt zu Loccum* (Göttingen 1925–29); F. Ranft, *Das katholisch-protestantische Problem* (Fulda 1947); M. P. Fleischer, *Katholische und lutherische Ireniker, unter besonderer Berücksichtigung des 19. Jh.* (Göttingen, Frankfurt and Zurich 1968); J. Müller, "Karl Ludwig und die Wiedervereinigung der Konfessionen," *Blätter für Pfälzische Kirchengeschichte* 29 (1962), 130–79; E. W. Zeeden, "Der ökumenische Gedanke in Veit Ludwig von Seckendorffs Historia Lutheranismi. Über die Idee einer religiösen Überwindung des intoleranten Konfessionalismus im späten 17. Jh.," *Festschr. für Gerhard Ritter zu seinem 60. Geburtstag* (Tübingen 1950); H. Schüßler, *Georg Calixt. Theologie und Kirchenpolitik. Eine Studie zur Ökumenizität des Luthertums* (Wiesbaden 1961); A. L. Veit, *Kirchliche Reunionsbestrebungen im ehemaligen Erzstift Mainz unter Erzbischof Johann Philipp von Schönborn 1647–1673* (Freiburg 1910); A. P. Brück, "Der Mainzer 'Unionsplan' aus dem Jahre 1660," *Jb. für das Bistum Mainz* 8 (1960), 148–62; H. Raab, "Der 'Discrete Catholische' des Landgrafen Ernst von Hessen-Rheinfels (1623–1693). Ein Beitrag zur Geschichte der Reunionsbemühungen und Toleranzbestrebungen im 17. Jh.," *AMrhKG* 12 (1960), 175–98; id., *Landgraf Ernst v. Hessen-Rheinfels* (St. Goar 1964); id., "Ernest, landgrave de Hesse-Rhinfels," *DHGE* XV (1963), 800–806; H. Wamper, *Das Leben der Brüder Adrian u. Peter van Walenburch aus Rotterdam und ihr Wirken in der Erzdiözese Köln bis zum Jahre 1649* (Cologne 1968); P. Wiedeburg, *Der junge Leibniz, das Reich und Europa,* Part 1: *Mainz* (Wiesbaden 1962); F. X. Kiefl, *Leibniz und die religiöse Wiedervereinigung Deutschlands* (Regensburg 1925); E. Benz, "Leibniz u. d. Wiedervereinigung der christlichen Kirchen," *ZRGG* 2 (1950), 97–113; L. Winterswyl, *Gottfried Wilhelm Leibniz. Über die Reunion der Kirchen. Auswahl und Übersetzung* (Freiburg 1939); F. Gaquère, *Le dialogue irénique Bossuet-Leibniz. La réunion des Églises en échec (1691–1702)* (Paris 1966); M. Prechtl, *Friedens-Benehmen zwischen Bossuet, Leibniz und Molanus* (1815); P. Hiltebrandt, *Die kirchlichen Reunionsverhandlungen in der zweiten Hälfte des 17. Jh.* (Rome 1922); H. Nottarp, *Zur "Communicatio in sacris cum haereticis"* (Halle 1933); S.J. T. Miller and J. P. Spielman, Jr., *Cristóbal Rojas y Spinola, Cameralist and Irenicist* (Philadelphia 1962); H. Tüchle, "Neue Quellen zu den Reunionsverhandlungen des Bischofs Spinola und seines Nachfolgers," *Einsicht und Glaube, Festschr. für Gottlieb Söhngen* (Freiburg 1962), 405–37; H. Raab, "De negotio Hannoveriano Religionis." Die Reunionsbemühungen des Bischofs Christoph de Rojas y Spinola im Urteil des Landgrafen Ernst von Hessen-Rheinfels," *Volk Gottes. Festschr. für Joseph Höfer* (Freiburg, Basel and Vienna 1967), 395–417; id., "Ad reuniendos dissidentes." Zur Gesch. der kirchlichen Reunionsbestrebungen im ausgehenden 18. und im beginnenden 19. Jh.," *Jb. für das Bistum Mainz* 8 (1960), 128–47; G. Richter, "Ein Fuldaer Plan zur Wiedervereinigung der christlichen Konfessionen in Deutschland," *Fuldaer Geschichtsblätter* 9 (1911), 1–7, 17–32, 57–64, 184–252; B. Menzel, "Der 'Fuldaer Plan' zur Kirchenunion und der Braunauer Abt Stefan Rautenstrauch (1779–1783)," *Heimat und Volk. Festschr. für Prof. Wilhelm Wostry* (Brünn 1937); G. Pfeilschifter, ed., *Korrespondenz des Fürstabtes Martin II. Gerbert von St. Blasien,* 2 vols. (Karlsruhe 1931–37); J. Hörmann, "Beda Mayer von Donauwörth, ein Ireniker der Aufklärungszeit," *Festgabe H. Knöpfler zur Vollendung des 70. Lebensjahres* (Freiburg 1917), 188–209; J. B. Blößner, *Maximilian Prechtl, der letzte Abt des Benediktinerklosters Michelfeld* (Kallmünz 1938). *Die Oberpfalz* 32, nos. 6–7; H. Graßl, "Ökumenisches Bayern," *Festschr. für M. Spindler* (Munich 1969), 529–52; U. im Hof, "Die Helvetische Überbrückung des konfessionellen Gegensatzes. Zur Frage der Begegnung zwischen katholischer und reformierter Schweiz im 18. Jh.," *Gottesreich und Menschenreich. Ernst Staehelin zum 80. Geburtstag* (Basel and Stuttgart 1969), 345–60; G. A. Benrath, "Die konfessionellen Unionsbestrebungen des Kurfürsten Karl Ludwig von der Pfalz (d. 1680)," *ZGObrh* 116 (1968), 187–252; G. May, *Interkonfessionalismus in der ersten Hälfte des 19. Jahrhunderts* (Paderborn 1969).

28. Ecclesiastical Learning in the Eighteenth Century—Theology of the Enlightenment and Pietism

Catholic Theology

GENERAL LITERATURE: Grabmann *G,* 179–212; Werner; Hurter IV–V: F. Stegmüller, "Barock, II. Theologie," *LThK* I, 1260–65; L. Scheffczyk, "Aufklärung, III. Theologie," *LThK* I, 1063–66.

LITERATURE: A. Anwander, *Die allgemeine Religionsgesch. im kath. Deutschland während der Aufklärung und der Romantik* (Salzburg 1932); M. Braubach, "Die kirchliche Aufklärung im kath. Deutschland im Spiegel des Journal von und für Deutschland," *HJ* 54 (1934), 1–63, 178–200; W. Forster, "Die kirchliche Aufklärung der Abtei Banz im Spiegel ihrer von 1772–98 herausgegebenen Zeitschrift," *SM* 63 (1951), 172–233; 64 (1952), 110–233; E. Tomek, *Kirchengesch. Österreichs III: Die Zeit der Aufklärung und des Absolutismus* (Innsbruck 1959); *Laurens. Ein Beitrag zur deutschen und französischen Aufklärung* (Berlin 1963); E. Winter, *Frühaufklärung. Der Kampf gegen den Konfessionalismus in Mittel- und Osteuropa und die deutsch-slawische Begegnung* (Berlin 1966); G. Otruba, "Kirche und Kultur in Aufklärung und Barock," *Jb. f. Landeskunde von Niederösterreich,* n.s. 31 (1934), 238–66; P. Kälin, *Die Aufklärung in Uri, Schwyz und Unterwalden im 18. Jahrhundert* (diss., Fribourg 1946); H. Wagner, "Die Aufklärung im Erzstift Salzburg," *Salzburger Universitätsreden* 26 (Salzburg and Munich 1968); A. Kraus, "Bürgerlicher Geist und Wissenschaft. Wissenschaftliches Leben in Zeitalter des Barock und der Aufklärung in Augsburg, Regensburg und Nürnberg," *Arch. f. Kulturgesch.* 49 (1967), 340–90; G. Groß, *Trierer Geistesleben unter dem Einfluß von Aufklärung und Romantik 1750–1850* (trier 1956), 15–110; F. Wetzel, *Geschichte der kath. Presse Deutschlands im 18. Jahrhundert* (diss., Heidelberg 1913); L. A. Veit, *Das Aufklärungsschrifttum des 18. Jahrhunderts und die deutsche Kirche* (Görres-Gesellschaft Vereinsschrift) (Cologne 1937); G. Schwaiger, "Die Aufklärung in kath. Sicht," *Concilium* 3 (1967), 559–66; B. Plongeron, "Recherches sur l'"Aufklärung' catholique en Europe occidentale (1770–1830)," *RHMC* 16 (1969), 555–605; R. van Dülmen, "Antijesuitismus und kath. Aufklärung in Deutschland," *HJ* 89 (1969), 52–80. For literature on individual theologians see: *LThK* and the following supplementary notes.

Systematic Theology: T. Müller, "Die Disentiser Barockscholastik," *ZSKG* 52 (1958), 1–26, 150–82.

Moral Theology: J. Klein, "Ursprung und Grenzen der Kasuistik," *Festschr. Fritz Tillmann* (Düsseldorf 1950), 229–45; H. Klomps, *Tradition und Fortschritt in der Moraltheologie. Die grundsätzliche Bedeutung der Kontroverse zwischen Jansenismus und Probabilismus* (Cologne 1963); W. Martens, *Die Botschaft der Tugend. Die Aufklärung im Spiegel der deutschen moralischen Wochenschriften* (Stuttgart 1968).

Pastoral Theology: A. Schrott, *Seelsorge im Wandel der Zeit* (Graz 1949); F. Dorfmann, *Die Ausgestaltung der Pastoraltheologie zur Universitätsdisziplin* (Vienna and Leipzig 1910; biblio.); R. Füglister, *Die Pastoraltheologie als Universitätsdisziplin* (Basel 1951); H. Schuster, "Die Gesch. der Pastoraltheologie," *Hdb. der Pastoraltheologie* I (Freiburg i. Brsg. 1964), 40–92; F. X. Arnold, *Grundsätzliches und Geschichtliches zur Theologie der Seelsorge* (Freiburg i. Brsg. 1949).

Catechetics: J. Schmitt, "Der Kampf um den Katechismus in der Aufklärungsperiode Deutschlands" (unpubl. diss., Munich 1935); L. Leutner, *Katechetik und Religionsunterricht in Österreich,* 2 vols. (Vienna 1955–59); J. Rabas, *Katechetisches Erbe der Aufklärungszeit, kritisch dargestellt am Lehrbuch der christkathol. Religion von J. F. Batz. Bamberg 1799* (Freiburg i. Brsg. 1963).

Church History: E. C. Scherer, *Gesch. und Kirchengesch. an den deutschen Universitäten. Ihre Anfänge im Zeitalter des Humanismus und ihre Ausbildung zur selbständigen Diszipln* (Freiburg i. Brsg. 1927); L. Scheffczyk, *F. L. Stolbergs "Gesch. der Religion Jesu Christi." Die Abwendung der kath. Kirchengeschichtsschreibung von der Aufklärung . . .* (Munich 1952); I. A. Endres, *Korrespondenz der Mauriner mit den Emmeramern* (Stuttgart and Vienna 1899); G. Pfeilschifter, *Die sanktblasische Germania sacra* (Kempten 1921); A. Pérez Goyena, "Los orígines del estudio de la Historia eclesiástica en España," *RF* 79 (1927); K. Zinke, *Zustände und Strömungen in der kath. Kirchengeschichtsschreibung des Aufklärungs-Zeitalters im deutschen Sprachgebiet* (diss., Breslau 1933); G. Heer, *Mabillon und die Schweizer Benediktinerklöster* (St. Gallen 1938); A. Walz, *Studi storiografici* (Rome 1940), 40–72; O. Köhler, "Der Gegenstand der Kirchengesch.," *HJ* 77 (1958), 254–69; T. Stowikowski, *Les opinions sur l'enseignement de l'histoire en Pologne au XVIIIe siècle et les conceptions didactiques de Joachim Lelcwel* (Polish) (Crakow 1960); A. Kraus, "Grundzüge barocker Geschichtsschreibung," *HJ* 88 (1968), 54–77.

SCHOLARSHIP IN ITALY: F. Venturi, "Le siècle des lumières en Italie," *Cahiers d'histoire* 5 (1960), 225–39; id., *Settecento riformatore. Da Muratori a Beccaria* (Turin 1969); A Prandi, *Religiosità e cultura nel '700 italiano* (Bologna 1966).

JANSENISM IN ITALY; SYNOD OF PISTOIA 1786: SOURCES: E. Codignola, *Carsteggi di giansenisti liguri,* 3 vols. (Florence 1941–42). LITERATURE: A. C. Jemolo, *Il giansenismo in Italia prima delle rivoluzioni* (Bari 1928); B. Matteucci, *Scipione de' Ricci* (Brescia 1941); E. Dammig, *Il movimento giansenista a Roma nella seconda metà del sec. XVIII* (Vatican City 1945); E. Codignola, *Il giansenismo toscano,* 2 vols. (Florence 1944); id., *Illuministi, giacobini e giansenisti nell'Italia del '700* (Florence 1947); F. Valsecchi, *Le riforme dell'assolutismo illuminato negli Stati italiani 1748–1789* (Milan 1953); G. Quazza, *Il problema italiano alla vigilia della riforme 1720–1738* (Rome 1954); P. de Leturia, "Il concetto di nazione italiana nel grande antigiansenista F. A. Zaccaria (1714–1795), secondo fonti dell'archivio di Loyola," *Analecta Gregoriana* 71 (1954), 231–57; P. de Leturia, *Nuove ricerche sul giansenismo* (Rome 1954); B. Matteucci, *Il giansenismo* (Rome 1954); G. Candelero, *Storia dell'Italia moderna I: Le origini del Risorgimento 1700–1815* (Milan 1956); G. Quazza, *Le riforme in Piemonte nella prima metà del Settecento,* 2 vols. (Modena 1957); E. W. Cochrane, "Le riforme Leopoldine in Toscana nella corrispondenza degli invitati francesi 1766–1791." *RSRis* 45 (1958), 199–218; M. Vaussard, *Jansénisme et gallicanisme aux origines religieuses du Risorgimento* (Paris 1959); E. Passerin d'Entréves, "La riforma 'giansenista' dell Chiesa e la lotta anticuriale in Italia nella seconda metà del Settecento," *Riv. Storica Italiana* 71 (1959), 209–34; F. Catalano, *Illuministi e giacobini del '700 italiano* (Milan 1959); M. Vaussard, *Correspondance Scipione de'Ricci-Henri Grégoire (1796–1807)* (Florence and Paris, 1963); A. Wandruszka, *Leopold II.*, 2 vols. (Vienna 1963–65); G. König, *Rom und die toskanische Kirchenpolitik 1765–1790* (diss., Cologne 1964); A. Wandruszka, F. Diaz, L. Dal Pane, and M. Rosa, "L'opera di Pietro Leopoldo, granduca di Toscana," *Rassegna storica toscana* 11 (1965), 179–300; C. Caristia, *Riflessi politici di giansenismo italiano* (Naples 1965); P. C. Cannarozzi, "I Collaboratori giansenisti di Pietro Leopoldo, granduca di Toscana," *Rassegna storica toscana* 12 (1966), 5–59; F. Diaz, *Francesco Maria Gianni. Dalla burocrazia alla politica sotto Pietro Leopoldo di Toscana* (Milan 1966); M. Rosa, *Riformatori e ribelli nell '700 religioso italiano* (Bari 1969); C. A. Belton, *Church Reform in 18th Century Italy (The Synod of Pistoia, 1786)* (The Hague 1969).

PROTESTANT THEOLOGY: SOURCES: W. Philipp, *Das Werden der Aufklärung in theologiegeschichtlicher Sicht* (Göttingen 1957) [texts]. LITERATURE: E. Hirsch, *Gesch. der neueren evangelischen Theologie,* 5 vols. (Gütersloh 1964); W. Kantzenbach, *Protestantisches Christentum im Zeitalter der Aufklärung* (Gütersloh 1965); A. Schlingensiepe-Pogge, *Das Sozialethos der lutherischen Aufklärungsteologie am Vorabend der industriellen Revolution* (Göttingen, Berlin and Frankfurt 1967); H. Hubschmid, *Gott. Mensch und Welt in der schweizerischen Aufklärung. Eine Untersuchung über Optimismus und Fortschrittsgedanken bei Joh. Jak. Scheuchzer, Joh. Heinrich Tschudi, Joh. Jak. Bodmer und Jakob Iselin* (Ph.D. diss., I Bern, Affoltern a. A. 1950); R. Bruch, "Das Verhältnis zwischen der kath. und prot. Moraltheologie zur Zeit der Aufklärung," *Festschrift Lorenz Jäger* (Paderborn 1962), 278–92; W. Nigg, *Die Kirchengeschichtsschreibung* (Munich 1934) [the title is misleading; Catholic historiography has been deliberately disregarded because, the author asserts, it does not contribute anything to the modern problem]; A. Klempt, *Die Säkularisierung der universalhistorischen Auffassung. Zum Wandel des Geschichtsdenkens im 16. und 17. Jh.* (Göttingen 1960) [important for the attention given to Protestant theology]; P. Meinhold, *Gesch. der kirchlichen Historiographie,* 2 vols. (Freiburg and Munich 1967) [sources and presentation].

UNIVERSITIES: LITERATURE: K. Goldman, *Verzeichnis der Hochschulen* (Neustadt an der Aisch 1967; contains precise catalog of all matriculations and their issues); *Les universités européennes du XIVe au XVIIIe siècle. Aspects et problemes. Actes du colloque int. à l'occasion du 6. centenaire de l'Univ. Jagelonne de Cracovie 6–8 mai 1964* (Geneva 1967); E. C. Scherer, *Gesch. und Kirchengesch. an den deutschen Universitäten* (Freiburg i. Brsg. 1927); R. Haaß, *Die geistige Haltung der katholischen Universitäten Deutschlands im 18. Jh.* (Freiburg i. Brsg. 1952) (accounts only for Germany within the borders of 1919 and investigates the position regarding the newly emerging philosopy); see additional literature under individual universities; M. Andrés, "Las facultades de teología en las universidades españolas (1396–1868)," *RET* 28 (1968), 319–58; H. Jedin, "Ein nicht realisierter Universitätsgründungsplan im 16. Jh.," *Festschr. L. Brandt* (Cologne 1969), 405–15 (beginning of denominationalism).

Bonn: M. Braubach, *Die erste Bonner Universität* (Bonn 1947); id., "Rheinische Aufklärung. Neue Funde zur Gesch. der l. Bonner Universität," *AHVNrh* 149/150 (1950/51), 74–180; 151/152 (1952), 257–348.

Dillingen: A. Biglmaier and F. Zoepfl. *Stadt und Universität Dillingen* (Dillingen 1950).

Freiburg: E. Säger, "Die Vertretung der Kirchengesch. in Freiburg von den Anfängen bis zur Mitte des 19. Jh," *Beiträge zur Freiburger Wissenschafts- und Universitätsgeschichte* 1 (1952); P. Diepgen 2nd E. T. Nauck, "Die Freidburger Medizinische Fakultät in der österreichischen Zeit," *Beiträge zur Freiburger Wissenschafts- und Universitätsgeschichte* 16 (1957); E. W. Zeeden, "Die Freiburger Philosophische Fakultät im Umbruch des 18. Jh.," *Beiträge zur Freiburger Wissenschafts- und Universitätsgeschichte* 17 (1957), 9–139; E. Zentgraf, ed., "Aus der Geschichte der Naturwissenschaften an der Universität Freiburg," *Beiträge zur Freiburger Wissenschafts- und Unversitätsgeschichte* 18 (1957); W. Müller, "Fünfhundert Jahre theologische Promotion an der Universität Freiburg," *Beiträge zur Freiburger Wissenschafts- und Universitätsgeschichte* 19 (1957); T. Kurrus, "Die Jesuiten an der Universität Freiburg 1620–1773," I: *Beiträge zur Freiburger Wissenschafts- und Universitätsgeschichte* 21 (1963); C. Schott, "Rat und Spruch der Juristenfakultät Freiburg i. Br.," *Beiträge zur Freiburger Wissenschafts- und Universitätsgeschichte* 30 (1965); T. Kurrus, "Zur Einführung der Experimentalphysik durch die Jesuiten an der Universität Freiburg," *Beiträge zur Freiburger Wissenschafts- und Universitätsgeschichte* 33 (1966), 119–24; F. Biesenbach, "Die Entwicklung der Nationalökonomie an der Universität Freiburg 1768–1896," *Beiträge zur Freiburger Wissenschafts- und Universitätsgeschichte* 36 (1969).

Fulda: W. A. Mühl, *Die Aufklärung an der Universität Fulda mit besonderer Berücksichtigung der philosophischen und juristischen Fakultät (1734–1805)* (Fulda 1961).

Graz: J. Matl, "Die Bedeutung der Universität Graz für die kulturelle Entwicklung des europäischen Ostens," *Festschr. Universität Graz* (Graz 1936), 167–226; A. Posch, "Die Bedeutung der Grazer theologischen Fakultät für den Südosten der ehemaligen Monarchie in der Zeit von 1773 bis 1827," *Festschr. Universität Graz* (Graz 1936), 105–19; id., "Die kirchliche Aufklärung in Graz und an der Grazer Hochschule," *Festschrift der Universität Graz* (1937).

Ingolstadt: R. Obermeier, *Die Universität Ingolstadt* (Ingolstadt 1959).

Innsbruck: *Forschungen zur Innsbrucker Universitätsgesch.* (Innsbruck 1960ff.); A. Haidacher, "Ein Gnadenstreit zwischen dem Stifte Wilten und der Universität Innsbruck aus dem Beginn des 18. Jh.," *APraem* 31 (1955), 100–135, 193–226; A. Mitterbacher, *Der Einfluß der Aufklärung an der theologischen Fakultät der Universität Innsbruck (1790–1823)* (Innsbruck 1962); F. Huter, "Die Anfänge der Innsbrucker Juristenfakultät (1671–1686)," *ASavRGgerm* 85 (1968), 223–47; G. Mraz, *Gesch. der Theologischen Fakultät der Universität Innsbruck von ihrer Gründung bis zum Jahre 1740* (Innsbruck 1968); *Die Matrikel der Universität Innsbruck,* Part 3: *Matricula Universitatis* I 1755/56–1763/64, revised by E. Weiler (Innsbruck 1968).

Louvain: J. Wils, *L'université de Louvain à travers 5 siècles* (Brussels 1927); R. Guelluye, "L'évolution des méthodes de théologie à Louvain d'Érasme à Jansenius," *RHE* 37 (1941), 31–144; L. van der Essen, *L'université de Louvain 1425–1940* (Brussels 1945); F. Claeys Bouuaert, *L'ancienne université de Louvain* (Louvain 1956).

Mainz: *Beiträge zur Gesch. der Universität Mainz* (Wiesbaden 1955ff.); A. P. Brück, *Die Mainzer Theologische Fakultät im 18. Jh.* (Wiesbaden 1955); L. Just, *Die alte Universität Mainz 1477–1798* (Wiesbaden 1957); L. Just and H. Mathy, *Die Universität Mainz* (Mainz 1965).

Münster: E. Hegel, *Die katholisch-theologische Fakultät Münster in ihrer geschichtlichen Entwicklung 1773 bis 1961* (Münster 1961).

Olmütz: G. Deutsch, *Die theologische Fakultät Olmütz* (Brünn 1885).

Osnabrück: C. Riepe, *Gesch. der Universität Osnabrück* (Osnabrück 1965).

Paderborn: K. Honselmann, *Die philosophisch-theologische Akademie in Paderborn und ihr Stiftungsvermögen* (Paderborn 1954).

Prague: R. Schreiber, *Studien zur Gesch. der Karls-Universität zu Prag* (Freilassing and Salzburg 1954).

Salzburg: A. Kalb, "Präsidium und Professorenkolleg der Benediktineruniv. Salzburg 1617–1743," *Mitt. der Ges. für Salzburger Landeskunde* 102 (1962), 117–66; M. Kaindl-Hoenig and K. H. Ritschel, *Die Salzburger Universität 1622–1964* (Salzburg 1964).

Vienna: A. Wappler, *Gesch. der theologischen Fakultät der k. k. Universität zu Wien* (Vienna 1884); R. Meister, *Entwicklung und Reformen des österreichischen Studienwesens,* 2 vols. (Vienna 1963).

ACADEMIES: LITERATURE: Especially: A. Kraus, *Vernunft und Geschichte. Die Bedeutung der deutschen Akademien für die Entwicklung der Geschichtswissenschaft im späten 18. Jh.* (Freiburg, Basel and Vienna 1963; with detailed biblio.); M. Maylender, *Storia delle Accademie d'Italia,* 5 vols. (Bologna and Turin 1926–30); V. Castañada y Alcover, *La Real Academia de la Historia 1735–1930* (Madrid 1930); E. W. Cochrane, *Tradition and Enlightenment in the Tuscan Academies* (Rome 1961); L. Hammermayer, "Die Benediktiner und die Akademiebewegung im katholischen Deutschland (1720–1770)," *SM* 70 (1959), 45–146; id., "Europäische Akademiebewegung und italienische Aufklärung," *HJ* 81 (1962), 247–63; P. Fuchs, *Palatinus Illustratus. Die historische Forschung an der kurpfälzischen Akademie der Wissenschaften* (Mannheim 1963); R. Rurup, "Die deutsche Geschichtswissenschaft im 18. Jh.," *ZGObrh* 113 (1965), 231–61.

EDUCATION: LITERATURE: J. Rößler, "Die kirchliche Aufklärung unter dem Speierer Fürstbischof August von Limburg-Stirum," *Mitt. des hist. Vereins der Pfalz* 34/35 (1915), 1–160; A. Messer, *Die Reform des Schulwesens im Kurfürstentum Mainz unter Emmerich Joseph 1763–1774* (Mainz 1897); P. Mauel, *Das Volksschulwesen des Hochstiftes Speyer im 18. Jh. 3.–4. Jahrb, des Vereins für christl. Erziehungswissenschaft 1910/11;* H. Hardewig, *Die Tätigkeit des Freiherrn Franz von Fürstenberg für die Schulen des Fürstbistums Münster* (Hildesheim 1912); E. Jehle, *Das niedere Schulwesen unter Limburg-Stirum* (Freiburg i. Brsg. 1923); N. Konrad, *Franz Ludwig von Erthal. Ein Organisator der Volksschule der Aufklärung* (Düsseldorf 1932); M. Schmidt, *Die Aufklärung im Fürstbistum Passau* (diss., Munich 1933): *Vh. des hist. Vereins˚für Nordbayern* 67/68 (1934, 1935); W. Roeßler, *Die Entstehung des modernen Erziehungswesens in Deutschland* (Stuttgart 1961); E. Schumacher, "Das kölnische Westfalen im Zeitalter der Aufklärung" (unpubl. diss., Bonn 1952); A. P. Brück, *Kurmainzer Schulgeschichte. Texte, Berichte. Memoranden* (Wiesbaden 1960); M. Renner, "Fuldaer Einfluß auf die Würzburger Schulreform Fürstbischofs Franz Ludwig von Erthal," *ZBLG* 28 (1965), 368–91; H. Flurschültz, *Die Verwaltung des Hochstiftes Würzburg unter Franz Ludwig von Erthal 1779–95* (Würzburg 1965); H. M. Elzer, ed., *Zwei Schriften der Kurmainzer Schulreform von 1770–1784* (Frankfurt, Berlin, Bonn and Munich 1967).

29. *Liturgy and Popular Piety—New Religious Orders*

LITERATURE

LITURGY: A. L. Mayer, "Liturgie, Aufklärung und Klassizismus," *JLW* 9 (1929), 67–127; A. Vierbach, *Die liturgischen Anschauungen des Vitus Anton Winter. Ein Beitrag zur Gesch. der Aufklärung* (Munich 1929); J. Schöttl, *Kirchliche Reformen des Salzburger Erzbischofs Hieronymus v. Colloredo im Zeitalter der Aufklärung* (Hirschenhausen 1939); W. Trapp, *Vorgeschichte und Ursprung der liturgischen Bewegung* (Regensburg 1940); A. L. Mayer, "Liturgie und Barock," *JLW* 15 (1941), 67–154; P. Salmon, *L'office divin.*

Histoire de la formation du bréviaire (Paris 1959); J. A. Jungmann, "Liturgisches Leben im Barock," J. A. Jungmann, *Erbe und Pastorale Gegenwart* (Innsbruck, Vienna and Munich 1960), 108–19; id., "Liturgische Erneuerung zwischen Barock und Gegenwart," *LJ* 12 (1962), 1–15; A.-G. Martimort, *Hdb. der Liturgiewissenschaft* I (Freiburg, Basel and Vienna 1963); B. Fischer, "Das Rituale Romanum (1614–1964)," *TThZ* 73 (1964), 257–71; W. Müller, "Wessenberg in heutiger Sicht," *ZSKG* 58 (1964), 293–308; T. Klauser, *Kleine abencländische Liturgiegeschichte* (Bonn 1965); A. Häußling, "Die Systematik der Väterlesungen in den Benediktinischen Reformbrevieren Frankreichs von 1777 und 1787," *ALW* 9 (1966), 418–24; A. Kurzeja, "Die Etappen in der Entwicklung des Stundengebets in der Trierer Kirche," *TThZ* 77 (1968), 104–19.

POPULAR PIETY: H. Schnell, *Der bairische Barock. Die volkliche, die geschichtliche und religiöse Grundlage* (Munich 1936); H. Hoffmann, "Die Frömmigkeit der deutschen Aufklärung," *Zs. f. Theol. u. Kirche* 16 (1906), 234–50; J. Hacker, "Die Messe in den deutschen Diözesan-Gesang- und Gebetbüchern von der Aufklärungszeit bis zur Gegenwart," *MthSt* (H) II. 1 (1950); K. Berger, *Barock und Aufklärung im geistl. Lied* (Marburg 1951); I. Müller, "Barocke Geistigkeit einer Benediktinerabtei," *ZSKG* 49 (1955), 257–87; L. A. Veit and L. Lenhart, *Kirche und Volksfrömmigkeit im Zeitalter des Barock* (Freiburg i. Brsg. 1956); A. Coreth, *Pietas Austriaca. Ursprung und Entwicklung barocker Frömmigkeit in Österreich* (Vienna 1959); A. Angyal, *Die slawische Barockwelt* (Leipzig 1961); P. Hankamer, *Deutsche Gegenreformation und deutscher Barock. Die deutsche Lit. im Zeitraum des 17. Jh.* (Stuttgart 1964); R. Alewyn, ed., *Deutsche Barockforschung* (Cologne and Berlin 1966); E. Krausen, "Die Verehrung römischer Katakombenheiliger in Altbayern im Zeitalter des Barock," *Bayer. Jb. für Volkskunde* 67 (1966), 37–47; B. Hubensteiner, *Vom Geist des Barock, Kultur und Frömmigkeit im alten Bayern* (Munich 1967); B. Goy, *Aufklärung und Volksfrömmigkeit in den Bistümern Würzburg und Bamberg* (Würzburg 1969).

THE SERMON: L. Signer, "Zur Forschungsgesch. der kath. Barockpredigt," *Kirche und Kanzel* XII (Paderborn 1929), 235–48; C. Schreiber, *Aufklärung und Frömmigkeit. Die katholische Predigt im deutschen Aufklärungszeitalter* (Munich 1940); B. v. Mehr, *Das Predigtwesen in Köln u. Rheinischen Kapuzinerprovinzen im 17. und 18. Jh.* (Rome 1945); B. Dreher, *Die Osterpredigt. Von der Reformation bis zur Gegenwart* (Freiburg i. Brsg. 1951); G. Lohmaier, *Bayerische Barockpredigt* (Munich 1961); L. Intorp, *Die westfälische Barockpredigt* (diss., Mainz 1962); E. Moser-Rath, *Predigtmärlein der Barockzeit* (Berlin 1964); R. Krause, *Die Predigt der späten deutschen Aufklärung 1770–1805* (Stuttgart 1965); J. B. Schneyer, "Wesenszüge des Barock in den Titeln seiner Predigtbücher," *MThZ* 19 (1968), 295–310.

THE RELIGIOUS ORDERS: Heimbucher; M. Escobar, *Ordini e Congregazioni religiose,* 2 vols. (Turin 1951–53); M. Vettori, "Die Tertiar-Schulschwestern in Süd- und Nordtirol. Ihr Werden und Wirken 1700–1955," *Schlern-Schriften* 141 (Innsbruck 1955); P. Hofmeister, "Die Verfassung der Benediktinerkongregationen," *SM* 66 (1955), 5–27; M. De Meulemeester, *Origines de la Congrégation du Très Saint Rédempteur* (Louvain 1957); I. Gautier, *Les Messieurs de Saint-Sulpice* (Paris 1957); L. J. Lekai, *Geschichte und Wirken der weißen Mönche* (Cologne 1958); M. de Meulemeester, *Histoire sommaire de la Congrégation du T. S. Rédempteur* (Louvain 1959); P. Schmitz, *Gesch. des Benediktinerordens* IV [from Trent to 1500] (Einsiedeln 1960); M. de C. Guendré, *Histoire de l'ordre des Ursulines en France;* II: *Les monastères d'Ursulines sous l'Ancien régime* (Paris 1960); C. Almeras, *S. Pablo de la Cruz, fundator de los Pasionistos* (Bilbao 1960); K. Zähringer, *Die Schulbrüder des hl. Joh. Bapt. de La Salle* (Fribourg 1962); C. Gérin, "Les Augustins en France avant 1789," *AAug* 24 (1961), 242–61; S. Leussen, *La Trappe, Schets van ontstaan en ontwikkeling 1664–1898* (Tilburg 1965); J. Salzgeber, *Die Klöster Einsiedeln und St. Gallen im Barockzeitalter* (Mürster 1967); O. Gregorio and A. Sampers, *Documenti interno alla regula della Congregazione de SS. Redentore 1725–1749 SHCSR* 16 (1968), 1–270; Alberto de la Virgen del Carmen, *Historia de la reforma Teresiana 1562–1962* (Madrid 1969); *Atlas geographicus ordinis FF. MM. Capuccinorum* (Rome 1968); A. Vernaschi, *Una istituzione originale. Le figlie della Carità di S. Vincenzo de' Paoli* (Rome 1968); M.-P. Desaing, *Die Ursulinen* (Fribourg 1968); G. Russotto, *San Giovanni di Dio e il suo ordine ospedaliero*, 2 vols. (Rome 1969); C. Catena, *Le Carmelitane. Storia e spiritualità* (Rome 1969); M. Arneth, *Das Ringen um Geist und Form der Priesterbildung im Säkularklerus des 17. Jh.* (Würzburg 1970).

SECTION THREE

The Papacy under the Increasing Pressure of the Established Church

30. *The Popes from Innocent XIII to Clement XII*

LITERATURE

F. Venturi, *Illuministi italiani. Riformatori lombardi, piemontesi e toscani* (Milan 1958); L. Dollot, "Conclaves et diplomatie française au XVIIIᵉ siècle," *Rev. d'Hist. diplom.* 75 (1961), 124–35; G. Caristia, "Riflessi politici del Giansenismo italiano IV. Il Giansenismo regalista," *AcTorino* 96 (1961/62), 665–776; L. Dal Pane, *Lo Stato Pontificio e il movimento riformatorio del Settecento* (Milan 1959); M. Andrieux, *La vie quotidienne dans la Rome pontificale au XVIIIᵉ siècle* (Paris 1962); F. Margiotta Broglio, "Appunti storiografici sul giansenismo italiano" *Scritti Jemolo* (Milan 1963), 781–849; F. Venturi, "Elementi e tentativi di riforme nello Stato Pontificio del Settecento," *RSIt* 75 (1963), 119–39; id. *Illuministi italiani. Riformatori napolitani* (Milan 1962); U. Marcelli, *Riforme e rivoluzione in Italia del secolo XVIII* (Bologna 1964); H. Benedikt, *Kaiseradler über den Apenninen. Die Österreicher in Italien 1700–1866* (Vienna 1964); G. Quazza, *Il problema italiano e l'equilibrio europea 1720–1738* (Turin 1965); G. Giarrizzo et al., *Illuministi Italiani. Riformatori delle antiche Repubbliche, dei Ducati, dello Stato Pontificio e delle Isole* (Milan 1965); V. E. Giuntella, "Roma nel Settecento," *StRom* 14 (1966), 269–91; F. Valsecchi, *Riformismo e antico regime nel secolo XVIII. Il riformismo borbonico a Napoli e a Parma, lo Stato della Chiesa* (Rome 1967); G. Schwaiger, "Die Geltung des Papsttums im 18. Jh.," *Festschr. Schmaus* (Munich 1967), 1153–69.

INNOCENT XIII: *BullRom Cocq* XI 2, 183–278; *BullRom* (ed. by Taur.) XXI, 867–958; *Hierarchia Catholica* V, 33f.; A. Mercati, *Raccolta*, 286–97; Ciaconius VI, 381–408; Pastor XV, 391–460; Seppelt V, 413–15; G. Schwaiger in *LThK* V, 695f.; M. v. Mayer, *Die Papstwahl I.'XIII.* (Vienna 1874); E. Michaud, "La fin de Clément XI et le commencement du pontificat d'I.," *Rev. internat. de théol.* 5 (Berne 1897), 42–60,

304–31; L. Wahrmund, "Die kaiserliche Exklusive im Konklave I.," *SAW* 170 (1912).

BENEDICT XIII: *BullRom Cocq* XI 2, 279–424; XII; *BullRom* (ed. by Taur.) XXII; *Opuscula varia* . . . (Rome 1726); *Concilium Romanum* . . . *celebratum anno 1725* (Rome 1725); *Collectio Lacensis* I, 341–466; *Hierarchia Catholica* V, 34–39; Quétif III, 471–81; Ciaconius VI, 409–572; A. Mercati, *Raccolta*, 297–311; G. B. Pittoni (Venice 1730); A. Borgia (Rome 1752); Pastor XV, 461–604; Seppelt V, 415–22; J. Carreyre: DHGE VIII, 163f.; P. Mikat in LThK II, 177; G. de Caro in *Dizionario biografico degli Italiani* VIII, 384–93; G. Vignato, *Storia di B.* (Milan 1953); G. Cardillo, "B. e il giansenismo," *Memorie Domenic.* 58 (1941), 217–22; 59 (1942), 38–43.

CLEMENT XII: *BullRom Cocq* XIII; XIV; *BullRom* (ed. by Taur.) XXIII–XXIV; *D*, 498–500; *Hierarchia Catholica* VI, 3–9; Ciaconius VI, 575–772; A. Mercati, *Raccolta*, 311–30; A. Fabroni, *De vita et rebus gestis* (Rome 1760); Pastor XV, 605–754; Seppelt V, 422–28; R. Mols in *DHGE* XII, 1361–81; H. Raab in *LThK* II, 1228f.; L. P. Raybaud. *Papauté et pouvoir temporel sous les pontificats de Clément XII et Benoît XIV* (Paris 1963); A. Zanelli, *Il conclave per elezione di Clemente* (Rome 1890); H. Hermelink, "Klemens XII. und die Kirchengüter in den protestantischen Ländern," *ZKG* 24 (1930), 609–15.

31. *Benedict XIV*

LITERATURE

Bullarium, 4 vols. (Rome 1746–57, Venice 1768); *Opera,* 12 vols. (Rome 1747–51); 15 vols. (Venice 1767); 18 vols. (Prato 1839–47); *Opera omnia in synopsim redacta ab E. de Azevedo,* 5 vols. (Rome 1766); *Opera inedita,* ed. by F. Heiner (Freiburg 1904); *D*, 500–513; E. de Heeckeren, *Correspondance* (Paris 1912; still significant until publication of Vol. 3 of the following edition); E. Morelli, ed., *Le lettere . . . al card. de Tencin,* 2 vols. (Rome 1955–65); L. Fresco, *Lettere inedite . . . a M. Querini* (Venice 1910); F. X. Kraus, *Briefe B.s an den Canon. P. F. Peggi* . . . (Freiburg 1888); *Hierarchia Catholica* VI, 10–18; A. Mercati, *Raccolta,* 330–81, 405–43; Pastor XVI/1, 1–439; Seppelt V, 428–55; J. Carreyre in *DHGE* VIII, 164–67; P. Mikat in *LThK* II, 177f.; M. Rosa in *Dizionario Biografico degli Italiani* VIII, 393–408; F. Montanari, *Il card. Lambertini fra la leggenda e la storia* (Milan 1943); P. Sighinolfi, *Il card. Lambertini* (Milan 1935); E. Morelli in *Tre Profili* (Rome 1955), 1–45; L. Dal Pane in *ASRomana* 10 (1958/59), 35–63; id. "Voti e speranze . . . per il conclave del 1740," *Accad. Bologna* 8 (1957/58), 140–63; R. Reinhardt, "Zur Kirchenpolitik B.s," *RQ* 60 (1965), 259–68; P. A. Kirsch, "Das von B. XIV . . . mit Spanien abgeschlossene Konkordat," *AkathKR* 80 (1900), 313–22; C. Bandi di Vesme," La pace di Aquisgrana (1748) . . . ," *Boll. Stor. Subalpino* 45 (1967), 249–314; 46 (1968), 103–74; A. A. Bettanini, *B. e la Repubblica di Venezia* (Padua 1966); L. Dal Pane, "La Congregazione economica . . . e la libertà di commercio," *Riv. Stor. Agricol.* 5 (1965), 371–418.

32. *Clement XIII and Clement XIV*

LITERATURE

F. Dörrer, "Der Schriftverkehr zwischen dem päpstl. Staatssekretariat und der Apost. Nuntiatur Wien . . . ," *RömHM* 4 (1960/61), 63–248; R. Olaechea, *Las relaciones hispano-romanas en la 2. mitad del XVIII* (Zaragoza 1965); A. C. Jemolo, *Il giansenismo in Italia prima della rivoluzione* (Bari 1928); E. Damming, *Il movimento giansenista a Roma nella seconda metà del sec. XVIII* (Rome 1945; reprint 1968); S. Traniello and E. Passerin d'Entrèves, "Ricerche sul tardo giansenismo italiano," *Riv. Storia e Letterat. Relig.* 3 (1967), 379–413; A. Melpignano, *L'anticurialismo napoletano sotto Carlo III* (Rome 1965); R. Mincuzzi, *B. Tanucci . . .* (Bari 1967).

CLEMENT XIII: *BullRom Continuatio* I–III; *D,* 513f.; *Hierarchia Catholica* VI, 19–24; A. Mercati, *Raccolta,* 381–85, 443–82; Pastor XVI/1, 441–1011; Seppelt V, 456–69; R. Mols in *DHGE* XII, 1381–1410; H. Raab in *LThK* II, 1229; X. de Ravignan, *Clément XIII et Clément XIV* (Paris 1854); G. Gonzi, *L'espulsione dei Gesuiti dai Ducati parmesi* (Parma 1967).

CLEMENT XIV: *BullRom Continuatio* IV; *Lettere ed altre opere* (Milan 1831); *Lettere, bolle e discorsi,* ed. by C. Frediani (Florence 1845); *Epistolae et brevia selectiora . . . ,* ed. by A. Theiner (Florence 1854); *D,* 514f.; *Hierarchia Catholica* VI, 25–28; Caraccioli, *Vita* (Florence 1776); A. v. Reumont, *Ganganelli . . . Seine Briefe und seine Zeit* (Berlin 1847); *Vita . . . e una lettera di Vincenzo Gioberti* (Rome 1847); J. Crétineau-Joly, *Clément et les jésuites* (Paris 1848); A. Theiner, *Geschichte des Pontificats . . .* (Leipzig and Paris 1853); J. Crétineau-Joly, *Lettre au P. A. Theiner* (Liège 1853); G. Boero, *Osservazioni sopra l'historia . . . scritta dal P. A. Theiner* (Monza 1854); Pastor XVI/2, 1–440; Seppelt V, 469–84; A. Mercati, *Raccolta,* 385–95, 484–92; E. Préclin in *DHGE* XII, 1411–23; H. Raab in *LThK* II, 1229f.; L. Cicchitto, *Il pontefice Clemente* (Rome 1934); W. Kratz, *Intorno al "Clemente XIV" del barone von Pastor* (Rome 1935); L. Berra, "Il diario del conclave di Clemente," *ASRomana* 85–86 (1962/63), 25–319; E. Duda, "Le Saint-Siège devant les événements politiques de Pologne . . . ," *SPM* 1, 139–207; G. C. Cordara, *De suppressione Societatis Jesu commentarii,* ed. by G. Albertotti (Padua 1925); id. *De suis ac suorum rebus . . . commentarii,* ed. by G. Albertotti (Turin 1933); E. Pacheco y de Leyva, "La intervención de Floridablanca . . . ," *Escuela española de arqueología e historia en Roma* 3 (1914), 37–198; H. Hoffmann, *Friedrich II. von Preußen und die Aufhebung . . .* (Leipzig 1962); R. van Dülmen, "Antijesuitismus und kath. Aufklärung in Deutschland," *HJ* 89 (1969), 52–80; A. Galessi, "La malattia e morte di Clemente," *Riv. Storia delle Scienze* 41 (1950), 153–65.

INDEX

Chantal, Jane Frances de 11
Charcas (Sucre), provincial synod (1629) 262
Charitas ille, bull (1777) 227
Charles I, king of England 13, 174f, 436
Charles II, king of England 179, 295, 348
Charles II, king of Spain 129, 168, 331
Charles III, king of Spain (later, as German
    emperor, Charles VI) 130f, 167, 171, 324,
    338, 369f, 575, 579
Charles IV, king of Spain 168, 171
Charles V, king of Spain 335
Charles VI, German emperor (earlier, as
    Charles III, king of Spain) 334, 337, 338,
    339, 448, 473, 490, 515, 568, 571
Charles VI, king of Spain 332
Charles VII, German emperor xv, 452ff, 493,
    568
—secularization project 482
Charles IX, king of Sweden 116
Charles of Anjou 341
Charles de Nevers 13
Charlier, Anne 422
Charron, Pierre 102
Chastel, Violante du 6
Chatel, Jean 58
Chaulnes, Charles, duke de 111, 331
Chelm 206
Chevalier, Abbé 389f
Cheyne, George 439
Chiemsee 146
Chiesa, Bernardino della 285
Chigi, Fabio, *see* Alexander VII
Chigi, Flavio, cardinal 118
Chile 250
Chiloé 250
China
—civilization 379
—mission 282, 303ff
— — missionaries of the *Padroado* 311
— — new orientation of missionary methods
    313
— — Propaganda missionaries 312
— — training of native priests 314ff
—persecution of Christians (1784/85) 307ff
China rapture 379
Chiquitos 253
Chiriguanos 250
Chlysty 203
Choiseul, Étienne François 411f, 579
Choiseul, Gilbert de 47
Christ, piety 552
Christian Brothers 84, 555
Christianity
—claim to absolute nature 345
—and Enlightenment 343ff
Christina, queen of Sweden 113, 115f, 125
Chrysanthos Notaras, patriarch of Jerusalem
    197, 214
Chumacero, Spanish ambassador 170
Chur 138, 151, 159, 160, 479
Church
—and contemporary culture 559

—and Enlightenment 108f
—loss of leadership 343
—reform xvii, 471
— — in the Church of the German Empire
    146ff
Church and state 170f, 559
—after Febronius 454ff
—in France 57ff
—in German religious legislation 451f, 470
— — after the Coblenz *gravamina* 458ff
Church history, historiography xix, 100f, 362,
    524, 529, 532, 543ff
—Protestant 536f
Church hymns 551
Cienfuegos, Álvaro 167, 525, 562
Cisalpine Club 182
Cistercians 17, 18
Cîteaux, abbey 17
Civil constitution 500
Clairvaux, abbey 17
Clarke, Samuel 536
Claudius, negus 221
Claver, Pedro 256
Clémencet, Dom 428
Clemens August, elector of Cologne 149,
    154, 495
Clemens Wenzeslaus of Saxony, elector of
    Trier 160, 456f, 459, 461, 464, 466, 469,
    478, 480, 495, 504, 507, 520
Clement VIII, pope 263
Clement IX (Giulio Rospigliosi), pope 56,
    114f, 282, 289, 330
Clement X (Emilio Altieri), pope xiv, xv,
    115ff, 119, 282, 331, 513, 561
Clement XI (Giovanni Francesco Albani),
    pope xv, 54ff, 92, 125, 129ff, 171, 311,
    331, 334, 337, 338f, 381ff, 385ff, 396,
    399f, 560, 562
—bull *Unigenitus* 381ff
—dispute with Philip V 338f
—Inquisition decree against Jansenism (1718)
    397
—and War of the Spanish Succession 129ff
Clement XII (Lorenzo Corsini), pope 340,
    563ff
Clement XIII (Carlo Rezzonico), pope 340,
    354, 411, 421, 435, 459, 475, 476, 573ff
—conflict with Bourbon courts 577
Clement XIV (Lorenzo Ganganelli), pope,
    xvi, 167, 206, 226, 411f, 551, 577ff
—and problem of Jesuits 579
Clément, Jacques 58
Clementine Peace (1668) 49ff, 67, 114
Clergy 59, 124
—in France 4ff
— —reform 20ff, 80, 84
—immunity 483f
Clermont-Tonnerre, bishop of Langres 383
Clerselier 106
Climent, José 164
Cluny, abbey 18f
Coadjutorships 146f

Romanus Pontifex, bull (1715) 339
Rome 534, 569
—concordat (1784) with Joseph II 480
—provincial council (1725) 563
Romero, Francisco 260
Rosa von Lima 259
Rosario, Constantino de 276
Rosenthal, Johannes 512
Rospiliosi, Cardinal 118
Rospigliosi, Giulio, *see* Clement IX
Rossi, Bernardo Maria de 525
Rostovski Feodosi 206
Roth, Heinrich 298
Rousse, Gérard 422
Rousseau, Jean-Baptiste 431
Rousseau, Jean-Jacques 265, 344, 346, 351, 357f, 364, 369f, 371, 380, 431
Rouvray 62
Royal Society 544
Rucellai, Giulio 342
Rue, de la 532
Ruggieri, Michele 310
Ruinart, Thierry 100
Ruiz, Felipe 162
Russia xix, 115, 207
—and ban of Jesuit order 581
—and Imperial Delegates Final Recess 503f
—Church and state 194ff
—development of state church 198f
—dissolution of Uniate Cátholic bishoprics 206
—Enlightenment 200f, 370f
—monastic reform 197
—new Church regulation 195ff
—Old Believers xix, 190f, 202
—Orthodox Church xix, 183ff
— — autocephaly 183
— — Baroque culture 216f
— — dependency on state 185ff
— — displacement from public life 200
— — dissolution of patriarchate and establishment of Holy Synod 193ff
— — ecclesiastical jurisdiction 190, 193
— — ecclesiastical organization 186, 192
— — internal reform 188f
— — internal threat by Enlightenment, rationalism, and Freemasonry 202
— — liturgy 188f
— — nationalization of Church property 200f
— — Old Believers and reform 189
— — priests, training 192
— — relaxation of tradition 192
— — Russian state church under Holy Synod 198ff
— — secularization 200
— — spiritual regulation 196
— — Tsar and Church 187ff, 203
—Protestants and Catholics in Russia 203ff
—regulation for Catholic Church of Latin and Uniate rites 207
—state church 198ff
—toleration edict of Peter I (1702) 203

Ruthenia, White 224f
Ruthenians (Carpatho-Ukrainians)
—union with Rome 225f
Ruysbroeck, Jan van 75, 95f

Sabatier, Pierre 529
Sacchetti, Giulio 109, 330
Sacramentals 550
Sacred Heart of Jesus devotion 78, 86, 166, 421, 432, 434, 436
Sacred Heart of Mary devotion 78
Sacy, *see* Lemaistre de Sacy, Isaac
Sahagun, Bernardino de 237
Sailer, Johann Michael 520, 523, 529, 531, 542
Saint-Amant 102
Saint-Amour, professor at Sorbonne 39f
Saint-Cyr, former abbey 84, 90
Saint-Cyran, abbey 8, 14
Saint-Cyran, *see* Duvergier de Hauranne
Sainte-Beuve, Madame de 10f
Saint-Georges de Marsay 439
Saint-Germain des Près, abbey 18, 98f
Saint-Hydulphe, Benedictine congregation 18
Saint-Jure, Jean-Baptiste de 79, 436, 440
Saint-Lazare 23
Saint-Lucien-lès-Beauvais, abbey 8
Saint-Magloire, seminary 22
Saint-Martin, de 312
Saint-Maur, abbey 97f, 100, 406
—*see also* Maurists
Saint-Sacrement, convent 30
Saint-Simon 397, 415
Saint-Sulpice 21, 78
Saint-Valéry, abbey 8
Saint-Vanne, Benedictine congregation 18f
Saints, veneration 552
Salas, Asensio 164
Saldanha, Cardinal 571, 574
Salesians 11, 555
Salignac, Marquis de 81f
Salle, Jean-Baptiste de la 84, 259
Salm-Salm, archbishop 144
Solomon Islands 324
Salusti, J. D. 307
Salzburg 143, 145, 148, 157, 458, 466, 478, 493, 497, 525
—congress of electoral Bavarian bishops (1770/71) 486
—synod (1569) 159
Salzinger, Ivo 526
Samuel Kapasulis, patriarch of Alexandria 213
Sandoval, Alonso de 256
Sanfelice, Cologne nuncio 139
San Marino 566
Santander, bishopric 162
Santarelli, Antonio 58, 60, 61
Santeul 430
Sanvitore, Diego Luis 324
Sanz, Pedro Martyr 308
Sao Paulo, bishopric 245
Sao Tomé, bishopric 271